ESSENTIALS OF

UNDERSTANDING
PSYCHOLOGY

ESSENTIALS OF
UNDERSTANDING PSYCHOLOGY

THIRD EDITION

Robert S. Feldman

University of Massachusetts at Amherst

The McGraw-Hill Companies, Inc.

New York   St. Louis   San Francisco   Auckland   Bogotá   Caracas
Lisbon   London   Madrid   Mexico City   Milan   Montreal   New Delhi
San Juan   Singapore   Sydney   Tokyo   Toronto

McGraw-Hill

A Division of The McGraw·Hill Companies

ESSENTIALS OF UNDERSTANDING PSYCHOLOGY

Acknowledgments appear on page 554 and on this page by reference.

This book is printed on acid-free paper.

1 2 3 4 5 6 7 8 9 0   VNH   VNH   9 0 9 8 7 6

ISBN 0-07-021479-4

This book was set in Life Roman by York Graphic Services, Inc.
The editors were Brian L. McKean and David A. Damstra;
the design was done by Initial Graphic Services, Inc.;
the production supervisor was Annette Mayeski.
The photo editor was Elyse Rieder.
Von Hoffman Press, Inc., was printer and binder.

Cover painting: Brian Dunning, *Animus*

Library of Congress Cataloging-in-Publication Data
Feldman, Robert S. (Robert Stephen) (date)
   Essentials of understanding psychology / Robert S. Feldman.—3rd ed.
      p.   cm.
   Abridged ed. of: Understanding psychology. 4th ed. c1996.
   ISBN 0-07-021479-4
   1. Psychology   I. Feldman, Robert S. (Robert Stephen) (date)
Understanding psychology.   II. Title.
BF121.F34   1997
150—dc20   96-12709

ABOUT THE AUTHOR

Robert S. Feldman is professor of psychology at the University of Massachusetts at Amherst, where he is director of undergraduate studies. A graduate of Wesleyan University and the University of Wisconsin–Madison, he is a former Fulbright Senior Research Scholar and Lecturer. He has been teaching introductory psychology for more than two decades and has taught courses at Mount Holyoke College, Wesleyan University, and Virginia Commonwealth University, in addition to the University of Massachusetts.

Dr. Feldman is a Fellow of the American Psychological Association and the American Psychological Society and author of more than 100 scientific articles, book chapters, and papers. He has also written or edited more than a dozen books, including *Fundamentals of Nonverbal Behavior* (Cambridge University Press) and *Applications of Nonverbal Behavioral Theories and Research* (Erlbaum). His research interests include nonverbal behavior and the social psychology of education.

His spare time is most often devoted to serious cooking and earnest, but unpolished, piano playing. He lives with his wife, also a psychologist, and three children, in a home overlooking the Holyoke mountain range in Amherst, Massachusetts.

To Ethel

CONTENTS IN BRIEF

CONTENTS

CHAPTER 12
PSYCHOLOGICAL DISORDERS   401

CHAPTER 13
TREATMENT OF PSYCHOLOGICAL DISORDERS   436

CHAPTER 14
SOCIAL PSYCHOLOGY   464

LIST OF BOXES

REVIEWERS

One of the most important features of *Essentials of Understanding Psychology* is the involvement of both professionals and students in the review process. The third edition of *Essentials of Understanding Psychology* has relied heavily—and profited substantially—from the advice of instructors and students from a range of backgrounds.

First, the manuscript was evaluated by traditional academic reviewers, who served in their capacity as content experts and teachers of psychology. These reviewers helped to ensure that this new edition was accurate and that it incorporated state-of-the-art research findings in psychology.

The second group of reviewers consisted of a panel of three students who assessed *Understanding Psychology,* literally line by line. Their insights and suggestions were invaluable to me in preparing this text.

Finally, dozens of students read parts of the manuscript to ensure that the material was clear and engaging. Their suggestions are incorporated throughout the text.

I am grateful to all these reviewers, who provided their time and expertise to help ensure that *Essentials of Understanding Psychology* reflects the best that psychology has to offer.

PROFESSIONAL REVIEWERS

Louis Banderet, Northeastern University and Quinsigamond Community College
Carol M. Batt, Sacred Heart University
Peggy Brooks, North Adams State College
Cynthia Crown, Xavier University
Ronald Finke, Texas A&M University
Lewis Harvey, University of Colorado, Boulder

Morton Hoffman, Metropolitan State University
Alfred D. Kornfeld, Eastern Connecticut State University
Barbara Lusk, Collin County Community College
Charles Miron, Catonsville Community College
Kenneth Oftenbacher, University of Nebraska, Omaha
Janet Proctor, Purdue University
Ina Samuels, University of Massachusetts, Boston
Norman Schorr, Montgomery College
Susan Shodahl, San Bernardino Valley College
Philip Stander, Kingsborough Community College
Annette Taylor, University of San Diego
Helen Taylor, Bellevue Community College
Charlene Wages, Francis Marion University

STUDENT IN-DEPTH REVIEW PANEL

Jonathan Fader   Jennifer Green   Giachary Lizarraga

STUDENT REVIEW COORDINATORS

Richard Klimeck, Montgomery College, Rockville Campus
Robert Kovaks, Camden Community College

PREFACE

The complexities and contradictions of human behavior defy easy explanation. We see good behavior and bad; we encounter rational and illogical conduct; and we find cooperation and violent competition among the peoples of the world.

The third edition of *Essentials of Understanding Psychology* reflects what psychologists have learned in their quest to understand and explain the behavior we see around us. The text is designed to provide a broad introduction to psychology. While focusing on the building blocks of the field, it also makes clear the relevance of psychology to people's everyday lives.

In revising *Essentials of Understanding Psychology*, I had four major goals:

▪ To provide broad coverage of the field of psychology, introducing the theories, research, and applications that constitute the discipline
▪ To serve as an impetus for readers to think critically about psychological phenomena, particularly those that have an impact on their everyday lives
▪ To illustrate the substantial diversity both within the field of psychology and in society as a whole by presenting material that reflects the discipline's increasing concern with cultural, gender, racial, and ethnic issues
▪ To arouse intellectual curiosity and build an appreciation of how psychology can increase students' understanding of the world around them

In short, *Essentials of Understanding Psychology* is meant not only to expose readers to the content—and promise—of psychology, but to do so in a way that will bring to life basic concepts and research findings and sustain interest in the discipline long after readers have completed their introductory course in psychology. My hope is that initial exposure to the realm of psychology will forge an ongoing enthusiasm and passion for the discipline, one that lasts a lifetime.

AN OVERVIEW OF *ESSENTIALS OF UNDERSTANDING PSYCHOLOGY*

Essentials of Understanding Psychology is based on the 19-chapter, widely used fourth edition of *Understanding Psychology,* a broad and comprehensive introduction to

the field of psychology. Like the book from which it is derived, *Essentials of Understanding Psychology* includes coverage of the traditional topical areas of psychology. It covers, for example, the biological foundations of behavior, sensation and perception, learning, cognition, development, personality, abnormal behavior, and the social psychological foundations of behavior.

Unlike its predecessor, however, *Essentials of Understanding Psychology* is a briefer volume. It focuses on the essence of psychology, providing an initial broad introduction to the field. The book also shows how the field's theories and research have an impact on readers' everyday lives.

There is considerable flexibility in the book's organizational structure. Each chapter is divided into between three and five manageable, self-contained units, permitting instructors to choose and omit sections according to their syllabus. In addition, because the applications material is well-integrated throughout, even in the chapters that cover the most traditional theoretical topics, the relationship between theory, research, and applications of psychology is addressed throughout the book.

In sum, the book reflects a combination of traditional core topics and contemporary applied subjects, providing a broad, eclectic—and current—view of the field of psychology. It draws from theoretical and applied approaches, and integrates the two with objective presentations of research that illustrate the way in which the science of psychology has evolved and grown. Indeed, the book exemplifies the view that a theory-application dichotomy is a false one. The text does not present applications as devoid of theory, but places them in a theoretical context, grounded in research findings. Likewise, when the text presents theoretical material, it draws practical implications from the theory.

WHAT'S NEW IN THE THIRD EDITION?

Much thought has gone into the changes incorporated into this edition of *Essentials of Understanding Psychology.* Because the basic structure and features of the first editions met with such a positive response from both students and professors, the fundamental attributes of the book remain intact. At the same time, additions and changes that reflect developments in the field of psychology have been incorporated.

Two major new features are found throughout the book. Every chapter includes a section called Exploring Diversity, which deals with an aspect of racial, ethnic, gender, or cultural diversity. For instance, the chapter on research discusses concerns of psychologists in choosing subjects that represent a broad sample of human behavior; the chapter on learning discusses the controversy over the existence of culturally based learning styles; and the chapter on memory considers whether there are differences in basic memory processes across cultures.

Furthermore, every chapter contains a Pathways through Psychology box. These boxes include biographical sketches of people who are making use of psychology in their work or professional pursuits.

Overall, a wealth of contemporary research is cited in this edition. Hundreds of new citations have been added, most published in the 1990s. Furthermore, an extensive array of new topics has been incorporated, along with information updating existing material. For instance, the new and revised topics featured in this edition include such subjects as psychology's role in preventing violence, distortions in surveys, brain lateralization, pheromones, cultural learning styles, the repressed memory controversy, bilingual education, measurement of intellectual ability, sexual harassment, cultural differences in academic performance, developmental changes in personality, *DSM-IV*, multiple personalities, Prozac, anger, collectivism and individualism, and aggression and culture.

LEARNING AIDS AND FEATURES OF *ESSENTIALS OF UNDERSTANDING PSYCHOLOGY*

Essentials of Understanding Psychology is designed with its ultimate consumer—the student—in mind. As you can see from the following full list of elements that are common to every chapter, the book incorporates several major educational features. These features are meant to make the book an effective learning device and, simultaneously, enticing and engaging:

■ *Chapter Outline.* Each chapter opens with an outline of the chapter structure. The outline helps orient readers to the chapter content and the relationships among topics.

■ *Prologue.* Each chapter starts with an account of an actual situation that demonstrates the relevance of basic principles and concepts of psychology to pertinent issues and problems. Each of these prologues is new to this edition and reflects current events.

■ *Looking Ahead.* A chapter overview follows the prologue. It articulates the key themes and issues covered within the chapter.

■ *Orienting Questions.* Each major section within the chapter begins with several broad questions, providing a framework for understanding and mastering the material that is to come.

■ *Psychology at Work.* The Psychology at Work boxes illustrate applications of current psychological theory and research findings to real-world problems.

PSYCHOLOGY AT WORK

Psychology and the Prevention of Violence

As he walks calmly through a Long Island Railroad car, Colin Ferguson shoots several rounds of ammunition from a handgun, killing five people and injuring twenty-three others.

A hired hitman smashes a portable nightstick into the knee of figure skater Nancy Kerrigan in an effort to keep her from competing in the winter Olympics.

A woman is killed by two teenage muggers during a robbery which nets the perpetrators less than $2.

It has been called the twentieth-century plague: violence in the United States. Surveys show that violence and crime rank at the top of any list of concerns for most

The epidemic of violence in the United States has extended into the schools, where metal detectors are sometimes used to prevent weapons from being brought to class.

gun used by a friend or acquaintance. The higher rate

that others' behavior was intended to upset them. The training resulted in a reduction of anger in the face of provocation (Graham & Hudley, 1992). One fact that has emerged quite clearly from this research is the requirement that programs be culturally, ethnically, and racially sensitive (Hammond & Yung, 1993).

• How prevalent is violence on television? It is clear that violence on television is common. One survey found that of ninety-four prime-time programs examined, forty-eight showed at least one act of violence, and they include fifty-seven people killed and ninety-nine assaulted (Hanson & Knopes, 1993). Furthermore,

■ **Pathways through Psychology.** These boxes, found in every chapter, provide biographical sketches of people working in professions that make use of the findings of psychology.

PATHWAYS THROUGH PSYCHOLOGY

Mary Garrett
San Francisco State College,
San Francisco, California

Born: 1947
Education: A.A., City College
of San Francisco; B.A., San
Francisco State College;
currently enrolled in M.A.
program, San Francisco State
Home: San Francisco, California

Most high school students have only a vague idea of what they want to do with their lives, but as far as Mary Garrett was concerned, there

Mary Garrett.

these effects in order to design effective psychosocial intervention," she said.

The impetus for the study was a similar project conducted by one of her professors. He had done an initial study on coping with AIDS, but he only used men in his sample. Garrett is interested in comparing how women and men deal with the disease.

"I want to find out if the coping strategies and processes are different for women. Women do have different stressors than men, such as being single mothers or being a black female in this society," she said.

The research, according to Garrett, will involve three phases

■ **Exploring Diversity.** Every chapter includes at least one section devoted to an aspect of racial, ethnic, gender, or cultural diversity. These sections highlight the way in which psychology informs (and is informed by) issues relating to the increasing multiculturalism of our global society.

 Exploring Diversity

Are There Cross-Cultural Differences in Memory?

Many travelers who have visited areas of the world in which there is no written language have returned with tales of people with phenomenal memories. Presumably because they have no written records, people in such cultures develop memories that can provide a kind of oral record keeping to keep track of important events in the society's history. For instance, storytellers in some preliterate cultures can recount long chronicles that recall the names and activities of people over many generations.

On the basis of such anecdotes, memory experts initially argued that people in preliterate society develop a different, and perhaps better, type of memory than those in cultures that employ a written language (Bartlett, 1932). They suggested that, in a society which lacks writing, people are going to be motivated to recall information with accuracy, particularly in terms of tribal histories and traditions that would otherwise be lost if not passed down orally from one generation to another.

■ **The Informed Consumer of Psychology.** Every chapter includes material designed to make readers more informed consumers of psychological information by giving them the ability to critically evaluate what the field of psychology offers.

 The Informed Consumer of Psychology

Effective Coping Strategies

How does one cope most effectively with stress? Researchers have made a number of recommendations for dealing with the problem. There is no universal solution, of course, since effective coping depends on the nature of the stressor and the degree to which control is possible. Still, some general guidelines can be followed (Folkman, 1984; Everly, 1989; Holahan & Moos, 1987, 1990):

■ *Turning threat into challenge.* When a stressful situation might be controllable, the best coping strategy is to treat the situation as a challenge, focusing on ways to control it. For instance, if you experience stress because your car is always breaking down, you might take an evening course in auto mechanics and learn to deal directly with the car's problems. Even if the repairs prove too difficult to do yourself, at least you'll be in a better position to understand what's wrong.

■ **Recap and Review.** Every chapter is divided into three or four sections, each of which concludes with a Recap and Review. The Recaps summarize the key points of the previous section, and the Reviews present a variety of questions for students to answer in order to test both recall and higher-level understanding of the material.

RECAP AND REVIEW

Recap
- People do not respond passively to visual stimuli; rather, they try to separate a given figure from the background.
- Among the gestalt laws of organization are closure, proximity, similarity, and simplicity.
- Feature analysis considers how people perceive a stimulus, break it down into the individual elements that make it up, and then use those elements to understand what they are seeing.
- Perception occurs through top-down and bottom-up processing.
- Depth perception occurs because of binocular disparity, motion parallax, and the relative size of images on the retina. Motion perception is the result of the movement of images across the retina, combined with information about head and eye movements.

- Visual illusions are physical stimuli that consistently produce errors in perception. Among the most common are the Poggendorf illusion and the Müller-Lyer illusion.
- Subliminal perception and extrasensory perception remain controversial.

Review
1. Match each of the following organizational laws with its meaning:
   1. Elements close together are grouped together.
   2. Patterns are perceived in the most basic, direct manner possible.
   3. Groupings are made in terms of complete figures.
   4. Elements similar in appearance are grouped together.
   a. Closure

■ **Running Glossary.** Key terms are highlighted in boldface type within the text where they are introduced and are defined in the margin of the page, with pronunciation guides for difficult words. There is also an end-of-book glossary.

■ **Looking Back.** To facilitate both the review and synthesis of the information covered, a numbered summary is included at the end of every chapter. The summary emphasizes the key points of the chapter and is organized according to the orienting questions posed at the beginning of every major section.

■ **Key Terms and Concepts.** A list of key terms and concepts, including the page numbers where they are introduced, is also provided at the end of each chapter.

ANCILLARY MATERIALS

The Third Edition of *Essentials of Understanding Psychology* is accompanied by an extensive, integrated set of supplemental materials designed to support the classroom teaching of both new and veteran instructors. Prepared under the supervision of Professor Mark Garrison, the student *Study Guide, Instructor's Manual,* and *Test Bank* are fully integrated to provide a consistent pedagogical framework for students and professors using *Understanding Psychology.*

The *Study Guide* has been completely revised and features an enhanced illustration program. The *Study Guide* opens with an introductory essay that provides the student with suggestions for how best to utilize the SQ3R study and review method (discussed in the next introductory section, To the Student). It also features a brief guide for nonnative speakers of English. Each *Study Guide* chapter contains a chapter outline with highlighted key terms, a detailed chapter summary, learning objectives keyed to page numbers in the text, and a set of self-study questions of various types and levels of difficulty.

The *Instructor's Manual* contains a wide variety of new lecture ideas, handouts, and resources. Designed to complement the *Study Guide* and *Test File,* each chapter in the *Instructor's Manual* includes a detailed chapter outline, a chapter summary, learning objectives, and a set of Lecture Resources including discussion topics, ideas for classroom demonstrations, a list of relevant films and videos, and suggestions for many new activities and projects that can be used both in and out of the classroom.

The *Test File* contains thousands of factual and conceptual multiple-choice and essay questions indexed to the text and keyed to the learning objectives. Computerized Test Banks are available in IBM (on both 5.25 and 3.5 disks) and Macintosh formats.

McGraw-Hill also provides a wide variety of audiovisual and computerized teaching aids. Available for the first time with this edition, *MICROGUIDE* offers a computerized version of the study guide with interactive testing and tutorial features.

Professors using *Essentials of Understanding Psychology* will receive a regular update, called *PsychFax,* written by this book's author. *PsychFax* will include reports of new psychological findings and will discuss the psychological implications of current events in the news. The update can be distributed to students or incorporated into lectures.

Finally, a toll-free, interactive reader comment line has been established for comments and queries. Users of *Essentials of Understanding Psychology* can call 1-800-223-6880, extension 29496, to have access to this line.

ACKNOWLEDGMENTS

As the list of reviewers on page xix attests, this book involved the efforts of many people. They lent their expertise to evaluate all or part of the manuscript, providing an unusual degree of quality control. Their careful work and thoughtful suggestions have improved the manuscript many times over from its first-draft incarnations. I am grateful to them all for their comments.

My thinking has been shaped by many teachers along the way. I was introduced to psychology at Wesleyan University, where several committed and inspiring teachers—in particular Karl Scheibe—conveyed their sense of excitement about the field and made its relevance clear to me. By the time I left Wesleyan I could envision no other career but that of psychologist. Although the nature of the University of Wisconsin, where I did my graduate work, could not have been more different from the much smaller Wesleyan, the excitement and inspiration were similar. Once again, a cadre of excellent teachers—led, especially, by the late Vernon Allen—molded my thinking and taught me to appreciate the beauty and science of the discipline of psychology.

My colleagues and students at the University of Massachusetts at Amherst provide ongoing intellectual stimulation, and I thank them for making the University a fine place to work. Several people also provided extraordinary research and editorial help. In particular, I am grateful to Erik Coats, a constant source of ideas and (more often than I wished) constructive criticism, and to John Graiff, who helped immeasurably on just about everything involving this book.

Every reader of this book owes a debt of gratitude to Rhona Robbin, senior developmental editor. Her relentless pursuit of excellence shaped the underlying quality of this book. Brian McKean, sponsoring editor of this edition, has brought innovation, creative energy, and a strong degree of commitment to the book, and I am very appreciative of his efforts.

Other people at McGraw-Hill were central to the design, production, and marketing process; these include editing supervisor David Damstra, designer Howard Leiderman, production supervisor Annette Mayeski, and photo editors Nancy Dyer and Elyse Rieder. I am also appreciative of Kim Hulbert and Annie Mitchell, whose marketing savvy informed the development of the third edition from its conception. I am proud to be a part of this world-class team.

Finally, I am, as always, indebted to my family. My parents, Leah Brochstein and the late Saul D. Feldman, provided a lifetime foundation of love and support, and I continue to see their influence in every corner of my life. My extended family also play a central role in my life. They include, more or less in order of age, my nieces and nephews, my brother, various brothers- and sisters-in-law, and Harry Brochstein. Finally, I am grateful to my aunt, Ethel Radler, to whom this book is dedicated, for her constant support and love.

Ultimately, my children, Jonathan, Joshua, and Sarah, and my wife, Katherine, remain the delight of my life. I thank them, with immense love.

Robert S. Feldman

TO THE STUDENT

STRATEGIES FOR EFFECTIVE STUDY AND CRITICAL THINKING

Essentials of Understanding Psychology has been written with the reader in mind, and it therefore includes a number of unique features intended to help you to maximize your learning of the basic concepts, principles, and theories that make up the field of psychology. To take advantage of these features, there are several steps you should take when reading and studying this book. By following these steps, not only will you get the most out of this book, but you will also develop study habits that will help you to learn more effectively from other texts and to think critically about new material that is presented. Among the most important steps to follow:

■ Familiarize yourself with the logic of the book's structure. Begin by reading the Table of Contents. It provides an overview of the topics that will be covered and gives a sense of the way in which the various topics are interrelated. Next, review the Preface, which describes the book's major features. Keep in mind that each chapter is divided into three to five self-contained units; these provide logical starting and stopping points for reading and studying.

Note, also, the major highlights of each chapter: a chapter-opening outline, a Prologue, a Looking Ahead section, Recaps and Reviews of key information following each of the major units, and—at the end of every chapter—a Looking Back section and a list of Key Terms and Concepts. The Looking Back summary is organized around the questions posed in the Looking Ahead section at the beginning of the chapter, thereby tying the chapter's contents together.

Because every chapter is structured in this same way, the book provides a set of familiar landmarks to help you chart your way through new material. This structure will help you in organizing each chapter's content.

Finally, there are certain styles of writing used by psychologists with which you should be familiar. In particular, citations to previous research are indicated by a name and date, typically set off in parentheses. Each of these names and dates refers to a book or article included in the Reference list at the end of this book.

■ Use a study strategy. Although we are expected to study and ultimately learn a wide range of material throughout our schooling, we are rarely taught any systematic strategies that permit us to study more effectively. Yet just as we wouldn't expect a physician to learn human anatomy by trial and error, it is the unusual student who is able to stumble upon a truly effective studying strategy.

Psychologists, however, have devised several excellent (and proven) techniques for improving study skills, two of which are described here. By employing one of these procedures—known by the initials "SQ3R" and "MURDER"—you can increase your ability to learn and retain information and to think critically, not just in psychology classes but in all academic subjects.

The SQ3R method includes a series of five steps, designated by the initials S-Q-R-R-R. The first step is to *survey* the material by reading the chapter outlines, chapter headings, figure captions, Recaps, and Looking Ahead and Looking Back sections, providing yourself with an overview of the major points of the chapter. The next step—the "Q" in SQ3R—is to *question*. Formulate questions—either aloud or in writing—before actually reading a section of the material. For instance, if you had first surveyed this section of the book, you might jot down in the margin, "What do 'SQ3R' and 'MURDER' stand for?" The queries posed at the start of the major sections and the reviews that end each part of the chapter are also good sources of questions. But it is important not to rely on them entirely; making up your own questions is critical. *Essentials of Understanding Psychology* has wide margins in which you can write your own questions. This process helps you to focus on the key points of the chapter, while at the same time putting you in an inquisitive frame of mind.

It is now time for the next, and most crucial, step: to *read* the material. Read carefully and, even more importantly, read actively and critically. For instance, while you are reading, answer the questions you have asked yourself. You may find yourself coming up with new questions as you read along; that's fine, since it shows you are reading inquisitively and paying attention to the material. Critically evaluate material by considering the implications of what you are reading, thinking about possible exceptions and contradictions, and examining the assumptions that lie behind the assertions made by the author.

The next step—the second "R"—is the most unusual. This "R" stands for *recite,* in which you look up from the book and describe and explain to yourself, or to a friend, the material you have just read and answer the questions you have posed earlier. Do it aloud; this is one time when talking to yourself is nothing to be embarrassed about. The recitation process helps you to clearly identify your degree of understanding of the material you have just read. Moreover, psychological research has shown that communicating material to others, or reciting it aloud to yourself, assists you in learning it in a different—and deeper—way than material that you do not intend to communicate. Hence, your recitation of the material is a crucial link in the studying process.

The final "R" refers to *review.* As we discuss in Chapters 5 and 6, reviewing is a prerequisite to fully learning and remembering material you have studied. Look over the information, reread the Recaps and Looking Back summaries, answer in-text review questions, and use any ancillary materials you may have available. (Both a traditional and a computerized student study guide are available to accompany *Essentials of Understanding Psychology.*) Reviewing should be an active process, in which you consider how different pieces of information fit together and develop a sense of the overall picture.

An alternative approach to studying—although not altogether dissimilar to SQ3R—is provided by the MURDER system (Dansereau, 1978). Despite the deadly connotations of its title, the MURDER system is a useful study strategy.

In MURDER, the first step is to establish an appropriate *mood* for studying by setting goals for a study session and choosing a time and place in which you will not be distracted. Next comes reading for *understanding,* in which careful attention is paid to the meaning of the material being studied. *Recall* is an immediate attempt to recall the material from memory, without referring to the text. *Digesting* the material comes next; you should correct any recall errors, and attempt to organize and store newly learned material in memory.

You should work next on *expanding* (analyzing and evaluating) new material and try to apply it to situations that go beyond the applications discussed in the text. By incorporating what you have learned into a larger information network in memory, you will be able to recall it more easily in the future. Finally, the last step is *review.* Just as with the SQ3R system, MURDER suggests that the systematic review of material is a necessary condition for successful studying.

Both the SQ3R and MURDER systems provide a proven means of increasing your study effectiveness. It is not necessary, though, to feel tied to a particular strategy; you might want to combine other elements into your own study system. For example, learning tips and strategies for critical thinking will be presented throughout *Essentials of Understanding Psychology,* such as in Chapter 6 when the use of mnemonics (memory techniques for organizing material to help its recall) is discussed. If these tactics help you to successfully master new material, stick with them.

The last aspect of studying that warrants mention is that *when* and *where* you study are in some ways as important as *how* you study. One of the truisms of the psychological literature is that we learn things better, and are able to recall them longer, when we study material in small chunks over several study sessions, rather than massing our study into one lengthy period. This implies that all-night studying just before a test is going to be less effective—and a lot more tiring—than employing a series of steady, regular study sessions.

In addition to carefully timing your studying, you should seek out a special location to study. It doesn't really matter where it is, as long as it has minimal distractions and is a place that you use *only* for studying. Identifying a special "territory" allows you to get in the right mood for study as soon as you begin.

A FINAL COMMENT

By using the proven study strategies presented above, as well as by making use of the pedagogical tools integrated in the text, you will maximize your understanding of the material in this book and will master techniques that will help you learn and think critically in all your academic endeavors. More importantly, you will optimize your understanding of the field of psychology. It is worth the effort: The excitement, challenge, and promise that psychology holds for you are significant.

CHAPTER 1
INTRODUCTION TO PSYCHOLOGY

The Making of a Terrorist

From all appearances, Ted Kaczynski's childhood and college life were remarkable only for the academic successes he achieved. Raised in what seemed to be an ordinary family, Kaczynski was always an excellent student, a math and science whiz kid. After skipping several grades during his public schooling, he enrolled at Harvard University at the age of 16. By the time he was in his early 20s he had received a Ph.D. in mathematics, and he was hired by the University of California at Berkeley for a prestigious teaching position.

At some point, however, his life departed radically from the norm. Suddenly quitting his teaching post, he retreated to a series of remote hideaways, where, according to the FBI, he took on a new and deadly pastime. In the next two decades, he allegedly sent bombs to a variety of people, injuring or killing almost two dozen victims. He was, according to Federal prosecutors, the Unabomber.

LOOKING AHEAD

We may never fully know what could have driven Ted Kaczynski to turn from professor to alleged terrorist. But it is clear that the case of the Unabomber raises a variety of issues for psychologists of several different orientations:

■ Psychologists studying the biology underlying behavior might examine whether some brain abnormality or chemical imbalance could account for the Unabomber's behavior.

■ Psychologists who study learning and thinking processes could consider how he developed the expertise to make bombs, as well as the reasoning employed in the lengthy statements he wrote describing his beliefs.

■ Those psychologists who specialize in the study of memory could investigate the accuracy of people's recollections of what the Unabomber looked like or their memories of the bombings.

■ Developmental psychologists, who study growth and change throughout life, might ask what clues could be found in the Unabomber's childhood to explain his adult behavior, and why his behavior differed so from other family members raised in the same environment.

Suspected Unabomber Ted Kaczynski was arrested in his remote cabin in the woods of Montana. The home was only 10 by 12 feet, and it lacked plumbing and electricity. What it did contain was a variety of explosives.

■ Health psychologists, who examine the relationship between physical and psychological factors, might focus on whether the surviving victims of the Unabomber faced unusual stress and illness as a result of their close encounter with death.

■ Clinical and counseling psychologists, who provide therapy for psychological disorders, would seek to identify whether the Unabomber had a recognizable psychological disorder

■ Social psychologists, who study how people's thoughts, feelings, and actions are affected by others, would try to understand what led the Unabomber to avoid human contact after he dropped out of society, and how he chose his victims.

Although the approaches that these different types of psychologists would take in studying the impact of the explosion are diverse, there is a common link: Each represents a specialty area within the general field of study called psychology. **Psychology** is the scientific study of behavior and mental processes.

Although this definition seems straightforward, it is deceptively simple. In fact, since the first stirrings of the discipline, psychologists have debated about just what should constitute the appropriate scope of the field. Should psychologists limit themselves to the study of outward, observable behavior? Is it possible to study internal thinking processes scientifically? Should the field encompass the study of such diverse topics as physical and mental health, perception, dreaming, and motivation? Is it appropriate to focus solely on human behavior, or should the behavior of nonhumans be included?

Most psychologists have answered these questions by taking a broad view, arguing that the field should be receptive to a variety of viewpoints and approaches. Consequently, the phrase "behavior and mental processes" in the definition must be understood to mean many things: It encompasses not just people's actions, but also their thoughts, feelings, perceptions, reasoning processes, memories, and even the biological activities that maintain bodily functioning.

When psychologists speak of "studying" behavior and mental processes, their perspective is equally broad. To psychologists, it is not enough simply to describe behavior. As with any science, psychology attempts to explain, predict, modify, and ultimately improve the lives of people and the world in which they live.

By using scientific methods, psychologists are able to find answers to questions about the nature of human behavior and thought processes that are far more valid and legitimate than those resulting from mere intuition and speculation. And what a variety and range of questions psychologists pose. Consider these examples: How do we see colors? What is intelligence? Can abnormal behavior be cured? How long can we go without sleep? Can aging be delayed? How does stress affect us? What is the best way to study? What is normal sexual behavior? How do we reduce violence?

These questions—which will be addressed in this book—provide just a hint of the various topics that will be presented as we explore the field of psychology. Our discussions will take us across the spectrum of what is known about behavior and mental processes. At times, we will leave the realm of humans to explore animal behavior, because many psychologists study nonhumans in order to determine general laws of behavior that pertain to *all* organisms. Animal behavior thus provides important clues to answering questions about human behavior. But we will always return to a consideration of the usefulness of psychology in helping to solve the everyday problems that confront all human beings.

In sum, this book will not only cover the breadth of the field of psychology, but try to convey its content in a way that arouses your interest and continuing curiosity about psychology. To that end, this text is intended to provide as close a facsimile to two people sitting down and discussing psychology as one can convey with the written word; when I write "we," I am talking about the two of us— reader and writer. To paraphrase an expression from the folks who spend much of their time with computers, the book is meant to be "reader-friendly."

Psychology: The scientific study of behavior and mental processes.

You will find out about how psychologists have been able to apply what they have learned to resolving practical problems that people encounter in everyday life (Psychology at Work boxes). You will meet people who have experienced first-hand how valuable a background in psychology can be in their professional lives (Pathways through Psychology boxes). You will learn about the contributions that psychology can make in enhancing our understanding of the multicultural world in which we live (Exploring Diversity sections).

Finally, you will find sections in each chapter that are intended to make you a more knowledgeable consumer of psychological information. These Informed Consumer of Psychology sections discuss concrete recommendations for incorporating psychology into your life. They are meant to enhance your ability to critically evaluate the contributions that psychologists can offer society.

The book itself has been designed to make it easier for you to learn the material we discuss. Based on principles developed by psychologists who specialize in learning and memory, information is presented in relatively small chunks, with each chapter including three to five major sections. Each of these segments starts with a few broad questions, and concludes with a Recap and Review section that lists the key points and poses a series of questions. Some questions provide a quick test of recall, with answers provided immediately following the review. Others, designated Ask Yourself, are broader in scope and are designed to elicit critical analysis of the information. These self-tests will help you in learning, and later recalling, the material. To further reinforce your understanding of important terms and concepts, each chapter ends with a comprehensive summary and list of key terms.

The framework of the book is embodied in this introductory chapter, which presents several topics that are central to an understanding of psychology. We begin by describing the different types of psychologists and the various roles they play. Next, we examine the major perspectives used to guide the work psychologists do. Finally, we identify the major issues that underlie psychologists' views of the world and human behavior, and discuss the way in which psychologists pose—and answer—questions about the world.

- *What is psychology, and why is it a science?*
- *What are the different branches of the field of psychology?*
- *Where are psychologists employed?*

PSYCHOLOGISTS AT WORK

Hunched over a laboratory table, the woman removes the adrenal glands from a brown Australian marsupial mouse. Male members of the species show a curious characteristic: After 5 to 12 hours of continuous copulation, they die. However, this behavior only occurs during a 2-week period. The woman believes that the adrenal glands trigger this furious sexual behavior in response to seasonal variations in the length of day and changes in temperature (Hunt, 1993; Nelson, Badura, & Goldman, 1990).

The middle-age man welcomes the participants in the study, who, more often than not, enter the room in pairs. This is hardly surprising since the point of the study is to examine twins. They have come to a testing site to meet with researchers who are studying similarities in the behavioral and personality traits of twins. By comparing twins who have lived together virtually all their lives with those who have been separated from birth, researchers are seeking to determine the relative influence of heredity and experience on human behavior.

Methodically—and painfully—retracing events of years before, the college student discloses a childhood secret that he has revealed previously to no one. The listener responds with support, suggesting to him that his concern is one shared by many people.

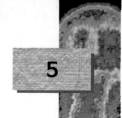

Although the last scene may be the only one that fits your image of what a psychologist does, each of these episodes describes work carried out by contemporary psychologists. The range and scope of psychology is remarkably broad.

The Branches of Psychology: Psychology's Family Tree

Psychology can be likened to a large extended family, with assorted nieces and nephews, aunts and uncles, and cousins who may not interact on a day-to-day basis, but who are related to one another in fundamental ways.

We will examine psychology's family tree by considering each of the major specialty areas of the field, describing them in the general order in which they are discussed in subsequent chapters of this book. Figure 1-1 depicts the proportion of psychologists who identify themselves as belonging to each of these major specialty areas.

The Biological Foundations of Behavior   In the most fundamental sense, people are biological organisms, and some psychologists investigate the ways in which the physiological functions and structures of our body work together to influence our behavior. *Biopsychology* is the branch of psychology that specializes in the biological bases of behavior. Studying a broad range of topics, biopsychologists focus on the operation of the brain and nervous system. For example, they may examine the ways in which specific sites in the brain are related to a disorder such as Parkinson's disease (see Chapter 2), or they may attempt to determine how our body's sensations are related to our emotions (see Chapter 9).

Sensing, Perceiving, Learning, and Thinking   If you have ever wondered how acute your vision is, how you sense pain, or how you can most effectively study, you have raised a question that is most appropriately answered by an experimental psychologist. *Experimental psychology* is the branch of psychology that studies the processes of sensing, perceiving, learning, and thinking about the world.

The work of experimental psychologists overlaps that done by biopsychologists, as well as by other types of psychologists. For this reason, the term "experimental psychologist" is somewhat misleading; psychologists in every specialty area use experimental techniques, and experimental psychologists do not limit themselves solely to experimental methods.

Several subspecialties have grown out of experimental psychology to become central branches of the field in their own right. One example of such a specialty

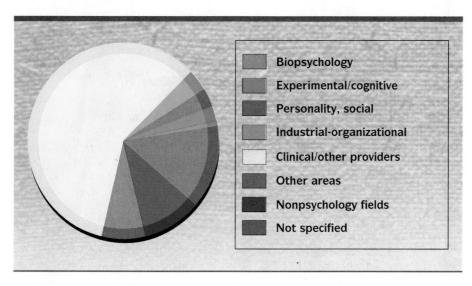

FIGURE 1-1   The percentage of psychologists falling into the major specialty areas of the field. *(Source: APA, research office, 1995, based on APA membership.)*

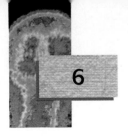
area is *cognitive psychology,* which focuses on the study of higher mental processes, including thinking, language, memory, problem solving, knowing, reasoning, judging, and decision making. Covering a wide range of human behavior, cognitive psychologists have, for instance, identified more efficient ways of remembering and better strategies for solving problems involving logic (discussed in Chapters 6 and 7).

Understanding Change and Individual Differences   A baby producing her first smile . . . taking her first step . . . saying her first word. These events, which can be characterized as universal milestones in development, are also singularly special and unique for each person. Developmental psychologists, whose work is discussed in Chapter 10, trace the physical, cognitive, social, and emotional changes that occur throughout life.

   Developmental psychology, then, is the branch of psychology that studies how people grow and change throughout the course of their lives. Another branch, *personality psychology,* attempts to explain both consistency and change in a person's behavior over time, as well as the individual traits that differentiate the behavior of one person from another when confronting the same situation. The major issues relating to the study of personality will be considered in Chapter 11.

Physical and Mental Health   If you have difficulty getting along with others, continuing unhappiness in your life, or a fear that prevents you from carrying out your normal activities, you might consult one of the psychologists who devote their energies to the study of physical or mental health: health psychologists, clinical psychologists, and counseling psychologists.

   Health psychology explores the relationship between psychological factors and physical ailments or disease. For instance, health psychologists are interested in how long-term stress (a psychological factor) can affect physical health. They are also concerned with identifying ways of promoting behavior related to good health (such as increased exercise) or discouraging unhealthy behavior such as smoking.

   For clinical psychologists, the focus of activity is on the treatment and prevention of psychological disturbance. *Clinical psychology* is the branch of psychology that deals with the study, diagnosis, and treatment of abnormal behavior. Clinical psychologists are trained to diagnose and treat problems ranging

Counseling psychologists who staff college centers advise students on career choices, methods of study, and strategies for coping with everyday problems.

from the everyday crises of life, such as grief due to the death of a loved one, to more extreme conditions, such as losing touch with reality. Some clinical psychologists also conduct research, investigating issues that range from identifying the early signs of psychological disturbance to studying the relationship between how family members communicate with one another and psychological disorder.

As we will see when we discuss abnormal behavior and its treatment in Chapters 12 and 13, the kinds of activities carried out by clinical psychologists are varied indeed. It is clinical psychologists who administer and score psychological tests and who provide psychological services in community mental health centers. Even sexual problems are often treated by clinical psychologists. ⅟

Like clinical psychologists, counseling psychologists deal with people's psychological problems, but they are problems of a particular sort. *Counseling psychology* is the branch of psychology that focuses primarily on educational, social, and career adjustment problems. Almost every college has a center staffed with counseling psychologists. This is where students can get advice on the kinds of jobs they might be best suited for, on methods of studying effectively, and on strategies for resolving everyday difficulties, such as problems with roommates and concerns about a specific professor's grading practices. Many large business organizations also employ counseling psychologists in order to help employees with work-related problems.

Two close relatives of counseling psychology are educational psychology and school psychology. *Educational psychology* considers how the educational process affects students. It is, for example, concerned with ways of understanding intelligence, developing better teaching techniques, and understanding teacher-student interaction. *School psychology,* in contrast, is the specialty area devoted to assessing children in elementary and secondary schools who have academic or emotional problems and developing solutions to such problems.

Understanding Our Social Networks   None of us lives in isolation; rather, we are all part of a complex network of social interrelationships. These networks with other people and with society as a whole are the focus of study for many different kinds of psychologists.

Social psychology, as we will see in Chapter 14, is the study of how people's thoughts, feelings, and actions are affected by others. Social psychologists focus on such diverse topics as human aggression, liking and loving, persuasion, and conformity. For instance, social psychologists ask, "Does observation of televised violence make people more aggressive?" "What is the role of physical attractiveness in choosing a spouse?" And "How are we influenced by salespeople?"

Industrial-organizational psychology is concerned with the psychology of the workplace. Specifically, it considers issues such as productivity, job satisfaction, and decision making. A related branch is *consumer psychology,* which analyzes people's buying habits and the effects of advertising on buyer behavior. An industrial-organizational psychologist might ask a question such as "How do you influence workers to improve the quality of products they produce?" while a consumer psychologist might ask the corresponding question of "How does product quality enter into decisions to purchase a specific product?"

Finally, *cross-cultural psychology* investigates the similarities and differences in psychological functioning in various cultures and ethnic groups. Psychologists specializing in cross-cultural issues investigate such questions as the following (Shweder & Sullivan, 1993): "How do the ways in which people in different cultures attribute their academic success or failures lead to differences in scholastic performance (a factor that may account for differences in academic achievement between American and Japanese students)?" "How do child-rearing practices, which are substantially different among various cultures, affect subsequent adult values and attitudes?" And "Why do cultures vary in their interpretation of what constitutes physical attractiveness?"

Forensic psychologists use mock juries, such as this one, to predict the outcome of actual jury trials.

Emerging Areas   As the field of psychology matures, the number of specialty areas continues to increase (Bower, 1993; Koch, 1993). For example, the study of the *psychology of women* concentrates on psychological factors relating to women's behavior and development. It focuses on a broad range of issues such as discrimination against women, the possibility that structural differences exist in men's and women's brains, the effects of hormones on behavior, and the causes of violence against women.

Another emerging area is *clinical neuropsychology*, which unites the areas of biopsychology and clinical psychology. It focuses on the way in which biological factors, such as brain dysfunctions, relate to psychological disorders.

Environmental psychology considers the relationship between people and their physical environment. Environmental psychologists have made significant progress in understanding how our physical environment affects the way we behave toward others, our emotions, and the amount of stress we experience in a particular setting. *Forensic psychology* focuses on legal issues, such as deciding what criteria determine whether a person is legally insane and whether larger or smaller juries make fairer decisions (Kempton, Darley, & Stern, 1992; Stern, 1992).

"Is there a home court advantage?" "Are there personality differences between people who participate in sports and exercise programs and those who don't?" "Does participation in sports reduce aggressive behavior?" "How can we motivate ourselves to perform at our optimum level?" These kinds of questions are addressed by *sport and exercise psychology*, the branch of the field that investigates the applications of psychology to athletic activity and exercise. It considers the role of motivation, the social aspects of sports, and even such physiological issues as the impact of training on muscle development.

Psychologists interested in *program evaluation* also constitute a growing body. They focus on assessing large-scale programs, usually run by the government, to determine whether the programs are effective in meeting their goals. For example, psychologists specializing in evaluation have examined the effectiveness of such governmental social services as the Head Start preschool program and Medicaid (Rossi & Freeman, 1993; Fink, 1993; Cook & Shadish, 1994).

Exploring Diversity

The Demographics of the Discipline

Wanted: Assistant professor at a small liberal arts college. Teach undergraduate courses in introductory psychology and courses in specialty areas of cognitive psychology, perception, and learning. Strong commitment to quality teaching and student advising necessary. The candidate must also provide evidence of scholarship and research productivity or potential.

Wanted: Industrial/organizational consulting psychologist. International firm is seeking psychologists for full-time career positions as consultants to management. Candidates must have the ability to establish a rapport with senior business executives and to assist them with innovative, practical, and psychologically sound solutions to problems concerning people and organizations.

Wanted: Clinical psychologist. Ph.D., internship experience, and license required. Comprehensive clinic seeks psychologist to work with children and adults, providing individual and group therapy, psychological evaluations, crisis intervention, and development of behavior treatment plans on multidisciplinary team. Broad experience with substance-abuse problems is desirable.

Psychology's Workplace   Given the diversity of roles that psychologists play, it is not surprising that they are employed in a variety of settings. Many are employed by institutions of higher learning (universities, 2- and 4-year colleges, and medical schools) or work as private practitioners treating clients. The next-most-frequent employment settings are hospitals, clinics, community mental-health centers, and counseling centers. Other settings include human-services organizations, research and consulting firms, and business and industry (ODEER, 1994).

Why are so many psychologists found in academic settings? The answer is that the three major roles played by psychologists in society—teacher, scientist, and clinical practitioner—are easily carried out in such an environment. Very often psychology professors are also actively involved in doing research or in serving clients. Whatever their particular job site, however, psychologists share a commitment to better both individual lives and society in general (Peterson, 1991; Coie et al., 1993; Rheingold, 1994).

Psychologists: A Statistical Portrait   Is there an "average" psychologist? Probably not. Just as the subfields of psychology are highly diversified, the kinds of people who make up the field are also quite varied. Some basic demographic statistics begin to tell the story. For example, about 60 percent of U.S. psychologists are men and about 40 percent women. Yet these figures are not static: By the year 2000 these percentages are expected to be about equal, and by the year 2010 the number of women in the field is predicted to exceed the number of men (APA, 1993; Fowler, 1993).

Furthermore, although most psychologists are found in the United States, the field extends well beyond the U.S. borders. A little more than one-third of the world's 500,000 psychologists are found in other parts of the world (Rosenzweig, 1992).

One issue of great concern to psychologists is the relative lack of diversity in terms of race and ethnic origin among psychologists within the United States. According to figures compiled by the American Psychological Association, of those psychologists who identify themselves by race and ethnic origin in surveys—and almost one-fifth don't respond to the question—the vast majority are white. Past discrimination and a lack of encouragement for minorities to enter the field have resulted in a situation in which less than 2 percent are Hispanic, 1.6 percent are African-American, 1.2 percent are Asian, and 0.5 percent are American Indian. Although the number of nonwhite psychologists currently in graduate school is higher, the numbers are still not representative of the proportion of minorities in society at large. In fact, the gains have not even kept up with the increasing growth of minority populations (APA, 1994).

The underrepresentation of racial and ethnic minorities among psychologists is significant for several reasons. First, the field of psychology may be diminished by a lack of the diverse perspectives and talents provided by minority-group members. Furthermore, minority-group psychologists serve as role models for members of minority communities. Their lack of representation within the profession may deter additional minority-group members from seeking to enter the field (King, 1993).

Finally, members of minority groups frequently prefer to receive psychological therapy and counseling from treatment providers of the same race or ethnic group as their own. The relative rarity of minority psychologists may therefore discourage some members of minority groups from seeking treatment. Consequently, both the American Psychological Association and individual graduate schools are vigorously seeking to increase the numbers of psychologists from underrepresented groups (Sue & Sue, 1990; Fowler, 1993; Allison et al., 1994).

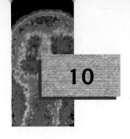
The Education of a Psychologist   How do people become psychologists? The most common route is a long one. Most psychologists have a doctoral graduate degree, in the form of either a Ph.D. or (less frequently) a Psy.D. The Ph.D. is a research degree, requiring a dissertation based on an original investigation, while the Psy.D. is a degree obtained by psychologists who wish to focus on the treatment of psychological disorders. Both the Ph.D. and Psy.D. typically take four or five years of work past the bachelor's level (Ellis, 1992).

Some fields of psychology involve education beyond the doctorate. For instance, doctoral-level clinical psychologists, who deal with people with psychological disorders, usually spend a year on an internship. They can be licensed by a state accreditation board.

Although most psychologists have a doctoral degree, not everyone who works in the field of psychology has a doctorate. About a third have a master's degree, which is earned following two or three years of graduate work. Masters-level psychologists may teach, conduct research under the supervision of a doctoral-level psychologist, or work in specialized programs dealing with drug abuse or crisis intervention (APA, 1993). Still, career opportunities are more limited for those with a master's degree than for those with a doctorate.

An undergraduate major in psychology provides worthwhile preparation for a variety of occupations, although it does not allow professional work in psychology per se. For instance, many people in business, nursing, law, social work, and other professions report that an undergraduate background in psychology has proved invaluable in their careers.

People other than psychologists also deal with psychological issues, but their training tends to differ from that of psychologists in significant ways. For instance, although psychiatrists deal with people with psychological disorders, they have medical degrees and have the capability of prescribing medicine. Trained initially as physicians, they often focus on the physical causes of psychological disorders. Consequently, they may be more apt to employ treatments involving drugs, rather than focusing on psychological causes. In addition, people in allied fields such as social work, marriage counseling, and school counseling often deal with psychological issues. However, their direct training in psychology is more limited than that attained by psychologists.

RECAP AND REVIEW

Recap

- Psychology is the scientific study of behavior and mental processes.
- Among the major kinds of psychologists are biopsychologists; experimental psychologists; cognitive psychologists; developmental and personality psychologists; health, clinical, and counseling psychologists; educational and school psychologists; and cross-cultural psychologists.
- Many psychologists are employed by institutions of higher learning, and the balance are employed by hospitals, clinics, and community health centers or are engaged in private practice.

Review

1. The foundation of psychology today lies in
   a. Intuition
   b. Observation and experimentation
   c. Trial and error
   d. Metaphysics

2. Match each branch of psychology with the issues or questions posed below.
   a. Biopsychology
   b. Experimental psychology
   c. Cognitive psychology
   d. Developmental psychology
   e. Personality psychology
   f. Health psychology
   g. Clinical psychology
   h. Counseling psychology
   i. Educational psychology
   j. School psychology
   k. Social psychology
   l. Industrial psychology
   m. Consumer psychology

   1. Joan, a college freshman, is panicking. She needs to learn better organizational skills and study habits to cope with the demands of college.

2. At what age do children generally begin to acquire an emotional attachment to their fathers?
3. It is thought that pornographic films that depict violence against women may prompt aggressive behavior in some men.
4. What chemicals are released in the human body as a result of a stressful event? What are their effects on behavior?
5. John is unique in his manner of responding to crisis situations, with an even temperament and a positive outlook.
6. The general public is more apt to buy products that are promoted by attractive and successful actors.
7. The teachers of 8-year-old Jack are concerned that he has recently begun to withdraw socially and to show little interest in schoolwork.
8. Janet's job is demanding and stressful. She wonders if her lifestyle is making her more prone to certain illnesses such as cancer and heart disease.
9. A psychologist is intrigued by the fact that some people are much more sensitive to painful stimuli than others.
10. A strong fear of crowds leads a young woman to seek treatment for her problem.
11. What mental strategies are involved in solving complex word problems?
12. What teaching methods most effectively motivate elementary school students to successfully accomplish academic tasks?
13. Jessica is asked by her company to develop a management strategy that will encourage safer work practices in an assembly plant.

Ask Yourself

Imagine you had a 7-year-old child who was having problems learning to read. Imagine further that you could consult as many psychologists as you wanted. How might each type of psychologist approach the problem?

Are intuition and common sense sufficient for understanding why people act the way they do? Why is a scientific approach appropriate for studying human behavior?

(Answers to review questions are on page 12.)

* *What are the historical roots of the field of psychology?*
* *What major approaches are used by contemporary psychologists?*
* *What is the future of psychology likely to hold?*

A SCIENCE EVOLVES: THE PAST, THE PRESENT, AND THE FUTURE

Some half-million years ago, primitive peoples assumed that psychological problems were caused by the presence of evil spirits. To allow these spirits to escape, ancient healers performed an operation called trephining. Trephining consisted of chipping away at the skull with crude stone instruments until a hole was cut through the bone. Because archaeologists have found skulls with signs of healing around the opening, we can assume that patients sometimes managed to survive the cure.

The famous Greek physician Hippocrates thought that personality was made up of four temperaments: sanguine (cheerful and active), melancholic (sad), choleric (angry and aggressive), and phlegmatic (calm and passive). These temperaments were influenced by the presence of "humors," or fluids, in the body. If one humor was out of balance, a physician would seek to either increase the deficient humor (through a medicinal potion) or decrease the excess (often through bloodletting).

According to the philosopher Descartes, nerves were hollow tubes through which "animal spirits" conducted impulses in the same way that water is transmitted through a pipe. When a person put a finger too close to the fire, the heat was transmitted via the spirits through the tube, directly into the brain.

Franz Josef Gall, a physician born in the 1700s, argued that a trained observer could discern intelligence, moral character, and other basic personality characteristics from the shape and number of bumps on a person's skull. His theory gave rise to the "science" of phrenology, employed by hundreds of devoted practitioners in the nineteenth century.

Descartes' assertion that the nerves were hollow tubes, through which impulses such as heat could flow, was once widely accepted.

11

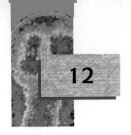
While these "scientific" explanations may sound farfetched, at one time they represented the most advanced thinking regarding what might be called the psychology of the era. Even without knowing much about modern-day psychology, you can surmise that our understanding of behavior has advanced tremendously since these earlier views were formulated. Yet most of the advances have been recent, for, as sciences go, psychology is one of the new kids on the block.

Although its roots can be traced back to the ancient Greeks and Romans, and although philosophers have argued for several hundred years about some of the same sorts of questions that psychologists grapple with today, the formal beginning of psychology is generally set at 1879. In that year, Wilhelm Wundt established the first laboratory devoted to the experimental study of psychological phenomena in Leipzig, Germany. At about the same time, the American William James was setting up his laboratory in Cambridge, Massachusetts.

Throughout its almost twelve decades of formal existence, psychology has led an active and dynamic life, gradually developing into a true science (Hilgard, Leary, & McGuire, 1991; Robinson, 1995). As part of this evolution, it has produced a number of conceptual perspectives, or *models*. These perspectives represent organized systems of interrelated ideas and concepts used to explain phenomena. Some of these perspectives have been discarded—as have the views of Hippocrates and Descartes—but others have been elaborated and provide a set of maps for psychologists to follow.

Each of the perspectives offers a distinctive outlook, emphasizing different factors. Just as we may employ not one but many maps to find our way around a particular geographical area—one map to show the roads, one the major landmarks, and one the topography of the hills and valleys—psychologists also find more than one approach useful in understanding behavior. Given the range and complexity of behavior, no single perspective or model will invariably provide an optimal explanation. Together, though, the differing perspectives provide us with a means to explain the extraordinary breadth of behavior.

The Roots of Psychology

When Wilhelm Wundt set up the first psychology laboratory in 1879, his aim was to study the building blocks of the mind. Considering psychology to be the study of conscious experience, he developed a model that came to be known as structuralism. **Structuralism** focused on the fundamental elements that form the foundation of thinking, consciousness, emotions, and other kinds of mental states and activities.

To come to an understanding of how basic sensations combined to produce our awareness of the world, Wundt and other structuralists used a procedure called **introspection** to study the structure of the mind. In introspection, people were presented with a stimulus—such as a bright green object or a sentence printed on a card—and asked to describe, in their own words and in as much detail as they could manage, what they were experiencing. Wundt argued that psychologists could come to understand the structure of the mind through the reports that people offered of their reactions.

Wundt's structuralism did not stand the test of time, however. Psychologists became increasingly dissatisfied with the assumption that introspection could unlock the fundamental elements of the mind. For one thing, people had difficulty describing some kinds of inner experiences, such as emotional responses. (Try to analyze and explain the primary elements of what you are feeling the next time you experience anger, for instance.)

Structuralism: An early approach to psychology which focused on the fundamental elements that form the foundation of thinking, consciousness, emotions, and other kinds of mental states and activities.

Introspection: A procedure used to study the structure of the mind, in which subjects are asked to describe in detail what they are experiencing when they are exposed to a stimulus.

ANSWERS TO PREVIOUS REVIEW
1. b **2.** h-1; d-2; k-3; a-4; e-5; m-6; j-7; f-8; b-9; g-10; c-11; i-12; l-13

Moreover, breaking down objects into their most basic mental units sometimes seemed to be a most peculiar undertaking. A book, for example, could not be described by a structuralist as merely a book, but instead had to be broken down into its various components, such as the material on the cover, the colors, the shapes of the letters, and so on. Finally, introspection was not a truly scientific technique. There were few ways in which an outside observer could verify the accuracy of the introspections that people did make. Such drawbacks led to the evolution of new models, which largely supplanted structuralism.

Interestingly, however, important remnants of structuralism still exist. As we shall see in Chapter 7, the past 20 years have seen a resurgence of interest in people's descriptions of their inner experience. Cognitive psychologists, who focus on higher mental processes such as thinking, memory, and problem solving, have developed innovative techniques for understanding people's conscious experience that overcome many of the difficulties inherent in introspection.

The model that largely replaced structuralism in the evolution of psychology was known as functionalism. Rather than focusing on the mind's components, **functionalism** concentrated on what the mind *does*—the functions of mental activity. Functionalists, whose model rose to prominence in the early 1900s, asked what roles behavior plays in allowing people to better adapt to their environments. Led by the American psychologist William James, the functionalists, rather than raising the more abstract questions about the processes of mental behavior, examined the ways in which behavior allows people to satisfy their needs (Johnson & Henley, 1990). By using functionalism, the famous American educator John Dewey developed the field of school psychology, proposing ways that students' educational needs could best be met.

Functionalism: An early approach to psychology that concentrated on what the mind does—the functions of mental activity—and the role of behavior in allowing people to adapt to their environments.

Another reaction to structuralism was the development of gestalt psychology in the early 1900s. **Gestalt psychology** is a model focusing on the study of how perception is organized. Instead of considering the individual parts that make up thinking, gestalt psychologists took the opposite tack, concentrating on how people consider individual elements together as units or wholes. Their credo was "The whole is different from the sum of its parts," meaning that, when considered together, the basic elements that compose our perception of objects produce something greater and more meaningful than those individual elements alone. As we shall see when we examine sensation and perception in Chapter 3, the contributions of gestalt psychologists to the understanding of perception are substantial.

Gestalt (geh SHTALLT) **psychology:** An approach to psychology that focuses on the organization of perception and thinking in a "whole" sense, rather than on the individual elements of perception.

Women in Psychology: Founding Mothers

Despite societal constraints that limited women's participation in many professions—and psychology was no exception—several women made major contributions to psychology in the early years of the field (Russo & Denmark, 1987). For example, in the early part of the century Leta Stetter Hollingworth coined the term "gifted" in reference to unusually bright children, and she wrote a book on adolescence that became a classic (Hollingworth, 1928). She was also one of the first psychologists to focus particularly on women's issues. For instance, she collected data to refute the view, popular in the early 1900s, that women's abilities regularly declined during parts of the menstrual cycle (Benjamin & Shields, 1990; Hollingworth, 1943/1990).

Another influential figure was June Etta Downey, who spearheaded the study of personality traits in the 1920s. She also developed a widely disseminated personality test and became the first woman to head a psychology department at a state university (Stevens & Gardner, 1982).

Despite the contributions of such women, psychology was largely a male-dominated field in its early years. However, the situation has been changing over the past decade, and as mentioned earlier, the number of women in the discipline has been increasing rapidly in recent years. Consequently, when future historians of science write about psychology in the 1990s, they are likely to be recording a history of men *and* women (Denmark, 1994).

Today's Perspectives

The early roots of psychology are complex and varied. It is not surprising, then, that the field is so diverse today. However, it is possible to encompass the breadth of psychology by using just a few basic perspectives: the biological, psychodynamic, cognitive, behavioral, and humanistic perspectives. Each of these broad perspectives, which continue to evolve, emphasizes different aspects of behavior and mental processes and steers the thinking of psychologists in somewhat different directions.

The Biological Perspective: Blood, Sweat, and Fears   When we get down to the basics, behavior is carried out by living creatures made of skin and guts. According to the **biological perspective,** the behavior of both people and animals should be considered in terms of their biological functioning: how the individual nerve cells are joined together, how the inheritance of certain characteristics from parents and other ancestors influences behavior, how the functioning of the body affects hopes and fears, what behaviors are due to instincts, and so forth. Even more complex kinds of behaviors, such as a baby's response to strangers, are viewed as having critical biological components by psychologists using the biological perspective.

Because every behavior can at some level be broken down into its biological components, the biological perspective has broad appeal. Psychologists who subscribe to this perspective have made major contributions to the understanding and betterment of human life, ranging from developing cures for certain types of deafness to identifying drugs to treat people with severe mental disorders.

The Psychodynamic Perspective: Understanding the Inner Person   To many people who have never taken a psychology course, psychology begins and ends with the psychodynamic perspective. Proponents of the **psychodynamic perspective** believe that behavior is motivated by inner forces and conflicts over which the individual has little awareness and control. Dreams and slips of the tongue are viewed as indications of what a person is truly feeling within a seething cauldron of unconscious psychic activity.

The psychodynamic view is intimately linked with one individual: Sigmund Freud. Freud was a Viennese physician in the early 1900s whose ideas about unconscious determinants of behavior had a revolutionary effect on twentieth-century thinking, not just in psychology but in related fields as well. Although many of the basic principles of psychodynamic thinking have been roundly criticized, the perspective that has grown out of Freud's work has provided a means not only for treating mental disorders but for understanding everyday phenomena such as prejudice and aggression.

The Cognitive Perspective: Comprehending the Roots of Understanding   The route to understanding behavior leads some psychologists straight into the mind. Evolving in part from structuralism, the **cognitive perspective** focuses on the processes that permit people to know, understand, and think about the world. The emphasis here is on learning how people understand and represent the outside world within themselves. Cognitive psychologists seek to explain how we process information and how our ways of thinking about the world influence our behavior.

Psychologists relying on this perspective ask questions ranging from whether a person can watch television and study at the same time (the answer is "proba-

Biological perspective: The psychological model that views behavior from the perspective of biological functioning.

Psychodynamic perspective: The psychological model based on the belief that behavior is motivated by inner forces over which the individual has little control.

Cognitive perspective: The psychological model that focuses on how people know, understand, and think about the world.

Sigmund Freud (1856–1939) provided the impetus for the psychodynamic perspective, which sees the roots of human behavior as residing in the unconscious.

bly not") to how people figure out for themselves the causes of others' behavior. The common elements that link cognitive approaches are an emphasis on how people understand and think about the world and a concern about describing the patterns and regularities of the operation of our minds.

The Behavioral Perspective: Observing the Outer Person   While the biological, psychodynamic, and cognitive approaches look inside the organism to determine the causes of its behavior, the behavioral perspective takes a very different approach. The **behavioral perspective** grew out of a rejection of psychology's early emphasis on the inner workings of the mind, suggesting instead that observable behavior should be the focus of the field.

John B. Watson was the first major American psychologist to advocate a behavioral approach. Working in the 1920s, Watson was adamant in his view that one could gain a complete understanding of behavior by studying and modifying the environment in which people operated. In fact, he believed rather optimistically that, by properly controlling a person's environment, one could elicit any desired sort of behavior. His own words make this philosophy clear: "Give me a dozen healthy infants, well-formed, and my own specified world to bring them up in and I'll guarantee to take any one at random and train him to become any type of specialist I might select—doctor, lawyer, artist, merchant-chief, and yes, even beggar-man and thief, regardless of his talents, penchants, tendencies, abilities, vocations and race of his ancestors" (Watson, 1924). In more recent times, the behavioral perspective was championed by B.F. Skinner, who, until his death in 1990, was the best-known contemporary psychologist. Much of our understanding of how people learn new behaviors is based on the behavioral perspective.

As we will see, the behavioral perspective crops up along every byway of psychology. Along with the influence it has had in the area of learning processes, this perspective has also made contributions in such diverse areas as the treatment of mental disorders, the curbing of aggression, the resolution of sexual problems, and even the halting of drug addiction.

The Humanistic Perspective: The Unique Qualities of *Homo sapiens*   Although it emerged several decades ago, the humanistic perspective is still considered the newest of the major approaches. Rejecting the views that behavior is determined largely by automatic biological forces, by unconscious processes, or solely by the environment, the **humanistic perspective** instead suggests that people are naturally endowed with the capacity to make decisions about their lives and to control their behavior.

Humanistic psychologists maintain that everyone has the power to develop higher levels of maturity and fulfillment. In their view, people will strive to reach their full potential if given the opportunity. The emphasis, then, is on **free will**, the human ability to make decisions about one's life.

The humanistic perspective assumes that people have the ability to make their own choices about their behavior, rather than relying on societal standards. In this view, someone who strives only for an unchallenging, menial job would be no worse—or no better—than a person who has higher aspirations.

More than any other approach, the humanistic perspective stresses the role of psychology in enriching people's lives and helping them to achieve self-fulfillment. While somewhat more limited than the other general perspectives, the humanistic perspective has had an important influence on psychologists, reminding them of their commitment to the individual person and society.

It is important not to let the abstract qualities of the humanistic perspective, as well as the other broad approaches we have discussed, lull you into thinking that they are purely theoretical: These perspectives underlie ongoing work of a practical nature as will be described throughout this book. As a start, consider the accompanying Psychology at Work box.

Behavioral perspective: The psychological model that suggests that observable behavior should be the focus of study.

John B. Watson (1878–1958), the originator of the behavioral perspective, in which observable responses to stimuli are emphasized.

Humanistic perspective: The psychological model that suggests that people are in control of their lives.

Free will: The human ability to make decisions about one's life.

PSYCHOLOGY AT WORK

Psychology and the Prevention of Violence

As he walks calmly through a Long Island Railroad car, Colin Ferguson shoots several rounds of ammunition from a handgun, killing five people and injuring twenty-three others.

A hired hitman smashes a portable nightstick into the knee of figure skater Nancy Kerrigan in an effort to keep her from competing in the winter Olympics.

A woman is killed by two teenage muggers during a robbery which nets the perpetrators less than $2.

It has been called the twentieth-century plague: violence in the United States. Surveys show that violence and crime rank at the top of any list of concerns for most Americans (New York Times/CBS News Poll, 1994).

Yet violence has not gone unchallenged. In fact, the field of psychology has come to play a key role in the fight against violence. Psychologists specializing in many areas, employing the major perspectives of the field, have made concerted efforts to quell the spread of the disease and to deal with its aftermaths (APA Public Interest Directorate, 1993; Farley, 1993). Their work is reflected in several questions being asked by psychologists:

• What measures can be taken to reduce the incidence of violence against minority-group members? Although violence represents a significant threat for all children and youth of both sexes, African-American males are particularly at risk. For example, the most frequent cause of death for male African-American adolescents is injuries stemming from a gun used by a friend or acquaintance. The higher rate of violence among African-American youth may be related to such factors as perpetrators' sense of hopelessness over

the future and exposure to a sub-culture of violence (Fingerhut, Ingram, & Feldman, 1992; Hammond & Yung, 1993).

Psychologists have devised several intervention programs targeted to African-American adolescents. For instance, one program taught social skills to be employed in situations in which conflicts are likely to lead to violence. After watching a series of videotapes using peer role models, participants in the program were less likely to fight and be arrested than nonparticipants (Hammond & Yung, 1991). In another approach, elementary-school-aged African-Americans were taught to modify their interpretations of others' actions. For example, they were taught to avoid leaping to the conclusion that others' behavior was intended to upset them. The training resulted in a reduction of anger in the face of provocation (Graham & Hudley, 1992). One fact that has emerged quite clearly from this research is the requirement that programs be culturally, ethnically, and racially sensitive (Hammond & Yung, 1993).

• How prevalent is violence on television? It is clear that violence on television is common. One survey found that of ninety-four prime-time programs examined, forty-eight showed at least one act of violence, and they included fifty-seven people killed and ninety-nine assaulted (Hansen & Knopes, 1993). Furthermore, the rate of violent crime depicted on television was almost twice as high as that found in real life in the United States. Children's television, too, features high rates of violence. In the 1992–1993 season, for instance, the frequency of violence in children's programs was eighteen violent scenes per hour (Gerbner, Morgan, & Signorielli, 1993; Waters, 1993).

Does observation of television violence promote real-world violence? Although they cannot be fully certain, most psychologists investigating aggression agree that observation of media aggression enhances the likelihood that viewers will act aggressively. Furthermore, it serves to desensitize viewers to displays of aggression, leading them to react with passivity to actual incidents of aggression (Berkowitz, 1993).

• Is there a hormonal link to aggression? Psychologist James Dabbs, Jr., thinks so, based on research in the areas of biopsychology and social psychology. He and his colleagues examined the level of testosterone, a male hormone, in almost 5000 U.S. Army veterans. Examining men with the highest and lowest levels of testosterone, Dabbs found that those in the high-testosterone group were more likely to be involved in a variety of aggressive and antisocial behaviors than were men in the low-testosterone group (Dabbs & Morris, 1990).

• Is there a cycle of violence, and how can we stop it? Child abusers have often been victims of abuse in their own childhood. According to the "cycle of-violence" explanation, abuse and neglect make children more likely to abuse and neglect their own children (Widom, 1989; Dodge, Bates, & Petit, 1990). This notion suggests that violence is perpetuated as each generation learns from the preceding one how to behave abusively.

Developmental psychologists, who study growth and change throughout the life span, have found a considerable amount of evidence to support the cycle-of-violence notion. However, such evidence does not tell the full story: Being abused does not inevitably lead to abuse of one's own children. Only one-third of people who have been abused or neglected as children go on to abuse their own children (Kaufman & Zigler, 1987). Current research is aimed at determining when a childhood history of abuse is most likely to result in adult violence, and how the cycle can be broken.

As we can see, psychologists are playing important and quite varied roles in combating violence. And violence is not the only societal problem for which psychologists are contributing their expertise in

an effort to alleviate human suffering. As we will explore in other Psychology at Work boxes, the basic principles of psychology are being used to address a wide range of social problems.

- *What are psychology's key issues and controversies?*
- *What is the future of psychology likely to hold?*

CONNECTIONS: PSYCHOLOGY'S UNIFYING THEMES

As you consider the many topical areas and perspectives that make up the field of psychology, you may find yourself thinking that you've embarked on a journey into a fragmented discipline that lacks cohesion. You may fear that psychology consists merely of a series of unrelated, separate subject areas, no closer to one another than physics is to chemistry. In fact, such a conclusion is not an unreasonable one, given that psychology covers so many diverse areas, ranging from topics as narrowly focused as the minute biochemical influences on behavior to social behavior in its broadest sense.

Yet despite the seeming disparity among the various topics and perspectives, the differences in some ways are more apparent than real. The field is actually more unified than a first glimpse may imply, in terms of both the links between psychology's branches and perspectives and the key issues that psychologists address.

The Links between Psychology's Branches and Perspectives

The field's five major perspectives play an important role in integrating the various branches of the discipline. Specifically, a psychologist from any given branch might choose to employ any one, or more, of the major perspectives.

For example, a developmental psychologist might subscribe to the psychodynamic perspective *or* the behavioral perspective *or* any of the other perspectives. Similarly, a clinical psychologist might use the behavioral perspective *or* the cognitive perspective *or* one of the other perspectives. The perspectives may be used in different ways by various psychologists, but the assumptions of a given perspective are similar regardless of the subfield to which it is applied.

Of course, not every branch of psychology is equally likely to employ a particular perspective. Historically, some kinds of psychologists have been more apt to rely on certain perspectives, and some perspectives have proved more useful than others when attempting to deal with a particular topical area.

For example, biopsychologists studying the brain are most likely to employ the biological perspective, given its emphasis on the biological foundations of behavior. At the same time, most biopsychologists reject the psychodynamic perspective's reliance on unconscious determinants of behavior. Similarly, social psychologists who are interested in explaining the roots of prejudice are more likely to find the cognitive perspective of use than the biological perspective.

TABLE 1-1 Positions Taken by Psychologists Using the Major Perspectives of Psychology

Issue	Perspective				
	Biological	Psychodynamic	Cognitive	Behavioral	Humanistic
Nature (heredity) vs. nurture (environment)	Nature (heredity)	Nature (heredity)	Both	Nurture (environment)	Nurture (environment)
Conscious vs. unconscious determinants of behavior	Unconscious	Unconscious	Both	Conscious	Conscious
Observable behavior vs. internal mental processes	Internal emphasis	Internal emphasis	Internal emphasis	Observable emphasis	Internal emphasis
Freedom vs. determinism	Determinism	Determinism	Freedom	Determinism	Freedom
Individual differences vs. universal principles	Universal emphasis	Universal emphasis	Individual emphasis	Both	Individual emphasis

Table 1-1 indicates which major models of psychology are most likely to be used by the different types of psychologists. Keep in mind, though, that at least in theory each of the models is available to any psychologist who chooses to employ it.

Psychology's Future

We've examined the foundations from which the field of psychology has evolved. But what does the future hold for the discipline? Although the course of scientific development is notoriously difficult to predict, several trends do seem likely to emerge in the not-so-distant future:

■ Psychology will become increasingly specialized. In a field in which practitioners must be experts on such diverse topics as the intricacies of the transmission of electrochemical impulses across nerve endings and the communication patterns of employees in large organizations, no one individual can be expected to master the field. Thus, it is likely that specialization will increase as psychologists delve into new areas (Bower, 1993; Koch, 1993).

■ New perspectives will evolve. As a growing, maturing science, psychology will develop new perspectives to supplant current approaches. Moreover, older perspectives may be merged to form new ones. We can be certain, then, that as psychologists accumulate more knowledge they will become increasingly sophisticated in their understanding of behavior and mental processes (Boneau, 1992; Gibson, 1994; Kimble, 1994).

■ Psychology will take the growing diversity of the country's population into account. As the population of the United States becomes more diverse, it will become more critical to consider racial, ethnic, linguistic, and cultural factors both when providing psychological services and when conducting research. The result will be a field that can provide an understanding of human behavior in its broadest sense (Goodchilds, 1991; Brislin, 1993; Lee, 1994).

■ Psychological treatment will become more accessible and socially acceptable as the number of psychologists increases. More psychologists will focus on prevention of psychological disturbance, rather than just on its treatment. In addition, they will act as consultants to the growing number of volunteer and self-help groups in an effort to assist the members of such groups to help themselves more effectively (Jacobs & Goodman, 1989; Fox, 1994).

■ Psychology's influence on issues in the public interest will grow. Each of the major problems of our time—such as the threat of nuclear war, racial and ethnic prejudice, poverty, environmental and technological disasters—has important psychological implications (Archer, Pettigrew, & Aronson, 1992; Calkins, 1993; Wiggins, 1994; Cowdry, 1995). While psychology alone will not solve these problems, its major accomplishments in the past (many of which are documented in other chapters of this book) foretell that psychologists will make important practical contributions toward their resolution.

RECAP AND REVIEW

Recap
- Traces of the early perspectives of structuralism, functionalism, and gestalt psychology can be seen in the major perspectives used by psychologists today.
- The dominant psychological perspectives encompass biological, psychodynamic, cognitive, behavioral, and humanistic approaches.
- In the future, the field of psychology is likely to become more specialized, to evolve new perspectives, to take the increasing diversity of the country's population into account more fully, and to become increasingly concerned with the public interest.

Review
1. Wundt described psychology as the study of conscious experience, a perspective he termed _Structuralism_.
2. Early psychologists studied the mind by asking people to describe what they were experiencing when exposed to various stimuli. This procedure was known as _introspection_.
3. The statement "In order to study human behavior, we must consider the whole of perception rather than its component parts" is one that might be made by a person subscribing to which perspective of psychology? _gestalt_
4. Jeanne's therapist asks her to recount a violent dream she had recently experienced in order to gain insight into the unconscious forces affecting her behavior. Jeanne's therapist is working from a _Psychodynamic_ perspective.

5. "It is behavior that can be observed which should be studied, not the suspected inner workings of the mind." This statement was most likely made by someone following the
   a. Cognitive perspective
   b. Biological perspective
   c. Humanistic perspective
   d. Behavioral perspective
6. "My therapist is wonderful! She always points out my positive traits. She dwells on my uniqueness and strength as an individual. I feel much more confident about myself—as if I'm really growing and reaching my potential." The therapist referred to above most likely practices from a _humanist_ perspective.
7. Each branch of psychology has a perspective unique to it. True or false?
8. Identify the perspective that suggests that abnormal behavior may be the result of largely unconscious forces. _Psychodynamic_
9. "Psychologists should only worry about behavior that is directly observable." This statement would most likely be made by a person using which psychological perspective?
   behavioral

Ask Yourself
How are today's major perspectives of psychology related to the earlier models of structuralism, functionalism, and gestalt psychology?

(Answers to review questions are on page 20.)

- *What is the scientific method, and how do psychologists use theory and research to answer questions of interest?*
- *What are the different research methods employed by psychologists?*
- *How do psychologists establish cause-and-effect relationships in research studies?*

RESEARCH IN PSYCHOLOGY

It was an image that few who saw the videotape would ever forget: As a large group of police officers and other bystanders watched, Rodney King received dozens of blows from police billy clubs. With the wire of a stun gun that had earlier delivered thousands of volts still wrapped around him, he was repeatedly kicked and pummeled. The beating continued for several minutes, as onlookers watched impassively or chatted with one another. King suffered several fractures, a shattered cheekbone, a ruptured eye socket, and a broken leg. Not one person intervened.

Of the two dozen police officers who were present at the beatings of Rodney King, only these four were brought to trial. The others stood by, unwilling to step in and try to stop the violence.

Why did no one come to King's rescue? The civilians observing the scene may have justified their behavior by rationalizing that the beating was a police matter, and thus a situation to be handled by law enforcement personnel. Yet even that weak excuse does not apply to those police officers who stood watch. In fact, several of the officers later admitted that, although they thought the beating was unjustifiable, they felt somehow unable to intervene. Consequently, they were merely passive bystanders as King received one incapacitating blow after another, in clear violation of police regulations.

The troubling question remains: Why did no one intervene?

Were this an isolated incident, we might be able to attribute the bystanders' inaction to something specific about the situation. However, events such as this one are all too common.

For example, in another famous case, a woman named Kitty Genovese was attacked by a man near an apartment building in New York City in the mid-1960s. At one point during the assault, which lasted 30 minutes, she managed to free herself and scream, "Oh, my God, he stabbed me. Please help me!" In the stillness of the night, no fewer than thirty-eight neighbors heard her screams. Windows opened and lights went on. One couple pulled chairs up to the window and turned off the lights so they could see better. Someone called out, "Let that girl alone." But shouts were not enough to scare off the killer. He chased her, stabbing her eight more times, and sexually molested her before leaving her to die. And how many of those thirty-eight witnesses came to her aid? As with Rodney King, not one person helped.

The cases of Rodney King and Kitty Genovese both remain dismaying—and puzzling—examples of "bad Samaritanism." The general public, as well as psychologists, found it difficult to explain how so many people could stand by without coming to the aid of helpless victims.

One easy explanation, supplied by many editorial writers, was that the incidents could be attributed to the basic shortcomings of "human nature." But such a supposition is woefully inadequate. For one thing, there are numerous examples of people who have placed their own lives at risk to help others in dangerous situations.

Clearly, then, "human nature" encompasses a wide range of both negative and positive responses. Consequently it does not provide a very satisfying explanation for the bystanders' unhelpful behavior. The mystery, then, of how to explain the lack of bystander intervention in both incidents remained unsolved.

Psychologists in particular puzzled over the problem for many years. After much research they finally reached an unexpected conclusion: Both Rodney King and Kitty Genovese might well have been better off had there been just a few people who heard their cries for help rather than the many that did. In fact, had there been just one bystander present in each instance, the chances of that person intervening might have been fairly high. For it turns out that the *fewer* witnesses present in a situation such as the two in question, the better the victim's chances of getting help.

How did psychologists come to such a curious conclusion? After all, logic and common sense clearly suggest that more bystanders would mean a greater likelihood that someone would help a person in need. This seeming contradiction— and the way psychologists resolved it—illustrates a central task for the field of psychology: the challenge of asking and answering questions of interest.

Posing Questions: Theories and Hypotheses

The challenge of appropriately framing those questions of interest to psychologists and properly answering them has been met through reliance on the scientific method. The **scientific method** is an approach used by psychologists, as well as researchers in other scientific disciplines, to better their understanding about the world (Hazen & Trefil, 1991). It consists of three main steps: (1) identifying questions of interest, (2) formulating an explanation, and (3) carrying out research designed to lend support to or refute the explanation.

Theories: Specifying Broad Explanations   In using the scientific method, psychologists start with the kinds of observations about behavior with which we are all familiar. If you have ever asked yourself why a particular teacher is so easily annoyed, why a friend is always late for appointments, or how your dog understands your commands, you have been formulating questions about behavior. Psychologists, too, ask questions about the nature and causes of behavior, although their questions are typically more precise.

Once a question has been formulated, the next step in the scientific method involves developing theories to explain the phenomenon that has been observed. **Theories** are broad explanations and predictions concerning phenomena of interest. They provide a framework for understanding the relationships among a set of otherwise unorganized facts or principles.

Growing out of the diverse perspectives of psychology as described earlier in this chapter, theories vary both in their breadth and in the particular level of detail they employ. For example, one theory might seek to explain and predict as broad a phenomenon as emotional experience in general. A more narrow theory might purport to predict how people display the emotion of fear nonverbally after receiving a threat. An even more specific theory might attempt to explain how the muscles of the face work in tandem to produce expressions of fear.

All of us have developed our own informal theories of human behavior, such as "People are basically good" or "People's behavior is usually motivated by self-interest" (Sternberg, 1985a). However, psychologists' theories are more formal and focused. They are established on the basis of a careful study of the psychological literature to identify relevant research conducted and theories formulated previously, as well as psychologists' general knowledge of the field.

Psychologists Bibb Latané and John Darley, responding specifically to the Kitty Genovese case, developed a theory based on a phenomenon they called *diffusion of responsibility* (Latané & Darley, 1970). According to their theory, the greater the number of bystanders or witnesses to an event that requires helping behavior, the more the responsibility for helping is perceived to be shared by all the bystanders. Because of this sense of shared responsibility, then, the more people present in an emergency situation, the less personally responsible each person feels—and the less likely it is that any single person will come forward to help.

Hypotheses: Crafting Testable Predictions   While such a theory makes sense, it represented only the beginning phase of Latané and Darley's investigative process. Their next step was to devise a way of testing their theory. To do this, they needed to derive a hypothesis. A **hypothesis** is a prediction stated in a way that allows it to be tested. Hypotheses stem from theories, helping to test the underlying validity of the theory.

Just as we have our own broad theories about the world, so do we develop hypotheses about events and behavior (ranging from trivialities, such as why our English professor is such an eccentric, to what is the best way for people to study). Although we rarely test them systematically, we do try to determine whether they are right or not. Perhaps we try cramming for one exam but study

Scientific method: The process of appropriately framing and properly answering questions, used by practitioners of psychology and those engaged in other scientific disciplines, to come to an understanding about the world.

Theories: Broad explanations and predictions concerning phenomena of interest.

Hypothesis (hy POTH eh sis): A prediction stated in a way that allows it to be tested.

The concept of diffusion of responsibilty helps explain why individuals in a crowd are not likley to assist strangers in distress; each bystander assumes that others will take the responsibility for helping.

over a longer period of time for another. By assessing the results, we have created a way to compare the two strategies.

Latané and Darley's hypothesis was a straightforward derivation from their more general theory of diffusion of responsibility: The more people who witness an emergency situation, the less likely it is that help will be given to a victim. They could, of course, have chosen another hypothesis (for instance, that people with greater skills related to emergency situations will not be affected by the presence of others), but their initial formulation seemed to offer the most direct test of the theory.

Psychologists rely on formal theories and hypotheses for many reasons. For one thing, theories and hypotheses allow psychologists to make sense of unorganized, separate observations and bits of information by permitting them to be placed within a structured and coherent framework. In addition, theories and hypotheses offer psychologists the opportunity to move beyond already known facts and principles and to make deductions about as yet unexplained phenomena. In this way, theories and hypotheses provide a reasoned guide to the direction that future investigation ought to take.

In sum, then, theories and hypotheses help psychologists pose the appropriate questions. How are such questions answered? As we shall see, the answers come from research, the systematic inquiry aimed at the discovery of new knowledge.

Finding Answers: Psychological Research

Just as we can develop several theories and hypotheses to explain particular phenomena, we also can use a considerable number of alternative means to carry out research. First, though, the hypothesis must be restated in a way that will allow it to be tested, a procedure known as operationalization. **Operationalization** is the process of translating a hypothesis into specific, testable procedures that can be measured and observed. There is no single way to go about operationalizing a hypothesis; it depends on logic, the equipment and facilities available, the psychological model being employed, and ultimately the ingenuity of the researcher (Creswell, 1994).

We will consider several of the major weapons in the psychologist's research arsenal. As we discuss these research methods, keep in mind that their relevance

Operationalization: The process of translating a hypothesis into specific testable procedures that can be measured and observed.

extends beyond testing and evaluating theories and hypotheses in psychology (Aronson et al., 1990). Even if they do not have a degree in psychology, for instance, people often carry out rudimentary forms of research on their own. For example, a boss may need to evaluate her employee's performance. A physician might systematically test the effects of different dosages of a drug on a patient. A salesperson may compare different persuasive strategies. Each of these situations calls for the use of the research practices we are about to discuss.

Archival Research   Suppose that, like psychologists Latané and Darley, you were interested in finding out more about emergency situations in which bystanders did not provide help. One of the first places to which you might turn would be historical accounts. By using newspaper records, for example, you might find support for the notion that a decrease in helping behavior has accompanied an increase in the number of bystanders.

Using newspaper articles is an example of archival research. In **archival research,** existing records, such as census data, birth certificates, or newspaper clippings, are examined to confirm a hypothesis. Archival research is a relatively inexpensive means of testing a hypothesis, since someone else has already collected the basic data. Of course, the use of already-existing data has several drawbacks. For one thing, the data may not be in a form that allows the researcher to fully test a hypothesis. The information may be incomplete, or it may have been collected haphazardly (Stewart & Kamins, 1993).

In most cases, though, archival research is stymied by the simple fact that records with the necessary information simply may not exist. In these instances, researchers often turn to another research method: naturalistic observation.

Naturalistic Observation   In **naturalistic observation,** the investigator simply observes some naturally occurring behavior and does not intervene in the situation. For example, a researcher investigating helping behavior might observe the kind of help given to victims in a high-crime area of a city. The important point to remember about naturalistic observation is that the researcher is passive and simply records what occurs (Erlandson et al., 1993).

While the advantage of naturalistic observation is obvious—we get a sample of what people do in their "natural habitat"—there is also an important drawback: the inability to control any of the factors of interest. For example, we might find so few naturally occurring instances of helping behavior that we would be unable to draw any conclusions. Because naturalistic observation prevents researchers from making changes in a situation, they must wait until appropriate conditions occur. Similarly, if people know that they are being watched, they may alter their reactions, resulting in behavior that is not truly representative of the group in question.

Survey Research   There is no more straightforward way of finding out what people think, feel, and do than by asking them directly. For this reason, surveys represent an important research method. In **survey research,** people chosen to represent some larger population are asked a series of questions about their behavior, thoughts, or attitudes. Survey methods have become so sophisticated that even using a very small sample is sufficient to infer with great accuracy how a larger group would respond. For instance, sampling just a few thousand voters is sufficient to predict within one or two percentage points who will win a presidential election—if the sample is chosen with care (Fowler, 1993).

Researchers investigating helping behavior might conduct a survey asking people to indicate their reasons for not wanting to come forward to help another individual. Similarly, researchers interested in learning about sexual practices have carried out surveys to learn which ones are common and which are not, and to chart changing notions of sexual morality over the past several decades.

Archival research: The examination of existing records for the purpose of confirming a hypothesis.

Naturalistic observation: Observation without intervention, in which the investigator records information about a naturally occurring situation.

Survey research: Sampling a group of people by assessing their behavior, thoughts, or attitudes, then generalizing the findings to a larger population.

A difficult but crucial task of survey researchers is the elimination of bias in the wording of their questions.

While asking people directly about their behavior seems in some ways like the most straightforward approach to understanding what people do, survey research has several potential drawbacks. For one thing, people may give inaccurate information because they don't really remember or because they don't want to let the researcher know what they really believe about a particular issue. Moreover, people sometimes offer responses they think the researcher wants to hear—or, in just the opposite instance, responses they assume the researcher *doesn't* want to hear. In some cases, unscrupulous pollsters ask biased questions deliberately designed to yield a particular result, either for commercial or for political purposes.

Case study: An in-depth investigation of an individual or small group.

The Case Study   When the police officers who participated in Rodney King's beating were arrested, many people found themselves wondering what it was about the officers' personalities or backgrounds that might have led to their conduct. In order to answer this question, psychologists might conduct a case study. In contrast to a survey, in which many people are studied, a **case study** is an in-depth, intensive investigation of an individual or small group of people. Case studies often include psychological testing, in which a carefully designed set of questions is used to gain some insight into the personality of the individual or group being studied.

When case studies are used as a research technique, the goal is often not only to learn about the few individuals being examined, but to use the insights gained to better understand people in general. However, any such generalizations must be made cautiously. For instance, the degree to which the police officers in the Rodney King case are representative of the general population is certainly open to question.

Correlational Research

In using the research methods that we have described, researchers often wish to determine the relationship between two behaviors or between responses to two questions on a questionnaire. For example, we might want to find out if people who report that they attend religious services regularly also report that they are more helpful to strangers in emergency situations. If we did find such a relationship, we could say that there was an association—or correlation—between attendance at religious services and helpfulness in emergencies.

Correlational research: Research to examine the relationship between two sets of factors to determine whether they are associated, or "correlated."

In **correlational research,** the relationship between two sets of factors is examined to determine whether they are associated, or "correlated." The strength of a relationship is represented by a mathematical score ranging from $+1.0$ to -1.0. A positive score indicates that, as the value of one factor increases, we can predict that the value of the other factor will also increase.

For example, if we predicted that, the *more* studying students do for a test the *higher* their subsequent grades on the test, and that the *less* studying they do the *lower* their test scores, we would expect to find a positive correlation. (Higher values of the factor of amount of time studying would be associated with higher values of the factor of test scores, and lower values of time spent studying would be associated with lower values of test scores.) The correlation, then, would be indicated by a score that was a positive number, and the closer the association between studying and grades, the closer the score would be to $+1.0$.

On the other hand, a correlation with a negative value tells us that, as the value of one factor increases, the value of the other decreases. For instance, we might predict that as the number of hours spent studying *increased* the number of hours spent in recreational activities would *decline*. Here, we are expecting a negative correlation, ranging between 0 and -1.0: More studying is associated with less recreation, and less studying is associated with more recreation. The stronger the association between study and play, the closer to -1.0 would be the score. For instance, a correlation of +.85 would indicate a strong positive association between recreation and studying; a correlation of −.02 or +.03 would indicate that there is virtually no association between them; and a correlation of −.80 would indicate a strong negative association.

Of course, it's quite possible that no relationship exists between two factors. For instance, we would probably not expect to find a relationship between number of hours studied and height. Lack of a relationship would be indicated by a correlation of close to 0; knowing how much someone studies does not tell us anything about how tall he or she is.

Correlation Does Not Imply Causation   When we find that two variables are strongly correlated with one another, it is tempting to presume that one factor causes the other. For example, if we find that more study time is associated with higher grades, we might guess that more studying *causes* higher grades. While not a bad guess, it remains just a guess—because finding that two factors are correlated does not mean that there is a causal relationship. Although the strong correlation suggests that knowing how much a person studies can help us predict how he or she will do on a test, it does not mean that the studying caused the test performance. It might be, for instance, that people who are interested in the subject matter tend to study more than those who are less interested, and that it is the lack of interest that predicts test performance, not the number of hours spent studying. Just because two factors occur together does not mean that one causes the other.

Another example illustrates the critical point that correlations tell us nothing about cause and effect but only provide a measure of the strength of a relationship between two factors. For instance, we might find that children who watch a lot of television programs featuring high levels of aggression are apt to demonstrate a relatively high degree of aggressive behavior, while those who watch few television shows that portray aggression are apt to exhibit a relatively low degree of such behavior (see Figure 1-2). We cannot say that the aggression is *caused* by the TV viewing, because several other explanations are possible.

For instance, it may be that children who have unusually high levels of energy seek out programs having aggressive content *and* are more aggressive. The children's energy levels, then, may be the true cause of the children's higher inci-

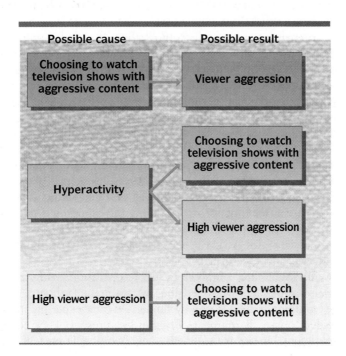

FIGURE 1-2   If we find that frequent viewing of television programs having aggressive content is associated with high levels of aggressive behavior, we might cite several plausible causes, as suggested in this figure. Correlational findings, then, do not permit us to determine causality.

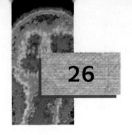

dence of aggression. Finally, it is also possible that people who are already highly aggressive choose to watch shows with high aggressive content *because* they are aggressive. Clearly, then, any number of causal sequences are possible—none of which can be ruled out by correlational research.

The inability of correlational research to demonstrate cause-and-effect relationships represents a crucial drawback to its use. There is, however, an alternative technique that does establish causality: the experiment.

Experimental Research

The *only* way that psychologists can establish cause-and-effect relationships through research is by carrying out an experiment. In a formal **experiment,** the relationship between two (or more) factors is investigated by deliberately producing a change in one factor in a situation and observing the effects of that change on other aspects of the situation. In an experiment, then, the conditions required to study a question of interest are created by an experimenter, who deliberately makes a change in those conditions in order to observe the effects of such change.

The change that is deliberately produced in a situation by an experimenter is called the **experimental manipulation.** Experimental manipulations are used to detect relationships between **variables**—behaviors, events, or other characteristics that can change, or vary, in some way.

There are several steps in carrying out an experiment, but the process typically begins with the development of one or more hypotheses for the experiment to test (Broota, 1990). Recall, for example, the hypothesis derived by Latané and Darley to test their theory of helping behavior: The more people who witness an emergency situation, the less likely it is that any of them will help a victim. We can trace the way they developed an experiment to test this hypothesis.

Their first step was to operationalize the hypothesis by conceptualizing it in such a way that it could be tested. Doing so required that Latané and Darley take into account the fundamental principle of experimental research mentioned earlier. There must be a manipulation of at least one variable in order to observe what effects the manipulation has on another variable. But this manipulation cannot be viewed by itself; if a cause-and-effect relationship is to be established, the effects of the manipulation must be compared with the effects of no manipulation or a different manipulation.

Experimental research requires, then, that the responses of at least two groups be compared with each other. One group will receive some special **treatment**—the manipulation implemented by the experimenter—while another group receives either no treatment or a different treatment. Any group receiving a treatment is called an **experimental group,** while a group that does not is called the **control group.** (In some experiments, however, there are multiple experimental and control groups, each of which is compared with the others.)

By employing both experimental and control groups in an experiment, researchers are able to rule out the possibility that something other than the experimental manipulation produced the results seen in the experiment. If we didn't have a control group, we couldn't be sure that some other factor, such as the temperature at the time we were running the experiment or the mere passage of time, wasn't causing the changes observed. Through the use of control groups, then, researchers can isolate specific causes for their findings—and cause-and-effect inferences can be drawn.

To Latané and Darley, a means of operationalizing their hypothesis was readily available. They decided they would create a bogus emergency situation that would require the aid of a bystander. As their experimental manipulation, they decided to vary the number of bystanders present. They could have just had an experimental group with, for instance, two people present, and a control group for

Experiment: A study carried out to investigate the relationship between two or more factors by deliberately producing a change in one factor and observing the effect that change has upon other factors.

Experimental manipulation: The change deliberately produced in an experiment to affect responses or behaviors in other factors to detect relationships between variables.

Variables: Behaviors or events that can change, or vary.

Treatment: The manipulation implemented by the experimenter to one group, while another group receives either no treatment or a different treatment.

Experimental group: Any group receiving a treatment.

Control group: The experimental group receiving no treatment.

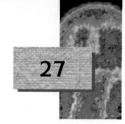

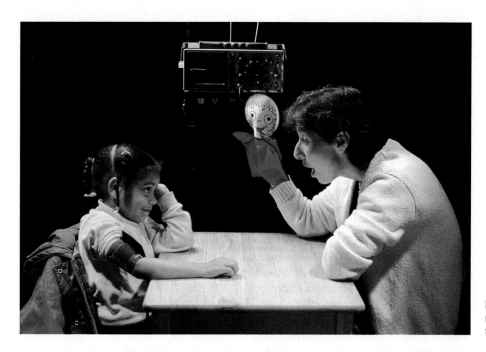

In this experiment, preschoolers' reactions to the puppet are monitored.

comparison purposes with just one person present. Instead, they settled on a more complex procedure in which three groups could be compared with one another, consisting of two, three, and six people.

Latané and Darley had now identified what is called the experimenter's **independent variable,** the variable that is manipulated. In this case, it was the number of people present. The next step was to decide how they were going to determine what effect varying the number of bystanders had on participants' behavior. Crucial to every experiment is the **dependent variable,** the variable that is measured and is expected to change as a result of the experimenter's manipulation. Experiments have, then, both an independent and a dependent variable. (To remember the difference, you might recall that a hypothesis predicts how a dependent variable *depends* on the manipulation of the independent variable.)

How, then, should the dependent measure be operationalized for Latané and Darley's experiment? One way might have been to use a simple yes-or-no measure of whether a **subject**—as a participant in research is known—helped or didn't help. But the two investigators decided they also wanted a measure that provided a more precise analysis of helping behavior, so they determined that they would measure the amount of time it took for a subject to provide help.

Latané and Darley now had all the components of an experiment. The independent variable, manipulated by them, was the number of bystanders present in an emergency situation. The dependent variable was whether the bystanders in each of the groups provided help and the amount of time it took for them to do so. *All* true experiments in psychology fit this straightforward model.

The Final Step: Random Assignment of Subjects To make the experiment a valid test of the hypothesis, the researchers needed to add a final step to the design: properly assigning subjects to receive a particular treatment.

The significance of this step becomes clear when we examine various alternative procedures. For example, the experimenters might have considered the possibility of assigning just males to the group with two bystanders, just females to the group with three bystanders, and both males and females to the group with six bystanders. Had they done so, however, it would have become clear that any differences they found in responsive behavior could not be attributed with any certainty solely to group size, since the differences might just as well be due to

Independent variable: The variable that is manipulated in an experiment.

Dependent variable: The variable that is measured and is expected to change as a result of experimenter manipulation.

Subject: A participant in research.

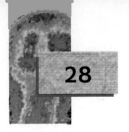
the makeup of the group. A more reasonable procedure would be to ensure that each group had the same composition in terms of gender; then the researchers would be able to make comparisons across groups with considerably more accuracy.

Subjects in each of the experimental groups ought to be comparable, and it is easy enough to create similar groups in terms of gender. The problem becomes a bit more tricky, though, when we consider other subject characteristics. How can we ensure that subjects in each experimental group will be equally intelligent, extroverted, cooperative, and so forth, when the list of characteristics—any one of which may be important—is potentially endless?

The solution to the problem is a simple but elegant procedure called random assignment to condition. In **random assignment to condition,** members of a group of subjects are assigned to a different experimental group or "condition" on the basis of chance and chance alone. The experimenter might, for instance, put the names of all potential subjects into a hat and draw names to make assignments to specific groups. The advantage of this technique is that subject characteristics have an equal chance of being distributed across the various groups. By using random assignment, the experimenter can be confident that each of the groups will have approximately the same proportion of intelligent people, cooperative people, extroverted people, males and females, and so on.

The following set of key elements is important to keep in mind as you consider whether a research study represents a true experiment:

■ An independent variable, the factor that is manipulated by the experimenter
■ A dependent variable, the variable that is measured by the experimenter and expected to change
■ A procedure that randomly assigns subjects to different experimental groups or "conditions" of the independent variable
■ A hypothesis that ties the independent and dependent variable together

Only if each of these elements is present can a research study be considered a true experiment in which cause-and-effect relationships can be determined. (For a summary of the different types of research that we've discussed, see Table 1-2.)

Random assignment to condition: The assignment of subjects to given groups on a chance basis alone.

TABLE 1-2 Research Strategies

Correlational Research		Experimental Research
	General process	
Researcher observes a previously existing situation but does not intervene		Researcher manipulates a situation in order to observe the outcome of the manipulation
	Intended result	
Identify associations between factors		Learn how changes in one factor cause changes in another
	Types	
Archival research (examines records to confirm a hypothesis)		Experiment (investigator produces a change in one factor to observe the effects of that change on other factors)
Naturalistic observation (observation of naturally occurring behavior, without intervention)		
Survey research (asking questions of people chosen to represent a larger population)		
Case study (intensive investigation of an individual or small group)		

Were Latané and Darley Right?   By now, you must be wondering whether Latané and Darley were right when they hypothesized that increasing the number of bystanders present in an emergency situation would lower the degree of helping behavior.

According to the results of the experiment they carried out, their hypothesis was right on target. In their test of the hypothesis, they used a laboratory setting in which subjects were told that the purpose of the experiment was to hold a discussion about personal problems associated with college. The discussion was to be held over an intercom supposedly in order to avoid the potential embarrassment of face-to-face contact. Chatting about personal problems was not, of course, the true purpose of the experiment, but subjects were told that it was, in order to keep their expectations about the experiment from biasing their behavior. (Consider how they would have been affected had they been told that their helping behavior in emergencies was being tested. The experimenters could never have gotten an accurate assessment of what the subjects would actually do in an emergency. By definition, emergencies are rarely announced in advance.)

The sizes of the discussion groups were two, three, and six people, which constituted the manipulation of the independent variable of group size. Subjects were randomly assigned to one of these groups upon their arrival at the laboratory.

As the subjects in each group were holding their discussion, they suddenly heard one of the other participants (in reality a trained **confederate,** or employee, of the experimenters) lapse into what sounded like an epileptic seizure:

I-er-um-I think I-I need-er-if-if- could-er-er-somebody er-er-er-er-er-er-er give me a little-er give me a little help here because-er-I-er-I'm-er-er-h-h- having a-a-a real problem-er-right now and I-er-if somebody could help me out it would-it-would- er-er s-s-sure be-sure be good . . . because- er-there-er-er-a cause I-er-I-uh-I've got a-a one of the-er-sei—er-er-things coming on and-and- and I could really-er-use some help so if somebody would-er-give me a little h-help-uh-er-er-er-er-er c-could somebody-er-er-help-er-us-us-us [choking sounds]. . . . I'm gonna die-er-er-I'm . . . gonna die-er-help-er-er-seizure-er-[choking sounds, then silence]. (Latané and Darley, 1970, p. 379)

The subjects' behavior was now what counted. The dependent variable was the time that elapsed from the start of the "seizure" to the time a subject began trying to help the "victim." If 6 minutes went by without a subject's offering help, the experiment was ended.

As predicted by the hypothesis, the size of the group had a significant effect on whether a subject provided help (Latané & Darley, 1970). In the two-person group (in which a subject thought he or she was alone with the victim), the average elapsed time was 52 seconds; in the three-person group (the subject, the victim, and one other person), the average elapsed time was 93 seconds; and in the six-person group (the subject, the victim, and four others), the average time was 166 seconds. Considering a simple yes-or-no measure of whether help was given confirms the elapsed-time pattern. In the two-person-group condition, 85 percent of the subjects helped; in the three-person-group condition, 62 percent helped; and in the six-person group, only 31 percent helped.

Because these results are so straightforward, it seems clear that the original hypothesis was confirmed. However, Latané and Darley could not be sure that the results were truly meaningful until they examined their data using formal statistical procedures. Statistical procedures—which entail several kinds of mathematical calculations—allow a researcher to determine precisely the likelihood that results are meaningful and not merely the outcome of chance.

The Latané and Darley study contains all the elements of an experiment: an independent variable, a dependent variable, random assignment to conditions, and multiple experimental groups. Because it does, we can say with some confidence that group size *caused* changes in the degree of helping behavior.

Of course, one experiment alone does not resolve forever the question of bystander intervention in emergencies. Psychologists require **replication** of findings,

Confederate: A participant in an experiment who has been instructed to behave in ways that will affect the responses of other subjects.

Replication: The repetition of an experiment in order to verify the results of the original experiment.

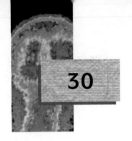

or that they be repeated, using other procedures in other settings, with other groups of subjects, before full confidence can be placed in the validity of any single experiment. [In this case, the experiment has stood the test of time. In a review of some fifty studies that were carried out in the 10 years following the original experiment, the finding that an increase in bystanders leads to decreased helping has been replicated in numerous other studies (Latané & Nida, 1981).]

In addition to replicating experimental results, psychologists need to test the limitations of their theories and hypotheses in order to determine under which specific circumstances they do and do not apply. It seems unlikely, for instance, that increasing numbers of bystanders *always* results in less helping. Therefore it is critical to understand the conditions in which exceptions to this general rule occur. For example, we might speculate that under conditions of shared outcomes, in which onlookers experience a sense that a victim's difficulties may later affect them in some way, help would be more readily forthcoming (Aronson, 1988). To test this hypothesis (for which, in fact, there is some support) requires additional experimentation.

Like any science, then, psychology increases our understanding in small, incremental steps, with each step building upon previous work. It is work carried

PATHWAYS THROUGH PSYCHOLOGY

Mary Garrett
San Francisco State College, San Francisco, California

Born: 1947
Education: A.A., City College of San Francisco; B.A., San Francisco State College; currently enrolled in M.A. program, San Francisco State
Home: San Francisco, California

Most high school students have only a vague idea of what they want to do with their lives, but as far as Mary Garrett was concerned, there was absolutely no question what she wanted. She yearned to be a psychologist.

The 48-year-old Garrett is finally making her dream come true. After a hiatus of many years in her education, she is now enrolled in a graduate program in research psychology at San Francisco State College.

"I've always been interested in people, in people's behavior, and why they do what they do," she said. "Even when I was in high school I wanted to be a psychologist, and now plan to teach and do research in psychology at the college level."

Mary Garrett

As part of her graduate studies, Garrett is planning to undertake an innovative and potentially significant study of African-American women with the AIDS virus. "The study is intended to increase our knowledge about the nature of the effects of stress on the mental and physical health of African-American women with HIV and AIDS, and the coping processes that mediate these effects in order to design effective psychosocial intervention," she said.

The impetus for the study was a similar project conducted by one of her professors. He had done an initial study on coping with AIDS, but he only used men in his sample. Garrett is interested in comparing how women and men deal with the disease.

"I want to find out if the coping strategies and processes are different for women. Women do have different stressors than men, such as being single mothers or being a black female in this society," she said.

The research, according to Garrett, will involve three phases: an initial exploratory study, in-depth interviews, and a written questionnaire. She attributes much of her ability to design the study to her undergraduate training as a psychology major. "It was in my methods class that I learned how to develop and give surveys. I'll also be using material I've learned from classes in statistics, methods, and aging and adult development," Garrett added. "All of my undergraduate work in psychology was instrumental in preparing for this current study.

out on many fronts, involving many people, like Mary Garrett, whose work is discussed in the Pathways through Psychology box.

RECAP AND REVIEW

Recap

- The scientific method used by psychologists proceeds in three steps: identifying questions of interest, formulating an explanation, and carrying out research that is designed to lend support to the explanation.
- Theories are broad explanations and predictions of phenomena of interest.
- Hypotheses grow out of theories, stating assumptions derived from a theory in a way that allows the assumptions to be tested through research.
- Key research methods include archival research, naturalistic observation, survey research, and the case study.
- In correlational research, the relationship between two variables is examined to determine whether they are associated, although cause-and-effect relationships cannot be established.
- In a formal experiment—which is the only means of determining cause-and-effect associations—the relationship between factors is investigated by deliberately producing a change in one factor and observing the change in the other.

Review

1. An explanation about a phenomenon of interest is known as a _____.
2. To test this explanation, it must be stated in terms of a testable question known as a _____.
3. An experimenter is interested in studying the relationship between hunger and aggression. He defines aggression as the number of times a subject will hit a punching bag. What is the process of defining this variable called?
4. Match the following forms of research to their definition:
   1. Archival research — b
   2. Naturalistic observation c
   3. Survey research — a
   4. Case study — d

a. Directly asking a sample of people questions about their behavior
b. Examining existing records to confirm a hypothesis
c. Looking at behavior in its true setting without intervening in the results
d. Doing an in-depth investigation of a person or small group

5. Match each of the following research methods with a problem basic to it:
   1. Archival research — c
   2. Naturalistic observation — b
   3. Survey research — d
   4. Case study — a
   a. May not be able to generalize to the population at large.
   b. People's behavior may change if they know they are being watched.
   c. The data may not exist or may be unusable.
   d. People may lie in order to present a good image.
6. A friend tells you that "Anxiety about speaking in public and performance are negatively correlated. Therefore, high anxiety must cause low performance." Is this statement true or false, and why?
7. A psychologist wants to study the effect of attractiveness on willingness to help a person with a math problem. Attractiveness would be the _independent_ variable, while amount of helping would be the _dependent_ variable.
8. The group in an experiment which receives no treatment is called the _Control_ group.

Ask Yourself

In running an experiment, you decide to take the first twenty available subjects and assign them to the experimental group and assign the next twenty to the control group. Why might this not be a good idea?

(Answers to review questions are on page 32.)

- ***What are the major issues that underlie the process of conducting research?***

RESEARCH CHALLENGES: EXPLORING THE PROCESS

It is probably apparent by now that there are few simple formulas that psychologists can follow as they carry out research. Choices must be made about the type of study to conduct, the measures to be taken, and the most effective way to analyze the results. Even after these essential decisions have been made, several critical issues still need to be considered. We turn first to the most fundamental of these issues: ethics.

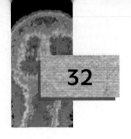

32

The Ethics of Research

Put yourself in the place of one of the subjects in the Latané and Darley experiment. How would you feel when you learned that the person who you thought was having a seizure was, in reality, a paid accomplice of the experimenter?

Although you might at first experience relief that there had been no real emergency, you might also feel some resentment that you had been deceived by the experimenter. And you might also experience concern that you had been placed in an unusual situation—one that may have dealt a blow to your self-esteem, depending on how you had behaved.

Most psychologists argue that the use of deception is sometimes necessary to avoid having subjects influenced by what they think is the study's true purpose. (If you knew the Latané and Darley study was actually concerned with your helping behavior, wouldn't you have automatically been tempted to intervene in the emergency?) To avoid such outcomes, researchers must occasionally use deception.

Nonetheless, because research has the potential to violate the rights of participants, psychologists are expected to adhere to a strict set of ethical guidelines aimed at protecting subjects (American Psychological Association, 1992). These guidelines advocate the following:

- Protection of subjects from physical and mental harm
- The right of subjects to privacy regarding their behavior
- The assurance that participation in research is completely voluntary
- The necessity of informing subjects about the nature of procedures prior to participation in the experiment

Although the guidelines do allow the use of deception, all experiments involving deception must be reviewed by an independent panel prior to their use—as must all research that uses human beings as subjects (Sieber, 1992; Rosnow et al., 1993; Rosenthal, 1994; Fisher & Fyrberg, 1994; Gurman, 1994).

One of the key ethical principles followed by psychologists is that of **informed consent.** Before participating in an experiment, subjects must sign a document affirming that they have been told the basic outlines of the study, that they know what their participation will involve, that they are aware of the risks the experiment may hold, and that they understand that their participation is purely voluntary and may be terminated at any time. The only time informed consent can be eliminated is in experiments in which the risks are minimal, as in a purely observational study on a street corner or other public location (Mann, 1994).

Informed consent: A document signed by subjects prior to an experiment in which the study and conditions and risks of participation are explained.

Exploring Diversity

Choosing Subjects That Represent the Scope of Human Behavior

When Latané and Darley, both college professors, decided who they should use as subjects in their experiment, they turned to the people who were most readily accessible to them: college students. In fact, college students are used so fre-

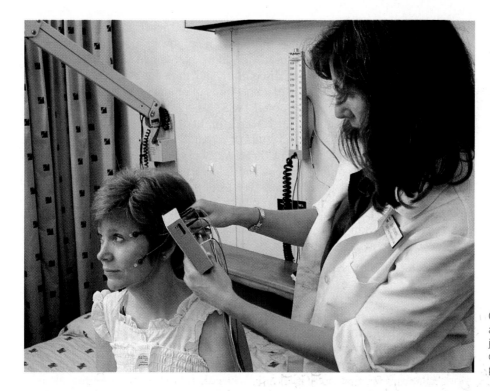

College students are readily available and widely used research subjects, but they may not be sufficiently representative of the general population.

quently in experiments that psychology has been called—somewhat contemptuously—the "science of the behavior of the college sophomore" (Rubenstein, 1982).

The use of college students as subjects has both advantages and drawbacks. The big benefit is their availability. Because most research occurs in university settings, college students are readily available. Typically, they participate for either extra course credit or a relatively small monetary payment, making the cost to the researcher minimal.

The problem with relying on college students for subjects is that they may not adequately represent the general population. College students tend to be younger and better educated than a significant percentage of the rest of the population of the United States. Moreover, their attitudes are likely to be less well formed, and they are apt to be more susceptible to social pressures from authority figures and peers than older adults (Sears, 1986).

Furthermore, college students are disproportionately white and middle-class. In fact, even research that does not employ college students tends to be based on white, middle-class subjects. In particular, the use of African-Americans as subjects not only is low, but has actually declined during the past 20 years (Graham, 1992).

When a science that purports to explain human behavior in general disregards a significant proportion of the population when it draws conclusions, something is amiss. Consequently, psychological researchers have become increasingly sensitive to the importance of using subjects who are fully representative of the general population (Youngstrom, 1994; Gannon et al., 1992; Bersoff, 1995).

Should Animals Be Used in Research?

It is not just psychologists working with humans who operate under strict ethical constraints; researchers who use animals as subjects have their own set of exacting guidelines to ensure that animals do not suffer (American Psychological Association, 1993). Specifically, they must make every effort to minimize discomfort, illness, and pain, and procedures subjecting animals to distress are used

only when an alternative procedure is unavailable and when the goal of research is justified by its prospective value. Moreover, there are federal regulations specifying how animals are to be housed, fed, and maintained. Not only must researchers strive to avoid physical discomfort, but they are also required to promote the *psychological* well-being of some kinds of animals, such as primates that are used in research (Novak & Suomi, 1988; Adler, 1991).

Why should animals be used for research in the first place? How can we dare to infer human behavior from the results of research employing rats, gerbils, and pigeons? The answer is that the 7 or 8 percent of psychological research that does employ animals has a different focus and is designed to answer different questions than research that uses humans. For example, the shorter life span of animals (rats live an average of 2 years) allows us to learn about the effects of aging in a much more rapid time frame than if we studied aging using human subjects. Moreover, the very complexity of human beings may obscure information about fundamental phenomena that can be more plainly identified in animals. Finally, some studies require large numbers of subjects who share similar backgrounds or who have been exposed to particular environments—conditions that could not practically be met with human beings (Gill et al., 1989).

Research using animals as subjects has provided psychologists with information that has profound benefits for humans (Miller, 1985b). For instance, animal research has furnished us with the keys to learning how to detect eye disorders in children early enough to prevent permanent damage, how to communicate more effectively with severely retarded children, and how to reduce chronic pain in people, to name just a few results (APA, 1988; Domjan & Purdy, 1995).

Despite the demonstrated value of research that uses animals as subjects, their use in psychological research remains controversial (Orlans, 1993; Devenport & Devenport, 1990; Ulrich, 1991; Plous, 1991), with some people calling for stringent restrictions or even a complete ban on the practice (Bowd & Shapiro, 1993). However, most psychologists believe that existing ethical guidelines are sufficiently stringent to provide protection for animals while still allowing valuable animal research to continue.

Threats to Experiments: Experimenter and Subject Expectations

Experimental bias: Factors that distort an experimenter's understanding of how the independent variable affected the dependent variable.

Even the best-laid experimental plans are susceptible to **experimental bias**—factors that distort an experimenter's understanding of how the independent variable *affected* the dependent variable. One of the most common forms of experimental bias that experimenters need to elude is *experimenter expectations*, whereby an experimenter unintentionally transmits cues to subjects about the way they are expected to behave in a given experimental condition (Harris, 1991; Blanck, 1993). The danger is that these expectations will bring about an "appropriate" behavior—one that may not have otherwise occurred. For example, if Latané and Darley had behaved toward subjects in the two-bystander condition as if they expected them to help, but let on that they had low expectations for helping in the six-person bystander condition, such variations in experimenter behavior—no matter how unintentional—might have affected the results.

A related problem is *subject expectations* about what is appropriate behavior. If you have ever been a subject in an experiment, you know that you quickly develop ideas about what is expected of you, and it is typical for people to develop their own hypotheses about what the experimenter hopes to learn from the study. If these expectations influence a subject's behavior, it becomes a cause for concern, since it is no longer the experimental manipulation producing an effect, but rather the subject's expectations.

To guard against the problem of subject expectations biasing the results of an experiment, the experimenter may try to disguise the true purpose of the experiment. Subjects who do not know that helping behavior is being studied, for example, are more apt to act in a "natural" way than if they are told their helping behavior is under scrutiny. Latané and Darley decided to misinform their subjects, telling them that the purpose of the experiment was to hold a discussion among college students about their personal problems. In doing so, they expected that their subjects would not suspect the true purpose of the experiment.

In some experiments, it is impossible to hide the actual purpose of the research. In cases such as these, other techniques are available. For example, suppose you were interested in testing the ability of a new drug to alleviate the symptoms of severe depression. If you simply gave the drug to half your subjects and not to the other half, subjects given the drug might report feeling less depressed merely because they knew they were getting a drug. Similarly, the subjects who got nothing might report feeling no better because they knew they were in a no-treatment control group.

To solve this problem, psychologists typically use a procedure in which subjects in the control group do receive a placebo treatment. A **placebo** is a bogus treatment such as a pill, "drug," or other substance without any significant chemical properties or active ingredient. Because members of both groups are kept in the dark about whether they are getting a real or a bogus treatment, any differences that are found can be attributed to the quality of the drug and not to the possible psychological effects of being administered a pill or other substance (Roberts et al., 1993).

There is still one more thing that a careful researcher must do in an experiment such as this. To overcome the possibility that experimenter expectations will affect the subject, the person who administers the drug shouldn't know whether it is actually the true drug or the placebo. By keeping both the subject and the experimenter who interacts with the subject "blind" to the nature of the drug being administered, researchers can more accurately assess the effects of the drug. This method is known as the *double-blind procedure.*

Placebo (pla SEE bo): A bogus treatment such as a pill, "drug," or other substance without any significant chemical properties or active ingredient.

The Informed Consumer of Psychology
Thinking Critically about Research

If you were about to purchase an automobile, it is unlikely that you would stop at the nearest car dealership and drive off with the first car a salesperson recommended. Instead, you would probably mull over the purchase, read about automobiles, consider the alternatives, talk to others about their experiences, and ultimately put in a fair amount of thought before you made such a major purchase.

In contrast, many of us are considerably less conscientious when it comes to the expenditure of intellectual assets than when we disperse our financial resources. People jump to conclusions on the basis of incomplete and inaccurate information, and it is relatively rare that they take the time to critically evaluate the research and data to which they are exposed.

Because the field of psychology is based on an accumulated body of research, it is crucial to scrutinize the methods, results, and claims of researchers thoroughly. Yet it is not just psychologists who need to know how to critically evaluate research; all of us are constantly exposed to the claims of others. Knowing how to approach research and data can be helpful in areas far beyond the realm of psychology.

Several basic questions can help us sort through what is valid and what is not. Among the most important to ask are the following:

■ What are the foundations of the research? Research studies should evolve from a clearly specified theory. Furthermore, the specific hypothesis that is being

tested must be taken into account. Unless we know what hypothesis is being examined, it is not possible to judge how successful a study has been. We need to be able to see how the hypothesis has been derived from an underlying theory, and in turn we need to consider how well the design of the study tests that hypothesis.

■ How well was the study conducted? Consider who the subjects were, how many of them there were, what methods were employed, and what problems in collecting the data the researcher encountered. For instance, there are important differences between a case study reporting the anecdotes of a handful of respondents and that of a careful survey collecting data from several thousand people.

■ What are the assumptions that lie behind the presentation of the results of the study? It is necessary to assess how well the statements being made reflect the actual data, as well as the logic of what is being claimed. For instance, the American Cancer Society announced in 1991 that a woman's odds of getting breast cancer had risen to 1 in 9. It turned out, though, that these were cumulative probabilities, reflecting the likelihood that a woman would develop breast cancer sometime between birth and age 110. For the vast majority of a woman's life, the odds of getting breast cancer are considerably lower. For instance, for women under the age of 50, the risk is closer to 1 in 1000 (Blakeslee, 1992; Kolata, 1993).

■ Is the logic of the claim reasonable? For instance, when the manufacturer of Brand X aspirin boasts that "no other aspirin is more effective in fighting pain than Brand X," this does not mean that Brand X is better than every other kind of aspirin. It just means that no other brand of aspirin works better, and that others may actually work just as well as Brand X. Expressed in the latter fashion, the finding doesn't seem worth bragging about.

These basic principles can help you assess the validity of research findings that you come across—both within and outside the field of psychology. The more you know how to evaluate research in general, the better you will be able to assess what the field of psychology has to offer.

RECAP AND REVIEW

Recap
- Among the major ethical issues faced by psychologists are deception in experiments and the use of animals as subjects.
- Threats to experiments include experimenter expectations and subject expectations.

Review
1. Ethical research begins with the concept of informed consent. Before signing up to participate in an experiment, subjects should be informed of
   a. the procedure of the study, stated generally
   b. the risks that may be involved
   c. their right to withdraw at any time
   d. all of the above

2. List three benefits of using animals in psychological research.
3. Experimenters can use deception as one means to try to eliminate subjects' expectations. True or false?
4. A procedure whereby the experimenter does not know whether subjects are receiving an actual treatment or not is known as the _____-_____ procedure.
5. A study is reported which shows that men differ from women in their preference of ice cream flavors. This study was based on a sample of two men and three women. What might be wrong with this study?

Ask Yourself
A psychologist tells you that because the results of his study involved a very large number of subjects, he can be sure that they are absolutely correct. Is he right or not, and why?

(Answers to review questions are on page 38.)

What is psychology, and why is it a science?

1. Although the definition of psychology—the scientific study of behavior and mental processes—is clear-cut, it is also deceptively simple, since "behavior" encompasses not just people's actions, but their thoughts, feelings, perceptions, reasoning, memory, and biological activities.

What are the different branches of the field of psychology?

2. Psychology includes a number of major specialty areas. Biopsychologists focus on the biological basis of behavior, while experimental psychologists study the processes of sensing, perceiving, learning, and thinking about the world. Cognitive psychology, an outgrowth of experimental psychology, considers the study of higher mental processes, including thinking, language, memory, problem solving, knowing, reasoning, judging, and decision making.

3. The branches of psychology that study change and individual differences are developmental and personality psychology. Developmental psychologists study how people grow and change throughout their life spans. Personality psychologists consider the consistency and change in an individual's behavior as he or she moves through different situations, as well as the individual differences that distinguish one person's behavior from another's when each is placed in the same situation.

4. Health, clinical, and counseling psychologists are primarily concerned with promoting physical and mental health. Health psychologists study psychological factors that affect physical disease, while clinical psychologists consider the study, diagnosis, and treatment of abnormal behavior. Counseling psychologists focus on educational, social, and career adjustment problems.

5. Educational psychologists investigate how the educational process affects students, while school psychologists specialize in assessing and treating children in elementary and secondary schools who have academic and/or emotional problems.

6. Social psychology is the study of how people's thoughts, feelings, and actions are affected by others. Industrial-organizational psychologists focus on how psychology can be applied to the workplace, while consumer psychologists consider the factors that influence people's buying habits. Cross-cultural psychology examines the similarities and differences among various cultures in psychological functioning. The newest areas of specialization include the psychology of women, clinical neuropsychology, environmental psychology, forensic psychology, sport and exercise psychology, and program evaluation.

Where are psychologists employed?

7. Psychologists are employed in a variety of settings. Although the primary employment sites are universities and colleges, many psychologists are found in hospitals, clinics, community mental-health centers, and counseling centers. Many also have practices in which they treat patients privately.

What are the historical roots of the field of psychology?

8. The foundations of psychology were established by Wilhelm Wundt in Germany in 1879. Early conceptual perspectives that guided the work of psychologists were structuralism, functionalism, and gestalt theory. Structuralism focused on identifying the fundamental elements of the mind, largely by using introspection. Functionalism concentrated on the functions performed by mental activities. Gestalt psychology focused on the study of how perception is organized into meaningful units.

What major approaches are used by contemporary psychologists?

9. The biological perspective focuses on the biological functioning of people and animals, reducing behavior to its most basic components. The psychodynamic perspective takes a very different approach. It suggests that there are powerful, unconscious inner forces and conflicts about which people have little or no awareness and which are primary determinants of behavior.

10. Cognitive approaches to behavior consider how people know, understand, and think about the world. Growing out of early work on introspection and later work by the gestaltists and functionalists, cognitive perspectives study how people understand and represent the world within themselves.

11. The behavioral perspective de-emphasizes internal processes and concentrates instead on observable behavior. It suggests that an understanding and control of a person's environment is sufficient to fully explain and modify behavior.

12. The humanistic perspective is the newest of the major perspectives of psychology. It emphasizes that people are uniquely inclined toward psychological growth and higher levels of functioning and that they will strive to reach their full potential.

What is the future of psychology likely to hold?

13. Several major trends seem to be emerging that may influence the future of psychology. Psychology will become increasingly specialized; it will evolve new perspectives; it will take the growing diversity of the country's population into account more fully; and it will become increasingly concerned with the public interest. In addition, psychological treatment is likely to become more accessible and socially acceptable.

What is the scientific method, and how do psychologists use theory and research to answer questions of interest?

14. The scientific method is an approach psychologists use to understand the unknown. It consists of three steps: identifying questions of interest, formulating an explanation, and carrying out research that is designed to lend support to the explanation.

15. Research in psychology is guided by theories (broad explanations and predictions of phenomena of interest) and hypotheses (derivations of theories that are predictions stated in a way that allows them to be tested).

What are the different research methods employed by psychologists?

16. Archival research uses existing records such as old newspapers or other documents to confirm a hypothesis. In naturalistic observation, the investigator acts mainly as an observer, making no change in a naturally occurring situation. In survey research, people are asked a series of questions about their behavior, thoughts, or attitudes. The case study represents an in-depth investigation and examination of one person or small group. These methods rely on correlational techniques that describe associations between various factors but cannot determine cause-and-effect relationships.

How do psychologists establish cause-and-effect relationships in research studies?

17. In a formal experiment, the relationship between factors is investigated by deliberately producing a change—called the experimental manipulation—in one of them and observing the change in the other. The factors that are changed are called variables—behaviors, events, or persons that can change, or vary, in some way. In order to test a hypothesis, it must be operationalized: The abstract concepts of the hypothesis are translated into the actual procedures used in the study.

18. In an experiment, at least two groups must be compared with each other to assess cause-and-effect relationships. The group receiving the treatment (the special procedure devised by the experimenter) is the experimental group, while the second group (which receives no treatment) is the control group.

There also may be multiple experimental groups, each of which is subjected to a different procedure and can then be compared with the others. The variable that is manipulated is the independent variable. The variable that is measured and expected to change as a result of manipulation of the independent variable is called the dependent variable.

19. In a formal experiment, subjects must be assigned to treatment conditions randomly so that subject characteristics are evenly distributed across the different conditions.

What are the major issues that underlie the process of conducting research?

20. One of the key ethical principles followed by psychologists is that of informed consent. Subjects must be told, prior to participation, the basic outline of the experiment and the risks and potential benefits of their participation. Researchers working with animals must also follow a rigid set of ethical guidelines for the protection of the animals.

21. Although the use of college students as subjects has the advantage of easy availability, there are drawbacks to their use. For instance, students do not necessarily represent the population as a whole. The use of animals as subjects also has costs in terms of generalizability, although the benefits of using animals in research have been profound.

22. Experiments are subject to a number of threats, or biases. Experimenter expectations occur when an experimenter unintentionally transmits cues to subjects about his or her expectations regarding their behavior in a given experimental condition. Subject expectations can also bias an experiment. To help eliminate bias, researchers use placebos and double-blind procedures.

KEY TERMS AND CONCEPTS

psychology (p. 3)
structuralism (p. 12)
introspection (p. 12)
functionalism (p. 13)
gestalt psychology (p. 13)
biological perspective (p. 14)
psychodynamic perspective (p. 14)
cognitive perspective (p. 14)
behavioral perspective (p. 15)
humanistic perspective (p. 15)
free will (p. 15)

scientific method (p. 21)
theories (p. 21)
hypothesis (p. 21)
operationalization (p. 22)
archival research (p. 23)
naturalistic observation (p. 23)
survey research (p. 23)
case study (p. 24)
correlational research (p. 24)
experiment (p. 26)
experimental manipulation (p. 26)
variables (p. 26)

treatment (p. 26)
experimental group (p. 26)
control group (p. 26)
independent variable (p. 27)
dependent variable (p. 27)
subject (p. 27)
random assignment to condition (p. 28)
confederate (p. 29)
replication (p. 29)
informed consent (p. 32)
experimental bias (p. 34)
placebo (p. 35)

ANSWERS TO PREVIOUS REVIEW
1. d **2.** (1) We can study simple phenomena in animals more easily than we can in people. (2) Large numbers of similar subjects can be easily obtained. (3) We can look at generational effects much more easily in animals with shorter life spans than we can with people. **3.** True **4.** double-blind **5.** There are far too few subjects. Without a larger sample, no valid conclusions can be drawn about ice cream preferences.

CHAPTER 2
THE BIOLOGY UNDERLYING BEHAVIOR

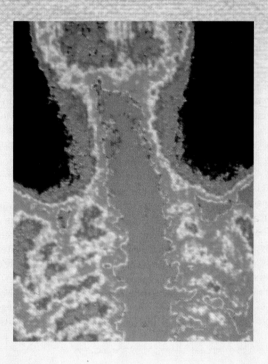

A Heart-Stopping Cure

After 5 hours on the operating table, the life began to ebb from Nancy Loiacono's body. Her respiration slowed to a crawl, and her heartbeat became increasingly faint. Finally, the lines on the monitor that charted her body signs went flat.

If this were the movies, the health care workers would have pulled a sheet over Loiacono's head and informed her next of kin of the death of their loved one. But this was real life, and the events transpiring on the table were just what the doctor ordered. An operation was taking place in order to cure a series of debilitating symptoms that had plagued Loiacono during the previous year. Starting with severe headaches, which had gradually worsened, she had eventually experienced hysteria, hallucinations, and vomiting as well.

The source of the problem had remained a mystery until physicians took a magnetic resonance image (MRI) of her brain. The MRI, a powerful computer-driven device that provides a detailed blueprint of the brain, showed that Loiacono had an aneurysm, a swollen, blood-filled bubble the size of a ping-pong ball, on the left side of her brain. Because the aneurysm could burst at any moment, leading to a disabling stroke or death, surgery was immediately ordered.

Using circulatory-arrest surgery, a pioneering procedure in use just a few years, physicians lowered Loiacono's body temperature 30 degrees below normal to temporarily stop her heart. As her heart's beating ceased, almost half of her body's blood was drained to reduce pressure within the circulatory system. The balloon-like aneurysm collapsed, permitting surgeons to seal it off through the installation of five clips that would remain in Loiacono's brain the rest of her life.

Once the delicate procedure was completed, Loiacono's blood was reheated, and her heart began to beat once again. The operation was a success: Her symptoms have disappeared, and her life has returned to normal (Breu, 1992).

LOOKING AHEAD

Nancy Loiacono's success story is mirrored in the stories of many others, as delicate surgery involving the recesses of the brain becomes more common. The results of operations like these are little short of miraculous. But the greater miracle is the object of the surgical procedure: the brain itself. As we shall see in this chapter, the brain, an organ roughly half the size of a loaf of bread, controls our behavior through every waking and sleeping moment. The brain and the nerves extending throughout the body constitute the human nervous system. Our movements, thoughts, hopes, aspirations, dreams—the very awareness that we are human—are all intimately related to this system.

Because the nervous system is vitally important in controlling behavior, and because human beings at their most basic level are biological entities, psychologists and researchers from other fields as diverse as computer science, zoology, and medicine have paid special attention to the biological underpinnings of behavior. These experts are collectively called *neuroscientists* (Lister & Weingartner, 1991; Churchland & Sejnowski, 1992; Gazzaniga, 1994).

Biopsychologists: Psychologists who study the ways biological structures and body functions affect behavior

Psychologists who specialize in considering the ways in which biological structures and functions of the body affect behavior are known as **biopsychologists.** These specialists seek to answer questions such as these: What are the bases for voluntary and involuntary functioning of the body? How are messages communicated from other parts of the body to the brain and from the brain to other parts of the body? What is the physical structure of the brain, and how does this structure affect behavior? Can the causes of psychological disorders be traced to biological factors, and how can such disorders be treated?

This chapter addresses such questions, focusing on those biological structures of the body of interest to biopsychologists. Initially, we discuss nerve cells, called neurons, which allow messages to travel through the brain and body. We learn that through their growing knowledge of neurons and the nervous system, psychologists are increasing their understanding of human behavior and are uncovering important clues in their efforts to cure certain kinds of diseases. The structure and main divisions of the nervous system are then presented, with explanations of how they work to control voluntary and involuntary behaviors. In the process we also examine how the various parts of the nervous system operate together in emergency situations to produce lifesaving responses to danger.

Next, we consider the brain itself, examining its major structures and the ways in which these affect behavior. We see how the brain controls movement, the five senses, and our thought processes. We also consider the fascinating notion that the two halves of the brain may have different specialties and strengths. Finally, we examine the chemical messenger system of the body, the endocrine system.

As we discuss these biological processes, it is important to keep in mind the rationale for doing so: Our understanding of human behavior cannot be complete without knowledge of the fundamentals of the brain and the rest of the nervous system. As we shall see, our behavior—our moods, motivations, goals, and desires—has a good deal to do with our biological makeup.

- *Why do psychologists study the brain and nervous system?*
- *What are the basic elements of the nervous system?*
- *How does the nervous system communicate electrical and chemical messages from one part to another?*

NEURONS: THE ELEMENTS OF BEHAVIOR

If you have ever watched the precision with which a well-trained athlete or dancer executes a performance, you may have marveled at the complexity—and wondrous abilities—of the human body. But even the most everyday tasks, such as picking up a pencil, writing, and speaking, require a sophisticated sequence of activities that is impressive. For instance, the difference between saying the words "dime" and "time" rests primarily on whether the vocal cords are relaxed or tense during a period lasting no more than one-hundredth of a second. Yet it is a distinction that almost everyone can make with ease.

The nervous system provides the pathways that permit us to carry out such precise activities. To understand how it is able to exert such exacting control over our bodies, we must begin by examining neurons, the most basic parts of the nervous system, and by considering the way in which nerve impulses are transmitted throughout the brain and body.

The Structure of the Neuron

The ability to play the piano, drive a car, or hit a tennis ball depends, at one level, merely on muscle coordination. But if we consider *how* the muscles involved in such activities are activated, we see that more fundamental processes are involved. It is necessary for the body to provide messages to the muscles and to coordinate those messages to enable the muscles to produce the complex movements that characterize successful physical activity.

Such messages are passed through specialized cells called **neurons,** the basic elements of the nervous system. Their quantity is staggering; some estimates suggest that there are as many as 100 or even 200 *billion* neurons in the brain alone. Although there are several types of neurons, each has a similar basic structure, as

Neurons: Specialized cells that are the basic elements of the nervous system that carry messages

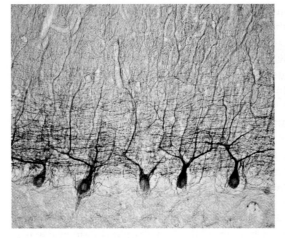

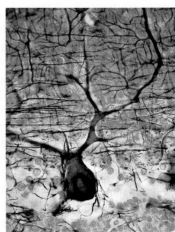

These two photographs, made with an electron microscope, show (left) a group of interconnected neurons in the cerebral cortex and (right) a close-up of a single neuron.

illustrated in Figure 2-1 (Levitan & Kaczmarek, 1991). Like all cells in the body, neurons have a cell body, containing a nucleus. The nucleus incorporates the inherited material that establishes how the cell will function.

In contrast to most other cells, however, neurons have a distinctive feature: the ability to communicate with other cells. As you can see in Figure 2-1, neurons have a cluster of fibers called **dendrites** at one end. These fibers, which look like the twisted branches of a tree, receive messages from other neurons. At the opposite end, neurons have a long, slim, tubelike extension called an **axon,** the part of the neuron that carries messages destined for other cells. The axon is considerably longer than the rest of the neuron. Although most axons are several millimeters in length, some may be as long as 3 feet. In contrast, the remainder of the neuron is only a fraction of the length of the axon. Finally, at the end of the axon are small branches ending in bulges called **terminal buttons** through which messages are relayed to other cells.

Dendrites: Cluster of fibers at one end of a neuron that receive messages from other neurons

Axon: A long extension from the end of a neuron that carries messages to other cells through the neuron

Terminal buttons: Small branches at the end of an axon that relay messages to other cells

FIGURE 2-1 The primary components of the specialized cell called the neuron, the basic element of the nervous system.

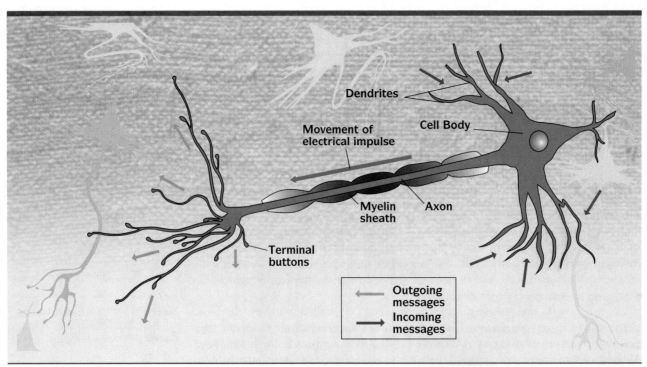

The messages that travel through the neuron are purely electrical in nature. Although there are exceptions, these electrical messages generally move across neurons as if they were traveling on a one-way street. They follow a route that begins with the dendrites, continues into the cell body, and leads ultimately down the tubelike extension, the axon. Dendrites, then, detect messages from other neurons; axons carry signals away from the cell body.

To prevent messages from short-circuiting one another, it is necessary for the axons to be insulated in some fashion (analogous to the way in which electrical wires must be insulated). In most axons, this is done with a protective coating known as the **myelin sheath,** made up of a series of specialized cells of fat and protein that wrap themselves around the axon.

Myelin sheath: An axon's protective coating, made of fat and protein

The myelin sheath also serves to increase the velocity with which the electrical impulses travel through the axons. Those axons that carry the most important and urgently required information have the greatest concentrations of myelin. If your hand touches a painfully hot stove, for example, the information regarding the pain is passed through axons in the hand and arm that contain a relatively large quantity of myelin, speeding the message of pain to the brain. In certain diseases, such as multiple sclerosis, the myelin sheath surrounding the axon deteriorates, exposing parts of the axon that are normally covered. The result is a kind of short circuit that causes a disturbance in messages between the brain and muscles and results in symptoms such as the inability to walk, vision difficulties, and general muscle impairment.

Although the electrical impulse moves across the neuron in a dendrite-to-cell body-to-axon sequence, certain substances travel through the neuron in the opposite direction. For instance, axons allow chemical substances needed for nourishment of the cell nucleus to move toward the cell body in a reverse flow. Certain diseases, such as amyotrophic lateral sclerosis (ALS)—also known as Lou Gehrig's disease for its most famous victim—may be caused by the inability of the neuron to transport vital materials in this reverse direction. When this occurs, the neuron eventually dies from starvation. Similarly, rabies is caused by the transmission of the rabies virus by reverse flow along the axon from the terminal buttons.

Lou Gehrig, of the New York Yankees, had a lifetime batting average of .340, and played in 2130 consecutive games before amyotrophic lateral sclerosis forced him out of the lineup. He died of the neural disorder—now familiarly known as Lou Gehrig's disease—at the age of 37.

Firing the Neuron

Like a gun, a neuron either fires or doesn't fire; there is no in-between stage. Pulling harder on the trigger is not going to make the bullet travel faster or more surely. Similarly, neurons follow an **all-or-none law.** They are either on or off; once triggered beyond a certain point, they will fire. When they are off—that is, in a **resting state**—there is a negative electrical charge of about −70 millivolts within the neuron (a millivolt is one-thousandth of a volt). This charge is caused by the presence of more negatively charged ions (a type of molecule) within the neuron than outside it. You might think of the neuron as one of the poles of a miniature car battery, with the inside of the neuron representing the negative pole and the outside of the neuron the positive pole (Koester, 1991).

All-or-none law: The principle governing the state of neurons, which are either on (firing) or off (resting)

Resting state: The nonfiring state of a neuron when the charge equals about −70 millivolts

However, when a message arrives, the cell walls in the neuron allow positively charged ions to rush in, at rates as high as 100 million ions per second. The sudden arrival of these positive ions causes the charge within that part of the cell to change momentarily from negative to positive. When the charge reaches a critical level, the "trigger" is pulled, and an electrical nerve impulse, known as an **action potential,** travels down the axon of the neuron (Siegelbaum & Koester, 1991; Neher, 1992; see Figure 2-2).

The action potential moves from one end of the axon to the other like a flame moves across a fuse toward an explosive. As the impulse travels along the axon, the movement of ions causes a sequential change in charge from negative to pos-

Action potential: An electric nerve impulse that travels through a neuron when it is set off by a "trigger," changing the cell's charge from negative to positive.

FIGURE 2-2 Changes in the electrical charge of a neuron during the passage of an action potential. In its normal resting state, a neuron has a negative charge of around −70 millivolts. When an action potential is triggered, however, the cell charge becomes positive, increasing to about +40 millivolts. Following the passage of the action potential, the charge becomes even more negative than it is in its typical state. It is not until the charge returns to its resting state that the neuron will be fully ready to be triggered once again.

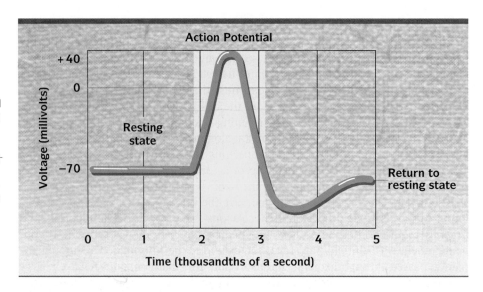

itive (see Figure 2-3). After the passage of the impulse, positive ions are pumped out of the axon, and the neuron charge returns to negative.

Just after an action potential has passed, the neuron cannot be fired again immediately, no matter how much stimulation it receives. It is as if the gun has to be painstakingly reloaded after each shot. There then follows a period in which, although it is possible to fire the neuron, it takes a stronger stimulus than that required if sufficient time had passed for the neuron to reach its normal resting state. Eventually, though, the neuron is ready to be fired once again.

These complex events may occur at dizzying speeds, although there is great variation among different neurons. The particular speed at which an action potential travels along an axon is determined by the axon's size and the thickness of the myelin sheath. Axons with small diameters carry impulses at about 2 miles per hour; longer and thicker ones can average speeds of more than 225 miles per hour.

In addition to varying according to how quickly an impulse moves across the axon, neurons differ in their potential rate of firing. Some neurons have the potential to fire as many as 1000 times per second; others have a maximum potential rate that is much lower. The intensity of a stimulus that provokes a neuron determines how much of this potential rate is reached. A strong stimulus, such as a bright light or a loud sound, leads to a higher rate of firing than a less intense stimulus does. Thus, while there are no differences in the strength or speed at which an impulse moves across a particular axon—as the all-or-none law sug-

FIGURE 2-3 Movement of an action potential across an axon. Just prior to time 1, positively charged ions enter the cell walls, changing the charge within that part of the cell from negative to positive. The action potential is thus triggered, traveling down the axon, as illustrated in the changes occurring from time 1 to time 3 (from top to bottom in this drawing). Following the passage of the action potential, positive ions are pumped out of the axon, restoring its charge to negative. The change in voltage illustrated at the top of the axon can be seen in greater detail in Figure 2-2.

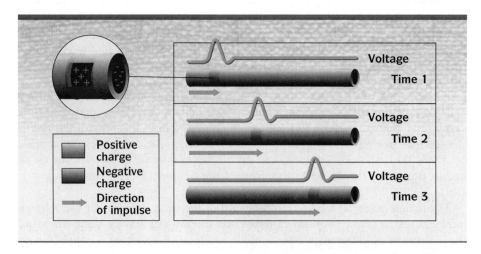

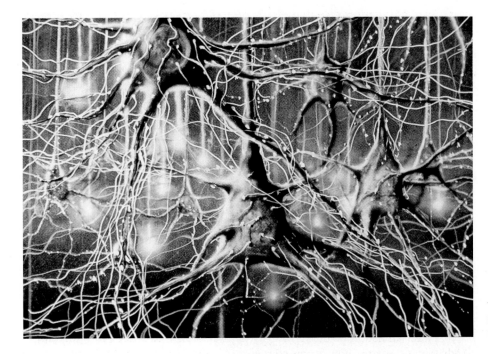

This color-enhanced micrograph illustrates the firing of multiple nerve cells.

gests—there is variation in the frequency of impulses, providing a mechanism by which we can distinguish the tickle of a feather from the weight of someone standing on our toe.

The structure, operation, and functions of the neuron illustrate how fundamental biological aspects of the body underlie several primary psychological processes. Our understanding of the way we sense, perceive, and learn about the world would be greatly restricted without the information that biopsychologists have acquired about the neuron.

Where Neuron Meets Neuron: Bridging the Gap

Did you ever put together a child's radio kit? If you have, you probably remember that the manufacturer supplied you with wires that had to be painstakingly connected to one another or to some other component of the radio; every piece had to be physically connected to something else.

The human brain and body are considerably more sophisticated than a radio, or any other manufactured apparatus, for that matter. Humans have evolved a neural transmission system that at some points has no need for a structural connection between its components. Instead, a chemical connection bridges the gap, known as a **synapse,** between two neurons. When a nerve impulse comes to the end of the axon and reaches a terminal button, the terminal button releases a chemical courier called a neurotransmitter.

Neurotransmitters are chemicals that carry messages across the synapse to the dendrite (and sometimes the cell body) of a receiver neuron. Like a boat that ferries passengers across a river, these chemical messengers move toward the shoreline of other neurons. The chemical mode of message transmission that occurs between neurons is strikingly different from the means by which communication occurs inside of neurons. It is important to remember, then, that although messages travel in electrical form within a neuron, they move *between* neurons through a chemical transmission system (see Figure 2-4a).

There are several types of neurotransmitters, and not all receiver neurons are capable of making use of the chemical message carried by a particular neurotransmitter. In the same way that a jigsaw puzzle piece can fit in only one spe-

Synapse: The gap between neurons through which chemical messages are communicated

Neurotransmitters: Chemicals that carry messages across the synapse to the dendrite (and sometimes the cell body) of a receiver neuron

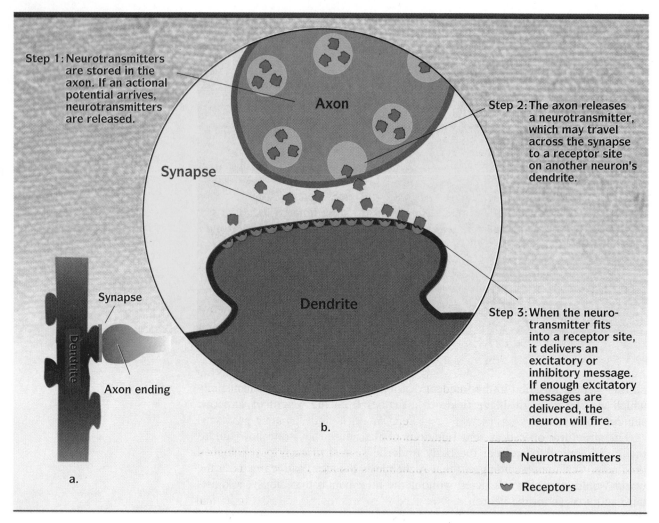

Step 1: Neurotransmitters are stored in the axon. If an actional potential arrives, neurotransmitters are released.

Step 2: The axon releases a neurotransmitter, which may travel across the synapse to a receptor site on another neuron's dendrite.

Axon

Synapse

Dendrite

Step 3: When the neuro- transmitter fits into a receptor site, it delivers an excitatory or inhibitory message. If enough excitatory messages are delivered, the neuron will fire.

Synapse

Dendrite

Axon ending

a.

b.

◆ Neurotransmitters

▽ Receptors

FIGURE 2-4 (*a*) A synapse is the junction between an axon and a dendrite. The gap between the axon and the dendrite is bridged by chemicals called neurotransmitters. (*b*) Just as the pieces of a jigsaw puzzle can fit in only one specific location in a puzzle, each kind of neurotransmitter has a distinctive configuration that allows it to fit into a specific type of receptor cell.

Excitatory message: A chemical secretion that makes it more likely that a receiving neuron will fire and an action potential will travel down its axon

Inhibitory message: A chemical secretion that prevents a receiving neuron from firing

cific location in a puzzle, so each kind of neurotransmitter has a distinctive configuration that allows it to fit into a specific type of receptor site on the receiving neuron (see Figure 2-4*b*). It is only when a neurotransmitter fits precisely into a receptor site that successful chemical communication is possible.

If a neurotransmitter does fit into a site on the receiving neuron, the chemical message it delivers is basically one of two types: excitatory or inhibitory. **Excitatory messages** make it more likely that a receiving neuron will fire and an action potential will travel down its axon. **Inhibitory messages,** in contrast, do just the opposite; they provide chemical information that prevents or decreases the likelihood that the receiving neuron will fire.

Because the dendrites of a neuron receive many messages simultaneously, some of which are excitatory and some inhibitory, the neuron must integrate the messages in some fashion. It does this by using a kind of chemical calculator. If the number of excitatory messages outweighs the number of inhibitory ones, the neuron will fire. On the other hand, if the number of inhibitory messages outweighs the excitatory ones, nothing will happen. The neuron will remain in its resting state.

If neurotransmitters remained at the site of the synapse, receptor neurons would be awash in a continual chemical bath, producing constant stimulation of the receptor neurons. If this were the case, effective communication across the synapse would no longer be possible. To solve this problem, neurotransmitters are either deactivated by enzymes or—more frequently—reabsorbed by the terminal buttons in an example of chemical recycling called **reuptake.** Like a vacuum cleaner sucking up dust, neurons reabsorb the neurotransmitters that are now clogging the synapse. All this activity occurs at lightning speed, with the process taking just several milliseconds (Kandel, Siegelbaum, & Schwartz, 1991).

Reuptake: The reabsorption of neurotransmitters by a terminal button

Neurotransmitters: Multitalented Chemical Couriers

Neurotransmitters represent a particularly important link between the nervous system and behavior. Not only are they important for maintaining vital brain and body functions, but having a deficiency or an excess of a neurotransmitter can produce severe behavior disorders.

So far, about fifty chemicals have been found to act as neurotransmitters, and many biopsychologists believe that dozens more may ultimately be identified (Shepherd, 1990). Neurotransmitters vary significantly in terms of how strong a concentration is required to trigger a neuron to fire. Furthermore, the effects of a given neurotransmitter vary, depending on the portion of the nervous system in which it is produced. The same neurotransmitter, then, can cause a neuron to fire when it is secreted in one part of the brain and can inhibit the firing of neurons when it is produced in another part. (The major neurotransmitters are shown in Table 2-1.)

One of the most common neurotransmitters is *acetylcholine* (or *ACh,* its chemical symbol), which is found throughout the nervous system. ACh is involved in our every move, as—among other things—it transmits messages relating to our skeletal muscles. ACh is also related to the drug curare, used on the tips of poison darts thrown by South American Indians. Curare keeps ACh from reaching receptor cells, thereby paralyzing the skeletal muscles and ultimately producing death by suffocation because the victim cannot breathe.

There is growing evidence that ACh is closely related to memory capabilities. And some scientists now suggest that Alzheimer's disease, the progressively degenerative disorder that ultimately produces loss of memory, confusion, and personality changes in its victims, is associated with a deficiency in the production of ACh. For example, some research shows that Alzheimer's patients have restricted production of ACh in portions of their brains. If this research is corroborated, it may lead to treatments in which production of ACh can be restored (Wolozin et al., 1986; Kosik, 1992).

Gamma-amino butyric acid (GABA), found in both the brain and the spinal cord, appears to be the nervous system's primary inhibitory neurotransmitter. It moderates a variety of behaviors, ranging from eating to aggression. The deadly poison strychnine produces convulsions by disrupting the transmission of GABA

TABLE 2-1	**Major Neurotransmitters**		
Name	Location	Functions	Effects
Adenosine triphosphate (ATP)	Throughout the nervous system	Excitatory	Memory
Acetylcholine (ACh)	Brain, spinal cord, peripheral nervous system, especially some organs of the parasympathetic nervous system	Excitatory in brain and autonomic nervous system; inhibitory elsewhere	Muscle movement; cognitive functioning
Dopamine (DA)	Brain	Inhibitory	Muscle disorders, mental disorders, Parkinson's disease
Endorphins	Brain, spinal cord	Primarily inhibitory, except in hippocampus	Pain suppression, pleasurable feelings, appetites, placebos
Gamma-amino butyric acid (GABA)	Brain, spinal cord	Main inhibitory neurotransmitter	Eating, aggression, sleeping

across synapses. Strychnine prevents GABA from carrying out its inhibitory role. It permits neurons to fire wildly, thereby producing convulsions. In contrast, some common substances, such as the tranquilizer Valium and alcohol, are effective because they permit GABA to operate more efficiently.

Another major neurotransmitter is *dopamine (DA).* The discovery that certain drugs can have a pronounced effect on dopamine release has led to the development of effective treatments for a wide variety of physical and mental ailments. For instance, Parkinson's disease, marked by varying degrees of muscular rigidity and shaking, seems to be caused by a deficiency of dopamine in the brain. As we'll discuss later in the chapter, techniques for increasing the production of dopamine in Parkinson's patients are proving effective (Yurek & Sladek, 1990; Weiss, 1990; Widner et al., 1992).

In some cases, overproduction of dopamine seems to produce negative consequences. For instance, researchers have hypothesized that schizophrenia and some other severe mental disturbances are affected or perhaps even caused by the presence of unusually high levels of dopamine (Wong et al., 1986; Wong et al., 1988; Seeman, Guan, & Van Tol, 1993). Drugs that block the reception of dopamine have been successful in reducing the abnormal behavior displayed by some people diagnosed with schizophrenia—as we will examine further when we consider abnormal behavior and its treatment in Chapters 12 and 13.

One of the newest neurotransmitters to be identified comes in the form of one of the body's most common substances: *adenosine triphosphate,* or *ATP.* Just as gasoline powers an automobile engine, ATP is the fuel used by the body to produce energy within cells, and it now appears that it plays an additional role as a neurotransmitter. Although research on ATP is in its infancy, biopsychologists speculate that it may play a major excitatory role. Furthermore, because it works very quickly, it may prove to have important therapeutic qualities and may be linked to several basic psychological processes. For example, some investigators hypothesize that ATP is essential in the formation of synapses vital to memory (Blakeslee, 1992; Evans, Derkach, & Surprenant, 1992; Edwards, Gibb, & Colquhoun, 1992).

Endorphins, another class of neurotransmitters, are a family of chemicals produced by the brain that are similar in structure to painkilling opiates. The production of endorphins seems to reflect the brain's effort to deal with pain. For instance, people who are afflicted with diseases that produce long-term, severe pain often develop large concentrations of endorphins in their brains—suggesting an effort by the brain to control the pain (Watkins & Mayer, 1982).

Endorphins may do more than provide mere pain reduction. They may also produce the euphoric feelings that joggers sometimes experience after long runs. It appears that the amount of exercise and perhaps even the pain involved in a long run stimulate the production of endorphins—ultimately resulting in what has been called a "runner's high" (Hathaway, 1984).

Endorphin release may also explain other phenomena that have long puzzled psychologists, such as the reasons that acupuncture and placebos (pills or other substances that contain no actual drugs but that patients *believe* will make them better) may be effective in reducing pain. Some biopsychologists speculate that both acupuncture and placebos induce the release of endorphins, which in turn, produce a positive bodily state (Bolles & Fanselow, 1982; Bandura et al., 1987).

Although it had been thought that all neurotransmitters are produced in the form of chemical liquids, surprising new evidence suggests that at least some chemical communication between neurons also may occur via nitric oxide, a gas. If this speculation is correct, it may mean that chemical gases are a supplementary form of interneuron communication—about whose existence we are just learning (Hoffman, 1991; Culotta & Koshland, 1992; Schuman & Madison, 1994). (For a profile of a person investigating the relationship between biology and behavior, see the Pathways through Psychology box.)

PATHWAYS THROUGH PSYCHOLOGY

Elaine Shen

Born: 1966
Education: B.A., Pacific Lutheran University, joint psychology and biology major; M.A., Oregon Health Sciences University, medical psychology; Ph.D. candidate
Home: Portland, Oregon

Elaine Shen believes that in the future the fields of psychology and biology will become increasingly intertwined. Her current academic work would certainly support that premise. A doctoral candidate at Oregon Health Sciences University in Portland, the 29-year-old Shen is doing research in what she considers a unique field.

"Currently I'm working in an area that combines psychology, biology, neuropsychology, pharmacology, and genetics. I'm interested in genetic components that may af-

Elaine Shen

fect behavioral responses to drugs of abuse such as alcohol, cocaine, and amphetamines," she said.

Shen completed her undergraduate studies with a dual B.A. in psychology and biology, but her expo-

sure to the field of neuropsychology sparked her interest in the more specialized field of medical psychology in which she is now working.

When asked what in her background led to her current studies, she described a class in neuropsychology. "After taking that course and discovering the link between biology and psychology, I wanted to explore it more," said Shen. "In contrast to basic biology where you can work in a very small area of a cell, psychology has taught me to look at the big picture, to consider what is relevant to behavior, and to examine how we function as people and socially adapt. The basic idea that behavior can be looked at in a scientific way, using scientific methodology, is very interesting to me.

RECAP AND REVIEW

Recap

- Neurons are the basic elements of the nervous system. They allow the transmission of messages that coordinate the complex activities of the human body.
- All neurons have a similar basic structure. They receive messages through the dendrites and transmit them through the axon to other neurons.
- Neurons fire according to an all-or-none law; they are either firing or resting.
- The specific site of transmission of messages from one neuron to another is called the synapse. Messages moving *across* synapses are chemical in nature, although they travel *within* neurons in an electrical form.
- Neurotransmitters are the specific chemicals that make the chemical connection at the synapse. These act either to excite other neurons into firing or to inhibit neurons from firing.

Review

1. The _____ is the fundamental element of the nervous system.
2. Messages move through the neuron in what direction?
   a. Dendrites ⟶ axon   b. Axon ⟶ dendrites
   c. Myelin ⟶ nucleus   d. Terminal button ⟶ brain
3. Just as electrical wires have an outer coating, so axons are insulated by a coating called the _____ _____ .
4. The electric nerve impulse that travels down a neuron is called a(n) _____ _____ .
5. The _____ law states that a neuron is either firing or resting.
6. The chemical connection between two neurons occurs at a gap known as a(n)
   a. axon   c. synapse
   b. terminal button   d. amino acid
7. _____ are chemical messengers that transmit between neurons.
8. Match the neurotransmitter with its function:
   1. Reduce the experience of pain
   2. Moderates eating and aggression
   3. Produces contractions of skeletal muscles

   a. ACh   b. GABA   c. Endorphins

Ask Yourself

What might be the advantage of neurons following the all-or-none law?

(Answers to review questions are on page 50.)

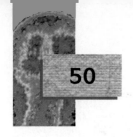

• *In what way are the structures of the nervous system tied together?*

THE NERVOUS SYSTEM

Given the complexity of individual neurons and the neurotransmission process, it should come as no surprise that the connections and structures formed by the neurons are complicated in their own right. Because just one neuron may be connected to 80,000 other neurons, the total number of possible connections is astonishing. For instance, some estimates of the number of neural connections within the brain fall in the neighborhood of 1 quadrillion—a 1 followed by 15 zeros—while some experts put the number even higher (Kolb & Whishaw, 1990; Estes, 1991; McGaugh, Weinberger, & Lynch, 1990; Eichenbaum, 1993).

Whatever the actual number of neural connections, the human nervous system has both a logic and an elegance. We turn now to its basic structures.

Central and Peripheral Nervous Systems

As you can see from the schematic representation in Figure 2-5, the nervous system is divided into two main parts: the central nervous system and the peripheral nervous system. The **central nervous system (CNS)** is composed of the brain and spinal cord. The **spinal cord,** about the thickness of a pencil, contains a bundle of nerves that leaves the brain and runs down the length of the back (see Figure 2-6). It is the main means for transmitting messages between the brain and the body.

However, the spinal cord is not just a communications conduit. It also controls some simple kinds of behaviors on its own, without any involvement of the brain. One example is the way that your knee jerks forward when it is tapped with a rubber hammer. Such behaviors, called **reflexes,** represent an automatic, invol-

Central nervous system (CNS): The system that includes the brain and the spinal cord

Spinal cord: A bundle of nerves running along the spine, carrying messages between the brain and the body

Reflexes: Automatic, involuntary responses to incoming stimuli

Sensory (afferent) neurons: Neurons that transmit information from the body to the central nervous system

Motor (efferent) neurons: Neurons that transmit information from nervous system to muscles and glands

Interneurons: Neurons that transmit information between sensory and motor neurons

FIGURE 2-5 A schematic diagram of the relationship of the parts of the nervous system.

The nervous system

Peripheral nervous system — Central nervous system

Somatic division (voluntary) — Autonomic division (invountary) — Brain — Spinal cord

Sympathetic (emergency activation) — Parasympathetic (calms body after emergency)

untary response to an incoming stimulus. Similarly, when you touch a hot stove and immediately withdraw your hand, a reflex is at work. Although the brain eventually analyzes and reacts to the situation ("ouch—hot stove—pull away!"), the initial withdrawal is directed only by neurons in the spinal cord.

Three sorts of neurons are involved in reflexes. **Sensory (afferent) neurons** transmit information from the perimeter of the body to the central nervous system. **Motor (efferent) neurons** communicate information from the nervous system to muscles and glands of the body. **Interneurons** connect sensory and motor neurons, carrying messages between the two.

The importance of the spinal cord and reflexes is illustrated by the outcome of accidents in which the cord is injured or severed. In one resulting injury, *paraplegia,* a person is unable to voluntarily move any muscles in the lower half of the body. However, even though the cord is severed, the undamaged area of the spinal cord is still able to produce some simple reflex actions, if stimulated appropriately. For instance, if a paraplegic's knee is tapped lightly, the lower leg will jerk forward slightly. Similarly, in some kinds of spinal cord injuries, people will move their legs in an involuntary response to a pinprick, even though they do not experience the sensation of pain.

As suggested by its name, the **peripheral nervous system** branches out from the spinal cord and brain and reaches the extremities of the body. Made up of long axons and dendrites, the peripheral nervous system encompasses all parts of the nervous system other than the brain and spinal cord. There are two major divisions, the somatic division and the autonomic division, both of which connect the central nervous system with the sense organs, muscles, glands, and other organs. The **somatic division** specializes in the control of voluntary movements—such as the motion of the eyes to read this sentence or of the hand to turn this page—and the communication of information to and from the sense organs. On the other hand, the **autonomic division** is concerned with the parts of the body that keep us alive—the heart, blood vessels, glands, lungs, and other organs that function involuntarily without our awareness. As you read now, the autonomic division of the peripheral nervous system is pumping blood through your body, pushing your lungs in and out, overseeing the digestion of the meal you had a few hours ago, and so on—all without a thought or care on your part.

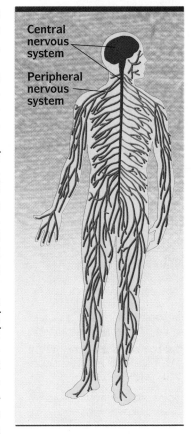

FIGURE 2-6 The central nervous system, consisting of the brain and spinal cord, and the peripheral nervous system.

Peripheral nervous system: All parts of the nervous system except the brain and the spinal cord (includes somatic and autonomic divisions)

Somatic division: The part of the nervous system that controls voluntary movements of the skeletal muscles

Autonomic division: The part of the nervous system that controls involuntary movement (the actions of the heart, glands, lungs, and other organs)

Actor Chistopher Reeve, shown here in his first public appearance following a severe riding injury, suffered damage to his spinal cord that left him paralyzed.

51

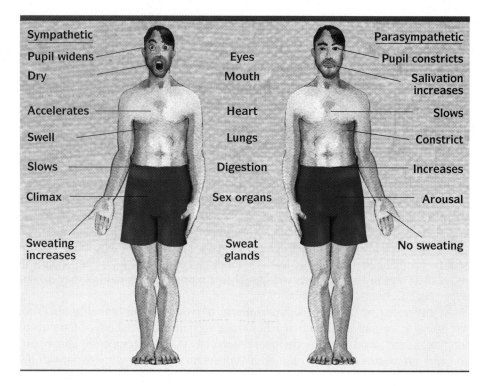

FIGURE 2-7 The major functions of the autonomic nervous system. The sympathetic division acts to prepare certain organs of the body for stressful emergency situations, and the parasympathetic division acts to calm the body after the emergency situation is resolved.

Activating the Autonomic Nervous System

The autonomic division plays a particularly crucial role during emergency situations. Suppose as you are reading you suddenly sense that a stranger is watching you through the window. As you look up, you see the glint of something that just might be a knife. As confusion races through your mind and fear overcomes your attempts to think rationally, what happens to your body? If you are like most people, you react immediately on a physiological level. Your heart rate increases, you begin to sweat, and you develop goose bumps all over your body.

The physiological changes that occur result from the activation of one of the two parts that make up the autonomic division: the **sympathetic division.** The sympathetic division acts to prepare the body in stressful emergency situations, engaging all the organism's resources to respond to a threat. This response often takes the form of "fight or flight." In contrast, the **parasympathetic division** acts to calm the body after the emergency situation is resolved. When you find, for instance, that the stranger at the window is actually your roommate who has lost his keys and is climbing in the window to avoid waking you, your parasympathetic division begins to predominate, lowering your heart rate, stopping your sweating, and returning your body to the state it was in prior to your fright. The parasympathetic division also provides a means for the body to maintain storage of energy sources such as nutrients and oxygen. The sympathetic and parasympathetic divisions work together to regulate many functions of the body (see Figure 2-7). For instance, sexual arousal is controlled by the parasympathetic division, while sexual orgasm is a function of the sympathetic division.

Sympathetic division: The part of the autonomic division of the peripheral nervous system that prepares the body to respond in stressful emergency situations

Parasympathetic division: The part of the autonomic division of the peripheral nervous system that calms the body, bringing functions back to normal after an emergency has passed

RECAP AND REVIEW

Recap

- The central nervous system (CNS) is made up of the brain and spinal cord, a thick bundle of nerves running from the brain down the length of the back.

- The peripheral nervous system includes all parts of the nervous system other than the brain and spinal cord. The peripheral nervous system has two major parts: the somatic division (for voluntary movements) and the autonomic division (for involuntary movements).

- The autonomic division, which itself has two parts (sympathetic and parasympathetic divisions), plays a major role during emergency situations.

Review

1. If you should put your hand on a red-hot piece of metal, the immediate response of pulling it away would be an example of a _____ .
2. The portion of your nervous system which controls functions such as breathing and digestion is known as the _____ division.

3. The peripheral nervous system includes nerves located in the arms, legs, and spinal cord. True or false?
4. Maria saw a young boy run into the street and get hit by a car. When she got to the fallen child, she was in a state of panic. She was sweating, and her heart was racing. Her biological state resulted from the activation of what division of the autonomic nervous system?
   a. Parasympathetic   c. Peripheral
   b. Somatic   d. Sympathetic

Ask Yourself

How might communication within the nervous system result in human consciousness?

(Answers to review questions are on page 54.)

- *How do researchers identify the major parts and functioning of the brain?*
- *What are the major parts of the brain, and what are the behaviors for which each part is responsible?*

THE BRAIN

It is not much to look at. Soft, spongy, mottled, and pinkish-gray in color, one could hardly say that it possesses much in the way of physical beauty. Despite its physical appearance, however, it ranks as the greatest natural marvel that we know and possesses a beauty and sophistication all its own.

The object to which this description applies: the brain. The brain is responsible for our loftiest thoughts—and our most primitive urges. It is the overseer of the intricate workings of the human body. If one were to attempt to design a computer to mimic the capabilities of the brain, the task would be nearly impossible; in fact, it has proved difficult even to come close (Hanson & Olson, 1990). The sheer quantity of nerve cells in the brain is enough to daunt even the most ambitious computer engineer. Many billions of nerve cells make up a structure weighing just 3 pounds in the average adult. However, it is not the number of cells that is the most astounding thing about the brain but its ability to allow human intellect to flourish as it guides our behavior and thoughts.

The brain is a three-pound mass of soft, spongy matter made up of billions of nerve cells that make all human achievement possible.

Studying the Brain's Structure and Functions: Spying on the Brain

The brain has posed a continual challenge to those wishing to study it. For most of history, its examination was possible only after an individual was dead. Only then could the skull be opened and the brain cut into without the risk of causing serious injury. While informative, such a limited procedure could hardly tell us much about the functioning of the healthy brain.

Today, however, important advances have been made in the study of the brain involving the use of brain scanning techniques. Using brain scanning, investigators can take a snapshot of the internal workings of the brain without having to cut surgically into a person's skull. The major scanning techniques, described below, are illustrated in Figure 2-8 (Hall, 1992; Maziotta, 1993; Raichle, 1994).

■ The *electroencephalogram (EEG)* records the electrical signals being transmitted inside the brain through electrodes placed on the outside of the skull. Although traditionally the EEG could produce only a graph of electrical wave pat-

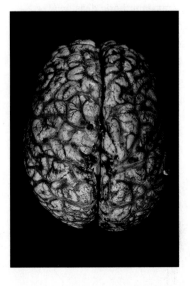

53

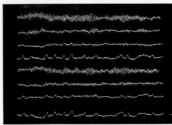
a. EEG

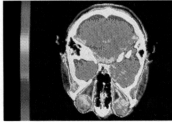
b. CAT scan

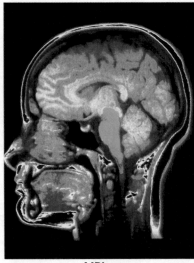
c. MRI scan

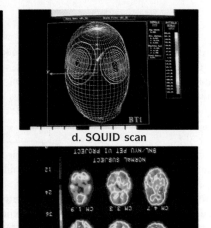
d. SQUID scan

e. PET scan

FIGURE 2-8 Brain scans produced by different techniques. (*a*) A computer-produced EEG image. (*b*) This CAT scan shows the structures of the brain. (*c*) The MRI scan uses a magnetic field to detail the parts of the brain. (*d*) The SQUID scan shows the neural activity of the brain. (*e*) The PET scan displays the functioning of the brain at a given moment and is sensitive to the person's activities.

terns, new techniques are now able to transform the brain's electrical activity into a pictorial representation of the brain that allows the diagnosis of such problems as epilepsy and learning disabilities.

■ The *computerized axial tomography (CAT)* scan uses a computer to construct an image of the brain by combining thousands of separate x-rays taken at slightly different angles. It is extremely useful for showing abnormalities in the structure of the brain, such as swelling and enlargement of certain parts, but does not provide information about brain activity.

■ The *magnetic resonance imaging (MRI)* scan produces a powerful magnetic field to provide a detailed, computer-generated image of brain structures. It is also capable of producing vivid images of individual bundles of nerves in other parts of the body, opening the way for improved diagnosis of such ailments as chronic back pain (Filler et al., 1993).

■ The *superconducting quantum interference device (SQUID)* scan is sensitive to tiny changes in magnetic fields that occur when neurons fire. Using SQUID, researchers can pinpoint the location of neural activity (e.g., Armstrong, Slaven, & Harding, 1991; Forss et al., 1993).

■ The *positron emission tomography (PET)* scan shows biochemical activity within the brain at a given moment. PET scans begin with the injection of radioactive (but safe) water into the bloodstream, which wends its way to the brain. By measuring the location of radiation within the brain, a computer can determine which are the more active regions, providing a striking picture of the brain at work.

Each of these techniques offers exciting possibilities not only for the diagnosis and treatment of brain disease and injuries but also for an increased understanding of the normal functioning of the brain (Gibbons, 1990; Martin, Brust, & Hilal, 1991; Posner, 1993; Crease, 1993).

The Central Core: Our "Old Brain"

While the capabilities of the human brain far exceed those of the brain of any other species, it is not surprising that the basic functions, such as breathing, eat-

---

ANSWERS TO PREVIOUS REVIEW
1. reflex   2. autonomic   3. False; the spinal cord belongs to the CNS.   4. d

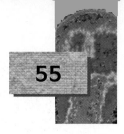
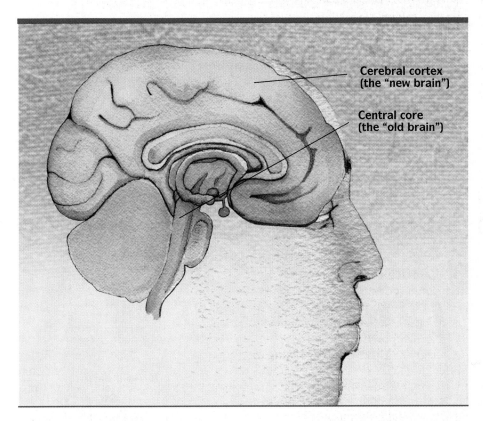

Cerebral cortex
(the "new brain")

Central core
(the "old brain")

FIGURE 2-9 The major divisions of the brain: the cerebral cortex and central core.

ing, and sleeping, that we share with more primitive animals are directed by a relatively primitive part of the brain. A portion of the brain known as the **central core** (see Figure 2-9) is quite similar to that found in all vertebrates (species with backbones). The central core is sometimes referred to as the "old brain" because its evolutionary underpinnings can be traced back some 500 million years to primitive structures found in nonhuman species.

If we were to move up the spinal cord from the base of the skull to locate the structures of the central core of the brain, the first part we would come to would be the *medulla* (see Figure 2-10). The medulla controls a number of critical body functions, the most important of which are breathing and maintenance of heartbeat. The *pons* comes next, joining the two halves of the cerebellum, which lies adjacent to it. Containing large bundles of nerves, the pons acts as a transmitter of motor information, coordinating muscles and integrating movement between the right and left halves of the body. It is also involved in the control of sleep.

The **reticular formation** extends from the medulla through the pons. Like an ever-vigilant guard, the reticular formation is made up of groups of nerve cells that can immediately activate other parts of the brain to produce general bodily arousal. If, for example, we are startled by a loud noise, our reticular formation can prompt a heightened state of awareness to determine whether a response is necessary. In addition, the reticular formation serves a different function when we are sleeping, seeming to filter out background stimuli to allow us to sleep undisturbed.

The **cerebellum** is found just above the medulla and behind the pons. Without the help of the cerebellum we would be unable to walk a straight line without staggering and lurching forward, for it is the job of the cerebellum to control bodily balance. It constantly monitors feedback from the muscles to coordinate their placement, movement, and tension. In fact, drinking too much alcohol seems to depress the activity of the cerebellum, leading to the unsteady gait and movement characteristic of drunkenness (Ghez, 1991).

Central core: The "old brain," which controls such basic functions as eating and sleeping and is common to all vertebrates

Reticular formation: A group of nerve cells in the brain that arouses the body to prepare it for appropriate action and screens out background stimuli

Cerebellum (ser uh BELL um): The part of the brain that controls bodily balance

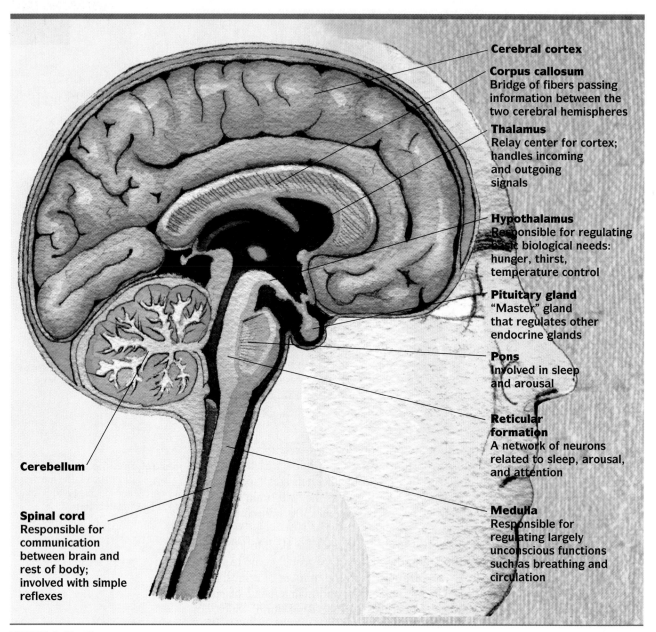

FIGURE 2-10 The structures within the brain.

Thalamus: The part of the brain's central core that transmits messages from the sense organs to the cerebral cortex and from the cerebral cortex to the cerebellum and medulla

Hypothalamus: A tiny part of the brain, located below the thalamus of the brain, that maintains homeostasis and produces and regulates vital, basic behavior such as eating, drinking, and sexual behavior

Hidden within the middle of the central core, the **thalamus** acts primarily as a busy relay station, mostly for information concerning the senses. Messages from the eyes, ears, and skin travel to the thalamus to be communicated upward to higher parts of the brain. The thalamus also integrates information from higher parts of the brain, sorting it out so that it can be sent to the cerebellum and medulla.

The **hypothalamus** is located just below the thalamus. Although tiny—about the size of a fingertip—the hypothalamus plays an inordinately important role. One of its major functions is to maintain *homeostasis*, a steady internal environment for the body. As we'll discuss further in Chapter 9, the hypothalamus helps provide a constant body temperature and monitors the amount of nutrients stored in the cells. A second major function is equally important: It produces and regulates behavior that is critical to the basic survival of the species—eating, drinking, sexual behavior, aggression, and nurturance of offspring (Kupfermann, 1991b).

56

Image labels:

Cerebral cortex

Corpus callosum
Bridge of fibers passing information between the two cerebral hemispheres

Thalamus
Relay center for cortex; handles incoming and outgoing signals

Hypothalamus
Responsible for regulating basic biological needs: hunger, thirst, temperature control

Pituitary gland
"Master" gland that regulates other endocrine glands

Pons
Involved in sleep and arousal

Reticular formation
A network of neurons related to sleep, arousal, and attention

Medulla
Responsible for regulating largely unconscious functions such as breathing and circulation

Cerebellum

Spinal cord
Responsible for communication between brain and rest of body; involved with simple reflexes

The Limbic System: Beyond the Central Core

In an eerie view of the future, some science fiction writers have suggested that people will someday routinely have electrodes implanted in their brains. These electrodes will permit them to receive tiny shocks that produce the sensation of pleasure by stimulating certain centers of the brain. When they feel upset, people will simply activate their electrodes to achieve an immediate high.

Although farfetched—and ultimately improbable—such a futuristic fantasy is based on fact. The brain does have pleasure centers in several areas, including some in the **limbic system.** Consisting of a series of interrelated structures, the limbic system borders the top of the central core and has connections with the cerebral cortex (located in Figure 2-9 roughly at the boundaries between the central core and cortex).

The structures of the limbic system jointly control a variety of basic functions relating to emotions and self-preservation, such as eating, aggression, and reproduction. Injury to the limbic system can produce striking changes in behavior. It can turn animals that are usually docile and tame into belligerent savages. Conversely, those that are usually wild and uncontrollable may become meek and obedient (Fanelli, Burright, & Donovick, 1983).

Research examining the effects of mild electric shocks to parts of the limbic system and other parts of the brain has produced some thought-provoking findings (Olds & Milner, 1954; Olds & Fobes, 1981). In one experiment, rats that pressed a bar received a mild electric jolt through an electrode implanted in their brain. Even starving rats on their way to food would stop to press the bar as many times as they could. Some rats would actually stimulate themselves literally thousands of times an hour—until they collapsed with fatigue (Routtenberg & Lindy, 1965).

The extraordinarily pleasurable quality of certain kinds of stimulation has also been experienced by humans, who, as part of treatment for certain kinds of brain disorders, have received electrical stimulation to certain areas of the limbic system. Although at a loss to describe just what it feels like, these people report the experience to be intensely pleasurable, similar in some respects to sexual orgasm.

The limbic system also plays an important role in learning and memory, a finding demonstrated in patients with epilepsy. In an attempt to stop their seizures, such patients have had portions of their limbic system removed. One unintended consequence of the surgery is that individuals sometimes have difficulty learning and remembering new information. In one case (discussed again when we focus on memory in Chapter 6), a patient who had undergone surgery was unable to remember where he lived, although he had resided at the same address for 8 years. Further, even though the patient was able to carry on animated conversations, he was unable, a few minutes later, to recall what had been discussed (Milner, 1966).

The limbic system, then, is involved in several important functions, including self-preservation, learning, memory, and the experience of pleasure. These functions are hardly unique to humans; in fact, the limbic system is sometimes referred to as the "animal brain" because its structures and functions are so similar to those of other mammals. To find that which is uniquely human, we need to turn to another part of the brain, the cerebral cortex.

Limbic system: The part of the brain located outside the "new brain" that controls eating, aggression, and reproduction

RECAP AND REVIEW

Recap

- Major brain scanning techniques include the electroencephalogram (EEG), the computerized axial tomography (CAT) scan, the magnetic resonance imaging (MRI) scan, the superconducting quantum interference device (SQUID) scan, and the positron emission tomography (PET) scan.

- The central core of the human brain is similar to that found in all vertebrates.
- Starting from the top of the spinal cord and moving up into the brain, first we find the medulla, which controls such functions as breathing and heartbeat. Next is the pons, which acts to transmit motor information.
- The reticular formation, extending from the medulla through the pons, arouses and activates the body but also censors outside stimulation during sleep. The cerebellum is involved in the control of motion.
- The thalamus acts primarily as a sensory-information relay center, whereas the hypothalamus maintains homeostasis, a steady internal environment for the body.
- The limbic system controls a variety of basic functions relating to emotions and self-preservation, such as eating, aggression, and reproduction.

Review

1. The EEG, CAT, MRI, PET, and SQUID are types of _____ _____ , procedures whereby a picture of the brain can be taken without opening the skull.
2. Match the name of each brain scan with the appropriate description:
   1. Powerful magnets produce magnetic fields in the brain that provide a computer-generated snapshot.
   2. Location of radioactive isotopes within the brain determines its active regions.
   3. Electrodes record the electrical signals transmitted through the brain.
   4. This scan measures tiny changes in magnetic fields that occur when neurons fire, pinpointing neural activity.
   5. Computer image combines thousands of x-ray pictures into one.

   a. EEG   d. PET
   b. CAT   e. SQUID
   c. MRI
3. Control of such functions as breathing and sleep is located in the recently developed "new brain." True or false?
4. Match the portion of the brain with its function:
   1. Maintains breathing and heartbeat
   2. Controls bodily balance
   3. Coordinates and integrates muscle movements
   4. Activates the brain to produce arousal

   a. Medulla   c. Cerebellum
   b. Pons   d. Reticular formation
5. You receive flowers from a friend. The color, smell, and feel of the flowers are relayed through what part of the brain?
6. The _____ , a fingertip-sized portion of the brain, is responsible for the maintenance of _____ , the regulation of the body's internal environment.
7. The hypothalamus is responsible for the production and regulation of behavior that is critical to the basic survival of the species, such as eating, drinking, sexual behavior, and aggression. True or false?

Ask Yourself

How would you answer the argument that "psychologists should leave the study of neurons and synapses and the nervous system to biologists"?

(Answers to review questions are on page 60.)

Cerebral cortex: The "new brain," responsible for the most sophisticated information processing in the brain; contains the lobes

Lobes: The four major sections of the cerebral cortex

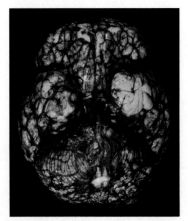

This view of the cerebral cortex shows the fissures that divide it into four lobes.

The Cerebral Cortex: Up the Evolutionary Ladder

As we have proceeded up the spinal cord and into the brain, our discussion has centered on the brain's areas that control functions similar to those found in less sophisticated organisms. But where, you may be asking, are the portions of the brain that enable humans to do what they do best, and that distinguish humankind from all other animals? Those unique features of the human brain—indeed, the very capabilities that allow you to come up with such a question in the first place—are embodied in the ability to think, evaluate, and make complex judgments. The principal location of these abilities, along with many others, is the **cerebral cortex.**

The cerebral cortex, which is sometimes referred to as the "new brain" because of its relatively recent evolution, is a mass of deeply folded, rippled, convoluted tissue. Although only about one-twelfth of an inch thick, it would, if flattened out, cover more than a 2-foot-square area. This configuration allows the surface area of the cortex to be considerably greater than if it were smoother and more uniformly packed into the skull. The mottled configuration also permits a high level of neuronal integration, allowing sophisticated processing of information.

The cortex has four major sections, called **lobes.** If we take a side view of the brain, the *frontal lobes* lie at the front center of the cortex, and the *parietal lobes* lie behind them. The *temporal lobes* are found in the lower center of the cortex, with the *occipital lobes* lying behind them. These four sets of lobes are physically separated by deep grooves called *sulci.* Figure 2-11a shows the four areas.

58

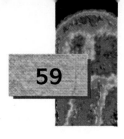

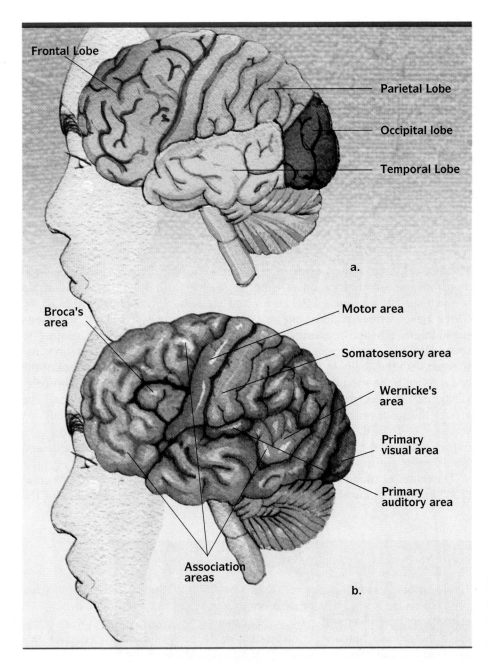

FIGURE 2-11 The cerebral cortex of the brain. (*a*) The major physical structures of the cerebral cortex are called lobes. (*b*) This figure illustrates the functions associated with particular areas of the cerebral cortex.

Another way of describing the brain is by considering the functions associated with a given area. Figure 2-11*b* shows the specialized regions within the lobes related to specific functions and areas of the body. Three major areas have been discovered: the motor areas, the sensory areas, and the association areas. Although we will discuss each of these areas as though they were separate and independent entities, keep in mind that this approach represents an oversimplification. In most instances, behavior is influenced simultaneously by several structures and areas within the brain, operating interdependently. Furthermore, even within a given area, additional subdivisions exist (Gibbons, 1990).

The Motor Area of the Cortex   If you look at the frontal lobe in Figure 2-11*b*, you will see a shaded portion labeled the **motor area.** This part of the cortex is largely responsible for the voluntary movement of particular parts of the body. Every portion of the motor area corresponds to a specific locale within the body.

Motor area: One of the major areas of the brain, responsible for voluntary movement of particular parts of the body

If we were to insert an electrode into a particular part of the motor area of the cortex and apply mild electrical stimulation, there would be involuntary movement in the corresponding part of the body (Kertesz, 1983). If we moved to another part of the motor area and stimulated it, a different part of the body would move.

The motor area has been so well mapped that it is possible to illustrate the amount and relative location of cortical tissue that is used to produce movement in specific parts of the human body. The control of body movements that are relatively large scale and require little precision, such as movement of a knee or a hip, is centered in a very small space in the motor area. On the other hand, movements that must be precise and delicate, such as facial expressions and finger movements, are controlled by a considerably larger portion of the motor area. In sum, the motor area of the cortex provides a clear guide to the degree of complexity and the importance of the motor capabilities of specific parts of the body (Barinaga, 1995).

The Sensory Area of the Cortex   Given the one-to-one correspondence between motor area and body location, it is not surprising to find a similar relationship between specific portions of the cortex and the senses. The **sensory area** of the cortex includes three regions: one that corresponds primarily to body sensations (including touch and pressure), one relating to sight, and a third relating to sound. For instance, the *somatosensory* area encompasses specific locations associated with the ability to perceive touch and pressure in a particular area of the body. As with the motor area, the amount of brain tissue related to a particular location on the body determines the degree of sensitivity of that location. The greater the space within the cortex, the more sensitive that area of the body. As you can see from the weird-looking individual in Figure 2-12, parts such as the fingers are related to proportionally more space in the somatosensory area and are the most sensitive.

The senses of sound and sight are also represented in specific areas of the cerebral cortex. An *auditory* area located in the temporal lobe is responsible for the

Sensory area: The site in the brain that corresponds to each of the senses, with the degree of sensitivity relating to the amount of brain tissue

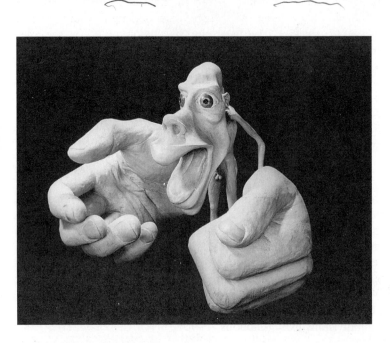

FIGURE 2-12   The greater the amount of tissue in the somatosensory area of the brain that is related to a specific body part, the more sensitive is that body part. If the size of our body parts reflected the corresponding amount of brain tissue, we would look like this strange creature.

ANSWERS TO PREVIOUS REVIEW

1. brain scans   **2.** 1-c; 2-d; 3-a; 4-e; 5-b   **3.** False; it is located in the central core, or "old brain."   **4.** 1-a; 2-c; 3-b; 4-d   **5.** Thalamus   **6.** hypothalamus; homeostasis   **7.** True

sense of hearing. If the auditory area is stimulated electrically, a person will hear sounds such as clicks or hums. It also appears that particular locations within the auditory area respond to specific pitches.

The *visual* area in the cortex, located in the occipital lobe, operates analogously to the other sensory areas. Stimulation by electrodes produces the experience of flashes of light or colors, suggesting that the raw sensory input of images from the eyes is received in this area of the brain and transformed into meaningful stimuli. The visual area also provides another example of how areas of the brain are intimately related to specific body areas: Particular areas of the eye's retina are related to particular parts of the cortex—with, as you might guess, more brain space given to the most sensitive portions of the retina (Miyashita, 1995).

The Association Areas of the Cortex   Consider the following case:

Twenty-five-year-old Phineas Gage, a railroad employee, was blasting rock one day in 1848 when an accidental explosion punched a 3-foot-long spike, about an inch in diameter, completely through his skull. The spike entered just under his left cheek, came out the top of his head, and flew into the air. Gage immediately suffered a series of convulsions, yet a few minutes later was talking with rescuers. In fact, he was able to walk up a long flight of stairs before receiving any medical attention. Amazingly, after a few weeks his wound healed, and he was physically close to his old self again. Mentally, however, there was a difference: Once a careful and hard-working person, Phineas now became enamored with wild schemes and was flighty and often irresponsible. As one of his physicians put it, "Previous to his injury, though untrained in the schools, he possessed a well-balanced mind, and was looked upon by those who knew him as a shrewd, smart businessman, very energetic and persistent in executing all his plans of operation. In this regard his mind was radically changed, so decidedly that his friends and acquaintances said he was 'no longer Gage.' " (Harlow, 1869, p. 14).

What had happened to the old Gage? Although there is no way of knowing for sure—science being what it was in the 1800s—we can speculate that the accident may have injured the association areas of Gage's cerebral cortex.

If you return one last time to our diagram of the cerebral cortex (Figure 2-11b), you will find that the motor and sensory areas take up a relatively small portion of the cortex; the remainder contains the association areas. The **association areas** are generally considered to be the site of higher mental processes such as thinking, language, memory, and speech.

Most of our understanding of the association areas comes from patients who have suffered some type of brain injury. In some cases the injury stemmed from natural causes such as a tumor or a stroke, either of which would block certain blood vessels within the cerebral cortex. In other cases, accidental causes were the culprits, as was true with Phineas Gage. In any event, damage to these areas can result in unusual behavioral changes, indicating the importance of the association areas to normal functioning (Kupfermann, 1991c).

Gage's case provides evidence that there is a specialized area for making rational decisions. When this area is damaged, people undergo personality changes that affect their ability to make moral judgments and to process emotions. At the same time, people with damage in this area are quite capable of reasoning logically, performing calculations, and recalling information (Damasio et al., 1994).

Injuries to other parts of the association areas can produce a condition known as apraxia. *Apraxia* occurs when an individual is unable to integrate activities in a rational or logical manner. For example, a patient asked to get a soda from the refrigerator might go to the refrigerator and open and close the door repeatedly, or might take bottle after bottle of soda out of the refrigerator, dropping each to the floor. Similarly, a person with apraxia who is asked to open a lock with a key may be unable to do so in response to the request—but, if simply left alone in a locked room, will unlock the door if he or she wishes to leave (Lechtenberg, 1982).

Association areas: One of the major areas of the brain, the site of the higher mental processes such as thought, language, memory, and speech

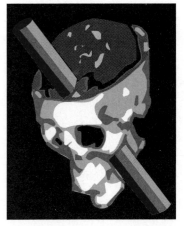

A model of the injury sustained by Phineas Gage. (Reprinted with permission of the author and publisher from *Science,* Volume 264, May 20, 1994, p.1104, Copyright 1994 American Association for the Advancement of Science.)

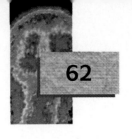
Apraxia is clearly not a muscular problem, since the person is capable of carrying out the individual components of the overall behavior. Moreover, if asked to perform the individual components of a larger behavioral pattern one at a time, a patient is often successful. It is only when asked to carry out a sequence of behaviors requiring a degree of planning and foresight that the patient shows deficits. It appears, then, that the association areas may act as "master planners," that is, organizers of actions.

Other difficulties that arise because of injury to the association area of the brain relate to the use of language. Problems with verbal expression, known as *aphasia,* can take many forms. In *Broca's aphasia* (caused by damage to the part of the brain first identified by a French physician, Paul Broca), speech becomes halting, laborious, and often ungrammatical. The speaker is unable to find the right words, in a kind of tip-of-the-tongue phenomenon that we all experience from time to time. In the case of people with aphasia, though, they grope for words almost constantly, eventually blurting out a kind of "verbal telegram." A phrase like "I put the book on the table" comes out as "I . . . put . . . book . . . table" (Lechtenberg, 1982; Cornell, Fromkin, & Mauner, 1993).

Wernicke's aphasia is a disorder named for its discoverer, Carl Wernicke. Wernicke's aphasia produces difficulties both in understanding others' speech and in producing language. Found in patients with damage to an area of the brain first identified by Wernicke, the disorder is characterized by speech that sounds fluent but makes no sense. For instance, one of Wernicke's patients, Philip Gorgan, was asked what brought him to the hospital. His rambling reply: "Boy, I'm sweating, I'm awful nervous, you know, once in a while I get caught up, I can't mention the tarripoi, a month ago, quite a little, I've done a lot well, I impose a lot, while, on the other hand, you know what I mean, I have to run around, look it over, trebbin and all that sort of stuff" (Gardner, 1975, p. 68).

Brain injuries, such as those that result in aphasia, and brain disorders due to disease and illness have given new impetus to scientists who are seeking to "map" the neural circuitry of the brain. Using sophisticated computer technology, researchers are seeking to create a data base encompassing every facet of the brain.

To further such research, the 1990s have been designated by the U.S. Congress as the "decade of the brain" in recognition of the importance of unraveling the brain's knotty mysteries. These efforts are beginning to pay off, in very practical ways, as we discuss in the Psychology at Work box.

- *How do the two halves of the brain operate interdependently?*
- *How can an understanding of the nervous system help us to find ways to alleviate disease and pain?*

The Specialization of the Hemispheres: Two Brains or One?

The most recent development, at least in evolutionary terms, in the organization and operation of our brain probably occurred in the last million years: a specialization of the functions controlled by the two sides of the brain, which has symmetrical left and right halves.

Specifically, the brain can be divided into two roughly similar mirror-image halves—just as we have two arms, two legs, and two lungs. Because of the way nerves are connected from the brain to the rest of the body, these two symmetrical left and right halves, called **hemispheres,** control the side of the body opposite to their location. The left hemisphere of the brain, then, generally controls the right side of the body, and the right hemisphere controls the left side of the body. Thus damage to the right side of the brain is typically indicated by functional difficulties in the left side of the body.

Hemispheres: Symmetrical left and right halves of the brain

PSYCHOLOGY AT WORK

Mending the Brain

Shortly after he was born, Jacob Stark's arms and legs started jerking every 20 minutes. Weeks later he could not focus his eyes on his mother's face. The diagnosis: uncontrollable epileptic seizures involving his entire brain.

His mother, Sally Stark, recalled: "When Jacob was two and a half months old, they said he would never learn to sit up, would never be able to feed himself. Nothing could be done to prevent profound retardation. They told us to take him home, love him and find an institution." (Blakeslee, 1992, p. C3)

Instead, the Starks brought Jacob to the University of California at Los Angeles for brain surgery when he was 5 months old. Surgeons removed 20 percent of his brain. The operation was a complete success. Three years later, Jacob seems normal in every way, with no sign of seizures.

Jacob's surgery is representative of increasingly daring approaches in the treatment of brain disorders. It also illustrates how our growing understanding of the processes that underlie brain functioning can be translated into solutions to difficult problems.

The surgery that helped Jacob was based on the premise that the diseased part of his brain was producing seizures throughout the entire brain. Surgeons reasoned that if they removed the misfiring portion, the remaining parts of the brain, which appeared intact in PET scans, would take over. They bet that Jacob could still lead a normal life following surgery, particularly because the surgery was being done at so young an age. Clearly, the gamble paid off.

The success of such surgery is in part related to new findings about the regenerative powers of the brain and nervous system. Although it has been known that the brain has the ability to shift functions to different locations following injury to a specific area, it had been assumed for decades that the neurons of the spinal cord and brain could never be replaced. However, new evidence is beginning to suggest otherwise. For instance, researchers have found that the cells from the brains of adult mice can produce new neurons, at least in a test-tube environment (Reynolds & Weiss, 1992; Barinaga, 1994).

The future also holds promise for people who suffer from the tremors and loss of motor control produced by Parkinson's disease. Because Parkinson's is caused by a gradual loss of cells that stimulate the production of dopamine in the brain, investigators reasoned that a procedure that would increase the supply of dopamine might be effective. They seem to be on the right track. When certain cells from human fetuses are injected directly into the brain of Parkinson's sufferers, the cells seem to take root, stimulating dopamine production. For most of those who have undergone this still experimental procedure, the preliminary results are promising, with some patients showing great improvement (Widner et al., 1992). (You'll note that this technique also raises some thorny ethical issues, given that the source of the implanted fetal tissue is aborted fetuses.)

As scientists learn more about the brain and other parts of the nervous system, it is certain that new treatment procedures will be developed for a variety of disorders. Clearly, our understanding of the biological foundations of human behavior holds significant promise for improving the quality of life for us all.

Yet the structural similarity between the two hemispheres of the brain is not reflected in all aspects of its functioning. It appears that certain activities are more likely to occur in one hemisphere than in the other. Early evidence for the functional differences between halves of the brain—called **lateralization**—came from studies of people with aphasia. Researchers found that people with the speech difficulties characteristic of aphasia tended to have physical damage to the left hemisphere of the brain. In contrast, physical abnormalities in the right hemisphere of the brain tended to produce far fewer problems with language. This finding led researchers to conclude that, for most people, language is lateralized, or located more in one hemisphere than the other—in this case, in the left side of the brain (Corina, Vaid, & Bellugi, 1992; Hellige, 1990).

It now seems clear that the two hemispheres of the brain are somewhat specialized in terms of the functions they carry out. The left hemisphere concentrates more on tasks that require verbal competence, such as speaking, reading, think-

Lateralization: The dominance of one hemisphere of the brain in specific functions

ing, and reasoning. The right hemisphere has its own strengths, particularly in nonverbal areas such as the understanding of spatial relationships, recognition of patterns and drawings, music, and emotional expression (Kitterle, 1991; Hellige, 1994; Zaidel, 1994.

In addition, the way in which information is processed is somewhat different in each hemisphere. The left hemisphere tends to consider information sequentially, one bit at a time, while the right hemisphere tends to process information globally, considering it as a whole (Gazzaniga, 1983; Springer & Deutsch, 1989).

On the other hand, it is important to keep in mind that the differences in specialization between the hemispheres are not great, and that the degree and nature of lateralization varies from one person to another. If, like most people, you are right-handed, the control of language is probably concentrated more in your left hemisphere. By contrast, if you are among the 10 percent of people who are left-handed or are ambidextrous (you use both hands interchangeably), it is much more likely that the language centers of your brain are located more in the right hemisphere or are divided equally between left and right hemispheres.

Researchers have also unearthed evidence that there may be subtle differences in brain lateralization patterns between males and females. In fact, some scientists have suggested that there are slight differences in the structure of the brain that may differ according to gender and culture. As we see next, such findings have led to a lively debate in the scientific community (Geschwind & Galaburda, 1987; Springer & Deutsch, 1989; Coren, 1992).

Exploring Diversity

Human Diversity and the Brain

The interplay of biology and environment is particularly evident when we consider evidence suggesting that there are both sex and cultural differences in brain structure and function. Let's consider sex first. According to recent evidence, males and females show some intriguing differences in brain lateralization, although the nature of those differences—or even their very existence—is the source of considerable controversy (Wood, Flowers, & Naylor, 1991; Kimura, 1992; Gur et al., 1995).

Some statements can be made with reasonable confidence. For instance, most males tend to show greater lateralization of language in the left hemisphere. For them, language is clearly relegated largely to the left side of the brain. In contrast, women display less lateralization, with language abilities apt to be more evenly divided between the two hemispheres (Gur et al., 1982). Such differences in brain lateralization may account, in part, for the superiority often displayed by females on certain measures of verbal skills, such as the onset and fluency of speech, and the fact that far more boys than girls have reading problems in elementary school (Kitterle, 1991).

Other research points to differences in brain structures between males and females, although here the evidence stands on much shakier ground. For example, part of the *corpus callosum,* a bundle of fibers that connects the hemispheres of the brain, is proportionally larger in women than men (Witelson, 1989). Studies conducted on rats, hamsters, and monkeys have also found size and structure differences in male and female brains (Allen et al., 1989; Ayoub, Greenough, & Juraska, 1983).

The meaning of such differences is far from clear. Consider one possibility related to differences in the proportion of the corpus callosum. Its increased proportion in women may permit stronger connections to develop between those parts of the brain that control speech. In turn, this would explain why speech tends to emerge slightly earlier in girls than in boys.

The brain's corpus callosum is proportionally larger in human females than in males, raising the possibility that structural differences in the brain may account in part for gender differences between males and females. However, the hypothesis remains highly speculative.

Before we rush to such a conclusion, though, it is important to consider an alternative hypothesis: It is plausible that the earlier emergence of verbal abilities in girls is due to the greater encouragement being given to them than to boys to verbalize as infants. In turn, this greater early experience may foster growth of certain parts of the brain. Hence, physical brain differences may be a *reflection* of social and environmental influences, rather than a *cause* of the differences in men's and women's behavior. At this point, it is impossible to confirm which of these two alternative hypotheses is correct.

The culture in which we are raised also may give rise to differences in brain lateralization. For example, native speakers of Japanese seem to process information regarding vowel sounds primarily in the brain's left hemisphere. In contrast, North and South Americans, Europeans, and individuals of Japanese ancestry who learn Japanese later handle vowel sounds principally in the right hemisphere.

The reason for such cultural difference in lateralization? One explanation may be that certain characteristics of the Japanese language, such as the ability to express complex ideas using only vowel sounds, result in the development of a specific type of brain lateralization in native speakers. Such a difference in lateralization may account for other dissimilarities between the way that native Japanese speakers and Westerners think about the world (Tsunoda, 1985).

In general, scientists are just beginning to understand the extent, nature, and meaning of sex and cultural differences in lateralization and brain structure. Furthermore, in evaluating the research on brain lateralization, it is important to keep in mind that the two hemispheres of the brain function in tandem. It is a mistake to think of particular kinds of information as being processed solely in the right or the left hemisphere. The hemispheres work interdependently in deciphering, interpreting, and reacting to the world. In addition, people (especially young children) who suffer brain damage to the left side of their brain and lose linguistic capabilities often recover the ability to speak, because the right side of the brain pitches in and takes over some of the functioning of the left side (Wiederhold, 1982). The brain, then, is remarkably adaptable and can modify its functioning, to some extent, in response to adverse circumstances (Kucharski & Hall, 1987; Hellige, 1993, 1994; Hoptman & Davidson, 1994; Singer, 1995).

The Split Brain: Exploring the Two Hemispheres

When the seizures first started, Cindy Gluccles hoped her physician would give her a drug that would prevent their recurrence. Her physician and her neurologist were both optimistic, maintaining that in most cases seizures could be controlled with the proper drugs. But the seizures got worse and more frequent, and no drug treatment seemed to help. Further examination revealed that the seizures were caused by remarkably large bursts of electrical activity that were starting in one hemisphere and moving to the other. Finally, her doctors prescribed a last-ditch measure: surgically cutting the corpus callosum, the bundle of nerves that connect the two hemispheres. Almost magically, the seizures stopped. The operation was clearly a success—but was Cindy the same person she had been before the operation?

That issue has evoked a great deal of interest on the part of brain researchers and has earned a Nobel Prize for Roger Sperry. Sperry, with a group of colleagues, explored the behavior of patients whose corpus callosum had been surgically cut. The research team found that in most ways there were no major changes in either personality or intelligence.

On the other hand, patients like Cindy Gluccles, called **split-brain patients,** did occasionally display some unusual behavior. For instance, one patient reported pulling his pants down with one hand and simultaneously pulling them up with the other. In addition, he mentioned grabbing his wife with his left hand and shaking her violently, while his right hand tried to help his wife by bringing his left hand under control (Gazzaniga, 1970).

Split-brain patients: People who suffer from independent functioning of the two halves of the brain, as a result of which the sides of their bodies work in disharmony

Interest in this occasional curious behavior, however, was peripheral to the rare opportunity that split-brain patients provided for researchers investigating the independent functioning of the two hemispheres of the brain, and Sperry developed a number of ingenious techniques for studying how each hemisphere operated (Sperry, 1982). In one experimental procedure, blindfolded subjects were allowed to touch an object with their right hand and were asked to name it. Because the right side of the body is connected to the left side of the brain—the hemisphere that is most responsible for language—the split-brain patient was able to name it. But if the blindfolded subject touched the object with his or her left hand, naming it aloud was not possible. However, the information had registered: When the blindfold was taken off, the subject was able to correctly choose the object that he or she had touched. Information could be learned and remembered, then, using only the right side of the brain. (By the way, this experiment won't work with you—unless you have had a split-brain operation—since the bundle of fibers connecting the two hemispheres of a normal brain immediately transfers the information from one hemisphere to the other.)

It is clear from experiments like this one that the right and left hemispheres of the brain specialize in handling different sorts of information. At the same time, it is important to realize that they are both capable of understanding, knowing, and being aware of the world, albeit in somewhat different ways. The two hemispheres, then, should be seen as different in terms of the efficiency with which they process certain kinds of information, rather than be viewed as two entirely separate brains. Moreover, in people with normal, nonsplit brains, the hemispheres work interdependently to allow the full range and richness of thought of which humans are capable (Hellige, 1993).

Brain Modules: The Architecture of the Brain

Think of the brain as a vast, sprawling factory in which workers carry out highly specialized tasks. In one wing, workers labor on plural verbs; in another part of the factory, others cope with right angles; and in yet another area of seemingly endless corridors, the workers deal with objects moving horizontally across the horizon. Yet ultimately all the disparate parts come together, producing a unique product: human thought and behavior.

This odd scenario reflects an increasingly popular view of the brain's architecture: in terms of the relationship between particular functions and structures of the brain, on the one hand, and complex cognitive processes such as thinking, understanding, perceiving, and awareness, on the other (Horgan, 1993; Wilson, Scalaidhe, & Goldman-Rakic, 1993).

Brain modules: Separate units of the brain that carry out specific tasks

According to an emerging view of how the brain operates, the brain is organized into a series of modules. **Brain modules** are separate units that carry out specific tasks. Like specialized factory workers, these modules are distributed throughout the brain and work interdependently and relatively simultaneously in processing information (Gazzaniga, 1989; Eichenbaum, 1993).

The basic notion behind the modular approach is that abilities that were once thought to be processed in a unitary manner are actually composed of many subtasks. Take, for example, the brain's ability to process information regarding vision. It was once believed that a single area within the brain controlled visual processing. However, as we will discuss when we consider vision in the next chapter, increasing evidence suggests that there are separate areas of the brain related to specific aspects of vision. For instance, one area of the brain seems to process information about color, another specializes in motion, and still another specializes in depth perception (Goldman-Rakic, 1988). Each of these aspects of vision is simultaneously processed by a separate module, and the information is then integrated to form a whole, intact visual image.

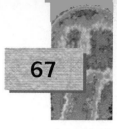

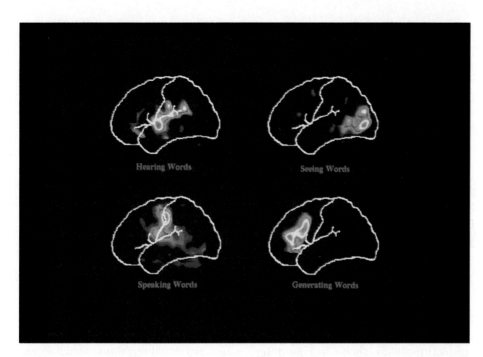

In support of a modular view of the functioning of the brain, these PET scans illustrate the different areas of the brain that are activated during various tasks involving language.

Recent research suggests that the degree of specialization of modules is remarkable (Hart & Gordon, 1992). For example, it now seems possible that the brain processes written and spoken language independently due to the existence of separate modules (Caramazza & Hillis, 1991). Instead of one system that learns the rules of a language, it may be that separate modules consider the way words sound, the manner in which words are written, the roots of words, parts of speech, and other aspects of language. Just as with vision, each of these properties of language is processed simultaneously and independently, and then the information is combined.

The growing evidence for the existence of independent, multiple modules within the brain provides a link between individual neurons and the broad consciousness we experience as human beings. Michael Gazzaniga, a well-known biopsychologist, has speculated that what provides people with a unified, conscious sense of the world is a module unique to human beings: an "interpreter" located in the left hemisphere of the brain (Gazzaniga, 1989).

According to Gazzaniga, this interpreter module permits us to build our own hypotheses about the meaning of our responses. The interpreter provides us with a means of developing and changing our beliefs about the world, and it gives us a way of understanding what is happening in our environment.

It is too early to tell if Gazzaniga's theory is correct. What is clear is that the human brain and nervous system are increasingly revealing their secrets to an array of biopsychologists, cognitive neuroscientists, and other investigators (Hellige, 1990; Estes, 1991).

The Endocrine System: Of Chemicals and Glands

One aspect of the brain that we have not yet considered is the **endocrine system,** a chemical communication network that sends messages throughout the nervous system via the bloodstream. Although not a structure of the brain itself, the endocrine system is intimately tied to the hypothalamus. The job of the endocrine

Endocrine system: A chemical communication network that sends messages throughout the nervous system via the bloodstream and secretes hormones that affect body growth and functioning

system is to secrete **hormones,** chemicals that circulate through the blood and affect the functioning and growth of other parts of the body (Crapo, 1985; Kravitz, 1988).

Like neurons, hormones transmit messages throughout the body, although the speed and mode of transmission are quite different. Whereas neural messages are measured in thousandths of a second, hormonal communications may take minutes to reach their destinations. Furthermore, neural messages move across neurons in specific lines (as with wires strung along telephone poles), whereas hormones travel throughout the entire body, similar to the way radio waves transmit across the entire landscape. Just as radio waves evoke a response only when a radio is tuned to the correct station, so hormones flowing through the bloodstream activate only those cells that are receptive and "tuned" to the appropriate hormonal message.

A major component of the endocrine system is the **pituitary gland,** found near—and regulated by—the hypothalamus. The pituitary gland has sometimes been called the "master gland," because it controls the functioning of the rest of the endocrine system. But the pituitary gland is more than just the taskmaster of other glands; it has important functions in its own right. For instance, hormones secreted by the pituitary gland control growth. Extremely short people—dwarfs— and unusually tall ones—giants—usually have pituitary gland deficiencies. Other endocrine glands, shown in Figure 2-13, affect emotional reactions, sexual urges, and energy levels.

Despite its designation as the "master gland," the pituitary is actually a servant of the brain, because the brain is ultimately responsible for the endocrine system's

FIGURE 2-13 Location and function of the major endocrine glands.

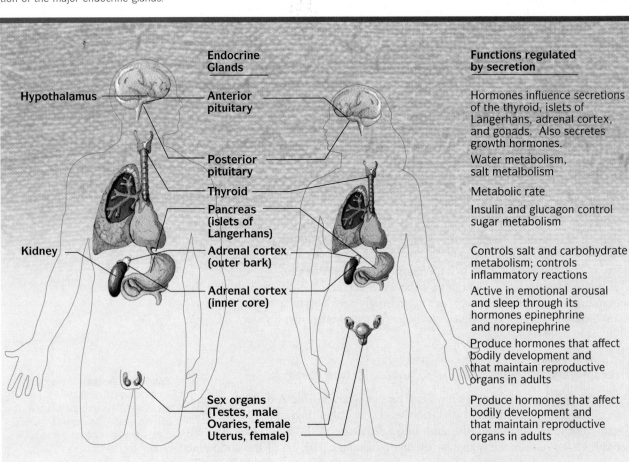

functioning. The brain regulates the internal balance of the body, ensuring that homeostasis is maintained through the hypothalamus. Yet the road from brain to endocrine system is not strictly a one-way street. Hormones may permanently modify the way in which brain cells are organized. For example, adult sexual behavior is thought to be affected by the production of hormones that modify cells in the hypothalamus.

Similarly, particular episodes in our lives can influence the production of hormones. For instance, one experiment in which college students played a computer game against a competitor found that individuals who were winning the game showed a rise in the production of testosterone—a hormone linked to aggressive behavior (Gladue, Boechler, & McCaul, 1989).

Individual hormones can wear many hats, depending on circumstances. For example, the hormone oxytocin is at the root of many of life's satisfactions and pleasures. In new mothers, oxytocin produces an urge to nurse newborn offspring. The same hormone also seems to stimulate cuddling between species members. And—at least in rodents—it encourages sexually active males to seek out females more passionately and females to be more receptive to males' sexual advances. One study showed that female mice administered oxytocin become 60 to 80 percent more energetic in seeking out males to mount them than a control group of mice who didn't receive any oxytocin (Angier, 1991).

The Informed Consumer of Psychology

Learning to Control Your Heart—and Mind— through Biofeedback

On a June evening in 1985, Tammy DeMichael was cruising along the New York State Thruway with her fiancé when he fell asleep at the wheel. The car slammed into the guardrail and flipped, leaving DeMichael with what the doctors called a "splattered C-6,7"—a broken neck and crushed spinal cord.

After a year of exhaustive medical treatment, she still had no function or feeling in her arms and legs. "The experts said I'd be a quadriplegic for the rest of my life, able to move only from the neck up," she recalls. "I wouldn't have wanted to keep living."

But DeMichael proved the experts wrong. Today, feeling has returned to her limbs, her arm strength is normal or better, and she no longer uses a wheelchair. "I can walk about 60 feet with just a cane, and I can go almost anywhere with crutches," she says. "I can bench-press 100 pounds, and I ride four miles daily on a stationary bike." (Morrow & Wolff, 1991, p. 64).

The key to DeMichael's astounding recovery: biofeedback. **Biofeedback** is a procedure in which a person learns to control through conscious thought internal physiological processes such as blood pressure, heart and respiration rate, skin temperature, sweating, and constriction of particular muscles. It had traditionally been thought that the heart, respiration rate, blood pressure, and other bodily functions are under the control of parts of the brain over which we have no influence. Yet psychologists are finding that what were once thought of as entirely involuntary biological responses are actually susceptible to voluntary control (Schwartz & Schwartz, 1993).

In biofeedback, a person is hooked up to electronic devices that provide continuous feedback relating to the physiological response in question. For instance, a person interested in controlling her blood pressure might be hooked up to an apparatus that constantly monitors and displays blood pressure. As she consciously thinks about altering the pressure, she receives immediate feedback on the measure of her success. In this way she can eventually learn to bring her pressure under control. Similarly, if an individual wanted to control headaches through biofeedback, he might have electronic sensors placed on certain muscles in his

Biofeedback: A technique for learning to control internal physiological processes through conscious thought

head and thereby learn to control the constriction and relaxation of those muscles. Then, when he felt a headache coming on, he could relax the relevant muscles and abort the pain.

In DeMichael's case, biofeedback was effective because not all of the nervous system's connections between the brain and her legs were entirely severed. Through biofeedback, she learned how to send messages to specific muscles, "ordering" them to move. Although it took more than a year, DeMichael was successful in restoring a large degree of her mobility.

While the control of physiological processes through the use of biofeedback is not easy to learn, it has been employed with success in a variety of ailments, including emotional problems (such as anxiety, depression, phobias, tension headaches, insomnia, and hyperactivity); medical problems with a psychological component (such as asthma, high blood pressure, ulcers, muscle spasms, and migraine headaches); and physical problems (such as DeMichael's injuries, strokes, cerebral palsy, and curvature of the spine).

Although biofeedback treatment cannot be successful in every case, it is clear that learning through biofeedback has opened up a number of exciting possibilities for treating people with physical and psychological problems (e.g., Kotses et al., 1991; Beckman et al., 1991). Moreover, some psychologists speculate that the use of biofeedback may one day become a part of everyday life.

For instance, one researcher has suggested that students whose minds wander during studying might be hooked up to an apparatus that gives them feedback on whether or not they are paying attention to the information they are studying (Ornstein, 1977). If they stop paying attention, the computer will alert them—putting them back on the right track.

RECAP AND REVIEW

Recap

- The cerebral cortex contains three major areas: the motor, sensory, and association areas. These areas control voluntary movement, the senses, and higher mental processes (including thought, language, memory, and speech), respectively.
- The two halves, or hemispheres, of the brain are structurally similar, but they seem to specialize in different functions. The left side of the brain is most closely related to language and verbal skills; the right side, to nonverbal skills such as mathematical and musical ability, emotional expression, pattern recognition, and the processing of visual information.
- The endocrine system secretes hormones, chemicals that affect the growth and functioning of the body.
- Biofeedback is a procedure by which a person learns to control certain internal physiological processes, thereby bringing relief from a variety of specific ailments.

Review

1. The _____ lobes lie behind the frontal lobes, and the _____ lobes lie behind the temporal lobes.
2. A surgeon places an electrode on a portion of your brain and stimulates it. Immediately, your right wrist involuntarily twitches. The doctor has most likely stimulated a portion of the _____ area of your brain.
3. The motor area of the brain is divided up into segments that control different body parts. The more precise the movements of these parts need to be, the larger the portion of the motor area devoted to that part. True or false?
4. The sensory areas of the brain are divided up according to the size of the sensory organ. Thus, since there is more skin on a person's back than on his fingertips, the portion of the sensory area that deals with sensations on the back will be larger than the fingertip section. True or false?
5. A man who has been asked to sharpen a pencil turns the sharpener for 5 minutes without putting the pencil into it. The condition that might be responsible for this type of behavior is called _____ .
6. Brain hemispheres control the side of the body they are located on. The left hemisphere controls the left side of the body, and the right hemisphere controls the right. True or false?
7. Nonverbal realms, such as emotions and music, are controlled primarily by the _____ hemisphere of the brain, while the _____ hemisphere is more responsible for speaking and reading.
8. Current theory suggests that the brain is actually organized into a set of _____ , each of which works interdependently on a task.

Could personal differences in terms of people's specialization of right and left hemispheres be related to occupational success?

Might an architect who relies on spatial skills have a different pattern of hemispheric specialization from a writer?

(Answers to review questions are on page 72.)

LOOKING BACK

Why do psychologists study the brain and nervous system?

1. A full understanding of human behavior requires knowledge of the biological influences underlying that behavior. This chapter reviews what biopsychologists (psychologists who specialize in studying the effects of biological structures and functions on behavior) have learned about the human nervous system.

What are the basic elements of the nervous system?

2. Neurons, the most basic elements of the nervous system, allow nerve impulses to pass from one part of the body to another. Information generally follows a route that begins with the dendrites, continues into the cell body, and leads ultimately down the tubelike extension, the axon.

How does the nervous system communicate electrical and chemical messages from one part to another?

3. Most axons are protected by a coating called the myelin sheath. When an axon receives a message to fire, it releases an action potential, an electric charge that travels through the neuron. Neurons operate according to an all-or-none law: Either they are at rest, or an action potential is moving through them. There is no in-between state.

4. Once a neuron fires, nerve impulses are carried to other neurons through the production of chemical substances, neurotransmitters, which actually bridge the gaps—known as synapses—between neurons. Neurotransmitters may be either excitatory, telling other neurons to fire, or inhibitory, preventing or decreasing the likelihood of other neurons firing. Among the major neurotransmitters are acetylcholine (ACh), which produces contractions of skeletal muscles, and dopamine, which has been linked to Parkinson's disease and certain mental disorders such as schizophrenia.

5. Endorphins, another type of neurotransmitter, are related to the reduction of pain. Endorphins aid in the production of natural painkillers and are probably responsible for creating the kind of euphoria that joggers sometimes experience after running.

In what way are the structures of the nervous system tied together?

6. The nervous system is made up of the central nervous system (the brain and spinal cord) and the peripheral nervous system (the remainder of the nervous system). The peripheral nervous system is made up of the somatic division, which controls voluntary movements and the communication of information to and from the sense organs, and the autonomic division, which controls involuntary functions such as those of the heart, blood vessels, and lungs.

7. The autonomic division of the peripheral nervous system is further divided into the sympathetic and parasympathetic divisions. The sympathetic division prepares the body in emergency situations, and the parasympathetic division helps the body return to its typical resting state.

How do researchers identify the major parts and functioning of the brain?

8. Brain scans take a "snapshot" of the internal workings of the brain without having to cut surgically into a person's skull. Major brain scanning techniques include the electroencephalogram (EEG), computerized axial tomography (CAT), magnetic resonance imaging (MRI), the superconducting quantum interference device (SQUID), and positron emission tomography (PET).

What are the major parts of the brain, and what are the behaviors for which each part is responsible?

9. The central core of the brain is made up of the medulla (which controls such functions as breathing and the heartbeat), the pons (which coordinates the muscles and the two sides of the body), the reticular formation (which acts to heighten awareness in emergencies), the cerebellum (which controls balance), the thalamus (which communicates messages to and from the brain), and the hypothalamus (which maintains homeostasis, or body equilibrium, and regulates basic survival behaviors). The functions of the central core structures are similar to those found in other vertebrates. This part of the brain is sometimes referred to as the "old brain."

10. The limbic system, found on the border of the "old" and "new" brains, is associated with eating, reproduction, and the experiences of pleasure and pain. The cerebral cortex—the "new brain"—has areas that control voluntary movement (the motor area); the senses (the sensory area); and thinking, reasoning, speech, and memory (the association areas).

How do the two halves of the brain operate interdependently?

11. The brain is divided into two halves, or hemispheres, each of which generally controls the opposite side of the body from that in which it is located. However, each hemisphere can be thought of as specialized in the functions it carries out: The left is best at verbal tasks, such as logical reasoning, speaking, and reading; the right is best at nonverbal tasks, such as spatial perception, pattern recognition, and emotional expression.

Some evidence also suggests that male and female brains may differ in structure in minor ways.

12. A growing body of evidence suggests that the brain is organized into a series of modules, separate units that carry out precise, specific functions. These modules, which are distributed throughout the brain, work interdependently and relatively simultaneously in processing information.

13. The endocrine system secretes hormones, allowing the brain to send messages throughout the nervous system via the bloodstream. A major component is the pituitary gland, which affects growth.

How can an understanding of the nervous system help us to find ways to alleviate disease and pain?

14. Biofeedback is a procedure by which a person learns to control internal physiological processes through conscious thought. By controlling what were previously considered involuntary responses, people are able to relieve anxiety, tension, migraine headaches, and a wide range of other psychological and physical problems.

KEY TERMS AND CONCEPTS

biopsychologists (p. 40)
neurons (p. 41)
dendrites (p. 42)
axon (p. 42)
terminal buttons (p. 42)
myelin sheath (p. 43)
all-or-none law (p. 43)
resting state (p. 43)
action potential (p. 43)
synapse (p. 45)
neurotransmitters (p. 45)
excitatory message (p. 46)
inhibitory message (p. 46)
reuptake (p. 47)
central nervous system (CNS) (p. 50)

spinal cord (p. 50)
reflexes (p. 50)
sensory (afferent) neurons (p. 51)
motor (efferent) neurons (p. 51)
interneurons (p. 51)
peripheral nervous system (p. 51)
somatic division (p. 51)
autonomic division (p. 51)
sympathetic division (p. 52)
parasympathetic division (p. 52)
central core (p. 55)
reticular formation (p. 55)
cerebellum (p. 55)
thalamus (p. 56)
hypothalamus (p. 56)

limbic system (p. 57)
cerebral cortex (p. 58)
lobes (p. 58)
motor area (p. 59)
sensory area (p. 60)
association areas (p. 61)
hemispheres (p. 62)
lateralization (p. 63)
split-brain patients (p. 65)
brain modules (p. 66)
endocrine system (p. 67)
hormones (p. 68)
pituitary gland (p. 68)
biofeedback (p. 69)

CHAPTER 3
SENSATION AND PERCEPTION

PROLOGUE

The Painful World of Jennifer Darling

It started innocently, when Jennifer Darling had hurt her right wrist during her gym class. At first it seemed like a simple sprain. But even though the initial injury healed, the excruciating, burning pain accompanying it did not go away. Instead, it spread to her other arm, and then to her legs. The pain, which Jennifer described as similar to "a hot iron on your arm," was unbearable, and normal painkillers proved ineffective.

The source of the pain turned out to be a rare condition known as "reflex sympathetic dystrophy syndrome," or RSDS for short. For a victim of RSDS, a stimulus as mild as a gentle breeze or the touch of a feather can produce agony. Even bright sunlight or a loud noise can trigger intense pain.

Although a precise explanation for RSDS eludes us, one theory is that messages of pain overwhelm and harm neurons in the nervous system. The body's natural mechanisms that moderate the experience of pain become increasingly less effective, and the brain begins to misinterpret even harmless stimuli such as light or heat as a sign of pain.

For Jennifer Darling, knowing the specific causes of RSDS is less important than finding a release from its ravages. Fortunately, she has found a way to gain at least temporary pain relief. Electrodes powered by battery have been implanted in her back and right arm. Using a computerized device, she is able to administer mild shocks, which neutralize the pain—at least temporarily. Although not a cure, it at least allows her to have something of a normal life (Bylinsky, 1993).

LOOKING AHEAD

Sensation: The process by which an organism's sense organs respond to a stimulus

Perception: The sorting out, interpretation, analysis, and integration of stimuli involving our sense organs and brain

Fortunately, few of us experience the extreme pain that Jennifer Darling does. Yet the distress of chronic pain sufferers is testimony to the profound effect our bodily sensations and perceptions have on our everyday behavior.

Pain is just one of the sensations to which we are sensitive. We also respond to light, sound, tastes, smells, and a variety of other stimulations. In this chapter we focus on the field of psychology concerned with the nature of information our body takes in through its senses and the way in which we interpret such information. We will explore both **sensation,** the process by which an organism's sense organs respond to a stimulus, and **perception,** the sorting out, interpretation, analysis, and integration of stimuli involving our sense organs and brain.

To a psychologist who is interested in understanding the causes of behavior, sensation and perception are fundamental topics, since our behavior is so much a reflection of how we react to and interpret stimuli from the world around us. Indeed, questions ranging from what processes enable us to see and hear, to how we know whether sugar or lemon is sweeter, to how we distinguish one person from another all fall into the realm of sensation and perception.

Although perception clearly represents a step beyond sensation, in practice it is sometimes difficult to distinguish the precise boundary between the two. Indeed, psychologists—and philosophers, as well—have argued for years over the distinction. The primary difference is that sensation can be thought of as an organism's first encounter with a raw sensory stimulus, while perception is the process by which the stimulus is interpreted, analyzed, and integrated with other sensory information. If, for example, we were considering sensation, we might ask how

74

loud a ringing fire alarm appears to be. On the other hand, if we were considering perception, we might ask whether someone recognizes the ringing sound as an alarm and its meaning.

The chapter begins with a discussion of the relationship between the nature of a physical stimulus and the kinds of sensory responses that are made to it. We then examine several of the major senses, including vision, hearing, balance, smell, taste, and the skin senses, which include touch and the experience of pain.

Next, the chapter explains how we organize the stimuli to which our sense organs are exposed. For instance, we consider a number of issues relating to perception, such as how we are able to perceive the world in three dimensions when our eyes are capable only of sensing two-dimensional images. Finally, we examine visual illusions, which provide us with important clues for understanding general perceptual mechanisms, and controversies surrounding subliminal and certain other forms of perception. As we explore these issues, we'll see how the senses work together to provide us with an integrated view and understanding of the world.

- *What is sensation, and how do psychologists study it?*
- *What is the relationship between the nature of a physical stimulus and the kinds of sensory responses that result from it?*

SENSING THE WORLD AROUND US

As she sat down to Thanksgiving dinner, Isabel reflected on how happy she was to be at her parents' home for the holiday. Exhausted from commuting between campus, her apartment, and her job, she was delighted to have someone else doing the cooking. She was especially sick of the tasteless lunches she bolted down at the campus cafeteria.

But these thoughts were soon interrupted when she saw her father carry the turkey in on a tray and place it squarely in the center of the table. The noise level, already high from the talking and laughter of family members, grew louder still. As Isabel picked up her fork, the smell of the turkey reached her and she felt her stomach growl hungrily. The sight and sound of her family around the table along with the smells and tastes of the holiday meal made Isabel feel more relaxed than she had since starting school in the fall.

Put yourself in this setting and consider how different it might be if any one of your senses were not functioning. What if you were blind and unable to see the faces of your family or the welcome shape of the succulent turkey? What if you had no sense of hearing and could not listen to the conversations of family members, or were unable to feel your stomach growl, or smell the dinner, or taste the food? Clearly, you would experience the dinner very differently from someone whose sensory apparatus was intact.

Moreover, the sensations mentioned above barely scratch the surface of sensory experience. Although most of us have been taught at one time or another that there are just five senses—sight, sound, taste, smell, and touch—this enumeration is too modest. Human sensory capabilities go far beyond the basic five senses. It is well established, for example, that we are sensitive not merely to touch, but to a considerably wider set of stimuli—pain, pressure, temperature, vibration, to name a few. In addition, the ear is responsive to information that allows us not only to hear but to keep our balance as well. Psychologists now believe that there are at least a dozen distinct senses, all of which are interrelated.

To consider how psychologists understand the senses and, more broadly, sensation and perception, we first need a basic working vocabulary. In formal terms, if any passing source of physical energy activates a sense organ, the energy is known as a stimulus. A **stimulus,** then, is energy that produces a response in a sense organ.

Stimulus: A source of physical energy that produces a response in a sense organ

Stimuli vary in both type and intensity. Different types of stimuli activate different sense organs. For instance, we can differentiate light stimuli, which activate our sense of sight and allow us to see the colors of a tree in autumn, from sound stimuli, which, through our sense of hearing, permit us to hear the sounds of an orchestra.

Each sort of stimulus that is capable of activating a sense organ can also be considered in terms of its strength, or *intensity*. Questions such as how intense a light stimulus needs to be before it is capable of being detected or how much perfume a person must wear before it is noticed by others relate to stimulus intensity.

The issue of how the intensity of a stimulus influences our sensory responses is considered a branch of psychology known as psychophysics. **Psychophysics** is the study of the relationship between the physical nature of stimuli and a person's sensory responses to them. Psychophysics played a central role in the development of the field of psychology. Many of the first psychologists studied issues related to psychophysics. It is easy to see why: Psychophysics bridges the physical world outside and the psychological world within (Geissler, Link, & Townsend, 1992).

Psychophysics: The study of the relationship between the physical nature of stimuli and a person's sensory reponses to them

Absolute Thresholds

Just when does a stimulus become strong enough to be detected by our sense organs? The answer to this question requires an understanding of the concept of absolute thresholds. An **absolute threshold** is the smallest intensity of a stimulus that must be present for it to be detected. Consider the following examples of absolute thresholds for the various senses (Galanter, 1962):

Absolute threshold: The smallest intensity of a stimulus that must be present for it to be detected

■ *Sight*: A candle flame can be seen 30 miles away on a dark, clear night.

■ *Hearing*: The ticking of a watch can be heard 20 feet away under quiet conditions.

■ *Taste*: Sugar can be discerned when 1 teaspoon is dissolved in 2 gallons of water.

■ *Smell*: Perfume can be detected when one drop is present in a three-room apartment.

■ *Touch*: A bee's wing falling from a distance of 1 centimeter can be felt on a cheek.

Such thresholds permit our sensory apparatus to detect a wide range of sensory stimulation. In fact, the capabilities of our senses are so fine-tuned that we might have problems if they were any more sensitive. For instance, if our ears were just slightly more acute, we would be able to hear the sound of air molecules in our ears knocking into our eardrum—a phenomenon that would surely prove distracting and might even prevent us from hearing sounds outside our bodies.

Of course, the absolute thresholds we have been discussing are measured under ideal conditions. Normally our senses cannot detect stimulation quite as well because of the presence of noise. *Noise,* as defined by psychophysicists, is background stimulation that interferes with the perception of other stimuli. Hence, noise refers not just to auditory stimuli, the most obvious example, but also to those stimuli that affect the other senses. Picture a talkative group of people crammed into a small, crowded, smoke-filled room at a party. The din of the crowd makes it hard to hear individual voices, and the smoke makes it difficult to see, or even taste, the food. In this case, the smoke and crowded conditions would be considered "noise," since they are preventing sensation at more discriminating levels.

The noise in a crowded bar, such as P.J. Clarke's in Chicago, is not just auditory. Smoke, crowding, and other conditions are also considered noise because they interfere with sensation.

Signal Detection Theory

Will an impending storm strike? Is this aircraft unfit to fly? Is that plane intending to attack this ship? Is this nuclear power plant malfunctioning? Is this assembly-line item flawed? Does this patient have the acquired immunodeficiency syndrome (AIDS) virus? Is this person lying? Is this football player using drugs? Will this school (or job) applicant succeed? (Swets, 1992, p. 522).

Questions such as these illustrate the range of decisions that people make. Yet for many of these questions, there is no black-and-white answer. Instead, the evidence in favor of or against a particular response is a matter of degree, making the response a matter of judgment.

Several factors influence how we answer such questions. For instance, physicians who are seeking to identify the presence of a tumor in an x-ray are influenced by their expectations, knowledge, and experience with patients. Clearly, then, the ability to detect and identify a stimulus is not just a function of the properties of the particular stimulus; it is also affected by psychological factors relating to the person making the judgment.

Signal detection theory is an outgrowth of psychophysics that seeks to explain the role of psychological factors in our ability to detect stimuli (Green & Swets, 1989; Greig, 1990; Swets, 1992). The theory acknowledges that, when attempting to detect a stimulus, observers may err in one of two ways: in reporting that a stimulus is present when it is not, or in reporting that a stimulus is not present when it actually is. By applying statistical procedures, psychologists using signal detection theory are able to obtain an understanding of how different kinds of decisions—which may involve such factors as observer expectations and motivation—relate to judgments about sensory stimuli in various situations. Statistical methods also allow psychologists to increase the reliability of predictions about what conditions will cause observers to be most accurate in their judgments (Commons, Nevin, & Davison, 1989).

Such findings have immense practical importance, such as in the case of radar operators who are charged with identifying and distinguishing incoming enemy missiles from the radar images of passing birds (Getty et al., 1988; Wickens, 1991). Another arena in which signal detection theory has practical implications is the judicial system (Buckhout, 1976). Witnesses who are asked to view a lineup find themselves in a classic signal detection situation, in which misidentification

Signal detection theory: The theory that addresses the role of psychological factors in our ability to identify stimuli

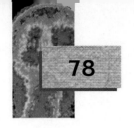

can have grave consequences for an individual (if an innocent person is incorrectly identified as a perpetrator) and for society (if a perpetrator is not detected). However, many witnesses have biases stemming from prior expectations about the socioeconomic status and race of criminals, attitudes toward the police and criminal justice system, and other viewpoints that impede accurate judgment. By using signal detection theory, psychologists have developed procedures that enhance people's chances of accurately identifying witnesses.

Just Noticeable Differences

Suppose a shopkeeper said you could choose six apples from a barrel, and you wanted to compare them to see which half dozen were the best—which were the biggest, which were the reddest, which tasted the sweetest. One approach to this problem would be to systematically compare one apple with another until you were left with a few so similar that you could not tell the difference between them. At that point, it wouldn't matter which ones you chose.

Difference threshold (or just noticeable difference): The smallest detectable difference between two stimuli

Psychologists have discussed this comparison problem in terms of the **difference threshold,** the smallest detectable difference between two stimuli, also known as a **just noticeable difference.** They have found that the stimulus value that constitutes a just noticeable difference depends on the initial intensity of the stimulus. For instance, you may have noticed that the light change that comes in a three-way bulb when you switch from 75 to 100 watts appears greater than when you switch from 100 to 125 watts, even though the wattage increase is the same in both cases. Similarly, when the moon is visible during the late afternoon, it appears relatively dim—yet against a dark night sky, it seems quite bright.

Weber's law: The principle which states that the just noticeable difference is a constant proportion of the intensity of an initial stimulus

The relationship between changes in the original value of a stimulus and the degree to which the change will be noticed forms one of the basic laws of psychophysics: Weber's law. **Weber's law** (with "Weber" pronounced "vay-ber") states that a just noticeable difference is a constant proportion of the intensity of an initial stimulus. Therefore, if a 1-pound increase in a 10-pound weight produces a just noticeable difference, it would take a 10-pound increase to produce a noticeable difference if the initial weight were 100 pounds. In both cases, the same proportional increase is necessary to produce a just noticeable difference—1:10 = 10:100. (Actually, Weber found the true proportional increase in weight that produces a just noticeable difference to be between 2 and 3 percent.) Similarly, the just noticeable difference distinguishing changes in loudness between sounds is larger for sounds that are initially loud than for sounds that are initially soft. This principle explains why a person in a quiet room is more apt to be startled by the ringing of a telephone than a person in a room that is already noisy. In order to produce the same amount of reaction in a noisy room, a telephone ring might have to approximate the loudness of cathedral bells.

Weber's law seems to hold up for all sensory stimuli, although its predictions are less accurate at extremely high or extremely low levels of stimulation (Sharpe et al., 1989). Moreover, the law helps explain psychological phenomena that lie beyond the realm of the senses. For example, imagine that you own a house you would like to sell for $150,000. You might be satisfied if you received an offer of $145,000 from a potential buyer, even though it was $5000 less than the asking price. On the other hand, if you were selling your car and asking $10,000 for it, an offer of $5000 less than your asking price would probably not make you happy. Although the absolute amount of money is the same in both cases, the psychological value of the $5000 is very different.

Sensory Adaptation

As the circus strongman carries a group of five acrobats across the circus tent, someone asks him if they aren't awfully heavy. He replies, "Not if you've just been carrying an elephant."

This story illustrates the phenomenon of **adaptation,** an adjustment in sensory capacity following prolonged exposure to stimuli. Adaptation occurs as people get used to a stimulus and change their frame of reference. Consequently, they do not respond to the stimulus in the way they did earlier.

One example of adaptation is the decrease in sensitivity that occurs after frequent exposure to a stimulus. If, for example, you were to repeatedly hear a loud tone, it would begin to sound softer after a while. This apparent decline in sensitivity to sensory stimuli is due to the inability of the sensory nerve receptors to constantly fire off messages to the brain. Because these receptor cells are most responsive to *changes* in stimulation, constant stimulation is not effective in producing a reaction.

Adaptation occurs with all the senses. For example, try to stare unblinkingly at the period at the end of this sentence. (You actually won't be able to do it very well because of minute, involuntary movements of your eye.) If you could stare long enough, the spot would eventually disappear as the visual neurons lost their ability to fire.

Judgments of sensory stimuli are also affected by the context in which the judgments are made. Carrying five acrobats seems insignificant to the strongman who has just carted an elephant around the tent. The reason is that judgments are made not in isolation from other stimuli, but in terms of preceding sensory experience.

You can demonstrate this for yourself by trying a simple experiment. Take two envelopes, one large and one small, and put fifteen nickels in each. Now lift the large envelope, put it down, and lift the small one. Which seems to weigh more? Most people report that the small one is heavier, although, as you know, the weights are nearly identical. The reason for this misconception is that the physical context of the envelope interferes with the sensory experience of weight. Adaptation to the context of one stimulus (the size of the envelope) alters responses to another stimulus (the weight of the envelope) (Coren & Ward, 1989).

Adaptation: An adjustment in sensory capacity following prolonged exposure to stimuli

---

RECAP AND REVIEW

Recap

- Although people have traditionally thought in terms of five senses, psychologists studying sensation have found that there are considerably more.
- Sensation is the process by which an organism responds to a stimulus. Perception is the sorting out, interpretation, analysis, and integration of stimuli by our sense organs.
- Psychophysics studies the relationship between the physical nature of stimuli and sensory responses that are made.
- An absolute threshold is the smallest amount of physical intensity by which a stimulus can be detected.
- Signal detection theory is used to predict the accuracy of sensory judgments.
- The difference threshold, or just noticeable difference, refers to the smallest detectable difference between two stimuli. According to Weber's law, a just noticeable difference is a constant proportion of the intensity of an initial stimulus.
- Sensory adaptation occurs when people are exposed to a stimulus for so long that they become used to it and therefore no longer respond to it.

Review

1. _____ is the stimulation of the sense organs; _____ is the sorting out, interpretation, analysis, and integration of stimuli by our sense organs.
2. The term "absolute threshold" refers to the largest amount of physical intensity of a stimulus that is detectable without being painful. True or false?
3. Signal detection theory states that people can err in making judgments in two ways. What are they?
4. The proposition stating that a just noticeable difference is a constant proportion of the intensity of an initial stimulus is known as _____ law.
5. After completing a very difficult rock climb in the morning, Carmella found the afternoon climb unexpectedly easy. This case illustrates the phenomenon of _____ .

Ask Yourself

Why is sensory adaptation essential for everyday psychological functioning?

(Answers to review questions are on page 80.)

- *What are the basic processes that underlie the sense of vision?*
- *How do we see colors?*

VISION: SHEDDING LIGHT ON THE EYE

When shown a drawing of an asparagus spear and asked what it is, the young man replies, "A rose twig with thorns." Yet when asked to, he can dash off an easily recognizable drawing of asparagus.

When shown a hand-drawn map of his native England with his birthplace marked, he can't identify it—even though he himself drew the map from memory.

Stranger still, the young man can write a letter—but he can't read it. (Bishop, 1993, p. 1).

Although the visual difficulties of C.K., as he is known in scientific literature, completely disrupted his life, the peculiar nature of his problem presented psychologists with an unusual opportunity to learn more about the operation of vision. C.K., a 33-year-old English immigrant, experienced brain damage as a result of an auto accident. In studying his condition, scientists discovered an unknown link between the eye and a particular area of the brain where images are stored (Behrmann, Winoiur, & Moscovitch, 1992).

C.K.'s case exemplifies the enormous intricacies of vision. These complexities begin with the very stimulus that produces vision: light. Although we are all familiar with light, its underlying physical qualities are more complex than is apparent.

The stimuli that register as light in our eyes are actually electromagnetic radiation waves to which our bodies' visual apparatus happens to be sensitive and capable of responding. As you can see in Figure 3-1, electromagnetic radiation is measured in wavelengths. The size of each wavelength corresponds to different types of energy. The range of wavelengths that humans are sensitive to—called the *visual spectrum*—is actually relatively small. Many nonhuman species have different capabilities. For instance, some reptiles and fish see longer wavelengths than humans, while certain insects see shorter wavelengths than humans.

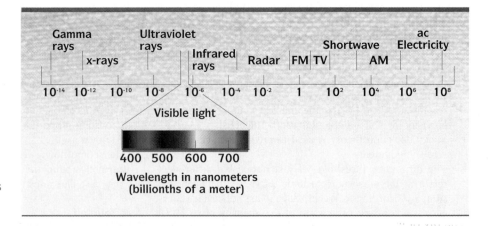

FIGURE 3-1 The visual spectrum—the range of wavelengths to which people are sensitive—represents only a small part of the kinds of wavelengths present in our environment.

ANSWERS TO PREVIOUS REVIEW
1. Sensation; perception. **2.** False; it is the smallest amount that is detectable.
3. A stimulus could be reported as present when it isn't, or it could be reported as absent when it is present. **4.** Weber's **5.** adaptation

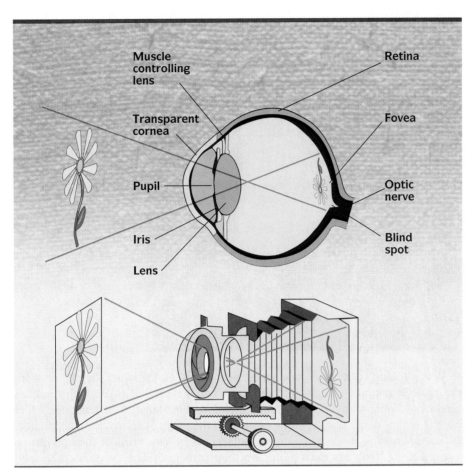

FIGURE 3-2 Although human vision is far more complicated than the most sophisticated camera, in some ways basic visual processes are analogous to those used in photography.

Light waves coming from some object outside the body (imagine the light reflected off the flower in Figure 3-2) first encounter the only organ that is capable of responding to the visual spectrum: the eye. Strangely enough, most of the eye is not involved with responding directly to light. Instead, its function is to shape the entering image into a form that can be used by the neurons that will serve as messengers to the brain. The neurons themselves take up a relatively small percentage of the total eye. In other words, most of the eye is a mechanical device, analogous in many respects to a camera without film, as you can see in Figure 3-2. At the same time, it is important to realize the limitations of this analogy. Vision involves processes that are far more complex and sophisticated than any camera is capable of mimicking. Once the image reaches the neuronal receptors of the eye, the analogy ends, for the processing of the visual image in the brain is more reflective of a computer than a camera.

Illuminating the Structure of the Eye

The ray of light we are tracing as it is reflected off the flower first travels through the *cornea,* a transparent, protective window that allows light to pass through. After moving through the cornea, the light traverses the pupil. The *pupil* is a dark hole found in the center of the *iris,* the colored part of the eye, which ranges in humans from a light blue to a dark brown. The size of the pupil opening depends on the amount of light in the environment. The dimmer the surroundings, the more the pupil opens in order to allow more light to enter.

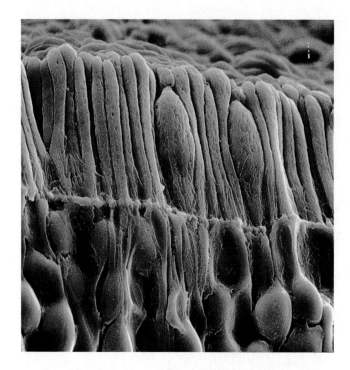

This electron micrograph clearly reveals the distinctive shapes of the eye's rods and cones.

Why shouldn't the pupil be opened all the way all the time, thereby allowing the greatest amount of light into the eye? The answer has to do with the basic physics of light. A small pupil greatly increases the range of distances at which objects are in focus. With a wide-open pupil, the range is relatively small, and details are harder to discern. (Camera buffs know this in terms of the aperture or f-stop setting that they must adjust on their cameras.) The eye takes advantage of bright light by decreasing the size of the pupil and thereby becoming more discerning. In dim light the pupil expands to enable us to view the situation better—but at the expense of visual detail. Perhaps one reason that candlelight dinners are often thought of as romantic is that the dimness of the light prevents one from seeing the details of a lover's flaws.

Once light passes through the pupil, it enters the *lens,* which is located directly behind the pupil. The lens acts to bend the rays of light so that they are properly focused on the rear of the eye. The lens focuses the light by changing its own thickness, a process called *accommodation.* The kind of accommodation that occurs depends on the location of the object in relation to the viewer's body. Distant objects require a relatively flat lens. In this case, the muscles controlling the lens relax, allowing the lens to flatten. In contrast, close objects are viewed best through a rounded lens. Here, then, the muscles contract, relieving tension and permitting the lens to become rounder.

Having traveled through the pupil and lens, our image of the flower finally reaches its ultimate destination in the eye—the **retina.** Here the electromagnetic energy of light is converted into messages that the brain can use. It is important to note that, because of the physical properties of light, the image reverses itself as it travels through the lens, and it reaches the retina upside down (relative to its original position). Although it might seem that this reversal would cause difficulties in understanding and moving about the world, this is not the case. The brain interprets the image in terms of its proper orientation.

The retina is actually a thin layer of nerve cells at the back of the eyeball (see Figure 3-3). Two kinds of light-sensitive receptor cells are found in the retina. The names they have been given describe their shapes: **rods,** which are long and cylindrical, and **cones,** which are short, thick, and tapered. The rods and cones are distributed unevenly throughout the retina. The greatest concentration of cones is on the part of the retina called the *fovea* (refer to Figure 3-2). The fovea

Retina: The part of the eye that converts the electromagnetic energy of light into useful information for the brain

Rods: Long, cylindrical, light-sensitive receptors in the retina that perform well in poor light but are largely insensitive to color and small details

Cones: Cone-shaped, light-sensitive receptor cells in the retina that are responsible for sharp focus and color perception, particularly in bright light

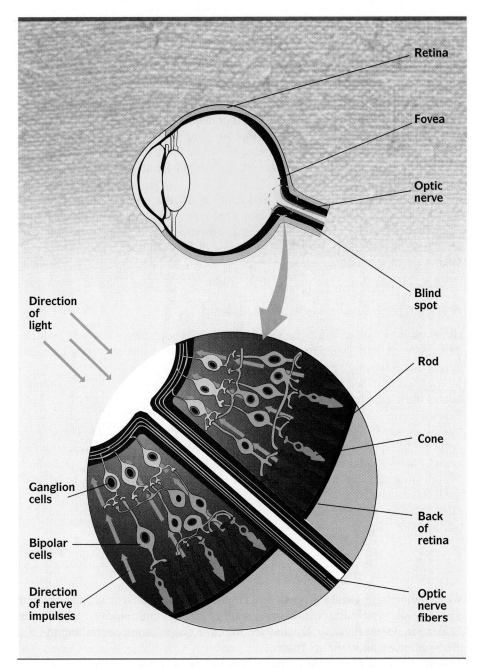

Retina

Fovea

Optic nerve

Blind spot

Direction of light

Rod

Cone

Ganglion cells

Bipolar cells

Direction of nerve impulses

Back of retina

Optic nerve fibers

FIGURE 3-3 The basic cells of the eye. Light entering the eye travels through the ganglion and bipolar cells and strikes the light-sensitive rods and cones located at the back of the eye. The rods and cones then transmit nerve impulses to the brain via the bipolar and ganglion cells.

is a particularly sensitive region of the retina. If you want to focus in on something of special interest, you will probably center the image from the lens onto the area of the fovea.

The density of cones declines just outside the fovea, although cones are found throughout the retina in lower concentrations. On the other hand, there are no rods in the very center of the fovea, but the density is greatest outside the fovea and then gradually declines toward the edges of the retina. Because the fovea covers only a small portion of the eye, there are fewer cones (about 7 million) than there are rods (about 125 million).

Not only are the rods and cones structurally dissimilar, but they play distinctly different roles in vision (Cohen & Lasley, 1986). Cones are primarily responsible for the sharply focused perception of color, particularly in brightly lit situations, while rods are related to vision in dimly lit situations and are largely in-

sensitive to color and to details as sharp as those the cones are capable of recognizing. The rods play a key role in *peripheral vision*—seeing objects that are outside the main center of focus—and in night vision. In both cases, the level of detail that can be discerned is far lower when the rods come into play than when the cones are activated, as you know from groping your way across a dark room at night. Although you may just dimly see the outlines of furniture, it is almost impossible to distinguish color and the other details of obstacles in your path. You may also have noticed that you can improve your view of a dim star at night by looking slightly away from it. The reason? If you shift your gaze off-center, the image from the lens falls not on the relatively night-blind cones of the fovea but on the more light-sensitive rods.

The distinctive abilities of rods and cones make the eye analogous to a camera that is loaded with two kinds of film. One type is a highly sensitive black-and-white film (the rods). The other type is a somewhat less sensitive color film (the cones). Remember, too, that these two types of film are distributed in the eye in different arrangements.

Adaptation: From Light to Dark

Have you ever walked into a movie theater on a bright, sunny day and stumbled into your seat, barely able to see at all? Do you also recall later getting up to buy popcorn and having no trouble navigating your way up the aisle?

Your ability to see relatively well after you've been in the theater for a while is due to **dark adaptation,** a heightened sensitivity to light that results from being in relative dimness. The speed at which dark adaptation occurs is a result of the rate of change in the chemical composition of the rods and cones. The changes occur at different speeds for the two kinds of cells, with the cones reaching their greatest level of adaptation in just a few minutes, but the rods taking close to 30 minutes to reach the maximum level. On the other hand, the cones never reach the level of sensitivity to light that the rods attain. When rods and cones are considered jointly, though, dark adaptation is complete in a darkened room in about half an hour (Tamura, Nakatani, & Yau, 1989).

Dark adaptation: A heightened sensitivity to light resulting from being in relative dimness

Sending the Message from the Eye to the Brain

When light energy strikes the rods and cones, it starts the first in a chain of events that transforms light into neural impulses that can be communicated to the brain. Before the neural message reaches the brain, however, some initial alteration of the visual information takes place.

What happens when light energy strikes the retina depends in part on whether it encounters a rod or a cone. Rods contain *rhodopsin,* a complex, reddish-purple substance whose composition changes chemically when energized by light and thereby sets off a reaction. The substance found in cone receptors is different, but the principles are similar. Stimulation of the nerve cells in the eye triggers a neural response that is transmitted to other nerve cells, called *bipolar cells* and *ganglion cells,* leading to the brain.

Bipolar cells receive information directly from the rods and cones. This information is then communicated to the ganglion cells. Ganglion cells collect and summarize visual information, which is gathered and moved out of the back of the eyeball through a bundle of ganglion axons called the **optic nerve** (Tessier-Lavigne, 1991; Yang & Masland, 1992).

Optic nerve: A bundle of ganglion axons that carry visual information

Because the opening for the optic nerve pushes through the retina, there are no rods or cones in the area, which creates a blind spot. Normally, however, this absence of nerve cells does not interfere with vision, because you automatically compensate for the missing part of your field of vision (Ramachandran, 1992).

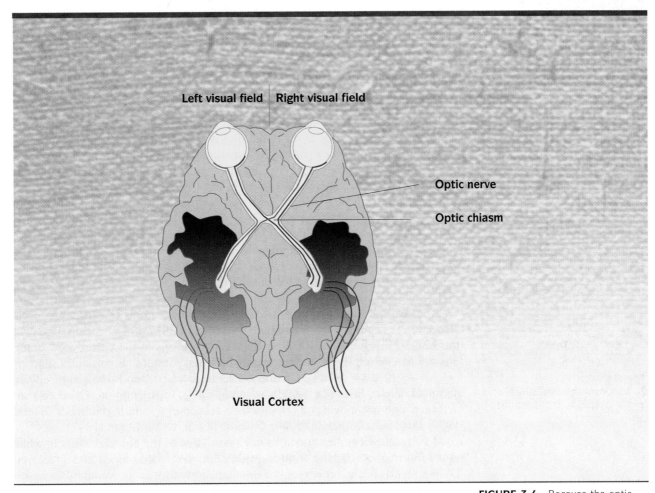

Left visual field   Right visual field

Optic nerve

Optic chiasm

Visual Cortex

FIGURE 3-4 Because the optic nerve coming from each eye splits at the optic chiasm, the image to a person's right is sent to the left side of the brain, and the image to the person's left is transmitted to the right side of the brain.

Once beyond the eye itself, the neural signals relating to the image move through the optic nerve. As the optic nerve leaves the eyeball, its path does not take the most direct route to the part of the brain right behind the eye. Instead, the optic nerves from each eye meet at a point roughly between the two eyes—called the *optic chiasm*—where each optic nerve then splits.

When the optic nerves split, the nerve impulses coming from the right half of each retina are sent to the right side of the brain, and the impulses arriving from the left half of each retina are sent to the left side of the brain. Because the image on the retina is reversed and upside down, however, those images coming from the right half of each retina are actually included in the field of vision to the left of a viewer, and images coming from the left half of the retina represent the field of vision to the right of the viewer (see Figure 3-4). In this way, our nervous system ultimately produces the phenomenon introduced in Chapter 2, in which each half of the brain is associated with the functioning of the opposite side of the body.

One of the most frequent causes of blindness is a restriction of the impulses across the optic nerve. *Glaucoma,* which strikes between 1 and 2 percent of those over age 40, occurs when pressure in the fluid of the eye begins to build up, either because it cannot be properly drained or because it is overproduced. When this first begins to happen, the nerve cells that communicate information about peripheral vision are constricted, leading to a decline in the ability to see anything outside a narrow circle directly ahead. This ensuing problem is called *tunnel vision.* Eventually, the pressure can become so great that all the nerve cells are con-

85

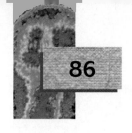

stricted, leading to total blindness. Fortunately, if detected early enough, glaucoma is highly treatable, either through medication that reduces the pressure in the eye or through surgery.

Processing the Visual Message

By the time a visual message reaches the brain, it has passed through several stages of processing. One of the initial sites is the ganglion cells (Yang & Masland, 1992). Each ganglion cell gathers information from a group of rods and cones in a particular area of the eye, and compares the amount of light entering the center of that area with the amount of light in the area around it. In some cases, ganglion cells are activated by light in the center (and darkness in the surrounding area). In other cases, the opposite is true. Some ganglion cells are activated when there is darkness in the center and light in the surrounding areas. The ultimate effect of this process is to maximize the detection of variations in light and darkness. The neural image that is passed on to the brain, then, is an enhanced version of the actual visual stimulus outside the body.

The ultimate processing of visual images takes place in the visual cortex of the brain, of course, and it is here that the most complex kinds of processing occur (Hurlbert & Poggio, 1988). Psychologists David Hubel and Torsten Wiesel won the Nobel Prize for their discovery that many neurons in the cortex are extraordinarily specialized, being activated only by visual stimuli of a particular shape or pattern—a process known as **feature detection.** They found that some cells are activated only by lines of a particular width, shape, or orientation. Other cells are activated only by moving, as opposed to stationary, stimuli (Hubel & Wiesel, 1979; Logothetis & Schall, 1989; Gallant, Braun, & VanEssen, 1993).

More recent work has added to our knowledge of the complex ways in which visual information coming from individual neurons is combined and processed. Different parts of the brain seem to simultaneously process nerve impulses in several individual systems. For instance, one system relates to shapes, one to colors, and others for movement, location, and depth (Zeki, 1993).

If separate neural systems exist for the processing of information about specific aspects of the visual world, how are all these data integrated by the brain? Although the exact process is not yet well understood, it seems likely that the brain makes use of information regarding the frequency, rhythm, and timing of the firing of particular sets of neural cells (Richmond et al., 1987). Furthermore, it appears that the brain's integration does not occur in any single step or location in the brain. Instead, integration of visual information is a process that seems to occur on several levels simultaneously (Zeki, 1993). The ultimate outcome, though, is indisputable: a vision of the world around us.

Color Vision and Color Blindness: The 7-Million-Color Spectrum

Although the range of wavelengths to which humans are sensitive is relatively narrow, at least in comparison to the entire electromagnetic spectrum, the portion to which we are capable of responding still allows us great flexibility in sensing the world. Nowhere is this clearer than in terms of the number of colors we can discern. A person with normal color vision is capable of distinguishing no less than 7 million different colors (Bruce & Green, 1990).

Although the variety of colors that people are generally able to distinguish is vast, there are certain individuals whose ability to perceive color is quite limited— the color-blind. Interestingly, the condition of these individuals has provided some of the most important clues for understanding how color vision operates (Nathans et al., 1986; Nathans et al., 1989; Shepard & Cooper, 1992).

Feature detection: The activation of neurons in the cortex by visual stimuli of specific shapes or patterns

a.

b.

c.

d.

FIGURE 3-5 These hot-air balloons appear as shown in (*a*) to someone with normal vision. (*b*) A person with red-green color blindness would see the scene like this, in hues of blue and yellow. (*c*) A person who is blue-yellow blind, conversely, would see it in hues of red and green. (*d*) To a monochromat, or person with total color blindness, it would look like this. (*Joe Epstein/Design Conceptions.*)

Before continuing, though, look at the photos shown in Figure 3-5. If you cannot see any difference in the series of photos, you probably are one of the 2 percent of men or 2 out of 10,000 women who are color-blind.

For most people who are color-blind, the world looks quite dull. Red fire engines appear yellow, green grass seems yellow, and the three colors of a traffic light all look yellow. In fact, in the most common form of color blindness, all red and green objects are seen as yellow. There are other forms of color blindness as well, but they are quite rare. In yellow-blue blindness, people are unable to tell the difference between yellow and blue, and in the most extreme case an individual perceives no color at all. To such a person the world looks something like the picture on a black-and-white television set.

To understand why some of us are color-blind, it is necessary to consider the basics of color vision. Two processes appear to be involved. The first process is explained by the **trichromatic theory of color vision.** It suggests that there are three kinds of cones in the retina, each of which responds primarily to a specific range of wavelengths. One is most responsive to blue-violet colors, one to green, and the other to yellow-red (Brown & Wald, 1964). According to trichromatic theory, perception of color is influenced by the relative strength with which each of the three kinds of cones is activated. If, for instance, we see a blue sky, the blue-violet cones are primarily triggered, while the others show less activity. The trichromatic theory provides a straightforward explanation of color blindness. It suggests that one of the three cone systems malfunctions, and colors covered by that range are perceived improperly (Nathans et al., 1989).

However, there are phenomena that the trichromatic theory is less successful at explaining. For instance, it cannot account for why pairs of colors can combine to form gray. The theory also does not explain what happens after you stare at something like the flag shown in Figure 3-6 for about a minute. Try this yourself, and then move your eyes to the white space below. You will see an image of the traditional red, white, and blue American flag. Where there was yellow, you'll see blue, and where there were green and black, you'll see red and white.

The phenomenon you have just experienced is called an *afterimage.* It occurs because activity in the retina continues even when you are no longer staring at the original picture. However, it also demonstrates that the trichromatic theory does not explain color vision completely. Why should the colors in the afterimage be different from those in the original?

Trichromatic theory of color vision: The theory which suggests that the retina has three kinds of cones, each responding to a specific range of wavelengths

FIGURE 3-6 If you stare at the dot in this flag for about a minute and then look at a piece of white paper, the afterimage phenomenon will make a traditional red, white, and blue flag appear.

Opponent-process theory of color vision: The theory which suggests that receptor cells are linked in pairs, working in opposition to each other

Because trichromatic processes do not provide a full explanation of color vision, vision researchers have developed an alternative explanation. According to the **opponent-process theory of color vision,** receptor cells are linked in pairs, working in opposition to each other. Specifically, there is a blue-yellow pairing, a red-green pairing, and a black-white pairing. If an object reflects light that contains more blue than yellow, it will stimulate the firing of the cells sensitive to blue, simultaneously discouraging or inhibiting the firing of receptor cells sensitive to yellow—and the object will appear blue. If, on the other hand, a light contains more yellow than blue, the cells that respond to yellow will be stimulated to fire while the blue ones are inhibited, and the object will appear yellow.

The opponent-process theory allows us to explain afterimages very directly. When we stare at the yellow in the figure, for instance, our receptor cells for the yellow component of the yellow-blue pairing become fatigued and are less able to respond to yellow stimuli. On the other hand, the receptor cells for the blue part of the pair are not tired, since they are not being stimulated. When we look at a white surface, the light reflected off it would normally stimulate both the yellow and the blue receptors equally. But the fatigue of the yellow receptors prevents

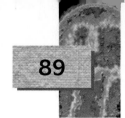

this from happening. They temporarily do not respond to the yellow, which makes the white light appear to be blue. Because the other colors in the figure do the same thing relative to their specific opponents, the afterimage produces the opponent colors—for a while. The afterimage lasts only a short time, since the fatigue of the yellow receptors is soon overcome, and the white light begins to be perceived more accurately.

It is now clear then that both opponent processes and trichromatic mechanisms are at work in allowing us to see color. However, they operate in different parts of the visual sensing system. Trichromatic processes work within the retina itself, while opponent mechanisms operate both in the retina and at later stages of neuronal processing (Leibovic, 1990; Gouras, 1991; De Valois & De Valois, 1993).

RECAP AND REVIEW

Recap

- The eyes are sensitive to electromagnetic radiation waves of certain wavelengths. These waves register as the sensation of light.
- As light enters the eye, it passes through the cornea, pupil, and lens and ultimately reaches the retina, where the electromagnetic energy of light is converted into nerve impulses usable by the brain. These impulses leave the eye via the optic nerve.
- The retina is composed of nerve cells called rods and cones, which play differing roles in vision and are responsible for dark adaptation.
- Humans are able to distinguish about 7 million colors. Color vision involves two processes: trichromatic mechanisms and an opponent-processing system.

Review

1. Light entering the eye first passes through the _____, a protective window.
2. The structure that converts light into usable neural messages is called the _____ .
3. Light is focused on the rear of the eye by the iris. True or false?
4. A woman with blue eyes could be described as having blue pigment in her _____ .
5. What is the process by which the thickness of the lens is changed in order to focus light properly?

6. The proper sequence of structures that light passes through in the eye is the _____ , _____ , _____ , and _____ .
7. Match each type of visual receptor with its function.
   1. Used for dim light, largely insensitive to color
   2. Detect color, good in bright light

   a. Rods
   b. Cones
8. Paco was to meet his girlfriend in the movie theater. As was typical, he was late and the movie had begun. He stumbled down the aisle, barely able to see. Unfortunately, the woman he sat down beside and attempted to put his arm around was not his girlfriend. He sorely wished he had given his eyes a chance and waited for _____ adaptation to occur.
9. _____ theory states that there are three types of cones in the retina, each of which responds primarily to a different color.

Ask Yourself

Why do you think the eye uses two distinct types of receptor cells, rods and cones? Why would the eye evolve so that the rods, which we rely on in low light, do not provide sharp images? Are there any advantages to this system?

(Answers to review questions are on page 90.)

- *What role does the ear play in the senses of sound, motion, and balance?*
- *How do smell and taste function?*
- *What are the skin senses, and how do they relate to the experience of pain?*

HEARING AND THE OTHER SENSES

The blast-off was easy compared with what the astronaut was experiencing now: space sickness. The constant nausea and vomiting were enough to make him wonder why he had

worked so hard to become an astronaut. Even though he had been warned that there was a 50 percent chance that his first experience in space would cause these symptoms, he wasn't prepared for how terribly sick he really felt.

Whether or not our fictional astronaut turns his rocket around and heads back to earth, his experience, a major problem for space travelers, is related to a basic sensory process centered in the ear: the sense of motion and balance. This sense allows people to navigate their bodies through the world and maintain an upright position without falling. Along with *hearing,* the process by which sound waves are translated into understandable and meaningful forms, the senses of motion and balance represent the major functions of the ear.

Sensing Sound

Although many of us think primarily of the outer ear when we consider hearing, this part functions simply as a reverse megaphone, designed to collect and bring sounds into the internal portions of the ear (see Figure 3-7). However, the location of the outer ears on different sides of the head helps with *sound localization,* the process by which we identify the origin of a sound. Wave patterns in the air enter each ear at a slightly different time, permitting the brain to use the discrepancy to locate the place from which the sound is originating. In addition, the two outer ears delay or amplify sounds of particular frequencies to different degrees (Butler, 1987; Middlebrooks & Green, 1991; Yost, 1992; Konishi, 1993).

Sound is the movement of air molecules brought about by the vibration of an object. Sounds travel through the air in wave patterns similar in shape to those made by a stone thrown into a still pond. When sounds, in the form of wave vibrations, arrive at the *outer ear,* they are funneled into the *auditory canal,* a tube-like passage that leads to the eardrum. The **eardrum** is aptly named because it operates like a miniature drum, vibrating when sound waves hit it. The more intense the sound, the more it vibrates. These vibrations are then transmitted into the *middle ear,* a tiny chamber containing just three bones called, because of their shapes, the *hammer,* the *anvil,* and the *stirrup.* These bones have one function: to transmit vibrations to the *oval window,* a thin membrane leading to the inner ear. Because of their shape, the hammer, anvil, and stirrup do a particularly effective job. Because they act as a set of levers, they not only transmit vibrations but actually increase their strength. Moreover, since the opening into the middle ear (the eardrum) is considerably larger than the opening out of it (the oval window), the force of sound waves on the oval window becomes amplified. The middle ear, then, acts as a tiny mechanical amplifier, making us aware of sounds that would otherwise go unnoticed.

The *inner ear* is the portion of the ear that changes the sound vibrations into a form that allows them to be transmitted to the brain. It also contains the organs that allow us to locate our position and determine how we are moving through space. When sound enters the inner ear through the oval window, it moves into the **cochlea,** a coiled tube filled with fluid that looks something like a snail. Inside the cochlea is the **basilar membrane,** a structure that runs through the center of the cochlea, dividing it into an upper and a lower chamber (see Figure 3-7). The basilar membrane is covered with **hair cells.** When these hair cells are bent by the vibrations entering the cochlea, a neural message is transmitted to the brain.

Sound: The movement of air molecules brought about by the vibration of an object

Eardrum: The part of the ear that vibrates when sound waves hit

Cochlea (KOKE lee uh): A coiled tube filled with fluid that receives sound via the oval window or through bone conduction

Basilar membrane: A structure dividing the cochlea into an upper and a lower chamber

Hair cells: Tiny cells covering the basilar membrane that, when bent by vibrations entering the cochlea, transmit neural messages to the brain

---

ANSWERS TO PREVIOUS REVIEW
1. cornea 2. retina 3. False; it is focused by the lens. 4. iris 5. Accommodation
6. cornea, pupil, lens, retina 7. 1-a; 2-b 8. dark 9. Trichromatic

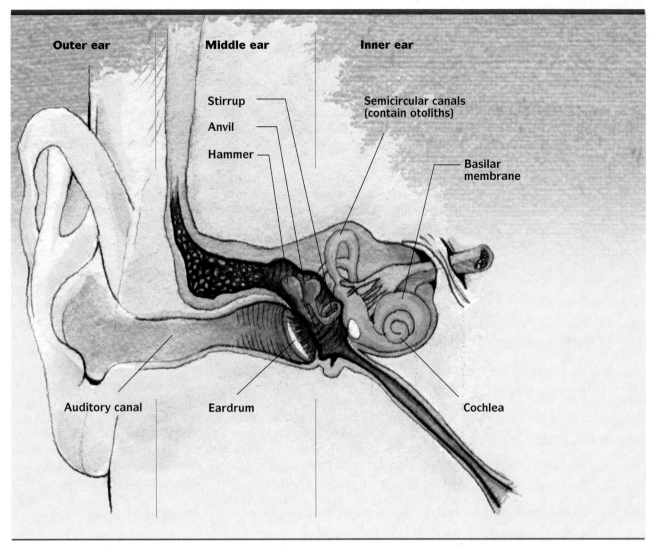

Outer ear   **Middle ear**   **Inner ear**

Stirrup

Anvil

Hammer

Semicircular canals
(contain otoliths)

Basilar
membrane

Auditory canal

Eardrum

Cochlea

FIGURE 3-7   The ear.

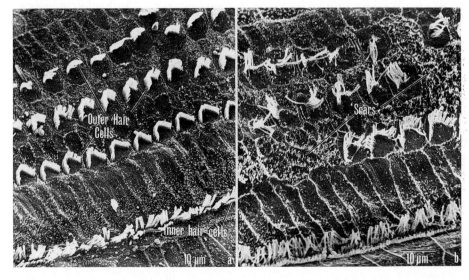

Outer Hair
Cells

Inner hair cells

10 μm   a

Scars

10 μm   b

At the left, the hair cells lining the
basilar membrane are upright.
When they are flattened by vibrations entering the cochlea, as at the
right, a neural message is transmitted to the brain, making hearing
possible.

Although sound typically enters the cochlea via the oval window, there is an additional method of entry: bone conduction. Because the ear rests on a maze of bones within the skull, the cochlea is able to pick up subtle vibrations that travel across the bones from other parts of the head (Lenhardt et al., 1991). For instance, one of the ways you hear your own voice is through bone conduction. This explains why you sound different to yourself than to other people who hear your voice. (Listen to yourself on a tape recorder sometime to hear what you *really* sound like!) The sound of your voice reaches you both through the air and via bone conduction and therefore sounds richer to you than to everyone else.

The Physical Aspects of Sound   As we mentioned earlier, what we refer to as sound is actually the physical movement of air molecules in regular, wavelike patterns caused by the vibration of an object (see Figure 3-8). Sometimes it is even possible to view these vibrations, as in the case of a stereo speaker that has no enclosure. If you have ever seen one, you know that, at least when the lowest notes are playing, you can see the speaker moving in and out. What is less obvious is what happens next: The speaker pushes air molecules into waves with the same pattern as its movement. These wave patterns soon reach your ear, although their strength has been weakened considerably during their travels. All other stimuli that produce sound work in essentially the same fashion, setting off wave patterns that move through the air to the ear. Air—or some other medium, such as water—is necessary to make the vibrations of objects reach us. This explains why there can be no sound in a vacuum.

We are able to see the speaker moving when low notes are played because of a primary characteristic of sound called frequency. *Frequency* is the number of wave crests that occur in a second. With very low frequencies there are relatively few, and therefore slower, up-and-down wave cycles per second. These are visible to the naked eye as vibrations in the speaker. Low frequencies are translated into a sound that is very low in pitch. (*Pitch* is the characteristic that makes sound "high" or "low.") The lowest frequency that humans are capable of hearing is 20 cycles per second. Higher frequencies translate into higher pitch. At the upper end of the sound spectrum, people can detect sounds with frequencies as high as 20,000 cycles per second.

While sound frequency allows us to enjoy the sounds of the high notes of a piccolo and the bass notes of a tuba, *intensity* is a feature of wave patterns that allows us to distinguish between loud and soft sounds. Intensity refers to the difference between the peaks and valleys of air pressure in a sound wave as it travels through the air. Waves with small peaks and valleys produce soft sounds, while those that are relatively large produce loud sounds.

We are sensitive to a broad range of sound intensity. The loudest sounds we are capable of hearing are about 10 million times as intense as the very weakest

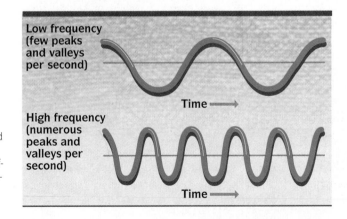

FIGURE 3-8 The waves produced by different stimuli are transmitted—usually through the air—in different patterns, with lower frequencies indicated by fewer peaks and valleys per second.

sound we can hear. This range is measured in *decibels,* which can be used to place everyday sounds along a continuum. When sounds get higher than 120 decibels, they become painful to the human ear. Exposure to such high levels can eventually result in hearing loss, as the hair cells of the basilar membrane lose their elasticity and bend and flatten. Such a loss of hearing is often permanent, although recent findings have shown that hair cells have the potential to repair themselves following damage (Travis, 1992).

Sorting Out Theories of Sound   How are our brains able to sort out wave-lengths of different frequencies and intensities? One clue comes from studies of the basilar membrane, the area within the cochlea that translates physical vibrations into neural impulses. It turns out that sounds affect different areas of the basilar membrane, depending on the frequency of the wave. The part of the basilar membrane nearest the oval window is most sensitive to high-frequency sounds, while the part nearest the cochlea's inner end is most sensitive to low-frequency sounds. This finding has led to the **place theory of hearing,** which says that different areas of the basilar membrane respond to different frequencies.

On the other hand, place theory does not tell the full story of hearing, since very-low-frequency sounds trigger neurons across such a wide area of the basilar membrane that no single site is involved. Consequently, an additional explanation for hearing has been proposed: frequency theory. The **frequency theory of hearing** suggests that the entire basilar membrane acts like a microphone, vibrating as a whole in response to a sound. According to this explanation, the nerve receptors send out signals that are tied directly to the frequency (the number of wave crests per second) of the sounds to which we are exposed, with the number of nerve impulses being a direct function of the sound's frequency. Thus, the higher the pitch of a sound (and therefore the greater the frequency of its wave crests), the greater the number of nerve impulses that are transmitted up the auditory nerve to the brain.

Most contemporary research indicates that both place theory and frequency theory explain at least some of the processes involved in hearing. However, neither explanation alone provides the full story (Levine & Shefner, 1991; Luce, 1993). Specifically, place theory provides a better explanation for the sensing of high-frequency sounds, whereas frequency theory explains what happens when low-frequency sounds are encountered. Medium-frequency sounds appear to incorporate both processes.

After an auditory message leaves the ear, it is transmitted to the auditory cortex of the brain through a complex series of neural interconnections. As the message is transmitted, it is communicated through neurons that respond to specific types of sounds. Within the auditory cortex itself, there are neurons that respond selectively to very specific sorts of sound features, such as clicks or whistles. Some neurons respond only to a specific pattern of sounds, such as a steady tone but not an intermittent one. Furthermore, specific neurons transfer information about a sound's location through their particular pattern of firing (Middlebrooks et al., 1994).

If we were to analyze the configuration of the cells in the auditory cortex, we would find that neighboring cells are responsive to similar frequencies. The auditory cortex, then, provides us with a "map" of sound frequencies, just as the visual cortex furnishes a representation of the visual field.

Our understanding of processes that underlie hearing has led to some important advances in the ability to restore lost hearing. At the same time though, as we discuss in the accompanying Psychology at Work box, this capability has raised some unexpected psychological issues for those who are eligible for hearing restoration.

Place theory of hearing: The theory which states that different areas of the basilar membrane respond to different frequencies

Frequency theory of hearing: The theory which suggests that the entire basilar membrane acts like a microphone, vibrating in response to sound

PSYCHOLOGY AT WORK

Restoring Hearing to the Deaf: A Mixed Blessing?

It would seem like nothing short of a miracle. By implanting a computerized device in the ear, many people, deaf from birth, are able to hear sounds such as automobile horns and doorbells for the first time.

The instrument that makes this possible is an electronic ear implant connected directly to the cochlea. The device works in certain cases of deafness in which the hair cells in the cochlea are damaged and unable to convert vibrations into the electrical impulses that the brain is able to use. A tiny microphone outside the ear is used to pick up sounds, which are then sent to a speech processor worn on a shoulder strap or belt that allows a user to squelch background noise with a button. An electronic signal produced by the processor is then sent to a transmitter behind the ear, which broadcasts a radio wave to a receiver implanted inside the skull. The implanted receiver is directly connected to the cochlea by twenty-two thin wires. The receiver emits electrical signals that stimulate the cochlea, sending a message to the brain that sound is being heard (Molotsky, 1984; Clark, 1987).

The device does not allow people to pick up words distinctly. Users report that the quality of speech heard is like that of Donald Duck. Nonetheless, about half the users of state-of-the-art implants are able to understand familiar voices and speak on the phone. Implants also enable users to detect changes in tone of voice and volume. Moreover, as the technology continues to improve, it is likely that improved hearing aids will make sound more distinct. For instance, by analyzing the frequency, rhythm, and loudness of sound, contemporary hearing aids can optimize speech and squelch background noises (Kirsch, 1989).

Although the restoration of hearing to a deaf person may seem like an unquestionably positive achievement, some advocates for the deaf suggest otherwise. The National Association of the Deaf has said in a formal statement that it imposes "invasive surgery on defenseless children, when the long-term physical, emotional and social effects on children from this irreversible procedure have not been scientifically established" (Barringer, 1993b, p. 1). Their point is that deafness represents a legitimate culture—no better or worse than the hearing culture—and that providing even limited hearing to deaf children robs them of their natural cultural heritage.

Not surprisingly, such a view is highly controversial. Proponents of cochlea implants argue that helping deaf children to hear enables them to avoid the stigma that comes from growing up as a member of a small minority group in a world where most people can hear. To keep people from hearing is to unnecessarily restrict their opportunities.

The arguments regarding the use of cochlea implants are unlikely to be resolved until research on the social adjustment of children who have received implants can be conducted. In the meantime, technological advances promise restoration of additional senses (Leutwyler, 1994). For example, laser technology often corrects nearsightedness, which occurs when the shape of the eye becomes distorted and the retina is unable to correctly focus the image entering the eye onto the retina (Selingman, 1991). By precisely removing a tiny slice of the cornea, the procedure changes the eye's configuration, allowing the image on the retina to be in focus. For nearsighted people, eyeglasses and contact lenses, then, may someday be considered relics of the past.

Balance: The Ups and Downs of Life

Nick Esasky had just signed a $5.7 million baseball contract with the Atlanta Braves when he began to run into trouble. In his words:

I felt great about playing in Atlanta, and I was in the best shape of my whole career. But about a week and a half into spring training, things started falling apart. Suddenly I began feeling weak and tired all the time. At first, I thought it was the flu and that it would go away. Then I began to get headaches and nausea, and I felt light-headed and dizzy. Soon it began to affect the way I was playing. At times it was hard for me to follow the ball. It looked hazy, as if it had a glow. I'd catch some off the end of my glove and miss others completely. Other times, a ball would land in my glove and I'd have no idea how it got there (Esasky, 1991, p. 62).

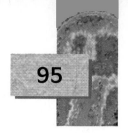

Esasky's problem would not go away, leading to a round of visits to specialists. Finally, after a variety of misdiagnoses, one doctor identified the source of Esasky's difficulty: his ear. Esasky was suffering from *vertigo,* a disorder of the inner ear resulting from a viral infection or head injury. He was forced to undergo a grueling program to bolster his sense of vision and the sense of touch in the soles of the feet, both of which could help compensate for his inner ear problems.

Several structures of the ear are related more to our sense of balance than to our hearing (J. P. Kelly, 1991). The **semicircular canals** of the inner ear consist of three tubes containing fluid that sloshes through them when the head moves, signaling rotational or angular movement to the brain. The pull on our bodies caused by the acceleration of forward, backward, or up-and-down motion, as well as the constant pull of gravity, is sensed by the **otoliths,** tiny, motion-sensitive crystals within the semicircular canals. When we move, these crystals shift like sands on a windy beach. The brain's inexperience in interpreting messages from the weightless otoliths is the cause of the space sickness commonly experienced by more than half of all space travelers (Flam, 1991; Weiss, 1992).

Semicircular canals: Part of the inner ear containing fluid that moves when the body moves to control balance

Otoliths: Crystals in the semicircular canals that sense body acceleration

Smell and Taste

When Audrey Warner returned home after a day's work, she knew that something was wrong the moment she opened her apartment door. A smell indicative of gas—a strong, sickening odor that immediately made her feel weak—permeated the apartment. She ran to the pay phone across the street and called the gas company. As she was explaining what she smelled, Warner heard a muffled explosion and then saw flames begin to shoot out of her apartment window. Her life had been saved by her ability to smell the gas.

Smell While there are few instances in which the sense of smell provides such drama, it is clear that our lives would be considerably less interesting if we could not smell freshly mowed hay, sniff a bouquet of flowers, or enjoy the aroma of an apple pie baking. Although many animals have keener abilities to detect odors than we do, since a greater proportion of their brains is devoted to the sense of smell than ours is, we are still able to detect more than 10,000 separate smells. We also remember smells, and long-forgotten events and memories can be brought back with the mere whiff of an odor associated with the memory (Schab, 1990, 1991; Bartoshuk & Beauchamp, 1994).

Results of "sniff tests" have shown that women generally have a better sense of smell than men do (Engen, 1987). People also seem to have the ability to distinguish males from females on the basis of smell alone. In one experiment, blindfolded students sniffed a sweating hand held ¹/₂ inch from their nose. The findings showed that male and female hands could be distinguished from one another with better than 80 percent accuracy (Wallace, 1977). Similarly, experimental subjects who were asked to sniff the breath of a male or female volunteer who was hidden from view were able to distinguish the sex of the donor at better than chance levels (Doty et al., 1982).

Our understanding of the mechanisms that underlie the sense of smell is just beginning to emerge. We do know that the sense of smell is sparked when the molecules of some substance enter the nasal passages and meet *olfactory cells,* the receptor cells of the nose. At least 1000 separate receptor cells have been identified so far. Each of these cells is so specialized that it responds only to a small band of different odors (Buck & Axel, 1991).

There's increasing evidence that in addition to olfactory cells, a parallel sensory system may provide an involuntary means of communication for humans. It has long been known that animals release *pheromones,* chemicals that produce a reaction in other members of the species, permitting them to send such messages as sexual availability. For instance, certain substances in the vaginal secretions of

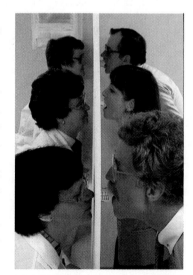

Intrepid volunteers such as those at the left demonstrate that it is possible to differentiate between men and women just by the smell of their breath.

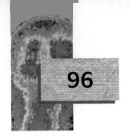
female monkeys contain pheromones that stimulate sexual interest in male monkeys.

Although it seems reasonable that humans might also communicate through the release of pheromones, the evidence is still scanty. Women's vaginal secretions contain chemicals similar to those found in monkeys, but the smells do not seem to be related to sexual activity in humans. On the other hand, the presence of these substances might explain why women who live together for long periods tend to show similarity in the timing of their menstrual cycles (Engen, 1982, 1987). In addition, women are able to identify their babies solely on the basis of smell just a few hours after birth (Porter, Cernich, & McLaughlin, 1983).

Surprising new evidence suggests that a tiny structure just inside each nostril may be the human version of the organ in animals that detects pheromones. Although the evidence is preliminary, it suggests that a pheromone sensory system may help motivate such basic human behavior as reproduction and child care (Takami et al., 1993; Getchell et al., 1993).

Taste   Unlike smell, which employs more than 1000 separate types of receptor cells, the sense of taste seems to make do with only a handful of fundamental types of receptors. Most researchers—although by no means all—suggest that particular receptor cells specialize in sweet, sour, salty, and bitter flavors. In their view, every other taste is simply a combination of these four basic qualities (McLaughlin & Margolskee, 1994).

The receptor cells for taste are located in *taste buds,* which are distributed across the tongue. However, the distribution is uneven, and certain areas of the tongue are more sensitive to particular fundamental tastes than others (Bartoshuk, 1971). As we can see in Figure 3-9, the tip of the tongue is most sensitive to sweetness. For example, a granule of sugar placed on the rear of the tongue will

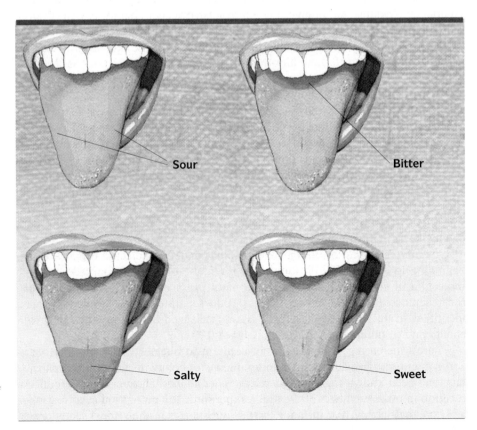

FIGURE 3-9   Particular portions of the tongue are sensitive to tastes that are bitter, sour, sweet, or salty.

hardly seem sweet at all. Similarly, only the sides of the tongue are very sensitive to sour tastes, and the rear specializes in bitter tastes.

The different taste areas on the tongue correspond to different locations in the brain. Neurons responding to sour and bitter tastes are located on one end of the area of the cortex corresponding to taste, whereas sweet tastes stimulate neurons on the opposite end of the cortex. In contrast, salty tastes stimulate neurons that are distributed across the entire taste area of the brain (Yamamoto, Yuyama, & Kawamura, 1981).

Of course, taste does not operate simply through the tongue, as anyone with a stuffy nose can confirm. The smell, temperature, texture, and even appearance of food and drink all affect our perception of flavor. Because of this, food and beverage manufacturers continually assess the quality of the taste, odor, and appearance of their products to ensure that quality is maintained. For example, the beer industry has developed a complex set of criteria to judge the caliber of its product.

The Skin Senses: Touch, Pressure, Temperature, and Pain

Consider the plight of this boy, born with an extremely rare inherited defect that made him insensitive to pain:

His arms and legs are deformed and bent, as though he had suffered from rickets. Several fingers are missing. A large open wound covers one knee, and the smiling lips are bitten raw. He looks, to all the world, like a battered child. . . . His fingers were either crushed or burned because he did not pull his hands away from things that were hot or dangerous. His bones and joints were misshapen because he pounded them too hard when he walked or ran. His knee had ulcerated from crawling over sharp objects that he could not feel. Should he break a bone or dislocate a hip, he would not feel enough to cry out for help. (Wallis, 1984, pp. 58, 60)

Clearly, the consequences of a painfree existence can be as devastating as those experienced by Jennifer Darling, whose chronic pain condition was described at the beginning of the chapter. If you never experienced pain, for instance, you might not notice that your arm had brushed against a hot pan, and you would likely suffer a severe burn. Similarly, without the warning sign of stomach pain that typically accompanies an inflamed appendix, your appendix might go on to rupture, spreading a fatal infection through your body. Such examples underscore the vital importance of the sense of pain.

In fact, all our **skin senses**—touch, pressure, temperature, and pain—play a critical role in survival, making us aware of potential danger to our bodies. Most of these senses operate through nerve receptor cells located at various depths throughout the skin, although they are not evenly distributed. When we consider receptors sensitive to touch, for example, some areas, such as the fingertips, have many more cells and as a consequence are notably sensitive. In contrast, areas with fewer cells, such as the middle of the back, are considerably less sensitive to touch (Kreuger, 1989).

Probably the most extensively researched skin sense is pain, and with good reason: People consult physicians and take medication for pain more than for any other symptom or condition. Nearly one-third of the population of the United States has problems with persistent or recurrent pain. And, as a result of pain, at any given moment some 2 million people in the United States are unable to function normally (Vlaeyen et al., 1990; Jessell & Kelly, 1991).

As with our other senses, the perception of pain is not a simple matter of a direct response to certain kinds of stimulation. Some kinds of pain, such as that experienced in childbirth, are moderated by the joyful nature of the situation. At the same time, even a minor stimulus can produce the perception of strong pain if it occurs in the context of an anxiety-tinged visit to the dentist. Clearly, then,

Skin senses: The senses that include touch, pressure, temperature, and pain

PATHWAYS THROUGH PSYCHOLOGY

Mark Jensen
Multi-Disciplinary Pain Center,
Seattle, Washington

Born: 1957
Education: B.A., McAllister College,
 St. Paul, Minnesota;
 Ph.D., Arizona State University
Home: Seattle, Washington

Mark Jensen

In high school, Mark Jensen came across published transcripts of therapy sessions conducted by Fritz Perls, founder of gestalt therapy. At that point he decided he wanted to be a therapist.

Twenty years later he has attained his goal. He is an attending psychologist at the Multi-Disciplinary Pain Center at the University of Washington Medical Center in Seattle, as well as associate professor in the department of rehabilitative medicine at the medical school.

Jensen's specific interest in pain began in graduate school. "To me it seemed interesting since there were so many unanswered questions. I thought it would be a rich area to research." His initial reasoning proved correct, and Jensen has spent his career investigating how people manage pain.

"Our primary interest is the association between what people believe about their bodies and how they manage pain symptoms and their functioning," he said. "What we found in our research is that there are important associations among these variables. We are exploring whether changes in beliefs and coping impact functioning. We're trying to identify the most important beliefs and coping strategies and alter them so that the individuals we treat can do more and feel better to fight the pain.

"One erroneous belief, for example, is that pain experience means that damage is occurring," Jensen explained. "For the most part this is not true for chronic pain. However, this belief may stop patients from engaging in coping strategies such as exercise because of the fear associated with the pain."

Approximately 150 patients, screened from 400 to 450 applicants, are treated every year at the center. As part of treatment, Jensen says he tries to have patients alter their beliefs that pain is a sign that physical damage is occurring. "We try to step back and look at all the coping strategies that can influence functioning," he said.

"Studies show that multidisciplinary programs work, with patients functioning better and reporting less pain," he added. "At this point we aren't sure why it's effective. That's why we are testing the hypothesis that the change comes from the patient changing beliefs and coping strategies. Although we're focusing on the basically psychological aspects of pain, you really can't separate the physiological aspects. When you change the psychological, you change the physiological reactions, and vice versa."

Gate-control theory of pain: The theory which suggests that particular nerve receptors lead to specific areas of the brain related to pain; when these receptors are activated by an injury or bodily malfunction, a "gate" to the brain is opened and pain is sensed

pain is a perceptual response that depends heavily on our emotions and thoughts (Fernandez & Turk, 1992; Cioffi & Holloway, 1993; Turk, 1994; Novy et al., 1995).

Some of the contradictions involved in our responses to stimulation capable of eliciting pain are explained by gate-control theory. The **gate-control theory of pain** suggests that particular nerve receptors lead to specific areas of the brain related to pain (Melzack & Wall, 1965; Wall & Melzack, 1989). When these receptors are activated because of some injury or problem with a part of the body, a "gate" to the brain is opened, allowing us to experience the sensation of pain.

However, another set of neural receptors is able, when stimulated, to close the "gate" to the brain, thereby reducing the experience of pain. The gate may be shut in two different ways. First, other impulses can overwhelm the nerve pathways relating to pain, which are spread throughout the brain (Talbot et al., 1991). In this case, nonpainful stimuli compete with and sometimes displace the neuronal message of pain, thereby shutting off the painful stimulus. This explains why rubbing the skin around an injury helps reduce pain. The competing stimuli from the rubbing may overwhelm the painful ones. Similarly, scratching is able to relieve itching (which is technically classified as a kind of pain stimulus).

Psychological factors account for the second way in which a gate may be activated (Turk, 1994). Depending on an individual's current emotions, interpretation of events, and previous experience, the brain may close a gate by sending a message down the spinal cord to an injured area, producing a reduction in or relief from pain. Thus soldiers who are injured in battle may experience no pain—the surprising situation in more than half of all combat injuries. The lack of pain probably occurs because a soldier experiences such relief at still being alive that his brain sends a signal to the injury site to shut down the pain gate (Sternbach, 1987; Willis, 1988; Baker & Kirsch, 1991).

Gate-control theory may also explain cultural differences in the experience of pain. Some of these variations are astounding. For example, in India people who participate in the "hook-swinging" ritual, to celebrate the power of the gods, have steel hooks embedded under the skin and muscles of their backs. During the ritual, they swing from a pole, suspended by the hooks. What would seem likely to induce excruciating pain instead produces a state of celebration and near-euphoria. In fact, when the hooks are later removed, the wounds heal quickly, and after 2 weeks almost no visible marks remain (Kosambi, 1967).

Gate-control theory suggests that the lack of pain is due to a message from the participant's brain, which shuts down the pain pathways. Gate-control theory may also explain the effectiveness of *acupuncture,* an ancient Chinese technique in which sharp needles are inserted into various parts of the body. The sensation from the needles may close the gateway to the brain, reducing the experience of pain. It is also possible that the body's own painkillers, the endorphins (discussed in Chapter 2), as well as positive and negative emotions, may play a role in opening and closing the gate (Wall & Melzack, 1984; Warga, 1987). (For a look at someone who deals professionally with pain, see the accompanying Pathways through Psychology box.)

RECAP AND REVIEW

Recap

- The senses of hearing, motion, and balance are centered in the ear.
- The major parts of the ear are the outer ear (which includes the auditory canal and eardrum), the middle ear (with the hammer, anvil, and stirrup), and the oval window leading to the inner ear. The inner ear contains the cochlea, basilar membrane, and hair cells.
- The physical aspects of sound include frequency and intensity. Both place and frequency processes are believed to operate in the transformation of sound waves into the experience of sound.
- The sense of balance is located in the ear's semicircular canals and otoliths.
- Less is known about the senses of smell and taste and the skin senses (touch, pressure, temperature, and pain) than about vision and hearing, although each is highly complex.

Review

1. The tubelike passage leading from the outer ear is known as the _____ _____ .

2. The purpose of the eardrum is to protect the sensitive nerves underneath it. It serves no purpose in actual hearing. True or false?

3. To what part of the ear do the three middle ear bones transmit their sound?

4. What theory of hearing states that the entire basilar membrane responds to a sound, vibrating more or less depending on the nature of the sound?

5. The three fluid-filled tubes in the inner ear which are responsible for our sense of balance are known as the

   _____ _____ .

6. Chemicals that produce a certain reaction in other members of the species are known as _____ .

7. _____-_____ theory states that when certain skin receptors are activated as the result of an injury, a "pathway" to the brain is opened, allowing pain to be experienced.

Ask Yourself

Much research has been done on repairing faulty sensory organs through such devices as cochlea implants, eyeglasses, and so forth. Do you think it would be feasible for science to attempt, via these same methods, to augment normal sensory capabilities beyond their "natural" range (such as increasing the capacity of the human visual or audio spectrum)? What benefits might this bring? What problems could it cause?

(Answers to review questions are on page 102.)

- *What principles underlie our organization of the visual world, allowing us to make sense of our environment?*
- *How are we able to perceive the world in three dimensions when our retinas are capable of sensing only two-dimensional images?*
- *What clues do visual illusions give us about our understanding of general perceptual mechanisms?*

PERCEPTUAL ORGANIZATION: CONSTRUCTING OUR VIEW OF THE WORLD

FIGURE 3-10 When the usual cues we use to distinguish figure from ground are absent, we may shift back and forth between different views of the same figure. If you look at each of these objects long enough, you'll probably experience a shift in what you're seeing. In (a), a designer used the figure-ground principle to create this vase that is meant to convey the profiles of Queen Elizabeth and Prince Philip of England. In (b), the shaded portion of the figure, called a Necker cube, can appear to be either the front or the back of the cube. Finally, in (c), you'll be able to see a face of a woman if you look at the drawing long enough.

Consider the vase shown in Figure 3-10a for a moment.

Or is it a vase? Take another look, and instead you may see the profile of two people.

Now that an alternative interpretation has been pointed out, you will probably shift back and forth between the two interpretations. Similarly, if you examine the shapes in Figure 3-10b and 3-10c long enough, you will probably experience a shift in what you're seeing. The reason for these reversals is this: Because each figure is two-dimensional, the usual means we employ for distinguishing the *figure* (the object being perceived) from the *ground* (the background or spaces within the object) do not work.

The fact that we can look at the same figure in more than one way illustrates an important point: We do not just passively respond to visual stimuli that happen to fall on our retinas. Instead, we actively try to organize and make sense of what we see.

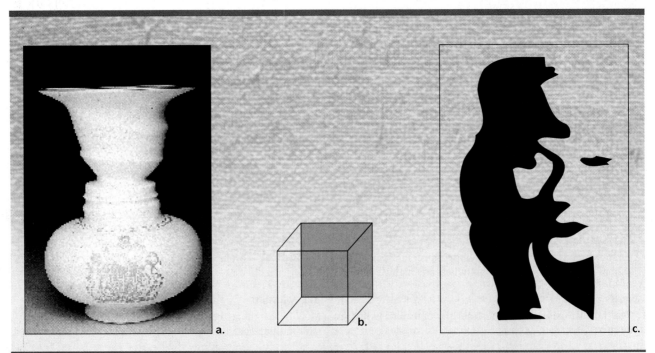

a.   b.   c.

We turn now from a focus on the initial response to a stimulus (sensation) to what our minds make of that stimulus—perception. Perception is a constructive process by which we go beyond the stimuli that are presented to us and attempt to construct a meaningful situation (Haber, 1983; Kienker et al., 1986).

The Gestalt Laws of Organization

Some of the most basic perceptual processes operate according to a series of principles that describe how we organize bits and pieces of information into meaningful wholes. These are known as **gestalt laws of organization,** set forth in the early 1900s by a group of German psychologists who studied patterns, or *gestalts* (Wertheimer, 1923). They discovered a number of important principles that are valid for visual (as well as auditory) stimuli:

Gestalt (geh SHTALLT) **laws of organization:** A series of principles that describe how we organize pieces of information into meaningful wholes; they include closure, proximity, similarity, and simplicity

■ *Closure.* Groupings are usually made in terms of enclosed or complete figures rather than open ones. We tend to ignore the breaks in the figure below and concentrate on the overall form.

■ *Proximity.* Elements that are closer together are grouped together. As a result, we tend to see pairs of dots rather than a row of single dots in the following pattern:

. . . .

■ *Similarity.* Elements that are similar in appearance are grouped together. We see, then, horizontal rows of dots and squares instead of vertical mixed columns below:

■ *Simplicity.* In a general sense, the overriding gestalt principle is one of simplicity: When we observe a pattern, we perceive it in the most basic, straightforward manner that we can (Hochberg, 1978).

Although gestalt psychology no longer plays a prominent role in contemporary psychology, its legacy endures. For instance, one fundamental gestalt principle, which remains influential, is that two objects considered together form a whole that is different from the simple combination of the objects. Gestalt psychologists argued—quite convincingly—that the perception of stimuli in our environment goes well beyond the individual elements that we sense. Instead, it represents an active, constructive process carried out within the brain. There, bits and pieces of sensations are put together to make something greater, and more meaningful, than the separate elements.

Feature Analysis: Focusing on the Parts of the Whole

A more recent approach to perception, **feature analysis,** considers how we perceive a shape, pattern, object, or scene by reacting first to the individual elements that make it up. These individual components are then used to understand the overall nature of what we are perceiving. Feature analysis begins with the evidence that individual neurons in the brain are sensitive to specific spatial configurations, such as angles, curves, shapes, and edges, as discussed earlier in the chapter. The presence of these neurons suggests that any stimulus can be broken down into a series of component features. For example, the letter "R" is a combination of a vertical line, a diagonal line, and a half circle (see Figure 3-11).

Feature analysis: Perception of a shape, pattern, object, or scene by responding to the individual elements that make it up

According to feature analysis, when we encounter a stimulus—such as a letter—our brain's perceptual processing system initially responds to its component

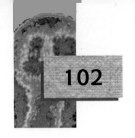

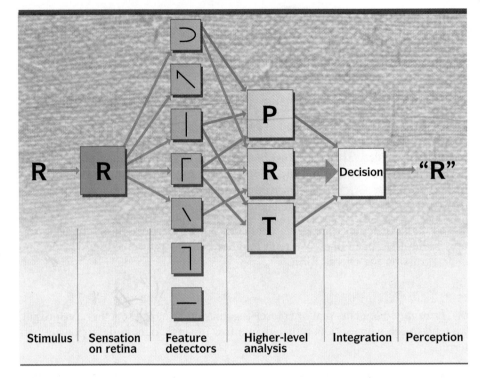

FIGURE 3-11 According to feature analysis approaches to perception, we break down stimuli into their component parts and then compare these parts to information that is stored in memory. When we find a match, we are able to identify the stimulus. In this example, the process by which we recognize the letter "R" is illustrated.

parts. Each of these parts is compared with information about components that is stored in memory. When the specific components we perceive match up with a particular set of components we have encountered previously, we are able to identify the stimulus (Spillmann & Werner, 1990).

According to some research, we perceive complex objects in a manner similar to the way in which we perceive simple letters, viewing them in terms of their component elements. For instance, just thirty-six fundamental components seem to be capable of producing over 150 million objects—more than enough to describe the 30,000 separate objects that the average person can recognize. Ultimately, these component features are combined into a representation of the whole object in the brain. This representation is compared with existing memories, thereby permitting us to identify the object (Biederman, 1987, 1990).

Psychologist Anne Treisman has a different perspective. She suggests that the perception of objects is best understood in terms of a two-stage process. In the *preattentive stage,* we focus on the physical features of a stimulus, such as its size, shape, color, orientation, or direction of movement. This initial stage takes little or no conscious effort. In the *focused-attention stage,* we pay attention to particular features of an object, choosing and emphasizing features that were initially considered separately (Treisman, 1988).

For example, take a look at the two upside-down photos in Figure 3-12. Probably, your first impression is that you're viewing two similar photos of the *Mona Lisa.* But now look at them rightside up, and you'll be surprised to note that one of the photos has distorted features. In Treisman's terms, your initial scanning of the photos took place at the preattentive stage. When you turned

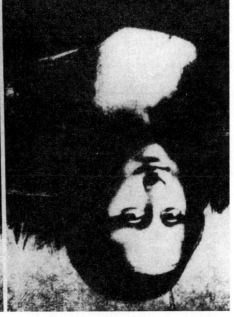

FIGURE 3-12 These pictures appear similar at first glance because only our preattentive process is active. When the pictures are seen upright, the true detail in the two faces is revealed. (*From Julesz, 1986.*)

them over, however, you immediately progressed into the focused-attention stage, where you were able to more carefully consider the actual nature of the stimuli.

Treisman's perspective and other approaches to feature analysis raise a puzzling question about the fundamental nature of perceptual processes: Is perception based mainly on consideration of the component parts of a stimulus, or is it grounded primarily in perception of the stimulus as a whole? It is an issue that we turn to next.

Top-Down and Bottom-Up Processing

Ca- yo- re-d t-is -en-en-e, w-ic- ha- ev-ry -hi-d l-tt-r m-ss-ng? It probably won't take you too long to figure out that it says, "Can you read this sentence, which has every third letter missing?"

If perception were based primarily on breaking down a stimulus into its most basic elements, understanding the sentence, as well as other ambiguous stimuli, would not be possible. The fact that you were probably able to recognize such an imprecise stimulus illustrates that perception proceeds along two different avenues, called top-down processing and bottom-up processing.

In **top-down processing,** perception is guided by higher-level knowledge, experience, expectations, and motivations. You were able to figure out the meaning of the sentence with the missing letters because you had prior reading experience and because written English contains redundancies. Not every letter of each word is necessary to decode its meaning. Moreover, your expectations played a role in your being able to read the sentence. You were probably expecting a statement that had *something* to do with psychology, and not the lyrics to a Grateful Dead song.

Top-down processing is illustrated by the importance of context in determining how we perceive objects (Biederman, 1981). Look, for example, at Figure 3-13. Most of us perceive that the first row consists of the letters "A" through "F," while the second contains the numbers 10 through 14. But take a more careful look, and you'll see that the "B" and the "13" are identical. Clearly, our perception is affected by our expectations about the two sequences—even though the two stimuli are exactly the same.

Top-down processing: Perception guided by knowledge, experience, expectations, and motivations

104

FIGURE 3-13 *The power of context is shown in this figure. Note how the "B" and the "13" are identical.*

Bottom-up processing: Recognizing and processing information about the individual components of a stimulus

Top-down processing, which takes our expectations and understanding of the situation into account, must take place in order for us to understand what we are perceiving. Yet top-down processing cannot occur on its own. Even though top-down processing allows us to fill in the gaps in ambiguous and out-of-context stimuli, we would be unable to perceive the meaning of such stimuli without bottom-up processing. **Bottom-up processing** consists of recognizing and processing information about the individual components of the stimuli. We would make no headway in our recognition of the sentence without being able to perceive the individual shapes that make up the letters. Some perception, then, occurs at the level of the patterns and features of each of the separate letters.

It should be apparent that top-down and bottom-up processing occur simultaneously, and interact with each other, in our perception of the world around us (Kimchi, 1992). It is bottom-up processing that permits us to process the fundamental characteristics of stimuli, whereas top-down processing allows us to bring our experience to bear on perception. And as we learn more about the complex processes involved in perception, we are developing a better understanding of how our brain continually interprets information from our senses and permits us to make responses appropriate to the environment.

Perceptual Constancy

Consider what happens as you finish a conversation with a friend and she begins to walk away from you. As you watch her walk down the street, the image on your retina becomes smaller and smaller. Do you wonder why she is shrinking?

Of course not. Despite the very real change in the size of the retinal image, you factor into your thinking the knowledge that your friend is moving farther away from you. No matter how far away she progresses, and no matter how small the retinal image becomes as a consequence of her distance, you still perceive her as the same size.

That your friend does not appear to shrink is due to perceptual constancy. *Perceptual constancy* is a phenomenon in which physical objects are perceived as unvarying and consistent, despite changes in their appearance or in the physical environment.

One of the most dramatic examples of perceptual constancy involves the rising moon. When the moon first appears at night, close to the horizon, it seems to be huge—considerably larger than when it is high in the sky later in the evening. You may have thought that the apparent size of the moon was caused by the moon's being physically closer to the earth when it first appears. In fact, though, this is not the case at all (Hershenson, 1989).

Instead, the moon appears to be larger when it is close to the horizon primarily because of a misapplication of perceptual constancy (Coren & Aks, 1990). When the moon is near the horizon, the perceptual cues of intervening terrain and objects such as trees on the horizon produce a misleading sense of distance. Because perceptual constancy leads us to take that distance into account when we view the moon, we perceive the moon as relatively large. On the other hand, when the moon is high in the sky, we see it by itself, and perceptual constancy leads us to perceive it as relatively small. To prove this, try looking at the moon when it is relatively low on the horizon through a paper-towel tube; the moon will suddenly appear to "shrink" back to normal size.

Although other factors help account for the moon illusion, perceptual constancy appears to be a primary ingredient in our susceptibility to the illusion (Coren, 1989; Coren & Aks, 1990; Suzuki, 1991). Furthermore, perceptual constancy occurs not just in terms of size (as with the moon illusion) but with shape and color as well (e.g., Brainard, Wandell, & Chichilnisky, 1993). The image on our retina varies as a plane approaches, flies overhead, and disappears, yet we do not perceive the plane as changing shape. Instead, we perceive it as unchanging, despite the physical variations that occur.

Depth Perception: Translating 2-D to 3-D

As sophisticated as the retina is, the images projected onto it are flat and two-dimensional (2-D). Yet the world around us is three-dimensional (3-D), and we perceive it that way. How do we make the transformation from 2-D to 3-D?

The ability to view the world in three dimensions and to perceive distance—a skill known as *depth perception*—is due largely to the fact that we have two eyes. Because there is a certain distance between the eyes, a slightly different image reaches each retina. The brain then integrates these two images into one composite view. But it does not ignore the difference in images, which is known as *binocular disparity.* The disparity allows the brain to estimate the distance of an object from us.

You can get a sense of binocular disparity for yourself. Hold a pencil at arm's length and look at it first with one eye and then with the other. There is little difference between the two views relative to the background. Now bring the pencil just 6 inches away from your face, and try the same thing. This time you will perceive a greater difference between the two views.

The fact that the discrepancy between the images in the two eyes varies according to the distance of objects that we view provides us with a means of determining distance. If we view two objects, and one is considerably closer to us than another, the retinal disparity will be relatively large and we will have a greater sense of depth between the two. On the other hand, if the two objects are a similar distance from us, the retinal disparity will be minor, and we will perceive them as being a similar distance from us.

Filmmakers, whose medium compels them to project images in just two dimensions, have tried to create the illusion of depth perception by using two cameras, spaced slightly apart, to produce slightly different images, each destined for a different eye. In a 3-D movie, the two images are projected simultaneously. This produces a double image, unless special glasses are worn to allow each image to be viewed by the eye for which it is intended. The special glasses—familiar to moviegoers since the first 3-D movie, *Bwana Devil,* appeared in 1952—provide a genuine sense of depth. Similar techniques are being developed to show 3-D movies on television (Rogers, 1988).

In some cases, certain cues permit us to obtain a sense of depth and distance with just one eye (Burnham, 1983). These cues are known as **monocular cues.** One monocular cue—*motion parallax*—is the change in position of an object on the retina as the head moves from side to side. The brain is able to calculate the distance of the object by the amount of change in the retinal image. Similarly, experience has taught us that, if two objects are the same size, the one that makes a smaller image on the retina is farther away than the one that provides a larger image—an example of the monocular cue of *relative size.*

Finally, anyone who has ever seen railroad tracks that seem to join together in the distance knows that distant objects appear to be closer together than nearer ones, a phenomenon called *linear perspective.* People use linear perspective as a

Monocular cues: Signals that allow us to perceive distance and depth with just one eye

monocular cue in estimating distance, allowing the two-dimensional image on the retina to record the three-dimensional world (Bruce & Green, 1990).

Motion Perception: As the World Turns

When a batter tries to hit a ball that has been pitched, the most important factor is the motion of the ball. How is a batter able to judge the speed and location of a target that is moving at some 90 miles per hour?

The answer rests, in part, on several cues that provide us with relevant information about the perception of motion (Movshon & Newsome, 1992). For one thing, the perceived movement of an object across the retina is typically made relative to some stable, unmoving background. Moreover, if the stimulus is heading toward us, the image on the retina may expand in size, filling more and more of the visual field. In such cases, we assume that the stimulus is approaching—and not that it is an expanding stimulus viewed at a constant distance.

It is not, however, just the movement of images across the retina that brings about the perception of motion. If it were, we would perceive the world as moving every time we moved our heads. Instead, one of the critical things we learn about perception is to factor information about head and eye movements along with information about changes in the retinal image.

In some cases, movement is so fast that we are unable to follow it. In those instances, we may be able to anticipate where an object will end up on the basis of our prior experience. For example, computer tracking of baseball pitches has shown that most fast balls thrown in major-league games travel too fast for the eye to follow. Indeed, if a batter tried to follow a fast ball from the moment it left a pitcher's hand, he would lose sight of it by the time it got about 5 feet from the plate (Bahill & Laritz, 1984). Research suggests that good hitters take their eyes off the ball during the middle of its trip and shift their vision closer to home plate, waiting for the ball's arrival and (hoped-for) impact with the bat. Thus, instead of relying on the raw sensory input from the traveling ball—the phenomenon of sensation—they employ perceptual processes, using what they have learned to expect about how balls travel.

Perceptual Illusions: The Deceptions of Perceptions

For sight follows gracious contours, and unless we flatter its pleasure by proportionate alternations of these parts (so that by adjustment we offset the amount to which it suffers illusions), an uncouth and ungracious aspect will be presented to the spectators (Vitruvius Pollio, 1960).

The phenomenon to which Vitruvius, a Greek architect who lived around 30 B.C., was referring in such elegant language is that people do not always view the world accurately. Consequently, Vitruvius argued that we must consider how people's eyes and brains perceive buildings when designing architectural works.

Consider the Parthenon, one of the most famous buildings of ancient Greece. Although it looks true and straight to the eye, it was actually built with a bulge on one side. This protrusion fools viewers into thinking it is straight. If it didn't have that bulge—and quite a few other "tricks" like it, such as columns that incline inward—it would look as if it were crooked and about to fall down.

The fact that the Parthenon appears to be completely upright, with straight lines and right angles at every corner, is the result of a series of visual illusions. **Visual illusions** are physical stimuli that consistently produce errors in perception. In the case of the Parthenon, the building appears to be completely square, as illustrated in Figure 3-14a. However, had it actually been built that way, it would look to us as it does in Figure 3-14b. The reason for this is the illusion illustrated in 3-14c, which makes angles placed above a line appear as if they were

Visual illusions: Physical stimuli that consistently produce errors in perception (often called optical illusions)

a.

c.

b.   d.

FIGURE 3-14 In building the Parthenon, the Greeks constructed an architectural wonder that looks perfectly straight, with right angles at every corner, as in (a). However, if it had been built with completely true right angles, it would have looked as it does in (b), due to the visual illusion illustrated in (c). To compensate for this illusion, the Parthenon was designed to have a slight upward curvature, as shown in (d). (*Coren & Ward, 1989, p. 5.*)

bent. To offset the illusion, the Parthenon was actually constructed as in Figure 3-14d, with a slight upward curvature.

Such perceptual insights did not stop with the Greeks. Modern-day architects and designers also take visual distortions into account in their planning. For example, the New Orleans Superdome makes use of several visual tricks. Its seats vary in color throughout the stadium to give the appearance, from a distance, that there is always a full house. The carpeting in some of the sloping halls has perpendicular stripes that make people slow their pace by producing the perception that they are moving faster than they actually are. The same illusion is used at toll booths on superhighways. Stripes painted on the pavement in front of the toll booths make drivers feel that they are moving more rapidly than they actually are and cause them to decelerate quickly.

The implications of visual illusions go beyond the attractiveness of buildings. For instance, suppose you were an air traffic controller watching a radar screen.

The suspected cause of this airplane crash, which killed 160 people in Columbia, was pilot error, possibly due to a visual illusion.

You might be tempted to sit back and relax as two planes drew closer together. If you did, however, the result might be an air disaster. Investigation has suggested that some 70 to 80 percent of all airplane accidents are caused by human errors of one sort or another (O'Hare & Roscoe, 1990).

The flight-path situation is an example of a well-known visual illusion called the *Poggendorf illusion.* The Poggendorf illusion is just one of many that consistently fool the eye (Perkins, 1983; Greist-Bousquet & Schiffman, 1986). Another is the one illustrated in Figure 3-15 called the *Müller-Lyer illusion.* Although the two lines are the same length, the one with the arrow tips pointing inward (Figure 3-15*a,* top) appears to be longer than the one with the arrow tips pointing outward (Figure 3-15*a,* bottom).

Although all kinds of explanations for visual illusions have been suggested, most concentrate either on the eye's visual sensory apparatus itself or on our interpretation of a given figure. Explanations for the Müller-Lyer illusion suggest, for example, that eye movements are greater when the arrow tips point inward, making us perceive the line as longer than when the arrow tips face outward.

Other evidence suggests that the illusion can be attributed to the brain's interpretive errors. For instance, one hypothesis assumes that the Müller-Lyer illusion is a result of the meaning we give to each of the lines (Gregory, 1978). When we see the top line in Figure 3-15*a,* we tend to perceive it as if it were the inside corner of a room extending away from us, as illustrated in Figure 3-15*b.* On the other hand, when we view the bottom line in Figure 3-15*a,* we perceive it as the relatively close outside corner of a rectangular object such as the building corner in Figure 3-15*c.* Because previous experience leads us to assume that the outside corner is closer than the inside corner, we make the further assumption that the inside corner must therefore be larger.

Given all the underlying assumptions, it may seem unlikely to you that this explanation is valid. However, there is a good degree of convincing evidence for it. One of the most telling pieces of support comes from cross-cultural studies that show that people raised in areas where there are few right angles—such as the

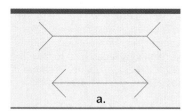

a.

FIGURE 3-15 (*a*) The Müller-Lyer illusion, in which the upper horizontal line appears longer than the lower one. (*b*) and (*c*) An explanation for the Müller-Lyer illusion suggests that the line with arrow points directed inward is interpreted as the inside corner of a rectangular room extending away from us (*b*), and the line with arrow points directed outward is viewed as the relatively close corner of a rectangular object, such as the building corner in (*c*). Our previous experience with distance cues leads us to assume that the outside corner is closer than the inside corner and that the inside corner must therefore be longer.

b.

c.

Zulu in Africa—are much less susceptible to the illusion than people who grow up where most structures are built using right angles and rectangles (Segall, Campbell, & Herskovits, 1966).

Exploring Diversity

Culture and Perception

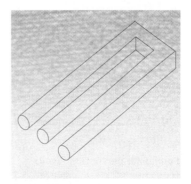

FIGURE 3-16 The "devil's tuning fork" has three prongs . . . or does it have two?

As the example of the Zulu indicates, the particular culture in which we are raised has clear consequences for the ways in which we perceive the world. Consider the drawing in Figure 3-16. Sometimes called the "devil's tuning fork," it is likely to produce a mind-boggling effect, as the center tine of the fork alternates between appearing and disappearing.

Now try to reproduce the drawing on a piece of paper. Chances are that the task is nearly impossible for you—unless you are a member of an African tribe with little exposure to Western cultures. For such individuals, the task is simple; they have no trouble reproducing the figure. The reason seems to be that Western people automatically interpret the drawing as something that cannot exist in three dimensions, and they are therefore inhibited from reproducing it. The African tribal members, on the other hand, do not make the assumption that the figure is "impossible" and instead view it in two dimensions, which enables them to copy the figure with ease (Deregowski, 1973).

Cultural differences are also reflected in depth perception. A Western viewer of Figure 3-17 would interpret the drawing as one in which the hunter is trying to spear the antelope in the foreground while an elephant stands under the tree in the background. A member of an isolated African tribe, however, interprets the scene very differently by assuming that the hunter is aiming at the elephant. Westerners use the difference in sizes between the two animals as a cue that the elephant is farther away than the antelope (Hudson, 1960).

The misinterpretations created by visual illusions are ultimately due, then, to errors in both fundamental visual processing and the way the brain interprets the information it receives. But visual illusions also illustrate something fundamental about perception that makes them more than mere psychological curiosities. There is a basic connection between our prior knowledge, needs, motivations, and expectations about how the world is put together and the way we perceive it. Our view of the world is very much a function, then, of fundamental psycholog-

FIGURE 3-17 Is the man about to spear the elephant or the antelope? Westerners assume that the differences in size between the two animals indicate that the elephant is farther away, and therefore the man is aiming for the antelope. On the other hand, members of some African tribes, not used to depth cues in two-dimensional drawings, assume that the man is aiming for the elephant. (*Drawing based on Deregowski, 1973.*)

ical factors. Furthermore, each of us perceives the environment in a way that is unique and personal—a fact that allows each of us to make our own special contribution to the world.

Subliminal Perception and Other Perceptual Controversies

Can you raise your self-esteem or improve your memory through subliminal perception? Probably not—although it may make you *think* you feel better and remember more.

Subliminal perception: The perception of messages about which a person has no awareness.

Subliminal perception refers to the perception of messages about which we have no awareness. The stimulus may be a word, a sound, or even a smell that activates the sensory system but is not intense enough to be reported as having been experienced by a person. For example, people may report being unable to perceive a word momentarily flashed on a screen in front of them. Later, though, they may behave in a way that indicates they actually saw it, providing evidence for subliminal perception. Specifically, experiments have shown that people who are exposed so briefly to a descriptive label that they cannot report seeing it later form impressions that are influenced by the label to which they were exposed (Bargh & Pietromonaco, 1982; Merikle, 1992).

Yet does this mean that subliminal messages can actually lead to significant changes in attitudes or behavior? Most recent evidence suggests not. In a well-controlled experiment, psychologist Anthony Greenwald and colleagues gave volunteers who wanted to improve either their self-esteem or their memories audiotapes that had been purchased from three manufacturers (Greenwald et al., 1991). The audible content of the tapes consisted of classical music, popular music, or sounds of the surf or woods. However, according to their manufacturers, subliminal audio messages relevant to either improved self-esteem or memory were repeated softly on the tapes.

To fully test the effects of the messages, the experimenters manipulated the labels on some of the tapes. Consequently, some participants who thought they were getting a self-esteem-enhancing tape were actually given a memory-improving tape, and others who received a tape labeled as if it were a memory-improving tape actually received one designed to enhance self-esteem. Some subjects, of course, received tapes that were correctly labeled.

The results were clear. After a month of use, neither the self-esteem nor the memory tape had any effect on actual self-esteem or memory. What did matter, though, was the label on the tape. Participants who thought they had received a self-esteem tape (whether it was really a self-esteem or a memory tape) tended to report an improvement in their self-esteem. Those who thought they had listened to a memory tape tended to report that their memory had improved, regardless of the true nature of the tape.

In sum, the subliminal messages contained on the tapes seemed to have no real consequences. This conclusion sums up the state of our knowledge about subliminal perception. Although we are able to perceive at least some kinds of information about which we are unaware, such information appears to have little consequential effect.

Still, claims about the effectiveness of subliminal messages continue to be made. For instance, the parents of two boys who committed suicide sued the rock band Judas Priest because of subliminal messages allegedly embedded in their music (Neely, 1990). The parents contended that their sons had killed themselves after listening repeatedly to a subliminal message saying "Do it!" in a song with lyrics discussing the hopelessness of life. The judge and jury disagreed, as would most psychologists.

Extrasensory Perception (ESP) Given the less-than-impressive evidence supporting subliminal perception, psychologists are even more skeptical of reports of *extrasensory perception,* or *ESP*—perception that does not involve our known senses. Most psychologists reject the existence of ESP, asserting that there is no sound documentation that the phenomenon exists (Swets & Bjork, 1990; Hyman, 1994).

However, a recent debate in one of the most prestigious psychology journals, *Psychological Bulletin,* has heightened interest in the area. According to an article by Daryl Bem and Charles Honorton, reliable evidence exists for what they call an "anomalous process of information transfer," or *psi,* a form of ESP (Bem & Honorton, 1994). Bem and Honorton argued that a cumulative body of research shows reliable support for the existence of psi when using a method called the "Ganzfeld procedure."

The Ganzfeld procedure employs a sender who is exposed to a stimulus, such as a work of art, a photo, or a videotaped sequence, for about 30 minutes. In another room, an isolated receiver is seated in a comfortable chair and is shielded from extraneous stimulation by eye coverings and earphones that play constant static. As senders concentrate on what they are seeing, receivers give a successive verbal account of their thoughts for the 30-minute period. At the end of the time period, receivers are typically presented with four stimuli and asked to choose which most closely matches what they experienced during the reception period. Because, over many Ganzfeld trials, some receivers successfully choose the correct stimulus at a rate that is slightly above what would be expected by chance alone, Bem and Honorton suggested that the evidence supports the existence of psi.

Their conclusion has been challenged on several counts. For example, one critic suggested that the research methodology in the studies they reviewed was inadequate, and that the specific experiments supporting psi do not include acceptable forms of randomization involving the presentation of stimuli (Hyman, 1994).

Because of questions about the quality of the research, as well as a lack of any credible theoretical explanation for how extrasensory perception might take place, most psychologists continue to believe that there is no reliable scientific support for ESP. Still, the recent exchange in *Psychological Bulletin* is likely to heighten the debate. More importantly, the renewed interest in ESP is likely to inspire more research, the only way that the issue can be resolved.

The Informed Consumer of Psychology
Managing Pain

Pain—whether it is a pounding, aching, stinging, soreness, or burning feeling— is one sensation that cannot be easily overlooked. When pain strikes, we are likely to seek whatever remedies are at hand, ranging from taking an aspirin to soaking in a hot bathtub.

For some sufferers, like Jennifer Darling (whose case we considered at the beginning of the chapter), the pain never ceases. Because of disease, injury, or medical procedures, or sometimes for unknown reasons, some people suffer from chronic, lingering pain. To fight chronic pain, as well as more common types, psychologists and medical specialists have devised several strategies of the sort mentioned earlier in the chapter in the Pathways through Psychology box describing the work of Mark Jensen.

Among the most important approaches to fighting chronic pain are the following (Druckman & Bjork, 1991; Turk & Melzack, 1992; Turk & Nash, 1993; Lang & Patt, 1994; Turk, 1994):

■ *Medication.* Painkilling drugs are the most popular treatment in fighting pain. They range from those that directly treat the source of the pain—such as reducing swelling in painful joints—to those that work on the symptoms of the pain. Moreover, pain-reducing medication is now sometimes routinely prescribed even before the onset of any pain in an effort to reduce its impact following surgery. Research suggests that in these instances patients actually end up taking less pain medication than those who wait until the pain takes hold (U.S. Public Health Service, 1992).

■ *Nerve and brain stimulation.* Pain relief can sometimes occur when a low-voltage electric current is passed through the specific part of the body that is in pain. In even more severe cases, electrodes can be surgically implanted directly into the brain, and a handheld battery pack can stimulate nerve cells to provide direct relief (Barbaro, 1988). This process, employed in the case of Jennifer Darling, is known as *transcutaneous electrical nerve stimulation,* or *TENS.*

■ *Hypnosis.* For those people who can be hypnotized, this method can produce a major degree of pain relief (Spiegel, 1987; Erickson, Hershman, & Secter, 1990).

■ *Biofeedback and relaxation techniques.* As we discussed in the previous chapter, biofeedback is a process in which people learn to control such "involuntary" functions as heartbeat and respiration. If the pain involves muscles, such as in tension headaches or back pain, biofeedback can be helpful (Dolce & Raczynski, 1985). Through biofeedback and the use of other techniques, people can be trained to relax their bodies systematically. Such relaxation is often effective in decreasing the pain caused by tension.

■ *Surgery.* One of the most extreme methods, surgery can be used to cut certain nerve fibers carrying pain messages to the brain. Still, because of the danger that other bodily functions will be affected, surgery is a treatment of last resort.

■ *Cognitive restructuring.* People who continually say to themselves, "This pain will never stop," "The pain is ruining my life," or "I can't take it any more" are likely to make their pain even worse. As we'll discuss in Chapter 13, by substituting more positive ways of thinking, people can increase their sense of control—and actually reduce the degree of pain they experience. Teaching people to rewrite the "script" that controls their reaction to pain through therapy can result in significant reductions in the perception of pain (Heyneman et al., 1990; Turk & Nash, 1993).

If you wish to learn more about chronic pain, you can consult the American Chronic Pain Association, P.O. Box 850, Rocklin, California 95677. In addition, many hospitals have pain clinics that specialize in the treatment of pain. Be sure, though, that the clinic you use is approved by the Commission for the Accreditation of Rehabilitative Facilities or the Joint Commission on the Accreditation of Health-Care Organizations.

RECAP AND REVIEW

Recap

- People do not respond passively to visual stimuli; rather, they try to separate a given figure from the background.
- Among the gestalt laws of organization are closure, proximity, similarity, and simplicity.
- Feature analysis considers how people perceive a stimulus, break it down into the individual elements that make it up, and then use those elements to understand what they are seeing.
- Perception occurs through top-down and bottom-up processing.

- Depth perception occurs because of binocular disparity, motion parallax, and the relative size of images on the retina. Motion perception is the result of the movement of images across the retina, combined with information about head and eye movements.
- Visual illusions are physical stimuli that consistently produce errors in perception. Among the most common are the Poggendorf illusion and the Müller-Lyer illusion.
- Subliminal perception and extrasensory perception remain controversial.

Review

1. Match each of the following organizational laws with its meaning:
   1. Elements close together are grouped together.
   2. Patterns are perceived in the most basic, direct manner possible.
   3. Groupings are made in terms of complete figures.
   4. Elements similar in appearance are grouped together.

   a. Closure
   b. Proximity
   c. Similarity
   d. Simplicity

2. _____ analysis deals with the way in which we break an object down into its component pieces in order to understand it.

3. Processing that takes into account higher functions such as expectations and motivations is known as _____-_____ processing, while processing that involves recognizing the individual components of a stimulus is known as _____-_____ processing.

4. When a car passes you on the road and appears to shrink as it gets farther away, what is the perceptual phenomenon that allows you to realize that the car does not get smaller, but rather farther away?

5. _____ _____ is the ability to view the world in three dimensions instead of two.

6. The eyes use a technique known as _____ _____ , which makes use of the differing images each eye sees to give three dimensions to sight.

7. Match the monocular cues with their definitions.
   1. Relative size
   2. Linear perspective
   3. Motion parallax

   a. Straight lines seem to join together as they become more distant.
   b. An object changes position on the retina as the head moves.
   c. If two objects are the same size, the one producing a smaller retinal image is farther away.

8. Which of the following has *not* been proposed as an explanation of why we perceive visual illusions?
   a. Variations in the eye's visual sensory apparatus
   b. Small distance between eyeballs
   c. Interpretive errors made by the brain
   d. Previous learning experience

Ask Yourself

As noted in our discussion of visual illusions, people from different cultures are not subject to the same illusions that we are, and we are not subject to some of their visual illusions. Armed with this information, you are asked to guide an Australian aborigine on a walking tour of Dallas. What kinds of problems might occur? How would you overcome them? Do you think you would gain anything from such an experience?

(Answers to review questions are on page 115.)

LOOKING BACK

What is sensation, and how do psychologists study it?

1. Sensation is the stimulation of the sense organs that comes from our initial encounter with stimuli (forms of energy that activate a sense organ). In contrast, perception is the process by which we sort out, interpret, analyze, and integrate stimuli to which our senses are exposed. Sensation has traditionally been investigated by the branch of psychology called psychophysics, which studies the relationship between the physical nature of stimuli and a person's sensory responses to them.

What is the relationship between the nature of a physical stimulus and the kinds of sensory responses that result from it?

2. One major area of psychophysics is the study of the absolute threshold, the smallest amount of physical intensity by which a stimulus can be detected. Although under ideal conditions absolute thresholds are extraordinarily sensitive, the presence of noise (background stimuli that interfere with other stimuli) reduces detection capabilities. Moreover, factors such as an individual's expectations and motivations affect success in detecting stimuli. Signal detection theory is now used to predict the accuracy of judgments by systematically taking into account two kinds of errors made by observers—reporting the presence of a stimulus when there is none and reporting the absence of a stimulus when one is actually present.

3. Difference thresholds relate to the smallest detectable difference between two stimuli, known as a just noticeable difference. According to Weber's law, a just noticeable difference is a constant proportion of the intensity of an initial stimulus.

4. Sensory adaptation occurs when we become accustomed to a constant stimulus and change our evaluation of it. Repeated exposure to a stimulus results in an apparent decline in sensitivity to it.

What are the basic processes that underlie the sense of vision?

5. Human sensory experience goes well beyond the traditional five senses, although most is known about just two: vision and hearing. Vision depends on sensitivity to light, electromagnetic waves that are reflected off objects outside the body. The eye shapes the light into an image that is transformed into nerve impulses and interpreted by the brain.

6. When light first enters the eye, it travels through the cornea and then traverses the pupil, a dark hole in the center of the iris. The size of the pupil opening adjusts according to the amount of light entering the eye. Light then enters the lens, which, by a process called accommodation, acts to focus light

rays onto the rear of the eye. On the rear of the eye is the retina, which is composed of light-sensitive nerve cells called rods and cones. The rods and cones are unevenly spaced over the retina, with the greatest concentration of cones occurring in an area called the fovea. Because of the phenomenon of adaptation, it takes time to adjust to situations that are darker than the previous environment.

7. The visual information gathered by the rods and cones is transferred via bipolar and ganglion cells through the optic nerve, which leads to the optic chiasm—the point where the optic nerve splits. Because the image on the retina is reversed and upside down, images from the right half of the retina are actually from the field of vision to the left of the person, and vice versa.

How do we see colors?

8. Color vision seems to be based on two processes described by the trichromatic theory and the opponent-process theory. The trichromatic theory suggests that there are three kinds of cones in the retina, each of which is responsive to a certain range of colors. The opponent-process theory presumes pairs of different types of cells in the eye. These cells work in opposition to each other.

What role does the ear play in the senses of sound, motion, and balance?

9. Sound, motion, and balance are centered in the ear. Sounds, in the form of vibrating air waves, enter the outer ear and travel through the auditory canal until they reach the eardrum. The vibrations of the eardrum are transmitted into the middle ear, which consists of three bones: the hammer, the anvil, and the stirrup. These bones transmit vibrations to the oval window, a thin membrane leading to the inner ear. In the inner ear, vibrations move into the cochlea, which encloses the basilar membrane. Hair cells on the basilar membrane change the mechanical energy of sound waves into nerve impulses that are transmitted to the brain. In addition to processing sound, the ear is involved in the sense of balance and motion through the semicircular canals and otoliths.

10. Sound has a number of important characteristics. One is frequency, the number of wave crests that occur in a second. Differences in the frequency of sound waves create different pitches. Another aspect of sound is intensity, the variations in pressure produced by a wave as it travels through the air. Intensity is measured in decibels. The place theory of hearing and the frequency theory of hearing explain the processes by which we distinguish sounds of varying frequency and intensity.

How do smell and taste function?

11. Considerably less is known about smell, taste, and the skin senses than about vision and hearing. Still, it is clear that smell employs olfactory cells (the receptor cells of the nose) and that taste is centered in the tongue's taste buds, which are capable of sensing combinations of sweet, sour, salty, and bitter flavors.

What are the skin senses, and how do they relate to the experience of pain?

12. The skin senses are responsible for the experiences of touch, pressure, temperature, and pain. We know the most about pain, which can be explained by the gate-control theory. The theory suggests that particular nerve receptors lead to specific areas of the brain related to pain. When these receptors are activated, a "gate" to the brain opens, allowing the sensation of pain to be experienced. In addition, another set of receptors, when stimulated, close the gate, thereby reducing the experience of pain. Endorphins, internal painkillers, may also affect the operation of the gate.

13. Among the techniques used most frequently to alleviate pain are administration of drugs, hypnosis, biofeedback, relaxation techniques, surgery, nerve and brain stimulation, and cognitive restructuring.

What principles underlie our organization of the visual world, allowing us to make sense of our environment?

14. Work on figure-ground distinctions shows that perception is a constructive process in which people go beyond the stimuli that are physically present and try to construct a meaningful situation. Perception follows the gestalt laws of organization. These laws provide a series of principles by which we organize bits and pieces of information into meaningful wholes, known as gestalts. Among the most important laws are those of closure, proximity, similarity, and simplicity. The gestalt psychologists demonstrated convincingly that perception follows the general rule: "The whole is greater than the sum of its parts."

15. Feature analysis pertains to how we consider a shape, pattern, object, or scene in terms of the individual elements that make it up. These component features are then combined into a representation of the whole object in the brain. Finally, this combination of features is compared against existing memories, permitting identification of the object.

16. Processing of perceptual stimuli occurs in both a top-down and a bottom-up fashion. In top-down processing, perception is guided by higher-level knowledge, experience, expectations, and motivations. In bottom-up processing, perception involves recognizing and processing information about the individual components of stimuli.

17. Perceptual constancy permits us to perceive stimuli as unvarying and consistent, despite changes in the environment or the appearance of the objects being perceived. Perceptual constancy occurs in terms of size, shape, and color constancy.

How are we able to perceive the world in three dimensions when our retinas are capable of sensing only two-dimensional images?

18. Depth perception is the ability to perceive distance and to view the world in three dimensions, even though the images projected on our retinas are two-dimensional. We are able to judge depth and distance as a result of binocular disparity (the difference in images as seen by each of the eyes) and monoc-

ular cues, such as motion parallax (the apparent movement of objects as one's head moves from side to side), the relative size of images on the retina, and linear perspective.

19. Motion perception depends on several cues. They include the perceived movement of an object across our retina and information about how the head and eyes are moving.

What clues do visual illusions give us about our understanding of general perceptual mechanisms?

20. Visual illusions are physical stimuli that consistently produce errors in perception, causing judgments that do not ac-

curately reflect the physical reality of the stimulus. Among the best-known illusions are the Poggendorf illusion and the Müller-Lyer illusion.

21. Visual illusions are usually the result of errors in the brain's interpretation of visual stimuli. Furthermore, the particular culture in which we are raised has clear consequences for the ways in which we perceive the world.

22. Subliminal perception refers to the perception of messages about which we have no awareness, while extrasensory perception does not involve our known senses. The reality of both phenomena is open to question and debate.

KEY TERMS AND CONCEPTS

sensation (p. 74)
perception (p. 74)
stimulus (p. 75)
psychophysics (p. 76)
absolute threshold (p. 76)
signal detection theory (p. 77)
difference threshold (p. 78)
just noticeable difference (p. 78)
Weber's law (p. 78)
adaptation (p. 79)
retina (p. 82)
rods (p. 82)
cones (p. 82)

dark adaptation (p. 84)
optic nerve (p. 84)
feature detection (p. 86)
trichromatic theory of color vision
  (p. 87)
opponent-process theory of color vision
  (p. 88)
sound (p. 90)
eardrum (p. 90)
cochlea (p. 90)
basilar membrane (p. 90)
hair cells (p. 90)
place theory of hearing (p. 93)

frequency theory of hearing (p. 93)
semicircular canals (p. 95)
otoliths (p. 95)
skin senses (p. 97)
gate-control theory of pain (p. 98)
gestalt laws of organization (p. 101)
feature analysis (p. 101)
top-down processing (p. 103)
bottom-up processing (p. 104)
monocular cues (p. 105)
visual illusions (p. 106)
subliminal perception (p. 110)

ANSWERS TO PREVIOUS REVIEW
1. 1-b; 2-d; 3-a; 4-c **2.** Feature **3.** top-down; bottom-up **4.** Perceptual constancy
5. Depth perception **6.** binocular disparity **7.** 1-c; 2-a; 3-b **8.** b

CHAPTER 4
STATES OF CONSCIOUSNESS

The Long Days and Short Life of Frank Ingulli

At 9:30 P.M. on May 19, Frank Ingulli, a third-year medical student working his 15th straight hour, was standing over an operating table and maneuvering a miniature abdominal camera as doctors finished off a gall bladder operation at the medical center.

Six hours later, Mr. Ingulli was stretched out on a table in the same hospital as some of the same doctors he had worked alongside were cutting his chest open and feverishly massaging his heart in a desperate effort—futile as it turned out—to revive him.

Mr. Ingulli, apparently driving to his nearby home to catch some sleep, had been crushed to death in a head-on collision after he mistakenly entered an exit ramp off Interstate 95 and found himself heading southbound on the northbound side of the bustling highway. (Berger, 1993, p. 29)

LOOKING AHEAD

The most likely cause of Frank Ingulli's lethal error: fatigue. His 15-hour day had followed two 12-hour days. And it had come in the midst of a three-month class for which he had to read a 2000-page principles of surgery text on which he was soon to be tested.

Although the consequences of fatigue are usually not as deadly as they were for Ingulli, most of us know all too well the feelings of exhaustion that follow from too little sleep. We know what it is like to fend off sleep, to try to stay alert and attentive, and the exquisite relief we experience when we finally can go to sleep.

But just what is sleep? And how, for that matter, can we explain our awareness during our waking hours? In this chapter, we consider consciousness. **Consciousness** is the awareness of the sensations, thoughts, and feelings being experienced at a given moment. Consciousness is our subjective understanding of both the environment around us and our private internal world, unobservable to outsiders.

Consciousness spans several dimensions, encompassing several levels of awareness. For instance, consciousness ranges from those perceptions we experience while wide awake, concentrating on performing well on a test or seeking to play well in a baseball game, to the minimal level of awareness we experience while sleeping. Consciousness thus varies from an active to a passive state (Hilgard, 1980; Milner & Rugg, 1992). In more active states, we systematically carry out mental activity, focusing our thoughts and absorbing the world around us. In more passive waking states, thoughts and images come to us more spontaneously; we daydream or drift from one thought to another. In the most passive states of consciousness, such as sleeping, we are only minimally aware of the stimuli around us. Still, we remain at least partially aware of events outside our bodies, because we still can be awakened by sufficiently strong stimuli—such as the ringing of a persistent alarm clock.

Because consciousness is so personal a phenomenon, psychologists have sometimes been reluctant to study it. After all, who can say that your consciousness is similar to or, for that matter, different from anyone else's? In fact, early psychologists suggested that the study of consciousness was out of bounds for the discipline. They argued that, because consciousness could be understood only by relying on the "unscientific" introspections of subjects about what they were experiencing at a given moment, its study was best left to disciplines such as philosophy. Proponents of this view suggested that philosophers could speculate at

Consciousness: A person's awareness of the sensations, thoughts, and feelings that he or she is experiencing at a given moment

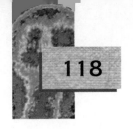
their leisure on such knotty issues as whether consciousness is separate from the physical body, how people know they exist, how the body and mind are related to each other, and how we identify what state of consciousness we are in at any given moment.

However, most contemporary psychologists reject the view that the study of consciousness is unsuitable for the field of psychology. They argue instead that there are several scientific approaches that permit its study. For example, biopsychologists can measure brain-wave patterns under varied conditions of consciousness, ranging from sleep to waking to hypnotic trances. Moreover, new understanding of the chemistry of drugs such as marijuana and alcohol has provided insights into the way they produce their pleasurable—as well as adverse—effects (Dennett, 1991; Leahey, 1994).

Another impetus for the study of consciousness is the realization that people throughout many different cultures routinely seek ways to alter their states of consciousness. These variations in states of consciousness have been found to share some basic characteristics (Ludwig, 1969; Martindale, 1981). One is an alteration in thinking, which may become shallow, illogical, or impaired in some way. In addition, people's sense of time may become disturbed, and their perceptions of the world and of themselves may be changed. They may experience losses of self-control, doing things they would never otherwise do. Finally, they may feel a sense of *ineffability*—the inability to understand an experience rationally or describe it in words.

This chapter considers several states of consciousness, beginning with two that we have all experienced: sleeping and dreaming. Next, we turn to states of consciousness found under conditions of hypnosis and meditation. Finally, we examine drug-induced states of consciousness.

- *What are the different states of consciousness?*
- *What happens when we sleep, and what are the meaning and function of dreams?*
- *How much do we daydream?*
- *What are the major sleep disorders and how can they be treated?*

SLEEP AND DREAMS

The crowd roared as running back Donald Dorff, age 67, took the pitch from his quarterback and accelerated smoothly across the artificial turf. As Dorff braked and pivoted to cut back over tackle, a huge defensive lineman loomed in his path. One hundred twenty pounds of pluck, Dorff did not hesitate. But let the retired grocery merchandiser from Golden Valley, Minnesota, tell it:

"There was a 280-pound tackle waiting for me, so I decided to give him my shoulder. When I came to, I was on the floor in my bedroom. I had smashed into the dresser and knocked everything off it and broke the mirror and just made one heck of a mess. It was 1:30 a.m." (Long, 1987, p. 787).

Dorff, it turned out, was suffering from a rare condition afflicting some older men. The problem occurs when the mechanism that usually shuts down bodily movement during dreams does not function properly. People suffering from the malady have been known to hit others, smash windows, punch holes in walls—all the while being fast asleep.

Donald Dorff's problem had a happy ending. With the help of clonazepam, a drug that suppresses movement during dreams, his malady vanished. He now sleeps through the night undisturbed.

Although sleeping is something we all do for a significant part of our lives, many myths and misconceptions about the topic abound. To test your own knowledge of sleep and dreams, try answering the following questions before reading further.

_____ 1. Some people never dream. True or false?

_____ 2. Most dreams are caused by bodily sensations such as an upset stomach. True or false?

_____ 3. It has been proved that eight hours of sleep is needed to maintain mental health. True or false?

_____ 4. When people do not recall their dreams, it is probably because they are secretly trying to forget them. True or false?

_____ 5. Depriving someone of sleep will invariably cause the individual to become mentally unbalanced. True or false?

_____ 6. If we lose some sleep, we will eventually make up all the lost sleep the next night or another night. True or false?

_____ 7. No one has been able to go for more than forty-eight hours without sleep. True or false?

_____ 8. Everyone is able to sleep and breathe at the same time. True or false?

_____ 9. Sleep enables the brain to rest since there is little brain activity taking place during sleep. True or false?

_____ 10. Drugs have been proved to provide a long-term cure for sleeping difficulties. True or false?

Scoring: This is an easy set of questions to score, for every item is false. But don't lose any sleep if you missed them; they were chosen to represent the most common myths regarding sleep. (Items were drawn from a questionnaire developed by Palladino & Carducci, 1984.)

FIGURE 4-1 Testing your knowledge of sleep and dreams. _(Adapted from Palladino & Carducci, 1984.)_

The success of Dorff's treatment illustrates just one of the recent advances that has occurred in our understanding of sleep. Yet there are still many unanswered questions, including why we sleep, how much sleep we need, what dreams mean and what their function is, and how we can avoid insomnia. (Before you read on, you might want to test your knowledge of sleep and dreams by answering the questions in Figure 4-1.)

The Stages of Sleep

Most of us consider sleep a time of quiet tranquillity, as we set aside the tensions of the day and spend the night in uneventful slumber. However, a closer look at sleep shows that a good deal of activity occurs throughout the night, and that what at first appears to be a unitary state is, in fact, quite diverse.

Much of our knowledge of what happens during sleep comes from the _electroencephalogram,_ or _EEG,_ a measurement of electrical activity within the brain (see Chapter 2). When probes from an EEG machine are attached to the surface

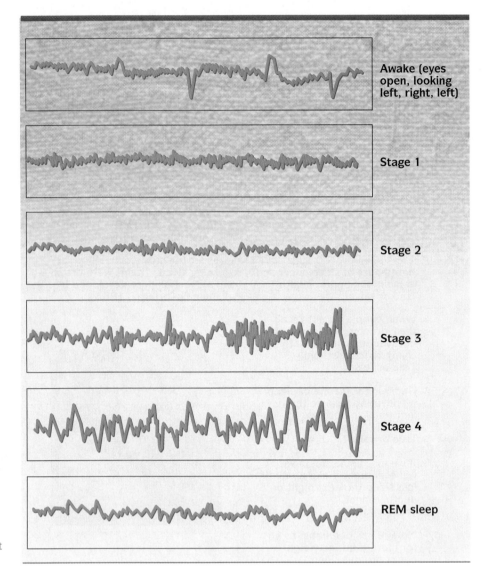

FIGURE 4-2 Brain-wave patterns (measured by an EEG apparatus) and eye movements in the different stages of sleep. *(Cohen, 1979.)*

of a sleeping person's scalp and face, it becomes readily apparent that instead of being dormant the brain is active throughout the night. It produces electrical discharges that form systematic, wavelike patterns that change in height (or amplitude) and speed (or frequency) in regular sequences. Instruments that measure muscle and eye movements also reveal a good deal of physical activity.

People progress through four distinct stages of sleep during a night's rest, moving through cycles lasting about 90 minutes. Each of these four sleep stages is associated with a unique pattern of brain waves, as shown in Figure 4-2. Moreover, there are specific biological indicators of dreaming.

When people first go to sleep, they move from a waking state in which they are relaxed with their eyes closed into **stage 1 sleep,** which is characterized by relatively rapid, low-voltage brain waves. This stage is actually a transition between wakefulness and sleep. During stage 1, images sometimes appear. It's as if we were viewing still photos. However, true dreaming does not occur during the initial entry into this stage.

As sleep becomes deeper, people enter **stage 2 sleep,** which is characterized by a slower, more regular wave pattern. However, there are also momentary interruptions of sharply pointed waves, called "sleep spindles" because of their configuration. It becomes increasingly difficult to awaken a person from stage 2

Stage 1 sleep: The state of transition between wakefulness and sleep, characterized by relatively rapid, low-voltage brain waves

Stage 2 sleep: A sleep deeper than that of stage 1, characterized by a slower, more regular wave pattern, along with momentary interruptions of "sleep spindles"

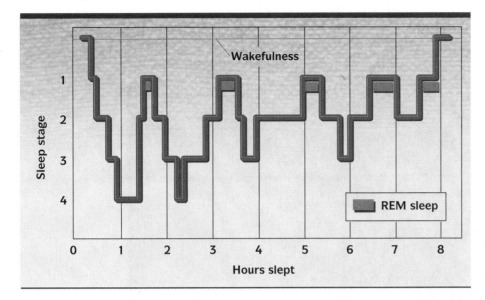

FIGURE 4-3 During the night, the typical sleeper passes through all four stages of sleep and several REM periods. *(Hartmann, 1967.)*

sleep, which makes up about half of the total sleep of those in their early twenties.

As people drift into **stage 3 sleep,** the next stage of sleep, the brain waves become slower, with an appearance of higher peaks and lower valleys in the wave pattern. By the time sleepers arrive at **stage 4 sleep,** the pattern is even slower and more regular, and people are least responsive to outside stimulation.

As you can see in Figure 4-3, stage 4 sleep is most likely to occur during the early part of the night. In addition to passing through regular transitions between stages of sleep, then, people tend to sleep less and less deeply over the course of the night. In the first half of the evening, our sleep is dominated by stages 3 and 4. The last half is characterized by lighter stages of sleep—as well as the phase of sleep during which dreams occur, as we discuss next (Dement & Wolpert, 1958; Ogilvie & Harsh, 1994).

Stage 3 sleep: A sleep characterized by slow brain waves, with greater peaks and valleys in the wave pattern

Stage 4 sleep: The deepest stage of sleep, during which we are least responsive to outside stimulation

REM Sleep: The Paradox of Sleep

Several times a night, while sleepers are in stage 1 sleep, something curious happens. Their heart rate increases and becomes irregular, their blood pressure rises, their breathing rate increases, and males—even male infants—have erections. Most characteristic of this period is the back-and-forth movement of the sleepers' eyes, as if they were watching an action-filled movie. This period of sleep is called **rapid eye movement,** or **REM, sleep.** REM sleep occupies a little over 20 percent of adults' total sleeping time.

Paradoxically, while all this activity is occurring, the major muscles of the body appear to be paralyzed—except in rare cases such as Donald Dorff's. For this reason, it is hard to awaken the sleeper. In addition, REM sleep is usually accompanied by dreams which, whether people remember them or not, are experienced by *everyone* during some part of the night.

Rapid eye movement (REM) sleep: Sleep occupying around 20 percent of an adult's sleeping time, characterized by increased heart rate, blood pressure, and breathing rate; erections; eye movements; and the experience of dreaming

One possible but still unproven explanation for rapid eye movements is that the eyes follow the action that is occurring in the dream (Dement, 1979; Kelly, 1991c). For instance, people who have reported dreaming about watching a tennis match just before they were awakened showed regular right-left-right eye movements, as if they were observing the ball flying back and forth across the net.

There is good reason to believe that REM sleep plays an important role in everyday human functioning. People deprived of REM sleep—by being awakened

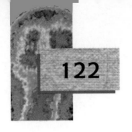

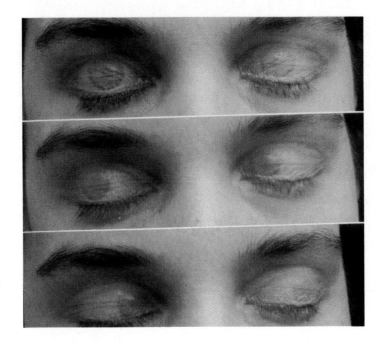

During REM sleep, our eyes flicker back and forth behind our closed eyelids as if we were watching the images in our dreams.

every time they begin to display the physiological signs of the stage—show a *rebound effect* when allowed to rest undisturbed. With this rebound effect, REM-deprived sleepers spend significantly more time in REM sleep than they normally would. It is as if the body requires a certain amount of REM sleep in order to function properly.

Is Sleep Necessary?

Sleep, in general, seems necessary for human functioning, although surprisingly enough this fact has not been firmly established (Webb, 1992). It is reasonable to expect that the body would require a tranquil "rest and relaxation" period in order to revitalize itself. However, several arguments suggest this is not the full explanation. For instance, most people sleep between 7 and 8 hours each night (Farley, 1993), but there is wide variability among individuals, with some people needing as little as 3 hours (see Figure 4-4).

Sleep requirements also vary over the course of a person's lifetime. As people age, they generally need less and less sleep. If sleep played a restorative function for the body, it is hard to see why the elderly would need less sleep than those who are younger.

Furthermore, people who participate in sleep deprivation experiments, in which they are kept awake for stretches as long as 200 hours, show no lasting effects. It's no fun—they feel weary and irritable, can't concentrate, and show a loss of creativity. They also show a decline in logical reasoning ability, although there are occasional increases at certain times of the day. However, after being allowed to sleep normally, they bounce back quickly and are able to perform at predeprivation levels after just a few days (Dement, 1976).

Those of us who worry, then, that long hours of study, work, or perhaps partying are ruining our health should feel heartened. As far as anyone can tell, most people suffer no permanent consequences of such sleep deprivation (Eckholm, 1988). At the same time, though, a lack of sleep may make us feel edgy, slow our reaction times, and lower our performance on academic tasks. Furthermore, we put ourselves at risk when we carry out routine activities, such as driving, when we're very sleepy. We certainly won't feel particularly good when we suffer from

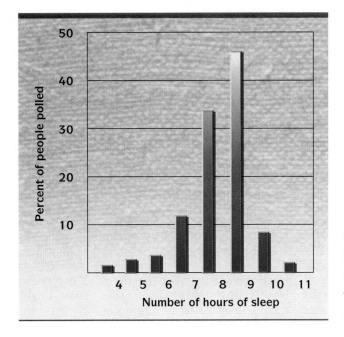

FIGURE 4-4 Although most people report sleeping between 8 and 9 hours per night, the amount varies a great deal. *[From Borbely, A. (1986). Secrets of sleep. New York: Basic Books; p. 43. Based on data of Kripke, D. F., et al., 1979.]*

sleep deprivation. In sum, a good night's rest is an appropriate goal (Angier, 1990; Webb, 1992).

Circadian Rhythms: Life Cycles

The fact that we cycle back and forth between wakefulness and sleep is one example of our body's circadian rhythms. **Circadian rhythms** (from the Latin *circa dies,* or "around a day") are biological processes that occur repeatedly on approximately a 24-hour cycle. Sleep and waking, for instance, occur naturally to the beat of an internal pacemaker that works on a cycle of about 25 hours. Several other bodily functions, such as body temperature, also work on circadian rhythms.

These circadian cycles are complex. For instance, sleepiness occurs not just in the evening, but throughout the day in regular patterns. Most of us tend to get drowsy in midafternoon—regardless of whether we have eaten a heavy lunch (Dement, 1989). By making an afternoon siesta part of their everyday habits, people in several cultures take advantage of the body's natural inclination to sleep at this time.

Circadian cycles are powerful—as anyone who has worked a night shift knows well (Mapes, 1990; Moore-Ede, 1993). Not only do night-shift workers have trouble staying awake, but they are less productive and more likely to have accidents than day workers (see the accompanying Psychology at Work box).

Although sleep operates on a 25-hour circadian cycle, other bodily rhythms operate on much longer cycles. For instance, some people experience *seasonal affective disorder,* a form of severe depression in which depression increases during the winter and lifts during the rest of the year. The disorder appears to be a result of the brevity and gloom of winter days. In fact, several hours of daily exposure to bright lights is sometimes sufficient to improve the mood of those with the disorder (Sack et al., 1990; Rosenthal, 1995).

Another periodic rhythm is women's menstrual cycles. Occurring on a 28-day schedule, the menstrual cycle is regulated by hormone production that ebbs and increases throughout the cycle as women's bodies prepare for the possibility of conception.

Are the physical changes that occur during the phases of the menstrual cycle

Circadian rhythms: Biological processes that occur repeatedly on approximately a 24-hour cycle

PSYCHOLOGY AT WORK

Resetting the Body's Internal Clock: Staying Up as the Sun Goes Down

- A meltdown nearly occurs at the Three Mile Island nuclear power plant with a crew that had only recently switched to the night shift. Time: 4:00 A.M.
- The Exxon Valdez strikes a reef in Alaska, resulting in a devastating oil spill. Time: 12:04 A.M.
- The Chernobyl reactor explodes. Time: 1:23 A.M.

Is it a coincidence that each of these disasters occurred during the wee hours of the night? Probably not, according to sleep researcher Martin Moore-Ede (1993). He has suggested the culprit is worker fatigue resulting from a schedule that is at odds with the body's natural circadian rhythms.

Happily, though, increasing evidence suggests it may be possible to alter circadian rhythms. One technique involves exposing people to bright lights during various parts of the day. The light tricks the parts of the brain associated with circadian rhythms (probably a part of the hypothalamus and the pineal gland) into thinking that night is actually day (Wever, 1989).

For instance, the San Diego Gas and Electric Company installed a computer-controlled lighting system in a power plant that gradually brightens and dims over the course of a shift. The exact pattern is tailored to employees' "light profiles," which are based on their specific sleeping patterns. The maximum brightness of the lights mimics the intensity of sunlight to a much greater extent than the light level found in the average office (Noble, 1993).

A similar procedure was used successfully by crews of the space shuttle *Columbia*. These astronauts were exposed to doses of bright lights over a period of 3 days. In just that time, their circadian rhythms shifted so radically that they were wide awake at night and craved sleep at dawn (Rosenthal, 1991; Czeisler et al., 1989; Czeisler, Johnson, & Duffy, 1990).

Such work has enormous practical implications for helping night-shift workers to synchronize their circadian rhythms with their job requirements. It has applications in other realms, as well. For example, it is conceivable that airlines could shine bright lights on passengers during long flights. This procedure could prepare them for the change in time zones at their destinations and help them avoid jet lag. Better still, people reaching a new destination might spend a few days at the beach, soaking up some rays, in order to reset their internal clocks (Nowak, 1994a).

Seasonal affective disorder can be relieved by several hours of exposure to special bright lights during the short days of winter.

accompanied by swings in mood? The answer is "probably not," despite the prevalence in the popular press of discussions of "premenstrual syndrome," or "PMS." PMS refers to a grab-bag of symptoms that include irritability, fatigue, anxiety, and volatility that are assumed to emerge just before menstruation. However, many members of the scientific community doubt the existence of this cluster, and question whether mood shifts in women are any more cyclical than those in men. For instance, studies that ask subjects to chart their mood on a daily basis show little relationship between menstrual cycle and mood. Indeed, when careful records are kept, men and women seem to show no differences in the variability of their moods. In sum, although a small proportion of women do suffer relatively intense periodic mood swings related to their menstrual cycle, most do not (McFarlane, Martin, & Williams, 1988; Cotton, 1993).

The Function and Meaning of Dreaming

I was sitting at my desk when I remembered that this was the day of my chemistry final! I felt awful. I hadn't studied a bit for it. In fact, I couldn't even remember where the class was held, and I had missed every lecture all semester. In a panic, I began running across campus desperately searching for the classroom so that I could beg the professor to give me another chance. But I had to stop at every classroom building, looking in one room after another, hoping to find the professor. It was hopeless; I knew I was going to fail and flunk out of college.

If you have had a dream similar to this—one that is surprisingly common among people involved in academic pursuits—you know how utterly convincing are the panic and fear that events in the dream can bring about. *Nightmares,* unusually frightening dreams, occur fairly often. In one survey, almost half of a group of college students who kept records of their dreams over a 2-week period reported having at least one nightmare. This works out to some twenty-four nightmares a year per person, on average (Wood & Bootzin, 1990; Berguier & Ashton, 1992).

On the other hand, most of the 150,000 dreams the average person experiences by the age of 70 are much less dramatic (Snyder, 1970; Webb, 1992). They typically encompass such everyday events as going to the supermarket, working at the office, or preparing a meal. Students dream about coming to class; professors dream about lecturing. Dental patients dream of getting their teeth drilled; dentists dream of drilling the wrong tooth. The English take tea with the queen in their dreams; in the United States, people go to a bar with the President (K. Wells, 1993; Solomon, 1993; see Figure 4-5, for the most common dreams).

But what, if anything, do all these dreams mean? Whether dreams have a specific significance and function is a question that scientists have considered for many years, developing several alternative theories.

Do Dreams Represent Unconscious Wish Fulfillment? Sigmund Freud viewed dreams as a guide to the unconscious (Freud, 1900). In his **unconscious wish fulfillment theory,** he proposed that dreams represent unconscious wishes that dreamers wish to see fulfilled. However, because these wishes are threatening to the dreamer's conscious awareness, the actual wishes—called the **latent content of dreams**—are disguised. The true subject and meaning of a dream, then, may have little to do with its overt story line, called by Freud the **manifest content of dreams.** To Freud, it was important to pierce the armor of a dream's manifest content to understand its true meaning. To do this, Freud tried to get people to discuss their dreams, associating symbols in the dreams to events in the past. He also suggested that there are certain common symbols with universal meanings that appear in dreams. For example, to Freud, dreams in which the person is flying symbolize a wish for sexual intercourse. (See Table 4-1, for other common dream symbols identified by Freud.)

Today many psychologists reject Freud's view that dreams typically represent

Unconscious wish fulfillment theory: A theory of Sigmund Freud, which proposes that dreams represent unconscious wishes that a dreamer wants to fulfill

Latent content of dreams: According to Freud, the "disguised" meanings of dreams, hidden by more obvious subjects

Manifest content of dreams: According to Freud, the overt story line of dreams

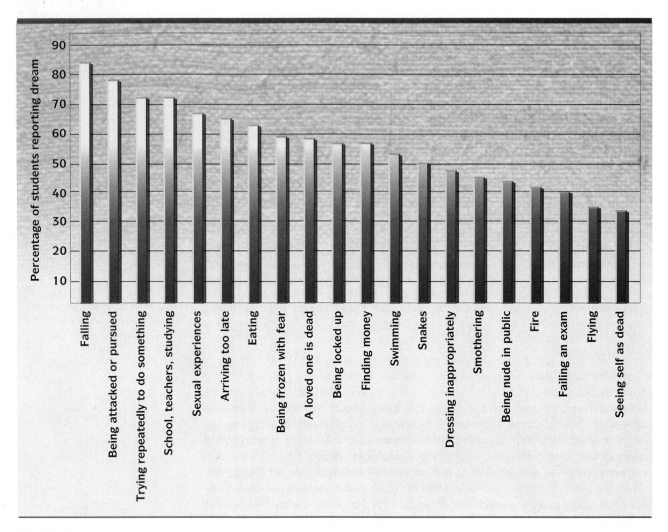

FIGURE 4-5 The twenty most common dreams reported by students. *(Griffith, Miyago, & Tago, 1958.)*

unconscious wishes and that particular objects and events in a dream are symbolic. Instead, the direct, overt action of a dream is considered the focal point in understanding its meaning. For example, a dream in which we are walking down a long hallway to take an exam for which we haven't studied does not relate to unconscious, unacceptable wishes. Instead, it simply means we are concerned about an impending test. Even more complex dreams can often be interpreted in terms of everyday concerns and stress (Cook, Caplan, & Wolowitz, 1990).

Moreover, we now know that some dreams reflect events occurring in the dreamer's environment as he or she is sleeping. For example, sleeping subjects in

TABLE 4-1 Dream Symbolism, According to Freud

Symbol (Manifest Content of Dream)	Interpretation (Latent Content)
Climbing up a stairway, crossing a bridge, riding an elevator, flying in an airplane, walking down a long hallway, entering a room, train traveling through a tunnel	Sexual intercourse
Apples, peaches, grapefruits	Breasts
Bullets, fire, snakes, sticks, umbrellas, guns, hoses, knives	Male sex organs
Ovens, boxes, tunnels, closets, caves, bottles, ships	Female sex organs

one experiment were sprayed with water while they were dreaming. These un-lucky volunteers reported more dreams involving water than a comparison group of subjects who were left to sleep undisturbed (Dement & Wolpert, 1958). Similarly, it is not unusual to wake up to find that the doorbell that was being rung in a dream is actually an alarm clock telling us it is time to get up.

Reverse-Learning Theory   Although the content of dreams can clearly be af-fected by environmental stimuli, the question of *why* we dream remains unre-solved. Several alternatives to Freud's theory have been proposed. According to the **reverse-learning theory,** for instance, dreams have no meaning whatsoever. Instead, they represent a kind of reverse learning, in which we flush away un-necessary information that we have accumulated during the day. In this view, dreaming simply represents the reverse learning of material that ultimately would prove to be confusing to us. Dreams, then, are a kind of mental housecleaning of the brain, but have no meaning in and of themselves (Crick & Mitchison, 1983).

Reverse-learning theory: A theory which proposes that dreams have no meaning in themselves, but in-stead function to rid us of unneces-sary information that we have accu-mulated during the day

Dreams-for-Survival Theory   The **dreams-for-survival theory** proposes yet an-other function for dreams. According to this theory, dreams permit information that is critical for our daily survival to be reconsidered and reprocessed during sleep. Dreaming is seen as an inheritance from our animal ancestors, whose small brains were unable to sift sufficient information during waking hours. Consequently, dreaming provided a mechanism that permitted the processing of information 24 hours a day.

Dreams-for-survival theory: A theory which proposes that dreams permit information critical for our daily survival to be reconsidered and reprocessed during sleep

According to this theory, dreams do have meaning. They represent concerns about our daily lives, illustrating our uncertainties, indecisions, ideas, and desires. Dreams are seen, then, as consistent with everyday living. Rather than being dis-guised wishes, as Freud suggested, they represent key concerns growing out of our daily experiences (Pavlides & Winson, 1989; Winson, 1990).

Recent research lends weight to the dreams-for-survival theory, suggesting that certain dreams permit people to focus on and consolidate memories, particularly those pertaining to "how-to-do-it" memories related to motor skills. For instance, in one experiment, subjects learned a visual memory task late in the day. They were then sent to bed, but awakened at certain times of the night. When people were awakened at times that did not interrupt dreaming, they typically showed the pattern of next-day improvement on their memory of the task. But when they were awakened during REM sleep—the stage of sleep when people dream—their performance declined. The conclusion: Dreaming may play a role in helping us to remember material to which we have been previously exposed (Karni et al., 1992, 1994; Wilson & McNaughton, 1994).

Activation-Synthesis Theory   The most influential current explanation for dreaming considers dreams as a byproduct of fundamental biological activity. According to psychiatrist J. Allan Hobson, who proposed the **activation-synthe-sis theory,** the brain produces random electrical energy during REM sleep, pos-sibly due to changes in the production of particular neurotransmitters. This elec-trical energy randomly stimulates memories lodged in various portions of the brain. Because we have a need to make sense of our world, even while asleep, the brain takes these chaotic memories and weaves them into a logical story line, fill-ing in the gaps to produce a rational scenario. In this view, then, dreams are closer to a self-generated game of Madlibs than to significant, meaningful psy-chological phenomena (Hobson & McCarley, 1977; Hobson, 1988).

Activation-synthesis theory: Hobson's theory that dreams are a result of random electrical energy stimulating memories lodged in vari-ous portions of the brain, which the brain then weaves into a logical story line

Yet Hobson does not entirely reject the view that dreams reflect unconscious wishes. He suggests that the particular scenario that a dreamer produces is not just random but instead is a clue to the dreamer's fears, emotions, and concerns. Hence, what starts out as a random process culminates in something meaningful.

Evidence that dreaming represents a response to random brain activity comes

from work with people who are injected with drugs similar to the neurotransmitter acetylcholine. Under the influence of the drug, people quickly enter REM sleep and have dreams similar in quality to those occurring during natural sleep (Schmeck, 1987). Still, such evidence as this does not confirm that these drug-induced dreams have psychological meaning.

The range of theories about dreaming (summarized in Table 4-2) clearly illustrates that dream researchers have yet to agree on the fundamental meaning of dreams. However, it does seem likely that the specific content of our dreams is unique to us and in some way represents meaningful patterns and concerns. Ultimately, dreams may provide clues about the experiences that on some level of consciousness are most important to us.

Daydreams: Dreams without Sleep

It is the stuff of magic: Our past mistakes can be wiped out and the future filled with noteworthy accomplishments. Fame, happiness, and wealth can be ours. In the next moment, though, the most horrible of tragedies can occur, leaving us devastated, alone, and penniless.

Daydreams: Fantasies people construct while awake

The source of these scenarios is **daydreams,** fantasies that people construct while awake. Unlike dreaming that occurs while sleeping, daydreams are more under people's control. Therefore their content is often more closely related to immediate events in the environment than is the content of the dreams that occur during sleep. Although they may include sexual content, daydreams also pertain to other activities or events relevant to a person's life.

Daydreams are a typical part of waking consciousness, although our awareness of the environment around us declines. People vary considerably in the amount of and their involvement in daydreaming. For example, around 2 to 4 percent of the population spend at least half their free time fantasizing. Although most people daydream much less frequently, almost everyone fantasizes to some degree. Studies that ask people to identify what they are doing at random times during the day have shown that they are daydreaming about 10 percent of the time. As for the content of fantasies, most concern such mundane, ordinary events as paying the telephone bill, picking up the groceries, or solving a romantic problem (Singer, 1975; Lynn & Rhue, 1988).

Although frequent daydreaming might seem to suggest psychological difficulties, there actually appears to be little relationship between psychological disturbance and daydreaming (Rhue & Lynn, 1987; Lynn & Rhue, 1988). Except in those rare cases in which a daydreamer is unable to distinguish a fantasy from reality (a mark of serious problems, as we discuss in Chapter 12), daydreaming seems to be a normal part of waking consciousness. Indeed, fantasy may con-

---

TABLE 4-2 Four Views of Dreams

Theory	Basic Explanation	Meaning of Dreams	Is Meaning of Dream Disguised?
Unconscious wish fulfillment theory (Freud)	Dreams represent unconscious wishes the dreamer wants to fulfill	Latent content reveals unconscious wishes	Yes, by manifest content of dreams
Reverse-learning theory	Unnecessary information is "unlearned" and removed from memory	None	No meaning
Dreams-for-survival theory	Information relevant to daily survival is reconsidered and reprocessed	Clues to everyday concerns about survival	Not necessarily
Activation-synthesis theory	Dreams are the result of random activation of various memories, which are tied together in a logical story line	Dream scenario that is constructed is related to dreamer's concerns	Not necessarily

tribute to the psychological well-being of some people by enhancing their creativity and by permitting them to use their imagination to understand what other people are experiencing.

Sleep Disturbances: Slumbering Problems

At one time or another, almost all of us have difficulty sleeping—a condition known as *insomnia*. It may be due to a particular situation such as the breakup of a relationship, concern about a test score, or the loss of a job. Some cases of insomnia, however, have no obvious causes. Some people are simply unable to fall asleep easily, or they go to sleep readily but wake up frequently during the night (Hauri, 1991). Insomnia is a problem that afflicts about a quarter of the population of the United States.

Other sleep problems are less common than insomnia, although they are still widespread (Kelly, 1991a; Reynolds & Kupfer, 1994). For instance, some 20 million people suffer from *sleep apnea,* a condition in which a person has difficulty breathing and sleeping simultaneously. The result is disturbed, fitful sleep, as the person is constantly reawakened when the lack of oxygen becomes great enough to trigger a waking response. In some cases, people with apnea wake as many as 500 times during the course of an evening, although they may not even be aware that they have wakened. Not surprisingly, such disturbed sleep results in complaints of fatigue the next day. Sleep apnea may account for *sudden infant death syndrome,* a mysterious killer of seemingly normal infants who die while sleeping.

Narcolepsy is an uncontrollable need to sleep for short periods during the day (Dement, 1976). No matter what the activity—holding a heated conversation, exercising, or driving—the narcoleptic will suddenly drift into sleep. People with narcolepsy go directly from wakefulness to REM sleep, skipping the other stages (Siegel et al., 1991). The causes of narcolepsy are not known, although there may be a genetic component, with narcolepsy running in some families.

We know relatively little about sleeptalking and sleepwalking, two fairly harmless sleep disturbances. Both occur during stage 4 sleep and are more frequent in children than in adults. In most cases, sleeptalkers and sleepwalkers have a vague consciousness of the world around them, and a sleepwalker may be able to walk

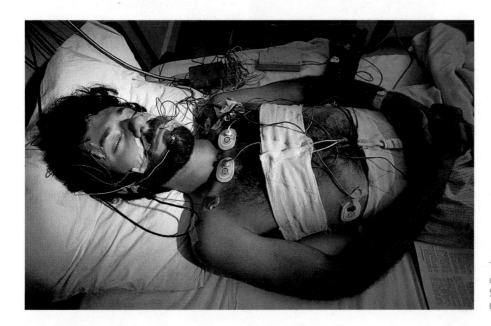

This man's physiological responses during sleep are being studied at Stanford University's Sleep Disorders Clinic in California.

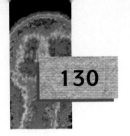

around obstructions in a crowded room in an agile fashion. Unless a sleepwalker wanders into a dangerous environment, sleepwalking typically poses little risk. Moreover, the conventional wisdom that it is dangerous to awaken sleepwalkers is wrong: No harm will come from waking them, although they will probably be quite confused. (For a discussion with a psychologist working in a sleep disorder clinic, see the accompanying Pathways through Psychology box.)

The Informed Consumer of Psychology

Sleeping Better

Fortunately, the most severe sleep disorder from which most of us suffer is insomnia. However, for the almost 40 million people in the United States who have difficulty sleeping, the fact that matters could be worse provides little solace (Holden, 1993).

For those of us who spend hours tossing and turning in bed, psychologists studying sleep disturbances have made a number of suggestions for overcoming insomnia (Jacobs, Benson, & Friedman, 1993). These include:

PATHWAYS THROUGH PSYCHOLOGY

Thomas Roth
Henry Ford Hospital, Detroit, Michigan

Born: 1942
Education: B.A., Hunter College; Ph.D., University of Cincinnati
Home: Detroit

Thomas Roth.

Although Thomas Roth began his undergraduate studies with a major in physiology, he found himself drawn to psychology. He became intrigued with experimental methodology and the experimental concepts. By the time he finished his undergraduate studies, he had decided to devote his career to psychology.

Today, Roth is the Chief of the Division of Sleep Medicine at the Henry Ford Hospital in Detroit, as well as a clinical professor in the Department of Psychology at the University of Michigan College of Medicine.

"The division has three main functions," explained Roth. "The first is to diagnose and treat patients with a variety of sleep disorders. The second function is research, which is a large part of the division. There is a variety of research that includes sleep disorder breathing, determinants of daytime sleeping, and diagnoses and management of insomnia.

"Our third function is educational. We teach residents in psy-chology, fellows in pulmonary medicine, and psychology interns," he added.

According to Roth, psychologists are the most logical practitioners for treating insomnia, which afflicts some 25 percent of the U.S. population. "Insomnia has as one of its major causes behavioral kinds of issues," he said. He adds that psychologists historically have been in the forefront of identifying the underlying causes of the disorder, and they also are in a good position to carry out research in the area.

Roth is involved in investigations of other types of sleep disorders. For instance, the Division of Sleep Disorders does extensive research on sleep apnea and on the safety and efficacy of drugs used to improve sleep. He noted that research on sleep is sorely needed. "Every year 200,000 Americans fall asleep at the wheel of a car and most are between the ages of 18 and 25. Why does this happen? The study of sleep is a terrific area of investigation, and requires more of our attention and understanding."

■ Exercise during the day and avoid naps. Not surprisingly, it helps to be tired before going to sleep! Moreover, learning systematic relaxation techniques and biofeedback (see Chapter 2) can help you unwind from the day's stresses and tensions (Woolfolk & McNulty, 1983).

■ Choose a regular bedtime, and then stick to it. Adhering to a habitual schedule helps your internal timing mechanisms to better regulate your body.

■ Don't use your bed as an all-purpose area; leave studying, reading, eating, watching TV, and other recreational activities to some other part of your living quarters. This lets your bed be a cue just for sleeping.

■ Avoid drinks with caffeine (such as coffee, tea, and some soft drinks) after lunch. Their effects can linger for as long as 8 to 12 hours after they are consumed.

■ Drink a glass of warm milk at bedtime. Your grandmother was right, although she probably didn't know why. (Milk contains the chemical tryptophan, which helps people get to sleep.)

■ Avoid sleeping pills. Although over $100 million a year is spent on sleeping pills in the United States, most of this money is wasted. They can be temporarily effective, but in the long run sleeping pills may cause more harm than good, since they disrupt the normal sleep cycle (McClusky, Milbank, & Switzer, 1991).

■ Try *not* to go to sleep. This advice, which sounds strange at first, actually makes a good deal of sense. Psychologists have found that part of the reason people have difficulty falling asleep is that they are trying so hard. A better strategy is one suggested by Richard P. Bootzin of the University of Arizona, who teaches people to recondition their sleeping habits. He tells them to go to bed only when they feel tired. If they don't get to sleep within 10 minutes, they should leave the bedroom and do something else, returning to bed only when they do feel tired. This process should be continued, all night if necessary. But in the morning, the patient must get up at his or her usual hour and must not take a nap during the day. After 3 to 4 weeks on this regimen, most people become conditioned to associate their beds with sleep—and fall asleep rapidly at night (Youkilis & Bootzin, 1981; Seltzer, 1986; Ubell, 1993).

Even if these techniques do not work to your satisfaction and you still feel that insomnia is a problem, there is one consolation. Many people who *think* they have sleeping problems may be mistaken. Observers find that patients who enter sleep laboratories for treatment actually sleep much more than they think they do (Trinder, 1988). For example, researchers have found that some people who report being up all night actually fall asleep in 30 minutes and stay asleep all night. Furthermore, some people with insomnia can accurately recall sounds they heard while they were asleep, which gives them the impression they were actually awake during the night (Engle-Friedman, Baker, & Bootzin, 1985).

The problem for many people with insomnia, then, is not an actual lack of sleep but rather faulty perceptions of their sleeping patterns. In many cases, just becoming aware of how long they really do sleep—and understanding the fact that the older they become the less sleep they need—is enough to "cure" people's perception that they have a sleep disorder.

RECAP AND REVIEW

Recap

- Consciousness refers to a person's awareness of the sensations, thoughts, and feelings being experienced at a given moment.
- There are four distinct stages of sleep, as well as REM (rapid eye movement) sleep. These stages recur in cycles during the course of a normal night's sleep.

- There are four major explanations of dreams. They include Freud's wish fulfillment theory, the reverse-learning theory, the dreams-for-survival theory, and the activation-synthesis theory.
- The major sleep disorders include insomnia, narcolepsy, and sleep apnea.

Review

1. _____ is the term used to describe our understanding of the world external to us, as well as our own internal world.
2. Contrary to popular belief, a great deal of neural activity goes on during sleep. True or false?
3. Dreams occur in what phase of sleep?
4. _____ _____ are internal bodily processes that occur on a daily cycle.
5. Freud's theory of unconscious _____ _____ states that the actual wishes that an individual expressed in dreams were disguised because they were threatening to the person's conscious awareness.
6. Match the theory of dreaming with its definition.
    1. Dreams-for-survival theory
    2. Reverse-learning theory
    3. Activation-synthesis theory

    a. Dreams permit necessary information to be reprocessed during sleep.
    b. Random energy produced during sleep stimulates the brain, which then weaves the activated memories into a story line.

c. Dreams "flush away" excess information gathered during the day.

7. Match the sleep problem with its definition.
    1. Insomnia
    2. Narcolepsy
    3. Sleep apnea

    a. Condition that makes breathing while sleeping difficult
    b. Difficulty in sleeping
    c. Uncontrollable need to sleep during the day

Ask Yourself

A new "miracle pill" has been developed. This pill, once taken, will allow a person to function with only 1 hour's sleep each night. Because of this short stretch of time, any individual who takes this pill will never dream again. Knowing what you do about the functions of sleep and dreaming, what would some of the advantages and drawbacks of such a pill be from a personal standpoint? What would some of the advantages and drawbacks of such a pill be from a societal standpoint? Would you take such a pill?

(Answers to review questions are on page 134.)

- *Are hypnotized people in a different state of consciousness, and can they be hypnotized against their will?*
- *What are the consequences of meditation?*

HYPNOSIS AND MEDITATION

You are feeling relaxed and drowsy. You are getting sleepier and sleepier. Your body is becoming limp. Now you are starting to become warm, at ease, more comfortable. Your eyelids are feeling heavier and heavier. Your eyes are closing; you can't keep them open any more. You are totally relaxed.

Now, as you listen to my voice, do exactly as I say. Place your hands above your head. You will find they are getting heavier and heavier—so heavy you can barely keep them up. In fact, although you are straining as hard as you can, you will be unable to hold them up any longer.

An observer watching the above scene would notice a curious phenomenon occurring. Many of the people listening to the voice would, one by one, drop their arms to their sides, as if they were holding heavy lead weights. The reason for this strange behavior? The people have been hypnotized.

Hypnosis: A Trance-Forming Experience?

Hypnosis: A state of heightened susceptibility to the suggestions of others

People under **hypnosis** are in a state of heightened susceptibility to the suggestions of others. In some respects, it appears that they are asleep. Yet other aspects of their behavior contradict this notion, for people are attentive to the hypnotist's suggestions and may carry out bizarre or silly suggestions.

Despite their compliance when hypnotized, people do not lose all will of their own. They will not perform antisocial behaviors, and they will not carry out self-destructive acts. People will not reveal hidden truths about themselves, and they are capable of lying. Moreover, people cannot be hypnotized against their will—despite popular misconceptions.

132

There are wide variations in people's susceptibility to hypnosis (Lynn et al., 1991; Kirsch & Council, 1995). About 5 to 20 percent of the population cannot be hypnotized at all, while some 15 percent are very easily hypnotized. Most people fall somewhere in between. Moreover, the ease with which a person is hypnotized is related to a number of other characteristics. People who are readily hypnotized are also easily absorbed while reading books or listening to music, becoming unaware of what is happening around them, and they often spend an unusual amount of time daydreaming. In sum, then, they show a high ability to concentrate and to become completely absorbed in what they are doing (Hilgard, 1974; Lynn & Snodgrass, 1987; Crawford, 1982; Rhue, Lynn, & Kirsch, 1993).

A Different State of Consciousness?   The issue of whether hypnosis represents a state of consciousness that is qualitatively different from normal waking consciousness has long been controversial among psychologists (Kirsh & Lynn, 1995).

Ernest Hilgard (1975) has argued convincingly that hypnosis does represent a state of consciousness that differs significantly from other states. He contended that particular behavioral characteristics clearly differentiate hypnosis from other states, encompassing higher suggestibility; increased ability to recall and construct images, including visual memories from early childhood; a lack of initiative; and the ability to accept uncritically suggestions that clearly contradict reality. For example, hypnotized people can be told that they are blind, and subsequently report an inability to see objects shown to them (Bryant & McConkey, 1990). Moreover, research has found changes in electrical activity in the brain that are associated with hypnosis, supporting the position that hypnotic states represent a state of consciousness different from that of normal waking (Spiegel, 1987).

Still, some theorists reject the notion that hypnosis represents a state of consciousness that differs significantly from normal waking consciousness (Spanos, 1986; Spanos & Chaves, 1989). They argue that altered brain-wave patterns are not sufficient to demonstrate that a hypnotic state is qualitatively different from everyday waking consciousness, given that there are no other specific physiological changes that occur when a person is in a trance.

Furthermore, some researchers have shown that people merely pretending to be hypnotized display behaviors that are nearly identical to those of truly hypnotized individuals, and that hypnotic susceptibility can be increased through training procedures (Gfeller, Lynn, & Pribble, 1987; Spanos et al., 1987). There is also little support for the contention that adults can accurately recall memories of childhood events while hypnotized (Nash, 1987). Such converging evidence suggests that there is nothing qualitatively special about the hypnotic trance (Barber, 1975; Lynn, Rhue, & Weekes, 1990; Spanos et al., 1991).

If hypnosis does not represent a state of consciousness distinct from normal waking consciousness, then why do people *appear* to be in an altered state? To Theodore Sarbin and colleagues, people who are hypnotized are in a heightened state of suggestibility, role-playing the state of hypnosis as they understand it. They are not "pretending" to be hypnotized. Instead, they believe they are hypnotized and are following the suggestions of the hypnotist in the same way they follow suggestions of employers, bosses, and other persons of authority (Sarbin, 1991).

The jury remains out, then, on whether hypnosis represents a truly unique state of consciousness. On the other hand, even if hypnosis proves to be merely a state of heightened suggestibility, hypnosis can still be used to solve practical problems that people experience. In fact, psychologists working in many different areas have found hypnosis to be a reliable, effective tool (Rhue, Lynn, & Kirsch, 1993). Among the range of applications are the following:

■ *Controlling pain.* Patients suffering from chronic pain may be given the sug-

134

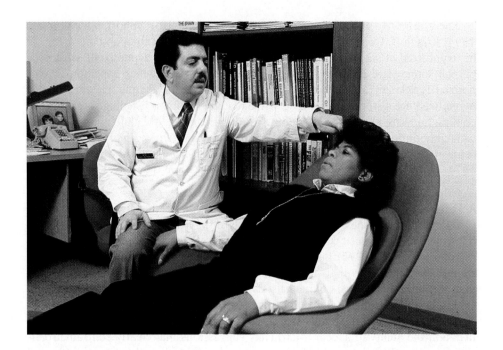

Hypnosis has been found to be an effective aid in certain cases, including pain relief and smoking cessation

gestion, while hypnotized, that their pain is eliminated or reduced. They can be told to feel that a painful area is hot, cold, or numb. They may also be taught to hypnotize themselves to relieve pain or to gain a sense of control over their symptoms. Hypnosis has proved to be particularly useful during childbirth and dental procedures (Erickson, Hershman, & Secter, 1990).

■ *Ending tobacco addiction.* Although it hasn't been successful in stopping drug and alcohol abuse, hypnosis is sometimes successful in helping people to stop unwanted behavior such as smoking. In some approaches, hypnotized smokers are given the suggestion that the taste and smell of cigarettes are unpleasant. Other techniques include teaching self-hypnosis to deal with cravings for cigarettes or suggesting during hypnosis that smokers owe their bodies protection from the ravages of smoking (Erickson, Hershman, & Secter, 1990).

■ *Treating psychological disorders.* Hypnosis is sometimes used during treatment for psychological disorders. For example, hypnosis may be used to heighten relaxation, increase expectations of success, or modify thoughts that are self-defeating. It can also be used to decrease anxiety (Weitzenhoffer, 1989).

■ *Recalling details of a crime.* Witnesses and victims are sometimes better able to recall details of a crime when hypnotized. In one well-known case, a witness to the kidnapping of a group of California schoolchildren was placed under hypnosis and was able to recall all but one digit of the license number on the kidnapper's vehicle (*Time,* 1976). On the other hand, the evidence regarding the accuracy of recollections obtained under hypnosis is decidedly mixed. In some cases, accurate recall of specific information increases—but so do the number of errors. Moreover, there is an increase in a person's confidence about the recollections obtained during hypnosis, even when the memories are inaccurate. The hypnotic state may simply make people more willing to report whatever they think they remember. Because of these questions about its usefulness, the legal status

ANSWERS TO PREVIOUS REVIEW
1. Consciousness **2.** True **3.** REM **4.** Circadian rhythms **5.** wish fulfillment
6. 1-a; 2-c; 3-b **7.** 1-b; 2-c; 3-a

of hypnosis has yet to be resolved (Dywan & Bowers, 1983; Nogrady, McConkey, & Perry, 1985; Council of Scientific Affairs, 1985; McConkey & Sheehan, 1995).

■ *Improving athletic performance.* Athletes sometimes turn to hypnosis to improve their performance. For example, championship boxer Ken Norton used hypnosis prior to a bout to prepare himself for the encounter, and baseball star Rod Carew used hypnotism to increase his concentration when batting (Udolf, 1981).

Hypnosis, then, has many potential applications. Of course, it is not invariably effective. For the significant number of people who cannot be hypnotized, it offers little help. But for people who make good hypnotic subjects, hypnosis may provide significant benefits.

Meditation: Regulating Our Own State of Consciousness

When traditional practitioners of the ancient eastern religion of Zen Buddhism want to achieve greater spiritual insight, they turn to a technique that has been used for centuries to alter their state of consciousness. This technique is called meditation.

Meditation is a learned technique for refocusing attention that brings about an altered state of consciousness. Although there is an exotic sound to it, some form of meditation is found within every major religion—including Christianity and Judaism. In the United States today, some of the major proponents of meditation are followers of Maharishi Mahesh Yogi, who practice a form of meditation called transcendental meditation, or TM, although many other groups teach various forms of meditation.

The specific meditative technique used in TM involves repeating a *mantra*—a sound, word, or syllable—over and over. In other forms of meditation, the focus is on a picture, flame, or specific part of the body. Regardless of the nature of the particular initial stimulus, in most forms of meditation the key to the procedure is concentrating on it so thoroughly that the meditator becomes unaware of any outside stimulation and reaches a different state of consciousness.

Following meditation, people report feeling thoroughly relaxed. They sometimes relate that they have gained new insights into themselves and the problems they are facing. The long-term practice of meditation may even improve health.

Meditation: A learned technique for refocusing attention that brings about an altered state of consciousness

(Drawing by Richter; © 1993 The New Yorker Magazine, Inc.)

A mantra commonly used in meditation is the syllable "om"

One study of a group of elderly residents found higher longevity for those who practiced TM over a 3-year period (Alexander et al., 1989).

Meditation brings about several physiological changes. For example, oxygen usage decreases, heart rate and blood pressure decline, and brain-wave patterns may change (Wallace & Benson, 1972). On the other hand, similar changes occur during relaxation of any sort, so whether these changes qualify as indicators of a true alteration in consciousness remains an open question (Holmes, 1985).

It *is* clear that most people can meditate without exotic trappings by using a few simple procedures developed by Herbert Benson, who has studied meditation extensively (Benson, 1993). The basics are similar in several respects to those developed as a part of Eastern religions, but they have no spiritual component. They include sitting in a quiet room with eyes closed, breathing deeply and rhythmically, and repeating a word or sound—such as the word "one"—over and over. Although the procedure is a bit more involved than this, most people find themselves in a deeply relaxed state after just 20 minutes. Practiced twice a day, Benson's meditative techniques seem to be just as effective in bringing about relaxation as more mystical methods (Benson & Friedman, 1985).

Exploring Diversity

Cross-Cultural Routes to Altered States of Consciousness

■ A group of Native American Sioux sit naked in a steaming sweat lodge, as a medicine man throws water on sizzling rocks to send billows of scalding steam into the air.

■ Aztec priests smear themselves with a mixture of crushed poisonous herbs, hairy black worms, scorpions, and lizards. Sometimes they drink the mixture.

■ During the sixteenth century, a devout Hasidic Jew lies across the tombstone of a celebrated scholar. As he murmurs the name of God repeatedly, he seeks to be possessed by the soul of the dead wise man's spirit. If successful, he will attain a mystical state, and the deceased's words will flow out of the follower's mouth.

Each of these rituals has a common goal: a suspension from the bonds of everyday awareness and access to an altered state of consciousness (Furst, 1977; Fine, 1994). Although they may seem curious and exotic from the vantage point of Western culture, they represent what seems to be a universal effort to alter consciousness. To members of other cultures, the use of meditation, alcohol, and other drugs in Western cultures to bring about a change in consciousness may seem equally peculiar.

Some scholars suggest that the quest to alter consciousness represents a basic human desire. For example, Ronald Siegel, who studies the biological basis of drugs, has argued that there is a universal need to alter mood or consciousness (Siegel, 1989). He even suggested that this need is as basic as requirements for sex, water, and food.

Whether or not one accepts such an extreme view, it is clear that different cultures have developed their own unique forms of consciousness-altering activities. Similarly, as we'll see when we discuss psychological disorders in Chapter 12, what is deemed "abnormal" behavior varies considerably from one culture to another.

Of course, realizing that efforts to produce altered states of consciousness are widespread throughout the world's societies does not answer a fundamental question: Is the experience of *normal,* unaltered states of consciousness similar across different cultures?

There are two possible responses to this question. Because humans share basic biological commonalities in the ways their brains and bodies are wired, we might assume that the fundamental experience of consciousness is similar across cultures. As a result, we could suppose that basic consciousness shows some common similarities across cultures.

On the other hand, the way in which certain aspects of consciousness are interpreted and viewed shows substantial differences among different cultures. For example, people in various cultures view the experience of the passage of time in varying ways. One study found, for instance, that Mexicans view time as passing more slowly than other North Americans do (Diaz-Guerrero, 1979).

Whatever the true nature of consciousness and why people seek to alter it, it is clear that people often seek the means to alter their everyday experience of the world. In some cases that need becomes overwhelming, as we see next when we consider the use of drugs.

RECAP AND REVIEW

Recap

- Hypnosis places people in a state of heightened susceptibility to the suggestions of others. People cannot be hypnotized against their will, and they vary in their susceptibility to hypnosis.
- One crucial question about hypnosis is whether or not it represents a separate state of consciousness. There is evidence on both sides of the issue.
- Meditation is a learned technique for refocusing attention and is meant to bring about an altered state of consciousness.
- Cultures differ in the routes they choose to bring about altered states of consciousness.

Review

1. _____ is a state of heightened susceptibility to the suggestions of others.

2. A friend tells you, "I once heard of a person who was murdered by being hypnotized and told to jump from the Golden Gate Bridge!" Could such a statement be true? Why or why not?

3. _____ is a learned technique for refocusing attention to bring about an altered state of consciousness.

4. Leslie repeats a unique sound, known as a _____, when she engages in transcendental meditation.

5. Meditation can be learned only by following procedures that include some spiritual component. True or false?

Ask Yourself

If meditation has psychological benefits, does this suggest that we are mentally overburdened in our normal state of consciousness?

(Answers to review questions are on page 138.)

- **What are the major classifications of drugs, and what are their effects?**

DRUG USE: THE HIGHS AND LOWS OF CONSCIOUSNESS

As the butane torch flame vaporized the cocaine in the bowl of a glass smoking pipe, Amir Vik-Kiv inhaled deeply, held the smoke in his expanded chest, then exhaled in a breathless rush. Suddenly, his eyes bulged and his hands trembled. Beads of sweat broke out on his forehead, and perspiration stains formed under his arms.

Moments earlier . . . the former television cameraman had "cooked" a gram of refined cocaine in the kitchen of his Northeast Washington apartment. Using a simple recipe of water and baking soda, he had reduced the substance to a potent, insidious form known as "crack."

Within an hour he had "burned" about $100 worth of the drug, but what had happened in his brain just seven seconds after taking the first hit was more like an explosion. Although he had not eaten food in a day or had sex in months, he was no longer hungry for either . . . .

What would happen when the dope ran out was another story. Before long Vik-Kiv would be crawling around the kitchen floor, searching for bits of cocaine that might have spilled. When he found anything white, he would take it—and gag at the taste of what could have been anything from a burning bread crumb to a moldering roach egg (Milloy, 1986, p. 1).

Although few people exhibit such extreme behavior, drugs are a part of almost all of our lives. From infancy on, most people take vitamins, aspirin, cold-relief medicine, and the like. These drugs have little effect on our consciousness, operating instead primarily on our biological functions.

On the other hand, some substances, known as psychoactive drugs, affect consciousness. **Psychoactive drugs** influence a person's emotions, perceptions, and behavior. Yet even these drugs are common in most of our lives. If you have ever had a cup of coffee or sipped a beer, you have taken a psychoactive drug.

A large number of individuals have used more potent—and dangerous—psychoactive drugs than coffee and beer. For instance, surveys find that 48 percent of high school seniors have used an illegal drug at least once in their lives, and the figures for the adult population are even higher (Johnston, Bachman, & O'Malley, 1995).

Of course, drugs vary widely in terms of the effects they have on users. The most dangerous ones are those that are addictive. **Addictive drugs** produce a biological or psychological dependence in the user, and their withdrawal leads to a craving for the drug that, in some cases, may be nearly irresistible. Addictions may be biologically based, in which case the body becomes so accustomed to functioning in the presence of a drug that it cannot function in its absence. Or addictions may be psychological, in which case people believe they need the drug in order to respond to the stresses of daily living. Although we generally associate addiction with drugs such as heroin, everyday sorts of drugs like caffeine (found in coffee) and nicotine (found in cigarettes) have addictive aspects as well.

We know relatively little about the reasons underlying addiction. One of the problems in identifying the causes is that different drugs (such as alcohol and cocaine) affect the brain in very different ways—and yet may be equally addicting. Furthermore, it takes longer to become addicted to some drugs than to others, even though the ultimate consequences of addiction may be equally grave (Julien, 1995; Lowinson et al., 1992).

Why do people take drugs in the first place? There are many reasons, ranging from the perceived pleasure of the experience itself, to the escape a drug-induced high affords from the everyday pressures of life, to an attempt to achieve a religious or spiritual state. But other factors, ones that have little to do with the nature of the experience itself, also lead people to try drugs (Glantz & Pickens, 1991).

For instance, the alleged drug use of well-known role models such as movie star River Pheonix or Marion Barry, mayor of Washington, DC, the easy availability of some illegal drugs, and the pressures of peers all play a role in the decision to use them (Graham, Marks, & Hansen, 1991; Jarvik, 1990). In some cases, the motive is simply the thrill of trying something new and perhaps flaunting the law (MacCoun, 1993). Regardless of the forces that lead a person to begin to use drugs, drug addiction is among the most difficult of all behaviors to modify, even with extensive treatment (Peele & Brodsky, 1991; Hawkins, Catalano, & Miller, 1992; Hser, Anglin, & Powers, 1993; Jarvis, Tebbutt, & Mattick, 1995; Washton, 1995).

Psychoactive drugs: Drugs that influence a person's emotions, perceptions, and behavior

Addictive drugs: Drugs that produce a physical or psychological dependence in the user

Jerry Garcia, lead guitarist of the Grateful Dead, died while in a clinic for drug and alcohol abusers.

ANSWERS TO PREVIOUS REVIEW
1. Hypnosis **2.** No; people who are hypnotized cannot be made to perform self-destructive acts. **3.** Meditation **4.** mantra **5.** False; some meditative techniques have no spiritual component.

Stimulants: Drug Highs

It's one o'clock in the morning, and you still haven't finished reading the last chapter of the text on which you are being tested in the morning. Feeling exhausted, you turn to the one thing that may help you stay awake for the next 2 hours: a cup of strong, black coffee.

If you have ever found yourself in such a position, you have been relying on a major **stimulant,** caffeine, to stay awake. *Caffeine* is one of a number of stimulants that affect the central nervous system by causing a rise in heart rate, blood pressure, and muscular tension. Caffeine is present not only in coffee; it is an important ingredient in tea, soft drinks, and chocolate as well (see Figure 4-6).

Caffeine produces several reactions (Rush, Sullivan, & Griffiths, 1994). The major behavioral effects of caffeine are an increase in attentiveness and a decrease in reaction time. Caffeine can also bring about an improvement in mood, most likely by mimicking the effects of a natural brain chemical, adenosine. Too much caffeine, however, can result in nervousness and insomnia. People can build up a biological dependence on the drug. If they suddenly stop drinking coffee, they may experience headaches or depression. Many people who drink large amounts of coffee on weekdays have headaches on weekends because of a sudden drop in the amount of caffeine they are consuming (Konner, 1988; Silverman et al., 1992; Strain, Mumford, & Griffiths, 1994).

Nicotine, found in cigarettes, is another common stimulant. The soothing effects of nicotine help explain why cigarette smoking is rewarding for smokers, many of whom continue to smoke despite clear evidence of its long-term health dangers. Smokers develop a dependence on nicotine, and those who suddenly stop smoking develop strong cravings for the drug (Murray, 1990). According to the former U.S. Surgeon General C. Everett Koop, who changed the designation of smoking from a "habit" to an "addiction" in 1988, the use of nicotine is "driven by strong, often irresistible urges and can persist despite . . . repeated efforts to quit" (Koop, 1988).

Cocaine   There is little doubt that the illegal drug that has posed the most serious problems in the last decade has been the stimulant *cocaine* and its derivative, *crack.* Cocaine is inhaled or "snorted" through the nose, smoked, or injected directly into the bloodstream. It is rapidly absorbed into the body, taking effect almost immediately.

Stimulant: A drug that affects the central nervous system, causing increased heart rate, blood pressure, and muscle tension

Caffeine and nicotine are two powerful, and widely used, drugs.

Cocaine is an illegal and highly addictive stimulant.

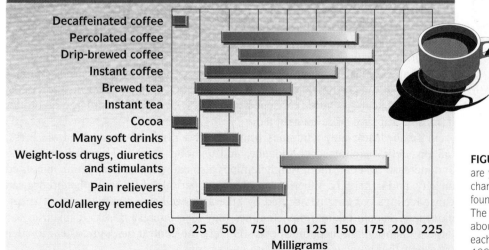

FIGURE 4-6 How much caffeine are you eating and drinking? This chart shows the range of caffeine found in common foods and drinks. The average American consumes about 200 milligrams of caffeine each day. *(The New York Times, 1991, p. C11.)*

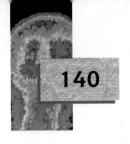
When used in relatively small quantities, cocaine produces feelings of profound psychological well-being, increased confidence, and alertness. (For a summary of the effects of cocaine and other illegal drugs, see Table 4-3.) Cocaine produces this "high" through the neurotransmitter dopamine. As you'll recall from Chapter 2, dopamine is one of the chemicals that transmit messages between neurons which are related to ordinary feelings of pleasure. Normally, when dopamine is released, excess amounts of the neurotransmitter are reabsorbed by the releasing neuron. However, when cocaine enters the brain, it blocks the reabsorption of leftover dopamine. As a result, the brain is flooded with dopamine-producing pleasurable sensations.

However, there is a steep price to be paid for the pleasurable effects of cocaine. The drug is psychologically and physically addictive, and users may grow obsessed with obtaining it. Cocaine addicts indulge in binge use, administering the drug every 10 to 30 minutes if it is available. During these binges, they think of nothing but cocaine, and eating, sleeping, family, friends, money, and even survival have no importance. Their lives become tied to the drug. Over time, users deteriorate mentally and physically, losing weight and growing suspicious of others. In extreme cases, cocaine can cause hallucinations. A common one is that insects are crawling over one's body. Ultimately, an overdose of cocaine can lead to death (Gawin & Ellinwood, 1988; Mendoza & Miller, 1992).

When cocaine is not available, abusers of the drug go through three distinct phases. In the first stage, users "crash" when the high subsides. They crave cocaine and feel depressed and agitated, and their anxiety intensifies. In the second stage, which begins from 9 hours to 4 days later, heavy users begin the process of "withdrawal." During this period, they initially crave cocaine less, feel bored and unmotivated, and experience little anxiety.

Later, though, cocaine abusers are highly sensitive to any cues that remind them of their prior cocaine use. These might be a person, event, location, or drug-abuse paraphernalia such as a glass pipe. When this happens, they are susceptible to resuming cocaine use if the drug is available. If addicts are able to pass through the withdrawal stage, they move into the third stage, in which craving for cocaine is further reduced and moods become relatively normal. However, they remain highly sensitive to cues related to cocaine use, and relapses are common. Cocaine abuse, then, has powerful, and lasting, consequences (Waldorf, Reinarman, & Murphy, 1991).

Almost one out of every two Americans between the ages of 25 and 30 has tried cocaine, and between 1 million and 3 million cocaine abusers are estimated to be in need of treatment. Furthermore, its use among high school students has increased slightly over the past few years, making the drug a major national problem (Gawin, 1991; National Institute of Drug Abuse, 1991; Johnston, Bachman, & O'Malley, 1995).

Amphetamines *Amphetamines* are strong stimulants such as Dexedrine and Benzedrine, popularly known as speed. When their use soared in the 1970s, the phrase "speed kills" became prevalent as the drug caused an increasing number of deaths. Although amphetamine use has declined from its peak in the 1970s, many drug experts believe that speed would quickly resurface in large quantities if cocaine supplies were interrupted.

In small doses, amphetamines bring about a sense of energy and alertness, talkativeness, heightened confidence, and a mood "high." They reduce fatigue and increase concentration. Amphetamines also cause a loss of appetite, increased anxiety, and irritability. When taken over long periods of time, amphetamines can cause feelings of being persecuted by others, as well as a general sense of suspiciousness. People taking amphetamines may lose interest in sex. If taken in too large a quantity, amphetamines overstimulate the central nervous system to such an extent that convulsions and death can occur.

TABLE 4-3 Drugs and Their Effects

Drug	Street Name	Effects	Withdrawal Symptoms	Adverse/Overdose Reactions
Stimulants				
Cocaine	Coke, blow, toot, snow, lady, crack	Increased confidence, mood elevation, sense of energy and alertness, decreased appetite, anxiety, irritability, insomnia, transient drowsiness, delayed orgasm	Apathy, general fatigue, prolonged sleep, depression, disorientation, suicidal thoughts, agitated motor activity, irritability, bizarre dreams	Elevated blood pressure, increase in body temperature, face-picking, suspiciousness, bizarre and repetitious behavior, vivid hallucinations, convulsions, possible death
Amphetamines				
Benzedrine	Speed			
Dexedrine	Speed			
Depressants				
Barbiturates				
Nembutal	Yellowjackets, yellows	Anxiety reduction, impulsiveness, dramatic mood swings, bizarre thoughts, suicidal behavior, slurred speech, disorientation, slowed mental and physical functioning, limited attention span	Weakness, restlessness, nausea and vomiting, headaches, nightmares, irritability, depression, acute anxiety, hallucinations, seizures, possible death	Confusion, decreased response to pain, shallow respiration, dilated pupils, weak and rapid pulse, coma, possible death
Seconal	Reds			
Phenobarbital				
Quaalude	Ludes, 714s			
Alcohol	Booze			
Narcotics				
Heroin	H, hombre, junk, smack, dope, horse, crap	Anxiety and pain reduction, apathy, difficulty in concentration, slowed speech, decreased physical activity, drooling, itching, euphoria, nausea	Anxiety, vomiting, sneezing, diarrhea, lower back pain, watery eyes, runny nose, yawning, irritability, tremors, panic, chills and sweating, cramps	Depressed levels of consciousness, low blood pressure, rapid heart rate, shallow breathing, convulsions, coma, possible death
Morphine	Drugstore dope, cube, first line, mud			
Hallucinogens				
Cannabis				
Marijuana	Bhang, Kif, ganja, dope, grass, pot, smoke, hemp, joint, weed, bone, Mary Jane, herb, tea	Euphoria, relaxed inhibitions, increased appetite, disoriented behavior	Hyperactivity, insomnia, decreased appetite, anxiety	Severe reactions are rare but include panic, paranoia, fatigue, bizarre and dangerous behavior, decreased testosterone over long term; immune-system effects
Hashish				
Hash oil				
LSD	Electricity, acid, quasey, blotter acid, microdot, white lightning, purple barrels	Fascination with ordinary objects, heightened aesthetic responses, vision and depth distortion, heightened sensitivity to faces and gestures, magnified feelings, paranoia, panic, euphoria	Not reported	Nausea and chills; increased pulse, temperature, and blood pressure; trembling; slow, deep breathing; loss of appetite; insomnia; longer, more intense "trips"; bizarre, dangerous behavior
Phencyclidine (PCP)	Angel dust, hog, rocket fuel, superweed, peace pill, elephant tranquilizer, dust, bad pizza	Increased blood pressure and heart rate, sweating, nausea, slowed reflexes, altered body image, altered perception of time and space, impaired memory	Not reported	Highly variable and possibly dose-related: disorientation; loss of recent memory; bizarre, violent behavior; hallucinations and delusions; coma

Depressants: Drugs that slow down the nervous system

Depressants: Drug Lows

In contrast to the initial effect of stimulants, which is an increase in arousal of the central nervous system, the effect of **depressants** is to impede the nervous system by causing the neurons to fire more slowly. Small doses result in at least temporary feelings of *intoxication*—drunkenness—along with a sense of euphoria and joy. When large amounts are taken, however, speech becomes slurred and muscle control becomes disjointed, causing difficulty of motion. Ultimately, consciousness may be lost entirely.

Alcohol   The most common depressant is *alcohol,* which is used by more people than any other drug. According to estimates based on liquor sales, the average person over the age of 14 drinks 2½ gallons of pure alcohol over the course of the year. This works out to more than 200 drinks per person. Although the amount of alcohol consumption has declined steadily over the last decade, surveys show that more than three-quarters of college students indicate they have had a drink within the last 30 days. Some 42 percent say that they have had five or more drinks within the past 2 weeks, and 16 percent of college students drink sixteen or more drinks per week (NIAAA, 1990; Carmody, 1990; Center on Addiction and Substance Abuse, 1994).

There are wide individual differences in alcohol consumption, as well as gender and cultural variations. For example, women are less likely to be drinkers and tend to be lighter drinkers than men, although the number of college women who abuse alcohol has tripled in the last two decades. Ironically, though, women tend to be more susceptible to the effects of alcohol, because their stomachs are less able to neutralize the drug and more alcohol goes directly into their bloodstreams (Hart & Sciutto, 1994; Eng, 1990; Center on Addiction and Substance Abuse, 1994).

There are also pronounced ethnic differences in alcohol consumption. For example, people of East Asian backgrounds who live in the United States tend to drink significantly less than whites or blacks, and their incidence of alcohol-related problems is lower. It appears that the physical reactions to drinking, which may include sweating, quickened heartbeat, and flushing, are more unpleasant for East Asians than for other groups (Akutsu et al., 1989).

Alcohol and driving are a deadly combination.

Although alcohol is a depressant, most people claim that it increases their sense of sociability and well-being. The discrepancy between the actual and the perceived effects of alcohol lies in its initial effects: release of tension and stress, feelings of happiness, and loss of inhibitions (Steele & Southwick, 1985; Steele & Josephs, 1990; Sayette, 1993). As the dose of alcohol increases, however, the depressive effects become more pronounced. People may feel emotionally and physically unstable. They also show poor judgment and may act aggressively. Moreover, their memories are impaired, their speech slurs, and they become incoherent. Eventually they may fall into a stupor and pass out. If they drink enough alcohol in a short time, they may die of alcohol poisoning (NIAAA, 1990; Bushman, 1993; Brown, 1995).

Although most people fall into the category of casual users, there are some 18 million alcoholics in the United States. *Alcoholics,* people with alcohol-abuse problems, come to rely on alcohol and continue to drink even though it causes serious difficulties. In addition, they become increasingly immune to the effects of alcohol. Consequently, alcoholics must drink progressively more in order to experience the initial positive feelings that alcohol brings about.

In some cases of alcoholism, people must drink constantly in order to feel well enough to function in their daily lives. In other cases, though, people drink inconsistently, but occasionally go on sporadic binges in which they consume large quantities of alcohol.

It is not clear why certain people become alcoholic and develop a tolerance for alcohol, while others do not. Some evidence suggests a genetic cause, although the question of whether there is a specific inherited gene that produces alcoholism is highly controversial (Blum et al., 1990; Bolos, Dean, & Rausburg, 1990). What is clear is that the chances of becoming alcoholic are considerably higher if alcoholics are present in earlier generations of a person's family. On the other hand, not all alcoholics have close relatives who are alcoholics. In these cases, environmental stressors are suspected of playing a large role (Frank, Jacobson, & Tuer, 1990; Holden, 1991; Greenfield et al., 1993b).

Barbiturates *Barbiturates,* which include such drugs as Nembutal, Seconal, and phenobarbital, are another form of depressant. Frequently prescribed by physicians to induce sleep or to reduce stress, barbiturates produce a sense of relaxation. Yet they too are psychologically and physically addictive, and when combined with alcohol, they can be deadly, since such a combination relaxes the muscles of the diaphragm to an extent that the user suffocates. The street drug known as Quaalude is closely related to the barbiturate family, and similar dangers are associated with it.

Narcotics: Relieving Pain and Anxiety

Narcotics are drugs that increase relaxation and relieve pain and anxiety. Two of the most powerful narcotics, *morphine* and *heroin,* are derived from the poppy seed pod. Although morphine is used medically to control severe pain, heroin is illegal in the United States. This has not prevented its widespread use.

Heroin users usually inject the drug directly into their veins with a hypodermic needle. The immediate effect has been described as a "rush" of positive feelings, similar in some respects to a sexual orgasm—and just as difficult to describe. After the rush, a heroin user experiences a sense of well-being and peacefulness that lasts 3 to 5 hours. When the drug's effects wear off, however, the user feels extreme anxiety and a desperate desire to repeat the experience. Moreover, larger amounts of heroin are needed each time to produce the same pleasurable effect. This leads to a cycle of biological and psychological addiction: The user is constantly either shooting up or trying to obtain ever-increasing amounts of the drug. Eventually, the life of the addict revolves around heroin.

Narcotics: Drugs that increase relaxation and relieve pain and anxiety

Because of the powerful positive feelings the drug produces, heroin addiction is particularly difficult to cure. One treatment that has shown some success is the use of methadone. *Methadone* is a synthetic chemical that satisfies a heroin user's physiological cravings for the drug without providing the "high" that accompanies heroin. When heroin users are placed on regular doses of methadone, they may be able to function relatively normally. The use of methadone has one substantial drawback, however. Although it removes the psychological dependence on heroin, it replaces the biological addiction to heroin with a biological addiction to methadone. Researchers are attempting to identify nonaddictive chemical substitutes for heroin, as well as substitutes for other addictive drugs, which do not replace one addiction with another (Waldrop, 1989).

Hallucinogens: Psychedelic Drugs

What do mushrooms, jimsonweed, and morning glories have in common? Besides being fairly common plants, each can be a source of a powerful **hallucinogen,** a drug that is capable of producing hallucinations, or changes in the perceptual process.

Hallucinogen (ha LOOS en o jen): A drug that is capable of producing changes in the perceptual process, or hallucinations

Marijuana   The most common hallucinogen in widespread use today is *marijuana,* whose active ingredient—tetrahydrocannabinol (THC)—is found in a common weed, cannabis. Marijuana is typically smoked in cigarettes, although it can be cooked and eaten. More than one-third of all Americans over the age of 12 have tried it at least once; among 18- to 25-year-olds, the figure is twice as high. Despite its illegality, marijuana use is so prevalent that about 35 percent of high school seniors say they have used the drug within the past year. Still, use of the drug is down considerably from its peak in 1972, when more than half of all high school students reported using the drug at least once within the prior year (National Institute of Drug Abuse, 1991; Johnston, Bachman, & O'Malley, 1995).

The effects of marijuana vary from person to person, but they typically consist of feelings of euphoria and general well-being. Sensory experiences seem more vivid and intense, and a person's sense of self-importance seems to grow. Memory may be impaired, causing the user to feel pleasantly "spaced out." On the other hand, the effects are not universally positive. Individuals who take marijuana when feeling depressed can end up even more depressed, since the drug tends to magnify both good and bad feelings.

Marijuana has the reputation of being a "safe" drug when used in moderation. There seems to be no scientific evidence that it is biologically addictive or that users "graduate" to more dangerous drugs. In fact, in certain cultures, the use of marijuana is routine. For instance, some people in Jamaica habitually drink a marijuana-based tea. In addition, marijuana has some proven medical uses; and sometimes it is legally prescribed for treating the eye disease of glaucoma and cases of severe asthma.

However, there are risks associated with long-term, heavy marijuana use. For instance, there is some evidence that heavy use at least temporarily decreases the production of the male sex hormone testosterone, potentially affecting sexual activity and sperm count (Jaffe, 1990). Similarly, heavy use affects the ability of the immune system to fight off germs and increases stress on the heart, although it is unclear how strong these effects are (Hollister, 1988). One negative consequence of smoking marijuana is unquestionable, though: The smoke can damage the lungs much the way cigarette smoke does, producing an increased likelihood of developing cancer and other lung diseases (Caplan & Brigham, 1990).

In sum, the *short-term* effects of marijuana use appear to be relatively minor— if users follow obvious cautions, such as avoiding driving or operating machinery. However, aside from lung damage, it is less clear whether there are harmful long-term consequences. Additional research is necessary before the question of its safety can be resolved.

LSD and PCP   Two of the strongest hallucinogens are *lysergic acid diethyl-amide,* or *LSD* (known commonly as acid), and *phencyclidine,* or *PCP* (often referred to as angel dust). Both drugs affect the operation of the neurotransmitter serotonin in the brain, causing an alteration in brain-cell activity and perception (Jacobs, 1987).

LSD produces vivid hallucinations. Perceptions of colors, sounds, and shapes are altered so much that even the most mundane experience—such as looking at the knots in a wooden table—can seem moving and exciting. Time perception is distorted, and objects and people may be viewed in a new way, with some users reporting that LSD increases their understanding of the world. For others, however, the experience brought on by LSD can be terrifying, particularly if users have had emotional difficulties in the past. Furthermore, people can experience flashbacks, in which they hallucinate long after the initial drug usage.

PCP also causes strong hallucinations. However, the potential side effects associated with its use make the drug even more dangerous than LSD. Large doses may cause paranoid and destructive behavior; in some cases users become violent toward themselves and others.

The Informed Consumer of Psychology

Identifying Drug and Alcohol Problems

In a society bombarded with commercials for drugs that are guaranteed to do everything from curing the common cold to giving new life to "tired blood," it is no wonder that drug-related problems represent a major social issue. Yet many people with drug and alcohol problems deny they have them, and even close friends and family members may fail to realize when occasional social use of drugs or alcohol has turned into abuse.

Certain signs, however, indicate when use becomes abuse (Brody, 1982; Gelman, 1989; NIAAA, 1990). Among them:

- Always getting high to have a good time
- Being high more often than not
- Getting high to get oneself going
- Going to work or class while high
- Missing or being unprepared for class or work because you were high
- Feeling bad later about something you said or did while high
- Driving a car while high
- Coming in conflict with the law because of drugs
- Doing something while high that you wouldn't otherwise do
- Being high in nonsocial, solitary situations
- Being unable to stop getting high
- Feeling a need for a drink or a drug to get through the day
- Becoming physically unhealthy
- Failing at school or on the job
- Thinking about liquor or drugs all the time
- Avoiding family or friends while using liquor or drugs

Any combination of these symptoms should be sufficient to alert you to the potential of a serious drug problem. Because drug and alcohol dependence are almost impossible to cure on one's own, people who suspect that they have a problem should seek immediate attention from a psychologist, physician, or counselor.

You can also get help from one of these national hotlines: For alcohol difficulties, call the National Council on Alcoholism at (800) 622-2255; for drug problems, call the National Institute on Drug Abuse at (800) 662-4357. You can also check your telephone book for a local listing of Alcoholics Anonymous or Narcotics Anonymous. Finally, you can write to the National Council on Alcoholism and Drug Dependence, 12 West 21st Street, New York, New York 10010, for help with alcohol and drug problems.

RECAP AND REVIEW

Recap
- Psychoactive drugs affect a person's emotions, perceptions, and behavior. The most dangerous drugs are those that are addictive—they produce a biological or psychological dependence.
- Stimulants produce an increase in the arousal of the central nervous system.
- Depressants decrease arousal in the central nervous system; they can produce intoxication.
- Narcotics produce relaxation, and relieve pain and anxiety.
- Hallucinogens produce hallucinations and other alterations of perception.

Review
1. What is the term for drugs that affect a person's consciousness?
2. Match the type of drug to an example of that type.
   1. Barbiturate
   2. Amphetamine
   3. Hallucinogen

a. LSD
b. Phenobarbital
c. Dexedrine

3. For each drug listed, classify it as a stimulant (S), depressant (D), hallucinogen (H), or narcotic (N):
   1. PCP _____
   2. Nicotine _____
   3. Cocaine _____
   4. Alcohol _____
   5. Heroin _____
   6. Marijuana _____
4. The effects of LSD may recur long after the drug has been taken. True or false?
5. _____ is a drug that has been used to cure people of heroin addiction.
6. What is the problem with the use of methadone treatment?

Ask Yourself
Why is the use of psychoactive drugs and the search for altered states of consciousness found in almost every culture?

(Answers to review questions are on page 148.)

LOOKING BACK

What are the different states of consciousness?
1. Consciousness refers to a person's awareness of the sensations, thoughts, and feelings being experienced at a given moment. It can vary in terms of how aware one is of outside stimuli—from an active to a passive state—and in terms of whether it is artificially induced or occurs naturally.

What happens when we sleep, and what are the meaning and function of dreams?
2. Using the electroencephalogram, or EEG, to study sleep, scientists have found that the brain is active throughout the night, and that sleep proceeds through a series of stages identified by unique patterns of brain waves. Stage 1 is characterized by relatively rapid, low-voltage waves, whereas stage 2 shows more regular, spindle patterns. In stage 3, the brain waves become slower, with higher peaks and lower valleys apparent. Finally, stage 4 sleep includes waves that are even slower and more regular.
3. REM (rapid eye movement) sleep is characterized by an in-

crease in heart rate, a rise in blood pressure, an increase in the rate of breathing, and, in males, erections. Most striking is the rapid movement of the eyes, which dart back and forth under closed eyelids. Dreams occur during this stage. REM sleep seems to be critical to human functioning, whereas other stages of sleep are less essential.
4. According to Freud, dreams have both a manifest content (their apparent story line) and a latent content (their true meaning). He suggested that the latent content provides a guide to a dreamer's unconscious, revealing unfulfilled wishes or desires. Many psychologists disagree with this view. They suggest that the manifest content represents the true import of the dream.
5. The reverse-learning theory suggests that dreams represent a process in which unnecessary information is "unlearned" and removed from memory. In this view, dreams have no meaning. In contrast, the dreams-as-survival theory suggests that information relevant to daily survival is reconsidered and reprocessed. Finally, the activation-synthesis theory proposes

that dreams are a result of random electrical energy. This electrical energy randomly stimulates different memories, which are then woven into a coherent story line.

How much do we daydream?

6. Daydreaming may occur 10 percent of the time, although wide individual differences exist in the amount of time devoted to it. There is little relationship between psychological disorders and a high incidence of daydreaming.

What are the major sleep disorders, and how can they be treated?

7. Insomnia is a sleep disorder characterized by difficulty sleeping. Sleep apnea is a condition in which people experience difficulties in sleeping and breathing at the same time. People with narcolepsy have an uncontrollable urge to sleep. Sleepwalking and sleeptalking are relatively harmless.

8. Psychologists and sleep researchers advise people with insomnia to consider the following: increasing exercise; choosing a regular bedtime; avoiding caffeine, sleeping pills, and using your bed for anything but sleep; drinking a glass of warm milk before bedtime; and avoiding *trying* to go to sleep.

Are hypnotized people in a different state of consciousness, and can they be hypnotized against their will?

9. Hypnosis produces a state of heightened susceptibility to the suggestions of the hypnotist. Although no physiological indicators distinguish hypnosis from normal waking consciousness, significant behavioral changes occur. These include increased concentration and suggestibility, heightened ability to recall and construct images, lack of initiative, and acceptance of suggestions that clearly contradict reality. However, people cannot be hypnotized unwillingly.

What are the consequences of meditation?

10. Meditation is a learned technique for refocusing attention that brings about an altered state of consciousness. In transcendental meditation, the most popular form practiced in the United States, a person repeats a mantra (a sound, word, or syllable) over and over, concentrating until he or she becomes unaware of any outside stimulation and reaches a different state of consciousness.

11. Different cultures have unique forms of altering states of consciousness. Some researchers speculate that a universal need exists for altered states of consciousness.

What are the major classifications of drugs, and what are their effects?

12. Drugs can produce altered states of consciousness. However, they vary in how dangerous they are and in whether or not they are addictive, producing a physical or psychological dependence. People take drugs for several reasons: to perceive the pleasure of the experience itself, to escape from everyday pressures, to attain religious or spiritual states, to follow the model of prestigious users or peers, or to experience the thrill of trying something new and perhaps illegal. Whatever the cause, drug addiction is one of the most difficult behaviors to modify.

13. Stimulants cause arousal in the central nervous system. Two common stimulants are caffeine (found in coffee, tea, and soft drinks) and nicotine (found in cigarettes). More dangerous are cocaine and amphetamines, or "speed." Although in small quantities stimulants bring about increased confidence, a sense of energy and alertness, and a "high," in larger quantities they may overload the central nervous system, leading to convulsions and death.

14. Depressants decrease arousal in the central nervous system, causing the neurons to fire more slowly. They may cause intoxication along with feelings of euphoria. The most common depressants are alcohol and barbiturates.

15. Alcohol is the most frequently used depressant. Although it initially releases tension and produces positive feelings, as the dose of alcohol increases, the depressive effects become more pronounced. Alcoholics develop a tolerance for alcohol and must drink alcoholic beverages in order to function. Both genetic causes and environmental stressors may lead to alcoholism.

16. Morphine and heroin are narcotics, drugs that produce relaxation and relieve pain and anxiety. Because of their addictive qualities, morphine and heroin are particularly dangerous.

17. Hallucinogens are drugs that produce hallucinations and other changes in perception. The most frequently used hallucinogen is marijuana; its use is common throughout the United States. Although occasional, short-term use of marijuana seems to be of little danger, long-term effects are less clear. The lungs can be damaged, there is the possibility that testosterone levels are lowered in males, and the immune system may be affected. Two other hallucinogens, LSD and PCP, affect the operation of neurotransmitters in the brain, causing an alteration in brain-cell activity and perception.

18. A number of signals indicate when drug use has become drug abuse. These include using drugs frequently, getting high in order to get to class or work, driving while high, developing legal problems, and getting high alone. A person who suspects that he or she has a drug problem should get professional help. People are almost never capable of solving drug problems on their own.

KEY TERMS AND CONCEPTS

consciousness (p. 117)
stage 1 sleep (p. 120)
stage 2 sleep (p. 120)
stage 3 sleep (p. 121)

stage 4 sleep (p. 121)
rapid eye movement (REM) sleep
   (p. 121)
circadian rhythms (p. 123)

unconscious wish fulfillment theory
   (p. 125)
latent content of dreams (p. 125)
manifest content of dreams (p. 125)

ANSWERS TO PREVIOUS REVIEW

1. Psychoactive **2.** 1-b; 2-c; 3-a **3.** 1-H; 2-S; 3-S; 4-D; 5-N; 6-H **4.** True
5. Methadone **6.** People become addicted to the methadone.

CHAPTER 5
LEARNING

Henrietta, Sue Strong's Lifeline

When she awoke following a terrifying car crash, Sue Strong found that she had lost almost all feeling and movement below the shoulders due to injury to her spinal cord. Overnight, she joined the ranks of the permanently physically challenged.

At first, Strong was completely dependent on other people. But that was before the arrival of Henrietta. "Having her completely changed my life. Before, I had to depend on people coming in to work, and worry about whether or not they'd show up on time. Now, if I'm up in my chair, and feeling OK, Henrietta and I can get along fine on our own" (MacFadyen, 1987, p. 132).

Henrietta is a capuchin monkey. Through careful, systematic training procedures she has become Strong's arms and legs. For instance, when Strong drops the mouth-stick she uses to work at a computer and answer the phone, she tells Henrietta to search for it. After locating it, Henrietta picks it up and carefully places it in Strong's mouth.

After Henrietta is sent to the kitchen to get some food, she quickly returns with a sandwich and places it where Strong can eat it. But when she can't stop herself from taking a small bite, she runs crying into her own quarters, overcome with guilt. It is not until Strong laughingly tells her it is all right to return that she comes back. She curls up at Strong's feet, looking apologetic. "Look at that, will you!" Strong says. "A face only a mother could love" (MacFadyen, 1987, p. 132).

LOOKING AHEAD

The same processes that allow trainers to harness and shape Henrietta's capabilities to benefit Sue Strong are at work in each of our lives, as we read a book,

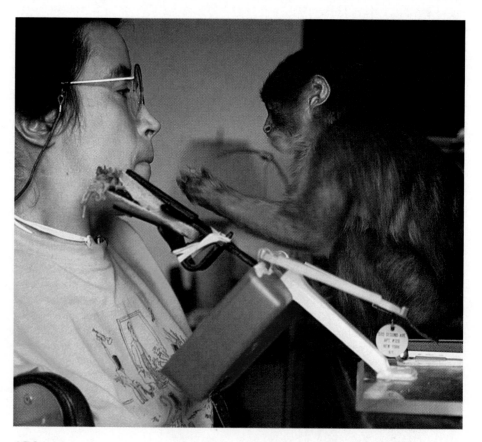

Sue Strong and her simian aide, Henrietta.

drive a car, play poker, study for a test, or perform any of the numerous activities that make up our daily routine. Like Henrietta, each of us must acquire and then refine our skills and abilities through learning.

A fundamental topic for psychologists, learning plays a central role in almost every specialty area of psychology, as we will see throughout this book. For example, a psychologist studying perception might ask, "How do we learn that people who look small from a distance are far away and not simply tiny?" A developmental psychologist might inquire, "How do babies learn to distinguish their mothers from other people?" A clinical psychologist might wonder, "Why do some people learn to be afraid when they see a spider?" A social psychologist might ask, "How do we learn to feel that we are in love?" Each of these questions, although drawn from very different fields of psychology, can be answered only with reference to learning processes.

What do we mean by learning? Although psychologists have identified a number of different types of learning, a general definition encompasses them all: **Learning** is a relatively permanent change in behavior brought about by experience. What is particularly important about this definition is that it permits us to distinguish between performance changes due to *maturation* (the unfolding of biologically predetermined patterns of behavior due simply to getting older) and those changes brought about by experience. For instance, children become better tennis players as they grow older partially because their strength increases with their size—a maturational phenomenon. Such maturational changes need to be distinguished from improvements due to learning, which are a consequence of practice.

Similarly, we must distinguish between short-term changes in behavior that are due to factors other than learning, such as declines in performance resulting from fatigue or lack of effort, and performance changes that are due to actual learning. For example, if Andre Agassi performs poorly in a tennis game because of tension or fatigue, this does not mean that he has not learned to play correctly or has forgotten how to play well.

The distinction between learning and performance is critical, and not always easy to make. To some psychologists, learning can only be inferred indirectly, by observing changes in performance. Because there is not always a one-to-one correspondence between learning and performance, understanding when true learning has occurred is difficult. (Those of us who have done poorly on an exam because we were tired and made careless mistakes can well understand this distinction.)

On the other hand, some psychologists have approached learning from a very different perspective. By considering learning simply as any change in behavior, they maintain that learning and performance are the same thing. Such an approach tends to dismiss the mental components of learning by focusing only on observable performance. As we will see, the degree to which learning can be understood without considering mental processes represents one of the major areas of disagreement among learning theorists of varying orientations.

In sum, we begin this chapter by examining the type of learning that underlies responses ranging from a dog salivating when it sees or hears its owner opening a can of dog food to the emotions we feel when our national anthem is played. We then discuss other theories that consider how learning is a consequence of rewarding circumstances. Finally, we examine approaches that focus on the cognitive aspects of learning.

Learning: A relatively permanent change in behavior brought about by experience

- *What is learning?*
- *How do we learn to form associations between stimuli and responses?*

CLASSICAL CONDITIONING

Does the mere sight of the golden arches in front of McDonald's make you feel pangs of hunger and think about hamburgers? If it does, then you are displaying a rudimentary form of learning called classical conditioning.

The processes that underlie classical conditioning explain such diverse phenomena as crying at the sight of a bride walking down the aisle at a wedding, fearing the dark, and falling in love with the boy or girl next door. To understand classical conditioning, however, it is necessary to move back in time and place to the early part of this century in Russia.

The Basics of Conditioning

Ivan Pavlov, a Russian physiologist, never intended to do psychological research. In 1904 he won the Nobel Prize for his work on digestion, testimony to his contribution to that field. Yet Pavlov is remembered not for his physiological research, but for his experiments on basic learning processes—work that he began quite accidentally.

Classical conditioning: A kind of learning in which a previously neutral stimulus comes to elicit a response through its association with a stimulus that naturally brings about the response

Pavlov had been studying the secretion of stomach acids and salivation in dogs in response to the ingestion of varying amounts and kinds of food. While doing so, he observed a curious phenomenon: Sometimes stomach secretions and salivation would begin when no food had actually been eaten. The mere sight of a food bowl, the individual who normally brought the food, or even the sound of that individual's footsteps was enough to produce a physiological response in the dogs. Pavlov's genius was his ability to recognize the implications of this rather basic discovery. He saw that the dogs were responding not only on the basis of a biological need (hunger), but also as a result of learning—or, as it came to be called, classical conditioning. In **classical conditioning,** an organism learns to respond to a neutral stimulus that normally does not bring about that response.

Ivan Pavlov is best known for his contributions to the field of classical conditioning.

To demonstrate and analyze classical conditioning, Pavlov conducted a series of experiments (Pavlov, 1927). In one, he attached a tube to the salivary gland of a dog, which allowed Pavlov to measure precisely the amount of salivation that occurred. He then sounded a tuning fork and, just a few seconds later, presented the dog with meat powder. This pairing, carefully planned so that exactly the same amount of time elapsed between the presentation of the sound and the meat powder, occurred repeatedly. At first the dog would salivate only when the meat powder itself was presented, but soon it began to salivate at the sound of the tuning fork. In fact, even when Pavlov stopped presenting the meat powder, the dog still salivated after hearing the sound. The dog had been classically conditioned to salivate to the tone.

As you can see in Figure 5-1, the basic processes of classical conditioning underlying Pavlov's discovery are straightforward, although the terminology he chose has a technical ring. Consider first the diagram in Figure 5-1*a*. Prior to conditioning, there are two unrelated stimuli: the sound of a tuning fork and meat powder. We know that the sound of a tuning fork leads not to salivation but to some irrelevant response such as perking of the ears or, perhaps, a startle reaction. The sound in this case is therefore called the **neutral stimulus** because it has no effect on the response of interest. We also have meat powder, which, because of the biological makeup of the dog, naturally leads to salivation—the response that we are interested in conditioning. The meat powder is considered an **unconditioned stimulus,** or **UCS,** because food placed in a dog's mouth automatically causes salivation to occur. The response that the meat powder elicits (salivation) is called an **unconditioned response,** or **UCR**—a response that is not associated with previous learning. Unconditioned responses are natural, innate responses that involve no training. They are always brought about by the presence of unconditioned stimuli.

Figure 5-1*b* illustrates what happens during conditioning. The tuning fork is repeatedly sounded just before presentation of the meat powder. The goal of conditioning is for the tuning fork to become associated with the unconditioned stimulus (meat powder) and therefore to bring about the same sort of response as the unconditioned stimulus. During this period, salivation gradually increases each time the tuning fork is sounded, until the tuning fork alone causes the dog to salivate.

When conditioning is complete, the tuning fork has evolved from a neutral stimulus to what is now called a **conditioned stimulus,** or **CS.** At this time, salivation that occurs as a response to the conditioned stimulus (tuning fork) is considered a **conditioned response,** or **CR.** This situation is depicted in Figure 5-1*c*. After conditioning, then, the conditioned stimulus evokes the conditioned response.

The sequence and timing of the presentation of the unconditioned stimulus and the conditioned stimulus are particularly important (Rescorla, 1988). Like a malfunctioning railroad warning light at a street crossing that does not go on until after a train has passed by, a neutral stimulus that follows an unconditioned stimulus has little chance of becoming a conditioned stimulus. On the other hand, just as a warning light works best if it goes on right before a train is about to go by, a neutral stimulus that is presented just before the unconditioned stimulus is most apt to result in successful conditioning. Research has shown that conditioning is most effective if the neutral stimulus (which will become a conditioned stimulus) precedes the unconditioned stimulus by between a half second and several seconds, depending on what kind of response is being conditioned.

The terminology employed by Pavlov to describe classical conditioning may at first seem confusing, but the following rules of thumb can help to make the relationships between stimuli and responses easier to understand and remember:

Neutral stimulus: A stimulus that, before conditioning, has no effect on the desired response

Unconditioned stimulus (UCS): A stimulus that brings about a response without having been learned

Unconditioned response (UCR): A response that is natural and needs no training (e.g., salivation at the smell of food)

Conditioned stimulus (CS): A once-neutral stimulus that has been paired with an unconditioned stimulus to bring about a response formerly caused only by the unconditioned stimulus

Conditioned response (CR): A response that, after conditioning, follows a previously neutral stimulus (e.g., salivation at the sound of a tuning fork)

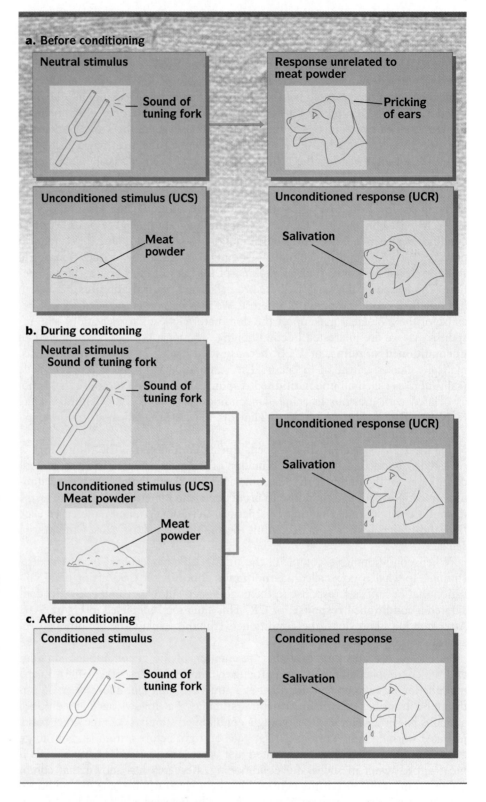

FIGURE 5-1 The basic process of classical conditioning. (a) Prior to conditioning, the sound of a tuning fork does not bring about salivation—making the tuning fork a neutral stimulus. On the other hand, meat powder naturally brings about salivation, making the meat powder an unconditioned stimulus and salivation an unconditioned response. (b) During conditioning, the tuning fork is sounded just before the presentation of the meat powder. (c) Eventually, the sound of the tuning fork alone brings about salivation. We can now say that conditioning has been accomplished: The previously neutral stimulus of the tuning fork is now considered a conditioned stimulus that brings about the conditioned response of salivation.

■ *Un*conditioned stimuli lead to *un*conditioned responses.

■ *Un*conditioned stimulus–*un*conditioned response pairings are *un*learned and *un*trained.

■ During conditioning, previously neutral stimuli are transformed into conditioned stimuli.

■ Conditioned stimuli lead to conditioned responses, and conditioned stimulus–conditioned response pairings are a consequence of learning and training.

■ Unconditioned responses and conditioned responses are similar (such as salivation in the example described above), but the conditioned response is learned, whereas the unconditioned response occurs naturally.

Applying Conditioning Principles to Human Behavior

Although the initial experiments were carried out with animals, classical conditioning principles were soon found to explain many aspects of everyday human behavior. Recall, for instance, the earlier illustration of how people may experience hunger pangs at the sight of McDonald's golden arches. The cause of this reaction is classical conditioning: The previously neutral arches have come to be associated with the food inside the restaurant (the unconditioned stimulus), causing the arches to become a conditioned stimulus that brings about the conditioned response of hunger.

Emotional responses are particularly likely to be learned through classical conditioning processes. For instance, how do some of us develop fears of mice, spiders, and other creatures that are typically harmless? In a now-famous case study designed to show that classical conditioning was at the root of such fears, an 11-month-old infant named Albert, who initially showed no fear of rats, heard a loud noise just as he was shown a rat (Watson & Rayner, 1920). The noise (the UCS) evoked fear (the UCR). After just a few pairings of noise and rat, Albert began to show fear of the rat by itself. The rat, then, had become a CS that brought about the CR, fear. Similarly, the pairing of the appearance of certain species (such as mice or spiders) with the fearful comments of an adult may cause children to develop the same fears their parents have. (By the way, we don't know what happened to the unfortunate Albert. Watson, the experimenter, has been condemned for using ethically questionable procedures.)

In adulthood, learning via classical conditioning occurs a bit more subtly. You may come to know that a job supervisor is in a bad mood when her tone of voice changes, if in the past you have heard her use that tone only when she was about to criticize someone's work. Likewise, you may not go to a dentist as often as you should because of prior associations with dentists and pain. Or you may have a particular fondness for the color blue because that was the color of your childhood bedroom. Classical conditioning, then, explains many of the reactions we have to stimuli in the world around us (Klein & Mowrer, 1989).

Extinction: Unlearning What We Have Learned

What do you think would happen if a dog, who had become classically conditioned to salivate at the sound of a bell, never again received food when the bell was sounded? The answer lies in one of the basic phenomena of learning: extinction. **Extinction** occurs when a previously conditioned response decreases in frequency and eventually disappears.

To produce extinction, one needs to end the association between conditioned and unconditioned stimuli. For instance, if we had trained a dog to salivate at the sound of a bell, we could produce extinction by ceasing to provide meat after the bell was sounded. At first the dog would continue to salivate when it heard the bell, but after a few such instances, the amount of salivation would probably decline, and the dog would eventually stop responding to the bell altogether. At that point, we could say that the response had been extinguished. In sum, extinction occurs when the conditioned stimulus is repeatedly presented without the unconditioned stimulus. We should keep in mind that extinction can be a helpful phenomenon. Consider, for instance, what it would be like if the fear you expe-

Extinction: The weakening and eventual disappearance of a conditioned response

rience after watching the famous shower scene in *Psycho* never was extinguished. You might well tremble with fright every time you even thought of showering.

As we will describe more fully in Chapter 13, psychologists have treated people with irrational fears, or phobias, using a form of therapy called systematic desensitization. The goal of *systematic desensitization* is to bring about the extinction of the phobia. For example, a therapist using systematic desensitization for a client who is afraid of dogs may repeatedly expose the client to dogs, starting with a less frightening aspect (a photo of a cute dog) and moving toward more feared ones (such as an actual encounter with a strange dog). As the negative consequences of exposure to the dog do not materialize, the fear eventually becomes extinguished.

Spontaneous Recovery: The Return of the Conditioned Response

Once a conditioned response has been extinguished, has it vanished forever? Not necessarily. Pavlov discovered this fact when he returned to his previously conditioned dog a week after the conditioned behavior had been extinguished. If he sounded a tuning fork, the dog once again salivated. Similarly, consider people who have been addicted to cocaine who manage to break the habit. Even though they are "cured," if they are subsequently confronted by a stimulus with strong connections to the drug—such as a white powder or a pipe used for smoking cocaine—they may suddenly experience an irresistible impulse to use the drug again, even after a long absence from drug use (Gawin, 1991).

Spontaneous recovery: The reappearance of a previously extinguished response after a period of time during which the conditioned stimulus has been absent

This phenomenon is called **spontaneous recovery**—the reappearance of a previously extinguished response after time has elapsed without exposure to the conditioned stimulus. Usually, however, responses that return through spontaneous recovery are weaker than they were initially and can be extinguished more readily than before.

Generalization and Discrimination

Despite differences in color and shape, to most of us a rose is a rose is a rose. The pleasure we experience at the beauty, smell, and grace of the flower is similar for different types of roses. Pavlov noticed an analogous phenomenon. His dogs often salivated not only at the sound of the tuning fork that was used during their original conditioning but at the sound of a bell or a buzzer as well.

Stimulus generalization: Response to a stimulus that is similar to but different from a conditioned stimulus; the more similar the two stimuli, the more likely generalization is to occur

Such behavior is the result of stimulus generalization. **Stimulus generalization** takes place when a conditioned response follows a stimulus that is similar to

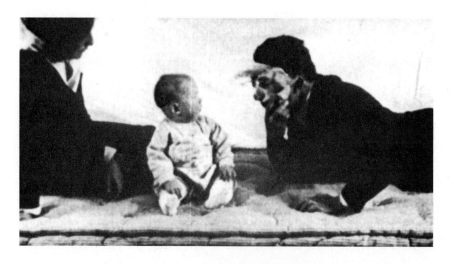

In John Watson's work with Albert, the infant's conditioned fear of white rats was generalized to other furry white objects, including the Santa Claus mask worn by Watson in this photograph.

the original conditioned stimulus. The greater the similarity between the two stimuli, the greater the likelihood of stimulus generalization. Baby Albert, who, as we mentioned earlier, was conditioned to be fearful of rats, was later found to be afraid of other furry white things as well. He was fearful of white rabbits, white fur coats, and even a white Santa Claus mask. On the other hand, according to the principle of stimulus generalization, it is unlikely that he would have been afraid of a black dog, since its color would differentiate it sufficiently from the original fear-evoking stimulus.

The conditioned response elicited by the new stimulus is usually not as intense as the original conditioned response, although the more similar the new stimulus is to the old one, the more similar the new response will be. It is unlikely, then, that Albert's fear of the Santa Claus mask was as great as his learned fear of a rat. Still, stimulus generalization permits us to know, for example, that we ought to brake at all red traffic signals, even if there are minor variations in size, shape, and shade of the light.

If stimuli are sufficiently distinct from one another so that the presence of one evokes a conditioned response but the other does not, we can say that **stimulus discrimination** has occurred. In stimulus discrimination, an organism learns to differentiate among different stimuli and restricts its responding to one stimulus rather than to others. Without the ability to discriminate between a red and a green traffic light, we would be mowed down by oncoming traffic; and if we could not discriminate a cat from a mountain lion, we might find ourselves in uncomfortable straits on a camping trip.

Stimulus discrimination: The process by which an organism learns to differentiate among stimuli, restricting its response to one in particular

Higher-Order Conditioning

Suppose a 4-year-old boy is knocked over a few times by his neighbor's large and ill-behaved dog, Rags. After a few such incidents, it would not be surprising that merely hearing the dog's name would produce a reaction of fear.

The unpleasant emotional reaction the child experiences on hearing "Rags" represents an example of higher-order conditioning. *Higher-order conditioning* occurs when a conditioned stimulus that has been established during earlier conditioning is then paired repeatedly with a neutral stimulus. If this neutral stimulus, by itself, comes to evoke a conditioned response similar to that of the original conditioned stimulus, higher-order conditioning has occurred. The original conditioned stimulus acts, in effect, as an unconditioned stimulus.

Our example of Rags can illustrate higher-order conditioning. The child has learned to associate the sight of Rags, who originally was a neutral stimulus, with rough behavior. The mere sight of Rags, then, has become a conditioned stimulus, which evokes the conditioned response of fear.

Later, however, the child makes the association that every time he sees Rags, its owner is calling the dog's name, saying, "Here, Rags." Because of this recurring pairing of the name of Rags (which was originally a neutral stimulus) with the sight of Rags (now a conditioned stimulus), the child becomes conditioned to experience a reaction of fear and loathing whenever he hears the name "Rags," even though he may be safely inside his house. The name "Rags," then, has become a conditioned stimulus because of its earlier pairing with the conditioned stimulus of the sight of Rags. Higher-order conditioning has occurred: The sound of Rags's name has become a conditioned stimulus evoking a conditioned response.

Some psychologists have suggested that higher-order conditioning may provide an explanation for the acquisition and maintenance of prejudice against members of racial and ethnic groups (Staats, 1975). Suppose, for instance, that every time a young girl's parents mentioned a particular racial group, they used such negative words as "stupid" and "filthy." Eventually, the girl might come to

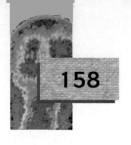

associate members of the group with the unpleasant emotional reaction that is evoked by the words "stupid" and "filthy" (reactions learned through prior classical conditioning). Although this is not a complete explanation for prejudice, as we shall see when we discuss it more fully in Chapter 14, it is likely that such higher-order conditioning is part of the process.

Beyond Traditional Classical Conditioning: Challenging Basic Assumptions

Theoretically, it ought to be possible to keep producing unlimited higher-order response chains, associating one conditioned stimulus with another. In fact, Pavlov hypothesized that all learning is nothing more than long strings of conditioned responses. However, this notion has not been supported by subsequent research, and it turns out that classical conditioning provides us with only a partial explanation of how people and animals learn (Rizley & Rescorla, 1972).

Some of the other fundamental assumptions of classical conditioning have also been questioned. For example, according to Pavlov, as well as to many contemporary proponents of the traditional view of classical conditioning, the process of linking stimuli and responses occurs in a mechanistic, unthinking way. In contrast to this perspective, learning theorists influenced by cognitive psychology have argued that there is more to classical conditioning than this mechanical view. They contend that learners actively develop an understanding and expectancy about what particular unconditioned stimuli are matched with specific conditioned stimuli. A sounding bell, for instance, gives a dog something to think about: the impending arrival of food. In a sense, this view suggests that the learner develops and holds an idea or image about how various stimuli are linked to one another (Rescorla, 1988; Turkkan, 1989; Baker & Mercier, 1989).

Traditional explanations of how classical conditioning operates have also been challenged by John Garcia, a leading researcher in learning processes. He disputes the supposition that optimum learning occurs only when the unconditioned stimulus *immediately* follows the conditioned stimulus (Garcia, Brett, & Rusiniak, 1989; Papini & Bitterman, 1990).

Like Pavlov, Garcia made his major contribution while studying a phenomenon unrelated to learning. He was initially concerned with the effects of exposure to nuclear radiation on laboratory animals. In the course of his experiments, he realized that rats in a radiation chamber drank almost no water, while in their home cage they drank it eagerly. The most obvious explanation—that it had something to do with the radiation—was soon ruled out. Garcia found that even when the radiation was not turned on, the rats still drank little or no water in the radiation chamber.

Initially puzzled by the rats' behavior, Garcia eventually figured out what was happening. He noticed that the drinking cups in the radiation chamber were made of plastic, thereby giving the water an unusual, plastic-like taste. In contrast, the drinking cups in the home cage were made of glass and left no abnormal taste.

After a series of experiments to rule out several alternative explanations, just one possibility remained: Apparently, the plastic-tasting water had become repeatedly paired with illness brought on by exposure to radiation, and had led the rats to form a classically conditioned association. The process began with the radiation acting as an unconditioned stimulus evoking the unconditioned response of sickness. With repeated pairings, the plastic-tasting water had become a conditioned stimulus that evoked the conditioned response of sickness (Garcia, Hankins, & Rusiniak, 1974).

The problem with this finding was that it violated one of the basic rules of classical conditioning—that an unconditioned stimulus should *immediately* follow the conditioned stimulus for optimal conditioning to occur. Instead, Garcia's findings showed that conditioning could occur even when there was an interval of as

long as 8 hours between exposure to the conditioned stimulus and the response of sickness. Furthermore, the conditioning persisted over very long periods and sometimes occurred after just one exposure to water that was followed later on by illness.

These findings have had important practical implications. For example, in order to prevent coyotes from killing their sheep, some ranchers now routinely lace a sheep carcass with a drug and leave the carcass in a place where coyotes will find it. The drug temporarily makes the coyotes quite ill, but it does not permanently harm them. After just one exposure to a drug-laden sheep carcass, coyotes tend to avoid sheep, which are normally one of their primary natural victims. The sheep, then, have become a conditioned stimulus to the coyotes. This approach is a far more humane one than shooting the coyotes, the traditional response of ranchers to predators (Gustavson et al., 1974).

RECAP AND REVIEW

Recap

- Learning is a relatively permanent change in behavior brought about by experience.
- Classical conditioning is a kind of learning in which an initially neutral stimulus, which does not evoke a relevant response, is paired repeatedly with an unconditioned stimulus. Eventually, the previously neutral stimulus evokes a response similar to that brought about by the unconditioned stimulus.
- Classical conditioning underlies many sorts of everyday learning, such as the acquisition of emotional responses.
- Among the basic phenomena of classical conditioning are extinction, spontaneous recovery, stimulus generalization and discrimination, and higher-order conditioning.

Review

1. _____ involves changes brought about by experience, whereas _____ describes changes due to biological development.
2. _____ is the name of the scientist responsible for discovering the learning phenomenon known as _____ conditioning, in which an organism learns a response to a stimulus to which it would not normally respond.

Refer to the passage below to answer questions 3 through 6:

The last three times Theresa has visited Dr. Noble for checkups, he has administered a painful preventive immuniza-

tion shot that has left her in tears. When her mother takes her for another checkup, Theresa begins to sob as soon as she comes face to face with Dr. Noble, even before the doctor has had a chance to say hello.

3. The painful shot that Theresa received during each visit was a(n) _____ _____, which elicited the _____ _____, her tears.
4. Dr. Noble is upset because his presence has become a(n) _____ _____ for Theresa's crying.
5. When elicited by Dr. Noble's presence alone, Theresa's crying is referred to as a(n) _____ _____.
6. Fortunately, Dr. Noble gave Theresa no more shots for quite some time. Over that time she gradually stopped crying and even came to like him. _____ had occurred.
7. _____ _____ occurs when a stimulus similar to, but not identical to, a conditioned stimulus produces a response. On the other hand, _____ _____ occurs when an organism does not produce a response to a stimulus that is distinct from the CS.

Ask Yourself

Theoretically, it should be possible to build an infinitely long chain of classically conditioned higher-order responses so that stimuli can be paired together indefinitely. What might prevent this from happening in humans?

(Answers to review questions are on page 160.)

• *What is the role of reward and punishment in learning?*

OPERANT CONDITIONING

Very good. . . . What a clever idea. . . . Fantastic. . . . I agree. . . . Thank you. . . . Excellent. . . . Super. . . . Right on. . . . This is the best paper you've ever written; you get an A. . . . You are really getting the hang of it. . . . I'm impressed. . . . Let me give you a hug. . . . You're getting a raise. . . . Have a cookie. . . . You look great. . . . I love you. . . .

Few of us mind being the recipient of any of the above comments. But what is especially noteworthy about them is that each of these simple statements can be used to bring about powerful changes in behavior and to teach the most complex tasks through a process known as operant conditioning. Operant conditioning forms the basis for many of the most important kinds of human, and animal, learning.

Operant conditioning: Learning in which a voluntary response is strengthened or weakened, depending on its positive or negative consequences; the organism operates on its environment in order to produce a particular result

Operant conditioning describes learning in which a voluntary response is strengthened or weakened, depending on its positive or negative consequences. Unlike classical conditioning, in which the original behaviors are the natural, biological responses to the presence of some stimulus such as food, water, or pain, operant conditioning applies to voluntary responses, which an organism performs deliberately, in order to produce a desirable outcome. The term "operant" emphasizes this point: The organism *operates* on its environment to produce some desirable result. For example, operant conditioning is at work when we learn that working industriously can bring about a raise or that studying hard results in good grades.

As with classical conditioning, the basis for understanding operant conditioning was laid by work with animals. We turn now to some of that early research, which began with a simple inquiry into the behavior of cats.

Thorndike's Law of Effect

FIGURE 5-2 Edward L. Thorndike devised this puzzle box to study the process by which a cat learns to press a paddle to escape the box and receive food. *(Thorndike, 1932.)*

If you placed a hungry cat in a cage and then put a small piece of food outside, chances are the cat would eagerly search for a way out of the cage. The cat might first claw at the sides or push against an opening. Suppose, though, that you had rigged things so that the cat could escape by stepping on a small paddle that released the latch to the door of the cage (see Figure 5-2). Eventually, as it moved around the cage, the cat would happen to step on the paddle, the door would open, and the cat would eat the food.

What would happen if you then returned the cat to the box? The next time, it would probably take a little less time for the cat to step on the paddle and escape. After a few trials, the cat would deliberately step on the paddle as soon as it was placed in the cage. What would have occurred, according to Edward L. Thorndike (1932), who studied this situation extensively, was that the cat would have learned that pressing the paddle was associated with the desirable consequence of getting food. Thorndike summarized that relationship by formulating the *law of effect,* which states that responses that are satisfying are more likely to be repeated, and those that are not satisfying are less likely to be repeated.

Thorndike believed that the law of effect operated as automatically as leaves falling off a tree in autumn. It was not necessary for an organism to understand that there was a link between a response and a reward. Instead, he thought that over time and through experience, the organism would make a direct connection between the stimulus and the response without any awareness that the connection existed.

The Basics of Operant Conditioning

Thorndike's early research served as the foundation for the work of one of the most influential psychologists, B. F. Skinner, who died in 1990. You may have

heard of the Skinner box (shown in one form in Figure 5-3), a chamber with a highly controlled environment used to study operant conditioning processes with laboratory animals. Whereas Thorndike's goal was to get his cats to learn to obtain food by leaving the box, animals in a Skinner box learn to obtain food by operating on their environment within the box. Skinner became interested in specifying how behavior varied as a result of alterations in the environment.

Skinner, whose work went far beyond perfecting Thorndike's earlier apparatus, is considered the father of a whole generation of psychologists studying operant conditioning (Delprato & Midgley, 1992; Bjork, 1993). To illustrate Skinner's contribution, let's consider what happens to a pigeon in the typical Skinner box.

Suppose you want to teach a hungry pigeon to peck a key that is located in its box. At first the pigeon will wander around the box, exploring the environment in a relatively random fashion. At some point, however, it will probably peck the key by chance, and when it does, it will receive a food pellet. The first time this happens, the pigeon will not learn the connection between pecking and receiving food and will continue to explore the box. Sooner or later the pigeon will again peck the key and receive a pellet, and in time the frequency of the pecking response will increase. Eventually, the pigeon will peck the key continually until it satisfies its hunger, thereby demonstrating that it has learned that the receipt of food is contingent on the pecking behavior.

Reinforcing Desired Behavior   Skinner called the process that leads the pigeon to continue pecking the key "reinforcement." **Reinforcement** is the process by which a stimulus increases the probability that a preceding behavior will be repeated. In other words, pecking is more likely to occur again due to the stimulus of food.

In a situation such as this one, the food is called a reinforcer. A **reinforcer** is any stimulus that increases the probability that a preceding behavior will occur

Reinforcement: The process by which a stimulus increases the probability that a preceding behavior will be repeated

Reinforcer: Any stimulus that increases the probability that a preceding behavior will be repeated

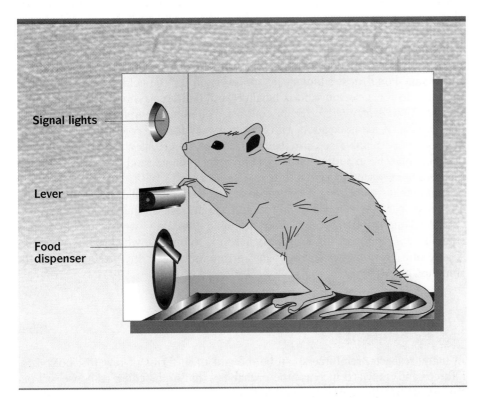

Signal lights

Lever

Food dispenser

FIGURE 5-3 A Skinner box, used to study operant conditioning. Laboratory animals learn to press the lever in order to obtain food, which is delivered in the tray.

*"Oh, not bad. The light comes on, I press the bar, they write me a check.
How about you?"*

Drawing by Cheney; © 1993 The New Yorker Magazine, Inc.

again. Hence, food is a reinforcer because it increases the probability that the behavior of pecking the key (formally referred to as the *response* of pecking) will
take place.

What kind of stimuli can act as reinforcers? Bonuses, toys, and good grades
can serve as reinforcers—if they strengthen a response that comes before their
introduction. In each case, it is critical that the organism learn that the delivery
of the reinforcer is contingent on the response occurring in the first place.

Of course, we are not born knowing that 75 cents can buy us a candy bar.
Rather, through experience we learn that money is a valuable commodity because
of its association with stimuli, such as food, drink, and shelter, that are naturally
reinforcing. This fact suggests a distinction that can be drawn regarding whether
something is a primary reinforcer or a secondary reinforcer. A *primary reinforcer*
satisfies some biological need and works naturally, regardless of a person's prior
experience. Food for the hungry person, warmth for the cold person, and cessation of pain for a person who is hurting would all be classified as primary reinforcers. A *secondary reinforcer,* in contrast, is a stimulus that becomes reinforcing because of its association with a primary reinforcer. For instance, we know
that money is valuable because we have learned that it allows us to obtain other
desirable objects, including primary reinforcers such as food and shelter. Money
thus becomes a secondary reinforcer.

What makes something a reinforcer depends on individual preferences. While
a Hershey bar may act as a reinforcer for one person, an individual who dislikes
chocolate might find 75 cents more desirable. The only way we can know if a
stimulus is a reinforcer for a given organism is to observe whether the rate of response of a previously occurring behavior increases after the presentation of the
stimulus.

Positive Reinforcers, Negative Reinforcers, and Punishment

In many respects, reinforcers can be thought of in terms of rewards; both a reinforcer and a reward increase the probability that a preceding response will occur again. But the term "reward" is limited to *positive* occurrences, and this is

where it differs from a reinforcer—for it turns out that reinforcers can be positive or negative.

A **positive reinforcer** is a stimulus added to the environment that brings about an increase in a preceding response. If food, water, money, or praise is provided following a response, it is more likely that that response will occur again in the future. The paycheck that workers get at the end of the week, for example, increases the likelihood they will return to their jobs the following week.

In contrast, a **negative reinforcer** refers to a stimulus that removes something unpleasant from the environment, leading to an increase in the probability that a preceding response will occur again in the future. For example, if you have cold symptoms that are relieved when you take medicine, you are more likely to take the medicine (a negative reinforcer) when you experience such symptoms again. Similarly, if the radio is too loud and hurts your ears, you are likely to find that turning it down relieves the problem. Lowering the volume is negatively reinforcing and you are more apt to repeat the action in the future. Negative reinforcement, then, teaches the individual that taking an action removes a negative condition that exists in the environment. Like positive reinforcers, negative reinforcers increase the likelihood that preceding behavior will be repeated.

Negative reinforcement occurs in two major forms of learning: escape conditioning and avoidance conditioning. In *escape conditioning,* an organism learns to make a response that brings about an end to an aversive situation. Escape conditioning is commonplace, and it often occurs quickly. For example, it doesn't take too long for children to learn to withdraw their hands from a hot radiator—an example of escape conditioning. Similarly, busy college students who take a day off to elude the stress of too heavy a workload are showing escape conditioning.

In contrast to escape conditioning, *avoidance conditioning* occurs when an organism responds to a signal of an impending unpleasant event in a way that permits its evasion. For example, a rat will readily learn to tap a bar to avoid a shock that is signaled by a tone. Similarly, automobile drivers learn to fill up their gas tanks in order to avoid running out of fuel.

It is important to note that, whether negative reinforcement consists of escape or avoidance conditioning, it is not the same as punishment. **Punishment** refers to unpleasant or painful stimuli that decrease the probability that a preceding behavior will occur again. In contrast, negative reinforcement is associated with the removal of an unpleasant or painful stimulus, which produces an *increase* in the behavior that brought an end to the unpleasant stimulus. If we receive a shock after behaving in a particular fashion, then, we are receiving punishment; but if we are already receiving a shock and do something to stop that shock, the behavior that stops the shock is considered to be negatively reinforced. In the first case, a specific behavior is apt to decrease because of the punishment; in the second, it is likely to increase because of the negative reinforcement (Azrin & Holt, 1966).

While punishment is typically considered in terms of applying some aversive stimulus—a spanking for misbehaving or 10 years in jail for committing a crime—it may also consist of the removal of something positive. For instance, when a teenager is told she will no longer be able to use the family car because of her poor grades, or when an employee is informed that he has been demoted with a cut in pay because of poor job evaluations, punishment in the form of the removal of a positive reinforcer is being administered.

The distinctions between the types of punishment, as well as positive and negative reinforcement, may appear confusing initially, but the following rules of thumb (and the summary in Table 5-1) can help you to distinguish these concepts from one another:

■ Reinforcement *increases* the behavior preceding it; punishment *decreases* the behavior preceding it.

Positive reinforcer: A stimulus added to the environment that brings about an increase in the response that preceded it

Negative reinforcer: A stimulus whose removal is reinforcing, leading to a greater probability that the response bringing about this removal will occur again

Punishment: An unpleasant or painful stimulus that is added to the environment after a certain behavior occurs, decreasing the likelihood that the behavior will occur again

Nature of Stimulus	Application	Removal or Termination
Positive (pleasant)	*Positive reinforcement* Example: Giving a raise for good performance Result: *Increase* in frequency of response (good performance)	*Punishment by removal* Example: Removal of favorite toy after misbehavior Result: *Decrease* in frequency of response (misbehavior)
Negative (unpleasant)	*Punishment by application* Example: Giving a spanking following misbehavior Result: *Decrease* in frequency of response (misbehavior)	*Negative reinforcement* Example: Terminating a headache by taking aspirin Result: *Increase* in frequency of response (taking aspirin)

TABLE 5-1   Types of Reinforcement and Punishment

■ The *application* of a *positive* stimulus brings about an increase in behavior and is referred to as positive reinforcement; the *removal* of a *positive* stimulus decreases behavior and is called punishment by removal.

■ The *application* of a *negative* stimulus decreases or reduces behavior and is called punishment by application; the *removal* of a *negative* stimulus that results in an increase in behavior is termed negative reinforcement.

The Pros and Cons of Punishment: Why Reinforcement Beats Punishment

Is punishment an effective means of modifying behavior? Punishment often presents the quickest route to changing behavior that, if allowed to continue, might be dangerous to an individual. For instance, a parent may not have a second chance to warn a child not to run into a busy street, so punishing the first incidence of this behavior might prove to be wise. Moreover, the use of punishment to suppress behavior, even temporarily, provides the opportunity to reinforce a person for subsequently behaving in a more desirable way.

There are some instances in which punishment may be the most humane approach to treating certain deep-seated psychological problems. For example, some children suffer from autism, a rare psychological disorder in which they may abuse themselves by tearing at their skin or banging their heads against the wall, injuring themselves severely in the process. In such cases, punishment in the form of a quick but intense electric shock has been used, sometimes with remarkable results, to prevent self-injurious behavior when all other treatments have failed (Lovaas & Koegel, 1973; Linscheid et al., 1990). Such punishment, however, is used only as a treatment of last resort to keep the child safe and to buy time until positive reinforcement procedures can be initiated.

Several disadvantages make the routine use of punishment questionable. For one thing, it is frequently ineffective, particularly if the punishment is not delivered shortly after the individual exhibits the unwanted behavior or if the individual is able to withdraw from the setting in which the punishment is being given. An employee who is reprimanded by the boss may quit; a teenager who loses the use of the family car may borrow a friend's instead. In such instances, then, the initial behavior that is being punished may be replaced by one that is even less desirable.

Even worse, physical punishment may convey to the recipient the idea that physical aggression is permissible and perhaps even desirable. A father who yells at and hits his son for misbehaving teaches the son that aggression is an appropriate, adult response. The son may soon copy his father's behavior by acting aggressively toward others. In addition, physical punishment is often administered

Despite its known disadvantages, punishment is frequently employed in a variety of situations.

by people who are themselves angry or enraged. It is unlikely that individuals in such an emotional state will be able to think through what they are doing or to carefully control the degree of punishment they are inflicting. Ultimately, those who resort to physical punishment run the risk that they will grow to be feared.

Another disadvantage of punishment is that unless people who are being punished can be made to understand the reasons for it (i.e., that the punishment is meant to change behavior and that it has nothing to do with the punishers' view of them as individuals), punishment may lead to lowered self-esteem.

Finally, punishment does not convey any information about what an alternative, more appropriate behavior might be. In order to be useful in bringing about more desirable behavior in the future, punishment must be accompanied by specific information about the behavior that is being punished, along with specific suggestions concerning a more desirable behavior. To punish a child for staring out the window in school may lead her to stare at the floor instead. Unless we teach her appropriate ways to respond, we have merely managed to substitute one undesirable behavior for another. If punishment is not followed up with reinforcement for subsequent behavior that is more appropriate, little will be accomplished.

In sum, reinforcing desired behavior is a more appropriate technique for modifying behavior than using punishment. Both in and out of the scientific arena, then, reinforcement usually beats punishment (Sulzer-Azaroff & Mayer, 1991).

Schedules of Reinforcement: Timing Life's Rewards

The world would be a different place if poker players folded for good at their first losing hand, fishermen returned to shore as soon as they missed a catch, or door-to-door salespeople stopped selling at the first house at which they were turned

away. The fact that such unreinforced behaviors continue, often with great frequency and persistence, illustrates that reinforcement need not be received continually in order for behavior to be learned and maintained. In fact, behavior that is reinforced only occasionally may ultimately be learned better than behavior that is always reinforced.

When we refer to the frequency and timing of reinforcement following desired behavior, we are talking about **schedules of reinforcement.** Behavior that is reinforced every time it occurs is said to be on a **continuous reinforcement schedule;** if it is reinforced some but not all of the time, it is on a **partial reinforcement schedule.** Although learning occurs more rapidly under a continuous reinforcement schedule, behavior lasts longer after reinforcement stops when it is learned under a partial reinforcement schedule.

Why should partial reinforcement schedules result in stronger, longer-lasting learning than continuous reinforcement schedules? We can answer the question by examining how we might behave when using a soda vending machine compared with a Las Vegas slot machine. When we use a vending machine, prior experience has taught us that every time we put in 75 cents, the reinforcement, a soda, ought to be delivered. In other words, the schedule of reinforcement is continuous. In comparison, a slot machine offers a partial reinforcement schedule. We have learned that after putting in 75 cents, most of the time we will not receive anything in return. At the same time, though, we know that we will occasionally win something.

Now suppose that, unbeknownst to us, both the soda vending machine and the slot machine are broken, so that neither one is able to dispense anything. It would not be very long before we stopped depositing coins into the broken soda machine. Probably at most we would try only two or three times before leaving the machine in disgust. But the story would be quite different with the broken slot machine. Here, we would drop in money for a considerably longer time, even though no response would be forthcoming.

In formal terms, we can see the difference between the two reinforcement schedules: Partial reinforcement schedules (such as those provided by slot machines) maintain performance longer than continuous reinforcement schedules (such as those established in soda vending machines) before extinction, the disappearance of the conditioned response, occurs.

Using a *cumulative recorder,* a device that automatically records and graphs the pattern of responses made in reaction to a particular schedule, learning psychologists have found that certain kinds of partial reinforcement schedules produce stronger and lengthier responding before extinction than others do (King & Logue, 1990). Although many different partial reinforcement schedules have been examined, they can most readily be put into two categories: schedules that consider the *number of responses* made before reinforcement is given, called fixed-ratio and variable-ratio schedules, and those that consider the *amount of time* that elapses before reinforcement is provided, called fixed-interval and variable-interval schedules.

Schedules of reinforcement: The frequency and timing of reinforcement following desired behavior

Continuous reinforcement schedule: The reinforcing of a behavior every time it occurs

Partial reinforcement schedule: The reinforcing of a behavior some but not all of the time

Fixed- and Variable-Ratio Schedules   In a **fixed-ratio schedule,** reinforcement is given only after a certain number of responses are made. For instance, a pigeon might receive a food pellet every tenth time it pecked a key; here, the ratio would be 1:10. Similarly, garment workers are generally paid on fixed-ratio schedules: They receive *x* dollars for every blouse they sew. Because a greater rate of production means more reinforcement, people on fixed-ratio schedules are apt to work as quickly as possible. Even when rewards are no longer offered, responding comes in bursts—although pauses between bursts become longer and longer until the response peters out entirely (see Figure 5-4).

In a **variable-ratio schedule,** reinforcement occurs after a varying number of responses rather than after a fixed number. Although the specific number of re-

Fixed-ratio schedule: A schedule whereby reinforcement is given only after a certain number of responses is made

Variable-ratio schedule: A schedule whereby reinforcement occurs after a varying number of responses rather than after a fixed number

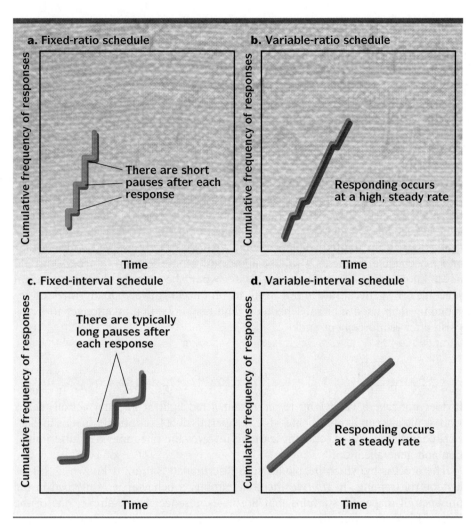

a. Fixed-ratio schedule

Cumulative frequency of responses

Time

There are short pauses after each response

b. Variable-ratio schedule

Cumulative frequency of responses

Time

Responding occurs at a high, steady rate

c. Fixed-interval schedule

Cumulative frequency of responses

Time

There are typically long pauses after each response

d. Variable-interval schedule

Cumulative frequency of responses

Time

Responding occurs at a steady rate

FIGURE 5-4 Typical outcomes of different reinforcement schedules. (*a*) In a fixed-ratio schedule, short pauses occur following each response. Because the more responses, the more reinforcement, fixed-ratio schedules produce a high rate of responding. (*b*) In a variable-ratio schedule, responding also occurs at a high rate. (*c*) A fixed-interval schedule produces lower rates of responding, especially just after reinforcement has been presented, since the organism learns that a specified time period must elapse between reinforcement. (*d*) A variable-interval schedule produces a fairly steady stream of responses.

sponses necessary to receive reinforcement varies, the number of responses usually hovers around a specific average. Probably the best example of a variable-ratio schedule is that encountered by a door-to-door salesperson. She may make a sale at the third, eighth, ninth, and twentieth houses she visits without being successful at any of the houses in between. Although the number of responses that must be made before making a sale varies, it averages out to a 20 percent success rate. Under these circumstances, you might expect that the salesperson would try to make as many calls as possible in as short a time as possible. This is the case with all variable-ratio schedules; they promote a high rate of response and a high degree of resistance to extinction.

Fixed- and Variable-Interval Schedules: The Passage of Time   In contrast to fixed- and variable-ratio schedules, in which the crucial factor is the number of responses, fixed-*interval* and variable-*interval* schedules focus on the amount of *time* that has elapsed since a person or animal was rewarded. One example of a fixed-interval schedule is a weekly paycheck. For people who receive regular, weekly paychecks, it typically makes little difference how much they produce in a given week—as long as they show up and do some work.

Because a **fixed-interval schedule** provides reinforcement for a response only if a fixed time period has elapsed, overall rates of response are relatively low. This is especially true in the period just after reinforcement when the time before another reinforcement is relatively great. Students' study habits often exemplify this

Fixed-interval schedule: A schedule whereby reinforcement is given at established time intervals

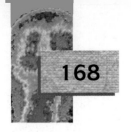

reality. If the periods between exams are relatively long (meaning that the opportunity for reinforcement for good performance is fairly infrequent), students often study minimally or not at all until the day of the exam draws near. Just before the exam, however, students begin to cram for it, signaling a rapid increase in the rate of their studying response (Mawhinney et al., 1971). As you might expect, immediately following the exam there is a rapid decline in the rate of responding, with few people opening a book the day after a test.

One way to decrease the delay in responding that occurs just after reinforcement, and to maintain the desired behavior more consistently throughout an interval, is to use a variable-interval schedule. In a **variable-interval schedule,** the time between reinforcements varies around some average rather than being fixed. For example, a professor who gives surprise quizzes that vary from one every 3 days to one every 3 weeks, averaging one every 2 weeks, is using a variable-interval schedule. Students' study habits would most likely be very different as a result of such an unpredictable schedule than those we observed with a fixed-interval schedule. Students would be apt to study more regularly since they would never know when the next surprise quiz would be coming. Variable-interval schedules, in general, are more likely to produce relatively steady rates of responding than fixed-interval schedules, with responses that take longer to extinguish after reinforcement ends.

> **Variable-interval schedule:** A schedule whereby reinforcement varies around some average rather than being fixed

Discrimination and Generalization in Operant Conditioning

It does not take a child long to learn that a red light at an intersection means stop, while a green light indicates that it is permissible to continue. Just as in classical conditioning, then, operant learning involves the phenomena of discrimination and generalization.

The process by which people learn to discriminate stimuli is known as stimulus control training. In *stimulus control training,* a behavior is reinforced in the presence of a specific stimulus, but not in its absence. For example, one of the most difficult discriminations many people face is determining when someone's friendliness is not mere friendliness, but a signal of romantic interest. People learn to make the discrimination by observing the presence of certain subtle nonverbal cues—such as increased eye contact and touching—that indicate romantic interest. When such cues are absent, people learn that no romantic interest is indicated. In this case, the nonverbal cue acts as a discriminative stimulus, one to which an organism learns to respond during stimulus control training. A *discriminative stimulus* signals the likelihood that reinforcement will follow a response. For example, if you wait until your roommate is in a good mood before you ask to borrow her favorite compact disc, your behavior can be said to be under stimulus control since you can discriminate between her moods.

Just as in classical conditioning, the phenomenon of stimulus generalization, in which an organism learns a response to one stimulus and then applies it to other stimuli, is also found in operant conditioning. If you have learned that being polite produces the reinforcement of getting your way in a certain situation, you are likely to generalize your response to other situations. Sometimes, though, generalization can have unfortunate consequences, such as when people behave negatively toward all members of a racial group because they have had an unpleasant experience with one member of that group.

Superstitious Behavior

■ At the University of Illinois, students taking exams in the auditorium of Lincoln Hall first rub the nose of a bust of Lincoln for good luck.

■ On exam days, students at Miami University avoid walking on a school seal that is embedded in the sidewalk.

■ One student at Albright College in Reading, Pennsylvania, was taking an introductory psychology class in a room that was partially underground. Whenever there was an exam, he entered the room by climbing through the window (Vyse, 1994).

While it is easy to sneer at such rituals, learning psychologists consider them as examples of an interesting class of responses called *superstitious behavior*. Such behavior can be explained in terms of the basic principles of reinforcement (Zimmer, 1984; Justice & Looney, 1990). As we have discussed, behavior that is followed by a reinforcer tends to be strengthened. Occasionally, however, the behavior that occurs prior to the reinforcement is entirely coincidental. Imagine, for instance, that a baseball player hits his bat against the ground three times in a row just before getting a single. The hit is, of course, coincidental to the batter's hitting the ground, but to the player it may be seen as somehow related. Because the player makes this association, he may hit the ground three times every time he is at bat in the future. And because he will be at least partially reinforced for this behavior—batters usually get a hit 25 percent of the time—his ground-hitting behavior will probably be maintained.

Do superstitions actually affect subsequent behavior? In fact, they do. According to some psychologists, superstitious behavior allows people to cope with anxiety by providing routines or rituals that can give them a sense of control over a situation (Zimmer, 1984). In this way, touching the nose of a statue may help calm a person—which, in fact, may lead to better performance when taking a test or going through a stressful interview. Our superstitions, then, may shape our subsequent behavior.

Superstitious behavior, such as being careful to avoid stepping on cracks in the sidewalk, may be the result of reinforcement that occurs coincidentally.

Shaping: Reinforcing What Doesn't Come Naturally

Consider the difficulty of using operant conditioning to teach people to repair an automobile transmission. If you had to wait until they fixed it perfectly before you provided them with reinforcement, the Model T might be back in style long before they ever mastered the repair process.

There are many complex behaviors, ranging from auto repair to zither playing, which we would not expect to occur naturally as part of anyone's spontaneous behavior. In cases such as these, in which there might otherwise be no opportunity to provide reinforcement for the particular behavior (since it never occurs in the first place), a procedure known as shaping is used. **Shaping** is the process of teaching a complex behavior by rewarding closer and closer approximations of the desired behavior. In shaping, any behavior that is at all similar to the behavior you want the person to learn is reinforced at first. Later, you reinforce only responses that are closer to the behavior you ultimately want to teach. Finally, you reinforce only the desired response. Each step in shaping, then, moves only slightly beyond the previously learned behavior, permitting the person to link the new step to the behavior learned earlier.

Shaping allows even nonhumans to learn complex responses that would never occur naturally, ranging from lions trained to jump through hoops to dolphins trained to rescue divers lost at sea. Shaping also underlies the learning of many complex human skills. For instance, the organization of most textbooks is based on the principles of shaping. Typically, information is presented so that new material builds on previously learned concepts or skills. Thus the concept of shaping could not be presented in this chapter until we had discussed the more basic principles of operant learning. (For a further discussion of the applications of psychological approaches to learning, see the accompanying Pathways through Psychology box).

Shaping: The process of teaching a complex behavior by rewarding closer and closer approximations of the desired behavior

The whale used in the movie "Free Willy" was trained using the principles of operant conditioning.

169

PATHWAYS THROUGH PSYCHOLOGY

Lynne Calero
Dolphin Research Center, Grassy Key, Florida

Born: 1951
Education: B.A. in psychology, George Washington University
Home: Big Pine Key, Florida

Many people have read about the possible connections between dolphins and humans in terms of both behavior and intellect, but for more than a decade Lynne Calero has seen these similarities firsthand.

Currently the medical director of the Dolphin Research Center in Grassy Key, Florida, Calero received her basic exposure to psychology as an undergraduate major at George Washington University in Washington, DC. "Our facility is a research education facility in which we do training to educate the public, as well as monitoring individual animals' health," she says.

Lynne Calero.

In training dolphins, Calero makes use of the basic principles of learning. "The whole basis of the training done with dolphins and sea lions is based on operant conditioning and positive reinforcement," she notes.

For instance, one specific type of training involves a series of steps to get the dolphin to learn to present its tail flukes, thereby permitting medical tests that require blood samples. "All the animals first learn the basics, such as responding to a whistle. The whistle then becomes a secondary reinforcer that is connected with feeding, giving attention, or a back rub.

"From there we gradually get them to position alongside of the dock," she explains, "followed by a series of approximations, as in training with any behavior. With each step we get closer to the tail flukes until the dolphin allows us to hold onto the flukes above the water surface."

Younger dolphins are easier to train, and it takes just a month of training before they will present their flukes. To Calero, this is one example of the unusual intelligence of dolphins. "Certainly their brain anatomy is very complicated. Overall, my impression is that dolphins are incredibly intelligent, as well as being intensely intuitive and wise."

Biological Constraints on Learning: You Can't Teach an Old Dog Just Any Trick

Keller and Marian Breland were pleased with their idea: As consultants to professional animal trainers, they came up with the notion of having a pig place a wooden disk into a piggy bank. With their experience in training animals through operant conditioning, they thought the task would be easy to teach, given that it was certainly well within the range of the pig's physical capabilities. Yet every time they tried out the procedure, it failed. Upon viewing the disk, the pigs were willing to do nothing but root the wooden disk along the ground. Apparently, the pigs were biologically programmed to push stimuli in the shape of disks along the ground.

Their lack of swine success led the Brelands to substitute a raccoon. Although the procedure worked fine with one disk, when two disks were used, the raccoon refused to deposit either of them and instead rubbed the two together, as if it were washing them. Once again, it appeared that the disks evoked biologically innate behaviors that were impossible to supplant with even the most exhaustive training (Breland & Breland, 1961).

The Brelands' difficulties illustrate an important point: Not all behaviors can be trained in all species equally well. Instead, there are *biological constraints,* built-in limitations, in the ability of animals to learn particular behaviors. In some cases, an organism will have a special bent that will aid in its learning a behavior

170

(such as behaviors that involve pecking in pigeons); in other cases, biological constraints will act to prevent or inhibit an organism from learning a behavior. In either instance, it is clear that animals have specialized learning mechanisms that influence how readily both classical and operant conditioning function, and each species is biologically primed to develop particular kinds of associations and to face obstacles in learning others (Hollis, 1984).

RECAP AND REVIEW

Recap

- Operant conditioning is a form of learning in which a voluntary response is strengthened or weakened, depending on its positive or negative consequences.
- Reinforcement is the process by which a stimulus increases the probability that a preceding behavior will be repeated.
- A positive reinforcer is a stimulus that is added to the environment to increase the likelihood of a response. A negative reinforcer is a stimulus that removes something unpleasant from the environment, leading to an increase in the probability that a preceding response will occur in the future.
- Punishment involves the administration of an unpleasant stimulus, following a response, which is meant to decrease or suppress behavior; it may also consist of the removal of a positive reinforcer.
- In punishment, the goal is to decrease or suppress undesired behavior by administering a stimulus; in negative reinforcement, the goal is to increase a desired behavior by removing a stimulus.
- Reinforcement need not be constant in order for behavior to be learned and maintained; partial schedules of reinforcement, in fact, lead to greater resistance to extinction than continuous schedules of reinforcement.
- Generalization, discrimination, and shaping are among the basic phenomena of operant conditioning.

Review

1. _____ conditioning describes learning that occurs as a result of reinforcement.
2. A hungry person would find food to be a _____ reinforcer, while a $10 bill would be a _____ reinforcer.
3. Match the type of operant learning with its definition:
   1. An unpleasant stimulus is presented to decrease behavior.
   2. An unpleasant stimulus is removed to increase behavior.
   3. A pleasant stimulus is presented to increase behavior.

   a. Positive reinforcement
   b. Negative reinforcement
   c. Punishment
4. Sandy had had a rough day, and his son's noisemaking was not helping him relax. Not wanting to resort to scolding, Sandy lowered his tone of voice and told his son in a serious manner that he was very tired and would like the boy to play quietly for an hour. This approach worked. For Sandy, the change in his son's behavior was
   a. positively reinforcing
   b. secondarily reinforcing
   c. punishing
   d. negatively reinforcing
5. Sandy was pleased. He had not been happy with himself a week earlier, when he had yelled loudly at his son. On that occasion he had halted his son's excessive noise through
   a. removal of a reinforcer
   b. punishment
   c. negative reinforcement
   d. extinction
6. In a _____ reinforcement schedule, behavior is reinforced some of the time, while in a _____ reinforcement schedule, behavior is reinforced all the time.
7. Match the type of reinforcement schedule with its definition.
   1. Reinforcement occurs after a set time period.
   2. Reinforcement occurs after a set number of responses.
   3. Reinforcement occurs after a varying time period.
   4. Reinforcement occurs after a varying number of responses.

   a. Fixed ratio
   b. Variable interval
   c. Fixed interval
   d. Variable ratio
8. Fixed reinforcement schedules produce greater resistance to extinction than variable reinforcement schedules. True or false?

Ask Yourself

B. F. Skinner believed that a person's entire life could be structured according to operant conditioning principles. Do you think this is possible? What benefits and problems would result?

George Steinbrenner, owner of the Yankees, is upset! He thinks that baseball star Wade Boggs, who displays a considerable amount of superstitious behavior on the playing field, should end his rituals. What techniques might you suggest to Steinbrenner to "cure" Boggs.

(Answers to review questions are on page 172.)

- *What is the role of cognition and thought in learning?*
- *What are some practical methods for bringing about behavior change, both in ourselves and in others?*

COGNITIVE APPROACHES TO LEARNING

Consider what happens when people learn to drive a car. They don't just get behind the wheel and stumble around until they randomly put the key into the ignition, and later, after many false starts, accidentally manage to get the car to move forward, thereby receiving positive reinforcement. Instead, they already know the basic elements of driving from prior experience as a passenger, in which they more than likely noticed how the key was inserted into the ignition, the car put in drive, and the gas pedal pressed for the car to go forward.

Clearly, not all learning is due to operant and classical conditioning. In fact, instances such as learning to drive a car imply that some kinds of learning must involve higher-order processes in which people's thoughts and memories and the way they process information account for their responses. Such situations argue against a perspective that regards learning as the unthinking, mechanical, and automatic acquisition of associations between stimuli and responses, as in classical conditioning. Or that it may be a consequence of the presentation of reinforcement, as in operant conditioning.

Cognitive learning theory: The study of the thought processes that underlie learning

Instead, some psychologists view learning in terms of the thought processes, or cognitions, that underlie it—an approach known as **cognitive learning theory.** Although psychologists using cognitive learning theory do not deny the importance of classical and operant conditioning, they have developed approaches that focus on the unseen mental processes that occur during learning, rather than concentrating solely on external stimuli, responses, and reinforcements.

In its most basic formulation, cognitive learning theory suggests that it is not enough to say that people make responses because there is an assumed link between a stimulus and a response due to a past history of reinforcement for the response. Instead, according to this point of view, people—and even animals—develop an *expectation* that they will receive a reinforcer upon making a response. Support for this point of view comes from several quarters.

Latent Learning

Latent learning: Learning in which a new behavior is acquired but not readily demonstrated until reinforcement is provided

Some of the most direct evidence regarding cognitive processes comes from a series of experiments that revealed a type of cognitive learning called latent learning. In **latent learning,** a new behavior is learned but is not demonstrated until reinforcement is provided for displaying it (Tolman & Honzik, 1930). In the studies, psychologists examined the behavior of rats in a maze such as the one shown in Figure 5-5a. In one representative experiment, a group of rats was allowed to wander around the maze once a day for 17 days without ever receiving any reward. Understandably, these rats made many errors and spent a relatively long time reaching the end of the maze. A second group, however, was always given food at the end of the maze. Not surprisingly, these rats learned to run quickly and directly to the food box, making few errors.

A third group of rats started out in the same situation as the unrewarded rats, but only for the first 10 days. On the eleventh day, a critical experimental ma-

---

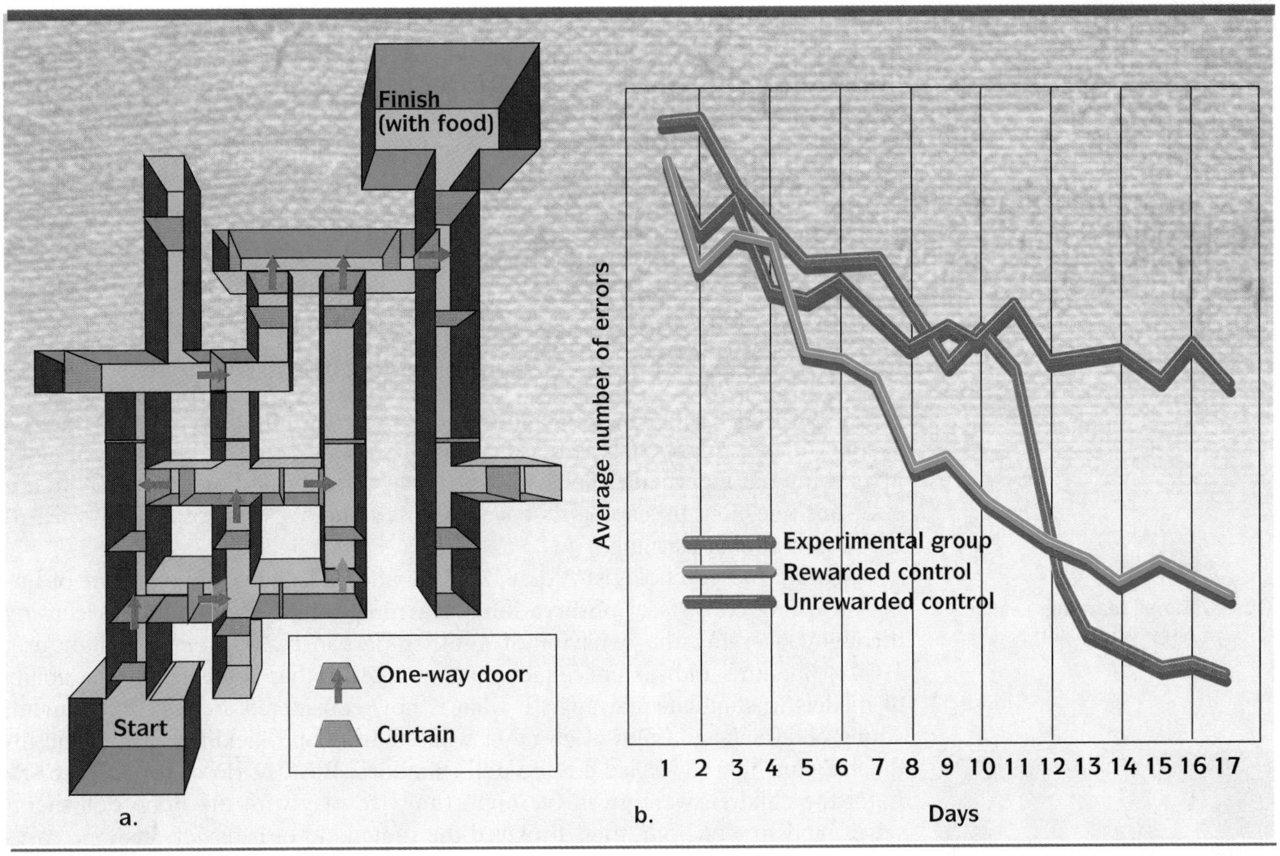
Finish
(with food)
Start
One-way door
Curtain
a.
Average number of errors
Experimental group
Rewarded control
Unrewarded control
1 2 3 4 5 6 7 8 9 10 11 12 13 14 15 16 17
b.
Days

FIGURE 5-5 *(a)* In an attempt to demonstrate latent learning, rats were allowed to roam through a maze of this sort once a day for 17 days. *(b)* Those rats that were never rewarded (the nonrewarded control condition) consistently made the most errors, whereas those that received food at the finish every day (the rewarded control condition) made far fewer errors. But the results also showed latent learning: Rats that were initially unrewarded but began to be rewarded only after the tenth day (the experimental group) showed an immediate reduction in errors and soon became similar to the error rate of the rats that had been consistently rewarded. According to cognitive learning theorists, the reduction in errors indicates that the rats had developed a cognitive map—a mental representation—of the maze. *(Tolman & Honzik, 1930.)*

nipulation was instituted: From that point on, the rats in this group were given food for completing the maze. The results of this manipulation were dramatic, as you can see from the graph in Figure 5-5*b*. The previously unrewarded rats, who had earlier seemed to wander about aimlessly, showed reductions in running time and declines in error rates such that their performance almost immediately matched that of the group that had received rewards from the start.

To cognitive theorists, it seemed clear that the unrewarded rats had learned the layout of the maze early in their explorations; they just never displayed their latent learning until the reinforcement was offered. The rats seemed to develop a **cognitive map** of the maze—a mental representation of spatial locations and directions.

Cognitive map: A mental representation of spatial locations and directions

People, too, develop cognitive maps of their surroundings, based primarily on particular landmarks (Garling, 1989). When they first encounter a new environment, their maps tend to rely on specific paths—such as the directions we might give someone unfamiliar with an area: "Turn right at the stop sign, make a left at the bridge, and then go up the hill." However, as people become more familiar with an area, they develop an overall conception of it—a cognitive map. Using such a map, they are eventually able to take shortcuts as they develop a broad understanding of the area (Gale et al., 1990).

Unfortunately, though, our cognitive maps are often riddled with errors, representing simplifications of the actual terrain. We tend to develop maps that ignore curving roads and instead conceive of areas in terms of straight grids of intersecting roadways (Tversky, 1981). Our cognitive maps, then, are imperfect versions of actual maps.

Despite their inadequacies, the possibility that we develop our cognitive maps through latent learning presents something of a problem for strict operant con-

ditioning theorists. If we consider the results of Tolman's maze experiment, for instance, it is unclear what the specific reinforcement was that permitted the rats that received no reward to initially learn about the layout of the maze, since there was no obvious reinforcer present. Instead, the results support a cognitive view of learning, in which learning may have resulted in changes in unobservable mental processes.

Observational Learning: Learning through Imitation

Let's return for a moment to the case of a person learning to drive. How can we account for instances such as these in which someone with no direct experience in carrying out a particular behavior learns the behavior and then does it? To answer this question, psychologists have proposed another form of cognitive learning: observational learning.

Observational learning: Learning through observations of others (models)

According to psychologist Albert Bandura and colleagues, a major part of human learning consists of **observational learning,** which they define as learning through observing the behavior of another person called a *model* (Bandura, 1977). Bandura and his colleagues demonstrated rather dramatically the ability of models to stimulate learning. In what is now considered a classic experiment, young children saw a film of an adult wildly hitting and kicking a 5-foot-tall inflatable punching toy called a Bobo doll (Bandura, Ross, & Ross, 1963a, 1963b). Later the children were given the opportunity to play with the Bobo doll themselves, and sure enough, they displayed the same kind of behavior, in some cases mimicking the aggressive behavior almost identically.

Not only negative behaviors are acquired through observational learning. In one experiment, for example, children who were afraid of dogs were exposed to a model—dubbed the Fearless Peer—playing with a dog (Bandura, Grusec, & Menlove, 1967). Following exposure, observers were considerably more likely to approach a strange dog than children who had not viewed the Fearless Peer.

According to Bandura, observational learning takes place in four steps: (1) paying attention and perceiving the most critical features of another person's behavior, (2) remembering the behavior, (3) reproducing the action, and (4) being motivated to learn and carry out the behavior. Instead of learning occurring through trial and error, then, with successes being reinforced and failures punished, many important skills are learned through observational processes (Bandura, 1986).

Observational learning is particularly important in acquiring skills in which shaping is inappropriate. Piloting an airplane and performing brain surgery, for example, would hardly be behaviors that could be learned using trial-and-error methods without grave cost—literally—to those involved in the learning.

Not all behavior that we witness is learned or carried out, of course. One crucial factor that determines whether we later imitate a model is the consequences of the model's behavior. If we observe a friend being rewarded for putting more time into her studies by receiving higher grades, we are more likely to model her behavior than if her behavior results in no improvement in her grades but rather greater fatigue and less of a social life. Models who are rewarded for behaving in a particular way are more apt to be mimicked than models who receive punishment. Interestingly, though, observing the punishment of a model does not necessarily stop observers from learning the behavior. Observers can still recount the model's behavior—they are just less apt to perform it (Bandura, 1977, 1986).

The photographs above are from the film used in Bandura's observational learning experiments: A model is shown kicking a Bobo doll. In the middle and bottom photos, a young boy and girl left alone with the doll imitate the behaviors they had seen in the film.

Observational learning is at the center of a controversy regarding the effects of exposure to violence and sex in the media. We discuss what psychologists have learned about this topic in the Psychology at Work box.

PSYCHOLOGY AT WORK

Violence on Television and Film: Does the Media's Message Matter?

Beavis and Butthead, MTV cartoon characters, discuss how much fun it is to set fires. On one occasion, one of them lights a fire in the other's hair by using aerosol spray cans and matches.

Later, 5-year-old Austin Messner, who had watched the cartoon, sets his bed on fire with a cigarette lighter. Although he and his mother escape the subsequent blaze, his younger sister dies.

In a scene from the 1993 film *The Program*, as cars and trucks speed by in both directions, a character lies down on the center line of a highway at night to demonstrate his toughness. In the movie, he walks away unscathed, proving that he's afraid of nothing.

Real life is a little different: Soon after watching the movie, several teenagers are killed in separate incidents in which they lay in the center of a darkened road and were run over by oncoming traffic. (Hinds, 1993)

Does observation of violence and antisocial acts in the media lead viewers to behave in similar ways? Because research on modeling shows that people frequently learn and imitate the aggression they observe, this question is among the most important ones being addressed by social psychologists.

Certainly, the amount of violence in the mass media is enormous. The average American child, between the ages of 5 and 15, is exposed to no fewer than 13,000 violent deaths on television; the number of fights and aggressive sequences that children view is still higher. Saturday mornings, once filled with relatively peaceful fare, now include cartoon programs, for example, that sport titles such as *Power Rangers* and *Robo Cop,* which include long sequences of aggressive action (Gerbner et al., 1978; Freedman, 1984; Liebert & Sprafkin, 1988).

Most research does, in fact, suggest that a significant association exists between watching such violent television programs and displaying aggressive behavior (Eron, 1982; Huesmann & Eron, 1986; Berkowitz, 1993). For example, one experiment showed that subjects who watched a lot of television as third-graders became more aggressive adults than those who didn't watch as much (Eron et al., 1972). Of course, these results cannot prove that viewing television caused the adult aggression. Some additional factors, such as particular personality characteristics of viewers, may have led both to high levels of viewing of aggressive shows and to high aggression.

Still, most experts agree that watching media violence can lead to a greater readiness to act aggressively (if not invariably to overt aggression) and to an insensitivity to the suffering of victims of violence (Linz, Donnerstein, & Penrod, 1988; Bushman & Geen, 1990; Comstock & Strasburger, 1990). Several factors help explain why the observation of media violence may provoke aggression. For one thing, viewing violence seems to lower inhibitions against the performance of aggression—watching television portrayals of violence makes aggression seem a legitimate response to particular situations.

Furthermore, viewing violence may distort our understanding of the meaning of others' behavior. We may, for example, be predisposed to view even nonaggressive acts by others as aggressive after watching media aggression, and subsequently may act upon these new interpretations by responding aggressively. Finally, a continual diet of aggression may leave us desensitized to violence, and what previously would have repelled us now produces little emotional response. Our sense of the pain and suffering brought about by aggression may be diminished, and we may find it easier to act aggressively ourselves (Geen & Donnerstein, 1983).

Given the probable links between violence and exposure to media aggression, psychologists are working on ways to reduce aggression in frequent viewers. One approach has been to explicitly teach children that televised violence is not representative of the real world, that the viewing of violence is objectionable, and that they should refrain from imitating behavior seen on television (Huesmann et al., 1983; Eron & Huesmann, 1985; Zillman, 1993).

The lessons appear to be effective: As a group, children who are given lessons act less aggressively than those who have not received lessons. For instance, in one experiment first- and third-grade students who tended to view a lot of television received several training sessions over a 9-month period (Huesmann et al., 1983). During the sessions, the students learned that the aggressive behavior on television does not approximate what happens in the real world. They were taught about camera techniques and special effects used to produce the illusion of aggression. Moreover, they learned that people generally used alternatives to aggression in seeking solutions to their problems. Finally, they were directly taught the undesirability of watching television violence and ways to avoid imitating aggression.

The program was highly successful. Compared with a control group of children who did not receive the training, the students who attended the classes were rated by their classmates as showing significantly lower levels of aggression. Furthermore, the students in the program perceived televised aggression much more negatively than those who did not participate. It seems, then, that the negative consequences of viewing media aggression can be reduced through training. Just as people learn through observation to act aggressively, they can learn to become less aggressive.

Exploring Diversity

Does Culture Influence How We Learn?

When a member of the Chilcotin Indian tribe teaches her daughter to prepare salmon, at first she only allows the daughter to observe the entire process. A little later, she permits her child to try out some basic parts of the task. Her response to questions is noteworthy. For example, when the daughter asks about how to do "the backbone part," the mother's response is to repeat the entire process with another fish. The reason? The mother feels that one cannot learn the individual parts of the task apart from the context of preparing the whole fish (Tharp, 1989).

It should not be surprising that children raised in the Chilcotin tradition, which stresses instruction that starts by communicating the entire task, might have difficulty with traditional western schooling. In the approach to teaching most characteristic of Western culture, tasks are broken down into their component parts. Only after each small step is learned is it thought possible to master the complete task.

Do the differences in teaching approaches between cultures affect how people learn? According to one school of thought, learners develop *learning styles,* characteristic ways of approaching material, based on their cultural background and unique pattern of abilities (Anderson & Adams, 1992).

Learning styles differ along several dimensions. For example, one central dimension is analytical versus relational approaches to learning (Anderson, 1988; Tharp, 1989). As illustrated in Table 5-2, people with a relational learning style

TABLE 5-2 Learning Styles

Relational Style	Analytical Style
1. Perceive information as part of total picture	1. Able to dis-embed information from total picture (focus on detail)
2. Exhibit improvisational and intuitive thinking	2. Exhibit sequential and structured thinking
3. More easily learn materials that have a human, social content and are characterized by experiential/cultural relevance	3. More easily learn materials that are inanimate and impersonal
4. Have a good memory for verbally presented ideas and information, especially if relevant	4. Have a good memory for abstract ideas and irrelevant information
5. Are more task-oriented concerning nonacademic areas	5. Are more task-oriented concerning academics
6. Are influenced by authority figures' expression of confidence or doubt in students' ability	6. Are not greatly affected by the opinions of others
7. Prefer to withdraw from unstimulating task performance	7. Show ability to persist at unstimulating tasks
8. Style conflicts with the traditional school environment	8. Style matches most school environments

Source: Anderson, J. A., & Adams, M. (1992). Acknowledging the learning styles of diverse student populations: Implications for instructional design. *New Directions for Teaching and Learning, 49,* 19–33.

master material best through exposure to a full unit or phenomenon. Parts of the unit can be comprehended only by understanding their relationship to the whole.

In contrast, people with an analytical learning style do best when they can carry out an initial analysis of the principles and components underlying a phenomenon or situation. By developing an understanding of the fundamental principles and components, they are best able to understand the full picture. (In certain respects, the distinction between relational and analytical learning styles is analogous to the distinction between top-down and bottom-up processing that we discussed in Chapter 3.)

Although research findings are mixed, some evidence suggests that particular minority groups within Western society display characteristic learning styles. For instance, James Anderson and Maurianne Adams (1992) argued that white females and African-American, Native American, and Hispanic-American males and females are more apt to use a relational style of learning than white and Asian-American males, who are more likely to employ an analytical style.

The conclusion that members of particular ethnic and gender groups have a similar learning style is controversial. Because there is so much diversity within each particular racial and ethnic group, critics argue that generalizations about learning style cannot be used to predict the style of any single individual regardless of group membership. Many psychologists contend that a discussion of group learning styles is a misguided undertaking. (This argument echoes a controversy about the usefulness of IQ tests that we will examine in Chapter 8.) Instead, they suggest that it is more fruitful to concentrate on determining each individual's particular learning style and pattern of academic and social strengths.

Still, it is clear that values about learning, which are communicated through a person's family and cultural background, have an impact on how successful students are in school. For instance, one theory suggests that learners who are members of minority groups who were voluntary immigrants are more apt to be successful in school than those who were brought into a majority culture against their will. For example, Korean children—the sons and daughters of voluntary immigrants—perform quite well, as a group, in U.S. schools. In contrast, Korean children tend to do poorly in Japan, where their parents had been made to immigrate during World War II, essentially as forced laborers. Presumably, children in the forced-immigration groups are less motivated to succeed than those in the voluntary-immigration groups (Ogbu, 1992; Gallagher, 1994).

The Unresolved Controversy of Cognitive Learning Theory

The degree to which learning is based on unseen internal factors rather than on external factors remains one of the major issues dividing learning theorists today (Amsel, 1988). Both classical conditioning and operant conditioning theories consider learning in terms of external stimuli and responses—a kind of "black box" analysis in which all that matters are the observable features of the environment, not what goes on inside a person's head. To the cognitive learning theorists, such an analysis misses the mark; what is crucial is the mental activity—the thoughts and expectations—that takes place.

Some psychologists argue that neither approach, by itself, is sufficient to explain all learning. Rather than viewing behavioral and cognitive approaches as contradictory, they see them as addressing different facets of learning. Such a theoretical outlook has allowed psychologists to make important advances in such areas as the treatment of certain kinds of abnormal behavior, as we will see in Chapter 13.

Still, while the controversy surrounding different approaches remains a major issue in psychology, tremendous advances are taking place in the practical application of principles derived from the various theories, as we shall see in the remainder of this chapter (Glaser, 1990).

The Informed Consumer of Psychology

Using Behavior Analysis and Behavior Modification

A couple who had been living together for 3 years began to fight more and more frequently. The issues of disagreement ranged from the seemingly petty, such as who was going to do the dishes, to the more profound, such as the quality of their love life and whether they found each other interesting. Disturbed about this increasingly unpleasant pattern of interaction, the couple went to a behavior analyst, a psychologist who specialized in behavior-modification techniques. After interviewing each of them alone and then speaking to them together, he asked them to keep detailed written records of their interactions over the next 2 weeks—focusing, in particular, on the events that preceded their arguments.

When they returned 2 weeks later, he carefully went over the records with them. In doing so, he noticed a pattern that the couple themselves had observed after they had started keeping their records: Each of their arguments had occurred just after one or the other had left some household chore undone. For instance, the woman would go into a fury when she came home from work and found that the man, a student, had left his dirty lunch dishes on the table and had not even started dinner preparations. The man would get angry when he found the woman's clothes draped on the only chair in the bedroom. He insisted it was her responsibility to pick up after herself.

Using the data that had been collected, the behavior analyst devised a system for the couple to try out. He asked them to list all of the chores that could possibly arise and assign each one a point value depending on how long it took to complete. Then he had them divide the chores equally and agree in a written contract to fulfill the ones assigned to them. If either failed to carry out one of the assigned chores, he or she would have to place $1 per point in a fund for the other to spend. They also agreed to a program of verbal praise, promising to verbally reward each other for completing a chore.

Although skeptical about the value of such a program, the couple agreed to try it for a month and to keep careful records of the number of arguments they had

Behavior modification for people who want to stop smoking may involve aversive conditioning, in which smoking and cues related to smoking are repeatedly paired with unpleasant stimuli.

during this period. To their surprise, the number declined rapidly, and even the more basic issues in their relationship seemed on the way to being resolved.

The case described above provides an illustration of **behavior modification,** a technique for promoting the frequency of desirable behaviors and decreasing the incidence of unwanted ones. Using the basic principles of learning theory, behavior-modification techniques have proved to be helpful in a variety of situations. Severely retarded people have learned the rudiments of language and, for the first time in their lives, have started dressing and feeding themselves. Behavior modification has also helped people to lose weight, give up smoking, and behave more safely (Bellack, Hersen, & Kazdin, 1990; Sulzer-Azaroff & Mayer, 1991; Malott, Whaley, & Malott, 1993).

The techniques used by behavior analysts are as varied as the list of processes that modify behavior. These include reinforcement scheduling, shaping, generalization training, discrimination training, and extinction. Participants in a behavior-change program do, however, typically follow a series of similar basic steps (Royer & Feldman, 1984). These steps include:

Identifying goals and target behaviors. The first step is to define "desired behavior." Is it an increase in time spent studying? A decrease in weight? An increase in the use of language? A reduction in the amount of aggression displayed by a child? The goals must be stated in observable terms and lead to specific targets. For instance, a goal might be "to increase study time," while the target behavior would be "to study at least two hours per day on weekdays and an hour on Saturdays."

Designing a data-recording system and recording preliminary data. In order to determine whether behavior has changed, it is necessary to collect data before any changes are made in the situation. This information provides a baseline against which future changes can be measured.

Selecting a behavior-change strategy. The most crucial step is to select an appropriate strategy. Since all the principles of learning can be employed to bring about behavior change, a "package" of treatments is normally used. This might include the systematic use of positive reinforcement for desired behavior (verbal praise or something more tangible, such as food), as well as a program of extinction for undesirable behavior (ignoring a child who throws a tantrum). Selecting the right reinforcers is critical; it may be necessary to experiment a bit to find out what is important to a given individual. It is best for participants to avoid threats, since they are merely punishing and ultimately not very effective in bringing about long-term changes in behavior.

Implementing the program. The next step is to institute the program. Probably the most important aspect of program implementation is consistency. It is also important to make sure that one is reinforcing the behavior he or she wants to reinforce. For example, suppose a mother wants her daughter to spend more time on her homework, but as soon as the child sits down to study, she asks for a snack. If the mother gets one for her, the mother is likely to be reinforcing her daughter's delaying tactic, not her studying. Instead, the mother might promise her daughter a snack after a certain time interval has gone by during which she has studied—thereby using the snack as a reinforcement for studying.

Keeping careful records after the program is implemented. Another crucial task is record keeping. If the target behaviors are not monitored, there is no way of knowing whether the program has actually been successful. Participants are advised not to rely on their memory, because it is all too easy for memory lapses to occur.

Evaluating and altering the ongoing program. Finally, the results of the program should be compared with preimplementation data to determine its effective-

Behavior modification: A technique for promoting the frequency of desirable behaviors and decreasing the incidence of unwanted ones

ness. If successful, the procedures employed can gradually be phased out. For instance, if the program called for reinforcing every instance of picking up one's clothes from the bedroom floor, the reinforcement schedule could be modified to a fixed-ratio schedule in which every third instance was reinforced. On the other hand, if the program had not been successful in bringing about the desired behavior change, consideration of other approaches might be advisable.

Behavior-change techniques based on these general principles have enjoyed wide success and have proved to be one of the most powerful means of modifying behavior (Greenwood et al., 1992). Clearly, it is possible to employ the basic notions of learning theory to improve our own lives.

RECAP AND REVIEW

Recap

- Cognitive learning theory focuses on the unseen, internal mental processes that are occurring within a person.
- Modeling consists of learning from the observation of others' behavior. The rewards that a model receives influences the extent to which the model will be imitated.
- Cultural factors are associated with the manner in which people learn.
- Behavior modification, a technique for promoting desirable behaviors and reducing undesirable ones, has been used successfully in changing both one's own and others' behavior.

Review

1. A distinguished scientist tells you "Learning can best be *cognitive learning theory* understood in terms of underlying thought processes." What theory is being described?
2. In cognitive learning theory, it is assumed that people develop a(n) *expectation* about receiving a reinforcer instead of basing behavior on past reinforcers.

3. *Latent* learning describes learning that takes place but is not shown until appropriate reinforcement is presented.
4. Bandura's theory of *observational* learning states that people learn through watching a *model*, which is another person displaying the behavior of interest. *mental processes*
5. Cognitive learning theorists are only concerned with overt behavior, not with its internal causes. True or *false*?
6. A man wishes to quit smoking. Upon the advice of a psychologist, he begins a program where he sets goals for his withdrawal, carefully records his progress, and rewards himself for not smoking during a certain period of time. What type of program is he following? *behavior modification*

Ask Yourself

How could a true experiment be devised that could confirm the long-term consequences of viewing aggression on television?

(Answers to review questions are on page 182.)

LOOKING BACK

What is learning?

1. Learning, a relatively permanent change in behavior due to experience, is a basic topic of psychology. However, it is a process that must be assessed indirectly—we can only assume that learning has occurred by observing performance, which is susceptible to such factors as fatigue and lack of effort.

How do we learn to form associations between stimuli and responses?

2. One major form of learning is known as classical conditioning. First studied by Ivan Pavlov, classical conditioning occurs when a neutral stimulus—one that brings about no relevant response—is repeatedly paired with a stimulus (called an unconditioned stimulus) that brings about a natural, untrained response. For instance, a neutral stimulus might be a buzzer;

an unconditioned stimulus might be a dish of ice cream. The response that ice cream might elicit in a hungry person—salivation—is called an unconditioned response; it occurs naturally, owing to the physical makeup of the individual being trained.

3. The actual conditioning occurs when the neutral stimulus is repeatedly presented just before the unconditioned stimulus. After repeated pairings, the neutral stimulus begins to bring about the same response as the unconditioned stimulus. When this occurs, we can say that the neutral stimulus is now a conditioned stimulus, and the response made to it is the conditioned response. For example, after a person has learned to salivate to the sound of the buzzer, we say the buzzer is a conditioned stimulus, and the salivation is a conditioned response.

4. Learning is not always permanent, however. Extinction occurs when a previously learned response decreases in frequency and eventually disappears.

5. Stimulus generalization occurs when a conditioned response follows a stimulus that is similar to the original conditioned stimulus. The greater the similarity between the two stimuli, the greater the likelihood of stimulus generalization; the closer the new stimulus to the old one, the more similar the new response. The converse phenomenon, stimulus discrimination, occurs when an organism learns to respond to one stimulus but not to another.

6. Higher-order conditioning occurs when an established conditioned stimulus is paired with a neutral stimulus, and the new neutral stimulus comes to evoke the same conditioned response as the original conditioned stimulus. The neutral stimulus becomes, then, another conditioned stimulus.

What is the role of reward and punishment in learning?

7. A second major form of learning is operant conditioning. Moving beyond Edward Thorndike's original work on the law of effect, which states that responses that produce satisfying results are more likely to be repeated than those that do not, B. F. Skinner carried out pioneering work on operant learning.

8. According to Skinner, the major mechanism underlying learning is reinforcement, the process by which a stimulus increases the probability that a preceding behavior will be repeated. We can determine whether a stimulus is reinforcing only by observing its effects upon behavior. If behavior increases, the stimulus is, by definition, a reinforcer. Primary reinforcers involve rewards that are naturally effective without prior exposure because they satisfy a biological need. Secondary reinforcers, in contrast, begin to act as if they were primary reinforcers through frequent pairings with a primary reinforcer.

9. Positive reinforcers are stimuli that are added to the environment and lead to an increase in a preceding response. Negative reinforcers are stimuli that remove something unpleasant from the environment, leading to an increase in the preceding response. Negative reinforcement occurs in two major forms. In escape conditioning, an organism learns to make a response that brings about an end to an aversive situation. In avoidance conditioning, an organism responds to a signal of an impending unpleasant event in a way that permits its evasion.

10. Punishment is the administration of an unpleasant stimulus following a response in order to produce a decrease in the incidence of that response. Punishment can also be characterized by the removal of a positive reinforcer. In contrast to reinforcement, in which the goal is to increase the incidence of behavior, punishment is meant to decrease or suppress behavior. Although there are some benefits to the use of punishment, its disadvantages usually outweigh its positive effects.

11. Schedules and patterns of reinforcement affect the strength and duration of learning. Generally, partial reinforcement schedules—in which reinforcers are not delivered on every trial—produce stronger and longer-lasting learning than continuous reinforcement schedules.

12. Among the major categories of reinforcement schedules are fixed- and variable-ratio schedules, which are based on the number of responses made, and fixed- and variable-interval schedules, which are based on the time interval that elapses before reinforcement is provided. Fixed-ratio schedules provide reinforcement only after a certain number of responses are made; variable-ratio schedules provide reinforcement after a varying number of responses are made—although the specific number typically settles around some average. In contrast, fixed-interval schedules provide reinforcement after a fixed amount of time has elapsed since the last reinforcement; variable-interval schedules provide reinforcement over varying amounts of time, although the times form a specific average.

13. Generalization and discrimination are phenomena that operate in operant conditioning as well as classical conditioning. Generalization occurs when an organism makes the same or a similar response to a new stimulus that it has learned to make in the past to a similar stimulus. Discrimination occurs when the organism responds to one stimulus, but does not respond to a similar (but different) stimulus.

14. Superstitious behavior results from the mistaken belief that particular ideas, objects, or behavior will cause certain events to occur. It occurs as a consequence of learning that is based on the coincidental association between a stimulus and subsequent reinforcement.

15. Shaping is a process for teaching complex behaviors by rewarding closer and closer approximations of the desired final behavior. Shaping forms the basis for learning many everyday skills and is central to presenting complicated information in textbooks.

16. There are biological constraints, or built-in limitations, on the ability of an organism to learn. Because of these constraints, certain behaviors will be relatively easy to learn, whereas other behaviors will be either difficult or impossible to learn.

What is the role of cognition and thought in learning?

17. Cognitive approaches consider learning in terms of thought processes, or cognition. Phenomena such as latent learning—in which a new behavior is learned but not performed until reinforcement is provided for its performance—and the apparent development of cognitive maps support cognitive approaches. Learning also occurs through the observation of behavior of others, known as models.

18. The major factor that determines whether an observed behavior will actually be performed is the nature of reinforcement or punishment a model receives.

19. Learning styles are characteristic ways of approaching material, based on a person's cultural background and unique pattern of abilities. One major dimension relates to analytical versus relational approaches to learning. People with relational learning styles master material best through exposure to a full unit or phenomenon. In contrast, people with analytical learning styles make an initial analysis of the principles and components underlying a phenomenon or situation.

What are some practical methods for bringing about behavior change, both in ourselves and in others?

20. Behavior modification is a method for formally using the principles of learning theory to promote the frequency of desired behaviors and to decrease or eliminate unwanted ones.

The typical steps in a behavior-change program are identifying goals and target behaviors, designing a data-recording system, recording preliminary data, selecting a behavior-change strategy, implementing the strategy, keeping careful records, and evaluating and altering the ongoing program.

KEY TERMS AND CONCEPTS

learning (p. 151)
classical conditioning (p. 152)
neutral stimulus (p. 153)
unconditioned stimulus (UCS) (p. 153)
unconditioned response (UCR) (p. 153)
conditioned stimulus (CS) (p. 153)
conditioned response (CR) (p. 153)
extinction (p. 155)
spontaneous recovery (p. 156)
stimulus generalization (p. 156)
stimulus discrimination (p. 157)

operant conditioning (p. 160)
reinforcement (p. 161)
reinforcer (p. 161)
positive reinforcer (p. 163)
negative reinforcer (p. 163)
punishment (p. 163)
schedules of reinforcement (p. 166)
continuous reinforcement schedule (p. 166)
partial reinforcement schedule (p. 166)
fixed-ratio schedule (p. 166)

variable-ratio schedule (p. 166)
fixed-interval schedule (p. 167)
variable-interval schedule (p. 168)
shaping (p. 169)
cognitive learning theory (p. 172)
latent learning (p. 172)
cognitive map (p. 173)
observational learning (p. 174)
behavior modification (p. 179)

CHAPTER 6
MEMORY

Memory on Trial: The Buckey Case

In the end, it came down to a question of memory: Should young children's recollections of abuse be trusted?

For prosecutors who charged Ray Buckey and his mother Peggy McMartin Buckey, owners of a once highly-regarded preschool, with sexual abuse, the answer was an unmistakable "yes." But for the defendants, who claimed that investigators had swayed and biased the children's memories during their investigation of the allegations, the case represented memory distortion gone wild.

During the trial, the children, now ten and eleven years old, provided graphic details of the Buckeys' alleged misdeeds years earlier. They accused the Buckeys of rape, sodomy, and conducting satanic rituals. However, many of the children's recollections were nothing short of bizarre. They recalled jumping out of airplanes and trips to cemeteries to dig up bodies.

We'll probably never know the real truth. What is clear is that the Buckeys' trial was the longest and most expensive in U.S. history, lasting 33 weeks and costing some $15 million. The jury deliberated for nine weeks as they considered the charge that the Buckeys had molested dozens of preschool-age children over the course of several years.

Ultimately, the jurors were simply unable to accept the truth of the children's recollections. They found the Buckeys not guilty on 52 counts of child sexual abuse and were deadlocked on an additional 13 counts. In the end, the Buckeys were freed. (Schindehette, 1990)

The Buckey case raises important questions about the nature and accuracy of memory in the context of the judicial system. But the issues involved in memory extend far beyond dramatic courtroom cases, for memory plays a central role in our everyday lives.

Our memory allows us to retrieve a vast amount of information to which we have been exposed. We are able to remember the name of a friend we haven't been in touch with for decades and to recall details of a picture that hung in our bedroom as a child. At the same time, though, memory failures are not uncom-

Peggy McMartin Buckey and her son Ray (at right) were acquitted of sexual abuse in a notorious trial. The key issue was the accuracy of children's memories of events that had allegedly happened years before, when they were very young.

mon. We may forget where we left the keys to the car or be unable to answer an exam question about material we studied (and understood) just a few hours earlier.

In this chapter, we address the topic of memory. We examine the ways in which information is stored and retrieved. We discuss approaches that suggest there are actually several separate types of memory, and we explain how each type functions in a somewhat different fashion. The problems of retrieving information from memory, the accuracy of memories, and the reasons information is sometimes forgotten are examined. We also consider the biological foundations of memory. Finally, we discuss some practical means of increasing memory capacity.

- *What is memory?*
- *Are there different kinds of memory?*

ENCODING, STORAGE, AND RETRIEVAL OF MEMORY

You are playing a game of Trivial Pursuit, and winning the game comes down to one question: On what body of water is Bombay located?

As you rack your brain for the answer, several fundamental processes relating to memory come into play. For instance, your difficulty in answering the question may be traced to the initial encoding stage of memory. *Encoding* refers to the process by which information is initially recorded in a form usable to memory. You may never, for instance, have been exposed to information regarding Bombay's location, or it simply may not have registered in a meaningful way if it had been pointed out to you.

On the other hand, even if you had been exposed to the information and originally knew the name of the body of water, you may still be unable to recall it because of a failure in the retention process. Memory specialists speak of *storage*, the maintenance of material saved in the memory system. If the material is not stored adequately, it cannot be recalled later.

Memory also depends on one last process: retrieval. In *retrieval*, material in memory storage is located, brought into awareness, and utilized. Your failure to recall Bombay's location, then, may rest on your inability to retrieve information that you learned earlier.

In sum, psychologists consider **memory** as the process by which we encode, store, and retrieve information (see Figure 6-1). Each of the three parts of this definition—encoding, storage, and retrieval—represents a different process, which you can think of as analogous to a computer's keyboard (encoding), disk (storage), and screen (retrieval). And only if all three processes have operated will you experience success and be able to recall the body of water on which Bombay is located: the Arabian Sea.

Memory: The process by which people encode, store, and retrieve information

FIGURE 6-1 Memory is built on these three basic processes.

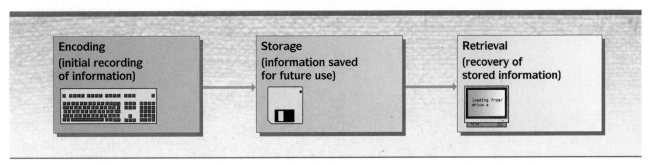

Encoding (initial recording of information)

Storage (information saved for future use)

Retrieval (recovery of stored information)

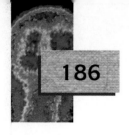

However, before continuing, we should keep in mind the value of memory *failures*. Forgetting is essential to the proper functioning of memory. The ability to forget inconsequential details about experiences, people, and objects allows us to avoid being burdened and distracted by trivial stores of meaningless data. Furthermore, forgetting permits us to combine similar recollections and form general impressions and recollections. For example, it would not be terribly useful to form separate memories of the way friends look every time we saw them. Consequently, we tend to forget their clothing, facial blemishes, and other transient features that change from one occasion to the next. Instead, our memories are based on a summarization of various critical features—a far more economical use of our memory capabilities. Forgetting unnecessary information is as essential to the proper functioning of memory as is remembering material.

Sensory memory: The initial, momentary storage of information, lasting only an instant

Short-term memory: The storage of information for 15 to 25 seconds

Long-term memory: The storage of information on a relatively permanent basis, although retrieval may be difficult

The Three Systems of Memory: Memory Storehouses

Although the processes of encoding, storing, and retrieving information are necessary for memory to operate successfully, they do not describe the specific manner in which material is entered into memory. Many psychologists studying memory suggest that there are different systems or stages through which information must travel if it is to be remembered.

According to one of the most influential theories, three kinds of memory storage systems exist. These types of storehouses vary in terms of their function and the length of time information is retained (Atkinson & Shiffrin, 1968, 1971).

As shown in Figure 6-2, **sensory memory** refers to the initial, momentary storage of information, lasting only an instant. It is recorded by the person's sensory system as a raw, nonmeaningful stimulus. **Short-term memory** holds information for 15 to 25 seconds. In this system, the information is stored in terms of its meaning rather than as mere sensory stimulation. The third type of storage is **long-term memory.** Information is stored as long-term memory on a relatively permanent basis, although it may be difficult to retrieve.

FIGURE 6-2 In this three-stage model of memory, information initially recorded by the person's sensory system enters sensory memory, which momentarily holds the information. It then moves to short-term memory, which stores the information for 15 to 25 seconds. Finally, the information can move into long-term memory, which is relatively permanent. Whether the information moves from short-term to long-term memory depends on the kind and amount of rehearsal of the material that is carried out. *(After Atkinson & Shiffrin, 1968.)*

Although we'll be discussing the three types of memory in terms of separate memory stores, keep in mind that these are not miniwarehouses located in particular portions of the brain. Instead, they represent three different types of abstract memory systems with different characteristics. Furthermore, although the three-part model dominated the field of memory for several decades, recent research has suggested several different approaches, as we'll discuss later. Still,

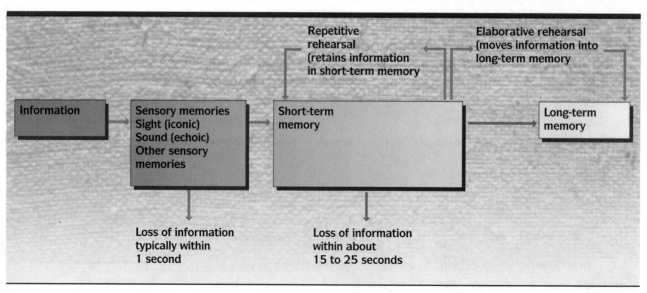

considering memory in terms of the three major kinds of stores has provided us with a useful framework for understanding how information is both recalled and forgotten.

Sensory Memory   A momentary flash of lightning, the sound of a twig snapping, and the sting of a pinprick all represent stimulations of exceedingly brief durations, but they may nonetheless provide important information that can require some response. Such stimuli are initially—and briefly—stored in sensory memory, the first repository of the information that the world presents to us. Actually, the term "sensory memory" encompasses several types of sensory memories, each related to a different source of sensory information. There is **iconic memory,** which reflects information from our visual system; **echoic memory,** which stores information coming from the ears; and corresponding memories for each of the other senses.

Regardless of the individual subtypes, sensory memory in general is able to store information for only a very short time. If material does not pass to short-term memory, that information is lost for good. For instance, iconic memory seems to last less than a second, although if the initial stimulus is very bright, the image may last a little longer (Long & Beaton, 1982). Echoic memory fades within 3 or 4 seconds (Darwin, Turvey, & Crowder, 1972). However, despite the brief duration of sensory memory, its precision is high: It is able to store an almost exact replica of each stimulus to which it is exposed.

If the storage capabilities of sensory memory are so limited and information stored within sensory memory so fleeting, it would seem almost impossible to find evidence for its existence; new information would constantly be replacing older information, even before a person could report its presence. Not until psychologist George Sperling (1960) conducted a series of clever and now-classic studies was sensory memory well understood. Sperling briefly exposed people to a series of twelve letters arranged in the following pattern:

F   T   Y   C
K   D   N   L
Y   W   B   M

When exposed to this array for just one-twentieth of a second, most people could accurately recall only four or five of the letters. Although they knew they had seen more, the memory of the rest of the letters had faded by the time they reported the first few letters. It was possible, then, that the information had initially been accurately stored in sensory memory, but during the time it took to verbalize the first four or five letters the memory of the other letters faded.

To test that possibility, Sperling conducted an experiment in which a high, medium, or low tone sounded just after a person had been exposed to the full pattern of letters. People were told to report the letters in the highest line if a high tone were sounded, the middle line if the medium tone occurred, or the lowest line at the sound of the low tone. Because the tone occurred after the exposure, people had to rely on their memory to report the correct row.

The results of the study clearly showed that people had been storing the complete pattern in memory. They were accurate in their recollection of the letters in the line that had been indicated by the tone, regardless of whether it was the top, middle, or bottom line. Obviously, *all* the lines they had seen had been stored in sensory memory. Despite its rapid loss, then, the information in sensory memory was an accurate representation of what people had seen.

By gradually lengthening the time between the presentation of the visual pattern and the tone, Sperling was able to determine with some accuracy the length of time that information was stored in sensory memory. The ability to recall a particular row of the pattern when a tone was sounded declined progressively as the period between visual exposure and tone increased. This decline continued

Iconic memory: The process that reflects information from our visual system

Echoic memory: The process that stores information coming from the ears

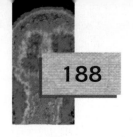
until the period reached about 1 second in duration, at which point the row could not be recalled accurately at all. Sperling concluded that the entire visual image was stored in sensory memory for less than a second.

In sum, sensory memory operates as a kind of snapshot that stores information—which may be of a visual, auditory, or other sensory nature—for a brief moment in time. But it is as if each snapshot, immediately after being taken, is destroyed and replaced with a new one. Unless the information in the snapshot is transferred to some other type of memory, it is lost.

Short-Term Memory: Our Working Memory   Because the information that is stored briefly in our sensory memory consists of representations of raw sensory stimuli, it is not meaningful to us. In order for us to make sense of it and to allow for the possibility of long-term retention, the information must be transferred to the next stage of memory, short-term memory. Short-term memory is the memory store in which material first has meaning, although the maximum length of retention is relatively short.

The specific process by which sensory memories are transformed into short-term memories is not yet clear. Some theorists suggest that the information is first translated into graphical representations or images, and others hypothesize that the transfer occurs when the sensory stimuli are changed to words (Baddeley & Wilson, 1985). What is clear, however, is that unlike sensory memory, which holds a relatively full and detailed—if short-lived—representation of the world, short-term memory has incomplete representational capabilities.

In fact, the specific amount of information that can be held in short-term memory has been identified: seven items, or "chunks," of information, with variations up to plus or minus two chunks. A **chunk** is a meaningful grouping of stimuli that can be stored as a unit in short-term memory. According to George Miller (1956), it could be individual letters, as in the following list:

C   N   Q   M   W   N   T

Each letter here qualifies as a separate chunk, and—as there are seven of them—they are easily held in short-term memory.

But a chunk might also consist of larger categories, such as words or other meaningful units. For example, consider the following list of twenty-one letters:

T W A C I A A B C C B S M T V U S A N B C

Clearly, because the list exceeds seven chunks, it is difficult to recall the letters after one exposure. But suppose they were presented to you as follows:

TWA   CIA   ABC   CBS   MTV   USA   NBC

In this case, even though there are still twenty-one letters, it would be possible to store them in memory, since they represent only seven chunks.

You can see how chunking works in terms of your own memory process by trying to memorize the shapes in Figure 6-3 after looking at them for just a few moments. Although it may at first seem to be an impossible task, just one hint will guarantee that you can easily memorize all the shapes: Each figure represents some part of a letter in the word "PSYCHOLOGY."

The reason the task suddenly became so simple was that the shapes could be grouped together into one chunk—a word that we all recognize. Rather than be-

Chunk: A meaningful grouping of stimuli that can be stored as a unit in short-term memory

FIGURE 6-3   Try looking at the shapes in this figure for a few moments, and memorize them in the exact sequence in which they appear.

If you consider this an impossible task, here's a hint that will guarantee that you can easily memorize all of them: They are the shapes of each part of the letters in the word "PSYCHOLOGY." The reason the task suddenly becomes simple is that the shapes can be grouped together into one chunk—a word that we all recognize. Rather than being considered as nineteen separate shapes, the symbols are recorded in the memory as just one chunk.

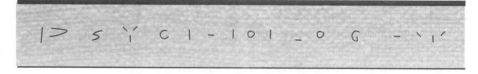

FIGURE 6-4 Look at the chessboard on the left for about 5 seconds, and then cover it with your hand. Now try to recreate the chess pieces on the blank board on the right. Unless you are an experienced chess player, you will probably have a good deal of difficulty recalling the configuration and types of chess pieces. On the other hand, expert chess players have little difficulty recreating the game board. *(Based on deGroot, 1966.)*

ing nineteen separate symbols with no meaning, they are recorded as just one chunk.

Chunks can vary in size from single letters or numbers to categories that are far more complicated. The specific nature of what constitutes a chunk varies according to one's past experience. You can see this for yourself by trying an experiment that was first carried out comparing expert and inexperienced chess players (deGroot, 1966).

Examine the chessboard at the left of Figure 6-4 for about 5 seconds, and then, after covering up the board, try to reproduce the position of the pieces on the blank chessboard to the right. Unless you are an experienced chess player, you are likely to have great difficulty carrying out such a task. Yet chess masters—the kind who win tournaments—do quite well: They are able to reproduce correctly 90 percent of the pieces on the board. In comparison, inexperienced chess players are typically able to reproduce only 40 percent of the board properly. The chess masters do not have superior memories in other respects; they generally test normally on other measures of memory. What they can do better than others is to see the board in terms of chunks or meaningful units and reproduce the position of the chess pieces by using these units.

Although it is possible to remember seven or so relatively complicated sets of information entering short-term memory, the information cannot be held there very long. Just how short term is short-term memory? Anyone who has looked up a telephone number at a pay phone, struggled to find coins, and forgotten the number at the sound of the dial tone knows that information in short-term memory does not remain there terribly long. Most psychologists believe that information in short-term memory is lost after 15 to 25 seconds—unless it is transferred to long-term memory.

Rehearsal   The repetition of information that has entered short-term memory is called **rehearsal**. Rehearsal accomplishes two things. First, as long as the information is repeated, it is kept alive in short-term memory. More important, however, rehearsal allows us to transfer the material into long-term memory.

Whether the transfer is made from short- to long-term memory seems to depend largely on the kind of rehearsal that is carried out. If the material is simply repeated over and over again—as we might do with a telephone number while we

Rehearsal: The transfer of material from short- to long-term memory via repetition

189

This young women is experiencing the limitations of short-term memory. Having just looked up a phone number, she has forgotten it as soon as she closed the directory. A brief period of rehearsal would have helped her to retain the number.

rush from the phone book to the telephone—it is kept current in short-term memory, but it will not necessarily be placed in long-term memory. Instead, as soon as we stop dialing, the number is likely to be replaced by other information and will be completely forgotten.

On the other hand, if the information in short-term memory is rehearsed using a process called elaborative rehearsal, it is much more likely to be transferred into long-term memory (Craik & Lockhart, 1972). *Elaborative rehearsal* occurs when the material is considered and organized in some fashion. The organization might include expanding the information to make it fit into a logical framework, linking it to another memory, turning it into an image, or transforming it in some other way. For example, vegetables to be purchased at a store could be woven together in memory as items being used to prepare an elaborate salad, they could be linked to the items bought on an earlier shopping trip, or they could be thought of in terms of the image of a farm with rows of each item.

By using organizational strategies called *mnemonics,* we can vastly improve our retention of information. Mnemonics (pronounced "neh MON ix") are formal techniques for organizing material in a way that makes it more likely to be remembered. For instance, when a musician learns that the spaces on the music staff spell the word "FACE" or when we learn the rhyme "Thirty days hath September, April, June, and November; all the rest have . . .," we are using mnemonics (Higbee & Kunihira, 1985; Mastropieri & Scruggs, 1991; Bellezza, Six, & Phillips, 1992).

Working Memory: The Components of Short-Term Memory   Although short-term memory has traditionally been considered as a single system, more recent evidence suggests that it may actually consist of several components. According to psychologist Alan Baddeley (1992, 1993), short-term memory is better thought of as a three-part **working memory**. In this view, one component is the *central executive,* which coordinates the material to focus on during reasoning and decision making. The central executive makes use of two subcomponents: the visuospatial sketch pad and the phonological loop. The *visuospatial sketch pad* concentrates on visual and spatial information, while the *phonological loop* is responsible for holding and manipulating material relating to speech, words, and numbers (Gathercole & Baddeley, 1993).

Working memory: Baddeley's theory that short-term memory comprises three components: the central executive, the visuospatial sketch pad, and the phonological loop

Drawing by R. Chast; © 1994; The New Yorker Magazine, Inc.

Some researchers suspect that a breakdown in the central executive may result in the memory losses that are characteristic of Alzheimer's disease, the progressively degenerative disorder that produces loss of memory and confusion (Baddeley, 1992). (We'll discuss Alzheimer's disease and other memory disorders at greater length later in the chapter.)

Long-Term Memory: The Final Storehouse Material that makes its way from short-term memory to long-term memory enters a storehouse of almost unlimited capacity. Like a new book delivered to a library, the information in long-term memory is filed and cataloged so that it can be retrieved when we need it.

Evidence of the existence of long-term memory, as distinct from short-term memory, comes from a number of sources. For example, people with certain kinds of brain damage have no lasting recall of new information following the damage, although people and events stored in memory prior to the injury remain intact (Milner, 1966). Because short-term memory following the injury appears to be operative—new material can be recalled for a very brief period—and because information encoded and stored prior to the injury is recalled, we can infer that there are two distinct types of memory—one for short-term and one for long-term storage.

Results from laboratory experiments are also consistent with the notion of separate short- and long-term memories. For example, in one set of studies people were asked to recall a relatively small amount of information (such as a set of three letters). Then, to prevent practice of the initial information, participants were required to recite some extraneous material aloud, such as counting backward by threes (Brown, 1958; Peterson & Peterson, 1959). By varying the amount of time between which the initial material was first presented and its recall was required, investigators found that recall was quite good when the interval was very short, but that it declined rapidly thereafter. After 15 seconds had gone by, recall hovered at around 10 percent of the material initially presented.

Although some of these people may not have ridden a bicycle in years., procedural memory enables them to resume riding with little practice.

Declarative memory: Memory for factual information: names, faces, dates, and the like

Procedural memory: Refers to memory for skills and habits such as riding a bike or hitting a baseball; sometimes referred to as "nondeclarative memory"

Semantic memory: Memory that stores general knowledge and facts about the world (e.g., mathematical and historical data)

Episodic memory: Memory for information relating to the biographical details of our individual lives

what happen to you

Apparently, the distraction of counting backward prevented almost all the initial material from reaching long-term memory. Initial recall was good because it was coming from short-term memory, but these memories were lost at a rapid rate. Eventually, all that could be recalled was the small amount of material that had made its way into long-term storage despite the distractions of counting backward.

The Modules of Memory   Although long-term memory initially was viewed as a unitary entity, most research now suggests that it is composed of several different components, or memory modules. Each of these modules is related to a separate memory system in the brain.

For instance, one major distinction is between declarative and procedural memory. **Declarative memory** is memory for factual information: names, faces, dates, and the like. In contrast, **procedural memory** (sometimes referred to as "nondeclarative memory") refers to memory for skills and habits such as riding a bike or hitting a baseball. Information *about* things is stored in declarative memory; information regarding *how* to do things is stored in procedural memory (Desimone, 1992; Squire, Knowlton, & Musen, 1993).

The facts in declarative memory can be further subdivided into semantic and episodic memory (Tulving, 1992). **Semantic memory** is memory for general knowledge and facts about the world, as well as memory for the rules of logic for deducing other facts (Martin, 1993). Because of semantic memory, we remember that $2 \times 2 = 4$, the ZIP code for Beverly Hills is 90210, and "memoree" is misspelled. Thus, semantic memory is similar to a kind of mental almanac of facts.

In contrast, **episodic memory** is memory for the biographical details of our individual lives. Our memories of what we have done and the kinds of experiences we have had constitute episodic memory. Consequently, when we recall our first date, the time we fell off our bicycle, or the way we felt when we graduated from high school, we are recalling episodic memories. (To help *your* long-term memory keep the distinctions between the different types of long-term memory straight, consider Figure 6-5.)

192

Episodic memories can be surprisingly detailed. Consider, for instance, how you'd respond if you were asked to identify what you were doing on a specific day 2 years ago. Impossible? You might think otherwise as you read the following exchange between a researcher and a subject who was asked, in a memory experiment, what he was doing "on Monday afternoon in the third week of September two years ago."

Subject: Come on. How should I know?
Experimenter: Just try it anyhow.
Subject: OK. Let's see: Two years ago . . . I would be in high school in Pittsburgh. . . . That would be my senior year. Third week in September—that's just after summer—that would be the fall term. . . . Let me see. I think I had chemistry lab on Mondays. I don't know. I was probably in chemistry lab. Wait a minute—that would be the second week of school. I remember he started off with the atomic table—a big fancy chart. I thought he was crazy trying to make us memorize that thing. You know, I think I can remember sitting. . . . (Lindsay & Norman, 1977)

Episodic memory, then, can provide information from events that happened long in the past (Reynolds & Takooshian, 1988).

But semantic memory is no less impressive, permitting us to dredge up tens of thousands of facts ranging from the date of one's birthday to the knowledge that $1 is less than $5. Many psychologists, using **associative models** of memory, argue that semantic memory consists of associations between mental representations of various pieces of information (e.g., Collins & Quillian, 1969; Collins & Loftus, 1975).

Associative models: A technique of recalling information by thinking about related information

The basic notion behind associative models is that, when we think about a particular concept, our semantic memory activates the recall of related concepts, bringing them more readily to mind. For example, thinking about a "robin" activates our recall of related concepts such as "eats worms" and "has a red breast." As a result, if we are trying to remember some specific bit of information (such as where we left our sunglasses), thinking about associated material may help us recollect it (such as where we were when we last wore the sunglasses).

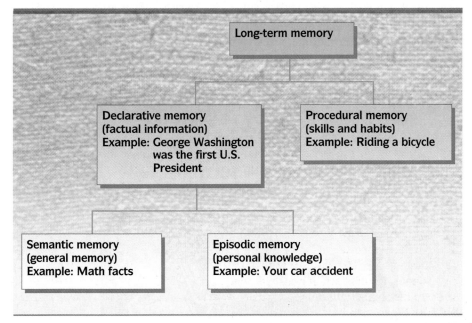

FIGURE 6-5 The different types of long-term memory.

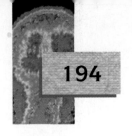
Priming: A technique of recalling information by having been exposed to related information at an earlier time

Explicit memory: Intentional or conscious recollection of information

Implicit memory: Memories of which people are not consciously aware, but which can affect subsequent performance and behavior

In such instances, related information helps prime us to recall information that we are otherwise unable to recollect. In **priming,** prior presentation of information subsequently makes it easier to recall related items, even when we have no conscious memory of the original information (Tulving & Schacter, 1990).

The typical experiment designed to illustrate priming helps clarify the phenomenon. In priming experiments, subjects are first presented with a stimulus such as a word, an object, or perhaps a drawing of a face. The second phase of the experiment is held after an interval ranging from several seconds to months later. At that point, subjects are exposed to incomplete perceptual information that is related to the first stimulus and asked whether they recognize it. For example, the new material may consist of the first letter of a word that had been presented earlier, or a part of a face that had been shown earlier. If subjects are able to identify the stimulus more readily than they identify stimuli that have not been presented earlier, priming has taken place.

Priming occurs even when subjects report no conscious awareness of having been exposed to a stimulus earlier. For instance, studies have found that people who are anesthetized during surgery can sometimes recall snippets of information that they heard during surgery—even though they have no conscious recollection of the surgery (Kihlstrom et al., 1990).

The discovery that people have memories about which they are unaware has been an important one. It has led to speculation that two forms of memory, explicit and implicit, may exist side by side. **Explicit memory** refers to intentional or conscious recollection of information. When we try to remember a name or date, we are using explicit memory.

In contrast, **implicit memory** refers to memories of which people are not consciously aware, but which can affect subsequent performance and behavior. When an event that we are unable to consciously recall affects our behavior, implicit memory is at work (Graf & Masson, 1993; Schacter, Chiu, & Ochsner, 1993).

There is considerable disagreement regarding the precise difference between implicit and explicit memory (Roediger, 1990; Lewandowsky, Dunn, & Kirsner, 1989; Schacter, 1992, 1993). Some researchers suggest that two distinct memory systems exist, one for implicit and one for explicit memory (e.g., Weiskrantz, 1989; Schacter, Chiu, & Ochsner, 1993). In contrast, other researchers have proposed that the two kinds of memory differ simply in the way that information is initially processed and retrieved, and do not demonstrate the existence of independent memory systems (e.g., Roediger, Weldon, & Challis, 1989).

It is still too early to tell which of these views will prevail in the memory research arena. Studies that support both sides of the argument are continuing to be conducted. In the meantime, research in several areas of psychology is demon-

Rob Rogers reprinted by permission of UFS, Inc.

strating that the influence of implicit memories on people's behavior may be consequential. For instance, social psychologists are investigating how we remember what others are like and how we subsequently act toward them. Similarly, psychologists specializing in learning are investigating how we can use implicit memory to teach skills more effectively. Such work should have important applications.

Levels of Processing

So far, we have relied on a model of memory which suggests that the processing of information in memory proceeds in three sequential stages, starting with sensory memory, advancing to short-term memory, and potentially ending in long-term memory. However, not all memory specialists agree with such a view. Some suggest that a single process accounts for how well information is remembered: the way in which material is first perceived, considered, and understood.

The **levels-of-processing theory** emphasizes the degree to which new material is mentally analyzed (Craik & Lockhart, 1972; Craik, 1990). In contrast to the view that there are sensory, short-term, and long-term memories, levels-of-processing theory suggests that the amount of information processing that occurs when material is initially encountered is central in determining how much of the information is ultimately remembered. According to this approach, the depth of processing during exposure to material—meaning the degree to which it is analyzed and considered—is critical; the greater the intensity of its initial processing, the more likely we are to remember it.

Because we do not pay close attention to much of the information to which we are exposed, typically only scant mental processing takes place, and we forget new material almost immediately. However, information to which we pay greater attention is processed more thoroughly. Thus, it enters memory at a deeper level—and is less apt to be forgotten than information processed at shallower levels.

The theory goes on to suggest that there are considerable differences in the way information is processed at various levels of memory. At shallow levels, information is processed merely in terms of its physical and sensory aspects. For example, we may pay attention only to the shapes that make up the letters in the word "dog." At an intermediate level of processing, the shapes are translated into meaningful units—in this case, letters of the alphabet. These letters are considered in the context of words, and a specific sound of the word may be attached to the letters.

At the deepest level of processing, information is analyzed in terms of its meaning. It may be seen in a wider context, and associations between the meaning of the information and broader networks of knowledge may be drawn. For instance, we may think of dogs not merely as animals with four legs and a tail, but in terms of their relationship to cats and other mammals. We may form an image of our own dog, thereby relating the concept to our own lives. According to the levels-of-processing approach, the deeper the initial level of processing of specific information, the longer the information will be retained. The approach suggests, then, that the best way to remember new information is to consider it thoroughly when you are first exposed to it—reflecting on how it relates to information that you currently know (McDaniel, Riegler, & Waddill, 1990).

The levels-of-processing theory considers memory as involving more active mental processes than the three-stage approach to memory. However, research has not been entirely supportive of the levels-of-processing approach. For example, in some cases material that is processed on a shallow level is remembered better than information processed on a deeper level (Baddeley, 1978; Cermak & Craik, 1979). Furthermore, no fully adequate means has been found for objectively measuring how deeply material is processed in the first place (Searleman & Herrmann, 1994).

In sum, neither the levels-of-processing model nor the three-stage model of

Levels-of-processing theory: The theory that emphasizes the degree to which new material is mentally analyzed

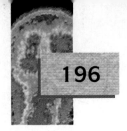

memory is able to account fully for all phenomena relating to memory. As a result, other models of memory have been proposed. For example, psychologist Nelson Cowan (1988) has suggested that the most accurate representation of memory is a model in which short-term storage is considered a part of long-term storage, rather than representing a separate stage. It is probably too early to tell—let alone remember—which of the multiple models of memory gives us the most accurate characterization of memory (Collins et al., 1993; Searleman & Herrmann, 1994).

RECAP AND REVIEW

Recap

- Memory is the process by which we encode, store, and retrieve information.
- Sensory memory contains a brief but accurate representation of physical stimuli to which a person is exposed. Each representation is constantly being replaced with a new one.
- Short-term memory has a capacity of seven (plus or minus two) chunks of information. Memories remain in short-term storage for 15 to 25 seconds and are then either transferred to long-term memory or lost.
- Long-term memory consists of declarative and procedural memory. Declarative memory is further subdivided into episodic and semantic memory.
- An alternative to the three-stage model of memory, the levels-of-processing approach suggests that information-is analyzed at different levels, with material processed at deeper levels being retained the longest.

Review

1. The process by which information is initially stored in memory is known as _____. _____ is the process by which elements of memory are brought into awareness and used.
2. Match the type of memory with its definition:
   1. Long-term memory
   2. Short-term memory
   3. Sensory memory

a. Holds information 15 to 25 seconds
b. Permanent storage, could be difficult to retrieve
c. Initial storage of information, lasts only a second
3. A _____ is a meaningful group of stimuli that can be stored together in short-term memory.
4. _____ are organizational strategies used to organize information.
5. There appear to be two types of declarative memory: _____ memory, which is memory for knowledge and facts, and _____ memory, which is memory for personal experiences.
6. _____ models of memory state that declarative memory is stored as associations between pieces of information.
7. You read an article stating that, the more a person analyzes a statement, the more likely he or she is to remember it later. What theory is this article describing?

Ask Yourself

Priming seems to occur without conscious awareness in most cases. How might this effect be used by advertisers and others to promote their products? What ethical principles are involved?

(Answers to review questions are on page 198.)

- **What causes difficulties and failures in remembering?**

RECALLING LONG-TERM MEMORIES

An hour after his job interview, Ricardo was sitting in a coffee shop, telling his friend Laura how well it had gone when the woman who had interviewed him walked in. "Well, hello, Ricardo. How are you doing?" Trying to make a good impression, Ricardo began to make introductions, but then realized he could not remember the interviewer's name. Stammering, he desperately searched his memory, but to no avail. "I *know* her name," he thought to himself, "but here I am, looking like a fool. I can kiss this job goodbye."

Have you ever tried to remember someone's name, convinced that you knew it, but unable to recall it no matter how hard you tried? This not infrequent occur-

The tip-of-the-tongue phenomenon is especially frustrating in situations where a person cannot recall the name of someone he or she has just met.

rence—known as the **tip-of-the-tongue phenomenon**—exemplifies the difficulties that can occur in retrieving information stored in long-term memory (Harris & Morris, 1986; A. S. Brown, 1991).

Retrieval Cues

One reason recall is not perfect is the sheer quantity of recollections that are stored in long-term memory. Although the issue is far from settled, many psychologists have suggested that the material that makes its way there is relatively permanent (Tulving & Psotka, 1971). If they are correct, this suggests that the capacity of long-term memory is vast, given the broad range of people's experiences and educational backgrounds. For instance, if you are like the average college student, your vocabulary includes some 50,000 words, you know hundreds of mathematical "facts," and you are able to conjure up images—such as the way your childhood home looked—with no trouble at all. In fact, simply cataloging all your memories would probably take years of work.

How do we sort through this vast array of material and retrieve specific information at the appropriate time? One of the major ways is through the use of retrieval cues. A *retrieval cue* is a stimulus that allows us to recall information that is located in long-term memory more easily (Tulving & Thompson, 1973). It may be a word, an emotion, a sound; whatever the specific cue, a memory will suddenly come to mind when the retrieval cue is present. For example, the smell of roasting turkey may evoke memories of Thanksgiving or family gatherings.

Retrieval cues guide people through the information stored in long-term memory in much the same way as the cards in a card catalog guide people through a library. They are particularly important when we are making an effort to *recall* information, as opposed to our being asked to *recognize* material stored in memory. In *recall,* a specific piece of information must be retrieved—such as that needed to answer a fill-in-the-blank question or write an essay on a test. In contrast, *recognition* occurs when people are presented with a stimulus and asked whether they have been exposed to it previously, or are asked to identify it from a list of alternatives.

As you might guess, recognition is generally a much easier task than recall. Recall is more difficult because it consists of a series of processes: a search through memory, retrieval of potentially relevant information, and then a decision regarding whether or not the information you have found is accurate. If it appears correct, the search is over, but if it does not, the search must continue. On the other hand, recognition is simpler since it involves fewer steps (Anderson & Bower, 1972; Miserando, 1991).

Tip-of-the-tongue phenomenon: The inability to recall information that one realizes one knows—a result of the difficulty of retrieving information from long-term memory

Naming the characters shown above (a recall task) is more difficult than solving the recognition problem posed alongside them.

Flashbulb Memories

Where were you on January 28, 1986? You will most likely draw a blank until this piece of information is added: January 28, 1986, was the date that the space shuttle *Challenger* exploded.

You probably have little trouble recalling your exact location and a variety of other trivial details that occurred when you heard the news, even though the accident happened years ago. The reason is a phenomenon known as **flashbulb memories.** Flashbulb memories are memories centered on a specific, important, or surprising event that are so vivid it is as if they represented a snapshot of the event.

Several types of flashbulb memories are common among college students. For example, involvement in a car accident, meeting one's roommate for the first time, and the night of high school graduation are all typical flashbulb memories (Rubin, 1985).

Flashbulb memories: Memories of a specific event that are so clear they seem like snapshots of the event

Flashbulb memory enables us to recall vivid details about important personal or historical events. Many Americans have flashbulb memories of the start of the Persian Gulf War.

ANSWERS TO PREVIOUS REVIEW
1. encoding; Retrieval **2.** 1-b; 2-a; 3-c **3.** chunk **4.** Mnemonics **5.** semantic; episodic **6.** Associative **7.** Levels-of-processing theory

Of course, flashbulb memories do not contain every detail of an original scene. For instance, I remember vividly that some three decades ago I was sitting in Mr. Sharp's tenth-grade geometry class when I heard that President Kennedy had been shot. Although I recall where I was sitting and how my classmates reacted to the news, I do not recollect what I was wearing or what I had for lunch that day. Flashbulb memories, then, are not complete, and just how much their essential nature differs from everyday memories remains an open question (McCloskey, Wible, & Cohen, 1988; Pillemer, 1990; Winograd & Neisser, 1992).

Still, flashbulb memories seem extraordinary because of the details they do include. An analysis of people's recollections of the Kennedy assassination found that their memories tended to have a number of features in common (Brown & Kulik, 1977). Most contained information regarding the place where the person heard the news, the person who told him or her about it, the event that was interrupted by the news, the emotions of the informant, the person's own emotions, and some personal details of the event (such as seeing a robin fly by while the information was being relayed).

On the other hand, we can't be sure that all the details recalled in flashbulb memories are accurate. For example, one day after the *Challenger* accident, psychologists Nicole Harsch and Ulric Neisser asked a group of college students how they had heard the news of the disaster. When they asked the same people the identical question 3 years later, most responded readily, providing reasonable responses. The trouble was that, in about one-third of the cases, their answers were completely wrong (Harsch & Neisser, 1989; Neisser & Harsch, 1992; Winograd & Neisser, 1992).

Flashbulb memories illustrate a more general phenomenon about memory: Memories that are exceptional are more easily retrieved (although not necessarily accurately) than those relating to events that are commonplace. We are more likely, for example, to recall a particular number if it appears in a group of twenty words than if it appears in a group of twenty other numbers. The more distinctive a stimulus, the more likely we are to recall it later (von Restorff, 1933; Walker & Jones, 1983).

Constructive Processes in Memory: Rebuilding the Past

As we have seen, although it is clear that we can have detailed recollections of significant and distinctive events, it is difficult to gauge the accuracy of such memories. In fact, it is apparent that our memories reflect, at least in part, **constructive processes,** processes in which memories are influenced by the meaning we give to events. When we retrieve information, then, the memory that is produced is affected not just by the direct prior experience we have had with the stimulus, but by our guesses and inferences about its meaning as well.

Constructive processes: Processes in which memories are influenced by the interpretation and meaning we give to events

The notion that memory is based on constructive processes was first put forward by Sir Frederic Bartlett, a British psychologist. He suggested that people tend to remember information in terms of **schemas,** general themes that contain relatively little specific detail (Bartlett, 1932). In a schema, unimportant details are omitted. Instead, memories consist of a general reconstruction of previous experience. Bartlett argued that such schemas were based not only on the specific material to which people are exposed, but also on their understanding of the situation, their expectations about the situation, and their awareness of the motivation underlying the behavior of others.

Schemas: General themes in memory that contain relatively little detail

In a demonstration of the operation of schemas, researchers have employed a process known as serial reproduction, in which information from memory is passed sequentially from one person to another. For an example of serial reproduction, look briefly at the drawing in Figure 6-6, and then try to describe it to someone else without looking back at it. Then ask that person to describe it to another person, and repeat the process with still one more person.

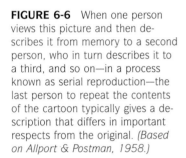

FIGURE 6-6 When one person views this picture and then describes it from memory to a second person, who in turn describes it to a third, and so on—in a process known as serial reproduction—the last person to repeat the contents of the cartoon typically gives a description that differs in important respects from the original. *(Based on Allport & Postman, 1958.)*

If you listen to the last person's report of the contents of the drawing, you are sure to find that it differs in important respects from the drawing itself. Many people recall the drawing as showing a razor in the hand of the African-American person—obviously an incorrect recollection, given that the razor is held by the white person (Allport & Postman, 1958).

This example, which is drawn from a classic experiment, illustrates the role of expectations in memory. The migration of the razor from the white person's hand to the African-American's hand in memory clearly indicates that expectations about the world—reflecting, in this case, the unwarranted prejudice that African-Americans may be more violent than whites and thus more apt to be holding a razor—have an impact upon how events are recalled.

Bartlett thought that schemas affected recall at the time of retrieval of information, and that the information had originally been entered into memory accurately. However, subsequent work has shown that our expectations and prior knowledge affect the way information is initially encoded in memory. For example, read and try to remember the following passage:

The procedure is actually quite simple. First you arrange items into different groups. Of course, one pile may be sufficient, depending on how much there is to do. If you have to go somewhere else due to lack of facilities, that is the next step; otherwise, you are pretty well set. It is important not to overdo things. That is, it is better to do too few things at once than too many. In the short run this may not seem important but complications can easily arise. A mistake can be expensive as well. At first, the whole procedure will seem complicated. Soon, however, it will become just another facet of life. It is difficult to foresee any end to the necessity for this task in the immediate future, but then one can never tell. After the procedure is completed, one arranges the materials into different groups again. Then they can be put into their appropriate places. Eventually, they will be used once more and the whole cycle will then have to be repeated. However, this is a part of life. (Bransford & Johnson, 1972, p. 722)

As the results of a study that used this passage revealed, your ability to recall it—as well as to understand it initially—would have been far greater if you had known prior to reading it that it referred to washing laundry (Bransford & Johnson, 1972). The way in which we understand information to which we are first exposed, then, can either assist or hinder our ability to remember it.

As noted, it is not just our expectations and prior knowledge that have an impact on what we recall. Our understanding of the motivations of others also contributes to constructive processes in memory. For example, in what has been

called the *soap opera effect,* knowledge about what motivates an individual can lead to elaborations in memory of earlier events involving that person.

The soap opera effect derives its name from soap opera characters who, at least in the eyes of occasional viewers, make seemingly innocent statements. However, to long-term viewers, who are aware of the characters' real motives, the same statements may be fraught with significance. In turn, this information will be remembered differently according to a person's understanding of the motivation behind the statement (Owens, Bower, & Black, 1979).

In sum, it is clear that our understanding of the motivations behind a person's behavior, as well as our expectations and knowledge, affects the reliability of our memories (Katz, 1989). In some cases, the imperfections of people's recollections can have profound implications, as we will see when we now consider memory in the legal realm.

Memory in the Courtroom: The Eyewitness on Trial

For William Jackson, the inadequate memories of two people cost him five years of his life. Jackson was the victim of mistaken identity during criminal proceedings. Two witnesses picked him out of a lineup as the perpetrator of a crime. On that basis, he was convicted and sentenced to serve fourteen to fifty years in jail.

Five years later the actual criminal was identified, and Jackson was released. For Jackson, though, it was too late. In his words, "They took away part of my life, part of my youth. I spend five years down there, and all they said was 'we're sorry.' " (*Time,* 1982)

Unfortunately, Jackson is not the only victim to whom apologies have had to be made; many cases of mistaken identity have occurred (Brandon & Davies, 1973). Research on eyewitness identification of suspects, as well as on memory for other details of crimes, has shown that witnesses are apt to make substantial errors when they try to recall details of criminal activity (Wells, 1993).

One reason is the impact of weapons used in crimes. When a criminal perpetrator displays a gun or knife, it acts like a perceptual magnet, with all witnesses' eyes being drawn to the weapon. As a consequence, less attention is paid to other details of the crime, and witnesses are less able to recall what actually occurred (Loftus, Loftus, & Messo, 1987).

Even when weapons are not involved, eyewitnesses are prone to errors relating to memory. For instance, viewers of a 12-second film of a mugging that was shown on a New York City television news program were later given the opportunity to pick out the assailant from a six-person lineup. Of some 2000 viewers who called the station after the program, only 15 percent were able to pick out the right person—a figure similar to random guessing (Buckhout, 1975).

One reason that eyewitnesses are prone to memory-related errors is that the specific wording of questions posed to them by police or attorneys can affect the way in which witnesses recall information, as a number of experiments illustrate. For example, in one experiment subjects were shown a film of two cars crashing into each other. Some were then asked the question, "About how fast were the cars going when they *smashed* into each other?" They estimated the speed to be an average of 40.8 miles per hour. In contrast, when another group of subjects was asked, "About how fast were the cars going when they *contacted* each other?" the average estimated speed was only 31.8 miles per hour (Loftus & Palmer, 1974).

The problem of memory reliability becomes even more acute when children are witnesses. Recent years have seen many instances in which children's recollections of sexual abuse are central to court cases, such as the Buckeys' case described at the start of this chapter. However, increasing evidence suggests that children's memories are highly vulnerable to the influence of others (Doris, 1991; Loftus & Ketcham, 1991; Loftus, 1993; Brainerd, Reyna, & Brandse, 1995).

For instance, in one experiment, 5- to 7-year-old girls who had just had routine physical examinations were shown an anatomically explicit doll. The girls were shown the doll's genital area and asked, "Did the doctor touch you here?" Three of the girls who did not have a vaginal or anal exam said that the doctor had in fact touched them in the genital area. And one of those three made up the detail, "The doctor did it with a stick" (Saywitz & Goodman, 1990).

Children's memories are especially susceptible to influence when the situation is highly emotional or stressful. For example, in the Buckey case, there was enormous pretrial publicity. Because the alleged victims were repeatedly questioned, often by untrained interviewers, their memories may have been influenced by the types of questions they were asked.

In sum, the memories of witnesses are far from infallible, and this is especially true when children are involved (Doris, 1991). The question of the accuracy of memories becomes even more complex, however, when we consider the triggering of memories of events that people at first don't even recall happening. As we discuss in the Psychology at Work box, this issue has raised considerable controversy.

Autobiographical Memory: Where Past Meets Present

Your memory of experiences in your own past might well be a fiction—or at least a distortion of what actually occurred. The same constructive processes that act to make us inaccurately recall the behavior of others also reduce the accuracy of autobiographical memories. **Autobiographical memories** refer to our recollections of circumstances and episodes from our own lives (Conway & Rubin, 1993; Friedman, 1993; Nelson, 1993; Rubin, 1995).

Autobiographical memories: Our recollections of circumstances and episodes from our own lives

For example, we tend to forget information about our past that is incompatible with the way in which we currently see ourselves. One study found that adults who were well adjusted but who had been treated for emotional problems during the early years of their lives tended to forget important but troubling childhood events. For instance, they forgot such difficult circumstances as their family's receiving welfare when they were children, being in foster care, and living in a home for delinquents (Robbins, 1988). Similarly, people who are depressed remember sad events from their past more easily than happy people do, and people who report being happy in adulthood remember more happy events than depressing ones (Bower & Cohen, 1982).

It is not just certain kinds of events that are distorted; particular periods of life are remembered more easily than others. For example, when people reach old age, they remember periods of life in which they experienced major transitions, such as attending college or working at a first job, better than their middle-age years (Rubin, 1985; Fitzgerald, 1988; Fromholt & Larsen, 1991).

Exploring Diversity

Are There Cross-Cultural Differences in Memory?

Many travelers who have visited areas of the world in which there is no written language have returned with tales of people with phenomenal memories. Presumably because they have no written records, people in such cultures develop memories that can provide a kind of oral record keeping to keep track of important events in the society's history. For instance, storytellers in some preliterate cultures can recount long chronicles that recall the names and activities of people over many generations.

PSYCHOLOGY AT WORK

Repressed Memories: Truth or Fiction?

Guilty of murder in the first degree. That was the jury's verdict in the case of George Franklin, Sr., who was charged with murdering his daughter's playmate. But this case was different from most other murder cases: It was based on memories that had been repressed for 20 years. Franklin's daughter claimed that she had forgotten everything she had once known about her father's crime until 2 years earlier, when she began to have flashbacks of the event. Initially, she had only a memory of her friend's look of betrayal. Over the next year, the memories became richer, and she recalled being together with her father and her friend. Then she remembered her father sexually assaulting her friend. She recalled his lifting a rock over his head, and then seeing her friend lying on the ground, covered with blood. On the basis of these memories, her father was arrested and ultimately convicted.

But just how accurate were these memories? Although the prosecutor and jury clearly believed Franklin's daughter, there is good reason to question the validity of *repressed memories,* recollections of events that are initially so shocking that the mind responds by pushing them into the unconscious. Supporters of the notion of repressed memory suggest that such memories may remain hidden, possibly throughout a person's lifetime, unless they are triggered by some current circumstance, such as the probing that occurs during psychological therapy.

However, psychologist Elizabeth Loftus maintains that so-called repressed memories may well be inaccurate or even wholly false. She notes how easy it is to plant memories that people believe are real. For example, in one experiment, a student named Jack wrote a story for his younger brother Chris, 14, to read. It described an event that never happened:

"It was 1981 or 1982. I remember that Chris was 5. We had gone shopping at the University City shopping mall in Spokane. After some panic, we found Chris being led down the mall by a tall, oldish man (I think he was wearing a flannel shirt). Chris was crying and holding the man's hand. The man explained that he had found Chris walking around crying his eyes out just a few moments before and was trying to help him find his parents."

Just a few weeks later, Chris was convinced the event had actually happened. He described the color of the old man's flannel shirt, his bald head, and how he felt "really scared." Even when informed that the event never happened, Chris clung to his memory, saying "Really? I thought I remembered being lost . . . and looking around for you guys. I do remember that, and then crying, and Mom coming up and saying, 'Where were you? Don't you . . . ever do that again' " (Loftus, 1993, p. 532).

Clearly, people are potentially susceptible to false memories. Why? Some false memories occur when people are unable to recall the source of a memory of a particular event about which they have only vague recollections (Schacter, 1994). When the source of the memory is unclear or ambiguous, people may begin to confuse whether they actually experienced the event or whether it was imagined. Ultimately, the memory begins to seem authentic, and people may come to believe that the event actually occurred.

In fact, some therapists have been accused of inadvertently encouraging people who come to them with psychological difficulties to recreate false chronicles of childhood sexual experiences. In addition, there have been many well-publicized declarations of repressed memories, such as those of Roseanne Barr, as well as parishioners of Catholic churches who remember being abused by a priest during their childhood. Such publicity makes the possibility of repressed memories seem more legitimate and may ultimately prime people to recall memories of events that never happened.

On the other hand, many psychologists see repressed memories as a very real phenomenon. Building upon a psychodynamic model of human behavior that we discussed in Chapter 1, they argue that it is reasonable to assume that some memories will be so painful that they are forced into the unconscious. They suggest that childhood sexual abuse is so traumatic that people are motivated to forget its occurrence. In support of their view, they point to cases in which it is possible to confirm once-repressed memories of childhood abuse (Frederickson, 1992).

The controversy regarding the legitimacy of repressed memories is unlikely to be resolved soon. Many psychologists, particularly those who provide therapy, give great weight to the reality of repressed memories. On the other side of the issue are many memory researchers, who maintain that there is no scientific support for the existence of such memories.

In the meantime, it seems clear that some recollections of childhood traumas may be temporarily forgotten and only recalled later in life. And it is equally true that certain memories of youth are inaccurate or even completely false. The challenge facing psychologists, members of juries, and others is to distinguish truth from fiction.

On the basis of such anecdotes, memory experts initially argued that people in preliterate society develop a different, and perhaps better, type of memory than those in cultures that employ a written language (Bartlett, 1932). They suggested that, in a society which lacks writing, people are going to be motivated to recall information with accuracy, particularly in terms of tribal histories and traditions that would otherwise be lost if not passed down orally from one generation to another.

However, more recent approaches to cultural differences suggest a different conclusion. For one thing, preliterate peoples don't have an exclusive claim on amazing memory feats. For instance, certain Hebrew scholars know the entire text of the Talmud, biblical commentaries, by heart. Not only have they memorized its thousands of pages, but they can recall what word is printed at a particular location when given a page number. Similarly, poetry singers in Yugoslavia know at least thirty songs from memory, each of which is several thousand lines long. Even in cultures in which written language exists, astounding feats of memory are possible (Neisser, 1982; Rubin, 1995).

Memory experts suggest that there are both similarities and differences in memory across cultures. According to psychologist Daniel Wagner, basic memory processes, such as short-term memory capacity and the structure of long-term memory, are universal and operate similarly in people of all cultures (Wagner, 1981). In contrast, cultural differences can be seen in the way in which information is acquired, rehearsed, and retrieved from memory. Consequently, culture determines how people consider and frame information initially, how much they practice learning and recalling it, and what strategies they use to try to recall it.

In sum, the association between culture and memory can be compared with the relationship between computer hardware and software. Basic memory processes, analogous to computer "hardware," are universal across cultures. On the other hand, the "software" of memory—the way information is initially acquired, rehearsed, and retrieved—is influenced by the nature of a specific culture.

RECAP AND REVIEW

Recap

- The tip-of-the tongue phenomenon refers to the inability to recall something that a person is sure he or she knows.
- Retrieval cues are particularly important when recalling information—as opposed to recognizing it.
- Flashbulb memories are memories that are centered on a specific, important event and are so clear it is as if they represent a snapshot of the event.
- Memories are affected, at least in part, by constructive processes, which influence the meaning we give to events. Autobiographical memory, for instance, can be distorted by constructive processes.
- Basic memory processes are universal, although the way in which information is initially acquired, rehearsed, and retrieved differs across cultures.

Review

1. While with a group of friends at a dance, Evita bumps into a man she dated last month. When she tries to introduce him to her friends, she cannot remember his name, though she is positive she knows it. What is the term for this occurrence?

2. _____ is used when a person is asked to retrieve a specific item from memory.

3. A friend of your mother tells you, "I know exactly where I was and what I was doing when I heard that Elvis died." What phenomenon explains this type of recollection?

4. The person described in question 3 could probably also accurately describe in detail what she was wearing when Elvis passed on, right down to the color of the ribbon on her blue suede shoes. True or false?

5. Retrieval of memories is influenced not only by objective reality, but also by our constructions of past events. True or false?

6. _____ are "themes," containing little specific detail, that are used to help us organize information in memory.

Ask Yourself

How might courtroom procedure be improved, knowing what you now know about memory errors and biases?

(Answers to review questions are on page 206.)

- *Why do we forget information?*
- *What are the biological bases of memory?*
- *What are the major memory impairments?*

FORGETTING: WHEN MEMORY FAILS

He could remember, quite literally, nothing—nothing, that is, that had happened since the loss of his brain's temporal lobes and hippocampus during experimental surgery to reduce epileptic seizures. Until that time, his memory had been quite normal. But after the operation he was unable to recall anything for more than a few minutes, and then the memory was seemingly lost forever. He did not remember his address, or the name of the person to whom he was talking. He would read the same magazine over and over again. According to his own description, his life was like waking from a dream and being unable to know where he was or how he got there. (Milner, 1966)

The difficulties faced by a person without a normal memory are legion, as the case described above attests. All of us who have experienced even routine instances of forgetting—such as not remembering an acquaintance's name or a fact on a test—understand the serious consequences of memory failure.

The first attempts to study forgetting were made by German psychologist Hermann Ebbinghaus about a hundred years ago. Using himself as his only subject, he memorized lists of three-letter nonsense syllables—meaningless sets of two consonants with a vowel in between, such as FIW and BOZ. By measuring how easy it was to relearn a given list of words after varying periods of time from initial learning had passed, he found that forgetting occurred systematically, as shown in Figure 6-7. As the figure indicates, the most rapid forgetting occurs in the first 9 hours, and particularly in the first hour. After 9 hours, the rate of forgetting slows and declines little, even after the passage of many days.

Despite his primitive methods, Ebbinghaus's research had an important influence on subsequent research, and his basic conclusions have been upheld (Wixted & Ebbeson, 1991). There is almost always a strong initial decline in memory, fol-

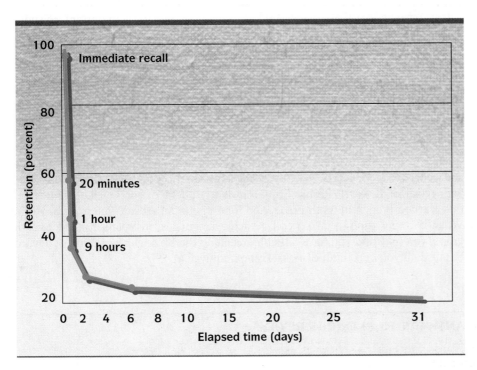

FIGURE 6-7 In his classic work, Ebbinghaus found that the most rapid forgetting occurs in the first 9 hours after exposure to new material. However, the rate of forgetting then slows down and declines very little even after many days have passed. *(Ebbinghaus, 1885/1913.)*

Decay: The loss of information through nonuse

Memory trace, or **engram:** A physical change in the brain corresponding to memory

lowed by a more gradual drop over time. Furthermore, relearning of previously mastered material is almost always faster than starting from scratch, whether the material is academic information or a motor skill such as serving a tennis ball.

Efforts at understanding the problem of *why* we forget have yielded two major solutions. One theory explains forgetting in terms of a process called **decay,** or the loss of information through its nonuse. This explanation assumes that when new material is learned, a **memory trace,** or **engram**—an actual physical change in the brain—occurs. In decay, the trace simply fades away with nothing left behind, because of the mere passage of time.

Although there is evidence that decay does occur, it does not seem to be the complete explanation for forgetting. Often there is no relationship between how long ago a person was exposed to information and how well it is recalled. If decay explained all forgetting, we would expect that, the longer time between the initial learning of information and our attempt to recall it, the harder it would be to remember it, since there would be more time for the memory trace to decay. Yet people who take several consecutive tests on the same material often recall more of the initial information when taking later tests than they did on earlier tests. If decay were operating, we would expect the opposite to occur (Payne, 1986).

Because decay does not fully account for forgetting, memory specialists have proposed an additional mechanism: **interference.** In interference, information in memory displaces or blocks out other information, preventing its recall.

Interference: The phenomenon by which recall is hindered because of other information in memory which displaces or blocks it out

To distinguish between decay and interference, think of the two processes in terms of a row of books on a library shelf. In decay, the old books are constantly crumbling and rotting away, leaving room for new arrivals. Interference processes suggest that new books knock the old ones off the shelf, where they become inaccessible.

Most research suggests that interference is the key process in forgetting (Potter, 1990). We mainly forget things because new memories interfere with the retrieval of old ones, not because the memory trace has decayed.

Although we may view interference negatively, it is important to remember that it may actually enhance our ability to understand and interact with the world around us. Interference assists us in developing general, summary memories of our experiences. For instance, rather than recalling every detail of every encounter with a particular professor, we tend to remember the most important episodes and forget those that are less meaningful. This ability allows us to draw a general, although not necessarily detailed or totally accurate, picture of what our encounters with the professor have been like in the past. Furthermore, it helps us to anticipate the course of future interactions (Potter, 1990).

Proactive and Retroactive Interference: The Before and After of Forgetting

There are actually two sorts of interference that influence forgetting: proactive and retroactive. In *proactive interference,* information learned earlier interferes with recall of newer material. Suppose, as a student of foreign languages, you first learned French in tenth grade, and then in eleventh grade you took Spanish. When it comes time to take a college achievement test in Spanish in the twelfth grade, you may find you have difficulty recalling the Spanish translation of a word because all you can think of is its French equivalent.

ANSWERS TO PREVIOUS REVIEW
1. Tip-of-the-tongue phenomenon **2.** Recall **3.** Flashbulb memory **4.** False; small details probably won't be remembered via flashbulb memory. **5.** True **6.** Schemas

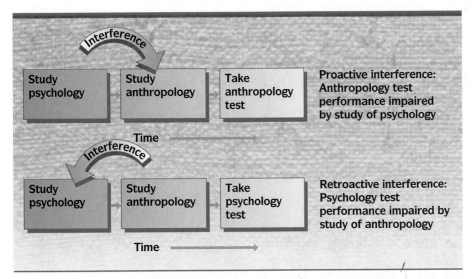

Proactive interference:
Anthropology test performance impaired by study of psychology

Retroactive interference:
Psychology test performance impaired by study of anthropology

FIGURE 6-8 Proactive interference occurs when material learned earlier interferes with recall of newer material. In this example, exposure to psychology prior to learning anthropology interferes with performance on an anthropology test. In contrast, retroactive interference exists when material learned after initial exposure to other material interferes with the recall of the first material. In this case, retroactive interference occurs when recall of psychology is impaired because of later exposure to anthropology.

On the other hand, *retroactive interference* refers to difficulty in recall of information because of later exposure to different material. If, for example, you have difficulty on a French achievement test because of your more recent exposure to Spanish, retroactive interference is the culprit. One way of remembering the difference between proactive and retroactive interference is to keep in mind that *pro*active interference moves forward in time—the past interferes with the present—whereas *retro*active interference retrogresses in time, working backward as the present interferes with the past. (See Figure 6-8.)

Although the concepts of proactive and retroactive interference suggest why material may be forgotten, they still do not explain whether forgetting due to interference is caused by the actual loss or modification of information or by problems in the retrieval of information. Most research suggests that material that has apparently been lost because of interference can eventually be recalled if appropriate stimuli are presented (Anderson, 1981; Tulving & Psotka, 1971), but the question has not been fully answered. In an effort to resolve the issue, some psychologists have begun to study the biological bases of memory in order to better understand what is remembered and what is forgotten—an increasingly important avenue of investigation that we turn to now.

The Biological Bases of Memory: The Search for the Engram

Where does memory reside? The search for the engram—the physical change in the brain that corresponds to the memory—has resulted in the development of several imaginative paths of research. This work has extended our knowledge of the biological underpinnings of memory in several directions.

Perhaps the most basic way to answer the question of where memory is "located" is to consider the level of individual neurons and their chemical interconnections. Most evidence suggests that particular memories produce biochemical changes at specific synapses between neurons. Research on the sea snail, a primitive organism that can learn simple responses, has shown that systematic changes occur in its synapses during learning. Specifically, the ability of a particular neuron to release its neurotransmitters increases or declines as a result of learning (Kandel & Schwartz, 1982; Mayford et al., 1992). If retention of the response is short term, the neuronal changes will be temporary. On the other hand, if long-term retention occurs, permanent structural changes in the neuronal connections will occur. Obviously, this difference between fleeting and permanent changes in the brain corresponds to the distinction between short- and long-term memory.

It is fair to ask just how much we can generalize from the lowly sea snail to humans. However, research using different species has produced results that suggest the underlying processes are similar. Furthermore, this work is consistent with research on *long-term potentiation,* long-lasting increases in the strength of the responsiveness at various synapses. Certain neural pathways seem to become easily excited as a response is learned, apparently as a memory is formed. It is as if we expanded the size of a garden hose in order to allow more water to be discharged (Lynch, Granger, & Staubli, 1991).

In sum, long-term potentiation increases the excitability of particular neurons and neural pathways. At the same time, changes also occur in the number of synapses, as dendrites branch out. These changes are known as *consolidation,* the process by which memories become fixed and stable in long-term memory. Consolidation takes some time to stabilize, which explains why long-term memories are not suddenly fixed in memory. Instead, consolidation may continue for days and even years (Squire, 1987).

The Site of the Engram   It is clear that memory produces changes on a neuronal level. But just where in the brain does all this activity take place?

This question has proved to be a major puzzle to psychologists interested in memory. The search began in the 1920s, when psychologist Karl Lashley ran a series of experiments in which he removed portions of the cortex of rats. He found that rats which were made to relearn a problem involving running a maze showed learning deficits in proportion to the extent of the damage to their cortex; when more material was removed from the cortex, greater learning difficulties took place.

More intriguing, however, was the finding that the time it took to relearn the problem was unrelated to the specific *location* of the injury. Regardless of the particular portion of the brain that had been removed, the degree of learning deficit was similar, suggesting that memory traces are somewhat evenly distributed across the brain. Results of Lashley's work—summarized in a famous paper titled "In Search of the Engram"—led to the view held for several decades that stored memories are widely and fairly equally distributed across the brain (Lashley, 1950).

Contemporary research on the biology of learning seems to suggest a different conclusion. Such research shows that separate, distinct areas of the cortex simultaneously process information about particular dimensions of the world, including visual, auditory, and other sensory stimuli. Because different areas of the brain are simultaneously involved in processing information about different aspects of a stimulus, it seems reasonable that information storage might be linked to the sites of processing and therefore located in those particular areas. According to this view, then, the location of an engram depends on the nature of the material that is being learned and the specific neural system that processed the information (Alkon, 1987; Matthies, 1989; Desimone, 1992; Squire, 1987; Squire, Knowlton, & Musen 1993).

How can we reconcile the growing contemporary view that memory is related to specific types of neural processing employed during learning when we consider Lashley's findings that memory deficits were unrelated to the location of injury to the cortex? One answer is that the contradiction between the two findings is more apparent than real. It is likely, for example, that Lashley's procedure of having rats run through a maze actually involves several kinds of information and learning—including visual information, spatial configuration, smells, and perhaps even sounds. Assuming this to be the case, learning and information processing must have been occurring in several modalities simultaneously, although presumably in different locations in the brain. If each of these processing modalities resulted in a separate memory trace, then removing any particular portion of the cortex would still leave the other memory traces intact—and produce the same

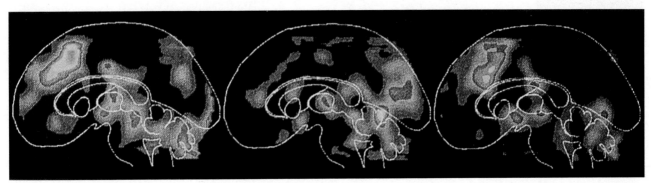

apparent deficit in performance regardless of which area of the cortex was removed.

In sum, it appears that memory is localized to specific areas in that a particular memory trace is related to a particular information processing system in the brain. But in a larger sense, memory traces are distributed throughout the brain, given that several brain processing systems are involved in any learning situation (Squire, 1987; Bear, Cooper, & Ebner, 1987; Cotman & Lynch, 1989).

Recent Work on the Biological Bases of Memory   Other investigators are following different paths to learn about the biological bases of memory. For instance, recent work suggests that the hippocampus plays a central role in the consolidation of memories, permitting them to be stored in the cerebral cortex of the brain (Zola-Morgan & Squire, 1990, 1993).

Investigators using PET scans, which measure biochemical activity in the brain, have recently found that neuronal memory traces are highly specialized. For instance, subjects in one experiment were given a list of nouns to read aloud. After reading each noun, they were asked to suggest a related verb. After reading the noun "dog," for example, they might have proposed the verb "bark."

Several distinct areas of the brain showed increased neural activity as subjects first did the task. However, if they repeated the task with the same nouns several times, the activity in the brain shifted to another area. Most interestingly, if they were given a new list of nouns, the activity in the brain returned to the areas that were initially activated.

The results suggest that a particular part of the brain is involved in the production of words, but another part takes over when the process becomes routine—in other words, when memory comes into play. It also suggests that memory is distributed in the brain not just in terms of its content, but in terms of its function (Horgan, 1993; Corbetta et al., 1993; Petersen & Fiez, 1993).

Furthermore, it appears that certain chemicals and neurotransmitters are linked to the formation, impairment, and improvement of memory (Kandel & Abel, 1995). In one study, for example, a group of chicks who received a drug that inhibited protein synthesis performed more poorly on a memory task than those who didn't receive the drug (Gibbs & Ng, 1977; McGaugh, 1989; Sawaguchi & Goldman-Rakic, 1991). Such work suggests a futuristic—although improbable—scenario in which people routinely take certain drugs in order to improve their memory. Ultimately, then, a trip down memory lane may start in the aisles of a drugstore (Flam, 1994).

Memory Dysfunctions: Afflictions of Forgetting

To a casual observer, Harold appears to be a brilliant golfer. He seems to have learned the game perfectly; his shots are almost flawless.

Yet anyone accompanying him on the course is bound to notice some startling incongruities. Although he is immediately able to size up a situation and hit the ball exactly where it should go, he cannot remember where the ball has just landed. At the end of each hole, he forgets the score. (Blakeslee, 1992, p. C1)

Harold's problem: He suffers from *Alzheimer's disease,* an illness that includes severe memory problems among its symptoms. Alzheimer's, discussed earlier in the chapter, is the fourth leading cause of death among U.S. adults. It strikes around 10 percent of people over the age of 65, and almost half of all people who live beyond 85 develop the disease (Gelman, 1989; Dickinson, 1991).

In its initial stages, Alzheimer's symptoms appear as simple forgetfulness of things like appointments and birthdays. As the disease progresses, memory loss becomes more profound, and even the simplest tasks—such as how to dial a telephone—are forgotten. Ultimately, victims can forget their own names or family members' faces. In addition, physical deterioration sets in, and language abilities may be lost entirely.

Although the causes of Alzheimer's disease are not fully understood, recent evidence suggests that it may be linked to a specific inherited defect (Dewji & Singer, 1996). The flaw leads to difficulties in the production of the protein beta amyloid, necessary for the maintenance of nerve-cell connections. When the manufacture of beta amyloid goes awry, it leads to the deterioration of nerve cells in the brain—producing the symptoms of Alzheimer's (Hardy et al., 1991). (For further discussion of Alzheimer's disease, see the Pathways through Psychology box.)

Alzheimer's disease is just one of several memory dysfunctions that plague their victims. Another is *amnesia,* memory loss that occurs without other mental difficulties. The classic case—immortalized in many a drama—is a victim who receives a blow to the head and is unable to remember anything from his or her past. In reality, amnesia of this type, known as retrograde amnesia, is quite rare. In *retrograde amnesia,* memory is lost for occurrences prior to a certain event. There is usually a gradual reappearance of lost memory, although it may take as long as several years for a full restoration to occur. In certain cases, some memories are lost forever. A second type of amnesia is exemplified by people who remember nothing of their current activities. In *anterograde amnesia,* loss of memory occurs for events following an injury. Information cannot be transferred from short-term to long-term memory, resulting in the inability to remember anything other than what was in long-term storage before the accident (Baddeley, 1982; Baddeley, Wilson, & Watts, 1995).

Amnesia is also displayed by people who suffer from *Korsakoff's syndrome,* a disease that afflicts long-term alcoholics who have also had an impaired diet, resulting in a thiamine deficiency. Although many of their intellectual abilities may be intact, they display a strange array of symptoms, including having hallucinations; repeating questions, even after being told the answer; and repeating the same story over and over.

Fortunately, most of us have memories that are intact, and the occasional failures we do suffer may actually be preferable to having a perfect memory. Consider, for instance, the case of a man who had total recall. After reading passages of the *Divine Comedy* in Italian—a language he did not speak—he was able to repeat them from memory even some 15 years later. He could memorize lists of fifty unrelated words and recall them at will more than a decade later. He could even repeat the same list of words backward, if asked (Luria, 1968).

Such a skill might at first seem to have few drawbacks, but it actually presented quite a problem. The man's memory became a jumble of lists of words, numbers, and names, and when he tried to relax, his mind was filled with images. Even reading was difficult, since every word evoked a flood of thoughts from the past that interfered with his ability to understand the meaning of what he was read-

Janice McGillick
Alzheimer's Association, St. Louis

Born: 1950
Education: University of Missouri at Columbia, B.A.; University of Chicago, M.A.
Home: St. Louis, Missouri

Growing up in a multigeneration family not only provided a real sense of family history for Janice McGillick; it also led her to work with those with Alzheimer's disease.

"While growing up, I had an intimate picture of my own great grandparents aging, and I was able to see how people may go from being productive, independent members of a community to being dependent," said McGillick, currently the education director of the St. Louis, Missouri, chapter of the Alzheimer's Association.

Having taken courses that ranged from the basic introduction to psychology as an undergraduate to courses in human development and aging in graduate school, McGillick credits her education in psychology with providing a strong foundation for her work in dealing with Alzheimer's patients in various stages of the disease.

Janice McGillick (on right).

She noted that the memory loss typical of Alzheimer's usually follows a set pattern. "People's memory for recent events is affected first. They tend to lose touch with events such as a granddaughter's graduation or a recent wedding anniversary," she noted. "At the same time, rituals and routines like prayers, songs, or a mother's name are the types of material that a patient tends to retain."

"In terms of everyday functioning, it means you can't remember what you had for lunch, carry out

basic calculations, balance a checkbook, or make the types of judgments we learn as adults. Eventually," she explains, "the disease progresses and affects long-term memory."

The process of working with an Alzheimer's patient is one that requires patience and sensitivity, according to McGillick. "In the early stages, you try to organize daily routines so the person can be successful in accomplishing them," she says.

As the disease progresses, though, caregivers must take on increasing responsibilities for the patient. "We have to modify our communication techniques by not speaking in compound sentences," she adds. "We have to keep things simple and have them do one task at a time. As the illness progresses, caregivers have to assume the responsibility of judgment, such as distinguishing hot from cold."

Alzheimer's patients require sensitivity and understanding, according to McGillick, even when memory losses lead people to tell the same story repeatedly. "You've got to let people tell a story, even though you may have heard it a thousand times. For them, it's important."

---

ing. Partially as a consequence of the man's unusual memory, psychologist A. R. Luria, who studied his case, found him to be a "disorganized and rather dull-witted person" (Luria, 1968, p. 65).

We may be grateful, then, that being somewhat forgetful plays a useful role in our lives.

The Informed Consumer of Psychology

Improving Your Memory

Apart from the advantages of forgetting, say, the details of a gruesome science fiction movie, most of us still would like to find ways of improving our memories. Given our understanding of memory, is it possible to find practical ways of

increasing our recall of information? Most definitely. Research has revealed a number of strategies that can be used to help us develop better memories (Higbee, 1988; Cohen, 1989; Hermann, 1991; Mastropieri & Scruggs, 1992). Among the best:

■ *The keyword technique.* Suppose you are taking a class in a foreign language and need to learn long lists of vocabulary words. One way of easing this process is to use the *keyword technique,* in which a foreign word is paired with a common English word that has a similar *sound.* This English word is known as the keyword. For example, to learn the Spanish word for duck (*pato,* pronounced *pot-o*), the keyword might be "pot"; for the Spanish word for horse (*caballo,* pronounced *cob-eye-yo*), the keyword might be "eye."

Once you have thought of a keyword, you form a mental image of it graphically "interacting" with the English translation of the word. For instance, you might envision a duck taking a bath in a pot to remember the word *pato,* or a horse with a large, bulging eye in the center of its head to recall *caballo.* This technique has produced considerably superior results in learning foreign language vocabulary than more traditional techniques involving memorization of the words themselves (Pressley & Levin, 1983; Pressley, 1987).

■ *Method of loci.* If you have ever had to give a talk in class, you know the difficulty of keeping in mind all the points you want to make. One technique that works quite effectively was developed by the ancient Greeks. When Greek orators sought to memorize long speeches, they used the *method of loci* (*loci* is the Latin word for places) to organize their recollections of what they wanted to say. With this technique, each part of a speech is imagined as "residing" in a different location of a building.

For instance, you might think of the preface of a talk as being in your house's entryway, the first major point being in the living room, the next major point residing in the dining room, and so forth, until the end of the speech is reached at the back bedroom of the house.

This technique can easily be adapted to learning lists of words; each word on the list is imagined as being located in a series of sequential locations. The method works best by using the most outlandish images possible: If you wanted to remember a list of groceries consisting of bananas, ketchup, and milk, for instance, you might think of a banana intertwined in the leaves of your living-room begonia, the ketchup spilled over the end table, and the milk spraying from the top of a table lamp. When you got to the supermarket, you could mentally "walk" through your living room, recalling the items easily.

■ *The encoding specificity phenomenon.* Some research suggests that we remember information best in an environment that is the same as or similar to where we initially learned it—a phenomenon known as *encoding specificity* (Tulving & Thompson, 1973). You may do better on a test, then, if you study in the same classroom in which the test is going to be given. On the other hand, if you must take tests in a different room from the one in which you studied, don't despair: The features of the test itself, such as the wording of the test questions, are sometimes so powerful they overwhelm the subtler cues relating to the original encoding of the material (Bjork & Richardson-Klarehn, 1989).

■ *Organization of text material.* Most of life's more important recall tasks involve not lists of words but rather texts that have been read. How can you facilitate recall of such material? One proven technique for improving recall of written material consists of organizing the material in memory as it is being read for the first time. To do this, you should first identify any advance information about the structure and content of the material—scanning by using the table of contents, chapter outline, headings, and even the end-of-chapter summary—before reading a given chapter. Understanding the structure of the material will enable you to recall it better.

Another technique is to ask yourself questions that integrate the material you have read, and then answer them. Asking questions will enable you to make connections and see relationships among the various facts, thereby promoting the processing of the material at a deeper level. As the levels-of-processing approach to memory that we discussed earlier suggests, doing so will aid later recall (Royer & Feldman, 1984). For example, you might at this moment ask yourself, "What are the major techniques for remembering material in textbooks?" and then try to answer the question.

■ *Organization of lecture notes.* "Less is more" is perhaps the best advice for taking lecture notes that aid in recall. Rather than trying to jot down every detail of a lecture, it is better to listen and think about the material, taking down the main points after you have considered them in a broader context. In effective note taking, thinking about the material initially is more important than writing it down. This is one reason that borrowing someone else's notes is a bad proposition, since you will have no framework in memory to use in understanding them (Peper & Mayer, 1978).

■ *Practice and rehearsal.* Although practice does not necessarily make perfect, it does help. By studying and rehearsing material past the point of initial mastery—a process called *overlearning*—people are able to show better long-term recall than if they stop practicing after their initial learning of the material.

Eventually, of course, practice has little or no effect; you probably already know your address so well that no amount of additional practice will make you recall it any better than you already do. But it is safe to say that, given the volume of material covered in most courses, academic material is rarely so securely retained, and you would generally be wise to review material a few times even after you feel you have learned it, in order to reach a true level of overlearning.

Research on the outcomes of elaborative rehearsal, discussed earlier in the chapter, also suggests the importance of asking and rehearsing the answers to questions in as active a manner as possible. In this way, the connections between the parts of the material are likely to become explicit, aiding in later recall by providing ample retrieval cues.

Finally, people who cram for tests should note that the best retention comes from practice that is distributed over many sessions, rather than left for one long session. Research clearly demonstrates that fatigue and other factors prevent long practice sessions from being as effective as distributed practice.

Most actors know that overlearning will improve long-term memory of their lines.

(Answers to review questions are on page 215.)

Recap

- Decay and interference are the primary explanations for forgetting.
- There are two kinds of interference: proactive interference (when information learned earlier interferes with recall of newer information) and retroactive interference (when new information interferes with recall of information learned earlier).
- The major memory dysfunctions include Alzheimer's disease, retrograde amnesia, anterograde amnesia, and Korsakoff's syndrome.
- Specific techniques for increasing the recall of information include the keyword technique, the method of loci, the use of encoding specificity, the organization of information in textbooks, good note taking, and practice and rehearsal.

Review

1. After learning the history of the Roman Empire for a class 2 years ago, you now find yourself unable to recall what you learned. A friend tells you that nonuse has caused you to lose the information. What is the formal name for this process?

2. A(n) _____ _____ is an actual physical change in the brain brought about by learning.

3. Memory that is difficult to access because of the presence of other information illustrates what phenomenon?

4. _____ interference occurs when older material is difficult to retrieve because of exposure to newer material. _____ interference refers to the difficulty in retrieving later material due to the interference of previous material.

5. Match the following memory disorders with the correct information:
   1. Affects alcoholics; thiamine deficiency
   2. Memory loss occurring without other mental problems
   3. Beta amyloid defect; progressive forgetting and physical deterioration

   a. Alzheimer's disease
   b. Korsakoff's syndrome
   c. Amnesia

Ask Yourself

How might biopsychology, especially the knowledge gained by the "search for the engram," aid in the treatment of memory disorders such as amnesia?

LOOKING BACK

What is memory?

1. Memory is the process by which we encode, store, and retrieve information. There are three basic kinds of memory storage: sensory memory, short-term memory, and long-term memory.

Are there different kinds of memory?

2. Sensory memory (made up of memories corresponding to each of the sensory systems) is the first place where information is saved, although the memories are very brief. For instance, iconic memory (made up of visual sensations) lasts less than a second, and echoic memory (corresponding to auditory sensations) lasts less than 4 seconds. Despite their brevity, sensory memories are very precise, storing almost an exact replica of each stimulus to which a person is exposed. Unless they are transferred to other types of memory, however, sensory memories appear to be lost.

3. Roughly seven (plus or minus two) chunks of information are capable of being transferred and held in short-term memory. A chunk is a meaningful bit of information, ranging in size from a letter or a single digit to more complicated categorizations. Information in short-term memory is held from 15 to 25 seconds and, if not transferred to long-term memory, is lost.

4. Memories are transferred into long-term storage through rehearsal. The most effective type is elaborative rehearsal, in which the material to be remembered is organized and expanded. Formal techniques for organizing material are called mnemonics.

5. Some theorists suggest that short-term memory is better thought of as a three-part working memory. In this view, there is a central executive, which coordinates the material to focus on during reasoning and decision making, and two subcomponents: the visuospatial sketch pad and the phonological loop.

6. If memories are transferred into long-term memory, they become relatively permanent. Long-term memory is composed of components or modules, each of which is related to separate memory systems in the brain. For instance, we can distinguish between declarative memory (memory for factual information: names, faces, dates, events in our lives, and the like) and procedural memory (memory for skills and habits such as riding a bike or hitting a baseball). Declarative memory is further subdivided into episodic memory (memories relating to our personal lives) and semantic memory (organized knowledge and facts).

7. Explicit memory refers to intentional or conscious recollection of information. In contrast, implicit memory refers to memories of which people are not consciously aware, but which can affect subsequent performance and behavior. Some researchers suggest that two distinct memory systems exist, one for implicit and the other for explicit memory. In contrast, other researchers have proposed that the two kinds of mem-

ory systems differ simply in the way that information is processed.

8. The levels-of-processing approach to memory suggests that the way in which information is initially perceived and analyzed determines the success with which the information is recalled. The deeper the initial processing, the greater the recall of the material.

What causes difficulties and failures in remembering?

9. The tip-of-the-tongue phenomenon refers to the experience of trying in vain to remember information that one is certain one knows. A major strategy for successfully recalling information is to use retrieval cues, stimuli that permit a search through long-term memory.

10. Flashbulb memories are memories centered on a specific, important event. These memories are so clear that they appear to represent a snapshot of the event. Flashbulb memories illustrate the broader point that, the more distinctive a memory, the more easily it can be retrieved.

11. Memory is a constructive process in which we relate memories to the meaning, guesses, and expectations that we give to the events each memory represents. Specific information is recalled in terms of schemas, or general themes that contain relatively little detail.

12. Eyewitnesses of crimes are apt to make substantial errors when they try to recall details of criminal activity. The problem of memory reliability becomes even more acute in cases where children are witnesses and in cases of repressed memories, recollections of events that initially are so shocking that the mind responds by pushing them into the unconscious.

13. Autobiographical memory, which refers to memories of circumstances and episodes from our own lives, is influenced by constructive processes. For example, people forget information about their pasts that is incompatible with the way they currently see themselves. In addition, although the basic structure of memory is similar across cultures, the way in which memory is acquired, rehearsed, and retrieved differs from one culture to another.

Why do we forget information?

14. Even with the use of retrieval cues, some information appears irretrievable, owing to decay or interference. Decay is the loss of information through its nonuse, whereas interference is the loss of material through the displacement of older material by new information. Interference seems to be the major cause of forgetting. There are two sorts of interference: proactive interference (when information learned earlier interferes with the recall of material to which one is exposed later) and retroactive interference (when new information interferes with the recall of information to which one was exposed earlier).

What are the biological bases of memory?

15. Current research on the biology underlying memory is concerned with the site of the engram, or memory trace. Certain drugs impair or aid memory in animals, suggesting that drugs may be used to improve the memory of people in the future.

What are the major memory impairments?

16. There are several memory dysfunctions. Among them are Alzheimer's disease, which leads to a progressive loss of memory, and amnesia, a memory loss that occurs without other mental difficulties and that can take two forms. In retrograde amnesia, there is loss of memory for occurrences prior to some event; in anterograde amnesia, there is loss of memory for events following an injury. Korsakoff's syndrome is a disease that afflicts long-term alcoholics, resulting in memory impairment.

17. Psychologists have developed a number of specific techniques to improve memory. These include using the keyword technique to memorize foreign vocabulary, applying the method of loci to learn lists, using the encoding specificity phenomenon, organizing text material and lecture notes, and practicing enough so that overlearning—studying and rehearsing past the point of initial mastery—occurs.

KEY TERMS AND CONCEPTS

memory (p. 185)
sensory memory (p. 186)
short-term memory (p. 186)
long-term memory (p. 186)
iconic memory (p. 187)
echoic memory (p. 187)
chunk (p. 188)
rehearsal (p. 189)
working memory (p. 190)

declarative memory (p. 192)
procedural memory (p. 192)
semantic memory (p. 192)
episodic memory (p. 192)
associative models (p. 193)
priming (p. 194)
explicit memory (p. 194)
implicit memory (p. 194)
levels-of-processing theory (p. 195)

tip-of-the-tongue phenomenon (p. 196)
flashbulb memories (p. 198)
constructive processes (p. 199)
schemas (p. 199)
autobiographical memories (p. 202)
decay (p. 206)
memory trace (p. 206)
engram (p. 206)
interference (p. 206)

ANSWERS TO PREVIOUS REVIEW
1. Decay **2.** memory trace (or engram) **3.** Interference **4.** Retroactive; Proactive
5. 1-b; 2-c; 3-a

CHAPTER 7
COGNITION AND LANGUAGE

Quick Fix in Space: The Hubble Telescope

It was a $1.5 billion mistake—a blunder on a grand scale. The finely-ground mirror of the Hubble space telescope, designed to provide an unprecedented glimpse into the vast reaches of the universe, was not so finely-ground after all.

Despite a variety of quality-control procedures intended to catch any flaws, there was a tiny blemish in the mirror that was not detected until the telescope had been launched into space and started to send back blurry photographs. By then, it seemed too late to fix the mirror.

Or was it? NASA engineers pondered the problem for months, devising, and discarding, one potential solution after another. Finally, they formulated a daring solution that involved sending a team of astronauts into space. Once there, a space-walking Mr. Goodwrench would install several new mirrors in the telescope, which could refocus the light and compensate for the original flawed mirror.

Although the engineers could not be certain that the $629 million plan would work, it seemed like a good solution, at least on paper. It was not until the first photos were beamed back to earth, though, that NASA knew their solution was A-OK. These photos provided spectacular views of galaxies millions of light years from earth. (Begley, 1993)

LOOKING AHEAD

The repair of the Hubble telescope proved to be a moment of problem-solving triumph for the National Aeronautic and Space Agency (NASA) engineers on the ground, as well as the astronauts in space. Overcoming the obstacles to a solution while working under enormous pressure, the engineers had succeeded in solving a difficult and risky problem. Their success illustrates how thoughtful and painstaking effort can lead to solutions in the face of formidable challenges.

Their accomplishment also raises a number of issues of central importance to psychologists: How do people use and retrieve information to devise innovative

Problem solving on a cosmic scale, as astronauts repair the Hubble telescope in space.

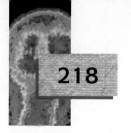

Cognitive psychology: The branch of psychology that specializes in the study of cognition

Cognition: The higher mental processes by which we understand the world, process information, make judgments and decisions, and communicate knowledge to others

solutions to problems? How is such knowledge transformed, elaborated upon, and utilized? More basically, how do people think about, understand, and, using language, describe the world?

In this chapter we consider **cognitive psychology,** the branch of psychology that focuses on the study of cognition. **Cognition** encompasses the higher mental processes of humans, including how people know and understand the world, process information, make judgments and decisions, and describe their knowledge and understanding to others. The realm of cognitive psychology is broad, then, and includes the research on memory examined in the previous chapter and much of the work on intelligence that we discuss in the next chapter (Massaro, 1991; Barsalou, 1992).

In this chapter we concentrate on three broad topics that are central to the field of cognitive psychology: thinking and reasoning, problem solving, and language. We first consider mental images and concepts (the building blocks of thinking) and various kinds of reasoning. Then we examine different strategies for approaching problems, means of generating solutions, and ways of making judgments about the usefulness and accuracy of solutions. Finally, in our focus on language, we consider the way language is developed and acquired, its basic characteristics, and the relationship between language and thought.

- *How do we think?*
- *What processes underlie reasoning and decision making?*

THINKING AND REASONING

Thinking

What is thinking?

The mere ability to pose such a question illustrates the distinctive nature of the human ability to think. No other species can contemplate, analyze, recollect, or plan in the manner that humans can. Yet knowing that we think and understanding what thinking is are two different things. Philosophers, for example, have argued for generations about the meaning of thinking, with some placing it at the core of human beings' understanding of their own existence.

Thinking: The manipulation of mental representations of information

To psychologists, **thinking** is the manipulation of mental representations of information. The representation may be a word, a visual image, a sound, or data in any other modality. What thinking does is to transform the representation of information into a new and different form for the purpose of answering a question, solving a problem, or aiding in reaching a goal.

Although a clear sense of what specifically occurs when we think remains elusive, the nature of the fundamental elements involved in thinking is becoming increasingly well understood (Newell, 1990). We begin by considering our use of mental images and concepts, the building blocks of thought.

Mental Images: Examining the Mind's Eye

Think of your best friend. Chances are that you "see" some kind of visual image when asked to think of her or him, or any other person or object, for that matter. To some cognitive psychologists, such mental images represent a major part of thinking.

Mental images: The images in the mind that resemble the object or event being represented

Mental images are representations in the mind that resemble the object or event being represented. They are not just visual representations; our ability to "hear" a tune in our head also represents a mental image. In fact, it may be that every sensory modality produces corresponding mental images (Paivio, 1971, 1975; Kosslyn, 1981; Kosslyn et al., 1990).

Research has found that our representations of mental images have many of the properties of the actual perception of objects being represented. For example, it takes more time to scan the mental visual representations of large objects than small ones, just as it takes more time to scan an actual large object than an actual small one. Similarly, we are able to manipulate and rotate mental visual images of objects, just as we are able to manipulate and rotate them in the real world (Kosslyn, 1981; Cooper & Shepard, 1984).

The production of mental images has been heralded by some as a way to improve performance of various skills. For instance, many athletes use mental imagery in training. Basketball players may try to produce vivid detailed images of the court, the basket, the ball, and the noisy crowd. They may visualize themselves taking a foul shot, watching the ball, and hearing the swishing sound as it goes through the net (May, 1989). Systematic evaluations of the use of mental imagery by athletes suggest that it is useful in providing a means for improving performance in the sports arena (Druckman & Bjork, 1991). Recent evidence suggests that mental imagery may produce improvements in other types of skills as well. For example, researcher Alvaro Pascual-Leone taught a group of people to play a five-finger exercise on the piano. One group practiced every day for five days, while a control group played without any training, just hitting the keys at random. Finally, the members of a third group were taught the exercise, but were not allowed to actually try it out on the piano. Instead, they rehearsed it mentally, sitting at the piano and looking at the keys, but not actually touching them.

When brain scans of people in the groups were compared, researchers found a distinct difference between those who actually manually practiced the exercise and those who just randomly hit keys. However, the most surprising finding came from the group that mentally rehearsed: Their brain scans were virtually identical to those of the people in the group who actually practiced the exercise. Apparently, the same network of brain cells involved in carrying out the task were involved in mentally rehearsing it (Chase, 1993; Pascual-Leone et al., in press).

Such research suggests that children whose parents nag them about practicing an instrument, or a dance routine, or some other skill that requires practice, can now employ a new excuse: They are practicing—in their mind.

Concepts: Categorizing the World

If someone asked you what was in your kitchen cabinet, you might answer with a detailed list of every item ("a jar of Skippy peanut butter, three packages of macaroni-and-cheese mix, six unmatched dinner plates," and so forth). More likely, though, you would respond by using some broader categories, such as "food" and "dishes."

The use of such categories reflects the operation of concepts. **Concepts** are categorizations of objects, events, or people that share common properties. By employing concepts, we are able to organize the complex phenomena into simpler, and therefore more easily usable, cognitive categories.

Concepts allow us to classify newly encountered objects on the basis of our past experience. For example, we are able to tell that a small rectangular box with buttons sitting on a chair near a television is probably a remote control—even if we have never encountered that specific brand before. Ultimately, concepts influence behavior; we would assume, for instance, that it might be appropriate to pet an animal, after determining that it is, in fact, a dog.

When cognitive psychologists first studied concepts, they focused on those that are clearly defined by a unique set of properties or features. For example, an equilateral triangle is a shape that has three sides of equal length. If an object has these characteristics, it is an equilateral triangle; if it does not, then it is not an equilateral triangle.

Concepts: Categorizations of objects, events, or people that share common properties

The categorization of objects is an important function of concepts.

TABLE 7-1   Prototypes of Four Natural Concepts

	Natural concept category			
Item	Furniture	Vehicle	Weapon	Vegetable
1	Chair	Car	Gun	Peas
2	Sofa	Truck	Knife	Carrots
3	Table	Bus	Sword	String beans
4	Dresser	Motorcycle	Bomb	Spinach
5	Desk	Train	Hand grenade	Broccoli
6	Bed	Trolley car	Spear	Asparagus
7	Bookcase	Bicycle	Cannon	Corn
8	Footstool	Airplane	Bow and arrow	Cauliflower
9	Lamp	Boat	Club	Brussels sprouts
10	Piano	Tractor	Tank	Lettuce
11	Cushion	Cart	Tear gas	Beets
12	Mirror	Wheelchair	Whip	Tomato
13	Rug	Tank	Ice pick	Lima beans
14	Radio	Raft	Fists	Eggplant
15	Stove	Sled	Rocket	Onion

Source: Rosch & Mervis, 1975.

Prototypes: Typical, highly representative examples of a concept

Other concepts—ones that often have the most relevance to our everyday lives—are more ambiguous and difficult to define. For instance, concepts such as "table" or "bird" share a set of general, relatively loose characteristic features, rather than unique properties that distinguish an example of the concept from a nonexample. When we consider these more ambiguous concepts, we usually think in terms of examples; these examples are called prototypes. **Prototypes** are typical, highly representative examples of a concept. For instance, a prototype of the concept "bird" is a robin; a prototype of "table" is a coffee table. Relatively high agreement exists among people about which examples of a concept are prototypes, as well as which examples are not. For instance, most people consider cars and trucks good examples of vehicles, whereas elevators and wheelbarrows are not viewed as terribly good examples. Consequently, cars and trucks are prototypes of the concept of vehicle (see Table 7-1).

Concepts enable us to think about and understand more readily the complex world in which we live. For example, the judgments we make about the reasons for other people's behavior are based on the ways in which we classify their behavior. Hence, our evaluation of a person who washes her hands twenty times a day could vary, depending on whether we place her behavior within the conceptual framework of a health-care worker or a mental patient. Similarly, physicians make diagnoses by drawing upon concepts and prototypes of symptoms they learned about in medical school. Finally, concepts and prototypes facilitate our efforts to draw suitable conclusions through the cognitive process we turn to next: reasoning.

Reasoning: Making Up Your Mind

Professors giving their students grades.

An employer determining whom to hire out of a pool of job applicants.

The President deciding whether the United States should go to war.

The common thread among these three circumstances: Each requires reasoning, the process by which information is used to draw a conclusion and make a decision.

Although philosophers and logicians have considered the foundations of reasoning for centuries, it is relatively recently that cognitive psychologists have begun to investigate how people reason and make decisions (Dominowski & Bourne, 1994; Evans, Newstead, & Byrne, 1994). Together, their efforts have contributed to our understanding of formal reasoning processes as well as the mental shortcuts we routinely use—shortcuts that may sometimes lead our reasoning capabilities astray.

Deductive and Inductive Reasoning   One approach taken by cognitive psychologists in their efforts to understand decision making is to examine how people use formal reasoning procedures. Two major forms exist: deductive reasoning and inductive reasoning (Rips, 1990, 1994; Bisanz, Bisanz, & Korpan, 1994).

In **deductive reasoning,** we draw inferences and implications from a set of assumptions and apply them to specific cases. Deductive reasoning begins with a series of assumptions or premises that are thought to be true, and then derives the implications of these assumptions. If the assumptions are true, then the conclusions must also be true.

Deductive reasoning: A reasoning process whereby inferences and implications are drawn from a set of assumptions and applied to specific cases

A major technique for studying deductive reasoning is through the use of asking subjects to evaluate syllogisms. A *syllogism* presents a series of two assumptions, or *premises,* that are used to derive a conclusion. By definition, the conclusion must be true if the assumptions or premises are true. For example, consider the following syllogism:

All men are mortal.   *[premise]*
Socrates is a man.   *[premise]*
Therefore, Socrates is mortal.   *[conclusion]*

In this case both premises are true, and so, then, is the conclusion. On the other hand, if either or both of the premises in a syllogism are not accurate, then there is insufficient support for the accuracy of the conclusion. Suppose, for example, you saw the following syllogism:

All people are good.   *[premise]*
Hitler is a person.   *[premise]*
Therefore, Hitler is good.   *[conclusion]*

Even though the conclusion is valid according to the rules of formal logic, you would most likely challenge the accuracy of the first premise.

The conclusion drawn from a set of statements, then, is only as justifiable as the accuracy of the premises involved. Unfortunately, in many instances the inaccuracy of a premise is not as obvious as it was in the example of Hitler, and we may accept a conclusion that is not logically valid. Consider the following examples of faulty reasoning:

Many brightly colored snakes are poisonous.   *[premise]*
The copperhead snake is not brightly colored.   *[premise]*
So the copperhead is not a poisonous snake.   *[conclusion]*

There is no doubt that some drugs are poisonous.   *[premise]*
All brands of beer contain the drug alcohol.   *[premise]*
Therefore, some brands of beer are poisonous.   *[conclusion]*

All poisonous things are bitter.   *[premise]*
Arsenic is not bitter.   *[premise]*
Therefore, arsenic is not poisonous.   *[conclusion]*

Deductive reasoning is widely used, not only in intellectual contexts but also in everyday situations, such as when a mechanic tries to figure out what is wrong with a car's engine.

Although each of the conclusions is unsound according to the rules of formal logic, you may find yourself thinking that the stated conclusion is valid—if you happen to agree with it. Experimental evidence suggests that people are more

apt to believe that arguments are logical when they agree with a conclusion than when they disagree with it (Janis & Frick, 1943; Solso, 1991). Consequently, a Democrat is considerably more likely than a Republican to agree with the following syllogism:

Democrats make great presidents.	*[premise]*
Bill Clinton was a Democrat.	*[premise]*
Therefore, Bill Clinton was a great president.	*[conclusion]*

Similarly, people's cultural experience has an impact on the nature of their logical thinking (Serpell & Boykin, 1994). Consider the following sequence, presented to a group of students in Russia:

Ivan and Boris always eat together.
Boris is eating.
What is Ivan doing?

Only one-fifth of the Russian students gave an answer based on traditional logic. Instead, the most frequent response was, "I don't know. I didn't see him." Although it is possible to conclude that the reasoning skills of the Russian students were less well developed than those of their American counterparts—who rarely get the answer wrong—such an interpretation is probably incorrect.

A more plausible explanation is one that takes into account the influence of the different cultural backgrounds of the two groups of students. People living in highly industrialized Western societies are likely to learn, through experience and perhaps direct instruction, to use abstract logic to draw conclusions about the world. On the other hand, because of their particular experiences, people in less industrialized societies may be more apt to rely on concrete modes of reasoning. Therefore, they may be more likely to use direct sensory experience as a basis for drawing conclusions, and may be less comfortable using abstract logic alone (Solso, 1991).

Ultimately, then, people's ability to use formal deductive reasoning may be compromised for several reasons. They may use inaccurate premises, draw erroneous conclusions, or simply fail to use formal logic in the first place. Using deductive reasoning does not ensure that everyone will draw the same conclusions.

The conceptual complement of deductive reasoning is inductive reasoning. In **inductive reasoning,** we infer a general rule from specific cases. Using our observations, knowledge, experiences, and beliefs about the world, we develop a summary conclusion. (You can recall the distinction between deductive and inductive reasoning in this way: In *de*ductive reasoning, the conclusion is *de*rived through the use of general rules, whereas in *in*ductive reasoning, a conclusion is *in*ferred from specific examples.)

Sherlock Holmes used inductive reasoning in his quest to solve mysteries. By amassing clues, he was ultimately able to determine the identity of the criminal. Similarly, we all use inductive reasoning, although typically in more ordinary situations. For instance, if the person in the apartment below you constantly plays Michael Jackson's music, you may begin to form an impression of what that individual is like, based on the sample of evidence available to you. Like Sherlock Holmes, you use pieces of evidence to draw a general conclusion.

The limitation of inductive reasoning is that any conclusions that are drawn may be biased if insufficient or invalid evidence is used. Psychologists know this well: The various scientific methods that they may employ in the collection of data to support their hypotheses are prone to several sorts of biases, such as using an inappropriate sample of subjects (see Chapter 1). Similarly, we may fail to draw appropriate conclusions about our neighbor if our impressions are based only on the music he or she plays and not on a broader sample of behavior.

Inductive reasoning: A reasoning process whereby a general rule is inferred from specific cases, using observation, knowledge, experience, and beliefs

Algorithms and Heuristics   When faced with a decision, we often turn to various kinds of mental shortcuts, known as algorithms and heuristics, to help us. An **algorithm** is a rule which, if followed, guarantees a solution to a problem. We can use an algorithm even if we do not understand why it works. For example, you may know that the length of the third side of a right triangle can be found using the formula $a^2 + b^2 = c^2$. You may not have the foggiest notion of the mathematical principles behind the formula, but this algorithm is always accurate and therefore provides a solution to a particular problem.

For many problems and decisions, however, no algorithm is available. In those instances, we may be able to use heuristics to help us. A **heuristic** is a rule of thumb or mental shortcut that may lead to a solution. Unlike algorithms, heuristics enhance the likelihood of success in coming to a solution but cannot ensure it. For example, chess players often follow the heuristic of attempting to gain control of the center of the board in determining what move to make. This tactic doesn't guarantee that they will win, but it does increase their chances of success. Similarly, some students follow the heuristic of preparing for a test by ignoring the assigned textbook reading and only studying their lecture notes—a strategy that may or may not pay off (Nisbett et al., 1993).

Although they may help people solve problems and make decisions, the use of certain kinds of heuristics may backfire. For example, we sometimes use the *representativeness heuristic,* a rule we apply when we judge people by the degree to which they represent a certain category or group of people. Suppose, for instance, you are the owner of a fast-food store and have been robbed many times by teenagers. The representativeness heuristic would lead you to raise your guard each time someone of this age group enters your store (even though, statistically, it is unlikely that any given teenager will rob you).

The *availability heuristic* involves judging the probability of an event by how easily the event can be recalled from memory (Tversky & Kahneman, 1974). According to this heuristic, we assume that events we remember easily are likely to have occurred more frequently in the past than those that are harder to remember. Furthermore, we assume that the same sort of event is more likely to occur in the future. For example, we are more apt to worry about being murdered than dying of diabetes, despite the fact that it is twice as likely that we will die of the disease. The reason we err is due to the ease with which we remember dramatic, highly publicized events like murder, leading us to overestimate the likelihood of their occurring.

Similarly, many people are more afraid of dying in a plane crash than in an auto accident—despite statistics showing that airplane travel is much safer than auto travel. The reason is that plane crashes receive far more publicity than auto wrecks, and are therefore more easily remembered. And so it is the availability heuristic that leads people to conclude that they are in greater jeopardy in an airplane than a car (Schwarz et al., 1991).

Algorithm: A rule that, if followed, guarantees a solution, though the reason why it works may not be understood by the person using it

Heuristic (hyur ISS tik): A rule of thumb that may bring about a solution to a problem but is not guaranteed to do so

RECAP AND REVIEW

Recap

- Cognitive psychologists specialize in the study of the higher mental processes of humans, including problem solving, knowing, reasoning, judging, and decision making.
- Thinking is the manipulation of mental representations of information.
- Mental images are representations in the mind that resemble the object or event being represented.
- Concepts are categorizations of objects, events, or people that share common properties.
- In deductive reasoning, we draw inferences and implica-

tions from a set of assumptions and apply them to specific cases; in inductive reasoning, we infer a general rule from specific cases.

- When making decisions, people frequently use algorithms (rules that, if followed, guarantee that a solution will be reached) and heuristics (rules of thumb that may lead to a solution).

Review

1. _____ _____ are representations in the mind that resemble the object or event being represented.

2. _____ are categorizations of objects that share common properties.

3. When you think of the term "chair," you immediately think of a comfortable easy chair. A chair of this type could be thought of as a _____ of the category "chair."

4. Match the type of reasoning with its definition:
   1. Deductive reasoning
   2. Inductive reasoning

   a. Deriving the conclusion from a set of premises
   b. Inferring a general rule from specific cases

5. When you ask your friend how best to study for your psychology final, he tells you, "I've always found it best to skim over the notes once, then read the book, then go over the notes again." What decision-making tool might this be an example of?

6. The _____ heuristic is used when one judges how likely an event is to occur by how easily it is retrieved from memory.

Ask Yourself

You are an expert computer programmer. You are given the task of designing a robot that can "learn" (through observation) to play the perfect game of chess and never lose. What knowledge of algorithms and heuristics would you bring to the task? What problems might you foresee?

(Answers to review questions are on page 226.)

- *How do people approach and solve problems?*
- *What are the major obstacles to problem solving?*

PROBLEM SOLVING

According to an old legend, a group of monks in Vietnam devote much of their time to attempting to solve a problem called the Tower of Hanoi puzzle. Should they succeed, the monks expect that it will bring an end to the world as we know it (Raphael, 1976). (Should you prefer that the world remain in its present state, there's no need for immediate concern: According to one estimate, the puzzle is so complex that it will take about a trillion years to reach a solution.)

In a simpler version of the puzzle, illustrated in Figure 7-1, there are three posts on which three disks are to be placed in the order shown. The goal of the puzzle is to move all three disks to the third post and arrange them in the same order, using as few moves as possible. But there are two restrictions: Only one disk can be moved at a time, and no disk can ever cover a smaller one during a move.

Why are cognitive psychologists interested in the Tower of Hanoi problem? The answer is that the way people go about solving this puzzle and simpler ones like it helps illuminate the processes by which people solve complex problems that they encounter in school and at work. For example, psychologists have found that problem solving typically involves three major steps: preparation for the creation of solutions, production of solutions, and judgment and evaluation of solutions that have been generated (Sternberg & Frensch, 1991).

FIGURE 7-1 The goal of the Tower of Hanoi puzzle is to move all three disks from the first post to the last and still preserve the original order of the disks, using the least number of moves possible while following the rules that only one disk at a time can be moved and no disk can cover a smaller one during a move. Try it yourself before you look at the solution, which is listed according to the sequence of moves. (Solution: Move C to 3, B to 2, C to 2, A to 3, C to 1, B to 3, and C to 3.)

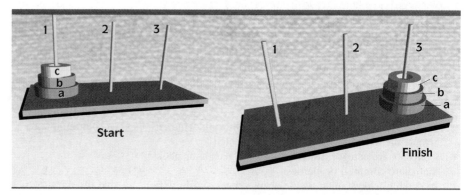

Preparation: Understanding and Diagnosing Problems

When approaching a problem like the Tower of Hanoi, most people begin by trying to ensure that they thoroughly understand the problem. If the problem is a novel one, they are likely to pay particular attention to any restrictions placed on coming up with a solution as well as the initial status of the components of the problem. If, on the other hand, the problem is a familiar one, they are apt to spend considerably less time in this stage.

Problems vary from well-defined to ill-defined (Reitman, 1965). For a *well-defined problem*—such as a mathematical equation or the solution to a jigsaw puzzle—both the nature of the problem itself and the information needed to solve it are available and clear. Thus, straightforward judgments can be made about whether a potential solution is appropriate. With an *ill-defined* problem, such as how to increase morale on an assembly line or bring peace to the Middle East, not only may the specific nature of the problem be unclear, but the information required to solve the problem may be even less obvious.

Kinds of Problems Problems typically fall into one of the three categories exemplified in Figure 7-2: arrangement, inducing structure, and transformation (Greeno, 1978). Each requires somewhat different kinds of psychological skills and knowledge to solve.

Arrangement problems require that a group of elements be rearranged or recombined in a way that will satisfy a certain criterion. There are usually several different possible arrangements that can be made, but only one or a few of the arrangements will produce a solution. Anagram problems and jigsaw puzzles represent arrangement problems.

> **Arrangement problems:** Problems whose solutions require the rearrangement of a group of elements in order to satisfy a certain criterion

In **problems of inducing structure,** a person must identify the relationships that exist among the elements presented and construct a new relationship among them. In such a problem, it is necessary to determine not only the relationships among the elements, but the structure and size of the elements involved. In the example shown in Figure 7-2, a person must first determine that the solution requires the numbers to be considered in pairs (14-24-34-44-54-64). It is only after that part of the problem is identified that the solution rule (the first number of each pair increases by one, while the second number remains the same) can be determined.

> **Problems of inducing structure:** Problems whose solutions require the identification of existing relationships among elements presented so as to construct a new relationship among them

The Tower of Hanoi puzzle represents a third kind of problem. **Transformation problems** consist of an initial state, a goal state, and a series of methods for changing the initial state into the goal state. In the Tower of Hanoi problem, the initial state is the original configuration; the goal state consists of the three disks on the third peg; and the method consists of the rules for moving the disks.

> **Transformation problems:** Problems to be solved using a series of methods to change an initial state into a goal state

Whether the problem is one of arrangement, inducing structure, or transformation, the initial stage of understanding and diagnosing is critical in problem solving because it allows us to develop our own cognitive representation of the problem and to place it within a personal framework. The problem may be divided into subparts, or some information may be ignored as we try to simplify the task. Winnowing out the unessential information is often a critical step in problem solving.

Representing and Organizing the Problem A crucial aspect of the initial encounter with a problem is the way in which we represent it to ourselves and organize the information presented to us (Brown & Walter, 1990). Consider the following problem:

A man climbs a mountain on Saturday, leaving at daybreak and arriving at the top near sundown. He spends the night at the top. The next day, Sunday, he leaves at daybreak and heads down the mountain, following the same path that he climbed the day before.

A. Arrangement problems

1. Anagrams: Rearrange the letters in each set to make an English word:

2. Two strings hang from a ceiling but are too far apart to allow a person to hold one and walk to the other. On the floor are a book of matches, screwdriver, and a few pieces of cotton. How could the strings be tied together?

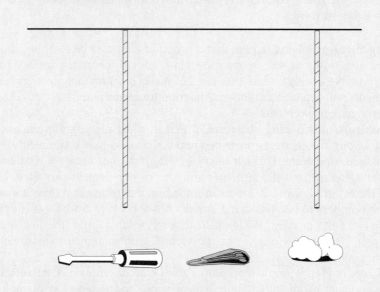

B. Problems of inducing structure

1. What number comes next in the series?

    1 4 2 4 3 4 4 4 5 4 6 4

2. Complete these analogies:

    baseball is to bat as tennis is to _____

    merchant is to sell as customer is to _____

FIGURE 7-2 The major categories of problems: (a) arrangement, (b) inducing structure, and (c) transformation. *Solutions appear on page 228. (Sources: Bourne et al., 1986; hobbit problem: Solso, 1991, p. 448)*

ANSWERS TO PREVIOUS REVIEW
1. Mental images **2.** Concepts **3.** prototype **4.** 1-a; 2-b **5.** Heuristic **6.** availability

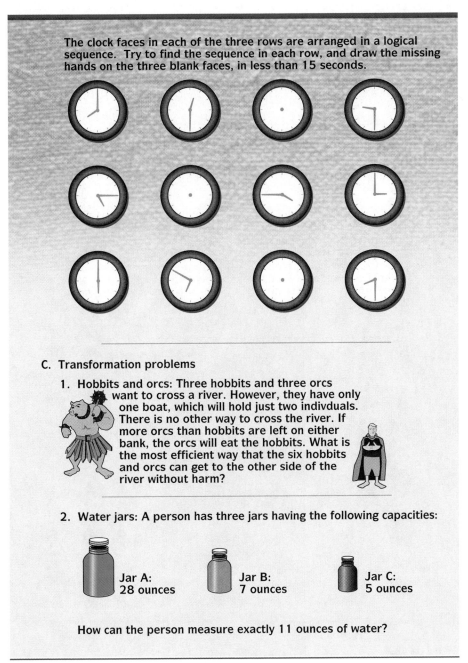

The clock faces in each of the three rows are arranged in a logical sequence. Try to find the sequence in each row, and draw the missing hands on the three blank faces, in less than 15 seconds.

C. Transformation problems

1. Hobbits and orcs: Three hobbits and three orcs want to cross a river. However, they have only one boat, which will hold just two indivduals. There is no other way to cross the river. If more orcs than hobbits are left on either bank, the orcs will eat the hobbits. What is the most efficient way that the six hobbits and orcs can get to the other side of the river without harm?

2. Water jars: A person has three jars having the following capacities:

Jar A: 28 ounces
Jar B: 7 ounces
Jar C: 5 ounces

How can the person measure exactly 11 ounces of water?

FIGURE 7-2 (continued)

The question is this: Will there be any time during the second day when he will be at exactly the same point on the mountain as he was at that time on the first day?

If you try to solve this problem by using algebraic or verbal representations, you will have a good deal of trouble. However, if you represent the problem with the kind of simple diagram illustrated in Figure 7-3, the solution becomes apparent.

Successful problem solving, then, requires that a person form an appropriate representation and organization of the problem. However, there is no one optimal way of representing and organizing material, since that depends on the nature of the problem. Sometimes simply restructuring a problem, from a verbal form to a pictorial or mathematical form for instance, can help point out a direct solution (Mayer, 1982).

A. Arrangement problems

1. FACET, NAIVE, DOUBT, ANVIL, THICK

2. The screwdriver is tied to one of the strings. This makes a pendulum that can be swung to reach the other string.

B. Problems of inducing structure

1. 7

2. racket; buy

3. The first blank face should show 5:00 (4½ hours added each time); the second one, 4:30 (45 minutes subtracted each time); the third one, 7:40 (50 minutes added each time).

C. Transformation problems

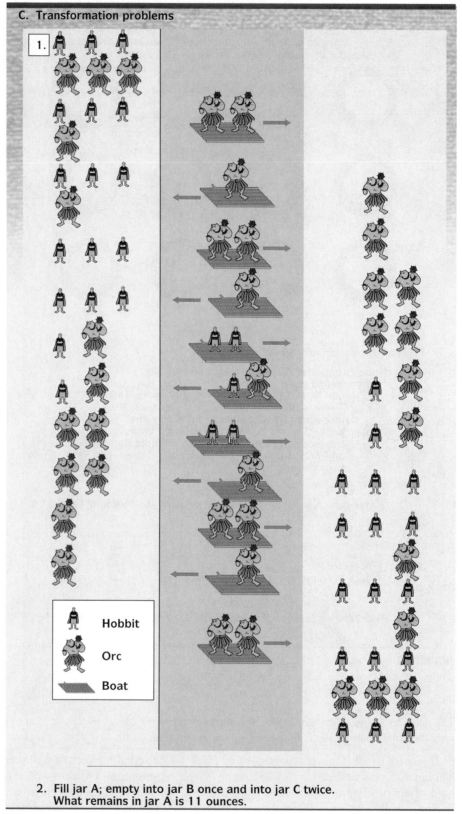

2. Fill jar A; empty into jar B once and into jar C twice. What remains in jar A is 11 ounces.

FIGURE 7-2 (continued)

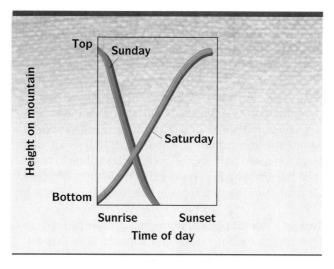

FIGURE 7-3 It is easy to solve the problem posed in the text by using a graph. Remember, the goal is not to determine the time, but just to indicate whether an exact time exists. *(Anderson, 1980.)*

Production: Generating Solutions

If a problem is relatively simple, a direct solution may already be stored in long-term memory, and all that is necessary is to retrieve the appropriate information. If the solution cannot be retrieved or is not known, we must instigate a process by which possible solutions can be generated and compared with information in long- and short-term memory.

Trial and Error At the most primitive level, solutions to problems can be obtained through trial and error. Thomas Edison was able to invent the light bulb only because he tried thousands of different kinds of materials for a filament before he found one that worked (carbon). The difficulty with trial and error, of course, is that some problems are so complicated it would take a lifetime to try out every possibility. For example, according to one estimate, there are some 10^{120} possible sequences of chess moves.

Means-Ends Analysis In place of trial and error, complex problem solving often involves the use of heuristics, which, as we discussed earlier, are rules of thumb that lead the way to solutions. Probably the most frequently applied heuristic in problem solving is a means-ends analysis. In a **means-ends analysis,** people repeatedly test for differences between the desired outcome and what currently exists. For example, people using a means-ends analysis to search for the correct sequence of roads to get to a city that they can see in the distance would analyze their solutions in terms of how much closer each individual choice of roadway brings them to the ultimate goal of arriving at the city. Such a strategy is only effective, though, if there is a direct solution to the problem. If the problem is such that indirect steps have to be taken which appear to *increase* the discrepancy between the current state and the solution, means-ends analyses can be counterproductive. In our example, if roadways are laid out in such a way that a person must temporarily move *away* from the city in order to reach it eventually, a means-ends analysis will keep the person from reaching the goal.

For some problems, the converse of a means-ends analysis is the most effective approach: working backward by beginning with the goal and moving toward the starting state. Instead of starting with the current situation and moving closer and closer to the solution, people can work in the opposite direction, starting with the goal and aiming to reach the beginning point (Bourne et al., 1986; Malin, 1979).

Means-ends analysis: Repeated testing for differences between the desired outcome and what currently exists

Subgoals   Another commonly used heuristic is to divide a problem into intermediate steps, or *subgoals,* and to solve each of those steps. For instance, if you return to the Tower of Hanoi problem, there are several obvious subgoals that could be chosen, such as moving the largest disk to the third post.

If solving a subgoal is a step toward the ultimate solution of a problem, then identifying subgoals is an appropriate strategy. There are cases, however, in which the formation of subgoals is not all that helpful and may actually take the problem solver longer to find a solution (Reed, 1988; Hayes, 1966). For example, some problems cannot be subdivided. Others are so difficult to subdivide that it takes longer to identify the appropriate subdivisions than to solve the problem by other means. Finally, even when a problem is divided into subgoals, it may be unclear what to do after a given subgoal has been reached.

Insight   Some approaches to problem solving focus less on step-by-step processes than on the sudden bursts of comprehension that one may experience during efforts to solve a problem. Just after World War I, German psychologist Wolfgang Köhler examined such problem-solving processes in chimps (Köhler, 1927). In his studies, Köhler exposed chimps to challenging situations in which the elements of the solution were all present; what was necessary was for the chimps to put the elements together.

For example, in one series of studies, chimps were kept in a cage in which boxes and sticks were strewn about, with a bunch of tantalizing bananas hanging high in the cage out of their reach. Initially, the chimps engaged in a variety of trial-and-error attempts at getting to the bananas: They would throw the stick at the bananas, jump from one of the boxes, or leap wildly from the ground. Frequently, they would seem to give up in frustration, leaving the bananas dangling temptingly overhead. But then, in what seemed like a sudden revelation, they

In an impressive display of insight, Sultan, one of the chimpanzees in Köhler's experiments in problem solving, sees a bunch of bananas that is out of his reach (a). He then carries over several crates (b), stacks them, and stands on them to reach the bananas (c).

a.   b.   c.

would abandon whatever activity they were involved in and stand on a box in order to be able to reach the bananas with a stick. Köhler called the cognitive processes underlying the chimps' behavior **insight,** a sudden awareness of the relationships among various elements that had previously appeared to be independent of one another.

Although Köhler emphasized the apparent suddenness with which solutions were revealed, subsequent research has shown that prior experience and initial trial-and-error practice in problem solving are prerequisites for "insight" (Metcalfe, 1986). One study demonstrated that only chimps who had experience in playing with sticks could successfully solve the problem; inexperienced chimps never made the connection between standing on the box and reaching the bananas (Birch, 1945). Some researchers have suggested that the behavior of the chimps represented little more than the chaining together of previously learned responses, no different from the way a pigeon learns, by trial and error, to peck a key (Epstein, 1987; Epstein et al., 1984). It is clear that insight depends on previous experience with the elements involved in a problem.

Insight: Sudden awareness of the relationships among various elements that had previously appeared to be independent of one another

Judgment: Evaluating the Solutions

The final step in problem solving is judging the adequacy of a solution. Often, this is a simple matter: If there is a clear solution—as in the Tower of Hanoi problem—we will know immediately whether we have been successful.

On the other hand, if the solution is less concrete, or if there is no single correct solution, evaluating solutions becomes more difficult. In such instances, we must decide which solution alternative is best. Unfortunately, we are often quite inaccurate in estimating the quality of our own ideas (Johnson, Parrott, & Stratton, 1968). For instance, a team of drug researchers working for a particular company may feel that their therapy for an illness is superior to all others, overestimating the likelihood of success and belittling the approaches of competing drug companies.

Theoretically, if the heuristics and information we rely on to make decisions are appropriate and valid, we can make accurate choices among problem solutions. However, as we see next, there are several kinds of obstacles to and biases in problem solving that affect the quality of the decisions and judgments we make.

Impediments to Problem Solving

Consider the following problem-solving test (Duncker, 1945):

You are presented with a set of tacks, candles, and matches in small boxes, and told your goal is to place three candles at eye level on a nearby door, so that wax will not drip on the floor as the candles burn (see Figure 7-4). How would you approach this challenge?

If you have difficulty solving the problem, you are not alone. Most people are unable to solve it when it is presented in the manner illustrated in the figure, in which the objects are located *inside* the boxes. On the other hand, if the objects were presented *beside* the boxes, just resting on the table, chances are you would solve the problem much more readily—which, in case you are wondering, requires tacking up the boxes and then placing the candles in the boxes (see Figure 7-6, on page 234).

The difficulty you probably encountered in solving the problem stems from its presentation and relates to the fact that you were misled at the initial preparation stage. Actually, significant obstacles to problem solving exist at each of the three major stages. Although cognitive approaches to problem solving suggest that thinking proceeds along fairly rational, logical lines as a person confronts a problem and considers various solutions, a number of factors act to hinder the development of creative, appropriate, and accurate solutions.

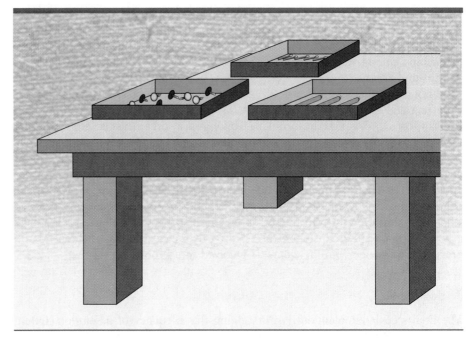

FIGURE 7-4 The problem here is to place three candles at eye level on a nearby door so that the wax will not drip on the floor as the candles burn—using only materials in the figure (tacks, candles, and matches in boxes). For a solution, turn to page 234, Figure 7-6.

Functional fixedness: The tendency to think of an object in terms of its most typical use

Mental set: The tendency for old patterns of problem solving to persist

Functional Fixedness and Mental Set   The reason that most people experience difficulty with the candle problem can be attributed to a phenomenon known as **functional fixedness,** the tendency to think of an object only in terms of its typical use. For instance, functional fixedness probably leads you to think of the book you are holding in your hands as something to read, as opposed to its value as a doorstop or as kindling for a fire. In the candle problem, functional fixedness occurs because the objects are first presented inside the boxes, which are then seen simply as containers for the objects they hold rather than as a potential part of the solution.

Functional fixedness is an example of a broader phenomenon known as **mental set,** the tendency for old patterns of problem solving to persist. Mental set can prevent us from seeing our way beyond the apparent constraints of a problem. For example, try to draw no more than four straight lines so that they pass through all nine dots in the grid below—without lifting your pen or pencil from the page:

$$
\begin{matrix}
\bullet & \bullet & \bullet \\
\bullet & \bullet & \bullet \\
\bullet & \bullet & \bullet
\end{matrix}
$$

If you had difficulty with the problem, it was probably because you felt compelled to keep your lines within the grid. If you had gone outside the boundaries, however, you would have succeeded with solutions such as those shown in Figure 7-5.

Inaccurate Evaluation of Solutions   When the nuclear power plant at Three Mile Island in Pennsylvania suffered its initial malfunction in 1979, a disaster that almost led to a nuclear meltdown, the plant operators were faced immediately with solving a problem of the most serious kind. Several monitors indicated contradictory information about the source of the problem: One suggested that the pressure was too high, leading to the danger of an explosion; others indicated that the pressure was too low, which could lead to a meltdown. Although the pressure was in fact too low, the supervisors on duty relied on the one monitor—which was faulty—that suggested the pressure was too high. Once they had made their decision and acted upon it, they ignored the contradictory evidence from the other monitors (Wickens, 1984).

One reason for the operators' mistake is the *confirmation bias,* in which initial hypotheses are favored and contradictory information supporting alternative hypotheses or solutions is ignored. Even when we find evidence that contradicts a solution we have chosen, we are apt to stick with our original hypothesis.

There are several reasons for the confirmation bias. One is that it takes cognitive effort to rethink a problem that appears to be solved already, so we are apt to stick with our first solution. Another is that evidence contradicting an initial solution may present something of a threat to our self-esteem, leading us to hold to the solutions that we have come up with first (Rasmussen, 1981; Fischoff, 1977).

Creativity and Problem Solving

Despite obstacles to problem solving, many people are adept at coming up with creative solutions to problems. One of the enduring questions that cognitive psychologists have tried to answer is what factors underlie **creativity,** which is usually defined as the combining of responses or ideas in novel ways (Glover, Ronning, & Reynolds, 1989; Isaksen & Murdock, 1993; Smith, Ward, & Finke, 1995).

Although being able to identify the stages of problem solving helps us to understand how people approach and solve problems, it does little to explain why some people come up with better solutions than others. Solutions to even the simplest of problems often show wide variations. Consider, for example, how you might respond to the question "How many uses can you think of for a newspaper?" Compare your own solution with this one proposed by a 10-year-old boy:

You can read it, write on it, lay it down and paint a picture on it. . . . You could put it in your door for decoration, put it in the garbage can, put it on a chair if the chair is messy. If you have a puppy, you put newspaper in its box or put it in your backyard for the dog to play with. When you build something and you don't want anyone to see it, put newspaper around it. Put newspaper on the floor if you have no mattress, use it to pick up something hot, use it to stop bleeding, or to catch the drips from drying clothes. You can

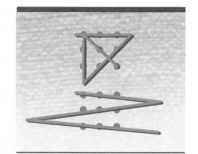

FIGURE 7-5 Solutions to the nine-dot problem require the use of lines drawn beyond the boundaries of the figure—something that our mental set may prevent us from easily seeing.

Creativity: The combining of responses or ideas in novel ways

The causes of creativity remain elusive.

use a newspaper for curtains, put it in your shoe to cover what is hurting your foot, make a kite out of it, shade a light that is too bright. You can wrap fish in it, wipe windows, or wrap money in it. . . . You put washed shoes in newspaper, wipe eyeglasses with it, put it under a dripping sink, put a plant on it, make a paper bowl out of it, use it for a hat if it is raining, tie it on your feet for slippers. You can put it on the sand if you had no towel, use it for bases in baseball, make paper airplanes with it, use it as a dustpan when you sweep, ball it up for the cat to play with, wrap your hands in it if it is cold. (Ward, Kogan, & Pankove, 1972)

It is obvious that this list shows extraordinary creativity. Unfortunately, it has proved to be considerably easier to identify *examples* of creativity than to determine its causes. Several factors, however, seem to be associated with creativity (Richards et al., 1988; Lubart, 1994).

One of these factors is divergent thinking. **Divergent thinking** refers to the ability to generate unusual, yet nonetheless appropriate, responses to problems or questions. This type of thinking contrasts with **convergent thinking,** which produces responses that are based primarily on knowledge and logic. For instance, someone relying on convergent thinking answers "You read it" to the query "What do you do with a newspaper?" In contrast, "You use it as a dustpan" is a more divergent—and creative—response (Runco, 1991; Baer, 1993).

Psychologists Robert Sternberg and Todd Lubart suggest that one important ingredient of creativity is the willingness to take risks that may result in potentially high payoffs (Sternberg & Lubart, 1992). In their view, creative people are similar to successful stock market investors, who follow the rule of "buying low and selling high." In an analogous fashion, creative individuals formulate and promote ideas that are, at least for the moment, out of synch with prevailing wisdom ("buying low"). Ultimately, though, highly creative people expect that their

Divergent thinking: The ability to generate unusual but appropriate responses to problems or questions

Convergent thinking: A type of thinking that produces responses based on knowledge and logic

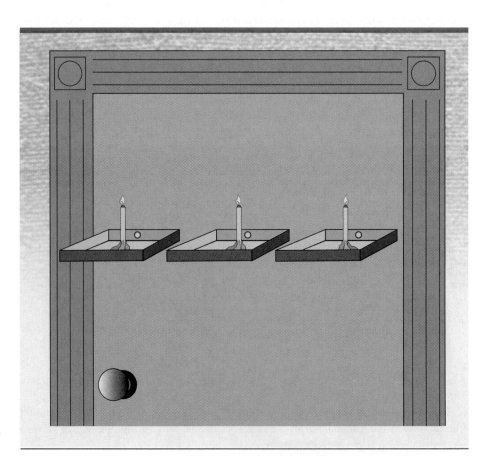

FIGURE 7-6 A solution to the problem posed in Figure 7-4 involves tacking the boxes to the door and placing the candles in the boxes.

ideas will rise in value and that others will ultimately find them of value and adopt them ("selling high").

Another ingredient of creativity is *cognitive complexity,* the use of and preference for elaborate, intricate, and complex stimuli and thinking patterns. Similarly, creative people often have a wider range of interests and are more independent and more interested in philosophical or abstract problems than less creative individuals are (Barron, 1990).

One factor that is *not* closely related to creativity is intelligence. Most items on intelligence tests focus on convergent thinking skills in that these questions are well defined and have only one acceptable answer. Creative people who are divergent thinkers may therefore find themselves at a disadvantage when taking such tests. This may explain why researchers consistently find that creativity is only slightly related to intelligence or school grades, particularly when intelligence is measured using typical intelligence tests (Barron & Harrington, 1981; Sternberg, 1988; Albert, 1992; Simonton, 1994).

The Informed Consumer of Psychology

Thinking Critically and Creatively

Can people be taught to be better thinkers? A growing body of evidence supports the notion that people can learn to perform better on decision-making and problem-solving tasks (Brown & Walter, 1990; Anderson, 1993). Abstract rules of logic and reasoning may be taught, and such training improves the way in which people are able to reason about the underlying causes of everyday life events. Ultimately, cognitive psychologists may routinely teach students not only to increase the skill with which they are able to solve problems, but to think more critically as well (Baron, 1993; Nickerson, 1994).

On the basis of the research we have discussed on problem solving, thinking, and creativity, there are several strategies that can help you think more critically and evaluate problems more creatively—whether they be the challenges of everyday life or more academically oriented problems such as determining the correct answer to a question on an exam. Suggestions for increasing critical thinking and creativity include the following (Baron & Sternberg, 1986; Coats, Feldman, & Schwartzberg, 1994; Hayes, 1989; Whimbey & Lochhead, 1991):

■ *Redefine problems.* The boundaries and assumptions you hold can be modified. For example, a problem can be rephrased at a more abstract or more concrete level, depending on how it is initially presented (Brown & Walter, 1990).

Use *fractionation,* in which an idea or concept is broken down into the parts that make it up. Through fractionation, each part can be examined for new possibilities and approaches, leading to a novel solution for the problem as a whole (deBono, 1967).

■ *Adopt a critical perspective.* Rather than passively accepting assumptions or arguments, critically evaluate material by considering its implications and thinking about possible exceptions and contradictions.

■ *Use analogies.* Analogies not only help us uncover new understanding; they provide alternative frameworks for interpreting facts. One particularly effective means of coming up with analogies is to look for them in the animal kingdom when the problem concerns people, and in physics or chemistry when the problem concerns inanimate objects. For instance, the idea for the unique packaging of Pringles potato chips reputedly arose when a manufacturer noticed that dry tree leaves, which normally crumble easily, could be packed together tightly if they were moistened slightly (Rice, 1984).

■ *Think divergently.* Instead of thinking in terms of the most logical or most common use for an object, consider how it might be of help if you were forbidden to use it in its usual way. Take the perspective of another person, one who either is involved in the situation or is a disinterested bystander. In doing so, you may gain a fresh view of the situation.

■ *Use heuristics.* As mentioned earlier, heuristics are rules of thumb that can help bring about a solution to a problem. If the nature of the problem is such that it has a single, correct answer, and a heuristic is available or can be constructed, using the heuristic frequently helps you to develop a solution more rapidly and effectively.

■ *Experiment with various solutions.* Don't be afraid to use different routes to find solutions for problems (verbal, mathematical, graphic, even acting out a situation). Try coming up with every conceivable idea you can, no matter how wild or bizarre it may seem at first. After you have come up with a list of solutions, you can review each one and try to think of ways of making what at first appeared impractical seem more feasible (Sinnott, 1989; Halpern, 1995).

RECAP AND REVIEW

Recap

- In solving problems, people typically pass through a series of three steps: preparation, production, and judgment.
- Insight is a sudden awareness of the relationships among various elements that had earlier seemed independent of one another.
- Among the obstacles to successful problem solving are mental set and functional fixedness, the faulty application of algorithms and heuristics, and the confirmation bias.
- Creativity is related to divergent thinking and cognitive complexity.
- Psychologists have devised several methods for enhancing critical thinking and creative problem solving.

Review

1. Three steps in problem solving studied by psychologists are _____ , _____ , and _____ .
2. Match the type of problem with its definition:
   1. Inducing structure
   2. Arrangement
   3. Transformation

   a. Changing the initial state to the goal state
   b. Rearranging elements to fit certain criteria
   c. Constructing a new relationship among elements

3. Solving a problem by trying to reduce the difference between the current state and the goal state is known as a _____-_____ _____ .
4. _____ is the term used to describe the sudden "flash" of revelation that often accompanies the solution to a problem.
5. Thinking of an object only in terms of its typical use is known as _____ _____ . A broader, related tendency for old problem-solving patterns to persist is known as a _____ _____ .
6. The _____ bias describes the phenomenon favoring an initial hypothesis and ignoring subsequent competing hypotheses.
7. Generating unusual but still appropriate responses to a question is known as _____ _____ .
8. Intelligence, as measured on standard intelligence tests, is highly correlated with measures of creativity. True or false?

Ask Yourself

If certain strategies that enhance creativity can indeed be taught, what potential benefits could this bring in the realms of business? Science? Working with the handicapped?

(Answers to review questions are on page 238.)

- *How do people use language?*
- *How does language develop?*

LANGUAGE

'Twas brillig, and the slithy toves   All mimsy were the borogoves,
Did gyre and gimble in the wabe: And the mome raths outgrabe.

Although few of us have ever come face to face with a tove, we have little difficulty in discerning that in Lewis Carroll's (1872) poem "Jabberwocky," the expression "slithy toves" represents an adjective, "slithy," and the noun it modifies, "toves."

Our ability to make sense out of nonsense, if the nonsense follows typical rules of language, illustrates both the sophistication of human language capabilities and the complexity of the cognitive processes that underlie the development and use of language. The way in which people are able to use **language**—the systematic, meaningful arrangement of symbols—clearly represents an important cognitive ability, one that is indispensable for communicating with others. But language is not only central to communication; it is also closely tied to the very way in which we think about and understand the world, for there is a crucial link between thought and language. It is not surprising, then, that psychologists have devoted considerable attention to studying the topic of language.

Language: The systematic, meaningful arrangement of symbols

Grammar: Language's Language

In order to understand how language develops, and what its relationship to thought is, we first need to review some of the formal elements that constitute language. The basic structure of language rests on grammar. **Grammar** is the system of rules that determine how our thoughts can be expressed.

Grammar deals with three major components of language: phonology, syntax, and semantics. **Phonology** refers to the study of the smallest units of sound, called **phonemes,** that affect the meaning of speech and to the way we use those sounds to produce meaning by placing them into the form of words. For instance, the "a" in "fat" and the "a" in "fate" represent two different phonemes in English (Halle, 1990).

Although English-speakers use just forty-two basic phonemes to produce words, the basic phonemes of other languages range from as few as fifteen to as many as eighty-five (Akmajian, Demers, & Harnish, 1984). Differences in phonemes are one reason people have difficulty in learning other languages: For example, to the Japanese-speaker, whose native language does not have an "r" phoneme, English words such as "roar" present some difficulty.

Syntax refers to the rules that indicate how words and phrases can be combined to form sentences. Every language has intricate rules that guide the order in which words may be strung together to communicate meaning. English-speakers have no difficulty in knowing that "Radio down the turn" is not an appropriate sequence, while "Turn down the radio" is. The importance of appropriate syntax is demonstrated by the changes in meaning that come from the differing orders of words in the following three sequences: "John kidnapped the boy," "John, the kidnapped boy," and "The boy kidnapped John" (Lasnik, 1990).

The third major component of language is semantics. **Semantics** refers to the rules governing the meaning of words and sentences (Larson, 1990; Hipkiss, 1995). Semantic rules allow us to use words to convey the subtlest of nuances. For instance, we are able to make the distinction between "The truck hit Laura" (which we would be likely to say if we had just seen the vehicle hitting Laura) and "Laura was hit by a truck" (which we would probably say if asked why Laura was missing class while she recuperated).

Despite the complexities of language, most of us acquire the basics of grammar without even being aware that we have learned its rules (Pinker, 1994). Moreover, even though we might have difficulty explicitly stating the rules of grammar that we employ, our linguistic abilities are so sophisticated that they enable us to utter an infinite number of different statements. We turn now to how such abilities are acquired.

Grammar: The system of rules that determine how our thoughts can be expressed

Phonology: The study of the smallest units of sound, called phonemes

Phonemes (FONE eems): The smallest units of sound used to form words

Syntax: The rules that indicate how words are joined to form sentences

Semantics: The rules governing the meaning of words and sentences

Language Development: Developing a Way with Words

To parents, the sounds of their infant babbling and cooing are music to their ears (except, perhaps, at three o'clock in the morning). These sounds also serve an important function: They mark the first step on the road to the development of language.

Babble: Speechlike but meaningless sounds

Children **babble**—make speechlike but meaningless sounds—from around the ages of 3 months through 1 year. While babbling they may produce, at one time or another, any of the sounds found in all languages, not just the one to which they are exposed. Even deaf children display their own form of babbling: Infants who are unable to hear and who are exposed to sign language from birth "babble," but they do it with their hands (Petitto & Marentette, 1991).

Babbling increasingly begins to reflect the specific language that is being spoken in the environment, initially in terms of pitch and tone and eventually in terms of specific sounds (Reich, 1986; Kuhl et al., 1992). By the time a child is approximately 1 year old, sounds that are not in the language disappear. It is then a short step to the production of actual words. In English, these are typically short words that start with a consonant such as "b," "d," "m," "p," or "t"—helping to explain why "mama" and "dada" are so often among babies' first words. Of course, even before they produce their first words, children are capable of understanding a fair amount of the language they hear. Language comprehension precedes language production.

After the age of 1 year, children begin to learn more complicated forms of language. They produce two-word combinations, which become the building blocks of sentences, and there is an acceleration in the number of different words they are capable of using. By the age of 2 years, the average child has a vocabulary of more than fifty words. Just 6 months later, that vocabulary has grown to several hundred words. At that time, children can produce short sentences, although they

A syllable in sign language, like the one illustrated here, occurs in the manual babbling of deaf infants as well as in the spoken babbling of hearing infants. The similarities suggest that language has biological roots.

ANSWERS TO PREVIOUS REVIEW

1. preparation, production, judgment **2.** 1-c; 2-b; 3-a **3.** means-ends analysis
4. Insight **5.** functional fixedness; mental set **6.** confirmation **7.** divergent thinking
8. False; intelligence, as measured on tests, is only slightly related to creativity.

use **telegraphic speech**—sentences that sound as if they were part of a telegram, in which words not critical to the message are left out. Rather than saying, "I showed you the book," a child using telegraphic speech might say, "I show book"; and "I am drawing a dog" might become "Drawing dog." As the child gets older, of course, the use of telegraphic speech declines and sentences become increasingly complex.

By the time children are 3 years of age, they learn to make plurals by adding "s" to nouns, and they are able to form the past tense by adding "ed" to verbs. This ability also leads to errors, since children tend to apply rules too inflexibly. This phenomenon is known as **overregularization,** whereby children apply rules even when the application results in an error. Thus, although it is correct to say "he walked" for the past tense of "walk," the "ed" rule doesn't work quite so well when children say "he runned" for the past tense of "run."

Much of children's acquisition of the basic rules of language is complete by the time they are 5. However, a full vocabulary and the ability to comprehend and use subtle grammatical rules are not attained until later. For example, a 5-year-old boy who is shown a blindfolded doll and asked, "Is the doll easy or hard to see?" would have great difficulty responding to the question. In fact, if he were asked to make the doll easier to see, he would probably try to remove the doll's blindfold. On the other hand, 8-year-olds have little difficulty understanding the question, realizing that the doll's blindfold has nothing to do with an observer's ability to see the doll (Chomsky, 1969).

Understanding Language Acquisition: Identifying the Roots of Language

While anyone who is around children will notice the enormous strides that are made in language development throughout childhood, the reasons for this rapid growth are less obvious. Two major explanations have been put forward: one based on learning theory and the other on innate processes.

The **learning-theory approach** suggests that language acquisition follows the principles of reinforcement and conditioning discussed in Chapter 5. For example, a child who utters the word "mama" is hugged and praised by her mother, thereby reinforcing the behavior and making its repetition more likely. This view suggests that children first learn to speak by being rewarded for making sounds that approximate speech. Ultimately, through a process of shaping, language becomes more and more like adult speech (Skinner, 1957).

The learning-theory approach is less successful when it comes to explaining the acquisition of language rules. Children are reinforced not only when they use proper language, but also when they respond incorrectly. For example, parents answer the child's "Why the dog won't eat?" as readily as they do the correctly phrased question "Why won't the dog eat?" Both sentences are understood equally well. Learning theory, then, does not seem to provide the full explanation for language acquisition.

An alternative model is provided by Noam Chomsky (1968, 1978, 1991), who argues that an *innate mechanism* plays an important role in language learning. He suggests that humans are born with an innate linguistic capability that emerges primarily as a function of maturation. According to his analysis, all the world's languages share a similar underlying structure called a **universal grammar.** Chomsky suggests that the human brain has a neural system, the **language-acquisition device,** which both permits the understanding of the structure of language and provides strategies and techniques for learning the unique characteristics of a given native language. According to this view, then, language is a uniquely human phenomenon made possible by the presence of the language-acquisition device.

Telegraphic speech: Sentences that sound as if they were part of a telegram, in which words not critical to the message are left out

Overregularization: Applying rules of speech in instances in which they are inappropriate

Learning-theory approach: Language acquisition follows the principles of reinforcement and conditioning (see Chapter 5)

Universal grammar: An underlying structure shared by all languages, the basis of Chomsky's theory that certain language characteristics are based in the brain's structure and are therefore common to all people

Language-acquisition device: A neural system of the brain hypothesized to permit understanding of language

Chomsky's view, as you might suspect, is not without its critics. For instance, learning theorists contend that the apparent ability of animals such as chimpanzees to learn the fundamentals of human language (as we discuss later in the chapter) argues against the innate view. The issue of how humans acquire language thus remains hotly contested (Rice, 1989; Pinker, 1990, 1994; Harley, 1995).

The Influence of Language on Thinking

Do Eskimos living in the frigid Arctic have a more expansive vocabulary to use in discussing snow than people living in more temperate climates? Contrary to conventional wisdom, probably not. Arguments that the Eskimo language has many more words than English for "snow" have been made since the early 1900s. At that time, linguist Benjamin Lee Whorf contended that because snow is so relevant to Eskimos' lives, they had developed a rich vocabulary to describe it—far richer than what we would find in other languages, such as English. As time went on, the supposed number of Eskimo words for snow took on mythic proportions, with one account suggesting that there were 400 distinct Eskimo terms for snow (Pinker, 1994; Martin & Pullum, 1991).

However, most psychologists now agree that such claims were based more on myth than reality. Eskimos have no more words for snow than English speakers. In fact, if you examine the English language closely, it is hardly impoverished when it comes to describing snow. (Consider sleet, slush, blizzard, dusting, and avalanche, for starters.)

The contention that the Eskimo language is particularly rich in snow-related terms was used as evidence for a controversial notion known as the linguistic-relativity hypothesis. According to the **linguistic-relativity hypothesis,** language shapes and, in fact, may determine the way people of a particular culture perceive and understand the world (Whorf, 1956; Lucy, 1992). According to this view, language provides us with categories that we use to construct our view of people and events in the world around us. Consequently, language shapes and produces thought.

Let's consider another possibility, however. Suppose that, instead of language being the *cause* of certain ways of thinking about the world, language is a *result* of thinking about and experiencing relevant stimuli in the environment. In this view, thought *produces* language. The only reason to expect that Eskimo language might have more words for snow than English is that snow is considerably more relevant to Eskimos than it is to people in other cultures.

Linguistic-relativity hypothesis:
The theory claiming that language shapes and may even determine the way people of a particular culture perceive and understand the world

Traveling in countries where a language other than our own is spoken raises the issue of the relationship between language and thought.

In an effort to determine which of the two descriptions (language produces thought versus thought produces language) provides the more accurate account, investigators have carried out a significant amount of research. In one important study, Eleanor Rosch (1974) compared the perception of colors by Americans and by members of the Dani tribe of New Guinea. The Dani have only two names for color: one for cold, dark colors and one for warm, lighter colors. In English, of course, there are hundreds of color names, but eleven of them represent major color categories (red, yellow, green, blue, black, gray, white, purple, orange, pink, and brown). Rosch argued that if the linguistic-relativity hypothesis were accurate, English-speakers should be more efficient at recognizing and distinguishing colors that represent the major categories than colors that are not members of major categories. In contrast, she reasoned that the Dani tribe members should show no difference in recognition between colors that are members of major or nonmajor categories since there are no words in their vocabulary to describe any of them.

However, the results did not support this hypothesis. There was no difference in the way that either English-speakers or Dani perceived the colors; both perceived colors in the major categories more efficiently than colors in the nonmajor categories. According to these results, then, language differences do not influence perception.

Subsequent research supports Rosch's findings and, by and large, does not support the linguistic-relativity hypothesis (R. Brown, 1986; Pinker, 1990). It seems most appropriate to conclude that, in general, cognition influences language and not the other way around.

On the other hand, language *does* affect thinking and cognition in certain respects. The manner in which information is stored in memory—and how well such information can subsequently be retrieved—is related to language (Cairns & Cairns, 1976). Similarly, our impressions and memories of others' personality and behavior are affected by the linguistic categories provided us by the language we speak (Hoffman, Lau, & Johnson, 1986). Furthermore, as we discuss in the Psychology at Work box, language may give us an edge—or hinder us—even in such seemingly unrelated areas as mathematics proficiency. Although language does not determine thought, then, it certainly influences it (Gerrig & Banaji, 1994).

Do Animals Use Language?

One of the enduring questions that has long puzzled psychologists is whether language is uniquely human or whether other animals are able to acquire it as well. It is clear that many animals communicate with one another in some rudimentary forms, such as fiddler crabs that wave their claws to signal, bees whose dance indicates the direction in which food will be found, or certain birds that say "zick, zick" during courtship and "kia" when they are about to fly away. But researchers have yet to demonstrate conclusively that these animals use true language, which is characterized in part by the ability to produce and communicate new and unique meanings following a formal grammar.

Psychologists have, however, been able to teach chimps to communicate at surprisingly high levels. For instance, Kanzi, a 9-year-old pygmy chimpanzee, has linguistic skills that some psychologists claim are close to those of a 2-year-old human being. Psychologist Sue Savage-Rumbaugh and colleagues, who have worked extensively with Kanzi, note that he can create sentences that are grammatically sophisticated and can even concoct new rules of syntax (Savage-Rumbaugh et al., 1993).

Despite the skills displayed by primates such as Kanzi, critics contend that the language the primates use still lacks a grammar and sufficiently complex and novel constructions to approach the realm of human capabilities (Seidenberg & Petitto, 1987). Instead, the critics maintain that the chimps are displaying a skill

Does Language Give the Chinese an Advantage in Math?

Can the difference between the time it takes to say "yi" versus "one" account for the greater proficiency of the Chinese over Americans in math?

In part, that's the hypothesis put forward by psychologist David Geary and colleagues. They suggest that children in China may do better in math than children in America because of differences in the language they use (Geary et al., 1993).

For example, it takes several hundred milliseconds less to pronounce "yi," the Chinese word for the number 1, than it does to say the English number "one." Other numbers are also shorter to say in Chinese than in English.

Because of these linguistic differences, Chinese children can hold more numbers in short-term memory than American children. For instance, one study comparing kindergarten-aged children in Hangzhou, China, and Columbia, Missouri, found that the Chinese children could hold 6.7 digits in short-term memory, compared with only 4.1 for the children in the United States.

Ultimately, differences between the Chinese and English languages seem to permit Chinese children to retrieve and mentally process numbers more rapidly. They also enable Chinese students to discontinue the use of counting on their fingers, a relatively primitive practice, at an earlier age than their American counterparts (Geary, Fan, & Bow-Thomas, 1992).

Although the differences between languages in the time it takes to say a number are tiny, the advantages apparently add up over time. Such differences may account for the fact that children in the United States show mathematics achievement that is consistently below that of children in China. The Chinese advantage starts even before children begin formal schooling in mathematics and continues throughout the course of formal schooling (Stevenson et al., 1990).

Of course, language differences do not fully account for the higher mathematics achievement of Chinese students. However, they do appear to play an important role. These findings also provide further evidence for the close relationship that exists between language and cognitive abilities.

no different from that of a dog that learns to lie down on command in order to get a reward. Furthermore, firm evidence is lacking that animals are able to recognize and respond to the mental states of others of their species, an important aspect of human communication (Cheney & Seyfarth, 1990; Seyfarth & Cheney, 1992).

Psychologist Sue Savage-Rumbaugh signs the word for "trailer" as she and chimp Kanzi take a water break.

Most evidence supports the contention that humans are better equipped than animals to produce and organize language in the form of meaningful sentences. But the issue of whether animals are capable of being taught to communicate in a way that resembles human language remains a controversial one (Seidenberg & Petitto, 1987; Savage-Rumbaugh, 1987; Gibbons, 1991). (To consider some of the practical implications of the work on animal language capabilities, see the Pathways through Psychology box.)

Exploring Diversity

Bilingual Education: Classrooms of Babel

For picture day at New York's P.S. 217, a neighborhood elementary school in Brooklyn, the notice to parents was translated into five languages. That was a nice gesture, but insufficient: More than 40 percent of the children are immigrants whose families speak any one of twenty-six languages, ranging from Armenian to Urdu. (Leslie, 1991, p. 56)

From the biggest cities to the most rural areas, the face—and voice—of education in the United States is changing. Children with names like Thong, Tariq, and Karachnicoff are becoming increasingly common as the wave of immigration during the 1980s, larger than that of the early 1900s, hits the country's schools. In seven states, including Texas, New York, and Colorado, more than one-quarter of the students are not native English speakers. For some 32 million Americans, English is their second language (U.S. Census Bureau, 1993).

How to deal appropriately and effectively with the increasing number of children who are not native English-speakers represents an important educational issue (Lam, 1992). Most educators suggest that a bilingual approach is best; with such an approach students are taught some subjects in their native language while they simultaneously learn English. Proponents of bilingualism maintain that it is necessary for students to develop a sound footing in basic subject areas and that, initially at least, instruction in their native language is the only way to provide them with that foundation. During this same period, they are to learn English, and the eventual goal is to shift all their instruction into English.

In contrast, some educators suggest that all instruction ought to be in English from the moment nonnative English-speakers enroll in school. To these educators, teaching students in a language other than English simply hinders integration of the nonnative English-speakers into society and ultimately does them a disservice.

While the issue is highly controversial, with strong political undercurrents, research has contributed several insights. In studying the relationship between bilingualism and cognition, psychologists have found that people who speak more than one language may well have some cognitive advantages over those who speak only one language.

For example, speakers of two languages show more cognitive flexibility. They have more linguistic possibilities at hand for contemplating situations they encounter because of their multiple-language abilities. In turn, this permits them to solve problems with greater creativity and flexibility.

Bilingual students are also more aware of the rules of language, and they may understand concepts more readily (Hakuta & Garcia, 1989). They may even score higher on intelligence tests. For example, one survey of schoolchildren in Canada found that students who spoke both French and English scored significantly higher on both verbal and nonverbal tests of intelligence than those who spoke only one language (Lambert & Peal, 1972).

The use of bilingual signs is commonplace in some parts of the United States, accommodating to the multicultural population.

PATHWAYS THROUGH PSYCHOLOGY

Rose Sevcik

Born: 1953
Education: A.B., John Carroll University; M.S., University of Connecticut; Ph.D., Georgia State University
Home: Atlanta, Georgia

Rose Sevcik and chimp.

For years, Sondra's future was considered bleak. Born deaf, mute, and mentally retarded, Sondra appeared to have no hope of ever speaking. Today, though, she is able to make simple requests using a computer-based language developed by a group of researchers who were initially interested in the language capabilities of chimpanzees.

Sondra's transformation came about as a result of a line of research being pursued by psychologist Rose Sevcik. As a member of the team of researchers seeking to refine our understanding of language development by studying both children and chimpanzees, Sevcik had the goal to develop a language system for children who, due to various disabilities, do not develop speech.

Sevcik began her pursuit of this goal at John Carroll University, a small liberal arts institution in Ohio, which provided the right blend of courses and faculty. "The school offered a lot of undergraduate requirements in all types of disciplines," said Sevcik. "I found a

course on research methods quite stimulating because I had the opportunity to learn about the neural sciences, and how the brain influences and affects behavior."

Graduating with an A.B. in psychology, Sevcik went on to the University of Connecticut and obtained a master's degree in experimental physiological psychology, followed by a doctorate in developmental comparative psychology at Georgia State University.

It was at the University of Connecticut, however, that she began to study how children and chimpanzees use and develop language. "I had the experience of taking courses that focused on the relationship between biology and behavior," said the 42-year-old researcher. "I developed my thesis on

the abilities of monkeys to perceive synthesized speech. What really got me into all of this was asking the question, 'Do these animals have any capacity to teach us something about how humans use and develop language?'

"When I came to Atlanta to continue my graduate studies, we used an artificial language developed in a study of how the great apes handle a systematic language system," Sevcik said. "My doctoral thesis was on how a rare species of infant pygmy chimps would develop a communication system when their only exposure was being shown the language."

Currently, Sevcik works in the morning with children and in the afternoon with chimps. "We are at work on a long-term project involving the use of microcomputer technology to develop an augmented system for kids who do not develop speech," she said. "We want to know if such children can be taught to speak, despite severe cognitive and linguistic disabilities. To answer this question, we need to determine how they proceed toward normal development and how they learn. We don't just want to look at the kids; we also want them to benefit." For developmentally disabled children such as Sondra, who may learn to communicate effectively for the first time, such work offers real promise.

Finally, evidence exists that there are common principles of language acquisition. Therefore, initial instruction in the native language may actually enhance the learning of English as a second language. There is certainly no evidence that children will be cognitively overwhelmed by instruction in both their native language and English (Lindholm, 1991).

In sum, research suggests that bilingual students actually have an advantage over students who speak just one language, suggesting that the wisest course might be to enhance language skills for bilingual students in both their original language *and* English. Furthermore, attention has recently begun to shift from the consequences of bilingualism to a broader question: What is the psychological impact of *biculturalism,* in which a person is a member of two cultures?

Some psychologists argue that society should promote an *alternation model* of bicultural competence. In an alternation model, members of minority cultures are supported in their efforts to maintain their original cultural identity, as well as in their integration into the dominant culture. The model promotes the view that a person can live as part of two cultures, with two cultural identities, without having to choose between them. Whether the alternation model becomes widely adopted remains to be seen (LaFromboise, Coleman, & Gerton, 1993).

RECAP AND REVIEW

Recap

- Language is characterized by grammar, a system of rules that determine how our thoughts can be expressed.
- Language acquisition proceeds rapidly from birth and is largely complete by the age of 5, although there are subsequent increases in vocabulary and sophistication.
- The learning-theory view suggests that language is learned through the principles of reinforcement and conditioning. In contrast, Chomsky's view suggests that language capabilities are innate, a result of the existence of a language-acquisition device in the brain.
- Issues involving the relationship between language and thought, animals' language abilities, and bilingual education are controversial.

Review

1. Match the component of grammar with its definition:
   1. Syntax
   2. Phonology
   3. Semantics

   a. Rules showing how words can be combined into sentences
   b. Rules governing the meaning of words and sentences
   c. The study of the sound units that affect speech

2. Language production and language comprehension develop in infants at approximately similar times. True or false?
3. _____ _____ refers to the phenomenon in which young children omit nonessential portions of sentences.
4. A child knows that adding "ed" to certain words puts them in the past tense. As a result, instead of saying "He came," the child says "He comed." This is an example of _____ .
5. _____ theory assumes that language acquisition is based on operant learning principles.
6. Chomsky argues that language acquisition is an innate ability tied to the structure of the brain. True or false?
7. Thought has been proved to influence language, but language does not seem to have an influence on thought. True or false?

Ask Yourself

Suppose you hear on the news tomorrow that a pair of chimpanzees have mastered English (via a computer console) at an eighth-grade level. What effect will this have on current theories of language acquisition? How might this knowledge be applied to humans?

(Answers to review questions are on page 247.)

LOOKING BACK

How do we think?

1. Cognitive psychologists study cognition, which encompasses the higher mental processes. These processes include the way people know and understand the world, process information, make decisions and judgments, and describe their knowledge and understanding to others.
2. Thinking is the manipulation of mental representations of information. Thinking transforms such representations into novel and different forms, permitting people to answer questions, solve problems, or reach goals.
3. Mental images are representations in the mind that resemble the object or event being represented. People's representations of mental images have many of the properties of actual perception of the objects being represented. For instance, it takes more time to scan the mental visual representations of large objects than small ones. Similarly, people are able to manipulate and rotate mental visual images of objects.

4. Concepts, one of the building blocks of thinking, are categorizations of objects, events, or people that share common properties. Some concepts are thought of in terms of prototypes, representative examples of the concept.

What processes underlie reasoning and decision making?

5. In deductive reasoning, people derive the implications of a set of assumptions that they know to be true. In inductive reasoning, in contrast, people infer a general rule from specific cases. Inductive reasoning allows people to use their observations, knowledge, experiences, and beliefs about the world to develop summary conclusions.
6. Decisions may be improved through the use of algorithms and heuristics. Algorithms are rules which, if followed, guarantee a solution, while heuristics are rules of thumb that may lead to a solution but are not guaranteed to do so.

7. There are several kinds of heuristics. In the representativeness heuristic, people decide whether a given example is a member of a particular category by evaluating how representative of that category the example is. The availability heuristic consists of judging the probability of an event by how easily other instances of the event can be recalled from memory.

How do people approach and solve problems?

8. Problem solving typically involves three major steps: preparation, production of solutions, and evaluation of solutions that have been generated. Preparation begins when people try to understand the problem. Some problems are well defined, with clear solution requirements; other problems are ill defined, with ambiguities in both the information required for a solution and the solution itself.

9. In arrangement problems, a group of elements must be rearranged or recombined in a way that will satisfy a certain criterion. In problems of inducing structure, a person must identify the relationships among the elements presented and construct a new relationship among them. Finally, transformation problems consist of an initial state, a goal state, and a series of methods for changing the initial state into the goal state.

10. A crucial aspect of the preparation stage is the representation and organization of the problem. Sometimes restructuring a problem from a verbal form to a pictorial or mathematical form can help point the way to the solution.

11. In the production stage, people try to generate solutions. The solutions to some problems may already be in long-term memory and can be directly retrieved. Alternatively, some problems may be solved through simple trial and error. More complex problems, however, require the use of heuristics.

12. In a means-ends analysis, a person will repeatedly test for differences between the desired outcome and what currently exists, trying each time to come closer to the goal. Another heuristic is to divide a problem into intermediate steps or subgoals and solve each of those steps.

13. One approach to problem solving is exemplified by Köhler's research with chimps, in which the elements of the situation had to be manipulated in a novel fashion in order for the chimps to solve the problem. Köhler called the cognitive processes underlying the chimps' behavior insight, a sudden awareness of the relationships among elements that had previously seemed independent.

What are the major obstacles to problem solving?

14. Several factors hinder effective problem solving. Functional fixedness (the tendency to think of an object only in terms of its most typical use) is an example of a broader phenomenon known as mental set. Mental set is the tendency for old patterns of problem solving to persist. The inappropriate use of algorithms and heuristics can also act as an obstacle to the production of solutions to problems. Finally, the confirmation bias, in which initial hypotheses are favored, can hinder the accurate evaluation of solutions to problems.

15. Creativity is the combining of responses or ideas in novel ways. Divergent thinking is the ability to generate unusual, but still appropriate, responses to problems or questions and is associated with creativity. Cognitive complexity, the use of and preference for elaborate, intricate, and complex stimuli and thinking patterns, is also related to creativity.

16. A growing body of evidence supports the idea that people can learn to perform better in problem-solving situations. By learning abstract rules of logic and reasoning, people are able to think critically about the underlying causes of everyday events.

17. Suggestions for solving problems creatively include redefining the problem, taking the perspective of another person, using analogies, thinking divergently, using heuristics, and experimenting with different solutions.

How do people use language?

18. Language is the systematic, meaningful arrangement of symbols. All languages have a grammar—a system of rules that determines how our thoughts can be expressed. Grammar encompasses the three major components of language: phonology, syntax, and semantics. Phonology refers to the study of the sounds (called phonemes) we make when we speak and to the use of those sounds to produce meaning; syntax refers to the rules that indicate how words are joined together to form sentences; and semantics refers to the rules governing the meaning of words and sentences.

How does language develop?

19. Language production, preceded by language comprehension, develops out of babbling (speechlike but meaningless sounds), which leads to the production of actual words. After a year, children use two-word combinations and their vocabulary increases. They first use telegraphic speech, in which words not critical to the message are dropped. By the age of 5, acquisition of language rules is relatively complete.

20. There are two major theories of language acquisition. Learning theorists suggest that language is acquired through reinforcement and conditioning. In contrast, Chomsky suggests that there is an innate language-acquisition device that guides the development of language.

21. The linguistic-relativity hypothesis suggests that language shapes and may determine the way people think about the world. Most evidence suggests that although language does not determine thought, it does affect how information is stored in memory and how well it can be retrieved.

22. The degree to which language is a uniquely human skill remains controversial. Although some psychologists contend that certain primates communicate at a high level but nonetheless do not use language, others suggest that they truly understand and produce language in the same way as humans.

23. People who speak more than one language may have a cognitive advantage over those who speak only one. Research suggests that they have greater cognitive flexibility, are more aware of the rules of language, and may understand concepts more readily.

KEY TERMS AND CONCEPTS

cognitive psychology (p. 218)
cognition (p. 218)

thinking (p. 218)
mental images (p. 218)

concepts (p. 219)
prototypes (p. 220)

ANSWERS TO PREVIOUS REVIEW

1. 1-a; 2-c; 3-b **2.** False; language comprehension precedes language production.
3. Telegraphic speech **4.** overregularization **5.** Learning **6.** True **7.** False; language
and thought seem to interact with each other in a variety of ways.

CHAPTER 8
INTELLIGENCE

PROLOGUE

Mindie Crutcher and Lenny Ng

When Mindie was born, physicians said she would always be hopelessly retarded, that she would never sit up, never walk, never speak. "She will never know you're her mother," they told 25-year-old Diane Crutcher. "Tell relatives your baby is dead."

Today, the child who would never sit up is a lively seventh-grader. The child who would never talk or know her own mother told a symposium of physicians she was "glad Mom and Dad gave me a chance."

Yet the experts were right about one thing: Mindie does have Down syndrome, a genetic disorder, one of the most common birth defects and the leading physical cause of mental retardation (Turkington, 1992, p. 42).

Imagine—and it takes some doing—Lenhard (Lenny) Ng, the older son of Cantonese immigrants who settled in Chapel Hill, N.C., where his father is a physics professor at the University of North Carolina. At 10, he scored a perfect 800 on the math SAT. He set a record by performing flawlessly, four years running, in the American High School Math Exam. Last year he won a gold medal at the math olympics in Moscow. He took honors in several violin and piano competitions and played on a championship little-league basketball team while earning all A's at UNC (he attended high school and college simultaneously).... This fall Ng will enter Harvard, probably as a sophomore. He is 16. It's enough to make you hate him—except that he is a genuinely nice kid.... And this will make you feel better: on his verbal SAT last year, Ng got a mere 780 (Beck & Wingert, 1993, p. 53).

Mindie Crutcher (top) and Lenhard Ng (bottom).

LOOKING AHEAD

Two different people, with very different intellectual capabilities and strengths. And yet, at their core, Mindie Crutcher and Lenny Ng share basic aspects of humanity and even, one could argue, intelligence, that ultimately make them more similar than different.

In this chapter, we consider intelligence in all its many varieties. Intelligence represents a focal point for psychologists intent on understanding how people are able to adapt their behavior to the environment in which they live. It also represents a key aspect of how individuals differ from one another in the way in which they learn about and understand the world.

We begin this chapter by considering the challenges involved in defining and measuring intelligence. If you are like most people, you have probably wondered how smart you are. Psychologists, too, have pondered the nature of intelligence. We will examine some of their conceptions of intelligence as well as efforts to develop and use standardized tests as a means of measuring intelligence.

We will also consider the two groups displaying extremes of individual differences in intelligence: the mentally retarded and the gifted. The special challenges of each population will be discussed along with special programs that have been developed to help individuals from both groups reach their full potential.

Finally, we will explore what are probably the two most controversial issues surrounding intelligence. First, we will consider the degree to which intelligence is influenced by heredity and by the environment. Then we will discuss whether traditional tests of intelligence are biased toward the dominant cultural groups in society—a difficult issue that has both psychological and social significance.

- *How do psychologists conceptualize and define intelligence?*
- *What are the major approaches to measuring intelligence?*

DEFINING INTELLIGENT BEHAVIOR

It is typical for members of the Trukese, a small tribe in the South Pacific, to sail a hundred miles in open ocean waters. Although their destination may be just a small dot of land less than a mile wide, the Trukese are able to sail unerringly toward it without the aid of a compass, chronometer, sextant, or any of the other sailing tools that are indispensable to modern Western navigation. They are able to sail accurately, even when prevailing winds do not allow a direct approach to the island and they must take a zigzag course (Gladwin, 1964).

How are the Trukese able to navigate so effectively? If you asked them, they could not explain it. They might tell you that they use a process that takes into account the rising and setting of the stars and the appearance, sound, and feel of the waves against the side of the boat. But at any given moment as they are sailing along, they could not identify their position or say why they are doing what they are doing. Nor could they explain their underlying navigational theory.

Some might say the inability of the Trukese to explain how their sailing technique works in Western terms is a sign of primitive or even unintelligent behavior. In fact, if we made Trukese sailors take a standardized Western test of navigational knowledge and theory, or, for that matter, a traditional test of intelligence, they might very well do poorly on it. Yet, as a practical matter, it is hard to accuse the Trukese of being unintelligent: Despite their inability to explain how they do so, they are able to navigate successfully through the open ocean waters.

The way in which the Trukese navigate points out the difficulty in coming to grips with what is meant by intelligence. To a Westerner, traveling in a straight line along the most direct and quickest route using a sextant and other navigational tools is likely to represent the most "intelligent" kind of behavior; a zigzag course, based on the "feel" of the waves, would not seem very reasonable. To the Trukese, who are accustomed to their own system of navigation, however, the use of complicated navigational tools might seem so overly

The Trukese people's effective method of navigation—which is done without maps or instruments—raises questions about the nature of intelligence.

complex and unnecessary that they might think of Western navigators as lacking in intelligence.

It is clear that the term "intelligence" can take on many different meanings (Lohman, 1989; Davidson, 1990). If, for instance, you lived in a remote African village, the way you differentiate between more intelligent and less intelligent people might be very different from the way that someone living in the heart of urban Miami would distinguish individual differences. To the African, high intelligence might be represented by exceptional hunting or other survival skills; to the Miamian, it might be exemplified by dealing effectively with a mass-transit system, by being "streetwise," or by avoiding being hustled.

Each of these conceptions of intelligence is reasonable, for each represents an instance in which more intelligent people are better able to use the resources of their environment than less intelligent people are, a distinction we would assume to be basic to any definition of intelligence. Yet it is also clear that these conceptions represent very different views of intelligence.

That two such different sets of behavior can exemplify the same psychological concept has long posed a challenge to psychologists. For years, they have grappled with the issue of devising a general definition of intelligence that would remain independent of a person's specific culture and other environmental factors. Interestingly, untrained laypersons have fairly clear conceptions of intelligence (Sternberg, 1985b). For example, in one survey that asked a group of people to define what they meant by intelligence, three major components of intelligence emerged (Sternberg et al., 1981). First, there was problem-solving ability: People who reason logically and identify more solutions to problems were seen as intelligent. Second, verbal abilities were thought to exemplify intelligence. Finally, social competence, the ability to show interest in others and interact effectively with them, was viewed as indicating intelligence.

The definition of intelligence that psychologists employ contains some of the same elements found in the layperson's conception. To psychologists, **intelligence** is the capacity to understand the world, think rationally, and use resources effectively when faced with challenges (Wechsler, 1975).

Intelligence: The capacity to understand the world, think rationally, and use resources effectively when faced with challenges

Unfortunately, neither the layperson's nor the psychologist's conception of intelligence is of much help when it comes to distinguishing, with any degree of precision, more intelligent people from less intelligent ones. To overcome this problem, psychologists who study intelligence have focused much of their attention on the development of batteries of tests, known, quite obviously, as **intelligence tests,** and have relied on such tests to identify a person's level of intelligence. These tests have proved to be of great benefit in identifying students in need of special attention in school, in diagnosing cognitive difficulties, and in helping people make optimal educational and vocational choices. At the same time, their use has proved quite controversial.

Intelligence tests: A battery of measures used to determine a person's level of intelligence

Measuring Intelligence

The first intelligence tests followed a simple premise: If performance on certain tasks or test items improved with age, then performance could be used to distinguish more intelligent people from less intelligent ones within a particular age group. Using this principle, Alfred Binet, a French psychologist, devised the first formal intelligence test, which was designed to identify the "dullest" students in the Paris school system in order to provide them with remedial aid.

Binet began by presenting tasks to same-age students who had been labeled "bright" or "dull" by their teachers. If a task could be completed by the bright students but not by the dull ones, he retained the task as a proper test item; otherwise it was discarded. In the end he came up with a test that distinguished between the bright and dull groups, and—with further work—one that distinguished among children in different age groups (Binet & Simon, 1916).

On the basis of the Binet test, children were assigned a score that corre-

Mental age: The typical intelligence level found for people at a given chronological age

Intelligence quotient (IQ) score: A measure of intelligence that takes into account an individual's mental and chronological ages

sponded to their **mental age,** the average age of children taking the test who achieved the same score. For example, if a 9-year-old boy received a score of 45 on the test and this was the average score received by 8-year-olds, his mental age would be considered to be 8 years. Similarly, a 14-year-old girl who scored an 88 on the test—matching the mean score for 16-year-olds—would be assigned a mental age of 16 years.

Assigning a mental age to students provided an indication of whether or not they were performing at the same level as their peers. However, it did not allow for adequate comparisons among people of different *chronological*, or *physical*, ages. By using mental age alone, for instance, we might assume that an 18-year-old responding at a 16-year-old's level would be as bright as a 5-year-old answering at a 3-year-old's level, when actually the 5-year-old would be displaying a much greater *relative* degree of slowness.

A solution to the problem came in the form of the **intelligence quotient,** or **IQ, score,** a measure of intelligence that takes into account an individual's mental *and* chronological ages. To calculate an IQ score, the following formula is used, in which MA stands for mental age and CA for chronological age:

$$\text{IQ score} = \frac{\text{MA}}{\text{CA}} \times 100$$

Using this formula, we can return to the earlier example of an 18-year-old performing at a mental age of 16 and calculate an IQ score of $(16 \div 18) \times 100 = 88.9$. In contrast, the 5-year-old performing at a mental age of 3 comes out with a considerably lower IQ score: $(3 \div 5) \times 100 = 60$.

As a bit of trial and error with the formula will show you, anyone who has a mental age equal to his or her chronological age will have an IQ equal to 100. Moreover, people with mental ages greater than their chronological ages will have IQs that exceed 100; and those with mental ages lower than their chronological ages will have IQs lower than 100.

Although the basic principles behind the calculation of an IQ score still hold, IQ scores are figured in a somewhat different manner today and are known as *deviation IQ scores.* First, the average test score for everyone of the same age who takes the test is determined, and this average score is assigned an IQ of 100. Then, with the aid of sophisticated mathematical techniques that calculate the differences (or "deviations") between each score and the average, IQ values are assigned to all the other test scores for this age group.

As you can see in Figure 8-1, approximately two-thirds of all individuals fall within 15 IQ points above and below the average score of 100. As scores increase or fall beyond that range, the percentage of people in a category falls considerably.

Tests of IQ   Just what is an IQ test like? It is probable that sometime during your academic career you have taken one; almost all of us are given IQ tests at one time or another.

Remnants of the original test are still with us, although it has been revised many times and in its modern incarnation bears little resemblance to the original version. Now called the *Stanford-Binet Test,* Fourth Edition, the measure was last revised in 1985 (Hagen, Sattler, & Thorndike, 1985; Thorndike, Hagen, & Sattler, 1986). It consists of a series of items that vary in nature according to the age of the person being tested. For example, young children are asked to copy figures or answer questions about everyday activities. Older people are asked to solve analogies, explain proverbs, and describe similarities that underlie sets of words.

The test is administered orally. An examiner begins by finding a mental age level at which the person is able to answer all questions correctly, and then moves on to successively difficult problems. When a mental age level is reached at which

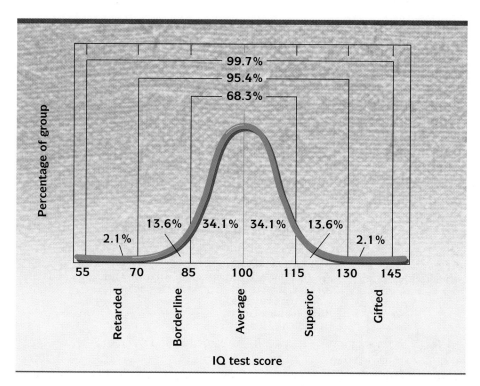

FIGURE 8-1 The average and most frequent IQ score is 100, and 68.3 percent of all people are within a 30-point range centered on 100. Some 95 percent of the population have scores that are between 70 and 130, and 99.7 percent have scores that are between 55 and 145.

no items can be answered, the test is over. By examining the pattern of correct and incorrect responses, the examiner is able to compute an IQ score for the person being tested.

The other IQ test frequently used in America was devised by psychologist David Wechsler and is known as the *Wechsler Adult Intelligence Scale—Revised*, or, more commonly, the *WAIS-R*. There is also a children's version, the *Wechsler Intelligence Scale for Children—III*, or *WISC-III*. Both the WAIS-R and the WISC-III have two major parts: a verbal scale and a performance (or nonverbal) scale. As you can see from the sample questions in Figure 8-2, the two scales include questions of very different types. Whereas verbal tasks consist of more traditional kinds of problems, including vocabulary definition and comprehension of various concepts, the nonverbal part involves assembling small objects and arranging pictures in a logical order. Although an individual's scores on the verbal and performance sections of the test are generally within close range of each other, the scores of a person with a language deficiency or a background of severe environmental deprivation may show a relatively large discrepancy between the two scores. By providing separate scores, the WAIS-R and WISC-III give a more precise picture of a person's specific abilities than a single score.

Because the Stanford-Binet, WAIS-R, and WISC-III all require individualized administration, it is relatively difficult and time-consuming to administer and score them on a wide-scale basis. Consequently, there are now a number of IQ tests that allow for group administration (Anastasi, 1988). Rather than having one examiner ask one person at a time to respond to individual items, group IQ tests are strictly paper-and-pencil measures, in which those taking the tests read the questions and provide their answers in writing. The primary advantage of group tests is their ease of administration.

There are, however, sacrifices made in group testing which, in some cases, may outweigh the benefits. For instance, group tests generally offer a more restricted range of questions than tests administered individually. Furthermore, people may be more motivated to perform at their highest ability level when working on a

FIGURE 8-2 Typical kinds of items found on the verbal and performance scales of the Wechsler Intelligence Scale for Children—III (WISC-III).

Types of Items found on the Wechsler Intelligence Scales for Children (WISC-III)

Name	Goal of Item	Example
Verbal scale		
Information	To assess general information	Where does milk come from?
Comprehension	To test understanding and evaluation of social norms and past experience	Why do we put food in the refrigerator?
Arithmetic	To assess math reasoning through verbal problems	Stacy had two crayons and the teacher gave her two more. How many did she have altogether?
Similarities	To test understanding of how objects or concepts are alike, tapping abstract reasoning	In what way are cows and horses alike?
Performance Scale		
Digit symbol	To assess speed of learning	Match symbols to numbers using the key
Picture completion	To identify missing parts, testing visual memory and attention	Identify what is missing
Object assembly	To test understanding of relationship of parts to wholes	Put pieces together to form a whole

Some intelligence tests include nonverbal items that assess the ability to copy a given pattern using blocks.

one-to-one basis with a test administrator than they are in a group. Finally, in some cases, it is simply impossible to employ group tests, particularly with young children or people with unusually low IQs.

Achievement and Aptitude Tests IQ tests are not the only kind of tests you have taken during the course of your schooling. Two other kinds of tests, related to intelligence but designed to measure somewhat different phenomena, are

achievement tests and aptitude tests. An **achievement test** is a test meant to ascertain a person's level of knowledge in a given subject area. Rather than measuring general ability as an intelligence test does, an achievement test concentrates on the specific material that a person has learned.

An **aptitude test** is designed to predict a person's ability in a particular area or line of work. Most of us take the most famous aptitude test in the process of pursuing admission to college: the Scholastic Assessment Test (SAT). The SAT is meant to predict how well people will do in college, and SAT scores have proved over the years to correlate moderately well with college grades.

Although in theory the distinction between intelligence, aptitude, and achievement tests can be precisely drawn, as a practical matter there is a good deal of overlap among them. For example, the SAT has been roundly criticized for being less of an aptitude test than one that actually measures achievement. It is difficult, then, to devise tests that predict future performance but do not rely on past achievement. The makers of the SAT have acknowledged this problem by recently changing the name of the SAT from its previous "Scholastic *Aptitude* Test" to the current "Scholastic *Assessment* Test."

One other change in the SAT involves the procedure by which it is presented to test-takers. The newest testing format eliminates paper and pencil altogether. Instead, examinees take the test on a computer, which provides them with a personalized version of the test, as we discuss in the accompanying Psychology at Work box.

Reliability and Validity   When we use a ruler, we expect to find that it measures an inch in the same way as the last time we used it. When we weigh ourselves on the bathroom scale, we hope that the variations we see on the scale are due to changes in our weight and are not errors on the part of the scale (unless the change in weight is in an unwanted direction!).

In the same way, we hope that psychological tests have **reliability**—that they consistently measure what they are trying to measure. We need to be sure that each time we administer the test, a person taking the test will achieve the same results—assuming that nothing about the person has changed relevant to what is being measured.

Suppose, for instance, that when you first took the SAT exams, you scored a 400 on the verbal section of the test. Then, after taking the test again a few months later, you scored a 700. Upon receiving your new score, you might well stop celebrating for a moment to question whether the test is reliable, for it is unlikely that your abilities could have changed enough to raise your score by 300 points.

But suppose your score changed hardly at all, and both times you received a score of about 400. You couldn't complain about a lack of reliability. However, if you knew your verbal skills were above average, you might be concerned that the test did not adequately measure what it was supposed to measure. In sum, the question has now become one of validity rather than of reliability. A test has **validity** when it actually measures what it is supposed to measure.

Knowing that a test is reliable is no guarantee that it is also valid. For instance, we could devise a very reliable means for measuring trustworthiness if we decided that trustworthiness is related to skull size. But there is certainly no guarantee that the test is valid, since one can reasonably assume that skull size has nothing to do with trustworthiness. In this case, then, we have reliability without validity.

On the other hand, if a test is unreliable, it cannot be valid. Assuming that all other factors—a person's motivation, knowledge of the material, health, and so forth—are similar, if someone scores high the first time she takes a specific test and low the second time, the test cannot be measuring what it is supposed to measure, and is therefore both unreliable and not valid.

Test validity and reliability are prerequisites for accurate assessment of intelli-

Achievement test: A test intended to determine a person's level of knowledge in a given subject area

Aptitude test: A test designed to predict ability in a particular area or line of work

Reliability: The concept that tests consistently measure what they are trying to measure

Validity: A test has validity when it actually measures what it is supposed to measure

PSYCHOLOGY AT WORK

Exchanging Pencils for Keyboards: Measuring Ability via Computer

If you were the kind of person who got the jitters just thinking about sharpening your No. 2 pencil before taking the SAT, you may be happy to learn that relief is in sight. Then again, the alternative might turn out to raise as many anxieties as its predecessor.

The Educational Testing Service (ETS)—the company that devises the SAT and the Graduate Record Exam (GRE), used for college and graduate school admission, respectively—has something new up its corporate sleeve: computerized administration. By 1996, the company planned to administer all GRE tests via a computer, and ultimately SAT administration will follow suit.

In the new computerized version, not only will the test questions be viewed and answered on a computer screen, but the test itself will be individualized. In what is known as adaptive testing, no two students will have an identical set of test questions. Instead, the computer will first present a randomly selected question of moderate dif-

ficulty. If the test-taker answers correctly, the computer will then present a randomly chosen item of slightly greater difficulty. If the answer is wrong, then the computer will present a slightly easier item. Each question becomes slightly harder or easier than the question preceding it, depending on whether the previous response is correct. Ultimately, the greater the number of difficult questions answered correctly, the higher the score.

Because the test is able to pinpoint a test-taker's level of proficiency fairly quickly, the total time spent taking the exam is shorter than it is when taking a traditional exam. Test-takers are not forced to spend a great deal of time answering questions that are either much easier or much harder than they can handle.

Computerized administration has another feature that may, or may not, be welcomed: presentation of an immediate test score. After completing the test, test-takers are given the option of nullifying the test if they think they did not do well. If they choose to proceed, however, the computer provides them with their scores, which then become part of a permanent record.

Computerized adaptive testing has its critics. Some observers suggest that the test discriminates against minorities, who may have limited access to computers and thus may have less practice with them or may be more intimidated by the testing medium (Winerip, 1993). However, ETS disputes the claim, although some of its own research shows that women and older test-takers show greater anxiety at the beginning of the test. Despite this anxiety, however, their performance ultimately is not affected.

Research also suggests that computerized adaptive testing provides scores equivalent to traditional paper-and-pencil measures for most types of testing. (The exception is for "speeded" tests, which involve many relatively easy items that must be completed in a relatively short time.) For tests such as the GRE, too, there appears to be no difference in scores that can be attributed to whether the test is administered traditionally or with a computer. Eventually, it is likely that the majority of tests will be administered via computer, ultimately making the No. 2 pencil a relic of times past.

gence—as well as for any other measurement task carried out by psychologists. Consequently, the measures of personality that we'll consider in Chapter 11, clinical psychologists' assessment of psychological disorders discussed in Chapter 13, and social psychologists' measures of attitudes described in Chapter 14 must meet the tests of validity and reliability in order for the results to be meaningful.

Assuming that a test is both valid and reliable, one further step is necessary in order to interpret the meaning of a particular test-taker's score: the establishment of norms. **Norms** are standards of test performance that permit the comparison of one person's score on the test to the scores of others who have taken the same test. For example, a norm permits test-takers to know that they have scored in the top 15 percent of those who have taken the test.

The basic scheme for developing norms is for test designers to calculate the average score for a particular group of people to whom the test is designed to be given. They can then determine the extent to which each person's score differs from those of the others who have taken the test in the past. Test-takers are then

Norms: Standards of test performance that permit the comparison of one person's score on a test to the scores of others who have taken the same test

able to consider the meaning of their raw scores relative to the scores of others who have taken the test, giving them a qualitative sense of their performance.

Obviously, the individuals who are employed in the establishment of norms are critical to the norming process. Those people used to determine norms must be representative of the individuals to whom the test is directed.

Alternative Formulations of Intelligence

Although Binet's procedure for measuring intelligence, exemplified by the modern Stanford-Binet and WAIS-R intelligence tests, remains one of the most frequently employed, some theorists argue that it lacks an underlying conception of what intelligence is. To Binet and his followers, intelligence was generally conceived of as a direct reflection of what score a person received on his or her test. That was an eminently practical approach, but one that depended not on an understanding of the nature of intelligence but primarily on comparing one person's performance with that of others. For this reason, the intelligence tests of Binet and his successors do little to increase our understanding of what intelligence means; they merely measure behavior assumed to exemplify intelligence.

This is not to say that researchers and theoreticians have ignored the issue of what intelligence really is (Carroll, 1992, 1993). One important question they have raised is whether intelligence is a single, unitary factor or whether it is made up of multiple components (Sternberg, 1990; Brody, 1993). The earliest psychologists interested in intelligence assumed that there was a general factor for mental ability, called **g,** or **g-factor** (Spearman, 1927). This factor was thought to underlie performance on every aspect of intelligence, and it was the g-factor that was presumably being measured on tests of intelligence.

More contemporary theoreticians have suggested that there are really two different kinds of intelligence: fluid intelligence and crystallized intelligence (Cattell, 1967, 1987). **Fluid intelligence** reflects reasoning, memory, and information processing capabilities. If we were asked to solve an analogy, group a series of letters according to some criterion, or remember a set of numbers, we would be using fluid intelligence.

In contrast, **crystallized intelligence** is the information, skills, and strategies that people have learned through experience and that they can apply in problem-solving situations. We would be likely to rely on crystallized intelligence, for instance, if we were asked to participate in a discussion about the causes of homelessness or to deduce the solution to a mystery: Such questions allow us to draw upon our own past experiences. The differences between fluid and crystallized intelligence become particularly evident in the elderly, who—as we will discuss further in Chapter 10—show declines in fluid, but not crystallized, intelligence (Horn, 1985).

Other theoreticians conceive of intelligence as encompassing even more components. For instance, by examining the talents of people who display unusual ability in certain areas, psychologist Howard Gardner has suggested that we have seven multiple intelligences, each relatively independent of the others (Gardner, 1983, 1993; Walters & Gardner, 1986). Specifically, he considers intelligence to include the seven spheres illustrated in Figure 8-3.

Although Gardner illustrates his conceptions of the specific types of intelligence with descriptions of well-known people, it is important to remember that each of us theoretically harbors the same kinds of intelligence. Moreover, although the seven are presented individually, Gardner suggests that these separate intelligences do not operate in isolation. Normally, any activity encompasses several kinds of intelligence working together.

Gardner's model has led to a number of advances in our understanding of the nature of intelligence. For example, one outgrowth of the model is the development of test items in which more than one answer can be correct, providing the

g, or **g-factor:** A theoretical single general factor accounting for mental ability

Fluid intelligence: Reflects reasoning, memory, and information-processing capabilities

Crystallized intelligence: The information, skills, and strategies that people have learned through experience and that can be applied in problem-solving situations

Playing a game like Trivial Pursuit and piloting an airplane call for differing degrees of fluid and crystallized intelligence.

1. Musical intelligence (skills in tasks involving music). Case example:

When he was 3, Yehudi Menuhin was smuggled into the San Francisco Orchestra concerts by his parents. The sound of Louis Persinger's violin so entranced the youngster that he insisted on a violin for his birthday and Louis Persinger as his teacher. He got them both. By the time he was 10 years old, Menuhin was an international performer.

2. Bodily kinesthetic intelligence (skills in using the whole body or various portions of it in the solution of problems or in the construction of products or displays, exemplified by dancers, athletes, actors, and surgeons). Case example:

Fifteeen-year old Babe Ruth played third base. During one game, his team's pitcher was doing very poorly and Babe loudly criticized him from third base. Brother Mathias, the coach, called out, "Ruth, if you know so much about it, *you* pitch!" Babe was surprised and embarrassed because he had never pitched before, but Brother Mathias insisted. Ruth said later that at the very moment he took the pitcher's mound, he *knew* he was supposed to be a pitcher.

3. Logical-mathematical intelligence (skills in problem-solving and scientific thinking). Case example:

Barbara McClintock won the Nobel Prize in medicine for her work in microbiology. She describes one of her breakthroughs, which came after thinking about a problem for half an hour . . .: "Suddenly I jumped and ran back to the (corn) field. At the top of the field (the others were still at the bottom) I shouted, 'Eureka, I have it!' "

4. Linguistic intelligence (skills involved in the production and use of language). Case example:

At the age of 10, T. S. Eliot created a magazine called *Fireside*, to which he was the sole contributor. In a three-day period during his winter vacation, he created eight complete issues.

5. Spatial intelligence (skills involving spatial configurations, such as those used by artists and architects). Case example:

Natives of the Caroline Islands navigate at sea without instuments. During the actual trip, the navigator must envision mentally a reference island as it passes under a particular star and from that he computes the number of segments completed, the proportion of the trip remaining, and any corrections in heading.

6. Interpersonal intelligence (skills in interacting with others, such as sensitivity to the moods, temperaments, motivations, and intentions of others). Case example:

When Anne Sullivan began instructing the deaf and blind Helen Keller, her task was one that had eluded others for years. Yet, just two weeks after beginning her work with Keller, Sullivan achieved a great success. In her words, "My heart is singing with joy this morning. A miracle has happened! The wild little creature of two weeks ago has been transformed into a gentle child."

7. Intrapersonal intelligence (knowledge of the internal aspects of oneself; access to one's own feelings and emotions). Case example:

In her essay "A Sketch of the Past," Virginia Woolf displays deep insight into her own inner life through these lines, describing her reaction to several specific memories from her childhood that still, in adulthood, shock her: "Though I still have the peculiarity that I receive these sudden shocks, they are now always welcome; after the first surprise, I always feel instantly that they are particularly valuable. And so I go on to suppose that the shock-receiving capacity is what makes me a writer."

FIGURE 8-3 Gardner's seven intelligences. *(Adapted from Walters & Gardner, 1986.)*

opportunity for test-takers to demonstrate creative thinking. According to these approaches, then, different kinds of intelligence may produce different—but equally valid—responses to the same question.

Is Information Processing Intelligence? Contemporary Approaches

The most recent contribution to understanding intelligence comes from the work of cognitive psychologists. Drawing on the research and theory that we discussed in Chapter 7, cognitive psychologists use an information-processing approach. They assert that the way people store material in memory and use the material to solve intellectual tasks provides the most accurate measure of intelligence. Consequently, cognitive psychologists do not focus on the structure of intelligence or its underlying content or dimensions. Instead, they examine the *processes* involved in producing intelligent behavior (Sternberg, 1990; Fagan, 1992).

By breaking tasks and problems into their component parts and identifying the nature and speed of problem-solving processes, researchers have noted distinct differences between those who score high on traditional IQ tests and those who score lower. Take, for example, a college student who is asked to solve the following analogy problem (Sternberg, 1982):

Lawyer is to client as doctor is to:
(a) *patient* or (b) *medicine*

According to Sternberg's theory, a student presented with this analogy tends to move through a series of stages in attempting to reach a solution (see Figure 8-4). First she will *encode* the initial information, which means providing each item with identifying cues that help retrieve relevant information buried in long-term memory. For instance, she may think of lawyer in terms of law school, the Supreme Court, *L.A. Law,* and a courtroom. Each of the other terms will be similarly encoded. Next, she will *infer* any possible relationship between lawyer and client. She may infer that the relevant relationship is that a client employs a lawyer, or, alternatively, that a lawyer gives services to a client.

Once she has inferred the relationship, she must *map* the higher-order relationship between the first half of the analogy and the second half—both deal with people who provide professional services for a fee. The crucial stage that follows is one of *application,* in which she tries out each answer option with the relationship she has inferred. She will presumably decide that a doctor provides professional services to a patient, not to medicine. Finally, the last component of solving the problem is *responding.*

By breaking problems into component parts in this manner, it is possible to identify systematic differences in both quantitative and qualitative aspects of problem solving, and to demonstrate that people with higher intelligence levels differ not only in the number of correct solutions they come up with, but in their method of solving problems. For instance, high scorers are apt to spend more time on the initial encoding stages of a problem, identifying the parts of the problem and retrieving relevant information from long-term memory. This initial emphasis on recalling relevant information pays off in the end; those who spend relatively less time on the initial stages tend to be less able to find a solution. People's use of such information-processing strategies, therefore, may underlie differences in intelligence.

Applying this cognitive approach to intelligence, psychologist Robert Sternberg (1985a, 1991) developed what he calls a triarchic theory of intelligence. The **triarchic theory of intelligence** suggests that there are three major aspects to intelligence: componential, experiential, and contextual (see Figure 8-5). The *componential* aspect focuses on the mental components involved in analyzing information to solve problems, particularly those processes operating when a person displays rational behavior. In contrast, the *experiential* aspect focuses on how a person's prior experiences affect intelligence, and how those experiences are brought to bear on problem-solving situations. Finally, the *contextual* aspect of intelligence takes into account how successful people are in facing the demands of their everyday environment.

Recent approaches to intelligence have focused most heavily on Sternberg's contextual aspect of intelligence. Several new theories emphasize *practical intelligence*—intelligence related to overall success in living, rather than to intellectual

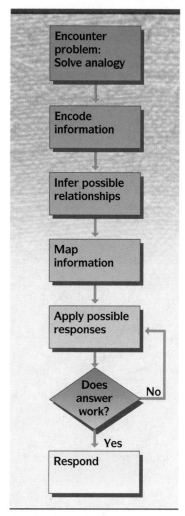

FIGURE 8-4 Information-processing stages in solving analogies. *(Sternberg, 1982.)*

Triarchic theory of intelligence: A theory suggesting three major aspects of intelligence: componential, experiential, and contextual

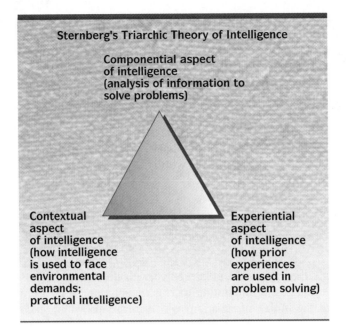

FIGURE 8-5 Sternberg's triarchic theory of intelligence. *(Based on Sternberg, 1985a, 1991.)*

and academic performance, as we discuss next (Sternberg & Detterman, 1986; Sternberg et al., 1995).

Practical Intelligence: Measuring Common Sense

Your year on the job has been generally favorable. Performance ratings for your department are at least as good as they were before you took over, and perhaps even a little better. You have two assistants. One is quite capable. The other just seems to go through the motions and is of little real help. Even though you are well liked, you believe that there is little that would distinguish you in the eyes of your superiors from the nine other managers at a comparable level in the company. Your goal is rapid promotion to an executive position. (Based on Wagner & Sternberg, 1985, p. 447)

What do you do to meet your goal? The way in which you answer this question may have a lot to do with your future success in a business career, according to its author, psychologist Robert J. Sternberg. The question is one of a series designed to help give an indication of your intelligence. It is not traditional intelligence that the question is designed to tap, but rather intelligence of a particular kind: practical intelligence for business (Wagner & Sternberg, 1991; Sternberg & Wagner, 1986, 1993).

The test that Sternberg has devised is one of several recent intelligence measures now taking shape. Each is designed to overcome one of the most glaring limitations of traditional IQ tests: the inability of traditional tests to accurately predict anything other than academic success.

For instance, although not all psychologists agree (e.g., Ree & Earles, 1992), most believe that IQ does not relate particularly well to *career success* (McClelland, 1993). For example, while it is clear that successful business executives usually score at least moderately well on IQ tests, the rates at which they advance and their ultimate business achievements are only minimally associated with their specific IQ scores.

Sternberg argues that career success requires a type of intelligence that is very different from that involved in academic success. Whereas academic success is based on knowledge of a particular information base obtained from reading and listening, practical intelligence is learned mainly through observation and model-

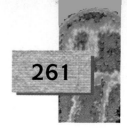
ing. People who are high in practical intelligence are able to learn general norms and principles and apply them appropriately.

Business is hardly the sole sphere in which this kind of practical intelligence is crucial, and some psychologists have suggested that practical intelligence is essential throughout everyday life. For example, psychologist Seymour Epstein has developed a test of what he terms "constructive thinking," which attempts to predict life success (Epstein & Meier, 1989; Epstein, 1994).

According to Epstein, constructive thinking underlies success in such domains as happiness with social relationships, job success, and even physical and emotional health. People who think constructively are able to manage their emotions effectively and deal with challenging situations in ways that promote success. Constructive thinkers, for instance, take action in objectionable situations, rather than just complaining about them. Epstein contends that constructive thinking is far more predictive of actual success in life than traditional IQ tests (Epstein, 1994).

In sum, it is clear that there are many ways to demonstrate—and measure—intelligence. A high IQ does not guarantee success in life, especially if it is accompanied by low practical intelligence.

The Informed Consumer of Psychology

Can You Do Better on Standardized Tests?

Even though psychologists disagree about the nature of intelligence, intelligence tests—as well as many other kinds of tests—are still widely used in a variety of situations. In school or on the job, almost all of us have had to cope with these formal, standardized tests—tests that have been formulated and verified with large representative samples. And most of us can probably understand the concern of students taking college entrance exams, such as the SAT, who worry that success in their future lives hangs on one morning's test results.

One outcome of the prevalence of tests in our society is the development of numerous coaching services meant to train people to raise their scores by reviewing basic skills and teaching test-taking strategies. But do they work?

The Educational Testing Service, the creators of the SAT, at one time suggested that coaching for the test was useless. Today, however, it acknowledges that the practice may have some beneficial consequences. In fact, most research verifies that coaching for the SAT exams produces small, but reliable, effects—usually in the range of 15- to 25-point increases each in verbal and math scores (Kulik, Bangert-Drowns, & Kulik, 1984; Becker, 1990; Powers, 1993).

On the other hand, most of the increase in scores following coaching may stem from increased familiarity with the test or from natural growth in cognitive abilities. Some research suggests that the coaching required to bring about average score increases of more than 20 to 30 points is so extensive that it would be the equivalent of going to school full time.

More research is needed before we can ascertain the true value of coaching. At the same time, there are certain steps you can take, without the benefit of coaching, to maximize your opportunity to score well on standardized tests. For example, the following four points provide good advice for taking traditional, noncomputerized tests (Crocetti, 1983):

■ *Preview each section.* Not only will it give you a chance to take a deep breath and prevent you from frantically rushing through a given section, but it will also alert you to any unexpected changes in the test format. Previewing will give you a sense of what to expect as you work through each problem.

■ *Time yourself carefully.* The computer that scores your test will not care how deeply you have thought out and considered each answer; all it notes is whether or not you have answered a problem correctly. Therefore, it is important not to spend too much time on initial problems at the expense of later ones. If you are unsure of an answer, try to narrow down the options; then guess and go on to the next problem. Perfection is not your goal; maximizing the number of correct responses is.

■ *Check the test-scoring policy to determine whether guessing is appropriate.* On some tests, wrong answers are subtracted from your score, making blind guessing a bad strategy. In comparison, many other tests do not penalize you for wrong answers. On tests with penalties for wrong answers, guess only if you can narrow the choices down to two or three. On the other hand, for tests in which wrong answers do not lower your score, it pays to guess, even if you have no idea of the correct response.

■ *Complete answer sheets accurately.* Obviously, it makes sense to check your answer sheet when you have finished the test. This can be done most efficiently if you have indicated your answers on the test booklet itself.

RECAP AND REVIEW

Recap

- Intelligence is the capacity to understand the world, think rationally, and use resources effectively when faced with challenges.
- The measure of intelligence used in tests is the intelligence quotient, or IQ.
- Tests must be reliable, measuring with consistency what they are trying to measure, and valid, measuring what is supposed to be measured
- There are a number of alternative formulations of intelligence.
- Coaching has some impact on improving test scores, although there is variability in its effectiveness.

Review

1. _____ is a measure of intelligence that takes into account both a person's chronological and mental ages.

2. _____ tests predict a person's ability in a specific area, while _____ tests determine the person's level of knowledge in a given area.

3. Some psychologists make the distinction between _____ intelligence, which reflects reasoning, memory, and information-processing capabilities, and _____ intelligence, which is the information, skills, and strategies that people have learned through experience.

4. Cognitive psychologists use an _____-_____ approach to measure intelligence.

Ask Yourself

How might fluid and crystallized intelligence be tested? What applications would each of these types of intelligence have?

(Answers to review questions are on page 264.)

- *How can the extremes of intelligence be differentiated?*
- *How can we help people to maximize their full potential?*

VARIATIONS IN INTELLECTUAL ABILITY

"Hey, hey, hey, Fact Track!" The 11-year-old speaker chose one of his favorite programs from the table next to the computer in his parents' dining room. He inserted the floppy disc, booted the system, and waited for the program to load.

"What is your name?" appeared on the monitor.

"Daniel Skandera," he typed. A menu scrolled up listing the program's possibilities. Daniel chose multiplication facts, Level 1.

"How many problems do you want to do?" the computer asked.

"20."

"Do you want to set a goal for yourself, Daniel?"

"Yes, 80 sec."

"Get ready!". . .

Randomly generated multiplication facts flashed on the screen: "4 × 6," "2 × 9," "3 × 3," "7 × 6." Daniel responded, deftly punching in his answers on the computer's numeric keypad. . . .

The computer tallied the results. "You completed 20 problems in 66 seconds. You beat your goal. Problems correct = 20. Congratulations Daniel!" And with that the 11-year-old retreated hastily to the TV room. The Lakers and 76ers were about to tip off for an NBA championship game, and Daniel wanted to see the first half before bedtime (Heward & Orlansky, 1988, p. 100).

If you view the mentally retarded as inept and dull, it is time to revise your beliefs. As in the case of Daniel, described above, individuals with deficits of intellectual abilities can lead full, well-rounded lives and in some cases even perform competently in certain kinds of academic endeavors.

More than 7 million people in the United States have been identified as having intelligence far enough below average for it to be regarded as a serious deficit. Both those people with low IQs, known as the mentally retarded, and those with unusually high IQs, referred to as the intellectually gifted, make up groups of individuals who require special attention to reach their full potential.

Mental Retardation

Although sometimes thought of as a rare phenomenon, mental retardation occurs in 1 to 3 percent of the population. There is wide variation among those labeled as mentally retarded, in large part because of the inclusiveness of the definition developed by the American Association on Mental Retardation. The association suggests that **mental retardation** exists when there is "significantly subaverage intellectual functioning," which occurs with related limitations in two or more of the skill areas of communication, self-care, home living, social skills, community use, self-direction, health and safety, functional academics, leisure, and work (AAMR, 1992).

While "subaverage intellectual functioning" can be measured in a relatively straightforward manner—using standard IQ tests—it is more difficult to determine how to gauge limitations in particular skill areas. Ultimately, this imprecision leads to a lack of uniformity in how experts apply the label of "mental retardation." Furthermore, it has resulted in significant variation in the abilities of people who are categorized as mentally retarded, ranging from those who can be taught to work and function with little special attention to those who virtually cannot be trained and who must receive institutional treatment throughout their lives (Matson & Mulick, 1991).

Most mentally retarded people have relatively minor deficits and are classified as having *mild retardation*. These individuals have IQ scores ranging from 55 to 69, and they constitute some 90 percent of all retarded individuals. Although their development is typically slower than that of their peers, they can function quite independently by adulthood and are able to hold jobs and have families of their own.

At greater levels of retardation—*moderate retardation* (IQs of 40 to 54), *severe retardation* (IQs of 25 to 39), and *profound retardation* (IQs below 25)— the difficulties are more pronounced. With the moderately retarded, deficits are obvious early, with language and motor skills lagging behind those of peers. Although these people can hold simple jobs, they need to have a moderate degree of supervision throughout their lives. The severely and profoundly retarded are generally unable to function independently. Often they have no language skills, poor motor control, and an inability to be toilet-trained; they are typically institutionalized for their entire lives.

Mental retardation: A significantly subaverage level of intellectual functioning which occurs with related limitations in two or more skill areas

Although defense lawyers argued that his low IQ prevented him from understanding his crime and the judicial proceedings adequately, Barry Lee Fairchild was executed for the murder of an Air Force nurse. His death raised important ethical issues.

What are the causes of mental retardation? In nearly one-third of the cases there is an identifiable biological reason. The most common biological cause of retardation is Down syndrome, exemplified by Mindie Crutcher at the start of the chapter. *Down syndrome,* which was once referred to as mongolism (because those with the disorder were viewed as having an Asian facial configuration), is caused by the presence of an extra chromosome (Cicchetti & Beeghly, 1990). In other cases of mental retardation, an abnormality occurs in the structure of a chromosome (Oberle et al., 1991; Yu et al., 1991). Birth complications, such as a temporary lack of oxygen, may also cause retardation.

The majority of cases of mental retardation are classified as familial retardation. In *familial retardation,* retarded people have no known biological defect, but do have a history of retardation within their families. Whether their families' backgrounds of retardation are caused by environmental factors, such as extreme continuous poverty leading to malnutrition, or by some underlying genetic factor is usually impossible to determine for certain. What is characteristic of familial retardation is the presence of more than one retarded person in the immediate family.

Regardless of the cause of mental retardation, important advances in the care and treatment of the mentally retarded have been made in the last two decades (Garber, 1988; Landesman & Ramey, 1989). Much of this change was instigated by the Education for All Handicapped Children Act of 1975 (Public Law 94-142). In this federal law, Congress ruled that the mentally retarded are entitled to a full education and that they must be educated and trained in the *least restrictive environment.* The law increased the educational opportunities for the retarded, facilitating their integration into regular classrooms as much as possible—a process known as *mainstreaming.*

The philosophy behind mainstreaming suggests that the interaction of retarded and nonretarded students in regular classrooms will improve the educational opportunities for the mentally retarded, increase their social acceptance, and facilitate their integration into society as a whole. The philosophy was once to segregate the retarded into special-education classes where they could learn at their own pace along with other handicapped students. Mainstreaming attempts to prevent the isolation inherent in special-education classes and to reduce the social stigma of retardation by allowing the handicapped to interact with their age peers as much as possible (Mastropieri & Scruggs, 1987).

Of course, there are still special-education classes; some retarded individuals function at too low a level to benefit from placement in regular classrooms. Moreover, retarded children mainstreamed into regular classes typically attend special classes for at least part of the day. Still, mainstreaming offers the promise of increasing the integration of the mentally retarded into society and allowing them to make their own contributions to the world at large. (To consider another application of mainstreaming, in which people with even severe forms of mental retardation are moved from institutions into the community, see the Pathways through Psychology box.)

The Intellectually Gifted

Intellectually gifted: Individuals characterized by higher-than-average intelligence, with IQ scores above 130

Another group of people—the intellectually gifted—differs as much from those with average intelligence as those who are mentally retarded, although in a different manner. Comprising 2 to 4 percent of the population, the **intellectually gifted** have IQ scores greater than 130.

PATHWAYS THROUGH PSYCHOLOGY

Rob Davies

Born: 1948
Education: B.A., State University of New York, New Paltz; M.B.A., State University of New York, Albany
Home: Albany, New York

Rob Davies.

Rob Davies has always been an activist, whether it was starting an environmental studies program while an undergraduate or applying a humanistic approach to psychology to provide a better life for the mentally retarded in the 1990s.

Davies is currently with the Bureau of Housing and Family Care for the New York Office of Mental Retardation and Developmental Disabilities. His goal is to move mentally retarded people out of institutions and into more natural environments such as group homes.

The 48-year-old Davies has spent most of his life giving those with little opportunity the chance to live a better life. After an undergraduate career that included courses in introductory and organizational psychology, he obtained a job working with juvenile delinquents and then ran a group home for the mentally retarded. It was while setting up a recreation program at a sheltered workshop that he realized the mentally retarded had the potential to control their own lives. "We set up an apartment program for the individuals, and at that time hired housewives who would teach them to budget, shop, and manage their own household," he said.

That experience ultimately led to his current position, where he helps in the selection of sites for group homes for the retarded within established neighborhoods. Much of his time is spent in dispelling people's prejudices about the mentally retarded. Although it is now standard practice to keep mentally retarded individuals involved in the community and to avoid institutionalization wherever possible, there are still drawbacks to the way in which the mentally retarded are treated.

"We still put limits on human potential," he notes. "In the 20 years I've been involved, I have never known anyone to predict human potential. I've heard many professionals say that the mentally retarded could never do certain things. But over the years all those predictions have been patently false, if the retarded are given the appropriate exposure and stimulation."

A member of a subcommittee of the President's Committee on Mental Retardation Housing, Davies focuses these days on giving the mentally retarded control of their lives. "People with disabilities need control over where they live, with whom they live, and control over who works with them," he said. "The whole concept is that people with disabilities should have equal opportunity for housing and jobs. It's basically a civil rights issue."

Although housing and money are important aspects in helping the mentally retarded, Davies notes that often the most modest activities produce some of the best results. "We often get off on complicated solutions when the simple, obvious solution is the best way," he says. "For instance, something like starting a circle of friends can be helpful. These are the things that give life quality—long-term relationships with friends, your house, your bed, a favorite cup. If you have a bad day at work, people without disabilities can come home and call a close friend or sit and relax. But if you have a bad day at a workshop for the mentally retarded, your supervisor will call your group home, and then they may get on your case. You don't have the same opportunities," he added.

Davies recalled an earlier time in his career when in an institution he approached a severely retarded woman lying on a bed staring at the ceiling. He went over and touched her forehead and noticed an immediate change in her face.

"There was a glow in her eye in which you could almost see her gratitude for being acknowledged. I still see that woman's eyes today," he recalled. "Sometimes seeing people with mental retardation is just recognizing a certain smile or a flicker of the eye. That seeing of people is how we communicate.

"In some ways, we all are disabled, since we don't have the skills to reach in and pull out the communications. That's the real challenge we have before us," he said.

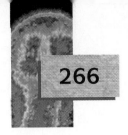
Although the stereotype associated with the gifted suggests that they are awkward, shy, social misfits unable to get along well with peers, most research indicates just the opposite is true. Like Lenny Ng, who was described at the start of the chapter, the intellectually gifted are most often outgoing, well-adjusted, popular people who are able to do most things better than the average person (Horowitz & O'Brien, 1987; Subotnik & Arnold, 1993, 1994).

For example, in a long-term study by Lewis Terman that started in the early 1920s and is still going on, 1500 children who had IQ scores above 140 were followed and examined periodically over the next sixty years (Sears, 1977; Terman & Oden, 1947). From the start, members of this group were physically, academically, and socially more able than their nongifted peers. They were generally healthier, taller, heavier, and stronger than average. Not surprisingly, they did better in school as well. They also showed better social adjustment than average. And all these advantages paid off in terms of career success: As a group, the gifted received more awards and distinctions, earned higher incomes, and made more contributions in art and literature than typical individuals. For example, by the time the members of the group were 40 years old, they had collectively written more than 90 books, 375 plays and short stories, and 2000 articles, and had registered more than 200 patents. Perhaps most important, they reported greater satisfaction in life than the nongifted.

On the other hand, the picture of these intellectually gifted people was not unvaryingly positive (Shurkin, 1992). Not every member of the group Terman studied was successful, and there were some notable failures. Moreover, other research suggests that high intelligence is not a homogeneous quality; a person with a high overall IQ is not necessarily gifted in every academic subject but may excel in just one or two (Stanley, 1980; Sternberg & Davidson, 1986). A high IQ, then, does not guarantee success in every endeavor.

Although special programs attempting to overcome the deficits of the mentally retarded abound, only recently have ways of encouraging the talents of the intellectually gifted been developed. This lack of special attention has been due in part to a persistent view that the gifted ought to be able to "make it on their own"; if they can't, then they really weren't gifted in the first place. More enlightened approaches, however, have acknowledged that without some form of special attention, the gifted may become bored and frustrated with the pace of their school-

Intellectually gifted children benefit from special education programs—when such classes are available, which is not often the case.

ing and may never reach their potential (Reis, 1989; Borland, 1989; Gallagher, 1993).

One particularly successful program for the intellectually gifted is a project called the Study of the Mathematically Precocious Youth. Within this program, seventh-graders who have shown unusual mathematical ability are enrolled in summer classes in which they are rapidly taught complex mathematical skills, culminating in college-level calculus. In addition, they receive instruction in a variety of other subjects, including the sciences and languages. The ultimate goal of the program, and others like it, is to provide enrichment for gifted students through an accelerated curriculum to allow their talents to flourish. Such programs increase the likelihood that the gifted will reach their maximum potential (Stanley, 1980; Southern, Jones, & Stanley, 1993).

RECAP AND REVIEW

Recap

- Mental retardation is defined by significantly subaverage levels of intellectual functioning along with deficits in adaptive behavior.
- The levels of retardation include mildly retarded (IQ of 55 to 69), moderately retarded (IQ of 40 to 54), severely retarded (IQ of 25 to 39), and profoundly retarded (IQ below 25).
- The most frequent causes of mental retardation are Down syndrome and familial influences.
- The intellectually gifted have IQs above 130 and comprise 2 to 4 percent of the population.

Review

1. Mental retardation refers specifically to those people with an IQ below 60. True or false?
2. _____ _____ is a disorder caused by an extra chromosome that is responsible for some cases of mental retardation.
3. _____ is the process by which mentally retarded stu-

dents are placed in normal classrooms to facilitate learning and reduce isolation.
4. Some forms of retardation can have a genetic basis and can be passed through families. True or false?
5. People with high intelligence are generally shy and socially withdrawn. True or false?

Ask Yourself

Suppose the federal government announced a $10 billion program designed to give aid to special schools in which gifted students can be enrolled. These schools will be designed to help gifted students achieve their maximum potential in specific areas in which they are the strongest. The schools will be offered free to such students, with a special tax being levied to pay for this project. The assumption behind these schools is that the productivity of such students in later years will more than make up for the expenditure of money in the present. What benefits could come from such a program? What drawbacks might occur?

(Answers to review questions are on page 268.)

- *Are traditional IQ tests culturally biased?*
- *Are there racial differences in intelligence?*
- *To what degree is intelligence influenced by the environment and to what degree by heredity?*

INDIVIDUAL DIFFERENCES IN INTELLIGENCE: HEREDITARY AND ENVIRONMENTAL DETERMINANTS

Kwang is often washed with a pleck tied to a:
(*a*) rundel
(*b*) flink
(*c*) pove
(*d*) quirj

If you found this kind of item on an intelligence test, you would probably complain that the test was totally absurd and had nothing to do with your intelligence or anyone else's. How could anyone be expected to respond to items presented in a language that was so unfamiliar?

But suppose you found the following item, which at first glance might look equally foreign:

Which word is most out of place here?
(*a*) splib
(*b*) blood
(*c*) gray
(*d*) spook

Just as absurd? On the contrary, there is considerably more reason to use this second question on an intelligence test than the first example, which was made up of nonsense syllables. Although this second example may appear as meaningless as the first to most of the white population of the United States, to urban African-Americans the question might be a reasonable test of their knowledge.

The second example is drawn from a test created by sociologist Adrian Dove, who tried to illustrate a problem that has plagued the developers of IQ tests from the beginning. By using terminology that would be familiar to urban African-Americans from inner-city backgrounds, but typically unfamiliar to whites (and to African-Americans raised within the dominant white culture), he dramatized the fact that cultural experience could play a critical role in determining intelligence test scores. (The answer to the item presented above, by the way, is *c*. To try your hand at other items drawn from Dove's test, see Table 8-1.)

The issue of devising fair intelligence tests that measure knowledge unrelated to cultural and family background and experience would be minor were it not for one important and persistent finding: Members of certain racial and cultural groups consistently score lower on intelligence tests than members of other groups (MacKenzie, 1984; Humphreys, 1992). For example, as a group, African-Americans tend to average 15 IQ points lower than whites. Does this reflect a true difference in intelligence, or are the questions biased in the kinds of knowledge they test? Clearly, if whites perform better because of their greater familiarity with the kind of information that is being tested, their higher IQ scores are not necessarily an indication that they are more intelligent than members of other groups.

There is good reason to believe that some standardized IQ tests contain elements that discriminate against minority-group members whose experiences differ from those of the white majority. Consider the question "What should you do if another child grabbed your hat and ran off with it?" Most white middle-class children answer that they would tell an adult, and this response is scored as "correct." On the other hand, a reasonable response might be to chase the person and fight to get the hat back, the answer that is chosen by many urban African-American children—but one that is scored as incorrect (Albee, 1978; Miller-Jones, 1989).

Furthermore, tests may include even more subtle forms of bias against minority groups. For example, psychologist Janet Helms (1992) argues that assessments of cognitive ability developed in the United States are sometimes constructed to favor responses that implicitly reflect North American or European

---

ANSWERS TO PREVIOUS REVIEW

1. False; the term is used to describe a wide range of people with various degrees of mental impairment. **2.** Down syndrome **3.** Mainstreaming **4.** True **5.** False; the gifted are generally more socially adept than those with a lower IQ.

TABLE 8-1   A Culture-*Unfair* Intelligence Test

If you have been raised within the dominant white culture, particularly in a suburban or rural environment, you may have difficulty in answering the following questions, which are designed to illustrate the importance of devising culture-fair intelligence tests.

1. Bird, or Yardbird, was the jacket that jazz lovers from coast to coast hung on
   (a) Lester Young
   (b) Peggy Lee
   (c) Benny Goodman
   (d) Charlie Parker
   (e) Birdman of Alcatraz

2. The opposite of square is
   (a) Round
   (b) Up
   (c) Down
   (d) Hip
   (e) Lame

3. If you throw the dice and 7 is showing on the top, what is facing down?
   (a) 7
   (b) Snake eyes
   (c) Boxcars
   (d) Little Joes
   (e) 11

4. Jazz pianist Ahmad Jamal took an Arabic name after becoming really famous. Previously he had what he called his "slave name." What was his previous name?
   (a) Willie Lee Jackson
   (b) LeRoi Jones
   (c) Wilbur McDougal
   (d) Fritz Jones
   (e) Andy Johnson

5. In C. C. Rider, what does "C. C." stand for?
   (a) Civil Service
   (b) Church Council
   (c) County Circuit Preacher
   (d) Country Club
   (e) Cheating Charley (the "Boxcar Gunsel")

Answers It is obvious how this test illustrates, in an exaggerated reverse fashion, the difficulties that an African-American from an inner-city background might have in responding to items on the typical intelligence test, which mirrors the dominant middle- and upper-class white culture. The correct answers are **1.** d; **2.** d; **3.** a; **4.** d; **5.** c. (Dove, 1968)

---

values, customs, or traditions. At the same time, such tests are biased against African and other cultural value systems.

More specifically, Helms suggests that the traditional Western value of "rugged individualism" means that correct answers to test items may require a test-taker to reason independently of a particular social context. In contrast, the African cultural value of communalism, in which one's group is valued more than individuals, may leave test-takers from that tradition unable to answer a question that provides no information about the social context.

The possibility of bias and discrimination against minority-group members in traditional IQ tests has led some jurisdictions to ban their use. For example, the state of California does not permit public schools to give African-American students IQ tests to decide whether they should be placed in special-education classes for what are called the "educable mentally retarded," although, in a complex legal interpretation, it will permit testing for certain other types of learning disabilities (Baker, 1987; Turkington, 1992). Ironically, because the ban on testing pertains only to African-American students, and not to whites, Hispanics, and other racial and ethnic groups, some people have argued that the ban itself is discriminatory.

Exploring Diversity

The Relative Influence of Heredity and of Environment

Culture-fair IQ test: A test that does not discriminate against members of any minority or cultural group

In an attempt to produce what has come to be called a **culture-fair IQ test,** one that does not discriminate against members of any minority or cultural group, psychologists have tried to devise test items that assess experiences common to all cultures or that emphasize questions that do not require language usage. However, test makers have found this difficult to do, and some culture-fair tests have produced even larger discrepancies between majority and minority groups than traditional tests that rely more heavily on verbal skills (Anastasi, 1988; Geisinger, 1992).

The efforts of psychologists to produce culture-fair measures of intelligence relate to a lingering controversy over differences in intelligence between members of minority and majority groups. In attempting to identify whether there are differences between such groups, psychologists have had to confront the broader issue of determining the relative contribution to intelligence of genetic factors (heredity) and experience (environment).

Richard Herrnstein, a psychologist, and Charles Murray, a sociologist, fanned the flames of the debate with the publication of their book, *The Bell Curve,* in 1994 (Herrnstein & Murray, 1994). They argued that an analysis of IQ differences between whites and African-Americans demonstrated that, although environmental factors played a role, there were also basic genetic differences between the two races. They based their argument on a number of findings. For instance, on average, whites score 15 points higher than African-Americans on traditional IQ tests even when socioeconomic class is taken into account. According to Herrnstein and Murray, middle- and upper-class African-Americans score lower than middle- and upper-class whites, just as lower-class African-Americans score lower on average than lower-class whites. Intelligence differences between African-Americans and whites, they concluded, cannot be attributed to environmental differences alone.

Heritability: A measure of the degree to which a characteristic is related to genetic, inherited factors, as opposed to environmental factors

Moreover, intelligence in general shows a high degree of **heritability,** a measure of the degree to which a characteristic is related to genetic, inherited factors (e.g., Bouchard et al., 1990). As can be seen in Figure 8-6, the closer the genetic link between two people, the greater the correspondence of IQ scores. Using data such as these, Herrnstein and Murray argued that differences between races in IQ scores were largely caused by genetically based differences in intelligence.

However, many psychologists reacted strongly to the arguments laid out in *The Bell Curve,* refuting several of the book's contentions (e.g., Nisbett, 1994). For one thing, even when socioeconomic conditions are supposedly held constant, wide variations remain among individual households, and no one can convincingly assert that living conditions of African-Americans and whites are identical even when their socioeconomic status is similar. Second, as we discussed earlier, there is reason to believe that traditional IQ tests may discriminate against lower-class urban African-Americans by asking for information pertaining to experiences they are unlikely to have had.

Moreover, there is direct evidence that African-Americans who are raised in enriched environments do not tend, as a group, to have lower IQ scores than

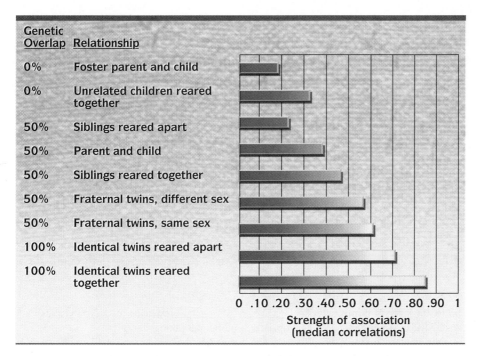

Genetic Overlap	Relationship
0%	Foster parent and child
0%	Unrelated children reared together
50%	Siblings reared apart
50%	Parent and child
50%	Siblings reared together
50%	Fraternal twins, different sex
50%	Fraternal twins, same sex
100%	Identical twins reared apart
100%	Identical twins reared together

0 .10 .20 .30 .40 .50 .60 .70 .80 .90 1
Strength of association
(median correlations)

FIGURE 8-6 *Summary findings on IQ and closeness of genetic relationship. The bars indicate the median correlations found across studies, while the percentages indicate the degree of genetic overlap within the relationship. Note, for example, that the median correlation for unrelated people reared apart is quite low, while the correlation for identical twins reared together is substantially higher. In general, the more similar the genetic and environmental background of two people, the greater the correlation. (Adapted from Bouchard & McGue, 1981.)*

whites in similar environments. For example, a study by Sandra Scarr and Richard Weinberg examined African-American children who were adopted at an early age by white middle-class families of above-average intelligence (Scarr & Weinberg, 1976). The IQ scores of the children averaged 106—about 15 points above the average IQ scores of unadopted African-American children reared in their own homes, and above the average scores of the general population. In addition, the younger a child's age at the time of adoption, the higher his or her IQ score tended to be. The evidence that genetic factors play the major role in determining racial differences in IQ, then, is not compelling, although the question still evokes controversy (Jacoby & Glauberman, 1995).

Ultimately, it is crucial to remember that IQ scores and intelligence have greatest relevance in terms of individuals, not groups. By far, the greatest discrepancies in IQ scores occur when comparing *individuals,* and not when comparing mean IQ scores of different *groups.* There are African-Americans who score high on IQ tests and whites who score low, just as there are whites who score high and African-Americans who score low. For the concept of intelligence to aid in the betterment of society, we must examine how *individuals* perform, not the groups to which they belong. We need to focus on the degree to which intelligence can be enhanced in a given person, not in members of a particular group (Angoff, 1988).

Other issues make the heredity-versus-environment debate somewhat irrelevant to practical concerns. For example, as we discussed earlier, there are multiple kinds of intelligence, and traditional IQ scores do not tap many of them. Furthermore, some psychologists argue that IQ scores are only weakly linked to intelligence, and that they are often inadequate predictors of ultimate academic and occupational success (Flynn, 1987). Finally, actual school achievement differences between whites and African-Americans appear to be narrowing (Jones, 1984). In sum, questions concerning differences in white and African-American intelligence levels may prove to be less pertinent than those relating to understanding individual differences in IQ, without regard to race.

Placing the Heredity-Environment Question in Perspective

There is no absolute resolution to the question of to what degree intelligence is influenced by heredity and by the environment. We are dealing with an issue for which experiments to determine cause and effect cannot be unambiguously devised. (A moment's thought about how we might experimentally assign infants to enriched or deprived environments will reveal the impossibility of devising ethically reasonable experiments!)

The more critical question to ask, then, is not whether it is primarily hereditary or environmental factors that underlie intelligence but whether there is anything we can do to maximize the intellectual development of each individual (Scarr & Carter-Saltzman, 1982; Angoff, 1988). We will then be able to make changes in the environment—which may take the form of enriched home and school environments—that can lead each person to reach his or her potential.

RECAP AND REVIEW

Recap

- The issue of whether IQ tests are biased in favor of dominant groups in society arises because African-Americans tend to average 15 IQ points lower than whites on standardized tests.
- Culture-fair IQ tests have been developed in an attempt to avoid discriminating against minority groups.
- Probably the most important issue concerning IQ is not the degree to which it is influenced by heredity or the environment, but what we can do to nurture and maximize the development of intelligence in all individuals.

Review

1. Intelligence tests may be biased toward the prevailing culture in such a way that minorities are put at a disadvantage when taking these tests. True or false?

2. A _____-_____ test tries to use only questions appropriate to all people taking the test.
3. IQ tests can accurately determine the intelligence of entire groups of people. True or false?
4. Intelligence can be seen as a reflection of a combination of _____ and _____ factors.

Ask Yourself

Industrial psychologists use a variety of tests to determine job hirings, promotions, etc. Armed with what you know about intelligence testing, you are asked to oversee the testing program for promotion to management positions at IBM. What recommendations would you make for this program?

(Answers to review questions are on page 273.)

LOOKING BACK

How do psychologists conceptualize and define intelligence?

1. Because intelligence can take many forms, defining it presents a challenge to psychologists. One commonly accepted view is that intelligence is the capacity to understand the world, think rationally, and use resources effectively when faced with challenges.

What are the major approaches to measuring intelligence?

2. Intelligence tests are used to measure intelligence. They provide a mental age which, when divided by a person's chronological age and then multiplied by 100, gives an IQ, or intelligence quotient, score. Specific tests of intelligence include the Stanford-Binet test, the Wechsler Adult Intelligence

Scale—Revised (WAIS-R), and the Wechsler Intelligence Scale for Children—III (WISC-III). In addition to intelligence tests, other standardized tests take the form of achievement tests (which measure level of knowledge in a given area) and aptitude tests (which predict ability in a given area).

3. Intelligence tests must have reliability and validity. Reliability refers to the consistency with which a test measures what it is trying to measure. A test has validity when it actually measures what it is supposed to measure.

4. Although intelligence tests are able to identify individual differences in intelligence, they do not provide us with an understanding of the underlying nature of intelligence. One of the major issues here is whether a single, unitary factor underlies intelligence or whether intelligence is made up of particular components.

5. The earliest psychologists interested in intelligence made the assumption that there was a general factor for mental ability called g. However, later psychologists disputed the view that intelligence was unidimensional.

6. Some researchers suggest that there are two kinds of intelligence: fluid intelligence and crystallized intelligence. Gardner's theory of multiple intelligences proposes that there are seven spheres of intelligence: musical, bodily kinesthetic, logical-mathematical, linguistic, spatial, interpersonal, and intrapersonal.

7. Information-processing approaches suggest that intelligence should be conceptualized as the way in which people represent and use material cognitively. Rather than focusing on the structure of intelligence, psychologists taking an information-processing approach examine the processes underlying intelligent behavior. One example of an information-processing approach is Sternberg's triarchic theory of intelligence, which suggests three major aspects of intelligence: componential, experiential, and contextual.

How can the extremes of intelligence be differentiated?

8. At the two extremes of intelligence are the mentally retarded and the intellectually gifted. The levels of mental retardation include mild retardation (IQ of 55 to 69), moderate retardation (IQ of 40 to 54), severe retardation (IQ of 25 to 39), and profound retardation (IQ below 25). About one-third of the cases of retardation have a known biological cause; Down syndrome is the most common. Most cases, however, are classified as ones of familial retardation, in which there is no known biological cause.

How can we help people to maximize their full potential?

9. There have been a number of recent advances in the treatment of both the mentally retarded and the intellectually gifted, particularly after federal law mandated that the mentally retarded be educated in the least restrictive environment. In mainstreaming, the mentally retarded are integrated into regular education classrooms as much as possible.

Are traditional IQ tests culturally biased?

10. Traditional intelligence tests have frequently been criticized for being biased in favor of the white middle-class population. That controversy has led to attempts to devise culture-fair tests, IQ measures that avoid questions that depend on a particular cultural background.

Are there racial differences in intelligence?

11. Issues of race and environmental and genetic influences on intelligence represent major controversies.

To what degree is intelligence influenced by the environment and to what degree by heredity?

12. Because individual IQ scores vary far more than group IQ scores, it is most critical to ask what we can do to maximize the intellectual development of each person.

KEY TERMS AND CONCEPTS

intelligence (p. 251)
intelligence tests (p. 251)
mental age (p. 252)
intelligence quotient (IQ) score (p. 252)
achievement test (p. 255)
aptitude test (p. 255)

reliability (p. 255)
validity (p. 255)
norms (p. 256)
g or g-factor (p. 257)
fluid intelligence (p. 257)
crystallized intelligence (p. 257)

triarchic theory of intelligence (p. 259)
mental retardation (p. 263)
intellectually gifted (p. 264)
culture-fair IQ test (p. 270)
heritability (p. 270)

ANSWERS TO PREVIOUS REVIEW

1. True **2.** culture-fair **3.** False; IQ tests are used to measure individual intelligence. Within any group there are wide variations in individual intelligence. **4.** hereditary; environmental

CHAPTER 9
MOTIVATION AND EMOTION

PROLOGUE

Jackie Fulton

It is the late 1970s. You are Jackie Fulton, an unmarried teenager attending DuSable High School in Chicago's south side, one of the toughest neighborhoods in the United States. Poverty-stricken and living in public housing, you've just given birth to a son. What do you do? If you're like thousands of other poor pregnant teenagers and young mothers, you may have no other choice but to drop out of school to raise your child, which in fact is what Jackie Fulton did.

Now fast-forward to the present. Visit DuSable High School, and you'll find Jackie Fulton, the parent of Gerald Fulton, who is a junior enrolled in the school. But Ms. Fulton is not visiting the school to check on her son's progress. Instead, she's a student herself. Enrolled in a special program for parents of students who attend the high school, Ms. Fulton is seeking to complete the high school education she was forced to cut short decades earlier. She takes tests, writes papers, and gets a report card—that her mother has to sign. If she's late, she gets detention. And if she does well, she can get on the honor roll.

It's not easy. Ms. Fulton attends class with people little more than half her age, and the other kids have sometimes teased her and her son. Studying is difficult for someone who has been out of school for so long, and reading problems that made studying difficult when she first started school still need to be overcome.

Does she ever think of quitting? In her words, "No. Because this is something that I wanted to do, and this is something that I need. This is one of my dreams. . . ." (Stahl, 1994, p. 13).

Jackie Fulton (right), highly motivated by the desire to obtain her diploma, attends the same Chicago high school as her son.

LOOKING AHEAD

What is it that motivates Ms. Fulton's determined quest for education? Is it the anticipation of getting a better-paying job? The reward of receiving good grades? The desire to leave public housing and move to a safer environment for her children? The joy of learning for learning's sake? The satisfaction of finally achieving a long-sought-after goal?

In this chapter, we consider the processes that underlie motivation, as well as the related topic of emotion. **Motivation** is concerned with the factors that direct and energize the behavior of humans and other organisms.

Psychologists who study motivation seek to discover the particular desired goals—the *motives*—that underlie behavior. Such motives may be exemplified by behavior as basic as drinking to satisfy thirst or as inconsequential as taking a stroll to obtain exercise. To the psychologist specializing in the study of motivation, underlying motives are assumed to steer one's choice of activities.

The study of motivation, then, consists of identifying why people seek to do the things they do. Psychologists studying motivation ask questions such as these: "Why do people choose particular goals for which to strive?" "What specific motives direct behavior?" "What individual differences in motivation account for the variability in people's behavior?" "How can we motivate people in particular ways, such as eating certain foods, quitting smoking, or engaging in safer-sex practices?"

Whereas motivation is concerned with the forces that direct future behavior, emotion pertains to the feelings we experience throughout the course of our lives. The study of emotions focuses on our internal experiences at any given moment. Most of us have felt a variety of emotions: happiness at getting an A on a difficult exam, sadness brought about by the death of a loved one, anger at being treated unfairly. Because emotions not only motivate our behavior but can also reflect our underlying motivation, they play a broad role in our lives.

In this chapter, we consider motivation and emotion. We begin by focusing on

Motivation: The factors that direct and energize behavior

the major conceptions of motivation, discussing how the different motives and needs people experience jointly affect behavior. We consider motives that are biologically based and universal in the animal kingdom, such as hunger and sex, as well as motives that are unique to humans, such as needs for achievement, affiliation, and power.

We then turn to the nature of emotional experience. We consider the roles and functions that emotions play in people's lives, discussing a number of theories meant to explain how people understand what emotion they are experiencing at a given moment.

Finally, the chapter ends with a look at stress. We consider the causes of stress, and discuss the various ways that people cope with it.

• *How does motivation direct and energize behavior?*

EXPLAINING MOTIVATION

In just an instant, John Thompson's life changed. That's all it took for an auger, an oversize, drill-like piece of farm equipment powered by a tractor, to rip off both of his arms when he slipped on the ice and fell against the rotating machinery.

Yet it was in the moments following the accident that Thompson demonstrated incredible bravery. Despite his pain and shock, he ran 400 feet to his house. Using the bone hanging from his left shoulder to open the door, he ran inside and dialed for help with a pen gripped in his teeth. When emergency crews arrived 30 minutes later, he told them where to find ice and plastic bags so that his severed arms could be packed for possible surgical reattachment. Thompson's rescuers came none too soon: By the time surgery could start, he had lost half his blood. (Nelson, 1992)

What explains John Thompson's enormous motivation to stay alive? Like many questions involving motivation, this one has no single answer. Clearly, biological aspects of motivation were at work: He obviously experienced a powerful drive to keep himself alive, before he lost so much blood that his life would drain away. But cognitive and social factors, such as his desire to see family and friends, also helped fuel his will to survive.

The complexity of motivation has led to the development of a variety of conceptual approaches. Although they vary in the degree to which they focus on biological, cognitive, and social factors, all seek to explain the energy that guides people's behavior in particular directions.

Instinct Approaches: Born to Be Motivated

When psychologists first sought to explain motivation, they turned to *instincts,* inborn patterns of behavior that are biologically determined rather than learned. According to an **instinct approach to motivation,** people and animals are born with preprogrammed sets of behaviors essential to their survival. These instincts provide the energy that channels behavior in appropriate directions. Hence, sex might be explained as a response to an instinct for reproduction, and exploratory behavior might be viewed as motivated by an instinct to examine one's territory.

There are several difficulties with such a conception, however. For one thing, psychologists have been unable to agree on what the primary instincts are. One early psychologist, William McDougall (1908), suggested that there are eighteen instincts, including pugnacity and gregariousness. Others found even more—with one sociologist claiming that there are exactly 5759 (Bernard, 1924). Clearly, such an extensive enumeration provides little more than labels for behavior.

No explanation based on the concept of instincts goes very far in explaining *why* a specific pattern of behavior, and not some other, has appeared in a given species. Furthermore, the variety and complexity of human behavior, much of

Instinct approach to motivation: The theory that says motivation is the result of an inborn pattern of behavior that is biologically determined

which is clearly learned, are difficult to explain if instincts are the primary motivational force. Therefore, conceptions of motivation based on instincts have been supplanted by newer explanations, although instinct approaches still play a role in certain theories. For example, in later chapters we will discuss Freud's work, which suggests that instinctual drives of sex and aggression motivate behavior. Moreover, many animal behaviors clearly have an instinctual basis.

Drive-Reduction Approaches: Satisfying Our Needs

In rejecting instinct theory, psychologists first proposed simple drive-reduction theories of motivation in its place (Hull, 1943). A **drive-reduction approach to motivation** suggests that when people lack some basic biological requirement such as water, a drive to obtain that requirement (in this case, the thirst drive) is produced.

Drive-reduction approach to motivation: The theory that claims that drives are produced to obtain our basic biological requirements

To understand this approach, we need to begin with the concept of drive. A **drive** is motivational tension, or arousal, that energizes behavior in order to fulfill some need. Many basic kinds of drives, such as hunger, thirst, sleepiness, and sex, are related to biological needs of the body or of the species as a whole. These are called *primary drives*. Primary drives contrast with *secondary drives*, in which no obvious biological need is being fulfilled. In secondary drives, needs are brought about by prior experience and learning. As we will discuss later, some people have strong needs to achieve academically and in their careers. We can say that their achievement need is reflected in a secondary drive that motivates their behavior.

Drive: A motivational tension, or arousal, that energizes behavior in order to fulfill a need

We usually try to satisfy a primary drive by reducing the need underlying it. For example, we become hungry after not eating for a few hours and may raid the refrigerator, especially if our next scheduled meal is not imminent. If the weather turns cold, we put on extra clothing or raise the setting on the thermostat in order to keep warm. If our body needs liquids in order to function properly, we experience thirst and seek out water.

Homeostasis The reason for such behavior is homeostasis, a basic motivational phenomenon underlying primary drives. **Homeostasis** is the maintenance of some optimal level of internal biological functioning by compensating for deviations from its usual, balanced, internal state. Although not all basic biological behaviors related to motivation fit a homeostatic model—sexual behavior is one example—most of the fundamental needs of life, including the need for food, water, maintenance of body temperature, and sleep, can be explained reasonably well by such an approach.

Homeostasis: The process by which an organism tries to maintain an internal biological balance, or "steady state"

Unfortunately, although drive-reduction theories provide a good explanation of how primary drives motivate behavior, they are inadequate when it comes to explaining behaviors in which the goal is not to reduce a drive, but rather to maintain or even to increase a particular level of excitement or arousal. For instance, some behaviors seem to be motivated by nothing more than curiosity (Loewenstein, 1994). Anyone who has rushed to pick up newly delivered mail, who avidly follows gossip columns in the newspaper, or who yearns to travel to exotic places knows the importance of curiosity in directing behavior. And it is not just human beings who display behavior indicative of curiosity: Monkeys will learn to press a bar just to be able to peer into another room, especially if something interesting (such as a toy train moving along a track) can be glimpsed (Butler, 1954). Monkeys will also expend considerable energy solving simple mechanical puzzles, even though their behavior produces no obvious reward (Harlow, Harlow, & Meyer, 1950; Mineka & Hendersen, 1985).

Similarly, many of us go out of our way to seek thrills through such activities as riding a roller coaster and steering a raft down the rapids of a river. Such be-

haviors certainly don't suggest that people seek only to reduce drives, as drive-reduction approaches would indicate.

Both curiosity and thrill-seeking behavior, then, shed doubt on drive-reduction approaches as a complete explanation for motivation. In both cases, rather than seeking to reduce an underlying drive, people and animals appear to be motivated to *increase* their overall level of stimulation and activity. In order to explain this phenomenon, psychologists have devised an alternative: the arousal approach to motivation.

Arousal Approaches: Beyond Drive Reduction

Arousal approach to motivation: The belief that we try to maintain certain levels of stimulation and activity, increasing or reducing them as necessary

Arousal approaches seek to explain behavior in which the goal is the maintenance of or an increase in excitement (Berlyne, 1967; Brehm & Self, 1989). According to an **arousal approach to motivation,** each of us tries to maintain a certain level of stimulation and activity. As with the drive-reduction model, if our stimulation and activity levels become too high, we try to reduce them. But in contrast to the drive-reduction model, the arousal model also suggests that if the levels of stimulation and activity are too low, we will try to *increase* them by seeking stimulation.

People vary widely in the optimal level of arousal they seek out, with some people having especially high levels of arousal (Mineka & Hendersen, 1985; Babbitt, Rowland, & Franken, 1990; Stacy, Newcomb, & Bentler, 1991). For example, psychologists have hypothesized that individuals such as comic John Belushi, DNA researcher Sir Francis Crick, daredevil Evel Knievel, and bank robbers Bonnie and Clyde exhibited a particularly high need for arousal (Farley, 1986). Such people may attempt to avoid boredom by seeking out challenging situations (Zuckerman, 1991).

One explanation of motivation holds that each peson behaves in such a way as to maintain a certain preferred level of arousal. As the practice of bungee jumping demonstrates, some people seem to need much more excitement than others.

TABLE 9-1   Do You Seek Out Sensation?

How much stimulation do you crave in your everyday life? You will have an idea after you complete the following questionnaire, which lists some items from a scale designed to assess your sensation-seeking tendencies. Circle either *A* or *B* in each pair of statements.

1. *A* I would like a job that requires a lot of traveling.
   B I would prefer a job in one location.
2. *A* I am invigorated by a brisk, cold day.
   B I can't wait to get indoors on a cold day.
3. *A* I get bored seeing the same old faces.
   B I like the comfortable familiarity of everyday friends.
4. *A* I would prefer living in an ideal society in which everyone was safe, secure, and happy.
   B I would have preferred living in the unsettled days of our history.
5. *A* I sometimes like to do things that are a little frightening.
   B A sensible person avoids activities that are dangerous.
6. *A* I would not like to be hypnotized.
   B I would like to have the experience of being hypnotized.
7. *A* The most important goal of life is to live it to the fullest and to experience as much as possible.
   B The most important goal of life is to find peace and happiness.
8. *A* I would like to try parachute jumping.
   B I would never want to try jumping out of a plane, with or without a parachute.
9. *A* I enter cold water gradually, giving myself time to get used to it.
   B I like to dive or jump right into the ocean or a cold pool.
10. *A* When I go on a vacation, I prefer the comfort of a good room and bed.
    B When I go on a vacation, I prefer the change of camping out.
11. *A* I prefer people who are emotionally expressive, even if they are a bit unstable.
    B I prefer people who are calm and even-tempered.
12. *A* A good painting should shock or jolt the senses.
    B A good painting should give one a feeling of peace and security.
13. *A* People who ride motorcycles must have some kind of unconscious need to hurt themselves.
    B I would like to drive or ride a motorcycle.

Scoring   Give yourself one point for each of the following responses: 1A, 2A, 3A, 4B, 5A, 6B, 7A, 8A, 9B, 10B, 11A, 12A, 13B. Find your total score by adding up the number of points and then use the following scoring key:

0–3   very low sensation seeking
4–5   low
6–9   average
10–11 high
12–13 very high

Keep in mind, of course, that this short questionnaire, for which the scoring is based on the results of college students who have taken it, provides only a rough estimate of your sensation-seeking tendencies. Moreover, as people get older, their sensation-seeking scores tend to decrease. Still, the questionnaire will at least give you an indication of how your sensation-seeking tendencies compare with those of others. (Source: Zuckerman, 1978.)

It is not just the celebrated who pursue arousal; many of us characteristically seek out relatively high levels of stimulation. You can get a sense of your own typical level of stimulation by completing the questionnaire in Table 9-1.

Incentive Approaches: Motivation's Pull

When a luscious dessert is brought to the table after a filling meal, its appeal has little or nothing to do with internal drives or with the maintenance of arousal. Rather, if we choose to eat the dessert, such behavior is motivated by the external stimulus of the dessert itself, which acts as an anticipated reward. This reward, in motivational terms, is an *incentive*.

Incentive approach to motivation: The theory explaining motivation in terms of external stimuli

An **incentive approach to motivation** attempts to explain why behavior is not always motivated by an internal need, such as the desire to reduce drives or to maintain an optimum level of arousal. Instead of focusing on internal factors, incentive theory explains motivation in terms of the nature of the external stimuli, the incentives that direct and energize behavior. In this view, properties of external stimuli largely account for a person's motivation.

Although the theory explains why we may succumb to an incentive (like a mouth-watering dessert) even though internal cues (like hunger) are lacking, it does not provide a complete explanation of motivation, since organisms seek to fulfill needs even when incentives are not apparent. Consequently, many psychologists believe that the internal drives proposed by drive-reduction theory work in tandem with the external incentives of incentive theory to "push" and "pull" behavior, respectively. Thus, at the same time we seek to satisfy our underlying hunger needs (the push of drive-reduction theory), we are drawn to food that appears particularly appetizing (the pull of incentive theory). Rather than contradicting each other, then, drives and incentives may work together in motivating behavior (Petri, 1991).

Cognitive Approaches: The Thoughts behind Motivation

Cognitive approach to motivation: The focus on the role of our thoughts, expectations, and understanding of the world

A **cognitive approach to motivation** focuses on the role of our thoughts, expectations, and understanding of the world. For instance, according to one cognitive approach, *expectancy-value theory,* two kinds of cognitions underlie our behavior. The first is our expectation that a behavior will cause us to reach a particular goal, and the second is our understanding of the value of that goal to us (Tolman, 1959). For example, the degree to which we are motivated to study for a test will be based jointly on our expectation of how well our studying will pay off (in terms of a good grade) and the value we place on getting a good grade. If both expectation and value are high, we will be motivated to study diligently; but if either one is low, our motivation to study will be relatively lower.

Intrinsic motivation: Motivation by which people participate in an activity for their own enjoyment, not for the reward it will get them

Extrinsic motivation: Motivation by which people participate in an activity for a tangible reward

Cognitive theories of motivation draw a key distinction between intrinsic and extrinsic motivation. **Intrinsic motivation** causes us to participate in an activity for our own enjoyment, rather than for any tangible reward that it will bring us. In contrast, **extrinsic motivation** causes us to do something for a tangible reward.

According to research on the two types of motivation, we are more apt to persevere, work harder, and produce work of higher quality when motivation for a task is intrinsic rather than extrinsic (Lepper & Greene, 1978; Deci & Ryan, 1985; Harackiewicz & Elliot, 1993). Some psychologists go farther, suggesting that providing rewards for desirable behavior may cause intrinsic motivation to decline and extrinsic motivation to increase. In one demonstration of this phenomenon, a group of nursery school students were promised a reward for drawing with magic markers (an activity for which they had previously shown high motivation). The reward served to reduce their enthusiasm for the task, for they later showed considerably less zeal for drawing (Lepper & Greene, 1978). It was as if the promise of reward undermined their intrinsic interest in drawing, turning what had been play into work.

Maslow's Hierarchy: Ordering Motivational Needs

What do Eleanor Roosevelt, Abraham Lincoln, and Albert Einstein have in common? Quite a bit, according to a model of motivation devised by psychologist Abraham Maslow: Each of them reached and fulfilled the highest levels of motivational needs underlying human behavior.

Maslow's model considers different motivational needs to be ordered in a hierarchy, and it suggests that before more sophisticated, higher-order needs can be met, certain primary needs must be satisfied (Maslow, 1970, 1987). The

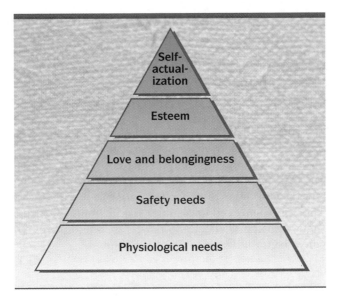

FIGURE 9-1 Maslow's hierarchy shows how our motivation progresses up the pyramid from a basis in the broadest, most fundamental biological needs to higher-order ones. *(After Maslow, 1970.)*

model can be conceptualized as a pyramid (see Figure 9-1) in which the more basic needs are at the bottom and the higher-level needs are at the top. In order for a particular need to be activated and thereby guide a person's behavior, the more basic needs in the hierarchy must be met first.

The most basic needs are those described earlier as primary drives: needs for water, food, sleep, sex, and the like. In order to move up the hierarchy, a person must have these basic physiological needs met. Safety needs come next in the hierarchy; Maslow suggests that people need a safe, secure environment in order to function effectively. Physiological and safety needs compose the lower-order needs.

Only when the basic lower-order needs are met can a person consider fulfilling higher-order needs, such as the need for love and a sense of belonging, esteem, and self-actualization. Love and belongingness needs include the need to obtain and give affection and to be a contributing member of some group or society. After these needs are fulfilled, the person strives for esteem. In Maslow's thinking, esteem relates to the need to develop a sense of self-worth by knowing that others are aware of one's competence and value.

Once these four sets of needs are fulfilled—no easy task—the person is ready to strive for the highest-level need, self-actualization. **Self-actualization** is a state of self-fulfillment in which people realize their highest potential. When Maslow first proposed the concept, he used it to describe just a few well-known individuals such as Eleanor Roosevelt, Lincoln, and Einstein. But self-actualization is not limited to the famous. A parent with excellent nurturing skills who raises a family, a teacher who year after year creates an environment that maximizes students' opportunities for success, and an artist who realizes her creative potential might all be self-actualized. The important thing is that people feel at ease with themselves and satisfied that they are using their talents to the fullest. In a sense, achieving self-actualization produces a decline in the striving and yearning for greater fulfillment that marks most people's lives and instead provides a sense of satisfaction with the current state of affairs (Jones & Crandall, 1991).

Unfortunately, research has not been able to validate the specific ordering of the stages of Maslow's theory, and it has proved difficult to measure self-actualization objectively (Haymes, Green, & Quinto, 1984; Weiss, 1991; Neher, 1991). However, Maslow's model is important for two reasons: It highlights the complexity of human needs, and it emphasizes that until more basic biological needs are met, people are going to be relatively unconcerned with higher-order needs.

Self-actualization: In Maslow's theory, a state of self-fulfillment in which people realize their highest potential

If people are hungry, their first interest will be in obtaining food; they will not be concerned with such needs as love and self-esteem. The model helps explain why victims of disasters such as famine and war may suffer the breakdown of normal family ties and be unconcerned with the welfare of anyone other than themselves.

Reconciling the Different Approaches to Motivation

Now that we have examined several different approaches to motivation, it is reasonable to wonder which of them provides the fullest account of motivational phenomena. Actually, many of the conceptual approaches are complementary, rather than contradictory, and it is often useful to employ several theories simultaneously in order to understand a particular motivational system (Deci, 1992). Thus, as we proceed to consider specific motives, such as the needs for food, sex, achievement, affiliation, and power, we will draw upon several of the theories to gain a better understanding of motivation.

RECAP AND REVIEW

Recap

- The study of motivation looks at the factors that energize and direct people's behavior.
- A drive is a motivational tension that energizes behavior to fulfill some need. Primary drives typically operate according to the principle of homeostasis, in which an organism strives to compensate for any deviations from a balanced, preferred internal state.
- Drive-reduction approaches propose that behavior is motivated by drives to reduce biological needs. Because they do not explain why people sometimes seek stimulation, arousal approaches have been devised.
- Cognitive approaches to motivation, exemplified by expectancy-value theory, suggest that people's thoughts, understanding, and interpretation of the world underlie their motivation.
- According to Maslow's motivational model, motivational needs progress in a hierarchy from the most basic to higher-order needs.

Review

1. _____ are forces that guide a person's behavior in a certain direction.
2. Biologically determined, inborn patterns of behavior are known as _____ .

3. Your psychology professor tells you, "Explaining behavior is easy! When we lack something, we are motivated to get it." What approach to motivation does your professor subscribe to?
4. By drinking water after running a marathon, a runner tries to keep his or her body at an optimal level of functioning. This process is called _____ .
5. Even though I am not thirsty, I am offered and accept a mug of beer. Assuming that I like beer very much, what theory of motivation would predict this behavior?
6. I help an elderly person across the street because doing a good deed makes me feel good. What type of motivation is at work here? What type of motivation would be at work if I were to help an elderly man across the street because he paid me $20?
7. According to Maslow, a person with no job, no home, and no friends can become self-actualized. True or false?

Ask Yourself

You have just been hired as a consultant at a large automobile plant. How might each of the approaches to motivation discussed in this section be put to use in the workplace to motivate workers?

(Answers to review questions are on page 284.)

- *What are the biological and social factors that underlie hunger?*
- *Why, and under what circumstances, do we become sexually aroused?*
- *How do people behave sexually?*
- *How are needs relating to achievement, affiliation, and power motivation exhibited?*

HUMAN NEEDS AND MOTIVATION: EAT, DRINK, AND BE DARING

To Bob, doing well in college meant that he would get into a good law school, which he saw as a stepping-stone to a successful future. Consequently, he never let up academically and always tried his best to do well in his courses. But his constant academic striving went well beyond the desire to get into law school; he tried not only to get good grades, but to get *better* grades than his classmates.

In fact, Bob was always trying to be the best at everything he did. He could turn the simplest activity into a competition. Bob couldn't even play poker without acting as if his winning the game was essential. There were, however, some areas in which he didn't compete. He was interested only if he thought he had a fighting chance to succeed; he ignored challenges that seemed too difficult as well as those that seemed too easy for him.

What is the motivation behind Bob's consistent striving to achieve? Moreover, why does he welcome some kinds of challenges and avoid others? To answer these questions, we must consider some of the specific kinds of needs that underlie behavior. In this section, then, we will examine several of the most important human needs. Because human beings are in a fundamental sense biological creatures, we first consider hunger and sex, primary drives that have received the most attention from researchers. Yet because much of human behavior has no clear biological basis, we will also examine the secondary drives—those uniquely human strivings, based on learned needs and past experience, that help explain behavior such as Bob's.

The Motivation behind Hunger and Eating

About one-third of the United States population suffers from **obesity,** defined as being more than 20 percent above the average weight for a person of a given height. Losing unwanted weight is something of an American obsession, as 60 to 80 *million* women and men struggle to achieve what they perceive to be an ideal weight and body shape—perceptions that are often inaccurate (Thompson, 1992; Brody, 1992). It is an increasingly losing battle: The percentage of individuals classified as obese increased by 31 percent from 1980 to 1991 (National Center for Health Statistics, 1994; Kuczmarski et al., 1994).

Ironically, what constitutes an ideal weight and body shape varies significantly across different cultures and from one time period to another within Western culture. For instance, contemporary societal views stressing the importance of slimness in women are relatively recent. In nineteenth-century Hawaii, the most attractive women were those who were the most overweight. Furthermore, for the rest of this century, except for the 1920s, the ideal female figure was relatively full (Silverstein et al., 1986). Even today, weight standards differ from one geographical area to another. Hence, some inner-city residents value "thick," or plump, bodies over leaner ones.

Eating behavior is clearly complex, involving a variety of mechanisms. In our discussion of what motivates us to eat, we'll start with the biological aspects of eating.

Biological Factors in the Regulation of Hunger In contrast to human beings, animals are unlikely to become obese. Most nonhuman species, when left in an environment in which food is readily available, do a good job of regulating their intake. You may have seen this with a pet who always has a dish of food available. Cats, for instance, will eat only until their immediate hunger is satisfied; they leave the remaining food untouched, returning to it only when internal cues tell them to eat once again.

Internal mechanisms seem to regulate not only the quantity of food intake in nonhumans, but also the kind of food that an animal desires. Hungry rats that

Obesity: The state of being more than 20 percent above the average weight for a person of a particular height

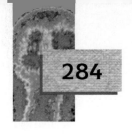

Following an operation in which the ventromedial nucleus of its hypothalamus was cut, this rat has eaten so much that it tips the scales at four times its normal weight.

have been deprived of particular foods tend to seek out alternatives that contain the specific nutrients their diet is lacking, and laboratory experiments show that animals given the choice of a wide variety of foods choose a fairly well-balanced diet (Rozin, 1977).

The mechanisms by which organisms know whether they require food or should stop eating are complex (Keesey & Powley, 1986). It's not just a matter of an empty stomach causing hunger pangs and a full one alleviating hunger. For example, people who have had their stomachs removed still experience the sensation of hunger (Ingelfinger, 1944). Consequently, regulation of eating goes beyond the fullness of one's stomach.

Some researchers suggest that changes in the chemical composition of the blood may be an important factor in controlling eating (Logue, 1991). For instance, experiments show that when glucose, a kind of sugar, is injected into the blood, hunger decreases and animals will refuse to eat. On the other hand, when insulin, a hormone involved in the conversion of glucose into stored fat, is introduced into the bloodstream, hunger increases (Rodin, 1985).

But what part of the body monitors changes in blood chemistry relating to eating behavior? The brain's *hypothalamus,* which we discussed in Chapter 2, appears to be primarily responsible for monitoring food intake (Kupfermann, 1991a). Injury to the hypothalamus has been shown to cause radical changes in eating behavior, depending upon the site of the injury. For example, rats whose *lateral hypothalamus* is damaged may literally starve to death. They refuse food when it is offered and, unless they are force-fed, eventually die. Rats with an injury to the *ventromedial hypothalamus* display the opposite problem: extreme overeating. Rats with this injury can increase in weight by as much as 400 percent. Similar phenomena occur in humans who have tumors of the hypothalamus.

Although it is clear that the hypothalamus plays an important role in regulating food intake, the exact way in which it operates is still unclear. Some re-

---

ANSWERS TO PREVIOUS REVIEW

1. Motives **2.** instincts **3.** Drive reduction **4.** homeostasis **5.** Incentive **6.** Intrinsic; Extrinsic **7.** False; lower-order needs must be fulfilled before self-actualization can occur.

searchers think it affects an organism's sense or perception of hunger; others hypothesize that it directly regulates the neural connections that control the muscles involved in eating behavior (Stricker & Zigmond, 1976; Kupfermann, 1991a).

One hypothesis suggests that injury to the hypothalamus affects the weight set point by which food intake is regulated (Nisbett, 1972). According to this hypothesis, the **weight set point** is the particular level of weight that the body strives to maintain. Acting as a kind of internal weight thermostat, the hypothalamus calls for either greater or less food intake.

In most cases, the hypothalamus does a good job. People who are not monitoring their weight show only minor weight fluctuations, in spite of substantial day-to-day variations in how much they eat and exercise. However, injury to the hypothalamus drastically raises or lowers the weight set point, and the organism then strives to meet its internal goal by increasing or decreasing its food consumption.

The weight set point may be determined, at least in part, by genetic factors. People seemed destined, through heredity, to have a particular **metabolism,** the rate at which food is converted to energy and expended by the body. Some people, with high metabolic rates, seem to be able to eat as much as they want without gaining weight, while others, with low metabolism, may eat literally half as much and yet gain weight readily (Roberts et al., 1988).

For instance, in one study, pairs of identical twins were placed on diets that contained an additional 1000 calories a day and forbidden to exercise. Over a 3-month period, each member of a twin pair gained virtually identical amounts of weight. However, when different pairs of twins were compared, the variation in weight gain was astounding. Some pairs gained three times as much weight as other pairs (Bouchard et al., 1990).

Social Factors in Eating   You've just finished a full meal and are completely stuffed. Suddenly, your host announces with great fanfare that he will be serving his "house specialty" dessert, bananas flambé, and that he has spent the better part of the afternoon preparing it. Even though you are full and don't even like bananas, you accept a serving of his dessert and eat it all.

Clearly, internal biological factors do not provide the full explanation for our eating behavior. External social factors, based on societal rules and conventions and on what we have learned about appropriate eating behavior, also play an important role. Take, for example, the simple fact that people customarily eat breakfast, lunch, and dinner at approximately the same times every day. Because we are accustomed to eating on schedule every day, we tend to feel hungry as the usual hour approaches, sometimes quite independently of what our internal cues are telling us.

Similarly, we tend to put roughly the same amount of food on our plates every day, even though the amount of exercise we may have had, and consequently our need for energy replenishment, varies from day to day. We also tend to prefer particular foods over others. Rats and dogs may be a delicacy in certain Asian cultures, but few people in Western cultures find them appealing, despite their potentially high nutritional value. In sum, cultural influences and our own individual habits play an important role in determining when, what, and how much we eat (Polivy & Herman, 1985; Boakes, Popplewell, & Burton, 1987).

Other social factors are related to our eating behavior as well. Some of us head toward the refrigerator after a difficult day, seeking solace in a pint of Heath Bar Crunch ice cream. Why? Perhaps when we were children, our parents gave us food when we were upset. Eventually, we may have learned, through the basic mechanisms of classical and operant conditioning, to associate food with comfort and consolation. Similarly, we may learn that eating provides an escape from unpleasant thoughts, as we focus instead on the immediate pleasures of eating. As

Weight set point: The particular level of weight the body strives to maintain

Metabolism: The rate at which food is converted to energy and expended by the body

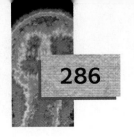

a consequence, we may eat when we experience distress (Davis, 1986; Heatherton, Herman, & Polivy, 1992; Greeno & Wing, 1994).

The Roots of Obesity   Given that eating behavior is influenced by both biological and social factors, determining the causes of obesity has proved to be a challenging task. Researchers have followed several paths.

Some psychologists suggest that an oversensitivity to external eating cues based on social convention, and a parallel insensitivity to internal hunger cues, produces obesity. Research has shown, for example, that obese people who are placed in a room next to an inviting bowl of crackers are apt to eat considerably more than nonobese people—even though they may have just finished a filling sandwich (Schachter, Goldman, & Gordon, 1968). In addition, obese individuals are less apt to eat if doing so involves any sort of work: In one experiment obese subjects were less likely to eat nuts that had to be shelled, but ate copious amounts of nuts that already had their shells removed. Nonobese people, in contrast, ate the same amount of nuts, regardless of whether or not the nuts had to be shelled (Nisbett, 1968; Schachter, 1971). Consequently, it appears that many obese people give undue attention to external cues, and are less aware of the internal cues that help nonobese people regulate their eating behavior.

On the other hand, many individuals who are highly reliant on external cues never become obese, and there are quite a few obese people who are relatively unresponsive to external cues (Herman, 1987; Rodin, 1981). Consequently, some psychologists have turned to weight-set-point theory as a plausible explanation for the cause of obesity.

Specifically, these researchers suggest that overweight people have higher set points than people of normal weight. Because their set points are unusually high, their attempts to lose weight by eating less may make them especially sensitive to external, food-related cues and therefore more apt to eat, perpetuating their obesity.

But why may some people's weight set point be higher than that of others? One factor may be the size and number of fat cells in the body, which increase as a function of weight increase. Because the set-point level seems to reflect the number of fat cells a person has, any increase in weight—which produces a rise in fat cells—may raise the set point. Furthermore, any loss of weight after the age of 2 does not decrease the number of fat cells in the body, although it may cause them to shrink in size (Knittle, 1975). Consequently, although fat babies are sometimes considered cute, obese children may have acquired so many fat cells that their weight set point is permanently too high.

In sum, according to the weight-set-point hypothesis, the presence of too many fat cells may result in the set point becoming "stuck" at a higher level than is desirable. Under such circumstances, losing weight becomes a difficult proposition, since one is constantly at odds with one's own internal set point when dieting.

Finally, growing evidence suggests that heredity plays a role in obesity. Several studies indicate that people who are prone to obesity may gain weight mainly because they inherit low rates of metabolism—and not because they overeat. Furthermore, researchers recently identified a particular gene that may be responsible for at least some kinds of obesity. A tendency to be obese, then, may be an inherited trait—one that we may well blame more on our ancestors than ourselves (J. Friedman et al., 1994).

Eating Disorders

It was widely reported that Princess Diana suffered from an eating disorder during the early years of her troubled marriage to Prince Charles of Great Britain.

A rice cake in the afternoon, an apple for dinner. That was Heather Rhodes's typical diet her freshman year at St. Joseph's College in Rensselaer, Indiana, when she began to nurture a fear (exacerbated, she says, by the sudden death of a friend) that she was gaining weight. But when Rhodes, now 20, returned home to Joliet, Illinois, for summer vacation a year and a half ago, her family thought she was melting away. "I could see the outline of her pelvis in her clothes . . ." says Heather's mother . . . , so she and the rest of the family confronted Heather one evening, placing a bathroom scale in the middle of the family room. "I told them they were attacking me and to go to hell," recalls Heather, who nevertheless reluctantly weighed herself. Her 5'7" frame held a mere 85 pounds—down 22 pounds from her senior year in high school. "I told them they rigged the scale," she says. It simply didn't compute with her self-image. "When I looked in the mirror," she says, "I thought my stomach was still huge and my face was fat" (Sandler, 1994, p. 56).

Heather suffered from the eating disorder anorexia nervosa. **Anorexia nervosa** is a severe eating disorder in which people may refuse to eat, while denying that their behavior and appearance—which can become skeletonlike—are unusual. Some 15 to 20 percent of anorexics literally starve themselves to death.

Anorexia nervosa afflicts mainly females between the ages of 12 and 40, although both men and women of any age may develop it. People with the disorder typically come from stable homes, and they are often successful, attractive, and relatively affluent. Their lives revolve around food: Although they eat little themselves, they may cook for others, go shopping for food frequently, or collect cookbooks (Hsu, 1990; Button, 1993).

A related problem, **bulimia,** is a disorder in which a person binges on incredibly large quantities of food. An entire gallon of ice cream and a whole pie may easily be consumed in a single sitting. Following such a binge, sufferers feel guilt and depression and typically induce vomiting or take laxatives to rid themselves of the food—behavior known as purging (Hinz & Williamson, 1987). Constant binging-and-purging cycles and the use of drugs to induce vomiting or diarrhea may create a chemical imbalance that can lead to heart failure. Typically, though, the weight of a person suffering from bulimia remains normal.

What causes anorexia nervosa or bulimia? Some researchers suspect a physiological cause such as a chemical imbalance in the hypothalamus or pituitary gland (Gold et al., 1986). Other psychologists believe the cause is rooted in societal expectations about the value of slenderness and the parallel notion that being obese is undesirable (Crandall & Biernat, 1990; Rothblum, 1990). They maintain that people with anorexia nervosa and bulimia become preoccupied with their weight, and take to heart the societal view that one can never be too thin. Consistent with such an explanation, clear standards exist on some college campuses about "appropriate" binging behavior, and the amount of binging is associated with a woman's popularity (Crandall, 1988). Finally, some psychologists suggest that the disorders occur as a consequence of overdemanding parents or other family problems (Logue, 1991).

The complete explanation for anorexia nervosa or bulimia remains elusive. The disorders probably stem from both biological and social causes, and successful treatment is likely to encompass several strategies, including therapy and dietary changes (Fichter, 1990; Schmidt & Treasure, 1993; Lask & Bryant-Waugh, 1993; Fairburn et al., 1993).

Anorexia nervosa: An eating disorder usually striking young women in which symptoms include self-starvation or near self-starvation in an attempt to avoid obesity

Bulimia: An eating disorder characterized by vast intake of food that may be followed by self-induced vomiting or by taking laxatives to rid themselves of the food

The Facts of Life: Human Sexual Motivation

Anyone who has seen two dogs mating knows that sexual behavior has a biological basis. Their sexual behavior appears to occur spontaneously, without much prompting on the part of others. In fact, a number of genetically controlled factors influence the sexual behavior of animals. For instance, animal behavior is affected by the presence of certain hormones in the blood. Moreover, females are receptive to sexual advances only at certain, relatively limited periods of time during the year (Short & Balaban, in press; D. Crews, 1993, 1994).

Human sexual behavior, by comparison, is more complicated, although the underlying biology is not all that different from that of related species. Consider the functions of the male and female **genitals,** or sex organs. In males, for example,

Genitals: The male and female sex organs

Androgens: Male sex hormones

Estrogen: A female sex hormone produced by the ovaries

Progesterone: A female sex hormone produced by the ovaries

Ovulation: The monthly release of an egg from an ovary

the *testes* secrete **androgens,** male sex hormones, at puberty. Not only do androgens produce secondary sex characteristics, such as the development of body hair and a deepening of the voice; they also increase the sex drive. Although there are long-term changes in the amount of androgens that are produced—with the greatest production occurring just after sexual maturity—their short-term production is fairly constant. Men, therefore, are capable of (and interested in) sexual activities without any regard to biological cycles. Given the proper stimuli leading to arousal, male sexual behavior can occur.

Women show a different, and more complex, pattern. When they reach maturity at puberty, the two *ovaries*, the female reproductive organs, begin to produce **estrogen** and **progesterone,** the female sex hormones. However, these hormones are not produced consistently; instead, their production follows a cyclical pattern. The greatest output occurs during **ovulation,** when an egg is released from the ovaries, making the chances of fertilization by a male sperm cell highest. While in nonhumans the period around ovulation is the only time that the female is receptive to sex, people are different. Although there are variations in reported sex drive, women are receptive to sex throughout their cycles, depending on the external stimuli they encounter in their environment (Hoon, Bruce, & Kinchloe, 1982).

Though biological factors "prime" people for sex, it takes more than hormones to motivate and produce sexual behavior. In animals it is the presence of a partner who provides arousing stimuli that leads to sexual activity. Humans are considerably more versatile; not only other people, but nearly any object, sight, smell, sound, or other stimulus can lead to sexual excitement. Because of prior associations, then, people may be turned on sexually by the smell of Chanel No. 5 or Brut, the sight of a bikini brief, or the sound of a favorite song, hummed softly in their ear. The reaction to a specific, potentially arousing stimulus, as we shall see, is a very individual one—what turns one person on may do just the opposite for another.

Sexual fantasies also play an important role in producing sexual arousal. Not only do people have fantasies of a sexual nature during their everyday activities, but about 60 percent of all people have fantasies during sexual intercourse. Interestingly, such fantasies often include having sex with someone other than one's partner of the moment.

Men's and women's fantasies differ little from each other in terms of content or quantity (Jones & Barlow, 1990). Thoughts of being sexually irresistible and of engaging in oral-genital sex are most common for both sexes (Sue, 1979; McCauley & Swann, 1980). It is important to note that fantasies are just that; in other words, they do not represent an actual desire to fulfill them in the real world. Thus, we should not assume from such data that females want to be sexually overpowered, nor should we assume that in every male lurks a potential rapist desirous of forcing sexual overtures on a submissive victim.

The Varieties of Sexual Experiences For most of recorded history, the vast variety of sexual practices remained shrouded in ignorance. However, in the late 1930s, biologist Albert Kinsey launched a series of surveys on the sexual behavior of Americans. The result was the first comprehensive look at sexual practices, highlighted by the publication of his landmark volumes, *Sexual Behavior in the Human Male* (Kinsey, Pomeroy, & Martin, 1948) and *Sexual Behavior in the Human Female* (Kinsey et al., 1953).

Kinsey's work set the stage for later surveys, although few comprehensive national surveys have been carried out since Kinsey did his initial work some 50 years ago. The reason: Investigations of sexual practices are always politically sensitive, and consequently large-scale surveys rarely receive governmental funding (Booth, 1989; McDonald, 1988; Gardner & Wilcox, 1993; Wyatt, 1994). However, by examining the common results gleaned from different samples of

subjects, we now have a reasonably complete picture of contemporary sexual practices—to which we turn next.

Masturbation   If you were to listen to physicians 50 years ago, you would have been told that **masturbation,** sexual self-stimulation, leads to a wide variety of physical and mental disorders, ranging from hairy palms to insanity. Had they been correct, however, most of us would be wearing gloves to hide the sight of our hair-covered palms—for masturbation is one of the most frequently practiced sexual activities. More than 90 percent of all males and almost two-thirds of all females have masturbated at least once. Among Americans aged 18 to 59, about 60 percent of the men and 40 percent of the women say they masturbated in the past year (Houston, 1981; Hunt, 1974; Michael et al., 1994).

Although masturbation is commonly considered an activity to engage in only if no other sexual outlets are available, this view bears little relationship to reality. Close to three-quarters of married men (aged 20 to 40) report masturbating an average of twenty-four times a year, and 68 percent of the married women in the same age group masturbate an average of ten times each year (Hunt, 1974; Michael et al., 1994).

Despite the high incidence of masturbation, attitudes toward it still reflect some of the negative views of yesteryear. For instance, one survey found that around 10 percent of the people who masturbated experienced feelings of guilt, and 5 percent of the males and 1 percent of the females considered their behavior perverted (Arafat & Cotton, 1974). Despite these negative attitudes, however, most experts on sex view masturbation not only as a healthy, legitimate—and harmless—sexual activity, but also as a means of learning about one's own sexuality.

Heterosexuality   People often believe that the first time they have sexual intercourse they have achieved one of life's major milestones. However, **heterosexuality,** sexual attraction and behavior directed to the opposite sex, consists of far more than just male-female intercourse. Kissing, petting, caressing, massaging, and other forms of sex play are all components of heterosexual behavior. Still, the focus of sex research has been on the act of intercourse, particularly in terms of its first occurrence and its frequency.

Premarital Sex   Until fairly recently, premarital sexual intercourse, at least for women, was considered one of the major taboos of our society. Traditionally, women have been warned by society that "nice girls don't do it"; men have been

Masturbation: Sexual self-stimulation

Heterosexuality: Sexual attraction and behavior directed to the opposite sex

Although the double standard has not died out completely, permissiveness with affection is now a widely accepted standard regarding premarital sex.

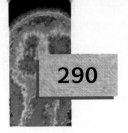

Double standard: The view that premarital sex is permissible for males but not for females

told that although premarital sex is OK for them, they should make sure they marry virgins. This view, that premarital sex is permissible for males but not for females, is called the **double standard.**

Although as recently as the 1960s the majority of adult Americans believed that premarital sex was always wrong, since that time there has been a dramatic change in public opinion. For example, in 1969 the majority of people thought it was wrong for a man and woman to have sexual intercourse before marriage. However, the 1991 figures show a shift; at that point, more people thought it was permissible than those who thought it was wrong.

Changes in attitudes toward premarital sex were matched by changes in actual rates of premarital sexual activity during the same period. For instance, the most recent figures show that just over one-half of women between the ages of 15 and 19 have had premarital sexual intercourse. These figures are close to double the percentage of women in the same age range who reported having intercourse in 1970 (CDC, 1991b, 1992). Clearly, the trend over the last several decades has been toward more women engaging in premarital sexual activity (Gerrard, 1988; Hofferth, Kahn, & Baldwin, 1987; CDC, 1991b, 1992).

Males, too, have shown an increase in the incidence of premarital sexual intercourse, although the increase has not been as dramatic as it has for females—probably because the rates for males were higher to begin with. For instance, the first surveys carried out in the 1940s showed an incidence of 84 percent across males of all ages; recent figures put the figure at closer to 95 percent. Moreover, the average age of males' first sexual experience has also been declining steadily. Some 60 percent of male high school students have had sexual intercourse; and by the time they reach the age of 20, 80 percent have had intercourse (Arena, 1984; CDC, 1992).

Marital Sex   To judge by the number of articles about sex in marriage, one would think that sexual behavior was the number 1 standard by which marital bliss is measured. Married couples are often concerned that they are having too little sex, too much sex, or the wrong kind of sex (Sprecher & McKinney, 1993).

Although there are many different dimensions against which sex in marriage is measured, one is certainly the frequency of sexual intercourse. What is typical? As with most other types of sexual activities, there is no easy answer to the question, since there are such wide variations in patterns between individuals. We do know that 43 percent of married couples have sexual intercourse a few times a month, and 36 percent have it two or three times a week (Michael et al., 1994). In addition, there are differences according to the number of years a couple has been together: the longer the marriage, the lower the frequency of sex.

The frequency of marital sexual intercourse also appears to be higher at this time than in other recent historical periods. A number of factors account for this increase. Increased availability of birth-control methods (including birth-control pills) and abortion have led couples to be less concerned about unwanted pregnancies. Moreover, several social changes are likely to have had an impact. As women's roles have changed, and the popular media have reinforced the notion that female sexuality is OK, the likelihood that a wife may initiate sex, rather than waiting for her husband's overture as in the former traditional scenario, has increased. As sex becomes more openly discussed in magazines, in books, and even on television shows, many married couples have come to believe that the frequency of sex is a critical index of the success of their marriage.

The consequences of the increase in marital intercourse are difficult to assess. It is clear that the degree of sexual satisfaction is related to overall satisfaction with a marriage. Yet the *frequency* of sexual intercourse does not appear to be associated with happiness in marriage. The rise in frequency of sexual intercourse does not suggest, then, that there will be an accompanying increase in marital satisfaction (Blumstein & Schwartz, 1983; Greeley, 1992).

Homosexuality and Bisexuality   Just as there seems to be no genetic or biological reason for heterosexual women to find men's buttocks particularly erotic, humans are not born with an innate attraction to the special characteristics of the opposite sex. We should not find it surprising, then, that some people, **homosexuals,** are sexually attracted to members of their own sex, while others, **bisexuals,** are sexually attracted to people of the same *and* the opposite sex. (Many male homosexuals prefer the term *gay,* and female homosexuals the label *lesbian,* which are seen as more positive.)

Although people often view homosexuality and heterosexuality as two completely distinct sexual orientations, the issue is not that simple. Pioneering sex researcher Alfred Kinsey acknowledged this when he considered sexual orientation along a scale, or continuum, with "exclusively homosexual" at one end and "exclusively heterosexual" at the other. In the middle were people who show both homosexual and heterosexual behavior. Updated by sociologist Martin S. Weinberg and colleagues (Weinberg, Williams, & Pryor, 1991), Kinsey's approach suggests that sexual orientation is dependent on a person's sexual feelings, sexual behaviors, and romantic feelings.

What determines people's sexual orientation? Although there are a number of theories, none has proved completely satisfactory. Some approaches are biological in nature, suggesting that there may be a genetic or hormonal reason for the development of homosexuality (Gladue, 1984; Hutchison, 1978; Bailey & Pillard, 1991). For example, some evidence suggests a difference in the structure of the anterior hypothalamus, an area of the brain that governs sexual behavior, between male homosexuals and heterosexuals (LeVay, 1991, 1993). Similarly, other research shows that, compared with heterosexual men or women, homosexual men have a larger anterior commissure, which is a bundle of neurons connecting the right and left hemispheres of the brain (Allen & Gorski, 1992).

Other theories of homosexuality have focused on the childhood and family background of homosexuals. For instance, Freud believed that homosexuality occurred as a result of inappropriate identification with the opposite-sex parent during development (Freud, 1922/1959). Similarly, other psychoanalysts suggest that the nature of the parent-child relationship can lead to homosexuality, and that male homosexuals frequently have overprotective, dominant mothers and passive, ineffective fathers (Bieber et al., 1962).

The problem with such theories is that there are probably as many homosexuals who were not subjected to the influence of such family dynamics as who were. The evidence does not support explanations that rely on child-rearing practices or on the nature of the family structure (Bell & Weinberg, 1978; Isay, 1990).

Another explanation for homosexuality rests on learning theory (Masters & Johnson, 1979). According to this view, sexual orientation is learned through rewards and punishments in much the same way that we might learn to prefer swimming over tennis. For example, a young adolescent who had a heterosexual experience whose outcome was unpleasant might learn to link unpleasant associations with the opposite sex. If that same person had a rewarding, pleasant homosexual experience, homosexuality might be incorporated into his or her sexual fantasies. If such fantasies are then used during later sexual activities—such as masturbation—they may be positively reinforced through orgasm, and the association of homosexual behavior and sexual pleasure might eventually cause homosexuality to become the preferred form of sexual behavior.

Although the learning-theory explanation is plausible, several difficulties rule out its being seen as a definitive one. Because our society tends to hold homosexuality in low esteem, one ought to expect that the punishments involved in homosexual behavior would outweigh the rewards attached to it. Furthermore, children growing up with a homosexual parent are statistically unlikely to become homosexual, thus contradicting the notion that homosexual behavior might be learned from others (Green, 1978).

Homosexuals: Persons who are sexually attracted to members of their own sex

Bisexuals: Persons who are sexually attracted to members of both sexes

The causes of homosexuality are still subject to debate, but research has established that gays and lesbians are as psychologically well adjusted as the general population.

Given the difficulty in finding a consistent explanation, the majority of researchers reject the notion that any single factor orients a person toward homosexuality. Most experts suspect that a combination of biological and environmental factors are at work (Money, 1987; McWhirter, Sanders, & Reinisch, 1990; Greene & Herek, 1993).

Although we don't know at this point exactly why people develop a particular sexual orientation, one thing is clear: There is no relationship between psychological adjustment and sexual preference. Bisexuals and homosexuals enjoy the same overall degree of mental and physical health as heterosexuals do. They hold equivalent ranges and types of attitudes about themselves, independent of sexual orientation. For such reasons, the American Psychological Association and most other mental health organizations have endorsed efforts to reduce discrimination against gay men and lesbians, such as revoking the ban against homosexuals in the military (Reiss, 1980; Bersoff & Ogden, 1991; Gonsiorek, 1991; Herek, 1993; Patterson, 1994).

Exploring Diversity

Female Circumcision: A Celebration of Culture—or Genital Mutilation?

In their living room in Atlanta, Hassan and Yasmin Ibrahim are having one of their nightly worried talks about their three little girls. Both want what is best for the children. But they cannot agree on a decision that will affect the girls every day of the rest of their young lives.

Mrs. Ibrahim seems a gentle woman. But she insists that each girl must in childhood have her clitoris removed.

In America, she says, it won't be as awful as back home in Somalia. She says here it can be done in a hospital, with a doctor and anesthetic—not in a hut, by a village headwoman, with the child awake to the knife and screaming.

Mr. Ibrahim, a certified public accountant, says he has "a big question mark" in his mind. He does not want his children to go through what their mother had to endure, like most Somali women.

But his wife says without the surgery no Somali man will marry them. They would be "different"—and she would be betraying her culture (Rosenthal, 1993, p. 13).

The operation in question—female circumcision—represents one of the most controversial procedures relating to sex throughout the world. In such an operation, the clitoris is removed, resulting in a permanent inability to experience sexual pleasure.

Some 80 million women, living mostly in Africa and Asia, have undergone female circumcision. For instance, more than 90 percent of Nigerian women have been circumcised during childhood, and more than 90 percent intend to circumcise their own daughters. Furthermore, in some cases, more extensive surgery is carried out, in which additional parts of the female genitals are removed or are sewn together with catgut or thorns (Ebomoyi, 1987; Rosenthal, 1993).

Those who practice female circumcision say it upholds an ancient societal tradition, no different from other cultural customs. Its purpose, they say, is to preserve virginity before marriage, to keep women faithful to their husbands after marriage, and to enhance a woman's beauty. Furthermore, proponents believe that it differs little from the common Western practice of male circumcision, in which the foreskin of the penis is surgically removed soon after birth.

Critics, on the other hand, argue that female circumcision is nothing less than female mutilation. Not only does the practice permanently eliminate sexual pleasure, but it can also lead to constant pain and infection, depending on the nature of the surgery. In fact, because the procedure is traditionally conducted in a ritualistic fashion without anesthetic, using a razor blade, sawtooth knife, or glass, the circumcision itself can be physically traumatic.

The procedure raises some difficult issues, which were brought to light in a recent court case. A Nigerian immigrant, living temporarily in the United States, went to court to argue that she should be allowed to remain permanently (Gregory, 1994). Her plea: If she and her young daughters were sent back to Nigeria, her daughters would face circumcision upon their return. (The court agreed and permitted her to stay indefinitely.) But others argue that circumcision is a valued cultural custom, and that no one, particularly someone using the perspective of another culture, should prevent people from carrying out the customs they think are important.

Lest we think that female circumcision is of remote interest to those living in Western cultures, keep this fact in mind: Just a few generations ago, some physicians in the United States suggested that a woman who showed "excessive" interest in sex should have her clitoris removed. Such a procedure, it was argued, would keep her sexual behavior under control (Hyde, 1994).

The Need for Achievement: Striving for Success

While hunger and sex may represent some of the most potent primary drives in our day-to-day lives, we are also motivated by powerful secondary drives that have no clear biological basis (McClelland, 1985; Geen, 1984). Among the most prominent of these is the need for achievement.

The **need for achievement** is a stable, learned characteristic in which satisfaction is obtained by striving for and attaining a level of excellence (McClelland et al., 1953). People with a high need for achievement seek out situations in which they can compete against some standard—be it grades, money, or winning at a game—and prove themselves successful. But they are not indiscriminate when it comes to picking their challenges: Like Bob, the would-be law student described earlier, they tend to avoid situations in which success will come too easily (which would be unchallenging) or those in which success is unlikely. Instead, people high in achievement motivation are apt to choose tasks that are of intermediate difficulty.

In contrast, people with low achievement motivation tend to be motivated primarily by a desire to avoid failure. As a result, they seek out easy tasks, being sure to avoid failure, or they seek out very difficult tasks for which failure has no negative implications, since almost anyone would fail at them. People with a high fear of failure will stay away from tasks of intermediate difficulty, since they may fail where others have been successful (Atkinson & Feather, 1966; Sorrentino, Hewitt, & Raso-Knott, 1992).

The outcomes of a high need for achievement are generally positive, at least in a success-oriented society such as our own (Heckhausen, Schmalt, & Schneider, 1985; Spence, 1985). For instance, people motivated by a high need for achievement are more likely to attend college than their low-achievement counterparts, and once in college they tend to receive higher grades in classes that are related to their future careers (Atkinson & Raynor, 1974). Furthermore, high-achievement motivation is associated with future economic and occupational success (McClelland, 1985).

Measuring Achievement Motivation How can we measure a person's need for achievement? The technique used most frequently is to administer a *Thematic Apperception Test (TAT)* (Spangler, 1992). In the TAT, people are shown a series of ambiguous pictures, such as the one in Figure 9-2. They are told to write a story that describes what is happening, who the people are, what led to the situation, what the people are thinking or wanting, and what will happen next. A stan-

Need for achievement: A stable, learned characteristic in which satisfaction comes from striving for and achieving a level of excellence

FIGURE 9-2 This ambiguous picture is similar to those used in the Thematic Apperception Test to determine people's underlying motivation. *(©1943 by the President and Fellows of Harvard College; 1971 by Henry A. Murray.)*

dard scoring system is then used to determine the amount of achievement imagery in people's stories. For example, someone who writes a story in which the main character is striving to beat an opponent, studying in order to do well at some task, or working hard in order to get a promotion shows clear signs of an achievement orientation. It is assumed that the inclusion of such achievement-related imagery in their stories indicates an unusually high degree of concern with—and therefore a relatively strong need for—achievement.

Other techniques have been developed for assessing achievement motivation on a societal level (Reuman, Alwin, & Veroff, 1984). For example, a good indication of the overall level of achievement motivation in a particular society can be found by assessing achievement imagery in children's stories or folk tales. Researchers who have examined children's reading books for achievement imagery over long periods have found correlations between the amount of imagery in the books and the economic activity in the society over the next few decades (DeCharms & Moeller, 1962). Whether stories incorporating achievement imagery actually influence children or simply reflect growing economic trends cannot be determined, of course. It is clear, though, that children might be learning more from their books than how to read—they may be acquiring an understanding of the level of achievement motivation that society expects of them.

Are There Racial Differences in Achievement Motivation? One sad fact of U.S. society is that the scholastic achievement of racial minorities often trails that of the white majority. Could these variations in educational attainment be attributed to differences in underlying achievement motivation?

According to a comprehensive review by psychologist Sandra Graham (1994), the answer is a firm "no." Summarizing decades of research, Graham found that there is little reliable evidence to suggest that African-Americans and whites differ in their underlying need for achievement. Furthermore, her analysis of a vast array of research suggests that African-Americans' expectations for future success in academic endeavors are relatively high, even after experiencing prior academic failure.

Graham's findings contradict a "deficit" view of African-American achievement motivation in which lower achievement is attributed to deficits in achievement motivation. They suggest that psychologists need to develop a fuller understanding of the particular circumstances and variables that influence the achievement strivings of both minority- and majority-group members (Graham, 1992; Betancourt & Lopez, 1993).

The Need for Affiliation: Striving for Friendship

Few of us choose to lead our lives as hermits. Why? One main reason is that most people have a **need for affiliation,** an interest in establishing and maintaining relationships with other people. Individuals with a high need for affiliation write TAT stories that emphasize the desire to maintain or reinstate friendships and show concern over being rejected by friends.

Need for affiliation: A need to establish and maintain relationships with other people

People who are higher in affiliation needs are particularly sensitive to relationships with others. They desire to be with their friends more of the time, and they want to be alone less often than people who are lower in their need for affiliation. At the same time, affiliation motivation may be less important than gender in determining how much time is actually spent with friends. According to the results of one study, regardless of their affiliative orientation, female students spend significantly more time with their friends and less time alone than male students do (Wong & Csikszentmihalyi, 1991).

The Need for Power: Striving for Impact on Others

If your fantasies include being elected President of the United States or running General Motors, they may be reflecting a high need for power. The **need for power,** a tendency to seek impact, control, or influence over others, and to be seen as a powerful individual, represents an additional type of motivation (Winter, 1973, 1987).

Need for power: A tendency to want to make an impression or have an impact on others in order to be seen as a powerful individual

As you might expect, people with a strong need for power are more apt to belong to organizations and seek office than those low in the need for power. They are also apt to be in professions in which their power needs may be fulfilled, such as business management and—you may or may not be surprised—teaching (Jenkins, 1994). In addition, they seek to display the trappings of power. Even in college, they are more apt to collect prestigious possessions, such as stereos and sports cars.

There are some significant sex differences in the display of the need for power. Men who are high in power needs tend to show unusually high levels of aggression, drink heavily, act in a sexually exploitative manner, and participate more frequently in competitive sports—behaviors that collectively represent somewhat extravagant, flamboyant behavior (Winter, 1973). In contrast, women display their power needs in a more restrained manner, congruent with traditional societal restraints on women's behavior. Women high in a need for power are more apt than men to channel their power needs in a socially responsible manner (such as by showing concern for others or through highly nurturant behavior) (Winter, 1988).

In common with other types of motivation, the need for power may express itself in several, quite diverse, ways (Spangler & House, 1991). How a particular need is manifested reflects a combination of people's skills, values, and the specific situations in which they find themselves. (See the Pathways through Psychology box (next page) for a discussion of how one psychologist applies some of the motivational concepts we've been discussing to the sports arena.)

PATHWAYS THROUGH PSYCHOLOGY

Thomas Tutko

Born: 1931
Education: B.A., Pennsylvania State University; M.S., Ph.D., Northwestern University
Home: San Jose, California

A correspondence course in psychology not only led Thomas Tutko toward a career in psychology, but paved the road for him to become one of the pioneers in the field of sports psychology.

"When I was serving in the Marines, I had a friend who was involved in a psychology correspondence course, and I was fascinated by it," said the 65-year-old Tutko, a native of Gallitzin, Pennsylvania. "After enrolling in a course by mail myself, I went on to college at Penn State. I have to say that taking that course was the single-most action that was responsible for changing my life."

Fresh out of Penn State in 1958 with an undergraduate degree in psychology, Tutko pursued his master's and doctorate degrees from Northwestern University. With an academic background in clinical psychology and research, he joined the faculty of San Jose State University and has been there ever since.

At San Jose, Tutko met Bruce

Thomas Tutko.

Ogilvie, who was counseling athletes having personal problems. Together they created the field of sports psychology. "In talking with Bruce, I suggested we do research to find out what a successful athlete looks like," Tutko said. "At that time we had some high-caliber athletes here such as John Carlos and Lee Evans whom we could work with."

In developing the field, Tutko said he and Ogilvie utilized a number of concepts already available in psychology, and modified and adapted them for use in sports. For instance, they help athletes build confidence by leading them to focus on what they do well rather than concentrating on what they do poorly. "Professional athletes are very serious, and sustaining their concentration is a major issue. We need to have them think positively to reinforce their behavior and to help with this we utilize various relaxation techniques."

Tutko notes further that motivation is a key concept for sports psychologists. "Whether or not an athlete is 'up' for a game is important. There is a maximum arousal point where the athlete is excited and thrilled and can be as efficient as possible. But it is also possible to be too aroused, and that can result in poor performance."

Tutko has worked with a variety of teams, including the Pittsburgh Pirates baseball team and the San Francisco 49ers, the Los Angeles Rams, and the Dallas Cowboys football teams. He is also involved in youth athletics, and he has written five books on psychology and sports. He teaches a sports psychology class, which, when he first introduced it, was one of the first in the nation. "The University said that if I didn't get at least 15 people enrolled, the course would be dropped. The first day we had 150 people show up. That proved to me there was a real need for sports psychology," he said.

RECAP AND REVIEW

Recap

- Hunger is affected by internal cues that regulate the amount and kind of food eaten. The hypothalamus is central in regulating food intake.
- People's weight set point, their sensitivity to external social cues, the number of fat cells they have, and genetic factors may all affect eating patterns.
- Although biological factors prime people for sex, other stimuli are necessary for sexual excitement to occur.
- Masturbation (sexual self-stimulation) is common among both men and women, although it is still viewed negatively by many people.

- The double standard has declined over the last few decades; tolerance for and actual acts of premarital sex have increased greatly.
- Among the major secondary drives are the needs for achievement, affiliation, and power.

Review

1. Laboratory animals, when deprived of certain nutrients, have been found to instinctively choose foods that contain the nutrients they are lacking. True or false?
2. Match the following terms with their definitions:

1. Hypothalamus
2. Lateral hypothalamic damage
3. Ventromedial hypothalamic damage

a. Leads to refusal of food and starvation
b. Responsible for monitoring food intake
c. Causes extreme overeating

3. The _____ _____ _____ is the particular level of weight the body strives to maintain.

4. _____ is the rate at which energy is produced and expended by the body.

5. _____ is an eating disorder characterized by binge eating, then purging the body by inducing vomiting. A person with the disorder of _____ _____ refuses to eat and denies that his or her behavior and appearance are unusual.

6. Men's and women's sexual fantasies are essentially similar to each other. True or false?

7. The work carried out by _____ in the 1930s was the first systematic study of sexual behavior ever undertaken.

8. Although the incidence of masturbation among young adults is high, once men and women become involved in intimate relationships with others, they typically cease masturbating. True or false?

9. Research comparing homosexuals and heterosexuals clearly demonstrates that there is no difference in the level of adjustment or psychological functioning between the two groups. True or false?

10. Jake is the type of person who constantly strives for excellence. He feels intense satisfaction when he is able to master a new task. Jake most likely has a high need for _____ .

Ask Yourself

Can traits such as the need for achievement, need for power, and need for affiliation be used to select workers for jobs? What other criteria, both motivational and personal, would need to be considered when making such a selection?

(Answers to review questions are on page 298.)

- *What are emotions, and how do we experience them?*
- *What are the functions of emotions?*

UNDERSTANDING EMOTIONAL EXPERIENCES

Karl Andrews held in his hands the envelope he had been waiting for. It could be the ticket to his future: an offer of admission to his first-choice college. But what was it going to say? He knew it could go either way; his grades were pretty good, and he had been involved in some extracurricular activities; but his SAT scores had been, to put it bluntly, lousy. He felt so nervous that his hands shook as he opened the thin envelope (not a good sign, he thought). Here it comes. "Dear Mr. Andrews," it read. "The President and Trustees of the University are pleased to admit you. . . ." That was all he needed to see. With a whoop of excitement, Karl found himself jumping up and down gleefully. A rush of emotion overcame him as it sank in that he had, in fact, been accepted. He was on his way.

At one time or another, all of us have experienced the strong feelings that accompany both very pleasant and very negative experiences. Perhaps it was the thrill of getting a sought-after job, the joy of being in love, the sorrow over someone's death, or the anguish of inadvertently hurting someone. Moreover, we experience such reactions on a less intense level throughout our daily lives: the pleasure of a friendship, the enjoyment of a movie, or the embarrassment of breaking a borrowed item.

Despite the varied nature of these feelings, they all represent emotions. Although everyone has an idea of what an emotion is, formally defining the concept has proved to be an elusive task. We'll use a general definition: **Emotions** are feelings that generally have both physiological and cognitive elements and that influence behavior.

Think, for example, about how it feels to be happy. First, we obviously experience a feeling that we can differentiate from other emotions. It is likely that we also experience some identifiable physical changes in our body: Perhaps our heart rate increases, or—as in the example earlier—we find ourselves "jumping for

Emotions: Feelings (such as happiness, despair, and sorrow) that generally have both physiological and cognitive elements and that influence behavior

297

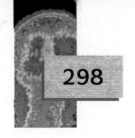
joy." Finally, the emotion probably encompasses cognitive elements; our understanding and evaluation of the meaning of what is happening prompts our feelings of happiness.

It is also possible, however, to experience an emotion without the presence of cognitive elements. For instance, we may react with fear to an unusual or novel situation (such as coming into contact with an erratic, unpredictable individual), or we may experience pleasure over sexual excitation without having cognitive awareness or understanding of what it is about the situation that is exciting.

Some psychologists argue that entirely separate systems govern cognitive responses and emotional responses. One controversy is whether the emotional response takes predominance over the cognitive response or vice versa. Some theorists suggest that we first respond to a situation with an emotional reaction and then later try to understand it (Zajonc, 1985). For example, we may enjoy a complex modern symphony without at first understanding it or knowing why we like it.

In contrast, other theorists propose that people first develop cognitions about a situation and then react emotionally. This school of thought suggests that it is necessary for us to first think about and understand a stimulus or situation, relating it to what we already know, before we can react on an emotional level (Lazarus, 1984, 1991a, 1991b).

Both sides of this debate can cite research to support their viewpoints, and so the question is far from resolved (Scheff, 1985; Frijda, 1988). It is possible that the sequence varies from situation to situation, with emotions predominating in some instances and cognitive processes occurring first in others.

The Functions of Emotions

Imagine what it would be like if we didn't experience emotion—no depths of despair, no depression, no remorse, but at the same time no happiness, joy, or love. Obviously life might be considerably less satisfying, and even dull, if we lacked the capacity to sense and express emotions.

But do emotions serve any purpose beyond making life interesting? Psychologists have identified a number of important functions that emotions play in our daily lives (Scherer, 1984). Among the most important of those functions are the following:

■ *Preparing us for action.* Emotions act as a link between events in the external environment and behavioral responses that an individual makes. For example, if we saw an angry dog charging toward us, the emotional reaction (fear) would be associated with physiological arousal of the sympathetic division of the autonomic nervous system (see Chapter 2). The role of the sympathetic division is to prepare us for emergency action, which presumably would get us moving out of the dog's way—quickly. Emotions, then, are stimuli that aid in the development of effective responses to various situations.

■ *Shaping our future behavior.* Emotions serve to promote learning of information that will assist us in making appropriate responses in the future. For example, the emotional response that occurs when a person experiences something unpleasant—such as a threatening dog—teaches that person to avoid similar circumstances in the future. Similarly, pleasant emotions act as reinforcement for prior behavior and therefore are apt to lead an individual to seek out similar situations in the future. Thus, the feeling of satisfaction that follows giving to a charity is likely to reinforce charitable behavior and make it more likely to occur in the future.

■ *Helping us to regulate social interaction.* As we shall discuss in detail later, the emotions we experience are frequently obvious to observers, as they are communicated through our verbal and nonverbal behaviors. These behaviors can act as a signal to observers, allowing them to better understand what we are experiencing and to predict our future behavior. In turn, this promotes more effective and appropriate social interaction. For instance, a mother who sees the terror on her 2-year-old son's face when he sees a frightening picture in a book is able to comfort and reassure him, thereby helping him to deal with his environment more effectively in the future.

Determining the Range of Emotions: Labeling Our Feelings

If we were to try to list the words in the English language that have been used to describe emotions, we would end up with at least 500 different examples (Averill, 1975). The list would range from such obvious emotions as "happiness" and "fear" to less common ones, such as "adventurousness" and "pensiveness."

One challenge for psychologists has been to try to sort through this list in order to identify the most important, fundamental emotions in our everyday lives, as well as to try to determine how our emotions are related to one another (Russell, 1991). One of the most comprehensive efforts has been carried out by Robert Plutchik (1984), who asked people to rate each of a large set of emotions along thirty-four different rating scales. Then, by mathematically combining the ratings, he was able to determine the relationships among the various emotions, as well as which emotions were most fundamental.

The results were clear: Eight different fundamental emotions (joy, acceptance, fear, surprise, sadness, disgust, anger, and anticipation) emerged, and they formed the pattern within the wheel shown in Figure 9-3. Furthermore, these primary emotions could be consolidated into the two-emotion combinations shown on the outside of the wheel. Emotions nearer one another in the circle are

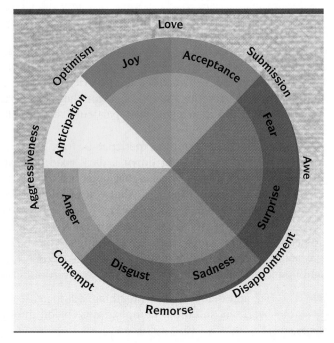

FIGURE 9-3 Plutchik's emotion wheel demonstrates how eight primary emotions are related to one another. *(Plutchik, 1980.)*

more closely related, while those opposite each other are conceptual opposites. For instance, sadness is opposite joy, and anticipation is opposite surprise.

While Plutchik's configuration of the basic emotions is reasonable, it is not the only plausible one. Other psychologists have come up with somewhat different lists, depending on the nature of the questions they have asked as well as the specific culture in which their research has been carried out. For instance, Germans report experiencing *schadenfreude*, a feeling of pleasure over another person's difficulties, while the Japanese experience *hagaii*, a mood of vulnerable heartache colored by frustration. In Tahiti, people experience *musu*, a feeling of reluctance to yield to unreasonable demands made by one's parents.

Finding *schadenfreude, hagaii,* and *musu* in a particular culture doesn't mean that inhabitants of other cultures are incapable of experiencing such emotions. It does suggest, though, that the existence of a linguistic category to describe a particular emotion may make it easier to discuss, contemplate, and perhaps experience the emotion more readily (Russell, 1991; Mesquita & Frijda, 1992).

Members of different cultures also experience emotions with differing degrees of intensity. For example, students in the United States report that their emotions last longer and are more intense than those of Japanese students. In addition, U.S. students say they react more positively to the experience of emotion than Japanese students (Matsumoto et al., 1988; Lee et al., 1992; Bond, 1993).

Because of the difficulties in identifying *the* unique set of primary emotions, some theorists reject entirely the notion that a small number of basic emotions exist. Instead, they suggest that emotions are best understood by breaking them down into their component parts (Ortony & Turner, 1990).

Still, while it has proved challenging for psychologists to produce a definitive, universal list of the primary emotions, each of us has little difficulty in identifying what we are experiencing at any given moment. The process by which we come to this understanding forms the basis of a number of theories of emotion, which we discuss next.

DECIPHERING OUR EMOTIONS

I've never been so angry; my heart is pounding, and I'm trembling all over. . . . I don't know how I'll get through the performance. I feel like my stomach is filled with butterflies. . . . That was quite a mistake I made! My face must be incredibly red. . . . When I heard the footsteps in the night, I was so frightened that I couldn't catch my breath.

If you examine our language, you will find that there are literally dozens of ways to describe how we feel when we are experiencing an emotion, and that the language we use to describe emotions is, for the most part, based on the physical symptoms that are associated with particular emotional experiences (Koveces, 1987).

Consider, for instance, the experience of fear. Pretend that it is late one New Year's Eve. You are walking down a dark road, and you hear a stranger approaching behind you. It is clear that he is not trying to hurry by but is coming directly toward you. You think of what you will do if the stranger attempts to rob you—or worse, hurt you in some way.

While these thoughts are running through your head, it is almost certain that something rather dramatic will be happening to your body. Among the most likely physiological reactions that may occur, which are associated with activation of the autonomic nervous system (see Chapter 2), are those listed here:

■ The rate and depth of your breathing will increase.
■ Your heart will speed up, pumping more blood through your circulatory system.

■ The pupils of your eyes will open wider, allowing more light to enter and thereby increasing your visual sensitivity.

■ Your mouth will become dry as your salivary glands, and in fact your entire digestive system, stop functioning. At the same time, though, your sweat glands may increase their activity, since increased sweating will help you rid yourself of excess heat developed by any emergency activity in which you engage.

■ As the muscles just below the surface of your skin contract, your hair may literally stand on end.

Of course, all these physiological changes are likely to occur without your awareness. At the same time, though, the emotional experience accompanying them will be obvious to you: You would most surely report being fearful.

Although it is a relatively straightforward matter to describe the general physical reactions that accompany emotions, the specific role that these physiological responses play in the experience of emotions has proved to be a major puzzle for psychologists. As we shall see, some theorists suggest that specific bodily reactions *cause* us to experience a particular emotion—we experience fear, for instance, *because* our heart is pounding and we are breathing deeply. In contrast, other theorists suggest that the physiological reaction is the *result* of the experience of an emotion. In this view, we experience fear, and this emotional experience causes our heart to pound and our breathing to deepen.

The James-Lange Theory: Do Gut Reactions Equal Emotions?

To William James and Carl Lange, who were among the first researchers to explore the nature of emotions, emotional experience is, very simply, a reaction to instinctive bodily events that occur as a response to some situation or event in the environment. This view is summarized in James's statement, ". . . we feel sorry because we cry, angry because we strike, afraid because we tremble" (James, 1890).

James and Lange took the view that the instinctive response of crying at a loss leads us to feel sorrow; that striking out at someone who frustrates us results in our feeling anger; that trembling at a menacing threat causes us to feel afraid. They suggested that for every major emotion there is an accompanying physiological, or "gut," reaction of internal organs—called a *visceral experience*. It is this specific pattern of visceral response that leads us to label the emotional experience.

In sum, James and Lange proposed that we experience emotions as a result of physiological changes that produce specific sensations. In turn, these sensations are interpreted by the brain as particular kinds of emotional experiences (see Figure 9-4). This view has come to be called the **James-Lange theory of emotion** (Izard, 1990; Laird & Bresler, 1990).

The James-Lange theory has some serious drawbacks, however. In order for the theory to be valid, visceral changes would have to occur at a relatively rapid pace, since we experience some emotions—such as fear upon hearing a stranger rapidly approaching on a dark night—almost instantaneously. Yet emotional experiences frequently occur even before there is time for certain physiological changes to be set into motion. Because of the slowness with which some visceral changes take place, it is hard to see how they could be the source of immediate emotional experience.

The James-Lange theory poses another difficulty: Physiological arousal does not invariably produce emotional experience. For example, a person who is jogging has an increased heartbeat and respiration rate, as well as many of the other physiological changes associated with certain emotions. Yet joggers do not typically think of such changes in terms of emotions. There cannot be a one-to-one

James-Lange theory of emotion: The belief that emotional experience is a reaction to bodily events occurring as a result of an external situation ("I feel sad because I am crying")

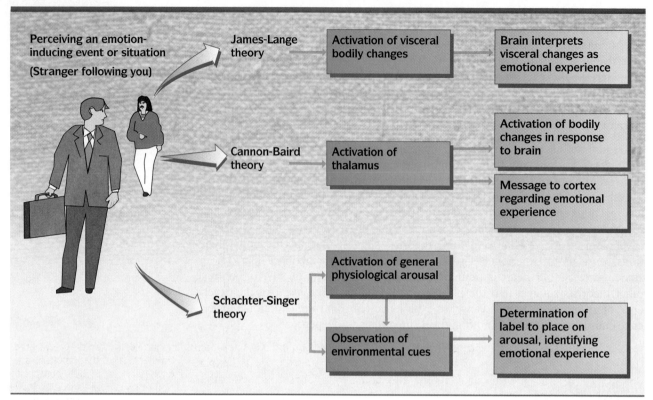

FIGURE 9-4 A comparison of three models of emotion.

correspondence, then, between visceral changes and emotional experience. Visceral changes by themselves may not be sufficient to produce emotion.

Finally, our internal organs produce a relatively limited range of sensations. Although some types of physiological changes are associated with specific emotional experiences (Levenson et al., 1992; Levenson, 1992), it is difficult to imagine how the range of emotions that people are capable of experiencing could be the result of unique visceral changes. Many emotions are actually associated with relatively similar sorts of visceral changes, a fact that contradicts the James-Lange theory.

The Cannon-Bard Theory: Physiological Reactions as the Result of Emotions

Cannon-Bard theory of emotion: The belief that both physiological and emotional arousal are produced simultaneously by the same nerve impulse

In response to the difficulties inherent in the James-Lange theory, Walter Cannon, and later Philip Bard, suggested an alternative view. In what has come to be known as the **Cannon-Bard theory of emotion,** they proposed the model illustrated in the middle part of Figure 9-4 (Cannon, 1929). The major thrust of the theory is to reject the view that physiological arousal alone leads to the perception of emotion. Instead, the theory assumes that both physiological arousal *and* the emotional experience are produced simultaneously by the same nerve impulse, which Cannon and Bard suggested emanates from the brain's thalamus.

According to the theory, after an emotion-inducing stimulus is perceived, the thalamus is the initial site of the emotional response. In turn, the thalamus sends a signal to the autonomic nervous system, thereby producing a visceral response. At the same time, the thalamus communicates a message to the cerebral cortex regarding the nature of the emotion being experienced. Hence, it is not necessary for different emotions to have unique physiological patterns associated with them—as long as the message sent to the cerebral cortex differs according to the specific emotion.

The Cannon-Bard theory seems to have been accurate in its rejection of the view that physiological arousal alone accounts for emotions. However, recent research has led to some important modifications of the theory. As you may recall from Chapter 2, we now understand that it is the hypothalamus and the limbic system, and not the thalamus, that play a major role in emotional experience. In addition, the simultaneity of the physiological and emotional responses, which is a fundamental assumption of the theory, has yet to be conclusively demonstrated (Pribram, 1984). This ambiguity has allowed room for yet another theory of emotions: the Schachter-Singer theory.

The Schachter-Singer Theory: Emotions as Labels

Suppose, as in our earlier example, you were walking down a dark street, fearful of the stranger who appeared to be following you. Additionally assume that you notice a woman on the other side of the street who also appears to be followed. However, suppose that the woman, instead of reacting with fear, begins to laugh and act gleeful. Might the reactions of this woman be sufficient to lay your own fears to rest? Might you, in fact, decide there is nothing to fear, and get into the spirit of the evening by beginning to feel glee yourself?

According to an explanation that focuses on the role of cognition, the **Schachter-Singer theory of emotion,** this might very well happen. This approach to explaining emotions emphasizes that we identify the emotion we are experiencing by observing our environment and comparing ourselves with others (Schachter & Singer, 1962).

Schachter-Singer theory of emotion: The belief that emotions are determined jointly by a nonspecific kind of physiological arousal and its interpretation, based on environmental cues

A classic experiment found evidence for this hypothesis. In the study, subjects were told that they would receive an injection of a vitamin called Suproxin. In reality, they were given epinephrine, a drug that causes an increase in physiological arousal, including higher heart and respiration rates and a reddening of the face, responses that typically occur during strong emotional reactions. Although one group of subjects was informed of the actual effects of the drug, another was left unaware.

Subjects in both groups were then individually placed in a situation where a confederate of the experimenter acted in one of two ways. In one condition, he acted angry and hostile, complaining that he would refuse to answer the personal questions on a questionnaire that the experimenter had asked him to complete. In the other condition, his behavior was quite the opposite. He behaved euphorically, flying paper airplanes and tossing wads of paper, in general acting in an exuberant manner.

The purpose of the experiment was to determine how the subjects would react emotionally to the confederate's behavior. When they were asked to describe their own emotional states at the end of the experiment, subjects who had been told of the effects of the drug were relatively unaffected by the behavior of the confederate. They thought their physiological arousal was due to the drug and therefore were not faced with the need to find a reason for their arousal. Hence, they reported experiencing relatively little emotion.

On the other hand, subjects who had not been told of the drug's real effects were influenced by the confederate's behavior. Those subjects exposed to the angry confederate reported that they felt angry, while those exposed to the euphoric confederate reported feeling happy. In sum, the results suggest that uninformed subjects turned to the environment and the behavior of others for an explanation of the physiological arousal they were experiencing.

The results of the Schachter-Singer experiment, then, support a cognitive view of emotions, in which emotions are determined jointly by a relatively nonspecific kind of physiological arousal *and* the labeling of the arousal based on cues from the environment (refer to the bottom part of Figure 9-4).

This is the high, swaying suspension bridge that was used to increase the physiological arousal of male subjects.

The Schachter-Singer theory of emotion has led to some clever experiments in several areas of psychology. For example, psychologists studying the determinants of interpersonal attraction have drawn applications from the theory. In one intriguing and imaginative experiment, an attractive, college-aged woman stood at the end of a swaying 450-foot suspension bridge that spanned a deep canyon. The woman was ostensibly conducting a survey, and she asked men who made it across the bridge a series of questions. She then gave them her telephone number, telling them that if they were interested in the results of the experiment they could contact her in the upcoming week.

In another condition, an attractive woman asked men who had just strolled across a stable bridge spanning a shallow stream 10 feet below to complete the same questionnaire. The results showed significant differences in the nature of the men's responses, depending on which bridge they had crossed. For instance, those who crossed the dangerous bridge showed significantly more sexual imagery in their survey responses than those who had crossed the less hazardous span. Furthermore, those crossing the dangerous span were significantly more likely to call the woman in the upcoming week, suggesting that their attraction to her was higher. The men whose arousal was increased by the dangerous bridge seemed to have searched for a reason for their physiological arousal—and ended up attributing the cause to the attractive woman (Dutton & Aron, 1974). Consistent with the Schachter-Singer theory, then, the men's emotional response was based on a labeling of their arousal.

Unfortunately, evidence gathered to confirm the Schachter-Singer theory has not always been so supportive (Reisenzein, 1983; Leventhal & Tomarken, 1986). Some research suggests that physiological arousal is not always essential for emotional experience to occur, and that physiological factors *by themselves* can account for one's emotional state in other instances (Marshall & Zimbardo, 1979; Chwalisz, Diener, & Gallagher, 1988). Furthermore, recent research suggests that the physiological arousal that accompanies certain emotions in fact may be specific to the emotion (Levinson, 1996).

Still, the Schachter-Singer theory of emotion represents a significant milestone in the study of emotions. The theory paved the way for recent investigations that have focused on the role of appraisal and unexplained physiological arousal. For instance, some work suggests that emotions are produced principally when we evaluate a situation as significant to our personal well-being (Mauro, Sato, & Tucker, 1992; Sinclair et al., 1994).

In sum, the Schachter-Singer theory of emotions is important because of its suggestion that, at least under some circumstances, emotional experiences are a joint function of physiological arousal and the labeling of that arousal. When the source of physiological arousal is unclear, we may look to our surroundings to determine just what it is we are experiencing.

Summing Up the Theories of Emotion

At this point, you have good reason to ask why there are so many theories of emotion and, perhaps even more important, which provides the most complete explanation. Actually, we have only scratched the surface. There are almost as many explanatory theories of emotion as there are individual emotions (e.g., Izard, 1990; Lazarus, 1991b; Oatley, 1992; Ekman & Davidson, 1994; Lazarus & Lazarus, 1994; Omdahl, 1995).

Why are theories of emotion so plentiful? The answer is that emotions are such complex phenomena that no single theory has been able to fully explain all facets of emotional experience. For each of the three major theories there is contradictory evidence of one sort or another, and therefore no theory has proved invariably accurate in its predictions.

PSYCHOLOGY AT WORK

The Truth about Lies: Using Emotional Responses to Separate the Dishonest from the Honest

Aldrich Ames, an employee of the U.S. Central Intelligence Agency, was given a routine lie-detector test twice during the last decade. On both occasions he passed the test. Yet at the same time that his truthfulness was being confirmed by the lie detector, he was allegedly involved in high-level espionage for the Russians.

Ames's case provoked little surprise among researchers who study the validity of lie-detector test results. Repeatedly, lie detectors have been proved to be unreliable indicators of when a person is lying.

A lie detector, or polygraph, is an electronic device designed to expose people who are telling lies. The basic assumption behind the apparatus is straightforward: The autonomic nervous system of people who are not being truthful becomes aroused as their emotionality increases. Polygraphs are designed to detect the physiological changes that are indicative of this arousal.

Actually, a number of separate physiological functions are measured simultaneously by a lie detector, including changes in breathing pattern, heart rate, blood pressure, and sweating. In theory, polygraph operators ask a series of questions, some of which they know will elicit verifiable, truthful responses. For instance, they may ask a person to provide his or her name and address. Then, when more critical questions are answered, operators can observe the nature of the physiological changes that occur. Answers whose accompanying physiological responses deviate significantly from those accompanying truthful responses are assumed to be false (Patrick & Iacono, 1991).

That's the theory, at least. The reality is something different: There is no foolproof technique for assessing the extent of the physiological changes that may indicate a lie. Even truthful responses may elicit physiological arousal if the question is emotion-laden (Waid & Orne, 1982). How many innocent people accused of a murder, for instance, would not respond emotionally when asked whether they committed the crime, since they know that their future may hang in the balance?

One further drawback of lie-detector tests is that people are capable of fooling the polygraph (Barland & Raskin, 1975; Honts, Raskin, & Kircher, 1987). For instance, biofeedback techniques (see Chapter 2) can be employed to produce emotional responses to accompany even truthful statements, meaning that the polygraph operator will be unable to differentiate between honest and dishonest responses. Even biting one's tongue or hiding a tack in a shoe and pressing on it as each question is answered may be sufficient to produce physiological arousal during each response, making truthful and deceptive responses indistinguishable (Honts, Hodes, & Raskin, 1985).

Because of these sources of error, lie-detector operators often make mistakes when trying to judge another person's honesty (Saxe, Dougherty, & Cross, 1985; Iacono, 1991; Saxe, 1994). The American Psychological Association has adopted a resolution stating that the evidence for the effectiveness of polygraphs "is still unsatisfactory" (APA, 1986). Even the major proponent of the use of polygraphs—the American Polygraph Association—admits an error rate between 4 and 13 percent, and critics suggest that research has given the actual rate as closer to 30 percent (Meyer & Macciocchi, 1989). Using such evidence, U.S. federal law bars employers from using polygraphs as screening devices for most jobs (Bales, 1988).

On the other hand, some recent evidence suggests that there may be one source of physiological information that may, in fact, increase the rate of accuracy: event-related brain potentials. Event-related brain potentials reflect tiny changes in electrical voltage that can be measured on a person's scalp. Some researchers have found that changes in event-related potentials occur when a person is being deceptive (Farwell & Donchin, 1991). So far, these results have been obtained solely in laboratory situations, and whether they will prove useful in real-life settings is still open to question (Bashore & Rapp, 1993).

In sum, there are good reasons to doubt that traditional polygraph tests can determine accurately whether someone is lying. Because of skepticism about the validity of lie detectors, many employers have turned instead to written "integrity tests" (Sackett, 1994). Such tests, designed to winnow out potentially honest employees from dishonest ones, have been widely adopted in industry. However, their validity has yet to be established. For now, then, you can be assured that any secrets you may harbor will remain hidden: No one has yet identified a foolproof way to distinguish people who are telling the truth from those who are lying (Saxe, 1994).

On the other hand, this abundance of theoretical approaches to emotions is not a cause for despair—or unhappiness, fear, or any other negative emotion. It simply reflects the fact that psychology is an evolving, developing science. As more evidence is gathered, the specific answers to questions about the nature of emotions will become clearer. Furthermore, even as our understanding of emotions continues to grow, there are ongoing efforts to apply our knowledge of emotions to some practical problems (see the Psychology at Work box on page 305).

RECAP AND REVIEW

Recap

- Emotions are feelings that generally have both a physiological component and a cognitive component.
- Emotions have several functions, including preparing us for action, shaping our future behavior, and regulating social interaction.
- A number of physiological changes accompany strong emotion, including rapid breathing and increased heart rate, opening of the pupils, dryness in the mouth, increase in sweating, and the sensation of hair "standing on end."
- The major theories of emotion are the James-Lange, Cannon-Bard, and Schachter-Singer theories.
- Polygraphs, designed to identify people who are lying on the basis of their physiological reactions, are not dependable.

Review

1. Emotions are always accompanied by a cognitive response. True or false?
2. The _____-_____ theory of emotions states that emotions are responses to instinctive bodily events.
3. Each emotion is accompanied by a unique set of physiological responses, thus proving the James-Lange emotion theory. True or false?
4. According to the _____-_____ theory of emotion, both an emotional response and physiological arousal are produced simultaneously by nerve impulses.
5. Your friend—a psychology major—tells you, "I was at a party last night. During the course of the evening, my general level of arousal increased. Since I was at a party where people were enjoying themselves, I assumed I must have felt happy." What theory of emotion does your friend subscribe to?
6. The _____, or "lie detector," is an instrument used to measure physiological responses associated with answers to questions.

Ask Yourself

Knowing what you do about physiological responses associated with emotions, do you think polygraphs should be used in criminal situations in order to determine a person's guilt or innocence? Should they be used in business to verify the truth of employees' statements on such topics as drug use or to decide hirings and firings?

(Answers to review questions are on page 308.)

- *What is stress, how does it affect us, and how can we best cope with it?*

STRESS AND COPING

It is now 10:26 a.m. Cathy Collins, a Teaneck, New Jersey, wife, mother, and administrative aide in a metropolitan hospital, has already been up for five hours, having left breakfast for her children and taken two buses to reach her tiny, windowless office.

She is standing with a phone cradled on her shoulder, contending with: a patient sitting at her desk, waiting to ask questions; a secretary with a question about another patient's chart; two calls on hold, and a buzzing intercom. On her desk are several forms to be completed, which she attempts to fill out between calls; a stack of paperwork three inches high in her "in" box; and a boss who has just walked out of his office and asked for something to be copied.

At this moment, a mechanism strapped to Cathy's waist and arm measures her blood pressure and heartbeat, finding that both are elevated 25 and 15 percent, respectively, over earlier readings. As it happened, this was not the biggest increase of the day for Collins. (Tierney, 1988)

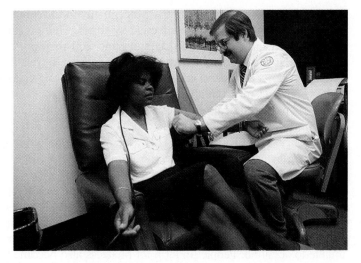

Cathy Collins, a volunteer subject in a study of stress in the workplace, is outfitted with the apparatus that will measure her stress levels.

Because Cathy Collins was participating in a hospital study of stress in the work-place, we know about her internal biological reactions to the events of the moment. And although no measurements were taken of her psychological reactions, few of us would have difficulty in guessing what she would report experiencing during this same period: stress.

Stress: Reacting to Threat and Challenge

Most of us need little introduction to the phenomenon of **stress,** formally defined as the response to events that threaten or challenge a person. Whether it be a pa-per or exam deadline, a family problem, or even a cumulative series of small events such as those faced by Cathy Collins on the job, life is full of circumstances and events, known as *stressors,* that produce threats to our well-being. Even pleas-ant events—such as planning a party or beginning a sought-after job—can pro-duce stress, although negative events result in greater detrimental consequences than positive ones (Sarason, Johnson, & Siegel, 1978; Brown & McGill, 1989).

All of us face stress in our lives. Some health psychologists believe that daily life actually involves a series of repeated sequences of perceiving threats, consid-ering ways to cope with them, and ultimately adapting to the threats, with greater or lesser success (Gatchel & Baum, 1983). Although adaptation is often minor and occurs without our being aware of it, in those cases in which the stress is more severe or longer-lasting, adaptation requires major effort and may produce physiological and psychological responses that result in health problems.

The High Cost of Stress Stress can take its toll in many ways, producing both biological and psychological consequences. Often the most immediate reaction to stress is a biological one. Exposure to stressors induces a rise in certain hormones secreted by the adrenal glands, an increase in heart rate and blood pressure, and changes in how well the skin conducts electrical impulses (Mason, 1975; Selye, 1976). On a short-term basis, these responses may be adaptive because they pro-duce an "emergency reaction," in which the body prepares to defend itself through activation of the sympathetic nervous system (see Chapter 2). These responses may allow more effective coping with the stressful situation.

However, continued exposure to stress results in a decline in the body's over-all level of biological functioning due to the constant secretion of the stress-re-lated hormones. Over time, stressful reactions can promote deterioration of body tissues such as blood vessels and the heart. Ultimately, we become more suscep-tible to disease as our ability to fight off germs is lowered (Kiecolt-Glaser & Glaser, 1986; Schneiderman, 1983; Cohen, Tyrrell, & Smith, 1993).

Stress: The response to events that are threatening or challenging

Psychosomatic (sy ko so MAT ik) **disorders:** Medical problems caused by an interaction of psychological, emotional, and physical difficulties

In addition to major health difficulties, many of the minor aches and pains we experience may be caused or worsened by stress. These include headaches, backaches, skin rashes, indigestion, fatigue, and constipation. Stress has even been linked to the common cold (Brown, 1984; Cohen, Tyrrell, & Smith, 1993).

Furthermore, a whole class of medical problems, known as **psychosomatic disorders,** often result from stress. These medical problems are caused by an interaction of psychological, emotional, and physical difficulties. Among the most common psychosomatic disorders are ulcers, asthma, arthritis, high blood pressure, and eczema (Shorter, 1991). In fact, the likelihood of the onset of any major illness seems to be related to the number and type of stressful events a person experiences (see Table 9-2).

On a psychological level, high levels of stress prevent people from coping with life adequately. Their view of the environment can become clouded (e.g., a minor criticism made by a friend is blown out of proportion). Moreover, at the greatest levels of stress, emotional responses may be so extreme that people are unable to act at all. People under a lot of stress also become less able to deal with new stressors. The ability to contend with future stress, then, declines as a result of past stress (Eckenrode, 1984; Glaser & Kiecolt-Glaser, 1994; Avison & Gotlib, 1994).

General adaptation syndrome (GAS): A theory developed by Selye that suggests that a person's response to stress consists of three stages: alarm and mobilization, resistance, and exhaustion

The General Adaptation Syndrome Model: The Course of Stress   The effects of stress are best illustrated by a model developed by Hans Selye (pronounced "sell-yea"), a major stress theorist (Selye, 1976). This model, the **general adaptation syndrome (GAS),** suggests that the same set of physiological reactions to stress occurs regardless of the particular cause of stress.

As shown in Figure 9-5, the model has three phases. The first stage, the *alarm and mobilization stage,* occurs when people become aware of the presence of a stressor. Suppose, for instance, you learned at the end of the first term of college that you were on academic probation because of your low grades. You would be likely to respond first with alarm, feeling concerned and upset. Subsequently, though, you would probably begin to mobilize your efforts, making plans and promises to yourself to study harder for the rest of the school year.

On a physiological level, the sympathetic nervous system is energized during the alarm and mobilization phase. Prolonged activation of this system may lead

FIGURE 9-5 The general adaptation syndrome suggests that there can be three major stages in people's response to stress. *(Selye, 1976.)*

Stressor

Alarm and mobilization
Meeting and resisting stressor.

Resistance
Coping with stress and resistance to stressor.

Exhaustion
Negative consequences of stress (such as illness) occur when coping is inadequate.

ANSWERS TO PREVIOUS REVIEW
1. False; emotions may occur without a cognitive response.   **2.** James-Lange   **3.** False; a wide number of emotions are related to similar bodily reactions.   **4.** Cannon-Bard
5. Schachter-Singer   **6.** polygraph

TABLE 9-2   **Predicting the Illness of the Future from the Stress of the Past**

Is there a stress-related illness in your future? Survey research has shown that the nature and number of stressors in a person's life is associated with the experience of a major illness (Rahe & Arthur, 1978).

To find out the degree of stress in your life, take the stressor value given beside each event you have experienced and multiply it by the number of occurrences over the past year (up to a maximum of four). Then add up these scores.

87 Experienced the death of a spouse
77 Married
77 Experienced the death of a close family member
76 Were divorced
74 Experienced a marital separation
68 Experienced the death of a close friend
68 Experienced pregnancy or fathered a pregnancy
65 Had a major personal injury or illness
62 Were fired from work
60 Ended a marital engagement or a steady relationship
58 Had sexual difficulties
58 Experienced a marital reconciliation
57 Had a major change in self-concept or self-awareness
56 Experienced a major change in the health or behavior of a family member
54 Became engaged to be married
53 Had a major change in financial status
52 Took on a mortgage or loan of less than $10,000
52 Had a major change in use of drugs
50 Had a major conflict or change in values
50 Had a major change in the number of arguments with your spouse
50 Gained a new family member
50 Entered college
50 Changed to a new school
50 Changed to a different line of work
49 Had a major change in amount of independence and responsibility
47 Had a major change in responsibilities at work
46 Experienced a major change in use of alcohol
45 Revised personal habits
44 Had trouble with school administration
43 Held a job while attending school
43 Had a major change in social activities
42 Had trouble with in-laws
42 Had a major change in working hours or conditions
42 Changed residence or living conditions
41 Had your spouse begin or cease work outside the home
41 Changed your choice of major field of study
41 Changed dating habits
40 Had an outstanding personal achievement
38 Had trouble with your boss
38 Had a major change in amount of participation in school activities
37 Had a major change in type and/or amount of recreation
36 Had a major change in religious activities
34 Had a major change of sleeping habits
33 Took a trip or vacation
30 Had a major change in eating habits
26 Had a major change in the number of family get-togethers
22 Were found guilty of minor violations of the law

Scoring   If your total score is above 1435, you are in a high-stress category, which, according to Marx, Garrity, and Bowers (1975), puts you at risk for experiencing a stress-related illness in the future. On the other hand, you should not assume that a high score destines you to a future illness. Because the research on stress and illness is correlational, major stressful events are best viewed as associated with illness—but they may not be its cause. Moreover, some research suggests that future illness is better predicted by the daily, ongoing hassles of life, rather than by the major events depicted in the questionnaire (Lazarus et al., 1985). Still, a high level of stressful events in one's life is a cause for concern, and so it makes sense to take measures to reduce stress (Marx, Garrity, & Bowers, 1975, p. 97; Maddi, Barone, & Puccetti, 1987; Crandall, 1992).

to problems of the blood circulatory system or stomach ulcers, and the body may become vulnerable to a host of diseases.

If the stressor persists, people move into the next stage of the model. In the *resistance stage,* people prepare themselves to fight the stressor. During resistance, people use various means to cope with the stressor—sometimes successfully—but at a cost of some degree of physical or psychological general well-being. For instance, in the case of your being placed on academic probation, resistance might take the form of devoting long hours to studying. You may ultimately be successful in raising your grades, but this achievement may come at the expense of a loss of sleep and hours of worry.

If resistance is not adequate, the last stage of the model, the *exhaustion stage,* is reached. During the exhaustion stage, a person's ability to adapt to the stressor declines to the point where negative consequences of stress appear: physical illness, psychological symptoms in the form of an inability to concentrate, heightened irritability, or, in severe instances, disorientation and a loss of touch with reality. In a sense, people wear out. For instance, if you become overwhelmed by pressure to perform well in your courses, you may get sick or find it impossible to study altogether.

Of course, not everyone reaches the exhaustion stage. If people can resist a stressor in the second stage, their physical resources are not drained and they can bounce back, thereby avoiding exhaustion.

How do people get beyond the third stage after they have entered it? In some cases, exhaustion allows people to avoid the stressor. For example, people who become ill from overwork may be excused from their duties for a time, thereby giving them a temporary respite from their responsibilities. At least for a time, then, the immediate stress is reduced.

The GAS model has had a substantial impact on our understanding of stress. By suggesting that the exhaustion of resources in the third stage of the model produces physiological damage, it has provided a specific explanation of how stress can lead to illness. Furthermore, the model can be applied to both people and nonhuman species.

On the other hand, some aspects of the GAS model have been questioned. One of the most important criticisms is directed at the theory's supposition about the sympathetic division's emergency reaction, activated during the alarm and mobilization phase. The theory proposes that the reaction is basically the same, regardless of the kind of stressor to which a person is exposed. However, some critics argue that certain stressors produce distinct physiological reactions, such as the secretion of specific hormones. Hence, stress reactions may be less similar to one another than the GAS implies (Mason, 1974; Hobfoll, 1989).

Furthermore, the model's reliance on physiological factors leaves little room for attention to psychological factors, particularly in terms of the way in which stressors are appraised differently by different people (Mikhail, 1981). Still, the model provides a basis for our understanding of stress.

The Nature of Stressors: My Stress Is Your Pleasure   As noted above, the general adaptation syndrome model is useful in explaining how people respond to stress, but it is not specific about what constitutes a stressor for a given person. Although certain kinds of events, such as the death of a loved one or participation in combat during a war, are universally stressful, other situations may or may not be stressful to a particular person (Fleming, Baum, & Singer, 1984; Lazarus & Cohen, 1977; Affleck et al., 1994).

Consider, for instance, bungee jumping. Some of us would find jumping off a bridge attached to a slender rubber tether to be extremely stressful. However, there are those who see such an activity as challenging and fun-filled. Whether or not bungee jumping is stressful depends in part, then, on individual perceptions of the activity.

For people to consider an event to be stressful, they must perceive it as threatening and must lack the resources to deal with it effectively (Folkman et al., 1986). Consequently, the same event may at times be stressful and at other times provoke no stressful reaction at all. For instance, a young man might experience stress when he is turned down for a date—if he attributes the refusal to his unattractiveness or unworthiness. But if he attributes it to some factor unrelated to his self-esteem, such as a previous commitment of the woman he asked, the experience of being refused might create no stress at all. Hence, cognitive factors relating to our interpretation of events play an important role in the determination of what is stressful.

A number of other variables also influence the severity of stress. For example, stress is greater when the importance and number of goals that are threatened are high, when the threat is immediate, or when the anticipation of the threatening event extends over a long period (Paterson & Neufeld, 1987).

Categorizing Stressors   What kinds of events tend to be seen as stressful? There are three general classes of events: cataclysmic events, personal stressors, and background stressors (Gatchel & Baum, 1983; Lazarus & Cohen, 1977).

Cataclysmic events are strong stressors that occur suddenly and affect many people simultaneously. Disasters such as tornadoes and plane crashes are examples of cataclysmic events that can affect hundreds or thousands of people simultaneously.

Cataclysmic events: Strong stressors that occur suddenly, affecting many people at once (e.g., natural disasters)

Although it might seem that cataclysmic events would produce potent, lingering stress, this is typically not the case. Such events are often less stressful in the long run than events that are initially less intense. One reason is that such events have a clear resolution. Once they are over and done with, people can look forward to the future knowing that the worst is behind them. Moreover, the stress induced by cataclysmic events is shared by others who have also experienced the disaster. This permits people to offer one another social support and a firsthand understanding of the difficulties the others are going through (Cummings, 1987; Pennebaker & Harber, 1993).

On the other hand, some victims of major catastrophes can experience **posttraumatic stress disorder,** or **PTSD,** in which the original events and the feelings associated with them are reexperienced in vivid flashbacks or dreams. Depending upon what statistics one employs, between 5 and 60 percent of the veterans of the Vietnam War suffer from PTSD. Even the Persian Gulf War, which ended quickly, produced the condition (Hobfoll et al., 1991; Sutker et al., 1993). Furthermore, those who have suffered child abuse or rape, rescue workers facing overwhelming situations, or victims of any sudden natural disaster or accident that produces feelings of helplessness and terror may suffer from the same disorder.

Posttraumatic stress disorder (PTSD): A phenomenon in which victims of major catastrophes reexperience the original stress event and associated feelings in vivid flashbacks or dreams

Symptoms of posttraumatic stress disorder include sleep difficulties, problems in relating to others, alcohol and drug abuse, and—in some cases—suicide. For instance, the suicide rate for Vietnam veterans is as much as 25 percent higher than for the general population (Pollock et al., 1990; Peterson, Prout, & Schwarz, 1991).

The second major category of stressor is that of personal stressor. **Personal stressors** include major life events such as the death of a parent or spouse, the loss of one's job, a major personal failure, or the diagnosis of a life-threatening illness. Typically, a personal stressor produces an immediate major reaction that soon tapers off. For example, stress arising from the death of a loved one tends to be greatest just after the time of death, but people begin to feel less stress and are better able to cope with the loss after the passage of time.

Personal stressors: Major life events, such as the death of a family member, that have immediate negative consequences which generally fade with time

In some cases, though, the effects of stress linger. Victims of rape sometimes suffer consequences long after the event, facing major difficulties in adjustment. Similarly, the malfunction of the Three Mile Island nuclear plant in Pennsylvania

Background stressors: Daily hassles, such as being stuck in traffic, that cause minor irritations but have no long-term ill effects, unless they continue or are compounded by other stressful events

Daily hassles: see Background stressors

in the early 1980s, which exposed people to the stressor of a potential nuclear meltdown, produced emotional, behavioral, and physiological consequences that lasted more than a year and a half (Baum, Gatchel, & Schaeffer, 1983).

Standing in a long line at a bank and getting stuck in a traffic jam are examples of the third major category of stressor: **background stressors,** or, more informally, **daily hassles** (Lazarus & Cohen, 1977). These stressors represent the minor irritations of life that we all face time and time again: delays, noisy cars and trucks, broken appliances, other people's irritating behavior, and so on. Another type of background stressor is a long-term, chronic problem such as being dissatisfied with school or job, being in an unhappy relationship, or living in crowded quarters without privacy.

By themselves, daily hassles do not require much coping or even responses on the part of the individual, although they certainly do produce unpleasant emotions and moods (Clark & Watson, 1988). Yet daily hassles add up—and ultimately they may produce as great a toll as a single, more stressful incident. In fact, there is an association between the number of daily hassles that people face and the number of psychological symptoms they report (Kanner et al., 1981; Zika & Chamberlain, 1987; Chamberlain & Zika, 1990). Even health problems (such as flu, sore throat, headaches, and backaches) have been linked to daily hassles (DeLongis, Folkman, & Lazarus, 1988; Jones, Brantley, & Gilchrist, 1988; Kohn, Lafreniere, & Gurevich, 1991).

Although the nature of daily hassles differs from day to day and from person to person, background stressors do have certain characteristics in common. One critical factor is related to the degree of control people have over aversive, unpleasant stimuli in the environment (Burger, 1992). When people feel they can control a situation and determine its outcome, stress reactions are reduced considerably. For instance, people exposed to high levels of noise suffer fewer adverse effects if they know they are able to control the noise than those exposed to the same amount of noise who are unable to control its intensity and duration (Glass & Singer, 1972).

Uplifts: Minor positive events that make one feel good

The flip side of hassles are **uplifts,** those minor positive events that make one feel good—even if only temporarily. As indicated in Figure 9-6, uplifts range from relating well to a companion to finding one's surroundings pleasing. What

The daily hassles of life, such as being required to wait in a long line, are minor stressors, but when they accumulate they can take a severe toll on a person's physical and psychological health.

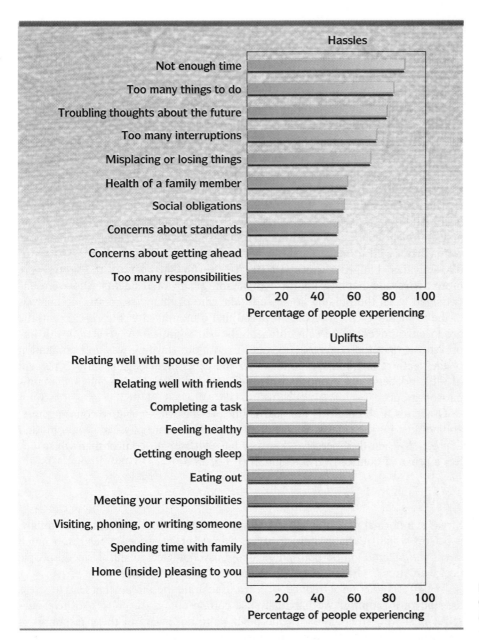

Hassles

Not enough time
Too many things to do
Troubling thoughts about the future
Too many interruptions
Misplacing or losing things
Health of a family member
Social obligations
Concerns about standards
Concerns about getting ahead
Too many responsibilities

0 20 40 60 80 100
Percentage of people experiencing

Uplifts

Relating well with spouse or lover
Relating well with friends
Completing a task
Feeling healthy
Getting enough sleep
Eating out
Meeting your responsibilities
Visiting, phoning, or writing someone
Spending time with family
Home (inside) pleasing to you

0 20 40 60 80 100
Percentage of people experiencing

FIGURE 9-6 The most common everyday hassles and uplifts. *(Hassles: Chamberlain & Zika, 1990; uplifts: Kanner et al., 1981.)*

is especially intriguing about these uplifts is that they are associated with people's psychological health in just the opposite way that hassles are: The greater the number of uplifts experienced, the fewer the psychological symptoms people later report.

Learned Helplessness   You've probably heard someone complaining about an intolerable situation that he couldn't seem to resolve, saying that he was tired of "hitting his head against the wall" and was giving up and accepting things the way they were. This example illustrates one of the possible consequences of being in an environment in which control over a situation is not possible—a state that produces learned helplessness. According to psychologist Martin Seligman, *learned helplessness* occurs when people conclude that unpleasant or aversive stimuli cannot be controlled—a view of the world that becomes so ingrained that they do not try to remedy the aversive circumstances, even if they actually can ex-

ert some influence (Seligman, 1975). Victims of the phenomenon of learned helplessness have decided that there is no link between the responses they make and the outcomes that occur.

Take, for example, what often happens to the elderly when they are placed in nursing homes or hospitals. One of the most striking features of their new environment is that they are no longer independent: They do not have control over the most basic activities in their lives. They are told what and when to eat, and told when they may watch TV or participate in recreational activities. In addition, their sleeping schedules are arranged by someone else. It is not hard to see how this loss of control can have negative effects upon people suddenly placed, often reluctantly, in such a situation.

The results of this loss of control and the ensuing stress are frequently poorer health and even a likelihood of earlier death. These outcomes were confirmed in an experiment conducted in a nursing home where elderly residents in one group were encouraged to make more choices and take greater control of their day-to-day activities (Langer & Janis, 1979). As a result, members of the group were more active and happier than a comparison group of residents who were encouraged to let the nursing home staff take care of them. Moreover, an analysis of the residents' medical records revealed that 6 months after the experiment, the group encouraged to be self-sufficient showed significantly greater health improvement than the comparison group. Even more startling was an examination of the death rate: Eighteen months after the experiment began, only 15 percent of the "independent" group had died—compared with 30 percent of the comparison group.

Other research confirms that learned helplessness has negative consequences, and not just for the elderly. People of all ages report more physical symptoms and depression when they perceive that they have little or no control than when they feel a sense of control over a situation (Peterson & Raps, 1984; Rodin, 1986).

Coping with Stress

Stress is a normal part of living. As Hans Selye has noted, to avoid stress totally, a person would probably have to cease living. Yet, as we have seen, too much stress can take its toll on both physical and psychological health. How do people deal with stress? Is there a way to reduce its negative effects?

The efforts to control, reduce, or learn to tolerate the threats that lead to stress are known as **coping.** We habitually use certain coping responses to help ourselves deal with stress. Most of the time, we're not aware of these responses—just as we may be unaware of the minor stressors of life until they build up to sufficiently aversive levels.

One means of dealing with stress that occurs on an unconscious level is the use of defense mechanisms. As we will discuss in Chapter 11, **defense mechanisms** are unconscious strategies that maintain a person's sense of control and self-worth by distorting or denying the actual nature of the situation. For example, one study examined California students who lived in dormitories close to a geological fault. Those who lived in dorms that were rated as being unlikely to withstand an earthquake were significantly more likely to doubt experts' predictions of an impending earthquake than those who lived in safer structures (Lehman & Taylor, 1988).

Another defense mechanism used to cope with stress is *emotional insulation,* in which a person stops experiencing any emotions at all, thereby remaining unaffected and unmoved by both positive and negative experiences. The problem with defense mechanisms, of course, is that they do not deal with reality but merely hide the problem.

People also use other, more direct and potentially more positive means for coping with stress (Aldwin & Revenson, 1987; Compas, 1987; Miller, Brody,

Coping: The efforts to control, reduce, or learn to tolerate the threats that lead to stress

Defense mechanisms: Unconscious strategies people use to reduce anxiety by concealing its source from themselves and others

& Summerton, 1988). Specifically, coping strategies fall into two categories: emotion-focused coping and problem-focused coping. *Emotion-focused coping* is characterized by the conscious regulation of emotions. Examples of emotion-focused coping include such strategies as accepting sympathy from others or looking at the bright side of a situation. In contrast, *problem-focused coping* attempts to manage the stressful problem or stimulus. Problem-focused strategies are intended to get the person who is experiencing stress to change his or her behavior, or to develop a plan of action to deal with the stress and follow it. Starting a study group to improve poor classroom performance is an example of problem-focused coping.

In most stressful incidents, people employ *both* emotion-focused and problem-focused strategies. However, they use emotion-focused strategies more frequently when they perceive circumstances as being unchangeable, and problem-focused approaches more often in situations they see as relatively modifiable (Folkman & Lazarus, 1980, 1988).

Coping Style: The Hardy Personality   Most of us cope with stress in a characteristic manner, employing a "coping style" that represents our general tendency to deal with stress in a specific way. For example, you may know people who habitually react to even the smallest amount of stress with hysteria, and others who calmly confront even the greatest stress in an unflappable manner. These kinds of people clearly have quite different coping styles (Taylor, 1991).

Among those who cope with stress most successfully are people with a coping style that has come to be called "hardiness." **Hardiness** is a personality characteristic associated with a lower rate of stress-related illness. It consists of three components: commitment, challenge, and control (Kobasa, 1979; Gentry & Kobasa, 1984).

Commitment is a tendency to throw ourselves into whatever we are doing with a sense that our activities are important and meaningful. Hardy people are also high in a sense of challenge, the second component; they believe that change, rather than stability, is the standard condition of life. To them, the anticipation of change serves as an incentive rather than a threat to their security. Finally, hardiness is marked by a sense of control—the perception that people can influence the events in their lives.

Hardiness seems to act as a buffer against stress-related illness. The hardy individual approaches stress in an optimistic manner and is apt to take direct action to learn about and deal with stressors, thereby changing stressful events into less threatening ones. As a consequence, a person with a hardy personality style is less likely to suffer the negative outcomes of high stress (Wiebe, 1991).

Hardiness: A personality characteristic associated with a lower rate of stress-related illness, consisting of three components: commitment, challenge, and control

The Informed Consumer of Psychology

Effective Coping Strategies

How does one cope most effectively with stress? Researchers have made a number of recommendations for dealing with the problem. There is no universal solution, of course, since effective coping depends on the nature of the stressor and the degree to which control is possible. Still, some general guidelines can be followed (Folkman, 1984; Everly, 1989; Holahan & Moos, 1987, 1990):

■   *Turning threat into challenge.* When a stressful situation might be controllable, the best coping strategy is to treat the situation as a challenge, focusing on ways to control it. For instance, if you experience stress because your car is al-

ways breaking down, you might take an evening course in auto mechanics and learn to deal directly with the car's problems. Even if the repairs prove too difficult to do yourself, at least you'll be in a better position to understand what's wrong.

■ *Making a threatening situation less threatening.* When a stressful situation seems to be uncontrollable, a different approach must be taken. It is possible to change one's appraisal of the situation, to view it in a different light, and to modify one's attitudes toward it (Smith & Ellsworth, 1987). The old truism "Look for the silver lining in every cloud" seems to be supported by research findings that show that people who discover something good in negative situations show less distress and better coping ability than those who do not (Silver & Wortman, 1980).

■ *Changing one's goals.* When a person is faced with an uncontrollable situation, another reasonable strategy is to adopt new goals that are practical in view of the particular situation. For example, a dancer who has been in an automobile accident and has lost full use of her legs may no longer aspire to a career in dance, but might modify her goals and try to become a dance instructor. Similarly, an executive who has lost his job may change his goal of becoming wealthy to that of obtaining a more modest, but secure, source of income.

■ *Taking physical action.* Another approach to coping with stress is to bring about changes in one's physiological reactions to it. For example, biofeedback, discussed in Chapter 2, can alter basic physiological processes, allowing people to reduce blood pressure, heart rate, and other consequences of heightened stress. In addition, exercise can be effective in reducing stress in several ways. For one thing, regular exercise reduces heart rate, respiration rate, and blood pressure (although these responses temporarily increase during exercise periods). Furthermore, exercise gives people a sense of control over their bodies, as well as a feeling of accomplishment (J. D. Brown, 1991).

Finally, sometimes a change in diet is helpful in coping with stress. For instance, people who drink large quantities of caffeine are susceptible to feeling jittery and anxious; simply decreasing the amount of caffeine they consume may be sufficient to reduce the experience of stress. Similarly, being overweight may itself be a stressor, and losing excess weight may be an effective measure for reducing stress—unless dieting itself becomes stressful.

■ *Preparing for stress before it happens.* A final strategy for coping with stress is *inoculation*: preparing for stress *before* it is encountered. First developed as a means of preventing postsurgical emotional problems among hospital patients, inoculation methods prepare people for stressful experiences—of either a physical or an emotional nature—by explaining, in as much detail as possible, the difficult events they are likely to encounter. As part of the process, people are asked to imagine how they will feel about the circumstances and to consider various ways of dealing with their reactions—all before the experiences have actually occurred. Probably the most crucial element, however, is providing individuals with clear, objective strategies for handling the situations, rather than simply telling them what to expect (Janis, 1984).

When carried out properly, inoculation works. People who have received inoculation treatments prior to facing stressful events cope more effectively with their situations than those who have not (Ludwick-Rosenthal & Neufeld, 1988; Register et al., 1991).

RECAP AND REVIEW

Recap

• Stress is the response to events that threaten an individual's ability to deal adequately with the situation.

• According to Selye's general adaptation syndrome model, stress follows three stages: alarm and mobilization, resistance, and exhaustion.

- The specific nature of stressors varies from person to person; what is stressful for one person may be invigorating to another. There are three general categories of stressors: cataclysmic events, personal stressors, and background stressors (or daily hassles).
- Perceptions of control typically reduce stress. In some instances, though, learned helplessness occurs—people perceive that aversive stimuli cannot be controlled.
- Coping devices may take the form of adopting defense mechanisms, turning threat into challenge, reducing the perception of threat, changing goals, taking physical action, or preparing for stress through inoculation.

Review

1. _____ is defined as a response to challenging or threatening events.
2. Match each portion of the GAS with its definition:
   1. Alarm
   2. Exhaustion
   3. Resistance

   a. Ability to adapt to stress diminishes; symptoms appear
   b. Activation of sympathetic nervous system
   c. Various strategies used to cope with a stressor

3. _____ _____ _____ occurs when the feelings associated with stressful events are relived after the event is over.
4. Stressors that affect a single person and produce an immediate major reaction are known as:
   a. Personal stressors
   b. Psychic stressors
   c. Cataclysmic stressors
   d. Daily stressors
5. Efforts to reduce or eliminate stress are known as _coping_.
6. People who exercise the personality characteristic of _____ seem to be more able to successfully combat stressors.

Ask Yourself

Given what you know about coping strategies related to stress, how would you go about training people to successfully avoid stress in their everyday lives? How would you use this information with a group of Gulf War veterans suffering from post-traumatic stress disorder?

(Answers to review questions are on page 319.)

LOOKING BACK

How does motivation direct and energize behavior?

1. The topic of motivation considers the factors that direct and energize behavior. Drive is the motivational tension that energizes behavior in order to fulfill a need. Primary drives relate to basic biological needs. Secondary drives are those in which no obvious biological need is fulfilled.

2. Motivational drives often operate under the principle of homeostasis, by which an organism tries to maintain an optimal level of internal biological functioning by making up for any deviations from its usual state.

3. A number of broad approaches to motivation move beyond explanations that rely on instincts. Drive-reduction approaches, though useful for primary drives, are inadequate for explaining behavior in which the goal is not to reduce a drive but to maintain or even increase excitement or arousal. In contrast, arousal approaches suggest that we try to maintain a particular level of stimulation and activity.

4. An alternative explanation of motivation—incentive approaches—focuses on the aspects of the environment that direct and energize behavior. Finally, cognitive approaches to motivation focus on the role of thoughts, expectations, and understanding of the world. One cognitive theory—expectancy-value theory—suggests that expectations that a behavior will accomplish a particular goal and our understanding of the value of that goal underlie behavior.

5. Maslow's hierarchy of needs suggests that there are five needs: physiological, safety, love and belongingness, esteem, and self-actualization. Only after the more basic needs are fulfilled is a person able to move toward higher-order needs.

What are the biological and social factors that underlie hunger?

6. Eating behavior is subject to homeostasis, since most people's weight stays within a relatively stable range. Organisms tend to be sensitive to the nutritional value of the food they eat, with the brain's hypothalamus being central to the regulation of food intake.

7. Social factors also play a role in the regulation of eating. For instance, mealtimes, cultural food preferences, the attractiveness of food, and other learned habits determine when and how much one eats. An oversensitivity to social cues and an insensitivity to internal cues may also be related to obesity. In addition, obesity may be caused by an unusually high weight set point—the weight at which the body attempts to maintain homeostasis—or by the rate of metabolism.

Why, and under what circumstances, do we become sexually aroused?

8. Although biological factors, such as the presence of androgens (male sex hormones) and estrogens and progesterone (female sex hormones) prime people for sex, almost any kind of stimulus can produce sexual arousal, depending on a person's prior experience. Fantasies are also important in producing arousal.

317

How do people behave sexually?

9. Masturbation is sexual self-stimulation. The frequency of masturbation is high, particularly for males. Although attitudes toward masturbation have become more liberal, they are still somewhat negative—even though no negative consequences regarding the act have been detected.

10. Heterosexuality, or the sexual attraction to members of the opposite sex, is the most common sexual orientation. In terms of premarital sex, the double standard, in which premarital sex is thought to be more permissible for men than for women, has declined, particularly among young people.

11. Homosexuals are sexually attracted to members of their own sex; bisexuals are sexually attracted to people of the same and the opposite sex. No explanation for why people become homosexual has been confirmed; among the possibilities are genetic or biological factors, childhood and family influences, and prior learning experiences and conditioning. What is clear is that there is no relationship between psychological adjustment and sexual preference.

How are needs relating to achievement, affiliation, and power motivation exhibited?

12. Need for achievement refers to the stable, learned characteristic in which a person strives to attain a level of excellence. People high in the need for achievement tend to seek out tasks that are of moderate difficulty, while those low in the need for achievement seek out only very easy and very difficult tasks. Need for achievement is usually measured through the Thematic Apperception Test (TAT), a series of pictures about which a person writes a story.

13. The need for affiliation is a concern with establishing and maintaining relationships with others, whereas the need for power is a tendency to seek to exert an impact on others.

What are emotions, and how do we experience them?

14. One broad definition of emotions views them as feelings that may affect behavior and generally have both a physiological and a cognitive component. What this definition does not do is address the issue of whether there are separate systems that govern cognitive and emotional responses, and whether one has primacy over the other.

What are the functions of emotions?

15. Among the functions of emotions are to prepare us for action, shape future behavior through learning, and help to regulate social interaction. Although the range of emotions is wide, according to one category system there are only eight primary emotions: joy, acceptance, fear, surprise, sadness, disgust, anger, and anticipation.

16. Among the general physiological responses to strong emotion are opening of the pupils, dryness of the mouth, and increases in sweating, rate of breathing, heart rate, and blood pressure. Because these physiological changes are not the full explanation of emotional experience, a number of distinct theories of emotion have been developed.

17. The James-Lange theory suggests that emotional experience is a reaction to bodily, or visceral, changes that occur as a response to an environmental event. These visceral experiences are interpreted as emotional responses. In contrast to the James-Lange theory, the Cannon-Bard theory contends that visceral movements are too slow to explain rapid shifts of emotion and visceral changes do not always produce emotions. Instead, the Cannon-Bard theory suggests that both physiological arousal *and* an emotional experience are produced simultaneously by the same nerve impulse. Therefore, the visceral experience itself does not necessarily differ among differing emotions.

18. The third explanation, the Schachter-Singer theory, rejects the view that the physiological and emotional responses are simultaneous. Instead, it suggests that emotions are determined jointly by relatively nonspecific physiological arousals and the subsequent labeling of those arousals. This labeling process uses cues from the environment to determine how others are behaving in the same situation.

What is stress, how does it affect us, and how can we best cope with it?

19. Stress is a response to threatening or challenging environmental conditions. People's lives are filled with stressors—the circumstances that produce stress—of both a positive and negative nature.

20. Stress produces immediate physiological reactions, including a rise in hormonal secretions, heart-rate and blood-pressure elevations, and changes in the electrical conductance of the skin. In the short term, these reactions may be adaptive, but in the long term they may have negative consequences, including the development of psychosomatic disorders. The consequences of stress can be explained in part by Selye's general adaptation syndrome (GAS), which suggests there are three stages to stress responses: alarm and mobilization, resistance, and exhaustion.

21. Stress factors are not universal—the way an environmental circumstance is interpreted affects whether it will be considered stressful. Still, there are general classes of events that tend to provoke stress: cataclysmic events, personal stressors, and background stressors, or daily hassles. Stress is reduced by the presence of uplifts, minor positive events that make people feel good—even if only temporarily.

22. Stress can be reduced by developing a sense of control over one's circumstances. In some cases, however, people develop a state of learned helplessness—a response to an uncontrollable situation that produces the feeling that no behavior will be effective in changing the situation; therefore no response is even attempted. Coping with stress can take a number of forms, including the unconscious use of defense mechanisms and the use of emotion-focused or problem-focused coping strategies.

KEY TERMS AND CONCEPTS

motivation (p. 275)

instinct approach to motivation (p. 276)

drive-reduction approach to motivation (p. 277)

drive (p. 277)

homeostasis (p. 277)

arousal approach to motivation (p. 278)

incentive approach to motivation (p. 280)

cognitive approach to motivation (p. 280)

intrinsic motivation (p. 280)

extrinsic motivation (p. 280)

self-actualization (p. 281)

obesity (p. 283)

weight set point (p. 285)

metabolism (p. 285)

anorexia nervosa (p. 287)

bulimia (p. 287)

genitals (p. 287)

androgens (p. 288)

estrogen (p. 288)

progesterone (p. 288)

ovulation (p. 288)

masturbation (p. 289)

heterosexuality (p. 289)

double standard (p. 290)

homosexuals (p. 291)

bisexuals (p. 291)

need for achievement (p. 293)

need for affiliation (p. 295)

need for power (p. 295)

emotions (p. 297)

James-Lange theory of emotion (p. 301)

Cannon-Bard theory of emotion (p. 302)

Schachter-Singer theory of emotion (p. 303)

stress (p. 307)

psychosomatic disorders (p. 308)

general adaptation syndrome (GAS) (p. 308)

cataclysmic events (p. 311)

posttraumatic stress disorder (PTSD) (p. 311)

personal stressors (p. 311)

background stressors (p. 312)

daily hassles (p. 312)

uplifts (p. 312)

coping (p. 314)

defense mechanisms (p. 314)

hardiness (p. 315)

ANSWERS TO PREVIOUS REVIEW

1. Stress **2.** 1-b; 2-a; 3-c **3.** Posttraumatic stress disorder **4.** a **5.** coping **6.** hardiness

CHAPTER 10
DEVELOPMENT

Against the Odds: Jamel Oeser-Sweat

Seventeen-year-old Jamel Oeser-Sweat has completed the requirements for Eagle Scout. He's president of a youth program called Supportive Children's Advocacy Network. He tutors elementary-school children twice a week. And he was named one of the 40 finalists in the Westinghouse Science Talent Search, out of some 1600 entrants.

Jamel Oeser-Sweat tutors a young girl.

Oeser-Sweat's achievements are impressive. What makes them truly remarkable, however, are the circumstances under which he accomplished so much.

For when Oeser-Sweat makes his way home each day, he must walk past prostitutes and drug dealers, who call out "What do you want? What do you want?" To reach his family's apartment, located in a public housing project, he sometimes must stand on his toes in the elevator to avoid stepping in puddles of urine.

Actually, the locale is a step up from his previous home: a grimy residence for the homeless, at which he can recall shootings in the lobby and drug addicts offering their underwear for sale.

Other aspects of his childhood were no less disadvantageous. His father died of cancer while he was a toddler, and at one point his mother was hospitalized because of psychological difficulties. During that period, he was placed in a group home for boys, while his younger brothers were placed in foster care.

Yet Oeser-Sweat not only managed to survive, but to thrive. Today, when he gets a call at his apartment on the newly installed telephone, it is quite likely to be a college recruiter. Both Harvard and Yale have urged him to apply. Although his grades and SAT scores are somewhat lower than those of the typical applicant to Ivy League schools, he thinks he has another quality that might compensate. "I think my biggest selling point is that I can endure through things." (Purdy, 1994, p. 36)

LOOKING AHEAD

What is the secret of Jamel Oeser-Sweat's endurance? How did he overcome a difficult social environment of the sort that waylays many others? What permitted him to achieve so much when the odds were so clearly stacked against him?

Oeser-Sweat's remarkable success story raises one of the most fundamental questions facing psychologists: How do hereditary and environmental factors interact to produce a unique individual? This question, among others, falls within the domain of developmental psychology.

Developmental psychology is the branch of psychology that studies the patterns of growth and change occurring throughout life. In large part, developmental psychologists study the interactions between the unfolding of biologically predetermined patterns of behavior and a constantly changing, dynamic environment. They ask how our genetic background affects our behavior throughout our lives, whether our potential is limited by heredity, and how our built-in biological programming affects our day-to-day development. Similarly, they are committed to understanding the way in which the environment works with—or against—our genetic capabilities, how the world we live in affects our development, and how we can be encouraged to develop our full potential.

Developmental psychology: The branch of psychology that studies people's growth and change over the lifespan

More than other psychologists, developmental psychologists consider the day-to-day patterns and changes in behavior that occur across the lifespan. In this chapter we will examine aspects of development during the entire lifespan, beginning with birth, moving through childhood and adolescence, and ending with adulthood, old age, and death.

We begin our discussion of development by examining the approaches that

have been used to understand and delineate the environmental and genetic factors that direct a person's development. Then we consider the very start of development, beginning with conception and the nine months of life prior to birth. We describe both genetic and environmental influences on the unborn individual, and explain how these can affect behavior throughout the life cycle.

Next, we examine the physical and perceptual developments that occur after birth, witnessing the enormous and rapid growth that takes place during the early stages of life. We also focus on the developing child's social world, indicating what draws the child into relationships with others and membership in society. We discuss cognitive growth during infancy and childhood, tracing changes in the way children think about the world.

We then examine development from adolescence through young adulthood, middle age, and old age. Our discussion of adolescence focuses on some of the major physical, emotional, and cognitive changes that occur during this transition from childhood to adulthood. Next, we consider early and middle adulthood, stages in which people are at the peak of their physical and intellectual abilities. We discuss the developmental changes people undergo during these periods and their relationship to work, families, and living patterns. Finally, in our discussion of old age, we examine the kinds of physical, intellectual, and social changes that occur as a consequence of the aging process, and see that aging may bring about both improvements and declines in various kinds of functioning. We end with a discussion of the ways in which people prepare themselves for death.

- *How do psychologists study the degree to which development is a joint function of hereditary and environmental factors?*
- *What is the nature of development prior to birth?*
- *What factors affect a child during the mother's pregnancy?*

NATURE AND NURTURE: A FUNDAMENTAL DEVELOPMENTAL ISSUE

How many bald, six-foot-six, 250-pound volunteer fire fighters are there in New Jersey who have droopy mustaches and aviator-style eyeglasses and wear key rings on the right side of their belts?

Gerald Levey and Mark Newman.

The answer is: two. Gerald Levey and Mark Newman are twins, separated at birth, who did not even know the other existed until they were reunited—in a fire station—by a fellow fire fighter who knew Newman and was startled to see Levey at a fire fighters' convention.

Their lives, although separate, took remarkably similar paths. Levey went to college, studying forestry; Newman planned to study forestry in college but instead took a job trimming trees. Both had jobs in supermarkets. One has a job installing sprinkler systems; the other installed fire alarms.

Both men are unmarried and find the same kind of woman attractive: "tall, slender, long hair." They share similar hobbies, enjoying hunting, fishing, going to the beach, old John Wayne movies, and professional wrestling. Both like Chinese food, and they drink the same brand of beer. Their mannerisms are also similar—for example, they both throw their heads back when they laugh. And, of course, there is one more thing: They share a passion for fighting fires. (Lang, 1987)

The similarities we see in twins Gerald Levey and Mark Newman vividly raise one of the fundamental questions posed by developmental psychologists: How can we distinguish between the causes of behavior that are _environmental_ (the influence of parents, siblings, family, friends, schooling, nutrition, and all the other experiences to which a child is exposed) and those causes that are _hereditary_ (those based on the genetic makeup of an individual that influence growth and development throughout life)? This question, which we first explored when we considered intelligence in Chapter 8, is known as the **nature-nurture issue.** In this context, nature refers to inherited factors and nurture to environmental influences.

The nature-nurture issue has philosophical roots. English philosopher John Locke argued in the 1600s that a newborn was, in effect, a blank slate, a _tabula rasa,_ on which the story of his or her individual experience could be written from scratch. In other words, he believed that the environment acted as the sole influence on development. In contrast, the French philosopher Jean Jacques Rousseau suggested a very different conception of development in the 1700s. He believed that people's "natural" characteristics (namely, genetic factors) were most influential, although subject to what Rousseau considered to be the corrupting influence of the environment.

Although the question was first posed as the nature-_versus_-nurture question, developmental psychologists today agree that _both_ nature and nurture interact to produce specific developmental patterns and outcomes. The question has changed from _which_ influences behavior to _how_ and to what degree environment and heredity produce their effects. No one grows up without being influenced by the environment, nor does anyone develop without being affected by his or her inherited genetic makeup. However, the debate over the relative influence of the two factors remains an ongoing one, with different approaches and theories of development emphasizing the environment or heredity to a greater or lesser degree.

For example, some developmental theories stress the role of learning in producing changes in behavior in the developing child, relying on the basic principles of learning discussed in Chapter 5. Such theories emphasize the role of environment in accounting for development. In contrast, other approaches emphasize the influence of one's physiological makeup and functioning on development. Such theories stress the role of heredity and _maturation_—the unfolding of biologically predetermined patterns of behavior—in producing developmental change. Maturation can be seen, for instance, in the development of sex characteristics (such as breasts or body hair) that occurs at the start of adolescence.

On some points, however, agreement exists among developmental psychologists of different theoretical persuasions. It seems clear that genetic factors not only provide the potential for particular behaviors or traits to emerge, but also place limitations on the emergence of such behavior or traits. For instance, hered-

Nature-nurture issue: The issue of the relative degrees to which environment and heredity influence behavior

TABLE 10-1 Characteristics with Strong Genetic Components		
Physical characteristics	Intellectual characteristics	Emotional characteristics and disorders
Height	Memory	Shyness
Weight	Ability as measured on intelligence tests	Extraversion
Obesity		Emotionality
Tone of voice	Age of language acquisition	Neuroticism
Blood pressure		Schizophrenia
Tooth decay	Reading disability	Anxiety
Athletic ability	Mental retardation	Alcoholism
Firmness of handshake		
Age of death		
Activity level		

Source: Papalia & Olds, 1988; Plomin, 1989.

ity defines people's general level of intelligence, setting an upper limit which—regardless of the quality of the environment—people cannot exceed. Heredity also provides limits on physical abilities; humans simply cannot run at a speed of 60 miles an hour, nor are they going to grow as tall as 10 feet, no matter what the quality of their environment (Plomin, 1990, 1994; Plomin & McClearn, 1993; Wachs, 1993).

Table 10-1 lists some of the characteristics that are most affected by heredity. As you consider these items, it is important to keep in mind that these characteristics are not *entirely* determined by heredity. Instead, the best evidence suggests to a relatively large extent that variations in these factors are due to the genetic makeup of an individual.

In most instances, environmental factors play a critical role in enabling people to reach those potential capabilities made possible by their genetic background. Had Albert Einstein received no intellectual stimulation as a child and not been sent to school, it is unlikely he would have reached his genetic potential. Similarly, a great athlete like basketball star Charles Barkley would have been unlikely to display much physical skill had he not been raised in an environment that nurtured his innate talent and gave him the opportunity to train and perfect his natural abilities.

In sum, developmental psychologists take an *interactionist* position on the nature-nurture issue, suggesting that a combination of hereditary and environmental factors influence development. The challenge facing developmental psychologists is to identify the specific kind and relative strength of each of these influences on the individual (Plomin & Neiderhiser, 1992; Wozniak & Fischer, 1993).

Addressing the Nature-Nurture Question

Developmental psychologists have tried to determine the relative influence of genetic and environmental factors on behavior in several different ways, although no technique is foolproof. Researchers can, for example, experimentally control the genetic makeup of laboratory animals by carefully breeding them for specific traits. Just as the people who raise Butterball turkeys have learned to produce a breed that grows especially quickly (so they can be brought to the marketplace less expensively), psychologists are able to breed strains of laboratory animals that share a similar genetic makeup. Observing animals with similar genetic back-

grounds in varied environments allows researchers to ascertain the effects of particular kinds of environmental stimulation. Ultimately, of course, there is the problem of generalizing the findings of animal research to a human population. However, these findings provide fundamental information that could not be obtained, for ethical reasons, by using human subjects.

Human twins also serve as an important source of information about the relative effects of genetic and environmental factors. If **identical twins** (those who are genetically identical) display different patterns of development, we have to attribute such differences to variations in the environment in which they were raised. The most useful data come from identical twins (such as Gerald Levey and Mark Newman) who are adopted at birth by different sets of foster parents and raised apart in differing environments. Studies of nontwin siblings who are raised in totally different environments also shed some light on the issue. Because they share relatively similar genetic backgrounds, siblings who show similarities as adults provide strong evidence for the importance of heredity (Lykken et al., 1993).

It is also possible to take the opposite tack. Instead of concentrating on people with similar genetic backgrounds who are raised in different environments, we may consider people raised in similar environments who have totally dissimilar genetic backgrounds. If we find, for example, that two adopted children—who have dissimilar genetic backgrounds—raised in the same family develop similarly, we have evidence for the importance of environmental influences on development. Moreover, it is possible to carry out research with animals with dissimilar genetic backgrounds; by experimentally varying the environment in which they are raised, we can determine the influence of environmental factors (independent of heredity) on development (Segal, 1993).

Identical twins: Twins with identical genetic makeup

Studying Development

The specific research methods used by developmental psychologists to consider the nature-nurture issue, as well as other questions of a developmental nature, tend to fall into two main categories: cross-sectional and longitudinal (Cohen & Reese, 1991, 1994). In **cross-sectional research,** people of different ages are compared at the same point in time. Cross-sectional studies provide information about differences in development between different age groups.

Suppose, for instance, we were interested in the development of intellectual ability in adulthood. To carry out a cross-sectional study, we might compare a sample of 25-, 45-, and 65-year-olds on an IQ test. We then can determine whether the average scores differ in each age group.

Cross-sectional research has limitations, however. For instance, we cannot be sure that any differences we find in IQ scores in our example are due just to age differences alone. Instead, they may reflect differences in educational attainment between the three age cohorts. (*Cohort* refers to a group of people who grow up at the same time in the same place.) Specifically, any age differences we find in our cross-sectional study may reflect that people in the older age group belong to a cohort that was less likely to attend college than those in the younger groups.

One way around the problem is to conduct a study employing the second major research strategy used by developmental psychologists: a longitudinal study. In **longitudinal research,** the behavior of one or more subjects is traced as the subjects age. Longitudinal studies assess *change* in intellectual ability over time, unlike cross-sectional studies, which assess *differences* among groups of people.

For instance, consider how we might investigate intellectual development during adulthood using a longitudinal research strategy. First, we might give IQ tests to a group of 25-year-olds. We'd then come back to them 20 years later and retest them at age 45. Finally, we'd return to them still once more when they were 65 years old and test them again.

Cross-sectional research: A research method in which people of different ages are compared at the same point in time

Longitudinal research: A research method that investigates behavior as subjects age

By examining changes over several points in time, we can clearly see how individuals develop. Unfortunately, there are also drawbacks to longitudinal research: It requires an enormous expenditure of time (as the researcher waits for the subjects to get older), and subjects who participate at an early stage may drop out, move away, or even die as the research continues. Moreover, subjects who take the same test at several points in time may become "testwise" and perform better each time they take it, having become more familiar with the test.

To make up for the limitations in cross-sectional and longitudinal research, investigators have devised an alternative strategy. Known as **cross-sequential research,** it combines cross-sectional and longitudinal approaches by taking a number of different age groups and examining them over several points in time. For example, investigators might use a group of 3-, 5-, and 7-year-olds, examining them every 6 months for a period of several years. This technique allows developmental psychologists to tease out the effects of age changes from other possibly influential factors.

The Start of Life: Conception and Beyond

Our understanding of the biology of the start of life—when a male's sperm cell penetrates a female's egg cell, marking the moment of *conception*—makes it no less of a miracle. At that single moment, an individual's genetic endowment is established for the rest of his or her life.

When the egg becomes fertilized by the sperm, the result is a one-celled entity called a **zygote** that immediately begins to develop. The zygote contains twenty-three pairs of **chromosomes,** rod-shaped structures that contain the basic hereditary information. One member of each pair is from the mother and the other is from the father. Each chromosome contains thousands of **genes**—smaller units through which genetic information is transmitted. Either individually or in combination, genes produce the particular characteristics of each person (Aitken, 1995).

While some genes are responsible for the development of systems common to all members of the human species—the heart, circulatory system, brain, lungs, and so forth—others control the characteristics that make each human unique, such as facial configuration, height, eye color, and the like. The child's sex is also determined by a particular combination of genes. Specifically, a child inherits an X chromosome from its mother, and either an X or Y chromosome from its father. With an XX combination, it is a female; with an XY combination, it develops as a male. Male development is triggered by a single gene on the Y chromosome, and without the presence of that specific gene, the individual will develop as a female (Roberts, 1988).

The zygote starts out as a microscopic speck. As it divides through an intricate preprogrammed system of cell division, it grows 10,000 times larger in just 4 weeks, to about one-fifth of an inch long (see Figure 10-1). At that point it is called an **embryo** and has developed a rudimentary heart (that beats), a brain, an intestinal tract, and a number of other organs. Although all these organs are at a primitive stage of development, they are clearly recognizable. Moreover, by the eighth week, the embryo is about an inch long, and has arms, legs, and a face that are discernible.

Following the eighth week, the embryo faces what is known as a **critical period,** the first of several stages in prenatal development in which specific kinds of growth must occur if the individual is to develop normally. For example, if the eyes and ears do not develop during this stage, they will never form later on, and if they form abnormally, they will be permanently damaged. During critical periods, organisms are particularly sensitive to environmental influences such as the presence of certain kinds of drugs, which, as we will see later, can have a devas-

Cross-sequential research: A research method that combines cross-sectional and longitudinal research by taking a number of different age groups and examining them over several points in time

Zygote: The one-celled product of fertilization

Chromosomes: Rod-shaped structures that contain basic hereditary information

Genes: The parts of a chromosome through which genetic information is transmitted

Embryo: A developed zygote that has a heart, a brain, and other organs

Critical period: The first of several stages of development in which specific kinds of growth must occur to enable further normal development

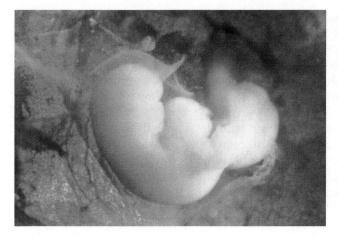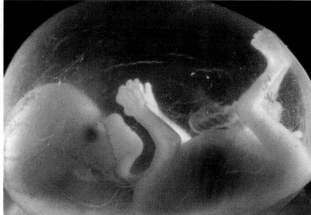

FIGURE 10-1 These remarkable photos of live fetuses display the degree of physical development at 4 and 15 weeks. [*(Left)* Lennart Nilsson, *A Child Is Born*/Dell Publishing, Inc.; *(Right)* Petit Format/ Science Source/Photo Researchers.]

tating effect on subsequent development (Bornstein & Krasnegor, 1989; Bornstein & Bruner, 1989).

Beginning in the ninth week and continuing until birth, the developing individual is called a **fetus.** At the start of this period, it begins to be responsive to touch; it bends its fingers when touched on the hand. At 16 to 18 weeks, its movements become strong enough for the mother to sense the baby. At the same time, hair may begin to grow on the baby's head, and the facial features become similar to those the child will display at birth. The major organs begin to function, although the fetus could not be kept alive outside the mother. In addition, a lifetime's worth of brain neurons are produced—although it is unclear whether the brain is capable of thinking in any real sense at this early stage.

By the twenty-fourth week, a fetus has many of the characteristics it will display as a newborn. In fact, when an infant is born prematurely at this age, it can open and close its eyes; suck; cry; look up, down, and around; and even grasp objects placed in its hands, although it is still unable to survive for long outside the mother.

The fetus continues to develop prior to birth. It begins to grow fatty deposits under the skin, and it gains weight. The fetus reaches the **age of viability,** the point at which it can survive if born prematurely, at about 28 weeks, although through advances in medical technology this crucial age is getting earlier. At 28 weeks, the fetus weighs about 3 pounds and is about 16 inches long. It may be capable of learning: One study found that the infants of mothers who had repeatedly read aloud the Dr. Seuss story *The Cat in the Hat* prior to birth preferred the sound of that particular story over other stories after they were born (Spence & DeCasper, 1982; Lecanuet, Grenier-Deferre, & Busnel, 1995).

In the final weeks of pregnancy, the fetus continues to gain weight and grow, becoming increasingly fit. At the end of the normal 38 weeks of pregnancy, the fetus typically weighs around 7 pounds and is about 20 inches in length.

Fetus: A developing child, from 9 weeks after conception until birth

Age of viability: The point at which a fetus can survive if born prematurely

Genetic Influences on the Fetus The process of fetal growth that we have just described reflects normal development, which occurs in 95 to 98 percent of all pregnancies. Some people are less fortunate, for in the remaining 2 to 5 percent of cases, children are born with serious birth defects. A major cause of such defects is faulty genes or chromosomes. Here are some of the most common genetic and chromosomal difficulties:

■ *Phenylketonuria.* A child born with the inherited disease phenylketonuria (PKU) cannot produce an enzyme that is required for normal development. This results in an accumulation of poisons that eventually cause profound mental retardation. The disease is treatable, however, if caught early enough. Most infants

today are routinely tested for PKU, and children with the disorder can be placed on a special diet that allows them to develop normally.

■ *Sickle-cell anemia.* About 10 percent of the African-American population has the possibility of passing on sickle-cell anemia, a disease that gets its name from the abnormal shape of the victims' red blood cells. Children with the disease may have poor appetites, swollen stomachs, and yellowish eyes; they frequently die during childhood.

■ *Tay-Sachs disease.* Children born with Tay-Sachs disease, a disorder that most often afflicts Jews of eastern European ancestry, usually die by the age of 3 or 4 because of the body's inability to break down fat. If both parents carry the genetic defect producing the fatal illness, their child has a one in four chance of being born with the disease (Navon & Proia, 1989).

■ *Down syndrome.* In Chapter 8, we discussed Down syndrome as a cause of mental retardation. Down syndrome is brought about not by an inherited trait passed on by the parents, but by a malfunction whereby the zygote receives an extra chromosome at the moment of conception, causing retardation and an unusual physical appearance (which led to an earlier label for the disease: mongolism). Down syndrome is related to the mother's and father's age; mothers over 35, in particular, stand a higher risk than younger women of having a child with the problem.

Prenatal Environmental Influences   Genetic factors are not the only causes of difficulties in fetal development; a number of environmental factors also have an effect on the course of development. The major prenatal environmental influences include:

■ *Mother's nutrition and emotional state.* What a mother eats during her pregnancy can have important implications for the health of her baby. Mothers who are seriously undernourished cannot provide adequate nutrition to the growing baby, and they are likely to give birth to underweight babies. Poorly nourished babies are also more susceptible to disease, and a lack of nourishment may have an adverse impact on mental development (Adams & Parker, 1990; Ricciuti, 1993).

Moreover, there is some evidence that the mother's emotional state affects the baby. Mothers who are anxious and tense during the last months of their pregnancies are more apt to have infants who are irritable and who sleep and eat poorly. The reason? One hypothesis is that the autonomic nervous system of the fetus becomes especially sensitive as a result of the chemical changes produced by the mother's emotional state (Kagan, Kearsley, & Zelazo, 1978).

■ *Illness of mother.* During 1964 and 1965 an epidemic of *rubella,* or German measles, in the United States resulted in the prenatal death or malformation of close to 50,000 children. Although the disease has relatively minor effects on the mother, it is one of a number of illnesses that can have devastating consequences for the developing fetus when contracted during the early part of a woman's pregnancy. Other maternal diseases that may produce a permanent effect on the fetus include syphilis, diabetes, and high blood pressure.

Acquired immune deficiency syndrome (AIDS) can be passed from mother to child prior to birth. Sadly, in many cases mothers may not even know they carry the disease and inadvertently transmit it to their children. The AIDS virus can also be passed on through breast feeding after birth (Heyward & Curran, 1988; HMHL, 1994a, 1994c).

■ *Mother's use of drugs.* Drugs taken by a pregnant woman can have a tragic effect on the unborn child. Probably the most dramatic example was thalidomide, a tranquilizer that was widely prescribed during the 1960s—until it was discovered that it caused severe birth defects such as the absence of limbs. Another example is the hormone diethylstilbestrol (DES), prescribed until the 1950s to prevent miscarriages. We now know that daughters whose mothers took DES during

TABLE 10-2 Environmental Factors Affecting Prenatal Development

Factor	Possible effect
Rubella (German measles)	Blindness, deafness, heart abnormalities, stillbirth
Syphilis	Mental retardation, physical deformities, maternal miscarriage
Addictive drugs	Low birth weight, addiction of infant to drug, with possible death, after birth, from withdrawal
Smoking	Premature birth, low birth weight and length
Alcohol	Mental retardation, lower-than-average birth weight, small head, limb deformities
Radiation from x-rays	Physical deformities, mental retardation
Inadequate diet	Reduction in growth of brain, smaller-than-average weight and length at birth
Mother's age—younger than 18 at birth of child	Premature birth, increased incidence of Down syndrome
Mother's age—older than 35 at birth of child	Increased incidence of Down syndrome
DES (diethylstilbestrol)	Reproductive difficulties and increased incidence of genital cancer in children of mothers who were given DES during pregnancy to prevent miscarriage
AIDS	Possible spread of AIDS virus to infant; facial deformities; growth failure

Source: Adapted from Schickendanz, Schickendanz, & Forsyth, 1982, p. 95.

pregnancy are at risk for developing abnormalities of the cervix and vagina and for developing cancer of the uterus. Sons whose mothers took DES have higher rates of infertility and reproductive problems.

Alcohol and nicotine are also dangerous to fetal development. For example, *fetal alcohol syndrome,* a condition resulting in mental and growth retardation, has been found in the children of mothers who consumed heavy or sometimes even moderate amounts of alcohol during pregnancy. Moreover, mothers who take physically addictive drugs such as cocaine run the risk of giving birth to babies who are similarly addicted. Their newborns suffer painful withdrawal symptoms after birth and sometimes show permanent physical and mental impairment as well (M. W. Miller, 1986; Waterson & Murray-Lyon, 1990; Lemoine & Lemoine, 1992; Meyer et al., 1996).

■ *Birth complications.* Although most births are routine, the process sometimes goes awry, resulting in injury to the infant. For example, the umbilical cord connecting the baby to the mother may become compressed, withholding oxygen from the child. If this occurs for too long, the child may suffer permanent brain damage.

A number of other environmental factors have an impact upon the child prior to and during birth (see Table 10-2). It is important to keep in mind, however, that development represents the interaction of environmental and genetic influences. Although we have been discussing the influences of genetics and environment separately, neither factor works alone. Moreover, while we have been emphasizing some of the ways in which development can go awry, the vast majority of births occur without difficulty. And in most instances, subsequent development also proceeds routinely, as we discuss next.

RECAP AND REVIEW

Recap

- A fundamental issue of developmental psychology is the nature-nurture question, which seeks to determine the relative influence of environmental and genetic factors on development.

- During the course of prenatal development, the one-cell zygote evolves into an embryo and subsequently a fetus. Birth typically occurs 38 weeks after conception.
- The major difficulties caused by genetic factors are sickle-cell anemia, phenylketonuria (PKU), Tay-Sachs disease, and Down syndrome. Among the primary environmental influences on prenatal development and newborn health are the mother's nutrition, state of health, and drug intake, and the nature of the baby's delivery.

Review

1. Developmental psychologists are interested in the effects of both _____ and _____ on development.
2. Environment and heredity both influence development, with genetic potentials generally establishing limits on environmental influences. True or false?
3. By observing genetically similar animals in differing environments, we can increase our understanding of the influences of hereditary and environmental factors in humans. True or false?

4. _____ research studies the same individuals over a period of time, while _____-_____ research studies people of different ages at the same time.
5. Match each of the following terms with its definition:
   1. Zygote
   2. Gene
   3. Chromosome

   a. Smallest unit through which genetic information is passed
   b. Fertilized egg
   c. Rod-shaped structure containing genetic information
6. Specific kinds of growth must take place during a _____ period if the embryo is to develop normally.

Ask Yourself

Given the possible effects of the environment on the developing child, do you think expectant mothers should be subject to legal prosecution for their use of alcohol and other drugs that may seriously harm their unborn children?

(Answers to review questions are on page 332.)

- *What are the major milestones of physical, perceptual, and social development after birth?*
- *How can we best describe cognitive development?*

PHYSICAL AND SOCIAL DEVELOPMENT

His head was molded into a long melon shape and came to a point at the back. . . . He was covered with a thick greasy white material known as "vernix," which made him slippery to hold, and also allowed him to slip easily through the birth canal. In addition to a shock of black hair on his head, his body was covered with dark, fine hair known as "lanugo." His ears, his back, his shoulders, and even his cheeks were furry. . . . His skin was wrinkled and quite loose, ready to scale in creased places such as his feet and hands. . . . His ears were pressed to his head in unusual positions—one ear was matted firmly forward on his cheek. His nose was flattened and pushed to one side by the squeeze as he came through the pelvis (Brazelton, 1969, p. 3).

What kind of creature is this? Although the description hardly fits that of the adorable babies seen in commercials, we are in fact talking about a normal, completely developed child just after the moment of birth. Called a **neonate,** the newborn presents itself to the world in a form that hardly meets the typical standards of beauty against which we normally measure babies. Yet ask any parent: No sight is more beautiful or exciting than the first glimpse of their newborn.

Neonate: A newborn child

The neonate's flawed appearance is brought about by a number of factors. The trip through its mother's birth canal may have squeezed the incompletely formed bones of the skull together and squashed the nose into the head. It is covered with *vernix,* a white, greasy material that is secreted to protect its skin prior to birth, and it may have *lanugo,* a soft fuzz, over its entire body. Its eyelids may be puffy with an accumulation of fluids because of its upside-down position during birth.

All this changes during the first 2 weeks of life, as the neonate takes on a more familiar appearance. Even more impressive are the capabilities that the neonate begins to display from the time it is born—capabilities that grow at an astounding rate over the ensuing months and years.

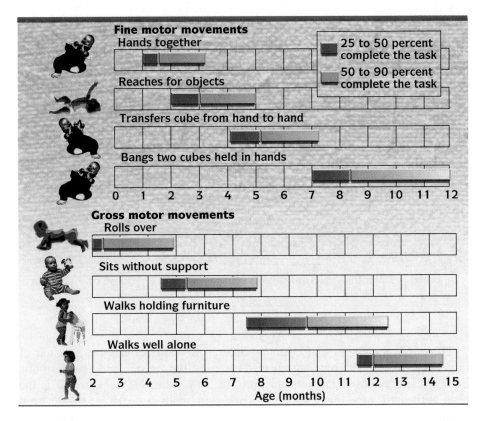

FIGURE 10-2 These landmarks of physical development illustrate the range of ages at which most infants are able to carry out various physical tasks. *(Frankenburg & Dodds, 1967.)*

The neonate is born with a number of **reflexes**—unlearned, involuntary responses that occur automatically in the presence of certain stimuli. Many of these reflexes are critical for survival and unfold naturally as a part of an infant's ongoing maturation. The *rooting reflex,* for instance, causes neonates to turn their heads toward things that touch their cheeks—such as a nipple of a mother's breast or a bottle. Similarly, a *sucking reflex* prompts the infant to suck at things that touch its lips. Among the other reflexes are a *gag reflex* (to clear its throat), the *startle reflex* (a series of movements in which the infant flings out its arms, fans its fingers, and arches its back in response to a sudden noise), and the *Babinski reflex* (the baby's toes fan out when the outer edge of the sole of its foot is stroked).

These primitive reflexes are lost after the first few months of life and replaced by more complex and organized behaviors. Although at birth the neonate is capable of only jerky, limited voluntary movements, during the first year of life the ability to move independently grows enormously. The typical baby is able to roll over by the age of 3 months; it can sit without support at 6 months, stand alone at about 11½ months, and walk by the time it is just over a year old. Not only does the ability to make large-scale movements improve during this time, but fine-muscle movements also become increasingly sophisticated (as illustrated in Figure 10-2).

Reflexes: Unlearned, involuntary responses to certain stimuli

Growth after Birth

Perhaps the most obvious sign of development is the physical growth of the child. During the first year of life, children typically triple their birth weight, and their height increases by about half. This rapid growth slows down as the child gets older—think how gigantic adults would be if that rate of growth were constant—and the average rate of growth from age 3 to the beginning of adolescence, around age 13, is a gain of about 5 pounds and 3 inches a year.

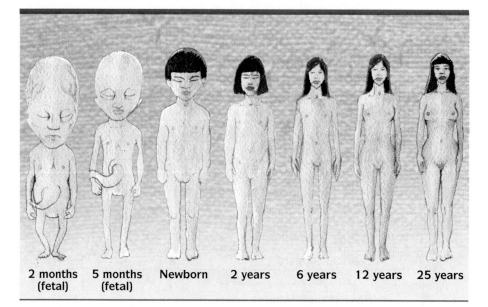

FIGURE 10-3 As development progresses, the relative size of the head—in relation to the rest of the body—decreases until adulthood is reached. *(Adapted from Robbins, 1929.)*

| 2 months (fetal) | 5 months (fetal) | Newborn | 2 years | 6 years | 12 years | 25 years |

The physical changes that occur as children develop are not just a matter of increasing growth; the relationship of the size of the various body parts to one another changes dramatically as children age. As you can see in Figure 10-3, the head of the fetus (and the newborn) is disproportionally large. However, the head soon becomes more proportional in size to the rest of the body as growth occurs mainly in the trunk and legs.

Development of Perception: Taking In the World

When proud parents pick up their neonate and peer into its eyes, is the child able to return their gaze? Although it was thought for some time that newborns could see only a hazy blur, most current findings indicate that the capabilities of neonates are far more impressive (Horowitz & Colombo, 1990). While their eyes have limited capacity to modify the shape of the lens, making it difficult to focus on objects that are not within a 7- to 8-inch distance from the face, neonates are able to follow objects moving within their field of vision. They also show the rudiments of depth perception, as they react by raising their hands when an object appears to be moving rapidly toward their face (Aslin & Smith, 1988; Colombo & Mitchell, 1990).

You might think that it would be hard to figure out just how well neonates are able to see, since their lack of both language and reading abilities clearly prevents them from saying what direction the "E" on a vision chart is facing. However, a number of ingenious methods, relying on biological responses and innate reflexes of the newborn, have been devised to test their perceptual skills (Koop, 1994).

For instance, infants who are shown a novel stimulus typically pay close attention to it, and as a consequence, their heart rates increase. But if they are repeatedly shown the same stimulus, their attention to it decreases, as indicated by a return to a slower heart rate. This phenomenon is known as **habituation,** the decrease in the response to a stimulus that occurs after repeated presentations of the same stimulus. By studying habituation, developmental psychologists can tell

Habituation: A decrease in response to repeated presentations of the same stimulus

---

ANSWERS TO PREVIOUS REVIEW
1. heredity; environment **2.** True **3.** True **4.** Longitudinal; cross-sectional
5. 1-b; 2-a; 3-c **6.** critical

when a stimulus can be detected and discriminated by a child too young to speak (Bornstein & Lamb, 1992).

Researchers have developed a number of other methods for measuring neonate and infant perception. One technique, for instance, involves babies sucking on a nipple attached to a computer. A change in the rate and vigor with which they suck is used to infer that they can perceive variations in stimuli. Other approaches include examining babies' eye movements and observing which way babies move their heads when presented with a visual stimulus (Milewski, 1976; Kolata, 1987; Bronson, 1990).

Using such research techniques, we now know that infants' visual perception is remarkably sophisticated from the start of life. At birth, babies show preferences for patterns with contours and edges over less distinct patterns, indicating that they are capable of responding to the configuration of stimuli. Furthermore, even newborns are aware of size constancy, apparently sensitive to the phenomenon that objects stay the same size even though the image on the retina may vary as their distance changes (Slater, Mattock, & Brown, 1990).

In fact, neonates have the ability to discriminate facial expressions—and even to imitate them (Field, 1982). As you can see in Figure 10-4, newborns exposed to an adult with a happy, sad, or surprised facial expression are able to produce a good imitation of the adult's expression. Even very young infants, then, can respond to the emotions and moods that their caregivers' facial expressions reveal. This capability provides the foundation for social interactional skills in children (Phillips et al., 1990).

Other visual abilities grow rapidly after birth. By the end of their first month, babies can distinguish some colors from others, and after 4 months they can readily focus on near or far objects. By 4 or 5 months, they are able to recognize two- and three-dimensional objects, and they can make use of the gestalt patterns we discussed in relation to adult perception in Chapter 3. Furthermore, there are

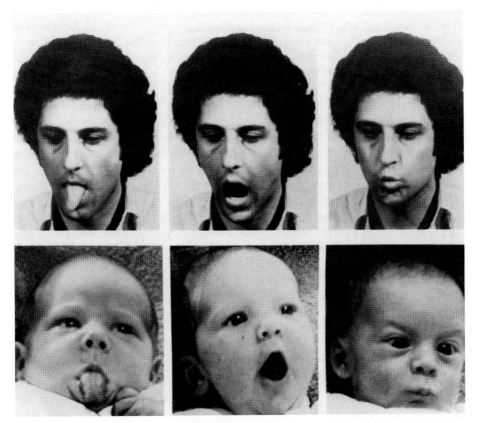

FIGURE 10-4 This newborn infant is clearly imitating the expressions of the adult model in these amazing photos. *(Courtesy of Andrew N. Meltzoff.)*

rapid improvements in perceptual abilities: Sensitivity to visual stimuli, for instance, becomes three to four times greater at 1 year of age than it was at birth (Aslin & Smith, 1988; Bower, 1989; Atkinson & Braddick, 1989).

In addition to vision, infants' other sensory capabilities are quite impressive (e.g., Trehub et al., 1991). Newborns can distinguish different sounds to the point of being able to recognize their own mothers' voices at the age of 3 days (DeCasper & Fifer, 1980). They are also capable of making subtle linguistic distinctions that underlie the language abilities described in Chapter 7. At 4 days of age, babies can discriminate between such closely related sounds as *ba* and *pa,* and they are soon able to distinguish between their native tongue and foreign languages (Jusczyk & Derrah, 1987; Jusczyk, 1986). By 6 months of age, they are capable of discriminating virtually any difference in sound that is relevant to the production of language (Aslin, 1987). Moreover, they are capable of discriminating different tastes and smells at a very early age (Steiner, 1979). There even seems to be something of a built-in sweet tooth: Neonates prefer liquids that have been sweetened with sugar over their unsweetened counterparts.

Development of Social Behavior: Taking On the World

As anyone who has seen an infant smiling at the sight of its mother can guess, at the same time that infants are growing physically and honing their perceptual abilities, they are also developing socially. The nature of a child's early social development provides the foundation for social relationships that will last a lifetime (Eisenberg, 1994).

Attachment, the positive emotional bond that develops between a child and a particular individual, is the most important form of social development that occurs during infancy (Greeberg, Cicchetti, & Cummings, 1990). One of the first investigators to demonstrate the importance and nature of attachment was psychologist Harry Harlow. Harlow found that when infant monkeys were given the choice of a wire "monkey" that provided food or a soft, terry-cloth "monkey" that was warm but did not provide food, they clearly preferred the cloth one, although they made occasional forays to the wire monkey to nurse (Harlow & Zimmerman, 1959). The cloth monkey provided greater comfort to the infants; food alone was insufficient to create attachment (see Figure 10-5).

Building on this initial work, other researchers have suggested that attachment grows through the responsiveness of infants' caregivers to the signals the babies provide, such as cries, smiles, reaching, and clinging. The greater the responsiveness of the caregiver to the child's signals, the more likely it is that the child will become securely attached. Full attachment eventually develops as a result of a complex series of interactions between caregiver and child known as the Attachment Behavioral System (Bell & Ainsworth, 1972). It is important to note that the infant plays as critical and active a role in the formation of a bond as the caregiver. Infants who respond positively to a caregiver promote more positive behavior on the part of the caregiver, which in turn elicits an even stronger degree of attachment from the child.

Measuring Attachment   Developmental psychologists have devised a quick and direct way of measuring attachment. Developed by Mary Ainsworth, the *Ainsworth strange situation* consists of a sequence of events involving a child and (typically) its mother. Initially, the mother and baby enter an unfamiliar room, and the mother permits the baby to explore while she sits down. An adult stranger then enters the room, after which the mother leaves. The mother then returns, and the stranger leaves. The mother then once again leaves the baby alone, and the stranger returns. Finally, the stranger leaves, and the mother returns (Ainsworth et al., 1978).

Attachment: The positive emotional bond that develops between a child and a particular individual

FIGURE 10-5 Although the wire "mother" dispensed milk to the hungry infant monkey, the soft, terry-cloth "mother" was preferred. *(Harry Harlow Primate Laboratory/ University of Wisconsin.)*

Babies' reactions to the strange situation vary drastically, depending, according to Ainsworth, on their degree of attachment to the mother. One-year-old children who are labeled "securely attached" employ the mother as a kind of home base, exploring independently but returning to her occasionally. When she leaves, they exhibit distress, and they go to her when she returns. Children termed "avoidant" do not cry when the mother leaves, but they seem to ignore her when she returns, appearing to be angry with her. Finally, "ambivalent" children display anxiety before they are separated and are upset when the mother leaves, but they may show ambivalent reactions to her return such as seeking close contact but simultaneously hitting and kicking her.

The nature of attachment between children and their mothers has far-reaching consequences for later development. For example, one study found that boys who were securely attached at age 1 showed fewer psychological difficulties when they were older than did avoidant or ambivalent youngsters (Lewis et al., 1984). Moreover, children who are securely attached to their mothers tend to be more socially and emotionally competent than their less securely attached peers, and they are viewed as more cooperative, capable, and playful (Sroufe, Fox, & Pancake, 1983; Ainsworth, 1989; Ainsworth & Bowlby, 1991; Holmes, 1994).

The significance of attachment in children's development raises an important question: Are children who attend day care less attached to their parents than children who are cared for by their parents at home? Because more than a million children, many still infants, are looked after by paid child-care workers in day-care centers outside the home, the issue has real practical significance (Booth, 1992). The research findings on the issue are inconsistent. Some evidence suggests that infants who are involved in outside care more than 20 hours a week in their first year show less attachment to their mothers than those who have not been in day care (Belsky & Rovine, 1988). On the other hand, most other research finds little or no difference in the strength of parental attachment bonds of infants and toddlers who have been in day care—regardless of the duration of their day-care experience—and those raised solely by their parents. Moreover, there is no evidence that children in day-care centers are more attached to the day-care workers than to their parents; in fact, they almost always appear to be

more attached to their parents (Rutter, 1982; Ragozin, 1980). In sum, most evidence suggests that children who are in day care are no less attached to their parents than those who are not in day care.

The Father's Role   For many years, the father stood in the shadows behind the mother—at least as far as developmental research was concerned. Because traditionally it was thought that the mother-infant bond was the most crucial in a child's life, researchers in earlier decades focused on the mother's relationship with her children. However, the last decade has seen an increase in studies that highlight the father's role in parenting (Lamb, 1987; Phares, 1992).

At the same time, the number of fathers who are primary caregivers for their children has grown. In 20 percent of families with children, the father is the parent that stays at home caring for preschoolers (O'Connell, 1993).

On the other hand, by and large, fathers still spend less time caring for and playing with their children than do mothers. However, the strength of attachment between fathers and their children can be as great as between mothers and their children. Although children can be simultaneously attached to both their parents (Lamb, 1982), the nature of attachment is not always identical between children and mothers and children and fathers. For instance, infants tend to prefer to be soothed by their mothers, even though fathers are just as adept at comforting and nurturing babies.

The reason for differences in attachment to mothers and fathers may be that mothers spend a greater proportion of their time feeding and directly nurturing their children, whereas fathers spend more time, proportionally, playing with them (Parke, 1981). Moreover, the quality of fathers' play is often different from that of mothers. Fathers engage in more physical, rough-and-tumble sorts of activities, whereas mothers play more verbally oriented games and traditional ones such as peekaboo. Such differences in play style are typically very pronounced, and occur even in the small minority of families in which the mother works to support the family and the father stays at home with the children (Field, 1978; Power & Parke, 1982).

Despite the differences between the behavior of fathers and mothers, each parent is an important attachment figure and plays a major role in the social development of a child. Furthermore, the sheer amount of time an adult spends with a child is often less important than the quality of that time (Hetherington & Parke, 1993).

Social Relationships with Peers

Anyone who watches a preschooler rush off to play with a neighborhood friend is aware of the enjoyment that children derive from being with their peers. Such friendships are crucial to a child's social development (Lewis & Feinman, 1991). According to developmental psychologist Willard Hartup, experience is necessary both in "vertical" relationships (those with people of greater knowledge and social power, such as parents) *and* in "horizontal" relationships (those with people who have the same amount of knowledge and social power) in order for children to develop social competence (Hartup, 1989; Hartup & Moore, 1993).

By the time they are 2 years old, children start to become less dependent on their parents and more self-reliant, increasingly preferring to play with friends. Initially, play is relatively independent: Even though they may be sitting side by side, 2-year-olds pay more attention to toys than to one another when playing. Later, however, children actively interact, modifying one another's behavior and later exchanging roles during play.

As children reach school age, their social interactions become increasingly formalized, as well as more frequent. They may engage in elaborate games involv-

At about age 2, children begin to become independent of their parents, preferring to play with friends—even though at that age they are more likely to play side by side than together.

ing complex scenarios. Play also becomes more structured, involving teams and games with rigid rules (Mueller & Lucas, 1975; Stambak & Sinclair, 1993).

It is important to realize that children's play serves purposes other than mere enjoyment (Asher & Parker, 1991; Cohen, 1993). It allows children to become increasingly competent in their social interactions with others. Through play they learn to take the perspective of other people and to infer others' thoughts and feelings, even when these are not being directly expressed. In sum, social interaction aids children in interpreting the meaning of others' behavior and developing the capacity to respond appropriately (Crick & Dodge, 1994).

Furthermore, children acquire physical and emotional self-control from play: They learn to avoid hitting an adversary who bests them, to be polite, and to control their emotional displays and facial expressions, such as smiling even when receiving a disappointing gift (Selman et al., 1983; Feldman, 1982, 1993; Fox, 1994). Situations that provide children with opportunities for social interaction, then, may enhance their social development. In fact, children learn a great deal from one another, as we discuss in the Psychology at Work box (next page).

Parenting Styles and Social Development

Although many advances in social development are prompted by peer interaction, parents' child-rearing patterns also shape their children's social competence. Psychologist Diana Baumrind (1971, 1980) found that parenting styles fall into three main categories. **Authoritarian parents** are rigid and punitive and value unquestioning obedience from their children. They have strict standards and discourage expressions of disagreement. **Permissive parents** give their children lax or inconsistent direction and, although warm, require little of them. Finally, **authoritative parents** are firm, setting limits for their children. As the children get older, these parents try to reason with and explain things to them. They also set clear goals and encourage their children's independence (see Table 10-3).

Authoritarian parents: Parents who are rigid and punitive, and who value unquestioning obedience from their children

Permissive parents: Parents who are lax, inconsistent, and undemanding, yet warm toward their children

Authoritative parents: Parents who are firm, set clear limits, and reason with and explain things to their children

TABLE 10-3 **Child-Rearing Patterns**		
Parental style	Parenting behavior	Children's behavior
Authoritarian	Rigid, punitive; strict standards	Unsociable, unfriendly, withdrawn
Permissive	Lax, inconsistent, undemanding	Immature, moody, dependent, low self-control
Authoritative	Firm, set limits and goals, use reasoning, encourage independence	Good social skills; likable, self-reliant, independent

Expert Infants: Babies Teaching Babies

It was during the blustery days of last March that 10-month-old Russell Ruud taught the other babies in his day-care group a lesson their parents may have wished he hadn't: how to unzip the Velcro chin straps of their winter hats.

"One day I went to pick Russell up and his teacher told me that the other mothers were complaining that their children had learned from him how to take off their hats," said Judith Ruud, Russell's mother. . . .

"I never showed Russell how to unzip the Velcro. . . . He learned it by trial and error, and the other kids saw him do it one day when they were getting dressed for an outing." (Goleman, 1993a, p. C10)

Russell's lesson to his classmates is just one example of how babies, some of whom are too young even to speak, may communicate knowledge about the world to one another. According to research conducted by developmental psychologists Elizabeth Hanna and Andrew Meltzoff, so-called expert babies are able to convey a remarkable amount of information to other infants (Hanna & Meltzoff, 1993). And the information sticks: What the other children learn from the "experts" is retained and later practiced.

In their research, Hanna and Meltzoff devised five toys with which a 1-year-old would enjoy playing. Although relatively simple, each required that it be played with in a specific manner in order for it to function properly. For instance, one was a plastic cup that would collapse if it was pushed in a certain way with the palm of the hand.

In the first part of the study, a group of infants watched an experimenter demonstrate how to play with one of the five toys. The infants were then permitted to play with the toy themselves, learning how to use it. In a later phase of the study, conducted at a day-care center, the now-expert babies played with a toy while other babies watched them, although the observers were not allowed to play with the toy themselves. However, 2 days later, the observer babies got their chance: They were given the opportunity to play with the toy in their own homes. The researchers found that almost three-quarters of the observer babies were able to play correctly with the toy.

Clearly, even young babies are capable of learning and remembering information to which they are exposed in day-care centers, even after a fair amount of time has gone by. Furthermore, this can happen even if they don't get the chance to immediately practice their skills.

These findings suggest that exposure to other children may have substantial benefits—a conclusion corroborated by research that examines the benefits of day care. For instance, children who attend high-quality child-care centers not only may do as well as children who stay at home with their parents, but in some respects may actually do better. As a result, children in child care are generally more considerate and sociable than other children, and they interact more positively with teachers. They may also be more compliant and regu-

late their own behavior more effectively (Howes, 1990; Clarke-Stewart, 1991; Clarke-Stewart, Gruber, & Fitzgerald, 1994).

In addition, especially for children from poor or disadvantaged homes, child care in specially enriched environments—those with many toys, books, a variety of children, and high-quality care providers—often proves to be more intellectually stimulating than the children's home environments. Such child care can lead to increased intellectual achievement in terms of higher IQ scores and better language development (Lee et al., 1990). In fact, some research suggests that children in child-care centers score higher on tests of cognitive abilities than those who are cared for by their mothers or by sitters or home day-care providers (Clarke-Stewart, 1991; Barnett, 1993).

Overall, there may be significant benefits from the social interaction and intellectual stimulation afforded by high-quality day-care centers. However, the key here is *high-quality* day care (which may not be easy to find). In contrast, low-quality day-care centers provide little or no advantage. Furthermore, we don't know yet whether the benefits of day care last through adulthood. Still, it is clear that participation in day care provides the opportunity for social interaction and stimulation that may prove to be beneficial (Zaslow, 1991; Zigler & Lang, 1991; Zigler & Styfco, 1993; Clarke-Stewart, Gruber, & Fitzgerald, 1994).

As you might expect, the three kinds of child-rearing styles are associated with very different kinds of behavior in children (although there are, of course, many exceptions). Children of authoritarian parents tend to be unsociable, unfriendly, and relatively withdrawn. In contrast, permissive parents' children are immature, moody, and dependent and have low self-control. The children of authoritative

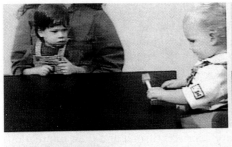

These photographs show a subject in the Hanna and Meltzoff (1993) study discussed in the box on page 338. In the top two photographs, a "trained" 14-month-old takes apart a toy as another, untutored baby watches from his mother's lap. After a five-minute delay, the second baby is allowed to play with the same toy. In the bottom two photographs, he succeeds in pulling the toy apart. This study provides vivid evidence that babies can teach other babies.

parents fare best: Their social skills are high—they are likable, self-reliant, independent, and cooperative.

Before we rush to congratulate authoritative parents and condemn authoritarian and permissive ones, it is important to note that in many cases authoritarian and permissive parents produce children who are perfectly well adjusted. Moreover, each child is born with a particular **temperament**—a basic, innate disposition. Some children are naturally warm and cuddly, whereas others are irritable and fussy. The kind of temperament a baby is born with may in part elicit particular kinds of parental child-rearing styles (Goldsmith et al., 1987; Goldsmith & Harman, 1994).

Temperament: Basic, innate disposition

Furthermore, the findings regarding child-rearing styles are chiefly applicable to American society, in which a dominant value is that children should learn to be independent and not rely too heavily on their parents. In contrast, Japanese parents encourage dependence in order to promote the values of cooperation and community life. These differences in cultural values result in very different philosophies of child rearing. For example, Japanese mothers believe it is a punishment to make a young child sleep alone, so many children sleep next to their mothers throughout infancy and toddlerhood (Kagan, Kearsley, & Zelazo, 1978; Miyake, Chen, & Campos, 1985).

In sum, a child's upbringing is a consequence of the child-rearing philosophy parents hold, the specific practices they employ, and the nature of their own and their child's personality. As is the case with other aspects of development, then, behavior is a function of a complex interaction of environmental and genetic factors (Maccoby, 1992; Darling & Steinberg, 1993; Smetana, 1995).

Erikson's Theory of Psychosocial Development

In trying to trace the course of social development, some theorists have considered how society and culture present challenges that change as the individual matures. Following this path, psychoanalyst Erik Erikson developed one of the most comprehensive theories of social development. According to Erikson (1963), the developmental changes occurring throughout our lives can be viewed as a series of eight stages of psychosocial development. **Psychosocial development** encompasses changes in our interactions with and understanding of one another as well as in our knowledge and understanding of ourselves as members of society.

Erikson suggests that passage through each of the stages necessitates resolu-

Psychosocial development: Development of individuals' interactions with and understanding of each other and of their knowledge and understanding of themselves as members of society

tion of a crisis or conflict. Accordingly, each of Erikson's eight stages is represented as a pairing of the most positive and most negative aspects of the crisis of the period. Although each crisis is never resolved entirely—life becomes increasingly complicated as we grow older—it needs to be resolved sufficiently so that we are equipped to deal with demands made during the following stage of development.

In the first stage of psychosocial development, the **trust-versus-mistrust stage** (birth to 1½ years), infants develop feelings of trust if their physical requirements and psychological needs for attachment are consistently met and their interactions with the world are generally positive. On the other hand, inconsistent care and unpleasant interactions with others can lead to the development of mistrust and leave an infant unable to meet the challenges required in the next stage of development.

In the second stage, the **autonomy-versus-shame-and-doubt stage** (1½ to 3 years), toddlers develop independence and autonomy if exploration and freedom are encouraged, or they experience shame, self-doubt, and unhappiness if they are overly restricted and protected. According to Erikson, the key to the development of autonomy during this period is for the child's caregivers to provide the appropriate amount of control. If parents provide too much control, children will be unable to assert themselves and develop their own sense of control over their environment; if parents provide too little control, children themselves become overly demanding and controlling.

The next crisis that children face is that of the **initiative-versus-guilt stage** (ages 3 to 6). In this stage, the major conflict is between a child's desire to initiate activities independently and the guilt that comes from the unwanted and unexpected consequences of such activities. If parents react positively to the child's attempts at independence, they help their child to resolve the initiative-versus-guilt crisis positively.

The fourth and last stage of childhood is the **industry-versus-inferiority stage** (ages 6 to 12). During this period, successful psychosocial development is characterized by increasing competency in all areas, be they social interactions or academic skills. In contrast, difficulties in this stage lead to feelings of failure and inadequacy.

Erikson's theory suggests that psychosocial development continues throughout life, and he proposes that there are four more crises to face past childhood (which we discuss later in this chapter). Although his theory has been criticized on several grounds—such as the imprecision of the concepts he employs and a greater emphasis on male development than female development—it remains influential and is one of the few that encompass the entire lifespan.

- *How can we best describe cognitive development?*
- *What can parents do to promote the competence of their children?*

COGNITIVE DEVELOPMENT

Suppose you had two drinking glasses of different shapes—one short and broad and one tall and skinny. Now imagine that you filled the short, broad one with soda about halfway and then poured the liquid from that glass into the tall one. The soda appears to fill about three-quarters of the second glass. If someone asked you whether there was more soda in the second glass than there had been in the first, what would you say?

You might think that such a simple question hardly deserves an answer; of course there is no difference in the amount of soda in the two glasses. However,

Trust-versus-mistrust stage: According to Erikson, the first stage of psychosocial development, occurring from birth to 18 months of age, during which time infants develop feelings of trust or lack of trust

Autonomy-versus-shame-and-doubt stage: The period during which, according to Erikson, toddlers (ages 18 months to 3 years) develop independence and autonomy if exploration and freedom are encouraged, or shame and self-doubt if they are restricted and overprotected

Initiative-versus-guilt stage: According to Erikson, the period during which children aged 3 to 6 years experience conflict between independence of action and the sometimes negative results of that action

Industry-versus-inferiority stage: According to Erikson, the period during which children aged 6 to 12 years may develop positive social interactions with others or may feel inadequate and become less sociable

most 4-year-olds would be likely to say that there is more soda in the second glass. If you then poured the soda back into the short glass, they would say there is now less soda than there was in the taller glass.

Why are young children confused by this problem? The reason is not immediately obvious. Anyone who has observed preschoolers must be impressed by how far they have progressed from the early stages of development. They speak with ease, know the alphabet, count, play complex games, use a tape player, tell stories, and communicate quite ably.

Yet, despite this outward sophistication, there are profound gaps in children's understanding of the world. Some theorists have suggested that children are incapable of understanding certain ideas and concepts until they reach a particular stage of **cognitive development**—the process by which a child's understanding of the world changes as a function of age and experience. In contrast to the theories of physical and social development discussed earlier (such as those of Erikson), theories of cognitive development seek to explain the quantitative and qualitative intellectual advances that occur during development.

Cognitive development: The process by which a child's understanding of the world changes as a function of age and experience

Piaget's Theory of Cognitive Development

No theory of cognitive development has had more impact than that of Swiss psychologist Jean Piaget. Piaget (1970) suggested that children throughout the world proceed through a series of four stages in a fixed order. He maintained that these stages differ not only in the *quantity* of information acquired at each stage, but in the *quality* of knowledge and understanding as well. Taking an interactionist point of view, he suggested that movement from one stage to the next occurred when the child reached an appropriate level of maturation *and* was exposed to relevant types of experiences. Without such experiences, children were assumed to be incapable of reaching their highest level of cognitive growth.

Piaget's four stages are known as the sensorimotor, preoperational, concrete operational, and formal operational stages (see Table 10-4). Let's examine each of them and the approximate ages they span.

Sensorimotor Stage: Birth to 2 Years   During the initial part of the **sensorimotor stage** the child has relatively little competence in representing the environment using images, language, or other kinds of symbols. Consequently, the infant has no awareness of objects or people who are not immediately present at a given moment, lacking what Piaget calls *object permanence*. **Object permanence** is the awareness that objects—and people—continue to exist even if they are out of sight.

How can we know that children lack object permanence? Although we cannot ask infants, we can observe their reaction when a toy they are playing with is hid-

Sensorimotor stage: According to Piaget, the stage from birth to 2 years during which a child has little competence in representing the environment using images, language, or other symbols

Object permanence: The awareness that objects do not cease to exist when they are out of sight

---

TABLE 10-4 **A Summary of Piaget's Stages of Cognitive Development**

Stage	Approximate age range	Major characteristics
Sensorimotor	Birth–2 years	Development of object permanence, development of motor skills, little or no capacity for symbolic representation
Preoperational	2–7 years	Development of language and symbolic thinking, egocentric thinking
Concrete operational	7–12 years	Development of conservation, mastery of concept of reversibility
Formal operational	12–adulthood	Development of logical and abstract thinking

den under a blanket. Until the age of about 9 months, children will make no attempt to locate the toy. However, soon after this age they will begin to actively search for the object when it is hidden, indicating that they have developed a mental representation of the toy. Object permanence, then, is a critical development during the sensorimotor stage.

Preoperational Stage: 2 to 7 Years   The most important development during the **preoperational stage** is the use of language, described in more detail in Chapter 7. Children develop internal representational systems that allow them to describe people, events, and feelings. They even use symbols in play, pretending, for example, that a book pushed across the floor is a car.

Although children's thinking is more advanced in this stage than it was in the earlier sensorimotor stage, it is still qualitatively inferior to that of adults. We see this when we observe the preoperational child engrossed in **egocentric thought,** a way of thinking in which the child views the world entirely from his or her own perspective. Preoperational children think that everyone shares their own perspective and knowledge. Thus, children's stories and explanations to adults can be maddeningly uninformative, as they are described without any context. For example, a preoperational child may start a story with "He wouldn't let me go," neglecting to mention who "he" is or where the storyteller wanted to go. Egocentric thinking is also seen when children at the preoperational stage play hiding games. For instance, 3-year-olds frequently hide with their faces against a wall, covering their eyes—although they are still in plain view. It seems to them that if *they* cannot see, no one else will be able to see them, since they assume that others share their view.

Another deficiency of preoperational children is demonstrated by their inability to understand the **principle of conservation,** which is the knowledge that quantity is unrelated to the arrangement and physical appearance of objects. Children who have not mastered this concept do not know that the amount, volume, or length of an object does not change when its shape or configuration is changed. The question about the two glasses—one short and broad, the other tall and thin, with which we began our discussion of cognitive development—illustrates this point quite clearly. Children who do not understand the principle of conservation invariably state that the amount of liquid changes as it is poured back and forth. They cannot comprehend that a transformation in appearance does not imply a transformation in amount. Instead, it seems just as reasonable to the child that there is a change in quantity as it does to the adult that there is no change.

There are a number of other ways, some quite startling, in which their failure to understand the principle of conservation affects children's behavior. Research demonstrates that principles that are obvious and unquestioned by adults may be completely misunderstood by children during the preoperational period, and that it is not until the next stage of cognitive development that children grasp the concept of conservation. (Several examples of conservation are illustrated in Figure 10-6.)

Concrete Operational Stage: 7 to 12 Years   The beginning of the **concrete operational stage** is marked by mastery of the principle of conservation. However, there are still some aspects of conservation—such as conservation of weight and volume—that are not fully understood for a number of years.

During the concrete operational stage, children develop the ability to think in a more logical manner, and they begin to overcome some of the egocentrism characteristic of the preoperational period. One of the major principles that children are able to grasp during this stage is reversibility, the idea that some changes can be undone by reversing an earlier action. For example, they can understand

Preoperational stage: According to Piaget, the period from 2 to 7 years of age that is characterized by language development

Egocentric thought: Viewing the world entirely from one's own perspective

Principle of conservation: The knowledge that quantity is unrelated to the arrangement and physical appearance of objects

Concrete operational stage: According to Piaget, the period from 7 to 12 years of age that is characterized by logical thought and a loss of egocentrism

Type of conservation	Modality	Change in physical appearance	Average age at which invariance is grasped
Number	Number of elements in a collection 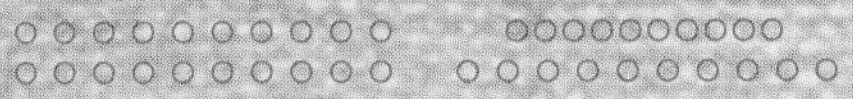	Rearranging or dislocating elements	6—7
Substance (mass)	Amount of a malleable substance (e.g., clay or liquid) 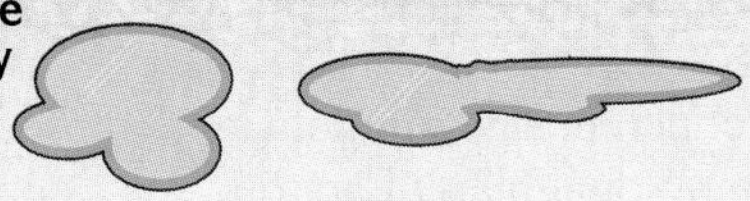	Altering shape	7—8
Length	Length of a line or object 	Altering shape or configuration	7—8
Area	Amount of surface covered by a set of plane figures 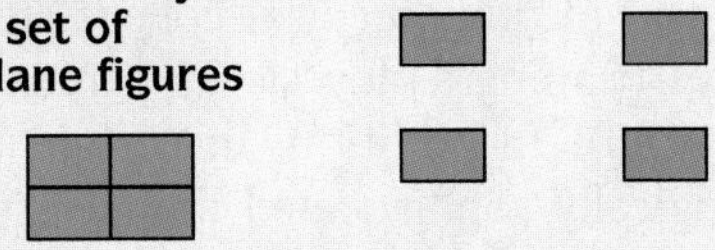	Rearranging the figures	8—9
Weight	Weight of an object	Altering shape	9—10
Volume	Volume of an object (in terms of water displacement) 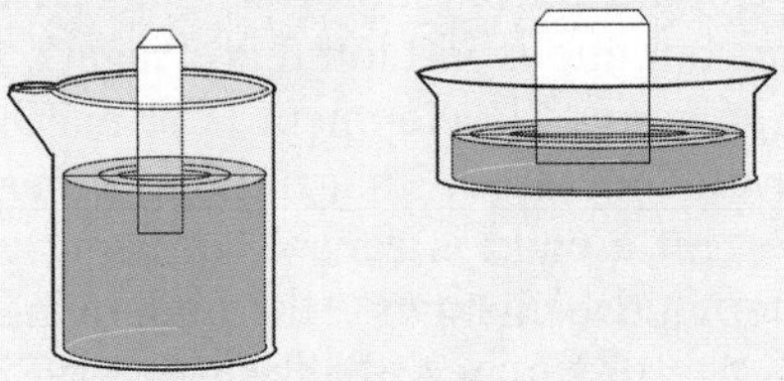	Altering shape	14—15

FIGURE 10-6 These tests are among those used most frequently to assess whether children have learned the principle of conservation across a variety of dimensions. *(Schickendanz, Schickendanz, & Forsyth, 1982.)*

that, when a ball of clay is rolled into a long sausage shape, it is possible to recreate the original ball by reversing the action. They can even conceptualize this principle in their heads, without having to see the action performed before them.

Although children make important advances in their logical capabilities during

the concrete operational stage, there is still one major limitation in their thinking: They are largely bound to the concrete, physical reality of the world. For the most part, they have difficulty understanding questions of an abstract or hypothetical nature.

Formal operational stage: According to Piaget, the period from age 12 to adulthood that is characterized by abstract thought

Formal Operational Stage: 12 Years to Adulthood   The **formal operational stage** produces a new kind of thinking—that which is abstract, formal, and logical. Thinking is no longer tied to events that are observed in the environment but makes use of logical techniques to resolve problems.

The emergence of formal operational thinking is illustrated by the way in which children approach the "pendulum problem," devised by Piaget (Piaget & Inhelder, 1958). The problem solver is asked to figure out what determines how fast a pendulum swings. Is it the length of the string, or the weight of the pendulum, or the force with which the pendulum is pushed? (For the record, the answer is the length of the string.)

Children in the concrete operational stage approach the problem haphazardly, without a logical or rational plan of action. For example, they may simultaneously change the length of the string *and* the weight on the string *and* the force with which they push the pendulum. Since they are varying all factors at once, they are unable to tell which factor is the critical one. In contrast, people in the formal operational stage approach the problem systematically. Acting as if they were scientists conducting an experiment, they examine the effects of changes in just one variable at a time. This ability to rule out competing possibilities is characteristic of formal operational thought.

Although formal operational thought emerges during the teenage years, this type of thinking is, in some cases, used only infrequently (Burbules & Linn, 1988). Moreover, it appears that many individuals never reach this stage at all; most studies show that only 40 to 60 percent of college students and adults fully reach it, with some estimates running as low as 25 percent in the general population (Keating & Clark, 1980). In addition, in certain cultures—particularly those that are less technologically sophisticated than Western societies—almost no one reaches the formal operational stage (Chandler, 1976; Super, 1980).

Stages Versus Continuous Development: Is Piaget Right?   No other theorist has given us as comprehensive a theory of cognitive development as Piaget. Still, many contemporary theorists suggest that a better explanation of how children develop cognitively can be provided by theories that do not subscribe to a stage approach. For instance, children are not always consistent in their performance of tasks that—if Piaget's theory were accurate—ought to be performed equally well at a given stage (Siegler, 1994).

Furthermore, some developmental psychologists suggest that cognitive development proceeds in a more continuous fashion than Piaget's stage theory implies. Instead, they propose that cognitive development is primarily quantitative in nature, rather than qualitative. They argue that although there are differences in when, how, and to what extent a child is capable of using given cognitive abilities—thereby reflecting quantitative changes—the underlying cognitive processes change relatively little with age (Gelman & Baillargeon, 1983; Case, 1991).

Another criticism leveled at Piaget is that he in some ways underestimated the age at which infants and children are able to understand specific concepts and principles; they seem to be more sophisticated in their cognitive abilities than he believed (Tomlinson-Keasey et al., 1979; Bornstein & Sigman, 1986). For instance, recent evidence suggests that infants as young as 5 months have rudimentary mathematical skills (Wynn, 1992).

Many developmental psychologists hold that cognitive development results from quantitative changes in children's ability to organize and use information.

Despite such criticisms, most developmental psychologists agree that, although the processes that underlie changes in cognitive abilities may not unfold in the manner suggested by his theory, Piaget has generally provided us with an accurate account of age-related changes in cognitive development. Moreover, the influence of his theory has been enormous (Ginsburg & Opper, 1988; Beilin & Pufall, 1992; Demetriou, Shayer, & Efklides, 1993). For example, Piaget suggests that increases in cognitive performance cannot be attained unless both cognitive readiness brought about by maturation *and* appropriate environmental stimulation are present. This view has been influential in determining the nature and structure of educational curricula and the way children are taught. Piaget's theory and methods have also been used to investigate issues surrounding animal cognition, such as whether primates show object permanence (they seem to; Dore & Dumas, 1987).

Information-Processing Approaches

If cognitive development does not proceed as a series of stages as suggested by Piaget, what *does* underlie the enormous growth in children's cognitive abilities that is apparent to even the most untutored eye? To many developmental psychologists, changes in **information processing,** the way in which people take in, use, and store information (Siegler, 1991) account for cognitive development.

According to this approach, quantitative changes occur in children's ability to organize and manipulate information. From this perspective, children are seen as becoming increasingly adept at information processing, analogous to the way a computer program might become more sophisticated as a programmer modifies it on the basis of experience. Information-processing approaches consider the kinds of "mental programs" that children invoke when approaching problems (Siegler, 1989; Mehler & Dupoux, 1994).

Several significant changes occur in children's information-processing capabilities. For one thing, speed of processing increases with age as some abilities become more automatic. The speed at which stimuli can be scanned, recognized, and compared with other stimuli increases with age. With increasing age, children can pay attention to stimuli longer, can discriminate between different stimuli more readily, and are less easily distracted (Kail, 1991; Jensen & Neff, 1993).

Memory also improves dramatically with age. You may recall from Chapter 6 that adults are able to keep seven, plus or minus two, chunks of information in short-term memory. In contrast, preschoolers can hold only two or three chunks; 5-year-olds can hold four; and 7-year-olds can hold five. The size of chunks also grows with age, as does the sophistication and organization of knowledge stored in memory (Bjorklund, 1985; Ornstein & Naus, 1988). Still, memory capabilities are impressive at a very early age: Even before they can speak, infants can remember events in which they were active participants for months, according to recent research (Rovee-Collier, 1993).

Finally, improvement in information processing is tied to advances in **metacognition,** an awareness and understanding of one's own cognitive processes. Metacognition involves the planning, monitoring, and revising of cognitive strategies. Younger children, who lack an awareness of their own cognitive processes, are often ignorant of their incapabilities, causing them to fail to recognize their own errors. It is only later, when metacognitive abilities become more sophisticated, that children are able to know when they *don't* understand. Such increasing sophistication reflects a change in children's *theory of mind*, their knowledge and beliefs about the way the mind operates (Flavell, Green, & Flavell, 1990; Moses & Chandler, 1992; Flavell, 1993).

Information processing: The way in which people take in, use, and store information

Metacognition: An awareness and understanding of one's own cognitive processes

Exploring Diversity

Supporting Children's School Achievement: The Asian Success Story

By the time they both complete public schooling, the average student in Japan achieves at a higher level than the average student in the United States. It doesn't start out that way: In first grade, only minor differences exist between Japanese and American student performance. However, by the time they both reach fifth grade, the average Japanese student has pulled ahead of his or her American counterpart and remains ahead through high school (Stevenson & Lee, 1990).

The school performance of Asian-American students as a group also reflects superior performance. For instance, Asian-American students in the San Diego area have higher grades than other students, and Asian-American students typically take more advanced courses than their classmates (Brand, 1987).

What accounts for the exceptional success of Asian students? One factor is that Asian children face greater cultural pressure to achieve in school. For instance, Japanese and Korean parents spend a great deal of time helping their children with schoolwork, and they stress that academic success is their children's most important task. Asian mothers also hold higher standards for their children's school performance than do American mothers.

Another reason for superior Asian performance rests on differences in how parents attribute their children's school success. Drawing on the writings of the great Chinese philosopher Confucius, Asian parents stress the importance of effort, hard work, and perseverance in school. At the same time, they minimize the effects of individual abilities. To the Asian parent, then, all children have pretty much the same level of underlying ability; what determines school success is how hard children work. American parents take a quite different view: They emphasize the importance of inborn ability, believing that children vary considerably in their abilities and that ability plays a primary role in school performance. At the same time, American parents downplay the role of effort in producing school success.

The impact of this philosophical difference is considerable. When students do not do well in school, parents in the United States may conclude that their children simply don't have sufficient ability. As a result, they do not push their children to work harder. In contrast, Asian children who perform poorly are typically

Many Asian-American students perform exceptionally well in school, in part because Asian cultures emphasize academic success and perseverance with schoolwork.

encouraged to work harder, because greater effort is seen as a means to overcome their academic difficulties (Stevenson, 1992; Stevenson & Stigler, 1992; Stevenson, Chen, & Lee, 1992).

In sum, the appearance of superior academic performance of Asian children seems to rest largely on cultural differences in how parents perceive the causes of school performance, on attitudes about the importance of education, and on the ways in which children are encouraged to succeed. If these cultural standards and values change, so too will the academic performance of students.

RECAP AND REVIEW

Recap

- The neonate is born with a number of reflexes, including the rooting, sucking, startle, and Babinski reflexes.
- Physical growth is initially rapid: During the first year, children typically triple their birth weight, and height increases by 50 percent. Rate of growth declines after age 3, averaging about 5 pounds and 3 inches a year until adolescence.
- The perceptual abilities of infants grow rapidly, although they are remarkably sophisticated at birth.
- Social development is demonstrated through the growth of attachment, the positive emotional bond that develops between a child and a particular individual. As a child ages, relationships with friends become increasingly important.
- Erikson's theory suggests that there are four stages of psychosocial development within childhood, with four other stages spanning the rest of life.
- A major theory of cognitive development—the way in which children's understanding of the world changes as a function of age and experience—is Piaget's theory. Piaget proposes four major stages: sensorimotor, preoperational, concrete operational, and formal operational.
- Although Piaget's description of what happens within the various stages of cognitive development has largely been upheld, some theorists argue that development is more gradual and continuous and due more to quantitative than to qualitative changes in cognition.
- Information-processing approaches to cognitive development focus on the quantitative changes that occur in the way in which people take in, use, and store information. Major changes occur with age in the speed of processing, length of attention span, memory, and metacognitive abilities.

Review

1. Researchers studying newborns use _____, or the decrease in the response to a stimulus that occurs after repeated presentations of the same stimulus, as an indicator of a baby's interest.
2. The emotional bond that develops between a child and its caregiver is known as _____ .

3. Children develop an attachment to their mothers only; the father's role is important, but children do not become attached to their fathers. True or false?
4. Match the parenting style with its definition:
   1. Permissive
   2. Authoritative
   3. Authoritarian

   a. Rigid; highly punitive; demand obedience
   b. Give little direction; lax on obedience
   c. Firm but fair; try to explain decisions
5. Similar child-rearing styles have been documented around the world. True or false?
6. Erikson's theory of _____ development involves a series of _____ stages, each of which must be resolved in order for a person to develop optimally.
7. _____ suggested four stages of cognitive development, each of which is dependent on maturational and environmental factors.
8. Match the stage of development with the thinking style characteristic of the stage:
   1. Egocentric thought
   2. Object permanence
   3. Abstract thinking
   4. Conservation; reversibility

   a. Sensorimotor   c. Preoperational
   b. Formal operational   d. Concrete operational
9. Current research suggests that child development may proceed in a continuous fashion, rather than in stages as suggested by Piaget. True or false?
10. _____-_____ theories of development suggest that the way in which a child handles information is critical to his or her development.

Ask Yourself

You are given a child to raise in an environment that you can shape totally to your liking. What would your optimal child-rearing environment be? What style of child rearing would you use? How do you think the child's temperamental style might influence or modify your choices?

(Answers to review questions are on page 349.)

• *What major physical, social, and cognitive transitions characterize adolescence?*

ADOLESCENCE: BECOMING AN ADULT

Turning 13 was an important period of my life. It was the time when I started to mature physically. It also was the time when more girls started to notice me. My personality changed a lot from a boring nerd to an energetic, funny and athletic kid.

As my year went on as a 13-year-old, as if things couldn't get better, they surprisingly did! My life as a child has ended. I was now a teenager. This just goes to show you that turning 13 meant turning into a new person.

Patrick Backer (Backer, 1993, p. 2)

As you go to school, things get harder. You sort of realize that you're getting older. Adults treat you like an adult and don't give you the breaks you got when you're a child.

To be 13 you have journeyed only half way to the *real* world. Then you notice that you're going to high school and think of the next four years and then college. Next you vote, a house, job and kids. It seems your life passes right before your eyes.

Mieko Ozeki (Ozeki, 1993, p. 2)

When I turned 13 it was like starting a new life. It was the year I was finally going to be allowed to do more things. For one thing I was able to hang out later. I wasn't a child anymore. I knew it and my parents knew it, too.

I really can't think of a more important birthday besides your first one.

Dmitri Ponomarev (Ponomarev, 1993, p. 2)

As these statements indicate, the thirteenth birthday has a significance that extends beyond simply marking the passage of another year. Instead, for many people, it is a moment that signifies the transition into adolescence.

Adolescence, the developmental stage between childhood and adulthood, is a critical period. It is a time of profound changes and, occasionally, turmoil. Considerable biological change occurs as adolescents attain sexual and physical maturity. At the same time, these physiological changes are rivaled by important social, emotional, and cognitive changes that occur as adolescents strive for independence and move toward adulthood.

Because many years of schooling precede most people's entry into the work force in Western society, the stage of adolescence is a fairly lengthy one, beginning just before the teenage years and ending just after them. No longer children, but considered by society to be not quite adults, adolescents face a period of rapid physical, cognitive, and social change that affects them for the rest of their lives.

Physical Development: The Changing Adolescent

If you think back to the start of your own adolescence, it is likely that the most dramatic changes you remember are of a physical nature. A spurt in height, the growth of breasts in girls, deepening voices in boys, the development of body hair, and intense sexual feelings are a source of curiosity, interest, and sometimes embarrassment for individuals entering adolescence.

The physical changes that occur at the start of adolescence are largely a result of the secretion of various hormones (see Chapter 2), and they affect virtually every aspect of the adolescent's life. Not since infancy has development been so dramatic. Weight and height increase rapidly due to a growth spurt that begins at around age 10 for girls and age 12 for boys. Adolescents may grow as much as 5 inches in a single year.

Puberty, the period at which maturation of the sexual organs occurs, begins at about age 11 or 12 for girls and 13 or 14 for boys. However, there are wide variations, and it is not uncommon for a girl to begin to menstruate—the first sign of sexual maturity in females—as early as age 8 or 9 or as late as age 16.

Adolescence: The developmental stage between childhood and adulthood during which many physical, cognitive, and social changes take place

Puberty: The period during which maturation of the sexual organs occurs

Furthermore, there are cultural variations in the timing of first menstruation. For example, the average Lumi girl in New Guinea does not begin menstruating until she is 18 (Eveleth & Tanner, 1976; Tanner, 1990).

In Western cultures, the average age at which adolescents reach sexual maturity has been steadily decreasing over the last century, most likely a result of better nutrition and medical care (Dreyer, 1982). Furthermore, girls living in affluent homes begin to menstruate at an earlier age than those from economically disadvantaged homes, in all regions of the world. The onset of puberty, then, provides a good illustration of how changes in the environment interact with heredity to affect development.

The age at which puberty begins has important implications for the way adolescents feel about themselves—as well as how others treat them. Early-maturing boys have a distinct advantage over later-maturing boys. They do better in athletics, are generally more popular with peers, and have more positive self-concepts (Peterson, 1985). On the other hand, they are more likely to have difficulties at school, to commit minor acts of delinquency, and to become involved with alcohol abuse. One reason for such behavior seems to be that early-maturing boys are more likely to become friends with older, and therefore more influential, boys, who may lead them into age-inappropriate activities. On balance, though, the consequences of early maturing for boys are basically positive; early maturers, compared with later maturers, are typically somewhat more responsible and cooperative in later life (Anderson & Magnusson, 1990).

The picture is different for girls. Although early-maturing girls are more sought after as dates and sometimes have better self-esteem than later-maturing girls, some of the consequences of their early physical maturation may be less positive.

The attitudes of a girl's peer group influence her reaction to early maturation.

ANSWERS TO PREVIOUS REVIEW

1. habituation **2.** attachment **3.** False; attachment to a father can be as strong as attachment to a mother. **4.** 1-b; 2-c; 3-a **5.** False; rearing styles are culture-specific.
6. psychosocial; eight **7.** Piaget **8.** 1-c; 2-a; 3-b; 4-d **9.** True **10.** Information-processing

For example, the development of such obvious characteristics as breasts may set them apart from their peers and be a source of ridicule (Simmons & Blyth, 1987).

The specific reactions to which girls are subjected as a result of early maturation are related in part to cultural norms and standards. In the United States, where the notion of female sexuality is regarded with a certain ambivalence, the consequences of early maturation may be primarily negative. In contrast, in countries in which attitudes toward sexuality are more open, the results of early maturation tend to be more positive. For instance, early-maturing girls in Germany have higher self-esteem than do early-maturing girls in the United States. And even in this country, reactions to early maturation may differ, depending on what community and peer group a girl is part of (Silbereisen et al., 1989; Richards et al., 1990).

Late maturation also produces certain psychological difficulties. Boys who are smaller and less coordinated than their more mature peers tend to be ridiculed and seen as less attractive. In time, they may come to view themselves in the same way. The consequences of late maturation may extend well into a male's thirties (Mussen & Jones, 1957). Similarly, late-maturing girls are at a disadvantage in junior high and high school. They hold a relatively low social status, and they may be overlooked in dating and other male-female activities (Apter et al., 1981; Clarke-Stewart & Friedman, 1987).

Clearly, the rate at which physical changes occur during adolescence can have significant effects on the way in which people are viewed by others and the way in which they view themselves. Just as important as physical changes, however, are the psychological and social changes that unfold during adolescence.

Moral and Cognitive Development: Distinguishing Right from Wrong

In Europe, a woman is near death from a special kind of cancer. The one drug that the doctors think might save her is a form of radium that a druggist in the same town has recently discovered. The drug is expensive to make, and the druggist is charging ten times the cost, or $2000, for a small dose. The sick woman's husband, Heinz, approaches everyone he knows in hopes of borrowing money, but he can get together only about $1000. He tells the druggist that his wife is dying and asks him to lower the price of the drug or let him pay later. The druggist says, "No, I discovered the drug and I'm going to make money from it." Heinz is desperate and considers breaking into the man's store to steal the drug for his wife.

What would you tell Heinz to do?

Kohlberg's Theory of Moral Development   In the view of psychologist Lawrence Kohlberg, the advice you give Heinz is a reflection of your level of moral development. According to Kohlberg, people pass through a series of stages in the evolution of their sense of justice and in the kind of reasoning they use to make moral judgments (Kohlberg, 1984). Largely because of the various cognitive deficits that Piaget described, preadolescent children tend to think either in terms of concrete, unvarying rules ("It is always wrong to steal" or "I'll be punished if I steal") or in terms of the rules of society ("Good people don't steal" or "What if everyone stole?").

Adolescents, however, are capable of reasoning on a higher plane, having typically reached Piaget's formal operational stage of cognitive development. Because they are able to comprehend broad moral principles, they can understand that morality is not always black and white and that conflict can exist between two sets of socially accepted standards.

Kohlberg (1984) suggests that the changes occurring in moral reasoning can

TABLE 10-5 Kohlberg's Levels of Moral Reasoning

Level	Stage	Sample moral reasoning of subjects	
		In favor of stealing	Against stealing
Level 1 Preconventional morality: At this level, the concrete interests of the individual are considered in terms of rewards and punishments.	Stage 1 Obedience and punishment orientation: At this stage, people stick to rules in order to avoid punishment, and obedience occurs for its own sake.	"If you let your wife die, you will get in trouble. You'll be blamed for not spending the money to save her, and there'll be an investigation of you and the druggist for your wife's death."	"You shouldn't steal the drug because you'll be caught and sent to jail if you do. If you do get away, your conscience will bother you thinking how the police will catch up with you at any minute."
	Stage 2 Reward orientation: At this stage, rules are followed only for a person's own benefit. Obedience occurs because of rewards that are received.	"If you do happen to get caught, you could give the drug back and you wouldn't get much of a sentence. It wouldn't bother you much to serve a little jail term, if you have your wife when you get out."	"You may not get much of a jail term if you steal the drug, but your wife will probably die before you get out, so it won't do much good. If your wife dies, you shouldn't blame yourself; it isn't your fault she has cancer."
Level 2 Conventional morality: At this level, people approach moral problems as members of society. They are interested in pleasing others by acting as good members of society.	Stage 3 "Good boy" morality: Individuals at this stage show an interest in maintaining the respect of others and doing what is expected of them.	"No one will think you're bad if you steal the drug, but your family will think you're an inhuman husband if you don't. If you let your wife die, you'll never be able to look anybody in the face again."	"It isn't just the druggist who will think you're a criminal; everyone else will too. After you steal the drug, you'll feel bad thinking how you've brought dishonor on your family and yourself; you won't be able to face anyone again."
	Stage 4 Authority and social-order-maintaining morality: People at this stage conform to society's rules and consider that "right" is what society defines as right.	"If you have any sense of honor, you won't let your wife die just because you're afraid to do the only thing that will save her. You'll always feel guilty that you caused her death if you don't do your duty to her."	"You're desperate and you may not know you're doing wrong when you steal the drug. But you'll know you did wrong after you're sent to jail. You'll always feel guilty for your dishonesty and lawbreaking."
Level 3 Postconventional morality: At this level, people use moral principles which are seen as broader than those of any particular society.	Stage 5 Morality of contract, individual rights, and democratically accepted law: People at this stage do what is right because of a sense of obligation to laws which are agreed upon within society. They perceive that laws can be modified as part of changes in an implicit social contract.	"You'll lose other people's respect, not gain it, if you don't steal. If you let your wife die, it will be out of fear, not out of reasoning. So you'll just lose self-respect and probably the respect of others too."	"You'll lose your standing and respect in the community and violate the law. You'll lose respect for yourself if you're carried away by emotion and forget the long-range point of view."
	Stage 6 Morality of individual principles and conscience: At this final stage, a person follows laws because they are based on universal ethical principles. Laws that violate the principles are disobeyed.	"If you don't steal the drug, and if you let your wife die, you'll always condemn yourself for it afterward. You won't be blamed and you'll have lived up to the outside rule of the law but you won't have lived up to your own standards of conscience."	"If you steal the drug, you won't be blamed by other people, but you'll condemn yourself because you won't have lived up to your own conscience and standards of honesty."

Source: Adapted from Kohlberg, 1969.

be understood best as a three-level sequence, which, in turn, is divided into six stages. These levels and stages, along with samples of subjects' reasoning at each stage, are described in Table 10-5. Note that arguments either in favor of or

against stealing the drug can be classified as belonging in the same stage of moral reasoning. It is the nature and sophistication of the argument that determine into what category it falls.

Kohlberg's theory assumes that people move through the six stages in a fixed order, and that they are not capable of reaching the highest stage until about the age of 13—primarily because of deficits in cognitive development that are not overcome until that age. However, many people never reach the highest level of moral reasoning. In fact, Kohlberg suggests that only about 25 percent of all adults rise above stage 4 of his model (Kohlberg & Ryncarz, 1990).

Extensive research has shown that the stages identified by Kohlberg generally provide a valid representation of moral development. Yet the research also raises several methodological issues. One major problem is that Kohlberg's procedure measures moral *judgments,* not *behavior.* Although Kohlberg's theory seems to be a generally accurate account of how moral reasoning develops, some research finds that moral reasoning is not always related to moral behavior (Snarey, 1985; Malinowski & Smith, 1985; Damon, 1988). At the same time, other investigators suggest that a relationship between moral judgments and behavior does exist. For example, one study found that students who were most likely to commit acts of civil disobedience were those whose moral judgments were at the highest levels (Candee & Kohlberg, 1987). Still, the evidence is mixed on this question; knowing right from wrong does not mean that we will always act in accordance with our judgments (Darley & Shultz, 1990; Denton & Krebs, 1990; Thoma, Rest, & Davison, 1991).

Moral Development in Women   Psychologist Carol Gilligan has identified an important shortcoming of Kohlberg's original research: It was carried out using only male subjects and is thus more applicable to them than to women. Furthermore, she argues convincingly that because of their distinctive socialization experiences, a fundamental difference exists in the manner in which men and women view moral behavior. According to Gilligan, men view morality primarily in terms of broad principles such as justice and fairness. In contrast, women see it in terms of responsibility toward individuals and willingness to make sacrifices to help a specific individual within the context of a particular relationship. Compassion for individuals is a more salient factor in moral behavior for women than it is for men (Gilligan, 1982; Gilligan, Ward, & Taylor, 1988; Gilligan, Lyons, & Hanmer, 1990).

Consequently, because Kohlberg's model conceives of moral behavior largely in terms of abstract principles such as justice and fairness, it is inadequate in describing the moral development of females. This factor accounts for the puzzling finding that women typically score at a lower level than men on tests of moral judgment using Kohlberg's stage sequence. In Gilligan's view, women's morality is centered on individual well-being and social relationships rather than on moral abstractions. For this reason, she maintains that the highest levels of morality are represented by compassionate concern for the welfare of others.

According to Gilligan's research, which investigated moral dilemmas such as deciding whether to have an abortion, women's moral development proceeds in three stages (see Table 10-6). In the first stage, termed "orientation toward individual survival," a woman concentrates on what is practical and best for her. During this stage, there is a transition from selfishness to responsibility, in which the woman thinks about what would be best for others.

At the second stage of moral development, termed "goodness as self-sacrifice," a woman begins to think that she must sacrifice her own wishes for the sake of what other people want. Ultimately, though, she makes the transition from "goodness" to "truth," in which she takes into account her own needs plus those of others.

In adolescence, the peer group becomes more important (relative to adults) as a sounding board for clarification of identity and as a source of social judgements.

TABLE 10-6 Gilligan's Stages of Moral Development

Stage	Major characteristics	Samples of reasoning used by women contemplating having an abortion
Stage 1 Orientation toward individual survival	Focus on what is practical, best for self; concern for survival	Having a baby would prevent her "from doing other things" but would be "the perfect chance to move away from home."
Stage 2 Goodness as self-sacrifice	Sacrifice of own wishes to help others	"I think what confuses me is a choice of either hurting myself or hurting other people around me. What is more important?"
Stage 3 Morality of nonviolence	Hurting anyone, including oneself, is immoral	"The decision has got to be, first of all, something that the woman can live with . . . and it must be based on where she is at and other significant people in her life are."

Source: Gilligan, 1982.

In the third stage, "morality of nonviolence," a woman comes to see that hurting anyone is immoral—including hurting herself. This realization establishes a moral equality between herself and others and represents, according to Gilligan, the most sophisticated level of moral reasoning.

As you can see, Gilligan's sequence of stages is very different from that presented by Kohlberg, and some psychologists have suggested that her rejection of Kohlberg's work is too sweeping (Colby & Damon, 1987). It is clear, though, that gender plays an important role in determining what is seen as moral. Furthermore, the differing conceptions of men and women over what constitutes moral behavior may lead them to regard the morality of a particular behavior in potentially contradictory ways. Ultimately, such divergent views may lead to disagreement, such as when a father and mother come to different conclusions about the necessity of disciplining a child (McGraw & Bloomfield, 1987; Handler, Franz, & Guerra, 1992).

Social Development: Finding Oneself in a Social World

"Who am I?" "How do I fit into the world?" "What is life all about?" Questions such as these assume particular significance during the teenage years, as adolescents seek to find their place in the broader social world. As we see, this quest takes adolescents along several routes.

Erikson's Theory of Psychosocial Development: The Search for Identity

Erikson's theory of psychosocial development emphasizes the search for identity during the adolescent years. As noted earlier, psychosocial development encompasses how people's understanding of themselves, one another, and the world around them changes during the course of development (Erikson, 1963).

The fifth stage of Erikson's theory (summarized, with the other stages, in Table 10-7) is labeled the **identity-versus-role-confusion stage** and encompasses adolescence. This stage is a time of major testing, as people try to determine what is unique and special about themselves. They attempt to discover who they are, what their strengths are, and what kinds of roles they are best suited to play for the rest of their lives—in short, their **identity.** Confusion over the most appropriate role to follow in life can lead to lack of a stable identity, adoption of a socially

Identity-versus-role-confusion stage: According to Erikson, a time in adolescence of testing to determine one's own unique qualities

Identity: The distinguishing character of the individual: who each of us is, what our roles are, and what we are capable of

TABLE 10-7 A Summary of Erikson's Stages

Stage	Approximate age	Positive outcomes	Negative outcomes
1. Trust-vs.-mistrust	Birth–1½ years	Feelings of trust from environmental support	Fear and concern regarding others
2. Autonomy-vs.-shame-and-doubt	1½–3 years	Self-sufficiency if exploration is encouraged	Doubts about self, lack of independence
3. Initiative-vs.-guilt	3–6 years	Discovery of ways to initiate actions	Guilt from actions and thoughts
4. Industry-vs.-inferiority	6–12 years	Development of sense of competence	Feelings of inferiority, no sense of mastery
5. Identity-vs.-role-confusion	Adolescence	Awareness of uniqueness of self, knowledge of role to be followed	Inability to identify appropriate roles in life
6. Intimacy-vs.-isolation	Early adulthood	Development of loving, sexual relationships and close friendships	Fear of relationships with others
7. Generativity-vs.-stagnation	Middle adulthood	Sense of contribution to continuity of life	Trivialization of one's activities
8. Ego-integrity-vs.-despair	Late adulthood	Sense of unity in life's accomplishments	Regret over lost opportunities of life

Intimacy-versus-isolation stage:
According to Erikson, a period during early adulthood that focuses on developing close relationships

Generativity-versus-stagnation stage: According to Erikson, a period in middle adulthood during which we take stock of our contributions to family and society

unacceptable role such as that of a social deviant, or difficulty in maintaining close personal relationships later in life (Kahn et al., 1985; Archer & Waterman, 1994).

During the identity-versus-role-confusion period, pressures to identify what one wants to do with one's life are acutely felt. Because these pressures come at a time of major physical changes as well as important changes in what society expects of them, adolescents can find the period a particularly difficult one. The identity-versus-role-confusion stage has another important characteristic: a decline in reliance on adults for information, with a shift toward using the peer group as a source of social judgments. The peer group becomes increasingly important, enabling adolescents to form close, adultlike relationships and helping them to clarify their personal identities.

According to Erikson, the identity-versus-role-confusion stage during adolescence marks a pivotal point in psychosocial development, paving the way for continued growth. For instance, during college, people move into the **intimacy-versus-isolation stage** (spanning the period of early adulthood, from around age 18 to age 30), in which the focus is on developing close relationships with others. Difficulties during this stage result in feelings of loneliness and a fear of relationships with others, while successful resolution of the crises of this stage results in the possibility of forming relationships that are intimate on physical, intellectual, and emotional levels.

Development continues during middle adulthood as people enter the **generativity-versus-stagnation stage.** Generativity refers to a person's contribution to his or her family, community, work, and society as a whole. Success in this stage results in positive feelings about the continuity of life, while difficulties lead to feelings of triviality regarding one's activities and a sense of stagnation or of having done nothing for upcoming generations. In fact, if a person has not successfully resolved the identity crisis of adolescence, he or she may still be floundering as far as identifying an appropriate career is concerned.

Finally, the last stage of psychosocial development, the period of **ego-integrity-versus-despair stage,** comprises later adulthood and continues until death. Success in resolving the difficulties presented by this stage of life is signified by a sense of accomplishment; difficulties result in regret over what might have been achieved, but was not.

One of the most noteworthy aspects of Erikson's theory is its suggestion that development does not stop at adolescence but continues throughout adulthood, a view that a substantial amount of research now confirms (Peterson & Stewart, 1993; Hetherington & Weinberger, 1993). For instance, a 22-year study by psychologist Susan Whitbourne found considerable support for the fundamentals of Erikson's theory, determining that psychosocial development continues through adolescence and adulthood (Whitbourne et al., 1992). In sum, adolescence is not an end point but rather a way station on the path of psychosocial development.

Ego-integrity-versus-despair stage: According to Erikson, a period from late adulthood until death during which we review life's accomplishments and failures

Stormy Adolescence: Myth or Reality?   Does puberty invariably foreshadow a stormy, rebellious period of adolescence? At one time most children entering adolescence were thought to be beginning a period fraught with stress and unhappiness, but psychologists are now finding that such a characterization is largely a myth. Most young people, it seems, pass through adolescence without appreciable turmoil in their lives (Peterson, 1988; Steinberg, 1993).

This is not to say that adolescence is completely tranquil (Laursen & Collins, 1994). There is clearly a rise in the amount of arguing and bickering in most families. Young teenagers, as part of their search for identity, tend to experience a degree of tension between their attempts to become independent from their parents and their actual dependence on them. They may experiment with a range of behaviors, flirting with a variety of activities that their parents, and even society as a whole, find objectionable. Happily, though, for the majority of families such tensions tend to stabilize during middle adolescence—around age 15 or 16—and eventually decline around age 18 (Montemayor, 1983; Galambos, 1992; Crockett & Crowter, 1995).

One reason for the increase in discord in adolescence appears to be the protracted period in which children stay at home with their parents. In prior historical periods—and in some non-Western cultures today—children leave home immediately after puberty and are considered adults. Today, however, sexually mature adolescents may spend as many as 7 or 8 years with their parents (Steinberg, 1989). Current statistics even foreshadow an extension of the conflicts of adolescence beyond the teenage years for a significant number of people. Some one-third of all unmarried men and one-fifth of unmarried women between the ages of 25 and 34 continue to reside with their parents (Gross, 1991).

Adolescence also introduces a variety of stresses outside the home. Typically, adolescents change schools at least twice (from elementary to middle or junior high, then to senior high school), and relationships with friends and peers are particularly volatile (Berndt, 1992). Many adolescents hold part-time jobs, increasing the demands of school, work, and social activities on their time. Such stressors can lead to tensions at home (Steinberg & Dornbusch, 1991). (For a discussion with someone whose work is directly involved with the period of adolescence, see the Pathways through Psychology box (next page.)

• *What are the principal kinds of physical, social, and intellectual changes that occur in early and middle adulthood, and what are their causes?*

EARLY AND MIDDLE ADULTHOOD: THE MIDDLE YEARS OF LIFE

Psychologists generally consider early adulthood to begin around age 20 and last until about age 40 to 45, and middle adulthood to last from about age 40 to 45 to around age 65. Despite the enormous importance of these periods of life—in terms of both the accomplishments that occur within them and their overall length (together they span some 40 years)—they have been studied less than any other stage by developmental psychologists. One reason is that the physical changes during these periods are less apparent and occur more gradually than do those at other times during the lifespan. In addition, the social changes are so diverse that they defy simple categorization. Still, there has been a recent upsurge of interest in adulthood among developmental psychologists, with a special focus

on the social changes that occur in terms of the family, marriage, divorce, and women's careers.

Physical Development: The Peak of Health

For most people, early adulthood marks the peak of physical health. From about 18 to 25 years of age, people's strength is greatest, their reflexes are quickest, and their chances of dying from disease are quite slim. Moreover, reproductive capabilities are at their highest level.

The changes that begin at age 25 are largely of a quantitative rather than a qualitative nature. The body begins to operate slightly less efficiently and becomes somewhat more prone to disease. Overall, however, ill health remains the exception; most people stay remarkably healthy. (Can you think of any machine other than the body that can operate without pause for so long a period?)

The major biological change that does occur pertains to reproductive capabilities during middle adulthood. On average, during their late forties or early fifties, women begin **menopause,** the point at which they stop menstruating and are no longer fertile. Because menopause is accompanied by a reduction in estrogen, a female hormone, women sometimes experience symptoms such as hot flashes, or sudden sensations of heat. However, most symptoms of menopause can be successfully treated with artificial estrogen, if the symptoms are severe enough to warrant medical intervention.

Menopause was once blamed for a host of psychological symptoms, including depression and memory loss. However, most research now suggests that such problems, if they do occur, are caused more by women's perceived reactions to reaching an "old" age in a society that highly values youth, rather than by menopause itself.

In fact, researchers have found that women's reactions to menopause vary significantly across cultures. According to anthropologist Yewoubdar Beyene, the more a society values old age, the less difficulty its women have during menopause. In her study of women in Mayan villages, she found that women looked forward to menopause, because they stopped having children. In addition, they didn't even experience some of the classic symptoms of menopause; hot flashes, for example, were unheard of. A society's attitudes, then, more than the physiological changes of menopause, may produce psychological difficulties (Ballinger, 1981; Beyene, 1989; Beck, 1992).

For men, the aging process during middle adulthood is somewhat subtler, since there are no physiological signals of increasing age equivalent to the end of menstruation in women. Moreover, men remain fertile and are capable of fathering children until well into old age. On the other hand, some gradual physical declines occur: Sperm production decreases, and the frequency of orgasm tends to decline. Once again, though, any psychological difficulties associated with these changes that men may experience are usually brought about not so much by physical deterioration as by the inability of the aging individual to meet the exaggerated standards of youthfulness held in high regard by our society.

Menopause: The point at which women stop menstruating, generally at around age 45

Social Development: Working at Life

Whereas physical changes during adulthood reflect development of a quantitative nature, social developmental transitions are more profound. It is during this period that people typically launch themselves into careers, marriage, and families.

Psychologist Daniel Levinson (1986) has proposed a model of adult development based on a comprehensive study of major events in the lives of a group of forty men. Although his initial sample was small and consisted only of white middle-class males, the study provided one of the first comprehensive descriptions of

the stages through which people pass following adolescence. Furthermore, based on more current research, Levinson contends that the life cycles of women and men are similar (Levinson, 1996).

According to Levinson, people pass through several stages from the entry into early adulthood through the end of middle adulthood. The stages in early adulthood relate to leaving one's family and entering the adult world. An individual envisions what Levinson calls "The Dream"—an all-encompassing vision about what goals are desired from life, be it writing the great American novel or becoming a physician. Career choices are made, and perhaps discarded, during early adulthood, until eventually long-term decisions are reached. This leads to a period of settling down in the late thirties, during which people establish themselves in a particular set of roles and begin to develop and work toward a vision of their own future.

In their early forties, people sometimes begin to question their lives as they enter a period called the **midlife transition,** and the idea that life is finite becomes paramount in their thinking. Rather than maintaining a future-oriented view of life, people begin to ask questions about their past accomplishments, assessing what they have done and how satisfying it has been to them (Gould, 1978). They realize that they will not accomplish everything they had hoped to before their lives end.

In some cases, people's assessments of their lives are negative, and they may enter what has been popularly labeled a **midlife crisis.** At the same time that they face signs of physical aging, they become aware that their careers are not going to progress considerably further. Even if they have attained the heights to which they aspired—be it company president or well-respected community leader—they find that the satisfaction derived from their accomplishments is not all that they had hoped it would be. As they look at their past, they may also be motivated to try to define what went wrong and how they can remedy previous dissatisfaction.

In most cases, though, the passage into middle age is relatively placid, and some developmental psychologists even question whether most people experience a midlife crisis (Whitbourne, 1986). Most 40-year-olds view their lives and accomplishments positively enough to have their midlife transition proceed relatively smoothly, and the forties and fifties are a particularly rewarding period of life. Rather than looking to the future, people at this stage concentrate on the present, and their involvement with their families, friends, and other social groups takes on new importance. A major developmental thrust of this period of life is learning to accept that the die has been cast, and that one must come to terms with one's circumstances.

Finally, during the last stages of middle adulthood—the fifties—people generally become more accepting of others and their lives and less concerned about issues or problems that once bothered them. Rather than being driven to achieve as they were in their thirties, they come to accept the realization that death is inevitable, and they try to understand their accomplishments in terms of the broader meaning of life (Gould, 1978). Although people may begin, for the first time, to label themselves as "old," many also develop a sense of wisdom and feel freer to enjoy life (Karp, 1988).

Because most work on the phases of social development in adulthood has been based on the study of men's lives, it is important to consider whether women's lives follow the same patterns. We might expect significant gender differences on several grounds. For one thing, women often play different roles in society than men, either by choice or because of societal expectations. Moreover, women's roles have undergone rapid social change in the last decade, as we shall discuss next, making generalizations about women's development during early and middle adulthood difficult (Gilligan, 1982; Gilligan, Lyons, & Hanmer, 1990; Mercer, Nichols, & Doyle, 1989).

Midlife transition: Beginning around the age of 40, a period during which we come to the realization that life is finite

Midlife crisis: The negative feelings that accompany the realization that we have not accomplished in life what we had hoped to

For these reasons, there is as yet no clear answer to the question of how women's social development differs from men's, since researchers have only begun to accumulate a large enough body of data focusing directly on women. Some recent research suggests, however, that there are both similarities and differences between men and women. Levinson (1996), for example, argues that women generally go through the same stages at the same ages as men, although disparities exist in the specific details of some of the stages. For instance, important differences appear during "The Dream," the stage in which people develop a vision of what their future life will encompass. Women often have greater difficulty than men in forming a clear dream, for they may experience conflict between the goals of working and of raising a family. For men, this conflict tends to be much less important, since a man who wishes to marry and have a family usually views employment as the means of taking care of his family.

Marriage, Children, and Divorce: Family Ties

In many a fairy tale, the typical ending has a dashing young man and a beautiful woman marrying, having children, and living happily ever after. Unfortunately, such a scenario is more common in fairy tales than real life. In most cases, it does not match the realities of love and marriage in the 1990s. Today, it is just as likely that the man and woman would first live together, then get married and have children—but ultimately end up getting divorced (Gottfried & Gottfried, 1994; Gottman, 1995).

According to census figures, the percentage of unmarried couples in U.S. households has increased dramatically over the last two decades, and the average age at which marriage takes place is higher than at any other time since the turn of the century (Barringer, 1989). When people do marry, the probability of divorce is high, particularly for younger couples. Even though divorce rates appear to be declining since they peaked in 1981, 60 percent of all first marriages still end in divorce. Two-fifths of children will experience the breakup of their parents' marriage before they are 18 years old. Moreover, the rise in divorce is not just a U.S. phenomenon: The divorce rate has accelerated over the last several decades in most industrialized countries except for Japan and Italy (Cherlin et al., 1991; Sorrentino, 1990; Cherlin, 1993; Goode, 1993).

Because of these matrimonial and divorce trends, society has witnessed more than a doubling of single-parent households over the past two decades. In 1990, some 28 percent of all family households had one parent, compared with just 13 percent in 1970. Some racial and ethnic groups have been particularly hard-hit by the phenomenon: More than half of all black children and almost one-third of Hispanic children lived in homes with only one parent in 1990. Furthermore, in most single-parent families, it is the mother, rather than the father, with whom the children reside—a phenomenon that is consistent across racial and ethnic groups throughout the industrialized world (U.S. Census Bureau, 1991; Burns & Scott, 1994).

Divorce and subsequent life in a single-parent household presents the potential for the development of several kinds of psychological difficulties, for both parents and children (Gottman, 1993; Guttman, 1993). Children may initially be exposed to high levels of parental conflict, leading to heightened anxiety and aggressive behavior. Later separation from one or the other parent is a painful experience and may result in obstacles to establishing close relationships throughout life. In many cases, good child care is hard to find, producing psychological stress and sometimes guilt over the arrangements working parents must, for economic reasons, make. Time is always at a premium in single-parent families (Whitehead, 1993).

On the other hand, little evidence suggests that children from single-parent families are less well adjusted than those from two-parent families (Barber &

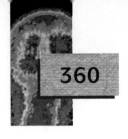

Eccles, 1992). Moreover, it is clear that children are more successful growing up in a relatively tranquil single-parent family than in a two-parent family in which the parents are engaged in continuous conflict with one another. In fact, the emotional and behavioral problems displayed by some children of divorced parents may stem more from family problems that existed prior to the divorce than from the divorce itself (Cherlin, 1993; Gottfried & Gottfried, 1994).

Do current statistics suggest that marriage is as obsolete as the horse and buggy? At first they may seem to, but a closer look reveals that this is not the case. For one thing, survey data show that most people want to get married at some time in their lives, and close to 95 percent eventually do. Even people who divorce are more likely than not to get remarried, some for three or more times—a phenomenon known as serial marriage. Finally, individuals who are married report being happier than those who are not (Brody, Neubaum, & Forehand, 1988; Strong, 1978; Glenn, 1987).

The Changing Face of Marriage   Marriage remains an important institution in Western culture, and identifying a mate is a critical issue for the majority of people during adulthood. On the other hand, the nature of marriage has changed over the last few decades, as the roles played by men and women have evolved. More women than ever before either want to or are forced by their economic situation to act simultaneously as wives, mothers, and wage earners—in contrast to women in traditional marriages, in which the husband is the sole wage earner and the wife assumes primary responsibility for caring for the home and children (Gottfried & Gottfried, 1988). In fact, close to three-quarters of all married women with school-aged children are working outside the home. More than 60 percent of mothers with infants and young children are employed (Clarke-Stewart, 1993; Lewin, 1995).

Although married women are more likely than they once were to be out of the house working, they are not free of household responsibilities. Even in marriages in which the spouses hold jobs of similar status and require similar hours, the distribution of household tasks between husbands and wives has not changed substantially. Working wives are still more likely to view themselves as responsible for the traditional homemaking tasks such as cooking and cleaning. In contrast, husbands of working wives still view themselves as responsible primarily for such household tasks as repairing broken appliances, putting up screens in the summer, and doing yard work (Schellhardt, 1990; Biernat & Wortman, 1991; Patterson, 1995).

On the other hand, not all couples divide responsibilities along traditional lines. For instance, husbands who strongly subscribe to feminist ideals are more likely to spend time taking care of their children. Moreover, homosexual couples tend to share domestic chores equitably, splitting tasks so that each partner carries out an equal number of different activities (Deutsch, Lussier, & Servis, 1993; Kurdek, 1993; Gilbert, 1993).

In addition, the way in which time is spent by married men and women during the average week is quite different. Although married men average slightly more work hours per week than married women, they spend considerably less time on household chores and child care. Overall, working women spend much more time than working men on combined job and family demands.

In fact, the number of hours put in by working mothers can be staggering. For instance, one survey found employed mothers of children under 3 years of age worked an average of 90 hours per week! Sociologist Arlie Hochschild refers to the additional work experienced by women as the "second shift." According to her analysis of national statistics, women who both work and are mothers put in an extra month of 24-hour days during the course of a year (Hochschild, with Machung, 1990; Hochschild, 1990). Furthermore, similar patterns are seen in

many developing societies throughout the world, with women working at full-time jobs and also having primary responsibilities for child care (Googans & Burden, 1987; Mednick, 1993).

In sum, many families in which both parents work still tend to view the mother as holding primary responsibility for child rearing. Consequently, rather than careers being a substitute for what women do at home, they often exist in addition to the role of homemaker. It is not surprising that some wives feel resentment toward husbands who spend less time on child care and housework than the wives had expected prior to the birth of children (Ruble et al., 1988; Williams & McCullers, 1983).

On the other hand, many wives report feeling relatively accepting of this unequal distribution. One reason is that traditional societal standards still provide relatively strong support for women who play a dominant role in child care and housework (Major, 1993). In addition, the benefits of work may outweigh the disadvantages of having major responsibilities in multiple roles for many women. For instance, women who work, particularly those in high-prestige occupations, report feeling a greater sense of mastery, pride, and competence than women who stay at home. The value of work, then, goes beyond merely earning a salary. Work provides personal satisfaction as well as a sense of contributing to society (Hoffman, 1989; Crosby, 1991; Barnett, Marshall, & Singer, 1992).

- ***How does the reality of old age differ from the stereotypes about the period?***
- ***How can we adjust to death?***

THE LATER YEARS OF LIFE: GROWING OLD

I've always enjoyed doing things in the mountains—hiking or, more recently, active cliff-climbing. When climbing a route of any difficulty at all, it's absolutely necessary to become entirely absorbed in what you're doing. You look for a crack that you can put your hand in. You have to think about whether the foothold over there will leave you in balance or not. Otherwise you can get trapped in a difficult situation. And if you don't remember where you put your hands or feet a few minutes before, then it's very difficult to climb down.

The more difficult the climb, the more absorbing it is. The climbs I really remember are the ones I had to work on. Maybe a particular section where it took two or three tries before I found the right combination of moves that got me up easily—and, preferably, elegantly. It's a wonderful exhilaration to get to the top and sit down and perhaps have lunch and look out over the landscape and be so grateful that it's still possible for me to do that sort of thing. (Lyman Spitzer, quoted in Kotre & Hall, 1990, pp. 358–359)

Lyman Spitzer. Age: 74.

If you can't quite picture a 74-year-old climbing rocks, some rethinking of your view of old age might well be in order. In spite of the societal stereotype of old age as a time of inactivity and physical and mental decline, *gerontologists*, specialists who study aging, are beginning to paint quite a different portrait of the elderly.

By focusing on the period of life that starts at around age 65, gerontologists are making important contributions in clarifying the capabilities of the elderly. Their work is demonstrating that significant developmental processes continue even during old age. And as life expectancy throughout the world increases, the number of people who reach old age will continue to grow substantially. Consequently, developing an understanding of the elderly has become a critical priority for psychologists (Cavanaugh & Park, 1993).

Jeanne Calment, who was certified as the oldest person in the world by the Guinness Book of Records, on her 120th birthday.

Physical Changes in the Elderly: The Old Body

Napping, eating, walking, conversing. It probably doesn't surprise you that these relatively unvigorous activities represent the typical pastimes of the elderly. But what is striking about this list is that these activities are identical to the most common leisure activities reported in a survey of college students. Although the students cited more active pursuits—such as sailing and playing basketball—as their favorite activities, in actuality they engaged in such sports relatively infrequently, spending most of their free time napping, eating, walking, and conversing (Harper, 1978).

Although the leisure activities in which the elderly engage may not differ all that much from those that younger people pursue, many physical changes are, of course, brought about by the aging process. The most obvious are those of appearance—hair thinning and turning gray, skin wrinkling and folding, and sometimes a slight loss of height as the size of the disks between vertebrae in the spine decreases—but there are also subtler changes in the body's biological functioning (DiGiovanna, 1994).

For example, sensory acuity decreases as a result of aging; vision and hearing are less sharp, and smell and taste are not as sensitive. Reaction time slows. There are changes in physical stamina. Because oxygen intake and heart-pumping ability decline, the body is unable to replenish lost nutrients as quickly—and therefore the rebound from physical activity is slower (Shock, 1962). Of course, none of these changes begins suddenly at age 65. Gradual declines in some kinds of functioning start earlier. It is in old age, however, that these changes become more apparent (Perlmutter, 1994).

What are the reasons for these physical declines? There are two major explanations: genetic preprogramming theories and wear-and-tear theories (Bergener, Ermini, & Stahelin, 1985; Whitbourne, 1986). **Genetic preprogramming theories of aging** suggest that there is a built-in time limit to the reproduction of human cells, and that after a certain time they are no longer able to divide (Hayflick, 1974). A variant of this idea is that some cells are genetically preprogrammed to become harmful to the body after a certain amount of time has gone by, causing the internal biology of the body to "self-destruct" (Pereira-Smith et al., 1988; Finch, 1990).

The second approach to understanding physical declines due to aging is based on the same factors that force people to buy new cars every so often: Mechanical devices wear out. According to **wear-and-tear theories of aging,** the mechanical functions of the body simply stop working efficiently. Moreover, waste byproducts of energy production eventually accumulate, and mistakes are made when cells reproduce. Eventually the body, in effect, wears out.

We do not know which of these theories provides a better explanation of the physical aging process; it may be that both contribute (Rusting, 1992). It is important to realize, however, that physical aging is not a disease, but rather a natural biological process. Many physical functions do not decline with age. For example, sex remains pleasurable well into old age (although the frequency of sexual activity decreases), and some elderly people even report that the pleasure they derive from sex increases (Lobsenz, 1975; Rowe & Kahn, 1987; Olshansky, Carnes, & Cassel, 1990; Ansberry, 1995).

Furthermore, neither genetic preprogramming theories nor wear-and-tear theories successfully explain a fact that is immediately apparent to anyone studying aging: Women live longer than men. Throughout the industrialized world, women outlive men by a margin of 4 to 10 years (Holden, 1987). The female advantage begins just after conception. Although more males are conceived than females, males have a higher rate of prenatal, infant, and childhood death, and by age 30 there are equal numbers of males and females. By age 65, 84 percent of females and 70 percent of males are still alive.

Genetic preprogramming theories of aging: Theories that suggest a built-in time limit to the reproduction of human cells

Wear-and-tear theories of aging: Theories suggesting that the body's mechanical functions cease efficient activity and, in effect, wear out

For many couples, growing older does not mean the end of sexual enjoyment.

Largely because of positive changes in men's health habits, including decreased smoking, greater consumption of foods that are low in cholesterol, and greater exercise, the gender gap is not increasing. But health habits do not provide the complete explanation for the difference, and a full explanation of why women live longer than men remains to be found. What is clear is that women, more often than men, must make the profound adjustments needed following the death of a spouse. Women's longer lives are something of a mixed blessing since women in their later years must frequently face life without a partner.

Cognitive Changes: Thinking About—and During—Old Age

Three women were talking about the inconveniences of growing old.

"Sometimes," one of them confessed, "when I go to my refrigerator, I can't remember if I'm putting something in or taking something out."

"Oh, that's nothing," said the second woman. "There are times when I find myself at the foot of the stairs wondering if I'm going up or if I've just come down."

"Well, my goodness!" exclaimed the third woman. "I'm certainly glad I don't have any problems like that"—and she knocked on wood. "Oh," she said, starting up out of her chair, "there's someone at the door." (Dent, 1984, p. 38)

At one time, many gerontologists would have agreed with the view—suggested by the story above—that the elderly are forgetful and confused. Today, however, most research tells us that this is far from an accurate assessment of elderly people's capabilities.

One reason for the change in view is the availability of more sophisticated research techniques for studying cognitive changes in the elderly. For example, if we were to give a group of elderly people an IQ test, we might find that the average score was lower than for a group of younger people. We might conclude that this signifies a decline in intelligence. Yet if we looked a little closer at the specific test, we might find that such a conclusion was unwarranted. For instance, many IQ tests include portions based on physical performance (such as arranging a group of blocks) or on speed. In such a case, poorer performance on the IQ test may be due to decrements in reaction time—a physical decline that accompanies old age—and have little or nothing to do with the intellectual capabilities of the elderly (Schaie, 1991).

Other difficulties hamper research into the cognitive functioning of the elderly. For example, the elderly are more likely than younger people to suffer from physical ill health. Some studies of IQ in the past inadvertently compared a group of

physically healthy younger people with a group of elderly people who were generally less healthy, with the finding of significantly lower scores for the elderly group. However, when only *healthy* elderly people are observed, intellectual declines are markedly less evident (Riegel & Riegel, 1972; Kausler, 1994). Furthermore, it is unfair to compare the test results of an elderly group with those of a younger group of subjects when the mean level of education is probably lower in the older group (for historical reasons) than in the younger one.

Similarly, declines in the IQ scores of the elderly may be caused by their having lower motivation to perform well on intelligence tests than younger people. Finally, traditional IQ tests may not be the most appropriate measures of intelligence in the elderly. For example, as we discussed in Chapter 8, some researchers contend that several kinds of intelligence exist, and others have found that the elderly perform better on tests of everyday problems and social competence than do younger individuals (Cornelius & Caspi, 1987; Willis & Schaie, 1994).

On the other hand, some declines in the intellectual functioning of the elderly have been found, even when using more sophisticated research methods. However, as can be seen in Figure 10-7, the pattern of age differences is not uniform for different types of cognitive abilities. Furthermore, the differences are not identical for men and women (Schaie, 1993, 1994).

In general, age-related changes in cognitive abilities can be summarized in terms of differences in fluid and crystallized intelligence. You may recall from Chapter 8 that *fluid intelligence* refers to reasoning, memory, and information-processing capabilities, while *crystallized intelligence* is intelligence based on the information, skills, and strategies that people have learned through experience and that can be applied in problem-solving situations.

Although fluid intelligence shows declines in old age, crystallized intelligence remains steady and in some cases actually improves (Baltes & Schaie, 1974; Schaie, 1993). For example, an elderly woman asked to solve a geometry problem (which taps fluid intelligence) might have greater difficulty than she once did,

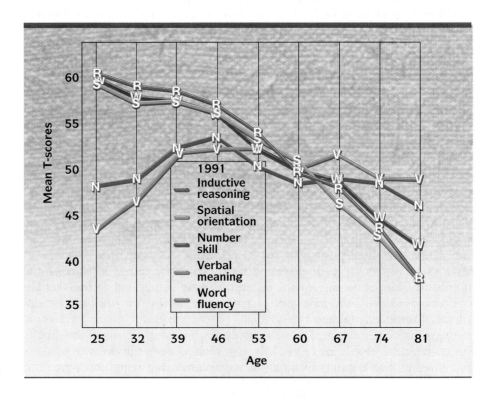

FIGURE 10-7 Age-related changes in intellectual skills vary according to the specific cognitive ability in question. *(Schaie, 1994.)*

but she might be better at solving verbal problems that require reasoned conclusions.

One reason for the developmental changes in intellectual functioning is that certain types of abilities may be more sensitive to changes in the nervous system than others. Another factor may be the degree to which the two kinds of intelligence are used during a person's lifetime. Whatever the reason, people compensate for the decline. They can still learn what they want to; it may just take more time (Storandt et al., 1984). Furthermore, teaching the elderly strategies for dealing with new problems can prevent declines in performance (Willis & Nesselroade, 1990).

Memory Changes in Old Age: Are the Elderly Forgetful? One of the characteristics most frequently attributed to the elderly is forgetfulness. How accurate is this assumption?

Most evidence suggests that memory change is *not* an inevitable part of the aging process. For instance, research shows that older people in cultures in which the elderly are held in high esteem, such as in mainland China, are less likely to show memory losses than those living in cultures in which the expectation is that memory declines are probable (Levy & Langer, 1994).

Even when elderly people do show memory declines, their deficits tend to be limited to particular types of memory. For instance, losses tend to be limited to *episodic memories,* which relate to specific experiences about our lives. Other types of memories, such as *semantic memories* (which refer to general knowledge and facts) and *implicit memories* (which are memories about which we are not consciously aware), are largely unaffected by age (Graf, 1990; Russo & Parkin, 1993).

Declines in episodic memories can often be traced to changes in the lives of the elderly. For instance, it is not surprising that a retired person, who may no longer face the same kind of consistent intellectual challenges encountered on the job, might well be less practiced in using memory or even be less motivated to remember things, leading to an apparent decline in memory. Even in cases in which long-term memory declines, the elderly person can usually profit from compensatory efforts. Training the elderly to use the kinds of mnemonic strategies described in Chapter 6 not only may prevent their long-term memory from deteriorating, but may actually improve it (Perlmutter & Mitchell, 1986; Brody, 1987; Ratner et al., 1987).

In the past, elderly people with severe cases of memory decline, accompanied by other cognitive difficulties, were viewed as suffering from senility. *Senility* is a broad, imprecise term typically applied to elderly people who experience progressive deterioration of mental abilities, including memory loss, disorientation to time and place, and general confusion. Once thought to be an inevitable state that accompanies aging, senility is now viewed by most gerontologists as a label that has outlived its usefulness. Rather than senility being the cause of certain symptoms, the symptoms are deemed to be caused by some other factor.

However, some cases of memory loss are produced by actual disease. For instance, *Alzheimer's disease* is the progressive brain disorder discussed in Chapter 6 which leads to a gradual and irreversible decline in mental abilities. In other cases, the symptoms of senility are caused by temporary anxiety and depression, which may be successfully treated, or may even be due to overmedication. The danger is that people suffering such symptoms may be labeled senile and left untreated, thereby continuing their decline—even though treatment would have been beneficial.

In sum, declines in cognitive functioning in old age are, for the most part, not unavoidable. The key to maintaining cognitive skills may lie in providing some

degree of intellectual stimulation. Like the rest of us, elderly people need a stimulating environment in order to hone and maintain their skills.

The Social World of the Elderly: Old but Not Alone

Just as the view that senility is an inevitable outcome of old age has proved to be wrong, so has the view that old age inevitably brings loneliness. The elderly most often see themselves as functioning members of society, with polls showing that just 12 percent of people 65 and over view loneliness as a serious problem (Harris Poll, 1975; Bond, Cutler, & Grams, 1995).

Still, the social patterns and behaviors of the elderly are different in some respects from those of younger individuals. Two major approaches have been suggested to explain elderly people's social environment: disengagement theory and activity theory. The **disengagement theory of aging** sees aging as a gradual withdrawal from the world on physical, psychological, and social levels (Cummings & Henry, 1961). Physically, lower energy levels produce less activity; psychologically, the focus shifts from others to the self; and socially, there is less interaction with others and a reduction in the level of participation in society at large. But rather than viewing this disengagement in a negative light, some theorists suggest that it should be seen positively. Such disengagement provides the opportunity for increased reflectiveness and decreased emotional investment in others at a time of life when social relationships will inevitably be ended by death.

Disengagement theory has been criticized because of its suggestion that disengagement is an automatic process, marking a sharp departure from earlier behavior patterns. Even more important are data showing that the elderly who report being the happiest are those who remain the most active (Havighurst, 1973). Such criticisms have led to the development of an alternative approach to describing social adjustment to aging. The **activity theory of aging** suggests that the elderly who age most successfully are those who maintain the interests and activities they pursued during middle age and who resist any decrease in the amount and kind of social interaction they have with others (Blau, 1973). According to activity theory, old age should reflect a continuation, as much as possible, of the activities in which people participated during the earlier part of their lives, as well as activities to replace those lost through changes such as retirement.

Activity theory is not without its critics. For instance, activity alone does not guarantee happiness. Rather, the *nature* of activities in which people engage is probably more critical (Gubrium, 1973). Furthermore, not all elderly people need a life filled with activities and social interaction to be happy; as in every stage of life, there are those who are just as satisfied leading a relatively inactive, solitary existence (Hansson & Carpenter, 1994; Baltes, 1995).

We cannot say whether disengagement theory or activity theory presents a more accurate view of the elderly, probably because there are vast individual differences in how people cope with the aging process. Clearly, however, the elderly are not just marking time until death. Rather, old age is a time of continued growth and development, as important as any other period of life.

Disengagement theory of aging: A theory suggesting that aging is a gradual withdrawal from the world on physical, psychological, and social levels

Activity theory of aging: A theory suggesting that the elderly who age most successfully are those who maintain the interests and activities they had during middle age

The Informed Consumer of Psychology

Adjusting to Death

At some time in your life, you will face death—certainly your own, as well as the deaths of friends and loved ones. Although there is nothing more inevitable in life than death, it remains a frightening, emotion-laden topic. There may be little that

is more stressful than the death of a loved one or the contemplation of your own imminent death, and preparing for death is likely to represent one of your most crucial developmental tasks.

Not too long ago, talk of death was taboo. The topic was never mentioned to dying people, and gerontologists had little to say about it. That changed, however, with the pioneering work of Elisabeth Kübler-Ross (1969), who brought the subject out into the open with her observation that those facing death tend to move through five broad stages.

(2δ)

■ *Denial.* In this first stage, people resist the idea that they are dying. Even if told that their chances for survival are small, they refuse to admit that they are facing death.

■ *Anger.* After moving beyond the denial stage, dying people are angry—angry at people around them who are in good health, angry at medical professionals for being ineffective, angry at God. They ask the question "Why me?" and are unable to answer it without feeling anger.

■ *Bargaining.* Anger leads to bargaining, in which the dying try to think of ways to postpone death. They may decide to dedicate their lives to religion if God saves them; they may say, "If only I can live to see my son married, I will accept death then." Such bargains are rarely kept, most often because the dying person's illness keeps progressing and invalidates any "agreements."

■ *Depression.* When dying people come to feel that bargaining is of no use, they move to the next stage: depression. They realize that death is inevitable, that they are losing their loved ones and that their lives really are coming to an end. They are experiencing what Kübler-Ross calls "preparatory grief" for their own death.

■ *Acceptance.* In this last stage, people are past mourning for the loss of their own lives, and they accept impending death. Usually, they are unemotional and uncommunicative; it is as if they have made peace with themselves and are expecting death without rancor.

Although not everyone experiences each of these stages in the same way, if at all, Kübler-Ross's theory remains our best description of people's reactions to their approaching demise. However, vast differences occur in how specific individuals react to impending death. The specific cause and duration of dying, as well as the person's sex, age, and personality and the type of support received from family and friends, all have an impact on how people respond to death (Zautra, Reich, & Guarnaccia, 1990; Stroebe, Stroebe, & Hansson, 1993).

Few of us enjoy the contemplation of death. Yet awareness of its psychological effects and consequences can make its coming less anxiety-producing and perhaps more understandable.

RECAP AND REVIEW

Recap

- Several critical physical changes occur during puberty. Early maturing is generally socially beneficial, whereas late maturing is usually disadvantageous.
- According to Kohlberg, moral development passes through a series of stages, each of which represents an increasingly sophisticated level. In Gilligan's contrasting view of moral development, women, more than men, focus on principles involving compassion toward the individual rather than on abstract principles of justice or fairness.
- During adolescence, people enter the crucial identity-

versus-role-confusion stage, which may include an identity crisis.
- Although adolescence was once thought of as a stormy, rebellious period, psychologists now believe that such a view reflects more myth than reality.
- According to a model developed by Levinson, social development during early and middle adulthood proceeds through a series of stages.
- Fluid intelligence and memory are affected by aging.
- The physical declines of the elderly are explained by two classes of theories: genetic preprogramming theories and wear-and-tear theories.

Review

1. Delayed maturation typically provides both males and females with a social advantage. True or false?

2. _____ proposed a set of six stages of moral development ranging from reasoning based on rewards and punishments, to abstract thinking involving concepts of justice.

3. Match each of Gilligan's stages of women's moral development with its definition:
   1. Morality of nonviolence
   2. Orientation toward individual survival
   3. Goodness as self-sacrifice

   a. Centered on what is best for the woman in particular.
   b. Woman must sacrifice her wants to what others want.
   c. Hurting anyone, including the self, is immoral.

4. Emotional and psychological changes that sometimes accompany menopause are probably not due to menopause itself. True or false?

5. Forty-year-old Rob recently found himself surveying his goals and accomplishments to date. Although he has accomplished a lot, he realizes that many of his goals will not be met in his lifetime. Levinson would term this stage in Rob's life as _____ _____ .

6. In households where both partners have similar jobs, the division of labor for household chores that generally occurs is the same as in "traditional" households where the husband works and the wife stays at home. True or false?

7. _____ _____ theories suggest that there is a maximum time limit in which cells are able to reproduce. This time limit explains the eventual breakdown of the body during old age.

8. During old age, a person's _____ intelligence continues to increase, while _____ intelligence may decline.

9. Lavinia feels that, in her old age, she has gradually decreased her social contacts and has become more self-oriented. A proponent of _____ theory interprets the situation as a result of Lavinia's not maintaining her past interests. A supporter of _____ theory views her behavior in a more positive light, suggesting that it is a natural process accompanied by enhanced reflectiveness and declining emotional investment.

10. In Kübler-Ross's _____ stage, people resist the idea of death. In the _____ stage, they attempt to make deals to avoid death, while in the _____ stage, they passively await death.

Ask Yourself

Many people today suffer from misconceptions about the elderly, thinking of them as senile, slow, lonely, and so forth. How might you go about proving these stereotypes wrong? What advantages might a change in our misconceptions have in terms of utilizing the elderly as a valuable resource?

(Answers to review questions are on page 370.)

LOOKING BACK

How do psychologists study the degree to which development is a joint function of hereditary and environmental factors?

1. Developmental psychology is the branch of psychology that studies growth and change throughout life. One fundamental question is how much developmental change is due to nature—hereditary factors—and how much to nurture—environmental factors. Most developmental psychologists believe that heredity defines the upper limits of our growth and change, whereas the environment affects the degree to which the upper limits are reached.

2. Cross-sectional research compares people of different ages with one another at the same point in time. In contrast, longitudinal research traces the behavior of one or more subjects as the subjects become older. Finally, cross-sequential research combines the two methods by taking several different age groups and examining them over several points in time.

What is the nature of development prior to birth?

3. At the moment of conception, a male's sperm cell and a female's egg cell unite, with each contributing to the new individual's genetic makeup. The new cell, a zygote, immediately begins to grow, becoming an embryo measuring about one-fifth of an inch long at 4 weeks. By the ninth week, the embryo is called a fetus and is responsive to touch and other stimulation. At about 28 weeks it reaches the age of viability, which means it may survive if born prematurely. A fetus is normally born after 38 weeks of pregnancy, weighing around 7 pounds and measuring about 20 inches in length.

What factors affect a child during the mother's pregnancy?

4. Genetic abnormalities produce birth defects such as phenylketonuria (PKU), sickle-cell anemia, Tay-Sachs disease, and Down syndrome. Among the prenatal environmental influences on fetal growth are the mother's nutritional status, illnesses, drug intake, and birth complications.

What are the major milestones of physical, perceptual, and social development after birth?

5. The newborn, or neonate, has many capabilities. Among them are the rooting reflex, the startle reflex, and the Babinski reflex. After birth, physical development is rapid; children typically triple their birth weight in a year. Perceptual abilities also increase rapidly; infants can distinguish color and depth soon after birth. Other sensory capabilities are also impressive at

birth; infants can distinguish sounds and discriminate tastes and smells. However, the development of more sophisticated perceptual abilities depends on increased cognitive abilities.

6. Social development in infancy is marked by the phenomenon of attachment—the positive emotional bond between a child and a particular individual. Attachment is measured in the laboratory using the Ainsworth strange situation and is related to later social and emotional adjustment.

7. As children become older, the nature of their social interactions with peers changes. Initially play occurs relatively independently, but it becomes increasingly cooperative. Play enhances social competence and self-control.

8. Different styles of child rearing result in differing outcomes. Authoritarian parents are rigid, punitive, and strict. Their children tend to be unsociable and withdrawn. Permissive parents, although warm, provide lax or inconsistent discipline. Their children tend to be immature, moody, dependent, and low in self-control. Finally, authoritative parents are firm, setting limits, but using reasoning and explanations. Their children tend to be likable, self-reliant, independent, and high in social skills. Of course, there are many exceptions, depending in part on the children's temperament and on the culture in which they are raised.

9. According to Erikson, eight stages of psychosocial development encompass people's changing interactions and understanding of themselves and others. During childhood, there are four stages, each of which relates to a crisis that requires resolution. These stages are labeled trust-versus-mistrust (birth to 18 months), autonomy-versus-shame-and-doubt (18 months to 3 years), initiative-versus-guilt (3 to 6 years), and industry-versus-inferiority (6 to 12 years).

How can we best describe cognitive development?

10. Piaget's theory suggests that cognitive development proceeds through four stages in which qualitative changes occur in thinking. In the sensorimotor stage (birth to 2 years), children develop object permanence, the awareness that objects and people continue to exist even if they are out of sight. In the preoperational stage (2 to 7 years), children display egocentric thought, but they do not yet understand the principle of conservation—the knowledge that quantity is unrelated to the arrangement and physical appearance of an object. The conservation principle is not fully grasped until the concrete operational stage (7 to 12 years), in which children begin to think more logically and to understand the concept of reversibility. In the final stage, the formal operational period (12 years to adulthood), thinking becomes abstract, formal, and fully logical.

11. Although Piaget's theory has had an enormous influence, some theorists suggest that the notion of developmental stages is inaccurate. They say that development is more continuous and that the changes occurring within and between stages are reflective of quantitative advances in cognitive development rather than in the quality of thought.

12. Information-processing approaches suggest that quantitative changes occur in children's ability to organize and manipulate information about the world, such as significant increases in speed of processing, attention span, and memory. In addition, there are advances in metacognition, the awareness and understanding of one's own cognitive processes.

What major physical, social, and cognitive transitions characterize adolescence?

13. Adolescence, the developmental stage between childhood and adulthood, is marked by the onset of puberty, the point at which sexual maturity occurs. The age at which puberty begins has implications for the way people view themselves and the way they are seen by others.

14. Moral judgments during adolescence increase in sophistication, according to Kohlberg's three-level, six-stage model. Although Kohlberg's stages are an adequate description of males' moral judgments, they do not seem to be as applicable in describing females' judgments. Specifically, Gilligan suggests that women view morality in terms of concern for individuals rather than in terms of broad, general principles of justice or fairness. In her view, moral development in women proceeds in three stages.

15. According to Erikson's model of psychosocial development, adolescence (the identity-versus-role-confusion stage) may be accompanied by an identity crisis, although this is by no means universal. Adolescence is followed by three stages of psychosocial development which cover the remainder of the lifespan.

What are the principal kinds of physical, social, and intellectual changes that occur in early and middle adulthood, and what are their causes?

16. Early adulthood marks the peak of physical health. Physical changes occur relatively gradually in men and women during adulthood, although one major change occurs at the end of middle adulthood for women: They begin menopause, after which they are no longer fertile. For men, the aging process is subtler, since they remain fertile.

17. Levinson's model of adult development begins with entry into early adulthood at around age 20 and ends at around age 60 or 65. One of the most critical transitions—at least for men—occurs during midlife (around age 40 to 45), when people typically experience a midlife transition in which the notion that life is not infinite becomes more important. In some cases this can lead to a midlife crisis; usually, however, the passage into middle age is relatively calm. Although Levinson suggests that women's lives follow basically the same pattern as men's, several gender differences are likely to occur.

18. As aging continues during middle adulthood, people realize in their fifties that their lives and accomplishments are fairly well set, and they try to come to terms with them.

How does the reality of old age differ from the stereotypes about the period?

19. Old age may bring marked physical declines. Although the activities of the elderly are not all that different from those of younger people, elderly people do experience decrements in reaction time, as well as sensory declines and a decrease in physical stamina. These declines might be caused by genetic preprogramming, which sets a time limit on the reproduction of human cells, or they may simply be due to wear and tear on the mechanical parts of the body.

20. Although intellectual declines were once thought to be an inevitable part of aging, most research suggests that this is not necessarily the case. Fluid intelligence does decline with age, and long-term memory abilities are sometimes impaired. In contrast, crystallized intelligence shows slight increases with age, and short-term memory remains at about the same level. **21.** Disengagement theory sees successful aging as a process accompanied by gradual withdrawal from the physical, psychological, and social worlds. In contrast, activity theory suggests that the maintenance of interests and activities from earlier years leads to successful aging. Because there are vast individual differences, it is unclear whether either of the two theories is completely accurate.

How can we adjust to death?

22. According to Kübler-Ross, dying people move through five stages as they face death: denial, anger, bargaining, depression, and acceptance. However, people's reactions to death vary significantly.

KEY TERMS AND CONCEPTS

developmental psychology (p. 321)
nature-nurture issue (p. 323)
identical twins (p. 325)
cross-sectional research (p. 325)
longitudinal research (p. 325)
cross-sequential research (p. 326)
zygote (p. 326)
chromosomes (p. 326)
genes (p. 326)
embryo (p. 326)
critical period (p. 326)
fetus (p. 327)
age of viability (p. 327)
neonate (p. 330)
reflexes (p. 331)
habituation (p. 332)
attachment (p. 334)
authoritarian parents (p. 337)
permissive parents (p. 337)

authoritative parents (p. 337)
temperament (p. 339)
psychosocial development (p. 339)
trust-versus-mistrust stage (p. 340)
autonomy-versus-shame-and-doubt
   stage (p. 340)
initiative-versus-guilt stage (p. 340)
industry-versus-inferiority stage (p. 340)
cognitive development (p. 341)
sensorimotor stage (p. 341)
object permanence (p. 341)
preoperational stage (p. 342)
egocentric thought (p. 342)
principle of conservation (p. 342)
concrete operational stage (p. 342)
formal operational stage (p. 344)
information processing (p. 345)
metacognition (p. 345)

adolescence (p. 348)
puberty (p. 348)
identity-versus-role-confusion
   stage (p. 353)
identity (p. 353)
intimacy-versus-isolation stage (p. 354)
generativity-versus-stagnation
   stage (p. 354)
ego-integrity-versus-despair
   stage (p. 355)
menopause (p. 357)
midlife transition (p. 358)
midlife crisis (p. 358)
genetic preprogramming theories
   of aging (p. 362)
wear-and-tear theories of aging (p. 362)
disengagement theory of aging (p. 366)
activity theory of aging (p. 366)

ANSWERS TO PREVIOUS REVIEW
1. False; both male and female adolescents may be hurt by delayed maturation. **2.** Kohlberg
3. 1-c; 2-a; 3-b **4.** True **5.** midlife transition **6.** True **7.** Genetic preprogramming
8. crystallized; fluid **9.** activity; disengagement **10.** denial; bargaining; acceptance

CHAPTER 11
PERSONALITY

River Phoenix

He was a strict vegetarian who ate no meat, seafood, or dairy products. Once he burst into tears when a companion ordered soft-shell crabs at a restaurant, upset because he was unable to convince the friend that meat "would kill you." He argued against violence, and in favor of universal love. He contributed generously to Earth Save, People for the Ethical Treatment of Animals, Greenpeace, and the Farm Animals Institute. He had plans for starting a school in Costa Rica and an ambitious national education project for U.S. high school students. He told friends he thought he had been chosen for a higher calling, and he had an innocence that made him seem far younger than his 23 years.

But there was another side to River Phoenix, star of such movies as *Stand By Me, My Own Private Idaho,* and *Running on Empty.* Although he tried to prevent photographers from taking his picture holding a cigarette, he was a chain smoker. He could be arrogant, boasting that songs he had written were "brilliant" and refusing to change a word. Friends sometimes found him distant and surly. He was drawn to the drug culture, and he found the mechanics of "spiking," or shooting up, fascinating. Trying morphine and heroin first in the early 1990s, he eventually moved on to a variety of other drugs.

In the end, the strict vegetarian, who admonished his friends to avoid meat for health reasons, became a victim of a lethal combination of cocaine, heroin, marijuana, and Valium. He died on a Los Angeles street, following 8 minutes of convulsions, at the age of 23. (Friend, 1994; Schindehette, 1994)

LOOKING AHEAD

Who was River Phoenix? Many people, like Phoenix, have different sides to their personalities, appearing one way in certain situations and quite differently in others. At the same time, you probably know people whose behavior is so consistent that you can easily predict how they are going to behave, no matter what the situation.

River Phoenix was a gifted actor who had several facets to his personality.

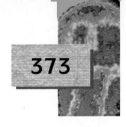
Psychologists who specialize in **personality** seek to understand the characteristic ways in which people behave. Personality encompasses the relatively enduring characteristics that differentiate people—those behaviors that make each of us unique. It is also personality that leads us to act in a consistent and predictable manner both in different situations and over extended periods of time.

In this chapter we consider a number of approaches to personality. We begin with the broadest and most comprehensive theory: Freud's psychoanalytic theory. Next, we turn to more recent theories of personality. We consider approaches that concentrate on identifying the most fundamental personality traits; theories that view personality as a set of learned behaviors; biological perspectives on personality; and approaches, known as humanistic theories, that highlight the uniquely human aspects of personality. We end our discussion by focusing on how personality is measured and how personality tests can be used.

Personality: The sum total of characteristics that differentiate people, or the stability in a person's behavior across different situations

- *How do psychologists define and use the concept of personality?*
- *What is the structure and development of personality according to Freud and his successors?*

PSYCHOANALYTIC APPROACHES TO PERSONALITY

Oscar Madison: sloppy, disheveled, unkempt.
Felix Unger: neat, precise, controlled.

As anyone who has seen the play or the old television series *The Odd Couple* can attest, Oscar and Felix are two people who could hardly seem to possess more dissimilar personalities. Yet to one group of personality theorists, *psychoanalysts,* the two men might actually be quite similar—at least in terms of the underlying part of personality that motivates their behavior. According to psychoanalysts, our behavior is triggered largely by powerful forces within our personality of which we are not aware. These hidden forces, shaped by childhood experiences, play an important role in energizing and directing our everyday behavior.

The most important theorist to hold such a view, and indeed one of the best-known figures in all psychology, is Sigmund Freud. An Austrian physician, Freud originated **psychoanalytic theory** in the early 1900s.

Psychoanalytic theory: Freud's theory that unconscious forces act as determinants of personality

Freud's Psychoanalytic Theory

The college student was intent on sounding smooth and making a good first impression on an attractive woman whom he had spotted across a crowded room at a party. As he walked toward her, he mulled over a line he had heard in an old movie the night before: "I don't believe we've been properly introduced yet." To his horror, what came out was a bit different. After threading his way through the crowded room, he finally reached the woman and blurted out, "I don't believe we've been properly seduced yet."

Although this statement may seem to be merely an embarrassing slip of the tongue, according to psychoanalytic theory such a mistake is not an error at all (Motley, 1987). Rather, it is an indication of deeply felt emotions and thoughts that are harbored in the **unconscious,** a part of the personality of which a person is not aware. The unconscious contains *instinctual drives:* infantile wishes, desires, demands, and needs that are hidden from conscious awareness because of the conflicts and pain they would cause us if they were part of our everyday lives. Many of life's experiences are painful, and the unconscious provides a "safe" haven for our recollections of such events. Uncomfortable memories can remain in our unconscious without continually disturbing us.

Unconscious: A part of the personality of which a person is unaware

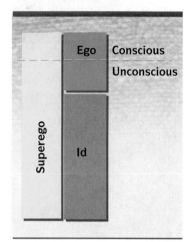

FIGURE 11-1 In Freud's model of personality, there are three major components: the id, the ego, and the superego. As the schematic shows, only a small portion of personality is conscious. This figure should not be thought of as an actual, physical structure, but rather as a model of the interrelationships among the parts of personality.

To Freud, conscious experience is just the tip of the psychological iceberg. Like the unseen mass of a floating iceberg, the material found in the unconscious dwarfs the information about which we are aware. Much of people's everyday behavior is viewed as being motivated by unconscious forces. For example, a child's concern over being unable to please her strict and demanding parents may lead her to have low self-esteem as an adult, even though she may be highly accomplished. Moreover, on a conscious level she may recall her childhood with great pleasure; it is her unconscious, in which the painful memories are held, that provokes the low self-evaluation.

According to Freud, to fully understand personality, it is necessary to illuminate and expose what is in the unconscious. But because the unconscious disguises the meaning of material it holds, it cannot be observed directly. It is therefore necessary to interpret clues to the unconscious—slips of the tongue, fantasies, and dreams—in order to understand the unconscious processes directing behavior. A slip of the tongue, such as the one quoted earlier, might be interpreted as revealing the speaker's underlying unconscious sexual desires.

If the notion of an unconscious does not seem so farfetched to most of us, it is only because Freudian theory has had such a widespread influence in Western culture, with applications ranging from literature to religion. In Freud's day, however, the idea that the unconscious could harbor painful material from which people were protecting themselves was revolutionary. The best minds of the time summarily rejected his ideas as being without basis and found the notion laughable. It is a tribute to the influence of Freud's theory that the concept of the unconscious is readily accepted by people today (Westen, 1990).

Structuring Personality: Id, Ego, and Superego To describe the structure of personality, Freud developed a comprehensive theory that held that personality consisted of three separate but interacting components: the id, the ego, and the superego. Freud suggested that the three structures can be depicted diagrammatically to show how they are related to the conscious and the unconscious (see Figure 11-1).

Although Freud described the three components of personality in very concrete terms, it is important to realize that they are not actual physical structures found in a certain part of the brain. Instead, they represent abstract conceptions of a general *model* of personality that describes the interaction of various processes and forces within one's personality that motivate behavior.

If personality consisted only of primitive, instinctual cravings and longings, it would have just one component: the id. The **id** is the raw, unorganized, inherited part of personality. Present from the time of birth, the sole purpose of the id is to reduce tension created by primitive drives related to hunger, sex, aggression, and irrational impulses. These drives are fueled by "psychic energy," or **libido,** as Freud called it. The id operates according to the *pleasure principle,* in which the goal is the immediate reduction of tension and the maximization of satisfaction.

Unfortunately for the id—but luckily for people and society—reality prevents the fulfillment of the demands of the pleasure principle in most cases. Instead, the world produces constraints: We cannot always eat when we are hungry, and we can discharge our sexual drives only when time and place allow—and a partner is willing. To account for this fact of life, Freud suggested a second component of personality, which he called the ego.

The **ego** provides a buffer between the id and the realities of the objective, outside world. In contrast to the pleasure-seeking nature of the id, the ego operates according to the *reality principle,* in which instinctual energy is restrained in order to maintain the safety of the individual and help integrate the person into society. In a sense, then, the ego is the "executive" of personality: It makes decisions, controls actions, and allows thinking and problem solving of a higher order

Id: The raw, unorganized, inherited part of personality whose purpose is to reduce tension created by biological drives and irrational impulses

Libido: According to Freud, the "psychic energy" that fuels the primary drives of hunger, sex, aggression, and irrational impulses

Ego: The part of personality that provides a buffer between the id and the outside world

than the id can achieve. The ego is also the seat of higher cognitive abilities such as intelligence, thoughtfulness, reasoning, and learning.

The **superego,** the final personality structure to develop, represents the rights and wrongs of society as handed down by a person's parents, teachers, and other important figures. It becomes a part of personality when children learn right from wrong and continues to develop as people begin to incorporate into their own standards the broad moral principles of the society in which they live.

The superego actually has two components, the *conscience* and the *ego-ideal.* The conscience prevents us from doing morally bad things, while the ego-ideal motivates us to do what is morally proper. The superego helps us to control impulses coming from the id, making our behavior less selfish and more virtuous.

Although on the surface the superego appears to be the opposite of the id, the two share an important feature: Both are unrealistic in that they do not consider the practical realities imposed by society. Thus the superego pushes the person toward greater virtue: If left unchecked, it would create perfectionists, unable to make the compromises that life requires. Similarly, an unrestrained id would create a primitive, pleasure-seeking, thoughtless individual, seeking to fulfill every desire without delay. The ego, then, must compromise between the demands of the superego and those of the id, thereby enabling a person to resist some of the gratification sought by the id while at the same time keeping the moralistic superego in check so that it does not prevent the person from obtaining any gratification at all.

Superego: The part of personality that represents the morality of society as presented by parents, teachers, and others

Developing Personality: A Stage Approach Freud also provided us with a view of how personality develops throughout a series of stages during childhood. What is especially noteworthy about the sequence he proposed is that it explains how experiences and difficulties during a particular childhood stage may predict specific sorts of idiosyncrasies in adult personality. The theory is also unique in focusing each stage on a major biological function, which Freud assumed to be the focus of pleasure in a given period.

In the first stage of development, called the **oral stage,** the baby's mouth is the focal point of pleasure (see Table 11-1 for a summary of the stages). During the first 12 to 18 months of life, children suck, mouth, and bite anything that will fit into their mouths. To Freud, this behavior suggested that the mouth was the primary site of a kind of sexual pleasure. If infants were either overly indulged (perhaps by being fed every time they cried) or frustrated in their search for oral gratification, they might become fixated at this stage. Displaying **fixation** means that an adult shows personality traits characteristic of an earlier stage of development due to an unresolved conflict stemming from the earlier period. For example, fixation at the oral stage might produce an adult who was unusually interested in

Oral stage: According to Freud, a stage from birth to 12–18 months, in which an infant's center of pleasure is the mouth

Fixation: Behavior in adulthood reflecting an earlier stage of development

---

TABLE 11-1 Freud's Stages of Personality Development

Stage	Age	Major characteristics
Oral	Birth to 12–18 months	Interest in oral gratification from sucking, eating, mouthing, biting
Anal	12–18 months to 3 years	Gratification from expelling and withholding feces; coming to terms with society's controls relating to toilet training
Phallic	3 to 5–6 years	Interest in the genitals; coming to terms with Oedipal conflict, leading to identification with same-sex parent
Latency	5–6 years to adolescence	Sexual concerns largely unimportant
Genital	Adolescence to adulthood	Reemergence of sexual interests and establishment of mature sexual relationships

According to psychoanalytic theory, toilet training is a crucial event in the formation of an individual's personality.

Anal stage: According to Freud, a stage, from 12–18 months to 3 years of age, in which a child's pleasure is centered on the anus

Phallic stage: According to Freud, a period beginning around age 3 during which a child's interest focuses on the genitals

Oedipal (ED ih pul) **conflict:** A child's sexual interest in his or her opposite-sex parent, typically resolved through identification with the same-sex parent

Latency period: According to Freud, the period, between the phallic stage and puberty, during which children's sexual concerns are temporarily put aside

Genital stage: According to Freud, a period from puberty until death, marked by mature sexual behavior (i.e., sexual intercourse)

overtly oral activities—eating, talking, smoking—or who showed symbolic sorts of oral interests: being either "bitingly" sarcastic or very gullible ("swallowing" anything).

From around 12 to 18 months until 3 years of age—where the emphasis in Western culture is on toilet training—the child enters the **anal stage.** At this point, the major source of pleasure changes from the mouth to the anal region, and children derive considerable pleasure from both retention and expulsion of feces. If toilet training is particularly demanding, the result may be fixation. If fixation occurs during the anal stage, Freud suggested that adults might show unusual rigidity, orderliness, punctuality—or extreme disorderliness or sloppiness, as in our earlier examples of Felix and Oscar.

At about age 3, the **phallic stage** begins, at which point there is another major shift in the primary source of pleasure for the child. This time, interest focuses on the genitals and the pleasures derived from fondling them. This is also the stage of one of the most important points of personality development, according to Freudian theory: the **Oedipal conflict.** As children focus their attention on their genitals, the differences between male and female anatomy become more salient. Furthermore, at this time Freud believed that the male begins to develop sexual interests in his mother, starts to see his father as a rival, and harbors a wish to kill his father—as Oedipus did in the ancient Greek tragedy. But because he views his father as too powerful, he develops a fear of retaliation in the form of "castration anxiety." Ultimately, this fear becomes so powerful that the child represses his desires for his mother and instead chooses *identification* with his father, trying to be as much like him as possible.

For girls, the process is different. Freud reasoned that girls begin to experience sexual arousal toward their fathers and—in a suggestion that was later to bring serious accusations that he viewed women as inferior to men—that they begin to experience *penis envy.* They wish they had the anatomical part that, at least to Freud, seemed most clearly "missing" in girls. Blaming their mothers for their lack of a penis, girls come to believe that their mothers are responsible for their "castration." As with males, though, they find that in order to resolve such unacceptable feelings, they must identify with the same-sex parent by behaving like her and adopting her attitudes and values. In this way, a girl's identification with her mother is completed.

At this point, the Oedipal conflict is said to be resolved, and Freudian theory assumes that both males and females move on to the next stage of development. If difficulties arise during this period, however, all sorts of problems are thought to occur, which include improper sex-role behavior and the failure to develop a conscience.

Following the resolution of the Oedipal conflict, typically at around age 5 or 6, children move into the **latency period,** which lasts until puberty. During this period, little of interest is occurring, according to Freud. Sexual concerns are more or less put to rest, even in the unconscious. Then, during adolescence, sexual feelings reemerge, marking the start of the final period, the **genital stage,** which extends until death. The focus during the genital stage is on mature, adult sexuality, which Freud defined as sexual intercourse.

Defense Mechanisms   Freud's efforts to describe and theorize about the underlying dynamics of personality and its development were motivated by very practical problems that his patients faced in dealing with *anxiety,* an intense, negative emotional experience. According to Freud, anxiety is a danger signal to the ego. Although anxiety may arise from realistic fears—such as seeing a poisonous snake about to strike—it may also occur in the form of *neurotic anxiety,* in which irrational impulses emanating from the id threaten to burst through and become uncontrollable. Because anxiety, naturally, is unpleasant, Freud believed that peo-

TABLE 11-2 Freud's Defense Mechanisms

Defense mechanism	Explanation	Example
Repression	Unacceptable or unpleasant impulses are pushed back into the unconscious	A woman is unable to recall that she was raped
Regression *go back to be a baby*	People behave as if they were at an earlier stage of development	A boss has a temper tantrum when an employee makes a mistake
Displacement	The expression of an unwanted feeling or thought is redirected from a more threatening, powerful person to a weaker one	A brother yells at his younger sister after a teacher gives him a bad grade
Rationalization	A distortion of reality in which a person justifies what happens	A person who is passed over for an award says she didn't really want it in the first place
Denial	Refusal to accept or acknowledge an anxiety-producing piece of information	A student refuses to believe that he has flunked a course
Projection	Attributing unwanted impulses and feelings to someone else	A man who is angry at his father acts lovingly to his father but complains that his father is angry with him
Sublimation	Diversion of unwanted impulses into socially approved thoughts, feelings, or behaviors	A person with strong feelings of aggression becomes a soldier

ple develop a range of defense mechanisms to deal with it. **Defense mechanisms** are unconscious strategies that people use to reduce anxiety by concealing the source from themselves and others (Cramer, 1987; Cooper, 1989). (Defense mechanisms are summarized in Table 11-2.)

The primary defense mechanism is *repression,* in which unacceptable or unpleasant id impulses are pushed back into the unconscious. Repression is the most direct method of dealing with anxiety; instead of handling an anxiety-producing impulse on a conscious level, one simply ignores it. For example, a college student who feels hatred for her mother might repress these personally and socially unacceptable feelings. They remain lodged within the id, since acknowledging them would provoke anxiety. This does not mean, however, that they have no effect: True feelings might be revealed through dreams, slips of the tongue, or symbolically in some other fashion. The student might, for instance, have difficulty with authority figures such as teachers and do poorly in school. Alternatively, she might join the military, where she could ultimately give harsh orders to others without having them questioned.

If repression is ineffective in keeping anxiety at bay, other defense mechanisms may be called upon. For example, *regression* might be used, whereby people behave as if they were at an earlier stage of development. By retreating to a younger age—for instance, by complaining and throwing tantrums—they might succeed in having fewer demands put upon them. For example, a student who is overwhelmed by exams might act in a childish, immature manner to escape his responsibilities.

Anyone who has ever been angered by the unfairness of a professor and then returned to the dorm and yelled at a roommate knows what displacement is all about. In *displacement,* the expression of an unwanted feeling or thought is redi-

Defense mechanisms:
Unconscious strategies people use to reduce anxiety by concealing its source from themselves and others

rected from a more threatening, powerful person to a weaker one. A classic case is yelling at one's secretary after being criticized by the boss.

Rationalization, another defense mechanism, occurs when we distort reality by justifying what happens to us. We develop explanations that allow us to protect our self-esteem. If you've ever heard someone say that he didn't mind being stood up for a date because he really had a lot of studying to do that evening, you have probably seen rationalization at work.

In *denial*, a person simply refuses to accept or acknowledge an anxiety-producing piece of information. For example, when told that his wife has died in an automobile crash, a husband may at first deny the tragedy, claiming that there must be some mistake, and only gradually come to conscious acceptance that she has actually been killed. In extreme cases, denial may linger; the husband may continue to expect that his wife will return home.

Projection is a means of protecting oneself by attributing unwanted impulses and feelings to someone else. For example, a man who feels sexually inadequate may complain to his wife that *she* is sexually inept.

Finally, one defense mechanism that Freud considered to be healthy and socially acceptable is sublimation. In *sublimation*, people divert unwanted impulses into socially approved thoughts, feelings, or behaviors. For example, a person with strong feelings of aggression may become a football player or karate instructor. Sublimation allows people the opportunity not only to release psychic tension but to do so in a way that is socially acceptable.

All of us employ defense mechanisms to some degree, according to Freudian theory, and they can serve a useful purpose by protecting us from unpleasant information. Yet some people use them to such an extent that a large amount of psychic energy must constantly be directed toward hiding and rechanneling unacceptable impulses. When this occurs, everyday living becomes difficult. In such cases, the result is what Freud called "neurosis," a mental disorder produced by anxiety.

Evaluating Freudian Theory   More than almost any other psychological theory we have discussed, Freud's personality theory presents an elaborate and complicated set of propositions—some of which are so removed from everyday explanations of behavior that they may appear difficult to accept (Crews, 1993). But laypeople are not the only ones to be concerned about the validity of Freud's theory; personality psychologists, too, have criticized its inadequacies.

Among the most compelling criticisms is the lack of scientific data to support the theory. Although there is a wealth of individual assessments of particular people that *seem* to support the theory, we lack definitive evidence showing that the personality is structured and operates along the lines Freud laid out. This is due, in part, to the fact that Freud's conception of personality is built on unobservable abstract conceptions. Moreover, while we can readily employ Freudian theory in after-the-fact explanations, it is extremely difficult to predict how certain developmental difficulties will be displayed in the adult. For instance, if a person is fixated at the anal stage, he might, according to Freud, be unusually messy—or he might be unusually neat. Freud's theory offers us no way to predict which manifestations of the difficulty will occur. It produces good history, then, but not such good science.

Finally, Freud made his observations—admittedly insightful ones—and derived his theory from a limited population. His theory was based almost entirely on upper-class Austrian women living in the strict, puritanical era of the early 1900s. How far one can generalize beyond this population is a matter of considerable debate. For instance, in some Pacific Island societies, the role of disciplinarian is played by a mother's oldest brother, not the father. In such a culture, it wouldn't make sense to argue that the Oedipal conflict would progress in the same way it did in Austrian society, where the father typically was the major disciplinarian—a view supported by studies in that society. In sum, cross-cultural research raises questions about the universality of Freud's view of personality development (Guthrie & Lonner, 1986; Brislin, 1993).

Despite these criticisms, which cannot be ignored, Freud's theory has had an enormous impact on the field of psychology—and indeed on all of Western thinking. The ideas of the unconscious, anxiety, defense mechanisms, and the childhood causes of adult psychological difficulties have permeated people's views of human behavior, including their understanding of the causes of their own behavior.

Furthermore, Freud's emphasis on the unconscious has been partially supported by some of the current research findings of cognitive psychologists. This work has revealed that mental processes about which people are unaware have an important impact on thinking and actions. In addition, experimental techniques derived from procedures used to study implicit memory (Chapter 6) allow the unconscious to be studied in a more scientifically sophisticated manner. The techniques help overcome the reliance of traditional Freudian approaches on single-subject case studies and unconfirmable theoretical interpretations of dreams and slips of the tongue for support (Kihlstrom, 1987; Westen, 1990; Jacoby & Kelley, 1992).

The importance of psychoanalytic theory is underscored by the fact that it spawned a significant—and enduring—method of treating psychological disturbances, as we will discuss further in Chapter 13. For a variety of reasons, then, Freud's psychoanalytic theory remains a significant contribution to our understanding of personality.

The Neo-Freudian Psychoanalysts

One particularly important outgrowth of Freud's theorizing was the work done by a series of successors who were trained in traditional Freudian theory but who later rejected some of its major points. These theorists are known as **neo-Freudian psychoanalysts.**

The neo-Freudians placed greater emphasis than Freud did on the functions of the ego, suggesting that it had more control than the id over day-to-day activities. They also paid greater attention to social factors and the effects of society and culture on personality development. Carl Jung (pronounced "yoong"), for example, who initially adhered closely to Freud's thinking, later rejected the notion of the primary importance of unconscious sexual urges—a key notion of Freudian theory. Instead he looked at the primitive urges of the unconscious more positively, suggesting that people had a **collective unconscious,** a set of influences we inherit from our own particular ancestors, the whole human race, and even animal ancestors from the distant past. This collective unconscious is shared by everyone and is displayed by behavior that is common across diverse cultures—such as love of mother, belief in a supreme being, and even behavior as specific as fear of snakes.

Jung went on to propose that the collective unconscious contains *archetypes,* universal symbolic representations of a particular person, object, or experience. For instance, a mother archetype, which contains reflections of our ancestors' relationships with mother figures, is suggested by the prevalence of mothers in art, religion, literature, and mythology. (Think of the Virgin Mary, Earth Mother, wicked stepmothers of fairy tales, Mother's Day, and so forth.)

To Jung, archetypes play an important role in determining our day-to-day reactions, attitudes, and values. For instance, Jung might explain the popularity of a movie such as *Batman* as being due to its use of broad archetypes of good (Batman), evil (the Joker), and innocence (Vicki Vail).

Alfred Adler, another important neo-Freudian psychoanalyst, also considered Freudian theory's emphasis on sexual needs to be misplaced. Instead, Adler pro-

Neo-Freudian psychoanalysts: Theorists who place greater emphasis than did Freud on the functions of the ego and its influence on our daily activities

Collective unconscious: A concept developed by Jung proposing that we inherit certain personality characteristics from our ancestors and the human race as a whole

In Jungian terms, Batman and the Joker are archetypes, or universally recognizable symbols, of good and evil.

Inferiority complex: According to Adler, a situation in which adults have not been able to overcome the feelings of inferiority they developed as children

posed that the primary human motivation was a striving for superiority, not in terms of superiority over others, but as a quest to achieve self-improvement and perfection. Adler used the term **inferiority complex** to describe cases in which adults have not been able to overcome the feelings of inferiority they developed as children, when they were small and limited in their knowledge about the world. Early social relationships with parents have an important effect on how well children are able to outgrow feelings of personal inferiority and instead orient themselves toward attaining more socially useful goals such as improving society.

Other neo-Freudians, such as Erik Erikson (whose theory we discussed in Chapter 10) and Karen Horney (1937), also focused less than Freud on inborn sexual and aggressive drives and more on the social and cultural factors behind personality. Horney, one of the first psychologists who championed women's issues, suggested that personality develops in terms of social relationships and depends particularly on the relationship between parents and child and how well the child's needs were met. She rejected Freud's suggestion that women have penis envy, asserting that what women envied most in men was not their anatomy but the independence, success, and freedom that women are often denied.

RECAP AND REVIEW

Recap

- Freud's psychoanalytic theory proposes that personality consists of three components: the id, the ego, and the superego.
- According to psychoanalytic theory, personality develops during a series of stages in which the focus of pleasure is on a particular part of the body.
- Defense mechanisms are unconscious strategies that people use to reduce anxiety by concealing its source. Among the most important are repression, regression, displacement, rationalization, denial, projection, and sublimation.
- Among the neo-Freudian psychoanalysts who built and

modified psychoanalytic theory are Jung, Adler, and Horney.

Review

1. _____ theory states that behavior is motivated primarily by unconscious forces.
2. Match each section of the personality (according to Freud) with its description:
   1. Ego
   2. Id
   3. Superego

a. Determines right from wrong on the basis of cultural standards

b. Operates according to the "reality principle"; energy is redirected to integrate the person into society

c. Seeks to reduce tension brought on by primitive drives

3. Within the superego, the _____-_____ motivates us to do what is right, while the _____ prevents us from doing what is unacceptable.

4. Which of the following represents the proper order of personality development according to Freud?

a. Oral, phallic, latency, anal, genital

b. Anal, oral, phallic, genital, latency

c. Oral, anal, phallic, latency, genital

d. Latency, phallic, anal, genital, oral

5. In the resolution of the _____ complex, Freud believed that boys learn to repress their desire for their mothers and identify with their fathers.

6. "_____ _____" is the term Freud used to describe unconscious strategies used to reduce anxiety.

Ask Yourself

A friend tells you that whenever he gets really angry, he goes to the gym and works out vigorously until he feels better. Which of Freud's defense mechanisms might this behavior represent?

(Answers to review questions are on page 382.)

• *What are the major aspects of trait, learning, biological, and humanistic approaches to personality?*

OTHER MAJOR APPROACHES TO PERSONALITY: IN SEARCH OF HUMAN UNIQUENESS

"Tell me about Nelson," said Johnetta.

"Oh, he's just terrific. He's the friendliest guy I know—goes out of his way to be nice to everyone. He hardly ever gets mad. He's just so even-tempered, no matter what's happening. And he's really smart, too. About the only thing I don't like is that he's always in such a hurry to get things done. He seems to have boundless energy, much more than I have."

"He sounds great to me, especially in comparison to Rico," replied Johnetta. "He is so self-centered and arrogant it drives me crazy. I sometimes wonder why I ever started going out with him."

Friendly, even-tempered, smart, energetic, self-centered, arrogant—this series of trait characterizations taken from the interchange above is used to describe the personalities of the boyfriends being discussed. In fact, most of our understanding of the reasons behind others' behavior is based on the premise that people possess certain traits that are assumed to be consistent across different situations. A number of formal theories of personality employ variants of this approach. We turn now to a discussion of these and other personality approaches, all of which provide alternatives to the psychoanalytic emphasis on unconscious processes in determining behavior.

Trait Approaches: Placing Labels on Personality

If someone were to ask you to characterize another person, it is probable that—like the two people in the conversation above—you would come up with a list of that individual's personal qualities, as you see them. But how would you know which of these qualities were most important to an understanding of that person's behavior?

Personality psychologists have asked similar questions themselves. In order to answer them, they have developed a model of personality known as **trait theory.** **Traits** are enduring dimensions of personality characteristics along which people differ.

Trait theory: A model that seeks to identify the basic traits necessary to describe personality

Traits: Enduring dimensions of personality characteristics differentiating people from one another

Trait theorists do not assume that some people have a trait and others do not; rather, they propose that all people possess certain traits, but that the degree to which a given trait applies to a specific person varies and can be quantified. For instance, you might be relatively friendly, whereas I might be relatively unfriendly. But we both have a "friendliness" trait, although your degree of "friendliness" would be higher than mine. The major challenge for trait theorists taking this approach has been to identify the specific primary traits necessary to describe personality. As we shall see, different theorists have come up with surprisingly different sets of traits.

Allport's Trait Theory: Identifying the Basics   When personality psychologist Gordon Allport systematically leafed through an unabridged dictionary, he came up with some 18,000 separate terms that could be used to describe personality. Although he was able to pare down the list to a mere 4500 descriptors after eliminating synonyms, he was obviously still left with a problem crucial to all trait approaches: Which of these were the most basic?

Allport answered this question by suggesting that there are three basic categories of traits: cardinal, central, and secondary (Allport, 1961, 1966). A **cardinal trait** is a single characteristic that directs most of a person's activities. For example, a totally selfless woman might direct all her energy toward humanitarian activities; an intensely power-hungry person might be driven by an all-consuming need for control.

Most people, however, do not develop all-encompassing cardinal traits. Instead, they possess a handful of central traits that make up the core of their personality. **Central traits,** such as honesty and sociability, are the major characteristics of an individual; they usually number from five to ten in any one person. Finally, **secondary traits** are characteristics that affect behavior in fewer situations and are less influential than central or cardinal traits. For instance, a preference for ice cream or a dislike of modern art would be considered a secondary trait.

The Theories of Cattell and Eysenck: Factoring Out Personality   More recent attempts to identify primary traits have centered on a statistical technique known as factor analysis. *Factor analysis* is a method of summarizing the relationships among a large number of variables into fewer, more general patterns. For example, a personality researcher might administer a questionnaire to many subjects, asking them to describe themselves by referring to an extensive list of traits. By statistically combining responses and computing which traits are associated with one another in the same person, a researcher can identify the most fundamental patterns or combinations of traits—called factors—that underlie subjects' responses.

Using factor analysis, personality psychologist Raymond Cattell suggested that the characteristics that can be observed in a given situation represent forty-six *surface traits,* or clusters of related behaviors. For example, you might encounter a friendly, gregarious librarian who goes out of his way to be helpful to you, and from your interactions with him decide that he possesses the trait of sociability—in Cattell's terms, a surface trait (Cattell, 1965; Cattell, Cattell, & Cattell, 1993).

However, such surface traits are based on people's perceptions and representations of personality; they do not necessarily provide the best description of the underlying personality dimensions that are at the root of all behavior. Carrying out further factor analysis, Cattell found that sixteen *source traits* represent the basic dimensions of personality. Using these source traits, he developed the

Cardinal trait: A single personality trait that directs most of a person's activities (e.g., greed, lust, kindness)

Central traits: A set of major characteristics that make up the core of a person's personality

Secondary traits: Less important personality traits (e.g., preferences for certain clothes or movies) that do not affect behavior as much as central and cardinal traits do

---

ANSWERS TO PREVIOUS REVIEW
1. Psychoanalytic   **2.** 1-b; 2-c; 3-a   **3.** ego-ideal; conscience   **4.** c   **5.** Oedipal
6. Defense mechanisms

Sixteen Personality Factor Questionnaire, or 16 PF, a measure that provides scores for each of the source traits.

Another trait theorist, psychologist Hans Eysenck (1973; Eysenck & Eysenck, 1985), also used factor analysis to identify patterns of traits, but he came to a very different conclusion about the nature of personality. He found that personality could best be described in terms of just two major dimensions: *introversion-extroversion* and *neuroticism-stability*. At one extreme of the introversion-extroversion dimension are the introverts (people who are quiet, passive, and careful), and at the other are the extroverts (outgoing, sociable, and active). Independently of this dimension, people can be rated as neurotic (moody, touchy, anxious) versus stable (calm, carefree, even-tempered). By evaluating people along these two dimensions, Eysenck has been able to predict behavior accurately in a variety of types of situations (see Figure 11-2).

The most recent research on traits suggests that five broad trait factors lie at the core of personality. The five factors, which have come to be called the "Big Five" by trait theorists, are *surgency* (extroversion and sociability), *neuroticism* (emotional stability), *intellect, agreeableness,* and *conscientiousness* (Digman, 1990; Funder, 1991; Goldberg, 1990; Costa & McCrae, 1995). Research conducted in countries as diverse as Canada, Finland, Poland, and the Philippines has helped produce a growing consensus that these five factors represent the best description of personality. Still, the evidence is not conclusive, and the specific number and kinds of traits that are considered fundamental remain a source of debate (and investigation) among trait theorists (Hofstee, de Raad, & Goldberg, 1992; Church & Burke, 1994; Katigbak & Akamine, 1994).

Evaluating Trait Approaches to Personality   Trait approaches have several virtues. They provide a clear, straightforward explanation of people's behavioral consistencies. Furthermore, traits allow us to readily compare one person with

Many people found it difficult to imagine that O. J. Simpson, shown here following the announcement of the "not guilty" verdict by the jury, could harbor personality traits that might lead him to murder his ex-wife and a male acquaintance.

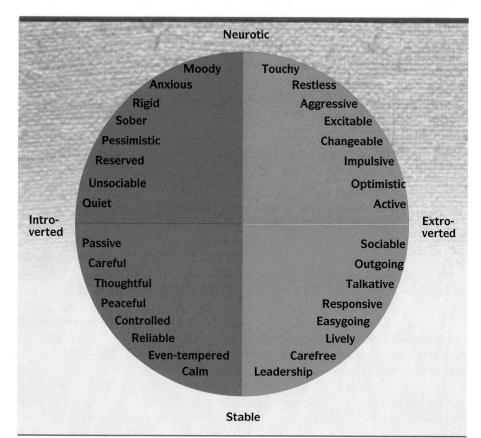

FIGURE 11-2 According to Eysenck, personality can be viewed as lying along two major dimensions: introversion-extroversion and neuroticism-stability. Other personality characteristics can be ordered along the circular figure depicted here. *(Eysenck, 1973.)*

In evaluating behavior, we must consider the extent to which the behavior is voluntary. The fact that a student is taking an introductory course, for example, doesn't necessarily reflect an interest in psychology if the course is a degree requirement.

another. Because of these advantages, trait conceptions of personality have had an important practical influence on the development of several personality measures discussed later in the chapter (Buss, 1989; Funder, 1991).

On the other hand, trait approaches have some drawbacks. For example, we have seen that various trait theories describing personality come to quite different conclusions about which traits are the most fundamental and descriptive. The difficulty in determining which of the theories is most accurate has led some personality psychologists to question the validity of trait conceptions of personality in general.

Actually, there is an even more fundamental difficulty with trait approaches. Even if we are able to identify a set of primary traits, we are left with little more than a label or description of personality—rather than an explanation of behavior. If we say that someone donates money to charity because he or she has the trait of generosity, we still do not know *why* the person became generous in the first place, or the reasons for displaying generosity in a given situation. In the view of some critics, then, traits do not provide explanations for behavior; they merely describe it.

Learning Approaches: We Are What We've Learned

The psychoanalytic and trait approaches we've discussed concentrate on the "inner" person—the stormy fury of an unobservable but powerful id or a hypothetical but critical set of traits. In contrast, learning approaches to personality focus on the "outer" person. To a strict learning theorist, personality is simply the sum of learned responses to the external environment. Internal events such as thoughts, feelings, and motivations are ignored. Although their existence is not denied, learning theorists say that personality is best understood by looking at features of a person's environment.

According to the most influential of the learning theorists, B. F. Skinner (whom we discussed first in terms of operant conditioning in Chapter 5), personality is a collection of learned behavior patterns (Skinner, 1975). Similarities in responses across different situations are caused by similar patterns of reinforcement that have been received in such situations in the past. If I am sociable both at parties and at meetings, it is because I have been reinforced previously for displaying social behaviors—not because I am fulfilling some unconscious wish based on experiences during my childhood or because I have an internal trait of sociability.

Strict learning theorists such as Skinner are less interested in the consistencies in behavior across situations, however, than in ways of modifying behavior. Their view is that humans are infinitely changeable. If one is able to control and modify the patterns of reinforcers in a situation, behavior that other theorists would view as stable and unyielding can be changed and ultimately improved. Learning theorists are optimistic in their attitudes about the potential for resolving personal and societal problems through treatment strategies based on learning theory—methods we will discuss in Chapter 13.

Social Cognitive Approaches to Personality Not all learning theories of personality take such a strict view in rejecting the importance of what is "inside" the person by focusing solely on the "outside." Unlike other learning approaches to personality, **social cognitive approaches** emphasize the influence of people's cognitions—their thoughts, feelings, expectations, and values—in determining personality. According to Albert Bandura, one of the main proponents of this point of view, people are able to foresee the possible outcomes of certain behaviors in a given setting without actually having to carry them out. This takes place mainly through the mechanism of *observational learning*—viewing the actions of others and observing the consequences (Bandura, 1977).

For instance, as we first discussed in Chapter 5, children who view a model behaving in, say, an aggressive manner tend to copy the behavior if the consequences of the model's behavior are seen to be positive. If, on the other hand, the model's aggressive behavior has resulted in no consequences or negative consequences, children are considerably less likely to act aggressively. According to social cognitive approaches, personality thus develops by repeated observation of the behavior of others.

Bandura places particular emphasis on the role played by *self-efficacy,* learned expectations that one is capable of carrying out a behavior or producing a desired outcome. Self-efficacy underlies people's faith in their ability to carry out a particular behavior. The greater a person's sense of self-efficacy, the more persistent he or she will be, and the more likely it is that the individual will be successful. For instance, students high in self-efficacy regarding scholastic accomplishments will be more likely to achieve academic success (Scheier & Carver, 1992).

Compared with other learning theories of personality, social cognitive approaches are distinctive in their emphasis on the reciprocity between individuals and their environments. Not only is the environment assumed to affect personality, but people's behavior and personalities are assumed to "feed back" and modify their environments—which in turn affects behavior in a web of reciprocity.

In fact, Bandura has suggested that reciprocal determinism is the key to understanding behavior. By *reciprocal determinism,* he was referring to how the interaction of environment, behavior, and individual ultimately causes people to behave in the ways they do (Bandura, 1981, 1986). For instance, a man with aggressive needs may get into a fight at a hockey game. He may later seek out hockey games in part to fulfill his enjoyment of fighting. At the same time, his drive to be aggressive may increase because of his fighting. In sum, the environment of the hockey game, the behavior of fighting, and the individual's characteristics interact with one another in a reciprocal fashion.

Evaluating Learning Approaches to Personality By ignoring the internal processes that are uniquely human, traditional learning theorists such as Skinner have been accused of oversimplifying personality to such an extent that the concept becomes meaningless. Reducing behavior to a series of stimuli and responses, and excluding thoughts and feelings from the realm of personality, leaves behaviorists practicing an unrealistic and inadequate form of science, in the eyes of their critics.

Of course, some of these criticisms are blunted by social cognitive approaches, which explicitly consider the role of cognitive processes in personality. Still, learn-

Social cognitive approaches: Theories that emphasize the influence of a person's cognitions—their thoughts, feelings, expectations, and values—in determining personality

ing approaches tend to share a highly *deterministic* view of human behavior, a view maintaining that behavior is shaped primarily by forces beyond the control of the individual. According to some critics, determinism disregards the ability of people to pilot their own course through life.

On the other hand, learning approaches have had a major impact in a variety of ways. For one thing, they have helped make the study of personality an objective, scientific venture by focusing on observable behavior and environment. In addition, learning approaches have produced important, successful means of treating personality disorders. The degree of success these treatments have enjoyed is testimony to the merits of learning-theory approaches to personality.

Biological Approaches: Are We Born with Personality?

Is personality inherited? That's the question raised by biological approaches to personality. *Biological approaches to personality* suggest that important components of personality are inherited, in much the same way that our height is determined in part by genetic contributions from our ancestors (Kupfermann, 1991d; Plomin & McClearn, 1993).

Temperament: The basic, innate disposition that emerges early in life

Temperament The study of **temperament,** the basic, innate disposition that emerges early in life, represents a biological approach to personality. For example, as early as 2 months of age, some infants show signs of shyness. They spontaneously frown, even while resting quietly—a rarity in young infants. Later, these same children are unusually fearful of the sight of an unfamiliar adult, and they fret when confronted with unfamiliar objects or new settings. By the time they are 3 or 4 years old, their parents and teachers label them as "shy."

To psychologist Jerome Kagan, such behavior is characteristic of the *inhibited* child. *Inhibited children,* who may represent as many as 10 percent of all children, are consistently shy and emotionally restrained in unfamiliar situations. When placed in a novel environment or when meeting people for the first time, they become noticeably quiet. When asked questions of just moderate difficulty by an unfamiliar adult in experiments, they become anxious, which has the effect of hindering their performance. They are more likely than other children to show unusual fears, such as fear of going into their bedrooms by themselves at night or of speaking aloud in class. In contrast, uninhibited children show little fear of strangers or of new situations, and act in a sociable and relaxed manner when encountering novel situations (Kagan, 1989b).

Inhibited children differ from uninhibited ones on a biological level. Inhibited children show higher muscle tension at age 5, particularly in the vocal cords and larynx. They tend to have more rapid resting heartbeats, and their heartbeats increase more when confronted with a new situation. There are also hormonal differences and variations in the excitability of the limbic system of the brain between inhibited and uninhibited children (Kagan & Snidman, 1991).

Based on this evidence, Kagan has suggested that the differences between inhibited and uninhibited children can be explained by the inhibited children's greater physiological reactivity—an inborn characteristic. According to this hypothesis, some infants, due to their genetic endowment, are more reactive to novel stimuli than others. Even the mildest stress raises their heartbeat, increases muscle tension, and causes changes in hormonal levels. It is this characteristic reactivity that ultimately leads most of the infants who show this pattern to later display shyness in social situations.

On the other hand, not all infants born with easily aroused nervous systems later become shy: About one-quarter overcome their biological predisposition and do not exhibit shyness in later years. It appears that certain kinds of environmental stress, such as parental marital strife or a chronic illness in the family, increase the likelihood that such infants will subsequently become shy children. It

According to the biological view of personality, characteristics of temperament are inborn. For example, an inhibited and consistently shy child may differ from other children on physiological reactivity.

is the interaction of heredity and environment, then, that determines whether a child will become shy.

Twin Studies   Other personality researchers, working from a biological perspective, have sought to determine whether genetic factors might explain additional personality characteristics. For example, personality psychologists Auke Tellegen and colleagues at the University of Minnesota have been examining the personality traits of some 350 pairs of twins (Tellegen et al., 1988). Forty-four of the pairs are genetically identical but raised apart from each other, providing the opportunity to determine the influence of genetic factors on personality. Each of the twins was given a battery of personality tests, including one that measured eleven key personality traits. The results of the tests indicated that in major respects the twins were quite similar in personality. Moreover, certain traits were more influenced by heredity than others. For example, social potency (the degree to which a person assumes mastery and leadership roles in social situations) and traditionalism (the tendency to follow authority) had particularly strong genetic components, whereas achievement and social closeness had relatively weak genetic components (see Figure 11-3, next page).

It seems, then, that heredity plays an important role in determining an individual's personality. Does this mean that parental influence and other environmental factors are of only minor importance? The answer is a clear "no," since parents and other figures in the child's environment shape the extent to which traits produced by heredity assert themselves (Loehlin, Willerman, & Horn, 1987; Rose et al., 1988; Bouchard, 1994). It is possible, for instance, to reduce the degree to which children high in self-absorption display that trait by exposing them to experiences with other children. Similarly, highly assertive children might be helped to temper their assertiveness through experiences that make them more aware of the feelings of others (Kagan, 1990).

Evaluating Biological Approaches to Personality   Current research clearly indicates that certain personality characteristics are influenced to some degree by biological factors. It seems natural to ask, "Just how much does biology matter?"

The answer is that we don't fully know. As we saw in our discussions of the inheritability of intelligence (Chapter 8) and the nature-nurture issue (Chapter 10), it is impossible to completely divorce genetic factors from environmental factors. Studies of identical twins raised in different environments are helpful. However, they cannot definitively answer the question, because it is impossible to maintain full control over environmental factors. Furthermore, estimates of the influence of genetics are just that—estimates—and they apply to groups, not individuals. Consequently, the findings shown in Figure 11-3 must be regarded as approximations.

In sum, although an increasing number of personality theorists are taking biological factors into account (e.g., DeKay & Buss, 1992), at the present time no comprehensive, unified theory that considers biological factors is widely accepted. Still, it is clear that certain personality traits have substantial genetic components, and heredity and environment interact to determine personality. Consequently, it is important to keep in mind that genes alone do not represent our destiny. Even if inherited factors predispose us to act in certain ways, these predispositions can be overcome. As Jerome Kagan put it, "Sometimes human behavior is the result of deliberation and will imposed on the invisible forces of biology and personal history" (Kagan, 1990, p. 5).

Humanistic Approaches: The Uniqueness of You

Where, in all these approaches to personality, is there an explanation for the saintliness of a Mother Teresa, the creativity of a Michelangelo, the brilliance and per-

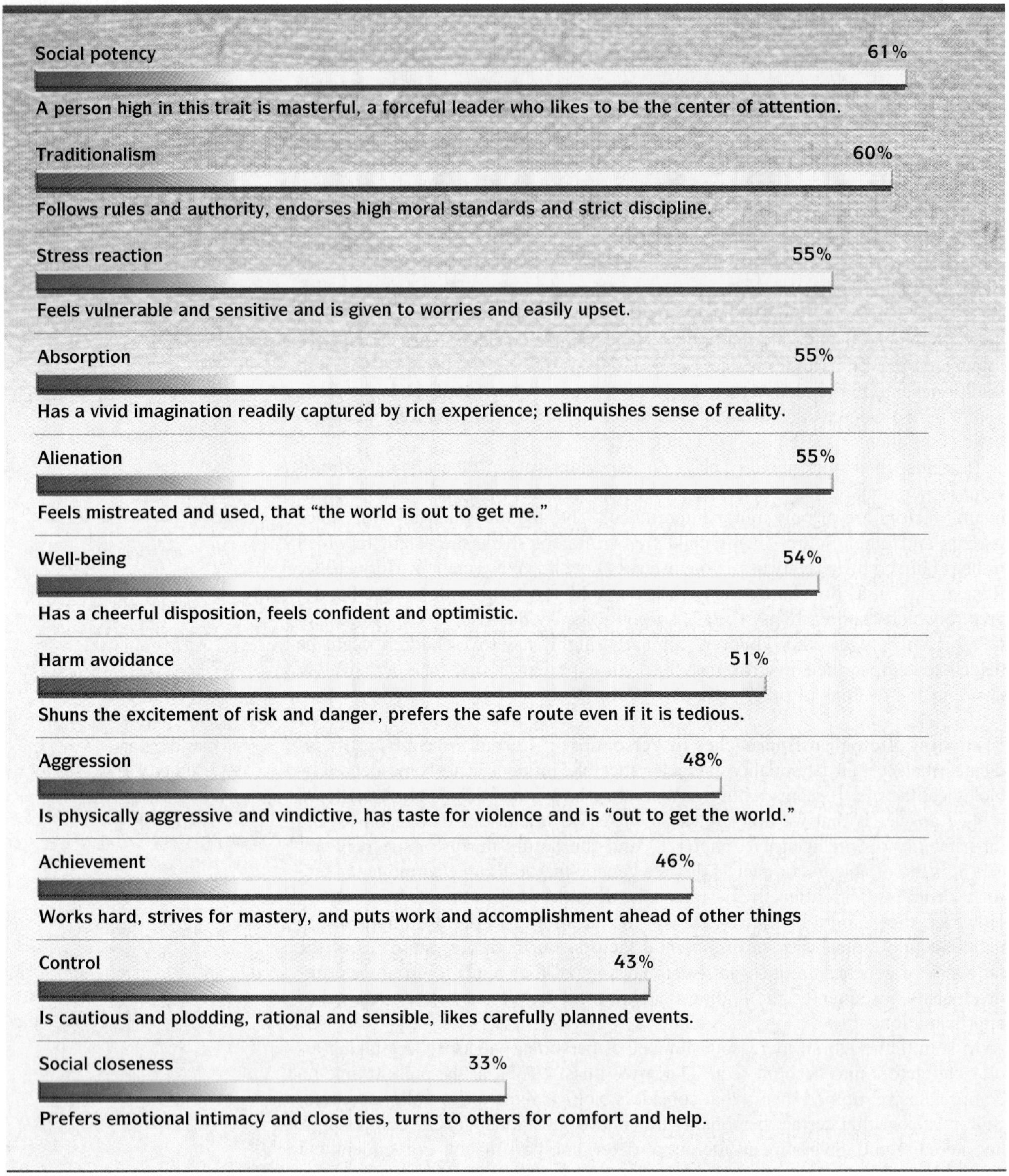

Social potency 61%

A person high in this trait is masterful, a forceful leader who likes to be the center of attention.

Traditionalism 60%

Follows rules and authority, endorses high moral standards and strict discipline.

Stress reaction 55%

Feels vulnerable and sensitive and is given to worries and easily upset.

Absorption 55%

Has a vivid imagination readily captured by rich experience; relinquishes sense of reality.

Alienation 55%

Feels mistreated and used, that "the world is out to get me."

Well-being 54%

Has a cheerful disposition, feels confident and optimistic.

Harm avoidance 51%

Shuns the excitement of risk and danger, prefers the safe route even if it is tedious.

Aggression 48%

Is physically aggressive and vindictive, has taste for violence and is "out to get the world."

Achievement 46%

Works hard, strives for mastery, and puts work and accomplishment ahead of other things

Control 43%

Is cautious and plodding, rational and sensible, likes carefully planned events.

Social closeness 33%

Prefers emotional intimacy and close ties, turns to others for comfort and help.

FIGURE 11-3 The roots of personality. The percentages indicate the degree to which eleven personality characteristics reflect the influence of heredity. *(Tellegen et al., 1988.)*

severance of an Einstein? An understanding of such unique individuals—as well as of more ordinary sorts of people who share some of the same attributes—comes from humanistic theory.

According to humanistic theorists, all of the approaches to personality that we have previously discussed share a fundamental misperception in their views of human nature. Instead of seeing people as controlled by unconscious, unseen forces (as do psychoanalytic approaches), a set of stable traits (trait approaches), situ-

ational reinforcements and punishments (learning theory), or inherited factors (biological approaches), **humanistic approaches to personality** emphasize people's basic goodness and their tendency to grow to higher levels of functioning. It is this conscious, self-motivated ability to change and improve, along with people's unique creative impulses, that make up the core of personality.

The major proponent of the humanistic point of view is Carl Rogers (1971). Rogers suggests that people have a need for positive regard that reflects a universal requirement to be loved and respected. Because others provide this positive regard, we grow dependent on them. We begin to see and judge ourselves through the eyes of other people, relying on their values.

According to Rogers, one outgrowth of placing import on the opinions of others is that there may be a conflict between people's actual experiences and their *self-concepts,* or self-impressions. If the discrepancies are minor, so are the consequences. But if they are great, they will lead to psychological disturbances in daily functioning, such as the experience of frequent anxiety.

Rogers suggests that one way of overcoming the discrepancy between experience and self-concept is through the receipt of unconditional positive regard from another person—a friend, a spouse, or a therapist. As we will discuss further in

Humanistic approaches to personality: Theories that emphasize people's basic goodness and their natural tendency to grow to higher levels of functioning

PSYCHOLOGY AT WORK

Personality Change during Adulthood: Will You Be a Different Person in the Future?

Will the personality you have now be the same in 20 years? It may not be. Although most approaches to personality suggest that our basic personality is relatively consistent once we reach adulthood, recent research suggests that basic aspects of personality may, in fact, not be as stable as once thought (Hetherington & Weinberger, 1993). In particular, it now appears that people undergo changes over the course of adulthood in the nature of their core personality, although the specific nature of those changes depends on gender.

According to psychologist Ravenna Helson and her colleagues, personality does change in significant ways during adulthood. In a study that examined a group of women and their male partners at the ages of 27 and 52, Helson found that there was significant personality change in both the men and women subjects, due largely to the major evolutions that had occurred in the participants' lives over the course of time (Wink

& Helson, 1993). At age 27, most men and women were in the "early parental period," in which they either had one or more children or were expecting a child. In contrast, men and women in their fifties were in the "postparental period." Only a minority of the postparental participants had children at home, most women and men had jobs and a few had retired.

Between the ages of 27 and 52, changing life conditions and roles led to significant personality changes. At age 27, the women were more emotionally dependent and concerned with promoting interpersonal relations than were the men, while the men reported feeling more competent (in the sense of being organized, thorough, efficient, and the like). In contrast, at age 52, these gender differences dispersed. Except for the fact that women showed somewhat more self-confidence than men, the personality profiles of men and women were quite similar at the later age. At the same time, both men's and women's personalities changed in several respects during the 25-year period. For instance, both groups showed an increase in self-discipline over the years.

In sum, both men's and women's personalities undergo change during adulthood, change that most likely reflects shifting circumstances and interests during different periods of life. Apparently, then, we're not destined to have the same personality throughout the course of life.

Not everyone agrees with the notion that personality undergoes significant change over the course of adulthood. Some researchers suggest that one's personality shows substantial stability over time and that significant changes are rare (McCrae & Costa, 1990). According to this point of view, if we look over a long enough period and sufficient situations, stable, significant behavioral consistencies can be identified (Epstein & O'Brien, 1985). To these scientists, fluctuations in basic personality, such as those identified by Helson, are only minor.

Given these differing views, the challenge for psychologists is to determine which specific characteristics are the most likely to persist and which are most apt to change.

TABLE 11-3 Aspects of Personality

	Dimension			
Theoretical approach	Conscious versus unconscious determinants of personality	Nature (genetic factors) versus nurture (environmental factors)	Freedom versus determinism	Stability versus modifiability
Psychoanalytic	Emphasizes the unconscious	Stresses the innate, inherited structure of personality	Stresses determinism, the view that behavior is directed and caused by factors outside one's control	Emphasizes the stability of characteristics throughout a person's life
Trait	Disregards both conscious and unconscious	Approaches vary	Stresses determinism, the view that behavior is directed and caused by factors outside one's control	Emphasizes the stability of characteristics throughout a person's life
Learning	Disregards both conscious and unconscious	Focuses on the environment	Stresses determinism, the view that behavior is directed and caused by factors outside one's control	Stresses that personality remains flexible and resilient throughout one's life
Biological	Disregards both conscious and unconscious	Stresses the innate, inherited structure of personality	Stresses determinism, the view that behavior is directed and caused by factors outside one's control	Emphasizes the stability of characteristics throughout a person's life
Humanistic	Stresses the conscious	Stresses the interaction between both nature and nurture	Stresses the freedom of individuals to make their own choices	Stresses that personality remains flexible and resilient throughout one's life

Self-actualization: A state of self-fulfillment in which people realize their highest potential

Chapter 13, *unconditional positive regard* refers to an attitude of acceptance and respect on the part of an observer, no matter what a person says or does. This acceptance, says Rogers, allows people the opportunity to evolve and grow both cognitively and emotionally and to develop more realistic self-concepts.

To Rogers and other humanistic personality theorists (such as Abraham Maslow, whose theory of motivation we discussed in Chapter 9), an ultimate goal of personality growth is self-actualization. **Self-actualization** is a state of self-fulfillment in which people realize their highest potential. This, Rogers would argue, occurs when their everyday experience and their self-concept are closely matched. People who are self-actualized accept themselves as they are in reality, which enables them to achieve happiness and fulfillment (Ford, 1991).

Evaluating Humanistic Approaches   Although humanistic theories suggest the value of providing unconditional positive regard toward people, unconditional positive regard toward humanistic theories has been less forthcoming from many personality theorists. The criticisms have centered on the difficulty of verifying the basic assumptions of the approach, as well as on the question of whether unconditional positive regard does, in fact, lead to greater personality adjustment.

Humanistic approaches have also been criticized for making the assumption that people are basically "good"—a notion that is unverifiable and, equally im-

portant, one in which nonscientific values are used to build supposedly scientific theories. Still, humanistic theories have been important in highlighting the uniqueness of human beings and in guiding the development of a significant form of therapy designed to alleviate psychological difficulties.

Comparing Approaches to Personality

Given the multiple approaches to personality that we have discussed, you may be wondering which of the theories provides the most accurate approach to personality. It is a question that cannot be answered with precision. Each theory holds distinct premises and looks at somewhat different aspects of personality. Furthermore, in many cases personality is most reasonably viewed from a number of perspectives simultaneously. Of course, someday there may be a unified theory of personality, but the field has not yet reached that point and is unlikely to do so in the near future.

In the meantime, the various theories highlight different aspects of personality. Table 11-3 compares them along several fundamental dimensions.

RECAP AND REVIEW

Recap

- Traits are relatively enduring dimensions along which people's personalities differ. Trait theorists have tried to identify the major traits that characterize personality.
- Learning theories of personality concentrate on how environmental factors shape personality. Among the most important approaches are Skinner's reinforcement theory and social cognitive approaches.
- Biological approaches focus on the degree to which personality characteristics are inherited.
- Humanistic theories view the core of personality as the ability to change, improve, and be creative in a uniquely human fashion.
- The major dimensions along which personality theories differ include the role of the unconscious versus the conscious, nature (genetic factors) versus nurture (environmental factors), freedom versus determinism, and stability versus modifiability of personality characteristics.

Review

1. Carl's determination to succeed is the dominant force in all his activities and relationships. According to Gordon Allport's theory, this is an example of a _____ trait. In contrast, Cindy's fondness for old western movies is an example of a _____ trait.
2. Which trait theorist used surface traits and source traits to explain behavior on the basis of sixteen personality dimensions?
   a. Hans Eysenck
   b. Walter Mischel
   c. Gordon Allport
   d. Raymond Cattell

3. What broad factors did Eysenck propose to describe personality?
4. A person who enjoys such activities as parties and hang gliding might be described by Eysenck as high on what trait?
5. Proponents of which approach to personality would be most likely to agree with the statement "Personality can be thought of as learned responses to a person's environment"?
   a. Humanistic approaches
   b. Biological approaches
   c. Learning approaches
   d. Trait approaches
6. A person who would make the statement "I know I can't do it" would be rated by Bandura as low on _____ _____.
7. Which approach to personality emphasizes the innate goodness of people and their desire to grow?
   a. Humanistic
   b. Psychoanalytic
   c. Learning
   d. Biological

Ask Yourself

Which of these theories of personality is most appealing to you? Which seems to make the most sense? If you were asked to write an essay providing "the definitive definition of personality," how would you use the information on personality we've been discussing to do it?

(Answers to review questions are on page 392.)

• *How can we most accurately assess personality?*
• *What are the major types of personality measures?*

ASSESSING PERSONALITY: DETERMINING WHAT MAKES US SPECIAL

You have a need for other people to like and admire you.

You have a tendency to be critical of yourself.

You have a great deal of unused potential that you have not turned to your advantage.

Although you have some personality weaknesses, you are generally able to compensate for them.

Relating to members of the opposite sex has presented problems to you.

While you appear to be disciplined and self-controlled to others, you tend to be anxious and insecure inside.

At times you have serious doubts about whether you have made the right decision or done the right thing.

You prefer a certain amount of change and variety and become dissatisfied when hemmed in by restrictions and limitations.

You do not accept others' statements without satisfactory proof.

You have found it unwise to be too frank in revealing yourself to others.

If you think these statements provide a surprisingly accurate account of your personality, you are not alone: Most college students think that the descriptions are tailored just to them. In fact, the statements are intentionally designed to be so vague as to be applicable to just about anyone (Forer, 1949; Russo, 1981).

The ease with which we can agree with such imprecise statements underscores the difficulty in coming up with accurate and meaningful assessments of people's personalities (Johnson et al., 1985; Prince & Guastello, 1990). Just as trait theorists were faced with the problem of determining the most critical and important traits, psychologists interested in assessing personality must be able to define the most meaningful ways of discriminating between one person's personality and another's. To do this, they use **psychological tests,** standard measures devised to assess behavior objectively. Such tests are used by psychologists to help people make decisions about their lives and understand more about themselves. They are also employed by researchers interested in the causes and consequences of personality (Groth-Marnat, 1990; Matarazzo, 1992).

Like the intelligence assessments that we discussed in Chapter 8, all psychological tests must have reliability and validity. *Reliability,* you may recall, refers to the measurement consistency of a test. If a test is reliable, it yields the same result each time it is administered to a given person or group. In contrast, unreliable tests give different results each time they are administered.

Tests also must be valid in order to draw meaningful conclusions. Tests have *validity* when they actually measure what they are designed to measure. If a test is constructed to measure sociability, for instance, we need to know that it actually measures sociability and not some other trait.

Psychological tests: Standard measures devised to assess behavior objectively

---

ANSWERS TO PREVIOUS REVIEW
1. cardinal; secondary **2.** d **3.** Introversion-extroversion and neuroticism-stability
4. Extroversion **5.** c **6.** self-efficacy **7.** a

Finally, psychological tests are based on *norms,* standards of test performance that permit the comparison of one person's score on the test with the scores of others who have taken the same test. For example, a norm permits test-takers to know they have scored in the top 10 percent of those who have taken the test.

Basically, norms are established by administering a particular test to a large number of people and determining the typical scores. It is then possible to compare a single person's score with the scores of the group, providing a comparative measure of test performance against others who have taken the test.

The establishment of appropriate norms is not a simple endeavor. For instance, the specific group that is employed to determine norms for a test has a profound effect on how an individual's performance is evaluated. Furthermore, as we discuss next, the process of establishing norms can take on political overtones.

Exploring Diversity

Should Race Be Used to Establish Norms?

The passions of politics may confront the objectivity of science when test norms are established, at least in the realm of tests that are meant to predict future job performance. In fact, a national controversy has developed regarding whether different norms should be established for members of various racial and ethnic groups (Kilborn, 1991; Brown, 1994; Sackett & Wilk, 1994).

At issue is the U.S. government's 50-year-old General Aptitude Test Battery, a test that measures a broad range of abilities from eye-hand coordination to reading proficiency. The problem that sparked the controversy is that African-Americans and Hispanics tend to score lower on the test, on average, than members of other groups. The lower scores are often due to a lack of relevant experience and prior job opportunities as a result of prejudice and discrimination.

To promote the employment of minority racial groups, the government developed a separate set of norms for African-Americans and Hispanics. Rather than using the pool of all people who took the test, the scores of African-American and Hispanic applicants were compared only with the scores of other African-Americans and Hispanics. Consequently, a Hispanic who scored in the top 20 percent of other Hispanics taking the test was considered to have received a score equivalent to a white job applicant who scored in the top 20 percent of the whites who took the test, even though the absolute score of the Hispanic might be lower than that of the white.

Critics of the adjusted norming system suggest that such a procedure is riddled with problems. According to them, not only is such a system unfair to white

These data-entry operators for the U.S. Census Bureau received their jobs by passing the General Aptitude Test Battery, which until recently was scored using a controversial race-norming system.

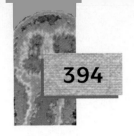

job applicants, but it fans the flames of racial bigotry. The practice was challenged legally, and with the passage of the Civil Rights Act in 1991, race norming on the General Aptitude Test Battery was discontinued.

However, proponents of race norming continue to argue that norming procedures that take race into account are an affirmative action tool that simply permits minority job-seekers to be placed on an equal footing with white jobseekers. Furthermore, a panel of the National Academy of Sciences concurred with the practice of adjusting test norms. It suggested that the unadjusted test norms are not terribly useful in predicting job performance, and that they would tend to screen out otherwise-qualified minority-group members.

Job testing is not the only area in which issues arise regarding norms and the meaning of test scores. As we saw in Chapter 8, when we discussed racial differences in IQ scores, the issue of how to treat racial differences in test scores is both a controversial and a divisive one. Clearly, race norming raises profound and intense feelings that may come into conflict with scientific objectivity, and the controversy is far from over (Geisinger, 1992; American Psychological Association, 1993).

The issue of establishing norms for tests is further complicated by the existence of a wide array of personality measures and approaches to assessment. We consider some of these measures, which have a variety of characteristics and purposes, next. (Also see the accompanying Pathways through Psychology box.)

Self-Report Measures of Personality

If someone wanted to assess your personality, one possible approach would be to carry out an extensive interview with you in order to determine the most important events of your childhood, your social relationships, and your successes and failures. Obviously, though, such a technique would be extraordinarily costly in terms of time and effort.

It is also unnecessary. Just as physicians draw only a small sample of your entire blood in order to test it, psychologists can utilize **self-report measures** that ask people about a relatively small sample of their behavior. This sampling of self-report data is then used to infer the presence of particular personality characteristics.

One of the best examples of a self-report measure, and the most frequently used personality test, is the **Minnesota Multiphasic Personality Inventory-2 (MMPI-2)** (Hathaway & McKinley, 1989; Butcher, 1990; Greene, 1991). Although the original purpose of the measure was to differentiate people with specific sorts of psychological difficulties from those without disturbances, it has been found to predict a variety of other behaviors. For instance, MMPI scores have been shown to be good predictors of whether college students will marry within 10 years and whether they will get advanced degrees (Dworkin & Widom, 1977). Police departments use the test to measure whether police officers are prone to use their weapons. Psychologists in the former Soviet Union even administered a modified form of the MMPI to their cosmonauts and Olympic athletes (Holden, 1986).

The test itself consists of a series of 567 items to which a person responds "true," "false," or "cannot say." The questions cover a variety of issues, ranging from mood ("I feel useless at times") to opinions ("people should try to understand their dreams") to physical and psychological health ("I am bothered by an upset stomach several times a week" and "I have strange and peculiar thoughts").

There are no right or wrong answers, of course. Instead, interpretation of the results rests on the pattern of responses. The test yields scores on ten separate scales, plus three scales meant to measure the validity of the respondent's answers. For example, there is a "lie scale" that indicates when people are falsifying their responses in order to present themselves more favorably (through items such

Self-report measures: A method of gathering data about people by asking them questions about a sample of their behavior

Minnesota Multiphasic Personality Inventory-2 (MMPI-2): A test used to identify people with psychological difficulties as well as to predict a variety of other behaviors

PATHWAYS THROUGH PSYCHOLOGY

Patricia Dyer
IBM, New York, New York

Patricia Dyer.

Education: B.A. in English, Pennsylvania State University; Ph. in personnel psychology, Columbia University
Born: 1940
Home: Manhattan, New York

When you receive 2 million employment applications a year and hire less than ½ percent of the applicants, how do you determine who is best suited to join your business?

This is where the expertise of Dr. Patricia Dyer, a psychologist who is a job-selection specialist at IBM, comes into play. As head of Testing and Assessment Services, she is responsible for developing tests that screen employees for the giant computer company.

Dyer and colleagues are developing a new generation of tests using the latest computer technology. "We are now working with different ways of getting at the skills and abilities using computerized multi-

media technology," she said. Test-takers are asked to solve a variety of problems faced by workers in a hypothetical manufacturing plant. These range from quality-control issues to specific kinds of work problems.

The test format has several advantages over traditional paper-and-pencil tests, according to Dyer, who has an undergraduate degree in English and a Ph.D. in personnel psychology. "For example, an on-the-job-training segment allows

candidates to build on what they have learned. That would be extraordinarily difficult with paper and pencil," she said (DeAngelis, 1994, p. 14).

While the methods of delivering the test via computer may be new, the basic procedures involved in developing the tests have been used for decades. Most are taught in almost any basic graduate assessment course, according to Dyer. "Testing has a long history and goes back to the turn of the century when Binet began to study school children," she said. "The idea of measuring abilities is not new.

"Two of the most important decisions an employer has to make are which people should be hired and what are the most effective ways to build an effective work force," said Dr. Dyer. "If the American economy is to succeed in the world market, we need a highly skilled and highly trained workforce to be competitive. Psychology has a lot to contribute to the process of identifying people who are best suited, and in terms of training and developing them once they are on board."

---

as "I can't remember ever having a bad night's sleep") (Butcher et al., 1990; Graham, 1990).

How did the authors of the MMPI determine what specific patterns of responses indicate? The procedure they used is typical of personality test construction—a process known as **test standardization.** To devise the test, groups of psychiatric patients with a specific diagnosis, such as depression or schizophrenia, were asked to complete a large number of items. The test authors then determined which items best differentiated members of these groups from a comparison group of normal subjects, and these specific items were included in the final version of the test. By systematically carrying out this procedure on groups with different diagnoses, the test authors were able to devise a number of subscales that identified different forms of abnormal behavior (see Figure 11-4).

When the MMPI is used for the purposes for which it was devised—identification of personality disorders—it does a reasonably good job. However, like other personality tests, it presents the opportunity for abuse. For instance, employers who use it as a screening tool for job applicants may interpret the results improperly, relying too heavily on the results of individual scales instead of taking into account the overall patterns of results, which require skilled interpreta-

Test standardization: A technique used to validate questions in personality tests by studying the responses of people with known psychological disorders

FIGURE 11-4 A sample profile on the MMPI-2 of a person who suffers from obsessional anxiety, social withdrawal, and delusional thinking. *[Based on data from Halgin & Whitbourne, 1994, p. 72; and Minnesota Multiphasic Personality Inventory-2. Copyright © by the Regents of the University of Minnesota, 1942, 1943 (renewed 1970, 1989).]*

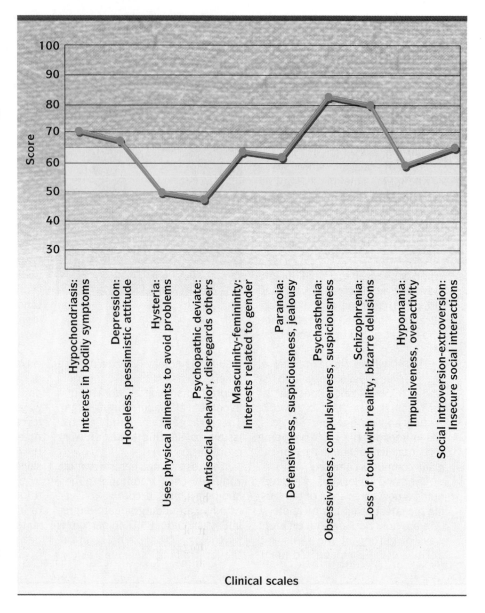

Projective personality test: A test in which a person is shown an ambiguous stimulus and asked to describe it or tell a story about it

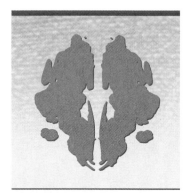

FIGURE 11-5 This inkblot is similar to the type used in the Rorschach personality test. What do you see in it?

tion. Furthermore, critics point out that the individual scales overlap, making their interpretation difficult. In sum, although the MMPI remains the most widely used personality test and has been translated into more than 100 different languages, it must be used with caution (Graham, 1990; Helmes & Reddon, 1993; Greene & Clopton, 1994).

Projective Methods

If you were shown the shape presented in Figure 11-5 and asked what it represented to you, you might not think that your impressions would mean very much. But to a psychoanalytic theoretician, your responses to such an ambiguous figure would provide valuable clues to the state of your unconscious, and ultimately to your general personality characteristics.

The shape in the figure is representative of inkblots used in **projective personality tests,** in which a person is shown an ambiguous stimulus and asked to describe it or tell a story about it. The responses are then considered to be "projections" of what the person is like.

The best-known projective test is the **Rorschach test.** Devised by Swiss psychiatrist Hermann Rorschach (1924), the test consists of showing a series of symmetrical stimuli, similar to the one in Figure 11-5, to people who are then asked what the figures represent to them. Their responses are recorded, and through a complex set of clinical judgments on the part of the examiner, people are classified into different personality types. For instance, respondents who see a bear in one inkblot are thought to have a strong degree of emotional control, according to the rules developed by Rorschach (Exner, 1993; Weiner, 1994; Aronow, Reznikoff, & Moreland, 1994).

The **Thematic Apperception Test (TAT)** is another well-known projective test. As noted when we discussed achievement motivation in Chapter 9, the TAT consists of a series of pictures about which a person is asked to write a story. The stories are then used to draw inferences about the writer's personality characteristics (Bellak, 1993).

Tests with stimuli as ambiguous as the Rorschach and TAT require particular skill and care in their interpretation. They are often criticized for requiring too much inference on the part of the examiner. However, they are widely used, particularly in clinical settings, and their proponents suggest that their reliability and validity are high.

Rorschach (ROAR shock) **test:** A test consisting of inkblots of indefinite shapes, the interpretation of which is used to assess personality characteristics

Thematic Apperception Test (TAT): A test consisting of a series of ambiguous pictures about which a person is asked to write a story, which is then taken to be a reflection of the writer's personality

Behavioral Assessment

If you were a psychologist subscribing to a learning approach to personality, you would be likely to object to the indirect nature of projective tests. Instead, you would be more apt to use **behavioral assessment**—direct measures of an individual's behavior used to describe characteristics indicative of personality. As with observational research (discussed in Chapter 1), behavioral assessment may be carried out naturalistically by observing people in their own settings: in the workplace, at home, or in school, for instance. In other cases, behavioral assessment occurs in the laboratory, under controlled conditions in which a psychologist sets up a situation and observes an individual's behavior.

Behavioral assessment: Direct measures of an individual's behavior used to describe characteristics indicative of personality

Regardless of the setting in which behavior is observed, an effort is made to ensure that behavioral assessment is carried out objectively, quantifying behavior as much as possible. For example, an observer might record the number of social contacts a person initiates, the number of questions asked, or the number of aggressive acts. Another method is to measure duration of events: the length of a temper tantrum in a child, the length of a conversation, the amount of time spent working, or the time spent in cooperative behavior.

Behavioral assessment is particularly appropriate for observing—and eventually remedying—specific behavioral difficulties, such as increasing socialization in shy children. It provides a means of assessing the specific nature and incidence of a problem and subsequently allows psychologists to determine whether intervention techniques have been successful.

Behavioral assessment techniques based on learning theories of personality have also made important contributions to the treatment of certain kinds of psychological difficulties. Indeed, the knowledge of normal personality provided by the theories we have discussed throughout this chapter has led to significant advances in our understanding and treatment of both physical and psychological disorders.

The Informed Consumer of Psychology

Assessing Personality Assessments

Wanted: People with "kinetic energy," "emotional maturity," and the ability to "deal with large numbers of people in a fairly chaotic situation."

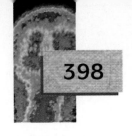

Although this job description may seem most appropriate for the job of co-host of *Wheel of Fortune,* in actuality it is part of an advertisement for managers for American MultiCinema's theaters (Dentzer, 1986). To find people with such qualities, AMC has developed a battery of personality measures for job applicants to complete. In developing its own tests, AMC joined scores of companies, ranging from General Motors to J. C. Penney, which employ personality tests to help determine who gets hired.

Individuals, too, have come to depend on personality testing. Many organizations will—for a hefty fee—administer a battery of personality tests that purport to steer people toward careers for which their personalities are particularly suited. Before relying too heavily on the results of such personality testing, in the role of either potential employee, employer, or consumer of testing services, several points should be kept in mind:

■ Understand what the test purports to measure. Standard personality measures are accompanied by information that discusses how the test was developed, to whom it is most applicable, and how the results should be interpreted. If possible, you should read the accompanying literature; it will help you understand the meaning of any results.

■ No decision should be based solely on the results of any one test. Test results should be interpreted in the context of other information—academic records, social interests, and home and community activities. Without these data, individual scores are relatively uninformative at best and may even be harmful.

■ Tests are not infallible. The results may be in error; the test may be unreliable or invalid. You may, for example, have had a "bad day" when you took the test, or the person scoring and interpreting the test may have made a mistake. You should not place undue stock in the results of the single administration of any test.

In sum, it is important to keep in mind the complexity of human behavior—particularly your own. No one test can provide an understanding of the intricacies of someone's personality without considering a good deal more information than can be provided in a single testing session.

RECAP AND REVIEW

Recap
- Psychological tests are standard measures used to assess behavior objectively. They must be reliable, measuring with consistency what they are trying to measure, and valid, measuring what is supposed to be measured.
- Self-report measures of personality ask people about a sample range of their behaviors. The results are then used to infer personality characteristics.
- Projective personality tests present ambiguous stimuli which the person is asked to describe or tell a story about. Responses are used as an indication of information about the individual's personality.
- Behavioral assessment employs direct measures of an individual's behavior to describe characteristics indicative of personality.

Review
1. _____ is the consistency of a personality test, while _____ is the ability of a test to actually measure what it is designed to measure.

2. _____ are standards used to compare scores of different people taking the same test.
3. Tests such as the MMPI-2, in which a small sample of behavior is assessed to determine larger trends, are examples of:
   a. Cross-sectional tests
   b. Projective tests
   c. Achievement tests
   d. Self-report tests
4. A person shown a picture and asked to make up a story about it would be taking a _____ personality test.

Ask Yourself
Should personality tests be used for personnel decisions? If you were asked to take such a test, what questions concerning test construction and validation would be important to you? If you were designing such a test, how would these concerns affect you?

(Answers to review questions are on page 400.)

How do psychologists define and use the concept of personality?

1. The behaviors that make people different from one another are those behaviors that psychologists consider to be at the root of personality. Personality refers to the relatively enduring characteristics that differentiate one person from another and that lead people to act in a consistent and predictable manner, both in different situations and over extended periods of time.

What is the structure and development of personality according to Freud and his successors?

2. According to psychoanalysts, much of behavior is caused by parts of personality which are found in the unconscious and of which we are unaware. Freud's theory suggests that personality is composed of the id, the ego, and the superego. The id is the unorganized, inborn part of personality whose purpose is to immediately reduce tensions relating to hunger, sex, aggression, and other primitive impulses. The ego restrains instinctual energy in order to maintain the safety of the individual and to help the person to be a member of society. The superego represents the rights and wrongs of society and consists of the conscience and the ego-ideal.

3. Freud's psychoanalytic theory suggests that personality develops through a series of stages, each of which is associated with a major biological function. The oral stage is the first period, occurring during the first year of life. Next comes the anal stage, lasting from approximately age 1 to age 3. The phallic stage follows, with interest focusing on the genitals. At age 5 or 6, near the end of the phallic stage, children experience the Oedipal conflict, a process through which they learn to identify with the same-sex parent by acting as much like that parent as possible. Then follows a latency period lasting until puberty, after which people move into the genital stage, a period of mature sexuality.

4. Defense mechanisms, used for dealing with anxiety relating to impulses from the id, provide people with unconscious strategies to reduce anxiety. The most common defense mechanisms are repression, regression, displacement, rationalization, denial, projection, and sublimation.

5. Freud's psychoanalytic theory has provoked a number of criticisms. These include a lack of supportive scientific data, the theory's inadequacy in making predictions, and its limitations owing to the restricted population on which it is based. Still, the theory remains a pivotal one. For instance, the neo-Freudian psychoanalytic theorists built on Freud's work, although they placed greater emphasis on the role of the ego and paid greater attention to social factors in determining behavior.

What are the major aspects of trait, learning, biological, and humanistic approaches to personality?

6. Trait approaches have tried to identify the most basic and relatively enduring dimensions along which people differ from one another—dimensions known as traits. For example, Allport suggested that there are three kinds of traits—cardinal, central, and secondary. Later theorists employed a statistical technique called factor analysis to identify the most crucial traits. Using this method, Cattell identified sixteen basic traits, while Eysenck found two major dimensions: introversion-extroversion and neuroticism-stability.

7. Learning approaches to personality concentrate on observable behavior. To the strict learning theorist, personality is the sum of learned responses to the external environment. In contrast, social cognitive approaches concentrate on the role of cognitions in determining personality. Social cognitive approaches pay particular attention to self-efficacy and reciprocal determinism in determining behavior.

8. Biological approaches to personality focus on how personality characteristics are inherited. For example, study of children's temperament suggests that a distinction exists between inhibited and uninhibited children which is reflected both in differences in biological reactivity and in shyness.

9. Humanistic approaches to personality emphasize the basic goodness of people. They consider the core of personality in terms of a person's ability to change and improve. Rogers' concept of the need for positive regard suggests that a universal requirement to be loved and respected underlies personality.

10. The major personality approaches differ along a number of important dimensions, including the role of the unconscious versus the conscious, nature versus nurture, freedom versus determinism, and stability versus modifiability of personality characteristics.

How can we most accurately assess personality?

11. Psychological tests are standard assessment tools that objectively measure behavior. They must be reliable, measuring what they are trying to measure consistently, and valid, measuring what they are supposed to measure.

What are the major types of personality measures?

12. Self-report measures ask people about a sample range of their behaviors. These reports are used to infer the presence of particular personality characteristics. The most commonly used self-report measure is the Minnesota Multiphasic Personality Inventory-2 (MMPI-2), designed to differentiate people with specific sorts of psychological difficulties from normal individuals.

13. Projective personality tests present an ambiguous stimulus; the observer's responses are then used to infer information about the observer. The two most frequently used projective tests are the Rorschach, in which reactions to inkblots are employed to classify personality types, and the Thematic Apperception Test (TAT), in which stories about ambiguous pictures are used to draw inferences about the storyteller's personality.

14. Behavioral assessment is based on the principles of learning theory. It employs direct measurement of an individual's behavior to determine characteristics related to personality.

KEY TERMS AND CONCEPTS

personality (p. 373)
psychoanalytic theory (p. 373)
unconscious (p. 373)
id (p. 374)
libido (p. 374)
ego (p. 374)
superego (p. 375)
oral stage (p. 375)
fixation (p. 375)
anal stage (p. 376)
phallic stage (p. 376)
Oedipal conflict (p. 376)
latency period (p. 376)
genital stage (p. 376)

defense mechanisms (p. 377)
neo-Freudian psychoanalysts (p. 379)
collective unconscious (p. 379)
inferiority complex (p. 380)
trait theory (p. 381)
traits (p. 381)
cardinal trait (p. 382)
central traits (p. 382)
secondary traits (p. 382)
social cognitive approaches (p. 385)
temperament (p. 386)
humanistic approaches to personality
    (p. 389)

self-actualization (p. 390)
psychological tests (p. 392)
self-report measures (p. 394)
Minnesota Multiphasic Personality
    Inventory-2 (MMPI-2) (p. 394)
test standardization (p. 395)
projective personality test (p. 396)
Rorschach test (p. 397)
Thematic Apperception Test (TAT)
    (p. 397)
behavioral assessment (p. 397)

CHAPTER 12
PSYCHOLOGICAL DISORDERS

Lori Schiller

Lori Schiller thinks it all began one night at summer camp when she was 15.

Suddenly, she was hearing voices, "You must die! Die! Die!" they screamed. The voices drove her from her bunk, out into the dark, where she thought she could escape. Camp officials found her jumping frantically on a trampoline, screaming. "I thought I was possessed," says Ms. Schiller, now 33. Terrified, she told no one about the voices when she first heard them. The camp sent her home sick. Says Nancy Schiller, her mother: "We thought she had the flu."

After Lori came home "sick" from summer camp, it was easy enough for everyone to shrug off the subtle changes in her personality. When she refused to make phone calls, her family wrote it off to adolescence. When she would lie on the sofa facing the wall as the rest of the family watched television, they figured she just wasn't interested in the show that was on. They didn't see it as a serious sign of withdrawal. . . .

In reality, she now says, she was frightened. Voices had begun sliding down the telephone wire; they were assaulting her from the TV screen. "The people on TV were telling me it was my responsibility to save the world, and if I didn't I would be killed," she says. . . .

Keeping her secret wasn't difficult at first. She could dodge the still-infrequent voices by taking a walk, or by retreating into sleep. But the voices were very real. "I was sure everyone else could hear them, and I was embarrassed because they were saying such bad things about me," she recalls.

Her behavior became erratic, wilder. On a whim one day, she hopped into her car, drove four hours home to Scarsdale, changed her mind and drove back. She went sky diving. She got stopped by police for speeding. She had fits of hysterical laughter. . . .

As time went on, Lori had more and more trouble concentrating, and more difficulty in controlling her impulses, one of which was to commit suicide. "I used to sit in the library, up all these stairs, and think about jumping," she recalls. Finally, in her senior year, she told her parents she "had problems" and asked to see a counselor. (Bennett, 1992, pp. A1, A10)

Although she had somehow managed to hide her disorder from everyone, Lori Schiller was losing her hold on reality. Less than a year after graduating from college, her parents convinced her to go to a private mental hospital. She would spend the next decade in and out of institutions, suffering from schizophrenia, one of the most severe psychological disorders.

Schiller's case raises several questions. What caused her disorder? Were genetic factors involved, or were environmental stressors primarily responsible for her disorder? Were there signs that others should have noticed earlier? Could her schizophrenia have been prevented from occurring? What were the specific symptoms of her abnormal behavior? And, more generally, how do we distinguish normal from abnormal behavior, and how can Lori's behavior be categorized and classified, pinpointing the specific nature of her problem?

We address the issues raised by Lori Schiller's case in this and the following chapter. We begin by discussing the distinction between normal and abnormal behavior, considering the subtle distinctions that must be made. We examine the various approaches that have been used to explain psychological disorders, ranging from explanations based on superstition to those based on contemporary, scientific approaches.

The heart of the chapter consists of a description of the various types of psychological disorders. Using a classification system employed by mental-health practitioners, we examine the most significant kinds of disorders. The chapter also includes a discussion of how to evaluate one's own behavior to determine whether it's advisable to seek help from a mental-health professional.

- *How can we distinguish normal from abnormal behavior?*
- *What are the major models of abnormal behavior used by mental-health professionals?*
- *What classification system is used to categorize abnormal behavior?*

NORMAL VERSUS ABNORMAL: MAKING THE DISTINCTION

Universally that person's acumen is esteemed very little perceptive concerning whatsoever matters are being held as most profitable by mortals with sapience endowed to be studied who is ignorant of that which the most in doctrine erudite and certainly by reason of that in them high mind's ornament deserving of veneration constantly maintain when by general consent they affirm that other circumstances being equal by no exterior splendour is the prosperity of a nation more efficaciously asserted than by the measure of how far forward may have progressed the tribute of its solicitude for that proliferent continuance which of evils the original if it be absent when fortunately present constitutes the certain sign of omnipollent nature's incorrupted benefaction.

It would be easy to conclude that these words were the musings of a madman. The passage does not seem to make any sense at all. But literary scholars would disagree. In actuality this passage is from James Joyce's classic *Ulysses,* which has been hailed as one of the major works of twentieth-century literature (Joyce, 1934, p. 377).

As this example illustrates, a cursory examination of a person's writing is insufficient to determine the degree to which he or she is "normal." But even when we consider more extensive samples of a person's behavior, we find that there may only be a fine line between behavior that is considered normal and that which is considered abnormal.

Defining Abnormality

The difficulty in distinguishing normal from abnormal behavior has inspired a diversity of approaches for devising a precise, scientific definition of "abnormal behavior." Over the years, such approaches have varied considerably. For instance, consider the following definitions:

■ *Deviation from the average.* This approach, perhaps the most obvious one, views abnormality as deviation from the average—a statistical definition. To determine abnormality, we simply observe what behaviors are rare or infrequent in a given society or culture and label these deviations from the norm as abnormal.

Although such a definition may be appropriate in some instances, its drawback is that some behaviors that are statistically rare clearly do not lend themselves to classification as abnormal. If most people prefer to have corn flakes for breakfast, but you prefer raisin bran, this hardly makes your behavior abnormal. Similarly, such a conception of abnormality would unreasonably label a person who has an unusually high IQ as abnormal, simply because it is statistically rare. A definition of abnormality that rests on deviation from the average, then, is insufficient by itself.

Was Yigal Amir, the assassin of Israeli Premier Yitzhak Rabin, abnormal according to the different psychological definitions?

■ *Deviation from the ideal.* An alternative approach to defining abnormality is one that measures behavior against the standard toward which most people are striving—the ideal. Under this sort of definition, behavior is considered abnormal if it deviates enough from some kind of ideal or cultural standards. Unfortunately, the definition suffers from even more difficulties than the deviation-from-the-average definition, since society has so few standards about which people agree. Moreover, the standards that do arise tend to change over time, making the deviation-from-the-ideal approach inadequate.

■ *Abnormality as a sense of subjective discomfort.* Given the drawbacks of both the deviation-from-the-average and deviation-from-the-ideal definitions of normality, we must turn to more subjective approaches. One of the most useful definitions of abnormal behavior concentrates on the psychological consequences of the behavior for the individual. In this approach, behavior is considered abnormal if it produces a sense of distress, anxiety, or guilt in an individual—or if it is harmful to others in some way.

Even a definition that relies on subjective discomfort has its drawbacks, for in some particularly severe forms of mental disturbance, people report feeling euphoric and on top of the world, even though their behavior seems bizarre to others. In this case, then, there is a subjective state of well-being, yet the behavior is within the realm of what most people would consider abnormal. This discrepancy suggests that a definition of abnormality that does not consider people's ability to function effectively is inadequate.

■ *Abnormality as the inability to function effectively.* Most people are able to feed themselves, hold a job, get along with others, and in general live as productive members of society. Yet there are those who are unable to adjust to the demands of society or function effectively.

According to this view of abnormality, people who are unable to function effectively and adapt to the demands of society are considered abnormal. For example, an unemployed, homeless woman living on the street might be considered unable to function effectively. Therefore her behavior would be viewed as abnormal, even had she made the choice to live in this particular fashion. Her inability to adapt to the requirements of society is what makes her "abnormal," according to this approach.

■ *Legal definitions of abnormality.* According to the jury that heard his case, Jeffery Dahmer, the mass murderer of scores of victims, who later was murdered himself, was perfectly sane when he killed his victims. Although you might question this view, it is a reflection of the way in which the law defines abnormal behavior. According to the law, the distinction between normal and abnormal behavior rests on the definition of "insanity," which is a legal, but not a psychological, term. The definition varies from one jurisdiction to another. In some states, insanity requires simply that the defendant cannot understand the difference between right and wrong at the time he or she commits a criminal act. In others, a person can be held "guilty, but mentally ill," of certain crimes, rather than the more stringent "not guilty by reason of insanity." Still other states consider whether defendants are substantially confused or unable to control themselves. And in three states—Idaho, Montana, and Utah—pleas of insanity are not allowed at all. Clearly, there is no commonly accepted legal definition of insanity, creating a confusing judicial situation (Simon & Aaronson, 1988).

Gradations of Abnormal and Normal Behavior: Drawing the Line on Abnormality Clearly, none of the previous definitions is broad enough to cover all instances of abnormal behavior. Consequently, the distinction between normal and abnormal behavior often remains somewhat ambiguous, even to trained professionals. Furthermore, the label "abnormal behavior" is influenced to a large extent by cultural expectations of what is considered to be normal behavior in a society.

Probably the best way to deal with this imprecision is to view abnormal and normal behavior as marking two ends of a continuum rather than as absolute states. As such, behavior should be evaluated in terms of gradations, ranging from completely normal functioning to extreme abnormal behavior. Obviously, behavior typically falls somewhere between these two extremes.

Models of Abnormality: From Superstition to Science

For much of the past, abnormal behavior was linked to superstition and witchcraft. People displaying abnormal behavior were accused of being possessed by the devil or some sort of demonic god (Howells & Osborn, 1984). Authorities felt justified in "treating" abnormal behavior by attempting to drive out the source of the problem. This typically involved whipping, immersion in hot water, starvation, or other forms of torture in which the cure was often worse than the affliction.

Contemporary approaches take a more enlightened view, and six major perspectives on abnormal behavior predominate: the medical model, the psychoanalytic model, the behavioral model, the cognitive model, the humanistic model, and the sociocultural model. These models suggest not only different causes of abnormal behavior but—as we shall see in the next chapter—different treatment approaches as well. (Table 12-1 summarizes the models and the way in which they can be applied to the case of Lori Schiller described in the Prologue.)

The Medical Model When a person displays the symptoms of tuberculosis, we generally find the tuberculin germ in his or her body tissue. In the same way, the **medical model of abnormality** suggests that, when an individual displays symptoms of abnormal behavior, the root cause will be found in a physical examina-

Medical model of abnormality: The model suggesting that when an individual displays symptoms of abnormal behavior, the cause is physiological

---

TABLE 12-1 The Models of Psychological Disorder: Applications to Lori Schiller's Case

In considering the case of Lori Schiller, discussed at the start of the chapter, we can employ each of the different models of abnormal behavior. Note, however, that given the nature of her psychological disorder, some of the models are considerably more applicable than others.

Model	Description	Possible application of model to Schiller's case
Medical model	Suggests that physiological causes are at the root of abnormal behavior	Examine Schiller for medical problems, such as a brain tumor, chemical imbalance in the brain, or disease
Psychoanalytic model	Abnormal behavior stems from childhood conflicts	Seek out information about Schiller's past, considering possible childhood conflicts
Behavioral model	Abnormal behavior is a learned response	Concentrate on rewards and punishments for Schiller's behavior, and identify environmental stimuli that reinforce her behavior
Cognitive model	Assumes cognitions (people's thoughts and beliefs) are central to abnormal behavior	Focus on Schiller's perceptions of herself and her environment
Humanistic model	Emphasizes people's control and responsibility for their own behavior	Consider Schiller's behavior in terms of the choices she has freely made
Sociocultural model	Assumes behavior is shaped by family, society, and culture	Focus on how societal demands contributed to Schiller's disorder

tion of the individual, be it a hormonal imbalance, a chemical deficiency, or a brain injury. Indeed, when we speak of mental "illness," the "symptoms" of abnormal behavior, and mental "hospitals," we are using terminology associated with the medical model.

Because many sorts of abnormal behaviors have been linked to biological causes, the medical model is a reasonable approach. Yet serious criticisms have been leveled against it. For one thing, there are many forms of abnormal behavior for which no biological cause has been identified. In addition, some critics have argued that the use of the term "illness" implies that people displaying abnormal behavior hold no responsibility for their actions (Szasz, 1982, 1994).

Still, recent advances in our understanding of the biological bases of behavior have supported the importance of considering physiological factors in abnormal behavior. For instance, we'll see later in the chapter that some of the most severe forms of psychological disturbance are the result of genetic factors, or malfunctions in the transmission of neurotransmitters (Resnick, 1992; Brunner et al., 1993).

The Psychoanalytic Model   Whereas the medical model suggests that biological causes are at the root of abnormal behavior, the **psychoanalytic model of abnormality** holds that abnormal behavior stems from childhood conflicts over opposing wishes regarding sex and aggression. As we discussed in Chapter 11, Freud believed that children pass through a series of stages in which sexual and aggressive impulses take different forms and stimulate conflicts that require resolution. If these childhood conflicts are not dealt with successfully, they remain unresolved in the unconscious and eventually bring about abnormal behavior during adulthood.

To understand the roots of a person's disordered behavior, the psychoanalytic model scrutinizes his or her early life history. However, because there is no conclusive way of linking people's childhood experiences with the abnormal behaviors they display as adults, we can never be sure that the mechanisms suggested by psychoanalytic theory are accurate. Moreover, psychoanalytic theory paints a picture of people as having little control over their behavior since it is guided by unconscious impulses.

On the other hand, the contributions of psychoanalytic theory have been significant. More than any other approach to abnormal behavior, this model highlights the fact that people can have a rich, involved inner life and that prior experiences can have a profound effect on current psychological functioning.

The Behavioral Model   Both the medical and the psychoanalytic models look at abnormal behaviors as *symptoms* of some underlying problem. In contrast, the **behavioral model of abnormality** looks at the behavior itself as the problem. Using the principles of learning discussed in Chapter 5, behavioral theorists see both normal and abnormal behaviors as responses to a set of stimuli, responses that have been learned through past experience and that are guided in the present by the stimuli one finds in one's environment. To explain why abnormal behavior occurs, one must analyze how an abnormal behavior has been learned and observe the circumstances in which it is displayed.

The emphasis on observable behavior represents both the greatest strength and the greatest weakness of the behavioral approach to abnormal behavior. Because of its emphasis on the present, this approach is the most precise and objective one in examining manifestations of abnormal behavior. Rather than hypothesizing elaborate underlying, unobservable mechanisms to explain abnormal behavior, behavioral theorists concentrate on immediate behavior. At the same time, though, critics charge that this focus ignores the rich inner world of thoughts, attitudes, and emotions that may contribute to abnormal behavior.

Psychoanalytic model of abnormality: The model suggesting that abnormality stems from childhood conflicts over opposing desires regarding sex and aggression

Behavioral model of abnormality: The model suggesting that the behavior itself is the problem to be treated, rather than viewing behavior as a symptom of some underlying medical or psychological problem

The Cognitive Model   The medical, psychoanalytic, and behavioral models view people's behavior as being caused by factors largely outside of their own control. To many critics, however, people's thoughts cannot be ignored.

In response to such concerns, some psychologists employ a **cognitive model of abnormality.** Rather than considering only external behavior, as in traditional behavioral approaches, the cognitive approach assumes that *cognitions* (people's thoughts and beliefs) are central to a person's abnormal behavior. A primary goal of treatment using the cognitive model is to explicitly teach new, more adaptive ways of thinking.

For instance, a student who has the erroneous cognition "This exam is crucial to my future" whenever taking an exam might be led, through therapy, to hold the more realistic thought: "My entire future is not dependent on this one exam." By changing cognitions in this way, psychologists working within a cognitive framework seek to allow people to free themselves from maladaptive thoughts and behaviors.

Cognitive model of abnormality: The model suggesting that people's thoughts and beliefs are central to abnormal behavior

The Humanistic Model   Psychologists who subscribe to the **humanistic model of abnormality** emphasize the control and responsibility that people have for their own behavior, even when such behavior is abnormal. The humanistic model of abnormality concentrates on what is uniquely human, viewing people as basically rational, oriented toward a social world, and motivated to get along with others (Rogers, 1980).

Humanistic approaches focus on the relationship of the individual to society, considering the ways in which people view themselves in relation to others and see their place in the world. People are viewed as having an awareness of life and of themselves that leads them to search for meaning and self-worth. Rather than assuming that a "cure" is required, the humanistic model suggests that individuals can, by and large, set their own limits of what is acceptable behavior. As long as they are not hurting others and do not feel personal distress, people should be free to choose the behaviors they engage in.

Although the humanistic model has been criticized for its reliance on unscientific, unverifiable information and its vague, almost philosophical, formulations, it offers a distinctive view of abnormal behavior. The model stresses the unique aspects of being human and provides a number of important suggestions for helping those with psychological problems.

Humanistic model of abnormality: The model suggesting that people are basically rational, and that they should set their own limits on acceptable behavior

The Sociocultural Model   The **sociocultural model of abnormality** makes the assumption that people's behavior—both normal and abnormal—is shaped by the kind of family group, society, and culture in which they live. According to this view, the kinds of relationships that evolve with others may support abnormal behaviors and even cause them to occur. Consequently, the kinds of stresses and conflicts people experience as part of their daily interactions with others in their environment can promote and maintain abnormal behavior.

Support for the position that sociocultural factors shape abnormal behavior comes from statistics that show that some kinds of abnormal behavior are far more prevalent among certain social classes than others. For instance, diagnoses of schizophrenia tend to be higher among members of lower socioeconomic classes than among members of more affluent groups. Proportionally more African-American individuals are involuntarily hospitalized for psychological disorders than are whites (Hollingshead & Redich, 1958; Keith, Regier, & Rae, 1991).

Furthermore, poor economic times tend to be linked to general declines in psychological functioning (Pines, 1981). In addition, social phenomena such as homelessness have been associated with psychological disorders (as discussed in the accompanying Pathways through Psychology box, next page).

Sociocultural model of abnormality: The model suggesting that people's behavior, both normal and abnormal, is shaped by family, society, and cultural influences

As with the other theories, the sociocultural model does not have unequivocal support. Alternative explanations abound for the association between abnormal behavior and social factors. For example, people from lower classes may be less likely than those from higher classes to seek help until their symptoms become relatively severe and warrant a more serious diagnosis (Gove, 1982). Furthermore, sociocultural explanations provide relatively little in the way of direct guidance for the treatment of individuals showing mental disturbance, since the focus is on broader societal factors.

Classifying Abnormal Behavior: The ABC's of *DSM*

Crazy. Nutty as a fruitcake. Loony. Insane. Neurotic. Psycho. Strange. Demented. Odd. Possessed. Wacko.

Society has long placed labels on people displaying abnormal behavior. Unfortunately, most of the time these labels have reflected intolerance, and they have been used with little thought as to what the label signifies.

Providing appropriate and specific names and classifications for abnormal behavior has presented a major challenge to psychologists. It is not too hard to understand why, given the difficulties discussed earlier in simply distinguishing normal from abnormal behavior. Yet classification systems are necessary in order to be able to describe and ultimately to diagnose abnormal behavior.

***DSM-IV:* Determining Diagnostic Distinctions**   Over the years many different classification systems have been used, varying in terms of how useful they are and how universally they have been accepted by mental-health workers. Today, however, one standard system, devised by the American Psychiatric Association, has emerged and is employed by most professionals to diagnose and classify abnor-

mal behavior (APA, 1994). The classification system is known as the ***Diagnostic and Statistical Manual of Mental Disorders*** **(4th ed.) *(DSM-IV)*.**

Published in 1994, *DSM-IV* presents comprehensive and relatively precise definitions for more than 200 separate diagnostic categories. By following the criteria presented in the system, diagnosticians can provide a clear description of the specific problem an individual is experiencing. (Table 12-2 provides a brief outline of the major diagnostic categories.)

DSM-IV evaluates behavior according to five separate dimensions, or *axes*. The first three axes assess the primary disorder, the nature of any long-standing personality problems in adults or any specific developmental problems in children and adolescents that may be relevant to treatment, and any physical disorders or illnesses that may also be present. The fourth and fifth axes take broader considerations into account. They focus on the severity of stressors present and on the person's general level of functioning over the past year in social relationships, work, and the use of leisure time.

One noteworthy feature of *DSM-IV* is that it is designed to be primarily descriptive and devoid of suggestions about the underlying causes of an individual's behavior and problems (Millon, 1991). Hence, the term "neurotic"—a label that is commonly used by people in their everyday descriptions of abnormal behavior—is not listed as a *DSM-IV* category. The reason is that "neurotic" derives directly from Freud's theory of personality (see Chapter 11). Because the term refers to problems associated with a specific cause and theoretical approach, neurosis is no longer listed as a category.

DSM-IV has the advantage, then, of providing a descriptive system that does not specify the cause or reason behind the problem. Instead, it paints a picture of the behavior that is being manifested. Why should this be important? For one

Diagnostic and Statistical Manual of Mental Disorders **(4th ed.) *(DSM-IV)*:** A manual that presents comprehensive definitions of more than 200 separate diagnostic categories for identifying problems and behaviors

---

TABLE 12-2 Major *DSM-IV* Diagnostic Categories

The following list of disorders represents the major categories from *DSM-IV,* presented in the order in which they are discussed in the text. This is only a partial list of the over 200 disorders found in *DSM-IV.*

Anxiety disorders (problems in which anxiety impedes daily functioning)
   Subcategories: generalized anxiety disorder, panic disorder, phobic disorder, obsessive-compulsive disorder, posttraumatic stress disorder

Somatoform disorders (psychological difficulties displayed through physical problems)
   Subcategories: hypochondriasis, conversion disorder

Dissociative disorders (the splitting apart of crucial parts of personality that are usually integrated)
   Subcategories: dissociative identity disorder (multiple personality), dissociative amnesia, dissociative fugue

Mood disorders (emotions of depression or euphoria that are so strong they intrude on everyday living)
   Subcategories: major depression, bipolar disorder

Schizophrenia (declines in functioning, thought and language disturbances, perception disorders, emotional disturbances, and withdrawal from others)
   Subcategories: disorganized, paranoid, catatonic, undifferentiated, residual

Personality disorders (problems that create little personal distress but that lead to an inability to function as a normal member of society)
   Subcategories: antisocial (sociopathic) personality disorder, narcissistic personality disorder

Sexual disorders (problems related to sexual arousal from unusual objects or problems related to sexual functioning)
   Subcategories: paraphilias, sexual dysfunction

Substance-related disorders (problems related to drug dependence and abuse)
   Subcategories: alcohol, cocaine, hallucinogens, marijuana

Delirium, dementia, amnesia, and other cognitive disorders

thing, it allows communication between mental-health professionals of diverse backgrounds and approaches. In addition, precise classification enables researchers to go forward and to explore the causes of a problem. If the manifestations of an abnormal behavior cannot be reliably described, researchers will be hard-pressed to find ways of investigating the disorder. Finally, *DSM-IV* provides a kind of conceptual shorthand through which professionals can describe the behaviors that tend to occur together in an individual (Widiger et al., 1990).

Classification Concerns   Like any classification system, *DSM-IV* has its drawbacks. For instance, critics charge that it relies too much on the medical model of psychological disorder. Because it was drawn up by psychiatrists—who are physicians—some condemn it for viewing abnormal behaviors primarily in terms of symptoms of some underlying physiological disorder. Moreover, other critics suggest that *DSM-IV* pigeonholes people into inflexible categories, and that it would be more reasonable to use systems that classify people in terms of gradations.

Other concerns with *DSM-IV* are more subtle, but equally important to consider. For instance, some critics argue that labeling an individual as abnormal provides a lifetime stigma that is dehumanizing. Furthermore, after an initial diagnosis is made, other diagnostic possibilities may be overlooked by mental-health professionals, who concentrate on the initial diagnostic category (Szasz, 1961, 1994; Kirk, 1992).

The notion that diagnostic categories provide rigid labels was illustrated in a now-classic experiment conducted in the early 1970s (Rosenhan, 1973). In the study, Rosenhan and seven of his colleagues presented themselves at the doors of separate mental hospitals across the United States and sought admission. The reason, they each stated, was that they were hearing voices—"unclear voices" that said "empty," "hollow," and "thud." Aside from changing their names and occupations, *everything* else they did and said was representative of their true behavior, including the responses they gave during extensive admission interviews and answers to the battery of tests they were asked to complete. In fact, as soon as they were admitted, they said they no longer heard any voices. In sum, each of the pseudopatients acted in a "normal" way.

One would assume that Rosenhan and his colleagues would have been quickly discovered as the impostors they were, but this was not the case. Instead, each of them was diagnosed as severely abnormal on the basis of observed behavior. Most were labeled as schizophrenic, and they were kept in the hospital from 3 to 52 days, with the average stay being 19 days. In most cases, they were not allowed to leave without the assistance of people outside the hospital. Even when they were discharged, most of the patients left with the label "schizophrenia—in remission," implying that the abnormal behavior had only temporarily subsided and could recur at any time. Most disturbing of all, none of the pseudopatients were identified by the staff of the hospitals as impostors. In sum, placing labels on people powerfully influences how their actions are perceived and interpreted.

Still, despite the drawbacks inherent in any labeling system, *DSM-IV* has had an important influence on the way in which mental-health professionals consider psychological disorders. It has increased both the reliability and validity of diagnostic categorization. In addition, it provides us with a logical way to organize our examination of the major types of mental disturbance, to which we turn next.

RECAP AND REVIEW

Recap

- Definitions of abnormality include those based on deviation from the average, deviation from the ideal, the psy-

chological consequences of the behavior for the individual, the individual's ability to function effectively and adapt as a member of society, and legal definitions.

- Abnormal and normal behavior may best be viewed in terms of gradations, ranging from completely normal functioning to extreme abnormal behavior.
- Current theories view abnormality in terms of six major models: the medical, psychoanalytic, behavioral, cognitive, humanistic, and sociocultural models.
- The *Diagnostic and Statistical Manual of Mental Disorders* (4th ed.) *(DSM-IV)* provides a description of over 200 separate diagnostic categories of psychological disorders.

Review

1. A problem in defining abnormal behavior is:
   a. Statistically rare behavior may not be abnormal.
   b. Not all abnormalities are accompanied by feelings of discomfort.
   c. Cultural standards are too general to use as a measuring tool.
   d. All of the above.
2. According to the definition of abnormality as experiencing subjective discomfort or causing harm to others, which of the following people is most likely to need treatment?
   a. An executive is afraid to accept a promotion because it would require moving from his ground-floor office to the top floor of a tall office building.
   b. A woman quits her job and chooses to live on the street.
   c. A man believes that friendly spacemen visit his house every Thursday.
   d. A photographer lives with nineteen cats in a small apartment.
3. Virginia's mother thinks that Virginia's behavior is clearly abnormal because, despite being offered admission to medical school, she decides to become a waitress. What approach is Virginia's mother using to define abnormal behavior?
4. Which of the following is a strong argument against the medical model?

a. Physiological abnormalities are almost always impossible to identify.
b. There is no conclusive way to link past experience and behavior.
c. The medical model rests too heavily on the effects of nutrition.
d. Assigning behavior to a physical problem takes responsibility away from the individual for changing his or her behavior.

5. Cheryl is painfully shy. According to the behavioral model, the best way to deal with her "abnormal" behavior is to:
   a. Treat the underlying physical problem.
   b. Use the principles of learning theory to modify her shy behavior.
   c. Express a great deal of caring.
   d. Uncover her negative past experiences through hypnosis.
6. Imagine that an acquaintance of yours was recently arrested for shoplifting a $10.95 necktie. Briefly explain this behavior in terms of *each* of the following:
   a. The medical model
   b. The psychoanalytic model
   c. The behavioral model
   d. The cognitive model
   e. The humanistic model
   f. The sociocultural model
7. *DSM-IV* is intended to both describe psychological disorders and suggest their underlying causes. True or false?

Ask Yourself

Do you agree or disagree that *DSM* should be updated every several years? What makes abnormal behavior so variable? Why can't there be one definition of abnormal behavior that is unchanging?

(Answers to review questions are on page 412.)

- *What are the major psychological disorders?*

THE MAJOR DISORDERS

Sally experienced her first panic attack out of the blue, three weeks after completing her senior year in college. She had just finished a job interview and was meeting some friends for dinner. In the restaurant, she began to feel dizzy. Within a few seconds, her heart was pounding, and she was feeling breathless, as though she might pass out. Her friends noticed that she did not look well and offered to drive her home. Sally suggested they stop at the hospital emergency room instead. Although she felt better by the time they arrived at the hospital, and tests indicated nothing wrong, Sally experienced a similar episode a week later while at a movie. . . .

Her attacks became more and more frequent. Before long, she was having several attacks per week. In addition, she constantly worried about having attacks. She began to avoid exercise and other activities that produced physical sensations. She also noticed the attacks were worse when she was alone. She began to avoid driving, shopping in large stores, and eating in all restaurants. Some weeks she avoided leaving the house completely. Sally stopped looking for work, fearing that she would be unable to stay at her job in the event of a panic attack (Antony, Brown, & Barlow, 1992, p. 79).

The diagnosis: Sally suffered from one of the major forms of psychological disturbance, known as an anxiety disorder.

Anxiety disorders represent just one of a number of major forms of abnormal behavior that we will consider. Keep in mind that we are focusing on those disorders that are most common, serious, or harmful to everyday functioning, and that many other types of disorders have been identified. It is also important to note that, although we'll be discussing these disturbances in a dispassionate manner, each represents a very human set of difficulties that influence, and in some cases wreak considerable havoc on, people's lives.

Anxiety Disorders

All of us, at one time or another, experience *anxiety*, a feeling of apprehension or tension, in reaction to stressful situations. There is nothing "wrong" with such anxiety; everyone feels it to some degree, and usually it is a reaction to stress that helps, rather than hinders, our daily functioning. Without anxiety, for instance, most of us would not be terribly motivated to study hard, to undergo physical exams, or to spend long hours at our jobs.

But some people experience anxiety in situations in which there is no external reason or cause. When anxiety occurs without external justification and begins to impede people's daily functioning, it is considered a psychological problem known as an **anxiety disorder.** There are four main types of anxiety disorders: generalized anxiety disorder, panic disorder, phobic disorder, and obsessive-compulsive disorder.

Anxiety disorder: The occurrence of anxiety without obvious external cause, intruding on daily functioning

Generalized Anxiety Disorder   As the name implies, **generalized anxiety disorder** refers to a disorder in which an individual experiences long-term, consistent anxiety without knowing why. Such people feel afraid of *something,* but are unable to articulate what it is. Because of their anxiety they are unable to function normally. They cannot concentrate, they cannot set their fears aside, and their lives become centered on their anxiety. Such anxiety may eventually result in the development of physiological problems. Because of heightened muscle tension and arousal, individuals with generalized anxiety disorder may begin to experience headaches, dizziness, heart palpitations, or insomnia.

Generalized anxiety disorder: The experience of long-term anxiety with no explanation

Panic Disorder   In another type of anxiety disorder, **panic disorder,** *panic attacks* occur that last from a few seconds to as long as several hours. During an attack, such as the ones experienced by Sally in the case described earlier, the anxiety that a person has been chronically experiencing suddenly rises to a peak, and the individual feels a sense of impending, unavoidable doom. Although symptoms differ from person to person, they may include heart palpitations, shortness of breath, unusual amounts of sweating, faintness and dizziness, an urge to urinate, gastric sensations and—in extreme cases—a sense of imminent death. After such an attack, it is no wonder that people tend to feel exhausted (Baker, 1989; Antony, Brown, & Barlow, 1992).

Panic disorder: Anxiety that manifests itself in the form of panic attacks that last from a few seconds to as long as several hours

---

ANSWERS TO PREVIOUS REVIEW
1. d **2.** a **3.** Deviation from the ideal **4.** d **5.** b **6.** Possible answers, which may vary, include the following: (a) A physiological problem may exist which causes him to behave irresponsibly. (b) Unresolved childhood conflicts led to the behavior. (c) He had enjoyed the immediate rewards of stealing in the past. (d) He holds inaccurate cognitions about the acceptability of stealing. (e) Stealing was an attempt to "discover" himself. (f) Stealing was caused by economic difficulties. **7.** False; *DSM-IV* is intended to be descriptive only.

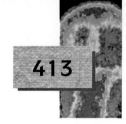

Phobic Disorder   Claustrophobia. Acrophobia. Xenophobia. Although these sound like characters in a Greek tragedy, they are actually members of a class of psychological disorders known as phobias. **Phobias** are intense, irrational fears of specific objects or situations. For example, claustrophobia is a fear of enclosed places, acrophobia a fear of high places, and xenophobia a fear of strangers. Although the objective danger posed by an anxiety-producing stimulus (which can be just about anything, as you can see from the list in Table 12-3) is typically small or nonexistent, to the individual suffering from the phobia it represents great danger, and a full-blown panic attack may follow exposure to the stimulus. Phobic disorders differ from generalized anxiety disorders and panic disorders in that there is a specific, identifiable stimulus that sets off the anxiety reaction.

Phobias may have only a minor impact on people's lives if those who suffer from them can avoid the things they fear. Unless one is a professional firefighter or tightrope walker, for example, a fear of heights may have little impact on one's daily life. On the other hand, a fear of strangers presents a more serious problem. In one extreme case, a Washington housewife left her home just three times in 30 years—once to visit her family, once to have an operation, and once to purchase ice cream for a dying companion (Adler, 1984).

Phobias: Intense, irrational fears of specific objects or situations

Obsessive-Compulsive Disorder   In **obsessive-compulsive disorder,** people are plagued by unwanted thoughts, called obsessions, or feel that they must carry out some actions, termed compulsions, against their will.

An **obsession** is a thought or idea that keeps recurring in one's mind. For example, a student may not be able to stop feeling that he has neglected to put his name on a test and may think about it constantly for the 2 weeks it takes to get the paper back. A man may go on vacation and wonder the whole time whether he locked his house. A woman may hear the same tune running through her head over and over again. In each case, the thought or idea is unwanted and difficult to put out of mind. Of course, many of us suffer from mild obsessions from time to time, but usually such thoughts persist for short periods only. For people with serious obsessions, however, the thoughts persist for days or months and may consist of bizarre, troubling images. In one classic case of an obsession, the patient complained of experiencing "terrible" thoughts:

Obsessive-compulsive disorder: A disorder characterized by obsessions or compulsions

Obsession: A thought or idea that keeps recurring

TABLE 12-3   Giving Fear a Proper Name

Phobia	Stimulus	Phobia	Stimulus
Acrophobia	Heights	Herpetophobia	Reptiles
Aerophobia	Flying	Hydrophobia	Water
Agoraphobia	Open spaces	Mikrophobia	Germs
Ailurophobia	Cats	Murophobia	Mice
Amaxophobia	Vehicles, driving	Mysophobia	Dirt or germs
Anthophobia	Flowers	Numerophobia	Numbers
Anthrophobia	People	Nyctophobia	Darkness
Aquaphobia	Water	Ochlophobia	Crowds
Arachnophobia	Spiders	Ophidiophobia	Snakes
Astraphobia	Lightning	Ornithophobia	Birds
Brontophobia	Thunder	Phonophobia	Speaking out loud
Claustrophobia	Closed spaces	Pyrophobia	Fire
Cynophobia	Dogs	Thanatophobia	Death
Dementophobia	Insanity	Trichophobia	Hair
Gephyrophobia	Bridges	Xenophobia	Strangers

When she thought of her boyfriend she wished he were dead; when her mother went down the stairs, she "wished she'd fall and break her neck"; when her sister spoke of going to the beach with her infant daughter, the patient "hoped that they would both drown." These thoughts "make me hysterical. I love them; why should I wish such terrible things to happen? It drives me wild, makes me feel I'm crazy and don't belong to society." (Kraines, 1948, p. 199)

Compulsions: Urges to repeatedly carry out an act that even the sufferer realizes is unreasonable

As part of an obsessive-compulsive disorder, people may also experience **compulsions,** urges to repeatedly carry out some act that seems strange and unreasonable, even to them. Whatever the compulsive behavior, people experience extreme anxiety if they cannot carry it out, even if it is something they want to stop. The acts involved may be relatively trivial, such as repeatedly checking the stove to make sure all the burners are turned off, or more unusual, such as a continuous need to wash oneself (Rachman & Hodgson, 1980). For example, consider this case report of a 27-year-old woman with a cleaning ritual:

Bess would first remove all of her clothing in a preestablished sequence. She would lay out each article of clothing at specific spots on her bed, and examine each one for any indications of "contamination." She would then thoroughly scrub her body, starting at her feet and working meticulously up to the top of her head, using certain washcloths for certain areas of her body. Any articles of clothing that appeared to have been "contaminated" were thrown into the laundry. Clean clothing was put in the spots that were vacant. She would then dress herself in the opposite order from which she took the clothes off. If there were any deviations from this order, or if Bess began to wonder if she had missed some contamination, she would go through the entire sequence again. It was not rare for her to do this four or five times in a row on certain evenings. (Meyer & Osborne, 1982, p. 156)

Unfortunately for those experiencing an obsessive-compulsive disorder, little or no reduction in anxiety results from carrying out a compulsive ritual. They tend to lead lives filled with unrelenting tension.

The Causes of Anxiety Disorders No single mechanism fully explains all cases of anxiety disorders, and each of the models of abnormal behavior that we discussed earlier has something to say about the causes. However, the medical, behavioral, and cognitive models have been particularly influential in psychologists' thinking.

The rituals of obsessive-compulsive disorder go far beyond mere tidiness. Often a ritual may preoccupy the person, and great anxiety ensues if the action cannot be carried out.

Biological approaches, stemming from the medical model, have shown that ge- netic factors play some role in anxiety disorders. For example, if one member of a pair of identical twins has panic disorder, there is a 30 percent chance that the other twin will have it also (Torgersen, 1983). Other evidence suggests that cer- tain chemical deficiencies in the brain may produce some kinds of anxiety disor- der. Specifically, low levels of several of the neurotransmitters discussed in Chapter 2 have been identified in individuals with obsessive-compulsive disorder (Gorman et al., 1989; Hoehn-Saric, 1993).

Psychologists employing the behavioral model have taken a different approach, emphasizing environmental factors. They consider anxiety to be a learned re- sponse to stress. For instance, suppose a young girl is bitten by a dog. When she sees a dog next, she is frightened and runs away—a behavior that relieves her anxiety and thereby reinforces her avoidance behavior. After repeated encounters with dogs in which she is reinforced for her avoidance behavior, she may develop a full-fledged phobia regarding dogs.

Finally, the cognitive model suggests that anxiety disorders are an outgrowth of inappropriate and inaccurate cognitions about circumstances in a person's world. For example, people with anxiety disorders may view a friendly puppy as a ferocious and savage pit bull, or they may see an air disaster looming every mo- ment they are in the vicinity of an airplane. According to the cognitive perspec- tive, it is people's faulty thinking about the world that is at the root of an anxiety disorder.

Somatoform Disorders: When the Psychological Leads to the Physical

Most of us know people who cannot wait to regale us with their latest physical problems; even an innocent "How are you?" brings a long list of complaints in response. People who consistently report physical problems, who have a preoc- cupation with their health, and who have unrealistic fears of disease may be ex- periencing a problem known as hypochondriasis. In *hypochondriasis* there is a constant fear of illness, and physical sensations are misinterpreted as signs of dis- ease. It is not that the "symptoms" are faked; hypochondriacs actually experience the aches and pains that most of us feel as we go through an active existence. It is the misinterpretation of these sensations as symptoms of some dread disease— often in the face of inarguable medical evidence to the contrary—that character- izes hypochondriasis (Costa & McCrae, 1985; Barsky et al., 1992).

Hypochondriasis is just one example of a class of disorders known as **so- matoform disorders,** psychological difficulties that take on a physical (somatic) form of one sort or another. Even though an individual with a somatoform dis- order reports physical symptoms, there is no underlying physical problem, or if a physical problem does exist, the person's reaction greatly exaggerates what would be expected from the medical problem alone. Only when a physical exam- ination rules out actual physiological difficulties can a diagnosis of somatoform disorder be made.

Somatoform disorders: Psychological difficulties that take on physical (somatic) form

In addition to hypochondriasis, the other major somatoform disorder is **con- version disorder.** Unlike hypochondriasis, in which there is no actual physical problem, conversion disorders involve an actual physical disturbance such as the inability to use a sensory organ or the complete or partial inability to move an arm or leg. The *cause* of such a physical disturbance is purely psychological. There is no biological reason for the problem. Some of Freud's classic cases in- volved conversion disorders. For instance, one patient of Freud's was suddenly unable to use her arm, without any apparent physiological cause. Later, just as abruptly, she regained its use.

Conversion disorder: A psychologi- cal disturbance characterized by ac- tual physical disturbances, such as the inability to speak or move one's arms

Conversion disorders are often characterized by their rapid onset. People wake up one morning blind or deaf, or they experience numbness that is restricted to

a certain part of the body. A person's hand, for example, might become entirely numb, while an area above the wrist—controlled by the same nerves—remains inexplicably sensitive to touch. Such a condition is referred to as "glove anesthesia," because the area that is numb is the part of the hand covered by a glove, and not a region related to pathways of the nervous system.

One of the most surprising characteristics frequently found in people experiencing conversion disorders is a lack of concern over symptoms that most of us would expect to be highly anxiety-producing (Ford & Folks, 1985). For instance, a person in good health who wakes up blind might react in a bland, matter-of-fact way. Considering how most of us would feel if we woke up in this condition, such a reaction hardly seems appropriate.

Conversion disorders occasionally occur on a large scale. In one instance, nearly one out of five student aviators enrolled at the U.S. Naval Aerospace Medical Institute began to suffer symptoms such as blurred vision, double vision, and the development of blind spots and focusing trouble (Mucha & Reinhardt, 1970). However, no underlying physical problem could be identified. Investigation revealed that the students found outright quitting an unacceptable response to the stress they were experiencing and instead developed physical responses that allowed them to avoid the demands of the program. Their stress was thus relieved through a face-saving physical problem.

Conversion disorders generally occur when an individual is under some kind of emotional stress that could be reduced by a physical symptom. The physical condition allows the person to escape or reduce the source of stress. An emotional problem is turned, then, into a physical ailment that acts to relieve the source of the original emotional problem.

Dissociative Disorders

Dissociative disorders: Psychological dysfunctions characterized by the splitting apart of critical personality facets that are normally integrated, allowing stress avoidance by escape

The most dramatic and celebrated cases of psychological dysfunction (although they are actually rare) have been **dissociative disorders.** The movie *The Three Faces of Eve,* the book *Sybil* (about a girl with sixteen personalities), and cases of people found wandering the streets with no notion of who they are or where they came from exemplify dissociative disorders. The key factor in such problems is the splitting apart (or dissociation) of critical parts of personality that are normally integrated and work together. This lack of integration acts to allow certain parts of a personality to avoid stress—since another part can be made to face it. By dissociating themselves from key parts of their personality, individuals with the disorder can eliminate anxiety (Ross et al., 1990).

Dissociative identity disorder, or **multiple personality:** A disorder in which a person displays characteristics of two or more distinct personalities

Three major types of dissociative disorders have been distinguished: dissociative identity disorder, dissociative amnesia, and dissociative fugue. A person with a **dissociative identity disorder,** or **multiple personality,** displays characteristics of two or more distinct personalities. Each personality has a unique set of likes and dislikes and its own reactions to situations. Some people with multiple personalities even carry several pairs of glasses because their vision changes with each personality (Braun, 1985). Moreover, each individual personality can be well adjusted when considered on its own (Ross, 1989).

The problem, of course, is that there is only one body available to the various personalities, forcing the personalities to take turns. Because there can be strong variations in personalities, the person's behavior—considered as a whole—can appear very inconsistent. For instance, in the famous case portrayed in *The Three Faces of Eve,* the meek, bland Eve White provided a stunning contrast to the dominant and carefree Eve Black (Sizemore, 1989).

Reports of multiple personality have increased dramatically over the last 15 years, with more cases being reported during a 5-year period in the 1980s than in the preceding 200 years (Putnam et al., 1986). As we discuss in the accompanying Psychology at Work box, the reason for this rise remains puzzling, and has produced unprecedented legal problems.

PSYCHOLOGY AT WORK

Multiple Personalities— or Multiple Fraud?

The man took the witness stand wearing a pink sweater, a skirt, high heels, and press-on nails. This was not the first time he had taken the stand in this trial. In fact, because he claimed to have 11 personalities, eight of whom knew something about the crime in question, the judge had allowed each of the personalities to testify separately. In his present personality, the man was a lesbian prostitute. (Scott, 1994)

This 1994 trial was not the first case in which a person claiming to have multiple personalities had been allowed to testify in court. In fact, in one case, a witness in a Wisconsin case testified while in the personality of a dog.

Such bizarre cases illustrate some of the thorny legal issues that have emerged in just the last decade in dealing with defendants and plaintiffs who may have dissociative identity disorder. For instance, if one of an individual's personalities commits a crime, while others are unaware of it, is the person guilty or innocent? What if one personality meets the legal definition of insanity, but the others don't? When testifying, should each separate personality be sworn in individually, or should once be enough?

These questions have taken on increasing urgency due to the fact that criminal defendants are increasingly claiming to suffer from multiple personalities. This permits

them to argue that they should not be held accountable for crimes committed when under the influence of an alternative, criminal personality. In some cases, though, such claims are fabricated. For instance, Kenneth Bianchi, the Hillside Strangler, used sham symptoms of dissociative identity disorder in an unsuccessful attempt to avoid criminal prosecution (Orne, Dinges, & Orne, 1984).

However, in other cases, the defense has been successful. One of the first of such cases occurred in 1978, when a man was found not guilty by reason of insanity in the rape of four women. He claimed to have ten personalities. Similarly, consider the following convoluted case:

Mark Peterson, a 31-year-old grocery worker from Oshkosh, Wisconsin, [defended] himself in court in November 1990, against a rape charge brought against him by Sarah, a woman with multiple personality disorder. He met 26-year-old "Franny" at a bar, and asked her for a date. Franny told Peterson about fun-loving 20-year-old "Jennifer" and reportedly, he summoned Jennifer and invited her to have sex with him. During intercourse, six-year-old "Emily" emerged; he reportedly told Jennifer to keep their activities secret from Sarah. But Franny and Emily told Sarah, who pressed charges against him. Although the jury voted to convict Peterson, the judge overturned the verdict on the grounds that the defense was not

allowed to have Sarah examined by a psychiatrist before the trial. (Halgin & Whitbourne, 1994, p. 205)

A large part of the problems arising from the use of dissociative identity disorder in court is that experts are unable to agree on the precise nature of the disorder. In fact, there is little understanding of why the incidence of the disorder has increased. Although one explanation for the increase is that diagnostic techniques have become more precise, some psychologists argue that the publicity accompanying well-known cases such as Sybil has led people to increasingly interpret psychological symptoms as signs of multiple personality. In turn, people may then describe their symptoms to therapists in a manner that predisposes therapists to view them as signs of multiple personality disorder. In sum, it is people's expectations about what they are experiencing that leads them to behave in a way that then supports their expectations (McHugh, 1993; Spanos, 1994).

Specialists can't agree on which of these two, quite contradictory, explanations accounts for the rise in cases of dissociative identity disorder. What is clear is that as more people report the symptoms of the disorder, it is becoming increasingly difficult to make clear-cut diagnoses—leading to continuing legal questions (North et al., 1993).

Dissociative amnesia, another dissociative disorder, is a failure or inability to remember past experiences. Dissociative amnesia is unlike simple amnesia, which, as we discussed in Chapter 6, involves an actual loss of information from memory, typically due to a physiological cause. In contrast, in cases of dissociative amnesia, the "forgotten" material is still present in memory—it simply cannot be recalled.

In the most severe forms, individuals cannot recall their names, are unable to recognize parents and other relatives, and do not know their addresses. In other respects, though, they may appear quite normal. Apart from an inability to remember certain facts about themselves, they may be able to recall skills and abilities that they developed earlier. For instance, even though a chef may not re-

Dissociative amnesia: A failure to remember past experience

member where he grew up and received training, he may still be able to prepare gourmet meals.

In some cases of dissociative amnesia, the memory loss is quite profound. For example, a woman—dubbed Jane Doe by her rescuers—was found by a Florida park ranger in the early 1980s. Incoherent, thin, and only partially clothed, Doe was unable to recall her name, her past, and even how to read and write. On the basis of her accent, authorities thought the woman was from Illinois, and interviews conducted while she was given tranquilizing drugs revealed that she had had a Catholic education. However, the childhood memories she revealed were so universal that her background could not be further pinpointed. In a desperate attempt to rediscover her identity, she appeared on the television show *Good Morning America,* and ultimately a couple from Roselle, Illinois, whose daughter had moved to Florida, stepped forward, saying that they were her parents. However, Jane Doe never regained her memory (Carson, Butcher, & Coleman, 1992).

Dissociative fugue: An amnesiac condition in which people take sudden, impulsive trips, sometimes assuming a new identity

A more unusual form of amnesia is a condition known as **dissociative fugue.** In this state, a person takes an impulsive, sudden trip, often assuming a new identity. After a period of time—days, months, or sometimes even years—the individual suddenly realizes that he or she is in a strange place and completely forgets the time spent wandering. The person's last memories are those from the time just before entering the fugue state.

What the dissociative disorders have in common is that they allow people to escape from some anxiety-producing situation. Either the person produces a new personality to deal with stress, or the situation that caused the stress is forgotten or left behind as the individual journeys to some new—and perhaps less anxiety-ridden—environment (Spiegel & Cardena, 1991).

RECAP AND REVIEW

Recap
- Anxiety disorders occur when anxiety is so great that it impedes people's everyday functioning.
- Somatoform disorders are psychological problems that take on a physical form.
- Dissociative disorders occur when normally integrated parts of personality split apart.

Review
1. Kathy is terrified of elevators. She is likely to be suffering from a(n):
   a. Obsessive-compulsive disorder
   b. Phobic disorder
   c. Panic disorder
   d. Generalized anxiety disorder
2. Carmen described an incident in which her anxiety suddenly rose to a peak and she felt a sense of impending doom. Carmen had experienced a(n) _____ _____ .

3. Troubling thoughts that persist for days or months are known as:
   a. Obsessions
   b. Compulsions
   c. Rituals
   d. Panic attacks
4. An overpowering urge to carry out a strange ritual is called a(n) _____ .
5. In what major way does conversion disorder differ from hypochondriasis?
6. The splitting apart of the personality, providing escape from stressful situations, is the key factor in _____ disorders.

Ask Yourself
Genetic factors have been found to play an important role in anxiety disorders. What other factors may contribute, and how can both the behavioral and cognitive models be used as a basis for treatment of anxiety disorders?

(Answers to review questions are on page 420.)

• *What are the most severe forms of psychological disorders?*

Mood Disorders: The Feeling Is Wrong

I do not care for anything. I do not care to ride, for the exercise is too violent. I do not care to walk, for walking is too strenuous. I do not care to lie down, for I should either

have to remain lying, and I do not care to do that, or I should have to get up again, and I do not care to do that either. . . . I do not care at all.

Did you ever apply for a job you really wanted, and for which you had a terrific interview, only to learn later that you didn't get it? Although your emotional reaction was probably not as strong as the one described above by the Danish philosopher Søren Kierkegaard, you probably experienced a feeling of depression, an emotional reaction of sadness and melancholy. Unlike Kierkegaard, though, who suffered from feelings of depression for extended periods, more than likely you returned to a more positive frame of mind relatively quickly.

We all experience mood swings. Sometimes we are happy, perhaps even euphoric; at other times we feel upset, saddened, or depressed. Such changes in mood are a normal part of everyday life. In some people, however, moods are so pronounced and so long-lasting that they interfere with the ability to function effectively. In extreme cases a mood may become life-threatening, and in others it may cause the person to lose touch with reality. Situations such as these represent **mood disorders,** disturbances in emotional feelings strong enough to intrude on everyday living.

Mood disorders: Disturbances in emotions and feelings severe enough to interfere with normal living

Major Depression   Moses. Rousseau. Dostoevsky. Queen Victoria. Lincoln. Tchaikovsky. Freud.

The common link among these people? Each is believed to have suffered from periodic attacks of **major depression,** one of the most common forms of mood disorders. Between 14 million and 15 million people in the United States suffer from major depression, and at any one time, between 6 and 10 percent of the U.S. population is clinically depressed. Depression is the most frequent problem diagnosed in outpatient clinics, affecting about one-third of the patients. The costs of depression to society are a staggering $43.7 *billion* a year (McGrath et al., 1990; Greenberg et al., 1993a, 1993b; Cronkite, 1994).

Women are twice as likely to experience major depression as men, with one-fourth of all females apt to encounter major depression at some point during their lives. Furthermore, although no one is quite sure why, the rate of depression is going up throughout the world. Results of in-depth interviews conducted in the mainland United States, Puerto Rico, Taiwan, Lebanon, Canada, Italy, Germany, and France indicate that the incidence of depression has increased significantly

Major depression: A severe form of depression that interferes with concentration, decision making, and sociability

In a tangle of chronic stomach pain, drug abuse, and persistent depression, Kurt Cobain of the rock group Nirvana committed suicide at the age of 27.

TABLE 12-4 A Test for Depression

This test was distributed by mental-health organizations during National Depression Screening Day in the early 1990s, a nationwide event that sought to identify people who suffered from depression severe enough to warrant psychological intervention. On the day of the screening, the organizations received some 30,000 inquiries (Hill, 1992).

To complete the questionnaire, count the number of statements with which you agree:

1. I feel downhearted, blue, and sad.
2. I don't enjoy the things that I used to.
3. I feel that others would be better off if I were dead.
4. I feel that I am not useful or needed.
5. I notice that I am losing weight.
6. I have trouble sleeping through the night.
7. I am restless and can't keep still.
8. My mind isn't as clear as it used to be.
9. I get tired for no reason.
10. I feel hopeless about the future.

Scoring If you agree with at least five of the statements, including either item 1 or 2, and if you have had these symptoms for at least 2 weeks, help from a professional is strongly recommended. If you answer yes to number 3, you should get help immediately.

---

over previous rates in every area. In fact, in some countries, the likelihood that individuals will suffer major depression at some point in their lives is three times higher than it was for earlier generations. The onset of major depression has become consistently higher, beginning at increasingly early ages (Weller & Weller, 1991; Weissman & Cross-National Collaborative Group, 1992; Compas, Ey, & Grant, 1993).

When psychologists speak of major depression, they do not mean the sadness that comes from experiencing one of life's disappointments. Some depression is normal following the breakup of a long-term relationship, the death of a loved one, or the loss of a job. It is even normal for less serious problems: doing badly in school or not getting into the college of one's choice.

People who suffer from major depression experience similar sorts of feelings, but the severity tends to be considerably greater. They may feel useless, worthless, and lonely and may despair over the future. Moreover, such feelings may continue for months and years. People with severe depression may have uncontrollable crying jags and disrupted sleep. The depth of such behavior and the length of time it lasts are the hallmarks of major depression. (Table 12-4 provides a quick assessment of the severity of depression.)

Mania and Bipolar Disorders: Ups and Downs While those with severe depression descend into depths of despair, another type of psychological disorder causes people to soar high emotionally, experiencing what is called mania. **Mania** refers to an extended state of intense euphoria and elation. People experiencing mania feel intense happiness, power, invulnerability, and energy. They may become involved in wild schemes, believing they will succeed at anything they attempt. There are many cases on record of people squandering all their money while in a state of mania. Consider, for example, the following description of an individual who experienced a manic episode:

Mania: An extended state of intense euphoria and elation

Mr. O'Reilly took a leave of absence from his civil service job. He purchased a large number of cuckoo clocks and then an expensive car, which he planned to use as a mobile showroom for his wares, anticipating that he would make a great deal of money. He proceeded to "tear around town" buying and selling clocks and other merchandise, and when he was not out, he was continuously on the phone making "deals." He rarely slept and, uncharacteristically, spent every evening in neighborhood bars drinking heavily and, according to him, "wheeling and dealing. . . ." He was $3000 in debt and had driven his family to exhaustion with his excessive activity and talkativeness. He said, however, that he felt "on top of the world." (Spitzer et al., 1983, p. 115)

Frequently, the same person sequentially experiences bouts of mania and depression. This alternation of mania and depression is called **bipolar disorder** (or, as it used to be known, manic-depressive disorder). The swings between highs and lows may occur as frequently as a few days apart, or they may alternate over a period of years. In addition, the periods of depression tend to be longer in most individuals than the periods of mania, although this pattern is reversed in some.

Ironically, some of society's most creative individuals may suffer from forms of bipolar disorder. The imagination, drive, excitement, and energy that they display during manic stages allow them to make unusually creative contributions. For instance, historical analysis of the composer Robert Schumann's music shows that he was most prolific during the periods of mania he suffered periodically. In contrast, his output dropped off drastically during periods of depression (Slater & Meyer, 1959; Goodwin & Jamison, 1990; Jamison, 1993).

Despite the creative fires that may be lit by mania, persons who experience this disorder often show a recklessness that produces self-injury, both emotionally and sometimes physically. They may alienate others with their talkativeness, inflated self-esteem, and indifference to the needs of others.

Causes of Mood Disorders   Because they represent a major mental-health problem, mood disorders—and, in particular, depression—have received a good deal of study. Several approaches have been used to explain the disorders. Psychoanalytic approaches, for example, see depression as the result of anger at oneself. In this view, people feel responsible for the bad things that happen to them and direct their anger inward.

On the other hand, convincing evidence has been found that both bipolar disorder and major depression have their roots in biological causes. For example, heredity plays a role in bipolar disorder; the affliction runs in some families (Egeland et al., 1987; Gershon et al., 1990). Furthermore, some researchers have found a chemical imbalance in the brains of some depressed patients. For instance, certain abnormalities have been identified in the brain's neurotransmitters (Goodwin & Jamison, 1990; Cooper, Bloom, & Roth, 1991; Horton & Katona, 1991).

Some explanations for mood disorders look to cognitive factors (Gotlib, 1992). Psychologist Martin Seligman suggests that depression is largely a response to **learned helplessness,** a state in which people perceive and eventually learn that there is no way to escape from or cope with stress. As a consequence, they simply give up fighting the stress and submit to it, thereby spawning depression (Seligman, 1975, 1988; Petersen, Maier, & Seligman, 1993). Building on Seligman's notions, other psychologists suggest that depression may be a result of hopelessness, a combination of learned helplessness and an expectation that negative outcomes in one's life are inevitable (Abramson, Metalsky, & Alloy, 1989).

Aaron Beck, a psychologist, has proposed that people's faulty cognitions underlie their depressed feelings. Specifically, his cognitive theory of depression suggests that depressed individuals typically view themselves as life's losers, blaming themselves whenever anything goes wrong. By focusing on the negative side

Bipolar disorder: A disorder in which a person alternates between euphoric feelings of mania and bouts of depression

Learned helplessness: A state in which people believe they cannot escape from or cope with stress, and they give up fighting it, leading to depression

of situations, they feel inept and unable to act constructively to change their environment. In sum, their negative cognitions lead to feelings of depression (Beck, 1976, 1982).

The various theories of depression have still not provided a complete answer to an elusive question that has dogged researchers: Why is the incidence of depression twice as high for women as for men? One explanation is that the stress experienced by women may be greater than that experienced by men at certain points in their lives—such as when a woman must simultaneously earn a living and be primary caregiver for her children. In addition, women have a higher risk for physical and sexual abuse, typically earn lower wages than men, and report greater unhappiness with their marriages (McGrath et al., 1990; Strickland, 1992; Nolen-Hoeksema & Girgus, 1994; Weissman & Olfson, 1995).

But biological factors may also explain some women's depression. For example, 25 to 50 percent of women who take oral contraceptives report symptoms of depression, and depression that occurs following the birth of a child is linked to hormonal changes (Strickland, 1992).

It is clear, ultimately, that researchers have discovered no definitive solutions to the puzzle of depression, and there are many alternative explanations. Most likely, mood disorders are caused by a complex interaction of several factors (Ingram, 1990; Wolman & Stricker, 1990).

Schizophrenia: When Reality Is Lost

I'm a doctor, you know. . . . I don't have a diploma, but I'm a doctor. I'm glad to be a mental patient, because it taught me how to be humble. I use Cover Girl creamy natural makeup. Oral Roberts has been here to visit me. . . . This place is where *Mad* magazine is published. The Nixons make Noson metal polish. When I was a little girl, I used to sit and tell stories to myself. When I was older, I turned off the sound on the TV set and made up dialogue to go with the shows I watched. . . . I'm a week pregnant. I have schizophrenia—cancer of the nerves. My body is overcrowded with nerves. This is going to win me the Nobel Prize for medicine. I don't consider myself schizophrenic anymore. There's no such thing as schizophrenia, there's only mental telepathy. I once had a friend named Camilla Costello. She was Abbott and Costello's daughter. . . . I'm in the Pentecostal Church, but I'm thinking of changing my religion. I have a dog at home. I love instant oatmeal. When you have Jesus, you don't need a diet. Mick Jagger wants to marry me. I want to get out of the revolving door. With Jesus Christ, anything is possible. I used to hit my mother. It was the hyperactivity from all the cookies I ate. I'm the personification of Casper the Friendly Ghost. I used to go outside asking the other kids to be my friend when I was little. California's the most beautiful state in the Union. I've been there once, by television. My name is Jack Warden, and I'm an actress. (Quoted in Sheehan, 1982, pp. 72–73)

This excerpt represents the efforts of a woman with schizophrenia, one of the most severe forms of mental disturbance, to hold a conversation. People with schizophrenia make up by far the largest percentage of those hospitalized for mental disorders. They are also in many respects the least likely to recover from their psychological difficulties.

Schizophrenia refers to a class of disorders in which severe distortion of reality occurs. Thinking, perception, and emotion may deteriorate; there may be a withdrawal from social interaction; and there may be displays of bizarre behavior. Although several types of schizophrenia (see Table 12-5) have been observed, the distinctions between them are not always clear-cut (e.g., Zigler & Glick, 1988; Fenton & McGlashan, 1991a). Moreover, the symptoms displayed by persons with schizophrenia may vary considerably over time, and people with schizophrenia show significant differences in the pattern of symptoms even when they are labeled with the same diagnostic category. Nonetheless, a number of characteristics reliably distinguish schizophrenia from other disorders. They include:

Schizophrenia: A class of disorders characterized by a severe distortion of reality, resulting in antisocial behavior, silly or obscene behavior, hallucinations, and disturbances in movement

TABLE 12-5 The Major Types of Schizophrenia

Type	Symptoms
Disorganized (hebephrenic) schizophrenia	Inappropriate laughter and giggling, silliness, incoherent speech, infantile behavior, strange and sometimes obscene behavior
Paranoid schizophrenia	Delusions and hallucinations of persecution or of greatness, loss of judgment, erratic and unpredictable behavior
Catatonic schizophrenia	Major disturbances in movement; in some phases, loss of all motion, with patient frozen into a single position, remaining that way for hours and sometimes even days; in other phases, hyperactivity and wild, sometimes violent, movement
Undifferentiated schizophrenia	Variable mixture of major symptoms of schizophrenia; classification used for patients who cannot be typed into any of the more specific categories
Residual schizophrenia	Minor signs of schizophrenia following a more serious episode.

■ *Decline from a previous level of functioning.* An individual can no longer carry out activities he or she was once able to do.

■ *Disturbances of thought and language.* Schizophrenics use logic and language in a peculiar way; their thinking does not make sense, and they do not follow conventional linguistic rules. Consider, for example, the following response to the question "Why do you think people believe in God?"

Uh, let's, I don't know why, let's see, balloon travel. He holds it up for you, the balloon. He don't let you fall out, your little legs sticking down through the clouds. He's down to

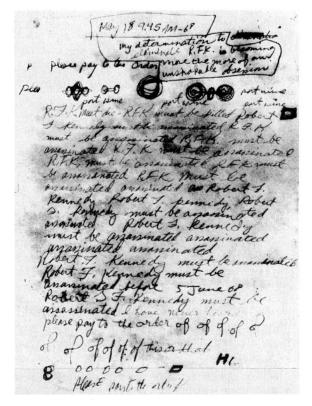

This excerpt from the diary of Sirhan Sirhan, the killer of Robert F. Kennedy, shows the disturbances of thought and language characteristic of schizophrenia.

the smokestack, looking through the smoke trying to get the balloon gassed up you know. Way they're flying on top that way, legs sticking out. I don't know, looking down on the ground, heck, that'd make you so dizzy you just stay and sleep you know, hold down and sleep there. I used to be sleep outdoors, you know, sleep outdoors instead of going home (Chapman & Chapman, 1973, p. 3).

As this selection illustrates, although the basic grammatical structure may be intact, the substance of schizophrenics' thinking is often illogical, garbled, and lacking in meaningful content.

■ *Delusions.* People with schizophrenia often have *delusions,* firmly held, unshakable beliefs with no basis in reality. Among the most frequent ones are the beliefs that they are being controlled by someone else, that they are being persecuted by others, and that their thoughts are being broadcast so that others are able to know what they are thinking.

■ *Perceptual disorders.* People with schizophrenia do not perceive the world as most other people do. They may see, hear, or smell things differently from others and do not even have a sense of their bodies in the way that others do. Some reports suggest that people with schizophrenia have difficulty determining where their own bodies stop and the rest of the world begins (Ritzler & Rosenbaum, 1974). They may also have *hallucinations,* the experience of perceiving things that do not actually exist (McGuire, Shah, & Murray, 1993).

■ *Emotional disturbances.* People with schizophrenia sometimes show a lack of emotion in which even the most dramatic events produce little or no emotional response. Conversely, they may display emotion that is inappropriate to a situation. For example, a schizophrenic might laugh uproariously at a funeral or may react with anger when being helped by someone.

■ *Withdrawal.* People with schizophrenia tend to have little interest in others. They tend not to socialize or hold real conversations with others, although they may talk *at* another person. In the most extreme cases they do not even acknowledge the presence of other people, appearing to be in their own isolated world.

The symptoms of schizophrenia follow two primary courses. In *process schizophrenia,* the symptoms develop relatively early in life, slowly and subtly. There may be a gradual withdrawal from the world, excessive daydreaming, a blunting of emotion, until eventually the disorder reaches the point where others cannot overlook it. In other cases, known as *reactive schizophrenia,* the onset of symptoms is sudden and conspicuous. The treatment outlook for reactive schizophrenia is relatively favorable; process schizophrenia has proved to be much more difficult to treat.

A relatively recent addition to the classifications used in schizophrenia distinguishes *positive-symptom schizophrenia* from *negative-symptom schizophrenia* (Opler et al., 1984; Andreasen, 1985). Negative-symptom schizophrenia means an absence or loss of normal functioning, such as social withdrawal or blunted emotions. In contrast, positive-symptom schizophrenia is indicated by the presence of disordered behavior such as hallucinations, delusions, and extremes of emotionality. The distinction, although controversial, is becoming increasingly important because it suggests that two different underlying processes may explain the roots of schizophrenia—which remains one of the greatest mysteries facing psychologists who deal with abnormal behavior (Fenton & McGlashan, 1991b; Heinrichs, 1993; Cromwell & Snyder, 1993).

Solving the Puzzle of Schizophrenia: Biological Evidence   Although it is clear that schizophrenic behavior departs radically from normal behavior, its causes are less apparent. It does appear, however, that schizophrenia has both biological and psychological components at its roots.

Let's first consider the evidence pointing to a biological cause of schizophrenia. Because schizophrenia is more common in some families than in others, ge-

This haunting art was created by an individual suffering from severe mental disturbance.

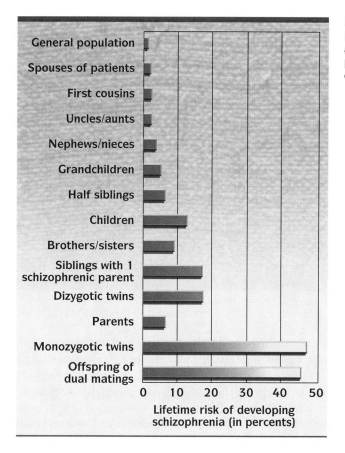

FIGURE 12-1 The closer the genetic links between two people, the greater the likelihood that if one experiences schizophrenia, so will the other. *(Gottesman, 1991.)*

The bar chart shows "Lifetime risk of developing schizophrenia (in percents)" on the x-axis (0 to 50) for the following groups:

- General population
- Spouses of patients
- First cousins
- Uncles/aunts
- Nephews/nieces
- Grandchildren
- Half siblings
- Children
- Brothers/sisters
- Siblings with 1 schizophrenic parent
- Dizygotic twins
- Parents
- Monozygotic twins
- Offspring of dual matings

netic factors seem to be involved in producing at least a susceptibility to or readiness for developing schizophrenia (Gottesman, 1991). For example, research has shown that the closer the genetic link between a person with schizophrenia and another individual, the higher the likelihood that the other person will experience the disorder (see Figure 12-1).

On the other hand, if genetics alone were responsible, then if one identical (monozygotic) twin has schizophrenia, the chance of the other twin having schizophrenia would be 100 percent, since identical twins share the same genetic makeup. Moreover, research that has sought to find a link between schizophrenia and a particular gene has been only partly successful (e.g., Crow, 1990; Crowe et al., 1991; Wang et al., 1993). Apparently schizophrenia is produced by more than genetic factors alone (Holzman & Matthysse, 1990; Iacono & Grove, 1993).

One of the most intriguing biological hypotheses to explain schizophrenia is that the brains of victims harbor either a biochemical imbalance or structural abnormality. For example, the *dopamine hypothesis* suggests that schizophrenia occurs when there is excess activity in those areas of the brain that use dopamine as a neurotransmitter (Wong et al., 1988; Seeman et al., 1993). This hypothesis came to light after the discovery that drugs that block dopamine action in brain pathways can be highly effective in reducing the symptoms of schizophrenia.

Unfortunately, the dopamine hypothesis does not provide the whole story. Drugs that block dopamine action produce a biological reaction in just a few hours after they're taken—yet the symptoms of schizophrenia do not subside for weeks. If the hypothesis were entirely correct, we would expect an immediate improvement in schizophrenic symptoms. Moreover, these drugs are effective in reducing symptoms not only in schizophrenics but also in those suffering from very different sorts of psychological problems such as mania and depression (Pickar,

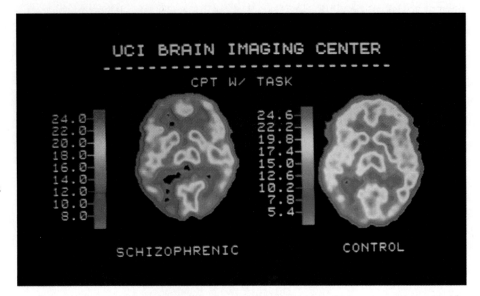

Compare these PET scans, which show differences in functioning between two people, one of whom has been diagnosed with schizophrenia. Both are performing a vigilance task. In the non-schizophrenic, the task increases prefrontal cortex metabolism (left). For the person with schizophrenia, however, this does not occur (right).

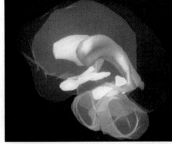

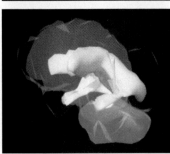

FIGURE 12-2 Structural changes in the brain have been found in people with schizophrenia. In the first magnetic resonance imaging (MRI) reconstruction of a patient with schizophrenia, the hippocampus (yellow) is shrunken, and the ventricles (gray) are enlarged and fluid-filled. In contrast, the brain of a person without the disorder appears structurally different. *(N. C. Andreasen, University of Iowa.)*

1988; Andreasen, 1989). Nevertheless, the dopamine hypothesis has provided a starting point in understanding biochemical factors in schizophrenia.

Other biological explanations for schizophrenia propose that structural abnormalities exist in the brains of people with the disorder. For example, the hippocampus and ventricles of the brains of those with schizophrenia differ in size from those who do not have the disorder (Suddath et al., 1990). Consistent with such research, the way in which the brain functions differs between people with schizophrenia and those who do not suffer from the disorder (Waddington, 1990; Anderson et al., 1994). The brain scans shown in Figure 12-2 illustrate some of these differences.

Psychological Perspectives on the Causes of Schizophrenia Although biological factors provide some pieces of the puzzle of schizophrenia, we still need to consider past and current experiences found in the environments of people who develop the disturbance. For instance, psychoanalytic approaches suggest that schizophrenia is a form of regression to earlier experiences and stages of life. Freud believed, for instance, that people with schizophrenia lack strong enough egos to cope with their unacceptable impulses. They regress to the oral stage—a time in which the id and ego are not yet separated. Therefore, individuals suffering from schizophrenia essentially lack an ego and act out impulses without concern for reality.

Although this reasoning is theoretically plausible, there is little evidence to support psychoanalytic explanations. Only slightly more convincing are theories that look toward the families of people with schizophrenia. For instance, such families often display abnormal communication patterns. These families may also differ on a number of other dimensions, including socioeconomic status, anxiety level, and general degree of stress present (Wynne et al., 1975; Lidz & Fleck, 1985).

Of course, the faulty communication patterns found in families of a person with schizophrenia may be as much a consequence of the schizophrenia as a cause. Still, theorists taking a behavioral perspective believe such communication problems support a *learned-inattention theory of schizophrenia* (Ullmann & Krasner, 1975). According to the learned-inattention view, schizophrenia is a learned behavior consisting of a set of inappropriate responses to social stimuli. Rather than respond to others, people with schizophrenia have learned to ignore appropriate stimuli. They pay attention instead to stimuli that are not related to normal social interactions. Because this results in bizarre behavior, others respond to them in a negative way, leading to social rejection and unpleasant interactions, and, ultimately, to an even less appropriate response by the individual. Eventually, the individual begins to "tune out" appropriate stimuli and develops schizophrenic characteristics.

The Multiple Causes of Schizophrenia   As we have seen, there is research supporting several different biological and psychological causes of schizophrenia. It is likely, then, that not just one but several causes jointly explain the onset of the problem. The predominant approach used today, the *predisposition model of schizophrenia,* considers a number of factors simultaneously (Zubin & Spring, 1977; Cornblatt & Erlenmeyer-Kimling, 1985; Fowles, 1992). This model suggests that individuals may inherit a predisposition or an inborn sensitivity to schizophrenia which makes them particularly vulnerable to stressful factors in the environment. The stressors may vary—social rejection or dysfunctional family communication patterns—but if they are strong enough and are coupled with a genetic predisposition, the result will be the onset of schizophrenia. Similarly, if the genetic predisposition is strong enough, schizophrenia may occur even when the environmental stressors are relatively weak.

In sum, schizophrenia is associated with several kinds of biological and psychological factors. It is increasingly clear, then, that schizophrenia is not produced by any single factor but by a combination of interrelated variables (Fowles, 1992; Straube & Oades, 1992; Carpenter & Buchanen, 1994).

Personality Disorders: Lacking Distress

I had always wanted lots of things; as a child I can remember wanting a bullet that a friend of mine had brought in to show the class. I took it and put it into my school bag and when my friend noticed it was missing, I was the one who stayed after school with him and searched the room, and I was the one who sat with him and bitched about the other kids and how one of them took his bullet. I even went home with him to help him break the news to his uncle, who had brought it home from the war for him.

But that was petty compared with the stuff I did later. I wanted a Ph.D. very badly, but I didn't want to work very hard—just enough to get by. I never did the experiments I reported; hell, I was smart enough to make up the results. I knew enough about statistics to make anything look plausible. I got my master's degree without even spending one hour in a laboratory. I mean, the professors believed anything. I'd stay out all night drinking and being with my friends, and the next day I'd get in just before them and tell 'em I'd been in the lab all night. They'd actually feel sorry for me. I did my doctoral research the same way, except it got published and there was some excitement about my findings. The research helped me get my first college teaching job. There my goal was tenure.

The rules at my university were about the same as at any other. You had to publish and you had to be an effective teacher. "Gathering" data and publishing it was never any problem for me, so that was fine. But teaching was evaluated on the basis of forms completed by students at the end of each semester. I'm a fair-to-good teacher, but I had to be sure that my record showed me as excellent. The task was simple. Each semester, I collected the evaluation forms, took out all the fair-to-bad ones and replaced them with doctored ones. It would take me a whole evening, but I'd sit down with a bunch of different colored pens and pencils and would fill in as many as 300 of the forms. Needless to say, I was awarded tenure. (Duke & Nowicki, 1979, pp. 309–310)

Before you begin to assume that all college professors are like this one, it should be stated that this person represents a clear example of someone with a personality disorder. A **personality disorder** is different from the other problems we have discussed in this chapter, because there is often little sense of personal distress associated with the psychological maladjustment of those affected. In fact, people with personality disorders frequently lead seemingly normal lives. However, just below the surface lies a set of inflexible, maladaptive personality traits that do

Personality disorder: A mental disorder characterized by a set of inflexible, maladaptive personality traits that keep a person from functioning appropriately in society

Antisocial, or **sociopathic, personality disorder:** A disorder in which individuals display no regard for moral and ethical rules or for the rights of others

not permit such individuals to function appropriately as members of society (Millon & Davis, 1995; Derksen, 1995).

The best-known type of personality disorder is the **antisocial, or sociopathic, personality disorder.** Individuals with this disturbance tend to display no regard for the moral and ethical rules of society or for the rights of others. Although they appear intelligent and are usually likable at first, they can be seen as manipulative and deceptive upon closer examination. Moreover, they lack a conscience, guilt, or anxiety over their wrongdoing. When those with an antisocial personality behave in a way that injures someone else, they understand intellectually that they have caused the harm but feel no remorse.

People with antisocial personalities are often impulsive, and they lack the ability to withstand frustration. Finally, they can be extremely manipulative. They may have excellent social skills, being charming and engaging and able to convince others to do what they want. Some of the best con men have antisocial personalities.

What causes such an unusual constellation of problems? A variety of factors have been suggested, ranging from a biologically induced inability to experience emotions appropriately to problems in family relationships (e.g., Newman & Kosson, 1986; Gillstrom & Hare, 1988; Nigg & Goldsmith, 1994). For example, in many cases of antisocial behavior, the individual has come from a home in which a parent has died or left, or one in which there is a lack of affection, a lack of consistency in discipline, or outright rejection. Other explanations concentrate on sociocultural factors, since an unusually high proportion of antisocial personalities come from lower socioeconomic groups. Some researchers have suggested that the breakdown of societal rules, norms, and regulations that may be found in severely deprived economic environments may encourage the development of antisocial personalities (Melges & Bowlby, 1969). Still, no one has been able to pinpoint the specific causes of antisocial personalities, and it is likely that some combination of factors is responsible (Hare, Hart, & Harpur, 1991).

Narcissistic personality disorder: A personality disorder characterized by an exaggerated sense of self-importance and an inability to experience empathy for others

Another example of a personality disturbance is the **narcissistic personality disorder,** characterized by an exaggerated sense of self-importance. Those with the disorder expect special treatment from others, while at the same time they disregard others' feelings. In some ways, in fact, the main attribute of the narcissistic personality is an inability to experience empathy for other people.

There are several other categories of personality disorder, ranging in severity from individuals who may simply be regarded by others as eccentric, obnoxious, or difficult, to people who act in a manner that is criminal and dangerous to others. Although they are not out of touch with reality in the way that schizophrenics are, people with personality disorders lead lives that are on the fringes of society.

RECAP AND REVIEW

Recap

- Mood disorders are characterized by disturbances in emotional feelings that are so great they impede daily living.

- Schizophrenia represents the most common diagnosis for those hospitalized for mental disturbance.

- People with personality disorders do not feel the personal distress associated with other disorders, but they do have maladaptive traits that prevent them from functioning appropriately as normal members of society.

Review

1. Henry's feelings of deep despair, worthlessness, and loneliness have persisted for months. His symptoms are indicative of:
   a. An adjustment reaction   c. Major depression
   b. Normal depression   d. Affective depression

2. States of extreme euphoria and energy paired with severe depression characterize _____ disorder.

3. Arthur's belief that his thoughts are being controlled by beings from outer space is an example of a _____.

4. _____ schizophrenia shows symptoms that are sudden and easily identifiable, while _____ schizophrenia develops gradually over a person's lifespan.

5. The _____ _____ states that schizophrenia may be caused by an excess of certain neurotransmitters in the brain.

6. Which of the following theories states that schizophrenia is caused by the combination of genetic and environmental stressors?
   a. Learned-inattention theory
   b. Predisposition model
   c. Dopamine hypothesis
   d. Learned-helplessness theory

7. The _____ personality disorder is characterized by a disregard for societal rules or others' rights.

Ask Yourself

Personality disorders are often characterized by a lack of visibility. Many people with personality disorders seem to live basically normal lives and are not a threat to others. Since these people can function well in society, why should they be considered "ill"?

(Answers to review questions are on page 430.)

• *What indicators signal a need for the help of a mental-health practitioner?*

BEYOND THE MAJOR DISORDERS: ABNORMAL BEHAVIOR IN PERSPECTIVE

The various forms of abnormal behavior described in *DSM-IV* cover much wider ground than we have been able to discuss in this chapter. Some we have considered in earlier chapters, such as *psychoactive substance-use disorder,* in which problems arise from the abuse of drugs (Chapter 4), and *sexual disorders,* in which one's sexual activity is unsatisfactory. Another important class of disorders we have previously touched upon is *organic mental disorders.* These are problems that have a purely biological basis. There are other disorders we have not mentioned at all, and each of the classes we have discussed can be divided into several subcategories.

Keep in mind that the specific nature of the disorders included in *DSM-IV* is a reflection of late-twentieth-century Western culture. The classification system is a snapshot of how its authors viewed mental disorder when it was published in 1994. In fact, the development of the latest version of *DSM* was a source of great controversy, in part reflecting issues that divide society.

For example, two disorders were particularly controversial during the revision process. One, known as the "self-defeating personality disorder," was a category that ultimately was removed from the appendix where it had appeared in the previous revision. The self-defeating personality disorder was meant to apply to cases in which a person remains in relationships in which they receive unpleasant and demeaning treatment without leaving or taking other action. It was typically used to describe people who remained in abusive relationships.

Although some clinicians argued that it was a valid category, one that they observed in their clinical practice, there ultimately seemed to be a lack of research evidence supporting its existence. Furthermore, some critics had complained that use of the label ended up condemning targets of abuse for their plight, a blame-the-victim phenomenon, and as a result, the category was removed from the manual.

A second and even more controversial category was "premenstrual dysphoric disorder." The disorder was characterized by severe, incapacitating mood changes or depression that are related to a woman's menstrual cycle. Some critics argue that including such a classification simply labels normal female behavior as a disorder. The former U.S. Surgeon General, Antonia Novello, suggested that what "in women is called PMS [premenstrual syndrome, a similar classification] in men is called healthy aggression and initiative" (Cotton, 1993, p. 270). Advocates

for including the disorder prevailed, however, and premenstrual dysphoric disorder was placed in the appendix of *DSM-IV.*

Such controversies underline that our understanding of abnormal behavior is a reflection of the society and culture in which we live. Future revisions of *DSM* may include a different catalog of disorders. Even now, other cultures might well include a list of disorders that look very different from the current one, as we discuss next.

Exploring Diversity

DSM and Culture—and the Culture of DSM

In most people's estimation, a person who hears voices of the recently deceased is probably a victim of some psychological disturbance. Yet members of the Plains Indian tribe routinely hear the voices of the dead calling to them from the afterlife.

This is but one example of the role that culture plays in the labeling of behavior as abnormal. In fact, of all the major adult disorders found within the *DSM* categorization, just four are found across all cultures of the world: schizophrenia, bipolar disorder, major depression, and anxiety disorders (Kleinman, 1991). *All* the rest are particular to North America and western Europe.

Take, for instance, anorexia nervosa, first discussed in Chapter 9. Anorexia nervosa is a disorder in which people, particularly young women, develop inaccurate views of their body appearance, become obsessed with their weight, and refuse to eat, sometimes starving in the process. This disorder occurs only in cultures holding the societal standard that slender female bodies are most desirable. Because for most of the world such a standard does not exist, anorexia nervosa does not occur. Interestingly, there is no anorexia nervosa in all of Asia, with two

In many cultures, including some Native American tribes, the ability to hear the voices of departed spirits is considered a devine gift. In modern, industrialized societies, however, hearing voices is viewed as a sign of psychological disturbance.

exceptions: the upper and upper-middle classes of Japan and Hong Kong, where Western influence tends to be great. It is also noteworthy that anorexia nervosa is a fairly recent disorder. In the 1600s and 1700s, it did not occur, because the ideal female body in Western society at that time was a plump one.

Similarly, dissociative identity disorder (multiple personality) only makes sense as a problem in societies in which a sense of self is fairly concrete. In places like India, the self is based more on external factors that are relatively independent of the person. There, when an individual displays symptoms of what people in Western society would call dissociative identity disorder, it is assumed that that person is possessed either by demons (which is viewed as a malady) or by gods (which is not a cause for treatment).

Furthermore, even though such disorders as schizophrenia are found throughout the world, the particular symptoms of the disorder are influenced by cultural factors. Hence, catatonic schizophrenia, in which unmoving patients appear to be frozen into the same position sometimes for days, is rare in North America and western Europe. In contrast, in India, 80 percent of those with schizophrenia are catatonic.

Other cultures have disorders that do not appear in the West. For example, in Malaysia, a behavior called "amok" is characterized by a wild outburst in which a person, usually quiet and withdrawn, kills or severely injures another. Another example is "koro," found in southeast Asian males who develop an intense panic that their penis is about to withdraw into their abdomen. Finally, a disorder sometimes found in rural Japan is "kitsunetsuki," in which those afflicted believe they have been possessed by foxes and display facial expressions characteristic of the animals (Carson, Butcher, & Coleman, 1992).

In sum, we should not assume that *DSM* provides the final word on psychological disorders. The disorders it includes are very much a creation and function of Western culture at a particular moment in time, and its categories should not be seen as universally applicable.

The Prevalence of Psychological Disorders: The Mental State of the Union

How common are the kinds of psychological disorders we've been discussing? Here's one answer: Every second person you meet is likely to suffer, at some point during his or her life, from a psychological disorder.

At least that's the conclusion from the most recent research on the prevalence of psychological disorders. In a massive study, researchers conducted face-to-face interviews with more than 8000 men and women between the ages of 15 and 54 years. The sample was designed to be representative of the population of the United States. According to results of the study, 48 percent of those interviewed experienced a disorder at some point in their lives. In addition, 30 percent experienced a disorder in any given year (Kessler et al., 1994).

The most common disorder was depression, with 17 percent of those surveyed reporting a major episode at least once in their lifetime (see Figure 12-3). Ten percent of those surveyed had suffered from depression during the current year. The next most frequent disorder was alcohol dependence, which occurred at a lifetime incidence rate of 14 percent. In addition, 7 percent of those interviewed had experienced alcohol dependence during the last year. Other frequent psychological disorders are drug dependence, disorders involving panic (such as an overwhelming fear of talking to strangers or terror of heights), and posttraumatic stress disorder.

The study also found some unexpected gender differences. For example, 12 percent of women experienced posttraumatic stress disorder—a rate twice as high as for men. The researchers conclude that posttraumatic stress disorder,

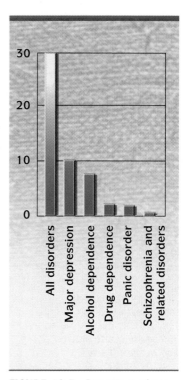

FIGURE 12-3 Percentage of people in the United States who reported a psychological disorder in the preceding year. *(Kessler et al., 1994.)*

which occurs following a sudden, severe psychological shock, represents a major psychological risk for women.

The results of the study highlight the extent of the need for mental-health services. For example, some 14 percent of those interviewed report having had three or more psychological disorders at some time during their lives. Statistically, the people making up this group, which is the segment of the population most in need of psychological services, tend to be low-income city-dwellers, poorly educated white women who are in their twenties and thirties.

Despite the relatively high prevalence of psychological disorders, the findings do not suggest that the country is on the verge of a collective breakdown. Although the results indicate that more people than expected experience the symptoms of psychological disorder, they do not indicate what effect they have had on people's family, schooling, or working situations. Furthermore, the study's finding that only 25 percent had ever sought professional help for their problems suggests that many people recover by themselves.

The Informed Consumer of Psychology

Deciding When You Need Help

After you consider the range and variety of psychological disturbances that can afflict people, it would not be surprising if you began to feel that you were suffering from one (or more) of the problems we have discussed. In fact, there is a name for this perception: *medical student's disease.* Although in the present case it might more aptly be labeled "psychology student's disease," the basic symptoms are the same: feeling that you suffer from the same sorts of problems you are studying.

Most often, of course, your concerns will be unwarranted. As we have discussed, the differences between normal and abnormal behavior are often so fuzzy that it is easy to jump to the conclusion that one has the same symptoms that are involved in serious forms of mental disturbance.

Before coming to such a conclusion, though, it is important to keep in mind that from time to time we all experience a wide range of emotions and subjective experiences, and it is not unusual to feel deeply unhappy, to fantasize about bizarre situations, or to feel anxiety about life's circumstances. It is the persistence, depth, and consistency of such behavior that sets normal reactions apart from abnormal ones. If you have not previously had serious doubts about the normality of your behavior, it is unlikely that reading about others' psychological disorders should prompt you to reevaluate your earlier conclusion.

On the other hand, many people do have problems that warrant concern, and in such cases it is important to consider the possibility that professional help is warranted. The following guidelines can help you determine if outside intervention might be useful (Engler & Goleman, 1922):

■ Long-term feelings of distress that interfere with your sense of well-being, competence, and ability to function effectively in daily activities
■ Occasions in which you experience overwhelmingly high stress, accompanied by feelings of inability to cope with the situation
■ Prolonged depression or feelings of hopelessness, particularly when they do not have any clear cause (such as the death of someone close)
■ Withdrawal from other people
■ A chronic physical problem for which no physical cause can be determined
■ A fear or compulsion that prevents you from engaging in everyday activities
■ Feelings that other people are out to get you or are talking about and plotting against you

■ The inability to interact effectively with others, preventing the development of friendships and loving relationships

The above criteria can serve as a rough set of guidelines for determining when the normal problems of everyday living are beyond the point that you are capable of dealing with them yourself. In such situations, the least reasonable approach would be to pore over the psychological disorders we have discussed in an attempt to pigeonhole yourself into a specific category. A more reasonable strategy is to consider seeking professional help—a possibility we discuss in the next chapter.

RECAP AND REVIEW

Recap
- Sexual disorders, psychoactive substance-use disorders, and organic mental disorders are other prevalent forms of abnormal behavior.
- What is considered abnormal behavior varies from one culture to another.
- Almost half of all people in the United States have experienced a psychological disorder at some point in their lives.
- Several guidelines can be used to determine when professional help is warranted for a psychological disorder.

Review
1. The latest version of *DSM* is considered to be the definitive guideline on defining mental disorders. True or false?
2. _____ _____ _____ , characterized by severe, incapacitating mood changes or depression related to a woman's menstrual cycle, was eventually added to the appendix of *DSM-IV* despite controversy surrounding its inclusion.
3. Match the disorder with the culture in which it is most common:

1. Amok
2. Anorexia nervosa
3. Kitsunetsuki
4. Catatonic schizophrenia

a. India
b. Malaysia
c. United States
d. Japan

4. Recent research on the prevalence of psychological disorders has found that _____ is the most common, with 17 percent of those surveyed reporting a major episode at least once in their lifetimes.

Ask Yourself
Society and culture can have a strong impact on determining what passes for normal and abnormal behavior. How would you "revise" *DSM-IV* to more accurately reflect cultural differences in determining psychological disorders?

(Answers to review questions are on page 435.)

LOOKING BACK

How can we distinguish normal from abnormal behavior?
1. The most satisfactory definition of abnormal behavior is one based on the psychological consequences of the behavior, which are thought of as abnormal if they produce a sense of distress, anxiety, or guilt or if they are harmful to others. Another useful definition considers people who cannot adapt to society and who are unable to function effectively to be abnormal. There are also legal definitions that focus on whether a person is "insane," which is a legal, not psychological, term.
2. No single definition is totally adequate. Therefore, it is reasonable to consider abnormal and normal behavior in terms of gradations, ranging from completely normal functioning to extremely abnormal behavior. Obviously, behavior typically falls somewhere between these two extremes.

What are the major models of abnormal behavior used by mental-health professionals?
3. The medical model of abnormal behavior views abnormality as a symptom of an underlying disease that requires a cure. Psychoanalytic models suggest that abnormal behavior is caused by conflicts in the unconscious stemming from past experience. In order to resolve psychological problems, people need to resolve the unconscious conflicts.
4. In contrast to the medical and psychoanalytic models, behavioral approaches view abnormal behavior not as a symptom of some underlying problem, but as the problem itself. To resolve the problem, one must change the behavior.
5. The cognitive approach, often referred to as the cognitive behavioral perspective, suggests that abnormal behavior is the result of faulty cognitions. In this view, abnormal behavior can

be remedied through a change in cognitions (thoughts and beliefs).

6. Humanistic approaches view people as rational and motivated to get along with others; abnormal behavior is seen as a difficulty in fulfilling one's needs. People are considered to be in control of their lives and able to resolve their own problems.

7. Sociocultural approaches view abnormal behavior in terms of difficulties arising from family and other social relationships. The sociocultural model concentrates on such factors as socioeconomic status and the social rules society creates to define normal and abnormal behavior.

What classification system is used to categorize abnormal behavior?

8. The system for classifying abnormal behavior that is used most widely today is *DSM-IV—Diagnostic and Statistical Manual of Mental Disorders* (4th ed.).

What are the major psychological disorders?

9. Anxiety disorders are present when a person experiences so much anxiety that it impedes daily functioning. Specific types of anxiety disorders include generalized anxiety disorder, panic disorder, phobic disorder, and obsessive-compulsive disorder. Generalized anxiety disorder occurs when a person experiences long-term anxiety with no apparent cause. Panic disorders are marked by panic attacks, which are sudden, intense feelings of anxiety. Phobic disorders are characterized by intense, irrational fears of specific objects or situations. People with obsessive-compulsive disorders display obsessions (recurring thoughts or ideas) or compulsions (repetitious, unwanted behaviors).

10. Somatoform disorders are psychological difficulties that are displayed through physical problems. An example is hypochondriasis, in which there is a constant fear of illness and a preoccupation with disease. Another somatoform disorder is conversion disorder, in which there is an actual physical difficulty that occurs without a physiological cause.

11. Dissociative disorders are marked by the splitting apart, or dissociation, of crucial parts of personality that are usually integrated. The three major kinds of dissociative disorders are dissociative identity disorder (multiple personality), dissociative amnesia, and dissociative fugue.

What are the most severe forms of psychological disorders?

12. Mood disorders are characterized by emotional states of depression or euphoria so strong that they intrude on everyday living. In major depression, people experience sorrow so deep that they may become suicidal. In bipolar disorder, stages of mania, in which there is an extended sense of elation and powerfulness, alternate with depression.

13. Schizophrenia is one of the severest forms of mental illness. The manifestations of schizophrenia include declines in functioning, thought and language disturbances, delusions, perceptual disorders, emotional disturbance, and withdrawal from others. There is strong evidence linking schizophrenia to genetic, biochemical, and environmental factors. According to the predisposition model, there is likely to be an interaction among various factors.

14. People with personality disorders experience little or no personal distress, but they do suffer from an inability to function as normal members of society. The best-known type of

personality disorder is the antisocial, or sociopathic, personality disorder, in which the moral and ethical rules of society are ignored. The narcissistic personality is characterized by an exaggerated sense of importance.

15. There are many other categories of disorders, including sexual disorders, psychoactive substance-use disorders, and organic mental disorders.

16. Students of psychology are susceptible to the same sort of "disease" that afflicts medical students: the perception that they suffer from the problems they are studying. Unless their psychological difficulties are persistent, have depth, and are consistent, however, it is unlikely that their concerns are valid.

What indicators signal a need for the help of a professional?

17. A number of signals indicate a need for professional help. These include long-term feelings of psychological distress, feelings of inability to cope with stress, prolonged feelings of hopelessness, withdrawal from other people, chronic physical problems with no apparent causes, phobias and compulsions, paranoia, and an inability to interact with others.

KEY TERMS AND CONCEPTS

medical model of abnormality (p. 405)
psychoanalytic model of abnormality (p. 406)
behavioral model of abnormality (p. 406)
cognitive model of abnormality (p. 407)
humanistic model of abnormality (p. 407)
sociocultural model of abnormality (p. 407)
Diagnostic and Statistical Manual of Mental Disorders (4th ed.) *(DSM-IV)* (p. 409)

anxiety disorder (p. 412)
generalized anxiety disorder (p. 412)
panic disorder (p. 412)
phobias (p. 413)
obsessive-compulsive disorder (p. 413)
obsession (p. 413)
compulsions (p. 414)
somatoform disorders (p. 415)
conversion disorder (p. 415)
dissociative disorders (p. 416)
dissociative identity disorder, or multiple personality (p. 416)

dissociative amnesia (p. 417)
dissociative fugue (p. 418)
mood disorders (p. 419)
major depression (p. 419)
mania (p. 420)
bipolar disorder (p. 421)
learned helplessness (p. 421)
schizophrenia (p. 422)
personality disorder (p. 427)
antisocial, or sociopathic, personality disorder (p. 428)
narcissistic personality disorder (p. 428)

ANSWERS TO PREVIOUS REVIEW

1. *False*; the development of the latest version of *DSM* was a source of great controversy, in part reflecting issues that divide society. **2.** Premenstrual dysphoric disorder **3.** 1-b, 2-c, 3-d, 4-a **4.** depression

CHAPTER 13
TREATMENT OF PSYCHOLOGICAL DISORDERS

Conquering Schizophrenia

For weeks they had practiced dance steps, shopped for formals, fretted about hairstyles and what on earth to say to their partners. Now the Big City band was pumping up the volume, and the whole ballroom was beginning to shake. Brandon Fitch, wearing a pinstripe suit and an ear-to-ear grin, shimmied with a high-stepping blonde. Daphne Moss, sporting a floral dress and white corsage, delighted her dad by letting him cut in. The usually quiet Kevin Buchberger leaped onto the dance floor and flat-out boogied for the first time in his life, while Kevin Namkoong grabbed an electric guitar and jammed with the band. The prom at Case Western Reserve University had hit full tilt.

But this was a prom that almost never was. Most of the 175 participants were in their 30s; they had missed the proms of their youth—along with other adolescent rites of passage. Don't ask where they were at 18 or 21. The memories are too bleak, too fragmented to convey. They had organized this better-late-than-never prom to celebrate their remarkable "awakening" to reality after many years of being lost in the darkness of schizophrenia. The revelers were, in a sense, the laughing, dancing embodiments of a new wave of drug therapy that is revolutionizing the way doctors are dealing with this most devilish of mental illnesses. . . .

Moss, Buchberger, Fitch and their fellow promgoers were awakened from their long nightmare of insanity by a remarkable drug called clozapine (brand name: Clozaril). The dinner dance, organized with help from psychiatrists and counselors at Case Western Reserve's affiliated University Hospitals, in Cleveland, served as a bittersweet celebration of shared loss and regained hope. "Those of us who are ill travel on a different road," said prom chairman Fitch in a welcoming address to his fellow refugees from madness. "We would have liked to have gone to our senior proms, but fate didn't give us that chance." (Wallis & Willwerth, 1992, p. 53)

LOOKING AHEAD

The drug that has brought new life to people like Daphne Moss, Kevin Buchberger, and Brandon Fitch is just one of many that, along with other new treatment approaches, have revolutionized the treatment of psychological disorders in the last

Brandon Fitch, a schizophrenic being successfully treated with clozapine, is finally able to enjoy the prom that his illness caused him to miss some fifteen years before.

437

several decades. Although there are literally hundreds of different treatment approaches, ranging from one-session informal counseling sessions to long-term drug therapy, all have a common objective: the relief of psychological disorders, with the ultimate aim of enabling individuals to achieve richer, more meaningful, and more fulfilling lives.

In this chapter, we explore a number of basic issues related to the treatment of abnormal behavior: How do we treat people with psychological disorders? Who is the most appropriate person to provide treatment? What is the future like for people with severe disturbances? What is the most reasonable therapeutic approach to use? Is one form of therapy better than the others? Does any therapy *really* work? How does one choose the "right" kind of therapy and therapist?

Most of the chapter focuses on the various approaches used by providers of treatment for psychological disturbances. Despite their diversity, these approaches fall into two main categories: psychologically based and biologically based therapy. Psychologically based therapy, or **psychotherapy,** is the process in which a patient (often referred to as the client) and a professional attempt to remedy psychological difficulties. In psychotherapy, the emphasis is on change as a result of discussions and interactions between therapist and client. In contrast, **biologically based therapy** relies on drugs and other medical procedures to improve psychological functioning.

As we describe the various approaches to therapy, it is important to keep in mind that, although the distinctions may seem clear-cut, there is a good deal of overlap in the classifications and procedures employed, and even in the training and titles of various kinds of therapists (see Table 13-1). In fact, many therapists today use a variety of methods with a given person, in what is referred to as an *eclectic approach to therapy.* Assuming that abnormal behavior is often the product of both psychological and biological processes, eclectic therapists may draw from several perspectives simultaneously, in an effort to address both the psychological and the biological aspects of a person's problems (Goldfried & Castonguay, 1992; Freedheim, 1992; Stricker & Gold, 1993).

Psychotherapy: The process in which a patient (client) and a professional attempt to remedy the client's psychological difficulties

Biologically based therapy: An approach to therapy that uses drugs and other medical procedures to improve psychological functioning

---

TABLE 13-1   Getting Help from the Right Person

Clinical psychologist
Ph.D. or Psy.D. who specializes in assessment and treatment of psychological difficulties

Counseling psychologist
Ph.D. who usually treats day-to-day adjustment problems in a counseling setting, such as a university mental-health clinic

Psychiatrist
Physician with postgraduate training in abnormal behavior who can prescribe medication as part of treatment

Psychoanalyst
Either a physician or a psychologist who specializes in psychoanalysis, the treatment technique first developed by Freud

Psychiatric social worker
Professional with a master's degree and specialized training in treating people in home and community settings

Each of these trained professionals could be expected to give helpful advice and direction, although the nature of the problem a person is experiencing may make one or another more appropriate. For example, a person who is suffering from a severe disturbance and has lost touch with reality will typically require some sort of biologically-based drug therapy. In that case, a psychiatrist—who is a physician—would clearly be the professional of choice. On the other hand, those suffering from milder disorders, such as difficulty in adjusting to the death of a family member, have a broader choice that might include any of the professionals listed above. The decision can be made easier by initial consultations with professionals in mental-health facilities in communities, colleges, and health organizations who often provide guidance in selecting an appropriate therapist.

- *What are the goals of psychologically and biologically based treatment approaches?*
- *What are the basic kinds of psychotherapies?*

PSYCHOTHERAPY: PSYCHOLOGICAL APPROACHES TO TREATMENT

ALICE: I was thinking about this business of standards. I somehow developed a sort of a knack, I guess, of—well—habit—of trying to make people feel at ease around me, or to make things go along smoothly. . . .

THERAPIST: In other words, what you did was always in the direction of trying to keep things smooth and to make other people feel better and to smooth the situation.

ALICE: Yes. I think that's what it was. Now the reason why I did it probably was— I mean, not that I was a good little Samaritan going around making other people happy, but that was probably the role that felt easiest for me to play. I'd been doing it around home so much. I just didn't stand up for my own convictions, until I don't know whether I have any convictions to stand up for.

THERAPIST: You feel that for a long time you've been playing the role of kind of smoothing out the frictions or differences or what not. . . .

ALICE: M-hm.

THERAPIST: Rather than having any opinion or reaction of your own in the situation. Is that it? (Rogers, 1951, pp. 152–153)

MARTHA: The basic problem is that I'm worried about my family. I'm worried about money. And I never seem to be able to relax.

THERAPIST: Why are you worried about your family? Let's go into that, first of all. What's to be concerned about? They have certain demands which you don't want to adhere to.

MARTHA: I was brought up to think that I mustn't be selfish.

THERAPIST: Oh, we'll have to knock *that* out of your head!

MARTHA: I think that that is one of my basic problems.

THERAPIST: That's right. You were brought up to be Florence Nightingale. . . .

MARTHA: And now I try to break away. For instance, they'll call up and say, "Why don't you come Sunday?" And if I say, "No, I'm busy," rather than saying "No, I'll come when it's convenient," they get terribly hurt, and my stomach gets all upset.

THERAPIST: Because you tell yourself, "There I go again. I'm a louse for not devoting myself to them!" As long as you tell yourself that crap, then your stomach or some other part of you will start jumping! But it's your *philosophy,* your *belief,* your *sentence* to yourself—"I'm no goddamned good! How could I do that lousy, stinking thing?" *That's* what's causing your stomach to jump. Now, that is a false sentence. Why are you no goddamned good because you prefer you to them? For that's what it amounts to. *Who* said you're no good—Jesus Christ? Moses? Who said so? The answer is: Your parents said so. And you believe it because they said so. But who the hell are they? (Ellis, 1974, pp. 223–286)

SANDY: My father . . . never took any interest in any of us. (Begins to weep.) It was my mother—rest her soul—who loved us, not our father. He worked her to death. Lord, I miss her. (Weeps uncontrollably.)—I must sound angry at my father. Don't you think I have a right to be angry?

THERAPIST: Do you think you have a right to be angry?

SANDY: Of course, I do! Why are you questioning me? You don't believe me, do you?

THERAPIST: You want me to believe you.

SANDY: I don't care whether you believe me or not. As far as I'm concerned, you're just a wall that I'm talking to—I don't know why I pay for this rotten therapy.—Don't you have any thought or feelings at all? I know what you're thinking—you think I'm crazy—you must be laughing at me—I'll probably be a case in your next book! You're just sitting there—smirking—making me feel like a bad person—thinking I'm wrong for being mad, that I have no right to be mad.

THERAPIST: Just like your father.

SANDY: Yes, you're just like my father.—Oh my God! Just now—I—I—thought I was talking to him. (Sue, Sue, & Sue, 1990, pp. 514–515)

As these excerpts from actual therapy sessions illustrate, therapy for psychological disorders is far from a uniform process. In the first case, the therapist painstakingly mirrors what Alice has said, reflecting back her observations. In contrast, the therapist in the second excerpt is considerably more active, prodding and inflaming the patient. Finally, the third case shows a therapist who says very little at all; the responses to Sandy's declarations are fundamentally noncommittal.

Although diverse in many respects, all psychological approaches see treatment as a way of solving psychological problems by modifying people's behavior and helping them gain a better understanding of themselves and their past, present, and future. We will consider four major kinds of psychotherapies: psychodynamic, behavioral, cognitive, and humanistic, all of which are based on the different models of abnormal behavior discussed in Chapter 12.

Psychodynamic Treatment: Piercing the Unconscious

Psychodynamic therapy: Therapy based on the notion, first suggested by Freud, that the basic sources of abnormal behavior are unresolved past conflicts and anxiety

Psychodynamic therapy is based on the premise, first suggested by Freud in his psychoanalytic approach to personality, that the primary sources of abnormal behavior are unresolved past conflicts and the possibility that unacceptable unconscious impulses will enter consciousness. To guard against this anxiety-provoking possibility, individuals employ *defense mechanisms,* psychological strategies that protect themselves from these unconscious impulses (see Chapter 11).

The most common defense mechanism is repression, in which threatening conflicts and impulses are pushed back into the unconscious. Although repression typically occurs, our unacceptable conflicts and impulses can never be completely buried. Therefore, some of the anxiety associated with them can produce abnormal behavior in the form of what Freud called *neurotic symptoms.*

How does one rid oneself of the anxiety produced by unconscious, unwanted impulses and drives? To Freud, the answer was to confront the conflicts and impulses by bringing them out of the unconscious part of the mind and into the conscious part. Freud assumed that this technique would reduce anxiety stemming from past conflicts and that the patient could then participate in his or her daily life more effectively.

The challenge facing a psychodynamic therapist, then, is how to facilitate patients' attempts to explore and understand their unconscious. The technique that has evolved has a number of components, but basically it consists of leading patients to consider and discuss their past experiences from the time of their first memories, in explicit detail. This process assumes that patients will eventually stumble upon long-hidden crises, traumas, and conflicts that are producing anxiety in their adult lives. They will then be able to "work through"—understand and rectify—these difficulties.

Psychoanalysis: Psychodynamic therapy that involves frequent sessions and often lasts for many years

Psychoanalysis: Freud's Therapy   Classic Freudian psychodynamic therapy, called **psychoanalysis,** tends to be a lengthy and expensive affair. Patients typically meet with their therapists an hour a day, 4 to 6 days a week, for several years. In their sessions, they often use a technique developed by Freud called *free association*. Patients are told to say aloud whatever comes to mind, regardless of its apparent irrelevance or senselessness. In fact, they are urged *not* to try to make sense of things or impose logic upon what they are saying, since it is assumed that the ramblings evoked during free association actually represent important clues to the unconscious, which has its own logic. It is the analyst's job to recognize and label the connections between what is being said and the patient's unconscious (Auld & Hyman, 1991).

Another important tool of the therapist is *dream interpretation*. As we discussed in Chapter 4, this is an examination of the patient's dreams to find clues to the unconscious conflicts and problems being experienced. According to Freud, dreams provide a close look at the unconscious because people's defenses tend to be lowered when they are asleep. But even in dreaming there is a censoring of thoughts; events and people in dreams are usually represented by symbols. Because of this phenomenon, one must move beyond the surface description of the dream, the *manifest content,* and consider its underlying meaning, the *latent content,* which reveals the true message of the dream.

The processes of free association and dream interpretation do not always move forward easily. The same unconscious forces that initially produced repression may work to keep past difficulties out of the conscious, producing resistance. *Resistance* is an inability or unwillingness to discuss or reveal particular memories, thoughts, or motivations. Resistance can be expressed in a number of ways. For instance, patients may be discussing childhood memories and suddenly forget what they were saying, or they may completely change the subject. It is the therapist's job to pick up instances of resistance and to interpret their meaning, as well as to ensure that patients return to the subject—which is likely to hold difficult or painful memories for them.

Because of the close, almost intimate interaction between patient and psychoanalyst, the relationship between the two often becomes emotionally charged and takes on a complexity unlike most others. Patients may come to see their analyst as symbolic of significant others in their past, perhaps a parent or a lover, and apply some of their feelings for that person to the analyst—a phenomenon known as *transference*.

Transference can be used by a therapist to help the patient re-create past relationships that were psychologically difficult. For instance, if a patient undergoing transference views his therapist as symbolic of his father—with whom he had a difficult relationship—the patient and therapist may "redo" an earlier interaction, this time including more positive aspects. Through this process, conflicts regarding the real father may be resolved. (Practitioners of psychoanalysis would see transference at work in Sandy's comment in the example of therapy earlier in this chapter that the therapist is "just like her father.")

Contemporary Alternatives to Psychoanalysis   Time and money: patients in psychoanalysis need a lot of both. As you can imagine, few people have the time, money, or patience that participating in years of traditional psychoanalysis requires. Moreover, there is no conclusive evidence that psychoanalysis, as originally conceived by Freud, works better than other, more contemporary versions of psychodynamic therapy. Today, for instance, psychodynamic therapy tends to be shorter, usually lasting no longer than 3 months or twenty sessions. The therapist takes a more active role than Freud would have liked, controlling the course of therapy and prodding and advising the patient with considerable directness. Finally, there is less emphasis on a patient's past history and childhood. Instead, a more here-and-now approach is used, in which the therapist concentrates on an individual's current relationships and specific complaints (MacKenzie, 1990; Ursano, Sonnenberg, & Lazar, 1991; HMHL, 1994b).

Even with its current modifications, psychodynamic therapy has its critics. It is still relatively time-consuming and expensive, especially in comparison with other forms of psychotherapy that we will discuss later. Moreover, certain kinds of patients tend to be well suited for this method, especially those who suffer from anxiety disorders and those who are highly articulate. These characteristics have been designated as a stereotype of the perfect patient known as YAVIS: a patient who is young, attractive, verbal, intelligent, and successful (Schofield, 1964).

Ultimately, the most important concern about psychodynamic treatment is whether it actually works, and here we find no pat answer. Psychodynamic treatment techniques have been controversial since Freud introduced them. Part of the problem is the difficulty in establishing whether or not patients have improved following psychodynamic therapy. One must depend on reports from the therapists or the patients themselves, reports that are obviously open to bias and subjective interpretation.

Critics have questioned the entire theoretical basis of psychodynamic theory, maintaining that there is no proof that such constructs as the unconscious exist. Despite the considerable criticism, though, the psychodynamic treatment approach has remained a viable one. To proponents, it not only provides effective treatment in many cases of psychological disturbance, but also permits the potential development of an unusual degree of insight into one's life (Fonagy & Moran, 1990; Crits-Cristoph, 1992; Shapiro & Emde, 1994).

Behavioral Approaches to Treatment

Perhaps, as a child, you were rewarded by your parents with an ice cream cone when you were especially good . . . or sent to your room if you misbehaved. As we saw in Chapter 5, the principles behind such a child-rearing strategy are valid: Good behavior is maintained by reinforcement, and unwanted behavior can be eliminated by punishment.

Behavioral treatment approaches: Approaches to treating abnormal behavior that assume that both normal and abnormal behaviors are learned and that appropriate treatment consists of learning new behavior or unlearning maladaptive behavior

These principles represent the basic underpinnings of **behavioral treatment approaches.** Building upon the fundamental processes of learning embodied in classical and operant conditioning, behavioral treatment approaches make a fundamental assumption: Both abnormal and normal behaviors are *learned.* People who display abnormal behavior either have failed to learn the skills needed to cope with the problems of everyday living or have acquired faulty skills and patterns that are being maintained through some form of reinforcement. To modify ab-

The relationship between therapist and patient that is characteristic of psychodynamic treatment is intimate and complex, and may be time-consuming and expensive.

normal behavior, then, behavioral approaches propose that people must learn new behavior to replace the faulty skills they have developed and unlearn their maladaptive behavior patterns (Bellack, Hersen, & Kazdin, 1990; Wilson & Agras, 1992; Bergin & Garfield, 1994).

To behavioral psychologists, it is not necessary to delve into people's pasts or their psyches. Rather than viewing abnormal behavior as a symptom of some underlying problem, they consider the abnormal behavior itself as the problem in need of modification. Changing people's behavior to allow them to function more effectively solves the problem—with no need for concern about the underlying cause. In this view, then, if you can change abnormal behavior, you've cured the problem.

Classical Conditioning Approaches   Suppose you bite into your favorite candy bar and then realize that it is infested with ants and that you've swallowed a bunch of them. You immediately become sick to your stomach and throw up. Your long-term reaction? You never eat that kind of candy bar again, and it may actually be months before you eat any type of candy.

This simple example hints at how classical conditioning might be used to modify behavior. Recall from our discussion in Chapter 5 that when a stimulus that naturally evokes a negative response (such as an unpleasant taste or a puff of air in the face) is paired with a previously neutral stimulus (such as the sound of a bell), the neutral stimulus can come to elicit a similar negative reaction by itself. Using this procedure, first developed by Ivan Pavlov, we may create unpleasant reactions to stimuli that previously were enjoyed—possibly to excess—by an individual. The technique, known as *aversive conditioning,* has been used in cases of alcoholism, drug abuse, and smoking.

The basic procedure in aversive conditioning is relatively straightforward. For example, a person with a drinking problem might be given an alcoholic drink along with a drug that causes severe nausea and vomiting. After these two are paired a few times, the alcohol alone becomes associated with the vomiting and loses its appeal. In fact, what typically happens is that just the sight or smell of alcohol triggers the aversive reaction.

Although aversion therapy works reasonably well to inhibit substance-abuse problems such as alcoholism and certain kinds of sexual disorders, its long-term effectiveness is questionable. Moreover, there are important ethical drawbacks to aversion techniques that employ such potent stimuli as electric shock—used only in the most extreme cases (for example, self-mutilation)—instead of drugs that merely induce gastric discomfort (Russo, Carr, & Lovaas, 1980). It is clear, though, that aversion therapy is an important procedure for eliminating maladaptive responses for some period of time—which provides, even if only temporarily, the opportunity to encourage more adaptive behavior patterns (Harris & Handleman, 1990).

The most successful treatment based on classical conditioning is known as systematic desensitization. In **systematic desensitization,** a person is taught to relax and then is gradually exposed to an anxiety-producing stimulus in order to extinguish the response of anxiety (Rachman & Hodgson, 1980; Wolpe, 1990; J. Smith, 1990).

Suppose, for instance, you were extremely afraid of flying. The very thought of being in an airplane made you begin to sweat and shake, and you'd never even been able to get yourself near enough to an airport to know how you'd react if you actually had to fly somewhere. Using systematic desensitization to treat your problem, you would first be trained in relaxation techniques by a behavior therapist (see Table 13-2), learning to relax your body fully—a highly pleasant state, as you might imagine.

The next step would involve the construction of a *hierarchy of fears*—a list, in

Systematic desensitization: A procedure in which a relaxation response is repeatedly paired with a stimulus that evokes anxiety in the hope that the anxiety will be alleviated

TABLE 13-2 How to Elicit the Relaxation Response

Step 1. Pick a focus word or short phrase that's firmly rooted in your personal belief system. For example, a nonreligious individual might choose a neutral word like *one* or *peace* or *love*. A Christian person desiring to use a prayer could pick the opening words of Psalm 23, *The Lord is my shepherd;* a Jewish person could choose *Shalom*.

Step 2. Sit quietly in a comfortable position.

Step 3. Close your eyes.

Step 4. Relax your muscles.

Step 5. Breathe slowly and naturally, repeating your focus word or phrase silently as you exhale.

Step 6. Throughout, assume a passive attitude. Don't worry about how well you're doing. When other thoughts come to mind, simply say to yourself, "Oh, well," and gently return to the repetition.

Step 7. Continue for 10 to 20 minutes. You may open your eyes to check the time, but do not use an alarm. When you finish, sit quietly for a minute or so, at first with your eyes closed and later with your eyes open. Then do not stand for one or two minutes.

Step 8. Practice the technique once or twice a day.

Source: Benson, 1993, p. 240.

order of increasing severity, of the things that are associated with your fears. For instance, your hierarchy might resemble this one:

- Watching a plane fly overhead
- Going to an airport
- Buying a ticket
- Stepping into the plane
- Seeing the plane door close
- Having the plane taxi down the runway
- Taking off
- Being in the air

Once this hierarchy had been developed and you had learned relaxation techniques, the two sets of responses would be associated with each other. To do this, your therapist might ask you to put yourself into a relaxed state and then to imagine yourself in the first situation identified in your hierarchy. After you were able to consider that first step while remaining relaxed, you would move on to the next

These participants in a systematic desensitization program have gradually overcome their fear of flying and are about to "graduate" by taking a brief flight.

situation, eventually moving up the hierarchy in gradual stages until you could imagine yourself being in the air without experiencing anxiety. In some cases, all this would take place in a psychologist's office, while in others, the client would actually be placed in the fear-evoking situation. Thus, it would not be surprising if you were brought, finally, to an airplane to use your relaxation techniques.

Systematic desensitization has proved to be an effective treatment for a number of problems, including phobias, anxiety disorders, and even impotence and fear of sexual contact (Karoly & Kanfer, 1982; Bellack, Hersen, & Kazdin, 1990). As you see, we can learn to enjoy the things we once feared.

Observational Learning and Modeling   If we had to be hit by a car in order to learn the importance of looking both ways before we cross the street, the world would probably suffer from a serious underpopulation problem. Fortunately, this is not necessary, for we learn a significant amount through **observational learning,** by modeling the behavior of other people.

Behavior therapists have used *modeling* to systematically teach people new skills and ways of handling their fears and anxieties. For example, some people have never learned fundamental social skills such as maintaining eye contact with those they are speaking to. A therapist can model the appropriate behavior and thereby teach it to someone deficient in such skills (Sarason, 1976). Children with dog phobias have also been able to overcome their fears by watching another child—called the "Fearless Peer"—repeatedly walk up to a dog, touch it, pet it, and finally play with it (Bandura, Grusec, & Menlove, 1967). Modeling, then, can play an effective role in resolving some kinds of behavior difficulties, especially if the model is rewarded for his or her behavior.

Operant Conditioning Approaches   Consider the A we get for a good paper . . . the raise for fine on-the-job performance . . . the gratitude for helping an elderly person cross the street. Such rewards for our behavior produce a greater likelihood that we will repeat that behavior in the future. Similarly, behavioral approaches using operant conditioning techniques (which demonstrate the effects of rewards and punishments on future behavior) are based on the notion that we should reward people for carrying out desirable behavior, and extinguish behavior that we wish to eliminate through either ignoring or punishing it (Kazdin, 1989).

Probably the best example of the systematic application of operant conditioning principles is the *token system,* whereby a person is rewarded with a token such as a poker chip or some kind of play money for desired behavior. The behavior may range from such simple things as keeping one's room neat to personal grooming to interacting with other people. The tokens that are earned for such behavior can then be exchanged for some desired object or activity, such as snacks, new clothes, or, in extreme cases, being able to sleep in one's own bed (as opposed to on the floor).

Although it is most frequently employed in institutional settings for individuals with relatively serious problems, the system is not unlike what parents do when they give children money for being well behaved—money they can later exchange for something they want. In fact, contingency contracting, a variant of the more extensive token system, has proved quite effective in producing behavior modification. In *contingency contracting,* a written agreement is drawn up between a therapist and a client (or teacher and student or parent and child). The contract states a series of behavioral goals the client hopes to attain. It also specifies the consequences for the client if the goals are reached—usually some explicit reward such as money or additional privileges. Contracts frequently state negative consequences if the goals are not met.

For instance, suppose a person is having difficulty quitting smoking. He and his therapist might devise a contract in which he would pledge that for every day

Observational learning: Learning by watching others' behavior and the consequences of that behavior

he went without a cigarette he would receive a reward. On the other hand, the contract could include punishments for failure. If the patient smoked on a given day, the therapist might send a check—written out in advance by the patient and given to the therapist to hold—to a cause the patient had no interest in supporting (for instance, to the National Rifle Association if the patient is a staunch advocate of gun control).

How Does Behavior Therapy Stack Up?   Behavior therapy is most helpful for certain kinds of problems. For instance, behavior therapy works well for treating phobias and compulsions, for establishing control over impulses, and for learning complex social skills to replace maladaptive behavior. More than any of the other therapeutic techniques, it has produced methods that can be employed by nonprofessionals to change their own behavior. Moreover, it tends to be economical in terms of time, since it is directed toward the solution of carefully defined problems (Wilson et al., 1987; Wilson & Agras, 1992).

On the other hand, behavior therapy is not always effective. For instance, it is not particularly successful in treating deep depression or personality disorders (Brody, 1990). In addition, it has been criticized for its emphasis on external behavior, and its consequent devaluation of internal thoughts and expectations. Finally, the long-term success of behavior therapy is sometimes less impressive that in the short run. Because of such concerns, some psychologists have turned to cognitive approaches.

Cognitive Approaches to Therapy

If you assumed that faulty, maladaptive cognitions lie at the heart of abnormal behavior, wouldn't the most direct treatment route be to teach people new, more adaptive modes of thinking? The answer is yes, according to psychologists taking a cognitive approach to treatment.

Cognitive approaches to therapy have as their goal a change in faulty cognitions that people hold about the world and themselves. Unlike traditional behavior therapists, who focus on modifying external behavior, cognitive therapists attempt to change the way people think (Beck, 1991; Kendall, 1991). Because they typically use basic principles of learning, the methods they employ are often referred to as the **cognitive-behavioral approach.**

Cognitive-behavioral approach: A process by which people's faulty cognitions about themselves and the world are changed to more accurate ones

Rational-emotive therapy: Psychotherapy based on Ellis's suggestion that the goal of therapy should be to restructure one's belief system into a more realistic, rational, and logical system

One of the best examples of cognitive-behavioral treatment is rational-emotive therapy. **Rational-emotive therapy** attempts to restructure a person's belief system into a more realistic, rational, and logical set of views. According to psychologist Albert Ellis (1987), many people lead unhappy and sometimes even psychologically disordered lives because they harbor such irrational, unrealistic ideas as these:

■ It is necessary to be loved or approved by virtually every significant other person for everything we do.
■ We should be thoroughly competent, adequate, and successful in all possible respects if we are to consider ourselves worthwhile.
■ It is horrible when things don't turn out the way we want them to.

In order to lead their clients to eliminate such maladaptive cognitions and adopt more effective thinking, rational-emotive therapists take an active, directive role during therapy, openly challenging patterns of thought that appear to be dysfunctional. (Martha's case excerpt earlier in the chapter is a good example of the approach.) For instance, a therapist might bluntly dispute the logic employed by a person in treatment by saying, "Why does the fact that your girlfriend left you mean that *you* are a bad person?" or "How does failing an exam indicate that you have *no* good qualities?" By pointing out the problems in clients' logic, therapists employing this form of treatment believe that people can come to adopt a more realistic view of themselves and their circumstances (Ellis & Dryden, 1987; Dryden & DiGiuseppe, 1990; Bernard & DiGiuseppe, 1993).

Another form of therapy that builds on a cognitive perspective is that of Aaron Beck (Beck, 1991). Like that of rational-emotive therapy, the basic goal of Beck's **cognitive therapy** is to change people's illogical thoughts about themselves and the world. However, cognitive therapy is considerably less confrontational and challenging than rational-emotive therapy. Instead of the therapist actively arguing with clients about their faulty cognitions, cognitive therapists are more apt to play the role of teacher. Clients are urged to obtain information on their own that will lead them to discard their inaccurate thinking. During the course of treatment, clients are helped to discover ways of thinking more appropriately about themselves and others (Beck & Haaga, 1992).

Cognitive approaches to therapy have proved successful in dealing with a broad range of disorders. Their ability to incorporate additional treatment approaches (e.g., combining cognitive and behavioral techniques in cognitive-behavioral therapy) has made cognitive therapy a particularly effective form of treatment (Whisman, 1993; Dobson & Shaw, 1994; Dobson & Craig, 1996).

Cognitive therapy: Psychotherapy based on Beck's goal to change people's illogical thoughts about themselves and the world

RECAP AND REVIEW

Recap

- Psychotherapy is psychologically based therapy in which the emphasis is on producing change through discussion and interaction between client and therapist. Biologically based therapy uses drugs and other medical procedures.
- Psychodynamic therapy is based on Freud's notion that psychological disorders are produced by unconscious conflicts and anxiety.
- Behavioral approaches to therapy assume that people who display abnormal behavior either have failed to acquire appropriate skills or have learned faulty or maladaptive skills.
- Cognitive approaches to therapy seek to change faulty cognitions that people hold about the world and themselves.

Review

1. A remedy for a psychological disorder that is based on discussion and interaction between therapist and client is known as _____ .
2. Match each of the following mental-health practitioners with the appropriate description:
   1. Psychiatrist
   2. Clinical psychologist
   3. Counseling psychologist
   4. Psychoanalyst

   a. Ph.D. specializing in treatment of psychological disorders
   b. Professional specializing in Freudian therapy techniques
   c. M.D. trained in abnormal behavior
   d. Ph.D. specializing in adjustment to day-to-day problems
3. According to Freud, people use _____ _____ as a means to ensure that unwanted impulses will not intrude on conscious thought.
4. In dream interpretation, a psychoanalyst must learn to distinguish between the _____ content of a dream, which is what appears on the surface, and the _____ content, its underlying meaning.
5. Which of the following treatments deals with phobias by gradual exposure to the item producing the fear?
   a. Systematic desensitization
   b. Partial reinforcement
   c. Behavioral self-management
   d. Ego control

Ask Yourself

In what situations might behavioral therapy be most useful? In what situations might a therapeutic technique that deals with thoughts rather than actions be more suitable?

(Answers to review questions are on page 448.)

- *What are humanistic and group therapy approaches to treatment?*
- *How effective is therapy, and which kind of therapy works best under a given circumstance?*

Humanistic Approaches to Therapy

As you know from your own experience, it is impossible to master the material covered in a course without some hard work, no matter how good the teacher

448

and the textbook are. You must take the time to study, to memorize the vocabulary, to learn the concepts. Nobody else can do it for you. If you choose to put in the effort, you'll succeed; if you don't, you'll fail. The responsibility is primarily yours.

Humanistic therapy draws upon this philosophical perspective of self-responsibility in developing treatment techniques. Although many different types of therapy fit into this category, the ideas that underlie them are the same: We have control of our own behavior; we can make choices about the kinds of lives we want to live; and it is up to us to solve the difficulties that we encounter in our daily lives.

Instead of being the directive figures that are in some psychodynamic and behavioral approaches, humanistic therapists view themselves as guides or facilitators. Therapists using humanistic techniques seek to lead people to realizations about themselves and to help them find ways to come closer to the ideal they hold for themselves. In this view, psychological disorders are the result of people's inability to find meaning in life and of feeling lonely and unconnected to others.

Humanistic approaches have spawned a number of therapeutic techniques. Among the most important are client-centered therapy, existential therapy, and gestalt therapy.

Client-Centered Therapy If you refer back to the case of Alice described earlier in the chapter, you'll see that the therapist's comments are not interpretations or answers to questions that the client has raised. Instead, they tend to clarify or reflect back what the client has said (e.g., "In other words, what you did . . ."; "You feel that . . ."; "Is that it?"). This therapeutic technique is known as *nondirective counseling*, and it is at the heart of client-oriented therapy. First practiced by Carl Rogers (1951, 1980), client-centered therapy is the best-known and most frequently used type of humanistic therapy.

The goal of **client-centered therapy** is to enable people to reach their potential for *self-actualization*. By providing a warm and accepting environment, therapists hope to motivate clients to air their problems and feelings, which, in turn, will enable the clients to make realistic and constructive choices and decisions about the things that bother them in their current lives. Instead of directing the choices clients make, then, the therapist provides what Rogers calls *unconditional positive regard*—expressing acceptance and understanding, regardless of the feelings and attitudes the client expresses. In doing so, the therapist hopes to create an atmosphere in which clients are able to come to decisions that can improve their lives.

Furnishing unconditional positive regard does not mean that the therapist must approve of everything the client says or does. Rather, it means that the therapist must convey that the client's thoughts and behaviors are seen as genuine reflections of what the client is experiencing (Lietaer, 1984).

It is relatively rare for client-centered therapy to be used today in its purest form. Contemporary approaches are apt to be somewhat more directive, with therapists nudging clients toward insights rather than merely reflecting back their statements. However, clients' insights are still seen as central to the therapeutic process.

Existential Therapy What is the meaning of life? Although we have probably all pondered this question, for some people it is a central issue in their daily lives.

Humanistic therapy: Therapy in which the underlying assumption is that people have control of their behavior, can make choices about their lives, and are essentially responsible for solving their own problems

Client-centered therapy: Therapy in which the therapist reflects back the patient's statements in a way that causes the patient to find his or her own solutions

---

For people who experience psychological problems as a result of difficulty in finding a satisfactory answer, existential therapy is particularly appropriate.

In contrast to other humanistic approaches that view humans' unique freedom and potential as a positive force, **existential therapy** is based on the premise that the inability to deal with such freedom can produce anguish, fear, and concern (May, 1969). In existential therapy, the goal is to allow individuals to come to grips with the freedom they have and to begin to understand how they fit in with the rest of the world. Existential therapists try to make their patients aware of the importance of free choice and the fact that they have the ultimate responsibility for making their own choices about their lives.

Therapists providing existential therapy are exceedingly directive, probing and challenging their clients' views of the world. In addition, therapists try to establish a deep and binding relationship with their clients. Their objective is to allow clients to see that they share in the difficulties and experiences that arise in trying to deal with the freedom that is part of being human (Bugental & Bracke, 1992; Bugental & McBeath, 1994).

Existential therapy: A humanistic approach that addresses the meaning of life and human freedom

Gestalt Therapy   Have you ever thought back to some childhood incident in which you were treated unfairly and again felt the rage you had experienced at that time? To therapists working in a gestalt perspective, the healthiest thing for you to do psychologically might be to act out that rage—by hitting a pillow, kicking a chair, or yelling in frustration. This sort of activity represents an important part of what goes on in gestalt therapy sessions, in which the client is encouraged to act out past conflicts and difficulties.

The rationale for this approach to treatment is that it is necessary for people to integrate their thoughts, feelings, and behaviors into a *gestalt,* the German term for "whole" (as we discussed in reference to perception in Chapter 3). According to Fritz Perls (1967, 1970), who developed **gestalt therapy,** the way to do this is for people to examine their earlier experience and complete any "unfinished business" from their past that still affects and colors present-day relationships. Specifically, Perls assumed that people should reenact during therapy the specific conflicts they experienced earlier. For instance, a client might first play the part of his angry father and then play himself when his father yelled at him. Gestalt therapists claim that, by increasing their perspective on a situation, clients are better able to understand the source of their psychological disorders. Ultimately, the goal is to experience life in a more unified and complete way (Korb, Gorrell, & VanDeRiet, 1989).

Gestalt therapy: An approach to therapy that attempts to integrate a client's thoughts, feelings, and behavior into a whole

Humanistic Approaches in Perspective   The notion that psychological disorders are the consequence of restricted growth potential is philosophically appealing to many people. Furthermore, the acknowledgment of humanistic therapists that the freedom we possess can lead to psychological difficulties provides an unusually supportive environment for therapy. In turn, this atmosphere can aid clients in finding solutions to difficult psychological problems.

On the other hand, the lack of specificity of the humanistic treatments is a problem that has troubled critics. Humanistic approaches are not very precise and are probably the least scientifically and theoretically developed type of treatment. Moreover, this form of treatment is best suited for the same kind of highly verbal client who profits most from psychoanalytic treatment. Still, humanistic treatment approaches have been influential.

Group Therapy

Although most treatment takes place between a single individual and a therapist, some forms of therapy involve groups of people seeking treatment. In **group ther-**

Group therapy: Therapy in which people discuss problems with a group

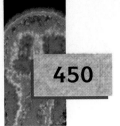

apy, several unrelated people meet with a therapist to discuss some aspect of their psychological functioning.

People typically discuss their problems with the group, which is often centered on a common difficulty, such as alcoholism or a lack of social skills. The other members of the group provide emotional support and dispense advice on ways in which they have coped effectively with similar problems (Lewis, 1987; Drum, 1990; Alonso & Swiller, 1993).

Groups vary greatly in terms of the particular model that is employed; there are psychoanalytic groups, humanistic groups, and groups corresponding to the other therapeutic approaches. Furthermore, groups also differ in the degree of guidance the therapist provides. In some, the therapist is quite directive, while in others, the members of the group set their own agenda and determine how the group will proceed (Flowers & Booraem, 1990; Ballinger & Yalom, 1994).

Because several people are treated simultaneously in group therapy, it is a much more economical means of treatment than individual psychotherapy. On the other hand, critics argue that group settings do not afford the individual attention inherent in one-to-one therapy, and especially shy and withdrawn individuals may not receive the necessary attention in a group.

Family therapy: An approach that focuses on the family as a whole unit to which each member contributes

Family Therapy   One specialized form of group therapy is family therapy. As the name implies, **family therapy** involves two or more members of the same family, one (or more) of whose problems led to treatment. But rather than focusing simply on members of the family who present the initial problem, family therapists consider the family as a whole unit, to which each member contributes. By meeting with the entire family simultaneously, family therapists attempt to obtain a sense of how the family members interact with one another (Sauber et al., 1993; Nichols & Schwartz, 1995).

Family therapists view the family as a "system," and they assume that the separate individuals in the family cannot improve without understanding the conflicts that are to be found in the interactions of the family members. Thus each member is expected to contribute to the resolution of the problem being addressed.

Many family therapists assume that family members fall into rigid roles or set patterns of behavior, with one person acting as the scapegoat, another as a bully, and so forth. In their view, family disturbances are perpetuated by this system of roles. One goal of this type of therapy, then, is to get the family members to adopt new, more constructive roles and patterns of behavior (Minuchin, 1974; Kaslow, 1991; Minuchin & Nichols, 1992).

In family therapy, the family system as a whole—not just one family member identified as having the "problem"—is treated.

Evaluating Psychotherapy: Does Therapy Work?

Your best friend at school, Ben, comes to you because he just hasn't been feeling right about things lately. He's upset because he and his girlfriend aren't getting along, but his difficulties go beyond that. He can't concentrate on his studies, he has a lot of trouble getting to sleep, and—this is what really bothers him—he's begun to think that people are ganging up on him, talking about him behind his back. It just seems that no one really cares about or understands him or makes any effort to see why he's become so miserable.

Ben is aware that he ought to get *some* kind of help, but he is not sure where to turn. He is fairly skeptical of psychologists, thinking that a lot of what they say is just mumbo-jumbo, but he's willing to put his doubts aside and try anything to feel better. He also knows there are many different types of therapy, and he doesn't have a clue about which would be best for him. He turns to you for advice, because he knows you are taking a psychology course. He asks, "Which kind of therapy works best?"

Is Therapy Effective?   Such a question requires a complex response, for there is no easy answer. In fact, identifying which form of treatment is most appropriate is a controversial, and still unresolved, task for psychologists specializing in abnormal behavior. For example, even before considering whether any one form of therapy works better than another, we need to determine whether therapy in *any* form is effective in alleviating psychological disturbances.

Until the 1950s most people simply assumed that therapy, on the face of it, was an effective strategy for resolving psychological difficulties. But in 1952 psychologist Hans Eysenck published an influential article reviewing the published literature on the subject, which challenged this widely held assumption. He claimed that people who received psychodynamic treatment and related therapies were no better off at the end of treatment than those people who were placed on a waiting list for treatment—but never received it. According to his analysis, about two-thirds of the people who reported suffering from "neurotic" symptoms believed that those symptoms had disappeared after 2 years, regardless of whether or not they had been in therapy. Eysenck concluded that people suffering from neurotic symptoms would go into **spontaneous remission,** recovery without treatment, if they were simply left alone—certainly a cheaper and simpler process.

As you can imagine, Eysenck's review was controversial from the start, and its conclusions were quickly challenged. Critics pointed to the inadequacy of the data he reviewed, suggesting that he was basing his conclusions on studies that contained a number of flaws.

Nevertheless, Eysenck's early review served to stimulate a continuing stream of better controlled, more carefully crafted studies on the effectiveness of psychotherapy, and today most psychologists agree: Therapy does work. Several recent comprehensive reviews indicate that therapy brings about greater improvement than no treatment at all, with the rate of spontaneous remission (recovery without treatment) fairly low. In most cases, then, the symptoms of abnormal behavior do not go away by themselves if left untreated—although the issue remains a hotly debated one (Weisz, Weiss, & Donenberg, 1992; Kazdin, 1993; Lipsey & Wilson, 1993).

Which Kind of Therapy Works Best?   Although most psychologists feel confident that psychotherapeutic treatment *in general* is more effective than no treatment at all, the question of whether any specific form of treatment is superior to any other has yet to be answered definitively (Persons, 1991; Jacobson & Truax, 1991; Bergin & Garfield, 1994).

For instance, one study comparing the effectiveness of various approaches found that, while there is some variation among the success rates of the various

Spontaneous remission: Recovery without treatment

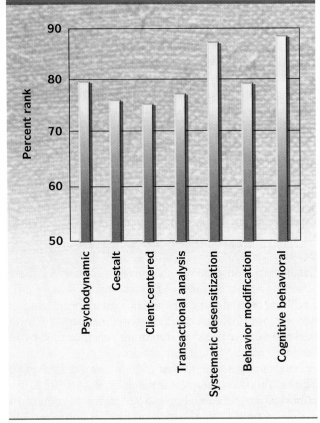

FIGURE 13-1 Estimates of the effectiveness of different types of treatment, in comparison to control groups of untreated people. The percentile score shows how much more effective a particular type of treatment is for the average patient than is no treatment. For example, people given psychodynamic treatment score, on average, more positively on outcome measures than about three-quarters of untreated people. *(Adapted from Smith, Glass, & Miller, 1980).*

treatment forms, most are fairly close to one another. As Figure 13-1 indicates, the success rates range from about 70 to 85 percent greater success for treated than for untreated individuals (Smith, Glass, & Miller, 1980). There is a slight tendency for behavioral approaches and cognitive approaches to be a bit more successful, but this may be due to differences in the severity of cases treated (Orwin & Condray, 1984). Other research, relying on *meta-analytic* procedures in which data from a large number of studies are statistically combined, yields similar general conclusions (Strupp & Binder, 1992; Giles, 1993).

In sum, we can draw several conclusions about the effectiveness of psychotherapy (Strupp & Binder, 1992; Seligman, 1995):

■ For most people, psychotherapy is effective. This conclusion holds over different lengths of treatment, specific kinds of psychological disorders, and types of treatment. Thus, the question "Does psychotherapy work?" seems to have been convincingly answered: It does (Lipsey & Wilson, 1993; Weisz, 1995).

■ On the other hand, psychotherapy doesn't work for everyone. As many as 10 percent of people show no improvement or actually deteriorate (Lambert, Shapiro, & Bergin, 1986; Luborsky, 1988).

■ Research has been unable to determine conclusively which of the many forms of therapy is most beneficial. Although some kinds of psychotherapy seem to work best for certain kinds of problems, generally the extent of the differences in impact is not substantial. Consequently, there is still no definitive answer to the question of which therapy works best—nor may one be found soon, due to the difficulties in sorting out the various factors that enter into the success of therapy.

Because no one type of psychotherapy is invariably effective, eclectic approaches to therapy are becoming increasingly popular. In an **eclectic approach**

Eclectic approach to therapy: An approach to therapy that uses techniques taken from a variety of treatment methods, rather than just one

to therapy, a therapist uses a variety of techniques, integrating several perspectives, to treat a person's problems. By using eclectic procedures, the therapist is able to choose the appropriate mix in accordance with the specific needs of the individual (Wells & Giannetti, 1990; Goldfried & Castonguay, 1992; Lazarus, Beutler, & Norcross, 1992).

Clearly, not every psychological disorder will be resolved equally well by every sort of therapy. Furthermore, therapists with certain personal characteristics may work better with particular individuals and types of treatments, and certain kinds of people may respond better to one form of therapy than another. For example, a behavioral approach may be more suitable for people who have difficulty expressing themselves verbally or who lack the patience or ability to engage in sustained introspection, qualities that are necessary for a psychodynamic approach (Crits-Christoph & Mintz, 1991). Similarly, racial and ethnic factors may be related to the success of treatment, as we discuss next.

Exploring Diversity

Racial and Ethnic Factors in Treatment: Should Therapists Be Color-Blind?

Consider the following description, written by a school counselor about a student:

Jimmy Jones is a 12-year-old Black male student who was referred by Mrs. Peterson because of apathy, indifference, and inattentiveness to classroom activities. Other teachers have reported that Jimmy does not pay attention, daydreams often, and frequently falls asleep during class. There is a strong possibility that Jimmy is harboring repressed rage that needs to be ventilated and dealt with. His inability to directly express his anger had led him to adopt passive aggressive means of expressing hostility, i.e., inattentiveness, daydreaming, falling asleep. It is recommended that Jimmy be seen for intensive counseling to discover the basis of the anger. (Sue & Sue, 1990, p. 44)

The counselor was wrong, however. After 6 months of therapy, the true cause of Jimmy's problems became evident: his impoverished and disorganized home environment. Because of the overcrowding at his house, he was often kept awake and thus was tired the next day. Frequently, he was also hungry. His problems, then, were due largely to the stresses arising from his impoverished environment and not to any deep-seated psychological problems.

This incident underscores the importance of taking people's environmental and cultural backgrounds into account during treatment for psychological disorders. In particular, some minority-group members, especially those who are also poor, have adopted behaviors that have been helpful in dealing with a society that discriminates against them on the basis of race or ethnic background. For instance, some behaviors that may signal psychological disorder in middle- and upper-class whites might simply be adaptive. A suspicious and distrustful African-American, then, might be displaying a survival strategy to protect himself from psychological as well as physical injury (Sue & Sue, 1990).

In fact, some of the most basic assumptions of much of psychotherapy must be questioned when dealing with racial, ethnic, and cultural minority-group members. For example, Asian and Hispanic cultures typically place much greater emphasis on the group, family, and society than the dominant culture, which focuses on the individual. When critical decisions are to be made, the family helps make them—suggesting that family members should play a role in psychological treatment.

Similarly, when traditional Chinese men and women feel depressed or anxious, they often are urged by others of their culture to avoid thinking about whatever upset them. Consider how this advice contrasts with the view of the treatment approaches that emphasize the value of insight.

Consequently, therapists *cannot* be "color-blind." Instead, they must take into account the racial, ethnic, cultural, and social-class backgrounds of their clients in determining the nature of a psychological disorder and the course of treatment (De La Cancela & Sotomayor, 1993; Casas, 1994; Allison et al., 1994; Aponte, Rivers, & Wohl, 1995).

RECAP AND REVIEW

Recap

- Humanistic approaches view therapy as a way to help people solve their own problems.
- In group therapy, several unrelated people meet with a therapist to discuss some aspect of their psychological functioning.
- A long-standing issue is whether psychotherapy is effective and, if it is, whether one kind is superior to others.
- Racial, ethnic, and cultural factors must be taken into account during treatment for psychological disorders.

Review

1. Match the names of the following treatment strategies with the corresponding statements you might expect to hear from a therapist.
   1. Gestalt therapy
   2. Group therapy
   3. Unconditional positive regard
   4. Behavioral therapy
   5. Nondirective counseling

   a. "In other words, you don't get along with your mother because she hates your girlfriend, is that right?"
   b. "I want you all to take turns talking about why you decided to come, and what you hope to gain from therapy."
   c. "I can understand why you wanted to wreck your friend's car after she hurt your feelings. Now, tell me more about the accident."

   d. "That's not appropriate behavior. Let's work on replacing it with something else."
   e. "Remember the anger you felt and scream until you feel better."

2. _____ therapies assume people are responsible for their own lives and the decisions they make.

3. _____ therapy emphasizes the integration of thoughts, feelings, and behaviors.

4. One of the major criticisms against humanistic therapies is that:
   a. They are too imprecise and unstructured.
   b. They treat only the symptom of the problem.
   c. The therapist dominates the patient-therapist interaction.
   d. They work well only on lower-class clients.

5. In a controversial study, Eysenck found that some people go into _____ _____, or recovery without treatment, if they are simply left alone instead of being treated.

6. Treatments that combine techniques from several theoretical approaches are called _____ procedures.

Ask Yourself

How can people be successfully treated in group therapy when individuals with the "same" problem are so different? What advantages might group therapy offer over individual therapy?

(Answers to review questions are on page 456.)

- *How are drug, electroconvulsive, and psychosurgical techniques used today in the treatment of psychological disorders?*

BIOLOGICAL TREATMENT APPROACHES: USING THE MEDICAL MODEL

If you get a kidney infection, you're given an antibiotic and, with luck, about a week later your kidney is as good as new. If your appendix becomes inflamed, a surgeon removes it and your body functions normally once more. Could an analogous approach, focusing on the body's physiology, be taken with psychological disturbances?

According to biological approaches to treatment, the answer is yes. Biologically based treatments are used routinely for certain kinds of problems. The basic model suggests that rather than focusing on a patient's psychological conflicts, past traumas, or environmental variables that may support abnormal behavior, it is more appropriate in certain cases to treat brain chemistry and other neurological factors directly. This can be done through the use of drugs, electric shock, or surgery.

Drug Therapy

Are we close to the day when we will take a pill each morning to maintain good psychological health, in the same way that we now take a vitamin pill to help us stay physically healthy? Although that day has not yet arrived, there are quite a few forms of **drug therapy** that successfully alleviate symptoms of a number of psychological disturbances.

Drug therapy: Control of psychological problems through drugs

Antipsychotic Drugs   Probably no greater change has occurred in mental hospitals than the successful introduction in the mid-1950s of **antipsychotic drugs**—drugs used to alleviate severe symptoms of disturbance, such as loss of touch with reality, agitation, and overactivity. Previously, mental hospitals typically fulfilled all the stereotypes of the insane asylum, with screaming, moaning, clawing patients displaying the most bizarre behaviors. Suddenly, in just a matter of days, the hospital wards became considerably calmer environments in which professionals could do more than just try to get the patients through the day without causing serious harm to themselves or others.

Antipsychotic drugs: Drugs that temporarily alleviate psychotic symptoms such as agitation and overactivity

This dramatic change was brought about by the introduction of a drug from the phenothiazine family called *chlorpromazine*. This drug, and others of similar types, rapidly became the most popular and successful treatment for schizophrenia. Today drug therapy is the preferred treatment for most cases of severely abnormal behavior and, as such, is used for most hospitalized patients with psychological disorders. For instance, the antipsychotic drug *clozapine* represents the current generation of antipsychotics. Clozapine was the drug used so successfully to treat those attending the prom described at the start of the chapter (Wallis & Willwerth, 1992; Meltzer, 1993).

How do antipsychotic drugs work? They function by regulating the production of dopamine at the brain's synapses, the sites where nerve impulses travel from one neuron to another (Zito, 1993). However, they do not produce a "cure" in the same way that, say, penicillin cures an infection. As soon as the drug is withdrawn, the original symptoms tend to reappear. Furthermore, such drugs can have long-term side effects, such as dryness of the mouth and throat, dizziness, and sometimes tremors and loss of muscle control that may continue even after drug treatments are stopped—a permanent condition called *tardive dyskinesia* (Kane, 1992).

Perhaps even more devastating than these physical side effects are the numbing effects of antipsychotic drugs on the emotional responses of some patients. For example, Mark Vonnegut (son of author Kurt Vonnegut) describes his reactions to the use of the antipsychotic drug Thorazine while he was institutionalized for schizophrenia:

What the drug is supposed to do is keep away hallucinations. What I think it does is just fog up your mind so badly you don't notice the hallucinations or much else.... On Thorazine everything's a bore. Not a bore, exactly. Boredom implies impatience. You can read comic books ... you can tolerate talking to jerks forever.... The weather is dull, the flowers are dull, nothing's very impressive. (Vonnegut, 1975, pp. 196–197)

Antidepressant Drugs   As you might guess from the name, **antidepressant drugs** are a class of medications used in cases of severe depression to improve the moods of patients. They were discovered quite by accident: It was found that patients suffering from tuberculosis who were given the drug iproniazid suddenly

Antidepressant drugs: Medications that improve a depressed patient's mood and feeling of well-being

Author William Styron was afflicted with major depression, which was treated effectively with antidepressant drugs.

Lithium (LITH ee um): a drug used in the treatment of bipolar disorders

Antianxiety drugs: Drugs that alleviate stress and anxiety

became happier and more optimistic. When the same drug was tested on people suffering from depression, a similar result occurred, and drugs became an accepted form of treatment for depression (McNeal & Cimbolic, 1986).

Most antidepressant drugs work by allowing an increase in the concentration of particular neurotransmitters in the brain (see Chapter 2). For example, tricyclic drugs modify the amounts of norepinephrine and serotonin at the synapses of neurons in the brain. Others, such as bupropion, operate by affecting the neurotransmitter dopamine (Zito, 1993).

Although antidepressant drugs may produce side effects such as drowsiness and faintness, their overall success rate is quite good. Unlike antipsychotic drugs, antidepressants can produce lasting, long-term recoveries from depression. In many cases, even after the drugs are no longer being taken, the depression does not return (Spiegel, 1989; Julien, 1995; Zito, 1993). (For a discussion of Prozac, one of the newest and already most widely known antidepressants, see the Psychology at Work box.)

Lithium   A drug that has been used very successfully in cases of bipolar disorders is **lithium,** a form of simple mineral salts. Although no one knows definitely why it works, it is effective in reducing manic episodes some 70 percent of the time. On the other hand, its effectiveness in resolving depression is not as impressive. It works only in certain cases, and like other antidepressants, it can produce a number of side effects (Coppen, Metcalfe, & Wood, 1982).

Lithium has a quality that sets it apart from other drug treatments: More than any other drug, it represents a *preventive* treatment, forestalling episodes of manic depression. Often, people who have been subject to manic-depressive episodes in the past can take a daily dose of lithium that prevents a recurrence of their symptoms. In contrast, most other drugs are useful only after symptoms of psychological disturbance occur.

Antianxiety Drugs   If the names Valium and Xanax sound familiar to you, you are not alone: They are among the drugs most frequently prescribed by physicians. Both are members of a class of drugs known as antianxiety drugs, which are prescribed—often by family physicians—to alleviate the stress and anxiety experienced by patients during particularly difficult periods. In fact, more than half of all Americans have a family member who has taken such a drug at one time or another.

As the name implies, **antianxiety drugs** reduce the level of anxiety experienced, essentially by reducing excitability and in part by increasing drowsiness. They are used not only to reduce general tension in people who are experiencing temporary difficulties but also to aid in the treatment of more serious anxiety disorders (Zito, 1993).

Although the popularity of antianxiety drugs suggests that they hold few risks, they can produce a number of potentially serious side effects. For instance, they can cause fatigue, and long-term use can lead to dependence. Moreover, taken in combination with alcohol, some antianxiety drugs can become lethal. But a more important issue concerns their use to suppress anxiety. Almost every approach to psychological disturbance views continuing anxiety as a signal of some sort of problem. Thus, drugs that mask anxiety may simply be hiding difficulties. Consequently, rather than confronting their underlying problems, people may simply be hiding from them through the use of antianxiety drugs.

ANSWERS TO PREVIOUS REVIEW

1. 1-e; 2-b; 3-c; 4-d; 5-a **2.** Humanistic **3.** Gestalt **4.** a **5.** spontaneous remission
6. eclectic

PSYCHOLOGY AT WORK

The Prozac Culture: Chasing Happiness in the Nineties

She has never suffered from depression, and she's not one to pop pills for fun. So why would a successful, 43-year-old public relations executive take Prozac? Helen Baker of Chicago (who wants to be identified by this pseudonym) takes it to give herself an edge. Like any busy professional, she often juggles competing priorities. Faced with looming deadlines and a dozen calls to return, she used to find herself paralyzed. "I would be unable to focus," she says. "I would end up waiting until the last moment to get things done." Now that she's on the antidepressant, she not only handles job pressures more gracefully but sports a more buoyant personality. She recently found her hand shooting up when a night-club comedian asked for a volunteer from the audience. "I couldn't believe I got up there and wasn't nervous," she says. "I was being open and making people laugh. In the past, I might have wanted to do it, but I wouldn't have done it without Prozac." (Crowley, 1994, p. 41)

Welcome to the last decade of the twentieth century, where drugs developed to treat psychological disorders have become as well-known as Ivory Soap—and used almost as much. The antidepressant Prozac, in particular, has graced the cover of magazines such as *Newsweek* and has been the topic of best-sellers like psychiatrist Peter Kramer's *Listening to Prozac* (Kramer, 1993).

Media hype aside, is the antidepressant fluoxetine, sold under the trade name of Prozac, truly as revolutionary as its proponents claim? In some respects, Prozac does merit accolades. Although it was introduced only in 1987, it is now the most frequently prescribed antidepressant. Despite its high expense, with each daily dose costing $2, it has significantly improved the lives of thousands of depressed individuals.

Prozac (and its cousins Zoloft and Paxil) works by blocking reabsorption of the neurotransmitter serotonin. Compared with other antidepressants, Prozac has relatively few side effects. Furthermore, many people who do not respond to other types of antidepressants do well on Prozac.

On the other hand, the drug has not been used long enough to know all of its potential side effects, and some reports suggest that Prozac may have a darker side. For example, between 20 and 30 percent of users report the side effects of nausea and diarrhea, and a smaller number report sexual dysfunctions (Barondes, 1994).

Furthermore, the reputation of Prozac as an all-purpose mood booster raises troublesome issues. The wave of publicity about the drug increases the likelihood that patients with mild forms of depression or even other disorders will forgo alternative, more suitable types of treatment such as psychotherapy. Instead, they may aggressively seek prescriptions for Prozac.

Many health providers are more than willing to oblige requests for the drug. Prozac is prescribed more than 1 million times a month, most often by practitioners who do not specialize in psychological disorders (Cowley, 1994). In one extreme case, a clinical psychologist in Washington State suggested the use of Prozac to more than 600 people in a town with a total population of 21,000—a practice, it should be added, that produced considerable condemnation (Egan, 1994).

The widespread use of Prozac, as well as the accolades it has attained, raises a more difficult, and ultimately philosophical, question: Are the positive changes in mood, attitudes, and outlook on life supposedly produced by Prozac completely desirable? Although proponents of the drug argue that it allows the "real person" to emerge, some observers argue that the personality that is seen when taking Prozac is less than genuine. They contend that people may not be better off, after all, in escaping from unpleasant feelings. To critics, people who take drugs such as Prozac may be unmotivated to seek the insights and experiences that can make life truly meaningful and worthwhile.

In sum, although Prozac has important benefits, it is not a wonder drug. Until the long-term biological and psychological effects of Prozac are known, its use requires caution.

Electroconvulsive Therapy

In the 1930s, a Hungarian physician concluded that people with epilepsy (a disorder characterized by seizures and convulsions) were immune to schizophrenia. Even though this conclusion was wrong, it led to further speculation that if epileptic-like convulsions could be induced in people with schizophrenia, they might relieve the disorder.

Electroconvulsive therapy (ECT):
Treatment involving the administration of an electric current to a patient's head to treat severe depression

Psychosurgery: Brain surgery, once used to alleviate symptoms of mental disorder but rarely used today

In a test of this hypothesis, several psychiatrists administered electric shocks to the heads of patients suffering from schizophrenia, thereby inducing convulsions. Surprisingly, although the reasoning that led to the test was flawed, patients did, in fact, experience some improvement, and electroconvulsive shock therapy was born (Bini, 1938).

The use of **electroconvulsive therapy (ECT)** has continued to the present, although the way in which it is administered has improved considerably. An electric current of 70 to 150 volts is briefly administered to a patient's head, causing a loss of consciousness and often seizures. Usually the patient is sedated and receives muscle relaxants prior to administration of the current, helping to prevent violent contractions. The typical patient receives about ten treatments in the course of a month, but some patients continue with maintenance treatments for months afterward (Weiner, 1982; Fink, 1990, 1994).

As you might expect, ECT is a controversial technique. Apart from the obvious distastefulness of a treatment that evokes images of capital punishment by electrocution, there are frequently side effects. For instance, following treatment, patients often experience disorientation, confusion, and sometimes memory loss that may remain for months. Moreover, many patients fear ECT, even though they are anesthetized during the actual treatment and thus experience no pain. Finally, we still do not know how or why ECT works, and some critics suggest that the treatment may produce permanent damage to the brain (Fisher, 1985).

Given the drawbacks to ECT, why is it used at all? The basic reason is that in many cases it seems to be an effective treatment for severe cases of depression. For instance, it may prevent depressed, suicidal individuals from committing suicide, and it can act more quickly than antidepressive medications, which may take longer to become effective. In fact, the use of ECT has risen in the last decade, with more than 100,000 people undergoing ECT each year. Still, ECT tends to be used only when other treatments have proved ineffective (Sackheim, 1985; Thienhaus, Margletta, & Bennett, 1990; APA Task Force, 1990; Coffey, 1993; Foderaro, 1993).

Psychosurgery

If ECT strikes you as a questionable procedure, the use of **psychosurgery**—brain surgery in which the object is to alleviate symptoms of mental disorder—is likely to appear even more so. A technique that is used only rarely today, psychosurgery was first introduced as a treatment of "last resort" in the 1930s. The procedure, a *prefrontal lobotomy,* consists of surgically destroying or removing certain parts of a patient's frontal lobes, which control emotionality. The rationale for this procedure was that destroying the connections between various parts of the brain would make patients less subject to emotional impulses, and their general behavior would improve.

Psychosurgery often did improve a patient's behavior—but not without drastic side effects. For along with remission of symptoms of mental disorder, patients sometimes suffered personality changes, becoming bland, colorless, and unemotional. In other cases, patients became aggressive and unable to control their impulses. In the worst cases, treatment resulted in the death of patients.

Despite these problems—and the obvious ethical questions regarding the appropriateness of forever altering someone's personality—psychosurgery was used in thousands of cases in the 1930s and 1940s. The process became so routine that in some clinics fifty patients a day were treated (Freeman, 1959).

With the advent of effective drug treatments, psychosurgery became nearly obsolete. However, it is still used in very rare cases when all other procedures have failed and the patient's behavior presents a high risk to self and others. For instance, psychosurgery may be employed in some highly unusual cases of obsessive-compulsive disorder or depression. It is also occasionally used in dying patients with severe, uncontrollable pain. Still, even these cases raise important ethical issues, and psychosurgery remains a highly controversial treatment (Valenstein, 1986; Chiocca & Martuza, 1990; Miller, 1994).

Biological Treatment in Perspective: Can Abnormal Behavior Be Cured?

In some respects, there has been no greater revolution in the field of mental health than that represented by the biological approaches to treatment. Mental hospitals have been able to concentrate more on actually helping patients and less on custodial functions, as previously violent, uncontrollable patients have been calmed by the use of drugs. Similarly, patients whose lives had once been disrupted by depression or manic-depressive episodes have been able to function normally, and other forms of drug therapy have also shown remarkable results.

On the other hand, biological therapies are not without their detractors. For one thing, critics charge that they merely provide relief of the *symptoms* of mental disorder; as soon as the drugs are withdrawn, the symptoms return. Although it is considered a major step in the right direction, biological treatment may not solve a patient's underlying problems that led him or her to therapy in the first place. Moreover, biological therapies can produce side effects, ranging from physical reactions to the development of *new* symptoms of abnormal behavior (Elkin, 1986). For these reasons, then, biologically based treatment approaches do not represent a cure-all for psychological disorders.

Community Psychology: Focus on Prevention

Each of the treatments that we have reviewed in this chapter has a common element: They are "restorative" treatments, aimed at alleviating psychological difficulties that already exist. However, a relatively new movement, dubbed **community psychology,** is geared toward a different aim: to prevent or minimize the incidence of psychological disorders.

Community psychology came of age in the 1960s, when plans were developed for a nationwide network of community mental-health centers. These centers were meant to provide low-cost mental-health services, including short-term therapy and community educational programs. Moreover, during the last 30 years, the population of mental hospitals has plunged, as drug treatments have made physical restraint of patients unnecessary. The influx of former mental patients into the community, known as **deinstitutionalization,** further spurred the community psychology movement, which was concerned with ensuring not only that the deinstitutionalized receive proper treatment but that their civil rights be maintained (Melton & Garrison, 1987).

Unfortunately, the original goals of the field of community psychology have not been met. For instance, the incidence of mental disorders has shown no decline. Many people who need treatment do not get it, and in some cases, care for people with psychological disorders has simply shifted from one type of treatment site to another (Kiesler & Simpkins, 1991, 1993).

However, the movement has yielded several encouraging byproducts. One of these is the installation of telephone "hot lines" in cities throughout the United States. People experiencing acute stress can dial a telephone number at any time of day or night and talk to a trained, sympathetic listener who can provide immediate—although obviously limited—treatment (Tolan et al., 1990).

The college crisis center is another innovation that grew out of the community psychology movement. Modeled after suicide prevention hot-line centers (places for potential suicide victims to call and speak to someone about their difficulties), campus crisis centers provide callers with the opportunity to discuss life crises with a sympathetic listener, who is most often a student volunteer.

Community psychology: A movement aimed toward preventing or minimizing psychological disorders in the community

Deinstitutionalization: The transfer of former mental patients from institutions into the community

Trained counselors who staff telephone hot lines offer advice to people in crisis and can make referrals to other agencies for longer-term treatment if needed.

PATHWAYS THROUGH PSYCHOLOGY

Gary Gollner

Gary Gollner

Born: 1945
Education: B.A. in psychology from the University of Nebraska at Lincoln; M.A. in social work from the University of Nebraska School of Social Work
Home: Lincoln, Nebraska

The war in Vietnam led Gary Gollner to the field of psychology. Although he initially planned a career in pharmacy, this goal had to be set aside when the Chicago native was drafted while in college. When his basic training ended, the Army administered a test to determine where his military future lay. The results: He was told he would become a "clinical psychology technician."

Although the decision made little sense to Gollner at the time, since he had only taken one psychology course in college, he was enrolled in an intensive 16-week training program. At its conclusion, he was sent to the Leavenworth Disciplinary Barracks in Kansas.

During his time at Leavenworth, he gained experience that he couldn't have obtained anywhere else. "At Leavenworth I was primarily responsible for testing prisoners. We would administer the MMPI, TATs, intelligence tests, and any other follow-up tests that were required," he said. "I also did some closely supervised therapy and was involved in behavior modification programs."

The work he was doing aroused his interest in psychology. "I really liked the work and felt it suited me," he said. When he returned to college after his tour of duty was over, he decided to pursue a career in psychology.

For the past 13 years, Gollner has been on the staff of the Counseling and Psychological Services at the University of Nebraska at Lincoln. "It is basically an outpatient clinic. Students come to us voluntarily, having already discovered that they are in psychological pain of one sort or another," he said. "Once here, we do a psychological intake evaluation where, among other things, we identify the problem, study the family history, and formulate a treatment plan.

"It's an extremely interesting place to work. We serve a bright, self-motivated group of college-age people, usually between the ages of 18 and 24," Gollner explained. "Generally speaking, they come in with very open minds and the ability to deal with abstract concepts and have an ability to be insightful and thoughtful. These capabilities are well suited to the cognitive and behavioral approaches we employ to help students with their problems.

"We see students with lots of relationship problems, early onset depression, some bipolar disorders, and some schizophrenia. But we tend to catch psychological disorders when they are most treatable," he said. "And that's very gratifying."

Although not professionals, the volunteers receive careful training in telephone counseling. They role-play particular problems and are told how to respond to the difficulties they may confront with callers. The volunteers also hold group meetings to discuss the kinds of problems they are encountering and to share experiences about the kinds of strategies that are most effective.

Because they are not professionals, the staff members of college crisis centers do not, of course, offer long-term therapy to those who contact them. But they are able to provide callers with a supportive, constructive response—often when it is most needed. They are also able to refer callers to appropriate agencies on and off campus to get the long-term help they need.

In addition to providing crisis centers, most colleges offer their students the opportunity to receive treatment in counseling or mental-health centers. The mission of such centers is to take preventive measures and to treat students who are undergoing psychological distress. (For more on this issue, see the accompanying Pathways through Psychology box.)

The Informed Consumer of Psychology

Choosing the Right Therapist

If you make the decision to seek therapy, you're faced with a daunting task. Choosing a therapist is no simple matter. There are, however, a number of guidelines that can help you determine if you've made the right choice (Engler & Goleman, 1992):

■ The relationship between client and therapist should be a comfortable one. You should not be intimidated by, or in awe of, a therapist. Instead, you should trust the therapist and feel free to discuss even the most personal issues without fearing a negative reaction. In sum, the "personal chemistry" should feel good.

■ Therapist and client should agree on what the goals are for treatment. These goals should be clear, specific, and attainable.

■ The therapist should have appropriate training and credentials for the type of therapy he or she is conducting and should be licensed by appropriate state and local agencies. Check the therapist's membership in national and state professional associations. In addition, the therapist should be queried about the cost of therapy, billing practices, and other business matters. It is no breach of etiquette to get these matters out on the table during an initial consultation.

■ Clients should feel they are making progress toward resolving their psychological difficulties after therapy has begun, despite occasional setbacks. Although there is no set timetable, the most obvious changes resulting from therapy tend to occur relatively early in the course of treatment. For instance, half of patients in psychotherapy improve by the eighth session and three-quarters by the twenty-sixth session (Howard et al., 1986a; Howard & Zola, 1988; Messer & Warren, 1995).

If a client has no sense of improvement after repeated visits, this issue should be frankly discussed, with an eye toward the possibility of making a change. Today, most therapy is of fairly brief duration, especially that involving college students—who average just five sessions (Nowicki & Duke, 1978; Koss & Butcher, 1986; Crits-Cristoph, 1992).

Clients should be aware that they will have to put in a great deal of effort in therapy. Although ours is a culture that promises quick cures for any problem—as anyone who has perused the self-help shelves of bookstores knows—in reality, solving difficult problems is not easy. People must be committed to making therapy work and should know that it is they, and not the therapist, who must do most of the work to resolve their problems. The potential is there for the effort to pay off handsomely—as people experience more positive, fulfilling, and meaningful lives.

RECAP AND REVIEW

Recap

- Biological treatment approaches encompass drug therapy, electric-shock therapy, and surgical therapy.
- Drug therapy has produced dramatic reductions in psychotic behavior. Among the medications used are antipsychotic drugs, antidepressant drugs, and antianxiety drugs.
- Electroconvulsive therapy (ECT) consists of passing an electric current through the brain of patients suffering from severe psychological disturbances, particularly from depression.

- The most extreme form of biological therapy is psychosurgery, in which patients undergo brain surgery. Although rarely used today, prefrontal lobotomies were once a common form of treatment.
- Community psychology aims to prevent or minimize psychological disorders.

Review

1. Antipsychotic drugs have provided effective, long-term, and complete cures for schizophrenia. True or false?

2. One of the most effective biological treatments for psychological disorders, used mainly to stop and prevent manic-depressive episodes, is:
a. Chlorpromazine   c. Librium
b. Lithium   d. Valium

3. Originally a treatment for schizophrenia, _____ _____ involves administering electric current to a patient's brain.

4. Psychosurgery has grown in popularity as a method of treatment as surgical techniques have become more precise. True or false?

5. The trend toward releasing more patients from mental hospitals into the community is known as _____ .

Ask Yourself
Are the techniques of ECT and psychosurgery ethical? Are there cases in which they should never be used? Does the fact that no one understands why ECT is effective mean that its use should be avoided? In general, should treatments that are seemingly effective, but for unknown reasons, be employed?

(Answers to review questions are on page 463.)

LOOKING BACK

What are the goals of psychologically and biologically based treatment approaches?
1. Although the specific treatment types are diverse, psychologically based therapy, known as psychotherapy, and biologically based therapy share the goal of resolving psychological problems by modifying people's thoughts, feelings, expectations, evaluations, and ultimately their behavior.

What are the basic kinds of psychotherapies?
2. Psychoanalytic treatment is based on Freud's psychodynamic theory. It seeks to bring unresolved past conflicts and unacceptable impulses from the unconscious into the conscious, where the problems may be dealt with more effectively. To do this, patients meet frequently with their therapists and use techniques such as free association and dream interpretation. The process can be a difficult one, because of patient resistance and transference, and there is no conclusive evidence that the process works.

3. Behavioral approaches to treatment view abnormal behavior itself as the problem, rather than viewing the behavior as a symptom of some underlying cause. To bring about a "cure," this view suggests that the outward behavior must be changed. In aversive conditioning, unpleasant stimuli are linked to a behavior that the patient enjoys but wants to stop. Systematic desensitization uses the opposite procedure. Relaxation is repeatedly paired with a stimulus that evokes anxiety in order to reduce that anxiety. Observational learning is another behavioral treatment used to teach new, more appropriate behavior, as are techniques such as token systems.

4. Cognitive approaches to treatment, which are often referred to as cognitive-behavioral therapy, suggest that the goal of therapy should be a restructuring of a person's belief system into a more realistic, rational, and logical view of the world. Two examples of cognitive treatments are Ellis's rational-emotive therapy and Beck's cognitive therapy.

What are humanistic and group therapy approaches to treatment?
5. Humanistic therapy is based on the premise that people have control of their behavior, that they can make choices about their lives, and that it is up to them to solve their own problems. Humanistic therapists take a nondirective approach, acting more as guides who facilitate a client's search for answers. One example of humanistic therapy is Carl Rogers's client-centered therapy, in which the goal is to enable people to make realistic and constructive choices and decisions about the things that bother them. Existential therapy helps people cope with the unique freedom and potential that human existence offers, whereas gestalt therapy is directed toward aiding people in the integration of their thoughts, feelings, and behavior.

How effective is therapy, and which kind of therapy works best under a given circumstance?
6. Most research suggests that, in general, therapy is more effective than no therapy, although how much more effective is not known. The answer to the more difficult question of which therapy works best is even less clear. It is indisputable, though, that particular kinds of therapy are more appropriate for some problems than for others.

How are drug, electroconvulsive, and psychosurgical techniques used today in the treatment of psychological disorders?
7. Biological treatment approaches suggest that therapy ought to focus on the physiological causes of abnormal behavior, rather than considering psychological factors. Drug therapy, the best example of biological treatments, has been effective in bringing about dramatic reductions in the appearance of severe signs of mental disturbance.

462

8. Antipsychotic drugs such as chlorpromazine are very effective in reducing psychotic symptoms, although they can produce serious side effects. Antidepressant drugs reduce depression. The antianxiety drugs are among the most frequently prescribed medications of any sort; they act to reduce the experience of anxiety.

9. Electroconvulsive therapy (ECT) consists of passing an electric current of 70 to 150 volts through the head of a patient, who loses consciousness and has a strong seizure. This procedure is an effective treatment for severe cases of depression. Another biological treatment is psychosurgery. The typi-

cal procedure consists of surgically destroying certain parts of a patient's brain in an operation known as a prefrontal lobotomy. Given the grave ethical problems and possible adverse side effects, the procedure is rarely used today.

10. Community psychology aims to prevent or minimize psychological disorders. The movement was spurred in part by deinstitutionalization, in which previously hospitalized mental patients were released into the community. A notable byproduct of the movement has been the installation of telephone hot lines and campus crisis centers.

KEY TERMS AND CONCEPTS

psychotherapy (p. 438)
biologically based therapy (p. 438)
psychodynamic therapy (p. 440)
psychoanalysis (p. 440)
behavioral treatment approaches
   (p. 442)
systematic desensitization (p. 443)
observational learning (p. 445)
cognitive-behavioral approach (p. 446)
rational-emotive therapy (p. 446)

cognitive therapy (p. 447)
humanistic therapy (p. 448)
client-centered therapy (p. 448)
existential therapy (p. 449)
gestalt therapy (p. 449)
group therapy (p. 449)
family therapy (p. 450)
spontaneous remission (p. 451)
eclectic approach to therapy (p. 452)
drug therapy (p. 455)

antipsychotic drugs (p. 455)
antidepressant drugs (p. 455)
lithium (p. 456)
antianxiety drugs (p. 456)
electroconvulsive therapy (ECT)
   (p. 458)
psychosurgery (p. 458)
community psychology (p. 459)
deinstitutionalization (p. 459)

ANSWERS TO PREVIOUS REVIEW

1. False; schizophrenia can be controlled, but not cured, by medication.   **2.** b
3. electroconvulsive therapy (ECT)   **4.** False; psychosurgery is now used only as a treatment of last resort.   **5.** deinstitutionalization

CHAPTER 14
SOCIAL PSYCHOLOGY

PROLOGUE

The Helping Hands

[Consider] Chris Renner, 26, who helped create Food Partnership Inc. outside Los Angeles. It troubled him that food banks were spending a fortune in transport fees to collect donations. With the help of the California Trucking Association and United Way, he worked out a method for trucks to transport food between donors and food banks when they were returning empty from a long haul. So far, the program has carried nearly 4 million pounds of food and saved the food banks $55,000 in trucking fees.

Or Pedro Jose Greer, a Miami physician who found his calling not only in hospitals but also under bridges and highways, where many of the city's homeless live. Four years ago, "Dr. Joe," 32, opened a clinic next to a shelter called Camillus House. He now has 130 volunteer doctors and medical personnel working on 40 patients a day. "There is so much talent among the poor, we must help them no matter what," he says. "We lose so much when we lose the people from the inner cities. . . ."

Or Suzanne Firtko, an architectural historian in New York City who invented the Street Sheet, instructions that direct homeless people to the nearest soup kitchens and clothes banks. She persuaded DuPont to donate waterproof, tear-resistant paper and designed the sheets with easy-to-understand graphics so those who cannot read well and non-English-speaking people could use them. The entire operation that first year cost $1,800. "Projects like mine become very expensive when they're done by established agencies," she says. "It's very cheap when you're doing it at your kitchen table." (Gibbs, 1989, p. 21)

Suzanne Firtko hands out copies of her *Street Sheet,* which directs homeless people to sources of food and clothing.

LOOKING AHEAD

Each of these people illustrates a side of human behavior that sometimes seems all too rare. The generosity of such individuals stands in sharp contrast to the aggression and violence that is so prevalent in our modern-day society.

In this chapter, we consider those aspects of human behavior that unite us, and separate us from one another, by focusing on social psychology. Social psychology is the study of how people's thoughts, feelings, and actions are affected by others. Social psychologists consider the nature and causes of individual behavior in social situations.

The broad scope of social psychology is conveyed by the kinds of questions social psychologists ask, such as: How can we convince people to change their attitudes or to adopt new ideas and values? In what ways do we come to understand what others are like? How are we influenced by what others do and think? Why do some people display such violence, aggression, and cruelty toward others that people throughout the world live in fear of annihilation? And why, on the other hand, do some people place their own lives at risk to help others?

In this chapter, we explore social psychological approaches to these and other issues. Not only do we examine those processes that underlie social behavior; we also discuss strategies and solutions to a variety of problems and issues that all of us face—ranging from achieving a better understanding of persuasive tactics to forming more accurate impressions of others and avoiding stereotypes and prejudice.

We begin with a look at attitudes, our evaluations of people and other stimuli. We examine how people form judgments about others and what causes their behavior. Next, we discuss social influence, the process by which the actions of an individual (or a group) affect the behavior of others.

Social psychology: The branch of psychology concerned with how people's thoughts, feelings, and actions are affected by others

The chapter continues with an examination of prejudice and discrimination. We look at how stereotypes influence our understanding of others, and consider the ways in which prejudice can be reduced. Finally, we consider examples of positive and negative social behavior. After examining what social psychologists have learned about the ways in which people become attracted to one another, form relationships, and fall in love, the chapter concludes with a look at the factors that underlie aggression and helping.

- *What are attitudes, and how are they formed, maintained, and changed?*
- *How do we form impressions of what others are like and of the causes of their behavior?*
- *What are the biases that influence the ways in which we view others' behavior?*

ATTITUDES AND SOCIAL COGNITION

What do Bill Cosby, Paula Abdul, and Michael Jordan have in common? Each has appeared in a television commercial, exhorting us to purchase some particular brand-name product.

These commercials were just a few of the thousands that appear on our screens, all designed to persuade us to purchase specific products. These attempts illustrate basic principles that have been articulated by social psychologists who study **attitudes,** learned predispositions to respond in a favorable or unfavorable manner to a particular person, behavior, belief, or thing (Eagly & Chaiken, 1993).

Our attitudes, of course, are not restricted to consumer products. We also develop attitudes toward specific individuals and to more abstract issues. For example, when you think of the various people in your life, you no doubt hold vastly

Attitudes: Learned predispositions to respond in a favorable or unfavorable manner to a particular object

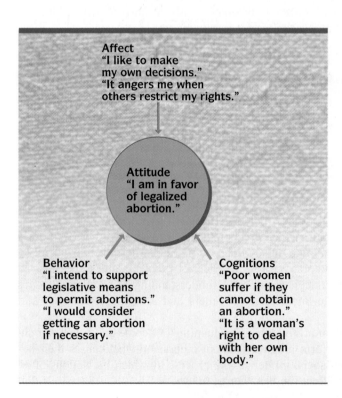

FIGURE 14-1 Like all attitudes, this attitude on abortion is composed of an affect component, behavioral component, and cognition component.

differing attitudes toward them, depending on the nature of your interactions with them. These attitudes may range from highly positive, as in the case of a lover, to extremely negative, as with a despised rival. Attitudes are also likely to vary in importance. Whereas our attitudes toward friends, family, and peers are generally central to our interactions in the social world, our attitudes toward, say, television newscasters may be relatively insignificant.

Social psychologists generally consider attitudes to follow the **ABC model of attitudes,** which suggests that an attitude has three components: affect, behavior, and cognition (Rajecki, 1989). The *affect component* encompasses our positive or negative emotions about something—how we feel about it. The *behavior component* consists of a predisposition or intention to act in a particular manner that is relevant to our attitude. Finally, the *cognition component* refers to the beliefs and thoughts we hold about the object of our attitude. For example, someone's attitude toward Paula Abdul may consist of a positive emotion (the affect component), an intention to buy her latest recording (the behavior component), and the belief that she is a good singer (the cognition component). (See Figure 14-1.)

Every attitude has these three interrelated components, although they vary in terms of which element predominates and in the nature of their relationships. All attitudes, however, develop according to the general principles that social psychologists have discovered about their formation, maintenance, and change—principles we discuss next.

ABC model of attitudes: The model suggesting that an attitude has three components: affect, behavior, and cognition

Forming and Maintaining Attitudes

Although people do not enter the world holding well-defined attitudes toward any particular person or object, anyone who has seen an infant smile at her parents knows that at least certain attitudes develop quickly. Interestingly, some of the same principles that govern how attitudes are acquired and develop in the youngest of children continue to operate throughout life.

Classical Conditioning and Attitudes   One of the basic processes underlying attitude formation and development can be explained on the basis of learning principles (McGuire, 1985; Cacioppo et al., 1992). The same classical conditioning processes that made Pavlov's dogs salivate at the sound of a bell can explain how attitudes are acquired. As we discussed in Chapter 5, people develop associations between various objects and the emotional reactions that accompany them. For example, many soldiers who were stationed in the Persian Gulf during the war with Iraq reported that they never wanted to sit on a sandy beach again. Put another way, the soldiers formed negative attitudes toward sand. Similarly, positive associations can develop through classical conditioning. We may come to hold a positive attitude toward a particular perfume because a favorite aunt wears it.

Advertisers make use of the principles of classical conditioning of attitudes by attempting to link a product they want consumers to buy with a positive feeling or event (Alsop, 1988). For instance, many advertisements feature young, attractive, healthy men and women using a product—even if it is one as uninteresting as toothpaste. The idea behind such advertisements is to create a classically conditioned response to the product, so that just glimpsing a tube of Crest toothpaste evokes a positive feeling.

Operant Conditioning Approaches to Attitude Acquisition   Another basic learning process, operant conditioning, also underlies attitude acquisition. Attitudes that are reinforced, either verbally or nonverbally, tend to be maintained. Conversely, a person who states an attitude that elicits ridicule from others may

modify or abandon the attitude. But it is not only direct reinforcement or punishment that can influence attitudes. *Vicarious learning,* in which a person learns something through the observation of others, can also account for attitude development—particularly when the individual has no direct experience with the object about which the attitude is held. It is through vicarious learning processes that children pick up the prejudices of their parents. For example, even if they have never met a blind person, children whose parents say that "blind people are incompetent" may adopt such attitudes themselves.

We also learn attitudes vicariously through television, films, and other media. For instance, movies that glorify violence reinforce positive attitudes regarding aggression, and portrayals of women as subservient to men shape and bolster sexist attitudes.

Persuasion: Changing Attitudes

Why did the makers of Pepsi conclude that endorsements by Ray Charles and Billy Crystal would lead people to drink more of their product? According to professionals working in the field of advertising, each of these celebrity endorsements is a carefully selected match between the product and the individual chosen to represent it. It is not just a matter of finding a well-known celebrity; the person must also be believable and trustworthy and reflect the qualities that advertisers want their particular product to project (Alwitt & Mitchell, 1985; Kanner, 1989).

The work of advertisers draws heavily upon findings from social psychology regarding persuasion. This research has identified a number of factors (see Figure 14-2) that promote effective persuasion—many of which you will recognize if you consider for a moment some of the advertisements with which you are most familiar (Johnson, 1991; Tesser & Shaffer, 1990).

Message Source   The individual who delivers a persuasive message, known as the attitude communicator, has a major impact on the effectiveness of that message. Communicators who are both physically and socially attractive seem to produce greater attitude change (Chaiken, 1979). Moreover, the expertise and trustworthiness of a communicator are related to the impact of a message—except in

FIGURE 14-2 In this model of the critical factors affecting persuasion, the message source and message characteristics are shown to influence the recipient or target of a persuasive message.

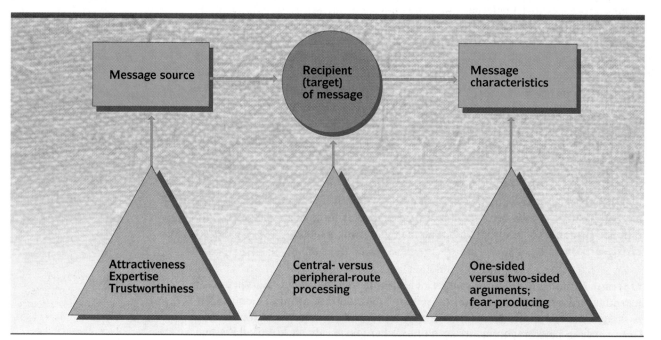

situations in which the communicator is believed to have an ulterior motive. If a prestigious communicator seems to be benefiting from persuading others, the message may be discounted (Hovland, Janis, & Kelly, 1953; Eagly, Wood, & Chaiken, 1978). For example, a prestigious scientist who argues in favor of opening a nuclear power plant would generally be a particularly influential source, unless it is revealed that the scientist owns stock in the power plant and stands to benefit financially from its opening (Kassin, 1983; Wu & Shaffer, 1987; Roskos-Ewoldsen & Fazio, 1992).

Characteristics of the Message   As you might expect, it is not just *who* delivers a message but *what* the message is like that affects attitude and behavior change. One-sided arguments—in which only the communicator's side is presented—are probably best if the communicator's message is already viewed favorably by the audience. But if the audience receives a message presenting an unpopular viewpoint, two-sided messages—which include both the communicator's position and the one he or she is arguing against—are more effective, probably because they are seen as more precise and thoughtful (Karlins & Abelson, 1979). In addition, fear-producing messages ("If you don't practice safer sex, you'll get AIDS") are generally effective, although not always. For instance, if the fear aroused is too strong, messages may evoke people's defense mechanisms and may be ignored. In such cases, fear appeals work best if they include precise recommendations for actions to avoid danger (Leventhal, 1970; Boster & Mongeau, 1985).

Characteristics of the Recipient or Target   Once a message has been communicated, the characteristics of the audience determine whether the message will be accepted. For example, it seems reasonable to assume that recipients' intelligence would be related to their persuasibility—and it is, although the relationship is complex. Specifically, high intelligence both aids and hinders persuasion. Because higher intelligence enables people to understand a message better and later recall it more easily, persuasion may be more likely. On the other hand, higher intelligence is associated with greater knowledge about a subject and more confidence in one's own opinions, and so messages of opposing viewpoints may be more likely to be rejected.

How do social psychologists reconcile these conflicting predictions? Most research suggests that highly intelligent people are more resistant to persuasion than those who are less intelligent. However, the question has not yet been fully resolved (Rhodes & Wood, 1992).

Some gender differences in persuasibility also seem to exist. For instance, social psychologist Alice Eagly (1989) has found that women are somewhat more easily persuaded than men, particularly when they have less knowledge of the message topic. However, the magnitude of the differences between men and women is not large.

One factor that clearly underlies whether a recipient is receptive to persuasive messages relates to the type of information processing they carry out. Social psychologists have discovered two primary information-processing routes to persuasion: central-route and peripheral-route processing (Petty & Cacioppo, 1986; Cialdini, 1984; Eagly, 1983). **Central-route processing** occurs when the recipient thoughtfully considers the issues and arguments involved in persuasion. **Peripheral-route processing,** in contrast, occurs when people are persuaded on the basis of factors unrelated to the nature or quality of the content of a persuasive message. Instead, they are influenced by factors that are irrelevant or extraneous to the attitude topic or issue, such as who is providing the message or how long the arguments are (Mackie, 1987; Petty & Cacioppo, 1986).

In general, central-route processing results in the most lasting attitude change. However, if central-route processing cannot be employed (for instance, if the tar-

Central-route processing: Message interpretation characterized by thoughtful consideration of the issues and arguments used to persuade

Peripheral-route processing: Message interpretation characterized by consideration of the source and related general information rather than of the message itself

get is inattentive, bored, or distracted), then the nature of the message becomes less important and peripheral factors more critical (Petty & Cacioppo, 1984).

Advertising that uses celebrities to sell a product, then, seeks to produce change through the peripheral route. In fact, it is possible that well-reasoned, carefully crafted messages will be *less* effective when delivered by a celebrity than by an anonymous source—if the target pays greater attention to the celebrity (leading to peripheral-route processing) than to the message (which would have led to central-route processing). On the other hand, since recipients of advertising messages are often in a fairly inattentive state, the use of celebrities is probably an excellent strategy. Advertisers are correct in their assumption that well-known individuals can have a significant persuasive impact.

Still other factors that advertisers take into account in considering targets of persuasive communications pertain to how readily targets can be influenced by particular messages. For instance, advertisers have begun to consider such basic characteristics as age, race, ethnicity, religion, income, and marital status in their advertising, using psychographic data. *Psychographics* is a technique for dividing people into lifestyle profiles that are related to purchasing patterns. For instance, the makers of Peter Pan peanut butter know through the use of psychographics that heavy users in the New York area tend to live in suburban and rural area households with children, headed by 18- to 54-year-olds; are frequent renters of home videos; go to theme parks; are below-average television viewers; and listen to radio at above-average rates (McCarthy, 1991). (Also see the Pathways through Psychology box.)

The Link between Attitudes and Behavior

Not surprisingly, attitudes influence behavior. If you like hamburgers (the affect component), are predisposed to eat at McDonald's or Burger King (the behavior component), and believe hamburgers are a good source of protein (the cognitive component), it is very likely that you will eat hamburgers frequently. The strength of the link between particular attitudes and behavior varies, of course, but generally people strive for consistency between their attitudes and their behavior. Furthermore, people tend to be fairly consistent in the different attitudes they hold. You would probably not hold the attitude that eating meat is immoral and still have a positive attitude toward hamburgers.

We tend to try to keep our attitudes and behavior consistent with one another. If we believe strongly in conserving natural resources and protecting the environment, we are likely to be conscientious about recycling.

PATHWAYS THROUGH PSYCHOLOGY

Karen Randolph

Education: B.A. in American history from Notre Dame University
Born: 1955
Home: Chicago

Karen Randolph

The next time you're in a grocery store, look around. You may find someone observing what you're putting in your grocery cart, seeking to learn the habits of the modern-day shopper.

This is one of the approaches used by Karen Randolph, a senior vice president for Consumer Resources at the Chicago advertising agency of Foote, Cone & Belding, to determine why people buy what they buy and ultimately to create effective product advertising.

"Our clients provide us with information and data on their products and we supplement it with what we call 'consumer immersion,' or observation work, which means getting in and living and breathing what your consumers live and breathe," said Randolph, whose initial exposure to psychology consisted of several courses in college.

Randolph, who has been with Foote, Cone & Belding for 19 years, said the firm makes it a point to hire people with psychology and social science backgrounds for the research work. "Our job is to understand what people are like and what they want, and give them a product that fits the description. We don't start with the product, we start with the consumer and what their needs and desires are," she added. "It's much easier to sell them what they want than trying to sell them something they don't want."

Randolph said the researchers go wherever a product is sold or used, be it a fast-food restaurant, a bar, or even people's homes. "We visit people in their homes and observe them doing laundry as well as asking them questions," she said. "It's not necessarily a structured interview. For instance, in a grocery store we would try to be unobtrusive, just watching and learning."

Randolph went on to say, "In addition, we might ask people why they chose to read the back of one package and not another, or why they spent so much time in a particular aisle, as well as what they were thinking when they picked up a particular item or looked at a display. We then get together and analyze the data."

Eventually, the results are used to produce persuasive advertising. But the research doesn't end there. After the advertising is created, more data are collected. "We have to test to assure that the advertising is communicating what it is supposed to and what the product is like," she said.

Interestingly, the consistency that leads attitudes to influence behavior sometimes works the other way around, for in some cases it is our behavior that shapes our attitudes. Consider, for instance, the following scenario:

You've just spent what you feel is the most boring hour of your life, turning pegs for a psychology experiment. Just as you're finally finished and about to leave, the experimenter asks you to do him a favor. He tells you that he needs a helper for future experimental sessions to introduce subsequent subjects to the peg-turning task. Your specific job would be to tell them that turning the pegs is an interesting, fascinating experience. Each time you tell this tale to another subject, you'll be paid $1.

If you agree to help out the experimenter, you may be setting yourself up for a state of psychological tension that is known as cognitive dissonance. According to a major social psychologist, Leon Festinger (1957), **cognitive dissonance** occurs when a person holds two attitudes or thoughts (referred to as *cognitions*) that contradict each other.

A subject in the situation just described is left with two contradictory thoughts: (1) I believe the task is boring, but (2) I said it was interesting with little justification ($1). According to the theory, dissonance should be aroused. How can

Cognitive dissonance: The conflict that arises when a person holds contradictory cognitions

471

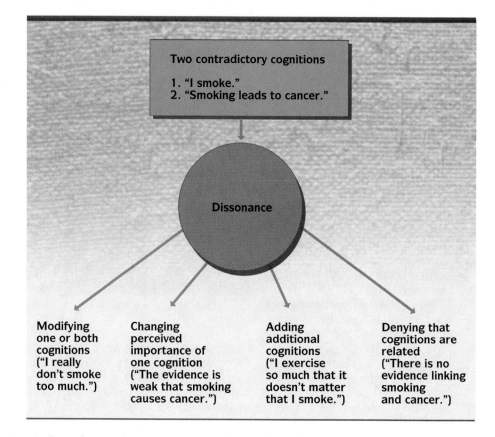

FIGURE 14-3 The presence of two contradictory cognitions ("I smoke" and "Smoking leads to cancer") produces dissonance, which may be reduced through several methods.

such dissonance be reduced? One can't very well deny having said that the task was interesting without making a fairly strong break with reality. But, relatively speaking, it is easy to change one's attitude toward the task—and thus the theory predicts that dissonance will be reduced as the subjects change their attitudes to be more positive.

This prediction was confirmed in a classic experiment (Festinger & Carlsmith, 1959). The experiment followed essentially the same procedure outlined earlier, in which subjects were offered $1 to describe a boring task as interesting. In addition, as a control, a condition was included in which other subjects were offered $20 to say that the task was interesting. The reasoning behind this condition was that $20 was so much money that subjects in this condition had a good reason to be conveying incorrect information; dissonance would *not* be aroused, and *less* attitude change would be expected. The results supported this notion. Subjects who were paid $1 changed their attitudes more (becoming more positive toward the peg-turning task) than subjects who were paid $20.

We now know that dissonance explains a number of everyday occurrences involving attitudes and behavior. For example, a smoker who knows that smoking leads to lung cancer holds contradictory cognitions: (1) I smoke, and (2) smoking leads to lung cancer. The theory predicts that these two thoughts will lead to a state of cognitive dissonance. More important, it predicts that the individual will be motivated to reduce such dissonance by one of the following methods: (1) modifying one or both of the cognitions, (2) changing the perceived importance of one cognition, (3) adding cognitions, or (4) denying that the two cognitions are related to each other. Hence the smoker might decide that he or she really doesn't smoke all that much (modifying the cognition), that the evidence linking smoking to cancer is weak (changing the importance of a cognition), that the amount of exercise he or she gets compensates for the smoking (adding cogni-

tions), or that there is no evidence linking smoking and cancer (denial). Whatever technique is used, the result is a reduction in dissonance (see Figure 14-3).

Social Cognition: Understanding Others

Regardless of whether they agreed with his policies and ideology, in spite of how much they felt he garbled the facts at news conferences, and irrespective of the trouble his subordinates found themselves in, most Americans genuinely *liked* former President Ronald Reagan. These problems, which might have been expected to reflect unfavorably upon him personally, never seemed to affect Reagan's popularity, and he was dubbed the "Teflon President" by the press. Perceived as a "nice guy," he remained one of the most popular Presidents of the century until the end of his second term.

Situations such as this one illustrate the power of our impressions and attest to the importance of determining how people develop an understanding of others. One of the dominant areas of study in social psychology during the last few years has focused on learning how we come to understand what others are like and how we explain the reasons underlying others' behavior (Fiske & Taylor, 1991; Devine, Hamilton, & Ostrom, 1994).

Understanding What Others Are Like   Consider for a moment the enormous amount of information about other people to which we are exposed. How are we able to decide what is important and what is not, and to make judgments about the characteristics of others? Social psychologists interested in this question study **social cognition**—the processes that underlie our understanding of the social world. They have learned that individuals have highly developed **schemas, sets of cognitions about people and social experiences.** These schemas organize information stored in memory; represent in our minds the way the social world operates; and give us a framework to categorize, store, remember, and interpret information relating to social stimuli (Fiske & Taylor, 1991; Fiske, 1992).

We typically hold schemas for particular types of people in our environments. Our schema for "teacher," for instance, generally consists of a number of characteristics: knowledge of the subject matter he or she is teaching, a desire to impart that knowledge, and an awareness of the student's need to understand what is being said. Or we may hold a schema for "mother" that includes the characteristics of warmth, nurturance, and caring. Regardless of their accuracy—and, as we shall see, very often their inaccuracy—schemas are important because they organize the way in which we recall, recognize, and categorize information about others. Moreover, they allow us to make predictions of what others are like on the basis of relatively little information, since we tend to fit people into schemas even when there is not much concrete evidence to go on (Snyder & Cantor, 1979; Smith, 1984).

Impression Formation   How do we decide that Gail is a flirt, or Andy is a jerk, or Jon is a really nice guy? The earliest work on social cognition was designed to examine *impression formation,* the process by which an individual organizes information about another person to form an overall impression of that person. In one classic study, for instance, students were told that they were about to hear a guest lecturer (Kelley, 1950). One group of students was told that the lecturer was "a rather warm person, industrious, critical, practical, and determined," while a second group was told that he was "a rather cold person, industrious, critical, practical, and determined."

The simple substitution of "cold" for "warm" was responsible for drastic differences in the way the students in each group perceived the lecturer, even though he gave the same talk in the same style in each condition. Students who had been

Social cognition: The processes that underlie our understanding of the social world

Schemas: Sets of cognitions about people and social experiences

474

told he was "warm" rated him considerably more positively than students who had been told he was "cold."

The findings from this experiment led to additional research on impression formation that focused on the way in which people pay particular attention to certain unusually important traits—known as **central traits**—to help them form an overall impression of others. According to this work, the presence of a central trait alters the meaning of other traits (Asch, 1946; Widmeyer & Loy, 1988). Hence the description of the lecturer as "industrious" presumably meant something different according to whether it was associated with the central trait "warm" or "cold."

Other work on impression formation has used information-processing approaches (see Chapter 7) to develop mathematically oriented models of how individual personality traits are combined to create an overall impression (Anderson, 1974). Generally, the results of this research suggest that in forming an overall judgment of a person, we use a psychological "average" of the individual traits we see, in a manner analogous to finding the mathematical average of several numbers (Kaplan, 1975; Anderson, 1991).

Of course, as we gain more experience with people and see them exhibiting behavior in a variety of situations, our impressions of them become more complex (Anderson & Klatzky, 1987; Casselden & Hampson, 1990). But because there are usually gaps in our knowledge of others, we still tend to fit them into personality schemas that represent particular "types" of people. For instance, we might hold a "gregarious person" schema, made up of the traits of friendliness, aggressiveness, and openness. The presence of just one or two of these traits might be sufficient to make us assign a person to a particular schema.

Unfortunately, the schemas we employ are susceptible to a variety of factors that affect the accuracy of our judgments (Kenny, 1991; Bernieri et al., 1994). For example, our mood affects how we perceive others. People who are happy form more favorable impressions and make more positive judgments than people who are in a bad mood (Forgas & Bower, 1987; Erber, 1991).

Even when schemas are not entirely accurate, they serve an important function. They allow us to develop expectations about how others will behave, permitting us to plan our interactions with others more easily and serving to simplify a complex social world.

Attribution Processes: Understanding the Causes of Behavior

When Barbara Washington, a new employee at the Ablex Computer Company, completed a major staffing project 2 weeks early, her boss, Yolanda, was delighted. At the next staff meeting, she announced how pleased she was with Barbara and explained that *this* was an example of the kind of performance she was looking for in her staff. The other staff members looked on resentfully, trying to figure out why Barbara had worked night and day to finish the project not just on time, but 2 weeks early. She must be an awfully compulsive person, they decided.

Most of us have, at one time or another, puzzled over the reasons behind someone's behavior. Perhaps it was in a situation similar to the one above, or it may have been under more formal circumstances, such as serving as a judge on a student judiciary board in a cheating case. In contrast to work on social cognition, which describes how people develop an overall impression about others' personality traits, **attribution theory** seeks to explain how we decide, on the basis of samples of an individual's behavior, what the specific causes of that person's behavior are (Weiner, 1985a, 1985b; Jones, 1990; White, 1992).

When trying to understand the causes that produce a given behavior, individuals typically try first to determine whether the cause is situational or dispositional (Heider, 1958). A **situational cause** is brought about by something in the

Central traits: The major traits considered in forming impressions of others

Attribution theory: The theory that seeks to explain how we decide, on the basis of samples of an individual's behavior, what the specific causes of that behavior are

Situational cause (of behavior): A cause of behavior that is based on environmental factors

environment. For instance, someone who knocks over a quart of milk and then cleans it up is probably doing so not because he or she is necessarily a terribly neat person, but because the *situation* is one that requires it. In contrast, a person who spends hours shining the kitchen floor is probably doing so because he or she *is* a neat person—hence, the behavior has a **dispositional cause,** prompted by the person's disposition (his or her internal traits or personality characteristics).

In our example involving Barbara, her fellow employees attributed her behavior to her disposition rather than to the situation. But from a logical standpoint, it is equally plausible that there was something about the situation that caused the behavior. If asked, Barbara might attribute her accomplishment to situational factors, explaining that she had so much other work to do that she just had to get the project out of the way, or that the project was not all that difficult and so it was easy to complete ahead of schedule. To her, then, the reason for her behavior might not be dispositional at all; it could be situational.

Biases in Attribution: To Err Is Human   Although attribution theory suggests that people rationally consider the causes of others' behavior, people do not always process information about others in a logical fashion (Funder, 1987; Gilbert, Jones, & Pelham, 1987). In fact, research shows that there tend to be consistent biases in the way attributions are made. Among the most typical:

■   *The fundamental attribution error.* One of the most common biases in people's attributions is the tendency to overattribute others' behavior to dispositional causes, and the corresponding failure to recognize the importance of situational causes. Known as the **fundamental attribution error,** this tendency is quite prevalent (Ross, 1977; Ross & Nisbett, 1991). We tend to exaggerate the importance of personality characteristics (dispositional causes) in producing others' behavior, minimizing the influence of the environment (situational factors).

Why should the fundamental attribution error be so common? One reason pertains to the nature of information that is available to the people making an attribution. When we view the behavior of another person in a particular setting, the information that is most conspicuous is the person's behavior itself. Because the individual's immediate surroundings are relatively unchanging, the person whose behavior we're considering is the center of our attention. In contrast, the person's environment is less attention-grabbing. Consequently, we are more likely to make attributions based on personal, dispositional factors and less likely to make attributions relating to the situation.

■   *The halo effect.* Harry is intelligent, kind, and loving. Is he also conscientious? If you were to hazard a guess, your most likely response would be yes. Your guess reflects the **halo effect,** a phenomenon in which an initial understanding that a person has positive traits is used to infer other uniformly positive characteristics (Cooper, 1981). The opposite would also hold true. Learning that Harry was unsociable and argumentative would probably lead you to assume he was lazy as well.

The reason for the halo effect is that we hold *implicit personality theories,* theories reflecting our notions of a combination of traits found in particular individuals. These theories are based on both experience and logic. Our perception of the world may be flawed, however, because application of our theory can be singularly inappropriate for a given individual, or it may simply be wrong. Most people have neither uniformly positive nor uniformly negative traits, but instead possess a combination of the two.

■   *Assumed-similarity bias.* How similar to you—in terms of attitudes, opinions, and likes and dislikes—are your friends and acquaintances? Most people believe that their friends and acquaintances are fairly similar to themselves. But this feeling goes beyond just people we know; there is a general tendency—known as the

Dispositional cause (of behavior): A cause of behavior that is based on internal traits or personality factors

Fundamental attribution error: A tendency to attribute others' behavior to dispositional causes and the failure to recognize the importance of situational causes

Halo effect: A phenomenon in which an initial understanding that a person has positive traits is used to infer other uniformly positive characteristics

assumed-similarity bias—to think of people as being similar to oneself, even when meeting them for the first time (Ross, Greene, & House, 1977; Hoch, 1987; Marks & Miller, 1987).

If other people are, in fact, different from oneself, the assumed-similarity bias reduces the accuracy of the judgments being made. Moreover, it suggests an interesting possibility: It may be that a judgment about another individual better defines the judge's characteristics than those of the person being rated. In some cases, then, the portrait we draw of another person—particularly one about whom we have little information—may in reality be a sketch of the way we view ourselves.

Assumed-similarity bias: The tendency to think of people as being similar to oneself

Exploring Diversity

Attributions in a Cultural Context: How Fundamental Is the Fundamental Attribution Error?

Some groups of Native Americans have a different sense of time from Caucasians of European extraction, potentially giving rise to cultural misunderstandings.

Not everyone is susceptible to attribution biases in the same way. The kind of culture in which we are raised clearly plays a role in the way we attribute others' behavior.

Take, for example, the fundamental attribution error, the tendency to overestimate the importance of personal, dispositional factors and underattribute situational causes when determining the causes of others' behavior. Although the error is pervasive in Western cultures, it seems to operate in a different way in Asian society.

Specifically, social psychologist Joan Miller (J. G. Miller, 1984) found that adult subjects in India were more likely to use situational attributions than dispositional ones in explaining events. These findings are the opposite of those based on subjects in the United States, and they contradict the fundamental attribution error.

Miller suggested that we can discover the reason for these results by examining the norms and values of Indian society, which emphasize social responsibility and societal obligations to a greater extent than in Western societies. Furthermore, she suggests that the particular language spoken in a culture may lead to different sorts of attributions. For instance, a tardy person using English might say "I am late," suggesting a personal, dispositional cause ("I am a tardy person"). In contrast, users of Spanish who are late say, "The clock caused me to be late." Clearly, the statement in Spanish implies that the cause is a situational one (Zebrowitz-McArthur, 1988).

In sum, people from different cultures explain behavior in different ways (Miller, Bersoff, & Harwood, 1990; Miller & Bersoff, 1992). Such differences in attributions may have profound implications. Recall, for instance, our discussion in Chapter 10 of the differences in the way people in Asian and Western cultures attribute school success. Asian parents tend to stress the importance of effort and hard work in producing good academic performance. In contrast, Western parents de-emphasize the role of effort. Instead, they attribute school success to innate ability. These discrepancies in attributional styles result in Asian students being pushed more to achieve and ultimately outperforming U.S. students in school (Stevenson, 1992; Stevenson & Stigler, 1992; Stevenson, Chen, & Lee, 1992).

RECAP AND REVIEW

Recap

- Attitudes are learned predispositions to respond in a favorable or unfavorable manner to a particular object. They

have three components: affect, behavior, and cognition.

- The major factors promoting persuasion relate to the message source, characteristics of the message, and characteristics of the recipient or target.

- People strive to fit their attitudes and behavior together in a logical framework, and they attempt to overcome any inconsistencies they perceive.
- Social cognition is concerned with the processes that underlie our understanding of the social world.
- Attribution theory explains the processes that underlie how we attribute the causes of others' behavior, particularly in terms of situational versus dispositional causes.

Review

1. A learned predisposition to respond in a favorable or an unfavorable manner to a particular object is called a(n) _attitude_

2. Match each component of the ABC model of attitudes with its definition:
   1. Affect — b
   2. Behavior — c
   3. Cognition — a
   a. Thoughts and beliefs
   b. Positive or negative emotions
   c. Predisposition to act a particular way

3. One brand of peanut butter advertises its product by describing its taste and nutritional value. It is hoping to persuade customers through _Central_-route processing. In ads for a competing brand, a popular actor is seen happily eating the product—but does not describe it. This approach hopes to persuade customers through _peripheral_ route processing.

4. Cognitive dissonance theory suggests that we commonly change our behavior to keep it consistent with our attitudes. True or False?

5. A _schema_ provides a mental framework for us to organize and interpret information about the social world.

6. Monica was happy to lend her textbook to a fellow student who seemed bright and friendly. She was surprised when her classmate did not return it. Her assumption that the bright and friendly student would also be responsible reflects the _halo_ effect.

Ask Yourself

Suppose you were assigned to develop a full advertising campaign for a product, including television, radio, and print ads. How might the theories in this chapter guide your strategy to suit the different media?

(Answers to review questions are on page 478.)

• What are the major sources and tactics of social influence?

SOCIAL INFLUENCE

You have just transferred to a new college and are attending your first class. When the professor enters, you find that your fellow classmates all rise, bow down, and then face the back of the room. You do not understand this behavior at all. Is it more likely that you will (1) jump up to join the rest of the class or (2) remain seated?

Based on what research has told us about **social influence,** the process by which the actions of an individual or group affect the behavior of others, the answer to such a question would almost always be the first option. As you undoubtedly know from your own experience, pressures to conform can be painfully strong, and they can bring about changes in behavior that, when considered in perspective, would otherwise never have occurred.

Social influence: The area of social psychology concerned with situations in which the actions of an individual or group affect the behavior of others

Conformity: Following What Others Do

Conformity is a change in behavior or attitudes brought about by a desire to follow the beliefs or standards of other people. The classic demonstration of pressure to conform comes from a series of studies carried out in the 1950s by Solomon Asch (Asch, 1951). In the experiments, subjects thought they were participating in a test of perceptual skills with a group of six other subjects. The subjects were shown one card with three lines of varying length and a second card which had a fourth line that matched one of the first three (see Figure 14-4). The task was seemingly straightforward: The subjects had to announce aloud which of the first three lines was identical in length to a "standard" line. Because the correct answer was always obvious, the task seemed easy to the participants.

Conformity: A change in behavior or attitudes brought about by a desire to follow the beliefs or standards of other people

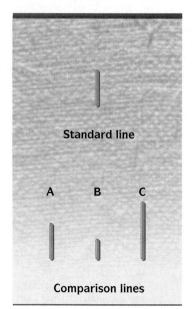

Standard line

A   B   C

Comparison lines

FIGURE 14-4 Subjects in Asch's conformity experiment were first shown a "standard" line and then asked to identify which of the three comparison lines was identical in length. As this example illustrates, there was always a correct answer.

Status: The social rank an individual holds within a group

Social supporter: A person who shares an unpopular opinion or attitude of another group member, thereby encouraging nonconformity

Indeed, since the subjects all agreed on the first few trials, the procedure appeared to be quite a simple one. But then something odd began to happen. From the perspective of the subject in the group who got to answer last, all of the first six subjects' answers seemed to be wrong—in fact, unanimously wrong. And this pattern persisted. Over and over again, the first six subjects provided answers that contradicted what the last subject believed to be the correct one. The dilemma that this situation posed for the last subject was whether to follow his or her own perceptions or to follow the group and repeat the answer that everyone else was giving.

As you might have guessed, the situation in the experiment was more contrived than it first appeared. The first six subjects were actually confederates of the experimenter and had been instructed to give unanimously erroneous answers in many of the trials. And the study had nothing to do with perceptual skills. Instead, the issue under investigation was conformity.

What Asch found was that, in about one-third of the trials, subjects conformed to the unanimous but erroneous group answer, with about 75 percent of all subjects conforming at least once. However, there were strong individual differences. Some subjects conformed nearly all the time, whereas others never did so.

Since Asch's pioneering work, literally hundreds of studies have examined the factors affecting conformity, and we now know a great deal about the phenomenon (Moscovici, 1985; Tanford & Penrod, 1984; Wood et al., 1994). Among the most important variables producing conformity are the following:

■ *The characteristics of the group.* The more attractive a group is to its members, the greater its ability to produce conformity (Hogg & Hardie, 1992). Furthermore, a person's relative **status,** the social rank held within a group, is critical: The lower a person's status in the group, the greater the power of the group over that person's behavior.

■ *The nature of the individual's response.* Conformity is considerably higher when people must make a response publicly than when they can respond privately, as our founding fathers noted when they authorized secret ballots in voting.

■ *The kind of task.* People working on tasks and questions that are ambiguous (having no clear answer) are more susceptible to social pressure. Someone asked to give an opinion, such as on what type of clothing is fashionable, is more likely to yield to conformist pressures than he or she would be if asked to answer a question of fact. Moreover, tasks at which an individual is less competent relative to the group create conditions in which conformity is more likely.

■ *Unanimity of the group.* Conformity pressures are most pronounced in groups that are unanimous in their support of a position. But what of the case in which people with dissenting views have an ally in the group, known as a **social supporter,** who agrees with them? Having just one person present who shares the unpopular point of view is sufficient to reduce conformity pressures (Allen, 1975; Levine, 1989). However, in some cases, pressures to conform are nearly irresistible.

Gender Differences in Conformity: Fact or Fiction? Are women more likely to conform than men? The answer to this question has seesawed back and forth for the last two decades.

For many years, the prevailing wisdom was that women were more easily influenced than men—a view that held until the late 1970s (Allen, 1965). At that

---

ANSWERS TO PREVIOUS REVIEW
1. attitude **2.** 1-b; 2-c; 3-a **3.** central; peripheral **4.** False; we typically change our attitudes, not our behavior, to reduce cognitive dissonance. **5.** schema **6.** halo

Thousands of Harley-Davidson motorcycle enthusiasts from all over the world met in Milwaukee, Wisconsin, to celebrate the company's anniversary. Such gatherings demonstrate that conformity to a group produces a sense of belonging in the individual members.

time, however, research began to suggest that the difference was not real. For example, it seemed that the tasks and topics employed in conformity experiments were often more familiar to men than to women. This unfamiliarity led women to conform more than men because of their feelings that they lacked expertise and not because of any ingrained susceptibility to conformity pressures (Eagly, 1978; Eagly & Carli, 1981).

More recent views, however, have supported the older conclusion: Women do seem to conform more to others than men, relatively independent of the topic at hand (Eagly, 1989). What causes them to conform are the traditional expectations society holds for women, which suggest that women should be concerned more than men in getting along well with others.

Consequently, research now suggests that women are more susceptible to social influence than men, but primarily under public conditions. In private, the differences between men's and women's conformity diminishes. Still, the topsy-turvy nature of the interpretation of the conformity research suggests that we have not heard the last word on this issue.

Compliance: Submitting to Direct Social Pressure

When we discuss conformity, we are usually talking about a phenomenon in which the social pressure is subtle or indirect. But in some situations social pressure is much more obvious, and there is direct, explicit pressure to endorse a particular point of view or to behave in a certain way. Social psychologists call the type of behavior that occurs in response to direct social pressure **compliance.**

Compliance: Behavior that occurs in response to direct social pressure

Several specific sales tactics represent attempts to gain compliance. Among the most frequently employed:

■ *The foot-in-the-door technique.* A salesperson comes to your door and asks you to accept a small sample. You agree, thinking you have nothing to lose. A little while later comes a larger request, which, because you have already agreed to the first one, you have a harder time turning down.

The salesperson in this case is employing a tried-and-true strategy that social psychologists call the foot-in-the-door technique. According to the *foot-in-the-*

door technique, you first ask that a person agree to a small request and later ask the person to comply with a more important one. It turns out that compliance with the ultimate request increases significantly when the person first agrees to the smaller favor.

The foot-in-the-door phenomenon was first demonstrated in a study in which a number of experimenters went door-to-door asking residents to sign a petition in favor of safe driving (Freedman & Fraser, 1966). Almost everyone complied with this small, benign request. However, a few weeks later, different experimenters contacted the residents again and made a much larger request: that they erect a huge sign reading "Drive Carefully" on their front lawns. The results were clear: 55 percent of those who had signed the petition agreed to the request, whereas only 17 percent of people in a control group who had not been asked to sign the petition agreed.

Subsequent research has confirmed the effectiveness of the foot-in-the-door technique (Beaman et al., 1983; Dillard, 1991). Why does it work? One reason is that involvement with the small request leads to an interest in an issue, and taking an action—any action—makes the individual more committed to the issue, thereby increasing the likelihood of future compliance. Another explanation revolves around people's self-perceptions. By complying with the initial request, individuals may come to see themselves as the kind of person who provides help when asked. Then, when confronted with the larger request, they agree in order to maintain the kind of consistency in attitudes and behavior that we described earlier. Although we don't know which of these two explanations is more accurate, it is clear that the foot-in-the-door strategy is effective (Dillard, 1991; Gorassini & Olson, 1995).

■ *The door-in-the-face technique.* A fund-raiser comes to your door and asks for a $500 contribution. You laughingly refuse, telling her that the amount is way out of your league. She then asks for a $10 contribution. What do you do? If you are like most people, you'll probably be a lot more compliant than if she hadn't asked for the huge contribution first. The reason lies in the *door-in-the-face technique,* in which a large request, refusal of which is expected, is followed by a smaller one. This strategy, which is the opposite of the foot-in-the-door approach, has also proved to be effective (Dillard, 1991; Reeves et al., 1991).

One example of its success was shown in a field experiment in which college students were stopped on the street and asked to agree to a substantial favor—acting as unpaid counselors for juvenile delinquents 2 hours a week for 2 years (Cialdini et al., 1975). Not surprisingly, no one agreed to make such an enormous commitment. But when they were later asked the considerably smaller favor of taking a group of delinquents on a two-hour trip to the zoo, half the people complied. In comparison, only 17 percent of a control group of subjects who had not first received the larger request agreed.

The use of this technique is widespread in everyday life. You may have used it at some point yourself, perhaps by asking your parents for a very large increase in your allowance and later settling for less. Similarly, television writers sometimes sprinkle their scripts with obscenities they know will be cut out by network censors, hoping to keep other key phrases intact (Cialdini, 1988).

■ *The that's-not-all technique.* In the *that's-not-all technique,* you're offered a deal at an inflated price. But immediately following the initial offer, the salesperson offers an incentive, discount, or bonus to clinch the deal.

Although it sounds transparent, such a practice can be quite effective. In one study, the experimenters set up a booth and sold cupcakes for 75 cents each. In one condition, customers were told directly that the price was 75 cents. But in another condition, they were told the price was $1, but had been reduced to 75 cents. As the that's-not-all technique would predict, more cupcakes were sold at the "reduced" price—even though it was identical to the price in the other experimental condition (Burger, 1986).

■ *The not-so-free sample.* If you're ever given a free sample, keep in mind that it comes with a psychological cost. Although they may not couch it in these terms, salespeople who provide samples to potential customers do so in order to instigate the norm of reciprocity. The *norm of reciprocity* is the well-accepted societal standard dictating that we should treat other people as they treat us. Receipt of a *not-so-free sample,* then, suggests the need for reciprocation—in the form of a purchase, of course (Cialdini, 1988).

Obedience: Obeying Direct Orders

Compliance techniques provide a means by which people are gently led toward agreement with another person's request. In some cases, however, requests are geared toward producing **obedience,** a change in behavior due to the commands of others. Although obedience is considerably less common than conformity and compliance, it does occur in several specific kinds of relationships. For example, we may show obedience to our boss, teacher, or parent merely because of the power the person holds to reward or punish us.

Obedience: A change in behavior due to the commands of others

To acquire an understanding of obedience, consider, for a moment, how you might respond if a stranger said to you:

I've devised a new way of improving memory. All I need is for you to teach people a list of words and then give them a test. The test procedure requires only that you give learners a shock each time they make a mistake on the test. To administer the shocks you will use a "shock generator" that give shocks ranging from 30 to 450 volts. You can see that the switches are labeled from "slight shock" through "danger: severe shock" at the top level, where there are three red X's. But don't worry; although the shocks may be painful, they will cause no permanent damage.

Presented with this situation, you would be likely to think that neither you nor anyone else would go along with the stranger's unusual request. Clearly, it lies outside the bounds of what we consider good sense.

Or does it? Suppose the stranger asking for your help were a psychologist conducting an experiment. Or suppose it were your teacher, your employer, or your military commander—all people in authority with some seemingly legitimate reason for their request.

If you still believe it unlikely that you would comply—think again, for the situation represented above describes a now-classic experiment conducted by social psychologist Stanley Milgram in the 1960s (Milgram, 1974). In the study, subjects were placed in a situation in which they were told by an experimenter to give increasingly strong shocks to another person as part of a study on learning (see Figure 14-5). In reality, the experiment had nothing to do with learning; the real issue under consideration was the degree to which subjects would comply with the experimenter's requests. In fact, the person supposedly receiving the shocks was actually a confederate who never really received any punishment.

Most people who hear a description of the experiment feel that it is unlikely that *any* subject would give the maximum level of shock—or, for that matter, any shock at all. Even a group of psychiatrists to whom the situation was described predicted that fewer than 2 percent of the subjects would fully comply and administer the strongest shocks. However, the actual results contradicted both experts' and nonexperts' predictions. Almost two-thirds of the subjects eventually used the highest setting on the shock generator to "electrocute" the learner.

Why did so many individuals comply fully with the experimenter's demands? Extensive interviews carried out with subjects following the experiment showed that they were obedient primarily because they believed that the experimenter would be responsible for any potential ill effects that befell the learner. The experimenter's orders were accepted, then, because the subjects thought that they personally could not be held accountable for their actions—they could always blame the experimenter.

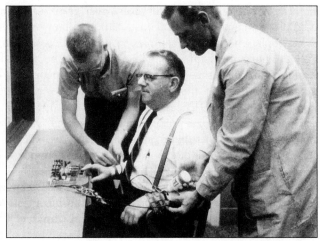

FIGURE 14-5 This impressive-looking "shock generator" was used to lead participants to believe they were administering electric shocks to another person, who was connected to the generator by electrodes that were attached to the skin. *(Copyright © 1965 by Stanley Milgram. From the film Obedience, distributed by the New York University Film Library and Pennsylvania State University, PCR.)*

Although the Milgram experiment has been criticized both on ethical grounds, for creating an extremely trying set of circumstances for the subjects, and on methodological grounds (A. G. Miller, 1986; Orne & Holland, 1968), it remains one of the strongest laboratory demonstrations of obedience (Blass, 1991; Blass & Krackow, 1991). We need only consider actual instances of obedience to authority to witness some frightening real-life parallels. A major defense of Nazi officers after World War II, for instance, was that they were "only following orders." Milgram's experiment, which was motivated in part by his desire to explain the behavior of everyday Germans during World War II, forces each of us to ask ourselves this question: Would we be able to withstand the intense power of authority?

RECAP AND REVIEW

Recap

- Social influence encompasses situations in which the actions of one individual or group affect the behavior of another.
- Conformity is a change in attitude or behavior brought about by a desire to follow the beliefs or standards of others.
- Compliance is a change in behavior made in response to more explicit social pressure. Obedience, in contrast, is a change in behavior resulting from a direct command.

Review

1. A _____ _____ , or person who agrees with the dissenting viewpoint, is likely to reduce conformity.
2. Who pioneered the study of conformity?
   a. Skinner
   b. Asch
   c. Milgram
   d. Fiala

3. Which of the following techniques asks a person to comply with a small initial request to enhance the likelihood that the person will later comply with a larger request?
   a. Door-in-the-face technique
   b. Foot-in-the-door technique
   c. Small-favor paradigm
   d. Low-balling technique
4. The _____-_____-_____-_____ technique begins with an outrageous request which then makes a smaller request seem reasonable.
5. _____ is a change in behavior that is due to another person's orders.

Ask Yourself

Given that persuasive techniques like those described in this section are so powerful, should there be laws against the use of such techniques? Should people be taught defenses against such techniques? Is the use of such techniques ethically and morally defensible?

(Answers to review questions are on page 484.)

- *What is the distinction between stereotypes, prejudice, and discrimination?*
- *How can we reduce prejudice and discrimination?*

PREJUDICE AND DISCRIMINATION

What do you think of when someone says, "He's African-American," or "She's Chinese," or "woman driver"? If you're like most people, you'll probably automatically jump to some sort of impression of what that individual is like. Such views represent **stereotypes,** beliefs and expectations about members of groups held simply on the basis of their membership in those groups.

Stereotypes can lead to **prejudice,** the negative (or positive) evaluations or judgments of members of a group that are based primarily on membership in the group rather than on the behavior of a particular individual. For instance, racial prejudice occurs when a member of a racial group is evaluated in terms of race and not because of his or her own characteristics or abilities.

The most common stereotypes and forms of prejudice have to do with racial, religious, and ethnic categorizations. Over the years, various groups have been called "lazy" or "shrewd" or "cruel" with varying degrees of regularity by non-group members (Katz & Braly, 1933; Weber & Crocker, 1983; Devine & Baker, 1991). Even today, despite major progress toward the reduction of legally sanctioned manifestations of prejudice such as school segregation, stereotypes remain.

For instance, although it might be comforting to think that prejudiced people in the United States are found primarily in groups such as the skinheads, neo-Nazis, and the Ku Klux Klan, the unfortunate reality is quite different: Racial, ethnic, and religious bigotry is commonplace.

This fact was brought home in a large-scale survey conducted in 300 communities throughout the United States, which found that expressions of prejudice were routine (T. W. Smith, 1990). The study used a careful and innovative measurement technique to assess stereotyping. People are often unwilling to express the prejudice they feel because such sentiments violate societal norms of politeness, so indirect assessments of stereotypes were necessary. To do this, participants in the survey were asked to indicate whether people in each of several groups were closer to one or the other end of a series of seven-point scales. For example, subjects were asked whether each racial group was closer to the end point of "hard-working" or the opposite end, "lazy." By comparing a particular group's ratings against ratings of other groups, it was possible to determine which groups were the most stereotyped.

The survey results revealed that stereotyping is alive and well. For example, around 80 percent of respondents believed that African-Americans were more likely than whites to "prefer to live off welfare." In general, African-Americans, Hispanics, and Asians were all assumed to be lazier, more violence-prone, less intelligent, and less patriotic than whites.

Furthermore, members of minority groups even stereotyped themselves. For instance, approximately one-third of African-Americans and Hispanics thought that members of their own group were less intelligent than whites. Such findings imply that members of minority groups are not immune to messages of prejudice when it is prevalent within a society.

Despite the civil rights advances of the past 25 years, stereotyping clearly remains all too common. Hispanics, Asians, and particularly African-Americans are viewed by whites in a negative manner. Until such stereotypes are dispelled, communities are likely to remain segregated, and their members wary of people from other racial and ethnic groups (Devine & Elliot, 1995).

But stereotypes are by no means confined to racial and ethnic groups. Sex and

Stereotypes: Beliefs and expectations about members of groups held simply on the basis of their membership in those groups

Prejudice: The negative (or positive) evaluations or judgments of members of a group that are based primarily on membership in the group rather than on the behavior of a particular individual

Ingroup-outgroup bias: The tendency to hold less favorable opinions about groups to which we do not belong (outgroups), while holding more favorable opinions about groups to which we do belong (ingroups)

Discrimination: Negative behavior toward members of a particular group

Self-fulfilling prophecy: An expectation about the occurrence of an event or behavior that increases the likelihood that the event or behavior will happen

age stereotyping are common as well (Swim et al., 1995). There is even a general stereotype relating to *any* group, known as the **ingroup-outgroup bias** (Wilder, 1986, 1990; Perdue et al., 1990). We tend to hold less favorable opinions about members of groups of which we are not a part (*outgroups*) and more favorable opinions about members of groups to which we belong (*ingroups*).

Although there is little evidence to support the accuracy of most stereotypes, they often have harmful consequences. When negative stereotypes are acted on, they result in **discrimination**—negative behavior toward members of a particular group. Discrimination can lead to exclusion from jobs, neighborhoods, or educational opportunities, and may result in members of particular groups receiving lower salaries and benefits (Lott & Maluso, 1995).

Stereotyping leads not only to overt discrimination; it can actually cause members of stereotyped groups to behave in ways that reflect the stereotype through a phenomenon known as the **self-fulfilling prophecy** (Archibald, 1974). Self-fulfilling prophecies are expectations about the occurrence of a future event or behavior that act to increase the likelihood that the event or behavior *will* occur. For example, if people think that members of a particular group are unambitious, they may treat them in a way that actually brings about their lack of ambition (Skrypnek & Snyder, 1982). Similarly, people holding a stereotype may be "primed" to interpret the behavior of the stereotyped group as representative of the stereotype, even when the behavior depicts something entirely different (Slusher & Anderson, 1987).

In some cases, knowing that others hold a stereotype about you may induce you to behave in line with the stereotype if you are striving to make a positive impression, even if such behavior is not representative of your typical behavior. For instance, researchers found that women interacting with an attractive, desirable male, whom they thought stereotyped women as passive and dependent, tended to espouse more passive and dependent views than women who thought the attractive male held nontraditional views of women. In contrast, when the male was unattractive, the women's behavior was not affected by the nature of the stereotype they thought he held. In sum, only when they felt motivated to make a good impression did they behave according to the stereotype (Zanna & Pack, 1974).

The Foundations of Prejudice

No one has ever been born disliking a particular racial, religious, or ethnic group. People learn to hate, in much the same way they learn the alphabet.

According to *social learning approaches* to stereotyping and prejudice, people's feelings about members of various groups are shaped by the behavior of parents, other adults, and peers (Zinberg, 1976; Kryzanowski & Stewin, 1985). For instance, bigoted parents may commend their children for expressing attitudes in favor of prejudice. Likewise, young children learn prejudice by imitating the behavior of adult models. Such learning starts at an early age, since children as young as 3 years of age begin to show preferences for members of their own race (Katz, 1976).

The mass media also provide a major source of information about stereotypes, not just for children, but for adults as well. Even today, some television shows, and movies, portray Italians as Mafia-like mobsters, Jews as greedy bankers, and African-Americans as bug-eyed, promiscuous, or lazy individuals who speak in jive. When such inaccurate portrayals are the primary source of information about minority groups, they can lead to the development and maintenance of unfavor-

---

ANSWERS TO PREVIOUS REVIEW
1. social supporter **2.** b **3.** b **4.** door-in-the-face **5.** Obedience

The tragic results of prejudice is reflected in the faces of these refugees who were forced to leave their homes during the Bosnian war.

able stereotypes (Jussim, Milburn, & Nelson, 1991; Hyler, Gabbard, & Schneider, 1991; Hammer, 1992; Evans, 1993).

Other explanations of prejudice and discrimination focus on how being a member of a particular group helps to magnify our sense of self-esteem. According to **social identity theory,** we use group membership as a source of pride and self-worth (Tajfel, 1982; Turner, 1987). Slogans such as "gay pride" and "black is beautiful" exemplify the argument that the groups to which we belong furnish us with a sense of self-respect.

However, there is an unfortunate outcome of the use of group membership to provide social respect. In an effort to maximize our sense of self-esteem, we may come to think that our own group is *better* than others. Consequently, we inflate the positive aspects of our own group—and, at the same time, devalue groups to which we do not belong. Ultimately, we come to view other groups as inferior to our own (Turner et al., 1992). The end result is prejudice toward members of groups of which we are not a part.

Neither social learning nor social identity approaches provide the full story of stereotyping and prejudice. For instance, some psychologists argue that prejudice results when there is competition for scarce societal resources. Thus, when competition exists for jobs or housing, members of majority groups may perceive (however unjustly) minority-group members as hindering their efforts to attain their goals, leading to prejudice (Simpson & Yinger, 1985). In addition, other explanations for prejudice emphasize human cognitive limitations that lead us to categorize people on the basis of visually conspicuous physical features such as race, sex, and ethnic group. Such categorization can lead to the development of stereotypes and ultimately discriminatory behavior (Brewer, 1988; Brewer & Lui, 1989).

Social identity theory: The theory that a person uses group membership as a source of pride and self-worth

Working to End Prejudice and Discrimination

How can we diminish the effects of prejudice and discrimination? Psychologists have developed several strategies that have proved effective. Among them:

■ *Increasing contact between the target of stereotyping and the holder of the stereotype.* Research has shown that increasing the amount of interaction between people can reduce negative stereotyping. But certain kinds of contact are more likely than others to foster the development of more accurate impressions of members of different groups. Situations where there is relatively intimate contact, where the individuals are of equal status, or where participants must cooperate with one another or are dependent on one another are most likely to bring about

Fighting Prejudice on Campus

One warm spring evening a few years back, an anonymous person—still unidentified—sent notes spewing racial hatred to four African-American students enrolled at Smith College, a small, women's liberal arts college in New England. The incident might well have been written off as just another case of racial bias, which has been on the rise on college campuses (as well as the country as a whole) for the last decade (U.S. Commission on Civil Rights, 1990). However, the college had already gone to some lengths to educate its students about the harmful consequences of prejudice, and the notes indicated that its efforts had not been particularly effective. The incident inspired demonstrations and protests on the college campus.

Ironically, the incident and the protests that followed led to research that spawned the development of a promising new technique for fighting racism. Social psychologist Fletcher Blanchard hired an experimenter to approach students on campus and say that she was conducting an opinion poll for a class (Blanchard, Lilly, & Vaughn,

1991). The purpose of the poll was ostensibly to learn how students felt the college should respond to the racial incident.

At the same time that the experimenter approached a potential subject, a confederate, posing as a student who happened to be passing by, was stopped so that her opinions could also be assessed. The experimenter asked both students how the college should respond to the notes. The confederate responded first and gave one of three prearranged responses. In one condition, she gave an unambiguously extreme antiracist response, endorsing the statement, "The person who is writing these notes should be expelled." In another condition, the confederate took a more moderate antiracist point of view, while in a third she took a lukewarm antiracist position.

The outcome was clear: When participants in the experiment heard another individual make strong antiracist responses, they were much more likely to express similar reactions than when hearing another person hold a position that was more accepting of racism. Even when subjects could respond secretly in writing, out of earshot

of the confederate, exposure to strong antiracist positions caused participants to espouse more antiracist views themselves.

In sum, hearing another person strongly condemn racism encourages others to denounce prejudice. Why? The primary reason is that public denunciations of racism make public standards, or norms, against racism more prominent. A few outspoken individuals, then, may create an atmosphere in which prejudice is viewed considerably more negatively than one in which others take no stand or take only weak stands.

One important lesson to be learned from the results of the study is that colleges and universities should vigorously promote a climate against racism, and students should be encouraged to publicly state their antiracist views. The research also suggests that institutions of higher learning should have aggressive antiracist policies and respond swiftly to acts of racism. By following such suggestions, norms against prejudice can become more visible, ultimately leading to less tolerance for acts of prejudice and discrimination.

a reduction of stereotyping. Such forms of contact seem to be particularly effective, since people's understanding of stereotyped groups becomes more detailed, individualized, and accurate as the amount of interaction increases. This finding provides part of the basis for such social practices as school integration and fair housing laws (Gaertner et al., 1990; Desforges et al., 1991).

■ *Making positive values more conspicuous.* It is not always necessary to rely on contact to change the nature of schemas and stereotypes. An alternative approach suggests that people who believe in equality and fair treatment of others but hold negative stereotypes should be made to understand that their views are inconsistent. For instance, research has shown that people who are made to see that the values they hold regarding equality and freedom are inconsistent with their negative perceptions of minority-group members are more likely to work actively against prejudice in the future (Rokeach, 1971).

■ *Providing information about the objects of stereotyping.* Probably the most direct means of changing schemas is through education, by teaching people to be

more aware of the positive characteristics of targets of stereotyping (Langer, Bashner, & Chanowitz, 1985). For instance, when the meaning of puzzling behavior is explained to people holding stereotypes, they may come to appreciate its significance—even though it may still appear foreign and perhaps even threatening (Fiedler, Mitchell, & Triandis, 1971; Landis et al., 1976).

Each of these strategies for forming more accurate impressions—although not invariably effective—serves to illustrate a major approach developed by social psychologists. In addition, new techniques to stem the tide of prejudice are still being developed, as we discuss in the Psychology at Work box.

RECAP AND REVIEW

Recap

- Stereotypes are beliefs and expectations about members of a group formed simply on the basis of their membership in that group.
- Prejudice is the negative (or positive) evaluation or judgment of members of a group that is based primarily on membership in the group rather than on the behavior of a particular individual.
- Among the ways of reducing stereotyping and prejudice are increasing contact, making positive values conspicuous, and providing information about the targets of stereotyping.

Review

1. Any expectation—positive or negative—about an individual based solely on that person's membership in a group can be a stereotype. True or false?

2. The tendency to think most favorably of communities to which we belong is known as:
   a. Stereotyping   c. Self-fulfilling prophecy
   b. Ingroup-outgroup bias   d. Discrimination
3. Paul is a store manager who does not expect women to succeed in business. He therefore offers important, high-profile responsibilities only to men. If the female employees fail to move up in the company, this could be an example of a _____-_____ prophecy.

Ask Yourself

We have seen that stereotypes can lead to harmful discrimination against a group of people—but that people can go too far in trying to avoid the appearance of bias, resulting in reverse discrimination. How would you try to teach people to recognize and avoid stereotyping, without overcompensating in this way?

(Answers to review questions are on page 488.)

- *Why are we attracted to certain people, and what is the progression that social relationships follow?*
- *What factors underlie aggression and prosocial behavior?*

POSITIVE AND NEGATIVE SOCIAL BEHAVIOR

Are people basically good or bad? Like philosophers and theologians, social psychologists have pondered the basic nature of humanity. Is it represented by the violence and cruelty we see throughout the world, or is there something special about human nature that permits loving, considerate, unselfish, and even noble behavior?

We turn to two routes that social psychologists have followed in seeking answers to these questions. We first consider what they have learned about the sources of our attraction to others, and we end the chapter with a look at two sides of the coin of human behavior: aggression and helping.

Liking and Loving: Interpersonal Attraction and the Development of Relationships

When nineteenth-century poet Elizabeth Barrett Browning wrote "How do I love thee? Let me count the ways," she was expressing feelings about a topic that is central to most people's lives—and one that has developed into a major subject of investigation by social psychologists: loving and liking. Known more formally as the study of **interpersonal attraction,** or close relationships, this topic encompasses the factors that lead to positive feelings for others.

Interpersonal attraction: Positive feelings for others; liking and loving

How Do I Like Thee? Let Me Count the Ways　By far the greatest amount of research has focused on liking, probably because it has always proved easier for investigators conducting short-term experiments to produce states of liking in strangers whom one has just met than to promote and observe loving relationships over long periods of time. Hence traditional studies have given us a good deal of knowledge about the factors that initially attract two people to each other (Berscheid, 1985; Fehr, 1995). Among the most important factors considered by social psychologists are the following:

■ *Proximity.* If you live in a dormitory or an apartment, consider the friends you made when you first moved in. Chances are you became friendliest with those who lived geographically closest to you. In fact, this is one of the most well-established findings in the interpersonal attraction literature: *Proximity* leads to liking (Festinger, Schachter, & Back, 1950; Nahome & Lawton, 1975).

■ *Mere exposure.* Repeated exposure to a person is often sufficient to produce attraction. Interestingly, repeated exposure to *any* stimulus—be it a person, picture, compact disc, or what have you—most frequently makes us like the stimulus more (Zajonc, 1968; Bornstein, 1989; Bornstein & D'Agostino, 1992). Becoming familiar with a stimulus can evoke positive feelings; these positive feel-

Friendships formed in college dormitories are a good example of how proximity leads to liking.

ings stemming from familiarity are then transferred to the stimulus itself. There are exceptions, though. In cases in which the initial interactions are strongly negative, repeated exposure is unlikely to cause us to like another person more; instead, the more we are exposed to him or her, the more we may dislike such an individual.

■ *Similarity.* Folk wisdom tells us that birds of a feather flock together. Unfortunately, it also maintains that opposites attract. Social psychologists have come up with a clear verdict regarding which of the two statements is correct: We tend to like those who are similar to us. Discovering that others are similar in terms of attitudes, values, or traits promotes liking for them. Furthermore, the more similar others are, the more we like them (Byrne, 1969; Hill & Stull, 1981; Carli, Ganley, & Pierce-Otay, 1991).

One reason similarity increases the likelihood of interpersonal attraction is that we assume that people with similar attitudes will evaluate us positively (Condon & Crano, 1988). Because there is a strong **reciprocity-of-liking effect** (a tendency to like those who like us), knowing that someone evaluates us positively will promote attraction to that person. In addition, we assume that when we like someone else, that person likes us in return (Metee & Aronson, 1974; Tagiuri, 1958).

Reciprocity-of-liking effect: The tendency to like those who like us

■ *Need complementarity.* We all know exceptions to the general rule that similarity is related to attraction. Some couples seem totally mismatched in terms of personality, interests, and attitudes, yet are clearly quite captivated with one another. Social psychologists have explained instances in which people are attracted to dissimilar others by considering the needs that their partners fulfill. According to this reasoning, we may be attracted to those people who fulfill the greatest number of needs for us. Thus a dominant person may seek out someone who is submissive; at the same time, the submissive individual may be seeking someone who is dominant. Although their dissimilarity often makes others expect them to be incompatible, by forming a relationship they are able to fulfill each other's complementary needs.

The hypothesis that people are attracted to others who fulfill their needs—dubbed the **need-complementarity hypothesis**—was first proposed in the late 1950s in a classic study that found that a sample of married couples appeared to have complementary needs (Winch, 1958). Although research attempting to support the concept since that time has been wildly inconsistent, it does seem that in some realms the hypothesis holds. For example, people with complementary abilities may be attracted to one another. In one study, schoolchildren developed friendships with others whose academic skills were in areas distinct from those in which they felt particularly competent, thereby allowing them to stand out in different subjects from their friends. A good mathematics student, then, might form a friendship with someone particularly good in English (Tessor, 1988).

Need-complementarity hypothesis: The hypothesis that people are attracted to others who fulfill their needs

In general, though, most evidence suggests that attraction is related more to similarity than to complementarity (e.g., Meyer & Pepper, 1977). Whether in the area of attitudes, values, or personality traits, similarity remains one of the best predictors of whether two people will be attracted to each other.

■ *Physical attractiveness.* For most people, the equation *beautiful = good* is a very real one. As a result, people who are physically attractive are more popular than those who are physically unattractive, if all other factors are equal. This finding, which contradicts the values that most people would profess, is apparent even in childhood—with nursery-school-age children rating popularity on the basis of attractiveness (Dion & Berscheid, 1974)—and continues into adulthood. Indeed, physical attractiveness may be the single most important element promoting initial liking in college dating situations, although its influence eventually decreases when people get to know each other better (Berscheid & Walster, 1974; Hatfield & Sprecher, 1986; Feingold, 1992).

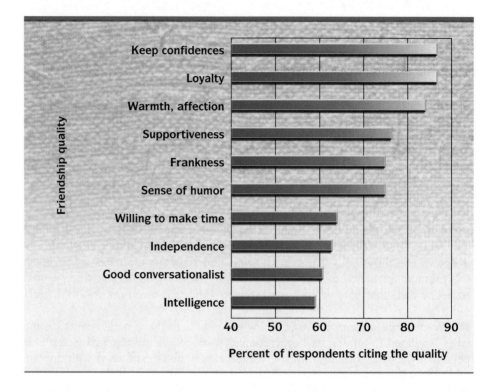

FIGURE 14-6 These are the key qualities looked for in a friend, according to some 40,000 respondents to a questionnaire.

The factors we have discussed are not, or course, the only constituents of liking. For example, survey research has sought to identify the factors critical in friendships. In a questionnaire answered by some 40,000 respondents, the qualities that were most valued in a friend were identified as the ability to keep confidences, loyalty, and warmth and affection, followed closely by supportiveness, frankness, and a sense of humor (Parlee, 1979). The results are summarized in Figure 14-6.

How Do I Love Thee? Let Me Count the Ways Whereas our knowledge of what makes people like one another is extensive, our understanding of love is more limited in scope and a relatively recent phenomenon. For some time, many social psychologists believed that love represented a phenomenon too difficult to observe and study in a controlled, scientific way. However, love is such a central issue in most people's lives that, in time, social psychologists could not resist its allure and became infatuated with the topic.

As a first step, researchers tried to identify the distinguishing characteristics between mere liking and full-blown love (Sternberg, 1987). Using this approach, they discovered that love is not simply liking of a greater quantity, but a qualitatively different psychological state (Walster & Walster, 1978). For instance, at least in its early stages, love includes relatively intense physiological arousal, an all-encompassing interest in another individual, fantasies about the other, and relatively rapid swings of emotion. Moreover, love—as distinct from liking—includes elements of passion, closeness, fascination, exclusiveness, sexual desire, and intense caring (Hendrick & Hendrick, 1989).

Several social psychologists have tried to capture the elusive nature of love using paper-and-pencil measures. For example, Zick Rubin (1970, 1973) tried to differentiate between love and liking using a paper-and-pencil scale. Keep a particular individual in mind as you answer these questions from his scale:

I feel I can confide in _____ about virtually everything.

I would do almost anything for _____ .

I feel responsible for _____'s well-being.

A positive response to each question provides an indication of love for the individual you have in mind. Now answer these questions, also drawn from Rubin's scale:

I think that _____ is unusually well adjusted.

I think that _____ is one of those people who quickly wins respect.

_____ is one of the most likable people I know.

These three questions are designed to measure liking, as opposed to loving. Researchers have found that couples scoring high on the love scale differ considerably from those with low scores. They gaze at each other more, and their relationships are more likely to be intact 6 months later than are the relationships of those who score low on the scale.

Other experiments have found evidence suggesting that the heightened physiological arousal hypothesized to be characteristic of loving is indeed present when a person reports being in love. Interestingly, though, it may not be just arousal of a sexual nature. Berscheid and Walster (1974) have theorized that when we are exposed to *any* stimulus that increases physiological arousal—such as danger, fear, or anger—we may label our feelings as love for another person present at the time of arousal. This is most likely to occur if there are situational cues that suggest that "love" is an appropriate label for the feelings being experienced. In sum, we perceive we are in love when instances of general physiological arousal are coupled with the thought that the cause of the arousal is most likely love.

This theory explains why a person who keeps being rejected or hurt by another can still feel "in love" with that person. If the rejection leads to physiological arousal, but the arousal still happens to be attributed to love—and not to rejection—then a person will still feel "in love."

Other researchers have theorized that there are several kinds of love (Hendrick, Hendrick, & Adler, 1988; Hendrick & Hendrick, 1992; Fehr & Russell, 1991). Some distinguish between two main types of love: passionate love and companionate love. **Passionate (or romantic) love** represents a state of intense absorption in someone. It includes intense physiological arousal, psychological interest, and care for the needs of another. In contrast, **companionate love** is the strong affection we have for those with whom our lives are deeply involved. The love we feel for our parents, other family members, and even some close friends falls into the category of companionate love.

According to psychologist Robert Sternberg (1986), an even finer differentiation between types of love is in order. He proposes that love is made up of three components: an *intimacy component,* encompassing feelings of closeness and connectedness; a *passion component,* made up of the motivational drives relating to sex, physical closeness, and romance; and a *decision/commitment component,* encompassing both the initial cognition that one loves someone and the longer-term feelings of commitment to maintain love.

Passionate (or romantic) love: A state of intense absorption in someone that is characterized by physiological arousal, psychological interest, and care for the needs of another

Companionate love: The strong affection we have for those with whom our lives are deeply involved

Tracing the Course of Relationships: The Rise and Fall of Liking and Loving
With more than one out of two marriages ending in divorce, and broken love affairs a common phenomenon, it is not surprising that social psychologists have begun to turn their attention increasingly toward understanding how relationships develop and are maintained—and, in some cases, dissolve (Clark & Reis, 1988; MacDermid, Huston, & McHale, 1990; Duck, 1994b).

The behavior of couples in developing relationships changes in fairly predictable patterns (Berscheid, 1985; Burgess & Huston, 1979). The most frequent pattern follows this course:

(35) The growth of the relationship

■ People interact more often, for longer periods of time, and in a widening array of settings.

■ They seek each other's company.

■ They increasingly "open up" to each other, disclosing secrets and sharing physical intimacies. They are more willing to share both positive and negative feelings and are increasingly willing to provide praise and criticism.

■ They begin to understand each other's point of view and way of looking at the world.

■ Their goals and behavior become more in tune, and they begin to share greater similarity in attitudes and values.

■ Their investment in the relationship—in terms of time, energy, and commitment—increases.

■ They begin to feel that their psychological well-being is tied to the well-being of the relationship. They come to see the relationship as unique and irreplaceable.

■ They start behaving like a couple, rather than like two separate individuals.

Although this sequence of transitions is typical, it is difficult to predict the exact point in a relationship when each will occur. One important reason is that, at the same time the relationship is evolving, the two individuals may be going through personal growth and change themselves. In addition, the people in the relationship may have differing goals for its outcome; one partner may be interested in marriage, while the other may only be looking for a relatively short-term relationship.

Finally, even if both partners have an underlying concern about finding a marriage partner, the kind of mate for whom one is looking may be very different from that sought by the other (Sprecher, Sullivan, & Hatfield, 1994). For instance, a survey of close to 10,000 individuals across the world found that people had considerably differing preferences regarding qualities in a mate, depending both on their culture and on their sex. For example, for people in the United States, mutual attraction and love were the most important characteristics. In contrast, men in China rated good health as most important, and women rated emotional stability and maturity as most important. In Zulu South Africa, males rated emotional stability first and females rated dependable character first (Buss et al., 1990; see Table 14-1).

Once a relationship has evolved, how can we distinguish successful ones from those that will ultimately fail? One approach is to examine the rate at which the various components of love develop. According to Sternberg's theory of love, the three individual components of love—intimacy, passion, and decision/commitment—vary in their influence over time and follow distinct courses. In strong loving relationships, for instance, the level of commitment peaks and then remains stable, while intimacy continues to grow over the course of a relationship (see Figure 14-7). Passion, on the other hand, shows a marked decline over time, reaching a plateau fairly early in a relationship. Still, it remains an important component of loving relationships.

The Decline of a Relationship   What is it that causes some relationships to flounder? Social psychologist George Levinger (1983) has speculated on the reasons behind the deterioration of relationships. One important factor appears to be a change in judgments about the meaning of a partner's behavior. Behavior that was once viewed as "charming forgetfulness" becomes seen as "boorish indifference," and the partner becomes less valued. In addition, communications may be disrupted. Rather than listening to what the other person is saying, each partner becomes bent on justifying himself or herself, and communication deteriorates. Eventually, a partner may begin to invite and agree with criticism of the other partner from people outside the relationship, and look to others for the fulfillment of basic needs that were previously met by the partner.

TABLE 14-1   Rank Ordering of Desired Characteristics in a Mate

	China		South Africa Zulu		United States	
	Males	Females	Males	Females	Males	Females
Mutual attraction—love	4	8	10	5	1	1
Emotional stability and maturity	5	1	1	2	2	2
Dependable character	6	7	3	1	3	3
Pleasing disposition	13	16	4	3	4	4
Education and intelligence	8	4	6	6	5	5
Good health	1	3	5	4	6	9
Sociability	12	9	11	8	8	8
Desire for home and children	2	2	9	9	9	7
Refinement, neatness	7	10	7	10	10	12
Ambition and industriousness	10	5	8	7	11	6
Good looks	11	15	14	16	7	13
Similar education	15	12	12	12	12	10
Good financial prospect	16	14	18	13	16	11
Good cook and housekeeper	9	11	2	15	13	16
Favorable social status or rating	14	13	17	14	14	14
Similar religious background	18	18	16	11	15	15
Chastity (no prior sexual intercourse)	3	6	13	18	17	18
Similar political background	17	17	15	17	18	17

Source: Buss et al., 1990.

Just as developing relationships tend to follow a common pattern, relationships that are on the decline conform to a pattern of stages (Duck, 1988). The first phase occurs when a person decides that he or she can no longer tolerate being in a relationship. During this stage, the focus is on the other person's behavior and an evaluation of the extent to which this behavior provides a basis for terminating the relationship.

In the next phase, a person decides to confront the partner and determines whether to attempt to repair, redefine, or terminate the relationship. For example, a redefinition might encompass a qualitative change in the level of the relationship. ("We can still be friends" might replace "I'll love you forever.")

FIGURE 14-7 The changing ingredients of love. The three components of love vary in strength over the course of a relationship. *(Sternberg, 1986.)*

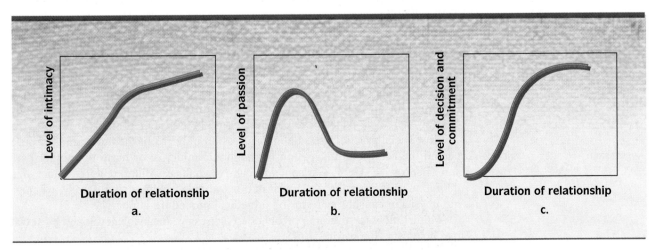

a.   Level of intimacy — Duration of relationship

b.   Level of passion — Duration of relationship

c.   Level of decision and commitment — Duration of relationship

494

step 3

If the decision is made to terminate the relationship, the person then enters a period in which there is public acknowledgment that the relationship is being dissolved and an accounting is made to others regarding the events that led to the termination of the relationship. The last stage is a "grave-dressing" phase, in which the major activity is to physically and psychologically end the relationship. One of the major concerns of this period is to rethink the entire relationship, making what happened seem reasonable and in keeping with one's self-perceptions.

Just how much distress do people experience when a relationship ends? The degree of anguish depends on what the relationship was like prior to its termination. In the case of undergraduate dating couples who break up, partners who report the most distress are those who had been especially close to one another over a long period and had spent a considerable amount of time exclusively together. They had participated in many activities with their partners and report having been influenced strongly by them. Finally, the degree of distress is related to holding the expectation that it will be difficult to find a new, replacement partner. If no alternatives are on the horizon, people are apt to look more longingly at what they once had (Simpson, 1987).

Aggression and Prosocial Behavior: Hurting and Helping Others

Drive-by shootings, car-jackings, and abductions are just some of the examples of violence that seem all too common. Yet we also find examples of generous, unselfish, thoughtful behavior that provide a more optimistic view of humankind. Consider, for instance, people who minister to the homeless, or individuals like Oscar Schindler, who helped Jews escape from Nazi death camps during World War II. Or contemplate the simple kindnesses of life: lending a valued compact disc, stopping to help a child who has fallen off her bicycle, or merely sharing a candy bar with a friend. Such instances of helping are no less characteristic of human behavior than the distasteful examples of aggression. In this last part of the chapter, we explore how social psychologists have sought to explain instances of both aggressive and helping behavior.

Hurting Others: Aggression   We need look no further than our daily paper or the nightly news to be bombarded with examples of aggression, both on a societal level (war, invasion, assassination) and on an individual level (crime, child abuse, and the many petty cruelties that humans are capable of inflicting on one another). Is such aggression an inevitable part of the human condition? Or is aggression primarily a product of particular circumstances that, if changed, could lead to its reduction?

The difficulty of answering such knotty questions becomes quickly apparent as soon as we consider how best to define the term "aggression." Depending on the way we define the word, many examples of inflicted pain or injury may or may not qualify as aggression (see Table 14-2). Although it is clear, for instance, that a rapist is acting aggressively toward his victim, it is less certain that a physician carrying out an emergency medical procedure without an anesthetic, thereby causing incredible pain to the patient, should be considered aggressive.

Aggression: The intentional injury of or harm to another person

Most social psychologists define aggression in terms of the intent and purpose behind the behavior. **Aggression** is intentional injury of or harm to another person (Berkowitz, 1993; Carlson, Marcus-Newhall, & Miller, 1989). Under this definition, it is clear that the rapist in our example is acting aggressively, whereas the physician causing pain during a medical procedure is not.

We turn now to several approaches to aggressive behavior developed by social psychologists (Berkowitz, 1993).

TABLE 14-2   Is This Aggression?

To see for yourself the difficulties involved in defining aggression, consider each of the following acts and determine whether it represents aggressive behavior—according to your own definition of aggression.

1. A spider eats a fly.
2. Two wolves fight for the leadership of the pack
3. A soldier shoots an enemy at the front line.
4. The warden of a prison executes a convicted criminal.
5. A man viciously kicks a cat.
6. A man, while cleaning a window, knocks over a flowerpot, which, while falling, injures a pedestrian.
7. Mr. X, a notorious gossip, speaks disparagingly of many people of his acquaintance.
8. A man mentally rehearses a murder he is about to commit.
9. An angry son purposely fails to write to his mother, who is expecting a letter and will be hurt if none arrives.
10. An enraged boy tries with all his might to inflict injury on his antagonist, a bigger boy, but is not successful in doing so. His efforts simply amuse the bigger boy.
11. A senator does not protest the escalation of bombing to which she is morally opposed.
12. A farmer beheads a chicken and prepares it for supper.
13. A hunter kills an animal and mounts it as a trophy.
14. A physician gives a flu shot to a screaming child.
15. A boxer gives his opponent a bloody nose.
16. A Girl Scout tries to assist an elderly woman but trips her by accident.
17. A bank robber is shot in the back while trying to escape.
18. A tennis player smashes her racket after missing a volley.
19. A person commits suicide.
20. A cat kills a mouse, parades around with it, and then discards it.

Source: Adapted from Benjamin, 1985, p. 41.

Instinct Approaches: Aggression as a Release   If you have ever punched an adversary in the nose, you may have experienced a certain satisfaction, despite your better judgment. Instinct theories, noting the prevalence of aggression in the human species and nonhuman animals as well, propose that aggression is primarily the outcome of innate—or inborn—urges.

The major proponent of the instinct approach is Konrad Lorenz, an ethologist (a scientist who studies animal behavior). He suggested that humans, along with members of other species, have a fighting instinct, which in earlier times ensured protection of food supplies and weeded out the weaker of the species (Lorenz, 1966, 1974). The controversial notion arising from Lorenz's instinct approach is that aggressive energy is constantly being built up within an individual until it is finally discharged in a process called **catharsis.** The longer the energy is built up, says Lorenz, the greater will be the magnitude of the aggression displayed when it is discharged.

Probably the most controversial idea to come out of instinct theories of aggression is Lorenz's proposal that society ought to provide acceptable means of catharsis through, for instance, participation in sports and games, in order to prevent its discharge in less socially desirable ways. Although the notion makes logical sense, there is no possible way to devise an adequate experiment to test it. Relatively little support exists for instinct theories in general, because of the difficulty in finding evidence for any kind of pent-up reservoir of aggression (Berkowitz, 1974; Geen & Donnerstein, 1983). Most social psychologists suggest that we should look to other approaches to explain aggression.

Catharsis: The process of discharging built-up aggression through violent acts

496

Frustration-Aggression Approaches: Aggression as a Reaction to Frustration
Suppose you've been working on a paper due in class early the next morning, and your word processor printer runs out of ink just before you can print out the paper. You rush to the store to buy more ink, only to find the salesclerk locking the door for the day. Even though the clerk can see you gesturing and literally begging him to open the door, he refuses, shrugging his shoulders and pointing to a sign that indicates when the store will open the next day. At that moment, the feelings you experience toward the salesclerk probably place you on the verge of real aggression, and you are undoubtedly seething inside.

Frustration-aggression theory tries to explain aggression in terms of events such as this one. When first put forward, the theory said flatly that frustration *always* led to aggression of some sort, and that aggression was *always* the result of some frustration, where **frustration** is defined as the thwarting or blocking of some ongoing, goal-directed behavior (Dollard et al., 1939). More recent formulations, however, have modified the original one, suggesting instead that frustration produces anger, leading to a *readiness* to act aggressively. Whether or not actual aggression occurs depends on the presence of *aggressive cues,* stimuli that have been associated in the past with actual aggression or violence and that will trigger aggression again (Berkowitz, 1984). In addition, frustration is assumed to produce aggression only to the extent that the frustration produces negative feelings (Berkowitz, 1989, 1990).

What kinds of stimuli act as aggressive cues? They can range from the most overt, such as the presence of weapons, to the subtlest, such as the mere mention of the name of an individual who has behaved violently in the past. For example, in one experiment, angered subjects behaved significantly more aggressively when in the presence of a rifle and revolver than in a comparable situation in which no guns were present (Berkowitz & LePage, 1967). Similarly, frustrated subjects in an experiment who had viewed a violent movie were more physically aggressive toward a confederate with the same name as the star of the movie than to a confederate with a different name (Berkowitz & Geen, 1966). It appears, then, that frustration does lead to aggression, at least when aggressive cues are present (Carlson, Marcus-Newhall, & Miller, 1990).

Observational Learning Approaches: Learning to Hurt Others Do we learn to be aggressive? The observational learning (sometimes called social learning) approach to aggression says we do. Taking an almost opposite view from instinct theories, which focus on innate explanations of aggression, observational learning theory (see Chapter 5) emphasizes that social and environmental conditions can teach individuals to be aggressive. Aggression is seen not as inevitable, but rather as a learned response that can be understood in terms of rewards and punishments (Bandura, 1973; Zillman, 1978).

Suppose, for instance, that a girl hits her younger brother when he damages one of her new toys. Whereas instinct theory would suggest that the aggression had been pent up and was now being discharged, and frustration-aggression theory would examine the girl's frustration at no longer being able to use her new toy, observational learning theory would look to a previous reinforcement that the girl had received for being aggressive. Perhaps she had learned that aggression resulted in her getting attention from her parents, or perhaps in the past her brother had apologized after being hit. In either case, observational learning theory views the aggression as a result of past rewards the girl had obtained for such behavior.

Observational learning theory pays particular attention not only to direct rewards and punishments that individuals themselves receive, but to the rewards and punishments that models—individuals who provide a guide to appropriate behavior—receive for their aggressive behavior. According to observational learning theory, people observe the behavior of models and the subsequent conse-

Frustration: A state produced by the thwarting or blocking of some ongoing, goal-directed behavior

quences of the behavior. If the consequences are positive, the behavior is likely to be imitated when the observer finds himself or herself in a similar situation.

This basic formulation of observational learning theory has received wide support. For example, nursery-school-age children who have watched an adult behave aggressively display the same behavior themselves if they have been previously angered (Bandura, Ross, & Ross, 1963a, 1963b). It turns out, though, that exposure to models typically leads to spontaneous aggression only if the observer has been angered, insulted, or frustrated after exposure (Bandura, 1973).

Helping Others: The Brighter Side of Human Nature

Turning away from aggression, we move now to the opposite—and brighter—side of the coin of human nature: helping behavior. Helping behavior, or **prosocial behavior** as it is more formally known, has been considered under many different conditions (McGuire, 1994). However, the question that psychologists have looked at most closely relates to bystander intervention in emergency situations. What are the factors that lead someone to help a person in need?

As we noted in Chapter 1, one critical factor is the number of others present. When more than one person bears witness to an emergency situation, there can be a sense of diffusion of responsibility among bystanders. **Diffusion of responsibility** is the tendency for people to feel that responsibility for acting is shared, or diffused, among those present. The more people that are present in an emergency, then, the less personally responsible each individual feels—and therefore the less help that is provided (Latané & Nida, 1981).

Although the majority of research on helping behavior supports the diffusion-of-responsibility formulation, other factors are clearly involved in helping behavior. According to a model developed by Latané and Darley (1970), the process of helping involves four basic steps:

■ *Noticing a person, event, or situation that may require help.*

■ *Interpreting the event as one that requires help.* Even if an event is noticed, it may be sufficiently ambiguous to be interpreted as a nonemergency situation (Shotland, 1985). It is here that the presence of others first affects helping behavior. The presence of inactive others may indicate to the observer that a situation does not require help—a judgment not necessarily made if the observer is alone.

■ *Assuming responsibility for taking action.* It is at this point that diffusion of responsibility is likely to occur if others are present. Moreover, a bystander's particular expertise is apt to play a role in whether helping occurs. For instance, if people with training in medical aid or lifesaving techniques are present, untrained bystanders are less apt to intervene because they feel they have less expertise. This point was well illustrated in a study by Jane and Irving Piliavin (1972), who conducted a field experiment in which an individual seemed to collapse in a subway car with blood trickling out of the corner of his mouth. The results of the experiment showed that bystanders were less likely to help when a person (actually a confederate) appearing to be an intern was present than when the "intern" was not present.

■ *Deciding on and implementing the form of assistance.* After an individual assumes responsibility for helping, the decision must be made about how assistance will be provided. Helping can range from very indirect forms of intervention, such as calling the police, to more direct forms, such as giving first aid or taking the victim to a hospital. Most social psychologists use a *rewards-costs approach* for helping to predict the nature of assistance that a bystander will choose to provide. The general notion is that the rewards of helping, as perceived by the bystander, must outweigh the costs if helping is to occur (Lynch & Cohen, 1978), and most research tends to support this notion.

Prosocial behavior: Helping behavior

Diffusion of responsibility: The tendency for people to feel that responsibility for helping is shared among those present

Altruism: Helping behavior that is beneficial to others while requiring sacrifice on the part of the helper

After the nature of assistance is determined, one step remains: the actual implementation of the assistance. A rewards-costs analysis suggests that the least costly form of implementation is the most likely to be used. However, this is not always the case: In some situations, people behave altruistically. **Altruism** is helping behavior that is beneficial to others but clearly requires self-sacrifice. For example, an instance in which a person runs into a burning house to rescue a stranger's child might be considered altruistic, particularly when compared with the alternative of simply calling the fire department (Batson, 1990, 1991; Dovidio, Allen, & Schroeder, 1990). (Figure 14-8 summarizes the basic steps of helping.)

Some research suggests that people who intervene in emergency situations tend to possess certain personality characteristics that differentiate them from nonhelpers. For example, Shotland (1984) suggests that helpers tend to be more self-assured. Other research has found that individuals who are characteristically high in *empathy*—a personality trait in which someone observing another person experiences the emotions of that person—and emotional understanding are more likely to respond to others' needs (Eisenberg & Fabes, 1991; Batson et al., 1991; Knight et al., 1994; Batson & Weeks, 1996).

Still, most social psychologists agree that no single set of attributes differentiates helpers from nonhelpers (Carlo et al., 1991). Temporary, situational factors play the predominant role in determining whether an individual intervenes in a situation requiring aid (e.g., Carlson, Charlin, & Miller, 1988).

For instance, our temporary moods help determine how helpful we are (Salovey, Mayer, & Roschman, 1991). Not surprisingly, being in a good mood encourages helping (Carlson, Charlin, & Miller, 1988). What doesn't make as much sense, at least at first, is the finding that bad moods, too, seem to encourage helping behavior (Eisenberg, 1991). There are some reasonable explanations, however, for this finding. For one thing, we may think that helping will enable us to view ourselves more positively, thereby raising our spirits and getting us out of our bad mood (Cialdini & Fultz, 1990). Similarly, if a bad mood causes us to focus on ourselves, the values we hold about helping may become more conspicuous—leading us to help more (Berkowitz, 1987).

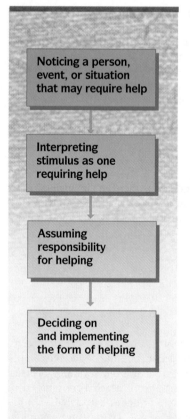

Noticing a person, event, or situation that may require help

↓

Interpreting stimulus as one requiring help

↓

Assuming responsibility for helping

↓

Deciding on and implementing the form of helping

FIGURE 14-8 The basic steps of helping. *(Based on Latané & Darley, 1970.)*

The Informed Consumer of Psychology

Dealing with Anger Effectively

At one time or another, almost everyone feels angry. The anger may have come as a result of a frustrating situation, or it may be due to the behavior of another individual. How we deal with such anger may determine the difference between a promotion and a lost job or a broken relationship and one that mends itself.

Social psychologists who have studied the topic suggest that there are several good ways to deal with anger, ones that maximize the potential for positive consequences (Novaco, 1975, 1986; Deffenbacher, 1988; Pennebaker, 1990). Among the most useful strategies are the following:

■ *Look at the situation that is producing anger from the perspective of others.* By taking others' point of view, you may be able to understand the situation better, and with increased understanding may become more tolerant of the apparent shortcomings of others.

■ *Reduce the importance of the situation.* Does it really matter that someone is driving too slowly and that you'll be late to an appointment as a result? Reinterpret the situation in a way that is less bothersome.

■ *Fantasize about getting even—but don't act on it.* Fantasy provides a safety valve. In your fantasies, you can yell at that unfair professor all you want and suffer no consequences. However, don't spend too much time brooding: Fantasize, but then move on.

■ *Relax.* By teaching yourself the kind of relaxation techniques used in systematic desensitization (see Table 13-2 in the previous chapter), you can help reduce your reactions to anger. In turn, your anger may dissipate.

No matter which of these strategies you try, above all don't ignore anger. People who always strive to suppress their anger may experience a variety of consequences, such as self-condemnation and even physical illness (Julius, 1990; Pennebaker, 1990).

RECAP AND REVIEW

Recap

- Studies of interpersonal attraction and close relationships consider liking and loving.
- Among the most important elements that affect liking are proximity, mere exposure, similarity, and physical attractiveness.
- Love is assumed to be distinct from liking in qualitative, as well as quantitative, respects. In addition, several different kinds of love can be distinguished.
- Aggression refers to intentional injury of or harm to another person.
- Helping in emergencies involves four steps.

Review

1. We tend to like those people who are similar to us. True or false?

2. _____ _____ predicts that we will be attracted to people whose needs fulfill our own.

3. According to Berscheid, a person can still feel in love with another even when constantly rejected if _____ is present and is misinterpreted as "love."

4. Which of the following three components of love were proposed by Sternberg?
   a. Passion, closeness, sexuality
   b. Attraction, desire, complementarity
   c. Passion, intimacy, commitment
   d. Commitment, caring, sexuality

5. According to survey research, people have similar preferences for a mate, relatively independent of their sex and cultural background. True or false?

6. Which hypothesis states that frustration produces anger, which in turn produces a readiness to act aggressively?
   a. Frustration-aggression
   b. Observational learning
   c. Catharsis
   d. Instinctual aggression

7. Based on the research evidence, which of the following might be the best way to reduce the amount of fighting a young boy does?
   a. Take him to the gym and let him work out on the boxing equipment.
   b. Take him to see *Pulp Fiction* several times in the hopes that it will provide catharsis.
   c. Reward him if he doesn't fight during a certain period.
   d. Ignore it and let it die out naturally.

8. If a person in a crowd does not help in an apparent emergency situation because of the other people present, that person is falling victim to the phenomenon of _____ _____ _____.

Ask Yourself

Can love be adequately studied? Is there an "intangible" quality to love that renders it at least partially unknowable? How would you define "falling in love"? How would you study it?

(Answers to review questions are on page 501.)

LOOKING BACK

What are attitudes, and how are they formed, maintained, and changed?

1. Social psychology is the study of the ways in which people's thoughts, feelings, and actions are affected by others, and the nature and causes of individual behavior in social situations.

2. Attitudes, a central topic of study in social psychology, are learned predispositions to respond in a favorable or unfavorable manner to a particular object. The ABC model of attitudes suggests that attitudes have three components: the affect component, the behavior component, and the cognition component. Attitudes can be acquired through several processes. They include classical conditioning, in which a previously neutral object begins to evoke the attitudes associated with another object due to repeated pairings, and operant conditioning, in which reinforcement acts to maintain an attitude.

3. A number of theories suggest that people try to maintain consistency between attitudes. Cognitive dissonance occurs

when two cognitions—attitudes or thoughts—contradict each other and are held simultaneously by an individual. To resolve the contradiction, the person may modify the cognition, change its importance, add cognitions, or deny the contradiction, thereby bringing about a reduction in dissonance.

How do we form impressions of what others are like and of the causes of their behavior?

4. Impressions of others are formed through social cognitions—the processes that underlie our understanding of the social world. People develop schemas, which organize information about people and social experiences in memory. Such schemas represent our social life and allow us to interpret and categorize information about others.

5. One of the ways in which people form impressions of others is through the use of central traits, personality characteristics that are given unusually heavy weight when an impression is formed. Information-processing approaches have found that we tend to average sets of traits to form an overall impression.

6. Attribution theory tries to explain how we understand the causes of behavior, particularly with respect to situational and dispositional factors.

What are the biases that influence the ways in which we view others' behavior?

7. Even though logical processes are involved, attribution is still prone to error. For instance, the fundamental attribution error is the tendency to overattribute others' behavior to dispositional causes, and the corresponding failure to recognize the importance of situational causes. Other biases include the halo effect, in which the initial understanding that a person has positive traits is used to infer other positive characteristics, and the assumed-similarity bias, the tendency to think of people as being similar to oneself.

What are the major sources and tactics of social influence?

8. Social influence is the area of social psychology concerned with situations in which the actions of an individual or group affect the behavior of others.

9. Conformity refers to changes in behavior or attitudes that occur as the result of a desire to follow the beliefs or standards of others. Among the factors affecting conformity are the nature of the group, the nature of the response required, the kind of task, and the unanimity of the group.

10. Compliance is behavior that occurs as a result of direct social pressure. Two means of eliciting compliance are the foot-in-the-door technique, in which people are initially asked to agree to a small request but are later asked to respond to a larger one, and the door-in-the-face procedure, in which a large request, designed to be refused, is followed by a smaller one. In contrast to compliance, obedience is a change in behavior in response to the commands of others.

What is the distinction between stereotypes, prejudice, and discrimination?

11. Stereotypes are beliefs and expectations about members of groups held on the basis of membership in those groups. Although they are most frequently used for racial and ethnic groups, stereotypes are also found in categorizations of sex- and age-group membership. Prejudice is the negative (or positive) evaluations or judgments of members of a group that are based primarily on membership in the group and not usually on the behavior of a particular individual.

12. Stereotyping and prejudice can lead to discrimination, negative behavior toward members of a particular group. They also can lead to self-fulfilling prophecies, expectations about the occurrence of future events or behaviors that act to increase the likelihood that the event or behavior will actually occur.

13. According to social learning approaches, people learn stereotyping and prejudice by observing the behavior of parents, other adults, and peers. In addition, social identity theory suggests that group membership is used as a source of pride and self-worth, which may lead people to think of their own group as better than others.

How can we reduce prejudice and discrimination?

14. Among the ways of reducing prejudice and discrimination are increasing contact, making positive values apparent, providing information about the target of the attribution or stereotype, and making norms against prejudice conspicuous.

Why are we attracted to certain people, and what is the progression that social relationships follow?

15. The study of interpersonal attraction, or close relationships, considers liking and loving. Among the primary determinants of liking are proximity, mere exposure, similarity, need complementarity, and physical attractiveness.

16. Loving is distinguished from liking by the presence of intense physiological arousal, an all-encompassing interest in another, fantasies about the other, rapid swings of emotion, fascination, sexual desire, exclusiveness, and strong feelings of caring. According to one approach, love can be categorized into two types: passionate and companionate.

17. Recent work has examined the development, maintenance, and deterioration of relationships. Relationships tend to move through stages, and the various components of love—intimacy, passion, and decision/commitment—vary in their influence over time.

What factors underlie aggression and prosocial behavior?

18. Aggression is intentional injury of or harm to another person. Instinct approaches suggest that humans have an innate drive to behave aggressively and that if aggression is not released in socially desirable ways, it will be discharged in some other form—a point for which there is relatively little research support. Frustration-aggression theory suggests that frustration produces a readiness to be aggressive—if aggressive cues are present. Finally, observational learning theory hypothesizes that aggression is learned through reinforcement—particularly reinforcement that is given to models.

19. Helping behavior in emergencies is determined in part by the phenomenon of diffusion of responsibility, which results in a lower likelihood of helping when more people are present. Deciding to help is the outcome of a four-stage process consisting of noticing a possible need for help, interpreting the situation as requiring aid, assuming responsibility for taking action, and deciding on and implementing a form of assistance.

KEY TERMS AND CONCEPTS

social psychology (p. 465)
attitudes (p. 466)
ABC model of attitudes (p. 467)
central-route processing (p. 469)
peripheral-route processing (p. 469)
cognitive dissonance (p. 471)
social cognition (p. 473)
schemas (p. 473)
central traits (p. 474)
attribution theory (p. 474)
situational cause (of behavior) (p. 474)
dispositional cause (of behavior)
  (p. 475)
fundamental attribution error (p. 475)

halo effect (p. 475)
assumed-similarity bias (p. 476)
social influence (p. 477)
conformity (p. 477)
status (p. 478)
social supporter (p. 478)
compliance (p. 479)
obedience (p. 481)
stereotypes (p. 483)
prejudice (p. 483)
ingroup-outgroup bias (p. 484)
discrimination (p. 484)
self-fulfilling prophecy (p. 484)

social identity theory (p. 485)
interpersonal attraction (p. 488)
reciprocity-of-liking effect (p. 489)
need-complementarity hypothesis
  (p. 491)
passionate (or romantic) love (p. 491)
companionate love (p. 491)
aggression (p. 494)
catharsis (p. 495)
frustration (p. 496)
prosocial behavior (p. 497)
diffusion of responsibility (p. 497)
altruism (p. 498)

ANSWERS TO PREVIOUS REVIEW
1. True **2.** Need complementarity **3.** arousal **4.** c **5.** False; they have distinct patterns of preferences. **6.** a **7.** c **8.** diffusion of responsibility

GLOSSARY

ABC model of attitudes: The model suggesting that an attitude has three components: affect, behavior, and cognition (Ch. 14)

Absolute threshold: The smallest intensity of a stimulus that must be present for it to be detected (Ch. 3)

Achievement test: A test intended to determine a person's level of knowledge in a given subject area (Ch. 8)

Action potential: An electric nerve impulse that travels through a neuron when it is set off by a "trigger," changing the cell's charge from negative to positive (Ch. 2)

Activation-synthesis theory: Hobson's theory that dreams are a result of random electrical energy stimulating memories lodged in various portions of the brain, which the brain then weaves into a logical story line (Ch. 4)

Activity theory of aging: A theory that suggests that the elderly who age most successfully are those who maintain the interests and activities they had during middle age (Ch. 10)

Adaptation: An adjustment in sensory capacity following prolonged exposure to stimuli (Ch. 3)

Addictive drugs: Drugs that produce a physical or psychological dependence in the user (Ch. 4)

Adolescence: The developmental stage between childhood and adulthood during which many physical, cognitive, and social changes take place (Ch. 10)

Age of viability: The point at which a fetus can survive if born prematurely (Ch. 10)

Aggression: The intentional injury of or harm to another person (Ch. 14)

Algorithm: A rule that, if followed, guarantees a solution, though the reason that it works may not be understood by the person using it (Ch. 7)

All-or-none law: The principle governing the state of neurons, which are either on (firing) or off (resting) (Ch. 2)

Altruism: Helping behavior that is beneficial to others while requiring sacrifice on the part of the helper (Ch. 14)

Anal stage: According to Freud, a stage, from 12–18 months to 3 years of age, in which a child's pleasure is centered on the anus (Ch. 11)

Androgens: Male sex hormones (Ch. 9)

Anorexia nervosa: An eating disorder usually striking young women in which symptoms include self-starvation or near self-starvation in an attempt to avoid obesity (Ch. 9)

Antianxiety drugs: Drugs that alleviate stress and anxiety (Ch. 13)

Antidepressant drugs: Medications that improve a depressed patient's mood and feeling of well-being (Ch. 13)

Antipsychotic drugs: Drugs that temporarily alleviate psychotic symptoms such as agitation and overactivity (Ch. 13)

Antisocial (sociopathic) personality disorder: A disorder in which individuals display no regard for moral and ethical rules or for the rights of others (Ch. 12)

Anxiety disorder: The occurrence of anxiety without obvious external cause, intruding on daily functioning (Ch. 12)

Aptitude test: A test designed to predict ability in a particular area or line of work (Ch. 8)

Archival research: The examination of existing records for the purpose of confirming a hypothesis (Ch. 1)

Arousal approaches to motivation: The belief that we try to maintain certain levels of stimulation and activity, increasing or reducing them as necessary (Ch. 9)

Arrangement problems: Problems whose solutions require the rearrangement of a group of elements in order to satisfy a certain criterion (Ch. 7)

Association areas: One of the major areas of the brain, the site of the higher mental processes such as thought, language, memory, and speech (Ch. 2)

Associative models: A technique of recalling information by thinking about related information (Ch. 6)

Assumed-similarity bias: The tendency to think of people as being similar to oneself (Ch. 14)

Attachment: The positive emotional bond that develops between a child and a particular individual (Ch. 10)

Attitudes: Learned predispositions to respond in a favorable or unfavorable manner to a particular object (Ch. 14)

Attribution theory: The theory that seeks to explain how we decide, on the basis of samples of an individual's behavior, what the specific causes of that behavior are (Ch. 14)

Authoritarian parents: Parents who are rigid and punitive, and who value unquestioning obedience from their children (Ch. 10)

Authoritative parents: Parents who are firm, set clear limits, and reason with and explain things to their children (Ch. 10)

Autobiographical memories: Our recollections of circumstances and episodes from our own lives (Ch. 6)

Autonomic division: The part of the nervous system that controls involuntary movement (the actions of the heart, glands, lungs, and other organs) (Ch. 2)

Autonomy-versus-shame-and-doubt stage: The period during which, according to Erikson, toddlers (ages 18 months to 3 years) develop independence and autonomy if exploration and freedom are encouraged, or shame and self-doubt if they are restricted and overprotected (Ch. 10)

Axon: A long extension from the end of a neuron that carries messages to other cells through the neuron (Ch. 2)

Babble: Speechlike but meaningless sounds (Ch. 7)

Background stressors: Daily hassles, such as being stuck in traffic, that cause minor irritations but have no long-term ill effects, unless they continue or are compounded by other stressful events (Ch. 9)

Basilar membrane: A structure dividing the cochlea into an upper and a lower chamber (Ch. 3)

Behavior modification: A technique for promoting the frequency of desirable behaviors and decreasing the incidence of unwanted ones (Ch. 5)

Behavioral assessment: Direct measures of an individual's behavior used to describe characteristics indicative of personality (Ch. 11)

Behavioral model of abnormality: The model suggesting that the behavior itself is the problem to be treated, rather than viewing behavior as a symptom of some underlying medical or psychological problem (Ch. 12)

Behavioral perspective: The psychological model that suggests that observable behavior should be the focus of study (Ch. 1)

Behavioral treatment approaches: Approaches to treating abnormal behavior that assume that both normal and abnormal behaviors are learned and that appropriate treatment consists of learning new behavior or unlearning maladaptive behavior (Ch. 13)

Biofeedback: A technique for learning to control internal physiological processes through conscious thought (Ch. 2)

Biological perspective: The psychological model that views behavior from the perspective of biological functioning (Ch. 1)

Biologically based therapy: An approach to therapy that uses drugs and other medical procedures to improve psychological functioning (Ch. 13)

Biopsychologists: Psychologists who study the ways biological structures and body functions affect behavior (Ch. 2)

Bipolar disorder: A disorder in which a person alternates between euphoric feelings of mania and bouts of depression (Ch. 12)

Bisexuals: Persons who are sexually attracted to members of both sexes (Ch. 9)

Bottom-up processing: Recognizing and processing information about the individual components of a stimulus (Ch. 3)

Brain modules: Separate units of the brain that carry out specific tasks (Ch. 2)

Bulimia: An eating disorder characterized by vast intake of food that may be followed by self-induced vomiting or by taking laxatives to rid one's self of the food (Ch. 9)

Cannon-Bard theory of emotion: The belief that both physiological and emotional arousal are produced simultaneously by the same nerve impulse (Ch. 9)

Cardinal trait: A single personality trait that directs most of a person's activities (e.g., greed, lust, kindness) (Ch. 11)

Case study: An in-depth investigation of an individual or small group (Ch. 1)

Cataclysmic events: Strong stressors that occur suddenly, affecting many people at once (e.g., natural disasters) (Ch. 9)

Catharsis: The process of discharging built-up aggression through violent acts (Ch. 14)

Central core: The "old brain," which controls such basic functions as eating and sleeping and is common to all vertebrates (Ch. 2)

Central nervous system (CNS): The system that includes the brain and the spinal cord (Ch. 2)

Central-route processing: Message interpretation characterized by thoughtful consideration of the issues and arguments used to persuade (Ch. 14)

Central traits: A set of major characteristics that make up the core of a person's personality (Ch. 11); the major traits considered in forming impressions of others (Ch. 14)

Cerebellum (ser uh BELL um): The part of the brain that controls bodily balance (Ch. 2)

Cerebral cortex: The "new brain," responsible for the most sophisticated information processing in the brain; contains the lobes (Ch. 2)

Chromosomes: Rod-shaped structures that contain basic hereditary information (Ch. 10)

Chunk: A meaningful grouping of stimuli that can be stored as a unit in short-term memory (Ch. 6)

Circadian rhythms: Biological processes that occur repeatedly on approximately a 24-hour cycle (Ch. 4)

Classical conditioning: A kind of learning in which a previously neutral stimulus comes to elicit a response through its association with a stimulus that naturally brings about the response (Ch. 5)

Client-centered therapy: Therapy in which the therapist reflects back the patient's statements in a way that causes the patient to find his or her own solutions (Ch. 13)

Cochlea (KOKE lee uh): A coiled tube filled with fluid that receives sound via the oval window or through bone conduction (Ch. 3)

Cognition: The higher mental processes by which we understand the world, process information, make judgments and decisions, and communicate knowledge to others (Ch. 7)

Cognitive approaches to motivation: The focus on the role of our thoughts, expectations, and understanding of the world (Ch. 9)

Cognitive-behavioral approach: A process by which people's faulty cognitions about themselves and the world are changed to more accurate ones (Ch. 13)

Cognitive development: The process by which a child's understanding of the world changes as a function of age and experience (Ch. 10)

Cognitive dissonance: The conflict that arises when a person holds contradictory cognitions (Ch. 14)

Cognitive learning theory: The study of the thought processes that underlie learning (Ch. 5)

Cognitive map: A mental representation of spatial locations and directions (Ch. 5)

Cognitive model of abnormality: The model suggesting that people's thoughts and beliefs are central to abnormal behavior (Ch. 12)

Cognitive perspective: The psychological model that focuses on how people know, understand, and think about the world (Ch. 1)

Cognitive psychology: The branch of psychology that specializes in the study of cognition (Ch. 7)

Cognitive therapy: Psychotherapy based on Beck's goal to change people's illogical thoughts about themselves and the world (Ch. 13)

Collective unconscious: A concept developed by Jung proposing that we inherit certain personality characteristics from our ancestors and the human race as a whole (Ch. 11)

Community psychology: A movement aimed toward preventing or minimizing psychological disorders in the community (Ch. 13)

Companionate love: The strong affection we have for those with whom our lives are deeply involved (Ch. 14)

Compliance: Behavior that occurs in response to direct social pressure (Ch. 14)

Compulsions: Urges to repeatedly carry out an act that even the sufferer realizes is unreasonable (Ch. 12)

Concepts: Categorizations of objects, events, or people that share common properties (Ch. 7)

Concrete operational stage: According to Piaget, the period from 7 to 12 years of age that is characterized by logical thought and a loss of egocentrism (Ch. 10)

Conditioned response (CR): A response that, after conditioning, follows a previously neutral stimulus (e.g., salivation at the sound of a tuning fork) (Ch. 5)

Conditioned stimulus (CS): A once-neutral stimulus that has been paired with an unconditioned stimulus to bring about a response formerly caused only by the unconditioned stimulus (Ch. 5)

Cones: Cone-shaped, light-sensitive receptor cells in the retina that are responsible for sharp focus and color perception, particularly in bright light (Ch. 3)

Confederate: A participant in an experiment who has been instructed to behave in ways that will affect the responses of other subjects (Ch. 1)

Conformity: A change in behavior or attitudes brought about by a desire to follow the beliefs or standards of other people (Ch. 14)

Consciousness: A person's awareness of the sensations, thoughts, and feelings that he or she is experiencing at a given moment (Ch. 4)

Constructive processes: Processes in which memories are influenced by the interpretation and meaning we give to events (Ch. 6)

Continuous reinforcement schedule: The reinforcing of a behavior every time it occurs (Ch. 5)

Control group: The experimental group receiving no treatment (Ch. 1)

Convergent thinking: A type of thinking that produces responses based on knowledge and logic (Ch. 7)

Conversion disorder: A psychological disturbance characterized by actual physical disturbances, such as the inability to speak or move one's arms (Ch. 12)

Coping: The efforts to control, reduce, or learn to tolerate the threats that lead to stress (Ch. 9)

Correlational research: Research to examine the relationship between two sets of factors to determine whether they are associated, or "correlated" (Ch. 1)

Creativity: The combining of responses or ideas in novel ways (Ch. 7)

Critical period: The first of several stages of development in which specific kinds of growth must occur to enable further normal development (Ch. 10)

Cross-sectional research: A research method in which people of different ages are compared at the same point in time (Ch. 10)

Cross-sequential research: A research method that combines cross-sectional and longitudinal research by taking a number of different age groups and examining them over several points in time (Ch. 10)

Crystallized intelligence: The information, skills, and strategies that people have learned through experience and that can be applied in problem-solving situations (Ch. 8)

Culture-fair IQ test: A test that does not discriminate against members of any minority or cultural group (Ch. 8)

Daily hassles: see Background stressors (Ch. 9)

Dark adaptation: A heightened sensitivity to light resulting from being in relative dimness (Ch. 3)

Daydreams: Fantasies people construct while awake (Ch. 4)

Decay: The loss of information through nonuse (Ch. 6)

Declarative memory: Memory for factual information: names, faces, dates, and the like (Ch. 6)

Deductive reasoning: A reasoning process whereby inferences and implications are drawn from a set of assumptions and applied to specific cases (Ch. 7)

Defense mechanisms: Unconscious strategies people use to reduce anxiety

by concealing its source from themselves and others (Ch. 9, 11)

Deinstitutionalization: The transfer of former mental patients from institutions into the community (Ch. 13)

Dendrites: Cluster of fibers at one end of a neuron that receive messages from other neurons (Ch. 2)

Dependent variable: The variable that is measured and is expected to change as a result of experimenter manipulation (Ch. 1)

Depressants: Drugs that slow down the nervous system (Ch. 4)

Developmental psychology: The branch of psychology that studies people's growth and change over the lifespan (Ch. 10)

***Diagnostic and Statistical Manual of Mental Disorders* (4th ed.) *(DSM-IV)*:** A manual that presents comprehensive definitions of more than 200 separate diagnostic categories for identifying problems and behaviors (Ch. 12)

Difference threshold (or just noticeable difference): The smallest detectable difference between two stimuli (Ch. 3)

Diffusion of responsibility: The tendency for people to feel that responsibility for helping is shared among those present (Ch. 14)

Discrimination: Negative behavior toward members of a particular group (Ch. 14)

Disengagement theory of aging: A theory that suggests that aging is a gradual withdrawal from the world on physical, psychological, and social levels (Ch. 10)

Dispositional cause (of behavior): A cause of behavior that is based on internal traits or personality factors (Ch. 14)

Dissociative amnesia: A failure to remember past experience (Ch. 12)

Dissociative disorders: Psychological dysfunctions characterized by the splitting apart of critical personality facets that are normally integrated, allowing stress avoidance by escape (Ch. 12)

Dissociative fugue: An amnesiac condition in which people take sudden, impulsive trips, sometimes assuming a new identity (Ch. 12)

Dissociative identity disorder, or **multiple personality:** A disorder in which a person displays characteristics of two or more distinct personalities (Ch. 12)

Divergent thinking: The ability to generate unusual but appropriate responses to problems or questions (Ch. 7)

Double standard: The view that premarital sex is permissible for males but not for females (Ch. 9)

Dreams-for-survival theory: A theory that proposes that dreams permit information critical for our daily survival to be reconsidered and reprocessed during sleep (Ch. 4)

Drive: A motivational tension, or arousal, that energizes behavior in order to fulfill a need (Ch. 9)

Drive-reduction approaches to motivation: The theory that claims that drives are produced to obtain our basic biological requirements (Ch. 9)

Drug therapy: Control of psychological problems through drugs (Ch. 13)

Eardrum: The part of the ear that vibrates when sound waves hit it (Ch. 3)

Echoic memory: The process that stores information coming from the ears (Ch. 6)

Eclectic approach to therapy: An approach to therapy that uses techniques taken from a variety of treatment methods, rather than just one (Ch. 13)

Ego-integrity-versus-despair stage: According to Erikson, a period from late adulthood until death during which we review life's accomplishments and failures (Ch. 10)

Ego: The part of personality that provides a buffer between the id and the outside world (Ch. 11)

Egocentric thought: Viewing the world entirely from one's own perspective (Ch. 10)

Electroconvulsive therapy (ECT): Treatment involving the administration of an electric current to a patient's head to treat severe depression (Ch. 13)

Embryo: A developed zygote that has a heart, a brain, and other organs (Ch. 10)

Emotions: Feelings (such as happiness, despair, and sorrow) that generally have both physiological and cognitive elements and that influence behavior (Ch. 9)

Endocrine system: A chemical communication network that sends messages throughout the nervous system via the bloodstream and secretes hormones that affect body growth and functioning (Ch. 2)

Episodic memory: Memory for information relating to the biographical details of our individual lives (Ch. 6)

Estrogen: A female sex hormone produced by the ovaries (Ch. 9)

Excitatory message: A chemical secretion that makes it more likely that a receiving neuron will fire and an action potential will travel down its axons (Ch. 2)

Existential therapy: A humanistic approach that addresses the meaning of life and human freedom (Ch. 13)

Experiment: A study carried out to investigate the relationship between two or more factors by deliberately producing a change in one factor and observing the effect that change has upon other factors (Ch. 1)

Experimental bias: Factors that distort an experimenter's understanding of how the independent variable affected the dependent variable (Ch. 1)

Experimental group: Any group receiving a treatment (Ch. 1)

Experimental manipulation: The change deliberately produced in an experiment to affect responses or behaviors in other factors to detect relationships between variables (Ch. 1)

Explicit memory: Intentional or conscious recollection of information (Ch. 6)

Extinction: The weakening and eventual disappearance of a conditioned response (Ch. 5)

Extrinsic motivation: Motivation by which people participate in an activity for a tangible reward (Ch. 9)

Family therapy: An approach that focuses on the family as a whole unit to which each member contributes (Ch. 13)

Feature analysis: Perception of a shape, pattern, object, or scene by responding to the individual elements that make it up (Ch. 3)

Feature detection: The activation of neurons in the cortex by visual stimuli of specific shapes or patterns (Ch. 3)

Fetus: A developing child, from nine weeks after conception until birth (Ch. 10)

Fixation: Behavior in adulthood reflecting an earlier stage of development

Fixed-interval schedule: A schedule whereby reinforcement is given at established time intervals (Ch. 5)

Fixed-ratio schedule: A schedule whereby reinforcement is given only after a certain number of responses is made (Ch. 5)

Flashbulb memories: Memories of a specific event that are so clear they seem like snapshots of the event (Ch. 6)

Fluid intelligence: Reflects reasoning, memory, and information-processing capabilities (Ch. 8)

Formal operational stage: According to Piaget, the period from age 12 to adulthood that is characterized by abstract thought (Ch. 10)

Free will: The human ability to make decisions about one's life (Ch. 1)

Frequency theory of hearing: The theory that suggests that the entire basilar membrane acts like a microphone, vibrating in response to sound (Ch. 3)

Frustration: A state produced by the thwarting or blocking of some ongoing, goal-directed behavior (Ch. 14)

Functional fixedness: The tendency to think of an object in terms of its most typical use (Ch. 7)

Functionalism: An early approach to psychology that concentrated on what the mind does—the functions of mental activity—and the role of behavior in allowing people to adapt to their environments (Ch. 1)

Fundamental attribution error: A tendency to attribute others' behavior to dispositional causes and the failure to recognize the importance of situational causes (Ch. 14)

g or g-factor: A theoretical single general factor accounting for mental ability (Ch. 8)

Gate-control theory of pain: The theory that suggests that particular nerve receptors lead to specific areas of the brain related to pain; when these receptors are activated by an injury or bodily malfunction, a "gate" to the brain is opened and pain is sensed (Ch. 3)

General adaptation syndrome (GAS): A theory developed by Selye that suggests that a person's response to stress consists of three stages: alarm and mobilization, resistance, and exhaustion (Ch. 9)

Generalized anxiety disorder: The experience of long-term anxiety with no explanation (Ch. 12)

Generativity-versus-stagnation stage: According to Erikson, a period in middle adulthood during which we take stock of our contributions to family and society (Ch. 10)

Genes: The parts of a chromosome through which genetic information is transmitted (Ch. 10)

Genetic preprogramming theories of aging: Theories that suggest a built-in time limit to the reproduction of human cells (Ch. 10)

Genital stage: According to Freud, a period from puberty until death, marked by mature sexual behavior (i.e., sexual intercourse) (Ch. 11)

Genitals: The male and female sex organs (Ch. 9)

Gestalt (geh SHTALLT) **laws of organization:** A series of principles that describe how we organize pieces of information into meaningful wholes; they include closure, proximity, similarity, and simplicity (Ch. 3)

Gestalt psychology: An approach to psychology that focuses on the organization of perception and thinking in a "whole" sense, rather than on the individual elements of perception (Ch. 1)

Gestalt therapy: An approach to therapy that attempts to integrate a client's thoughts, feelings, and behavior into a whole (Ch. 13)

Grammar: The system of rules that determine how our thoughts can be expressed (Ch. 7)

Group therapy: Therapy in which people discuss problems with a group (Ch. 13)

Habituation: A decrease in response to repeated presentations of the same stimulus (Ch. 10)

Hair cells: Tiny cells covering the basilar membrane that, when bent by vibrations entering the cochlea, transmit neural messages to the brain (Ch. 3)

Hallucinogen (ha LOOS en o jen): A drug that is capable of producing changes in the perceptual process, or hallucinations (Ch. 4)

Halo effect: A phenomenon in which an initial understanding that a person has positive traits is used to infer other uniformly positive characteristics (Ch. 14)

Hardiness: A personality characteristic associated with a lower rate of stress-related illness, consisting of three components: commitment, challenge, and control (Ch. 9)

Hemispheres: Symmetrical left and right halves of the brain (Ch. 2)

Heritability: A measure of the degree to which a characteristic is related to genetic, inherited factors, as opposed to environmental factors (Ch. 8)

Heterosexuality: Sexual attraction and behavior directed to the opposite sex (Ch. 9)

Heuristic (hyur ISS tik): A rule of thumb that may bring about a solution to a problem but is not guaranteed to do so (Ch. 7)

Homeostasis: The process by which an organism tries to maintain an internal biological balance, or "steady state" (Ch. 9)

Homosexuals: Persons who are sexually attracted to members of their own sex (Ch. 9)

Hormones: Chemicals that circulate throughout the blood and affect the functioning and growth of parts of the body (Ch. 2)

Humanistic approaches to personality: Theories that emphasize people's basic goodness and their natural tendency to grow to higher levels of functioning (Ch. 11)

Humanistic model of abnormality: The model suggesting that people are basically rational, and that they should set their own limits on acceptable behavior (Ch. 12)

Humanistic perspective: The psychological model that suggests that people are in control of their lives (Ch. 1)

Humanistic therapy: Therapy in which the underlying assumption is that people have control of their behavior, can make choices about their lives, and are essentially responsible for solving their own problems (Ch. 13)

Hypnosis: A state of heightened susceptibility to the suggestions of others (Ch. 4)

Hypothalamus: A tiny part of the brain, located below the thalamus of the brain, that maintains homeostasis and produces and regulates vital, basic behavior such as eating, drinking, and sexual behavior (Ch. 2)

Hypothesis (hy POTH eh sis): A prediction stated in a way that allows it to be tested (Ch. 1)

Iconic memory: The process that reflects information from our visual system (Ch. 6)

Id: The raw, unorganized, inherited part of personality whose purpose is to reduce tension created by biological drives and irrational impulses (Ch. 11)

Identical twins: Twins with identical genetic makeup (Ch. 10)

Identity: The distinguishing character of the individual: who each of us is, what our roles are, and what we are capable of (Ch. 10)

Identity-versus-role-confusion stage: According to Erikson, a time in adolescence of testing to determine one's own unique qualities (Ch. 10)

Implicit memory: Memories of which people are not consciously aware, but which can affect subsequent performance and behavior (Ch. 6)

Incentive approaches to motivation: The theory explaining motivation in terms of external stimuli (Ch. 9)

Independent variable: The variable that is manipulated in an experiment (Ch. 1)

Inductive reasoning: A reasoning process whereby a general rule is inferred from specific cases, using observation, knowledge, experience, and beliefs (Ch. 7)

Industry-versus-inferiority stage: According to Erikson, the period during which children aged 6 to 12 years may develop positive social interactions with others or may feel inadequate and become less sociable (Ch. 10)

Inferiority complex: According to Adler, a situation in which adults have not been able to overcome the feelings of inferiority they developed as children (Ch. 11)

Information processing: The way in which people take in, use, and store information (Ch. 10)

Informed consent: A document signed by subjects prior to an experiment in which the study and conditions and risks of participation are explained (Ch. 1)

Ingroup-outgroup bias: The tendency to hold less favorable opinions about groups to which we do not belong (outgroups), while holding more favorable opinions about groups to which we do belong (ingroups) (Ch. 14)

Inhibitory message: A chemical secretion that prevents a receiving neuron from firing (Ch. 2)

Initiative-versus-guilt stage: According to Erikson, the period during which children aged 3 to 6 years experience conflict between independence of action and the sometimes negative results of that action (Ch. 10)

Insight: Sudden awareness of the relationships among various elements that had previously appeared to be independent of one another (Ch. 7)

Instinct approaches to motivation: The theory that says motivation is the result of an inborn pattern of behavior that is biologically determined (Ch. 9)

Intellectually gifted: Individuals characterized by higher-than-average intelligence, with IQ scores above 130 (Ch. 8)

Intelligence: The capacity to understand the world, think rationally, and use resources effectively when faced with challenges (Ch. 8)

Intelligence quotient (IQ) score: A measure of intelligence that takes into account an individual's mental and chronological ages (Ch. 8)

Intelligence tests: A battery of measures used to determine a person's level of intelligence (Ch. 8)

Interference: The phenomenon by which recall is hindered because of other information in memory which displaces or blocks it out (Ch. 6)

Interneurons: Neurons that transmit information between sensory and motor neurons (Ch. 2)

Interpersonal attraction: Positive feelings for others; liking and loving (Ch. 14)

Intimacy-versus-isolation stage: According to Erikson, a period during early adulthood that focuses on developing close relationships (Ch. 10)

Intrinsic motivation: Motivation by which people participate in an activity for their own enjoyment, not for the reward it will get them (Ch. 9)

Introspection: A procedure used to study the structure of the mind, in which subjects are asked to describe in detail what they are experiencing when they are exposed to a stimulus (Ch. 1)

James-Lange theory of emotion: The belief that emotional experience is a reaction to bodily events occurring as a result of an external situation ("I feel sad because I am crying") (Ch. 9)

Language: The systematic, meaningful arrangement of symbols (Ch. 7)

Language-acquisition device: A neural system of the brain hypothesized to permit understanding of language (Ch. 7)

Latency period: According to Freud, the period, between the phallic stage and puberty, during which children's sexual concerns are temporarily put aside (Ch. 11)

Latent content of dreams: According to Freud, the "disguised" meanings of dreams, hidden by more obvious subjects (Ch. 4)

Latent learning: Learning in which a new behavior is acquired but not readily demonstrated until reinforcement is provided (Ch. 5)

Lateralization: The dominance of one hemisphere of the brain in specific functions (Ch. 2)

Learned helplessness: A state in which people believe they cannot escape from or cope with stress, and they give up fighting it, leading to depression (Ch. 12)

Learning: A relatively permanent change in behavior brought about by experience (Ch. 5)

Learning-theory approach: Language acquisition follows the principles of reinforcement and conditioning (see Chapter 5) (Ch. 7)

Levels-of-processing theory: The theory that emphasizes the degree to which new material is mentally analyzed (Ch. 6)

Libido: According to Freud, the "psychic energy" that fuels the primary drives of hunger, sex, aggression, and irrational impulses (Ch. 11)

Limbic system: The part of the brain located outside the "new brain" that controls eating, aggression, and reproduction (Ch. 2)

Linguistic-relativity hypothesis: The theory claiming that language shapes and may even determine the way people of a particular culture perceive and understand the world (Ch. 7)

Lithium (LITH ee um)**:** A drug used in the treatment of bipolar disorders (Ch. 13)

Lobes: The four major sections of the cerebral cortex (Ch. 2)

Long-term memory: The storage of information on a relatively permanent basis, although retrieval may be difficult (Ch. 6)

Longitudinal research: A research method that investigates behavior as subjects age (Ch. 10)

Major depression: A severe form of depression that interferes with concentration, decision making, and sociability (Ch. 12)

Mania: An extended state of intense euphoria and elation (Ch. 12)

Manifest content of dreams: According to Freud, the overt story line of dreams (Ch. 4)

Masturbation: Sexual self-stimulation (Ch. 9)

Means-ends analysis: Repeated testing for differences between the desired outcome and what currently exists (Ch. 7)

Meditation: A learned technique for refocusing attention that brings about an altered state of consciousness (Ch. 4)

Memory: The process by which people encode, store, and retrieve information (Ch. 6)

Memory trace or Engram: A physical change in the brain corresponding to memory (Ch. 6)

Menopause: The point at which women stop menstruating, generally at around age 45 (Ch. 10)

Mental age: The typical intelligence level found for people at a given chronological age (Ch. 8)

Mental image: The images in the mind that resemble the object or event being represented (Ch. 7)

Mental retardation: A significantly subaverage level of intellectual functioning which occurs with related limitations in two or more skill areas (Ch. 8)

Mental set: The tendency for old patterns of problem solving to persist (Ch. 7)

Metabolism: The rate at which food is converted to energy and expended by the body (Ch. 9)

Metacognition: An awareness and understanding of one's own cognitive processes (Ch. 10)

Midlife crisis: The negative feelings that accompany the realization that we have not accomplished in life what we had hoped to (Ch. 10)

Midlife transition: Beginning around the age of 40, a period during which we come to the realization that life is finite (Ch. 10)

Minnesota Multiphasic Personality Inventory-2 (MMPI-2): A test used to identify people with psychological difficulties as well as to predict a variety of other behaviors (Ch. 11)

Monocular cues: Signals that allow us to perceive distance and depth with just one eye (Ch. 3)

Mood disorders: Disturbances in emotions and feelings severe enough to interfere with normal living (Ch. 12)

Motivation: The factors that direct and energize behavior (Ch. 9)

Motor area: One of the major areas of the brain, responsible for voluntary movement of particular parts of the body (Ch. 2)

Motor (efferent) neurons: Neurons that transmit information from nervous system to muscles and glands (Ch. 2)

Myelin sheath: An axon's protective coating, made of fat and protein (Ch. 2)

Narcissistic personality disorder: A personality disorder characterized by an exaggerated sense of self-importance and an inability to experience empathy for others (Ch. 12)

Narcotics: Drugs that increase relaxation and relieve pain and anxiety (Ch. 4)

Naturalistic observation: Observation without intervention, in which the investigator records information about a naturally occurring situation (Ch. 1)

Nature-nurture issue: The issue of the relative degrees to which environment and heredity influence behavior (Ch. 10)

Need-complementarity hypothesis: The hypothesis that people are attracted to others who fulfill their needs (Ch. 14)

Need for achievement: A stable, learned characteristic in which satisfaction comes from striving for and achieving a level of excellence (Ch. 9)

Need for affiliation: A need to establish and maintain relationships with other people (Ch. 9)

Need for power: A tendency to want to make an impression or have an impact on others in order to be seen as a powerful individual (Ch. 9)

Negative reinforcer: A stimulus whose removal is reinforcing, leading to a greater probability that the response bringing about this removal will occur again (Ch. 5)

Neo-Freudian psychoanalysts: Theorists who place greater emphasis than did Freud on the functions of the ego and its influence on our daily activities (Ch. 11)

Neonate: A newborn child (Ch. 10)

Neurons: Specialized cells that are the basic elements of the nervous system that carry messages (Ch. 2)

Neurotransmitter: A chemical that carries messages across the synapse to the dendrite (and sometimes the cell body) of a receiver neuron (Ch. 2)

Neutral stimulus: A stimulus that, before conditioning, has no effect on the desired response (Ch. 5)

Norms: Standards of test performance that permit the comparison of one person's score on a test to the scores of others who have taken the same test (Ch. 8)

Obedience: A change in behavior due to the commands of others (Ch. 14)

Obesity: The state of being more than 20 percent above the average weight for a person of a particular height (Ch. 9)

Object permanence: The awareness that objects do not cease to exist when they are out of sight (Ch. 10)

Observational learning: Learning through observations of others (models) (Ch. 5, 13)

Obsession: A thought or idea that keeps recurring (Ch. 12)

Obsessive-compulsive disorder: A disorder characterized by obsessions or compulsions (Ch. 12)

Oedipal (ED ih pul) **conflict:** A child's sexual interest in his or her opposite-sex parent, typically resolved through identification with the same-sex parent (Ch. 11)

Operant conditioning: Learning in which a voluntary response is strengthened or weakened, depending on its positive or negative consequences; the organism operates on its environment in order to produce a particular result (Ch. 5)

Operationalization: The process of translating a hypothesis into specific testable procedures that can be measured and observed (Ch. 1)

Opponent-process theory of color vision: The theory that suggests that receptor cells are linked in pairs, working in opposition to each other (Ch. 3)

Optic nerve: A bundle of ganglion axons that carry visual information (Ch. 3)

Oral stage: According to Freud, a stage from birth to 12–18 months, in which an infant's center of pleasure is the mouth (Ch. 11)

Otoliths: Crystals in the semicircular canals that sense body acceleration (Ch. 3)

Overregularization: Applying rules of speech in instances in which they are inappropriate (Ch. 7)

Ovulation: The monthly release of an egg from an ovary (Ch. 9)

Panic disorder: Anxiety that manifests itself in the form of panic attacks that last from a few seconds to as long as several hours (Ch. 12)

Parasympathetic division: The part of the autonomic division of the peripheral nervous system that calms the body, bringing functions back to normal after an emergency has passed (Ch. 2)

Partial reinforcement schedule: The reinforcing of a behavior some but not all of the time (Ch. 5)

Passionate (or romantic) love: A state of intense absorption in someone that is characterized by physiological arousal, psychological interest, and care for the needs of another (Ch. 14)

Perception: The sorting out, interpretation, analysis, and integration of stimuli involving our sense organs and brain (Ch. 3)

Peripheral nervous system: All parts of the nervous system except the brain and the spinal cord (includes somatic and autonomic divisions) (Ch. 2)

Peripheral-route processing: Message interpretation characterized by consideration of the source and related general information rather than of the message itself (Ch. 14)

Permissive parents: Parents who are lax, inconsistent, and undemanding, yet warm toward their children (Ch. 10)

Personal stressors: Major life events, such as the death of a family member, that have immediate negative consequences which generally fade with time (Ch. 9)

Personality: The sum total of characteristics that differentiate people, or the stability in a person's behavior across different situations (Ch. 11)

Personality disorder: A mental disorder characterized by a set of inflexible, maladaptive personality traits that keep a person from functioning appropriately in society (Ch. 12)

Phallic stage: According to Freud, a period beginning around age 3 during which a child's interest focuses on the genitals (Ch. 11)

Phobias: Intense, irrational fears of specific objects or situations (Ch. 12)

Phonemes (FONE eems): The smallest units of sound used to form words (Ch. 7)

Phonology: The study of the smallest units of sound, called phonemes (Ch. 7)

Pituitary gland: The "master gland," the major component of the endocrine system, which secretes hormones that control growth (Ch. 2)

Place theory of hearing: The theory that states that different areas of the basilar membrane respond to different frequencies (Ch. 3)

Placebo (pla SEE bo)**:** A bogus treatment such as a pill, "drug," or other substance without any significant chemical properties or active ingredient (Ch. 1)

Positive reinforcer: A stimulus added to the environment that brings about an increase in the response that preceded it (Ch. 5)

Posttraumatic stress disorder (PTSD): A phenomenon in which victims of major catastrophes reexperience the original stress event and associated feelings in vivid flashbacks or dreams (Ch. 9)

Prejudice: The negative (or positive) evaluations or judgments of members of a group that are based primarily on membership in the group rather than on the behavior of a particular individual (Ch. 14)

Preoperational stage: According to Piaget, the period from 2 to 7 years of age that is characterized by language development (Ch. 10)

Priming: A technique of recalling information by having been exposed to related information at an earlier time (Ch. 6)

Principle of conservation: The knowledge that quantity is unrelated to the arrangement and physical appearance of objects (Ch. 10)

Problems of inducing structure: Problems whose solutions require the identification of existing relationships among elements presented so as to construct a new relationship among them (Ch. 7)

Procedural memory: Refers to memory for skills and habits such as riding a bike or hitting a baseball. Sometimes referred to as "nondeclarative memory" (Ch. 6)

Progesterone: A female sex hormone produced by the ovaries (Ch. 9)

Projective personality test: A test in which a person is shown an ambiguous stimulus and asked to describe it or tell a story about it (Ch. 11)

Prosocial behavior: Helping behavior (Ch. 14)

Prototypes: Typical, highly representative examples of a concept (Ch. 7)

Psychoactive drugs: Drugs that influence a person's emotions, perceptions, and behavior (Ch. 4)

Psychoanalysis: Psychodynamic therapy that involves frequent sessions and often lasts for many years (Ch. 13)

Psychoanalytic model of abnormality: The model suggesting that abnormality stems from childhood conflicts over opposing desires regarding sex and aggression (Ch. 12)

Psychoanalytic theory: Freud's theory that unconscious forces act as determinants of personality (Ch. 11)

Psychodynamic perspective: The psychological model based on the belief that behavior is motivated by inner forces over which the individual has little control (Ch. 1)

Psychodynamic therapy: Therapy based on the notion, first suggested by Freud, that the basic sources of abnormal behavior are unresolved past conflicts and anxiety (Ch. 13)

Psychological tests: Standard measures devised to assess behavior objectively (Ch. 11)

Psychology: The scientific study of behavior and mental processes (Ch. 1)

Psychophysics: The study of the relationship between the physical nature of stimuli and a person's sensory responses to them (Ch. 3)

Psychosocial development: Development of individuals' interactions with and understanding of each other and of their knowledge and understanding of themselves as members of society (Ch. 10)

Psychosomatic (sy ko so MAT ik) **disorders:** Medical problems caused by an interaction of psychological, emotional, and physical difficulties (Ch. 9)

Psychosurgery: Brain surgery, once used to alleviate symptoms of mental disorder but rarely used today (Ch. 13)

Psychotherapy: The process in which a patient (client) and a professional attempt to remedy the client's psychological difficulties (Ch. 13)

Puberty: The period during which maturation of the sexual organs occurs (Ch. 10)

Punishment: An unpleasant or painful stimulus that is added to the environment after a certain behavior occurs, decreasing the likelihood that the behavior will occur again (Ch. 5)

Random assignment to condition: The assignment of subjects to given groups on a chance basis alone (Ch. 1)

Rapid eye movement (REM) sleep: Sleep occupying around 20 percent of an adult's sleeping time, characterized by increased heart rate, blood pressure, and breathing rate; erections; eye movements; and the experience of dreaming (Ch. 4)

Rational-emotive therapy: Psychotherapy based on Ellis's suggestion that the goal of therapy should be to restructure one's belief into a more realistic, rational, and logical system (Ch. 13)

Reciprocity-of-liking effect: The tendency to like those who like us (Ch. 14)

Reflexes: Unlearned, automatic involuntary responses to certain stimuli (Ch. 2, 10)

Rehearsal: The transfer of material from short- to long-term memory via repetition (Ch. 6)

Reinforcement: The process by which a stimulus increases the probability that a preceding behavior will be repeated (Ch. 5)

Reinforcer: Any stimulus that increases the probability that a preceding behavior will be repeated (Ch. 5)

Reliability: The concept that tests consistently measure what they are trying to measure (Ch. 8)

Replication: The repetition of an experiment in order to verify the results of the original experiment (Ch. 1)

Resting state: The nonfiring state of a neuron when the charge equals about 270 millivolts (Ch. 2)

Reticular formation: A group of nerve cells in the brain that arouses the body to prepare it for appropriate action and screens out background stimuli (Ch. 2)

Retina: The part of the eye that converts the electromagnetic energy of light into useful information for the brain (Ch. 3)

Reuptake: The reabsorption of neurotransmitters by a terminal button (Ch. 2)

Reverse-learning theory: A theory that proposes that dreams have no meaning in themselves, but instead function to rid us of unnecessary information that we have accumulated during the day (Ch. 4)

Rods: Long, cylindrical, light-sensitive receptors in the retina that perform well in poor light but are largely insensitive to color and small details (Ch. 3)

Rorschach (ROAR shock) **test:** A test consisting of inkblots of indefinite shapes, the interpretation of which is used to assess personality characteristics (Ch. 11)

Schachter-Singer theory of emotion: The belief that emotions are determined jointly by a nonspecific kind of physiological arousal and its interpretation, based on environmental cues (Ch. 9)

Schedules of reinforcement: The frequency and timing of reinforcement following desired behavior (Ch. 5)

Schemas: General themes in memory that contain relatively little detail (Ch. 6); sets of cognitions about people and social experiences (Ch. 14)

Schizophrenia: A class of disorders characterized by a severe distortion of reality, resulting in antisocial behavior, silly or obscene behavior, hallucinations, and disturbances in movement (Ch. 12)

Scientific method: The process of appropriately framing and properly answering questions, used by practitioners of psychology and those engaged in other scientific disciplines, to come to an understanding about the world (Ch. 1)

Secondary traits: Less important personality traits (e.g., preferences for certain clothes or movies) that do not affect behavior as much as central and cardinal traits do (Ch. 11)

Self-actualization: In Maslow's theory, a state of self-fulfillment in which people realize their highest potential (Ch. 9, 11)

Self-fulfilling prophecy: An expectation about the occurrence of an event or behavior that increases the likelihood that the event or behavior will happen (Ch. 14)

Self-report measures: A method of gathering data about people by asking them questions about a sample of their behavior (Ch. 11)

Semantic memory: Memory that stores general knowledge and facts about the world (e.g., mathematical and historical data) (Ch. 6)

Semantics: The rules governing the meaning of words and sentences (Ch. 7)

Semicircular canals: Part of the inner ear containing fluid that moves when the body moves to control balance (Ch. 3)

Sensation: The process by which an organism's sense organs respond to a stimulus (Ch. 3)

Sensorimotor stage: According to Piaget, the stage from birth to 2 years during which a child has little competence in representing the environment using images, language, or other symbols (Ch. 10)

Sensory (afferent) neurons: Neurons that transmit information from the body to the central nervous system (Ch. 2)

Sensory area: The site in the brain that corresponds to each of the senses, with the degree of sensitivity relating to the amount of brain tissue (Ch. 2)

Sensory memory: The initial, momentary storage of information, lasting only an instant (Ch. 6)

Shaping: The process of teaching a complex behavior by rewarding closer and closer approximations of the desired behavior (Ch. 5)

Short-term memory: The storage of information for 15 to 25 seconds (Ch. 6)

Signal detection theory: The theory that addresses the role of psychological factors in our ability to identify stimuli (Ch. 3)

Situational cause (of behavior): A cause of behavior that is based on environmental factors (Ch. 14)

Skin senses: The senses that include touch, pressure, temperature, and pain (Ch. 3)

Social cognition: The processes that underlie our understanding of the social world (Ch. 14)

Social cognitive approaches: Theories that emphasize the influence of a person's cognitions—their thoughts, feelings, expectations, and values—in determining personality (Ch. 11)

Social identity theory: The theory that a person uses group membership as a source of pride and self-worth (Ch. 14)

Social influence: The area of social psychology concerned with situations in which the actions of an individual or group affect the behavior of others (Ch. 14)

Social psychology: The branch of psychology concerned with how people's thoughts, feelings, and actions are affected by others (Ch. 14)

Social support: A mutual network of caring, interested others (Ch. 9)

Social supporter: A person who shares an unpopular opinion or attitude of another group member, thereby encouraging nonconformity (Ch. 14)

Sociocultural model of abnormality: The model suggesting that people's behavior, both normal and abnormal, is shaped by family, society, and cultural influences (Ch. 12)

Somatic division: The part of the nervous system that controls voluntary movements of the skeletal muscles (Ch. 2)

Somatoform disorders: Psychological difficulties that take on physical (somatic) forms (Ch. 12)

Sound: The movement of air molecules brought about by the vibration of an object (Ch. 3)

Spinal cord: A bundle of nerves running along the spine, carrying messages between the brain and the body (Ch. 2)

Split-brain patient: A person who suffers from independent functioning of the two halves of the brain, as a result of which the sides of the body work in disharmony (Ch. 2)

Spontaneous recovery: The reappearance of a previously extinguished response after a period of time during which the conditioned stimulus has been absent (Ch. 5)

Spontaneous remission: Recovery without treatment (Ch. 13)

Stage 1 sleep: The state of transition between wakefulness and sleep, characterized by relatively rapid, low-voltage brain waves (Ch. 4)

Stage 2 sleep: A sleep deeper that than of stage 1, characterized by a slower, more regular wave pattern, along with momentary interruptions of "sleep spindles" (Ch. 4)

Stage 3 sleep: A sleep characterized by slow brain waves, with greater peaks and valleys in the wave pattern (Ch. 4)

Stage 4 sleep: The deepest stage of sleep, during which we are least responsive to outside stimulation (Ch. 4)

Status: The social rank an individual holds within a group (Ch. 14)

Stereotypes: Beliefs and expectations about members of groups held simply on the basis of their membership in those groups (Ch. 14)

Stimulants: Drugs that affect the central nervous system, causing increased heart rate, blood pressure, and muscle tension (Ch. 4)

Stimulus: A source of physical energy that produces a response in a sense organ (Ch. 3)

Stimulus discrimination: The process by which an organism learns to differentiate among stimuli, restricting its response to one in particular (Ch. 5)

Stimulus generalization: Response to a stimulus that is similar to but different from a conditioned stimulus; the more similar the two stimuli, the more likely generalization is to occur (Ch. 5)

Stress: The response to events that are threatening or challenging (Ch. 9)

Structuralism: An early approach to psychology which focused on the fundamental elements that form the foundation of thinking, consciousness, emotions, and other kinds of mental states and activities (Ch. 1)

Subject: A participant in research (Ch. 1)

Subliminal perception: The perception of messages about which a person has no awareness (Ch. 3)

Superego: The part of personality that represents the morality of society as presented by parents, teachers, and others (Ch. 11)

Survey research: Sampling a group of people by assessing their behavior, thoughts, or attitudes, then generalizing the findings to a larger population (Ch. 1)

Sympathetic division: The part of the autonomic division of the peripheral nervous system that prepares the body to respond in stressful emergency situations (Ch. 2)

Synapse: The gap between neurons through which chemical messages are communicated (Ch. 2)

Syntax: The rules that indicate how words are joined to form sentences (Ch. 7)

Systematic desensitization: A procedure in which a relaxation response is repeatedly paired with a stimulus that evokes anxiety in the hope that the anxiety will be alleviated (Ch. 13)

Telegraphic speech: Sentences that sound as if they were part of a telegram, in which words not critical to the message are left out (Ch. 7)

Temperament: The basic, innate disposition that emerges early in life (Ch. 10, 11)

Terminal buttons: Small branches at the end of an axon that relay messages to other cells (Ch. 2)

Test standardization: A technique used to validate questions in personality tests by studying the responses of people with known psychological disorders (Ch. 11)

Thalamus: The part of the brain's central core that transmits messages from the sense organs to the cerebral cortex and from the cerebral cortex to the cerebellum and medulla (Ch. 2)

Thematic Apperception Test (TAT): A test consisting of a series of ambiguous pictures about which a person is asked to write a story, which is then taken to be a reflection of the writer's personality (Ch. 11)

Theories: Broad explanations and predictions concerning phenomena of interest (Ch. 1)

Thinking: The manipulation of mental representations of information (Ch. 7)

Tip-of-the-tongue phenomenon: The inability to recall information that one realizes one knows—a result of the difficulty of retrieving information from long-term memory (Ch. 6)

Top-down processing: Perception guided by knowledge, experience, expectations, and motivations (Ch. 3)

Trait theory: A model that seeks to identify the basic traits necessary to describe personality (Ch. 11)

Traits: Enduring dimensions of personality characteristics differentiating people from one another (Ch. 11)

Transformation problems: Problems to be solved using a series of methods to change an initial state into a goal state (Ch. 7)

Treatment: The manipulation implemented by the experimenter in regard to one group, while another group receives either no treatment or a different treatment (Ch. 1)

Triarchic theory of intelligence: A theory suggesting three major aspects of intelligence: componential, experiential, and contextual (Ch. 8)

Trichromatic theory of color vision: The theory that suggests that the retina has three kinds of cones, each responding to a specific range of wavelengths (Ch. 3)

Trust-versus-mistrust stage: According to Erikson, the first stage of psychosocial development, occurring from birth to 18 months of age, during which time infants develop feelings of trust or lack of trust (Ch. 10)

Unconditioned response (UCR): A response that is natural and needs no training (e.g., salivation at the smell of food) (Ch. 5)

Unconditioned stimulus (UCS): A stimulus that brings about a response without having been learned (Ch. 5)

Unconscious: A part of the personality of which a person is unaware (Ch. 11)

Unconscious wish fulfillment theory: A theory of Sigmund Freud, which proposes that dreams represent unconscious wishes that a dreamer wants to fulfill (Ch. 4)

Universal grammar: An underlying structure shared by all languages, the basis of Chomsky's theory that certain language

characteristics are based in the brain's structure and are therefore common to all people (Ch. 7)

Uplifts: Minor positive events that make one feel good (Ch. 9)

Validity: A test has validity when it actually measures what it is supposed to measure (Ch. 8)

Variable: A behavior or event that can change, or vary (Ch. 1)

Variable-interval schedule: A schedule whereby reinforcement varies around some average time interval rather than being fixed (Ch. 5)

Variable-ratio schedule: A schedule whereby reinforcement occurs after a varying number of responses rather than after a fixed number (Ch. 5)

Visual illusion: A physical stimulus that consistently produces errors in perception (often called an optical illusion) (Ch. 3)

Wear-and-tear theories of aging: Theories that suggest that the body's mechanical functions cease efficient activity and, in effect, wear out (Ch. 10)

Weber's law: The principle that states that the just noticeable difference is a constant proportion of the intensity of an initial stimulus (Ch. 3)

Weight set point: The particular level of weight the body strives to maintain (Ch. 9)

Working memory: Baddeley's theory that short-term memory comprises three components: the central executive, the visuospatial sketch pad, and the phonological loop (Ch. 6)

Zygote: The one-celled product of fertilization (Ch. 10)

REFERENCES

AAMR (American Association of Mental Retardation). (1992). *Definition of mental retardation.* Washington, DC: American Association of Mental Retardation.

Abramson, L. Y., Metalsky, G. I., & Alloy, L. B. (1989). Hopelessness depression: A theory-based subtype. *Psychological Review, 96,* 358–372.

Adams, B., & Parker, J. D. (1990). Maternal weight gain in women with good pregnancy outcome. *Obstetrics and Gynecology, 76,* 1–7.

Adler, J. (1984, April 23). The fight to conquer fear. *Newsweek,* pp. 66–72.

Adler, T. (1991, June). Primate rules focus on mental well-being. *APA Monitor, 6.*

Affleck, G., Tennen, H., Urrows, S., & Higgins, P. (1994). Person and contextual features of daily stress reactivity: Individual differences in relations of undesirable daily events with mood disturbance and chronic pain intensity. *Journal of Personality and Social Psychology, 66,* 329–340.

Ainsworth, M. D. S. (1989). Attachments beyond infancy. *American Psychologist, 44,* 709–716.

Ainsworth, M. D. S., Blehar, M. C., Waters, E., & Wall, S. (1978). *Patterns of attachment: A psychological study of the strange situation.* Hillsdale, NJ: Erlbaum.

Ainsworth, M. D. S., & Bowlby, J. (1991). An ethological approach to personality development. *American Psychologist, 46,* 333–341.

Aitken, R. J. (1995, July 7). The complexities of conception. *Science, 269,* 39–40.

Akmajian, A., Demers, R. A., & Harnish, R. M. (1984). *Linguistics.* Cambridge, MA: MIT Press.

Akutsu, P. D., Sue, S., Zane, N. W. S., & Nakamura, C. Y. (1989). Ethnic differences in alcohol consumption among Asians and Caucasians in the United States: An investigation of cultural and physiological factors. *Journal of Studies on Alcohol, 50,* 261–267.

Albee, G. W. (1978, February 12). I.Q. tests on trial. *The New York Times,* p. E13.

Albert, R. S. (Ed.). (1992). *The social psychology of creativity and exceptional achievement* (2nd ed.). New York: Pergamon Press.

Aldwin, C. M., & Revenson, T. A. (1987). Does coping help? A reexamination of the relation between coping and mental health. *Journal of Personality and Social Psychology, 53,* 337–348.

Alexander, C. N., Langer, E. J., Newman, R. I., Chandler, H. M., & Davies, J. L. (1989). Transcendental meditation, mindfulness, and longevity: An experimental study with the elderly. *Journal of Personality and Social Psychology, 57,* 950–964.

Alkon, D. L. (1987). *Memory traces in the brain.* New York: Cambridge University Press.

Allen, L. S., & Gorski, R. A. (1992). Sexual orientation and the size of the anterior commissure in the human brain. *Proceedings of the National Academy of Sciences, 89,* 7199.

Allen, L. S., Hines, M., Shryne, J. E., & Gorski, R. A. (1989). Two sexually dimorphic cell groups in the human brain. *Journal of Neuroscience, 9,* 497–506.

Allen, V. L. (1965). Situational factors in conformity. In L. Berkowitz (Ed.), *Advances in experimental social psychology* (Vol. 1). New York: Academic Press.

Allen, V. L. (1975). Social support for nonconformity. In L. Berkowitz (Ed.), *Advances in experimental and social psychology* (Vol. 8). New York: Academic Press.

Allison, K. W., Crawford, I., Echemendia, R., Robinson, L., & Knepp, D. (1994). Human diversity and professional competence: Training in clinical counseling psychology revisited. *American Psychologist, 49,* 792–796.

Allport, G. W. (1961). *Pattern and growth in personality.* New York: Holt, Rinehart and Winston.

Allport, G. W. (1966). Traits revisited. *American Psychologist, 21,* 1–10.

Allport, G. W., & Postman, L. J. (1958). The basic psychology of rumor. In E. D. Maccoby, T. M. Newcomb, & E. L. Hartley (Eds.), *Readings in social psychology* (3rd ed.). New York: Holt, Rinehart and Winston.

Alonso, A., & Swiller, H. I. (Eds.). (1993). *Group therapy in clinical practice.* Washington, DC: American Psychiatric Press.

Alsop, R. (1988, May 13). Advertisers put consumers on the couch. *Wall Street Journal,* p. 21.

Alwitt, L., & Mitchell, A. A. (1985). *Psychological processes and advertising effects: Theory, research, and applications.* Hillsdale, NJ: Erlbaum.

American Psychological Association. (1992). *Ethical principles of psychologists and code of conduct.* Washington, DC: American Psychological Association.

American Psychological Association. (1993, January/February). Subgroup norming and the Civil Rights Act. *Psychological Science Agenda, 5,* 6.

American Psychological Association. (1995). *Diagnostic and statistical manual of mental disorders* (4th ed.) *(DSM-IV).* Washington, DC: American Psychological Association.

Amsel, A. (1988). *Behaviorism, neobehaviorism, and cognitivism in learning theory.* Hillsdale, NJ: Erlbaum.

Anastasi, A. (1988). *Psychological testing* (6th ed.). New York: Macmillan.

Anderson, B. F. (1980). *The complete thinker: A handbook of techniques for creative and critical problem solving.* Englewood Cliffs, NJ: Prentice-Hall.

Anderson, J. (1988). Cognitive styles and multicultural populations. *Journal of Teacher Education, 39,* 2–9.

Anderson, J. A., & Adams, M. (1992). Acknowledging the learning styles of diverse student populations: Implications for instructional design. *New Directions for Teaching and Learning, 49,* 19–33.

Anderson, J. R. (1981). Interference: The relationship between response latency and response accuracy. *Journal of Experimental Psychology: Human Learning and Memory, 7,* 311–325.

Anderson, J. R. (1993). Problem solving and learning. *American Psychologist, 48,* 35–44.

Anderson, J. R., & Bower, G. H. (1972). Recognition and retrieval processes in free recall. *Psychological Review, 79,* 97–123.

Anderson, N. H. (1974). Cognitive algebra integration theory applied to social attribution. In L. Berkowitz (Ed.), *Advances in experimental social psychology* (Vol. 7, pp. 1–101). New York: Academic Press.

Anderson, N. H. (Ed.). (1991). *Contributions to information integration theory: Vol. 2. Social.* Hillsdale, NJ: Erlbaum.

Anderson, S. M., & Klatzky, R. L. (1987). Traits and social stereotypes: Levels of categorization in person perception. *Journal of Personality and Social Psychology, 53,* 235–246.

Anderson, T., & Magnusson, D. (1990). Biological maturation in adolescence and the development of drinking habits and alcohol abuse among young males: A prospective longitudinal study. *Journal of Youth and Adolescence, 19,* 33–42.

Andreasen, N. C. (1985). Positive vs. negative schizophrenia: A critical evaluation. *Schizophrenia, 11,* 380–389.

Andreasen, N. C. (1989). Neural mechanisms of negative symptoms. *British Journal of Psychiatry, 155,* 93–98.

Andreasen, N. C., Arndt, S., Swayze, V., II, Cizadlo, T., Flaum, M., O'Leary, D., Ehrhardt, J. C., & Yuh, W. T. C. (1994, October 14). Thalamic abnormalities in schizophrenia visualized through magnetic resonance image averaging. *Science, 266,* 294–298.

Angier, N. (1990, May 15). Cheating on sleep: Modern life turns America into the land of the drowsy. *The New York Times,* pp. C1, C8.

Angier, N. (1991, January 22). A potent peptide prompts an urge to cuddle. *The New York Times,* p. C1.

Angoff, W. H. (1988). The nature-nurture debate, aptitudes, and group differences. *American Psychologist, 43,* 713–720.

Ansberry, C. (1995, February 14). After seven decades, couple still finds romance in the 90s. *Wall Street Journal,* pp. A1, A17.

Antony, M. M., Brown, T. A., & Barlow, D. H. (1992). Current perspectives on panic and panic disorder. *Current Directions in Psychological Science, 1,* 79–82.

APA (American Psychological Association). (1986, March). Council resolution on polygraph tests. *APA Monitor.*

APA (American Psychological Association). (1988). *Behavioral research with animals.* Washington, DC: American Psychological Association.

APA (American Psychological Association) (1993). *Employment survey.* Washington, DC: American Psychological Association.

APA (American Psychological Association). (1994). *Careers in psychology.* Washington, DC: American Psychological Association.

APA (American Psychiatric Association) Task Force on Electroconvulsive Therapy. (1990). *The practice of electroconvulsive therapy: Recommendations for treatment, training, and privileging.* Washington, DC: American Psychiatric Association.

APA Public Interest Directorate. (1993, August 10). *Violence and youth: Psychology's response.* Washington, DC: American Psychological Association.

Aponte, J. F., Rivers, R. Y., & Wohl, J. (Eds.). (1995). *Psychological interventions and cultural diversity.* Boston: Longwood.

Apter, A., Galatzer, A., Beth-Halachmi, N., & Laron, Z. (1981). Self-image in adolescents with delayed puberty and growth retardation. *Journal of Youth and Adolescence, 10,* 501–505.

Arafat, I., & Cotton, W. L. (1974). Masturbation practices of males and females. *Journal of Sex Research, 10,* 293–307.

Aronow, E., Reznikoff, M., & Moreland, K. (1994). *The Rorschach technique: Perceptual basics, content interpretation, and applications.* Boston: Longwood.

Archer, D., Pettigrew, T. F., & Aronson, E. (1992). Making research apply. *American Psychologist, 47,* 1233–1236.

Archer, S. L., & Waterman, A. S. (1994). Adolescent identity development: Contextual perspectives. In C. B. Fisher & R. M. Lerner (Eds.), *Applied developmental psychology.* New York: McGraw-Hill.

Archibald, W. P. (1974). Alternative explanations for the self-fulfilling prophecy. *Psychological Bulletin, 81,* 74–84.

Arena, J. M. (1984, April). A look at the opposite sex. *Newsweek on Campus,* p. 21.

Armstrong, R. A., Slaven, A., & Harding, G. F. (1991). Visual evoked magnetic fields to flash and pattern in 100 normal subjects. *Vision Research, 31,* 1859–1864.

Aronson, E. (1988). *The social animal* (3rd ed.). San Francisco: Freeman.

Aronson, E., Ellsworth, P. C., Carlsmith, J. M., & Gonzales, M. H. (1990). *Methods of research in social psychology* (2nd ed.). New York: McGraw-Hill.

Asch, S. E. (1946). Forming impressions of personality. *Journal of Abnormal and Social Psychology, 41,* 258–290.

Asch, S. E. (1951). Effects of group pressure upon the modification and distortion of judgments. In H. Guetzkow (Ed.), *Groups, leadership, and men.* Pittsburgh: Carnegie Press.

Asher, S. R., & Parker, J. G. (1991). Significance of peer relationship problems in childhood. In B. H. Schneider, G. Attili, J. Nadel, & R. P. Weissberg (Eds.), *Social competence in developmental perspective.* Amsterdam: Kluwer Academic Publishing.

Aslin, R. N., & Smith, L. B. (1988). Perceptual development. *Annual Review of Psychology, 39,* 435–473.

Atkinson, J., & Braddick, O. (1989). Development of basic visual functions. In A. M. Slater & J. G. Bremner (Eds.), *Infant development.* Hillsdale, NJ: Erlbaum.

Atkinson, J. W., & Feather, N. T. (1966). *Theory of achievement motivation.* New York: Krieger.

Atkinson, J. W., & Raynor, J. O. (Eds.). (1974). *Motivation and achievement.* Washington, DC: Winston.

Atkinson, R. C., & Shiffrin, R. M. (1968). Human memory: A proposed system and its control processes. In K. W. Spence and J. T. Spence (Eds.), *The psychology of learning and motivation: Advances in research and theory* (Vol. 2, pp. 80–195). New York: Academic Press.

Auld, F., & Hyman, M. (1991). *Resolution of inner conflict: An introduction to psychoanalytic therapy.* Washington, DC: American Psychological Association.

Averill, J. R. (1975). A semantic atlas of emotional concepts. *Catalog* of Selected Documents in Psychology, 5, 330.

Avison, W. R., & Gotlib, I. H. (Eds.). (1994). *Stress and mental health.* New York: Plenum Press.

Ayoub, D. M., Greenough, W. T., & Juraska, J. M. (1983). Sex differences in dendritic structure in the preoptic area of the juvenile macaque monkey brain. *Science, 219,* 197–198.

Azrin, N. H., & Holt, N. C. (1966). Punishment. In W. A. Honig (Ed.), *Operant behavior: Areas of research and application* (pp. 380–447). New York: Appleton.

Babbitt, T., Rowland, G., & Franken, R. (1990). Sensation seeking and participation in aerobic exercise classes. *Personality and Individual Differences, 11,* 181–184.

Backer, P. (1993, February 28). On turning 13: Reports from the front lines. *The New York Times,* Sec. 4, p. 2.

Baddeley, A. (1982). *Your memory: A user's guide.* New York: Macmillan.

Baddeley, A. (1992, January 31). Working memory. *Science, 255,* 556–559.

Baddeley, A. (1993). Working memory and conscious awareness. In A. F. Collins, S. E. Gathercole, M. A. Conway, & P. E. Morris (Eds.), *Theories of memory.* Hillsdale, NJ: Erlbaum.

Baddeley, A. D. (1978). The trouble with levels: A reexamination of Craik and Lockhart's framework for memory research. *Psychological Review, 85,* 139–152.

Baddeley, A., & Wilson, B. (1985). Phonological coding and short-term memory in patients without speech. *Journal of Memory and Language, 24,* 490–502.

Baddeley, A., Wilson, B., & Watts, F. (Eds.). (1995). *Handbook of memory disorders.* New York: Wiley.

Baer, J. (1993). *Creativity and divergent thinking: A task-specific approach.* Hillsdale, NJ: Erlbaum.

Bailey, J. M., & Pillard, R. C. (1991). A genetic study of male sexual orientation. *Archives of General Psychiatry, 48,* 1089–1096.

Baker, A. G., & Mercier, P. (1989). Attention, retrospective processing and evolution of a structured connectionist model of Pavlovian conditioning (AESOP). In S. B. Klein & R. R. Mowrer (Eds.), *Contemporary learning theories: Vol. I. Pavlovian conditioning and the status of traditional learning theory.* Hillsdale, NJ: Erlbaum.

Baker, J. N. (1987, July 27). Battling the IQ-test ban. *Newsweek,* p. 53.

Baker, R. (Ed.). (1989). *Panic disorder: Theory, research and therapy.* New York: Wiley.

Baker, S. L., & Kirsch, I. (1991). Cognitive mediators of pain perception and tolerance. *Journal of Personality and Social Psychology, 61,* 504–510.

Bales, J. (1988, April). Polygraph screening banned in Senate bill. *APA Monitor, 10.*

Ballinger, B., & Yalom, I. (1994). Group therapy in practice. In B. Bongar & L. E. Beutler (Eds.), *Comprehensive textbook of psychotherapy: Theory and practice.* New York: Oxford University Press.

Ballinger, C. B. (1981). The menopause and its syndromes. In J. G. Howells (Ed.), *Modern perspectives in the psychiatry of middle age* (pp. 279–303). New York: Brunner/Mazel.

Baltes, M. M. (1995). Dependency in old age: Gains and losses. *Current Directions in Psychological Science, 4,* 14–19.

Baltes, P. B., & Schaie, K. W. (1974, March). The myth of the twilight years. *Psychology Today,* pp. 35–38ff.

Bandura, A. (1973). *Aggression: A social learning analysis.* Englewood Cliffs, NJ: Prentice-Hall.

Bandura, A. (1977). *Social learning theory.* Englewood Cliffs, NJ: Prentice-Hall.

Bandura, A. (1981). In search of pure unidirectional determinants. *Behavior Therapy, 12,* 30–40.

Bandura, A. (1986). *Social foundations of thought and action: A social cognitive theory.* Englewood Cliffs, NJ: Prentice-Hall.

Bandura, A., Grusec, J. E., & Menlove, F. L. (1967). Vicarious extinction of avoidance behavior. *Journal of Personality and Social Psychology, 5,* 16–23.

Bandura, A., O'Leary, A., Taylor, C. B., Gauthier, J., & Gossard, D. (1987). Perceived self-efficacy and pain control: Opioid and non-opioid mechanism. *Journal of Personality and Social Psychology, 53,* 563–571.

Bandura, A., Ross, D., & Ross, S. (1963a). Imitation of film-mediated aggressive models. *Journal of Abnormal and Social Psychology, 66,* 3–11.

Bandura, A., Ross, D., & Ross, S. (1963b). Vicarious reinforcement and imitative learning. *Journal of Abnormal and Social Psychology, 67,* 601–607.

Barbaro, N. M. (1988). Studies of PAG/PVG stimulation for pain relief in humans. *Progress in Brain Research, 77,* 165–173.

Barber, B. L., & Eccles, J. S. (1992). Long-term influence of divorce and single parenting on adolescent family- and work-related values, behaviors, and aspirations. *Psychological Bulletin, 111,* 108–126.

Barber, T. X. (1975). Responding to "hypnotic" suggestions: An introspective report. *American Journal of Clinical Hypnosis, 18,* 6–22.

Bargh, J., & Pietromonaco, P. (1982). Automatic information processing and social perception: The influence of trait information presented outside of conscious awareness on impression formation. *Journal of Personality and Social Psychology, 43,* 437–449.

Barinaga, M. (1994, December 2). Watching the brain remake itself. *Science, 226,* 1475–1476.

Barinaga, M. (1995, June 23). Remapping the motor cortex. *Science, 268,* 1696–1698.

Barland, G. H., & Raskin, D. C. (1975). An evaluation of field techniques in detection of deception. *Psychophysiology, 12,* 321–330.

Barnett, R. C., Marshall, N. L., Raudenbush, S. W., & Brennan, R. T. (1993). Gender and the relationship between job experiences and psychological distress: A study of dual-earner couples. *Journal of Personality and Social Psychology, 64,* 794–806.

Barnett, R. C., Marshall, N. L., & Singer, J. D. (1992). Job experiences over time, multiple roles, and women's mental health: A longitudinal study. *Journal of Personality and Social Psychology, 67,* 634–644.

Barnett, W. S. (1993). Benefit-cost analysis of preschool education: Findings from a 25-year follow-up. *Journal of Orthopsychiatry, 63,* 500–508.

Baron, J. (1993). Why teach thinking?—An essay. *Applied Psychology: An International Review, 42,* 191–237.

Baron, J. B., & Sternberg, R. J. (1986). *Teaching thinking skills.* New York: Freeman.

Barondes, S. H. (1994, February 25). Thinking about Prozac. *Science, 263,* 1102–1103.

Barringer, F. (1989, June 9). Doubt on "trial marriage" raised by divorce rates. *The New York Times,* pp. 1, 28.

Barringer, F. (1993a, April 1). Viral sexual diseases are found in 1 of 5 in U.S. *The New York Times,* pp. A1, B9.

Barringer, F. (1993b, May 16). Pride in a soundless world: Deaf oppose a hearing aid. *The New York Times,* pp. 1, 22.

Barron, F. (1990). *Creativity and psychological health: Origins of personal vitality and creative freedom.* Buffalo, NY: Creative Education Foundation.

Barron, F., & Harrington, D. M. (1981). Creativity, intelligence, and personality. *Annual Review of Psychology, 32,* 439–476.

Barsalou, L. W. (1992). *Cognitive psychology: An overview for cognitive scientists.* Hillsdale, NJ: Erlbaum.

Barsky, A. J., Cleary, P. D., Wyshak, G., Spitzer, R. L., Williams, J. B. W., & Klernan, G. L. (1992). A structure diagnostic interview for hypochondriasis: A proposed criterion standard. *Journal of Nervous and Mental Disease, 180,* 20–27.

Bartlett, F. (1932). *Remembering: A study in experimental and social psychology.* Cambridge, England: Cambridge University Press.

Bartoshuk, L. M. (1971). The chemical senses: I. Taste. In J. N. Kling & L. A. Riggs (Eds.), *Experimental psychology* (3rd ed.). New York: Holt, Rinehart and Winston.

Bartoshuk, L. M., & Beauchamp, G. K. (1994). Chemical senses. *Annual Review of Psychology, 45,* 419–449.

Bashore, T. R., & Rapp, P. E. (1993). Are there alternatives to traditional polygraph procedures? *Psychological Bulletin, 113,* 3–22.

Batson, C. D. (1990). How social an animal? The human capacity for caring. *American Psychologist, 45,* 336–346.

Batson, C. D. (1991). *The altruism question: Toward a social-psychological answer.* Hillsdale, NJ: Erlbaum.

Batson, C. D., Batson, J. G., Slingsby, J. K., Harrell, K. L., Peekna, H. M., & Todd, R. M. (1991). Empathic joy and the empathy-altruism hypothesis. *Journal of Personality and Social Psychology, 61,* 413–426.

Batson, C. D., & Weeks, J. L. (1996). Mood effects of unsuccessful helping: Another test of the empathy-altruism hypothesis. *Personality and Social Psychology Bulletin, 22,* 148–157.

Baum, A., Gatchel, R. J., & Schaeffer, M. A. (1983). Emotional, behavioral, and physiological effects of chronic stress at Three Mile Island. *Journal of Consulting and Clinical Psychology, 51,* 565–572.

Baumrind, D. (1971). Current patterns of parental authority. *Developmental Psychology Monographs, 4,* (1, pt. 2).

Baumrind, D. (1980). New directions in socialization research. *Psychological Bulletin, 35,* 639–652.

Beaman, A. L., Cole, C. M., Preston, M., Klentz, B., & Steblay, N. M. (1983). Fifteen years of foot-in-the-door research: A meta-analysis. *Personality and Social Psychology Bulletin, 9,* 181–196.

Bear, M. F., Cooper, L. N., & Ebner, F. F. (1987). A physiological basis for a theory of synapse modification. *Science, 237,* 42–48.

Beck, A. T. (1976). *Cognitive therapy and emotional disorders.* New York: International Universities Press.

Beck, A. T. (1982). Cognitive theory of depression: New perspectives. In P. Clayton & J. Barrett (Eds.), *Treatment of depression: Old controversies and new approaches.* New York: Raven.

Beck, A. T. (1991). Cognitive therapy: A 30-year perspective. *American Psychologist, 46,* 368–375.

Beck, A. T., & Emery, G. (with Greenberg, R. L.). (1985). *Anxiety disorders and phobias: A cognitive perspective.* New York: Basic Books.

Beck, A. T., & Haaga, D. A. F. (1992). The future of cognitive therapy. *Psychotherapy, 29,* 34–38.

Beck, M. (1992, May 25). Menopause. *Newsweek,* pp. 71–79.

Beck, M., & Wingert, P. (1993, June 23). The young and the gifted. *Newsweek,* pp. 52–53.

Becker, B. J. (1990). Coaching for the Scholastic Aptitude Test: Further synthesis and appraisal. *Review of Educational Research, 60,* 373–417.

Beckman, J. C., Keefe, F. J., Caldwell, D. S., & Brown, C. J. (1991). Biofeedback as a means to alter electromyographic activity in a total knee replacement patient. *Biofeedback and Self Regulation, 16,* 23–35.

Begley, S. (1993, December 20). "We slam-dunked it": NASA's shuttle mission fixes Hubble Telescope. *Newsweek,* pp. 100–102.

Behrmann, M., Winocur, G., & Moscovitch, M. (1992). Dissociation between mental imagery and object recognition in a brain-damaged patient. *Nature, 359,* 636–637.

Beilin, H., & Pufall, P. (Eds.). (1992). *Piaget's theory: Prospects and possibilities.* Hillsdale, NJ: Erlbaum.

Bell, A., & Weinberg, M. S. (1978). *Homosexuality: A study of diversities among men and women.* New York: Simon & Schuster.

Bell, S. M., & Ainsworth, M. D. S. (1972). Infant crying and maternal responsiveness. *Child Development, 43,* 1171–1190.

Bellack, A. S., Hersen, M., & Kazdin, A. E. (1990). *International handbook of behavior modification and therapy.* New York: Plenum Press.

Bellak, L. (1993). *The T.A.T., C.A.T., and S.A.T. in clinical use* (5th ed.). Boston: Longwood.

Bellezza, F. S., Six, L. S., & Phillips, D. S. (1992). A mnemonic for remembering long strings of digits. *Bulletin of the Psychonomic Society, 30,* 271–274.

Belsky, J., & Rovine, M. (1988). Nonmaternal care in the first year of life and infant-parent attachment security. *Child Development, 59,* 157–167.

Bem, D. J., & Honorton, C. (1994). Does psi exist? Replicable evidence for an anomalous process of information transfer. *Psychological Bulletin, 115,* 4–18.

Benjamin, Jr., L. T. (1985, February). Defining aggression: An exercise for classroom discussion. *Teaching of Psychology, 12* (1), 40–42.

Benjamin, Jr., L. T., & Shields, S. A. (1990). Foreword. In H. Hollingworth, *Leta Stetter Hollingworth: A biography.* Bolton, MA: Anker Publishing.

Bennett, A. (1992, October 14). Lori Schiller emerges from the torments of schizophrenia. *Wall Street Journal,* pp. A1, A10.

Benson, H. (1993). The relaxation response. In D. Goleman & J. Guerin (Eds.), *Mind-body medicine: How to use your mind for better health.* Yonkers, NY: Consumer Reports Publications.

Benson, H., & Friedman, R. (1985). A rebuttal to the conclusions of Davis S. Holme's article, "Meditation and somatic arousal reduction." *American Psychologist, 40,* 725–726.

Bergener, M., Ermini, M., & Stahelin, H. B. (Eds.). (1985, February). *Thresholds in aging.* The 1984 Sandoz Lectures in Gerontology, Basel, Switzerland.

Berger, J. (1993, May 30). The long days and short life of a medical student. *The New York Times,* p. B4.

Bergin, A. E., & Garfield, S. L. (Eds.). (1994). *Handbook of psychotherapy and behavior change* (4th ed.). New York: Wiley.

Berguier, A., & Ashton, R. (1992). Characteristics of the frequent nightmare sufferer. *Journal of Abnormal Psychology, 101*, 246–250.

Berkowitz, L. (1974). Some determinants of impulsive aggression: The role of mediated associations with reinforcements for aggression. *Psychological Review, 81*, 165–176.

Berkowitz, L. (1984). Aversive conditioning as stimuli to aggression. In R. J. Blanchard & C. Blanchard (Eds.), *Advances in the study of aggression* (Vol. 1). New York: Academic Press.

Berkowitz, L. (1987). Mood, self-awareness, and willingness to help. *Journal of Personality and Social Psychology, 52*, 721–729.

Berkowitz, L. (1989). Frustration-aggression hypothesis. *Psychological Bulletin, 106*, 59–73.

Berkowitz, L. (1990). On the formation and regulation of anger and aggression: A cognitive-neoassociationistic analysis. *American Psychologist, 45*, 494–503.

Berkowitz, L. (1993). *Aggression: Its causes, consequences, and control.* New York: McGraw-Hill.

Berkowitz, L., & Green, R. G. (1966). Film violence and the cue properties of available targets. *Journal of Personality and Social Psychology, 3*, 525–530.

Berkowitz, L., & LePage, A. (1967). Weapons as aggression-eliciting stimuli. *Journal of Personality and Social Psychology, 7*, 202–207.

Berlyne, D. (1967). Arousal and reinforcement. In D. Levine (Ed.), *Nebraska symposium on motivation.* Lincoln: University of Nebraska Press.

Bernard, M. E., & DiGiuseppe, R. (Eds.). (1993). *Rational-emotive consultation in applied settings.* Hillsdale, NJ: Erlbaum.

Berndt, T. J. (1992). Friendship and friends' influence in adolescence. *Current Directions in Psychological Science, 1*, 156–159.

Bernieri, F. J., Zuckerman, M., Koestner, R., & Rosenthal, R. (1994). Measuring person perception accuracy: Another look at self-other agreement. *Personality and Social Psychology Bulletin, 20*, 367–378.

Berscheid, E. (1985). Interpersonal attraction. In G. Lindzey & E. Aronson (Eds.), *Handbook of social psychology* (3rd ed.). New York: Random House.

Berscheid, E., & Walster, E. (1974). Physical attractiveness. In L. Berkowitz (Ed.), *Advances in experimental social psychology* (Vol. 7, pp. 157–215). New York: Academic Press.

Bersoff, D. N. (1995). *Ethical conflicts in psychology.* Washington, DC: American Psychological Association.

Bersoff, D. N., & Ogden, D. W. (1991). APA Amicus Curiae briefs: Furthering lesbian and gay male civil rights. *American Psychologist, 46*, 950–956.

Betancourt, H., & Lopez, S. R. (1993). The study of culture, ethnicity, and race in American psychology. *American Psychologist, 48*, 1586–1596.

Beyene, Y. (1989). *From menarche to menopause: Reproductive lives of peasant women in two cultures.* Albany: State University of New York Press.

Bieber, I., et al. (1962). *Homosexuality: A psychoanalytic study.* New York: Basic Books.

Biederman, I. (1987). Recognition-by-components: A theory of human image understanding. *Psychological Review, 94*, 115–147.

Biederman, I. (1990). Higher-level vision. In D. N. Osherson, S. Kosslyn, & J. Hollerbach (Eds.), *An invitation to cognitive science: Visual cognition and action.* Cambridge, MA: MIT Press.

Biernat, H., & Wortman, C. B. (1991). Sharing of home responsibilities between professionally employed women and their husbands. *Journal of Personality and Social Psychology, 60*, 844–860.

Binet, A., & Simon, T. (1916). *The development of intelligence in children (The Binet-Simon Scale).* Baltimore: Williams & Wilkins.

Bini, L. (1938). Experimental research on epileptic attacks induced by the electric current. *American Journal of Psychiatry (Suppl. 94),* 172–183.

Birch, H. G. (1945). The role of motivation factors in insightful problem solving. *Journal of Comparative Psychology, 38*, 295–317.

Birchwood, M., Hallett, L., & Preston, R. (1989). In M. Birchwood et al., *Schizophrenia: An integrated approach to research and treatment.* New York: New York University Press.

Bisanz, J., Bisanz, G. L., & Korpan, C. A. (1994). Inductive reasoning. In R. J. Sternberg (Ed.), *Thinking and problem-solving.* San Diego, CA: Academic Press.

Bishop, J. E. (1993, September 30). The knowing eye: One man's acci-dent is shedding new light on human perception. *Wall Street Journal,* pp. A1, A8.

Bjork, D. W: (1993). *B. F. Skinner: A life.* New York: Basic Books.

Bjork, R. A., & Richardson-Klarehn, A. (1989). On the puzzling relationship between environmental context and human memory. In C. Izawa (Ed.), *Current issues in cognitive processes: The Tulane-Floweree symposium on cognition.* Hillsdale, NJ: Erlbaum.

Bjorklund, D. F. (1985). The role of conceptual knowledge in the development of organization in children's memory. In C. J. Brainerd & M. Pressley (Eds.), *Basic process in memory development.* New York: Springer-Verlag.

Blakeslee, S. (1992, August 11). Finding a new messenger for the brain's signals to the body. *The New York Times,* p. C3.

Blanchard, F. A., Lilly, R., & Vaughn, L. A. (1991). Reducing the expression of racial prejudice. *Psychological Science, 2*, 101–105.

Blanck, P. D. (Ed.). (1993). *Interpersonal expectations: Theory, research and applications.* Cambridge, England: Cambridge University Press.

Blass, T. (1991). Understanding behavior in the Milgram obedience experiment: The role of personality, situations, and their interactions. *Journal of Personality and Social Psychology, 60*, 398–413.

Blass, T., & Krackow, A. (1991, June). *The Milgram obedience experiments: Students' views vs. scholarly perspectives and actual findings.* Paper presented at the annual meeting of the American Psychological Society, Washington, D.C.

Blau, Z. S. (1973). *Old age in a changing society.* New York: New Viewpoints.

Blum, K., Noble, E. P., Sheridan, P. J., Montgomery, A., Ritchie, T., Jagadeeswaran, P., Nogami, H., Briggs, A. H., & Cohn, J. B. (1990, April 18). Allelic association of human dopamine D2 Receptor gene in alcoholism. *Journal of the American Medical Association, 263*, 2055–2059.

Blumstein, P. W., & Schwartz, P. (1983). *American couples.* New York: Morrow.

Boakes, R. A., Popplewell, D. A., & Burton, M. J. (Eds.) (1987). *Eating habits: Food, physiology, and learned behaviour.* New York: Wiley.

Bolger, N., & Eckenrode, J. (1991). Social relationships, personality, and anxiety during a major stressful event. *Journal of Personality and Social Psychology, 61,* 440–449.

Bolles, R. C., & Fanselow, M. S. (1982). Endorphins and behavior. *Annual Review of Psychology, 33,* 87–101.

Bolos, A. M., Dean, M., & Rausburg, M. (1990, December 26). Population and pedigree studies reveal a lack of association between the dopamine D2 Receptor gene and alcoholism. *Journal of the American Medical Association, 264,* 3156.

Bond, L. A., Cutler, S. J., & Grams, A. E. (1995). *Promoting successful and productive aging.* Newbury Park, CA: Sage.

Bond, M. H. (1993). Emotions and their expression in Chinese culture. *Journal of Nonverbal Behavior, 17,* 245–263.

Boneau, C. A. (1992). Observations of psychology's past and future. *American Psychologist, 47,* 1586–1596.

Booth, A. (Ed.). (1992). *Child care in the 1990s: Trends and consequences.* Hillsdale, NJ: Erlbaum.

Booth, W. (1989). Asking America about its sex life. *Science, 243,* 304.

Borbely, A. (1986). *The secrets of sleep.* New York: Basic Books.

Borland, J. H. (1989). *Planning and implementing programs for the gifted.* New York: Teachers College Press.

Bornstein, M. H. (1989). Sensitive periods in development: Structural characteristics and causal interpretations. *Psychological Bulletin, 105,* 179–197.

Bornstein, M. H., & Bruner, J. S. (Eds.). (1989). *Interaction on human development: Crosscurrents in contemporary psychology services.* Hillsdale, NJ: Erlbaum.

Bornstein, M. H., & Krasnegor, N. A. (Eds.) (1989). *Stability and continuity in mental development: Behavioral and biological perspectives.* Hillsdale, NJ: Erlbaum.

Bornstein, M. H., & Lamb, M. E. (1992). *Development in infancy* (3rd ed.). New York: McGraw-Hill.

Bornstein, M. H., & Sigman, M. D. (1986). Continuity in mental development from infancy. *Child Development, 57,* 251–274.

Bornstein, R. F., & D'Agostino, P. R. (1992). Stimulus recognition and the mere exposure effect. *Journal of Personality and Social Psychology, 63,* 545–552.

Boster, F. J., & Mongeau, P. (1985). Fear-arousing persuasive messages. In R. N. Bostrom (Ed.), *Communi-cation yearbook* (Vol. 8) Beverly Hills, CA: Sage.

Bouchard, C., Tremblay, A., Despres, J. P., Nadeau, A., et al. (1990, May 24). The response to long-term overfeeding in identical twins. *New England Journal of Medicine, 322,* 1477–1482.

Bouchard, T. J., & McGue, M. (1981). Familial studies of intelligence: A review. *Science, 212,* 1055–1059.

Bouchard, Jr., T. J. (1994, June 17). Genes, environment, and personality. *Science, 264,* 1700–1701.

Bourne, L. E., Dominowski, R. L., Loftus, E. F., & Healy, A. F. (1986). *Cognitive processes* (2nd ed.). Englewood Cliffs, NJ: Prentice-Hall.

Bowd, A. D., & Shapiro, K. J. (1993). The case against laboratory animal research in psychology. *Journal of Social Issues, 49,* 133–142.

Bower, G., & Cohen, P. R. (1982). Emotional influences in memory and thinking: Data and theory. In M. S. Clark & S. T. Fiske (Eds.), *Affect and cognition.* Hillsdale, NJ: Erlbaum.

Bower, G. H. (1993). The fragmentation of psychology? *American Psychologist, 48,* 905–907.

Bower, T. (1989). The perceptual world of the newborn child. In A. M. Slater & J. G. Bremner (Eds.), *Infant development.* Hillsdale, NJ: Erlbaum.

Brainard, D. H., Wandell, B. A., & Chichilnisky, E. (1993). Color constancy: From physics to appearance. *Current Directions in Psychological Science, 2,* 165–170.

Brainerd, C. J., Reyna, V. F., & Brandse, E. (1995). Are children's false memories more persistent than their true memories? *Psychological Science, 6,* 359–364.

Brand, D. (1987, August 31). The new whiz kids. *Time,* pp. 42–51.

Brandon, R., & Davies, C. (1973). *Wrongful imprisonment: Mistaken convictions and their consequences.* Hamden, CT: Archon Books.

Bransford, J. D., & Johnson, M. K. (1972). Contextual prerequisites for understanding: Some investigations of comprehension and recall. *Journal of Verbal Learning and Verbal Behavior, 11,* 717–721.

Braun, B. (1985, May 21). Interview by D. Goleman: New focus on multiple personality. *The New York Times,* p. C1.

Brazelton, T. B. (1969). *Infants and mothers: Differences in development.* New York: Dell.

Brehm, J. W., & Self, E. A. (1989). The intensity of motivation. *Annual Review of Psychology, 40,* 109–131.

Breland, K., & Breland, M. (1961). Misbehavior of organisms. *American Psychologist, 16,* 681–684.

Breu, G. (1992, November 23). A heart stopper. *People Weekly,* pp. 87–88.

Brewer, M. B. (1988). A dual process model of impression formation. In T. K. Srull & R. S. Wyer, Jr. (Eds.), *Advances in social cognition* (Vol. 1, pp. 1–36). Hillsdale, NJ: Erlbaum.

Brewer, M. B., & Lui, L. L. (1989). The primacy of age and sex in the structure of person categories. *Social Cognition, 7,* 262–274.

Brislin, R. (1993). *Understanding culture's influence on behavior.* Fort Worth, TX: Harcourt Brace Jovanovich.

Brody, G. H., Neubaum, E., & Forehand, R. (1988). Serial marriage: A heuristic analysis of an emerging family form. *Journal of Personality and Social Psychology, 103,* 211–222.

Brody, J. (1982). *New York Times guide to personal health.* New York: Times Books.

Brody, J. E. (1987, November 19). Encouraging news for the absent-minded: Memory can be improved, with practice. *The New York Times,* p. C1.

Brody, J. E. (1992, November 23). For most trying to lose weight, dieting only makes things worse. *The New York Times,* pp. A1, A8.

Brody, N. (1990). Behavior therapy versus placebo: Comment on Bowers and Clum's meta-analysis. *Psychological Bulletin, 107,* 106–109.

Brody, N. (1993). Intelligence and the behavioral genetics of personality. In R. Plomin & G. E. McClearn (Eds.), *Nature, nurture, and psychology.* Washington, DC: American Psychological Association.

Bronson, G. W. (1990). The accurate calibration in infants' scanning records. *Journal of Experimental Child Psychology, 49,* 79–100.

Broota, K. D. (1990). *Experimental design in behavioral research.* New York: Wiley.

Brown, A. S. (1991). A review of the tip-of-the-tongue experience. *Psychological Bulletin, 109,* 204–223.

Brown, D. C. (1994). Subgroup norming: Legitimate testing practice or reverse discrimination? *American Psychologist, 49,* 927–928.

Brown, J. D. (1991). Staying fit and staying well: Physical fitness as a moderator of life stress. *Journal of*

Personality and Social Psychology, 60, 555–561.

Brown, J. D., & McGill, K. L. (1989). The cost of good fortune: When positive life events produce negative health consequences. *Journal of Personality and Social Psychology, 57*, 1103–1110.

Brown, P. K., & Wald, G. (1964). Visual pigments in single rod and cones of the human retina. *Science, 144*, 45–52.

Brown, R. (1958). How shall a thing be called? *Psychological Review, 65*, 14–21.

Brown, R. (1986). *Social psychology* (2nd ed.). New York: Macmillan.

Brown, R., & Kulik, J. (1977). Flashbulb memories. *Cognition, 5*, 73–99.

Brown, S. (Ed.). (1995). *Treating alcoholism.* San Francisco: Jossey-Bass.

Brown, S. I., & Walter, M. I. (Eds.). (1990). *The art of problem posing* (2nd ed.). Hillsdale, NJ: Erlbaum.

Bruce, V., & Green, P. R. (1990). *Visual perception: Physiology, psychology and ecology* (2nd ed.). Hillsdale, NJ: Erlbaum.

Brunner, H. G., Nelen, M., Breakefield, X. O., Ropers, H. H., & van Oost, B. A. (1993, October 22). Abnormal behavior associated with a point mutation in the structural gene for monoamine oxidase A. *Science, 262*, 578–580.

Bryant, R. A., & McConkey, K. M. (1990). Hypnotic blindness and the relevance of cognitive style. *Journal of Personality and Social Psychology, 59*, 756–761.

Buck, L., & Axel, R. (1991, April 5). A novel multigene family may encode odorant receptors: A molecular basis for odor recognition. *Cell, 65*, 167–175.

Buckhout, R. (1974). Eyewitness testimony. *Scientific American, 231*, 23–71.

Buckhout, R. (1976). Eyewitness testimony. In R. Held & W. Richards (Eds.), *Recent progress in perception.* San Francisco: Freeman.

Buckhout, R., Figueroa, D., & Hoff, E. (1975). Eyewitness identification: Effects of suggestion and bias in identification from photographs. *Bulletin of the Psychonomic Society, 6*, 71–74.

Bugental, J. F. T., & Bracke, P. E. (1992). The future of existential-humanistic psychotherapy. *Psychotherapy, 29*, 28–33.

Bugental, J. F. T., & McBeath, B. (1994). Depth existential therapy: Evolution since World War II. In B.

Bongar & L. E. Beutler (Ed.), *Comprehensive textbook of psychotherapy: Theory and practice.* New York: Oxford University Press.

Burbules, N. C., & Linn, M. C. (1988). Response to contradiction: Scientific reasoning during adolescence. *Journal of Educational Psychology, 80*, 67–75.

Burger, J. M. (1986). Increasing compliance by improving the deal: The that's-not-all technique. *Journal of Personality and Social Psychology, 51*, 277–283.

Burger, J. M. (1992). *Desire for control: Personality, social and clinical perspectives.* New York: Plenum Press.

Burgess, R. L., & Huston, T. L. (Eds.). (1979). *Social exchanges in developing relationships.* New York: Academic Press.

Burnham, D. K. (1983). Apparent relative size in the judgment of apparent distance. *Perception, 12*, 683–700.

Burns, A., & Scott, C. (1994). *Mother-headed families and why they have increased.* Hillsdale, NJ: Erlbaum.

Bushman, B. J. (1993). Human aggression while under the influence of alcohol and other drugs: An integrative research review. *Current Directions in Psychological Science, 2*, 148–152.

Bushman, B. J., & Geen, R. G. (1990). Role of cognitive-emotional mediators and individual differences in the effects of media violence on aggression. *Journal of Personality and Social Psychology, 58*, 156–163.

Buss, A. H. (1989). Personality as traits. *American Psychologist, 44*, 1378–1388.

Buss, D. M., et al. (1990). International preferences in selecting mates: A study of 37 cultures. *Journal of Cross-Cultural Psychology, 21*, 5–47.

Butcher, J. N. (1990). *The MMPI-2 in psychological treatment.* New York: Oxford University Press.

Butcher, J. N., Graham, J. R., Dahlstrom, W. G., & Bowman, E. (1990). The MMPI-2 with college students. *Journal of Personality Assessment, 54*, 1–15.

Butler, R. A. (1954). Incentive conditions which influence visual exploration. *Journal of Experimental Psychology, 48*, 19–23.

Butler, R. A. (1987). An analysis of the monaural displacement of sound in space. *Perception & Psychophysics, 41*, 1–7.

Button, E. (1993). *Eating disorders: Personal construct theory and change.* New York: Wiley.

Bylinsky, G. (1993, March 22). New gains in the fight against pain. *Fortune,* pp. 107–118.

Byrne, D. (1969). Attitudes and attraction. In L. Berkowitz (Ed.), *Advances in experimental social psychology* (Vol. 4, pp. 35–89). New York: Academic Press.

Cacioppo, J. T., Marshall-Goodell, B. S., Tassinary, L. G., & Petty, R. E. (1992). Rudimentary determinants of attitudes: Classical conditioning is more effective when prior knowledge about the attitude stimulus is low than high. *Journal of Experimental Social Psychology, 28*, 207–233.

Cairns, H. S., & Cairns, C. E. (1976). *Psycholinguistics: A cognitive view of language.* New York: Holt, Rinehart and Winston.

Calkins, B. J. (1993). *Advancing the science: A psychologist's guide to advocacy.* Washington, DC: American Psychological Association.

Candee, D., & Kohlberg, L. (1987). Moral judgment and moral action: A reanalysis of Haan, Smith, and Block's (1968) free-speech data. *Journal of Personality and Social Psychology, 52*, 554–564.

Cannon, W. B. (1929). Organization for physiological homeostatics. *Physiological Review, 9*, 280–289.

Caplan, G. A., & Brigham, B. A. (1990). Marijuana smoking and carcinoma of the tongue: Is there an association? *Cancer, 66*, 1005–1006.

Caramazza, A., & Hillis, A. E. (1991, February 28). Lexical organization of nouns and verbs in the brain. *Nature, 349*, 788–790.

Carli, L. L., Ganley, R., & Pierce-Otay, A. (1991). Similarity and satisfaction in roommate relationships. *Personality and Social Psychology Bulletin, 17*, 419–426.

Carlo, G., Eisenberg, N., Troyer, D., Switzer, G., & Speer, A. L. (1991). The altruistic personality: In what contexts is it apparent? *Journal of Personality and Social Psychology, 61*, 450–458.

Carlson, M., Charlin, V., & Miller, N. (1988). Positive mood and helping behavior: A test of six hypotheses. *Psychological Bulletin, 55*, 211–229.

Carlson, M., Marcus-Newhall, A., & Miller, N. (1989). Evidence for a general construct of aggression. *Per-*

sonality and Social Psychology Bulletin, 15, 377–389.

Carlson, M., Marcus-Newhall, A., & Miller, N. (1990). Effects of situational aggression cues: A quantitative review. *Journal of Personality and Social Psychology, 58,* 622–633.

Carmody, D. (1990, March 7). College drinking: Changes in attitude and habit. *The New York Times,* p. C11.

Carpenter, Jr., W. T., & Buchanan, R. W. (1994, March 10). Medical progress: Schizophrenia. *New England Journal of Medicine, 330,* 681–690.

Carroll, J. B. (1992). Cognitive abilities: The state of the art. *Psychological Science, 3,* 266–270.

Carroll, J. B. (1993). *Human cognitive abilities: A survey of factor-analytic studies.* Cambridge, England: Cambridge University Press.

Carson, R. C., Butcher, J. N., & Coleman, J. C. (1992). *Abnormal psychology and modern life* (9th ed.). New York: HarperCollins.

Casas, J. M. (1994). Counseling and psychotherapy with racial/ethnic minority groups in theory and practice. In B. Bongar & L. E. Beutler (Eds.), *Comprehensive textbook of psychotherapy: Theory and practice.* New York: Oxford University Press.

Case, R. (Ed.). (1991). *The mind's staircase: Exploring the conceptual underpinnings of children's thought and knowledge.* Hillsdale, NJ: Erlbaum.

Casselden, P. A., & Hampson, S. E. (1990). Forming impressions from incongruent traits. *Journal of Personality and Social Psychology, 59,* 353–362.

Cattell, R. B. (1965). *The scientific analysis of personality.* Chicago: Aldine.

Cattell, R. B. (1967). *The scientific analysis of personality.* Baltimore: Penguin.

Cattell, R. B. (1987). *Intelligence: Its structure, growth, and action.* Amsterdam: North-Holland.

Cattell, R. B., Cattell, A. K., & Cattell, H. E. P. (1993). *Sixteen personality factor questionnaire* (5th ed.). San Antonio, TX: Harcourt Brace.

Cavanaugh, J. C., & Park, D. C. (1993, December). The graying of America: An aging revolution in need of a national research agenda. *American Psychologist Observer,* p. 3.

CDC (Centers for Disease Control). (1991). *Incidence of sexually transmitted disease.* Atlanta, GA: Centers for Disease Control.

CDC (Centers for Disease Control). (1992). *Most students sexually active: Survey of sexual activity.* Atlanta, GA: Centers for Disease Control.

Center on Addiction and Substance Abuse. (1994). *Report on college drinking.* New York: Columbia University.

Cermak, L. S., & Craik, F. I. M. (Eds.). (1979). *Levels of processing in human memory.* Hillsdale, NJ: Erlbaum.

Chaiken, S. (1979). Communicator physical attractiveness and persuasion. *Journal of Personality and Social Psychology, 37,* 1387–1397.

Chamberlain, K., & Zika, S. (1990). The minor events approach to stress: Support for the use of daily hassles. *British Journal of Psychology, 81,* 469–481.

Chandler, M. J. (1976). Social cognition and life-span approaches to the study of child development. In H. W. Reese & L. P Lipsitt (Eds.), *Advances in child development and behavior* (Vol. 11). New York: Academic Press.

Chapman, L. J., & Chapman, J. P. (1973). *Disordered thought in schizophrenia.* New York: Appleton-Century-Crofts.

Chase, M. (1993, October 13). Inner music: Imagination may play role in how the brain learns muscle control. *Wall Street Journal,* pp. A1, A6.

Cheney, D. L., & Seyfarth, R. M. (1990). *How monkeys see the world: Inside the mind of another species.* Chicago: University of Chicago Press.

Cherlin, A. (1993). *Marriage, divorce, remarriage.* Cambridge, MA: Harvard University Press.

Cherlin, A. J., Furstenberg, Jr., F. F., Chase-Lansdale, P. L., Kiernan, K. E., Robins, P. K., Morrison, D. R., & Teitler, J. O. (1991, June 7). Longitudinal studies of effects of divorce on children in Great Britain and the United States. *Science, 252,* 1386–1389.

Chiocca, E. A., & Martuza, R. L. (1990). Neurosurgical therapy of the patient with obsessive-compulsive disorder. In M. A. Jenike, L. Baer, & W. E. Minichiello (Eds.), *Obsessive compulsive disorders: Theory and management* (2nd ed.). Chicago: Yearbook Medical Publishers.

Chomsky, N. (1968). *Language and mind.* New York: Harcourt Brace Jovanovich.

Chomsky, N. (1969). *The acquisition of syntax in children from five to ten.* Cambridge, MA: MIT Press.

Chomsky, N. (1978). On the biological basis of language capacities. In G. A. Miller & E. Lennenberg (Eds.), *Psychology and biology of language and thought* (pp. 199–220). New York: Academic Press.

Chomsky, N. (1991). Linguistics and cognitive science: Problems and mysteries. In A. Kasher (Ed.), *The Chomskyan turn.* Cambridge, MA: Blackwell.

Church, A. T., & Burke, P. J. (1994). Exploratory and confirmatory tests of the big five and Tellegen's three- and four-dimensional models. *Journal of Personality and Social Psychology, 66,* 93–114.

Churchland, P. S., & Sejnowski, T. J. (1992). *The computational brain.* Cambridge, MA: Bradford.

Chwalisz, K., Diener, E., & Gallagher, D. (1988). Autonomic arousal feedback and emotional experience: Evidence from the spinal-cord injured. *Journal of Personality and Social Psychology, 54,* 820–828.

Cialdini, R. B. (1984). *Social influence.* New York: William Morrow.

Cialdini, R. B. (1988). *Influence: Science and practice* (2nd ed.). Glenview, IL: Scott, Foresman.

Cialdini, R., & Fultz, J. (1990). Interpreting the negative mood-helping literature via "Mega"-analysis: A contrary view. *Psychological Bulletin, 107,* 210.

Cialdini, R. B., Schaller, M., Houlihan, D., Arps, K., Fultz, J., & Beaman, A. L. (1975). Reciprocal concessions procedure for inducing compliance: The door-in-the-face technique. *Journal of Personality and Social Psychology, 31,* 206–215.

Cialdini, R. B., Schaller, M., Houlihan, D., Arps, K., Fultz, J., & Beaman, A. L. (1987). Empathy-based helping: Is it selflessly or selfishly motivated? *Journal of Personality and Social Psychology, 52,* 749–758.

Cicchetti, D., & Beeghly, M. (Eds.). (1990). *Children with Down syndrome.* Cambridge, England: Cambridge University Press.

Cioffi, D., & Holloway, J. (1993). Delayed costs of suppressed pain. *Journal of Personality and Social Psychology, 64,* 274–282.

Clark, L. A., & Watson, D. (1988). Mood and the mundane: Relations between daily life events and self-reported mood. *Journal of Personality and Social Psychology, 54,* 296–308.

Clark, M. (1987, November 9). Sweet music for the deaf. *Newsweek,* p. 73.

Clark, M. S., & Reis, H. T. (1988). Interpersonal processes in close relationships. *Annual Review of Psychology, 39,* 609–672.

Clarke-Stewart, K. A. (1991). A home is not a school: The effects of child care on children's development. *Journal of Social Issues, 47,* 105–123.

Clarke-Stewart, K. A. (1993). *Daycare.* Cambridge, MA: Harvard University Press.

Clarke-Stewart, K. A., & Friedman, S. (1987). *Child development: Infancy through adolescence.* New York: Wiley.

Clarke-Stewart, K. A., Gruber, C. P., & Fitzgerald, L. M. (1994). *Children at home and in day care.* Hillsdale, NJ: Erlbaum.

Coats, E. J., Feldman, R. S., & Schwartzberg, S. (1994). *Critical thinking: General principles and case studies.* New York: McGraw-Hill.

Coffey, C. E. (1993). *The clinical science of electroconvulsive therapy.* Washington, DC: American Psychiatric Press.

Cohen, D. (1993). *The development of play* (2nd ed.). London: Routledge.

Cohen, D. B. (1979). *Sleep and dreaming: Origins, nature, and functioning.* New York: Pergamon Press.

Cohen, G. (1989). *Memory in the real world.* Hillsdale, NJ: Erlbaum.

Cohen, S., Tyrrell, D. A., & Smith, A. P. (1993). Negative life events, perceived stress, negative affect, and susceptibility of the common cold. *Journal of Personality and Social Psychology, 64,* 131–140.

Cohen, S. H., & Reese, H. W. (Eds.). (1991). *Life-span developmental psychology: Methodological innovations.* Hillsdale, NJ: Erlbaum.

Cohen, S. H., & Reese, H. W. (Eds.). (1994). *Life-span developmental psychology: Methodological contributions.* Hillsdale, NJ: Erlbaum.

Cohen, T. E., & Lasley, D. J. (1986). Visual sensitivity. In M. R. Rosenzweig & Porter (Eds.), *Annual Review of Psychology, 37,* 103–112.

Coie, J. D., Watt, N. F., West, S. G., Hawkins, J. D., Asarnow, J. R., Markman, H. J., Ramey, S. L., Shure, M. B., & Long, B. (1993). The science of prevention: A conceptual framework and some directions for a national research program. *American Psychologist, 48,* 1013–1022.

Colby, A., & Damon, W. (1987). Listening to a different voice: A review of Gilligan's *In a different voice.* In M. R. Walsh (Ed.), *The psychology of women.* New Haven, CT: Yale University Press.

Collins, A. F., Gathercole, S. E., Conway, M. A., & Morris, P. E. (Eds.). (1993). *Theories of memory.* Hillsdale, NJ: Erlbaum.

Collins, A. M., & Loftus, E. F. (1975). A spreading-activation theory of semantic processing. *Psychological Review, 82,* 407–428.

Collins, A. M., & Quillian, M. R. (1969). Retrieval times from semantic memory. *Journal of Verbal Learning and Verbal Behavior, 8,* 240–247.

Colombo, J., & Mitchell, D. W. (1990). Individual differences in early visual attention. In J. Colombo & J. W. Fagen (Eds.), *Individual differences in infancy: Reliability, stability, and prediction.* Hillsdale, NJ: Erlbaum.

Commons, M. L., Nevin, J. A., & Davison, M. C. (Eds.). (1989). *Signal detection: Mechanism, models and applications.* Hillsdale, NJ: Erlbaum.

Compas, B. E. (1987). Coping with stress during childhood and adolescence. *Psychological Bulletin, 101,* 393–403.

Compas, B. E., Ey, S., & Grant, K. E. (1993). Taxonomy, assessment, and diagnosis of depression during adolescence. *Psychological Bulletin, 114,* 323–344.

Comstock, G., & Strasburger, V. C. (1990). Deceptive appearances: Television violence and aggressive behavior. Conference: Teens and television (1988, Los Angeles, California). *Journal of Adolescent Health Care, 11,* 31–44.

Condon, J. W., & Crano, W. D. (1988). Inferred evaluation and the relation between attitude similarity and interpersonal attraction. *Journal of Personality and Social Psychology, 54,* 789–797.

Conway, M., & Rubin, D. (1993). The structure of autobiographical memory. In A. F. Collins, S. E. Gathercole, M. A. Conway, & P. E. Morris (Eds.), *Theories of memory.* Hillsdale, NJ: Erlbaum.

Cook, C. A. L., Caplan, R. D., & Wolowitz, H. (1990). Nonwaking responses to waking stressors: Dreams and nightmares. *Journal of Applied Social Psychology, 20,* 199–226.

Cook, T. D., & Shadish, W. R. (1994). Social experiments: Some developments over the past fifteen years. *Annual Review of Psychology, 45,* 545–580.

Cooper, I. S. (1981). *Living with chronic neurological disease.* New York: Norton.

Cooper, J. R., Bloom, F. E., & Roth, R. H. (1991). *The biochemical basis of neuropharmacology.* New York: Oxford University Press.

Cooper, L. A., & Shepard, R. N. (1984, December). Turning something over in the mind. *Scientific American,* pp. 106–114.

Cooper, S. H. (1989). Recent contributions to the theory of defense mechanism: A comparative view. *Journal of the American Psychoanalytic Association, 37,* 865–892.

Coppen, A., Metcalfe, M., & Wood, K. (1982). Lithium. In E. S. Paykel (Ed.), *Handbook of affective disorders.* New York: Guilford Press.

Corbetta, M., Miezin, F. M., Shulman, G. L., & Petersen, S. E. (1993, March). A PET study of visuospatial attention. *Journal of Neuroscience, 13,* 1202–1226.

Coren, S. (1989). The many moon illusions: An integration through analysis. In M. Hershenson (Ed.), *The moon illusion.* Hillsdale, NJ: Erlbaum.

Coren, S. (1992). *The left-handed syndrome.* New York: The Free Press.

Coren, S., & Aks, D. J. (1990). Moon illusion in pictures: A multimechanism approach. *Journal of Experimental Psychology: Human Perception and Performance, 16,* 365–380.

Coren, S., Porac, C., & Ward, L. M. (1984). *Sensation and perception* (2nd ed). New York: Academic Press.

Coren, S., & Ward, L. M. (1989). *Sensation and perception* (3rd ed.). San Diego, CA: Harcourt Brace Jovanovich.

Corina, D. P., Vaid, J., & Bellugi, U. (1992). The linguistic basis of left hemisphere specialization. *Science, 255,* 1258.

Cornblatt, B., & Erlenmeyer-Kimling, L. E. (1985). Global attentional deviance in children at risk for schizophrenia: Specificity and predictive validity. *Journal of Abnormal Psychology, 94,* 470–486.

Cornelius, S. W., & Caspi, A. (1987). Everyday problem solving in adulthood and old age. *Psychology and Aging, 2,* 144–153.

Cornell, T. L., Fromkin, V. A., & Mauner, G. (1993). A linguistic approach to language processing in Broca's aphasia: A paradox resolved. *Current Directions in Psychological Science, 2,* 47–52.

Costa, Jr., P. T., & McCrae, R. R. (1985). Hypochondriasis, neuroticism, and aging. *American Psychologist, 40,* 19–28.

Costa, Jr., P. T., & McCrae, R. R. (1995). Solid ground in the wetlands of personality: A reply to Block. *Psychological Bulletin, 117,* 216–220.

Cotman, C. W., & Lynch, G. S. (1989). The neurobiology of learning and memory. *Cognition, 33,* 201–241.

Cotton, P. (1993, July 7). Psychiatrists set to approve DSM-IV. *Journal of the American Medical Association, 270,* 13–15.

Council of Scientific Affairs (1985, April 5). Scientific status of refreshing recollection by the use of hypnosis. *Journal of the American Medical Association, 253.*

Cowan, N. (1988). Evolving conceptions of memory storage, selective attention, and their mutual constraints within the human information-processing system. *Psychological Bulletin, 104,* 163–191.

Cowdry, R. W. (1995). Basic behavioral science research for mental health: A national investment. A report of the National Advisory Mental Health Council Behavioral Science Task Force. *Psychological Science, 6,* 192–199.

Cowley, G. (1994, February 7). The culture of Prozac. *Newsweek,* pp. 41–42.

Craik, F. I., & Lockhart, R. S. (1972). Levels of processing: A framework for memory research. *Journal of Verbal Behavior, 11,* 671–684.

Craik, F. I. M. (1990). Levels of processing. In M. E. Eysenck (Ed.), *The Blackwell dictionary of cognitive psychology.* London: Blackwell.

Cramer, P. (1987). The development of defense mechanisms. *Journal of Personality, 55,* 597–614.

Crandall, C., & Biernat, M. (1990). The ideology of anti-fat attitudes. *Journal of Applied Social Psychology, 20,* 227–243.

Crandall, C. S. (1988). Social contagion of binge eating. *Journal of Personality and Social Psychology, 55,* 588–598.

Crandall, C. S. (1992). Psychophysical scaling of stressful life events. *Psychological Science, 3,* 256–258.

Crapo, L. (1985). *Hormones: Messengers of life.* New York: Freeman.

Crawford, H. J. (1982). Hypnotizability, daydreaming styles, imagery vividness, and absorption: A multidimensional study. *Journal of Personality and Social Psychology, 42,* 915–926.

Crease, R. P. (1993, July 30). Biomedicine in the age of imaging. *Science, 261,* 554–561.

Creswell, J. W. (1994). *Research design.* Newbury Park, CA: Sage.

Crews, D. (1993). The organizational concept and vertebrates without sex chromosomes. *Brain, Behavior, and Evolution, 42,* 202–214.

Crews, D. (1994, January). Animal sexuality. *Science, 263,* 108–114.

Crews, F. (1993, November 18). The unknown Freud. *New York Review,* pp. 55–66.

Crick, F., & Mitchison, G. (1983). The function of dream sleep. *Nature, 304,* 111–114.

Crick, N. R., & Dodge, K. A. (1994). A review and reformulation of social information-processing mechanisms in children's social adjustment. *Psychological Bulletin, 115,* 74–101.

Crits-Christoph, P. (1992). The efficacy of brief dynamic psychotherapy: A meta-analysis. *American Journal of Psychiatry, 149,* 151–158.

Crits-Christoph, P., & Mintz, J. (1991). Implications of therapist effects for the design and analysis of comparative studies of psychotherapies. *Journal of Consulting and Clinical Psychology, 59,* 20–26.

Crocetti, G. (1983). *GRE: Graduate record examination general aptitude test.* New York: Arco.

Crockett, L. J., & Crouter, A. C. (Eds.). (1995). *Pathways through adolescence: Individual development in relation to social contexts.* Hillsdale, NJ: Erlbaum.

Cromwell, R. L., & Snyder, C. R. (1993). *Schizophrenia: Origins, processes, treatment, and outcome.* New York: Oxford University Press.

Cronkite, K. (1994). *On the edge of darkness: Conversations about depression.* New York: Doubleday.

Crosby, F. J. (1991). *Juggling: The unexpected advantages of balancing career and home for women, their families, and society.* New York: The Free Press.

Crow, T. J. (1990). The continuum of psychosis and its genetic origins: The sixty-fifth Maudsley lecture. *British Journal of Psychiatry, 156,* 788–797.

Crowe, R. R., Black, D. W., Wesner, R., Andreasen, N. C., Cookman, A., & Roby, J. (1991). Lack of linkage to chromosome 5q11-q13 in six schizophrenia pedigrees. *Archives of General Psychiatry, 48,* 357–361.

Croyle, R. T., & Hunt, J. R. (1991). Coping with health threat: Social influence processes in reactions to medical test results. *Journal of Personality and Social Psychology, 60,* 382–389.

Culotta, E., & Koshland, Jr., D. E. (1992, December 18). No news is good news. *Science, 258,* 1862–1865.

Cummings, E., & Henry, W. E. (1961). *Growing old.* New York: Basic Books.

Cummings, J. (1987, October 6). An earthquake aftershock: Calls to mental health triple. *The New York Times,* p. A1.

Czeisler, C. A., Johnson, M. P., & Duffy, J. F. (1990, May 3). Exposure to bright light and darkness to treat physiological maladaption to night work. *New England Journal of Medicine, 322,* 1253.

Czeisler, C. A., Kronauer, R. E., Allan, J. S., Duffy, J. F., Jewett, M. E., Brown, E. N., & Ronda, J. M. (1989, June 16). Bright light induction of strong (Type O) resetting of the human circadian pacemaker. *Science, 244,* 1328–1333.

Dabbs, J. M., Jr., & Morris, R. (1990) Testosterone, social class, and antisocial behavior in a sample of 4,462 men. *Psychological Science, 1,* 209–211.

Damasio, H., Grabowski, T., Frank, R., Galaburda, A. M., & Damasio, A. R. (1994, May 20). The return of Phineas Gage: Clues about the brain from the skull of a famous patient. *Science, 264,* 1102–1105.

Damon, W. (1988). *The moral child.* New York: The Free Press.

Dana, R. H. (1993). *Multicultural assessment perspectives for professional psychology.* Boston: Allyn & Bacon.

Darley, J. M., & Shultz, T. R. (1990). Moral rules: Their content and acquisition. *Annual Review of Psychology, 41,* 525–556.

Darling, N., & Steinberg, L. (1993). Parenting style as context: An integrative model. *Psychological Bulletin, 113,* 487–496.

Darwin, C. J., Turvey, M. T., & Crowder, R. G. (1972). An auditory analogue of the Sperling partial-report procedure: Evidence for brief auditory storage. *Cognitive Psychology, 3,* 255–267.

Davidson, J. E. (1990). Intelligence recreated. *Educational Psychologist, 25,* 337–354.

Davis, R. (1986). Assessing the eating disorders. *The Clinical Psychologist, 39,* 33–36.

De La Cancela, V., & Sotomayer, G. M. (1993). Rainbow warriors: Reducing institutional racism in mental health. *Journal of Mental Health Counseling, 15,* 55–71.

De Valois, R. L., & De Valois, K. K. (1993). A multi-stage color model. *Vision Research, 33,* 1053–1065.

DeAngelis, T. (1994, June). New test allows takers to tackle real-life problems. *APA Monitor,* p. 14.

DeBono, E. (1967). *The five day course in thinking.* New York: Basic Books.

DeCasper, A. J., & Fifer, W. D. (1980). Of human bonding: Newborns prefer their mothers' voices. *Science, 208,* 1174–1176.

DeCharms, R., & Moeller, G. H. (1962). Values expressed in American children's readers, 1800–1950. *Journal of Abnormal and Social Psychology, 64,* 136–142.

Deci, E. L. (1992). On the nature and functions of motivation theories. *Psychological Science, 3,* 167–176.

Deci, E. L., & Ryan, R. M. (1985). *Intrinsic motivation and self-determination in human behavior.* New York: Plenum Press.

Deffenbacher, J. L. (1988). Cognitive relaxation and social skills treatments of anger: A year later. *Journal of Consulting Psychology, 35,* 309–315.

DeGroot, A. D. (1966). Perception and memory versus thought: Some old ideas and recent findings. In B. Kleinmuntz (Ed.), *Problem solving: Research, method, and theory.* New York: Wiley.

DeKay, W. T., & Buss, D. M. (1992). Human nature, individual differences, and the importance of context: Perspectives from evolutionary psychology. *Current Directions in Psychological Science, 1,* 184–189.

DeLongis, A., Folkman, S., & Lazarus, R. S. (1988). The impact of daily stress on health and mood: Psychological social resources as mediators. *Journal of Personality and Social Psychology, 54,* 486–495.

Delprato, D. J., & Midgley, B. D. (1992). Some fundamentals of B. F. Skinner's behaviorism. *American Psychologist, 47,* 1507–1520.

Dement, W. (1989). *Sleep and alertness: Chrono-biological, behavioral and medical aspects of napping.* New York: Raven Press.

Dement, W. C. (1976). *Some must watch while some must sleep.* New York: Norton.

Dement, W. C. (1979). Two kinds of sleep. In D. Goleman & R. J. Davidson (Eds.), *Consciousness: Brain, states of awareness, and mysticism* (pp. 72–75). New York: Harper & Row.

Dement, W. C., & Wolpert, E. A. (1958). The relation of eye movements, body mobility, and external stimuli to dream content. *Journal of Experimental Psychology, 55,* 543–553.

Demetriou, A., Shayer, M., & Efklides, A. (1993). *Neo-Piagetian theories of cognitive development.* London: Routledge.

Denmark, F. L. (1994). Engendering psychology. *American Psychologist, 49,* 329–334.

Dennett, D. C. (1991). *Consciousness explained.* Boston: Little, Brown.

Dent, J. (1984, March). *Reader's Digest, 124,* 38.

Denton, K., & Krebs, D. (1990). From the scene of the crime: The effect of alcohol and social context on moral judgment. *Journal of Personality and Social Psychology, 59,* 242–248.

Dentzer, S. (1986, May 5). Can you pass the job test? *Newsweek,* pp. 46–53.

Deregowski, J. B. (1973). Illusion and culture. In R. L. Gregory & G. H. Combrich (Eds.), *Illusion in nature and art* (pp. 161–192). New York: Scribner.

Derksen, J. J. L. (1995). *Personality Disorders: Clinical and social perspectives.* New York: Wiley.

Desforges, D. M., Lord, C. G., Ramsey, S. L., Mason, J. A., VanLeeuwen, M. D., West, S. C., & Lepper, M. R. (1991). Effects of structured cooperative contact on changing negative attitudes toward stigmatized social groups. *Journal of Personality and Social Psychology, 60,* 531–544.

Desimone, R. (1992, October 9). The physiology of memory: Recordings of things past. *Science, 258,* 245–255.

Deutsch, F. M., Lussier, J. B., & Servis, L. J. (1993). Husbands at home: Predictors of paternal participation in childcare and housework. *Journal of Personality and Social Psychology, 65,* 1154–1166.

Devenport, L. D., & Devenport, J. A. (1990). The laboratory animal dilemma: A solution in our backyards. *Psychological Science, 1,* 215–216.

Devine, P. G., & Baker, S. M. (1991). Measurement of racial stereotype subtyping. *Personality and Social Psychology Bulletin, 17,* 44–50.

Devine, P. G., & Elliot, A. J. (1995). Are racial stereotypes *really* fading? The Princeton trilogy revisited. *Personality and Social Psychology Bulletin, 21,* 1139–1150.

Devine, P. G., Hamilton, D. L., & Ostrom, T. M. (Eds.). (1994). *Social cognition: Impact on social psychology.* San Diego, CA: Academic Press.

Dewji, N. N., & Singer, S. J. (1996, January 12). Genetic clues to Alzheimer's disease. *Science, 271,* 159–160.

Diaz-Guerrero, R. (1979). Culture and personality revisited. *Annals of the New York Academy of Sciences, 285,* 119–130.

Dickinson, A. (1991, September). Helpless to save her sister from Alzheimer's, an anguished actress provides what comfort she can. *People Weekly,* 75–78.

DiClemente, C. C. (1993). Changing addictive behaviors: A process perspective. *Current Directions in Psychological Science, 2* (4), 101–106.

Diener, E., Sandvik, E., & Larsen, R. J. (1985). Age and sex effects for emotional intensity. *Developmental Psychology, 21,* 542–546.

DiGiovanna, A. G. (1994). *Human aging: Biological perspectives.* New York: McGraw-Hill.

Digman, J. M. (1990). Personality structure: Emergence of the five-factor model. *Annual Review of Psychology, 41,* 417–440.

Dillard, J. P. (1991). The current status of research on sequential-request compliance techniques. Special issue: Meta-analysis in personality and social psychology. *Personality and Social Psychology Bulletin, 17,* 283–288.

Dion, K. K., & Berscheid, E. (1974). Physical attractiveness and peer perception among children. *Sociometry, 37,* 1–12.

Dobson, K. S., & Craig, K. D. (Eds.). (1996). *Advances in cognitive-behavioral therapy.* Newbury Park, CA: Sage.

Dobson, K. S., & Shaw, B. F. (1994). Cognitive therapies in practice. In B. Bongar & L. E. Beutler (Eds.), *Comprehensive textbook of psychotherapy: Theory and practice.* New York: Oxford University Press.

Dodge, K. A., Bates, J. E., & Petit, G. S. (1990, December 20). Mechanisms in the cycle of violence. *Science, 250,* 1678–1683.

Dolce, J. J., & Raczynski, J. M. (1985). Neuromuscular activity and electromyography in painful backs: Psychological and biomechanical models in assessment and treatment. *Psychological Bulletin, 97,* 502–520.

Dollard, J., Doob, L., Miller, N., Mower, O. H., & Sears, R. R.

(1939). *Frustration and aggression.* New Haven, CT: Yale University Press.

Dominowski, R. L., & Bourne, Jr., L. E. (1994). History of research on thinking and problem-solving. In R. J. Sternberg (Ed.), *Thinking and problem-solving.* San Diego, CA: Academic Press.

Domjan, M., & Purdy, J. E. (1995). Animal research in psychology: More than meets the eye of the general psychology student. *American Psychologist, 50,* 496–503.

Dore, F. Y., & Dumas, C. (1987). Psychology of animal cognition: Piagetian studies. *Psychological Bulletin, 102,* 219–233.

Doris, J. (Ed.). (1991). *The suggestibility of children's recollections: Implications for eyewitness testimony.* Hyattsville, MD: American Psychological Association.

Doty, R. L., Green, P. A., Ram, C., & Yankell, S. L. (1982). Communication of gender from human breath odors: Relationship to perceived intensity and pleasantness. *Hormones and Behavior, 16,* 13–22.

Dove, A. (1968, July 15). Taking the chitling test. *Newsweek.*

Dovidio, J. F., Allen, J. L., & Schroeder, D. A. (1990). Specificity of empathy-induced helping: Evidence for altruistic motivation. *Journal of Personality and Social Psychology, 59,* 249–260.

Dreyer, P. H. (1982). Sexuality during adolescence. In B. B. Wolman (Ed.), *Handbook of developmental psychology.* Englewood Cliffs, NJ: Prentice-Hall.

Druckman, D., & Bjork, R. A. (1991). *In the mind's eye: Enhancing human performance.* Washington, DC: National Academy Press.

Drum, D. J. (1990). Group therapy review. *Counseling Psychologist, 18,* 131–138.

Dryden, W., & DiGiuseppe, R. (1990). *A primer on rational-emotive therapy.* Champaign, IL: Research Press.

Duck, S. (Ed.). (1984). *Personal relationships.* New York: Academic Press.

Duck, S. (1988). *Relating to others.* Chicago: Dorsey.

Duke, M., & Nowicki, S., Jr. (1979). *Abnormal psychology: Perspectives on being different.* Monterey, CA: Brooks/Cole.

Duncker, K. (1945). On problem solving. *Psychological Monographs, 58* (5, whole no. 270).

Dutton, D. G., & Aron, A. P. (1974). Some evidence for heightened sexual attraction under conditions of high anxiety. *Journal of Personality and Social Psychology, 30,* 510–517.

Dworkin, R. H., & Widom, C. S. (1977). Undergraduate MMPI profiles and the longitudinal prediction of adult social outcome. *Journal of Consulting and Clinical Psychology, 45,* 620–625.

Dywan, J., & Bowers, K. (1983). The use of hypnosis to enhance recall. *Science, 222,* 184–185.

Eagly, A. (1978). Sex differences in influenceability. *Psychological Bulletin, 85,* 86–116.

Eagly, A. (1989, May). Meta-analysis of sex differences. Annual conference on adversity, University of Massachusetts, Amherst.

Eagly, A., & Chaiken, S. (1993). *The psychology of attitudes.* Fort Worth, TX: Harcourt Brace Jovanovich.

Eagly, A. H. (1983). Gender and social influence: A social psychological analysis. *American Psychologist, 38,* 971–981.

Eagly, A. H., & Carlie, L. L. (1981). Sex of researchers and sex-typed communications as determinants of sex differences in influenceability: A meta-analysis of social influence studies. *Psychological Bulletin, 90,* 1–20.

Eagly, A. H., Wood, W., & Chaiken, S. (1978). Causal inferences about communicators and their effect on opinion change. *Journal of Personality and Social Psychology, 36,* 424–435.

Ebbinghaus, H. (1885/1913). *Memory: A contribution to experimental psychology* (H. A. Roger & C. E. Bussenius, Trans.). New York: Columbia University Press.

Ebomoyi, E. (1987). Prevalence of female circumcision in two Nigerian communities. *Sex Roles, 17,* 13–152.

Eckenrode, J. (1984). Impact of chronic and acute stressors on daily reports of mood. *Journal of Personality and Social Psychology, 46,* 907–918.

Eckholm, E. (1988, April 17). Exploring the forces of sleep. *The New York Times Magazine,* pp. 26–34.

Edwards, F. A., Gibb, A. J., & Colquhoun, D. (1992, September 5). ATP receptor-mediated synaptic currents in the central nervous system. *Nature, 359,* 144–147.

Egan, T. (1994, January 30). A Washington city full of Prozac. *The New York Times,* p. A16.

Egeland, J. A., Gerhard, D. S., Pauls, D. L., Sussex, J. N., Kidd, K. K., **Allen, C. R., Hostetter, A. M., & Housman, D. E.** (1987). Bipolar affective disorders linked to DNA markers on chromosome 11. *Nature, 325,* 783–787.

Eichenbaum, H. (1993, August 20). Thinking about brain cell assemblies. *Science, 261,* 993–994.

Eisenberg, N. (1991). Meta-analytic contributions to the literature on prosocial behavior. *Personality and Social Psychology Bulletin, 17,* 273–282.

Eisenberg, N. (1994). *Social development.* Newbury Park, CA: Sage.

Eisenberg, N., & Fabes, R. A. (1991). Prosocial behavior and empathy: A multimethod developmental perspective. In M. S. Clark (Ed.), *Prosocial behavior.* Newbury Park, CA: Sage.

Ekman, P., & Davidson, R. J. (1994). *The nature of emotion: Fundamental questions.* New York: Oxford University Press.

Elkin, I. (1986, May). *NIMH treatment of depression: Collaborative research program.* Paper presented at the annual meeting of the American Psychiatric Association, Washington, DC.

Ellis, A. (1974). *Growth through reason.* Hollywood, CA: Wilshire Books.

Ellis, A. (1987). The impossibility of achieving consistently good mental health. *American Psychologist, 42,* 364–375.

Ellis, A., & Dryden, W. (1987). *The practice of rational-emotive therapy (RET).* New York: Springer.

Ellis, H. C. (1992). Graduate education in psychology: Past, present, and future. *American Psychologist, 47,* 570–576.

Eng, R. C. (Ed.). (1990). *Women: Alcohol and other drugs.* Dubuque, IA: Kendall/Hunt.

Engen, T. (1982). *Perception of odors.* New York: Academic Press.

Engen, T. (1987, September-October). Remembering odors and their names. *American Scientist, 75,* 497–503.

Engle-Friedman, M., Baker, A., & Bootzin, R. R. (1985). Reports of wakefulness during EEG identified stages of sleep. *Sleep Research, 14,* 152.

Engler, J., & Goleman, D. (1992). *The consumer's guide to psychotherapy.* New York: Simon & Schuster.

Epstein, R., Kirshnit, C. E., Lanza, R. P., & Rubin, L. C. (1984). Insight in the pigeon: Antecedents and determinants of intelligent performance. *Nature, 308,* 61–62.

Epstein, S. (1994). An integration of the cognitive and the psychodynamic unconscious. *American Psychologist, 49,* 709–724.

Epstein, S., & Meier, P. (1989). Constructive thinking: A broad coping variable with specific components. *Journal of Personality and Social Psychology, 57,* 332–350.

Epstein, S., & O'Brien, E. J. (1985). The person-situation debate in historical and current perspective. *Psychological Bulletin, 98,* 513–537.

Erber, R. (1991). Affective and semantic priming: Effects of mood on category accessibility and inference. *Journal of Experimental Social Psychology, 27,* 480.

Erickson, M. H., Hershman, S., & Secter, I. I. (1990). *The practical application of medical and dental hypnosis.* New York: Brunner/Mazel.

Erikson, E. H. (1963). *Childhood and society* (2nd ed.). New York: Norton.

Erlandson, D. A., Harris, E. L., Skipper, B. L., & Allen, S. D. (1993). *Doing naturalistic inquiry: A guide to methods.* Newbury Park, CA: Sage.

Eron, L. D. (1982). Parent-child interaction, television violence, and aggression of children. *American Psychologist, 37,* 197–211.

Eron, L. D., & Huesmann, L. R. (1985). The control of aggressive behavior by changes in attitude, values, and the conditions of learning. In R. J. Blanchard & C. Blanchard (Eds.), *Advances in the study of aggression.* New York: Academic Press.

Eron, L. D., Huesmann, L. R., Lefkowitz, M. M., & Walden, L. O. (1972). Does television cause aggression? *American Psychologist, 27,* 253–263.

Esasky, N. (1991, March). His career threatened by dizzying attacks of vertigo: A ballplayer struggles to regain his field of dreams. *People Weekly,* pp. 61–64.

Estes, W. K. (1991). Cognitive architectures from the standpoint of an experimental psychologist. *Annual Review of Psychology, 42,* 1–28.

Evans, D. L. (1993, March 1). The wrong examples. *Newsweek,* p. 10.

Evans, J. S. B. T., Newstead, S. E., & Byrne, R. M. E. (1994). *Human reasoning: The psychology of deduction.* Hillsdale, NJ: Erlbaum.

Evans, R. J., Derkach, V., & Surprenant, A. (1992, June 11). ATP (adenosine triphosphate) mediates fast synaptic transmission in mammalian neurons. *Nature, 357,* 503–505.

Eveleth, P., & Tanner, J. (1976). *World-wide variation in human growth.* New York: Cambridge University Press.

Everly, G. S., Jr. (1989). *A clinical guide to the treatment of the human stress response.* New York: Plenum Press.

Exner, Jr., J. E. (1993). *The Rorschach: A comprehensive system.* New York: Wiley.

Eysenck, H. J. (1973). *Eysenck on extroversion.* New York: Wiley.

Eysenck, H. J. (1985). Race, social class, and individual differences in IQ. *Personality and Individual Differences, 6,* 287.

Eysenck, H. J., & Eysenck, M. W. (1985). *Personality and individual differences: A natural science approach.* New York: Plenum Press.

Fagan, J. F., III. (1992). Intelligence: A theoretical viewpoint. *Current Directions in Psychological Science, 1,* 82–86.

Fairburn, C. C., Jones, R., Peveler, R. C., et al. (1993). Psychotherapy and bulimia nervosa. *Archives of General Psychiatry, 50,* 419–428.

Fanelli, R. J., Burright, R. G., & Donovick, P. J. (1983). A multivariate approach to the analysis of genetic and septal lesion effects on maze performance in mice. *Behavioral Neuroscience, 97,* 354–369.

Farley, C. F. (1993, April 19). CNN/Time national poll. *Time,* p. 15.

Farley, F. (1986, May). The big T in personality. *Psychology Today,* pp. 44–52.

Farwell, L. A., & Donchin, E. (1991). The truth will out: Interrogative polygraphy ("lie detection") with event-related brain potentials. *Psychophysiology, 28,* 531–547.

Fehr, B. (1995). *Friendship processes.* Newbury Park, CA: Sage.

Fehr, B., & Russell, J. A. (1991). The concept of love viewed from a prototype perspective. *Journal of Personality and Social Psychology, 60,* 425–438.

Feingold, A. (1992). Good-looking people are not what we think. *Psychological Bulletin, 111,* 304–341.

Feldman, R. S. (Ed.). (1982). *Development of nonverbal behavior in children.* New York: Springer-Verlag.

Feldman, R. S. (Ed.). (1993). *Applications of nonverbal behavioral theories and research.* Hillsdale, NJ: Erlbaum.

Fenton, W. S., & McGlashan, T. H. (1991a). Natural history of schizophrenia subtypes: I. Longitudinal study of paranoid, hebephrenic, and undifferentiated schizophrenia. *Archives of General Psychiatry, 48,* 969–977.

Fenton, W. S., & McGlashan, T. H. (1991b). Natural history of schizophrenia subtypes: II. Positive and negative symptoms and long-term course. *Archives of General Psychiatry, 48,* 978–986.

Fernandez, E., & Turk, D. C. (1992). Sensory and affective components of pain: Separation and synthesis. *Psychological Bulletin, 112,* 205–217.

Festinger, L. (1957). *A theory of cognitive dissonance.* Stanford, CA: Stanford University Press.

Festinger, L., & Carlsmith, J. M. (1959). Cognitive consequences of forced compliance. *Journal of Abnormal and Social Psychology, 58,* 203–210.

Festinger, L., Schachter, S., & Back, K. W. (1950). *Social pressure in informal groups.* New York: Harper.

Fichter, M. M. (Ed.). (1990). *Bulimia nervosa: Basic research, diagnosis and therapy.* New York: Wiley.

Fiedler, F. E., Mitchell, R., & Triandis, H. C. (1971). The culture assimilator: An approach to cross-cultural training. *Journal of Applied Psychology, 55,* 95–102.

Field, T. (1982). Individual differences in the expressivity of neonates and young infants. In R. S. Feldman (Ed.), *Development of nonverbal behavior in children.* New York: Springer-Verlag.

Field, T. M. (1978). Interaction of primary versus secondary caretaker fathers. *Developmental Psychology, 14,* 183–184.

Filler, A. G., Howe, F. A., Hayes, C. E., Kliot, M., Winn, H. R., Bell, B. A., Griffiths, J. R., & Tsuruda, J. S. (1993, March 13). Magnetic resonance neurography. *The Lancet, 341,* 659–661.

Finch, C. E. (1990). *Longevity, senescence, and the genome.* Chicago: University of Chicago Press.

Fine, L. (1994). Personal communication.

Fingerhut, L., Ingram, D., & Feldman, J. (1992). Firearm and nonfirearm homicide among persons 15 through 19 years of age. *Journal of the American Medical Association, 267,* 3048–3053.

Fink, A. (1993). *Evaluation fundamentals.* Newbury Park, CA: Sage.

Fink, M. (1990, April). Continuation of ECT. *Harvard Medical School Mental Health Letter, 6,* 8.

Fink, M. (1994, May). Can ECT be an effective treatment for adolescents? *Harvard Mental Health Letter, 10,* 8.

Fischoff, B. (1977). Perceived informativeness of facts. *Journal of Experimental Psychology: Human Perception and Performance, 3,* 349–358.

Fisher, C. B., & Fyrberg, D. (1994). Participant partners: College students weigh the costs and benefits of deceptive research. *American Psychologist, 49,* 417–427.

Fisher, K. (1985, March). ECT: New studies on how, why, who. *APA Monitor,* pp. 18–19.

Fiske, S. T. (1992). Thinking is for doing: Portraits of social cognition from Daguerreotype to laserphoto. *Journal of Personality and Social Psychology, 63,* 877–889.

Fiske, S. T., & Taylor, S. E. (1991). *Social cognition* (2nd ed.). New York: McGraw-Hill.

Fitzgerald, J. M. (1988). Vivid memories and the reminiscence phenomenon: The role of a self narrative. *Human Development, 31,* 261–273.

Flam, F. (1991, June 14). Queasy riders. *Science, 252,* 1488.

Flam, F. (1994, October 14). Will a new type of drug make memory-making easier? *Science, 266,* 218–219.

Flavell, J. H. (1993). Young children's understanding of thinking and consciousness. *Current Directions in Psychological Science, 2,* 40–43.

Flavell, J. H., Green, F. L., & Flavell, E. R. (1990). Developmental changes in young children's knowledge about the mind. *Cognitive Development, 5,* 1–27.

Fleming, R., Baum, A., & Singer, J. E. (1984). Toward an integrative approach to the study of stress. *Journal of Personality and Social Psychology, 46,* 939–949.

Flowers, J. V., & Booraem, C. D. (1990). The effects of different types of interventions on outcome in group therapy. *Group, 14,* 81–88.

Flynn, J. R. (1987). Massive IQ gains in 14 nations: What IQ tests really measure. *Psychological Bulletin, 101,* 171–191.

Foderaro, L. W. (1993, July 19). With reforms in treatment, shock therapy loses shock. *The New York Times,* pp. A1, B2.

Folkman, S. (1984). Personal control and stress and coping processes: A theoretical analysis. *Journal of Personality and Social Psychology, 46,* 839–852.

Folkman, S., & Lazarus, R. S. (1980). An analysis of coping in a middle-aged community sample. *Journal of Health and Social Behavior, 21,* 219–239.

Folkman, S., & Lazarus, R. S. (1988). Coping as a mediator of emotion. *Journal of Personality and Social Psychology, 54,* 466–475.

Folkman, S., Lazarus, R. S., Dunkel-Schetter, C., DeLongis, A., & Green, R. J. (1986). Dynamics of a stressful encounter: Cognitive appraisal, coping, and encounter outcome. *Journal of Personality and Social Psychology, 50,* 992–1003.

Fonagy, P., & Moran, G. S. (1990). Studies of the efficacy of child psychoanalysis. *Journal of Consulting and Clinical Psychology, 58,* 684–695.

Ford, C. V., & Folks, D. G. (1985). Conversion disorders: An overview. *Psychosomatics, 26,* 371–383.

Ford, J. G. (1991). Rogers's theory of personality: Review and perspectives. In A. Jones & R. Crandall (Eds.), *Handbook of self-actualization* [Special issue]. *Journal of Social Behavior and Personality, 6,* 19–44.

Forer, B. (1949). The fallacy of personal validation: A classroom demonstration of gullibility. *Journal of Abnormal and Social Psychology, 44,* 118–123.

Forgas, J. P., & Bower, G. H. (1987). Mood effects on person-perception judgments. *Journal of Personality and Social Psychology, 53,* 53–60.

Forss, N., Makela, J. P., McEvoy, L., & Hari, R. (1993). Temporal integration and oscillatory responses of the human auditory cortex revealed by evoked magnetic fields to click trains. *Hearing Research, 68,* 89–96.

Fowler, R. D. (1993). New stats add weight to member director. *APA Monitor,* p. 2.

Fowles, D. C. (1992). Schizophrenia: Diathesis-stress revisited. *Annual Review of Psychology, 43,* 303–336.

Fox, N. (Ed.). (1994). The development of emotion regulation: Biological and behavioral consideration. *Monographs of the SRCD.*

Frank, S. J., Jacobson, S., & Tuer, M. (1990). Psychological predictors of young adults' drinking behaviors. *Journal of Personality and Social Psychology, 59,* 770–780.

Frankenburg, W. K., & Dodds, J. B. (1967). The Denver developmental screening test. *Journal of Pediatrics, 71,* 181–191.

Frederickson, R. (1992). *Repressed memories: A journey to recovery from sexual abuse.* New York: Fireside Books.

Freedheim, D. K. (Ed.). (1992). *History of psychotherapy: A century of change.* Washington, DC: American Psychological Association.

Freedman, J. L. (1984). Effects of television violence on aggressiveness. *Psychological Bulletin, 96,* 227–246.

Freedman, J. L., & Fraser, S. C. (1966). Compliance without pressure: The foot-in-the-door technique. *Journal of Personality and Social Psychology, 4,* 195–202.

Freeman, W. (1959). Psychosurgery. In *American handbook of psychiatry* (Vol. 2, pp. 1521–1540). New York: Basic Books.

Freud, S. (1922/1959). *Group psychology and the analysis of the ego.* London: Hogarth.

Friedman, H. S., Tucker, J. S., Tomlinson-Keasey, C., Schwartz, J., et al. (1993). Does childhood personality predict longevity? *Journal of Personality and Social Psychology, 65,* 176–185.

Friedman, J., et al. (1994, December). Obesity gene. *Nature, 367,* 732–735.

Friedman, W. J. (1993). Memory for the time of past events. *Psychological Bulletin, 113,* 44–66.

Friend, T. (1994, March). River, with love and anger. *Esquire,* pp. 108–117.

Frijda, N. H. (1988). The laws of emotion. *American Psychologist, 43,* 349–358.

Fromholt, P., & Larsen, S. F. (1991). Autobiographical memory in normal, aging and primary degenerative dementia (dementia of Alzheimer type). *Journal of Gerontology, 46,* 85–91.

Funder, D. C. (1991). Global traits: A neo-Allportian approach to personality. *Psychological Science, 2,* 31–39.

Funder, D. C. F. (1987). Errors and mistakes: Evaluating the accuracy of social judgment. *Psychological Bulletin, 101,* 75–90.

Furst, P. T. (1977). "High states" in culture-historical perspective. In N. E. Zinberg (Ed.), *Alternate states of consciousness.* New York: The Free Press.

Gaertner, S. L., Mann, J. A., Dovidio, J. F., Murrell, A. J., & Pomare, M. (1990). How does cooperation reduce intergroup bias? *Journal of Personality and Social Psychology, 59,* 692–704.

Galambos, N. L. (1992). Parent-adolescent relations. *Current Directions in Psychological Science, 1,* 146–149.

Galanter, E. (1962). Contemporary psychophysics. In R. Brown, E. Galanter, E. Hess, & G. Maroler (Eds.), *New directions in psychology* (pp. 87–157). New York: Holt.

Gale, N., Golledge, R. G., Pellegrino, J. W., & Doherty, S. (1990). The acquisition and integration of route knowledge in an unfamiliar neighborhood. *Journal of Environmental Psychology, 10,* 3–25.

Gallagher, J. J. (1993). Current status of gifted education in the United States. In K. A. Heller, F. J. Monks, & A. H. Passow (Eds.), *International handbook of research and development of giftedness and talent.* Oxford, England: Pergamon Press.

Gallagher, J. J. (1994). Teaching and learning: New models. *Annual Review of Psychology, 45,* 171–195.

Gallant, J. L, Braun, J., & VanEssen, D. C. (1993, January 1). Selectivity for polar, hyperbolic, and cartesian gratings in macaque visual cortex. *Science, 259,* 100–103.

Gallup Poll. (1969, 1978, 1991). Poll on sexual intercourse before marriage. Gallup Poll.

Gannon, L., Luchetta, T., Rhodes, K., Pardie, L., & Segrist, D. (1992). Sex bias in psychological research. *American Psychologist, 47,* 389–396.

Garber, H. L. (1988). *The Milwaukee Project: Preventing mental retardation in children at risk.* Washington, DC: American Association on Mental Retardation.

Garcia, J., Brett, L., & Rusiniak, K. (1989). Limits of Darwinian conditioning. In S. B. Klein & R. R. Mowrer (Eds.), *Contemporary learning theories* (Vol. 2). Hillsdale, NJ: Erlbaum.

Garcia, J., Hankins, W. G., & Rusiniak, K. W. (1974). Behavioral regulation of the milieu intern in man and rat. *Science, 185,* 824–831.

Gardner, H. (1975). *The shattered mind: The person after brain damage.* New York: Knopf.

Gardner, H. (1983). *Frames of mind: The theory of multiple intelligences.* New York: Basic Books.

Gardner, H. (1993). *Multiple intelligences.* New York: Basic Books.

Gardner, W., & Wilcox, B. L. (1993). Political intervention in scientific peer review. *American Psychologist, 48,* 972–983.

Garfield, S. L. (1990). Issues and methods in psychotherapy process research. *Journal of Consulting and Clinical Psychology, 58,* 273–280.

Garling, T. (1989). The role of cognitive maps in spatial decisions. *Journal of Environmental Psychology, 9,* 269–278.

Gatchel, R. J., & Baum, A. (1983). *An introduction to health psychology.* Reading, MA: Addison-Wesley.

Gathercole, S. E., & Baddeley, A. D. (1993). *Working memory and language processing.* Hillsdale, NJ: Erlbaum.

Gawin, F. H. (1991, March 29). Cocaine addiction: Psychology and neurophysiology. *Science, 251,* 1580–1586.

Gawin, F. H., & Ellinwood, E. H. (1988). Cocaine and other stimulants: Actions, abuse, and treatment. *New England Journal of Medicine, 318,* 1173.

Gazzaniga, M. S. (1970). *The bisected brain.* New York: Plenum Press.

Gazzaniga, M. S. (1983). Right-hemisphere language following brain bisection: A twenty-year perspective. *American Psychologist, 38,* 525–537.

Gazzaniga, M. S. (1989, September 1). Organization of the human brain. *Science, 245,* 947–952.

Gazzaniga, M. S. (Ed.). (1994). *The cognitive neurosciences.* Cambridge, MA: MIT Press.

Geary, D. C., Bow-Thomas, C. C., Fan, L., & Siegler, R. S. (1993). Even before formal instruction, Chinese children outperform American children in mental addition. *Cognitive Development, 8,* 517–529.

Geary, D. C., Fan, L., & Bow-Thomas, C. C. (1992). Numerical cognition: Loci of ability differences comparing children from China and the United States. *Psychological Science, 3,* 180–185.

Geen, R. G. (1984). Human motivation: New perspectives on old problems. In A. M. Rogers & C. J. Scheirer (Eds.), *The G. Stanley Hall Lecture Series* (Vol. 4). Washington, DC: American Psychological Association.

Geen, R. G., & Donnerstein, E. (1983). *Aggression: Theoretical and empirical reviews.* New York: Academic Press.

Geisinger, K. F. (Ed.). (1992). *Psychological testing of Hispanics.* Washington, DC: American Psychological Association.

Geissler, H., Link, S. W., & Townsend, J. T. (1992). *Cognition, information processing, and psychophysics.* Hillsdale, NJ: Erlbaum.

Gelman, D. (1989, February 20). Roots of addiction. *Newsweek,* pp. 52–57.

Gelman, R., & Baillargeon, R. (1983). A review of some Piagetian concepts. In J. H. Flavell & E. M. Markman (Eds.), *Handbook of child psychology: Vol. 3. Cognitive development* (4th ed.). New York: Wiley.

Gentry, W. D., & Kobasa, S. C. O. (1984). Social and psychological resources mediating stress-illness relationships in humans. In W. D. Gentry (Ed.), *Handbook of behavioral medicine.* New York: Guilford Press.

Gerbner, G., Gross, L., Jackson-Beeck, M., Jeffries-Fox, S., & Signorielli, N. (1978). Cultural indicators: Violence profile No. 9. *Journal of Communication, 28,* 176–207.

Gerbner, G., Morgan, M., & Signorielli, N. (1993). *Television violence.* Unpublished study, University of Pennsylvania, Philadelphia.

Gerrard, M. (1988). Sex, sex guilt, and contraceptive use revisited: The 1980s. *Journal of Personality and Social Psychology, 57,* 973–980.

Gerrig, R. J., & Banaji, M. R. (1994). Language and thought. In R. J. Sternberg (Ed.), *Thinking and problem-solving.* San Diego, CA: Academic Press.

Gershon, E. S., Martinez, M., Goldin, L. R., & Gejman, P. V. (1990). Genetic mapping of common disease: The challenges of manic-depressive illness and schizophrenia. *Trends in Genetics, 6,* 282–287.

Geschwind, N., & Galaburda, A. M. (1987). *Cerebral lateralization: Biological mechanism, associations, and pathology.* Cambridge, MA: MIT Press.

Getchell, T. V., Chen, Y., Strotmann, J., Breer, H., & Getchell, M. L. (1993). Expression of a mucociliary-specific epitome in human olfactory epithelium. *Neuroreport, 4,* 623–626.

Getty, D. J., Pickett, R. M., D'Orsi, C. J., & Swets, J. A. (1988). Enhanced interpretation of diagnostic images. *Investigative Radiology, 23,* 240–252.

Gfeller, J. D., Lynn, S. J., & Pribble, W. E. (1987). Enhancing hypnotic susceptibility: Interpersonal and rapport factors. *Journal of Personality and Social Psychology, 52,* 586–595.

Ghez, C. (1991). The cerebellum. In E. R. Kandel, J. H. Schwartz, & T. M. Jessell (Eds.), *Principles of neural science* (3rd ed.). New York: Elsevier.

Gibbons, A. (1990, July 13). New maps of the human brain. *Science, 249,* 122–123.

Gibbons, A. (1991, March 29). Deja vu all over again: Chimp-language wars. *Science, 251,* 1561–1562.

Gibbs, M. E., & Ng, K. T. (1977). Psychobiology of memory: Towards a model of memory formation. *Behavioral Reviews, 1,* 113–136.

Gibbs, N. (1989, January 9). For goodness' sake. *Time,* pp. 20–24.

Gibson, E. J. (1994). Has psychology a future? *Psychological Science, 5,* 69–76.

Gilbert, D. T., Jones, E. E., & Pelham, B. W. (1987). Influence and inference: What the active perceiver overlooks. *Journal of Personality and Social Psychology, 52,* 861–870.

Gilbert, L. A. (1993). *Two careers/one family: The promise of gender equality.* Newbury Park, CA: Sage.

Giles, T. R. (Ed.). (1993). *Handbook of effective psychotherapy.* New York: Plenum Press.

Gill, Jr., T. J., Smith, G. J., Wissler, R. W., & Kunz, H. W. (1989, July 29). The rat as an experimental animal. *Science, 245,* 269–276.

Gilligan, C. (1982). *In a different voice: Psychological theory and women's development.* Cambridge, MA: Harvard University Press.

Gilligan, C., Lyons, N. P., & Hanmer, T. J. (Eds.). (1990). *Making connections.* Cambridge, MA: Harvard University Press.

Gilligan, C., Ward, J. V., & Taylor, J. M. (Eds.). (1988). *Mapping the moral domain: A contribution of women's thinking to psychological theory and education.* Cambridge, MA: Harvard University Press.

Gillstrom, B. J., & Hare, R. D. (1988). Language-related hand gestures in psychopaths. *Journal of Personality Disorders, 1,* 21–27.

Ginsburg, H. P., & Opper, S. (1988). *Piaget's theory of intellectual development* (3rd ed.). Englewood Cliffs, NJ: Prentice-Hall.

Gladue, B. (1984). Hormone markers for homosexuality. *Science, 225,* 198.

Gladue, B. A., Boechler, M., & McCaul, K. D. (1989). Hormonal response to competition in human males. *Aggressive Behavior, 15,* 409–422.

Gladwin, T. (1964). Culture and logical process. In N. Goodenough (Ed.), *Explorations in cultural anthropology: Essays in honor of George Peter Murdoch.* New York: McGraw-Hill.

Glantz, M., & Pickens, R. (Eds.). (1991). *Vulnerability to drug abuse.* Washington, DC: American Psychological Association.

Glaser, R. (1990). The reemergence of learning theory within instructional research. *American Psychologist, 45,* 29–39.

Glaser, R., & Kiecolt-Glaser, J. (Eds.). (1994). *Handbook of human stress and immunity.* San Diego, CA: Academic Press.

Glass, D. C., & Singer, J. E. (1972). *Urban stress.* New York: Academic Press.

Glenn, N. D. (1987, October). Marriage on the rocks. *Psychology Today,* pp. 20–21.

Glover, J. A., Ronning, R. R., & Reynolds, C. R. (Eds.). (1989). *Handbook of creativity.* New York: Plenum Press.

Gold, P. W., Gwirtsman, H., Avgerinos, P. C., Nieman, L. K., Gallucci, W. T., Kaye, W., Jimerson, D., Ebert, M., Rittmaster, R., Loriaux, L., & Chrousos, G. P. (1986). Abnormal hypothalamic-pituitary-adrenal function in anorexia nervosa. *New England Journal of Medicine, 314,* 1335–1342.

Goldberg, L. R. (1990). An alternative "Description of Personality": The big-five factor structure. *Journal of Personality and Social Psychology, 59,* 1216–1229.

Goldfried, M. R., & Castonguay, L. G. (1992). The future of psychotherapy integration. *Psychotherapy, 29,* 4–10.

Goldman-Rakic, P. S. (1988). *Neurobiology of neocortex.* New York: Wiley.

Goldsmith, H. H., Buss, A. H., Plomin, R., Rothbart, M. K., Thomas, A., Chess, S., Hinde, R. A., & McCall, R. B. (1987). Roundtable: What is temperament? Four approaches. *Child Development, 58,* 505–529.

Goldsmith, H. H., & Harman, C. (1994). Temperament and attachment; individuals and relationships. *Current Directions in Psychological Science, 3,* 53–56.

Goleman, D. (1985, February 5). Mourning: New studies affirm its benefits. *The New York Times,* pp. C1–C2.

Goleman, D. (1993a, July 21). "Expert" babies found to teach others. *The New York Times,* p. C10.

Gonsiorek, J. C. (1991). The empirical basis for the demise of the illness model of homosexuality. In J. Gonsiorek & J. Weinrich (Eds.), *Homosexuality: Research implications for public policy.* Newbury Park, CA: Sage.

Goodchilds, J. D. (Ed.). (1991). *Psychological perspectives on human diversity in America.* Washington, DC: American Psychological Association.

Goode, W. J. (1993). *World changes in divorce patterns.* New Haven, CT: Yale University Press.

Goodwin, F. K., & Jamison, K. R. (1990). *Manic-depressive illness.* New York: Oxford University Press.

Googans, B., & Burden, D. (1987). Vulnerability of working parents: Balancing work and home roles. *Social Work, 32,* 295–300.

Gorassini, D. R., & Olson, J. M. (1995). Does self-perception change explain the foot-in-the-door effect? *Journal of Personality and Social Psychology, 69,* 91–105.

Gorman, J. M., Liebowitz, M. R., Fyer, A. J., & Stein, J. (1989). A neuroanatomical hypothesis for panic disorder. *American Journal of Psychiatry, 146,* 148–161.

Gotlib, I. H. (1992). Interpersonal and cognitive aspects of depression. *Current Directions in Psychological Science, 1,* 149–154.

Gottesman, I. I. (1991). *Schizophrenia genesis: The origins of madness.* New York: Freeman.

Gottfried, A. E., & Gottfried, A. W. (Eds.). (1988). *Maternal employment and children's development.* New York: Plenum Press.

Gottfried, A. E., & Gottfried, A. W. (Eds.). (1994). *Redefining families.* New York: Plenum Press.

Gottman, J. M. (1993). *What predicts divorce? The relationship between marital processes and marital outcomes.* Hillsdale, NJ: Erlbaum.

Gottman, J. M. (Ed.). (1995). *What predicts divorce? The measures.* Hillsdale, NJ: Erlbaum.

Gould, R. L. (1978). *Transformations.* New York: Simon and Schuster.

Gouras, P. (1991). Color vision. In E. R. Kandel, J. H. Schwartz, & T. M. Jessell (Eds.), *Principles of neural science* (3rd ed.). New York: Elsevier.

Gove, W. R. (1982). Labeling theory's explanation of mental illness: An update of recent evidence. *Deviant Behavior, 3,* 307–327.

Graf, P. (1990, Spring). Life-span changes in implicit and explicit memory. *Bulletin of the Psychosomatic Society, 28,* 353–358.

Graf, P., & Masson, M. E. J. (Eds.). (1993). *Implicit memory: New directions in cognition, development,* and neuropsychology. Hillsdale, NJ: Erlbaum.

Graham, J. R. (1990). *MMPI-2: Assessing personality and psychopathology.* New York: Oxford University Press.

Graham, J. W., Marks, G., & Hansen, W. B. (1991). Social influence processes affecting adolescent substance use. *Journal of Applied Psychology, 76,* 291–298.

Graham, S. (1992). "Most of the subjects were white and middle class": Trends in published research on African Americans in selected APA journals, 1970–1989. *American Psychologist, 47,* 629–639.

Graham, S. (1994). Motivation in African Americans. *Review of Educational Research, 64,* 55–117.

Graham, S., & Hudley, C. (1992). An attributional approach to aggression in African-American children. In D. Schunk & J. Meece (Eds.), *Student perceptions in the classroom.* Hillsdale, NJ: Erlbaum.

Greeberg, M. T., Cicchetti, D., & Cummings, E. M. (Eds.). (1990). *Attachment in the preschool years: Theory, research, and intervention.* Chicago: University of Chicago Press.

Greeley, A. M. (1992, Oct. 4). Happiest couples in study have sex after 60. *The New York Times,* p. 13.

Green, D. M., & Swets, J. A. (1989). *A signal detection theory and psychophysics.* Los Altos, CA: Peninsula.

Green, R. (1978). Sexual identity of 37 children raised by homosexual or transsexual parents. *American Journal of Psychiatry, 135,* 687–692.

Greenberg, P., Stiglin, L. E., Finkelstein, S. N., & Berndt, E. R. (1993a). The economic burden of depression in 1990. *Journal of Clinical Psychiatry, 54,* 405–418.

Greenberg, P., Stiglin, L. E., Finkelstein, S. N., & Berndt, E. R. (1993b). Depression: A neglected major illness. *Journal of Clinical Psychiatry, 54,* 419–424.

Greene, R. L. (1991). *The MMPI-2/MMPI: An interpretive manual.* Boston: Longwood.

Greene, R. L., & Clopton, J. R. (1994). Minnesota Multiphasic Personality Inventory-2. In M. E. Maruish (Ed.), *The use of psychological tests for treatment planning and outcome assessment.* Hillsdale, NJ: Erlbaum.

Greeno, C. G., & Wing, R. R. (1994). Stress-induced eating. *Psychological Bulletin, 115,* 444–464.

Greeno, J. G. (1978). Natures of problem-solving abilities. In W. K. Estes (Ed.), *Handbook of learning and cognitive processes.* Hillsdale, NJ: Erlbaum.

Greenwald, A. G., Spangenberg, E. R., Pratkanis, A. R., & Eskenzai, J. (1991). Double-blind tests of subliminal self-help audiotapes. *Psychological Science, 2,* 119–122.

Greenwood, C. R., Carta, J. J., Hart, B., Kamps, D., Terry, B., Arreaga-Mayer, C., Atwater, J., Walker, D., Risley, T., & Delquadri, J. C. (1992). Out of the laboratory and into the community: 26 years of applied behavior analysis at the Juniper Gardens children's project. *American Psychologist, 47,* 1464–1474.

Gregory, R. L. (1978). *The psychology of seeing* (3rd ed.). New York: McGraw-Hill.

Gregory, S. S. (1994, March 21). At risk of mutilation. *Time,* pp. 45–46.

Greig, G. L. (1990). On the shape of energy-detection ROC curves. *Perception & Psychophysics, 48,* 77–81.

Greist-Bousquet, S., & Schiffman, H. R. (1986). The basis of the Poggendorff effect: An additional clue for Day and Kasperczyk. *Perception and Psychophysics, 39,* 447–448.

Griffith, R. H., Miyago, O., & Tago, A. (1958). The universality of typical dreams: Japanese vs. Americans. *American Anthropologist, 60,* 1173–1179.

Griffiths, R., et al. (1994). Caffeine. *Psychopharmacology.*

Gross, J. (1991, June 16). More young single men hang onto apron strings. *The New York Times,* pp. 1, 18.

Grossman, M., & Wood, W. (1993). Sex differences in intensity of emotional experience: A social role interpretation. *Journal of Personality and Social Psychology, 65,* 1010–1022.

Groth-Marnat, G. (1990). *Handbook of psychological assessment* (2nd ed.). New York: Wiley.

Gubrium, J. G. (1973). *The myth of the golden years: A socioenvironmental theory of aging.* Springfield, IL: Thomas.

Gur, R. C., Gur, R. E., Obrist, W. D., Hungerbuhler, J. P., Younkin, D., Rosen, A. D., Skilnick, B. E., & Reivich, M. (1982). Sex and handedness differences in cerebral blood flow during rest and cognitive activity. *Science, 217,* 659–661.

Gur, R. C., Mozley, L. H., Mozley, P. D., Resnick, S. M., Karp, J. S., Alavi, A., Arnold, S. E., & Gur, R. E. (1995, January 27). Sex differences in regional glucose metabolism during a resting state. *Science, 267,* 528–531.

Gurman, E. B. (1994). Debriefing for all concerned: Ethical treatment of human subjects. *Psychological Science, 5,* 139.

Gustavson, C. R., Garcia, J., Hankins, W. G., & Rusniak, K. W. (1974). Coyote predation control by aversive conditioning. *Science, 184,* 581–583.

Guthrie, G., & Lonner, W. (1986). Assessment of personality and psychopathology. In W. Lonner & J. Berry (Eds.), *Field methods in cross-cultural research.* Newbury Park, CA: Sage.

Guttman, J. (1993). *Divorce in psychosocial perspective: Theory and research.* Hillsdale, NJ: Guttmann.

Haber, R. N. (1983). Stimulus information processing mechanisms in visual space perception. In J. Beck, B. Hope, & A. Rosenfeld (Eds.), *Human and machine vision.* New York: Academic Press.

Hagen, E., Sattler, J. M., & Thorndike, R. L. (1985). *Stanford-Binet test.* Chicago: Riverside.

Hakuta, K. U., & Garcia, E. E. (1989). Bilingualism and education. *American Psychologist, 44,* 374–379.

Halgin, R. P., & Whitbourne, S. K. (1994). *Abnormal psychology.* Fort Worth, TX: Harcourt Brace.

Hall, S. S. (1992). *Mapping the next millennium.* New York: Random House.

Halle, M. (1990). Phonology. In D. N. Osherson & H. Lasnik (Eds.), *Language.* Cambridge, MA: MIT Press.

Halpern, D. F. (1995). *Thought & knowledge: An introduction to critical thinking* (3rd ed.). Hillsdale, NJ: Erlbaum.

Hammer, J. (1992, October 26). Must Blacks be buffoons? *Newsweek,* pp. 70–71.

Hammond, R., & Yung, B. (1991). Preventing violence in at-risk African-American youth. *Journal of Health Care for the Poor and Underserved, 2,* 359–373.

Hammond, W. R., & Yung, B. (1993). Psychology's role in the public health response to assaultive violence among young African-American men. *American Psychologist, 48,* 142–154.

Handler, A., Franz, C. E., & Guerra, H. (1992, April). *Sex differences in moral orientation in midlife adults: A longitudinal study.* A paper presented at the meeting of the Eastern Psychological Association, Boston.

Hanna, E., & Meltzoff, A. N. (1993). Peer imitation by toddlers in laboratory, home, and day-care contexts: Implications for social learning and memory. *Developmental Psychology, 29*, 701–710.

Hansen, B., & Knopes, C. (1993, July 6). Prime time tuning out varied culture. *USA Today*, pp. 1A, 3D.

Hanson, S. J., & Olson, C. R. (Eds.). (1990). *Connectionist modeling and brain function.* Cambridge, MA: MIT Press.

Harackiewicz, J. M., & Elliot, A. J. (1993). Achievement goals and intrinsic motivation. *Journal of Personality and Social Psychology, 65*, 904–915.

Hare, R. D., Hart, S. D., & Harpur, T. J. (1991). Psychopathy and the DSM-IV criteria for antisocial personality disorder. *Journal of Abnormal Psychology, 100*, 391–398.

Harley, T. A. (1995). *The psychology of language: From data to theory.* Hillsdale, NJ: Erlbaum.

Harlow, H. F., Harlow, M. K., & Meyer, D. R. (1950). Learning motivated by a manipulation drive. *Journal of Experimental Psychology, 40*, 228–234.

Harlow, H. F., & Zimmerman, R. R. (1959). Affectional responses in the infant monkey. *Science, 130*, 421–432.

Harlow, J. M. (1869). Recovery from the passage of an iron bar through the head. *Massachusetts Medical Society Publication, 2*, 329–347.

Harper, T. (1978, November 15). It's not true about people 65 or over. *Green Bay (Wis.) Press-Gazette*, p. D-1.

Harris, J. E., & Morris, P. E. (1986). *Everyday memory and action and absent mindedness.* New York: Academic Press.

Harris, M. J. (1991). Controversy and cumulation: Meta-analysis and research on interpersonal expectancy effects. *Personality and Social Psychology Bulletin, 17*, 316–322.

Harris Poll: National Council on the Aging (1975). *The myth and reality of aging in America.* Washington, DC: National Council on the Aging.

Harris, S. L., & Handleman, J. S. (1990). *Aversive and nonaversive interventions.* New York: Springer.

Harsch, N., & Neisser, U. (1989). *Substantial and irreversible errors in flashbulb memories of the Challenger explosion.* Poster presented at the meeting of the Psychonomic Society, Atlanta.

Hart, Jr., J., & Gordon, B. (1992, September 3). Neural subsystems for object knowledge. *Nature, 359*, 60–64.

Hart, K. E., & Sciutto, M. J. (1994, April). *Gender differences in alcohol-related problems.* Paper presented at the annual meeting of the Eastern Psychological Association, Providence, RI.

Hartmann, E. (1967). *The biology of dreaming.* Springfield, IL: Thomas.

Hartup, W. W. (1989). Social relationships and their developmental significance. *American Psychologist, 44*, 120–126.

Hartup, W. W., & Moore, S. G. (1993). Early peer relations: Developmental significance and prognostic implications. *Early Childhood Research Quarterly, 5*, 1–17.

Hatfield, E., & Sprecher, S. (1986). *Mirror, mirror: The importance of looks in everyday life.* Albany: State University of New York Press.

Hathaway, B. (1984, July). Running to ruin. *Psychology Today*, pp. 14–15.

Hathaway, S. R., & McKinley, J. C. (1989). *MMPI-2: Minnesota Multiphasic Personality Inventory-2.* Minneapolis: University of Minnesota Press.

Hauri, P. J. (Ed.). (1991). *Case studies in insomnia.* New York: Plenum Press.

Havighurst, R. J. (1973). Social roles, work, leisure, and education. In C. Eisdorfer & M. P. Lawton (Eds.), *The psychology of adult development and aging.* Washington, DC: American Psychological Association.

Hawkins, D. J., Catalano, R. F., & Miller, J. Y. (1992). Risk and protective factors for alcohol and other drug problems in adolescence and early adulthood: Implications for substance abuse prevention. *Psychological Bulletin, 112*, 64–105.

Hayes, J. R. (1966). Memory, goals, and problem solving. In B. Kleinmuntz (Ed.), *Problem solving: Research, method, and theory.* New York: Wiley.

Hayes, J. R. (1989). *The complete problem solver* (2nd ed.). Hillsdale, NJ: Erlbaum.

Hayflick, L. (1974). The strategy of senescence. *Journal of Gerontology, 14*, 37–45.

Haymes, M., Green, L., & Quinto, R. (1984). Maslow's hierarchy, moral development, and prosocial behavioral skills within a child psychiatric population. *Motivation and Emotion, 8*, 23–31.

Hazen, R. M., & Trefil, J. (1991). *Science matters: Achieving scientific literacy.* New York: Doubleday.

Heatherton, T. F., Herman, C. P., & Polivy, J. (1992). Effects of distress on eating: The importance of ego-involvement. *Journal of Personality and Social Psychology, 62*, 801–803.

Heckhausen, H., Schmalt, H. D., & Schneider, K. (1985). *Achievement motivation in perspective* (M. Woodruff & R. Wicklund, Trans.). Orlando, FL: Academic Press.

Heinrichs, R. W. (1993). Schizophrenia and the brain: Conditions for neuropsychology of madness. *American Psychologist, 48*, 221–233.

Hellige, J. B. (1990). Hemispheric asymmetry. *Annual Review of Psychology, 41*, 55–80.

Hellige, J. B. (1993). Unity of thought and action: Varieties of interaction between the left and right cerebral hemispheres. *Current Directions in Psychological Science, 2*, 21–25.

Hellige, J. B. (1994). *Hemispheric asymmetry: What's right and what's left.* Cambridge, MA: Harvard University Press.

Helmes, E., & Reddon, J. R. (1993). A perspective on developments in assessing psychopathology: A critical review of the MMPI and MMPI-2. *Psychological Bulletin, 113*, 453–471.

Helms, J. E. (1992). Why is there no study of cultural equivalence in standardized cognitive ability testing? *American Psychologist, 47*, 1083–1101.

Hendrick, S. S., & Hendrick, C. (1992). *Romantic love.* Newbury Park, CA: Sage.

Hendrick, S. S., Hendrick, C., & Adler, N. L. (1988). Romantic relationships: Love, satisfaction, and staying together. *Journal of Personality and Social Psychology, 54*, 980–988.

Herek, G. M. (1993). Sexual orientation and military service: A social science perspective. *American Psychologist, 48*, 538–549.

Herman, C. P. (1987). Social and psychological factors in obesity: What we don't know. In H. Weiner & A. Baum (Eds.), *Perspectives in behavioral medicine: Eating regulation and discontrol.* Hillsdale, NJ: Erlbaum.

Hermann, D. J. (1991). *Super memory.* Emmaus, PA: Rodale Press.

Herrnstein, R. J., & Murray, D. (1994). *The bell curve.* New York: The Free Press.

Hershenson, M. (Ed.). (1989). *The moon illusion.* Hillsdale, NJ: Erlbaum.

Hetherington, E. M., & Parke, R. D. (1993). *Child psychology: A contemporary viewpoint* (4th ed.). New York: McGraw-Hill.

Hetherington, T. F., & Weinberger, J. (Eds.). (1993). *Can personality change?* Washington, DC: American Psychological Association.

Heward, W. L., & Orlansky, M. D. (1988). *Exceptional children* (3rd ed.). Columbus, OH: Merrill.

Heyneman, N. E., Fremouw, W. J., Gano, D., Kirkland, F., & Heiden, L. (1990). Individual differences and the effectiveness of different coping strategies for pain. *Cognitive Therapy and Research, 14,* 63–77.

Heyward, W. L., & Curran, J. W. (1988, October). The epidemiology of AIDS in the U.S. *Scientific American,* pp. 72–81.

Higbee, K. L. (1988). *Your memory: How it works and how to improve it.* New York: Paragon House.

Higbee, K. L., & Kunihira, S. (1985). Cross-cultural applications of Yodni mnemonics in education. *Educational Psychologist, 20,* 57–64.

Hilgard, E. R. (1974). Imaginative involvement: Some characteristics of the highly hypnotizable and the non-hypnotizable. *International Journal of Clinical and Experimental Hypnosis, 22,* 138–156.

Hilgard, E. R. (1975). Hypnosis. *Annual Review of Psychology, 26,* 19–44.

Hilgard, E. R. (1980). Consciousness in contemporary psychology. *Annual Review of Psychology, 31,* 1–26.

Hilgard, E. R., Leary, D. E., & McGuire, G. R. (1991). The history of psychology: A survey and critical assessment. *Annual Review of Psychology, 42,* 79–107.

Hill, C. T., & Stull, D. E. (1981). Sex differences in effects of social and value similarity in same-sex friendship. *Journal of Personality and Social Psychology, 41,* 488–502.

Hill, W. (1992). Personal communication. Public Affairs Network Coordinator for the American Psychiatric Association.

Hinds, M. C. (1993, October 19). Not like the movie: A dare leads to death. *The New York Times,* p. A11.

Hinz, L. D., & Williamson, D. A. (1987). Bulimia and depression: A review of the affective-variant hypothesis. *Psychological Bulletin, 102,* 150–158.

Hipkiss, R. A. (1995). *Semantics: Defining the discipline.* Hillsdale, NJ: Erlbaum.

HMHL. (1994a, January). AIDS and mental health—Part I. *Harvard Mental Health Letter, 10,* 1–4.

HMHL. (1994b, March). Brief psychodynamic therapy—Part I. *Harvard Mental Health Letter,* p. 10.

HMHL. (1994c, February). AIDS and Mental health—Part II. *Harvard Mental Health Letter, 10,* 1–4.

Hobfoll, S. E. (1989). Conservation of resources: A new attempt at conceptualizing stress. *American Psychologist, 44,* 513–524.

Hobfoll, S. E., Spielberger, C. D., Breznitz, S., Figley, C., Folkman, S., Lepper-Green, B., Meichenbaum, D., Milgram, N. A., Sandler, I., Sarason, I., & van der Kolk, B. (1991). War-related stress: Addressing the stress of war and other traumatic events. *American Psychologist, 46,* 848–855.

Hobson, J. A. (1988). *The dreaming brain.* New York: Basic Books.

Hobson, J. A., & McCarley, R. W. (1977). The brain as a dream state generator: An activation-synthesis hypothesis of the dream process. *American Journal of Psychiatry, 134,* 1335–1348.

Hoch, S. J. (1987). Perceived consensus and predictive accuracy: The pros and cons of projection. *Journal of Personality and Social Psychology, 53,* 221–234.

Hochberg, J. E. (1978). *Perception.* Englewood Cliffs, NJ: Prentice-Hall.

Hochschild, A. R. (1990). The second shift: Employed women and putting in another day of work at home. *Utne Reader, 38,* 66–73.

Hoehn-Saric, R. (Ed.). (1993). *Biology of anxiety disorders.* Washington, DC: American Psychiatric Association.

Hofferth, S. L., Kahn, J. R., & Baldwin, W. (1987). Premarital sexual activity among U.S. teenage women over the past three decades. *Family Planning Perspectives, 19,* 46–53.

Hoffman, C., Lau, I., & Johnson, D. R. (1986). The linguistic relativity of person cognition: An English-Chinese comparison. *Journal of Personality and Social Psychology, 51,* 1097–1105.

Hoffman, L. W. (1989). Effects of maternal employment in the two-parent family. *American Psychologist, 44,* 283–292.

Hoffman, M. (1991, June 28). A new role for gases: Neurotransmission. *Science, 252,* 1788.

Hofstee, W. K. B., de Raad, B., & Goldberg, L. R. (1992). Integration of the big five and circumflex approaches to trait structure. *Journal of Personality and Social Psychology, 63,* 146–163.

Hogg, M. A., & Hardie, E. A. (1992). Prototypicality, conformity and depersonalized attraction: A self-categorization analysis of group cohesiveness. *British Journal of Social Psychology, 31,* 41–56.

Holahan, C. J., & Moos, R. H. (1987). Personal and contextual determinants of coping strategies. *Journal of Personality and Social Psychology, 52,* 946–955.

Holahan, C. J., & Moos, R. H. (1990). Life stressors, resistance factors, and improved psychological functioning: An extension of the stress resistance paradigm. *Journal of Personality and Social Psychology, 58,* 909–917.

Holden, C. (1987, October 9). Why do women live longer than men? *Science, 238,* 158–160.

Holden, C. (1991, January 11). Probing the complex genetics of alcoholism. *Science, 251,* 163–164.

Holden, C. (1993, January 15). Wake-up call for sleep research. *Science, 259,* 305.

Hollingshead, A. B., & Redich, F. C. (1958). *Social class and mental illness.* New York: Wiley.

Hollingworth, H. L. (1990). *Leta Stetter Hollingworth: A biography.* Boston, MA: Anker Publishing. (Originally published 1943)

Hollingworth, L. S. (1928). *The psychology of the adolescent.* New York: Appleton.

Hollis, K. L. (1984). The biological function of Pavlovian conditioning: The best defense is a good offense. *Journal of Experimental Psychology: Animal Behavior Processes, 10,* 413–425.

Hollister, L. E. (1988). Cannabis-1988. *Acta Psychiatry Scandinavia, 78* (Suppl. 345), 108–118.

Holmes, D. S. (1985). To meditate or rest? The answer is rest. *American Psychologist, 40,* 728–731.

Holmes, J. (1994). *John Bowlby and attachment theory.* New York: Routledge.

Holyoak, K. J. (1990). Problem solving. In D. N. Osherson & E. E. Smith (Eds.), *Thinking.* Cambridge, MA: MIT Press.

Holzman, P. S., & Matthysse, S. (1990). The genetics of schizophrenia: A review. *Psychological Science, 1,* 279–286.

Honts, C. R., Hodes, R. L., & Raskin, D. C. (1985). Effects of physical countermeasures on the physiological detection of deception. *Journal of Applied Psychology, 70,* 177–187.

Honts, C. R., Raskin, D. C., & Kircher, J. C. (1987). Effects of physical countermeasure and their electromyographic detection during polygraphy tests for deception. *Journal of Psychophysiology, 1,* 241–247.

Hoon, P. W., Bruce, K., & Kinchloe, B. (1982). Does the menstrual cycle play a role in sexual arousal? *Psychophysiology, 19,* 21–26.

Hoptman, M. J., & Davidson, R. J. (1994). How and why do the two cerebral hemispheres interact? *Psychological Bulletin, 116,* 195–219.

Horgan, J. (1993, December). Fractured functions: Does the brain have a supreme integrator? *Scientific American,* pp. 36–37.

Horn, J. L. (1985). Remodeling old models of intelligence. In B. B. Wolman (Ed.), *Handbook of intelligence.* New York: Wiley.

Horney, K. (1937). *Neurotic personality of our times.* New York: Norton.

Horowitz, F. D., & Colombo, J. (Eds.). (1990). *Infancy research: A summative evaluation and a look to the future.* Detroit: Wayne State University.

Horowitz, F. D., & O'Brien, M. (Eds.). (1987). *The gifted and talented: Developmental perspectives.* Washington, DC: American Psychological Association.

Horton, R., & Katona, C. (Eds.). (1991). *Biological aspects of affective disorders.* San Diego: Academic Press.

House, J. S., Landis, K. R., & Umberson, D. (1989, July 29). Social relationships and health. *Science, 241,* 540–545.

Houston, L. N. (1981). Romanticism and eroticism among black and white college students. *Adolescence, 16,* 263–272.

Hovland, C., Janis, I., & Kelly, H. H. (1953). *Communication and persuasion.* New Haven, CT: Yale University Press.

Howard, A., Pion, G. M., Gottfredson, G. D., Flattau, P. E., Oskamp, S., Pfafflin, S. M., Bray, D. W., & Burstein, A. D. (1986). The changing face of American psychology: A report from the committee on employment and human resources. *American Psychologist, 41,* 1311–1327.

Howard, K. I., & Zola, M. A. (1988). Paper presented at the annual meeting of the Society for Psychotherapy Research.

Howells, J. G., & Osborn, M. L. (1984). *A reference companion to the history of abnormal psychology.* Westport, CT: Greenwood Press.

Howes, C. (1990). Can the age of entry into child care and the quality of child care predict adjustment in kindergarten? *Developmental Psychology, 26,* 292–303.

Hser, Y., Anglin, M. D., & Powers, K. (1993). A 24-year follow-up of California narcotics addicts. *Archives of General Psychiatry, 50,* 577–584.

Hsu, L. K. G. (1990). *Eating disorders.* New York: Guilford Press.

Hubel, D. H., & Wiesel, T. N. (1979). Brain mechanisms of vision. *Scientific American,* pp. 150–162.

Hudson, W. (1960). Pictorial depth perception in subcultural groups in Africa. *Journal of Social Psychology, 52,* 183–208.

Huesmann, L. R., & Eron, L. D. (Eds.). (1986). *Television and the aggressive child: A cross-national comparison.* Hillsdale, NJ: Erlbaum.

Huesmann, L. R., Eron, L. D., Klein, R., Brice, P., & Fischer, P. (1983). Mitigating the imitation of aggressive behaviors by changing children's attitudes about media violence. *Journal of Personality and Social Psychology, 5,* 899–910.

Hull, C. L. (1943). *Principles of behavior.* New York: Appleton-Century-Crofts.

Humphreys, L. G. (1992). Commentary: What both critics and users of ability tests need to know. *Psychological Science, 3,* 271–274.

Hunt, M. (1974). *Sexual behaviors in the 1970s.* New York: Dell.

Hunt, M. (1993). *The story of psychology.* New York: Doubleday.

Hurlburt, A. C., & Poggio, T. A. (1988, January 29). Synthesizing a color algorithm from examples. *Science, 239,* 482–485.

Hutchison, J. B. (Ed.). (1978). *Biological determinants of sexual behavior.* New York: Wiley.

Hyde, J. S. (1994). *Understanding human sexuality* (5th ed.). New York: McGraw-Hill.

Hyler, S. E., Gabbard, G. O., & Schneider, I. (1991). *Homicidal maniacs and narcissistic parasites: Stigmatization of mentally ill persons in the movies.* Paper presented at the annual meeting of the American Psychiatric Association, San Francisco. *Hospital and Community Psychiatry, 42,* 1044–1048.

Hyman, R. (1994). Anomaly or artifact? Comments on Bem and Honorton. *Psychological Bulletin, 115,* 19–24.

Iacono, W. G. (1991). Can we determine the accuracy of polygraph tests? In P. K. Ackles, J. R. Jennings, & M. G. H. Coles (Eds.), *Advances in psychophysiology* (Vol. 4). Greenwich, CT: JAI Press.

Iacono, W. G., & Grove, W. M. (1993). Schizophrenia reviewed: Toward an integrative genetic model. *Psychological Science, 4,* 273–276.

Ingelfinger, F. J. (1944). The late effects of total and subtotal gastrectomy. *New England Journal of Medicine, 231,* 321–377.

Ingram, R. E. (Ed.). (1990). *Contemporary psychological approaches to depression: Theory, research, and treatment.* New York: Plenum Press.

Isaksen, S. G., & Murdock, M. C. (1993). The emergence of a discipline: Issues and approaches to the study of creativity. In S. G. Isaksen, M. C. Murdock, R. L. Firestein, & D. J. Treffinger (Eds.), *The emergence of a discipline* (Vol. 1). Norwood, NJ: Ablex.

Isay, R. A. (1990). *Being homosexual: Gay men and their development.* New York: Avon.

Izard, C. E. (1990). Facial expressions and the regulation of emotions. *Personality and Social Psychology Bulletin, 58,* 487–498.

Jacobs, B. L. (1987, July–August). How hallucinogenic drugs work. *American Scientist, 75,* 386–392.

Jacobs, G. D., Benson, H., & Friedman, R. (1993). Home-based central nervous system assessment of a multifactor behavioral intervention for chronic sleep-onset insomnia. *Behavior Therapy, 24,* 159–174.

Jacobs, M. K., & Goodman, G. (1989). Psychology and self-helping groups: Predictions on a partnership. *American Psychologist, 44,* 536–545.

Jacobson, N. S., & Truax, P. (1991). Clinical significance: A statistical approach to defining meaningful change in psychotherapy research. *Journal of Consulting and Clinical Psychology, 59,* 12–19.

Jacoby, L. L., & Kelley, C. M. (1992). A process-dissociation framework for investigating unconscious influences: Freudian slips, projective tests, subliminal perception, and signal detection theory. *Current Direc-*

tions in *Psychological Science, 1,* 174–179.

Jacoby, R., & Glauberman, N. (Eds.). (1995). *The bell curve debate.* New York: Times Books/Random House.

Jaffe, J. W. (1990). Drug addiction and drug abuse. In A. G. Gilman, T. W. Rall, A. S. Nies, & P. Taylor (Eds.), *Goodman and Gilman's The pharmacological basis of therapeutics* (8th ed.). New York: Pergamon Press.

James, W. (1890). *The principles of psychology.* New York: Holt.

Jamison, K. R. (1993). *Touched with fire: Manic depressive illness and the artistic temperament.* New York: The Free Press.

Janis, I. (1984). Improving adherence to medical recommendations: Descriptive hypothesis derived from recent research in social psychology. In A. Baum, J. E. Singer, & S. E. Taylor (Eds.), *Handbook of medical psychology* (Vol. 4). Hillsdale, NJ: Erlbaum.

Janis, I. L., & Frick, F. (1943). The relationship between attitudes toward conclusions and errors in judging logical validity of syllogisms. *Journal of Experimental Psychology, 33,* 73–77.

Jarvik, M. E. (1990, October 19). The drug dilemma: Manipulating the demand. *Science, 250,* 387–392.

Jarvis, T. J., Tebbutt, J., & Mattick, R. P. (1995). *Treatment approaches for alcohol and drug dependence.* New York: Wiley.

Jensen, J. K., & Neff, D. L. (1993). Development of basic auditory discrimination in preschool children. *Psychological Science, 4,* 104–107.

Jessell, T. M., & Kelly, D. D. (1991). Pain and analgesia. In E. R. Kandel, J. H. Schwartz, & T. M. Jessell (Eds.), *Principles of neural science* (3rd ed.). New York: Elsevier.

Johnson, B. T. (1991). Insights about attitudes: Meta-analytic perspectives. *Personality and Social Psychology Bulletin, 17,* 289–299.

Johnson, D. M., Parrott, G. R., & Stratton, R. P. (1968). Production and judgment of solutions to five problems. *Journal of Educational Psychology Monograph Supplement, 59* (6, pt. 2).

Johnson, J. T., Cain, L. M., Falke, T. L., Hayman, J., & Perillo, E. (1985). The "Barnum Effect" revisited: Cognitive and motivational factors in the acceptance of personality descriptions. *Journal of Person-*

ality and Social Psychology, 49, 1378–1391.

Johnson, M. G., & Henley, T. (1990). *Reflections on the principles of psychology.* Hillsdale, NJ: Erlbaum.

Johnston, L., Bachman, J., & O'Malley, P. (1994). *Monitoring the future: A continuing study of the lifestyles and values of youth.* Ann Arbor, MI: University of Michigan Institute of Social Research.

Johnston, L., Bachman, J., & O'Malley, P. (1995). *Monitoring the future study.* Ann Arbor, MI: University of Michigan.

Jones, A., & Crandall, R. (Eds.). (1991). Handbook of self-actualization. *Journal of Social Behavior and Personality, 6,* 1–362.

Jones, E. E. (1990). *Interpersonal perception.* New York: Freeman.

Jones, G. N., Brantley, P. J., & Gilchrist, J. C. (1988, August). *The relation between daily stress and health.* Paper presented at the annual meeting of the American Psychological Association, Atlanta.

Jones, J. C., & Barlow, D. H. (1990). Self-reported frequency of sexual urges, fantasies, and masturbatory fantasies in heterosexual males and females. *Archives of Sexual Behavior, 19,* 269–279.

Jones, L. V. (1984). White-black achievement differences: The narrowing gap. *American Psychologist, 39,* 1207–1213.

Joyce, J. (1934). *Ulysses.* New York: Random House.

Julesz, B. (1986). Stereoscopic vision. *Vision Research, 26,* 1601–1612.

Julien, R. M. (1995). *Primer of drug action* (6th ed.). New York: Freeman.

Julius, M. (1990). Paper presented at the Gerontological Society of America on women who suppress their anger.

Jusczyk, P. W. (1986). Toward a model of the development of speech perception. In J. S. Perkell & D. H. Klatt (Eds.), *Invariance and variability in speech processes.* Hillsdale, NJ: Erlbaum.

Jusczyk, P. W., & Derrah, C. (1987). Representation of speech sounds by young infants. *Developmental Psychology, 23,* 648–654.

Jussim, L., Milburn, M., & Nelson, W. (1991). Emotional openness: Sex-role stereotypes and self-perceptions. *Representative Research in Social Psychology, 19,* 35–52.

Justice, T. C., & Looney, T. A. (1990). Another look at "superstitions" in

pigeons. *Bulletin of the Psychonomic Society, 28,* 64–66.

Kagan, J. (1989). *Unstable ideas: Temperament, cognition, and self.* Cambridge, MA: Harvard University Press.

Kagan, J. (1990). Temperament and social behavior. *Harvard Medical School Mental Health Letter, 6,* 4–5.

Kagan, J., Kearsley, R., & Zelazo, P. R. (1978). *Infancy: Its place in human development.* Cambridge, MA: Harvard University Press.

Kagan, J., & Snidman, N. (1991). Infant predictors of inhibited and uninhibited profiles. *Psychological Science, 2,* 40–44.

Kahn, S., Zimmerman, G., Csikszentmihalyi, M., & Getzels, J. W. (1985). Relations between identity in young adulthood and intimacy at midlife. *Journal of Personality and Social Psychology, 49,* 1316–1322.

Kail, R. (1991). Processing time declines exponentially during childhood and adolescence. *Developmental Psychology, 27,* 259–266.

Kandel, E., & Abel, T. (1995, May 12). Neuropeptides, adenylyl cyclase, and memory storage. *Science, 268,* 825–826.

Kandel, E. R., & Schwartz, J. H. (1982). Molecular biology of learning: Modulation or transmitter release. *Science, 218,* 433–442.

Kandel, E. R., Siegelbaum, S. A., & Schwartz, J. H. (1991). Synaptic transmission. In E. R. Kandel, J. H. Schwartz, & T. M. Jessell (Eds.), *Principles of neural science* (3rd ed.). New York: Elsevier.

Kane, J. M. (1992). *Tardive dyskinesia.* Washington, DC: American Psychiatric Association Press.

Kanner, A. D., Coyne, J. C., Schaefer, C., & Lazarus, R. (1981). Comparison of two modes of stress measurement: Daily hassles and uplifts versus major life events. *Journal of Behavioral Medicine, 4,* 14.

Kanner, B. (1989, May 8). Mind games. *New York Magazine,* pp. 34–40.

Kaplan, M. F. (1975). Information integration in social judgment: Interaction of judge and informational components. In M. Kaplan & S. Schwartz (Eds.), *Human development and decision processes.* New York: Academic Press.

Karlins, M., & Abelson, H. I. (1979). *How opinions and attitudes are changed.* New York: Springer-Verlag.

Karni, A., Tanne, D., Rubenstein, B. S., Askenasy, J. J. M., & Sagi, D. (1992, October). No dreams—no memory: The effect of REM sleep deprivation on learning a new perceptual skill. *Society for Neuroscience Abstracts, 18,* 387.

Karni, A., Tanne, D., Rubenstein, B. S., Askenasy, J. J. M., & Sagi, D. (1994, July 29). Dependence on REM sleep of overnight improvement of a perceptual skill. *Science, 265,* 679–682.

Karoly, P., & Kanfer, F. H. (1982). *Self-management and behavior change.* New York: Pergamon Press.

Karp, D. A. (1988). A decade of remembrances: Changing age consciousness between fifty and sixty years old. *The Gerontologist, 28,* 727–738.

Kaslow, F. W. (1991). The art and science of family psychology: Retrospective and perspective. *American Psychologist, 46,* 621–626.

Kassin, S. M. (1983). Deposition testimony and the surrogate witness: Evidence for a "messenger effect" in persuasion. *Personality and Social Psychology Bulletin, 9,* 281–288.

Katigbak, M. S., & Akamine, T. X. (1994, August). *Relating indigenous Philippine dimension to the big five model.* Paper presented at the 102nd Annual Convention of the American Psychological Association, Los Angeles.

Katz, A. N. (1989). Autobiographical memory as a reconstructive process: An extension of Ross's hypothesis. *Canadian Journal of Psychology, 43,* 512–517.

Katz, D., & Braly, K. W. (1933). Racial stereotypes of 100 college students. *Journal of Abnormal and Social Psychology, 4,* 280–290.

Katz, P. A. (Ed.). (1976). *Towards the elimination of racism.* New York: Pergamon Press.

Kaufman, J., & Zigler, E. (1987). Do abused children become abusive parents? *American Journal of Orthopsychiatry, 57,* 186–192.

Kausler, D. H. (1994). *Learning and memory in normal aging.* San Diego, CA: Academic Press.

Kazdin, A. E. (1989). *Behavior modification in applied settings* (4th ed.). Pacific Grove, CA: Brooks/Cole.

Kazdin, A. E. (1993). Psychotherapy for children and adolescents: Current progress and future research directions. *American Psychologist, 48,* 644–657.

Keating, D. P., & Clark, L. V. (1980). Development of physical and social reasoning in adolescence. *Developmental Psychology, 16,* 23–30.

Keesey, R. E., & Powley, T. L. (1986). The regulation of body weight. *Annual Review of Psychology, 37,* 109–133.

Keith, S. J., Regier, D. A., & Rae, D. S. (1991). Schizophrenic disorders. In L. N. Robins & D. A. Regier (Eds.), *Psychiatric disorders in America.* New York: The Free Press.

Kelley, H. (1950). The warm-cold variable in first impressions of persons. *Journal of Personality and Social Psychology, 18,* 431–439.

Kelly, D. D. (1991a). Disorders of sleep and consciousness. In E. R. Kandel, J. H. Schwartz, & T. M. Jessell (Eds.), *Principles of neural science* (3rd ed.). New York: Elsevier.

Kelly, D. D. (1991b). Sexual differentiation of the nervous system. In E. R. Kandel, J. H. Schwartz, & T. M. Jessell (Eds.), *Principles of neural science* (3rd ed.). New York: Elsevier.

Kelly, D. D. (1991c). Sleep and dreaming. In E. R. Kandel, J. H. Schwartz, & T. M. Jessell (Eds.), *Principles of neural science* (3rd ed.). New York: Elsevier.

Kelly, J. P. (1991). The sense of balance. In E. R. Kandel, J. H. Schwartz, & T. M. Jessell (Eds.), *Principles of neural science* (3rd ed.). New York: Elsevier.

Kempton, W., Darley, J. M., & Stern, P. C. (1992). Psychological research for the new energy problems: Strategies and opportunities. *American Psychologist, 47,* 1213–1223.

Kendall, P. C. (Ed.). (1991). *Child and adolescent therapy: Cognitive-behavioral procedures.* New York: Guilford Press.

Kenny, D. A. (1991). A general model of consensus and accuracy in interpersonal perception. *Psychological Review, 98,* 155–163.

Kertesz, A. E. (1983). Cyclofusion and stereopsis. *Perception and Psychophysics, 33,* 99–101.

Kessler, R. C., McGonagle, K. A., Zhao, S., Nelson, C. B., Hughes, M., Eshleman, S., Wittchen, H., & Kendler, K. S. (1994). Lifetime and 12 month prevalence of DSM-III-R psychiatric disorders in the United States. *Archives of General Psychiatry, 51,* 8–19.

Kiecolt-Glaser, J. K., & Glaser, R. (1986). Behavioral influences on immune function: Evidence for the interplay between stress and health. In T. Field, P. McCabe, & N. Schneiderman (Eds.), *Stress and coping* (Vol. 2). Hillsdale, NJ: Erlbaum.

Kienker, P. K., Sejnowski, T. J., Hinton, G. E., & Schumacher, L. E. (1986). Separating figure from ground with a parallel network. *Perception, 15,* 197–216.

Kiesler, C. A., & Simpkins, C. (1991, June). The de facto national system of psychiatric inpatient care. *American Psychologist, 46,* 579–584.

Kiesler, C. A., & Simpkins, C. G. (1993). *The unnoticed majority in psychiatric inpatient care.* New York: Plenum Press.

Kihlstrom, J. F. (1987, September 18). The cognitive unconscious. *Science, 237,* 1445–1452.

Kihlstrom, J. F., Schacter, D. L., Cork, R. C., Hurt, C. A., & Behr, S. E. (1990). Implicit and explicit memory following surgical anesthesia. *Psychological Science, 1,* 303–306.

Kilborn, P. T. (1991, May 15). "Race norming" tests become a fiery issue. *The New York Times.*

Kimble, G. A. (1994). A frame of reference for psychology. *American Psychologist, 49,* 510–519.

Kimchi, R. (1992). Primacy of holistic processing and global/local paradigm: A critical review. *Psychological Bulletin, 112,* 24–38.

Kimura, D. (1992, September). Sex differences in the brain. *Scientific American,* pp. 119–125.

King, G. R., & Logue, A. W. (1990). Humans' sensitivity to variation in reinforcer amount: Effects of the method of reinforcer delivery. *Journal of the Experimental Analysis of Behavior, 53,* 33–46.

King, S. H. (1993). The limited presence of African-American teachers. *Review of Educational Research, 63,* 114–149.

Kinsey, A. C., Pomeroy, W. B., & Martin, C. E. (1948). *Sexual behavior in the human male.* Philadelphia: Saunders.

Kinsey, A. C., Pomeroy, W. B., Martin, C. E., & Gebhard, P. H. (1953). *Sexual behavior in the human female.* Philadelphia: Saunders.

Kirk, S. A. (1992). *The selling of DSM: The rhetoric of science in psychiatry.* Hawthorne, NY: Aldine de Gruyter.

Kirsch, B. (1989, October 8). Breaking the sound barrier. *The New York Times Magazine,* pp. 64–66, 68–70.

Kirsch, I., & Council, J. R. (in press). Situational and personality correlates of suggestibility. In E. Fromm & M. Nash (Eds.), *Contemporary perspectives in hypnosis research.* New York: Guilford Press.

Kirsch, I., & Lynn, S. J. (1995). The altered state of hypnosis: Changes in the theoretical landscape. *American Psychologist, 50*, 846–858.

Kitterle, F. L. (Ed.). (1991). *Cerebral laterality: Theory and research.* Hillsdale, NJ: Erlbaum.

Klein, S. B., & Mowrer, R. R. (1989). *Contemporary learning theories, instrumental conditioning theory and the impact of biological constraints on learning.* Hillsdale, NJ: Erlbaum.

Kleinman, A. (1991, July). The psychiatry of culture and culture of psychiatry. *Harvard Mental Health Letter.*

Knight, G. P., Johnson, L. G., Carlo, G., & Eisenberg, N. (1994). A multiplicative model of the dispositional antecedents of prosocial behavior: Predicting more of the people more of the time. *Journal of Personality and Social Psychology, 66*, 178–183.

Knittle, J. L. (1975). Early influences on development of adipose tissue. In G. A. Bray (Ed.), *Obesity in perspective.* Washington, DC: U.S. Government Printing Office.

Kobasa, S. C. (1979). Stressful life events, personality, and health: An inquiry into hardiness. *Journal of Personality and Social Psychology, 37*, 1–11.

Koch, S. (1993). "Psychology" or "The psychological studies"? *American Psychologist, 48*, 902–904.

Koester, J. (1991). Membrane potential. In E. R. Kandel, J. H. Schwartz, & T. M. Jessell (Eds.), *Principles of neural science* (3rd ed.). New York: Elsevier.

Kohlberg, L. (1969). Stage and sequence: The cognitive-developmental approach to socialization. In D. Goslin (Ed.), *Handbook of socialization theory and research.* Chicago: Rand McNally.

Kohlberg, L. (1984). *The psychology of moral development: Essays on moral development* (Vol. 2). San Francisco: Harper & Row.

Kohlberg, L., & Ryncarz, R. A. (1990). Beyond justice reasoning: Moral development and consideration of a seventh stage. In C. N. Alexander & E. J. Langer (Eds.), *Higher stages of human development: Perspectives on adult growth.* New York: Oxford University Press.

Köhler, W. (1927). *The mentality of apes.* London: Routledge & Kegan Paul.

Kohn, P. M., Lafreniere, K., & Gurevich, M. (1991). Hassles, health, and personality. *Journal of Personality and Social Psychology, 61*, 478–482.

Kolata, G. (1987, May 15). Early signs of school-age IQ. *Science, 236*, 774–775.

Kolata, G. (1993, February 28). Rethinking the statistics of "epidemic" breast cancer. *The New York Times.*

Kolb, B., & Whishaw, I. Q. (1990). *Fundamentals of human neuropsychology* (3rd ed.). New York: Freeman.

Konishi, M. (1993, April). Listening with two ears. *Scientific American,* pp. 66–73.

Konner, M. (1988, January 17). Caffeine high. *The New York Times Magazine,* pp. 47–48.

Koop, C. E. (1988). *The health consequences of smoking.* Washington, DC: Government Printing Office.

Koop, C. B. (1994). Infant assessment. In C. B. Fisher & R. M. Lerner (Eds.), *Applied developmental psychology.* New York: McGraw-Hill.

Korb, M. P., Gorrell, J., & VanDeRiet, V. (1989). *Gestalt therapy: Practice and theory* (2nd ed.). New York: Pergamon Press.

Kosambi, D. D. (1967). Living prehistory in India. *Scientific American,* p. 105.

Kosik, K. S. (1992, May 8). Alzheimer's disease: A cell biological perspective. *Science, 256*, 780–783.

Koss, M. P., & Butcher, J. N. (1986). Research on brief psychotherapy. In S. L. Garfield & A. E. Bergin (Eds.), *Handbook of psychotherapy and behavior change* (3rd ed.). New York: Wiley.

Kosslyn, S. M. (1981). The medium and the message in mental imagery. *Psychological Review, 88*, 46–66.

Kosslyn, S. M., Seger, C., Pani, J. R., & Hillger, L. A. (1990). When is imagery used in everyday life? A diary study. *Journal of Mental Imagery, 14*, 131–152.

Kostses, H., et al. (1991). Long-term effects of biofeedback-induced facial relaxation on measures of asthma severity in children. *Biofeedback and Self-Regulation, 16*, 1–22.

Koveces, Z. (1987). *The container metaphor of emotion.* Paper presented at the University of Massachusetts, Amherst.

Kotre, J., & Hall, E. (1990). *Seasons of life.* Boston: Little, Brown.

Kraines, S. H. (1948). *The therapy of the neuroses and psychoses* (3rd ed.). Philadelphia: Lea & Febiger.

Kramer, P. (1993). *Listening to Prozac.* New York: Viking.

Kravitz, E. A. (1988). Hormonal control of behavior: Amines and the biasing of behavioral output in lobsters. *Science, 241*, 1775–1782.

Kreuger, L. E. (1989). *The world of touch.* Hillsdale, NJ: Erlbaum.

Kryzanowski, E., & Stewin, L. (1985). Developmental implications in youth counseling: Gender socialization. *International Journal for the Advancement of Counseling, 8*, 265–278.

Kübler-Ross, E. (1969). *On death and dying.* New York: Macmillan.

Kucharski, D., & Hall, W. G. (1987). New routes to early memories. *Science, 238*, 786–788.

Kuczmarski, R. J., Flegal, K. M., Campbell, S. M., & Johnson, C. L. (1994, July 20). Increasing prevalence of overweight among US adults. *Journal of the American Medical Association, 272*, 205–211.

Kuhl, P. K., Williams, K. A., Lacerda, F., Stevens, K. N., & Lindblom, B. (1992, January 31). Linguistic experience alters phonetic perception in infants by 6 months of age. *Science, 255*, 606–608.

Kulik, J. A., Bangert-Drowns, R. L., & Kulik, C. C. (1984). Effectiveness of coaching for aptitude tests. *Psychological Bulletin, 95*, 179–188.

Kupfermann, I. (1991a). Hypothalamus and limbic system: Motivation. In E. R. Kandel, J. H. Schwartz, & T. M. Jessell (Eds.), *Principles of neural science* (3rd ed.). New York: Elsevier.

Kupfermann, I. (1991b). Hypothalamus and limbic system: Petidergic neurons, homeostatis, and emotional behavior. In E. R. Kandel, J. H. Schwartz, & T. M. Jessell (Eds.), *Principles of neural science* (3rd ed.). New York: Elsevier.

Kupfermann, I. (1991c). Localization of higher cognitive and affective functions: The association cornices. In E. R. Kandel, J. H. Schwartz, & T. M. Jessell (Eds.), *Principles of neural science* (3rd ed.). New York: Elsevier.

Kupfermann, I. (1991d). Genetic determinants of behavior. In E. R. Kandel, J. H. Schwartz, & T. M. Jessell (Eds.), *Principles of neural science* (3rd ed.). New York: Elsevier.

Kurdek, L. A. (1993). The allocation of household labor in gay, lesbian, and heterosexual married couples. *Journal of Social Issues, 49*, 127–139.

LaFromboise, T., Coleman, H. L., & Gerton, J. (1993). Psychological impact of biculturalism: Evidence and theory. *Psychological Bulletin, 114*, 395–412.

Laird, J. D., & Bresler, C. (1990). William James and the mechanisms of emotional experience. *Personality and Social Psychology Bulletin, 16,* 636–651.

Lam, T. C. M. (1992). Review of practices and problems in the evaluation of bilingual education. *Review of Educational Research, 62,* 181–203.

Lamb, M. (1982). The bonding phenomenon: Misinterpretations and their implications. *Journal of Pediatrics, 101,* 555–557.

Lamb, M. E. (Ed.). (1987). *The father's role.* Hillsdale, NJ: Erlbaum.

Lambert, M. J., Shapiro, D. A., & Bergin, A. E. (1986). The effectiveness of psychotherapy. In S. L. Garfield & A. E. Bergin (Eds.), *Handbook of psychotherapy and behavior change* (3rd ed.). New York: Wiley.

Lambert, W. E., & Peal, E. (1972). The relation of bilingualism to intelligence. In A. S. Dil (Ed.), *Language, psychology, and culture.* Stanford, CA: Stanford University Press.

Landesman, S., & Ramey, C. (1989). Developmental psychology and mental retardation: Integrating scientific principles with treatment practices. *American Psychologist, 44,* 409–415.

Landis, D., Day, H. R., McGrew, P. L., Thomas, J. A., & Miller, A. B. (1976). Can a black "culture assimilator" increase racial understanding? *Journal of Social Issues, 32,* 169–183.

Lang, J. S. (1987, April 13). Happiness is a reunited set of twins. *U.S. News and World Report,* pp. 63–66.

Lang, S. S., & Patt, R. B. (1994). *You don't have to suffer.* New York: Oxford University Press.

Langer, E., & Janis, I. (1979). *The psychology of control.* Beverly Hills, CA: Sage.

Larsen, R. J., & Diener, E. (1987). Affect intensity as an individual characteristic: A review. *Journal of Research in Personality, 21,* 1–39.

Larson, R. K. (1990). Semantics. In D. N. Osherson & H. Lasnik (Eds.), *Language.* Cambridge, MA: MIT Press.

Lashley, K. S. (1950). In search of the engram. *Symposia of the Society for Experimental Biology, 4,* 454–482.

Lask, B., & Bryant-Waugh, R. (Eds.). (1993). *Childhood onset of anorexia nervosa and related eating disorders.* Hillsdale, NJ: Erlbaum.

Lasnik, H. (1990). Syntax. In D. N. Osherson & H. Lasnik (Eds.), *Language.* Cambridge, MA: MIT Press.

Latané, B., & Darley, J. M. (1970). *The unresponsive bystander: Why doesn't he help?* New York: Appleton-Century-Crofts.

Latané, B., & Nida, S. (1981). Ten years of research on group size and helping. *Psychological Bulletin, 89,* 308–324.

Laursen, B., & Collins, W. A. (1994). Interpersonal conflict during adolescence. *Psychological Bulletin, 115,* 197–209.

Lazarus, A. A., Beutler, L. E., & Norcross, J. C. (1992). The future of technical eclecticism. *Psychotherapy, 29,* 11–20.

Lazarus, R. S. (1984). On the primacy of cognition. *American Psychologist, 39,* 124–129.

Lazarus, R. S. (1991a). Cognition and motivation in emotion. *American Psychologist, 46,* 352–367.

Lazarus, R. S. (1991b). *Emotion and adaptation.* New York: Oxford University Press.

Lazarus, R. S., & Cohen, J. B. (1977). Environmental stress. In I. Altman & J. F. Wohlwill (Eds.), *Human behavior and the environment: Current theory and research* (Vol. 2). New York: Plenum Press.

Lazarus, R. S., DeLongis, A., Folkman, S., & Gruen, R. (1985). Stress and adaptational outcomes: The problem of confounded measures. *American Psychologist, 40,* 770–779.

Lazarus, R. S., & Lazarus, B. N. (1994). *Passion and reason: Making sense of our emotions.* New York: Oxford University Press.

Leahey, T. H. (1994). Is this a dagger I see before me? Four theorists in search of consciousness. *Contemporary Psychology, 39,* 575–581.

Lecanuet, J.-P., Granier-Deferre, C., & Busnel, M. C. (1995). Human fetal auditory perception. In J.-P. Lecanuet, W. P. Fifer, N. A. Krasnegor, & W. P. Smotherman (Eds.), *Fetal development: A psychobiological perspective.* Hillsdale, NJ: Erlbaum.

Lechtenberg, R. (1982). *The psychiatrist's guide to diseases of the nervous system.* New York: Wiley.

Lee, M. E., Matsumoto, D., Kobayashi, M., Krupp, D., Maniatis, E. F., & Roberts, W. (1992). Cultural influences on nonverbal behavior in applied settings. In R. S. Feldman (Ed.), *Applications of nonverbal behavioral theory and research.* Hillsdale, NJ: Erlbaum.

Lee, V. E., Brooks-Gunn, J., Schnur, E., & Liaw, F. (1990). Are Head Start effects sustained? A longitudinal follow-up comparison of disadvantaged children attending Head Start, no preschool, and other preschool programs. *Child Development, 61,* 495–507.

Lee, Y. (1994). Why does American psychology have cultural limitations? *American Psychologist, 49,* 524.

Lehman, D. R., & Taylor, S. E. (1988). Date with an earthquake: Coping with a probable, unpredictable disaster. *Personality and Social Psychology Bulletin, 13,* 546–555.

Leibovic, K. N. (Ed.). (1990). *Science of vision.* New York: Springer-Verlag.

Lemoine, P., & Lemoine, P. (1992). Outcome of children of alcoholic mothers (study of 105 cases followed to adult age) and various prophylactic findings. *Annals of Pediatrics—Paris, 39,* 226–235.

Lenhardt, M. L., Skellett, R., Wang, P., & Clarke, A. M. (1991, July 5). Human ultrasonic speech perception. *Science, 253,* 82–85.

Lepper, M. R., & Greene, D. (Eds.). (1978). The hidden costs of reward. Hillsdale, NJ: Erlbaum.

Leslie, C. (1991, February 11). Classrooms of Babel. *Newsweek,* pp. 56–57.

Leutwyler, K. (1994, March). Prosthetic vision. *Scientific American,* p.108.

LeVay, S. (1991). A difference in hypothalamic structure between heterosexual and homosexual men. *Science, 253,* 1034–1037.

LeVay, S. (1993). *The sexual brain.* Cambridge, MA: MIT Press.

Levenson, R. W. (1992). Autonomic nervous system differences among emotions. *Psychological Science, 3,* 23–27.

Levenson, R. W., Ekman, P., Heider, K., & Friesen, W. V. (1992). Emotion and autonomic nervous system activity in the Minangkabau of West Sumatra. *Journal of Personality and Social Psychology, 62,* 972–988.

Leventhal, H. (1970). Findings and theory in the study of fear communications. In L. Berkowitz (Ed.), *Advances in experimental social psychology* (Vol. 5). New York: Academic Press.

Leventhal, H., & Tomarken, A. J. (1986). Emotion: Today's problems. *Annual Review of Psychology, 37,* 565–610.

Levine, J. M. (1989). Reaction to opinion deviance in small groups. In P. B. Paulus (Ed.), *Psychology of* group influence (2nd ed.). Hillsdale, NJ: Erlbaum.

Levine, M. W., & Shefner, J. M. (1991). *Fundamentals of sensation and perception* (2nd ed.). Pacific Grove, CA: Brooks/Cole.

Levinger, G. (1983). Development and change. In H. H. Kelley et al., *Close relationships*. San Francisco: Freeman.

Levinson, D. (1996). *The seasons of a woman's life.* New York: Knopf.

Levinson, D. J. (1986). A conception of adult development. *American Psychologist, 41,* 3–13.

Levitan, I. B., & Kaczmarek, L. K. (1991). *The neuron: Cell and molecular biology.* New York: Oxford University Press.

Levy, B. L., & Langer, E. (1994). Aging free from negative stereotypes: Successful memory in China and among the American deaf. *Journal of Personality and Social Psychology, 66,* 989–997.

Lewandowsky, S., Dunn, J. C., & Kirsner, R. (Eds.). (1989). *Implicit memory: Theoretical issues.* Hillsdale, NJ: Erlbaum.

Lewin, T. (1995, May 11). Women are becoming equal providers: Half of working women bring home half the household income. *The New York Times,* p. A14.

Lewis, M., & Feinman, S. (Eds.). (1991). *Social influences and socialization in infancy.* New York: Plenum Press.

Lewis, M., Feiring, C., McGuffog, C., & Jaskir, J. (1984). Predicting psychopathology in six-year-olds from early social relations. *Child Development, 55,* 123–136.

Lewis, P. (1987). Therapeutic change in groups: An interactional perspective. *Small Group Behavior, 18,* 548–556.

Lidz, T., & Fleck, S. (1985). *Schizophrenia and the family* (2nd ed.). New York: International Universities Press.

Liebert, R. M., & Sprafkin, J. (1988). *The early window: Effects of television on children and youth* (3rd ed.). New York: Pergamon.

Lietaer, G. (1984). Unconditional positive regard: A controversial basic attitude in client-centered therapy. In R. F. Levant & L. M. Shlien (Eds.), *Client-centered therapy and the person-centered approach.* New York: Praeger.

Lindholm, K. J. (1991). Two-way bilingual/immersion education: Theory, conceptual issues, and pedagogical implications. In R. V. Padilla & A. Benavides (Eds.), *Critical per-*

spectives on bilingual education research. Tempe, AZ: Bilingual Review Press.

Lindsay, P. H., & Norman, D. A. (1977). *Human information processing* (2nd ed.). New York: Academic Press.

Linscheid, T. R., Iwata, B. A., Ricketts, R. W., Williams, D. E., & Griffin, J. C. (1990). Clinical evaluation of the self-injurious behavior inhibiting system (SIBIS). *Journal of Applied Behavior Analysis, 23,* 53–78.

Linz, D. G., Donnerstein, E., & Penrod, S. (1988). Effects of long-term exposure to violent and sexually degrading depictions of women. *Journal of Personality and Social Psychology, 55,* 758–768.

Lipsey, M. W., & Wilson, D. B. (1993). The efficacy of psychological, educational, and behavioral treatment: Confirmation from meta-analysis. *American Psychologist, 48,* 1181–1209.

Lister, R. G., & Weingartner, H. J. (Eds.). (1991). *Perspectives on cognitive neuroscience.* New York: Oxford University Press.

Lobsenz, M. M. (1975). *Sex after sixty-five* (Public Affairs Pamphlet #519). New York: New York Public Affairs Committee.

Locke, D. C. (1992). *Increasing multicultural understanding.* Newbury Park, CA: Sage.

Loehlin, J. C., Willerman, L., & Horn, J. M. (1987). Personality resemblance in adoptive families: A 10-year follow-up. *Journal of Personality and Social Psychology, 53,* 961–969.

Loewenstein, G. (1994). The psychology of curiosity: A review and reinterpretation. *Psychological Bulletin, 116,* 75–98.

Loftus, E. F. (1993). Psychologists in the eyewitness world. *American Psychologist, 48,* 550–552.

Loftus, E. F., & Ketcham, K. (1991). *Witness for the defense: The accused, the eyewitness who puts memory on trial.* New York: St. Martin's.

Loftus, E. F., Loftus, G. R., & Messo, J. (1987). Some facts about "weapon focus." *Law and Human Behavior, 11,* 55–62.

Loftus, E. F., & Palmer, J. C. (1974). Reconstruction of automobile destruction: An example of the interface between language and memory. *Journal of Verbal Learning and Verbal Behavior, 13,* 585–589.

Logothetis, N. K., & Schall, J. D. (1989, August 18). Neuronal cor-

relates of subjective visual perception. *Science, 245,* 761–763.

Logue, A. W. (1991). *The psychology of eating and drinking* (2nd ed.). New York: Freeman.

Lohman, D. F. (1989). Human intelligence: An introduction to advances in theory and research. *Review of Educational Research, 59,* 333–373.

Long, A. (1987, December). What is this thing called sleep? *National Geographic, 172,* 786–821.

Long, G. M., & Beaton, R. J. (1982). The case for peripheral persistence: Effects of target and background luminance on a partial-report task. *Journal of Experimental Psychology: Human Perception and Performance, 8,* 383–391.

Lorenz, K. (1966). *On aggression.* New York: Harcourt Brace Jovanovich.

Lorenz, K. (1974). *Civilized man's eight deadly sins.* New York: Harcourt Brace Jovanovich.

Lott, B., & Maluso, D. (Eds.). (1995). *The social psychology of interpersonal discrimination.* New York: Guilford Press.

Lovaas, O. I., & Koegel, R. (1973). Behavior therapy with autistic children. In C. Thoreson (Ed.), *Behavior modification and education.* Chicago: University of Chicago Press.

Lowinson, J. H., Ruiz, P., Millman, R. B., & Langrod, J. G. (1992). *Substance abuse: A comprehensive textbook* (2nd ed.). Baltimore: Williams and Wilkins.

Lubart, T. I. (1994). Creativity. In R. J. Sternberg (Ed.), *Thinking and problem-solving.* San Diego, CA: Academic Press.

Luborsky, L. (1988). *Who will benefit from psychotherapy?* New York: Basic Books

Luce, R. D. (1993). *Sound and hearing.* Hillsdale, NJ: Erlbaum.

Luchins, A. S. (1946). Classroom experiments on mental set. *American Journal of Psychology, 59,* 295–298.

Lucy, J. A. (1992). *Language diversity and thought: A reformulation of the linguistic relativity hypothesis.* Cambridge, England: Cambridge University Press.

Ludwick-Rosenthal, R., & Neufeld, R. W. J. (1988). Stress management during noxious medical procedures: An evaluative review of outcome studies. *Psychological Bulletin, 104,* 326–342.

Ludwig, A. M. (1969). Altered states of consciousness. In C. T. Tart

(Ed.), *Altered states of consciousness*. New York: Wiley.

Luria, A. R. (1968). *The mind of a mnemonist*. Cambridge, MA: Basic Books.

Lykken, D. T., McGue, M., Tellegen, A., & Bouchard, Jr., T. J. (1993). Emergenesis: Genetic traits that may not run in families. *American Psychologist, 47*, 1565–1577.

Lynch, G., Granger, R., & Staubli, U. (1991). Long-term potentiation and the structure of memory. In W. C. Abraham, M. C. Corballis, & K. G. White (Eds.), *Memory mechanisms: A tribute to G. V. Goddard*. Hillsdale, NJ: Erlbaum.

Lynch, Jr., J. G., & Cohen, J. L. (1978). The use of subjective expected utility theory as an aid to understanding variables that influence helping behavior. *Journal of Personality and Social Psychology, 36*, 1138–1151.

Lynn, S. J., & Rhue, J. W. (1988). Fantasy-proneness: Hypnosis, developmental antecedents, and psychopathology. *American Psychologist, 43*, 35–44.

Lynn, S. J., Rhue, J. W., & Weekes, J. R. (1990). Hypnotic involuntariness: A social cognitive analysis. *Psychological Review, 97*, 169–184.

Lynn, S. J., & Snodgrass, M. (1987). Goal-directed fantasy, hypnotic susceptibility, and expectancies. *Journal of Personality and Social Psychology, 53*, 933–938.

Lynn, S. J., Weekes, J. R., Neufeld, V., Zivney, O., Brentar, J., & Weiss, F. (1991). Interpersonal climate and hypnotizability level: Effects on hypnotic performance, rapport, and archaic involvement. *Journal of Personality and Social Psychology, 60*, 739–743.

Maccoby, E. E. (1992). The role of parents in the socialization of children: An historical overview. *Developmental Psychology, 28*, 1006–1017.

MacCoun, R. J. (1993). Drugs and the law: A psychological analysis of drug prohibition. *Psychological Bulletin, 113*, 497–512.

MacDermid, S. M., Huston, T. L., & McHale, S. M. (1990). Changes in marriage associated with the transition to parenthood: Individual differences as a function of sex-role attitudes and changes in division of labor. *Journal of Marriage and the Family, 52*, 475–486.

MacFadyen, J. T. (1987, November). Educated monkeys help the disabled help themselves. *Smithsonian*, pp. 125–133.

MacKenzie, B. (1984). Explaining race differences in IQ: The logic, the methodology, and the evidence. *American Psychologist, 39*, 1214–1233.

MacKenzie, E. K. R. (1990). *Introduction to time-limited group psychotherapy*. Washington, DC: American Psychiatric Press.

Mackie, D. M. (1987). Systematic and nonsystematic processing of majority and minority persuasive communications. *Journal of Personality and Social Psychology, 53*, 41–52.

Maddi, S. R., Barone, P. T., & Puccetti, M. C. (1987). Stressful events are indeed a factor in physical illness: Reply to Schroeder and Costa (1984). *Journal of Personality and Social Psychology, 52*, 833–843.

Major, B. (1993). Gender, entitlement, and the distribution of family labor. *Journal of Social Issues, 49*, 141–159.

Malin, J. T. (1979). Information-processing load in problem solving by network search. *Journal of Experimental Psychology: Human Perception and Performance, 5*, 379–390.

Malinowski, C. I., & Smith, C. P. (1985). Moral reasoning and moral conduct: An investigation prompted by Kohlberg's theory. *Journal of Personality and Social Issues, 49*, 1016–1027.

Malott, R. W., Whaley, D. L., & Malott, M. E. (1993). *Elementary principles of behavior* (2nd ed.). Englewood Cliffs, NJ: Prentice-Hall.

Mann, T. (1994). Informed consent for psychological research: Do subjects comprehend consent forms and understand their legal rights? *Psychological Science, 5*, 140–143.

Manuck, S. B., Kaplan, J. R., Adams, M. R., & Clarkson, T. B. (1989). Behaviorally elicited heart rate reactivity and atherosclerosis in female cynomolgus monkeys *(Macaca fascicularis)*. *Psychosomatic Medicine, 51*, 306–318.

Mapes, G. (1990, April 10). Beating the clock: Was it an accident Chernobyl exploded at 1:23 in the morning? *Wall Street Journal*, pp. Al, A16.

Marks, G., & Miller, N. (1987). Ten years of research on the false-consensus effect: An empirical and theoretical review. *Psychological Bulletin, 102*, 72–90.

Marshall, G., & Zimbardo, P. (1979). The affective consequences of "inadequately explained" physiological arousal. *Journal of Personality and Social Psychology, 37*, 970–988.

Martin, J. (1993). Episodic memory: A neglected phenomenon in the psychology of education. *Educational Psychologist, 28*, 169–183.

Martin, J. H., Brust, J. C. M., & Hilal, S. (1991). Imaging the living brain. In E. R. Kandel, J. H. Schwartz, & T. M. Jessell (Eds.), *Principles of neural science* (3rd ed.). New York: Elsevier.

Martin, L., & Pullum, G. K. (1991). *The great Eskimo vocabulary hoax*. Chicago: University of Chicago Press.

Martindale, C. (1981). *Cognition and consciousness*. Homewood, IL: Dorsey.

Marx, M. B., Garrity, T. F., & Bowers, F. R. (1975). The influence of recent life experience on the health of college freshmen. *Journal of Psychosomatic Research, 19*, 87–98.

Maslow, A. H. (1970). *Motivation and personality* (2nd ed.). New York: Harper & Row.

Maslow, A. H. (1987). *Motivation and personality* (3rd ed.). New York: Harper & Row.

Mason, J. W. (1974). Specificity in the organization of neuroendocrine response profiles. In P. Seeman and G. M. Brown (Eds.), *Frontiers in neurology and neuroscience research*. First International Symposium of the Neuroscience Institute. Toronto: University of Toronto Press.

Mason, J. W. (1975). A historical view of the stress field. *Journal of Human Stress, 1*, 6–12, 22–37.

Mason, M. (1994). *The making of Victorian sexual attitudes* (Vol. 2). New York: Oxford University Press.

Massaro, D. (1991). Psychology as a cognitive science. *Psychological Science, 2*, 302–306.

Masters, W. H., & Johnson, V. E. (1979). *Homosexuality in perspective*. Boston: Little, Brown.

Mastropieri, M. A., & Scruggs, T. (1987). *Effective instruction for special education*. Boston: College-Hill Press/Little, Brown.

Mastropieri, M. A., & Scruggs, T. E. (1991). *Teaching students ways to remember: Strategies for learning mnemonically*. Cambridge, MA: Brookline Books.

Mastropieri, M. A., & Scruggs, T. E. (1992). Science for students with disabilities. *Review of Educational Research, 62*, 377–411.

Matarazzo, J. D. (1992). Psychological testing and assessment in the 21st century. *American Psychologist, 47*, 1007–1018.

Matsumoto, D., Kudoh, T., Schjerer, K., & Wallbot, H. G. (1988).

Emotion antecedents and reactions in the U.S. and Japan. *Journal of Cross-Cultural Psychology, 19,* 267–286.

Matthies, H. (1989). Neurobiological aspects of learning and memory. *Annual Review of Psychology, 40,* 381–404.

Mauro, R., Sato, K., & Tucker, J. (1992). The role of appraisal in human emotions: A cross-cultural study. *Journal of Personality and Social Psychology, 62,* 301–317.

Mawhinney, V. T., Boston, D. E., Loaws, O. R., Blumenfeld, G. T., & Hopkins, B. L. (1971). A comparison of students' studying behavior produced by daily, weekly, and three-week testing schedules. *Journal of Applied Behavior Analysis, 4,* 257–264.

May, R. (1969). *Love and will.* New York: Norton.

Mayer, R. E. (1982). Different problem-solving strategies for algebra word and equation problems. *Journal of Experimental Psychology: Learning, Memory, and Cognition, 8,* 448–462.

Mayford, M., Barzilai, A., Keller, F., Schacher, S., & Kandel, E. R. (1992). Modulation of an NCAM-related adhesion molecule with long-term synaptic plasticity in aplasia. *Science, 256,* 638–644.

Maziotta, J. (1993, June). *History and goals of the human brain project.* Paper presented at the annual meeting of the American Psychological Society, Chicago.

McCarthy, M. J. (1991, March 18). Marketers zero in on their customers. *Wall Street Journal,* p. B1.

McCauley, C., & Swann, C. P. (1980). Sex differences in the frequency and functions of fantasies during sexual activity. *Journal of Research in Personality, 14,* 400–411.

McClelland, D. C. (1985). How motives, skills, and values determine what people do. *American Psychologist, 40,* 812–825.

McClelland, D. C. (1993). Intelligence is not the best predictor of job performance. *Current Directions in Psychological Research, 2,* 5–8.

McClelland, D. C., Atkinson, J. W., Clark, R. A., & Lowell, E. L. (1953). *The achievement motive.* New York: Appleton-Century-Crofts.

McCloskey, M., Wible, C. G., & Cohen, N. J. (1988). Is there a special flashbulb-memory mechanism? *Journal of Experimental Psychology: General, 117,* 171–181.

McClusky, H. Y., et al. (1991). Efficacy of behavioral versus triazolam treatment in persistent sleep-onset insomnia. *American Journal of Psychiatry, 148,* 121–126.

McConkey, K. M., & Sheehan, P. W. (1995). *Hypnosis, memory, and behavior in criminal investigation.* New York: Guilford Press.

McCrae, R. R., & Costa, Jr., P. T. (1990). *Personality in adulthood.* New York: Guilford Press.

McDaniel, M. A., Riegler, G. L., & Waddill, P. J. (1990). Generation effects in free recall: Further support for a three-factor theory. *Journal of Experimental Psychology: Learning, Memory, and Cognition, 16,* 789.

McDonald, K. (1988, March). Sex under glass. *Psychology Today,* pp. 58–59.

McDougall, W. (1908). *Introduction to social psychology.* London: Methuen.

McFarlane, J., Martin, C. L., & Williams, T. M. (1988). Mood fluctuations: Women versus men and menstrual versus other cycles. *Psychology of Women Quarterly, 12,* 201–223.

McGaugh, J. L., (1989). Involvement of hormonal and neuromodulatory systems in the regulation of memory storage. *Annual Review of Neuroscience, 12,* 255–287.

McGaugh, J. L., Weinberger, N. M., & Lynch, G. (Eds.). (1990). *Brain organization and memory: Cells, systems, and circuits.* New York: Oxford University Press.

McGrath, E., Keita, G. P., Strickland, B. R., & Russo, N. F. (Eds.). (1990). *Women and depression: Risk factors and treatment issues.* Washington, DC: American Psychological Association.

McGraw, K. M., & Bloomfield, J. (1987). Social influence on group moral decisions: The interactive effects of moral reasoning and sex-role orientation. *Journal of Personality and Social Psychology, 53,* 1080–1087.

McGuire, A. M. (1994). Helping behaviors in the natural environment: Dimensions and correlates of helping. *Personality and Social Psychology Bulletin, 120,* 45–56.

McGuire, P. K., Shah, G. M. S., & Murray, R. M. (1993, September 18). Increased blood flow in Broca's area during auditory hallucinations in schizophrenia. *Lancet, 342,* 703–706.

McGuire, W. J. (1985). Attitudes and attitude change. In G. Lindzey & E. Aronson (Eds.), *Handbook of social psychology* (Vol. 2, 3rd ed.). New York: Random House.

McHugh, P. R. (1993, September). Multiple personality disorder. *Harvard Medical School Letter,* pp. 4–6.

McLaughlin, S., & Margolskee, R. F. (1994, November–December). The sense of taste. *American Scientist, 82,* 538–545.

McNeal, E. T., & Cimbolic, P. (1986). Antidepressants and biochemical theories of depression. *Psychological Bulletin, 99,* 361–374.

McWhirter, D. P., Sanders, S., & Reinisch, J. M. (1990). *Homosexuality, heterosexuality: Concepts of sexual orientation.* New York: Oxford University Press.

Mednick, A. (1993). World's women familiar with a day's double shift. *APA Monitor,* p. 32.

Mehler, J., & Dupoux, E. (1994). *What infants know: The new cognitive science of early development.* Cambridge, MA: Blackwell.

Melges, F. T., & Bowlby, J. (1969). Types of hopelessness in psychopathological process. *Archives of General Psychiatry, 70,* 690–699.

Melton, G. B., & Garrison, E. G. (1987). Fear, prejudice, and neglect: Discrimination against mentally disabled persons. *American Psychologist, 42,* 1007–1026.

Meltzer, H. Y. (1993, August). Clozapine: A major advance in the treatment of schizophrenia. *Harvard Mental Health Letter, 10,* 4–6.

Melzack, R., & Wall, P. D. (1965). Pain mechanisms: A new theory. *Science, 150,* 971–979.

Mendolia, M., & Kleck, R. E. (1993). Effects of talking about a stressful event on arousal: Does what we talk about make a difference? *Journal of Personality and Social Psychology, 64,* 283–292.

Mendoza, R., & Miller, B. L. (1992, July). Neuropsychiatric disorders associated with cocaine use. *Hospital and Community Psychiatry, 43,* 677–680.

Mercer, R. T., Nichols, E. G., & Doyle, G. C. (1989). *Transitions in a woman's life: Major life events in developmental context.* New York: Springer.

Merikle, P. M. (1992). Perception without awareness: Critical issues. *American Psychologist, 47,* 792–795.

Mesquita, B., & Frijda, N. H. (1992). Cultural variations in emotions: A review. *Psychological Bulletin, 112,* 179–204.

Messer, S. B., Warren, C. S. (1995). *Models of brief psychodynamic therapy.* New York: Guilford Press.

Metcalfe, J. (1986). Premonitions of insight predict impending error. *Journal of Experimental Psychology: Learning, Memory, and Cognition, 12,* 623–634.

Metee, D. R., & Aronson, E. (1974). Affective reactions to appraisal from others. In T. L. Huston (Ed.), *Foundations of interpersonal attraction* (pp. 235–283). New York: Academic Press.

Meyer, J. P., & Pepper, S. (1977). Need compatibility and marital adjustment in young married couples. *Journal of Personality and Social Psychology, 35,* 331–342.

Meyer, R. G., & Macciocchi, S. N. (1989). The context of self-disclosure, the polygraph, and deception. *Forensic Reports, 2,* 295–303.

Meyer, R. G., & Osborne, Y. V. H. (1987). *Case studies in abnormal behavior* (2nd ed.). Boston: Allyn & Bacon.

Michael, R. T., Gagnon, J. H., Laumann, E. O., & Kolata, G. (1994). *Sex in America: A definitive survey.* Boston: Little, Brown.

Middlebrooks, J. C., Clock, A. E., Xu, L., & Green, D. M. (1994, May 6). A panoramic code for sound location by cortical neurons. *Science, 264,* 842–844.

Middlebrooks, J. C., & Green, D. M. (1991). Sound localization by human listeners. *Annual Review of Psychology, 42,* 135–159.

Mikhail, A. (1981). Stress: A psychophysiological conception. *Journal of Human Stress, 7,* 9–15.

Milewski, A. E. (1976). Infants' discrimination of internal and external pattern elements. *Journal of Experimental Child Psychology, 22,* 229–246.

Milgram, S. (1974). *Obedience to authority.* New York: Harper & Row.

Miller, A. G. (1986). *The obedience experiments: A case study of controversy in social science.* New York: Praeger.

Miller, G. A. (1956). The magical number seven, plus or minus two: Some limits on our capacity for processing information. *Psychology Review, 63,* 81–97.

Miller, J. G. (1984). Culture and the development of everyday social explanation. *Journal of Personality and Social Psychology, 46,* 961–978.

Miller, J. G., & Bersoff, D. M. (1992). Culture and moral judgment: How are conflicts between justice and interpersonal responsibilities resolved? *Journal of Personality and Social Psychology, 62,* 541–554.

Miller, J. G., Bersoff, D. M., & Harwood, R. L. (1990). Perceptions of social responsibility in India and in the United States: Moral imperatives or personal decisions? *Journal of Personality and Social Psychology, 58,* 33–47.

Miller, M. W. (1986, September 19). Effects of alcohol on the generation and migration of cerebral cortical neurons. *Science, 2133,* 1308–1310.

Miller, M. W. (1994, December 1). Brain surgery is back in a limited way to treat mental ills. *Wall Street Journal,* p. 1.

Miller, N. E. (1985a, February). Rx: Biofeedback. *Psychology Today,* pp. 54–59.

Miller, N. E. (1985b). The value of behavioral research on animals. *American Psychologist, 40,* 423–440.

Miller, S. M., Brody, D. S., & Summerton, J. (1988). Styles of coping with threat: Implications for health. *Journal of Personality and Social Psychology, 54,* 142–148.

Miller-Jones, D. (1989). Culture and testing. *American Psychologist, 44,* 360–366.

Millon, T., & Davis, R. D. (1995). *Disorders of personality: DSM-IV and beyond* (2nd ed.). New York: Wiley.

Milloy, C. (1986, June 22). Crack user's highs, lows. *Washington Post,* p. A-1.

Milner, A. D., & Rugg, M. D. (Eds.). (1992). *The neuropsychology of consciousness.* San Diego, CA: Academic Press.

Milner, B. (1966). Amnesia following operation on temporal lobes. In C. W. M. Whitty & P. Zangwill (Eds.), *Amnesia.* London: Butterworth.

Mineka, S., & Henderson, R. W. (1985). Controllability and predictability in acquired motivation. Annual Review of *Psychology, 36,* 495–529.

Minuchin, S. (1974). *Families and family therapy.* Cambridge, MA: Harvard University Press.

Minuchin, S., & Nichols, M. P. (1992). *Family healing.* New York: Free Press.

Miserando, M. (1991). Memory and the seven dwarfs. *Teaching of Psychology, 18,* 169–171.

Miyake, K., Chen, S., & Campos, J. J. (1985). Infant temperament, mother's mode of interaction, and attachment in Japan: An interim report. *Monographs of the Society for Research in Child Development, 50,* 276–297.

Miyashita, Y. (1995, June 23). How the brain creates imagery: Projection to primary visual cortex. *Science, 268,* 1719–1720.

Molotsky, I. (1984, November 30). Implant to aid the totally deaf is approved. *The New York Times,* pp. 1, B10.

Money, J. (1987). Sin, sickness, or status? Homosexuality, gender identity, and psychoneuroendocrinology. *American Psychologist, 42,* 384–399.

Montemayor, P. (1983). Parents and adolescents in conflict: All families some of the time and some families most of the time. *Journal of Early Adolescence, 3,* 83–103.

Moore-Ede, M. (1993). *The twenty-four hour society.* Boston: Addison-Wesley.

Morrow, J., & Wolff, R. (1991, May). Wired for a miracle. *Health,* pp. 64–84.

Moscovici, S. (1985). Social influence and conformity. In G. Lindzey & E. Aronson (Eds.), *Handbook of social psychology* (3rd ed.). New York: Random House.

Moses, L. J., & Chandler, M. J. (1992). Traveler's guide to children's theories of mind. *Psychological Inquiry, 3,* 286–301.

Motley, M. T. (1987, February). What I meant to say. *Psychology Today,* pp. 25–28.

Movshon, J. A., & Newsome, W. T. (1992). Neural foundations of visual motion perception. *Current Directions in Psychological Science, 1,* 35–39.

Mueller, E., & Lucas, T. (1975). A developmental analysis of peer interaction among toddlers. In M. Lewis & L. A. Rosenblum (Eds.), *Friendship and peer relations.* New York: Wiley-Interscience.

Murray, J. B. (1990). Nicotine as a psychoactive drug. *Journal of Psychology, 125,* 5–25.

Mussen, P. H., & Jones, M. C. (1957). Self-conceptions, motivations, and interpersonal attitudes of late- and early-maturing boys. *Child Development, 28,* 243–256.

Nahome, L., & Lawton, M. P. (1975). Similarity and propinquity in friendship formation. *Journal of Personality and Social Psychology, 32,* 205–213.

Nash, M. (1987). What, if anything, is regressed about hypnotic age regression? A review of the empirical literature. *Psychological Bulletin, 102,* 42–52.

Nathans, J., Davenport, C. M., Maumenee, I. H., Lewis, R. A., Hejtmancik, J. F., Litt, M.,

Lovrien, E., Weleber, R., Bachynski, B., Zwas, F., Klingaman, R., & Fishman, G. (1989, August 25). Molecular genetics of human blue cone monochromacy. *Science, 245,* 831–838.

Nathans, J., Piantanidu, T. P., Eddy, R. L., Shows, T. B., & Hogness, D. S. (1986, April 11). Molecular genetics of inherited variation in human color vision. *Science, 232,* 203–210.

National Center for Health Statistics. (1994). *Report on obesity in the United States.* Washington, DC: National Center for Health Statistics.

National Institute of Drug Abuse. (1991). *National survey results on drug use.* Washington, DC: U.S. Department of Health and Human Services.

Navon, R., & Proia, R. L. (1989, March 17). The mutations in Ashkenazi Jews with adult G(M2) Gangliosidosis, the adult form of Tay-Sachs disease. *Science, 243,* 1471–1474.

Neely, K. (1990, October 4). Judas Priest gets off the hook. *Rolling Stone,* p. 39.

Neher, A. (1991). Maslow's theory of motivation: A critique. *Journal of Humanistic Psychology, 31,* 89–112.

Neher, E. (1992, April 24). Ion channels for communication between and within cells. *Science, 256,* 498–502.

Neisser, U. (1982). *Memory observed.* San Francisco: Freeman.

Neisser, U., & Harsch, N. (1992). Phantom flashbulbs: False recollections of hearing the news about Challenger. In E. Winograd & U. Neisser (Eds.), *Affect and accuracy in recall: Studies of "flashbulb" memories.* New York: Cambridge University Press.

Nelson, K. (1993). The psychological and social origins of autobiographical memory. *Psychological Science, 4,* 7–14.

Nelson, M. (1992, February 3). Too tough to die. *People Weekly,* pp. 30–33.

Nelson, R. J., Badura, L. L., & Goldman, B. D. (1990). Mechanisms of seasonal cycles of behavior. *Annual Review of Psychology, 41,* 81–108.

New York Times/CBS News Poll. (1994, February 20). Respondents citing each problem as the most important facing the country. *The New York Times,* p. E3.

The New York Times. (1991, August 7). Levels of caffeine. *The New York Times,* p. C11.

Newell, A. (1990). *Unified theories of cognition.* Cambridge, MA: Harvard University Press.

Newman, J. P., & Kosson, D. S. (1986). Passive avoidance learning in psychopathic and nonpsychopathic offenders. *Journal of Abnormal Psychology, 95,* 252–256.

NIAAA (National Institute on Alcohol Abuse and Alcoholism). (1990). *Alcohol and health.* Washington, DC: U.S. Government Printing Office.

Nichols, M. P., & Schwartz, R. C. (1995). *Family therapy: Concepts and methods* (3rd ed.). Boston: Longwood.

Nickerson, R. S. (1994). Teaching of thinking and problem-solving. In R. J. Sternberg (Ed.), *Thinking and problem-solving.* San Diego, CA: Academic Press.

Nigg, J. T., & Goldsmith, H. H. (1994). Genetics of personality disorders: Perspectives from personality and psychopathology research. *Psychological Bulletin, 115,* 346–380.

Nisbett, R. E. (1968). Taste, deprivation, and weight determinants of eating behavior. *Journal of Personality and Social Psychology, 10,* 107–116.

Nisbett, R. E. (1972). Hunger, obesity and the ventromedial hypothalamus. *Psychological Review, 79,* 433–453.

Nisbett, R. (1994, October 31). Blue genes. *New Republic, 211,* 15.

Nisbett, R. E., Krantz, D. H., Jepson, D., & Kunda, Z. (1993). The use of statistical heuristics in everyday reasoning. In R. E. Nisbett (Ed.), *Rules for reasoning.* Hillsdale, NJ: Erlbaum.

Noble, B. P. (1993, June 13). Staying bright-eyed in the wee hours. *The New York Times,* p. F11.

Nogrady, H., McConkey, K. M., & Perry, C. (1985). Enhancing visual memory: Trying hypnosis, trying imagination, and trying again. *Journal of Abnormal Psychology, 94,* 105–204.

Nolen-Hoeksema, S., & Girgus, J. S. (1994). The emergence of gender differences in depression during adolescence. *Psychological Bulletin, 115,* 424–443.

North, C. S., Ryall, J. M., Wetzel, R. D., & Ricci, D. A. (1993). *Multiple personalities, multiple disorders.* New York: Oxford University Press.

Novaco, R. W. (1975). *Anger control: The development and evaluation of an experimental treatment.* Lexington, MA: Lexington Books.

Novak, M. A., & Suomi, S. J. (1988). Psychological well-being of primates in captivity. *American Psychologist, 43,* 765–773.

Novy, D. M., Nelson, D. V., Francis, D. J., & Turk, D. C. (1995). Perspectives of chronic pain: An evaluation comparison of restrictive and comprehensive models. *Psychological Bulletin, 118,* 238–247.

Nowak, R. (1994, March 4). Chronobiologists out of sync over light therapy patents. *Science, 263,* 1217–1218.

Nowicki, S., & Duke, M. (1978). An examination of counseling variables within a social learning framework. *Journal of Counseling Psychology, 25,* 1–7.

NSFH (National Survey of Families and Households). (1993, August). Married fathers with preschoolers. *American Demographics,* p. 25.

Oatley, K. (1992). *Best laid schemes: The psychology of emotions.* Cambridge, MA: Cambridge University Press.

Oberle, I., Rousseau, F., Heitz, D., Kretz, C., Devys, D., Hanauer, A., Boue, J., Bertheas, M. F., & Mandel, J. L. (1991, May 24). Instability of a 550–base pair DNA segment and abnormal methylzatin in fragile X syndrome. *Science, 252,* 1097–1102.

Office of Demographic, Employment, and Educational Research. (1994). *Demographic characteristics of members by type of APA membership.* Washington, DC: American Psychological Association.

Ogbu, J. (1992). Understanding cultural diversity and learning. *Educational Researcher, 21,* 5–14.

Ogilvie, R., & Harsh, J. (1994). *Sleep onset: Normal and abnormal processes.* Washington, DC: American Psychological Association.

O'Hare, D., & Roscoe, S. (1990). *Flightdeck performance: The human factor.* Ames: Iowa State University Press.

Olds, J., Milner, P. (1954). Positive reinforcement produced by electrical stimulation of septal area and other regions of rat brain. *Journal of Comparative and Physiological Psychology, 47,* 411–427.

Olds, M. E., & Fobes, J. L. (1981). The central basis of motivation: Intracranial self-stimulation studies. *Annual Review of Psychology, 32,* 123–129.

Olshansky, S. J., Carnes, B. A., & Cassel, C. (1990, November 2). In search of Methuselah: Estimating the upper limits to human longevity. *Science, 250,* 634–639.

Omdahl, B. (1995). *Cognitive appraisal, emotion, and empathy.* Hillsdale, NJ: Erlbaum.

Opler, L. A., Kay, S. R., Rosado, V., & Lindenmayer, J. P. (1984). Positive and negative syndromes in chronic schizophrenic in patients. *Journal of Nervous and Mental Disease, 172,* 317–325.

Orlans, F. B. (Ed.). (1993). *In the name of science: Issues in responsible animal experimentation.* New York: Oxford University Press.

Orne, M. T., Dinges, D. F., & Orne, E. C. (1984). On the differential diagnosis of multiple personality in the forensic context. *International Journal of Clinical and Experimental Hypnosis, 32,* 118–169.

Orne, M. T., & Holland, C. C. (1968). On the ecological validity of laboratory deceptions. *International Journal of Psychiatry, 6,* 282–293.

Ornstein, P. A., & Naus, M. J. (1988). Effects of the knowledge base on children's memory strategies. In H. W. Reese (Ed.), *Advances in child development and behavior* (Vol. 19). New York: Academic Press.

Ornstein, R. E. (1977). *The psychology of consciousness* (2nd ed.). New York: Harcourt Brace Jovanovich.

Ortony, A., & Turner, T. J. (1990). What's basic about basic emotions? *Psychological Review, 97,* 315–331.

Orwin, R. G., & Condray, D. S. (1984). Smith and Glass' psychotherapy conclusions need further probing: On Landman and Dawes' re-analysis. *American Psychologist, 39,* 71–72.

Owens, J., Bower, G. H., & Black, J. (1979). The "soap opera" effect in story recall. *Memory & Cognition, 7,* 185–191.

Ozeki, M. (1993, February 28). On turning 13: Reports from the front lines. *The New York Times,* sec. 4, p. 2.

Paivio, A. (1971). *Imagery and verbal processes.* New York: Holt, Rinehart & Winston.

Paivio, A. (1975). Perceptual comparison through the mind's eye. *Memory & Cognition, 3,* 635–647.

Palladino, J. J., & Carducci, B. J. (1984). Students' knowledge of sleep and dreams. *Teaching of Psychology, 11,* 189–191.

Palmer, S. F. (1975). The effects of contextual scenes on the identification of objects. *Memory & Cognition, 3,* 519–526.

Papalia, D., & Olds, S. (1989). *Human development* (4th ed.). New York: McGraw-Hill.

Papini, M. R., & Bitterman, M. E. (1990). The role of contingency in classical conditioning. *Psychological Review, 97,* 396–403.

Parke, R. D. (1981). *Fathers.* Cambridge, MA: Harvard University Press.

Parlee, M. B. (1979, October). The friendship bond. *Psychology Today,* pp. 43–45.

Participant. (1994). *Young lives in the balance.* Washington, DC: Teachers Insurance and Annuity Association.

Pascual-Leone, Alvaro, et al. (in press). Bethesda, MD: National Institutes of Neurological Disorders and Stroke, U.S. Department of Health and Human Services.

Paterson, R. J., & Neufeld, R. W. J. (1987). Clear danger: Situational determinants of the appraisal of threat. *Psychological Bulletin, 101,* 404–416.

Patrick, C. J., & Iacono, W. G. (1991). Validity of the control question polygraph test: The problem of sampling bias. *Journal of Applied Psychology, 76,* 229–238.

Patterson, C. J. (1994). Lesbian and gay families. *Current Directions in Psychological Science, 3,* 62–64.

Patterson, C. J. (1995). Families of the baby boom: Parents' division of labor and children's adjustment. Special Issue: Sexual orientation and human development. *Developmental Psychology, 31,* 115–123.

Pavlides, C., & Winson, J. (1989). Influences of hippocampal place cell firing in the awake state on the activity of these cells during subsequent sleep episodes. *Journal of Neuroscience, 9,* 2907–2918.

Pavlov, I. P. (1927). *Conditioned reflexes.* London: Oxford University Press.

Payne, D. G. (1986). Hyperamnesia for pictures and words: Testing the recall level hypothesis. *Journal of Experimental Psychology: Learning, Memory, and Cognition, 12,* 16–29.

Peele, S., & Brodsky, A. (1991). *The truth about addiction and recovery.* New York: Simon & Schuster.

Penfield, W., & Rasmussen, T. (1950). *The cerebral cortex of man.* New York: Macmillan.

Pennebaker, J., & Roberts, T. A. (1992). Toward a his and hers theory of emotion: Gender differences in visceral perception. *Journal of Social and Clinical Psychology, 11,* 199–212.

Pennebaker, J. W. (1990). *Opening up: The healing power of confiding in others.* New York: Morrow.

Pennebaker, J. W., & Harber, K. D. (1993). A social stage model of collective coping: The Loma Prieta earthquake and the Persian Gulf War. *Journal of Social Issues, 49,* 125–145.

Peper, R. J., & Mayer, R. E. (1978). Note taking as a generative activity. *Journal of Educational Psychology, 70,* 514–522.

Perdue, C. W., Dovidio, J. F., Gurtman, H. B., & Tyler, R. B. (1990). Us and them: Social categorization and the process of intergroup bias. *Journal of Personality and Social Psychology, 59,* 475–486.

Pereira-Smith, O., Smith, J., et al. (1988, August). Paper presented at the annual meeting of the International Genetics Congress, Toronto.

Perkins, D. N. (1983). Why the human perceiver is a bad machine. In J. Beck, B. Hope, & A. Rosenfeld (Eds.), *Human and machine vision.* New York: Academic Press.

Perlmutter, M. (1994). Cognitive skills within the context of adult development and old age. In C. B. Fisher & R. M. Lerner (Eds.), *Applied developmental psychology.* New York: McGraw-Hill.

Perlmutter, M., & Mitchell, D. B. (1986). The appearance and disappearance of age differences in adult memory. In I. M. Craik & S. Trehub (Eds.), *Aging and cognitive processes.* New York: Plenum Press.

Perls, F. S. (1967). Group vs. individual therapy. *ETC: A Review of General Semantics, 34,* 306–312.

Perls, F. S. (1970). *Gestalt therapy now: Therapy, techniques, applications.* Palo Alto, CA: Science and Behavior Books.

Persons, J. B. (1991). Psychotherapy outcome studies do not accurately represent current models of psychotherapy: A proposed remedy. *American Psychologist, 46,* 99–106.

Petersen, C., Maier, S. F., & Seligman, M. E. P. (1993). *Learned helplessness.* New York: Oxford University Press.

Petersen, S. E., & Fiez, J. A. (1993). The processing of single words studied with positron emission tomography. *Annual Review of Neuroscience, 16,* 509–530.

Peterson, A. (1985). Pubertal development as a cause of disturbance: Myths, realities, and unanswered questions. *Genetic, Social and General Psychology Monographs, 111,* 205–232.

Peterson, A. C. (1988, September). Those gangly years. *Psychology Today*, pp. 28–34.

Peterson, B. E., & Stewart, A. J. (1993). Generativity and social motives in young adults. *Journal of Personality and Social Psychology, 65*, 186–198.

Peterson, C., & Raps, C. S. (1984). Helplessness and hospitalization: More remarks. *Journal of Personality and Social Psychology, 46*, 82–83.

Peterson, D. R. (1991). Connection and disconnection of research and practice in the education of professional psychologists. *American Psychologist, 46*, 422–429.

Peterson, K. C., Prout, M. F., & Schwarz, R. A. (1991). *Posttraumatic stress disorder: A clinician's guide*. New York: Plenum Press.

Peterson, L. R., & Peterson, M. J. (1959). Short-term retention of individual items. *Journal of Experimental Psychology, 58*, 193–198.

Petri, H. L. (1991). *Motivation: Theory, research, and applications* (3rd ed.). Belmont, CA: Wadsworth.

Pettito, L. A., & Marentette, P. F. (1991, March 22). Babbling in the manual mode: Evidence for the ontogeny of language. *Science, 251*, 1493–1496.

Petty, R. E., & Cacioppo, J. T. (1984). The effects of involvement on responses to argument quantity and quality: Central and peripheral routes to persuasion. *Journal of Personality and Social Psychology, 46*, 69–81.

Petty, R. E., & Cacioppo, J. T. (1986). The elaboration likelihood model of persuasion. In L. Berkowitz (Ed.), *Advances in experimental social psychology* (Vol. 10). New York: Academic Press.

Phares, V. (1992). Where's poppa? The relative lack of attention to the role of fathers in child and adolescent psychopathology. *American Psychologist, 47*, 656–664.

Phillips, R. D., Wagner, S. H., Fells, C. A., & Lynch, M. (1990). Do infants recognize emotion in facial expressions? Categorical and "metaphorical" evidence. *Infant Behavior and Development, 13*, 71–84.

Piaget, J. (1970). Piaget's theory. In P. H. Mussen (Ed.), *Carmichael's manual of child psychology* (Vol. I, 3rd ed.). New York: Wiley.

Piaget, J., & Inhelder, B. (1958). *The growth of logical thinking from childhood to adolescence* (A. Parsons & S. Seagrin, Trans.). New York: Basic Books.

Pickar, D. (1988). Perspectives on a time-dependent model of neuroleptic action. *Schizophrenia Bulletin, 14*, 255–265.

Piliavin, J. A., & Piliavin, I. M. (1972). Effect of blood on reactions to a victim. *Journal of Personality and Social Psychology, 23*, 353–362.

Pillemer, D. B. (1990). Clarifying the flashbulb memory concept: Comment on McCloskey, Wible, and Cohen (1988). *Journal of Experimental Psychology: General, 119*, 92–96.

Pines, M. (1981, April 16). Recession is linked to far-reaching psychological harm. *The New York Times*, p. C1.

Pinker, S. (1990). Language acquisition. In D. N. Osherson & H. Lasnik (Eds.), *Language*. Cambridge, MA: MIT Press.

Pinker, S. (1994). *The language instinct*. New York: William Morrow.

Plomin, R. (1989). Environment and genes: Determinants of behavior. *American Psychologist, 44*, 105–111.

Plomin, R. (1990, April 13). The role of inheritance in behavior. *Science, 248*, 183–188.

Plomin, R., & McClearn, G. E. (Eds.). (1993). *Nature, nurture, and psychology*. Washington, DC: American Psychological Association.

Plomin, R., & Neiderhiser, J. M. (1992). Genetics and experience. *Current Directions in Psychological Science, 1*, 160–163.

Plous, S. (1991). An attitude survey of animal rights activists. *Psychological Science, 2*, 194–196.

Plutchik, R. (1980). *Emotion, a psychorevolutionary synthesis*. New York: Harper & Row.

Plutchik, R. (1984). Emotion. In K. Scherer & P. Ekman (Eds.), *Approaches to emotion*. Hillsdale, NJ: Erlbaum.

Polivy, J., & Herman, C. P. (1985). Dieting and binging: A causal analysis. *American Psychologist, 40*, 193–201.

Pollock, D. A., Rhodes, P., Boyle, C. A., Decoufle, P., & McGee, D. L. (1990). Estimating the number of suicides among Vietnam veterans. *American Journal of Psychiatry, 147*, 772–776.

Ponomarev, D. (1993, February 28). On turning 13: Reports from the front lines. *The New York Times*, sec. 4, p. 2.

Porter, R. H., Cernich, J. M., & McLaughlin, F. J. (1983). Maternal recognition of neonates through olfactory cues. *Physiology and Behavior, 30*, 151–154.

Posner, M. I. (1993). Seeing the mind. *Science, 262*, 673–674.

Potter, M. C. (1990). Remembering. In D. N. Osherson & E. E. Smith (Eds.), *Thinking*. Cambridge, MA: MIT Press.

Power, T. G., & Parke, R. D. (1982). Play as a context for early learning: Lab and home analyses. In L. M. Laosa & I. E. Sigal (Eds.), *The family as a learning environment*. New York: Plenum Press.

Powers, D. E. (1993). Coaching for the SAT: A summary of the summaries and an update. *Educational Measurement Issues and Practice, 12*, 24–30, 39.

Pressley, M. (1987). Are keyword method effects limited to slow presentation rates? An empirically based reply to Hall and Fuson (1986). *Journal of Educational Psychology, 79*, 333–335.

Pressley, H., & Levin, J. R. (1983). *Cognitive strategy research: Psychological foundations*. New York: Springer-Verlag.

Price, R. (1992). Psychosocial impact of job loss on individuals and families. *Current Directions in Psychological Science, 1*, 9–14.

Prince, R. J., & Guastello, S. J. (1990). The Barnum effect in a computerized Rorschach interpretation system. *Journal of Personality, 124*, 217–222.

Psychinfo. (1991, January). The PsychINFO Basic Workshop. *Psychological Bulletin, 107*, 210–214.

Purdy, M. (1994, January 30). Budding scientist's success breaks the mold. *The New York Times*, pp. A1, A36.

Putnam, F. W., Guroff, J. J., Silberman, E. K., Barban, L., et al. (1986). The clinical phenomenology of multiple personality disorder: Review of 100 recent cases. *Journal of Clinical Psychiatry, 47*, 285–293.

Rachman, S., & Hodgson, R. (1980). *Obsessions and compulsions*. Englewood Cliffs, NJ: Prentice-Hall.

Ragozin, A. S. (1980). Attachment behavior of day care children: Naturalistic and laboratory observations. *Child Development, 51*, 409–415.

Raichle, M. E. (1994). Images of the mind: Studies with modern imaging techniques. *Annual Review of Psychology, 45*, 333–356.

Rajecki, D. W. (1989). *Attitudes* (2nd ed.). Sunderland, MA: Sinauer.

Ramachandran, V. S. (1992). Filling in gaps in perception: Part 1. *Current Directions in Psychological Science, 1*, 199–205.

542

Raphael, B. (1976). *The thinking computer.* San Francisco: Freeman.

Rasmussen, J. (1981). Models of mental strategies in process control. In J. Rasmussen & W. Rouse (Eds.), *Human detection and diagnosis of system failures.* New York: Plenum Press.

Ratner, H. H., Schell, D. A., Crimmins, A., Mittelman, D., et al. (1987). Changes in adults' prose recall: Aging or cognitive demands? *Developmental Psychology, 23,* 521–525.

Ree, M. J., & Earles, J. A. (1992). Intelligence is the best predictor of job performance. *Current Directions in Psychological Research, 1,* 86–89.

Reed, S. K. (1988). *Cognition: Theories and applications* (2nd ed.). Monterey, CA: Brooks/Cole.

Reeves, R. A., Baker, G. A., Boyd, J. G., & Cialdini, R. B. (1991). The door-in-the-face technique: Reciprocal concessions vs. self-presentational explanations. *Journal of Social Behavior and Personality, 6,* 545–558.

Register, A. C., Beckham, J. C., May, J. G., & Gustafson, D. F. (1991). Stress inoculation bibliotherapy in the treatment of test anxiety. *Journal of Counseling Psychology, 38,* 115–119.

Reich, P. A. (1986). *Language development.* Englewood Cliffs, NJ: Prentice-Hall.

Reis, S. M. (1989). Reflections on policy affecting the education of gifted and talented students. *American Psychologist, 44,* 399–408.

Reisenzein, R. (1983). The Schachter theory of emotion: Two decades later. *Psychological Bulletin, 94,* 239–264.

Reiss, B. F. (1980). Psychological tests in homosexuality. In J. Marmor (Ed.), *Homosexual behavior* (pp. 296–311). New York: Basic Books.

Reitman, J. S. (1965). *Cognition and thought.* New York: Wiley.

Rescorla, R. A. (1988). Pavlovian conditioning: It's not what you think it is. *American Psychologist, 43,* 151–160.

Resnick, S. M. (1992). Positron emission tomography in psychiatric illness. *Current Directions in Psychological Science, 1,* 92–98.

Reuman, D. A., Alwin, D. F., & Veroff, J. (1984). Assessing the validity of the achievement motive in the presence of random measurement error. *Journal of Personality and Social Psychology, 47,* 1347–1362.

Reynolds, B. A., & Weiss, S. (1992, March 27). Generations of neurons and astrocytes from isolated cells of the adult mammalian central nervous system. *Science, 255,* 1707–1710.

Reynolds, C. F., III, & Kupfer, D. J. (1994). Sleep disorders. In J. M. Oldham & M. B. Riba. (Eds.), *Review of Psychiatry, 13.* Washington, DC: American Psychiatric Press.

Reynolds, R. I., & Takooshian, H. (1988, January). Where were you August 8, 1985? *Bulletin of the Psychonomic Society, 26,* 23–25.

Rheingold, H. L. (1994). *The psychologist's guide to an academic career.* Washington, DC: American Psychological Association.

Rhodes, N., & Wood, W. (1992). Self-esteem and intelligence affect influenceability: The mediating role of message reception. *Psychological Bulletin, 111,* 156–171.

Rhue, J. W., Lynn, S. J., & Kirsch, I. (Eds.). (1993). *Handbook of clinical hypnosis.* Washington, DC: American Psychological Association.

Ricciuti, H. N. (1993). Nutrition and mental development. *Current Directions in Psychological Science, 2,* 43–46.

Rice, A. (1984, May). Imagination to go. *Psychology Today,* pp. 48–52.

Rice, M. L. (1989). Children's language acquisition. *American Psychologist, 44,* 149–156.

Richards, M., Boxer, A., Petersen, A., & Albrecht, R. (1990). Relation of weight to body image in pubertal girls and boys from two communities. *Developmental Psychology, 26,* 313–321.

Richards, R., Kinney, D. K., Benet, M., & Merzel, A. P. C. (1988). Assessing everyday creativity: Characteristics of the lifetime creativity scales and validation with three large samples. *Journal of Personality and Social Psychology, 54,* 476–485.

Richmond, B. J., Optican, L. M., Podell, M., & Spitzer, H. (1987). Temporal encoding of two-dimensional patterns by single units in primate inferior temporal cortex. 1. Response characteristics. *Journal of Neurophysiology, 57,* 132–146.

Riegel, K. F., & Riegel, R. M. (1972). Development, drop, and death. *Developmental Psychology, 6,* 306–319.

Rips, L. J. (1990). Reasoning. *Annual Review of Psycholoy, 41,* 321–353.

Rips, L. J. (1994). Deductive reasoning. In R. J. Sternberg (Ed.), *Thinking and problem-solving.* San Diego, CA: Academic Press.

Ritzler, B., & Rosenbaum, G. (1974). Proprioception in schizophrenics and normals: Effects of stimulus intensity and interstimulus interval. *Journal of Abnormal Psychology, 83,* 106–111.

Rizley, R. C., & Rescorla, R. A. (1972). Associations in higher order conditioning and sensory preconditioning. *Journal of Comparative and Physiological Psychology, 81,* 1–11.

Robbins, T. W. (1988). Arresting memory decline. *Nature, 336,* 207–208.

Robbins, W. J. (1929). *Growth.* New Haven, CT: Yale University Press.

Roberts, A. H., Kewman, D. G., Mercier, L., & Hovell, M. (1993). The power of nonspecific effects in healing: Implications for psychosocial and biological treatments. *Clinical Psychology Review, 13,* 375–391.

Roberts, L. (1988, January 1). Zeroing in on the sex switch. *Science, 239,* 21–23.

Roberts, S. B., Savage, J., Coward, W. A., Chew, B., & Lucas, A. (1988, February 25). Energy expenditure and intake in infants born to lean and overweight mothers. *New England Journal of Medicine, 318,* 461–466.

Robinson, D. N. (1995). *An intellectual history of psychology* (3rd ed.). Madison, WI: University of Wisconsin Press.

Rodin, J. (1981). Current status of the internal-external hypothesis of obesity: What went wrong? *American Psychologist, 34,* 361–372.

Rodin, J. (1985). Insulin levels, hunger, and food intake: An example of feedback loops in body-weight regulation. *Health Psychology, 4,* 1–18.

Rodin, J. (1986, September 19). Aging and health: Effects of the sense of control. *Science, 233,* 1271–1276.

Roediger, III., H. L. (1990). Implicit memory: Retention without remembering. *American Psychologist, 45,* 1043–1056.

Roediger, H. L, Weldon, M. S., & Challis, B. H. (1989). Explaining dissociations between implicit and explicit measures of retention: A processing account. In H. L. Roediger & F. I. M. Craik (Eds.), *Varieties of memory and consciousness: Essays in honour of Endel Tulving.* Hillsdale, NJ: Erlbaum.

Rogers, C. R. (1951). *Client-centered therapy.* Boston: Houghton-Mifflin.

Rogers, C. R. (1971). A theory of personality. In S. Maddi (Ed.), *Per-*

spectives on personality. Boston: Little, Brown.

Rogers, C. R. (1980). *A way of being.* Boston: Houghton Mifflin.

Rogers, M. (1988, February 15). The return of 3-D movies—on TV. *Newsweek*, pp. 60–62.

Rokeach, M. (1971). Long-range experimental modification of values, attitudes, and behavior. *American Psychologist, 26,* 453–459.

Rorschach, H. (1924). *Psychodiagnosis: A diagnostic test based on perception.* New York: Grune and Stratton.

Rosch, E. (1974). Linguistic relativity. In A. Silverstein (Ed.), *Human communication: Theoretical explorations* (pp. 95–121). New York: Halstead Press.

Rosch, E., & Mervis, C. B. (1975). Family resemblances: Studies in the internal structure of categories. *Cognitive Psychology, 7,* 573–605.

Rose, R. J., Koskenvuo, M., Kaprio, J., Sarna, S., & Langinvainio, H. (1988). Shared genes, shared experiences, and similarity of personality: Data from 14,288 adult Finnish co-twins. *Journal of Personality and Social Psychology, 54,* 161–171.

Rosenhan, D. L. (1973). On being sane in insane places. *Science, 179,* 250–258.

Rosenthal, A. M. (1993, July 27). The torture continues. *The New York Times,* p. A13.

Rosenthal, E. (1991, April, 23). Pulses of light give astronauts new rhythms. *The New York Times,* pp. C1, C8.

Rosenthal, N. E. (1995, March). Light and biological rhythms in psychiatry. *The Harvard Mental Health Letter,* pp. 5–6.

Rosenthal, R. (1994). Science and ethics in conducting, analyzing, and reporting psychological research. *Psychological Science, 5,* 127–134.

Rosenzweig, M. R. (1992). Psychological science around the world. *American Psychologist, 47,* 718–722.

Roskos-Ewoldsen, D. R., & Fazio, R. H. (1992). The accessibility of source likability as a determinant of persuasion. *Personality and Social Psychology Bulletin, 18,* 19–25.

Rosnow, R. L., Rotheram-Borus, M. J., Ceci, S. J., Blanck, P. D., & Koocher, G. P. (1993). The institutional review board as a mirror of scientific and ethical standards. *American Psychologist, 48,* 821–826.

Ross, C. A. (1989). *Multiple personality disorder: Diagnosis, clinical features and treatment.* New York: Wiley.

Ross, C. A., Miller, S. D., Reagor, P., Bjornson, L., Fraser, G. A., & Anderson, G. (1990). Structured interview data on 102 cases of multiple personality disorder from four centers. *American Journal of Psychiatry, 147,* 596–601.

Ross, L. (1977). The intuitive psychologist and his shortcomings: Distortions in the attribution process. In L. Berkowitz (Ed.), *Advances in experimental social psychology* (Vol. 10, pp. 174–221). New York: Academic Press.

Ross, L., Greene, D., & House, P. (1977). The false consensus effect: An egocentric bias in social perception and attribution processes. *Journal of Experimental Social Psychology, 13,* 279–301.

Ross, L., & Nisbett, R. E. (1991). *The person and the situation.* New York: McGraw-Hill.

Rossi, P. H., & Freeman, H. E. (1993). *Evaluation* (5th ed.). Newbury Park, CA: Sage.

Rothblum, E. D. (1990). Women and weight: Fad and fiction. *Journal of Psychology, 124,* 5–24.

Routtenberg, A., & Lindy, J. (1965). Effects of the availability of rewarding septal and hypothalamic stimulation on bar pressing for food under conditions of deprivation. *Journal of Comparative and Physiological Psychology, 60,* 158–161.

Rovee-Collier, C. (1993). The capacity for long-term memory in infancy. *Current Directions in Psychological Science, 2,* 130–135.

Rowe, J. W., & Kahn, R. L. (1987, July 10). Human aging: Usual and successful. *Science, 237,* 143–149.

Royer, J. M., & Feldman, R. S. (1984). *Educational psychology: Applications and theory.* New York: Knopf.

Rozin, P. (1977). The significance of learning mechanisms in food selection: Some biology, psychology and sociology of science. In L. M. Barker, M. R. Best, & M. Donijan (Eds.), *Learning mechanisms in food selection.* Waco, TX: Baylor University Press.

Rubenstein, C. (1982, July). Psychology's fruit flies. *Psychology Today,* pp. 83–84.

Rubin, D. C. (1985, September). The subtle deceiver: Recalling our past. *Psychology Today,* pp. 39–46.

Rubin, D. C. (1995a). *Memory in oral traditions.* New York: Oxford University Press.

Rubin, D. C. (Ed.). (1995b). *Remembering our past: Studies in autobiographical memory.* New York: Cambridge University Press.

Rubin, Z. (1970). Measurement of romantic love. *Journal of Personality and Social Psychology, 16,* 265–273.

Rubin, Z. (1973). *Liking and loving.* New York: Holt, Rinehart and Winston.

Ruble, D. N., Fleming, A. S., Hackel, L. S., & Stangor, C. (1988). Changes in the marital relationship during the transition to first-time motherhood: Effects of violated expectations concerning division of household labor. *Journal of Personality and Social Psychology, 55,* 78–87.

Runco, M. A. (1991). *Divergent thinking.* Norwood, NJ: Ablex.

Russell, J. A. (1991). Culture and the categorization of emotion. *Psychological Bulletin, 110,* 426–450.

Russo, D. C., Carr, E. G., & Lovaas, O. I. (1980). Self-injury in pediatric populations. *Comprehensive handbook of behavioral medicine* (Vol. 3: Extended applications and issues). Holliswood, NY: Spectrum.

Russo, N. (1981). In L. T. Benjamin, Jr., & K. D. Lowman (Eds.), *Activities handbook for the teaching of psychology.* Washington, DC: American Psychological Association.

Russo, N. F., & Denmark, F. L. (1987). Contribution of women to psychology. *Annual Review of Psychology, 38,* 279–298.

Russo, R., & Parkin, A. J. (1993). Age differences in implicit memory: More apparent than real. *Memory & Cognition, 21,* 73–80.

Rusting, R. L. (1992, December). Why do we age? *Scientific American,* pp. 130–141.

Rutter, M. (1982). Social-emotional consequences of day-care for preschool children. In E. F. Zigler & E. W. Gordon (Eds.), *Day-care: Scientific and social policy issues.* Boston: Auburn House.

Sack, R. L., Lewy, A. J., White, D. M., Singer, C. M., Fireman, M. J., & Vandiver, R. (1990). Morning vs. evening light treatment for winter depression: Evidence that the therapeutic effects of light are mediated by circadian phase shift. *Archives of General Psychiatry, 47,* 343–351.

Sackett, P. R. (1994). Integrity testing for personnel selection. *Current Directions in Psychological Science, 3,* 73–76.

Sackett, P. R., & Wilk, S. L. (1994). Within-group norming and other forms of score adjustment in preemployment testing. *American Psychologist, 49,* 929–954.

Sackheim, H. A. (1985, June). The case for E.C.T. *Psychology Today,* pp. 36–40.

Salovy, P., Mayer, J. D., & Rosenhan, D. L. (1991). Mood and helping: Mood as a motivator of helping and helping as a regulator of mood. In M. S. Clark (Ed.), *Prosocial behavior.* Newbury Park, CA: Sage.

Sandler, B. (1994, January 31). First denial, then a near-suicidal plea: "Mom, I need your help." *People Weekly,* pp. 56–58.

Sarason, B. R., Sarason, I. G., & Pierce G. R. (1990). *Social support: An interactional view.* New York: Wiley.

Sarason, I. G. (1976). A modeling and informational approach to delinquency. In E. Ribes-Inesta & A. Bandura (Eds.), *Analysis of delinquency and aggression.* Hillsdale, NJ: Erlbaum.

Sarason, S., Johnson, J. H., & Siegel, J. M. (1978). Assessing the impact of life changes: Development of the Life Experiences Survey. *Journal of Consulting and Clinical Psychology, 46,* 932–946.

Sarbin, T. R. (1991). Hypnosis: A fifty year perspective. *Contemporary Hypnosis, 8,* 1–15.

Sauber, S. R., L'Abate, L., Weeks, G. R., & Buchanan, W. L. (1993). *The dictionary of family psychology and family therapy* (2nd ed.). Newbury Park, CA: Sage.

Savage-Rumbaugh, E. S., Murphy, J., Sevcik, R. A., Williams, S., Brakke, K., & Rumbaugh, D. M. (1993). Language comprehension in ape and child. *Monographs of the Society for Research in Child Development, 58,* nos. 3 & 4.

Savage-Rumbaugh, S. (1987). Communication, symbolic communication, and language: Reply to Seidenberg and Petitto. *Journal of Experimental Psychology: General, 116,* 288–292.

Sawaguchi, T., & Goldman-Rakic, P. S. (1991, February 22). D1 Dopamine receptors in prefrontal cortex: Involvement in working memory. *Science, 251,* 947–950.

Saxe, L. (1994). Detection of deception: Polygraphy and integrity tests. *Current Directions in Psychological Science, 3,* 69–73.

Saxe, L., Dougherty, D., & Cross, T. (1985). The validity of polygraph testing. *American Psychologist, 40,* 355–366.

Sayette, M. A. (1993). An appraisal-disruption model of alcohol's effects on stress responses in social drinkers. *Psychological Bulletin, 114,* 459–476.

Saywitz, K., & Goodman, G. (1990). Unpublished study reported in Goleman, D. (1990, November 6). Doubts rise on children as witnesses. *The New York Times,* pp. C1, C6.

Scarr, S., & Carter-Saltzman, L. (1982). Genetics and intelligence. In R. J. Sternberg (Ed.), *Handbook of human intelligence* (pp. 792–896). Cambridge, England: Cambridge University Press.

Scarr, S., & Weinberg, R. A. (1976). I.Q. test performance of black children adopted by white families. *American Psychologist, 31,* 726–739.

Schab, F. R. (1990). Odors and the remembrance of things past. *Journal of Experimental Psychology: Learning, Memory, and Cognition, 16,* 648–655.

Schab, F. R. (1991). Odor memory: Taking stock. *Psychological Bulletin, 109,* 242–251.

Schachter, S. (1971). Some extraordinary facts about obese humans and rats. *American Psychologist, 26,* 129–144.

Schachter, S., Goldman, R., & Gordon, A. (1968). Effects of fear, food deprivation, and obesity on eating. *Journal of Personality and Social Psychology, 10,* 91–97.

Schachter, S., & Singer, J. E. (1962). Cognitive, social, and physiological determinants of emotional state. *Psychological Review, 69,* 379–399.

Schacter, D. (1993). Understanding implicit memory: A cognitive neuroscience approach. In A. F. Collins, S. E. Gathercole, M. A. Conway, & P. E. Morris (Eds.), *Theories of memory.* Hillsdale, NJ: Erlbaum.

Schacter, D. L. (1992). Understanding implicit memory. *American Psychologist, 47,* 559–569.

Schacter, D. L. (1994, May). Harvard conference on false memories. Cambridge, MA.

Schacter, D. L., Chiu, C.-Y. P., & Ochsner, K. N. (1993). Implicit memory: A selective review. *Annual Review of Neuroscience, 16,* 159–182.

Schaie, K. W. (1991). Developmental designs revisited. In S. H. Cohen & H. W. Reese (Eds.), *Life-span developmental psychology: Methodological innovations.* Hillsdale, NJ: Erlbaum.

Schaie, K. W. (1993). The Seattle longitudinal studies of adult intelligence. *Current Directions in Psychological Science, 2,* 171–175.

Schaie, K. W. (1994). The course of adult intellectual development. *American Psychologist, 49,* 304–313.

Scheff, T. J. (1985). The primacy of affect. *American Psychologist, 40,* 849–850.

Scheier, M. F., & Carver, C. S. (1992). Effects of optimism on psychological and physical well-being: Theoretical overview and empirical update. Special issue: Cognitive perspectives in health psychology. *Cognitive Therapy and Research, 16,* 201–228.

Schellhardt, T. D. (1990, September 19). It still isn't dad at home with sick kids. *Wall Street Journal,* p. B1.

Scherer, K. R. (1984). Les motions: Fonctions et composantes. [Emotions: Functions and components.] *Cahiers de psychologie cognitive, 4,* 9–39.

Schickedanz, J. A., Schickedanz, D. I., & Forsyth, P. D. (1982). *Toward understanding children.* Boston: Little, Brown.

Schindehette, S. (1990, February 5). After the verdict, solace for none. *People Weekly,* pp. 76–80.

Schindehette, S. (1994, January 17). High life. *People Weekly,* pp. 57–66.

Schmeck, Jr., H. M. (1987, December 29). New light on the chemistry of dreams. *The New York Times,* pp. C1, C2.

Schmidt, U., & Treasure, J. (1993). *Getting better bit(e) by bit(e): A survival kit for sufferers of bulimia nervosa and binge eating disorders.* Hillsdale, NJ: Erlbaum.

Schneiderman, N. (1983). Animal behavior models of coronary heart disease. In D. S. Krantz, A. Baum, & J. E. Singer (Eds.), *Handbook of psychology and health* (Vol. 3). Hillsdale, NJ: Earlbaum.

Schofield, W. (1964). *Psychotherapy: The purchase of friendship.* Englewood Cliffs, NJ: Prentice-Hall.

Schuman, E. M., & Madison, D. V. (1994, January 28). Locally distributed synaptic potentiation in the hippocampus. *Science, 263,* 532–536.

Schwartz, M. S., & Schwartz, N. M. (1993). Biofeedback: Using the body's signals. In D. Goleman & J. Gurin (Eds.), *Mind-body medicine.* Yonkers, NY: Consumer Reports Books.

Schwarz, N., Bless, H., Strack, F., Klumpp, G., et al. (1991). Ease of retrieval as information: Another look at the availability heuristic. *Journal of Personality and Social Psychology, 61,* 195–202.

Scott, J. (1994, March 11). Multiple-personality cases perplex legal system. *The New York Times*, pp. A1, B6.

Searleman, A., & Herrmann, D. (1994). *Memory from a broader perspective.* New York: McGraw-Hill.

Sears, D. O. (1986). College sophomores in the laboratory: Influences of a narrow data base on social psychology's view of human nature. *Journal of Personality and Social Psychology, 51,* 515–530.

Sears, R. R. (1977). Sources of life satisfaction of the Terman gifted men. *American Psychologist, 32,* 119–128.

Seeman, P., Guan, H. C., & Van Tol, H. H. (1993). Dopamine D4 receptors elevated in schizophrenia. *Nature, 347,* 441.

Segal, N. L. (1993). Twin, sibling, and adoption methods: Tests of evolutionary hypotheses. *American Psychologist, 48,* 943–956.

Segall, M. H., Campbell, D. T., & Herskovits, M. J. (1966). *The influence of culture on visual perception.* New York: Bobbs-Merrill.

Seidenberg, M. S., & Petitto, L. A. (1987). Communication, symbolic communication, and language: Comment on Savage-Rumbaugh, McDonald, Sevcik, Hopkins, & Rupert (1986). *Journal of Experimental Psychology: General, 116,* 279–287.

Seligman, M. E. P. (1975). *Helplessness: On depression, development, and death.* San Francisco: Freeman.

Seligman, M. E. P. (1988, October). Baby boomer blues. *Psychology Today,* p. 54.

Seligman, M. E. P. (1995). The effectiveness of psychotherapy: The *Consumer Reports* study. *American Psychologist, 50,* 965–974.

Seligmann, J. (1991, June 17). A light for poor eyes. *Newsweek,* p. 61.

Selman, R. L., Schorin, M. Z., Stone, C. R., & Phelps, E. (1983). A naturalistic study of children's social understanding. *Developmental Psychology, 19,* 82–102.

Seltzer, L. (1986). *Paradoxical strategies in psychotherapy.* New York: Wiley.

Selye, H. (1976). *The stress of life.* New York: McGraw-Hill.

Serpell, R., & Boykin, A. W. (1994). Cultural dimensions of thinking and problem-solving. In R. J. Sternberg (Ed.), *Thinking and problem-solving.* San Diego, CA: Academic Press.

Seyfarth, R. M., & Cheny, D. L. (1992, December). Meaning and mind in monkeys (vocalizations and intent). *Scientific American, 267,* 122–128.

Shapiro, T., & Emde, R. N. (Eds.). (1994). *Research in psychoanalysis: Process, development, outcome.* Madison, CT: International Universities Press.

Sharpe, L. T., Fach, C., Nordby, K., & Stockman, A. (1989, April 21). *Science, 244,* 354–356.

Sheehan, S. (1982). *Is there no place on earth for me?* Boston: Houghton Mifflin.

Shepard, R., & Metzler, J. (1971). Mental rotation of three dimensional objects. *Science, 171,* 701–703.

Shepard, R. N., & Cooper, L. A. (1992). Representation of colors in the blind, color-blind, and normally sighted. *Psychological Science, 3,* 97–104.

Shepherd, G. M. (Ed.). (1990). *The synaptic organization of the brain* (3rd ed.). New York: Oxford University Press.

Shock, N. W. (1962, January). The physiology of aging. *Scientific American,* pp. 100–110.

Short, R. V., & Balaban, E. (Eds.). (1994). *The differences between the sexes.* Cambridge, England: Cambridge University Press.

Shorter, E. (1991). *From paralysis to fatigue: A history of psychosomatic illness in the modern era.* New York: The Free Press.

Shotland, R. L. (1984, March). Paper presented at the Catherine Genovese Memorial Conference on Bad Samaritanism, Fordham University, New York

Shurkin, J. N. (1992). *Terman's kids: The groundbreaking study of how the gifted grow up.* Boston: Little, Brown.

Shweder, R. A., & Sullivan, M. A. (1993). Cultural psychology: Who needs it. *Annual Review of Psychology, 44,* 497–523.

Sieber, J. E. (1992). *Planning ethically responsible research.* Newbury Park, CA: Sage.

Siegel, J. M. (1990). Stressful life events and use of physician services among the elderly: The moderating role of pet ownership. *Journal of Personality and Social Psychology, 58,* 1081–1086.

Siegel, J. M., Nienhuis, R., Fahringer, H. M., Paul, R., Shiromani, P., Dement, W. C., Mignot, E., & Chiu, C. (1991, May 31). Neuronal activity in narcolepsy: Identification of cataplexyrelated cells in the medial medulla. *Science, 252,* 1315–1318.

Siegel, R. K. (1989). *Life in pursuit of artificial paradise.* New York: Dutton.

Siegelbaum, S. A., & Koester, J. (1991). Ion channels. In E. R. Kandel, J. H. Schwartz, & T. M. Jessell (Eds.), *Principles of neural science* (3rd ed.). New York: Elsevier.

Siegler, R. S. (1991). *Children's thinking* (2nd ed.). Englewood Cliffs, NJ: Prentice-Hall.

Siegler, R. S. (1994). Cognitive variability: A key to understanding cognitive development. *Current Directions in Psychological Science, 3,* 1–5.

Silbereisen, R., Petersen, A., Albrecht, H., & Kracke, B. (1989). Maturational timing and the development of problem behavior: Longitudinal studies in adolescence. *Journal of Early Adolescence, 9,* 247.

Silver, R. L., & Wortman, C. B. (1980). Coping with undesirable life events. In J. Barber & M. E. P. Seligman (Eds.), *Human helplessness: Theory and application.* New York: Academic Press.

Silverman, K., Evans, S. M., Strain, E. C., & Griffiths, R. R. (1992, October 15). Withdrawal syndrome after the double-blind cessation of caffeine consumption. *New England Journal of Medicine, 327,* 1109–1114.

Silverstein, B., Perdue, L., Peterson, B., & Kelly, E. (1986). The role of the mass media in promoting a thin standard of bodily attractiveness for women. *Sex Roles, 14,* 519–532.

Simmons, R., & Blyth, D. (1987). *Moving into adolescence.* New York: Aldine de Gruyter.

Simon, R. J., & Aaronson, E. E. (1988). *The insanity defense: A critical assessment of law and policy in the post-Hinckley era.* New York: Praeger.

Simonton, D. K. (1994). *Greatness: Who makes history and why.* New York: Guilford Press.

Simpson, G. E., & Yinger, J. M. (1985). *Racial and cultural minorities: An analysis of prejudice and discrimination* (5th ed.). New York: Harper & Row.

Simpson, J. A. (1987). The dissolution of romantic relationships: Factors involved in relationship stability and emotional distress. *Journal of Personality and Social Psychology, 53,* 683–692.

Sinclair, R. C., Hoffman, C., Mark, M. M., Martin, L. L., & Pickering, T. L. (1994). Construct accessibility and the misattribution of arousal: Schachter and Singer revisited. *Psychological Science, 5,* 15–19.

Singer, J. L. (1975). *The inner world of daydreaming.* New York: Harper & Row.

546

Singer, W. (1995, November 3). Development and plasticity of cortical processing architectures. *Science, 270,* 758–764.

Sinnott, J. D. (Ed.). (1989). *Everyday problem solving: Theory and applications.* New York: Praeger.

Sizemore, C. C. (1989). *A mind of my own: The woman who was known as Eve tells the story of her triumph over multiple personality disorder.* New York: Morrow.

Skinner, B. F. (1957). *Verbal behavior.* New York: Appleton-Century-Crofts.

Skinner, B. F. (1975). The steep and thorny road to a science of behavior. *American Psychologist, 30,* 42–49.

Skrypnek, B. J., & Snyder, M. (1982). On the self-perpetuating nature of stereotypes about women and men. *Journal of Experimental Social Psychology, 18,* 277–291.

Slater, A., Mattock, A., & Brown, E. (1990). Size constancy at birth: Newborn infants' responses to retinal and real size. *Journal of Experimental Child Psychology, 49,* 314–322.

Slater, E., & Meyer, A. (1959). Contributions to a pathography of the musicians. *Confinia Psychiatrica.* Reprinted in K. R. Jamison, *Touched with fire: Manic-depressive illness and the artistic temperament.* New York: The Free Press.

Slusher, M. P., & Anderson, C. A. (1987). When reality monitoring fails: The role of imagination in stereotype maintenance. *Journal of Personality and Social Psychology, 52,* 653–662.

Smetana, J. G. (1995). Parenting styles and conceptions of parental authority during adolescence. *Child Development, 66,* 299–316.

Smith, C. A., & Ellsworth, P. C. (1987). Patterns of appraisal and emotion related to taking an exam. *Journal of Personality and Social Psychology, 52,* 475–488.

Smith, E. R. (1984). Attributions and other inferences: Processing information about the self versus others. *Journal of Experimental Social Psychology, 20,* 97–115.

Smith, J. (1990). *Cognitive-behavioral relaxation training.* New York: Springer.

Smith, M. L., Glass, G. V., & Miller, T. J. (1980). *The benefits of psychotherapy.* Baltimore: Johns Hopkins.

Smith, S. M., Ward, T. B., & Finke, R. A. (Eds.). (1995). *The creative cognition approach.* Cambridge, MA: Bradford.

Smith, T. W. (1990, December). *Ethnic images.* (GSS Topical Report No. 19). Chicago: National Opinion Research Center.

Smith, T. W. (1991). Adult sexual behavior in 1989: Number of partners, frequency of intercourse, and risk of AIDS. *Family Planning Perspectives, 23,* 102–107.

Snarey, J. R. (1985). Cross-cultural universality of social-moral development: A critical review of Kohlbergian research. *Psychological Bulletin, 97,* 202–232.

Snyder, F. (1970). The phenomenology of dreaming. In L. Madow & L. H. Snow (Eds.), *The psychodynamic implications of the physiological studies on dreams.* Springfield, IL: Thomas.

Snyder, M., & Cantor, N. (1979). Testing hypotheses about other people: The use of historical knowledge. *Journal of Experimental Social Psychology, 15,* 330–343.

Solomon, C. (1993, December 21). Having nightmares? Chances are they are about your job. *Wall Street Journal,* pp. A1, A4.

Solso, R. L. (1991). *Cognitive psychology* (3rd ed.). Boston: Allyn & Bacon.

Sorrentino, C. (1990). The changing family in international perspective. *Monthly Labor Review, 113,* 41–58.

Sorrentino, R. M., Hewitt, E. C., & Raso-Knott, P. A. (1992). Risk-taking in games of chance and skill: Informational and affective influences on choice behavior. *Journal of Personality and Social Psychology, 62,* 522–533.

Southern, W. T., Jones, E. D., & Stanley, J. C. (1993). Acceleration and enrichment: The context and development of program options. In K. A. Heller, F. J. Monks, & A. H. Passow (Eds.), *International handbook of research and development of giftedness and talent.* Oxford, England: Pergamon.

Spangler, W. D. (1992). Validity of questionnaire and TAT measures of need for achievement: Two meta-analyses. *Psychological Bulletin, 112,* 140–154.

Spangler, W. D., & House, R. J. (1991). Presidential effectiveness and the leadership motive profile. *Journal of Personality and Social Psychology, 60,* 439–455.

Spanos, N. P. (1986). Hypnotic behavior: A social psychological interpretation of amnesia, analgesia, and "trance logic." *Behavioral and Brain Science, 9,* 449–467.

Spanos, N. P. (1994). Multiple identity enactments and multiple personality disorder: A sociocognitive perspective. *Psychological Bulletin, 116,* 143–165.

Spanos, N. P., & Chaves, J. F. (Eds.). (1989). *Hypnosis: The cognitive-behavioral perspective.* Buffalo, NY: Prometheus Books.

Spanos, N. P., Cross, W. P., Menary, E. P., Brett, P. J., & deGroic, M. (1987). Attitudinal and imaginal ability predictors of social cognitive skill-training enhancements in hypnotic susceptibility. *Personality and Social Psychology Bulletin, 13,* 379–398.

Spanos, N. P., Menary, E., Gabora, N. J., DuBreuil, S. C., & Dewhirst, B. (1991). Secondary identity enactments during hypnotic past-life regression: A sociocognitive perspective. *Journal of Personality and Social Psychology, 61,* 308–320.

Spearman, C. (1927). *The abilities of man.* London: Macmillan.

Spence, J. T. (1985, August). *Achievement American style: The rewards and costs of individualism* (Presidential address). 93rd Annual Convention of the American Psychological Association, Los Angeles.

Spence, M. J., & DeCasper, A. J. (1982, March). *Human fetuses perceive maternal speech.* Paper presented at the meeting of the International Conference on Infant Studies, Austin, TX.

Sperling, G. (1960). The information available in brief visual presentation. *Psych Monographs, 74,* (whole no. 498).

Sperry, R. (1982). Some effects of disconnecting the cerebral hemispheres. *Science, 217,* 1223–1226.

Spiegel, D., & Cardena, E. (1991). Disintegrated experience: The dissociative disorders revisited. *Journal of Abnormal Psychology, 100,* 366–378.

Spiegel, H. (1987). The answer is: Psychotherapy plus. Special issue: Is hypnotherapy a placebo? *British Journal of Experimental and Clinical Hypnosis, 4,* 163–164.

Spiegel, R. (1989). *Psychopharmacology: An introduction.* New York: Wiley.

Spillman, L., & Werner, J. (Eds.). (1990). *Visual perception: The neurophysiological foundations.* San Diego, CA: Academic Press.

Spitzer, R. L., Skodol, A. E., Gibbon, M., & Williams, J. B. W. (1983). *Psychopathology: A case book.* New York: McGraw-Hill.

Sprecher, S., & McKinney, K. (1993). *Sexuality.* Newbury Park, CA: Sage.

Sprecher, S., Sullivan, Q., & Hatfield, E. (1994). Mate selection preferences: Gender differences examined in a national sample. *Journal of Personality and Social Psychology, 66,* 1074–1080.

Springer, S. P., & Deutsch, G. (1989). *Left brain, right brain* (3rd ed.). New York: Freeman.

Squire, L. (1987). *Memory and brain.* New York: Oxford University Press.

Squire, L. R., Knowlton, B., & Musen, G. (1993). The structure and organization of memory. *Annual Review of Psychology, 44,* 453–495.

Sroufe, L. A., Fox, N. E., & Pancake, V. R. (1983). Attachment and dependency in a developmental perspective. *Child Development, 54,* 1615–1627.

Staats, A. W. (1975). *Social behaviorism.* Homewood, IL: Dorsey Press.

Stacy, A. W., Newcomb, M. D., & Bentler, P. M. (1991). Social psychological influences on sensation seeking from adolescence to adulthood. *Personality and Social Psychology Bulletin, 17*(6), 701–708.

Stahl, L. (1994, February 13). *Sixty minutes: Changing the odds.* Livingston, NJ: Burrelle's Information Services.

Stambak, M., & Sinclair, H. (Eds.). (1993). *Pretend play among 3-year-olds.* Hillsdale, NJ: Erlbaum.

Stanley, J. C. (1980). On educating the gifted. *Educational Researcher, 9,* 8–12.

Steele, C. M., & Josephs, R. A. (1990). Alcohol myopia: Its prized and dangerous effects. *American Psychologist, 45,* 921–933.

Steele, C. H., & Southwick, L. (1985). Alcohol and social behavior I: The psychology of drunken excess. *Journal of Personality and Social Psychology, 48,* 18–34.

Steinberg, L. (1989). *Adolescence* (2nd ed.). New York: Knopf.

Steinberg, L. (1993). *Adolescence* (3rd ed). New York: McGraw-Hill.

Steinberg, L., & Dornbusch, S. (1991). Negative correlates of part-time employment during adolescence: Replication and elaboration. *Developmental Psychology, 27,* 304.

Steiner, J. E. (1979). Human facial expressions in response to taste and smell stimulation. In H. Reese & L. P. Lipsitt (Eds.), *Advances in child development and behavior* (Vol. 13). New York: Academic Press.

Stern, P. C. (1992). What psychology knows about energy conservation. *American Psychologist, 47,* 1224–1232.

Sternbach, R. A. (Ed.). (1987). *The psychology of pain.* New York: Raven Press.

Sternberg, R. J. (1982). Reasoning, problem solving, and intelligence. In R. J. Sternberg (Ed.), *Handbook of human intelligence* (pp. 225–307). Cambridge, MA: Cambridge University Press.

Sternberg, R. J. (1985a). *Beyond IQ: A triarchic theory of human intelligence.* New York: Cambridge University Press.

Sternberg, R. J. (1985b). Implicit theories of intelligence, creativity, and wisdom. *Journal of Personality and Social Psychology, 49,* 607–627.

Sternberg, R. J. (1986). Triangular theory of love. *Psychological Review, 93,* 119–135.

Sternberg, R. J. (1987). Liking versus loving: A comparative evaluation of theories. *Psychological Bulletin, 102,* 331–345.

Sternberg, R. J. (1988). *The nature of creativity.* Cambridge, England: Cambridge University Press.

Sternberg, R. J. (1990). *Metaphors of mind: Conceptions of the nature of intelligence.* Cambridge, England: Cambridge University Press.

Sternberg, R. J. (1991). Theory-based testing of intellectual abilities: Rationale for the Sternberg Triarchic abilities test. In H. A. H. Rowe (Ed.), *Intelligence: Reconceptualization and measurement.* Hillsdale, NJ: Erlbaum.

Sternberg, R. J., Conway, B. E., Ketron, J. L., & Bernstein, M. (1981). Peoples' conceptions of intelligence. *Journal of Personality and Social Psychology, 41,* 37–55.

Sternberg, R. J., & Davidson, J. E. (Eds.). (1986). *Conceptions of giftedness.* New York: Cambridge University Press.

Sternberg, R. J., & Detterman, D. (1986). *What is intelligence?* Norwood, NJ: Ablex.

Sternberg, R. J., & Frensch, P. A. (1991). *Complex problem solving: Principles and mechanisms.* Hillsdale, NJ: Erlbaum.

Sternberg, R. J., & Lubart, T. I. (1992). Buy low and sell high: An investment approach to creativity. *Current Directions in Psychological Science, 1,* 1–5.

Sternberg, R. J., & Wagner, R. K. (Eds.). (1986). *Practical intelligence: Nature and origins of competence in the everyday world.* New York: Cambridge University Press.

Sternberg, R. J., & Wagner, R. K. (1993). The g-ocentric view of intelligence and job performance is wrong. *Current Directions in Psychological Science, 2,* 1–5.

Sternberg, R. J., Wagner, R. K., Williams, W. M., & Horvath, J. A. (1995). Testing common sense. *American Psychologist, 50,* 912–927.

Stevens, G., & Gardner, S. (1982). *The women of psychology: Pioneers and innovators* (Vol. 1). Cambridge, MA: Schenkman.

Stevenson, H. W. (1992, December). Learning from Asian schools. *Scientific American,* pp. 70–75.

Stevenson, H. W., Chen, C., & Lee, S.-Y. (1992). A comparison of the parent-child relationship in Japan and the United States. In J. L. Roopnarine & D. B. Carter (Eds.), *Parent-child socialization in diverse cultures.* Norwood, NJ: Ablex.

Stevenson, H. W., & Lee, S.-Y. (1990). Contexts of achievement: A study of American, Chinese, and Japanese children. *Monographs of the Society for Research in Child Development,* no. 221, 55, nos. 1–2.

Stevenson, H. W., Lee, S.-Y., Chen, C., Lummis, M., Stigler, J., Fan, L., & Ge, F. (1990). Mathematics achievement of children in China and the United States. *Child Development, 61,* 1053–1066.

Stevenson, H. W., & Stigler, J. W. (1992). *The learning gap: Why our schools are failing and what we can learn from Japanese and Chinese education.* New York: Summit.

Stewart, D. W., & Kamins, M. A. (1993). *Secondary research: Information sources and methods* (2nd ed.). Newbury Park, CA: Sage.

Storandt, M., et al. (1984). Psychometric differentiation of mild senile dementia of the Alzheimer type. *Archives of Neurology, 41,* 497–499.

Straube, E. R., & Oades, R. D. (1992). *Schizophrenia: Empirical research and findings.* San Diego, CA: Academic Press.

Stricker, E. M., & Zigmond, M. J. (1976). Recovery of function after damage to catecholamine-containing neurons: A neurochemical model for hypothalamic syndrome. In J. M. Sprague & A. N. Epstein (Eds.), *Progress in psychobiology and physiological psychology* (Vol. 6). New York: Academic Press.

Stricker, G., & Gold, J. R. (Eds.). (1993). *Comprehensive handbook of psychotherapy integration.* New York: Plenum Press.

Strickland, B. R. (1992). Women and depression. *Current Directions in Psychological Science, 1,* 132–135.

Stroebe, M. S., Stroebe, W., & Hansson, R. O. (Eds.). (1993).

Handbook of bereavement: Theory, research, and intervention. Cambridge, England: Cambridge University Press.

Strong, L. D. (1978). Alternative marital and family forms: Their relative attractiveness to college students and correlates of willingness to participate in nontraditional forms. *Journal of Marriage and the Family, 40,* 493–503.

Strupp, H. H., & Binder, J. L. (1992). Current developments in psychotherapy. *The Independent Practitioner, 12,* 119–124.

Subotnik, R. F., & Arnold, K. D. (1993). Longitudinal studies of giftedness: Investigating the fulfillment of promise. In K. A. Heller, F. J. Monks, & A. H. Passow (Eds.), *International handbook of research and development of giftedness and talent.* Oxford, England: Pergamon Press.

Subotnik R. F., & Arnold, K. D. (1994). *Beyond Terman: Contemporary longitudinal studies of giftedness and talent.* Norwood, NJ: Ablex.

Suddath, R. L., Christison, G. W., Torrey, E. F., Casanova, M. F., & Weinberger, D. R. (1990, March 22). Anatomical abnormalities in the brains of monozygotic twins discordant for schizophrenia. *New England Journal of Medicine, 322,* 789–794.

Sue, D. (1979). Erotic fantasies of college students during coitus. *Journal of Sex Research, 15,* 299–305.

Sue, D. W., & Sue, D. (1990). *Counseling the culturally different: Theory and practice* (2nd ed.). New York: Wiley.

Sue, D. W., Sue, D., & Sue, S. (1990). *Understanding abnormal behavior* (3rd ed.). Boston: Houghton-Mifflin.

Sulzer-Azaroff, B., & Mayer, R. (1991). *Behavior analysis and lasting change.* New York: Holt.

Super, C. M. (1980). Cognitive development: Looking across at growing up. In C. M. Super & S. Harakness (Eds.), *New directions for child development: Anthropological perspectives on child development* (pp. 59–69). San Francisco: Jossey-Bass.

Sutker, P. B., Uddo, M., Brailey, K., & Allain, Jr., A. N. (1993). Warzone trauma and stress-related symptoms in Operation Desert Shield/Storm (ODS) returnees. *Journal of Social Issues, 49,* 33–49.

Suzuki, K. (1991). Moon illusion simulated in complete darkness: Planetarium experiment reexamined.

Perception & Psychophysics, 49, 349–354.

Swets, J. A. (1992). The science of choosing the right decision threshold in high-stakes diagnostics. *American Psychologist, 47,* 522–532.

Swets, J. A., & Bjork, R. A. (1990). Enhancing human performance: An evaluation of 'new age' techniques considered by the U.S. Army. *Psychological Science, 1,* 85–96.

Swim, J. K., Aikin, K. J., Hall, W. S., & Hunter, B. A. (1995). Sexism and racism: Old-fashioned and modern prejudices. *Journal of Personality and Social Psychology, 68,* 199–214.

Szasz, T. (1982). The psychiatric will: A new mechanism for protecting persons against "psychosis" and psychiatry. *American Psychologist, 37,* 762–770.

Szasz, T. S. (1961). *The myth of mental illness.* New York: Harper & Row.

Szasz, T. S. (1994). *Cruel compassion: Psychiatric control of society's unwanted.* New York: Wiley.

Tagiuri, R. (1958). Social preference and its perception. In R. Tagiuri & L. Petrullo (Eds.), *Person, perception, and interpersonal behavior* (pp. 316–336). Stanford, CA: Stanford University Press.

Tajfel, H. (1982). *Social identity and intergroup relations.* London: Cambridge University Press.

Takami, S., Getchell, M. L., Chen, Y., Monti-Bloch, L., Berliner, D. L., Stensaas, L. J., & Getchell, T. V. (1993). Vomeronasal epithelial cells of the adult human express neuron-specific molecules. *Neuroreport, 4,* 375–378.

Talbot, J. D., Marrett, S., Evans, A. C., Meyer, E., Bushnell, M. C., & Duncan, G. H. (1991, March 15). Multiple representations of pain in human cerebral cortex. *Science, 251,* 1355–1358.

Tamura, T., Nakatani, K., & Yau, K.-W. (1989, 18 August). Light adaptation in cat retinal rods. *Science, 245,* 755–758.

Tanford, S., & Penrod, S. (1984). Social influence model: A formal integration of research on majority and minority influence processes. *Psychological Bulletin, 95,* 189–225.

Tanner, J. M. (1978). *Education and physical growth* (2nd ed.). New York: International Universities Press.

Tanner, J. M. (1990). *Foetus into man: Physical growth from conception to maturity. Revised.* Cam-

bridge, MA: Harvard University Press.

Taylor, A. (1991, April 8). Can Iacocca fix Chrysler—again? *Fortune,* pp. 50–54.

Taylor, S. E., Buunk, B. P., & Aspinwall, L. G. (1990). Social comparison, stress, and coping. *Personality and Social Psychology Bulletin, 16,* 74–89.

Tellegen, A., Lykken, D. T., Bouchard, Jr., T. J., Wilcox, K. J., Segal, N. L., & Rich, S. (1988). Personality similarity in twins reared apart and together. *Journal of Personality and Social Psychology, 54,* 1031–1039.

Terman, L. M., & Oden, M. H. (1947). *Genetic studies of genius, IV: The gifted child grows up.* Stanford, CA: Stanford University Press.

Tesser, A. (1988). Toward a self-evaluation maintenance model of social behavior. In L. Berkowitz (Ed.), *Advances in experimental social psychology* (Vol. 21). New York: Academic Press.

Tesser, A., & Shaffer, D. R. (1990). Attitudes and attitude change. *Annual Review of Psychology, 41,* 479–523.

Tessier-Lavigne, M. (1991). Phototransduction and information processing in the retina. In E. R. Kandel, J. H. Schwartz, & T. M. Jessell (Eds.), *Principles of neural science* (3rd ed.). New York: Elsevier.

Tharp, R. G. (1989). Psychocultural variables and constants: Effects on teaching and learning in schools. Special issue: Children and their development: Knowledge base, research agenda, and social policy application. *American Psychologist, 44,* 349–359.

Thienhaus, O. J., Margletta, S., & Bennett, J. A. (1990). A study of the clinical efficacy of maintenance ECT. *Journal of Clinical Psychiatry, 51,* 141–144.

Thoma, S. J., Rest, J. R., & Davison, M. L. (1991). Describing and testing a moderator of the moral judgment and action relationship. *Journal of Personality and Social Psychology, 61,* 659–669.

Thompson, J. K. (1992). *Journal of Social Behavior and Personality.*

Thorndike, E. L. (1932). *The fundamentals of learning.* New York: Teachers College.

Thorndike, R. L., Hagan, E., & Sattler, J. (1986). *Stanford-Binet* (4th ed.). Chicago: Riverside.

Tierney, J. (1988, May 15). Wired for stress. *The New York Times Magazine,* pp. 49–85.

Time. (1976, September). Svengali squad: L.A. police. *Time*, p. 76.

Time. (1982, October 4). "We're sorry: A case of mistaken identity." *Time*, p. 45.

Tolan, P., Keys, C., Chertok, F., & Jason, L. (1990). *Researching community psychology.* Washington, DC: American Psychological Association.

Tolman, E. C. (1959). Principles of purposive behavior. In S. Koch (Ed.), *Psychology: A study of a science* (Vol. 2). New York: McGraw-Hill.

Tolman, E. C., & Honzik, C. H. (1930). Introduction and removal of reward and maze performance in rats. *University of California Publications in Psychology, 4,* 257–275.

Tomlinson-Keasey, C. (1985). *Child development: Psychological, sociological, and biological factors.* Homewood, IL: Dorsey.

Tomlinson-Keasey, C., Eisert, D. C., Kahle, L. R., Hardy-Brown, K., & Keasey, B. (1979). The structure of concrete operations. *Child Development, 50,* 1153–1163.

Torgersen, S. (1983). Genetic factors in anxiety disorders. *Archives of General Psychiatry, 40,* 1085–1089.

Travis, J. (1992, September 4). Can "hair cells" unlock deafness? *Science, 257,* 1344–1345.

Trehub, S. E., Schneider, B. A., Thorpe, L. A., & Judge, P. (1991). Observational measures of auditory sensitivity in early infancy. *Developmental Psychology, 27,* 40–49.

Treisman, A. (1988). Features and objects: The Fourteenth Bartlett Memorial Lecture. *Quarterly Journal of Experimental Psychology, 40,* 201–237.

Trinder, J. (1988). Subjective insomnia without objective findings: A pseudodiagnostic classification. *Psychological Bulletin, 107,* 87–94.

Tsunoda, T. (1985). *The Japanese brain: Uniqueness and universality.* Tokyo, Japan: Taishukan Publishing.

Tulving, E. (1993). What is episodic memory? *Current Directions in Psychological Science, 2,* 67–70.

Tulving, E., & Psotka, J. (1971). Retroactive inhibition in free recall: Inaccessibility of information available in the memory store. *Journal of Experimental Psychology. 87,* 1–8.

Tulving, E., & Schacter, D. L. (1990, January 19). Priming and human memory systems. *Science, 247,* 301–306.

Tulving, E., & Thompson, D. M. (1973). Encoding specificity and retrieval processes in episodic mem-

ory. *Psychological Review, 80,* 352–373.

Turk, D. C. (1994). Perspectives on chronic pain: The role of psychological factors. *Current Directions in Psychological Science, 3,* 45–49.

Turk, D. C., & Melzack, R. (Eds.). (1992). *Handbook of pain assessment.* New York: Guilford Press.

Turk, D. C., & Nash, J. M. (1993). Chronic pain: New ways to cope. In D. Goleman & J. Guerin (Eds.), *Mind-body medicine: How to use your mind for better health.* Yonkers, NY: Consumer Reports Publications.

Turkington, C. (1992, December). Ruling opens door—a crack—to IQ-testing some black kids. *APA Monitor*, pp. 28–29.

Turkkan, J. S. (1989). Classical conditioning: The new hegemony. *Behavioral & Brain Sciences, 12,* 121–179.

Turner, J. C. (1987). *Rediscovering the social group: A self-categorization theory.* New York: Basil Blackwell.

Turner, M. E., Pratkanis, A. R., Probasco, P., & Leve, C. (1992). Threat, cohesion, and group effectiveness: Testing a social identity maintenance perspective on groupthink. *Journal of Personality and Social Psychology, 63,* 781–796.

Tversky, A., & Kahneman, D. (1974). Judgment under uncertainty: Heuristics and biases. *Science, 185,* 1124–1131.

Tversky, B. (1981). Distortions in memory for maps. *Cognitive Psychology, 13,* 407–433.

Ubell, E. (1993, January 10). Could you use more sleep? *Parade*, pp. 16–18.

Udolf, R. (1981). *Handbook of hypnosis for professionals.* New York: Van Nostrand.

Ullman, L. P., & Krasner, L. (1975). *A psychological approach to abnormal behavior* (2nd ed.). Englewood Cliffs, NJ: Prentice-Hall.

Ulrich, R. E. (1991). Animal rights, animal wrongs and the question of balance. *Psychological Science, 2,* 197–201.

Ursano, R. J., Sonnenberg, S. M., & Lazar, S. (1991). *Concise guide to psychodynamic psychotherapy.* Washington, DC: American Psychiatric Press.

U.S. Census Bureau. (1991). *Household and family characteristics, March 1990 & 1989.* (Current Population Reports). Washington, DC: U.S. Census Bureau.

U.S. Census Bureau. (1993). *The top 25 languages.* Washington, DC: U.S. Census Bureau.

U.S. Commission on Civil Rights. (1990). *Intimidation and violence: Racial and religious bigotry in America.* Washington, DC: U.S. Commission on Civil Rights Clearinghouse.

U.S. Public Health Service. (1992). *Pain control after surgery.* Washington, DC: U.S. Public Health Service.

Valenstein, E. S. (1986). *Great and desperate cures: The rise and decline of psychosurgery and other radical treatments for mental illness.* New York: Basic Books.

Vlaeyen, J. W. S., Geurts, S. M., Kole-Snijders, A. M. J., Schuerman, J. A., Groenman, N. H., & van Eek, H. (1990). What do chronic pain patients think of their pain? Towards a pain cognition questionnaire. *British Journal of Clinical Psychology, 29,* 383–394.

von Restorff, H. (1933). Uber die wirking von bereichsbildungen im Spurenfeld. In W. Kohler & H. von Restorff, *Analyse von vorgangen in Spurenfeld. I. Psychologische forschung, 18,* 299–342.

Vonnegut, M. (1975). *The Eden express.* New York: Bantam.

Vyse, S. A. (1994, February 27). Unpublished e-mail message. Connecticut College.

Wachs, T. D. (1993). The nature-nurture gap: What we have here is a failure to collaborate. In R. Plomin & G. E. McClearn (Eds.), *Nature, nurture, and psychology.* Washington, DC: American Psychological Association.

Waddington, J. L. (1990). Sight and insight: Regional cerebral metabolic activity in schizophrenia visualized by positron emission tomography, and competing neurodevelopmental perspectives. *British Journal of Psychiatry, 156,* 615–619.

Wagner, D. A. (1981). Culture and memory development. In H. C. Triandis & A. Heron (Eds.), *Handbook of cross-cultural psychology: Vol. 4. Developmental psychology.* Boston: Allyn & Bacon.

Wagner, R., & Sternberg, R. (1985). Alternate conceptions of intelligence and their implications for education. *Review of Educational Research, 54,* 179–223.

Wagner, R. K., & Sternberg, R. J. (1991). *Tacit knowledge inventory.* San Antonio, TX: The Psychological Corporation.

Waid, W. M., & Orne, M. T. (1982). The physiological detection of deception. *American Scientist, 70,* 402–409.

Waldorf, D., Reinarman, C., & Murphy, S. (1991). *Cocaine changes: The experience of using and quitting.* Philadelphia: Temple University Press.

Waldrop, M. W. (1989, September 29). NIDA aims to fight drugs with drugs. *Science, 245,* 1443–1444.

Walker, N., & Jones, P. (1983). Encoding processes and the recall of text. *Memory & Cognition, 11,* 275–282.

Wall, P. D., & Melzack, R. (Eds.). (1984). *Textbook of pain.* Edinburgh: Churchill Livingstone.

Wall, P. D., & Melzack, R. (Eds.). (1989). *Textbook of pain* (2nd ed.). New York: Churchill Livingstone.

Wallace, P. (1977). Individual discrimination of humans by odor. *Physiology and Behavior, 19,* 577–579.

Wallace, R. K., & Benson, H. (1972, February). The physiology of meditation. *Scientific American,* pp. 84–90.

Wallis, C. (1984, June 11). Unlocking pain's secrets. *Time,* pp. 58–60.

Wallis, C., & Willwerth, J. (1992, July 6). Schizophrenia: A new drug brings patients back to life. *Time,* pp. 52–57.

Walster, E., & Walster, G. W. (1978). *Love.* Reading, MA: Addison-Wesley.

Walters, J. M., & Gardner, H. (1986). The theory of multiple intelligences: Some issues and answers. In R. J. Sternberg & R. K. Wagner (Eds.), *Practical intelligence.* Cambridge, England: Cambridge University Press.

Wang, Z. W., Black, D., Andreasen, N. C., & Crowe, R. R. (1993). A linkage study of Chromosome 11q in schizophrenia. *Archives of General Psychiatry, 50,* 212–216.

Ward, W. C., Kogan, N., & Pankove, E. (1972). Incentive effects in children's creativity. *Child Development, 43,* 669–677.

Warga, C. (1987, August). Pain's gatekeeper. *Psychology Today,* pp. 51–56.

Washton, A. M. (Ed.). (1995). *Psychotherapy and substance abuse: A practitioner's handbook.* New York: Guilford Press.

Waters, H. F. (1993, July 12). Networks under the gun. *Newsweek,* pp. 64–66.

Waterson, E. J., & Murray-Lyon, I. M. (1990). Preventing alcohol-related birth damage: A review. *Social Science and Medicine, 30,* 349–364.

Watkins, L. R., & Mayer, D. J. (1982). Organization of endogenous opiate and nonopiate pain control systems. *Science, 216,* 1185–1192.

Watson, J. B. (1924). *Behaviorism.* New York: Norton.

Watson, J. B., & Rayner, R. (1920). Conditioned emotional reactions. *Journal of Experimental Psychology, 3,* 1–14.

Webb, W. B. (1992). *Sleep: The gentle tyrant* (2nd ed.). Boston, MA: Anker.

Weber, R., & Crocker, J. (1983). Cognitive processes in the revision of stereotypic beliefs. *Journal of Personality and Social Psychology, 45,* 961–977.

Wechsler, D. (1975). Intelligence defined and undefined. *American Psychologist, 30,* 135–139.

Weinberg, M. S., Williams, C. J., & Pryor, D. W. (1991, February 27). Personal communication. Indiana University, Bloomington.

Weiner, B. (1985a). "Spontaneous" causal thinking. *Psychological Bulletin, 97,* 74–84.

Weiner, B. (1985b). *Human motivation.* New York: Springer-Verlag.

Weiner, I. B. (1994). Rorschach assessment. In M. E. Maruish (Ed.), *The use of psychological tests for treatment planning and outcome assessment.* Hillsdale, NJ: Erlbaum.

Weiner, R. (1982). Another look at an old controversy. *Contemporary Psychiatry, 1,* 61–62.

Weiskrantz, L. (1989). Remembering dissociations. In H. L. Roediger & F. I. M. Craik (Eds.), *Varieties of memory and consciousness: Essays in honour of Endel Tulving.* Hillsdale, NJ: Erlbaum.

Weiss, A. S. (1991). The measurement of self-actualization: The quest for the test may be as challenging as the search for the self. *Journal of Social Behavior and Personality, 6,* 265–290.

Weiss, R. (1990, February 3). Fetal-cell recipient showing improvements. *Science News,* p. 70.

Weiss, R. (1992, April 28). Travel can be sickening; now scientists know why. *The York Times,* pp. C1, C11.

Weissman, M., & the Cross-National Collaborative Group. (1992, December 2). Changing rates of major depression. *Journal of the American Medical Association, 262,* 3098–3105.

Weissman, M. M., & Olfson, M. (1995, August 11). Depression in women: Implications for health care research. *Science, 269,* 799–801.

Weisz, J. R., Weiss, B., & Donenberg, G. R. (1992). The lab versus the clinic: Effects of child and adolescent psychotherapy. *American Psychologist, 47,* 1578–1585.

Weisz, J. R., Weiss, B., Han, S. S., Granger, D. A., & Morton, T. (1995). Effects of psychotherapy with children and adolescents revisited: A meta-analysis of treatment outcome studies. *Psychological Bulletin, 117,* 450–468.

Weitzenhoffer, A. M. (1989). *The practice of hypnotism.* New York: Wiley.

Weller, E. B., & Weller, R. A. (1991). Mood disorders in children. In G. J. Wiener (Ed.), *Textbook of child and adolescent psychiatry.* Washington, DC: American Psychiatric Press.

Wells, G. L. (1993). What do we know about eyewitness identification? *American Psychologist, 48,* 553–571.

Wells, G. L., Luus, C. A. E., & Windschitl, P. D. (1994). Maximizing the utility of eyewitness identification evidence. *Current Directions in Psychological Science, 3,* 194–197.

Wells, K. (1993, July 30). Night court: Queen is often the subject of subjects' dreams. *Wall Street Journal,* pp. A1, A5.

Wells, R. A., & Giannetti, V. J. (1990). *Handbook of the brief psychotherapies.* New York: Plenum Press.

Wertheimer, M. (1923). Untersuchungen zur Lehre von der Gestalt. II. *Psychol. Forsch., 5,* 301–350. In Beardsley and M. Wertheimer (Eds.) (1958), *Readings in perception.* New York: Van Nostrand.

Westen, D. (1990). Psychoanalytic approaches to personality. In L. A. Pervin (Ed.), *Handbook of personality: Theory and research.* New York: Guilford Press.

Wever, R. A. (1989). Light effects on human circadian rhythms: A review of recent experiments. *Journal of Biological Rhythms, 4,* 161–185.

Whimbey, A., & Lochhead, J. (1991). *Problem solving and comprehension* (5th ed.). Hillsdale, NJ: Erlbaum.

Whisman, M. A. (1993). Mediators and moderators of change in cognitive therapy of depression. *Psychological Bulletin, 114,* 248–265.

Whitbourne, S. K. (1986). *Adult development* (2nd ed.). New York: Praeger.

Whitbourne, S. K., Zuschlag, M. K., Elliot, L. B., & Waterman, A. S. (1992). Psychosocial development in adulthood: A 22-year sequential study. *Journal of Personality and Social Psychology, 63,* 260–271.

White, P. A. (1992). The anthropomorphic machine: Causal order in nature and the world view of common sense. *British Journal of Psychology, 83,* 61–96.

Whitehead, B. D. (1993, April). Dan Quayle was right. *Atlantic Monthly,* pp. 47–84.

Whorf, B. L. (1956). *Language, thought, and reality.* New York: Wiley.

Wickens, C. D. (1984). *Engineering psychology and human performance.* Columbus, OH: Merrill.

Wickens, C. D. (1991). *Engineering psychology and human performance* (2nd ed.) New York: HarperCollins.

Widiger, T. A., Frances, A. J., Pincus, H. A., & Davis, W. W. (1990). DSM-IV literature reviews: Rationale, process, and limitations. *Journal of Psychopathology and Behavioral Assessment, 12,* 189–202.

Widmeyer, W. N., & Loy, J. W. (1988). When you're hot, you're hot! Warm-cold effects in first impressions of persons and teaching effectiveness. *Journal of Educational Psychology, 80,* 118–121.

Widner, H., Tetrud, J., Rehncrona, S., Snow, B., Brundin, P., Gustavii, B., Bjorklund, A., Lindvall, O., & Langston, J. W. (1992, November 26). Bilateral fetal mesencephalic grafting in two patients with Parkinsonism induced by 1–methyl–4–phenyl–1,2,3,6–tetrahydropyridine (MPTP). *New England Journal of Medicine, 327,* 1591–1592.

Widom, C. S. (1989). Does violence beget violence? A critical examination of the literature. *Psychological Bulletin, 106,* 3–28.

Wiebe, D. J. (1991). Hardiness and stress moderation: A test of proposed mechanisms. *Journal of Personality and Social Psychology, 60,* 89–99.

Wiederhold, W. C. (Ed.). (1982). *Neurology for non-neurologists.* New York: Academic Press.

Wiggins, Jr., J. G. (1994). Would you want your child to be a psychologist? *American Psychologist, 49,* 485–492.

Wilder, D. A. (1986). Social categorization: Implications for creation and reduction of intergroup bias. In L. Berkowitz (Ed.), *Advances in experimental social psychology* (Vol. 19). San Diego, CA: Academic Press.

Wilder, D. A. (1990). Some determinants of the persuasive power of ingroups and out-groups: Organization of information and attribution of independence. *Journal of Personality and Social Psychology, 59,* 1202–1213.

Williams, S. W., & McCullers, J. C. (1983). Personal factors related to typicalness of career and success in active professional women. *Psychology of Women Quarterly, 7,* 343–357.

Willis, S. L., & Nesselroade, C. S. (1990). Long-term effects of fluid ability training in old-old age. *Developmental Psychology, 26,* 905–910.

Willis, S. L., & Schaie, K. W. (1994). In C. B. Fisher & R. M. Lerner (Eds.), *Applied developmental psychology.* New York: McGraw-Hill.

Willis, Jr., W. D. (1988). Dorsal horn neurophysiology of pain. *Annals of the New York Academy of Science, 531,* 76–89.

Wilson, F. A. W., O Scalaidhe, S. P., & Goldman-Rakic, P. S. (1993, June 25). Dissociation of object and spatial processing domains in primate prefrontal cortex. *Science, 260,* 1955–1958.

Wilson, G. T., & Agras, W. S. (1992). The future of behavior therapy. *Psychotherapy, 29,* 39–43.

Wilson, G. T., Franks, C. M., Kendall, P. C., & Foreyt, J. P. (1987). *Review of behavior therapy: Theory and practice* (Vol. 11). New York: Guilford Press.

Wilson, M. A., & McNaughton, B. L. (1994, July 29). Reactivation of hippocampal ensemble memories during sleep. *Science, 265,* 676–679.

Winch, R. F. (1958). *Mate selection: A study of complementary needs.* New York: Harper & Row.

Winerip, M. (1993, November 15). No. 2 pencil fades as graduate exam moves to computer. *The New York Times,* pp. A1, B9.

Wink, P., & Helson, R. (1993). Personality change in women and their partners. *Journal of Personality and Social Psychology, 65,* 597–605.

Winograd, E., & Neisser, E. (Eds.). (1992). *Affect and accuracy in recall: Studies in "flashbulb memories."* Cambridge, England: Cambridge University Press.

Winson, J. (1990, November). The meaning of dreams. *Scientific American,* pp. 86–96.

Winter, D. G. (1973). *The power motive.* New York: The Free Press.

Winter, D. G. (1987). Leader appeal, leader performance, and the motive profile of leaders and followers: A study of American presidents and elections. *Journal of Personality and Social Psychology, 52,* 196–202.

Winter, D. G. (1988). The power motive in women—and men. *Journal of Personality and Social Psychology, 54,* 510–519.

Witelson, S. (1989, March). *Sex differences.* Paper presented at the annual meeting of the New York Academy of Sciences, New York.

Wixted, J. T., & Ebbesen, E. B. (1991). On the form of forgetting. *Psychological Science, 2,* 409–415.

Wolman, B. B., & Stricker, G. (Eds.). (1990). *Depressive disorders: Facts, theories, and treatment methods.* New York: Wiley.

Wolozin, B. L., Pruchnicki, A., Dickson, D. W., & Davies, P. (1986). A neuronal antigen in the brains of Alzheimer patients. *Science, 232,* 648–650.

Wolpe, J. (1990). *The practice of behavior therapy.* Boston: Allyn & Bacon.

Wong, D. F., Gjedde, A., Wagner, Jr., H. M., Dannals, R. F., Links, J. M., Tune, L. E., & Pearlson, G. D. (1988, February 12). Response to Zeeberg, Gibson, and Reba. *Science, 239,* 790–791.

Wong, D. F., Wagner, Jr., H. N., Tune, L. E., Dannals, R. F., Pearlson, G. D., Links, J. M., Tamminga, C. A., Broussolle, E. P., Ravert, H. T., Wilson, A. A., Toung, T., Malat, J., Williams, J. A., O'Tuama, L. A., Snyder, S. H., Kuhar, M. J., & Gjedde, A. (1986, December 19). Positron emission tomography reveals elevated D2 Dopamine receptors in drug-naive schizophrenics. *Science, 234,* 1558–1563.

Wong, M. M., & Csikszentmihalyi, M. (1991). Affiliation motivation and daily experience: Some issues on gender differences. *Journal of Personality and Social Psychology, 60,* 154–164.

Wood, F. B., Flowers, D. L., & Naylor, C. E. (1991). Cerebral laterality in functional neuroimaging. In F. L. Kitterle (Ed.), *Cerebral laterality: Theory and research.* Hillsdale, NJ: Erlbaum.

Wood, J. M., & Bootzin, R. (1990). The prevalence of nightmares and their independence from anxiety. *Journal of Abnormal Psychology, 99,* 64–68.

Wood, W., Lundgren, S., Ouellette, J. A., Busceme, S., & Blackston, T. (1994). Minority influence: A meta-analytic review of social-influence processes. *Psychological Bulletin, 115,* 323–345.

Woolfolk, R. L., & McNulty, T. F. (1983). Relaxation treatment for insomnia: A component analysis. *Journal of Consulting and Clinical Psychology, 4,* 495–503.

World Bank. (1994). *Life expectancy at birth.* Washington, DC: World Bank.

Wozniak, R. H., & Fischer, K. W. (Eds.). (1993). *Development in context: Acting and thinking in specific environments.* Hillsdale, NJ: Erlbaum.

Wu, C., & Shaffer, D. R. (1987). Susceptibility to persuasive appeals as a function of source credibility and prior experience with the attitude object. *Journal of Personality and Social Psychology, 52,* 677–688.

Wyatt, G. E. (1994). The sociocultural relevance of sex research: Challenges for the 1990s and beyond. *American Psychologist, 49,* 748–754.

Wynn, K. (1992, August 27). Addition and subtraction by human infants. *Nature, 358,* 749–750.

Wynne, L. C., Singer, M. T., Bartko, J. J., & Toohey, M. L. (1975). *Schizophrenics and their families: Recent research on parental communication.* Psychiatric Research: The Widening Perspective. New York: International Universities Press.

Yamamato, T., Yuyama, N., & Kawamura, Y. (1981). Cortical neurons responding to tactile, thermal and taste stimulations of the rat's tongue. *Brain Research, 22,* 202–206.

Yang, G., & Masland, R. H. (1992, December 18). Direct visualization of the dendritic and receptive fields of directionally selective retinal ganglion cells. *Science, 258,* 1949–1952.

Yost, W. A. (1992). Auditory perception and sound source determination. *Current Directions in Psychological Science, 1,* 179–184.

Youkilis, H., & Bootzin, R. R. (1981). A psychophysiological perspective on the etiology and treatment of insomnia. In S. M. Haynes & L. A. Gannon (Eds.), *Psychosomatic disorders: A psychophysiological approach to etiology and treatment.* New York: Praeger.

Youngstrom, N. (1994). Adapt to diversity or risk irrelevance, field warned. *APA Monitor.*

Yu, S., Pritchard, H., Kremer, E., Lynch, M., Nancarrow, J., Baker, E., Holman, K., Mulley, J. C., Warren, S. T., Schlessinger D., Sutherland, G. R., & Richards, R. I. (1991, May 24). Fragile X genotype characterized by an unstable region of DNA. *Science, 252,* 1179–1181.

Yurek, D. M., & Sladek, Jr., J. R. (1990). Dopamine cell replacement: Parkinson's disease. *Annual Review of Neuroscience, 13.*

Zaidel, D. W. (1994). Worlds apart: Pictorial semantics in the left and right cerebral hemispheres. *Current Directions in Psychological Science, 3,* 5–8.

Zajonc, R. B. (1968). The attitudinal effects of mere exposure. *Journal of Personality and Social Psychology, 9,* 1–27.

Zajonc, R. B. (1985). Emotion and facial efference: A theory reclaimed. *Science, 228,* 15–21.

Zajonc, R. B., & McIntosh, D. N. (1992). Emotions research: Some promising questions and some questionable promises. *Psychological Science, 3,* 70–74.

Zanna, M. P., & Pack, S. J. (1974). On the self-fulfilling nature of apparent sex differences in behavior. *Journal of Experimental Social Psychology, 11,* 583–591.

Zaslow, M. J. (1991). Variation in child care quality and its implications for children. *Journal of Social Issues, 47,* 125–138.

Zautra, A. J., Reich, J. W., & Guarnaccia, C. A. (1990). Some everyday life consequences of disability and bereavament for older adults. *Journal of Personality and Social Psychology, 59,* 550–561.

Zebrowitz-McArthur, L. (1988). Person perception in cross-cultural perspective. In M. H. Bond (Ed.), *The cross-cultural challenge to social psychology.* Newbury Park, CA: Sage.

Zeki, S. (1992, September). The visual image in mind and brain. *Scientific American, 267,* 68–76.

Zigler, E., & Glick, M. (1988). Is paranoid schizophrenia really camouflaged depression? *American Psychologist, 43,* 284–290.

Zigler, E. F., & Lang, M. E. (1991). *Child care choices: Balancing the needs of children, families, and society.* New York: The Free Press.

Zigler, E., & Styfco, S. J. (1993). *Head start and beyond: A national plan for extended childhood intervention.* New Haven, CT: Yale University Press.

Zika, S., & Chamberlain, K. (1987). Relation of hassles and personality to subjective well-being. *Journal of Personality and Social Psychology, 53,* 155–162.

Zillman, D. (1978). *Hostility and aggression.* Hillsdale, NJ: Erlbaum.

Zillman, D. (1993). Mental control of angry aggression. In D. M. Wegner & J. W. Pennebaker (Eds.), *Handbook of mental control.* Englewood Cliffs, NJ: Prentice-Hall.

Zimmer, J. (1984). Courting the gods of sport: Athletes use superstition to ward off the devils of injury and bad luck. *Psychology Today,* pp. 36–39.

Zinberg, N. E. (1976). Normal psychology of the aging process, revisited (I): Social learning and self-image in aging. *Journal of Geriatric Psychiatry, 9,* 131–150.

Zito, J. M. (1993). *Psychotherapeutic drug manual* (3rd ed., rev.). New York: Wiley.

Zola-Morgan, S. M., & Squire, L. R. (1990, October 12). The primate hippocampal formation: Evidence for a time-limited role in memory storage. *Science, 250,* 288–290.

Zola-Morgan, S., & Squire, L. R. (1993). The neuroanatomy of memory. *Annual Review of Neuroscience, 16,* 547–563.

Zubin, J., & Spring, B. (1977). Vulnerability: New view of schizophrenia. *Journal of Abnormal Psychology, 86,* 103–126.

Zuckerman, M. (1978). The search for high sensation. *Psychology Today,* pp. 30–46.

Zuckerman, M. (1991). One person's stress is another person's pleasure. In C. D. Spielberger, I. G. Sarason, Z. Kulczar, & G. L. Van Heck (Eds.), *Stress and emotion: Anxiety, anger, and curiosity.* New York: Hemisphere.

ACKNOWLEDGMENTS

Figure 1-1 adapted from (1995). Profile of all APA members: 1995. 1993 Directory Survey, with new member updates for 1994 and 1995. Compiled by the American Psychological Association Research Office, Washington, DC. Copyright 1995 American Psychological Association.

Figure 2-10 adapted from Nauta, W. J. H., and Feirtag, M. The Organization of the Brain. *Scientific American.* Copyright 1979 by Scientific American, Inc. All rights reserved.

Figure 2-11 adapted from Gerschwind, N. Specializations of the Human Brain. *Scientific American.* Copyright 1979 by Scientific American, Inc. All rights reserved.

Figure 2-13 adapted from Rosenzweig, M. R., and Leiman, A. L. *Physiological Psychology,* 1982.

Figure 3-4 from Lindsey, P. H., and Norman, D. A. *Human Information Processing* (2nd ed.), 1977. Orlando, FL: Harcourt Brace Jovanovich.

Figure 3-10 adapted from Shepard, Roger C. (1990). *Mind sights.* New York: W. H. Freeman. Reprinted with permission of W. H. Freeman. Copyright © 1990.

Figure 3-11 from Goldstein, E. B. (1984). *Sensation and perception* (2nd ed.). Pacific Grove, CA: Brooks-Cole Publishing.

Figure 3-13 from Coren, S., Porac, C., & Ward, L. M. *Sensation and perception* (3rd ed.), 1989. Copyright © by Harcourt Brace Jovanovich, Inc. Used by permission of the publisher.

Figure 3-14 from Coren, S., Porac, C., & Ward, L. M. *Sensation and perception* (2nd ed.), 1984. Orlando, FL: Harcourt Brace Jovanovich.

Figure 3-17 reprinted with the permission of Gerald Duckworth & Co. from *Illusion in nature and art* by R. L. Gregory and E. H. Gombrich.

Figure 4-3 adapted from Hartmann, E., *The biology of dreaming,* 1967. Springfield, IL: Charles C Thomas.

Figure 4-4 adapted from *Secrets of sleep* by Alexander Borbely. Copyright © 1984 by Deutsch Verlag-Anstalt GmbH. English translation copyright 1986 by Basic Books, Inc., reprinted by permission of Basic Books, a division of HarperCollins Publishers.

Figure 4-5 reproduced by permission of the American Anthropological Association. From Griffith, R. M., Otoya, M., & Tago, A. (1958). The universality of typical dreams. *American Anthropologist, 60,* pt. 1. Adaptation of the twenty most common dreams.

Figure 4-6 copyright © 1991 by The New York Times Company. Reprinted by permission.

Figure 6-2 adapted from Atkinson, R. C., & Shiffrin, R. M., Human memory: A proposed system and its control processes. In K. W. Spencer & J. T. Spencer (eds.), *The psychology of learning and motivation: Advances in research and theory* (Vol. 4), 1968. Orlando, FL: Harcourt Brace Jovanovich.

Figure 7-2 adapted from Solso, R. L., *Cognitive Psychology,* 3rd ed., 1991. Used by permission from Allyn & Bacon Publishers.

Figure 7-2 from Poncin, M. (1990). *Brain fitness.* New York: Random House.

Figure 7-3 adapted from *The complete thinker,* Barry F. Anderson. Copyright © 1980. Used by permission of Prentice-Hall, a Division of Simon & Schuster, Englewood Cliffs, NJ.

Figure 8-3 adapted from Walters, E., & Gardner, H. (1986). The theory of multiple intelligences: Some issues and answers. In R. J. Sternberg, & R. K. Wagner (eds.), *Practical intelligence.* New York: Cambridge University Press.

Figure 8-5 adapted from Sternberg, R. J. (1985). *Beyond IQ: A triarchic theory of human intelligence.* New York: Cambridge University Press.

Table 9-1 adapted from Zuckerman, M. Abridged sensation-seeking questionnaire. *Psychology Today, 11,* February 1978. Reprinted with permission from Psychology Today magazine. Copyright © 1978.

Figure 9-1 adapted from *Motivation and personality* by Abraham H. Maslow. Copyright © 1954 by Harper & Row, Publishers, Inc. Copyright © 1970 by Abraham H. Maslow. Reprinted by permission of HarperCollins Publishers.

Figure 9-3 adapted from Plutchik, R., Emotion. In *Approaches to Emotion,* K. Scherer and D. Ekman (eds.). Copyright © 1984 by Lawrence Erlbaum Associates. Reprinted with permission of the publisher.

Figure 9-6 adapted from Kanner, A. D., Coyen, J. C., Schaefer, C., & Lazarus, R. (1981). Comparison of two modes of stress measurement: Daily hassles and uplifts versus major life events. *Journal of Behavioral Medicine, 4,* p. 14.

Figure 9-6 adapted from Chamberlain, K., & Zika, C. (1990). *British Journal of Psychology, 81,* 469–481. Used by permission of Kerry Chamberlain.

Figure 10-2 adapted from Frankenburg, W. K., and Dodds, J. B. (1967). The Denver Development Screening Test. *Journal of Pediatrics, 71,* 181–191.

Figure 10-7 adapted from Tanner, J. M. (1978). *Education and physical growth* (2nd ed.). New York: International Universities Press.

Table 10-3 adapted from Kohlberg, L., Stage and sequence: The cognitive development approach to socialization. In D. A. Goslin (ed.), *Handbook of socialization theory and research.* Copyright © 1969 by Houghton Mifflin Company. Reprinted with permission.

Figure 10-8 reprinted by permission of Harvard University Press from *Constancy and change in human development,* Orville G. Brim and Jerome Kagan (eds.). Cambridge, MA: Harvard University Press. Copyright 1980 by the President and Fellows of Harvard College.

Figure 10-13 adapted from Schaie, K. W. (1994). The course of adult intellectual development. *American Psychologist, 49,* 304–313. Copyright © 1994 the American Psychological Association.

Figure 11-2 adapted from Catell, Eber, and Tatsuoka. Copyright © 1970 by the Institute for Personality and Ability Testing. Reproduced by permission.

Figure 11-3 adapted from Eysenck, H. J. (1973). *Eysenck on Extroversion.* Collins Professional and Technical Books, Ltd.

Figure 12-1 from Beck, A. T., and Emery, G., *Anxiety disorders and phobias: A cognitive perspective.* Copyright © 1985 by Basic Books, Inc. New York. Used by permission of publisher.

Figure 12-6 adaptation from Gottesman, I. I. (1991). *Schizophrenia genesis.* New York: W. H. Freeman.

Figure 12-9 adapted from Kesler, R. C., et al. (1994). Lifetime and 12-month prevalence of DSM-III-R psychiatric disorders in the U.S. *Archives of General Psychiatry, 51,* 8–19.

Table 13-2 from Benson, H., *The relaxation response.* Copyright © 1975 William Morrow and Co., Inc., New York. Used by permission of publisher.

Figure 14-6 from Parlee, M. B. The friendship bond. *Psychology Today,* October 3, 1979. Reprinted with permission from Psychology Today. Copyright © 1979.

Table 14-1 adapted from Buss, D. M. et al., International preferences in selecting mates: A study of 37 cultures. *Journal of Cross-Cultural Psychology, 21,* 1990. Used by permission of Sage Publications, Inc.

Figure 14-7 adapted from Sternberg, R. J. (1986). Triangular theory of love. *Psychological Review, 93,* 119. Copyright © 1986 by the American Psychological Association. Reprinted by permission of the publisher and the author.

Table 14-2 adapted from Benjamin, L. T., Jr., Defining aggression: An exercise for the classroom. *Teaching Psychology, 12* (1), February 1985. Copyright 1985, Lawrence Erlbaum Associates, Hillsdale, NJ.

PHOTO CREDITS

Chapter 1: Chapter opening photo: David Madison; p. 2: AP/Wide World Photos; p. 6: Howard Dratch/Image Works; p. 8: Bob Daemmrich/Stock, Boston; p. 11: Bettmann; p. 14: Bettmann; p. 15: Culver; p. 20: AP/Wide World Photos; p. 22: Robert Brenner/PhotoEdit; p. 23: Rhoda Sidney/Photo Edit; p. 27: James Wilson/Woodfin Camp & Associates; p. 33: B. W. Hoffmann/Unicorn Stock Photos.

Chapter 2: Chapter opening photo: Howard Sochurek/Stock Market; p. 42: (left and right): Manfred Kage/Peter Arnold; p. 43: AP/Wide World Photos; p. 45: John Allison/Peter Arnold; p. 51: Arthur Grace/Sygma; p. 53: A. Glauberman/Photo Researchers; p. 58: A. Glauberman/Photo Researchers; p. 61: Courtesy of Antonio Damasio/Science; p. 64: David Young-Wolff/Photo Edit; p. 67: Marcus E. Raichle, M.D., Washington University School of Medicine.

Chapter 3: Chapter opening photo: Ken Lax/Photo Researchers; p. 77: Michael L. Abramson/Woodfin Camp & Associates; p. 82: Lennart Nilsson. Behold Man. Little, Brown & Co./Bonnier-Alba; p. 87: Joe Epstein/Design Conceptions; p. 91: Courtesy J. E. Hawkins; p. 95: Louis Psihoyos/Contact Press Images; p. 100: Courtesy Kaiser Porcelain, Ltd.; p. 103: Courtesy Dr. Bela Julesz, Lab of Vision Research, Rutgers University; p. 107: John G. Gross/Photo Researchers; p. 108: Espectador/Gamma Liaison; p. 108: Innervisions; p. 108: Innervisions.

Chapter 4: Chapter opening photo: Vega/Photo Researchers; p. 122: Alan J. Hobson/Photo Researchers; p. 124: William McCoy/Rainbow; p. 129: Dan McCoy/Rainbow; p. 134: John Ficara/Woodfin Camp & Associates; p. 138: AP/Wide World Photos; p. 139: D. Ogust/Image Works; p. 139: Mark C. Burnett/Photo Researchers; p. 142: Jeff Greenberg/Picture Cube.

Chapter 5: Chapter opening photo: Stephen Frisch/Stock, Boston; p. 150: José Azel/Aurora; p. 152: Culver; p. 156: Courtesy of Dr. Benjamin Harris, University of Wisconsin-Kenosha; p. 165: Jim Daniels/Picture Cube; p. 169: Freda Leinwand/Monkmeyer; p. 174: Courtesy of Albert Bandura; p. 178: Lester Sloan/Woodfin Camp & Associates.

Chapter 6: Chapter opening photo: Jeff Isaac Greenberg/Photo Researchers; p. 184: AP/Wide World Photos; p. 190: Joel Gordon; p. 192: Jeffrey Muir Hamilton/Stock, Boston; p. 197: Town McCarthy Photos/Picture Cube; p. 198: © Walt Disney Productions; p. 198: AP/Wide World Photos; p. 209: Washington University from: Scientific American, December 1993; p. 213: Bill Bachmann/Stock South.

Chapter 7: Chapter opening photo: MacDonald Photography/Picture Cube; p. 217: NASA; p. 219: Bob Daemmrich/Stock, Boston; p. 221: Tony Freeman/PhotoEdit; p. 230 (a-c): SuperStock, Inc; p. 233: Robert Clay/Monkmeyer; p. 238: Courtesy of Dr. Laura Ann Petitto © 1991. Photo by Robert Lamarche; p. 240: Deni McIntyre/Photo Researchers; p. 242: Georgia State University's Language Research Center; p. 243: M. Vintoniv/Stock, Boston.

Chapter 8: Chapter opening photo: Joseph Nettis/Photo Researchers; p. 249 (top): James S. Douglass; p. 249 (bottom): Pat Harbron/Outline; p. 250: David Hiser/Aspen; p. 254: Suzanne Szasz/Photo Researchers; p. 257: Sepp Seitz/Woodfin Camp & Associates; p. 257: Bob Daemmrich/The Image Works; p. 263: AP/Wide World Photos; p. 266: Joel Gordon.

Chapter 9: Chapter opening photo: Jean Marc Barey/Photo Researchers; p. 275: Todd Buchanan/NYT Pictures; p. 278: Peter Southwick/Stock, Boston; p. 284: Courtesy of Neal E. Miller, Dept. of Psychology, Yale University; p. 286: J. Fincher/Gamma Liaison; p. 289: Jeff Greenberg/Unicorn Stock Photos; p. 291: Owen Franken/Stock, Boston; p. 294: © 1943 by the President and Fellows of Harvard College; © 1971 by Henry A. Murray; p. 303: Courtesy of Donald E. Dutton; p. 307: © 1986 Andy Levin; p. 312: Vanessa Vick/Photo Researchers.

Chapter 10: Chapter opening photo: Emily Strong/Picture Cube; p. 321: Suzanne DeChillo/NYT Pictures; p. 322: Peter Byron; p. 333: Courtesy Andrew N. Meltzoff; p. 337: The Photo Works/Photo Researchers; p. 339: © Hanna & Meltzoff; p. 344: Chuck O'Rear/Woodfin Camp & Associates; p. 346: Mark S. Wexler/Woodfin Camp & Associates; p. 349: Catherine Karnow/Woodfin Camp & Associates; p. 352: Mary Kate Denny/PhotoEdit; p. 361: Jean-Michel Turpin/Gamma Liaison; p. 363: Tom McCarthy Photos/Picture Cube; p. 356: © 1994 Susan Muniak.

Chapter 11: Chapter opening photo: Myrleen Ferguson Cate/PhotoEdit; p. 372: Westenberger/Gamma Liaison; p. 376: Margaret Miller/Photo Researchers; p. 380 (both): AP/Wide World Photos; p. 383: AP/Wide World Photos; p. 384: Arni Katz/Stock South/Atlanta; p. 386: David Young-Wolff/PhotoEdit; p. 393: Bob Daemmrich/Image Works.

Chapter 12: Chapter opening photo: Will & Deni McIntyre/Photo Researchers; p. 403: Photos ©: 5096/Gamma Liaison; p. 408: Andrew N. Meltzoff; p. 414: The Photo Works; p. 419: Frank Micelotta/Outline; p. 426 (both top photos): Nancy Andreasen/University of Iowa Hospitals & Clinics; p. 426 (bottom): Monte S. Buchsbaum, M.D., Mount Sinai Medical Center; p. 430: Kal Muller/Woodfin Camp & Associates.

Chapter 13: Chapter opening photo: Janice Sheldon/Photo 20-20; p. 437: Lynn Johnson/Black Star; p. 442: Jim Wilson/Woodfin Camp & Associates; p. 444: Rick Friedman/Black Star; p. 450: David Young-Wolff/PhotoEdit; p. 456: Dominique Nabokov/Gamma Liaison; p. 459: Mary Kate Denny/PhotoEdit.

Chapter 14: Chapter opening photo: Kevin Forest/Image Bank; p. 465: © Stefan Maria Rother, Courtesy Street Sheet; p. 470: David R. Frazier/Photo Researchers; p. 476: Lowell Georgia/Photo Researchers; p. 479: David Burnett/Contact Press Images; p. 485: Michel Euler/AP/Wide World Photos; p. 488: Florent Flipper/Unicorn Stock Photos; p. 471: © Karen I. Hirsch.

NAME INDEX

SUBJECT INDEX

Need for power, 295
Negative reinforcers, 163, 164
Negative-symptom schizophrenia, 424
Nembutal, 141, 143
Neo-Freudian psychoanalysis, 379–380, 441–442
Neonates:
    development of, 329, 330–334
    and perceptual development, 332–334
Nervous system, 50–52
    central (CNS), 50–51, 140
    peripheral, 51–52, 328
    (See also Brain; Neurons)
Neurons, 41–48
    and brain modules, 67
    connections between, 45–48
    firing of, 43–45
    and memory, 207–209
    motor (efferent), 51
    and neurotransmitters, 45–48, 140, 145, 415
    sensory (afferent), 51
    structure of, 41–43
Neuroscientists, 40
Neurosis, 378, 383, 440
Neurosurgery, 63, 65–66
Neuroticism-stability, 383
Neurotransmitters, 45–48, 140, 145, 415
Neutral stimulus, 153
Nicotine, 134, 138, 139, 329
    (See also Smoking)
Nightmares, 125
Noise, 76
Nondirective counseling, 448
Norepinephrine, 456
Norm of reciprocity, 481
Norms, 256–257, 393–394
Not-so-free samples, 481
Notetaking, and memory, 213
Nurture (see Nature-nurture issue)

Obedience, 481–482
Obesity, 283, 286
Object permanence, 341
Observational learning, 174, 385, 445, 496–497
Obsessions, 413–414
Obsessive-compulsive disorder, 413–414
Occipital lobes, 58–59
Oedipal conflict, 376
Oklahoma City bombing incident, 2
Old age, 361–367
    cognitive changes in, 363–365
    and death, 366–367
    and learned helplessness, 314
    memory changes in, 365–366
    physical changes in, 362–363
    social world in, 366
"Old brain" (central core), 54–56
Olfactory cells, 95–96
Operant conditioning, 159–171, 384
    and attitudes, 467–468
    basics of, 160–162
    and biological constraints on learning, 170–171
    discrimination in, 168
    generalization in, 168
    and law of effect, 160
    punishment in, 163–165
    reinforcement in, 161–164, 165–168
    shaping in, 169, 239
    and superstitious behavior, 168–169
    treatment based on, 445–446
Operationalization, 22–23
Opponent-process theory of color vision, 88–89
Optic chiasm, 85
Optic nerve, 84–86
Oral stage, 375–376
Organic mental disorders, 429
Otoliths, 91, 95
Outer ear, 90, 91
Ovaries, 288
Overlearning, 213
Overregularization, 239
Ovulation, 288
Oxytocin, 69

Pain, 97–99
    gate-control theory of, 98–99
    reflex sympathetic dystrophy syndrome (RSDS), 74
Pain management, 74, 98, 111–112, 133–134
Panic disorder, 412
Paraplegia, 51
Parasympathetic division, of autonomic nervous system, 52
Parents:
    infant attachment to, 334–336
    and parenting styles, 337–339
    in single-parent households, 359–360
    and stormy adolescence, 355
    (See also Fathers; Marriage; Mothers)
Parietal lobes, 58–59
Parkinson's disease, 48, 63
Partial reinforcement schedule, 166
Passionate (romantic) love, 491
Paxil, 457
Peer relationships, 336–337
Penis envy, 376, 380
Perception, 74–75, 100–111
    bottom-up processing in, 104
    constancy of, 104–105
    and culture, 109–110
    depth, 105–106
    development of, 332–334
    extrasensory (ESP), 110–111
    feature analysis in, 101–103
    and gestalt laws of organization, 101
    illusions of, 106–109
    motion, 106
    and schizophrenia, 424
    subliminal, 110
    top-down processing in, 103
Perceptual constancy, 104–105
Perceptual disorders, 424
Peripheral nervous system, 51–52, 328
Peripheral-route processing, 469–470
Peripheral vision, 84
Permissive parents, 337–339
Personal stressors, 311–312
Personality, 372–398
    adult, changes in, 389
    biological approaches to, 386–387, 390
    and four temperaments, 11
    hardy, 315
    humanistic approaches to, 387–391
    learning approaches to, 384–386, 390, 397
    multiple, 416–417, 431
    psychoanalytic approaches to, 373–380, 390
    trait approaches to, 381–384, 390
Personality assessment, 392–398
    behavioral, 397
    evaluation of, 397–398
    norms in, 393–394
    projective personality tests in, 293–294, 396–397
    self-report measures in, 394–396
Personality development:
    adult, 389
    child, 376
    infant, 375–376
Personality disorders, 409, 427–428
Personality psychology, 6
Persuasion, 468–470
Phallic stage, 375, 376
Phencyclidine (PCP; angel dust), 141, 145
Phenobarbital, 141, 143
Phenylketonuria (PKU), 327–328
Pheromones, 95–96
Phobias, 155–156, 413
Phobic disorder, 413
Phonemes, 237
Phonological loop, 190
Phonology, 237
Phrenology, 11
Physical development:
    in adolescence, 348–350
    in adulthood, 357
    in infancy, 330–334
    neonatal, 329, 330–334

in old age, 362–363
at start of life, 326–329
Pineal gland, 124
Pitch, 92
Pituitary gland, 56, 68–69, 287
Place theory of hearing, 93
Placebos, 35, 48
Play, and "expert" babies, 338
Pleasure:
    and limbic system, 57
    and narcotics, 143–144
    and phallic stage, 375, 376
Pleasure principle, 374
Poggendorf illusion, 108
Polygraphs, 305
Pons, 55, 56
Positive reinforcers, 163, 164
Positive-symptom schizophrenia, 424
Positron emission tomography (PET) scans, 54, 63, 67, 209, 426
Posttraumatic stress disorder (PTSD), 311, 431–432
Power, need for, 295
Practical intelligence, 259–261
Practice, 189–190, 213, 219
Preattentive stage, 102
Predisposition model of schizophrenia, 427
Prefrontal lobotomy, 458–459
Pregnancy, 326–329
Prejudice and discrimination, 483–487
    fighting, 485–487
    foundations of, 484–485
    as higher-order conditioning, 157–158
    in intelligence tests, 267–272
    stereotypes in, 483–484, 485–486
    (See also Discrimination)
Premarital sex, 289–290
Premenstrual syndrome (PMS), 125, 429–430
Premises, 221–222
Preoperational stage, 342
Primary drives, 277
Primary reinforcers, 162
Priming, 194
Principle of conservation, 342, 343
Proactive interference, 206, 207
Problem-focused coping, 315
Problem solving, 217–218, 224–236
    creativity and, 233–235
    evaluating solutions in, 231
    and formal operational stage, 344
    generating solutions in, 229–231
    impediments to, 231–233
    and intelligence, 250–251
    kinds of problems and, 225–228
    preparation for, 225–228
    representing and organizing problems, 225–227
Problems of inducing structure, 225, 226–227, 228
Procedural memory, 192
Process schizophrenia, 424
Progesterone, 288
Program evaluation, 8
Projection, 377, 378
Projective personality tests, 293–294, 396–397
Prosocial behavior, 497–498
Prototypes, 220
Proximity, 101
Prozac, 456, 457
Psi, 111
Psychiatry, 438
Psychoactive drugs, 138, 141, 429
    (See also Drug use and abuse)
Psychoanalysis, 373, 438, 440–441, 442
Psychoanalytic model of abnormality, 405, 406
Psychoanalytic theory, 373–380, 390
    Freudian, 373–379, 406, 426, 440–441, 442
    neo-Freudian, 379–380, 441–442
Psychodynamic perspective, 14, 18
Psychodynamic therapy, 440–442
Psychographics, 470
Psychological disorders, 402–433
    anxiety, 409, 412–415, 456
    classification of, 408–410, 429–431
    dissociative, 409, 416–418, 431